MYSOCLAB

MYSOCLAB for *Mastering Sociology* provides all the tools you need to engage every student before, during, and after class. An assignment calendar and gradebook allow you to assign specific activities with due dates and to measure your students' progress throughout the semester.

The **PEARSON ETEXT** lets students access their textbook anytime, anywhere, and anyway they want, including listening online. The eText for *Mastering Sociology* features integrated videos, Social Explorer activities, additional readings and interactive self-quizzes.

A **PERSONALIZED STUDY PLAN** for each student, based on Bloom's Taxonomy, arranges activities from those that require less complex thinking—like remembering and understanding—to more complex critical thinking—like applying and analyzing. This layered approach promotes better critical thinking skills, helping students succeed in the course and beyond.

MYSOCLAB

SOCIAL EXPLORER

activities connect with topics from the text, engaging students with data visualizations, comparisons of change over time, and data localized to their own communities.

STUDENT PERSPECTIVES VIDEOS

begin and conclude each chapter. Students share their experiences and perspectives on sociological topics. These videos are designed to engage viewers and encourage them to build a sociological perspective relevant to their own lives.

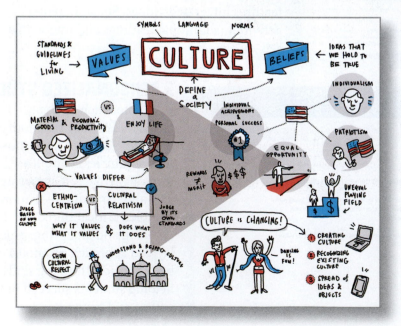

CORE CONCEPTS VIDEOS

introduce students to key concepts and terminology needed to succeed in the introductory course. Designed to supplement the instruction in the book, the Core Concept Videos provide a quick reference for review.

MYSOCLIBRARY

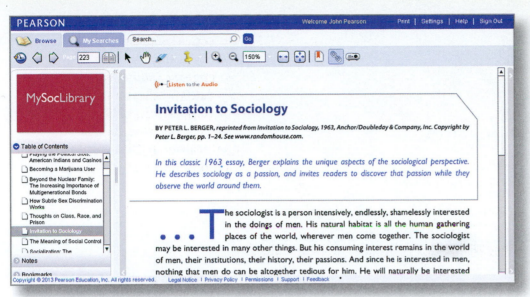

available in the Pearson eText 200 classic and contemporary articles that enable students to explore the discipline more deeply. Multiple-choice questions for each reading help students review what they've learned—and allow instructors to monitor their performance.

SOCIOLOGY IN FOCUS

(www.sociologyinfocus.com) is a blog by sociologists for students that highlights a sociological perspective on current events, pop culture, and everyday life. Updated at least twice a week, Sociology in Focus is a terrific way to bring current examples into the classroom.

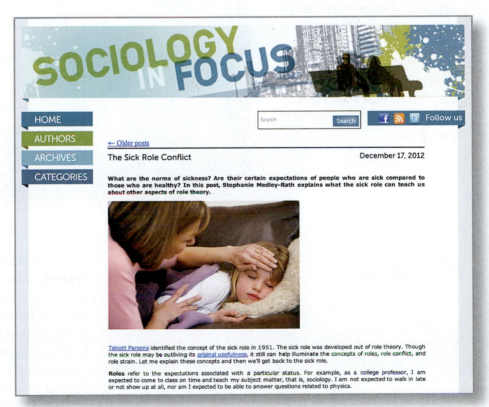

MASTERING SOCIOLOGY

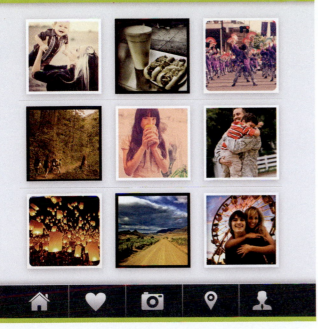

MASTERING
SOCIOLOGY

JAMES M. HENSLIN

MASTERING SOCIOLOGY

JAMES M. HENSLIN
SOUTHERN ILLINOIS UNIVERSITY, EDWARDSVILLE

PEARSON

Boston   Columbus   Indianapolis   New York   San Francisco   Upper Saddle River
Amsterdam   Cape Town   Dubai   London   Madrid   Milan   Munich   Paris   Montréal   Toronto
Delhi   Mexico City   São Paulo   Sydney   Hong Kong   Seoul   Singapore   Taipei   Tokyo

Editorial Director: Craig Campanella
Editor in Chief: Dickson Musslewhite
Senior Acquisitions Editor: Brita Mess
Assistant Editor: Seanna Breen
Director of Marketing: Brandy Dawson
Executive Marketing Manager: Maureen Prado Roberts
Managing Editor: Denise Forlow
Senior Production Project Manager: Marianne Peters-Riordan
Senior Operations Supervisor: Mary Fischer
Operations Specialist: Alan Fischer
Art Director: Anne Bonanno Nieglos
Interior Design: Riezebos Holzbaur/Brieanna Hattey

Cover Designer: Cliff Alejandro/Creative Circle
Cover Photo Credits (clockwise from top left): Layland Masuda/Getty Images; blackwater images/Getty Images; KevinRuss/Getty Images; Ariel Skelley/Getty Images; Simone Becchetti/Getty Images; Radu Razvan/Shutterstock; Daniel Osterkamp/Getty Images; andipantz/Getty Images; Rubberball/Mike Kemp/Getty Images
Digital Media Editor: Rachel Comerford
Development Editor: Jennifer Auvil
Production Development: Dusty Friedman
Full-Service Project Management: Jared Sterzer
Composition: PreMediaGlobal
Printer/Binder: RR Donnelley
Text Font: 10/12 Minion Pro Regular

Credits and acknowledgments borrowed from other sources and reproduced, with permission, in this textbook appear on appropriate page within text (or on page 522).

Library of Congress Cataloging-in-Publication Data
Henslin, James M.
    Mastering sociology / James M. Henslin.
        pages cm
    ISBN-13: 978-0-205-20678-0
    ISBN-10: 0-205-20678-6
1. Sociology. I. Title.
    HM585.H448 2013
301—dc23
V092

2012049591

10 9 8 7 6 5 4
V011

Student Version:
ISBN 10: 0205206743
Á la carte Version:
ISBN 10: 0205206883

To my fellow instructors of sociology, who strive for creative teaching and the development of their students' sociological perspective.

With my sincere admiration and appreciation,

Jim Henslin

BRIEF CONTENTS

Part I
THE SOCIOLOGICAL PERSPECTIVE

CHAPTER 1 The Sociological Perspective   1

CHAPTER 2 Research and Theory in Sociology   18

CHAPTER 3 Culture   46

CHAPTER 4 Socialization   77

CHAPTER 5 Social Structure and Social Interaction   105

CHAPTER 6 Deviance and Social Control   145

Part II
SOCIAL INEQUALITY

CHAPTER 7 Social Stratification   181

CHAPTER 8 Race and Ethnicity   226

CHAPTER 9 Sex and Gender   269

Part III
SOCIAL INSTITUTIONS

CHAPTER 10 Politics and the Economy   305

CHAPTER 11 Marriage and Family   350

CHAPTER 12 Education and Religion   388

Part IV
SOCIAL CHANGE

CHAPTER 13 Population and Urbanization   425

CHAPTER 14 Social Change and the Environment   465

CONTENTS

TO THE STUDENT   xix

TO THE INSTRUCTOR   xxi

ABOUT THE AUTHOR   xxvii

Part I
THE SOCIOLOGICAL PERSPECTIVE

Chapter 1
The Sociological Perspective   1

Unit 1.1 **Seeing the Social Context**	2
Unit 1.2 **Origins of Sociology**	5
Tradition Versus Science	5
Auguste Comte and Positivism	5
Herbert Spencer and Social Darwinism	6
Karl Marx and Class Conflict	6
Emile Durkheim and Social Integration	7
Max Weber and the Protestant Ethic	7
Unit 1.3 **Sociology in North America: Social Reform Versus Social Analysis**	10
Sexism at the Time: Women in Early Sociology	10
Racism at the Time: W. E. B. Du Bois	12
Jane Addams and Social Reform	12
Talcott Parsons and C. Wright Mills: Theory versus Reform	13
The Tension Today: Basic, Applied, and Public Sociology	13
Pulling It All Together	16
Did I Learn It? Answers	17

Chapter 2
Research and Theory in Sociology   18

Unit 2.1 **Doing Research: The Need**	19
Unit 2.2 **Doing Research: The Model**	20
A Research Model	20
Unit 2.3 **Doing Research: The Methods**	24
Surveys	24
Secondary Analysis	26

Analysis of Documents	26
Experiments	27
Unobtrusive Measures	28
Participant Observation (Fieldwork)	28
Gender in Sociological Research	28
Unit 2.4 **Why Research Needs Theory: A Very Brief Introduction**	31
Unit 2.5 **Theoretical Perspectives: Symbolic Interactionism**	32
Applying Symbolic Interactionism	33
Unit 2.6 **Theoretical Perspectives: Functional Analysis**	35
Robert Merton and Functionalism	35
Applying Functional Analysis	36
Unit 2.7 **Theoretical Perspectives: Conflict Theory**	38
Karl Marx and Conflict Theory	38
Conflict Theory Today	38
Feminists and Conflict Theory	38
Applying Conflict Theory	39
Unit 2.8 **Putting the Perspectives Together: Macro and Micro**	40
Which Theory Is the Right One?	40
Levels of Analysis: Macro and Micro	40
Pulling It All Together	42
Did I Learn It? Answers	44

Chapter 3
Culture   46

Unit 3.1 **What Is Culture?**	47
Unit 3.2 **Culture and Orientations to Life**	49
"Culture within Us": Our Lens for Viewing Life	49
Ethnocentrism and Orientations to Life	50
Unit 3.3 **Symbolic Culture: Language**	
Language	

Unit 3.4	**Symbolic Culture: Gestures**	57
Unit 3.5	**Symbolic Culture: Values, Norms, Sanctions, Folkways, and Mores**	59
	Values, Norms, and Sanctions	59
	Folkways and Mores	60
Unit 3.6	**Many Cultural Worlds**	61
	Subcultures	61
	Countercultures	61
Unit 3.7	**Values in U.S. Society**	65
	An Overview of U.S. Values	65
	Value Clusters	66
	Values as Distorting Lenses	66
	"Ideal" Versus "Real" Culture	66
Unit 3.8	**Changing Values**	67
	Value Contradictions	67
	When Values Clash	67
	Emerging Values	67
Unit 3.9	**Cultural Universals**	69
Unit 3.10	**Technology in the Global Village**	70
	The New Technology	70
	Cultural Lag and Cultural Change	70
	Technology and Cultural Leveling	71
	Pulling It All Together	73
	Did I Learn It? Answers	75

Chapter 4
Socialization
77

Unit 4.1	**Extremes in Socialization**	78
	Feral Children	78
	Isolated Children	78
	Isolated Animals	80
	Institutionalized Children	80
Unit 4.2	**Socialization into the Self and Mind**	83
	Cooley and the Looking-Glass Self	83
	Mead and Role Taking	83
Unit 4.3	**Socialization into Emotions**	86
	Expressing Emotions: Biology	86
	Expressing Emotions: "Feeling Rules"	86
	What We Feel	87
Unit 4.4	**Getting the Message: Learning Gender**	88
	Learning the Gender Map	89
	Gender Messages in the Family	89
	Gender Messages from Peers	89
	Gender Messages in the Mass Media	90
Unit 4.5	**Agents of Socialization**	92
	The Family	92
	Day Care	93
	The School and Peer Groups	94
	The Workplace	94
Unit 4.6	**Resocialization**	95
	Total Institutions	96
Unit 4.7	**Socialization through the Life Course**	97
	Childhood (from birth to about age 12)	97
	Adolescence (ages 13–17)	98
	Transitional Adulthood (ages 18–29)	99
	The Middle Years (ages 30–65)	99
	The Older Years (about age 65 on)	99
	Pulling It All Together	101
	Did I Learn It? Answers	103

Chapter 5
Social Structure and Social Interaction
105

Unit 5.1	**Levels of Sociological Analysis: Macrosociology and Microsociology**	106
	Macrosociology and Microsociology: A Brief Overview	106
	THE MACROSOCIOLOGICAL PERSPECTIVE	108
Unit 5.2	**The Macrosociological Perspective: Social Structure**	108
	The Sociological Significance of Social Structure	108
Unit 5.3	**The Components of Social Structure: Culture, Social Class, Groups, Social Status, and Roles**	110
	Culture	110
	Social Class	111
	Groups	111
	Social Status	111
	Roles	113
Unit 5.4	**Another Component of Social Structure: Social Institutions**	115
	What Social Institutions Are	116
Unit 5.5	**Comparing Functionalist and Conflict Perspectives**	117
	The Functionalist Perspective	117
	The Conflict Perspective	118
Unit 5.6	**What Holds Society Together?**	120
	Mechanical and Organic Solidarity	120
	Gemeinschaft and *Gesellschaft*	121
	Changes in Social Structure	121
Unit 5.7	**The Microsociological Perspective: Social Interaction in Everyday Life**	123
	The Microsociological Perspective	123
	Symbolic Interaction	123

THROUGH THE AUTHOR'S LENS:
Vienna: Social Structure and
Social Interaction   124

Unit 5.8   **Dramaturgy: The Presentation of
Self in Everyday Life**   127
Introducing Dramaturgy   127

Unit 5.9   **Ethnomethodology: Uncovering
Background Assumptions**   133
Introducing Ethnomethodology   133

Unit 5.10   **The Social Construction of Reality**   135
Introducing the Social Construction
of Reality   135

 THROUGH THE AUTHOR'S LENS:
When a Tornado Strikes: Social
Organization Following a Natural Disaster   138

Pulling It All Together   140
Did I Learn It? Answers   143

**Chapter 6
Deviance and Social
Control**   **145**

Unit 6.1   **What Is Deviance?**   146
How Norms Make Social Life Possible   147
Sanctions   147

Unit 6.2   **Comparing Sociobiology, Psychology,
and Sociology**   149
Explanations for Violating Norms   149

Unit 6.3   **The Symbolic Interactionist Perspective**   151
Differential Association Theory   151

Control Theory   152
Labeling Theory   153

Unit 6.4   **The Functionalist Perspective**   155
Can Deviance Really Be Functional
for Society?   155
Strain Theory: How Mainstream
Values Produce Deviance   156
Illegitimate Opportunity Structures:
Social Class, Gender, and Crime   157

Unit 6.5   **The Conflict Perspective**   161
Class, Crime, and the Criminal
Justice System   161
The Law as an Instrument
of Oppression   161

Unit 6.6   **Reactions to Deviance: Prisons**   162
Street Crime and Prisons   163
Street Crime and the "Three-Strikes"
Laws   164
The Decline in Violent Crime   165
Recidivism   165

Unit 6.7   **Reactions to Deviance: The Death Penalty**   167
The Death Penalty and Serial Killers   167
Bias in the Death Penalty   168

Unit 6.8   **On Laws and Crime Statistics**   171
The Trouble with Crime Statistics   171

Unit 6.9   **The Medicalization of Deviance**   173
Neither Mental Nor Illness?   173

Unit 6.10   **The Need for a More Humane Approach**   176
A More Humane Approach   176

Pulling It All Together   177
Did I Learn It? Answers   179

Part II
SOCIAL INEQUALITY

 **Chapter 7
Social Stratification**   **181**

Unit 7.1   **Global Stratification: From Slavery
to Social Class**   182
Slavery   182
Caste   183
Social Class   185
Global Stratification and the Status
of Females   185

Unit 7.2   **Three Worlds of Stratification**   186
The Most Industrialized Nations   187
The Industrializing Nations   187
The Least Industrialized Nations   187

 THROUGH THE AUTHOR'S LENS:
The Dump People: Working and Living and Playing
in the City Dump of Phnom Penh, Cambodia   188
Cutting across the Three Worlds:
The New Global Superclass   190

Unit 7.3   **How Did the World's Nations
Become Stratified?**   191
Colonialism   191
World System Theory   192
Culture of Poverty   192
Evaluating the Theories   193

Unit 7.4   **Why Is Social Stratification Universal?**   193
The Functionalist View: Motivating
Qualified People   193
The Conflict Perspective: Class
Conflict and Scarce Resources   197

Unit 7.5 **What Determines Social Class?** 198
Karl Marx: The Means of Production 199
Max Weber: Property, Power,
and Prestige 199

Unit 7.6 **Social Class in the United States** 201
Property 201
Power 204
Prestige 204
Status Inconsistency 205

Unit 7.7 **A Social Class Model** 207
The Capitalist Class 207
The Upper Middle Class 209
The Lower Middle Class 209
The Working Class 209
The Working Poor 209
The Underclass 209

Unit 7.8 **Consequences of Social Class** 211
Physical Health 211
Mental Health 212
Family Life 212
Education 212
Religion 213
Politics 213
Crime and Criminal Justice 213

Unit 7.9 **Social Mobility** 214
Three Types of Social Mobility 214
Women in Studies of Social Mobility 215

Unit 7.10 **Poverty** 216
Drawing the Poverty Line 216
Stereotypes of the Poor 217
Race–Ethnicity and Poverty 218
Suburbanization of Poverty 218
Children of Poverty 218
The Penalties of Poverty 219
Where Is Horatio Alger? The Social
Functions of a Myth 220
Pulling It All Together 221
Did I Learn It? Answers 223

**Chapter 8
Race and Ethnicity** 226

Unit 8.1 **Race: Myth and Reality** 227
Human Variety 227
Ethnic Groups 229

Unit 8.2 **Minority Groups and Dominant Groups** 230
How Dominant Groups Treat
Minority Groups 231

Unit 8.3 **Prejudice and Discrimination** 236
Learning Prejudice 237
Groups Based on Prejudice 238
Individual and Institutional
Discrimination 238

Unit 8.4 **Theories of Prejudice** 240
Psychological Perspectives 240
Sociological Perspectives 241

Unit 8.5 **Racial–Ethnic Relations:
European Americans** 245
White Anglo Saxon Protestants 246

Unit 8.6 **Racial–Ethnic Relations:
Latinos (Hispanics)** 248
Numbers, Origins, and Location 248

Unit 8.7 **Racial–Ethnic Relations:
African Americans** 252
Rising Expectations and Civil Strife 253

Unit 8.8 **Racial–Ethnic Relations:
Asian Americans** 256
A Background of Discrimination 256

Unit 8.9 **Racial–Ethnic Relations:
Native Americans** 258
Diversity of Groups 259
From Treaties to Genocide and
Population Transfer 259

Unit 8.10 **Looking Toward the Future** 261
The Immigration Debate 262
Affirmative Action 263
Toward a True Multicultural Society 263
Pulling It All Together 265
Did I Learn It? Answers 267

**Chapter 9
Sex and Gender** 269

Unit 9.1 **Differences between Sex and Gender** 270
Sex and Gender 270

Unit 9.2 **Human Behavior: Biological or Social
Factors?** 273
The Dominant Position in Sociology 273
The Minority Position in Sociology 274
The Vietnam Veterans Study 274

Unit 9.3 **How Females Became a Minority Group** 276
Females as a Minority Group 276
How Did Females Become a
Minority Group? 276

Unit 9.4 **Fighting Back: The Rise of Feminism** 279
Cultural Supports to Maintain
Dominance 279
The Struggle 280

Unit 9.5 **Global Inequality in the World of Work** 282
Sex Typing of Work around the World 283
Gender and the Prestige of Work 283

THROUGH THE AUTHOR'S LENS:
Work and Gender:
Women at Work in India 284

Unit 9.6 **Gender Inequality in the
American Workplace** 287
The Pay Gap 287
The Slowly Cracking Glass Ceiling 289

Unit 9.7 **Sexual Harassment** 290
From Personal to Structural 291

Unit 9.8 **Gender Inequality in Everyday Life
and Health Care** 292
Gender Inequality in Everyday Life 292
Gender Inequality in Health Care 293

Unit 9.9 **Violence against Women** 294
Violence against Women on a
Global Level 295
Violence against Women in the
United States 295

Unit 9.10 **The Changing Face of Politics** 298
Cultural Supports of Gender
Discrimination 298
Women's Potential Political Power 298

Pulling It All Together 300
Did I Learn It? Answers 302

Part III
SOCIAL INSTITUTIONS

**Chapter 10
Politics and the
Economy** 305

POLITICS: ESTABLISHING LEADERSHIP 306

Unit 10.1 **Power, Authority, and Violence** 306
Authority and Legitimate Violence 306
Traditional Authority 307
Rational–Legal Authority 307
Charismatic Authority 308
The Transfer of Authority 309

Unit 10.2 **Types of Government** 311
Monarchies: The Rise of the State 311
Democracies: Citizenship as a
Revolutionary Idea 311
Dictatorships and Oligarchies:
The Seizure of Power 312

Unit 10.3 **The U.S. Political System** 315
Political Parties and Elections 315
Voting Patterns 316
Lobbyists and Special-Interest Groups 318

Unit 10.4 **Who Rules the United States?** 321
The Functionalist Perspective: Pluralism 321
The Conflict Perspective:
The Power Elite 322
Which View Is Right? 323

Unit 10.5 **War and Terrorism: Implementing
Political Objectives** 324
Why Countries Go to War 324
Terrorism 325

THE ECONOMY: WORK IN THE GLOBAL VILLAGE 327

Unit 10.6 **The Transformation of Economic Systems** 327
Preindustrial Societies: The Birth
of Inequality 328
Industrial Societies: The Birth
of the Machine 328
Postindustrial Societies: The Birth
of the Information Age 329
Biotech Societies: Is a New Type
of Society Emerging? 330

Unit 10.7 **Principles and Criticisms of Capitalism
and Socialism** 331
Capitalism 332
Socialism 333
Criticisms of Capitalism and Socialism 333

Unit 10.8 **Belief Systems and the Convergence
of Capitalism and Socialism** 335
Belief Systems of Capitalism
and Socialism 335
The Convergence of Capitalism
and Socialism 335

Unit 10.9 **The Globalization of Capitalism** 337
A New Global Structure 337
Stagnant Paychecks 338

The New Economic System and the
Old Divisions of Wealth 339

 THROUGH THE AUTHOR'S LENS:
Small Town USA: Struggling to Survive 340
The Global Superclass 342

Unit 10.10 A New World Order? 343
Trends Toward Unity 343
Strains in the Global System 344
Pulling It All Together 345
Did I Learn It? Answers 347

Chapter 11 Marriage and Family

350

Unit 11.1 Marriage and Family in Global Perspective 351
What Is a Family? 351
What Is Marriage? 351
Common Cultural Themes 352

**Unit 11.2 Marriage and Family in Theoretical
Perspective** 355
The Functionalist Perspective:
Functions and Dysfunctions 355
The Conflict Perspective: Struggles
between Husbands and Wives 356
The Symbolic Interactionist Perspective:
Gender, Housework, and Child Care 356

Unit 11.3 Love and Marriage 358
Love and Courtship in Global Perspective 359
Marriage 360

Unit 11.4 Family Transitions 361
Childbirth 362
Child Rearing 362
Staying Home Longer 364
Widowhood 364

Unit 11.5 Racial–Ethnic Diversity 366
African American Families 366
Latino Families 367
Asian American Families 368
Native American Families 368

Unit 11.6 More Diversity 369
One-Parent Families 369
Couples without Children 370
Blended Families 370
Gay and Lesbian Families 371

Unit 11.7 Current Trends 372
Postponing Marriage and Childbirth 372
Cohabitation 372

Unit 11.8 Divorce and Remarriage 375
Ways of Measuring Divorce 375
Children of Divorce 376
Grandchildren of Divorce 377
Fathers' Contact with Children
after Divorce 377
The Ex-Spouses 378
Remarriage 378

Unit 11.9 Two Sides of Family Life 380
The Dark Side of Family Life:
Spouse Battering, Child Abuse,
and Incest 380
The Bright Side of Family Life:
Successful Marriages 381

Unit 11.10 The Future of Marriage and Family 383
Pulling It All Together 384
Did I Learn It? Answers 386

Chapter 12 Education and Religion

388

**EDUCATION: TRANSFERRING KNOWLEDGE
AND SKILLS** 389

Unit 12.1 Education in Global Perspective 389
Education in the Most Industrialized
Nations: Japan 389
Education in the Industrializing
Nations: Russia 390
Education in the Least Industrialized
Nations: Egypt 391

**Unit 12.2 The Functionalist Perspective: Providing
Social Benefits** 392
Teaching Knowledge and Skills 392
The Transmission of Mainstream Values 392
Social Integration 393
Gatekeeping (Social Placement) 393
Replacing Family Functions 394

**Unit 12.3 The Conflict Perspective: Perpetuating
Social Inequality** 395
Stacking the Deck: Unequal Funding 395
Tilting the Tests: Discrimination by IQ 395
The Bottom Line: Family Background 396

Unit 12.4 The Symbolic Interactionist Perspective: Teacher Expectations 398
The Rist Research 398
How Do Teacher Expectations Work? 399

Unit 12.5 Problems in U.S. Education—And Their Solutions 400
Mediocrity 401
Violence 403

RELIGION: ESTABLISHING MEANING 404

Unit 12.6 Religion in Global Perspective 404
What Is Religion? 404

Unit 12.7 The Functionalist Perspective 406
Functions of Religion 406
Dysfunctions of Religion 407

Unit 12.8 The Conflict Perspective 408
Opium of the People 408
Legitimating Social Inequalities 409

Unit 12.9 The Symbolic Interactionist Perspective 410
Religious Symbols 410
Beliefs 411
Rituals 411

THROUGH THE AUTHOR'S LENS:
Holy Week in Spain 412
Religious Experience 414

Unit 12.10 Religion in the United States 415
Types of Religious Groups 415
Cult (New Religion) 415
Sect 416
Church 416
Ecclesia (State Religion) 416
Characteristics of Religious Groups 417
The Future of Religion 419
Pulling It All Together 420
Did I Learn It? Answers 423

Part IV
SOCIAL CHANGE

**Chapter 13
Population and
Urbanization** 425

POPULATION IN GLOBAL PERSPECTIVE 426

UNIT 13.1 A Planet with No Space for Enjoying Life? 426
The New Malthusians 427
The Anti-Malthusians 427
Who Is Correct? 429

Unit 13.2 Why Are People Starving? 430

Unit 13.3 How Populations Grow 432
Why Do the Least Industrialized Nations Have So Many Children? 433
Implications of Different Rates of Growth 433

Unit 13.4 The Three Demographic Variables 436
Problems in Forecasting Population Growth 438

URBANIZATION 440

Unit 13.5 The Development of Cities 441

THROUGH THE AUTHOR'S LENS:
Medellin, Colombia: A Walk Through El Tiro 442
The Process of Urbanization 444

Unit 13.6 U.S. Urban Patterns 446
The United States 446
The Rural Rebound 448

Unit 13.7 Models of Urban Growth 450
The Concentric Zone Model 450
The Sector Model 450
The Multiple-Nuclei Model 450
The Peripheral Model 451
Critique of the Models 451

Unit 13.8 City Life: From Alienation to Community 452
Alienation in the City 453
Community in the City 453
Who Lives in the City? 454

Unit 13.9 The Diffusion of Responsibility 455

Unit 13.10 Urban Problems and Social Policy 456

THROUGH THE AUTHOR'S LENS:
Community in the City 457
Suburbanization 458
Disinvestment and Deindustrialization 458
The Potential of Urban Revitalization 458
Pulling It All Together 460
Did I Learn It? Answers 462

**Chapter 14
Social Change
and the Environment** 465

Unit 14.1 How Social Change Transforms Social Life 466
The Four Social Revolutions 466
From *Gemeinschaft* to *Gesellschaft* 466
The Industrial Revolution 466

Unit 14.2 **Global Politics: Power and Conflict**   468

Unit 14.3 **Theories and Processes of Social Change**   470
     Evolution from Lower to Higher   470
     Natural Cycles   470
     Conflict over Power   471

Unit 14.4 **Ogburn's Theory**   473

Unit 14.5 **Networking, Facebook, and Technology**   475
     The Facebook of Revolution   476
     The Changing Face of War   477

Unit 14.6 **The Growth Machine Versus the Earth**   479
     Environmental Problems and
     Industrialization   479

Unit 14.7 **The Environmental Movement**   483

Unit 14.8 **Environmental Sociology**   485
     The Environment and Sociology   485
Pulling It All Together   487
Did I Learn It? Answers   488

EPILOGUE   490
GLOSSARY   492
REFERENCES   501
CREDITS   522
NAME INDEX   527
SUBJECT INDEX   533

WELCOME TO SOCIOLOGY! I've loved sociology since I was in my teens, and I hope you enjoy it, too. Sociology is fascinating because it is about human behavior, and many of us find that it holds the key to understanding social life.

If you like to watch people and try to figure out why they do what they do, you will like sociology. Sociology pries open the doors of society so you can see what goes on behind them. *Mastering Sociology* stresses how profoundly our society and the groups to which we belong influence us. Social class, for example, sets us on a particular path in life. For some, the path leads to more education, interesting jobs, higher income, and better health, but for others it leads to dropping out of school, dead-end jobs, poverty, and even a higher risk of illness and disease. These paths are so significant that they affected your chances of making it to your first birthday, as well as of getting in trouble with the police. If you marry, they will even influence how you relate to your spouse, how many children you will have, and how you will rear them.

When I took my first course in sociology, I was "hooked." Seeing how marvelously my life had been influenced by these larger social forces opened my eyes to a new world, one that has been fascinating to explore. I hope that you will have this experience, too.

From how people become homeless to how they become presidents, from why people commit suicide to why women are discriminated against in every society around the world—all are part of sociology. This breadth is what makes sociology so intriguing. We can place the sociological lens on broad features of society, such as social class, gender, and race–ethnicity, and then immediately turn our focus on the smaller, more intimate level. If we look at two people interacting—whether quarreling or kissing—we see how these broad features of society are being played out in their lives.

One of sociology's many pleasures is that as you study life in groups (which can be taken as a definition of sociology), whether those groups are in some far-off part of the world or in some nearby corner of your own society, you gain new insights into who you are and how you got that way. As you see how *their* customs affect *them,* the effects of your own society on yourself become more visible.

This book, then, can be part of your intellectual journey, an adventure that can lead you to a new way of looking at your social world—and in the process, help you to better understand both society and yourself.

I wish you the very best in college—and in your career afterward. It is my sincere desire that *Mastering Sociology* will contribute to that success.

Jim Henslin
Department of Sociology
Southern Illinois University, Edwardsville

P.S. I enjoy communicating with students, so feel free to comment on your experiences with this text. Because I travel a lot, it is best to reach me by e-mail: henslin@aol.com

I am pleased that you have chosen *Mastering Sociology*, a new approach to teaching sociology. From the beginning to the end, this book is a learning-centered text. It is designed to *teach* students, not simply to present information. You will be pleased at how well your students learn from this text and how well it complements your teaching.

Let me tell you why I wrote this book and then give you an overview of how it is laid out.

I have taught intro students for decades—with an enthusiasm for sociology that stays with me and that you should see shining through in this text. I always enjoyed the intro course, as the students responded favorably to innovative teaching. And I was always experimenting, finding new ways of reaching students. As I did this, I didn't hold back on the content, as it was my responsibility to teach sociology. I felt that if I approached teaching in this way, students would learn. And they did. And we both enjoyed the course.

But two things bothered me. First, students often asked me, "What should I learn in this chapter?" and my answer was, "Learn it all." And, of course, when I said this, the students would leave perplexed. *Mastering Sociology* solves this problem. From the way I have designed this book, the students will know precisely what they are expected to learn—*and* they will know if they learned it.

Second, I taught at an average college, with students whose backgrounds were highly diverse. Some students were highly qualified academically, while others had difficulty with basic academics. Many of these latter students would do poorly, and I kept thinking that there must be a way to reach *all* students, no matter their level of preparation. But how?

Mastering Sociology solves this problem, too. Built upon solid pedagogical principles, this text is an exceptionally effective teaching tool. You, of course, are the judge as you use this book in the classroom. I certainly hope that your experience matches my expectations and confirms these goals.

Today's students are not the same as the students of previous decades. They have no less ability, but they have grown up in an instantaneous world. Their experience is that of quick snapshots of events swirling around them. Their way of thinking is built around short bursts. Instead of lamenting this orientation, this book is designed to capture the approach that students have to their world.

As will become apparent as you teach from this text, I have not sacrificed sociological content. Students will learn sociology, not just some puffery trying to pass itself off as sociology, a masquerade that most of us find quite distasteful.

You now have the "why," the "who," and the "what." Let's get an overview of the "how," so you can see how this book works and precisely what makes it so different. I expect that you will find this text to be the most effective you have ever used. This is a bold statement, but I think this will be the result that you will have the pleasure of enjoying. Let's see why I expect you to have such a positive teaching experience.

The Modular Approach

The modular approach is not new, but combined with the personalization of sociology in this text, along with the reviews I have built into the chapters, your students *will* learn well.

I have broken each chapter into short, coherent units, which enhance learning by matching the students' approach to thinking. Each unit is self-contained, so after students complete a unit, they can take a break and do something else if they prefer. Following each unit is a series of questions that are an essential part of the learning process. Sequential with the unit's presentation, the questions do not just let students know how they are doing, but they also teach. Repeating the unit's main points, the questions are a form of review. These questions are such an essential part of the learning process that I have written each one myself. If they were the usual add-on, I would have had the publisher get someone to write them. Writing the questions so they would accomplish this teaching/learning goal was highly time-consuming, but this form of evaluative review is essential to the goal of *Mastering Sociology*.

But I get ahead of myself. Let me back up and give you an overview of the book, starting with how the chapters are laid out.

Getting Started

This short opening to each chapter is designed to arouse the students' interest by showing how the coming chapter is relevant to their life.

Unit Heading

Each unit heading is marked clearly by its unit number and title. The title indicates the topic that follows.

What Am I Supposed to Learn?

Here I spell out the unit's learning objectives. Each learning objective is numbered and written clearly. Students will know precisely what they are to learn.

The Narrative

After the learning objectives comes the presentation of the sociological materials. I have written the narrative clearly, directing it in a personal fashion to the student. Students should gain the impression that I am talking to them directly, as this is precisely what I am trying to do. If teaching/learning is to be successful, it is important to engage the students in the process, which is what the narrative does.

To attain clarity of learning objectives and to personalize the presentation of sociological concepts and research, it is not necessary to sacrifice sociological content. Although *Mastering Sociology* makes learning both easy and enjoyable, what the students learn in this text matches the content of standard courses. Students will be introduced to sociology's major ideas, theories, and research. *Mastering Sociology* changes the form, not the content.

Testing Myself: Did I Learn It?

Following the content of each unit comes a self-test. I have written these questions both to match the learning objectives and to provide a review of the unit. The questions are direct and straightforward, designed to measure learning. After studying a unit, students should have little trouble answering these questions correctly. If students miss a question, they will be able to spot their weakness and go back to the unit to learn that particular material.

Everything in this text revolves around learning, including these self-test questions. As I said earlier, these questions are such an essential part of the learning process that I have written them myself. They are a way to help students attain mastery of the learning objectives.

This sequence repeats throughout each chapter: Getting Started, the unit number and title, the learning objectives, the sociological narrative, and the self-test.

Pulling It All Together

The last unit of each chapter is followed by *Pulling It All Together*. Here I again reinforce the students' learning by reviewing the chapter's learning goals. I have written a brief summary for each learning objective, answers that are inadequate for students to memorize, but that serve as a solid review.

Five Additional Features that Enhance Learning

These additional features are:

MAKING IT PERSONAL

This is probably my favorite feature of the entire book, the one whose writing gave me the most pleasure. In this feature, I have picked up some element of the sociological presentation and have related it directly to the students' life. To point out how directly sociology is connected to what the students are experiencing in society lets them see that sociology is not something that belongs only in the classroom. By personalizing sociology, students not only learn more but they do so in a much more enjoyable way.

You will find that *Making It Personal* enhances your teaching. Students will grasp sociological concepts and ideas in a new, refreshing way. This feature, which helps students see how society has impacted their lives, even their intimate orientations to life, truly helps make sociology come alive. *Making It Personal* can also serve as an essential tool to stimulate provocative discussions that enliven your classroom.

FROM ANOTHER STUDENT

Many students have written me over the years, pointing out how my text has helped them in one way or another. The content of *Mastering Sociology* is the same, so in this feature I reproduce some of these notes, always with permission of the students who wrote them. The intention of this feature is simple, to encourage students to read the text and learn sociology.

IF YOU WANT TO LEARN MORE

This feature points to items that I have written on particular topics. As students read these one-page pieces online, they will better see how their world is immersed in sociology. Because these short analyses are built on interesting events, you might want to incorporate some of them into your course. They feature local, national, and international events, as well as other matters of human interest. In them, I make the sociology explicit, so the student can see the connection between life events and sociology. These items are available free to students in the **SocLab** that Allyn and Bacon provides.

THE PHOTOS AND CAPTIONS

You can take photos for granted, as all texts have them. But in *Mastering Sociology*, I have chosen each photo myself and have written each caption. Each photo illustrates some particular sociological content, and the caption makes a photo's purpose explicit.

In addition, I have designed the captions not only to inform students but also to engage them. Many captions ask students to apply sociological content. Since the photos and captions are so integrated in the text, you can use them to promote discussion in your classroom.

THROUGH THE AUTHOR'S LENS

In personalizing this text with the goal of making sociology come alive for students, I have developed photo essays called *Through the Author's Lens*. These photo essays let your students look over my shoulder as I take them on sociological journeys—from a visit to people who live and work in a dump in Cambodia to people in the USA who are putting their lives together after a tornado devastated their neighborhood. Some of the photos I took challenge common assumptions. In the photo essay on India, for example, students will see women doing extremely hard labor on construction crews. This caused me to rethink gender, and might do the same for your students.

Some Final Remarks

You will find the pedagogy of this text sound. Its learning-centered principles are based on reinforcement. I have designed the text to help all students learn sociology, including students whose academic background is considerably less than ideal. A more advanced student who read a sample chapter said, "I wish I had had this to learn from. The units make it so clear and easy!" This was music to my ears, as I want to reach all students.

I know that having your students do well is your goal in teaching. This text is designed specifically to help you reach this goal. The principle I followed as I wrote this text is: Students can learn and do well. They just need the right materials to help them achieve.

My goal is for students, after studying a unit and taking the self-test, to say, "Yes, I can do it. I learned this. I'm going to make it in college!"

I say this from personal experience, having come from a family in which I was the first college graduate. My mother dropped out of high school in the 11th grade, while my father didn't even make it to high school, dropping out after the 7th grade. I know the self-doubts that students bring with them to college and the obstacles they face. I designed *Mastering Sociology* as a tool to help students overcome their self-doubts, a major obstacle to their success. As they learn, they will know they can succeed.

I eagerly await your reaction to using this text with your class. You can write me at the following address. I would appreciate it if you would share your experience with me. This will help me to better meet the needs of students, my continuous goal.

Jim Henslin

Jim Henslin
henslin@aol.com

I want to thank the hard-working, creative team I have had the privilege of working with at Allyn and Bacon. I especially want to thank Brita Mess, who has supported this project from the manuscript stage to the printed page; Jenn Auvil, who coordinated many aspects in the book's initial stages; Dusty Freedman, who stepped in on an unexpected basis and valiantly saw the book through its latter stages; Kate Cebic, for some photo research; and the many people behind the scenes who checked manuscript and did innumerable tasks of which I am only dimly aware. A hearty and heartfelt thanks to them all.

I also want to thank my fellow sociology instructors who were kind enough to share their reactions to the *Mastering Sociology* manuscript. It has been my privilege to follow many of their suggestions.

Reviewers of the First Edition

Karen Done, *Coahoma Community College*

Richard Ellefritz, *Oklahoma State University*

Sara Fisch, *Scottsdale Community College*

Tammie Foltz, *Des Moines Area Community College*

Patricia Gleich, *Pensacola State College*

Marta Henriksen, *Central New Mexico Community College*

Amy Holzgang, *Cerritos College*

William Kimberlin, *Lorain County Community College*

Michele Marion, *Paradise Valley Community College*

Charles Post, *Borough of Manhattan Community College-CUNY*

Mona Scott, *Mesa Community College*

Rachel Stehle, *Cuyahoga Community College*

Brooke Strahn-Koller, *Kirkwood Community College*

Connie Veldink, *Everett Community College*

Karl Wielgus, *Anoka Ramsey Community College*

I was born in a rented room in a little town on the bitterly cold Canadian border in Minnesota. My mother hadn't completed high school, and my father hadn't even made it beyond the 7th grade. From the rented room, we moved to a house, a converted garage that didn't have indoor plumbing. One of my colder memories goes back to age 11 when I froze my nose while delivering newspapers in my little northern village. I was elated at age 16 when my parents packed up the car and moved to sunny California, where I graduated from high school and junior college. During the summer following high school graduation, while working as a laborer on construction projects, I took a correspondence course in Greek from the University of California at Berkeley. Indiana was where I graduated from college. I was awarded scholarships at Washington University in St. Louis, Missouri, where I earned my master's and doctorate in sociology. After winning a competitive postdoctoral fellowship from the National Institute of Mental Health, I spent a challenging year studying how people adjust to the suicide of a family member.

My primary interests in sociology are the sociology of everyday life, deviance, and international relations. One of my main goals in sociology is to make sociological concepts and research findings down to earth. Among my books are *Sociology: A Down-to-Earth Approach* (Pearson), in its 11th edition; *Down to Earth Sociology: Introductory Readings* (Free Press), going into its fifteenth edition; and *Social Problems* (Allyn and Bacon), now in its 11th edition. I have published widely in sociology journals, including *Social Problems* and *American Journal of Sociology*. The topics range from the esoteric ethnomethodological locationalities to the everyday nitty-gritty of cabdrivers shooting midnight craps in St. Louis alleys.

While a graduate student, I taught at the University of Missouri at St. Louis. After completing my doctorate, I joined the faculty at Southern Illinois University, Edwardsville, where I am Professor Emeritus of Sociology. I've always enjoyed teaching the introductory course. What a pleasure to see students' faces light up when they first glimpse the sociological perspective and begin to see how society has become an essential part of how they view the world!

I enjoy reading (obviously), but also fishing, kayaking, and a little weight lifting. My two favorite activities are writing and traveling. I especially enjoy visiting other cultures, even living in them. This brings me face to face with behaviors and ways of thinking that challenge my perspectives, begging me to explore why they and I view the world so differently. These cultural excursions take me beyond the

Photo by Anita Henslin

standard research and make sociological principles come alive. In the photo essays in this book, I am able to share some of these experiences with you.

My mother once told me that I had "gypsy blood" in me. She was speaking figuratively, of course, but I can't seem to settle in any one spot. The "other side" keeps beckoning, and I can't get rid of this urge to explore it. Hitchhiking around northern Africa and Europe was one way that I have satisfied this desire. I recently married a woman from Latvia, an Eastern European country formerly dominated by the Soviet Union. There, I became an immigrant, certainly an eye-opening experience for me. I later gave up the immigrant status, but while in Latvia I observed how people were struggling to adjust to capitalism. I also interviewed aged political prisoners who had survived the Soviet gulag. After this, I moved to Spain, where I was able to observe how people adjust to a deteriorating economy and their reactions to the immigration of people from contrasting cultures. (Of course, for this I didn't need to leave the United States.) To better round out my cultural experiences, which I find fascinatingly enjoyable and which keep my writing down to earth, I am making plans for extended stays in India and South America. There, and wherever else my sociological odyssey may take me, I expect to do more photo essays to reflect contrasting cultures. In the meantime, I'm back in the States, where among other activities I am documenting our economic crisis and deteriorating infrastructure.

I am grateful to be able to live in such exciting social, technological, and geopolitical times—and to have access to portable broadband Internet while I pursue my sociological imagination.

CHAPTER 1
THE SOCIOLOGICAL PERSPECTIVE

Watch the **Video** in **mysoclab**

((•●—**Listen** to the **Chapter Audio** in **mysoclab**

GETTING STARTED

You are in for an exciting and eye-opening experience. Sociology offers a fascinating view of social life. The *sociological perspective* opens a window onto unfamiliar worlds—and offers a fresh look at familiar ones. In this text, you will find yourself in the midst of Nazis in Germany and warriors in South America. Sociology is broad, and your journey will even take you to a group that lives in a city dump. (If you want to jump ahead, on pages 188–189 you can see the photos I took of the people who live—and work and play—in a dump in Cambodia.) You will also find yourself looking at your own world in a different light. As you view other worlds—or your own—the sociological perspective enables you to gain a different way of looking at social life. This is what many find appealing about sociology.

Get ready for a fascinating journey. But be warned: As you observe other groups, you might end up questioning your assumptions about life. This is what happened to me when I took my introductory course in sociology as a freshman in college.

Gush Katif beach, Israel

UNIT 1.1
Seeing the Social Context

WHAT AM I SUPPOSED TO LEARN?

After you have read this unit, you should be able to

1 Explain what the sociological perspective is.

2 Understand how both history and biography are essential elements of the sociological perspective.

3 Apply the sociological perspective to your own life.

At the center of sociology is the **sociological perspective.** This simply means that to explain people's behavior, sociologists stress the social contexts in which people live. They look at how these contexts influence people's lives. Sociologists want to know how groups influence people, especially how people are influenced by their **society**—a group of people who share a culture and a territory.

 Watch the **Video**
The Basics: What is Sociology?
in **mysoclab**

To find out why people do what they do, sociologists look at **social location,** the corners in life that people occupy because of their place in a society. They want to know how such things as jobs, income, education, gender, race–ethnicity, and age affect people's ideas and behavior.

Look at the items I just mentioned: jobs, income, education, gender, race–ethnicity, and age. You can see that sociology gets personal. In a recurring feature of this text, you will be able to apply sociological ideas to yourself. Let's go to the first *Making It Personal.*

MAKING IT PERSONAL

Putting Yourself in the Sociological Perspective

Let's take a quick start at doing sociology. I don't want you to simply memorize terms. This is not what the introductory course in sociology is all about. Sociology is about people's lives—and this includes *your* life. So let's get started by applying the *sociological perspective,* which can be rather abstract to learn. Please reflect on the following:

When you were growing up, how did being identified with a group called *females* or with a group called *males* shape your ideas of who you are today? Consider how this has influenced how you feel about yourself. How has it helped to form your ideas of what you should attain in life? How is it part of the ways that you relate to other people? As you consider this, even briefly, you will start to see how your *group memberships* (social location) are vital in producing the *you* that you are. Seeing this is the beginning of the sociological perspective.

To apply the sociological perspective to these students at the University of Virginia, you would include such concepts as football game, fan, gender, and college student. What other social contexts would you add?

Let's look at this in a little more detail. Sociologist C. Wright Mills (1959), who calls the sociological perspective the sociological imagination, put it this way: *"The sociological imagination enables us to grasp the connection between history and biography."* By *history,* Mills meant that each society is located in a broad stream of events. This gives each society specific characteristics—such

sociological perspective understanding human behavior by placing it within its broader social context; also called the *sociological imagination*

society people who share a culture and a territory

social location the group memberships that people have because of their location in history and society

as its ideas about how men and women should act, what they should wear, and how they should relate to one another. By *biography,* Mills referred to our specific experiences in society, which give us our orientations to life.

In short, you don't do what you do because you inherited some internal mechanism, such as instincts. Rather, *external* influences—your experiences—become part of your attitudes, thinking, and motivation. The society in which you grow up, and your particular location in that society, lie at the center of what you do and how you think.

Let's apply this idea in *Making It Personal.*

Let's make one more point before closing this first unit, that you are influenced by two hugely different levels: a globalizing world and your own small corners in life. Your ancestors lived on isolated farms and in small towns. They grew their own food and made their own clothing. They bought only sugar, coffee, and a few other items that they couldn't produce. Beyond the borders of their small communities lay a world they perceived only dimly. What a contrast with your life. Consider the labels on your clothing (likely from Hong Kong to Italy), as well as the

many other imported products that have become part of your daily life. You are personally experiencing how the world has shrunk into a global village.

Even though you are surrounded by imports from all over the world and you can pick up a telephone or use the Internet to communicate instantly with people anywhere on the planet, you continue to occupy your own little corners of life. Like those of your ancestors, your worlds, too, are marked by differences in family background, religion, gender, race–ethnicity, and social class. In these corners, you continue to learn distinctive ways of viewing the world.

One of the beautiful—and fascinating—aspects of sociology is that it enables you to look at both parts of your current reality: being part of a global network *and* your unique experiences in your smaller corners of life. This text reflects both of these worlds, each so vital in understanding who you are. I think you will enjoy the process of self-discovery that sociology offers.

Read the **Document**
"Invitation to Sociology" by Peter L. Berger in **mysoclab**

MAKING IT PERSONAL

Society in You

The sociological perspective is so significant to this course that I want to make sure you're learning what it is. So let's apply it to your life once more.

Consider when you were just a newborn baby, a crying little thing that had just emerged from your mother. If someone had kidnapped you and brought you to the Yanomamö Indians in the jungles of South America, a year or so later when you began to talk, would your first words be in English? You know the answer.

Now extend this just a little bit. You also know that you would not think like an American. You would not grow up wanting credit cards, for example—or a car, a cell phone, and an iPad. You would take your place in Yanomamö society— perhaps as a food gatherer or a hunter—and you would not even know about the world left behind at birth. You would also grow up assuming that it is natural to want many children, not debating whether to have one, two, or three children.

Do you see just some of the influences of your society, how it has produced not just your language but also even what you want out of life? If you are thinking along with me, you can see that even your *personal, intimate* desires—such as what you expect about marriage and children—are related to society.

The shorthand term for this is *society in you.*

(If you are an immigrant or were reared in another culture, apply the same ideas to yourself. The specifics about language and certain goals in life such as number of children might differ, but the idea is exactly the same.)

Although the norms of this Yanomamo teenager in the jungles of Brazil differ from your norms, they guide her behavior the same as yours guide you.

UNIT 1.1 // TESTING MYSELF
DID I LEARN IT? ANSWERS ARE AT THE END OF THE CHAPTER

Don't skip this self-test or any that follow. These self-tests are designed to let *you* know how *you* are doing. The questions are not meant to be tricky. On the contrary, they are an essential part of helping you learn and do well in this course.

These questions are a way for you to pause and review the main points you have just read. This reinforces your learning. You will also immediately spot areas you didn't master. If you don't know an answer or if you miss a question, go back to that section and find the answer. This will help you look up any question you missed and master the material.

I think you will find that these little reviews help you learn sociology. And your instructor and I want you to do well in this course. Go through the *Testing Myself* slowly and think along with each question. I have designed them to help you learn.

1. At the heart of the sociological perspective is understanding how people
   a. are all alike under the skin
   b. can never fully understand who they really are
   c. change their minds over little things
   d. are influenced by society

2. When sociologists apply the sociological perspective, they
   a. use their own experiences to interpret what people tell them
   b. keep in mind that all people are the same under the skin
   c. look at the influences of social location
   d. find that people will give different answers if they are listening to different types of music

3. Jobs, income, education, gender, race–ethnicity, and age are all examples of what goes into the
   a. ideal way that people relate to one another
   b. sociological perspective
   c. production of the gross national product
   d. deterioration and renewal of a society

4. C. Wright Mills used this term to refer to the sociological perspective
   a. sociological imagination
   b. crafting knowledge independently of external influences
   c. historical variables
   d. life changes and life chances

5. In reference to the sociological imagination (perspective), C. Wright Mills used the word history. By this term, he meant that
   a. corrupt politics is destroying our society
   b. the schools do an inadequate job of teaching current events
   c. power differences among societies make wars inevitable
   d. each society is located in a broad stream of events that gives specific characteristics to its people

6. In reference to the sociological imagination (perspective), C. Wright Mills used the word biography. By this term, he meant that
   a. the education channel does not do adequate background research on its topics
   b. although the death of individuals is inevitable, society itself continues
   c. our specific experiences in society give us our orientations to life
   d. life is ever changing, and each person influences others

7. Sociologists view human behavior primarily as the outcome of
   a. instincts
   b. external influences
   c. internal mechanisms
   d. inherited tendencies

8. Mentioned in the text are these two levels of influence on our behavior and thinking
   a. a globalizing world and our small corners in life
   b. job insecurity and inflation
   c. education and home life
   d. communication and transportation

9. To apply the sociological perspective to myself, I would
   a. consider mental influences on my behavior and ideas
   b. look primarily to my country's history
   c. watch videos and movies
   d. consider how my experiences have influenced my behavior and ideas

Now that you have taken the first of the little quizzes that run through this book, you can see how they review the main points that you just read. *Testing Myself* really does help you learn. Again, for any questions that you missed, please go back and review the section where the answer is so you can learn that point. This prepares you for the next unit. As you continue doing this, you will master sociology.

We'll do this together, as I have kept you in mind continuously as I prepared this text. Even though I don't know you personally, and have never even met you, I know what it is like to start college and to have so many new ideas swirling around in your head. After some of the confusion wears off, you will find it to be a wondrous experience, and sociology will be an important part of it.

Let's go on to the second unit. You will see that this unit is a little longer and we cover a little more ground.

UNIT 1.2 Origins of Sociology

You are going to learn about the general historical background that produced sociology and be introduced to five early sociologists. All five are important for the origin of sociology, but three of them—Durkheim, Weber, and Marx—became so significant that students around the world still study their ideas.

Watch the **Video**
The Big Picture: What is Sociology? in
mysoclab

Tradition Versus Science

Just how did sociology begin? Even in ancient times, people asked questions about why war exists, why some people become more powerful than others, and why some are rich but others are poor. However, they often based their answers on superstition, myth, or even the position of the stars. They did not *test* their assumptions.

Science, in contrast, requires theories that can be tested by research. Measured by this standard, sociology emerged about the middle of the 1800s when social observers began to use scientific methods to test their ideas.

Sociology was born in social upheaval. The *Industrial Revolution* had just begun, and masses of people were moving to cities in search of work. This broke their ties to the land—and to a culture that had provided ready answers to the difficult questions

Sociology began with research and theorizing on broad questions about social change and what holds society together. Today's sociologists do research on almost all aspects of human behavior.

1.2

WHAT AM I SUPPOSED TO LEARN?

After you have read this unit, you should be able to

1 Summarize the origins of sociology.

2 Explain why Durkheim's research on suicide is essential to understanding sociology.

of life. The cities greeted them with horrible working conditions: low pay, long hours, and dangerous work. Families lived on the edge of starvation, and children worked alongside the adults. Life no longer looked the same, and tradition, which had provided the answers to social life, no longer could be counted on.

Explore the **Concept**
The Development of American Society in **mysoclab**

Tradition suffered further blows. With the success of the American and French revolutions, new ideas swept out the old. As the idea that people don't belong to a king and that they possess inalienable rights caught fire, many traditional Western monarchies gave way to more democratic forms of government. This stimulated new perspectives.

About this time, the **scientific method**—using objective, systematic observations to test theories—was being tried out in chemistry and physics. This approach opened many secrets that had been concealed in nature. With traditional answers falling, the next step was to apply the scientific method to questions about social life. The result was the birth of sociology.

Auguste Comte and Positivism

The bloody French Revolution had just taken place, where the crowds had cheered at the public execution of the king and queen of France. With this still fresh in his mind, Auguste Comte (1798–1857) started to wonder what holds society together. Why do we have social order instead of anarchy or chaos? he asked. And when society becomes set on a particular course, what causes it to change?

The way to answer such questions, Comte decided, was to apply the scientific method to the social world, a process known as **positivism.** Just as the scientific method had revealed the law of gravity, so, too, it would uncover the laws that

science the application of systematic methods to obtain knowledge and the knowledge obtained by those methods

scientific method the use of objective, systematic observations to test theories

positivism the application of the scientific approach to the social world

sociology the scientific study of society and human behavior

Auguste Comte (1798–1857), who is credited as the founder of sociology, began to analyze the bases of the social order. Although he stressed that the scientific method should be applied to the study of society, he did not apply it himself

underlie society. Comte called this new science **sociology**—"the study of society" (from the Greek word *logos,* "study of," and the Latin word *socius,* "companion," or "being with others"). Comte wanted this new science not only to discover social principles but also to apply them to social reform. He developed a grandiose view: Sociologists would reform the entire society, making it a better place to live.

Comte did not do what we today call research, and his conclusions have been abandoned. Nevertheless, his insistence that we must observe and classify human activities to uncover society's fundamental laws is well taken. Because he coined the term *sociology,* Comte often is credited with being the founder of sociology.

Herbert Spencer and Social Darwinism

Herbert Spencer (1820–1903), who grew up in England, is sometimes called the second founder of sociology. Spencer disagreed sharply with Comte. He said that sociologists should keep their hands off social reform: Societies are evolving, and we shouldn't interfere with them. In a natural process, societies go from a lower form to a higher form. As Spencer put it, societies change from "barbarian" to "civilized." This process takes many generations, and during this time a society's most capable and intelligent members ("the fittest") survive, while the less capable die out. These fittest members produce a more advanced society—unless misguided do-gooders get in the way and help the less fit (the lower classes) survive.

Spencer called this principle *the survival of the fittest.* Although Spencer coined this phrase, it usually is attributed to his contemporary, Charles Darwin. Where Spencer proposed that societies evolve over time as the fittest adapt to their environment, Darwin applied this idea to organisms. Because Darwin is better known, Spencer's idea is called *social Darwinism.* History is fickle, and if fame had gone the other way, we might be speaking of "biological Spencerism."

Like Comte, Spencer did not conduct scientific studies, and his ideas, too, were discarded.

Karl Marx and Class Conflict

You might be surprised to see the name Karl Marx (1818–1883) in our discussion of the origins of sociology since he is known primarily as a communist and is demonized in the United States. Sociologists include him because he left a lasting understanding of how society is put together. He said that society is made up of two social classes: the **bourgeoisie** (boo-shwa-ZEE) (the *capitalists,* who own the capital, land, factories, and machines) and the **proletariat** (the exploited workers). You can look at history in various ways, but the theme running through it all, said Marx, is **class conflict,** the conflict between these two natural enemies.

Like Comte, Marx thought that people should try to improve society. Unlike Comte, Marx's proposal for change was radical: revolution. Marx claimed that eventually, the workers would unite and break the chains that held them to the bourgeoisie. The workers' revolution would be bloody, but it would usher in a classless society, one free of exploitation. People would then work according to their abilities and receive goods and services according to their needs (Marx and Engels 1848/1967). It doesn't take too much imagination to see why the people in power in Germany weren't too pleased with these ideas. They threw Marx out of

bourgeoisie Marx's term for capitalists, those who own the means of production

proletariat Marx's term for the exploited class, the mass of workers who do not own the means of production

class conflict Marx's term for the struggle between capitalists and workers

Herbert Spencer (1820–1903), sometimes called the second founder of sociology, coined the term "survival of the fittest." Spencer thought that helping the poor was wrong, that this merely helped the "less fit" survive.

Karl Marx (1818–1883) believed that the roots of human misery lay in class conflict, the exploitation of workers by those who own the means of production. Social change, in the form of the workers overthrowing the capitalists was inevitable from Marx's perspective. Although Marx did not consider himself a sociologist, his ideas about conflicting class interests have influenced many sociologists, particularly conflict theorists.

the country, and he settled in London, where he did most of his research.

It is important to stress that Marxism is not the same as communism. Marx proposed revolution as the way for workers to gain control of society, but he did not develop the political system called *communism*. This is a later application of his ideas. Marx himself was disgusted when he heard debates about his analysis of social life. After listening to some of the positions attributed to him, he shook his head and said, "I am not a Marxist" (Dobriner 1969b:222; Gitlin 1997:89).

Emile Durkheim and Social Integration

Until the time of Emile Durkheim (1858–1917), sociology was viewed as part of history and economics. Durkheim, who grew up in France, wanted to get sociology recognized as a separate academic discipline (Coser 1977). He achieved this goal in 1887 when the University of Bordeaux awarded him the world's first academic appointment in sociology.

Durkheim's second goal was to show how social forces affect people's behavior. To accomplish this, he conducted rigorous research. One of his more interesting studies was on suicide. When Durkheim (1897/1966) compared the suicide rates of European countries, he found that each country had a different rate of suicide—and that these rates remain about the same year after year. He also found that different groups within a country have different suicide rates and that these, too, remain stable from year to year: Males are more likely than females to kill themselves, Protestants more likely than Catholics or Jews, and the unmarried more than the married. From these observations, Durkheim concluded that suicide is not what it appears—individuals here and there deciding to take their lives for personal reasons. Instead, *social factors underlie suicide,* which is why a group's rate remains fairly constant year after year.

The key social factor in suicide, Durkheim found, is **social integration,** the degree to which people are

social integration
the degree to which members of a group or a society feel united by shared values and other social bonds; also known as social cohesion

tied to their social group: *People who have weaker social ties are more likely to commit suicide.* Consider Protestants, males, and the unmarried. Why do they have higher suicide rates? The Protestant religion encourages more independent thinking and action; males are more independent than females; and the unmarried lack the ties that come with marriage. Another way of putting this is to say that members of these groups have fewer of the social ties that keep people from committing suicide. In Durkheim's term, they have less social integration.

Despite the many years that have passed since Durkheim did his research, the principle he uncovered still applies: People who are less socially integrated have higher rates of suicide. More than a century later, in our own society these same groups that Durkheim identified—Protestants, males, and the unmarried— are more likely to kill themselves.

It is important to stress the principle that was central in Durkheim's research: *Human behavior cannot be understood only in terms of the individual; we must always examine the social forces that affect people's lives.* Suicide, for example, appears to be such an intensely individual act that psychologists should study it, not sociologists. If we look at human behavior only in reference to the individual, we miss its *social* basis.

Let's apply what Durkheim said in *Making It Personal* on the next page.

Max Weber and the Protestant Ethic

Max Weber (Mahx VAY-ber) (1864–1920), a German sociologist and a contemporary of Durkheim, also became a professor in the new academic discipline of sociology. With Durkheim and Marx, Weber is one of the three most influential of all sociologists. To introduce Weber, let's consider an issue he raised that remains controversial today.

RELIGION AND THE ORIGIN OF CAPITALISM

Weber wanted to uncover the origin of capitalism, which was transforming society. His conclusion was surprising: Changes in religion brought about capitalism. Here's how it works. Roman

*The French sociologist **Emile Durkheim** (1858–1917) contributed many important concepts to sociology. His comparison of the suicide rates of several countries revealed an underlying social factor: People are more likely to commit suicide if their ties to others in their communities are weak. Durkheim's identification of the key role of social integration in social life remains central to sociology today.*

***Max Weber** (1864–1920) was another early sociologist who left a profound impression on sociology. He used crosscultural and historical materials to trace the causes of social change and to determine how social groups affect people's orientations to life.*

MAKING IT PERSONAL

Applying Durkheim

Did you know that 29,000 whites and 2,000 African Americans will commit suicide this year? Of course not. And you probably are wondering if anyone can know something like this *before* it happens. Sociologists can. How? Sociologists look at *patterns of behavior,* recurring characteristics or events.

Do you want even more specific predictions? Look at Figure 1.1. There you can see the methods by which African Americans and whites commit suicide. I'm sure you are struck by how similar they are. This indicates something far beyond the individuals who kill themselves. But there is more than

this. These patterns are so consistent that we can predict with high certainty that of the 29,000 whites about 15,500 will use guns to kill themselves. We can also predict that of the 2,000 African Americans 60 to 70 will jump to their deaths.

Isn't this amazing! Suicide—one of the most intense, personal, individualistic acts in the world is vitally influenced by social forces. These patterns—both the numbers of people who kill themselves and the ways they take their lives—recur year after year. As Durkheim would say, this indicates that suicide reflects conditions of society. But what conditions? To be frank with you, we sociologists are weak here. I can point out that the popularity and accessibility of guns are part of it, but these patterns of suicide also reflect many conditions that we don't understand. Someone is going to find these patterns so intriguing that he or she will investigate them. Could it be you? (Go back to page 7.)

FIGURE 1.1

How Americans Commit Suicide

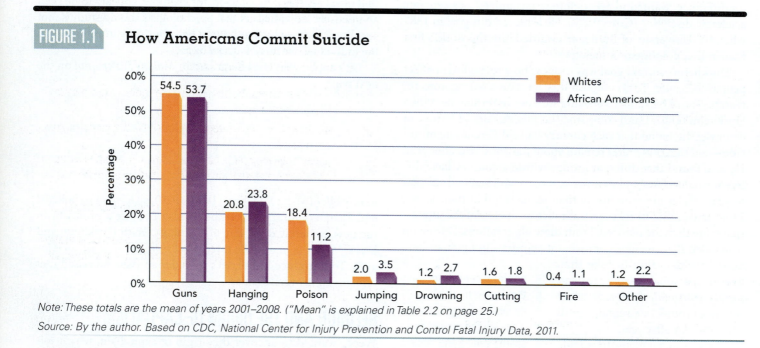

Note: These totals are the mean of years 2001–2008. ("Mean" is explained in Table 2.2 on page 25.)

Source: By the author. Based on CDC, National Center for Injury Prevention and Control Fatal Injury Data, 2011.

Catholics are taught that because they are church members they are on the road to heaven. This encourages them to hold on to traditional ways of life. Protestants, in contrast, those of the Calvinist tradition, are told that they won't know if they are saved until Judgment Day. Understandably, this teaching made them a little uncomfortable, and they started to look for "signs" that they were in God's will. What did the Calvinists conclude? That financial success is a blessing from God. It indicates that God is on their side. As you can understand, this motivated them to bring about this "sign" and receive spiritual comfort. They began to live frugal lives, saving their money, and investing it in order

to make even more. A surprising result of religious teaching, then, was the birth of capitalism.

Weber (1904/1958) called this self-denying approach to life the *Protestant ethic.* He termed the desire to invest capital in order to make more money the *spirit of capitalism.* To test his theory, Weber compared the extent of capitalism in Roman Catholic and Protestant countries. He found that capitalism was more likely to flourish in Protestant countries. Weber's conclusion that religion was the key factor in the rise of capitalism was controversial when he made it, and it continues to be debated today (Cantoni 2009).

As you probably noticed, this is a lot of material to cover in a short space. Don't be surprised if you don't know the answers to all 10 questions in this *Testing Myself*. There is no reason to expect that you will learn everything in the first reading. Now it's time to find out if there are gaps in what you learned, and then go back and fill in those gaps. You are laying a foundation here, so be thorough.

1. Sociology arose when traditional answers were no longer satisfactory. One of the background factors that upset society, stimulating the development of sociology, was the
   a. global warming of the 1700s
   b. entrance of women into the workforce
   c. Industrial Revolution
   d. war between France and Germany

2. The term scientific method refers to
   a. using objective, systematic observations to test theories
   b. applying observations of the social world to the physical world
   c. applying observations of the physical world to the social world
   d. methods to change society

3. This term refers to the process of applying the scientific method to the social world
   a. rapport
   b. rapprochement
   c. negativism
   d. positivism

4. Auguste Comte, who developed the term sociology and is associated with positivism, developed a grandiose view of sociology. He said that sociologists should
   a. analyze all societies on earth
   b. not limit their analysis to the earth, but search for extraterrestrial societies as well
   c. reform the entire society, making it a better place to live
   d. study the religious influences on people

5. Herbert Spencer developed the term the survival of the fittest. Spencer's idea that societies evolve, changing from lower to higher forms and that the less fit, primarily the poor, die as the more fit survive, is called social Darwinism. Spencer disagreed with

Comte. He said that because societies are evolving, with the fittest surviving, sociologists should
   a. do solid social research
   b. stay away from social reform
   c. be examples to others by having solid marriages
   d. encourage people to postpone marriage and get an education

6. Karl Marx, who developed the concept class conflict, said there are two social classes, and they are natural enemies. These classes are the
   a. bourgeoisie and the proletariat
   b. upper and the lower
   c. principled and the unprincipled
   d. ruly and the unruly

7. Emile Durkheim, who did research on suicide in Europe, found that Protestants, males, and the unmarried are more likely to commit suicide than are Roman Catholics, females, and the married. He said this is because they
   a. have less education
   b. are less successful economically
   c. are less integrated into society
   d. are more likely to be escapists

8. Durkheim's research on suicide revealed this basic sociological principle:
   a. People who are more integrated in society are more likely to commit suicide.
   b. Human behavior cannot be understood only in terms of the individual; we must always examine the social forces that affect people's lives.
   c. Recognizing human rights is a basic principle that helps societies advance.
   d. If human rights are trampled on, no matter how much education is stressed, a society cannot advance in ways that really count.

Max Weber's 1904 analysis of how and why Protestants started capitalism remains a matter of controversy today.

9. Max Weber wrote a book called *The Protestant Ethic and the Spirit of Capitalism*. By the term *Protestant ethic*, Weber referred to

  a. a religious orientation that denies the reality of suffering

  b. the unity of religion and science

  c. attaining more education in order to get a better job

  d. a self-denying approach to life

10. By the term *spirit of capitalism*, Weber referred to

  a. the people who developed windmills which increased production

  b. the supremacy of capitalism to socialism

  c. the desire to invest capital in order to make more money

  d. profits becoming the motivator in offering private education, including long distance learning

UNIT 1.3

Sociology in North America: Social Reform Versus Social Analysis

WHAT AM I SUPPOSED TO LEARN?

After you have read this unit, you should be able to

1 Explain how sexism and racism were part of early sociology in North America.

2 Summarize the tension in sociology between social analysis and social reform.

Let's turn to how sociology developed in North America. As we do so, we shall focus on some of the social conditions of this period and the controversy between social reform and social theory.

Sexism at the Time: Women in Early Sociology

As you may have noticed, all the sociologists we have discussed are men. In the 1800s, sex roles were rigid, with women assigned the roles of daughter, wife, and mother. In the classic German phrase, women were expected to devote themselves to the four K's: *Kirche, Küche, Kinder, und Kleider* (church, cooking, children, and clothes). Trying to break out of this mold meant risking severe disapproval.

FROM ANOTHER STUDENT

I am in my 50's and am in about my 3rd year of college and have been putting off taking Sociology because I always thought of it as learning about welfare or people on welfare! I really am enjoying your text, easily read and understood. Thank you so much for all you've opened up for me.

Kathy Stone
Ozarks Technical Community College

At this time, many people had no formal education at all, not even the first grade. For most of those who had gone to school, their learning was limited to basic reading, writing, and adding and subtracting. Higher education was rare and reserved primarily for men. Of the handful of women who were able to pursue higher education, some became prominent in early sociology. Marion Talbot, for example, was an associate editor of the *American Journal of Sociology* for thirty years, from its founding in 1895 to 1925. Some early female sociologists had an infuence that went far beyond sociology. Frances Perkins was the first woman to hold a cabinet position, serving twelve years as U.S. Secretary of Labor under President Franklin Roosevelt. Grace Abbott became chief of the U.S. government's Children's Bureau. The photo wheel on the next page portrays some of these early sociologists.

The early female sociologists were on Comte's side, viewing sociology as a way to improve society. They looked for ways to stop lynching, integrate immigrants into society, and improve the conditions of workers. As sociology developed in North America, a debate arose: Should the purpose of sociology be to reform society or to do objective research on society? Those who held the university positions—which were men—won the debate. They feared that advocating for the poor would jeopardize the reputation of sociology—and their own university positions. It was these men who wrote the history of sociology. Distancing themselves from the social reformers, they ignored the early female sociologists (Lengermann and Niebrugge 2007). Now that women have regained their voice in sociology—and have begun to rewrite its history—early female sociologists are again, as here, being acknowledged.

FIGURE 1.2   ## Photo Wheel of Women Sociologists

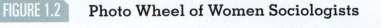

Beatrice Potter Webb
(1858–1943)
Self–educated

Alice Paul
(1885–1977)
American University
D.C.L. 1928

Marion Talbot
(1858–1948)
MIT
B.S. 1888

Anna Julia Cooper
(1858–1964)
University of Paris
Ph.D. 1925

Frances Perkins
(1880–1965)
Columbia University
M.A. 1910

Grace Abbott
(1878–1939)
University of Chicago
M.Phil. 1909

The Forgotten Sociologists

Early North American sociologists combined the roles of social analysis and social reform. As sociology became a respected academic subject and sociology departments developed across the United States, academic sociologists began to emphasize social research and theory. From this orientation, the academic sociologists wrote the history of sociology. They designated non-academic activists as social workers, not sociologists, effectively writing them out of the history of sociology. The women shown here, among the forgotten sociologists of this period, are gradually regaining a place in the history of sociology.

Florence Kelley
(1859–1932)
Northwestern University
J.D. 1895

Emily Greene Balch
(1867–1961)
Bryn Mawr College
B.A. 1889

Ida B. Wells-Barnett
(1862–1931)
Attended Fisk
University 1882–1884

Charlotte Perkins Gilman
(1860–1935)
Attended Rhode Island
School of Design 1878–1880

Photo wheel copyright 2012 © James M. Henslin

A classic example of how early female sociologists were ignored is Harriet Martineau (1802–1876). Although Martineau was from England, she is included here because she did extensive analyses of U.S. social customs. Sexism was so pervasive that when Martineau first began to analyze social life, she would hide her writing beneath her sewing when visitors arrived, for writing was "masculine" and sewing "feminine" (Gilman 1911/1971:88). Despite her acclaimed research on social life in both Great Britain and the United States, until recently Martineau was known primarily for translating Comte's ideas into English.

*Interested in social reform, **Harriet Martineau** (1802–1876) turned to sociology, where she discovered the writings of Comte. She became an advocate for the abolition of slavery, traveled widely, and wrote extensive analyses of social life.*

IF YOU WANT TO LEARN MORE about what society was like, especially gender relations, when Martineau did her research on the United States

Read more from the author: Harriet Martineau and U.S. Customs: Listening to an Early Feminist in **mysoclab**

Racism at the Time: W. E. B. Du Bois

Not only was sexism assumed to be normal during this early period of sociology, but so was racism. This made life difficult for African American professionals such as W. E. B. Du Bois (1868–1963). Du Bois, who became the first African American to earn a doctorate at Harvard, also studied at the University of Berlin, where he attended lectures by Max Weber. In 1897, Du Bois began teaching at Atlanta University, where he remained for most of his career.

It is difficult to grasp how racist society was at this time. As Du Bois passed a butcher shop in Georgia one day, he saw the fingers of a lynching victim displayed in the window (Aptheker 1990). When Du Bois went to national meetings of the American Sociological Society, restaurants and hotels would not allow him to eat or room with the white sociologists. How times have changed. Today, sociologists not only would boycott such establishments anywhere, but they would also refuse to hold meetings in that state. At that time, however, racism, like sexism, prevailed throughout society.

Du Bois did extensive research. For about twenty years, he published a book a year on black–white relations. He was also a social activist. Along with Jane Addams and others, Du Bois founded the National Association for the Advancement of Colored People (NAACP). Continuing to battle racism both as a sociologist and as a journalist, Du Bois eventually embraced revolutionary Marxism. He became such an outspoken critic of racism that for years the U.S. State Department, fearing he would criticize the United States in other countries, refused to issue him a passport (Du Bois 1968). At age 93, dismayed that so little improvement had been made in race relations, Du Bois moved to Ghana, where he died and was buried (Stark 1989).

IF YOU WANT TO LEARN MORE about what society was like, especially race relations, when DuBois was starting out

Read more from the author: W.E.B Du Bois: The Souls of Black Folk in **mysoclab**

Jane Addams and Social Reform

Although many North American sociologists combined the role of sociologist with that of social reformer, none was as successful as Jane Addams (1860–1935). Like Harriet Martineau, Addams came from a background of wealth and privilege. She attended the Women's Medical College of Philadelphia, but dropped out because of illness (Addams 1910/1981). On one of her trips to Europe, Addams was impressed with work being done to help London's poor. From then on, she worked tirelessly for social justice.

In 1889, Addams co-founded Hull-House, located in Chicago's notorious slums. Hull-House was open to people who needed refuge—to immigrants, the sick, the aged, the poor. Sociologists from the nearby University of Chicago were frequent visitors at Hull-House. Addams used her piercing insights into the social classes, especially the ways in which workers were exploited and peasant immigrants adjusted to city life, to try to bridge the gap between the powerful and the powerless. With Du Bois, Addams was one of the founders of the NAACP. She was also one of the founders of the American Civil Liberties Union. She fought for the eight-hour work day and for laws against child labor. Her efforts at social reform were so outstanding that in 1931, Addams was a co-winner of the Nobel Prize for Peace. She and Emily Greene Balch (in 1946) are the only sociologists to have won this coveted award.

***W(illiam) E(dward) B(urghardt) Du Bois**
(1868–1963) spent his lifetime studying relations between African Americans and whites. Like many early North American sociologists, Du Bois combined the role of academic sociologist with that of social reformer.*

***Jane Addams** (1860–1935), a recipient of the Nobel Prize for Peace, worked on behalf of poor immigrants. With Ellen G. Starr, she founded Hull-House, a center to help immigrants in Chicago. She was also a leader in women's rights (women's suffrage), as well as the peace movement of World War I.*

Talcott Parsons and C. Wright Mills: Theory versus Reform

Like Du Bois and Addams, many early North American sociologists worked toward the reform of society, but by the 1940s the emphasis had shifted to social theory. A major sociologist of this period, Talcott Parsons (1902–1979), developed abstract models of society that influenced a generation of sociologists. C. Wright Mills (1916–1962), who deplored Parsons' theoretical abstractions and the general dry analyses of this period, urged sociologists to get back to social reform. He said that sociologists were missing the point. Our freedom, he stated, was threatened by the coalescing interests of a group he called the *power elite*—the top leaders of business, politics, and the military. Shortly after Mills' death came the turbulent late 1960s and early 1970s. This precedent-shaking era sparked interest in social reform, making Mills' ideas popular among a new generation of sociologists.

C. Wright Mills *(1916–1962) was a controversial figure in sociology because of his analysis of the role of the power elite in U.S. society. Today, his analysis is taken for granted by many sociologists and members of the public.*

The Tension Today: Basic, Applied, and Public Sociology

BASIC SOCIOLOGY

As we have seen, two contradictory aims—analyzing society versus working toward its reform—have run through North American sociology since its founding. This tension is still with us today. Some sociologists see their proper role as doing **basic sociology,** analyzing some aspect of society, with no goal other than gaining knowledge. To this, others reply, "Knowledge for what?" They argue that gaining knowledge through research is not enough. Sociologists, they stress, need to use their expertise to help reform society, to help bring justice and better conditions to the poor and oppressed.

APPLIED SOCIOLOGY

As Figure 1.3 below shows, one attempt to go beyond basic sociology is **applied sociology,** using sociology to solve problems. Applied sociology takes us back to the roots of sociology, for as you will recall, sociologists helped to found the NAACP.

Today's applied sociologists lack the broad vision that the early sociologists had of reforming society, but their application of sociology is wide-ranging. Some work for business firms to solve problems in the workplace, while others investigate social problems such as pornography, rape, pollution, or the spread of AIDS. Sociology is even being applied to find ways to disrupt terrorist groups (Sageman 2008a, 2008b).

From *Careers in Sociology* on the next page, you can also see that a Ph.D. is helpful but not essential to be an applied sociologist.

> **basic sociology** sociological research for the purpose of making discoveries about life in human groups, not for making changes in those groups

> **applied sociology** the use of sociology to solve problems—from the micro level of classroom interaction and family relationships to the macro level of crime and pollution

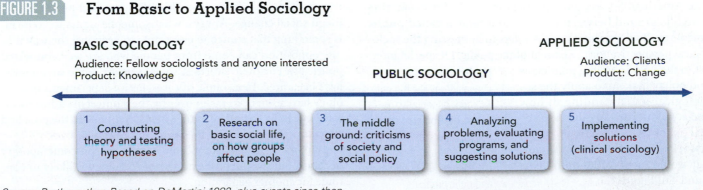

FIGURE 1.3	**From Basic to Applied Sociology**

BASIC SOCIOLOGY
Audience: Fellow sociologists and anyone interested
Product: Knowledge

PUBLIC SOCIOLOGY

APPLIED SOCIOLOGY
Audience: Clients
Product: Change

1 Constructing theory and testing hypotheses

2 Research on basic social life, on how groups affect people

3 The middle ground: criticisms of society and social policy

4 Analyzing problems, evaluating programs, and suggesting solutions

5 Implementing solutions (clinical sociology)

Source: By the author. Based on DeMartini 1982, plus events since then.

Careers in Sociology: What Applied Sociologists Do

Most sociologists teach in colleges and universities, sharing sociological knowledge with students, as your instructor is doing with you in this course. Applied sociologists, in contrast, work in a wide variety of areas—from counseling children to studying how diseases are transmitted. To give you an idea of this variety, let's look over the shoulders of four applied sociologists.

Leslie Green, who does marketing research at Vanderveer Group in Philadelphia, Pennsylvania, earned her bachelor's degree in sociology at Shippensburg University. She helps develop strategies to get doctors to prescribe particular drugs. She sets up the meetings, locates moderators for the discussion groups, and arranges payments to the physicians who participate in the research. "My training in sociology," Green says, "helps me in 'people skills.' It helps me to understand the needs of different groups, and to interact with them."

Stanley Capela, whose master's degree is from Fordham University, works as an applied sociologist at HeartShare Human Services in New York City. He evaluates how children's programs—such as ones that focus on housing, AIDS, group homes, and preschool education—actually work, compared with how they are supposed to work. He spots problems and suggests solutions. One of his assignments was to find out why it was taking so long to get children adopted, even though there was a long list of eager adoptive parents. Capela pinpointed how the paperwork got bogged down as it was routed through the system and suggested ways to improve the flow of paperwork.

Laurie Banks, who received her master's degree in sociology from Fordham University, analyzes statistics for the New York City Health Department. As she examined death certificates, she noticed that a Polish neighborhood had a high rate of stomach cancer. She alerted the Centers for Disease Control and Prevention, which conducted interviews in the neighborhood. Scientists from the CDC traced the cause to eating large amounts of sausage. In another case, Banks compared birth certificates with school records. She found that problems at birth—low birth weight, lack of prenatal care, and birth complications—were linked to low reading skills and behavior problems in school.

Daniel Knapp, who earned a doctorate from the University of Oregon, applied sociology by going to the city dump. Moved by the idea that urban wastes could be recycled and reused, he first tested this idea by scavenging in a small way—at the city dump at Berkeley, California. After starting a company called Urban Ore, Knapp (2005) did research on how to recycle urban wastes and worked to change waste disposal laws. As a founder of the recycling movement in the United States, Knapp's application of sociology continues to influence us all.

From just these few examples, you can catch a glimpse of the variety of work that applied sociologists do. Some work for corporations, some are employed by government and private agencies, and others run their own businesses. You can also see that you don't need a doctorate in order to work as an applied sociologist.

IF YOU WANT TO LEARN MORE about why the lines between basic, applied, and public sociology are not always firm, how basic sociology can morph into public sociology

Read more from the author: Unanticipated Public Sociology: Studying Job Discrimination in **mysoclab**

Watch the **Video**
Sociology on the Job:
What is Sociology? in
mysoclab

PUBLIC SOCIOLOGY

The American Sociological Association (ASA) is promoting a middle ground between research and reform called **public sociology.** By this term, the ASA refers to harnessing the sociological perspective for the benefit of the public. Of special interest to the ASA is getting politicians and policy makers to apply the sociological understanding of how society works as they develop social policy (American Sociological Association 2004). Public sociology would incorporate both items 3 and 4 of Figure 1.3.

public sociology applying sociology for the public good; especially the use of the sociological perspective (how things are related to one another) to guide politicians and policy makers

SOCIAL REFORM IS RISKY

As some sociologists have found, promoting social reform is risky, especially if they work with oppressed people to demand social change. Always, what someone wants to "reform" is something that someone else wants to keep just the way it is. The opposition can come from people who are well connected politically. For their efforts at social reform, some sociologists have been fired. In a couple of cases, entire departments of sociology have even been taken over by their university administrators for "taking sociology to the streets," siding with the poor and showing them how to use the law to improve their lives.

With roots that go back a century or more, this contemporary debate about the purpose and use of sociology is likely to continue for another generation.

UNIT 1.3 // TESTING MYSELF
DID I LEARN IT? ANSWERS ARE AT THE END OF THE CHAPTER

Again, don't let it bother you if you didn't learn everything the first time through. Just go back and review the specific areas that this *Testing Myself* shows you missed.

1. Frances Perkins was the first woman to hold a cabinet position, serving twelve years as Secretary of Labor under President Franklin Roosevelt. Perkins was mentioned as an example of
   a. the first case of affirmative action
   b. an early female sociologist whose influence went far beyond sociology
   c. tokenism
   d. how socialism began to erode the American way of life

2. In early sociology in North America, controversy arose about the purpose of sociology. The issue was whether
   a. sociologists should work to reform society or do objective research on society
   b. women should be allowed to be sociologists
   c. African Americans should be allowed to be sociologists
   d. sociologists should take the side of the poor or of the wealthy

3. In early sociology in North America, women generally took the position that the purpose of sociology was to
   a. improve family life
   b. get the poor to give birth to fewer children
   c. do objective research on society
   d. reform society

4. The men who held the university positions won the debate about the purpose of sociology. When they wrote the history of sociology, female sociologists
   a. picketed the Department of Sociology at Princeton University, the publishers of this history
   b. founded WISDOM, Women in Sociology Daring to Outdo Men
   c. were mostly written out of that history
   d. resigned en masse from colleges and universities and went into social work

5. The experiences of W. E. B. Du Bois illustrate the racism in society during the time of early sociology in North America. When Du Bois, one of the founders of the NAACP (National Association for the Advancement of Colored People) and a prolific researcher on race relations, went to national meetings of the American Sociological Society
   a. restaurants and hotels would not allow him to eat or room with the white sociologists
   b. the association refused to let him speak
   c. the U.S. State Department hid microphones in his hotel room
   d. he was so poor that he brought canned goods from home to eat in his hotel room

6. Jane Addams was a sociologist who fought for the eight-hour work day and for laws against child labor. To help immigrants, the sick, the aged, and the poor, Addams also founded an organization in the slums of Chicago called Hull-House. Her efforts at social reform were so successful that she was
   a. elected mayor of Chicago
   b. awarded a million dollar grant by the state of Illinois
   c. appointed Ambassador to Sweden
   d. a co-winner of the Nobel Prize for Peace

7. Sociologist Talcott Parsons developed abstract models of society. Sociologist C. Wright Mills said that instead of doing this, sociologists should
   a. do more research on the lives of the poor
   b. use more advanced statistical techniques to analyze research
   c. get back to social reform
   d. open up centers to help the poor, like Jane Addams did with Hull-House in Chicago

8. The tension between sociological analysis and social reform that showed up in early sociology in North America continues today. To illustrate this ongoing tension, basic, applied, and public sociology are contrasted. The term basic sociology refers to doing research on
   a. fundamentals of social life, such as learning language
   b. some aspect of society, with no goal other than gaining knowledge
   c. the medical institution in order to improve patient care
   d. schools to improve teaching and learning

9. To illustrate the continuing tension between sociological analysis and social reform, basic, applied, and public sociology are contrasted. The term applied sociology refers to
   a. using sociology to solve problems
   b. doing research on the purpose of society
   c. analyzing the basic philosophical questions of existence
   d. trying to understand why at this historical point in time capitalism has become the world's dominant economic system

10. To illustrate the continuing tension between sociological analysis and social reform, basic, applied, and public sociology are contrasted. The term public sociology refers to
   a. the study of international relations
   b. research on the fundamentals of an organization, such as boot camp in the military
   c. research on social interaction that occurs in public settings, such as parks
   d. harnessing the sociological perspective for the benefit of the public

PULLING IT ALL TOGETHER REVIEWING THE LEARNING GOALS

You have just been introduced to the sociological perspective and to the broad context that produced sociology. Congratulations on completing this chapter!

Before you close the text, however, it is time for a quick overview of what you have learned. This is one more way of "locking it all in," so review this final section slowly and keep asking yourself, "Do I understand this?" If something isn't clear, go back to the section where it was presented. As I mentioned in the previous units, it's OK not to get everything the first time. It is the same with this review. You might have forgotten some things. Now is the time to find out. Also, the end-of-chapter reviews are excellent to use before you take in-class tests.

Unit 1.1 The Sociological Perspective: Seeing the Social Context

1. Explain what the sociological perspective is.
   - The sociological perspective is understanding how people are influenced by their social location (their social experiences, the social contexts that influence them).

2. Understand how both history and biography are essential elements of the sociological perspective.
   - The broad stream of events of history gives our society its specific characteristics—such as its ideas about how men and women should act and how they should relate to one another. Within our history-shaped society, we have specific experiences, our own biography. Both give us our orientations to life.

3. Apply the sociological perspective to your own life.
   - This is unique to you: Think about how your social locations have influenced your behavior and ideas.

Watch the **Video**
The Basics: What is Sociology? in **mysoclab**

Read the **Document**
"Invitation to Sociology" by Peter L. Berger in **mysoclab**

Unit 1.2 Origins of Sociology

1. Summarize the origins of sociology.
   - Sociology developed when social change undermined traditional explanations of life. Main

figures in sociology's development are Auguste Comte, Herbert Spencer, Karl Marx, Emile Durkheim, and Max Weber. You should know their basic ideas.

2. State why Durkheim's research on suicide reveals the essence of sociology.
   - Durkheim's research revealed that each country has its own suicide rate, as do groups within a country. That these rates recur year after year indicates that suicide is more than individuals here and there deciding to kill themselves, that social conditions underlie suicide.

Watch the **Video**
The Big Picture: What is Sociology? in **mysoclab**

Explore the **Concept**
The Development of American Society in **mysoclab**

Unit 1.3 Sociology in North America: Social Reform Versus Social Analysis

1. Explain how sexism and racism were part of early sociology in North America.
   - At this time in history, sexism and racism were assumed to be a natural part of social life. For the most part, women and African Americans were pushed to the side and kept out of the mainstream of sociology.

2. Summarize the tension in sociology between social analysis and social reform.
   - The debate about sociology's purpose—to do research on social life or to reform society—was won by the men who held university positions. As they wrote the history of sociology, they ignored the contributions of the social reformers. The debate continues today.

Watch the **Video**
Sociology on the Job: What is Sociology? in **mysoclab**

UNIT 1.1 // TESTING MYSELF
DID I LEARN IT? ANSWERS

1. **d** are influenced by society

2. **c** look at the influences of social location

3. **b** sociological perspective

4. **a** sociological imagination

5. **d** each society is located in a broad stream of events that gives specific characteristics to its people

6. **c** our specific experiences in society give us our orientations to life

7. **b** external influences

8. **a** a globalizing world and our small corners in life

9. **d** consider how my experiences have influenced my behavior and ideas

UNIT 1.2 // TESTING MYSELF
DID I LEARN IT? ANSWERS

1. **c** Industrial Revolution

2. **a** using objective, systematic observations to test theories

3. **d** positivism

4. **c** reform the entire society, making it a better place to live

5. **b** stay away from social reform

6. **a** bourgeoisie and the proletariat

7. **c** are less integrated into society

8. **b** Human behavior cannot be understood only in terms of the individual; we must always examine the social forces that affect people's lives.

9. **d** a self-denying approach to life

10. **c** the desire to invest capital in order to make more money

UNIT 1.3 // TESTING MYSELF
DID I LEARN IT? ANSWERS

1. **b** an early female sociologist whose influence went far beyond sociology

2. **a** sociologists should work to reform society or do objective research on society

3. **d** reform society

4. **c** were mostly written out of that history

5. **a** restaurants and hotels would not allow him to eat or room with the white sociologists

6. **d** a co-winner of the Nobel Prize for Peace

7. **c** get back to social reform

8. **b** some aspect of society, with no goal other than gaining knowledge

9. **a.** using sociology to solve problems

10. **d** harnessing the sociological perspective for the benefit of the public

CHAPTER 2
RESEARCH AND THEORY IN SOCIOLOGY

((•— Listen to the **Chapter Audio** in **mysoclab**

GETTING STARTED

In this chapter, you will get an understanding of what sociology is. In this chapter, I'll lay the basic foundation. I'll ask—and answer—three main questions: Why do sociologists do research? How do sociologists do research? And how do sociologists interpret their research?

And on the way to these answers you'll learn a few other things, from why love weakens marriage (yes, weakens it) to research that put a graduate student's life in danger. I'll also share with you the time during my own research that I unintentionally stumbled into a strange woman's bedroom.

👁— Watch the **Video** in **mysoclab**

"Million Women Rise" march in London, England

TOGETHER WE CAN END MALE VIOLENCE AGAINST WOMEN

MILLIONWOMENRISE.COM

UNIT 2.1

Doing Research: The Need

WHAT AM I SUPPOSED TO LEARN?

After you have read this unit, you should be able to

1 Explain why common sense is not adequate to understand social life.

Throughout this text, you are going to read about what sociologists have found in their research. The shorthand term for this is "research findings." You will find some of the research findings to be eye-opening, but about some of the others you'll probably say "I already knew that." So before we get started in this unit, we ought to ask why we even need sociological research. Why isn't common sense enough?

The short answer is this. Common sense consists of assumptions about the way the world "is." These assumptions, the things that "everyone knows are true," may or may not be true. It takes research to find out.

Let's run a quick check on *your* common sense. How do you think it stacks up with research findings? Let's find out. What do you think the answers are to these five questions? Mark each as true or false.

1. More U.S. students are killed in school shootings now than ten or fifteen years ago.

2. The earnings of U.S. women have just about caught up with those of U.S. men.

3. With life so rushed and more women working for wages, today's parents spend less time with their children than parents of previous generations did.

4. A large percentage of terrorists are mentally ill.

5. Couples who lived together before marriage are usually more satisfied with their marriage than couples who did not live together before marriage.

Some of the answers probably seemed obvious to you. It is only common sense, for example, that parents are spending less time with their children today, or that terrorists are mentally ill. Now look at the answers.

1. More students were shot to death at U.S. schools in the early 1990s than now (Henslin 2013).

2. Over the years, the wage gap has narrowed, but only slightly. On average, women earn only about 72 percent of what men earn. This low figure is actually an improvement over earlier years. See Chapter 9.

3. Today's parents actually spend more time with their children (Bianchi et al. 2006). To see how this could be, see Chapter 11.

4. Extensive testing of Islamic terrorists shows that they actually tend to score more "normal" on psychological tests than most "normal" people do. As a group, they are in *better* mental health than the rest of the population. See Chapter 10.

5. The opposite is true. Couples who cohabit before marriage are more likely to divorce. To see why, see Chapter 11. (But this is changing.)

That's right. All five statements are false. Parents are spending *more* time with their children, and those people who blow themselves up turn out to have good mental health. Hard to figure. But I think you get the point. We can't depend on common sense to know what is true and what isn't. We need solid research to find out. So let's look at how sociologists do research.

Since we have common sense to interpret people and interaction, such as that depicted in this photo, why do we need sociological research?

UNIT 2.1 // TESTING MYSELF
DID I LEARN IT? ANSWERS ARE AT THE END OF THE CHAPTER

This is a very short unit. Here are just three questions.

1. This is the shorthand term for the results of sociological research
   a. research examinings
   b. research attempts
   c. research conclusions
   d. research findings

2. The reason that common sense is not enough, and why we need sociological research, is
   a. there is not enough of it to go around
   b. the genetic structures are changing
   c. common sense may or may not be true
   d. common sense is manipulated by politicians

3. Common sense consists of
   a. ideas that are foolish
   b. assumptions about the way the world "is"
   c. attempts to improve the human species
   d. research findings

UNIT 2.2

Doing Research: The Model

Sociological research methods range from interviewing people and doing participant observation to examining archives of historical data.

WHAT AM I SUPPOSED TO LEARN?

After you have read this unit, you should be able to

1 Summarize the research model and know its basic terms.

You have seen the need for social research. Now let's look at how sociologists actually do their research.

A Research Model

Figure 2.1 on the next page shows the model that sociologists follow as they do their research. Sometimes the steps shown in this model run together, and in some research not all the steps apply. In general, though, this is an accurate overview of the research process. Let's assume that you are going to do research. How would you apply these eight steps?

A lot of new terms follow, so go over these eight steps slowly.

1. *Selecting a topic.* First, what do you want to know more about? Let's suppose that you have chosen spouse abuse as your topic.

2. *Defining the problem.* Your next step is to narrow the topic. Spouse abuse is too broad; you need to focus on a specific area. For example, you may want to know why men are more likely than women to be the abusers. Or perhaps you want to know what can be done to reduce domestic violence.

3. *Reviewing the literature.* You must review the literature to find out what has been published on the problem. You don't want to waste your time rediscovering what is already known.

4. *Formulating a hypothesis.* Now you need to develop a **hypothesis,** a statement of

hypothesis a statement of how variables are expected to be related to one another, often according to predictions from a theory

The Research Model

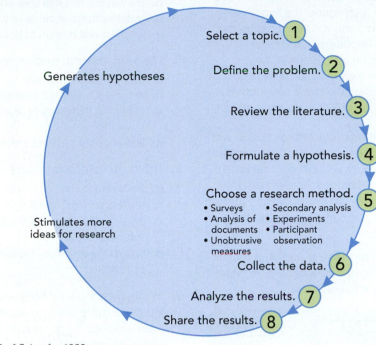

- Select a topic. ①
- Define the problem. ②
- Review the literature. ③
- Formulate a hypothesis. ④
- Choose a research method. ⑤
  - Surveys
  - Analysis of documents
  - Unobtrusive measures
  - Secondary analysis
  - Experiments
  - Participant observation
- Collect the data. ⑥
- Analyze the results. ⑦
- Share the results. ⑧

Generates hypotheses

Stimulates more ideas for research

Source: Adapted from Figure 2.2 of Schaefer 1989.

what you expect to find. Let's suppose that you came up with this hypothesis: "Men who are more socially isolated are more likely to abuse their wives than are men who are more socially integrated."

As you can see, a hypothesis predicts a relationship between **variables,** things that *vary*, or are different, from one person or situation to another. Look at your hypothesis. You have three variables: social isolation, social integration, and spouse abuse. Your hypothesis states how you think these variables are related to one another—that more isolated men are more likely to be abusers.

How are you going to measure these variables? The ways you measure them are called **operational definitions.** For this research, you would need ways to measure social isolation, social integration, and spouse abuse.

5. *Choosing a research method.* The term **research method** (also called *research design*)

variable a factor that can vary (or change) from one person or situation to another

operational definition the way in which a researcher measures a variable

research method (or research design) one of six procedures that sociologists use to collect data: surveys, secondary analysis, analysis of documents, experiments, unobtrusive measures, and participant observation

refers to how you collect your data. You have six basic research methods to choose from. I will explain these in the next unit.

6. *Collecting the data.* Here is where your operational definitions come into play. You have to make certain that they have **validity.** That is, your operational definitions must measure what they are intended to measure—social isolation, social integration, and spouse abuse—and not something else. Spouse abuse, for example, seems to be obvious. But it isn't. Not everyone agrees that a particular act is abuse. Some say it is, and some say it isn't. Which will you choose? Your operational definitions must be so precise that no one has any question about what you are measuring.

Your data must also be reliable. **Reliability** means that if other researchers use your operational definitions, their findings will be consistent with yours. If you use sloppy operational definitions, husbands who have done the same violent act might be included in some research but not in other research. This would produce erratic results. You might show a 5 percent rate of spouse abuse, for example, while another

validity the extent to which an operational definition measures what it is intended to measure

reliability the extent to which research produces consistent or dependable results

researcher concludes that it is 30 percent. This would make your research unreliable.

7. *Analyzing the results.* To analyze the data you gather, you can choose from a variety of techniques. If a hypothesis has been part of your research, you will test it during this step. Some research has no hypothesis. Sociologists who use participant observation (discussed in the next unit), for example, usually are exploring some setting, and they do not use hypotheses (the plural of hypothesis) or even specify the variables before they do the research.

8. *Sharing the results.* To wrap up your research, you will write a report to share your findings with the scientific community. You will report how you did your research, including your operational definitions. You will also show how your findings fit in with the published literature and how they support or disagree with the theories that apply to your topic.

Before you test yourself, turn to the next page and look at Table 2.1 Sociologists often summarize their findings in tables, and this example will help you learn to read them.

UNIT 2.2 // TESTING MYSELF
DID I LEARN IT? ANSWERS ARE AT THE END OF THE CHAPTER

I'm sure you'll agree that this is a lot to pack into one short unit. I don't know anyone who learns it all the first time through. Remember that you need to *study* these materials, not simply read them. Again, use this *Testing Myself* to identify your strong and weak areas and then go back and make the weak areas strong.

1. This unit presented a model of sociological research. As sociologists do research, the eight steps of this model
   a. sometimes run together
   b. are rigorously separated from one another
   c. are usually skipped
   d. are generally expanded into ten steps

2. A hypothesis is
   a. something that varies or changes from one person or situation to another
   b. an idea that turns out to be wrong
   c. a carryover variable from previous research that is being applied in a new setting
   d. a statement of what you expect to find; how you think variables are related to one another

3. A variable is something that
   a. is quite costly
   b. sociologists find as they do their research
   c. varies or changes from one person or situation to another
   d. manages to escape the notice of sociological researchers

4. The term operational definition refers to
   a. something that varies or changes from one person or situation to another
   b. the way you measure a variable
   c. variables that turn out to be wrong
   d. variables that turn out to be right

5. The term research method (or research design) refers to
   a. how you collect your data
   b. the way you measure a variable
   c. something that varies or changes from one person or situation to another
   d. how you think variables are related to one another

6. The term validity refers to
   a. being able to draw conclusions from research
   b. researchers locating the right subjects to study
   c. researchers overcoming the challenge of changing circumstances
   d. operational definitions measuring what they are intended to measure

7. In this hypothesis, "Men who are more socially isolated are more likely to abuse their wives than are men who are more socially integrated," social isolation is an example of
   a. a variable   b. an operational definition
   c. validity   d. reliability

8. Two sociologists wanted to do research on spouse abuse. They decided to interview men who had been arrested for domestic violence. "Arrested for domestic violence" is
   a. an example of validity   b. an example of reliability
   c. a research method   d. an operational definition

9. Sociologists in St. Louis decided to repeat a study on spouse abuse that other sociologists had done. They used the same operational definitions. They found similar rates of spouse abuse by age and race–ethnicity. This is an example of
   a. validity   b. a variable
   c. reliability   d. a research method

10. Three sociologists were discussing research they were going to do at a boys' school. They were concerned that their research findings would not apply to girls. In this discussion "boys" and "girls" are
    a. reliable   b. variables
    c. operational definitions   d. a hypothesis

TABLE 2.1   How to Read a Table

Tables summarize information. Because sociological findings are often presented in tables, it is important to understand how to read them. Tables contain six elements: title, headnote, headings, columns, rows, and source. When you understand how these elements fit together, you know how to read a table.

(1) The *title* states the topic. It is located at the top of the table. What is the title of the table to the right? Please determine your answer before looking at the correct answer at the bottom of this page.

(2) The *headnote* is not always included in a table. When it is present, it is located just below the title. Its purpose is to give more detailed information about how the data were collected or how data are presented in the table. What are the first eight words of the headnote for this table?

(3) The *headings* tell what kind of information is contained in the table. There are three headings in this table. What are they? In the second heading, what does *n* = 25 mean?

(4) The *columns* present information arranged vertically. What is the fourth number in the second column and the second number in the third column?

(5) The *rows* present information arranged horizontally. In the fourth row, which husbands are more likely to have less education than their wives?

(6) The *source* of a table, usually listed at the bottom, provides information on where the data in the table originated. Often, as in this instance, the information is specific enough for you to consult the original source. What is the source for this table?

Comparing Violent and Nonviolent Husbands

Based on interviews with 150 husbands and wives in a Midwestern city who were getting a divorce.

Husband's Achievement and Job Satisfaction	Violent Husbands (n = 25)	Nonviolent Husbands (n = 125)
He started but failed to complete high school or college.	44%	27%
He is very dissatisfied with his job.	44%	18%
His income is a source of constant conflict.	84%	24%
He has less education than his wife.	56%	14%
His job has less prestige than his father-in-law's.	37%	28%

Source: Modification of Table 1 in O'Brien 1975.

Some tables are much more complicated than this one, but all follow the same basic pattern. To apply these concepts to a table with more information, see Table 8.1, in the chapter on race and ethnicity.

ANSWERS

1. Comparing Violent and Nonviolent Husbands
2. Based on interviews with 150 husbands and wives
3. Husband's Achievement and Job Satisfaction, Violent Husbands, Nonviolent Husbands. The *n* is an abbreviation for number, and *n* = 25 means that 25 violent husbands were in the sample.
4. 56%, 18%
5. Violent Husbands
6. A 1975 article by O'Brien (listed in the References section of this text).

UNIT 2.3

Doing Research: The Methods

In this unit, we will look at the research methods sociologists use. We will review a lot of materials. There are even books written on each of the six methods you are going to learn about. You might want to stop at some point and take the *Testing Myself* to the point that you've read. If you want to do this, I suggest that you break after Surveys. Although this is just the first research method, it is

How do you think sociologists might research what happened to this woman? Keep this photo in mind as you study research methods.

WHAT AM I SUPPOSED TO LEARN?

After you have read this unit, you should be able to

1 Summarize the six research methods.

2 Explain how to measure "average," how to select good samples, what closed and open-ended questions are, what rapport is, and how gender can affect research.

the longest and most detailed, with a lot of terms to learn. It is important to understand these research methods, as they are foundational to sociology.

As we review the six research methods (or *research designs*) that sociologists use, we will continue our example of spouse abuse. You will see that the method you choose depends on the questions you want to answer. To analyze what you find in your research, you will want to know what "average" is. Table 2.2 on the next page discusses ways to measure average.

Surveys

Let's suppose that you want to know how many wives are abused each year. Some husbands also are abused, of course, but let's assume that you are going to focus on wives. An appropriate method for this purpose would be the **survey,** in which you ask people a series of questions. Before you begin your research, however, you must deal with some practical matters that face all researchers. Let's look at these issues.

SELECTING A SAMPLE

You might want to learn about all wives in the world, but, obviously, your resources will not let you do this. You will have to narrow your **target population,** the group that you are going to study.

Let's assume that your resources (money, assistants, time) allow you to investigate spouse abuse only on your campus. Let's also assume that your college enrollment is large, so you won't be able to survey all the married women who are enrolled. How do you solve this? You select a **sample,** individuals from among your population.

survey the collection of data by having people answer a series of questions

target population a target group to be studied

sample the individuals intended to represent the population to be studied

TABLE 2.2   Three Ways to Measure "Average"

The Mean	The Median	The Mode
The term *average seems* clear enough. As you learned in grade school, to find the average you add a group of numbers and then divide the total by the number of cases that you added. Assume that the following numbers represent men convicted of battering their wives.	To compute the second average, the *median*, first arrange the cases in order—either from the highest to the lowest or the lowest to the highest. This produces the following distribution.	The third measure of average, the *mode*, is simply the cases that occur the most often. In this instance the mode is 57, which is way off the mark.

The Mean

EXAMPLE
321
229
57
289
136
57
1,795

The total is 2,884. Divided by 7 (the number of cases), the average is 412. Sociologists call this form of average the *mean.*

The mean can be deceptive because it is strongly influenced by extreme scores, either low or high. Note that six of the seven cases are less than the mean.

Two other ways to compute averages are the median and the mode.

The Median

EXAMPLE

57	1,795
57	321
136	289
229	229
289	136
321	57
1,795	57

Then look for the middle case, the one that falls halfway between the top and the bottom. That number is 229, for three numbers are lower and three numbers are higher. When there is an even numbers of cases, the median is the halfway mark between the two middle cases.

The Mode

EXAMPLE
57
57
136
229
289
321
1,795

Because the mode is often deceptive, and only by chance comes close to either of the other two averages, sociologists seldom use it. In addition, not every distribution of cases has a mode. And if two or more numbers appear with the same frequency, you can have more than one mode.

It is important that you select the right sample, for your choice will affect your research findings. As you know, courses in sociology and courses in engineering might appeal to students who have different experiences in life. If so, surveying just one or the other would produce skewed results.

You are going to want to generalize your findings to all the married women enrolled in your college. This means that you need a sample that accurately *represents* these women on your campus. How can you get a **representative sample**?

The best way is to use a **random sample.** This does *not* mean that you stand on some campus corner and ask questions of any woman who happens to walk by. *In a random sample, everyone in your target population has the same chance of being included in the study.* In this case, every married woman enrolled in your college—whether first-year or graduate student, full- or part-time—must have the same chance of being included in your sample.

How can you get a random sample? First, you need a list of all the married women enrolled in your college. Then you assign a number to each name on the list. Using a table of random numbers, you then determine which of these women will become part of your sample. (Tables of random numbers are available in statistics books and online, or they can be generated by a computer.)

A random sample will represent your study's target population fairly—in this case, married women enrolled at your college. This means that you can generalize your findings to *all* the married women students on your campus, even if they were not included in your sample.

ASKING NEUTRAL QUESTIONS

After you have decided on your target population and sample, your next task is to make certain that your questions are neutral. Your questions must allow **respondents,** the people who answer your questions, to express their own opinions. For example, if you were to ask, "Don't you think that men who beat their wives should go to prison?" you would be tilting the answer toward agreement with a prison sentence. The *Doonesbury* cartoon on the next page illustrates a blatant example of biased questions.

TYPES OF QUESTIONS

You must also decide whether to use closed- or open-ended questions. **Closed-ended questions** are followed by a list of possible answers. Closed-ended questions would work if you want to know someone's age

representative sample a sample that represents the target population

random sample a sample in which everyone in the target population has the same chance of being included in the study

respondents people who respond to a survey, either in interviews or by self-administered questionnaires

closed-ended questions questions that are followed by a list of possible answers to be selected by the respondent

Improperly worded questions can steer respondents toward answers that are not their own, which produces invalid results.

(possible ages would be listed), but not for many other items. For example, how could you list all the opinions that people have about what should be done to spouse abusers? The answers provided for closed-ended questions can miss your respondent's opinions.

As Table 3 below illustrates, the alternative is **open-ended questions,** which let people answer in their own words. Although open-ended questions allow you to tap the full range of people's opinions, they make it difficult to compare answers. For example, how would you compare these answers to this question: "Why do you think men abuse their wives?"

"They're sick."
"The wife probably deserved it."
"I think they must have had problems with their mother."
"We ought to string them up!"

ESTABLISHING RAPPORT

You might be wondering, "Will women who have been abused really give honest answers to strangers?" If you were to walk up to women on the street and ask if their husbands have ever beaten them, there would be little reason to take your findings seriously—if you had any findings other than being shoved away. If, however, you establish **rapport** ("ruh-POUR"), a feeling of trust, with your respondents,

victims will talk about sensitive matters. A good example is rape. Each year, researchers interview a random sample of 100,000 Americans. They ask whether these individuals have been victims of burglary, robbery, and other crimes. After establishing rapport, the researchers then ask about rape—and rape victims do talk about their experiences. From this national crime victimization survey, we learn that the number of completed rapes is close to the number reported to the police—but that most attempted rapes are not reported. There are about *ten* times more attempted rapes than the total that shows up in the official statistics (*Statistical Abstract* 2012:Tables 314, 315).

Secondary Analysis

In **secondary analysis,** researchers analyze data that others have collected. For example, if you were to analyze the original data from a study of women who had been abused by their husbands, you would be doing secondary analysis.

Analysis of Documents

Documents, or written sources, include books, newspapers, bank records, immigration records, and so on. To study spouse abuse, you might examine police reports to find out how many men in your community have been arrested for abuse. You might also use court records to find out how many of those men were charged, convicted, or put on probation. If you want to learn about the social and emotional adjustment of the victims, however, these documents would tell you nothing. Other documents, though, might provide

open-ended questions questions that respondents answer in their own words

rapport (ruh-POUR) a feeling of trust between researchers and the people they are studying

secondary analysis the analysis of data that have been collected by other researchers

documents in its narrow sense, written sources that provide data; in its extended sense, archival material of any sort, including photographs, movies, videos, CDs, DVDs, and so on

TABLE 2.3	Closed- and Open-Ended Questions	

A. Closed-Ended Question	B. Open-Ended Question
Which of the following best fits your idea of what should be done to someone who has been convicted of spouse abuse? 1. Probation 2. Jail time 3. Community service 4. Counseling 5. Divorce 6. Nothing—It's a family matter	What do you think should be done to someone who has been convicted of spouse abuse?

Analyzing documents is a research skill useful not only for sociologists but also for almost everyone who goes on to higher education, a skill that can be transferred to the workplace.

those answers. For example, a crisis intervention center might have records that contain key information—but gaining access to them is almost impossible. Perhaps an unusually cooperative center might ask victims to keep diaries that you could study.

Experiments

Do you think there is a way to change a man who abuses his wife into a loving husband? No one has made this claim, but a lot of people say that abusers need therapy. Despite what people say, no one knows if therapy works. Because **experiments** are useful for determining cause and effect, let's suppose that

experiment the use of control and experimental groups and dependent and independent variables to test causation

you propose an experiment to a judge and she lets you study men who have been arrested for spouse abuse. As in Figure 2.2 below, you would divide the men randomly into two groups. This helps to ensure that their individual characteristics (attitudes, number of arrests, severity of crimes, education, race–ethnicity, age, and so on) are distributed between the groups. You then would arrange for the men in the **experimental group** to receive some form of therapy. The men in the **control group** would not get this therapy.

Your **independent variable,** something that causes another variable to change, would be therapy. Your **dependent variable,** the variable that might be changed, would be the men's behavior: whether they abuse women after they get out of jail. Unfortunately, your operational definition of the men's behavior will be sloppy: either reports from the wives or records indicating which men were rearrested for abuse. This is sloppy because some of the women will not report the abuse, and of those who do, some of the men will not be arrested. Yet it might be the best you can do.

Let's assume that you choose rearrest as your operational definition. If you find that the men who received therapy are *less* likely to be rearrested for abuse, you can conclude that therapy made the difference. If you find *no difference* in rearrest rates, you can conclude that the therapy was ineffective. And if you find that the men who received the therapy have a *higher* rearrest rate, you can conclude that the therapy backfired, that it increased abuse. This could happen. We have a severe need for scientific research on this topic.

experimental group the group of subjects in an experiment who are exposed to the independent variable

control group the subjects in an experiment who are not exposed to the independent variable

independent variable a factor that causes a change in another variable, called the dependent variable

dependent variable a factor in an experiment that is changed by an independent variable

---

FIGURE 2.2   **The Experiment**

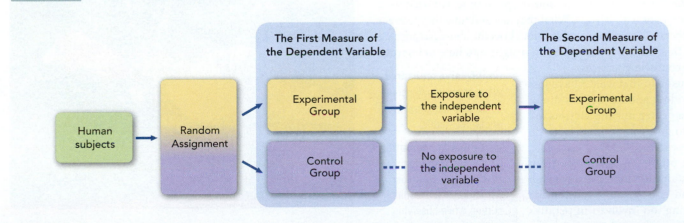

Source: By the author.

Unobtrusive Measures

Some researchers use **unobtrusive measures.** They study the behavior of people who are not aware that they are being studied. To determine whisky consumption in a town that was legally "dry," researchers counted the empty bottles in trashcans (Lee 2000). Some researchers have also gone high-tech. When you shop, cameras can follow you from the minute you enter a store to the minute you hit the checkout counter, recording each item you touch—as well as every time you pick your nose (Rosenbloom 2010; Singer 2010). Some Web coupons are embedded with bar codes that record your name and Facebook information.

As you probably have noticed, unobtrusive measures raise ethical issues of invasion of privacy. For this reason, we cannot use most unobtrusive measures to research spouse abuse. But you could analyze 911 calls. Or you could analyze articles abused women have written. Or if abused or abusing spouses held a public forum on the Internet, you could record and analyze their online conversations. Sociologists disagree on the ethics of unobtrusive research, but this is the general point of view: It is considered acceptable to secretly record people's behavior in public settings, such as a crowd, but not in private settings.

Participant Observation (Fieldwork)

If you do **participant observation** (also called **fieldwork**), you *participate* in a research setting while you *observe* what is happening in that setting. Obviously, this method does not mean that you would sit around and watch someone being abused. But if you want to learn how abuse affects the victims' hopes and goals, their dating patterns, or their marriages, you could use participant observation.

> **Read** the **Document**
> "The Promise and Pitfalls of Going Into the Field" by Patricia A. Adler and Peter Adler in **mysoclab**

For example, if your campus has a crisis intervention center, with permission of the director of the center and the victims, you might be able to observe the counseling sessions. If the rapport is really good, you might even be able to spend time with victims at their homes or with friends. What they say and how they interact with others will help you to understand how the abuse has affected them. This, in turn, could give you insight into how to improve college counseling services.

I must add that what I have just said is ideal, and neither the director of a center nor the victims are likely to give you permission to do such research.

You might be able to see from this example that this research method can ignite the dilemma of getting too involved in people's lives. If you "spend time with the victims at their homes or with their

unobtrusive measures ways of observing people so they do not know they are being studied

participant observation (or fieldwork) research in which the researcher participates in a research setting while observing what is happening in that setting

friends," would it be too emotionally draining for you? Would you even get involved in activities that bother you? For a report on fascinating participant observation in which the researcher had to deal with these dilemmas—and which could have cost him his life—read the Gang Leader for a Day box.

Gender in Sociological Research

One of the issues that comes up in social research, is gender—and for good reason. Gender is so significant in social life and the topic of spouse abuse is so sensitive that you might be wondering if a man could interview women who have been beaten by a man. Could he even do participant observation of them? Technically, the answer is yes. But because the women have been victimized by men, they might be less likely to share their experiences and feelings with men. If so, women would be better suited to conduct this research and more likely to achieve valid results. The supposition that these victims will be more open with women than with men, however, is just that—a supposition. Research alone will verify or refute this assumption.

Gender issues can pop up in unexpected ways in sociological research. I vividly recall an incident in San Francisco.

> *The streets were getting dark, and I was still looking for homeless people. When I saw someone lying down, curled up in a doorway, I approached the individual. As I got close, I began my opening research line, "Hi, I'm Dr. Henslin from … ." The individual began to scream and started to thrash wildly. Startled by this sudden, high-pitched scream and by the rapid movements, I quickly backed away. When I later analyzed what had happened, I concluded that I had intruded into a woman's bedroom.*

This incident also holds another lesson. Researchers do their best, but they make mistakes. Sometimes these mistakes are minor, and even humorous. The woman sleeping in the doorway wasn't frightened. It was only just getting dark, and there were many people on the street. She was just assertively marking her territory and letting me know in no uncertain terms that I was an intruder. If we make a mistake in research, we pick up and go on.

To do research on these people, what research method do you think would be best to use?

GANG LEADER FOR A DAY: ADVENTURES OF A ROGUE SOCIOLOGIST

Next to the University of Chicago is an area of poverty so dangerous that the professors warn students to avoid it. One of the graduate students in sociology, Sudhir Venkatesh, the son of immigrants from India, decided to ignore the warning.

With clipboard in hand, Sudhir entered "the projects." Ignoring the glares of the young men standing around, he went into the lobby of a high-rise. Seeing a gaping hole where the elevator was supposed to be, he decided to climb the stairs, where he was almost overpowered by the smell of urine. After climbing five flights, Sudhir came upon some young men shooting craps in a dark hallway. One of them jumped up, grabbed Sudhir's clipboard, and demanded to know what he was doing there.

Sudhir blurted, "I'm a student at the university, doing a survey, and I'm looking for some families to interview."

One man took out a knife and began to twirl it. Another pulled out a gun, pointed it at Sudhir's head, and said, "I'll take him."

Then came a series of rapid-fire questions that Sudhir couldn't answer. He had no idea what they meant: "You flip right or left? Five or six? You run with the Kings, right?"

Grabbing Sudhir's bag, two of the men searched it. They could find only questionnaires, pen and paper, and a few sociology books. The man with the gun then told Sudhir to go ahead and ask him a question.

Sweating despite the cold, Sudhir read the first question on his survey, "How does it feel to be black and poor?" Then he read the multiple-choice answers: "Very bad, somewhat bad, neither bad nor good, somewhat good, very good."

As you might surmise, the man's answer was too obscenity-laden to be printed here.

As the men deliberated Sudhir's fate ("If he's here and he don't get back, you know they're going to come looking for him"), a powerfully built man with a few glittery gold teeth and a sizable diamond earring appeared. The man, known as J.T., who, it turned out, directed the drug trade in the building, asked what was going on. When the younger men mentioned the questionnaire, J.T. turned to Sudhir and said to ask him a question.

Amidst an eerie silence, Sudhir asked, "How does it feel to be black and poor?"

Sudhir Venkatesh, who now teaches at Columbia University, New York City.

"I'm not black," came the reply.

"Well, then, how does it feel to be African American and poor?"

"I'm not African American either. I'm a nigger."

Sudhir was left speechless. Despite his naïveté, he knew better than to ask, "How does it feel to be a nigger and poor?"

As Sudhir stood with his mouth agape, J.T. added, "Niggers are the ones who live in this building. African Americans live in the suburbs. African Americans wear ties to work. Niggers can't find no work."

Not exactly the best start to a research project.

But this weird and frightening beginning turned into several years of fascinating research. Over time, J.T. guided Sudhir into a world that few outsiders ever see. Not only did Sudhir get to know drug dealers, crackheads, squatters, prostitutes, and pimps, but he also was present at beatings by drug crews, drive-by shootings done by rival gangs, and armed robberies by the police.

How Sudhir got out of his predicament in the stairwell, his immersion into a threatening underworld—the daily life for many people in "the projects"—and his moral dilemma at witnessing so many crimes are part of his fascinating experience in doing participant observation of the Black Kings.

Sudhir, who was reared in a middle-class suburb in California, even took over this Chicago gang for a day. This is one reason that he calls himself a rogue sociologist—the decisions he made that day were serious violations of law, felonies that could bring years in prison. There are other reasons, too: During the research, he kicked a man in the stomach, and he was present as the gang planned drive-by shootings.

Sudhir eventually completed his Ph.D., and he now teaches at Columbia University.

Based on Venkatesh 2008.

UNIT 2.3 // TESTING MYSELF
DID I LEARN IT? ANSWERS ARE AT THE END OF THE CHAPTER

As you noticed, this is a highly compact unit. After identifying your weak areas in this *Testing Myself*, you might want to read the entire unit again and retake this *Testing Myself*. This will help you learn these basic materials.

1. This research method consists of asking a series of questions
   a. unobtrusive measures   **b.** secondary analysis
   c. participant observation   **d.** survey

2. If you do a survey, the group you study is called your
   a. study group   **b.** research group
   c. target population   **d.** experimental group

3. In, Mythville, Tennessee, a town of 35,000 people, you are going to do research on the attitudes of grade school children toward male and female action figures. Since you can't interview all grade school children, you need a smaller number from this target group. This smaller number is called your
   a. secondary group   **b.** sample
   c. random group   **d.** survey group

4. You want to do research on drug use by students at your college For everyone in your target population to have the same chance of being included in your research, you need a
   a. primary sample   **b.** secondary sample
   c. survey sample   **d.** random sample

5. For your research on drug use to be successful, it is essential that you develop rapport with the students. Rapport refers to
   a. feelings of trust between researcher and respondent
   b. emotional support that a respondent gives a researcher
   c. emotional support that a researcher gives a respondent
   d. unanticipated changes that occur during the research process that affect your research findings

6. If you were to analyze the data other researchers had gathered on drug use, you would be doing
   a. an experiment   **b.** an unobtrusive measure
   c. participant observation   **d.** secondary analysis

7. You are going to conduct an experiment to find factors that cause violence to increase or decrease. You test your subjects and use techniques to divide them randomly into two groups. You have one group watch a movie that contains scenes of violence. You then test all the subjects again. The group that watched the movie is called the
   a. control group   **b.** experimental group
   c. trial group   **d.** enhanced learning group

8. In the experiment you are conducting on violence (question 7), the group that did not watch the movie is called the
   a. control group   **b.** experimental group
   c. fallback group   **d.** reserve group

9. You find that a library has a chest of diaries and bank records of immigrants from Latvia. You then analyze these records to learn about the ways that immigrants adjust to American life. You did this kind of research:
   a. analysis of documents   **b.** secondary materials
   c. participant observation   **d.** closed-ended sources

10. You decide to do research on softball players. To do this research, you join a softball team. You are doing this type of research
    a. participant observation   **b.** survey
    c. rapport building   **d.** secondary analysis

FROM ANOTHER STUDENT

I just want you to know that I scored a 95% on my first Sociology exam. Being out of school for thirty years and learning so well is a great feeling.

Happy Trails,
Ella Lipchik
Community College of Allegheny County

UNIT 2.4

Why Research Needs Theory: A Very Brief Introduction

After you have read this unit, you should be able to

1 Explain why research needs theory.

2 Explain why you are a theorist.

Why does research need theory? Because without theory, research findings are simply a collection of "facts." There must be a way to tie research findings together, and this is where theory comes in.

Don't let the word *theory* scare you. It might surprise you, but you yourself are already a theorist. That is, you "do theory" all the time. Theory is a way to interpret something by fitting it into a "framework of ideas." This "framework of ideas" connects items and lets you see how they are related to one another. For example, if you enter a class for the first time, you will immediately start to think about what your fellow students are like and what your teacher is like. You will fit what you see going on in the classroom into your "framework of ideas"—what you already know about people and about classroom behavior. "Students do certain things because …" "Teachers act a little differently. They do certain things because …" "So I expect these particular things to happen."

This doesn't mean that you are right. Something might be different in this case. But you are using a framework of ideas to interpret what you see. You are "doing theory," and you do this regularly, as part of your everyday life.

Sociologists do the same thing. Their theory is on a higher or more abstract level than the example I just gave, but the principle is the same. A **theory** is a statement about how some parts of the world fit together and how they work. It is an explanation of how two or more "facts" are related to one another.

Sociologists have developed three main "frameworks of ideas" that they use to interpret research findings. Each of these theories—symbolic interactionism, functional analysis, and conflict theory—is like a lens through which we can view social life. We will examine the main elements of each theory. But instead of leaving things hanging, we will apply each theory to the U.S. divorce rate, to see why it is so high.

theory a statement about how some parts of the world fit together, how two or more facts, conditions, or variables are related to one another

> **Watch** the **Video** The Basics: Sociological Theory and Research in **mysoclab**

UNIT 2.4 // TESTING MYSELF
DID I LEARN IT? ANSWERS ARE AT THE END OF THE CHAPTER

1. "I myself use theory in everyday life." This statement means that as a part of my everyday life, I regularly fit my experiences into the way I have of thinking about life. "The way I have of thinking about life" is called my
   a. relational universe
   b. framework of ideas
   c. objective reality
   d. systemic reality

2. Without theory, research findings are
   a. haphazard
   b. not proven
   c. not true
   d. a collection of facts

3. A theory
   a. applies ideas learned in one setting to another setting
   b. consists of biased assumptions
   c. ties research findings together
   d. is fine for some purposes, especially ideas, but when it comes to practical matters it seldom works

4. A framework of ideas that connects items is one definition of
   a. the scientific method
   b. theory
   c. research methods
   d. operational definitions

5. A definition of theory is
   a. a statement about how some parts of the world fit together and how they work
   b. the transcripts of recorded interviews
   c. biased assumptions
   d. research in action

6. Here is another definition of theory:
   a. assumptions of the best research method to apply to a research problem
   b. research findings
   c. the transfer of ideas of the way things work to the actual testing of those ideas
   d. an explanation of how two or more "facts" are related to one another

UNIT 2.5

Theoretical Perspectives: Symbolic Interactionism

The central idea of **symbolic interactionism** is that *symbols*—things to which we attach meaning—are the key to understanding how we view the world and communicate with one another. This perspective was brought to sociology by Charles Horton Cooley (1864–1929), William I. Thomas (1863–1947), and George Herbert Mead (1863–1931). I would like to introduce this theory in a slightly different way. Take a look at *Making It Personal*.

symbolic interactionism a theoretical perspective in which society is viewed as composed of symbols that people use to establish meaning, develop their views of the world, and communicate with one another

MAKING IT PERSONAL

Symbols in Your Everyday Life

Without symbols, your social life would be so limited that it would be unlike anything you know. It would be so different that—and this is going to sound really strange—without symbols you would have no aunts or uncles or brothers and sisters. I know this may sound unbelievable, but follow along with me. It is symbols that define your relationships. There would still be reproduction, but no symbols to tell you how you are related to whom. You would not know to whom you owe respect and obligation, or from whom you can expect privileges—two elements that lie at the essence of your relationships.

I know this is vague. What does it mean to say that symbols tell you how you are related to others and how you should act toward them? I think this example is going to get the point across.

After you have read this unit, you should be able to

1 Summarize symbolic interactionism.

2 Use symbolic interactionism to explain why the U.S. divorce rate is high.

Suppose that you have fallen head over heels in love. Finally, after what seems forever, it is the night before your wedding. As you contemplate tomorrow's bliss, your mother comes to you in tears. Sobbing, she tells you that she had a child before she married your father, a child that she gave up for adoption. Breaking down, she says that she has just discovered that the person you are going to marry is this child.

What that person means to you (the symbol) will change overnight! And I'm sure you can see that your behavior will change, too!

The symbols "boyfriend" and "brother"—or "girlfriend" and "sister"—are certainly different from one another. And each symbol points to remarkably different behavior.

Are you catching a glimpse of how your relationships depend on symbols?

Now let's take this a step further. Not only do relationships depend on symbols, but so does society itself. Without symbols, we could not coordinate our actions with those of others. We could not make plans for a future day, time, and place. Unable to specify times, materials, sizes, or goals, we could not build bridges and highways. Without symbols, we would have no movies or music, no hospitals, no government, no religion. The class you are taking could not exist—nor could this text. On the positive side, there would be no war.

Why do symbolic interactionists say that symbols are the essence of social life? Like this couple in India who just married, what symbols do you use to communicate meaning?

FIGURE 2.3 U.S. Marriage, U.S. Divorce

Source: By the author. Based on Statistical Abstract of the United States 1998:Table 92 and 2011:Tables 78, 129; earlier editions for earlier years. The broken lines indicate the author's estimates.

Applying Symbolic Interactionism

Look at Figure 2.3, which shows U.S. marriages and divorces over time. Let's see how symbolic interactionists would use changing symbols to explain this figure. For background, you should understand that marriage used to be a *lifelong commitment*. A hundred years ago (and less) getting divorced was viewed as immoral, a flagrant disregard for public opinion, and the abandonment of adult responsibilities. Let's see what changed.

THE MEANING OF MARRIAGE

In 1933, sociologist William Ogburn reported that young people were placing more emphasis on the personality of their potential mates. Just a dozen years later, in 1945, sociologists Ernest Burgess and Harvey Locke noted that couples were expecting more affection, understanding, and compatibility in marriage. In addition, fewer and fewer people were viewing marriage as a lifelong commitment based on duty and obligation, which had been the traditional view. As marriage came to be viewed as an arrangement based on attraction and feelings, it became one that could be broken when feelings changed.

THE MEANING OF DIVORCE

As divorce became more common, its meaning changed. Rather than being a symbol of failure and sin, divorce came to indicate freedom and new beginnings. Removing the stigma from divorce shattered a strong barrier that had prevented husbands and wives from breaking up.

THE MEANING OF PARENTHOOD

Parents used to have little responsibility for their children beyond providing food, clothing, shelter, and moral guidance. And they needed to do this for only a short time, because children began to contribute to the support of the family early in life. Among many people, parenthood is still like this. In Colombia, for example, children of the poor often are expected to support themselves by the age of 8 or 10. In our society, however, we assume that children are vulnerable beings who must depend on their parents for financial and emotional support for many years—often until they are well into their 20s. The greater responsibilities that we now assign to parenthood place heavy burdens on today's couples and, with them, more strain on marriage.

THE MEANING OF LOVE

And we can't overlook the love symbol. As surprising as it may sound, to have love as the main reason for marrying weakens marriage. In some depth of our being, we expect "true love" to deliver constant emotional highs—or at least "heartfelt understanding" from our spouse. This expectation sets people up for crushed hopes, as dissatisfactions in marriage are inevitable. When problems arise, spouses tend to blame one another for failing to deliver the expected satisfaction.

IN SUM: Symbolic interactionists look at how changing ideas (or symbols) of marriage, divorce, parenthood, and love put pressure on married couples. No single change is *the* cause of our

divorce rate, but, taken together, these changes provide a push toward divorce. And the more common divorce has become, the more acceptable it has become.

UNIT 2.5 // TESTING MYSELF
DID I LEARN IT? ANSWERS ARE AT THE END OF THE CHAPTER

1. The definition of symbol is
   a. an object in our social world that has personal meaning
   b. an object in our natural world that has personal meaning
   c. an object in our natural world that has social meaning
   d. something to which we attach meaning and use to communicate with one another

2. The central idea of symbolic interactionism is that
   a. human interaction contains hidden meanings that researchers must discover
   b. few people understand the secret nature of human interaction
   c. symbols—things to which we attach meaning—are the key to understanding how we view the world and communicate with one another
   d. there is a natural meaning to objects, called symbols, that sociologists study

3. This statement, "Without symbols we would have no aunts or uncles, employers or teachers—or even brothers and sisters," sounds like an exaggeration. To illustrate what this statement means, and how symbols underlie our orientation and actions, an example of a couple who was going to get married was used. This example contrasts these terms
   a. natural parents versus adopted parents
   b. boyfriend and girlfriend versus brother and sister
   c. natural children versus adopted children
   d. teacher and student versus boss and employee

4. A hundred years or so ago, divorce was considered
   a. immoral
   b. the best way out of a bad marriage
   c. a course of action open only for women
   d. illegal during the first five years of marriage

5. In 1933, sociologist William Ogburn reported that young people were placing more emphasis on the personality of their potential mates. Then in 1945,

sociologists Ernest Burgess and Harvey Locke noted that couples were expecting more affection, understanding, and compatibility in marriage. The implication of these changes for divorce is that
   a. divorce decreased at that time because more affection and understanding led to husbands and wives being more compatible
   b. marriage was more easily broken as it became more of an agreement based on attraction and feelings, rather than a commitment based on duty and obligation
   c. divorce became more common as understanding and compatibility decreased
   d. divorce declined as people's personalities improved

6. It may sound strange, but to have love as the main reason for marrying
   a. makes the Hollywood depictions of romance more accurate than most people think
   b. makes marriage about the same as a college education
   c. weakens marriage
   d. contributes to the emotional instability of teenagers

7. Symbolic interactionists stress that symbols give meaning to what people do and provide direction to their lives. Changing symbols also underlie the high U.S. divorce rate. Changing ideas of parenthood contributed to the high divorce rate by
   a. requiring that parents give allowances to their children
   b. increasing the responsibilities of parents, placing more stress on couples
   c. making it almost impossible to give birth at home
   d. instituting a tracking system through government agencies

8. Symbolic interactionists stress that changing ideas of love contributed to the high divorce rate by
   a. replacing duty and obligation as the basis for marriage with feelings, which are changeable
   b. making people confront uncomfortable "self-messages"
   c. bringing unrealistic images to teenagers, who seek self-fulfillment in another person rather than in personal growth and accomplishments
   d. placing a greater emphasis on material wealth

9. Symbolic interactionists stress that changing ideas of divorce contributed to the high divorce rate by
   a. removing the need to be married in order to survive in the new economic order
   b. placing greater responsibility on parents for taking care of their children
   c. encouraging couples to look for love "in all the wrong places"
   d. removing many of the negative meanings that had been attached to divorce

10. The bottom line regarding symbolic interactionism and our high divorce rate is that
    a. changes in one part of society affect other parts of society
    b. none of us is safe in marriage
    c. marriage, like the rest of society, is held together by symbols, which changed and led to an increase in divorce
    d. the customs of one generation are not the customs of another generation

UNIT 2.6

Theoretical Perspectives: Functional Analysis

WHAT AM I SUPPOSED TO LEARN?

After you have read this unit, you should be able to

1 Summarize functional analysis.

2 Use functional analysis to explain why the U.S. divorce rate increased.

The central idea of **functional analysis** is that society is a whole unit, made up of interrelated parts that work together. Functional analysis (also known as *functionalism* and *structural functionalism*) is rooted in the origins of sociology. Auguste Comte and Herbert Spencer viewed society as a kind of living organism. Just as a person or animal has organs that function together, they wrote, so does society. And like an organism, if society is to function smoothly, its parts must work together in harmony.

Emile Durkheim also viewed society as being composed of many parts, each with its own function. When the parts of society fulfill their functions, society is in a

functional analysis a theoretical perspective in which society is viewed as composed of various parts. Each part has a function that, when fulfilled, contributes to society's equilibrium; also known as *functionalism* and *structural functionalism*

"normal" state. If the parts do not fulfill their functions, society is in an "abnormal" or "pathological" state. To understand society, then, functionalists say that we need to analyze both *structure* (how the parts of a society fit together to make the whole) and *function* (what each part does, how it contributes to society).

Robert Merton and Functionalism

Robert Merton (1910–2003) dropped the organic analogy, but he kept the image of society as a whole that is composed of parts that work together. Merton used the term *functions* to refer to the beneficial consequences of people's actions, the things that people do that help keep a group (society, social system) going. These acts can be anything, such as parents going to work and supporting their children. In contrast, *dysfunctions* are the harmful consequences of people's actions. They undermine a system, reducing the capacity of its parts to work well together. As Merton put it, they reduce the group's equilibrium.

Functions can be either manifest or latent. If an action is *intended* to help some part of a system, it is a *manifest function*. For example, suppose that our nation's birth rate drops so low that the population begins to shrink. Congress grows alarmed and offers a $10,000 bonus for every child born to a married couple. As you can see, the intention, or manifest function, of the bonus is to increase childbearing within the family unit. But there are also *latent functions* of people's actions. That is, they can have *unintended* consequences that help some part of a system. Let's suppose that the bonus works. As the birth rate jumps, so does the sale of diapers and baby furniture. Because the benefits to these businesses were not the intended consequences, they are latent functions of the bonus.

Human actions can also hurt a system, of course. Because such consequences usually are unintended, Merton called them *latent dysfunctions*. Let's assume that the government fails to specify a "stopping point" with regard to its bonus system. To collect more bonuses, some people keep on having children. The more children they have, however, the more they need the next bonus to survive. Large families become common, and poverty increases. Welfare is reinstated, taxes jump, and the nation erupts in protest. Because these results were not intended and because they harmed the social system, they would be latent dysfunctions of the bonus program.

IN SUM: Society is a functioning unit, with each part related to the whole. When we study a part of society, we need to see how it is related to the larger unit. We do this by looking for its functions and dysfunctions. Functional analysis can be applied to any social group, whether it is an entire society, a college, or even a group as small as a family.

Applying Functional Analysis

Now let's apply functional analysis to explain the high U.S. divorce rate. Functionalists stress that industrialization weakened the traditional functions of the family. Before industrialization, the family formed an economic team. On the farm, where most people lived, each family member had jobs or "chores" to do. The wife was in charge not only of household tasks but also of collecting eggs, milking cows, churning butter, and raising small animals, such as chickens. She also did the cooking, baking, canning, sewing, darning, washing, and cleaning. The daughters helped her. The husband was responsible for caring for large animals, such as horses and cattle, for planting and harvesting, and for maintaining buildings and tools. The sons helped him.

This certainly doesn't sound like life today! But what does it have to do with divorce? These many functions of the husband, wife, and children united them into a strong social unit. Simply put, the husband and wife depended on each other for survival—and there weren't many alternatives.

Many other functions also bound family members to one another: educating the children, teaching them religion, providing

From the functionalist perspective, why is the divorce rate lower in agricultural societies?

home-based recreation, and caring for the sick and elderly. To further see how sharply family functions have changed, look at this example from the 1800s:

> *When Phil became sick, Ann, his wife, cooked for him, fed him, changed the bed linens, bathed him, read to him from the Bible, and gave him his medicine. (She did this in addition to doing the housework and taking care of their six children.) Phil was also surrounded by the children, who shouldered some of his chores while he was sick. When Phil died, the male relatives made the casket while Ann, her sisters, and mother washed and dressed the body. Phil was "laid out" in the front parlor (the formal living room), where friends, neighbors, and relatives paid their last respects. From there, friends moved his body to the church for the final message and then to the grave they themselves had dug.*

Perhaps this example, something I experienced in a deep way, will also help.

> *In Spain, where the divorce rate is low and where the family still has more functions that tie them together than do most families in the United States, a dying person is sent home from the hospital so he or she can die surrounded by family members. I had made friends with Severino, who ran a restaurant with his wife and two sons. They worked together daily seven days a week. Severino came down with brain cancer, and after futile surgery, the hospital sent him home to die. During these last few days, he was surrounded constantly by family and friends who expressed their love and concern. When his body started to shut down, and he lost consciousness during the two days before his death, his two sons would lie on the bed next to him, hugging him, crying, and telling him how much they loved him.*

IN SUM: When the family loses functions, it becomes more fragile, making an increase in divorce inevitable. The changes in economic production from family to office and factory illustrate how the family has lost functions. No longer is making a living a cooperative, home-based activity, where husband and wife depend on one another for their interlocking contributions to this mutual endeavor. Instead, husbands and wives today earn individual paychecks and increasingly function as separate components in an impersonal, multinational, and even global system. The fewer functions that family members share, the fewer are their "ties that bind"—and these ties are what help husbands and wives get through the problems they inevitably experience.

UNIT 2.6 // TESTING MYSELF
DID I LEARN IT? ANSWERS ARE AT THE END OF THE CHAPTER

1. The central idea of functional analysis is that
   a. if the people who are in control of society functioned better, society would be better
   b. we need to work to improve the functioning of society
   c. criminals should be rehabilitated so they do not interfere with the smooth functioning of society
   d. society is a whole unit, made up of interrelated parts that work together

2. Emile Durkheim said that when the parts of society fulfill their functions, society is in a "normal" state. If they do not fulfill their functions, society
   a. needs to change
   b. can last after its parts stop functioning, but for only about 20 years or so
   c. is in an "abnormal" or "pathological" state
   d. becomes like a wild animal that looks for victims

3. To understand society, functionalists say that we need to look at both structure and function. By structure, they are referring to
   a. how children learn to become adults who contribute to the well-being of society
   b. how the parts of a society fit together to make the whole
   c. how the government looks out for the welfare of its citizens
   d. what each part of society does

4. To understand society, functionalists say that we need to look at both structure and function. By function, they mean
   a. what each part does, how it contributes to society
   b. what the government does to help the poor
   c. that we need to learn ways to make our groups more functional, so they contribute to the well-being of society
   d. how the parts of a society fit together to make the whole

5. Suppose that the Federal Reserve Board raises interest rates in order to reduce inflation, and it works. The reduction of inflation is
   a. a manifest function
   b. a latent function
   c. a secret means to help the power elite and Wall Street financiers
   d. an example of how the government is trying to take over the affairs of citizens

6. Suppose that the Federal Reserve Board raises interest rates in order to reduce inflation. It works, and inflation drops. With the higher interest rates, more of the elderly receive higher income from their investments, and more of them leave welfare. The reduced welfare among the elderly is
   a. a manifest function
   b. an interference by the government in the normal working of a free market economy
   c. a latent function
   d. a latent dysfunction

7. Suppose that the Federal Reserve Board raises interest rates in order to reduce inflation. It works, and inflation drops. But because of the higher interest rates fewer people can buy houses, and the housing market collapses. The collapse of the housing market is
   a. about what you can expect when the Federal Reserve Board puts its hands on things
   b. part of an economic system gone bad
   c. a manifest function
   d. a latent dysfunction

8. To apply functional analysis to explain the high U.S. divorce rate, functionalists would stress that industrialization and urbanization
   a. were developments whose roots go far back in history
   b. weakened the traditional functions of the family
   c. were connected to the rise of the power of central governments, which connect many parts of society into a whole
   d. are new to the social scene, have brought many negative consequences, and are changing as society develops more effective means for regulating itself

9. To apply functional analysis to explain the high U.S. divorce rate, functionalists would stress that
   a. the traditional functions that held couples together have been weakened
   b. marriage isn't what it used to be
   c. the love symbol weakened marriage by placing emphasis on self-fulfillment
   d. this was just temporary and marriage is now getting stronger

10. The bottom line regarding functionalism and our high divorce rate is that
    a. changes in one part of society affect other parts of society
    b. none of us is safe in marriage
    c. when the family loses functions, it becomes more fragile, increasing the divorce rate
    d. the customs of one generation are not the customs of another generation

UNIT 2.7

Theoretical Perspectives: Conflict Theory

WHAT AM I SUPPOSED TO LEARN?

After you have read this unit, you should be able to

1 Summarize conflict theory.

2 Use conflict theory to explain why the U.S. divorce rate is high.

Conflict theory provides a third perspective on social life. Unlike the functionalists, who view society as a harmonious whole with its parts working together, conflict theorists stress that society is composed of groups that are competing with one another for scarce resources. The surface might show alliances or cooperation, but scratch that surface and you will find a struggle for power.

Karl Marx and Conflict Theory

Karl Marx, the founder of conflict theory, witnessed the Industrial Revolution that transformed Europe. He saw that peasants who left the land to work in cities earned barely enough to eat. Things were so bad that the average worker died at age 30, the average wealthy person at age 50 (Edgerton 1992:87). Shocked by this suffering and exploitation, Marx began to analyze society and history. As he did so, he developed **conflict theory.** He concluded that the key to human history is *class conflict*. In each society, some small group controls the means of production and exploits those who are not in control. In industrialized societies, the struggle is between the *bourgeoisie,* the small group of capitalists who own the means to produce wealth, and the *proletariat,* the mass of workers who are exploited by the bourgeoisie. The

> **conflict theory** a theoretical perspective in which society is viewed as composed of groups that are competing for scarce resources

capitalists (owners) control the legal and political system: If the workers rebel, the capitalists call on the power of the state to subdue them.

 Explore the **Concept** Income Inequality in **mysoclab**

When Marx made his observations, capitalism was in its infancy and workers were at the mercy of their employers. Workers had none of what many workers take for granted today—minimum wage, eight-hour days, coffee breaks, five-day work weeks, paid vacations and holidays, medical benefits, sick leave, unemployment compensation, Social Security, and, for union workers, the right to strike. Marx's analysis reminds us that these benefits came not from generous hearts, but by workers forcing concessions from their employers.

Conflict Theory Today

Today's sociologists extend conflict theory beyond the relationship of capitalists and workers. They examine how opposing interests are part of every layer of society—whether that is a small group, an organization, a community, or the entire society. For example, when police, teachers, and parents try to enforce conformity, this creates resentment and resistance. It is the same when a teenager tries to "change the rules" to gain more independence, or when a wife or husband wants more say in the family decisions. Throughout society, then, there is a constant struggle to determine who has authority or influence and how far that dominance goes (Turner 1978; Leeson 2006; Piven 2008).

Sociologist Lewis Coser (1913–2003) pointed out that conflict is most likely to develop among people who are in close relationships. These people have worked out ways to distribute power and privilege, responsibilities and rewards. Any change in this arrangement can lead to hurt feelings, resentment, and conflict. Even in intimate relationships, then, people are in a constant balancing act, with conflict lying uneasily just beneath the surface.

Feminists and Conflict Theory

Just as Marx examined conflict between capitalists and workers, many feminists analyze conflict between men and women. Their primary focus is the historical, contemporary, and global

From a conflict perspective, what is likely happening here?

inequalities of men and women—and how the traditional dominance by men can be overcome to bring about equality of the sexes. Feminists are not united by the conflict perspective, however. They tackle a variety of topics and use whatever theory applies.

Applying Conflict Theory

To explain why the U.S. divorce rate is high, conflict theorists focus on how men's and women's relationships have changed. For millennia, men dominated women, and women had few alternatives other than to accept their exploitation. As industrialization transformed the world, it brought women the ability to meet their basic survival needs without being dependent on a husband. This new ability gave them the power to refuse to bear burdens that earlier generations accepted as inevitable. The result is that today's women are likely to dissolve a marriage that becomes intolerable—or even just unsatisfactory.

IN SUM: The dominance of men over women was once considered natural and right. As women gained education and earnings, they first questioned and then rejected this assumption. As wives strove for more power and grew less inclined to put up with relationships that they defined as unfair, the divorce rate increased. From the conflict perspective, then, the high divorce rate in the United States does not mean that marriage has weakened, but, rather, that women are making headway in their historical struggle with men.

UNIT 2.7 // TESTING MYSELF
DID I LEARN IT? ANSWERS ARE AT THE END OF THE CHAPTER

1. The essence of conflict theory is that
   a. the symbols given us by society lie at the root of our thoughts and relationships
   b. none of us is really free
   c. the groups of society work together in a harmonious whole
   d. society is composed of groups that are competing with one another for scarce resources

2. As developed by Karl Marx, in classic conflict theory the key to human history is
   a. ever changing
   b. class conflict
   c. education
   d. the ideas that the proletariat develop as they struggle for justice

3. The classic focus of conflict theory is on class conflict. This is conflict between the bourgeoisie and the proletariat. The proletariat are the
   a. students who study sociology and social change
   b. top leaders—military, political, and business
   c. workers who are exploited by the bourgeoisie
   d. students who advocate for social change

4. The classic focus of conflict theory is on class conflict. This is conflict between the bourgeoisie and the proletariat. The bourgeoisie are
   a. those who are demanding social change
   b. the small group of capitalists who own the means to produce wealth
   c. the downtrodden of society, the poor, the unemployed, and the homeless
   d. the women who not only have entered traditional male occupations but also have become leaders in these fields

5. Today's sociologists extend conflict theory beyond the relationship of capitalists and workers. They examine how
   a. opposing interests run throughout society—whether that is a small group, an organization, a community, or the entire society
   b. people from the bottom layers of society who make it to the top make peace with the conditions they previously viewed as negative
   c. society changes, bringing one group after another into different positions
   d. societies are born, go through a vigorous youthful period, reach a plateau of power and energy (called the stage of maturity), and then slowly decline

6. Today's sociologists extend conflict theory beyond the relationship of capitalists and workers. They examine how
   a. the educational system is divided into layers of prominence
   b. college degrees are a ticket to high-paying jobs
   c. rapid communications through satellite connections are changing school and the workplace
   d. there is a constant struggle throughout society to determine who has authority or influence and how far that dominance goes

7. The primary focus of feminists who use conflict theory is the
   a. changes in the educational system and its impact on the work world of women
   b. changes in political leadership and the division of political privileges
   c. historical, contemporary, and global inequalities of men and women—and how the traditional dominance by men can be overcome to bring about equality of the sexes
   d. way that men have given up leadership roles

8. To explain why the U.S. divorce rate is high, conflict theorists focus on
   a. the changing role of religion in today's society
   b. how men's and women's relationships have changed

c. how women, having secured voting rights in 1920, used their new power to challenge the traditional role of men in the family

d. international relations, especially changes in global stratification

9. From the conflict perspective, our country's high divorce rate
   a. indicates that women are making headway in their historical struggle with men

b. is a sign that society is deteriorating

c. indicates that the social institutions need to work together to strengthen families

d. is just a temporary situation, and in about 10 years the divorce rate should decline

---

UNIT 2.8
Putting the Perspectives Together: Macro and Micro

WHAT AM I SUPPOSED TO LEARN?

After you have read this unit, you should be able to

1 Explain why we need all three theoretical perspectives.

2 Summarize macro and micro approaches in sociology and associate these levels with the theoretical perspectives.

Congratulations on getting through this second chapter! Or I should say almost through. It is time to wrap this chapter up and in this very short, final unit introduce you to a couple more ideas.

Which Theory Is the Right One?

Which of these theoretical perspectives is the *right* one? As you have seen, each produces a contrasting picture of divorce. The pictures that emerge are quite different from the commonsense understanding that two people are simply "incompatible." *Because each theory focuses on different features of social life, each produces a distinct interpretation. Consequently, we need to use all three theoretical lenses to analyze human behavior. By combining the contributions of each, we gain a more comprehensive picture of social life.*

Levels of Analysis: Macro and Micro

Watch the **Video** The Big Picture: Sociological Theory and Research in **mysoclab**

A major difference among the three theoretical perspectives is their level of analysis. Functionalists and conflict theorists focus on the **macro-level;** that is, they examine large-scale patterns of society, such as unemployment. In contrast, symbolic interactionists usually focus on the **micro-level,** on **social interaction**—what people do when they are in one another's presence. These levels are summarized in Table 2.4.

To make this distinction between micro and macro levels clearer, let me mention the research I did of the homeless. I used participant observation, staying in homeless shelters in a dozen different cities in the United States. There I ate with the men, observed them, and interviewed them. Because my theoretical perspective was symbolic interactionism, I focused on the *micro* level. I analyzed what homeless people did when they were in shelters and on the streets. I paid attention to what they said, as well as to their **nonverbal interaction,** how they used gestures and space. I was struck by how silent it was at meals. While hundreds of men ate together in the homeless shelters, they sat there silently, each engrossed in his own problems. Unlike college students who would be talking animatedly with one another, these men had nothing to look forward to—and little to talk about. No one wanted to listen to someone talk about collecting cans or begging.

This micro level, however, would not interest functionalists and conflict theorists. They would not be interested in how the men chip in to buy a bottle of wine and how they share that bottle. Instead, functionalists and conflict theorists would focus on the *macro* level. They would look at how major changes in society have produced homelessness. Functionalists would stress how unskilled jobs have dried up, reducing the need for these men's labor. They would also stress that millions of jobs have been transferred to workers overseas. They might also focus on how the family has changed, that because divorce is high and families are smaller many people who can't find

macro-level large scale patterns of society

micro-level small scale patterns of society

social interaction what people do when they are in each other's presence

nonverbal interaction communication without words—through gestures, use of space, silence, and so on

TABLE 2.4 **Three Theoretical Perspectives in Sociology**

Theoretical Perspective	Usual Level of Analysis	Focus of Analysis	Key Terms	Applying the Perspective to the U.S. Divorce Rate
Symbolic Interactionism	Microsociological: examines small-scale patterns of social interaction	Face-to-face interaction, how people use symbols to create social life	Symbols Interaction Meanings Definitions	Industrialization and urbanization changed marital roles and led to a redefinition of love, marriage, children, and divorce.
Functional Analysis (also called functionalism and structural functionalism)	Macrosociological: examines large-scale patterns of society	Relationships among the parts of society; how these parts are functional (have beneficial consequences) or dysfunctional (have negative consequences)	Structure Functions (manifest and latent) Dysfunctions Equilibrium	As social change erodes the traditional functions of the family, family ties weaken, and the divorce rate increases.
Conflict Theory	Macrosociological: examines large-scale patterns of society	The struggle for scarce resources by groups in a society; how the elites use their power to control the weaker groups	Inequality Power Conflict Competition Exploitation	When men control economic life, the divorce rate is low because women find few alternatives to a bad marriage. The high divorce rate reflects a shift in the balance of power between men and women.

work don't have a family to fall back on. For their part, conflict theorists would stress the struggle between social classes. They would be interested in how international elites make decisions about global production and trade, and how these decisions affect the local job market and homelessness. They would also want to know about the power behind the scenes, how the elite use it to their own advantage.

Each theoretical perspective is like a spotlight shined onto a dark area. Each illuminates part of that area through its specific framework for interpreting social life. Each produces remarkably contrasting pictures of the world. Part of the enjoyment of sociology is seeing the different pictures that emerge as we look at social life through these theoretical lenses.

As we explore what sociologists do, you will read about research on the macro level, from racism and sexism to the globalization of capitalism. You will also read about research at the micro level of face-to-face interaction—talking, touching, and gestures. This beautiful variety in sociology—and the contrast of going from the larger picture to the smaller picture and back again—is part of the reason that sociology holds such fascination for me. I hope that you also will find this variety appealing.

What different "pictures" of this scene emerge if you apply each of the theoretical perspectives to this event? Which is the right one?

◉ **Watch** the **Video**
Sociology on the Job: Sociological Theory and Research in **mysoclab**

UNIT 2.8 // TESTING MYSELF
DID I LEARN IT? ANSWERS ARE AT THE END OF THE CHAPTER

1. None of the three theoretical perspectives is the *right* one. Rather, we need to use all three because
   a. we cannot take sides in sociology
   b. to use just one of the perspectives would offend the other theorists
   c. there are just too many to choose from

d. each theory, focusing on specific features of social life, produces a distinct interpretation; by combining the contributions of each, we gain a more comprehensive picture of social life

2. The term macro level refers to
   a. how societies change
   b. the economic conflict between power elites that threatens world peace
   c. large-scale social patterns, such as unemployment, economic conflict, and international relations
   d. how businesspeople seek a "niche" in the market, where they can establish sales for their products

3. The term micro level refers to
   a. changes in voting patterns in national elections
   b. small-scale social patterns, such as what people say to one another
   c. how inventions have changed entire societies.
   d. changes in the unemployment rate

4. The term nonverbal interaction refers to
   a. the ways people use space, the looks on their faces as they talk, and how they gesture
   b. actions of the government that are not put into words

c. the unstated goals of classroom teachers
d. two people kissing (yes, but one of the other answers is more complete)

5. A sociologist is doing research on the struggle between social classes. This sociologist is probably a
   a. graduate student   b. symbolic interactionist
   c. functionalist   d. conflict theorist

6. A sociologist is doing research on how people make bids at auctions, how they signal their intentions. She is also studying the ways that auctioneers pick up and respond to these signals. This sociologist is probably a
   a. graduate student   b. symbolic interactionist
   c. functionalist   d. conflict theorist

7. A sociologist is doing research on how changes in the economy are leading to different types of work and how this is having an impact on contributions to charitable organizations. This sociologist is probably a
   a. graduate student   b. symbolic interactionist
   c. functionalist   d. conflict theorist

✓ ●─[**Study** and **Review** in **mysoclab**

PULLING IT ALL TOGETHER REVIEWING THE LEARNING GOALS

In this broad, sweeping review of research methods and theory, we've covered a tremendous amount of ground. Good for you for completing this chapter!

Again, before you close the text, take a quick overview of what you have read. Remember that this is not an actual test; rather, it is a way to review and lock in what you have learned. As you review this final section, be sure to keep asking yourself, "Do I understand this?" And if something isn't clear, go back to the section where it was presented. As I have stressed, it really is OK not to get everything the first time.

If you have learned most everything up to this point, you are doing well.

Unit 2.1   Doing Research: The Need

1. Explain why common sense is not adequate to understand social life.
   ● We need social research because common sense is based on limited, untested experiences and can be wrong.

Unit 2.2   Doing Research: The Model

1. Summarize the research model and know its basic terms.
   ● The eight steps of research are selecting a topic, defining the problem, reviewing the literature, formulating a hypothesis, choosing a research method, collecting the data, analyzing the findings, and sharing the findings. The basic terms are *hypothesis*, *variable*, *operational definition*, *research method*, *validity*, and *reliability*.

Unit 2.3   Doing Research: The Methods

1. Summarize the six research methods.
   ● The six basic research methods are surveys, secondary analysis, analysis of documents, experiments, unobtrusive measures, and participant observation. The outline of each is sketched in the text.

2. State how to measure "average," how to select good samples, what closed- and open-ended questions are, what rapport is, and how gender can affect research.

Three ways to measure average are mean, median, and mode. In the best sample, a random sample, everyone in the target population has an equal chance of being part of the sample. Closed-ended questions have specific answers to choose from. In open-ended questions respondents reply in their own words. Rapport is trust between researcher and those being researched. People being studied can react to the sex of the researcher.

> **Read** the **Document**
> "The Promise and Pitfalls of Going Into the Field" by Patricia A. Adler and Peter Adler in **mysoclab**

Unit 2.4 Why Research Needs Theory: A Very Brief Introduction

1. Explain why research needs theory.

- Without theory, research findings are simply a collection of loose, unorganized facts. Theory is a way of tying research findings together. Theory is used to interpret research findings.

2. Explain why you are a theorist.

- You "do theory" all the time. As a regular part of your life, you interpret things that happen to you—and things you see or that people tell you. Your world is not a buzzing mass of confusing, disconnected items. You use "frameworks of thought," or categories, to interpret events. By doing this, you are using theory. Your "theories," though they help you get through everyday life, are inconsistent, biased, and not rigorously tested.

> **Watch** the **Video** The Basics: Sociological Theory and Research in **mysoclab**

Unit 2.5 Theoretical Perspectives: Symbolic Interactionism

1. Summarize symbolic interactionism.

- The central idea of symbolic interactionism is that symbols—things to which we attach meaning—are the key to understanding how we view the world and communicate with one another.

2. Use symbolic interactionism to explain why the U.S. divorce rate is high.

- The symbols that made marriage long-lasting were duty and life-long commitment. Marriage was weakened when love and emotional fulfillment became the reasons for marriage, since these are of a changing nature. The change in the meaning of parenting (more obligations for a longer time) and divorce (losing much of its negative meaning) also undermined marriage.

Unit 2.6 Theoretical Perspectives: Functional Analysis

1. Summarize functional analysis.

- The central idea of functional analysis is that society is a whole unit, made up of interrelated parts that work together. Like an organism, if society is to function smoothly, its parts must work together in harmony. To understand society, we need to analyze both structure (how the parts of a society fit together to make the whole) and function (what each part does, how it contributes to society). To do this, we can analyze functions and dysfunctions (manifest and latent).

2. Use functional analysis to explain why the U.S. divorce rate increased.

- As industrialization moved production away from the family, it weakened ties that had held husbands and wives together.

Unit 2.7 Theoretical Perspectives: Conflict Theory

1. Summarize conflict theory.

- Society is composed of groups that are competing with one another for scarce resources. This competition, or class conflict, between the bourgeoisie (capitalists) and the proletariat (workers) is the key to human history. Today's conflict theorists extend the analysis of conflict to other groups in society.

2. Use conflict theory to explain why the U.S. divorce rate is high.

- Marriage has been a place of conflict for women and men for millennia, with men traditionally dominant and women dependent on men. The high divorce rate indicates that women are exercising their growing independence, less willing to put up with the dominance of men.

> **Explore** the **Concept**
> Income Inequality in **mysoclab**

Unit 2.8 Putting the Perspectives Together: Macro and Micro

1. State why we need all three theoretical perspectives.

- Because each theoretical perspective focuses on specific features of social life, each produces a distinct interpretation. Combining the contributions of each yields a more comprehensive picture of social life.

2. Summarize macro and micro approaches in sociology and associate these levels with the theoretical perspectives.

- The macro approach focuses on larger-scale aspects of society, such as unemployment. The micro approach focuses on small-scale social patterns, on social interaction. Symbolic interactionists are likely to follow the micro approach. Functionalists and conflict theorists are likely to focus on macro aspects of society.

◉ Watch the Video The Big Picture: Sociological Theory and Research in **mysoclab**

◉ Watch the Video Sociology on the Job: Sociological Theory and Research in **mysoclab**

UNIT 2.1 // TESTING MYSELF
DID I LEARN IT? ANSWERS

1. **d** research findings

UNIT 2.2 // TESTING MYSELF
DID I LEARN IT? ANSWERS

1. **a** sometimes run together

2. **d** a statement of what you expect to find; how you think variables are related to one another

3. **c** varies or changes from one person or situation to another

4. **b** the way you measure a variable

UNIT 2.3 // TESTING MYSELF
DID I LEARN IT? ANSWERS

1. **d** survey

2. **c** target population

3. **b** sample

4. **d** random sample

UNIT 2.4 // TESTING MYSELF
DID I LEARN IT? ANSWERS

1. **b** framework of ideas

2. **d** a collection of facts

3. **c** ties research findings together

UNIT 2.5 // TESTING MYSELF
DID I LEARN IT? ANSWERS

1. **d** something to which we attach meaning and use to communicate with one another

2. **c** common sense may or may not be true

3. **b** assumptions about the way the world "is"

5. **a** how you collect your data

6. **d** operational definitions measuring what they are intended to measure

7. **a** a variable

8. **d** an operational definition

9. **c** reliability

10. **b** variables

5. **a** feelings of trust between researcher and respondent

6. **d** secondary analysis

7. **b** experimental group

8. **a** control group

9. **a** analysis of documents

10. **a** participant observation

4. **b** theory

5. **a** a statement about how some parts of the world fit together and how they work

6. **d** an explanation of how two or more "facts" are related to one another

2. **c** symbols—things to which we attach meaning—are the key to understanding how we view the world and communicate with one another

3. **b** boyfriend and girlfriend versus brother and sister

4. **a** immoral

5. **b** marriage was more easily broken as it became more of an agreement based on attraction and feelings, rather than a commitment based on duty and obligation

6 **c.** weakens marriage

7 **b.** increasing the responsibilities of parents, placing more stress on couples

8 **a** replacing duty and obligation as the basis for marriage with feelings, which are changeable

9 **d** removing many of the negative meanings that had been attached to divorce

10 **c** marriage, like the rest of society, is held together by symbols, which changed and led to an increase in divorce

UNIT 2.6 // TESTING MYSELF
DID I LEARN IT? ANSWERS

1. **d** society is a whole unit, made up of interrelated parts that work together

2. **c** is in an "abnormal" or "pathological" state

3. **b** how the parts of a society fit together to make the whole

4. **a** what each part does, how it contributes to society

5. **a** a manifest function

6. **c** a latent function

7. **d** a latent dysfunction

8. **b** weakened the traditional functions of the family

9. **a** the traditional functions that held couples together have been weakened

10. **c** when the family loses functions, it becomes more fragile, increasing the divorce rate

UNIT 2.7 // TESTING MYSELF
DID I LEARN IT? ANSWERS

1. **d** society is composed of groups that are competing with one another for scarce resources

2. **b** class conflict

3. **c** workers who are exploited by the bourgeoisie

4. **b** the small group of capitalists who own the means to produce wealth

5. **a** opposing interests run throughout every layer of society—whether that is a small group, an organization, a community, or the entire society

6. **d** there is a constant struggle throughout society to determine who has authority or influence and how far that dominance goes

7. **c** historical, contemporary, and global inequalities of men and women—and how the traditional dominance by men can be overcome to bring about equality of the sexes

8. **b** how men's and women's relationships have changed

9. **a** indicates that women are making headway in their historical struggle with men

3. **b** small-scale social patterns, such as what people say to one another

4. **a** the ways people use space, the looks on their faces as they talk, and how they gesture

5. **d** conflict theorist

6. **b** symbolic interactionist

7. **c** functionalist

UNIT 2.8 // TESTING MYSELF
DID I LEARN IT? ANSWERS

1. **d** each theory, focusing on specific features of social life, produces a distinct interpretation; by combining the contributions of each, we gain a more comprehensive picture of social life

2. **c** large-scale social patterns, such as unemployment, economic conflict, and international relations

CHAPTER 3
CULTURE

◉ **Watch** the **Video** in **mysoclab**

((•━ **Listen** to the **Chapter Audio** in **mysoclab**

GETTING STARTED

What do you think about bullfighting? Do you think it is a brutal example of animal cruelty? I can't say for sure, of course, but this is probably your attitude—if you were reared in the United States. But this is not the attitude of most people in Spain, where bullfighting is celebrated as a majestic art, a heroic confrontation between a man who withstands the fury of an enraged bull—who usually, but not always, wins.

Why such a wide gulf in attitudes? There is a one-word answer for it: *culture*. And this is what we are going to look at in this chapter. You are going to see how culture has shaped *your* ideas about the world. And what an extensive shaping it is, forming not simply your desire for an education but also reaching right into your heartfelt convictions and even your world of private thoughts.

I think you are going to enjoy this little excursion.

Hong Kong, China

UNIT 3.1

What Is Culture?

WHAT AM I SUPPOSED TO LEARN?

After you have read this unit, you should be able to

1 State what culture is.

2 Explain the difference between material culture and nonmaterial culture.

Let's begin by asking what culture is. The concept is sometimes easier to grasp by description than by definition, so I'd like to tell you what happened when I was in Morocco.

I had been hitchhiking through Europe during a summer vacation. I was on a limited budget—actually a skimpy one—but I was finding free places to sleep, eating yogurt, cheese, and grapes, and thoroughly enjoying myself. These days of freedom took me to Morocco.

I found the sights that greeted me exotic—not unlike the scenes in Casablanca or Raiders of the Lost Ark. The men, women, and even the children really did wear those white robes that reached down to their feet. What was especially striking was that the women were almost totally covered. Despite the heat, they wore not only full-length gowns but also head coverings that reached down over their foreheads with veils that covered their faces from the nose down. You could see nothing but their eyes.

As the only blue-eyed, blond, 6-foot-plus person around, and the only one who was wearing jeans and a pullover shirt, in a world of white-robed short people, I stood out like a creature from another planet. Everyone stared. No matter where I went, they stared. I tried staring back, but this had no effect. It was so different from home, where, if you caught someone staring at you, that person would look embarrassed and immediately glance away.

And standing in line? Not like home either. Buying a ticket for a bus or train meant pushing and shoving toward the ticket man (always a man—no women were visible in any public position), who took the money from whichever outstretched hand he decided on.

And germs? That notion didn't seem to exist here either. Flies swarmed over the food in the restaurants and the unwrapped loaves of bread in the stores. Shopkeepers would considerately shoo the flies off before handing me a loaf. They also offered home delivery. I watched a bread vendor deliver a loaf to a woman who was standing on a second-floor balcony. She first threw her money to the man, and he then threw the unwrapped bread up to her. Unfortunately, his throw was off. The bread bounced off the wrought-iron balcony railing and landed in the street, which was filled with people, wandering dogs, and the ever-present urinating and defecating donkeys. The vendor simply picked up the unwrapped loaf and threw it again. This certainly wasn't his day, for he missed again. But he made it on his third attempt. The woman smiled as she turned back into her apartment, apparently to prepare the noon meal for her family.

The culture I was surrounded with in northern Africa was strikingly different from mine, and intriguing to me as a sociologist. I could see it in people's clothing, jewelry, and hairstyles. I heard it in people's speech. I saw it in their gestures. When I talked to people, culture became apparent in their beliefs about relationships and what is valuable in life. All of these characteristics indicate **culture**—a group's language, beliefs, values, norms, behaviors, and even material objects that they pass from one generation to the next.

culture The language, beliefs, values, norms, behaviors, and even material objects that characterize a group and are passed from one generation to the next

Photo taken in Morocco.

The **material culture**—such things as jewelry, art, buildings, weapons, machines, and even eating utensils, makeup, hairstyles, and clothing—provided a sharp contrast to what I was used to seeing. There is nothing inherently "natural" about material culture. That is, it is no more natural (or unnatural) to wear gowns on the street than it is to wear jeans.

I also found myself immersed in an unfamiliar **nonmaterial culture,** that is, a group's ways of *thinking* (its beliefs, values, and other assumptions about the world) and *doing* (its common patterns of behavior, including language, gestures, and other forms of interaction). North African assumptions that it is acceptable to stare at others in public and to push people aside to buy tickets are examples of nonmaterial culture. So are U.S. assumptions that it is wrong to do either of these things. Like material culture, neither custom is "right." People simply become comfortable with the customs they learn during childhood, and—as when I visited northern Africa—uncomfortable when their assumptions about life are challenged.

material culture The material objects that distinguish a group of people, such as their art, buildings, weapons, utensils, machines, hairstyles, clothing, and jewelry

nonmaterial culture A group's ways of thinking (including its beliefs, values, and other assumptions about the world) and doing (its common patterns of behavior, including language and other forms of interaction); also called *symbolic culture*

UNIT 3.1 // TESTING MYSELF
DID I LEARN IT? ANSWERS ARE AT THE END OF THE CHAPTER

1. The term culture refers to a group's
   a. language, beliefs, and values
   b. values, norms, and behaviors
   c. material objects
   d. language, beliefs, values, norms, behaviors, and material objects

2. Culture is divided into these two types
   a. language and material objects
   b. language and values
   c. material and nonmaterial
   d. beliefs and behaviors that are passed from one generation to the next

3. "The woman I met from India was wearing the most beautiful gold necklace I've ever seen."

The person who said this was referring to the woman's
   a. nonmaterial culture
   b. material culture
   c. wealth
   d. beauty

4. The guest speaker, a man from Turkmenistan, described to the audience one of the country's ethnic group's belief in reincarnation. He told a funny story about a guy who came back as a woman. The speaker was referring to the group's
   a. nonmaterial culture
   b. material culture
   c. transformational culture
   d. negative view of the world

5. If a group's norms permit staring at others in public, the staring is an example of
   a. material culture
   b. transformative culture
   c. nonmaterial culture
   d. rudeness

6. One group has the custom of lining up one behind the other to buy tickets, and another group has the custom of pushing to get to the ticket seller. Both the lining up and the pushing are examples of
   a. material culture
   b. ways to buy tickets
   c. nonmaterial culture
   d. normative exchange

7. Maria spent her junior year in France, where she attended a girls' high school. She was intrigued by the way her classmates used makeup. When she returned home, her friends remarked about how different she looked. The makeup is an example of
   a. material culture
   b. transformational culture
   c. nonmaterial culture
   d. informational culture

8. I assume that you had no problem with question number 7. Now think this one through carefully. When Maria spent her junior year in France, she learned a different way to use makeup. The makeup is an example of material culture, but ideas about who should and should not use makeup and what makeup is appropriate for what occasions are an example of
   a. material culture
   b. transformational culture
   c. nonmaterial culture
   d. informational culture

UNIT 3.2 Culture and Orientations to Life

"Culture within Us": Our Lens for Viewing Life

Explore the **Concept**
The Asian American Population of the United States – The Diversity of Cultures in **mysoclab**

Anthropologist Ralph Linton (1936) once said, "The last thing a fish would ever notice would be water." This sounds like a strange statement, but it makes sense. It simply means that we tend to take the world we are reared in for granted. Our culture—except in unusual circumstances—remains below our radar. We take *our* speech, *our* gestures, *our* beliefs, and *our* customs for granted. We assume that they are "normal," even "natural," and we almost always follow them without question.

Culture's influence on you is so profound that it touches almost every aspect of who and what you are. You came into this life without a language; without values and morality; with no ideas about religion, war, money, love, use of space, and so on. You possessed none of these fundamental orientations that are so essential in determining the type of person you have become. Yet they now are an essential part of you, and, like the fish and the water, you take them for granted.

Sociologists call this *culture within us*. These learned and shared ways of believing and of doing (another definition of culture) that penetrate us at an early age become our taken-for-granted assumptions about what normal life is. *Culture becomes the lens through which we perceive and evaluate what is going on around us.* Seldom do we question these assumptions, for, like water to a fish, the lens through which we view life remains largely beyond our perception.

Watch the **Video**
Sociology on the Job: Culture in **mysoclab**

In rare instances these assumptions are challenged, which can be quite upsetting. As a sociologist I should be able to look at my own culture "from the outside," but my trip to Africa revealed how fully I had internalized my culture. My upbringing in Western culture had given me assumptions about social life that had become rooted deeply in my being—eye contact, hygiene, and the use of space. These are an essential part of the way I get through everyday life in the States. But in this part of Africa these assumptions were useless in helping me navigate everyday life. No longer could I count on people to stare tactfully, to take precautions against invisible microbes, or to stand in line, one behind the other.

WHAT AM I SUPPOSED TO LEARN?

After you have read this unit, you should be able to

1 Explain how culture is the lens through which you view life.

2 Know what culture shock, ethnocentrism, and cultural relativism are.

I found these unfamiliar behaviors unsettling, for they violated my basic expectations of "the way people *ought* to be." I did not even realize how firmly I held these expectations until they were challenged in this unfamiliar setting. When my nonmaterial culture failed me—when it no longer helped me to make sense out of the world—I experienced a disorientation known as **culture shock.** In the case of buying tickets, being several inches taller than most Moroccans let me outreach others. But I never got used to the idea that pushing ahead of others was "right." I always felt guilty when I used my size to receive better treatment.

> *IF YOU WANT TO LEARN MORE* about culture shock, as it was experienced by the Hmong when they were abruptly transported from Laotian villages to the United States,
>
> **Read** more from the author: Culture Shock: The Arrival of the Hmong in **mysoclab**

IN SUM: To avoid losing track of the ideas we are discussing, let's pause for a moment to summarize and, in some instances, clarify the principles we have covered.

1. There is nothing "natural" about material culture. Arabs wear gowns on the street and feel that it is natural to do so. Americans do the same with jeans.

2. There is nothing "natural" about nonmaterial culture. It is just as arbitrary to stand in line as to push and shove.

3. Culture penetrates deeply into our thinking, becoming a taken-for-granted lens through which we see the world.

4. Culture provides implicit instructions that tell us what we ought to do and how we ought to think. It establishes a fundamental basis for making our decisions.

5. We view what people do as right or wrong according to the culture we internalize. (I, for example, believed deeply

culture shock the disorientation that people experience when they come in contact with a fundamentally different culture and can no longer depend on their taken-for-granted assumptions about life

This photo of passengers riding outside a train because the inside is packed illustrates how the norms of India differ from those of the United States.

that it was wrong to push and shove to get ahead of others.)

6. Coming into contact with a radically different culture challenges our basic assumptions of life. (I experienced culture shock when I discovered that my deeply ingrained cultural ideas about hygiene and the use of personal space no longer applied.)

7. Culture itself is universal. All people have culture, for a society cannot exist without developing shared, learned ways of dealing with the challenges of life. The specifics of those cultures, though, differ from one group of people to another.

Ethnocentrism and Orientations to Life

Read the **Document**
"Body Ritual Among the Nacirema" by Horace Miner in **mysoclab**

"Culture within us" brings **ethnocentrism,** a tendency to judge others by the way our own group does things. All of us learn that the ways of our own group are good and right, even superior to other ways of life. As sociologist William Sumner (1906), who developed this concept, said, "One's own group is the center of everything, and all others are scaled and rated with reference to it." The results of ethnocentrism are both positive and negative. On the positive side, it creates in-group loyalties. On the negative side, ethnocentrism leads to discrimination against people whose ways differ from ours.

ethnocentrism the use of one's own culture as a yardstick for judging the ways of other individuals or groups, generally leading to a negative evaluation of their values, norms, and behaviors

To counter our tendency to use our own culture as the standard by which we judge other cultures, we can practice **cultural relativism;** that is, we can try to understand a culture on its own terms. This means looking at how the elements of a culture fit together, without judging those elements as better or worse than our own way of life.

With our own culture embedded so deeply within us, however, practicing cultural relativism can be a challenge. A little while ago, I asked how you felt about bullfighting. From the perspective of U.S. culture, it is wrong to raise bulls for the purpose of stabbing them to death in front of crowds that shout "Olé!" If we use cultural relativism, however, we will view bullfighting from the perspective of the culture in which it takes place. We will look at *its* history, *its* folklore, *its* ideas of bravery, and *its* ideas of sex roles.

You may still regard bullfighting as wrong, of course, especially if your culture, which is part of you, has no history of bullfighting. We all possess culturally specific ideas about cruelty to animals, ideas that have evolved slowly and match other elements of our culture. In the United States, for example, practices that once were common in some areas—cockfighting, dogfighting, bear–dog fighting, and so on—have been gradually eliminated.

No matter how hard we try, none of us can be entirely successful at practicing cultural relativism. Our own culture is too deeply engrained in us for this to occur. We just can't help thinking that our ways are superior. To see what I mean, consider the foods discussed in *Making It Personal* on page 52.

I think you'll find the next attempt to apply cultural relativism a bit easier. Look at the photos on the next page. As you view them, try to appreciate the cultural differences they illustrate about standards of beauty.

ATTACK ON CULTURAL RELATIVISM

Although cultural relativism can help us avoid cultural smugness, this view has come under attack. In a provocative book, *Sick Societies* (1992), anthropologist Robert Edgerton suggests that we should develop a scale for evaluating cultures on their "quality of life," much as we do for U.S. cities. He asks why we should consider cultures that practice female circumcision, gang rape, or wife beating, or cultures that sell little girls into prostitution, as morally equivalent to those that do not. Cultural values that result in exploitation, he says, are inferior to those that enhance people's lives.

Edgerton's sharp questions and challenging examples bring us to a topic that comes up repeatedly in this text: the disagreements that arise among scholars as they confront contrasting views of reality. It is difficult to argue against Edgerton. I find myself nodding my head immediately. Yet I fear ethnocentrism—that the standards for judging a culture's "quality of life" will reflect the culture of those who do the judging. The matter is complicated, with arguments on both sides. Such questioning of assumptions keeps sociology interesting.

cultural relativism not judging a culture but trying to understand it on its own terms

Standards of Beauty

Standards of beauty vary so greatly from one culture to another that what one group finds attractive, another may not. Yet, in its ethnocentrism, each group thinks that its standards are the best—that the appearance reflects what beauty "really" is.

As indicated by these photos, around the world men and women aspire to their group's norms of physical attractiveness. To make themselves appealing to others, they try to make their appearance reflect their culture's standards.

Ecuador

United States

Thailand

China

Kenya

Cameroon

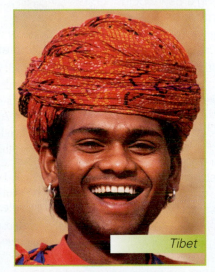
Tibet

New Guinea

Roasted guinea pigs for sale in Lima, Peru.

MAKING IT PERSONAL

Bon Appétit. Would You Eat These Foods?

You probably know that the French like to eat snails. Would you?

Or how about this? A friend, Dusty Friedman, told me that when she was traveling in Sudan, she was served and ate raw baby camel liver. She also ate camel milk cheese patties that had been cured in dry camel dung.

Could you eat these things, prepared in this way, which are assumed to be natural within that culture?

If you are still nodding your head, and judging these things as fine despite your culture, then try this one. In parts of Thailand, scorpions are on the menu of restaurants. So are crickets, beetles, even flies (Gampbell 2006).

Did you handle those okay? I doubt it, but let's try one more. In some Asian cultures, chubby dogs and cats are considered a delicacy. ("I'll take the one wagging its tail. Lightly browned with a little puppy sauce, please.")

Why is it that we have difficulty with these types of foods? It is *not* because of the food. It is because of our culture. We have learned that certain things are "food" and other things are "not food." ("Puppies are supposed to be cute pets, not food.") This is *culture within us*.

You "learned food" at such a young age that this might be difficult to accept. It's the same for everyone in the world. This becomes clearer if we turn the situation around. Marston Bates (1967), a zoologist, was in the llanos of Colombia sharing a dish of toasted ants. When he and his host began to talk about what people eat or do not eat, he remarked that in the United States people eat the legs of frogs. He reported that "the very thought of this filled my ant-eating friends with horror. It was as though I had mentioned some repulsive sex habit."

Cultural relativism is an attempt to refocus our cultural lens so we can appreciate other ways of life rather than simply asserting "Our way is right." But you can see how difficult this is.

UNIT 3.2 // TESTING MYSELF
DID I LEARN IT? ANSWERS ARE AT THE END OF THE CHAPTER

1. When Ralph Linton said, "The last thing a fish would ever notice would be water," he meant that
   a. like fish, we don't observe much about our world
   b. fish have bad eyesight
   c. water in its pure form is so clear it is practically invisible
   d. we tend to take the culture we are reared in for granted

2. Culture—the learned and shared ways of believing and doing—penetrates us at an early age, and
   a. is highly questioned by most us during our teen years
   b. is the source of rebellion for those who get in trouble with the law
   c. becomes our taken-for-granted assumptions about what normal life is
   d. is difficult to transfer

3. The phrase culture within us means that
   a. culture is the lens through which we perceive and evaluate the world
   b. culture is like food to our bodies
   c. we do not eat foods that are not part of our culture
   d. if you want to study culture, you have to study people

4. The term ethnocentrism refers to our tendency to
   a. find fault with others as we encourage them to live up to our standards
   b. be culturally relative
   c. avoid foods that are not like those we learned to eat during childhood
   d. judge others by the way our own group does things

5. There are two right answers here. Choose the broadest. The term culture shock refers to the disorientation people feel when they
   a. are exposed to a culture that differs fundamentally from their own

b. try to discover new ways of doing things

c. sit down to eat a meal and learn that they are being served dog

d. face their worst fears

6. The positive side of ethnocentrism is that it
   a. provides a way to overcome our prejudices
   b. is never far from being a good guide to everyday life
   c. creates in-group loyalties
   d. is a source of goodwill among people

7. The negative side of ethnocentrism is that it
   a. can disappear practically overnight
   b. leads to discrimination
   c. seldom turns out to be right
   d. is a foolish choice to make

8. The term cultural relativism refers to
   a. our tendency to be ethnocentric
   b. an effort to find something good in another culture even when it is bad
   c. trying to understand a culture on its own terms
   d. the culture that we internalize becoming the "right" way of doing things

9. From the Making It Personal on food customs, it would be fair to say that
   a. we are like cows when it comes to food; our bodies tell us what we should eat
   b. items viewed as food in one culture can be seen as repulsive in another culture
   c. everyone views food in about the same way
   d. there is good reason that hamburgers have become popular around the world

10. Robert Edgerton's attack on cultural relativism centers on the idea that
    a. cultures that try to reform themselves are better than those that do not
    b. there are a lot of ways to develop a quality of life
    c. the quality of life of a culture cannot be established
    d. cultures that have less exploitation represent a better quality of life

UNIT 3.3

Symbolic Culture: Language

WHAT AM I SUPPOSED TO LEARN?

After you have read this unit, you should be able to

1 Explain how language is the basis of culture and even makes a past and future possible.

2 Summarize the Sapir-Whorf hypothesis and know how language contains ways of viewing the world.

The problem with the term *nonmaterial culture,* developed by anthropologists, is that it refers to what this part of culture is *not.* The term says that nonmaterial culture is *not* its material part. This is okay, but sociologists prefer to use a term that refers to what it *is,* so they usually call it **symbolic culture.** They chose this term because nonmaterial culture consists of the symbols that people use. A **symbol** is something to which we attach meaning and use to communicate with one another.

For a group to exist, it is essential that its members be able to communicate with one another. Talk, as you know, is our usual form of communicating, so let's suppose that you are listening and watching people who are talking. What do you hear and see? You hear language and see gestures, two of the main elements of *symbolic culture.* To start our exploration of symbolic culture, then, let's begin with how we communicate with one another.

Language

Language consists of symbols that can be combined in an infinite number of ways for the purpose of communicating abstract thought. Each word is actually a symbol, a sound to which we have

symbolic culture another term for nonmaterial culture

symbol something to which people attach meaning and then use to communicate with others

language a system of symbols that can be combined in an infinite number of ways and can represent not only objects but also abstract thought

attached meaning. Although all human groups have language, there is nothing universal about the meanings given to particular sounds. In two cultures, the same sound may mean something entirely different—or may have no meaning at all. In German, for example, *gift* means "poison," so if you give a box of chocolates to a non-English-speaking German and say, "Gift, Eat" . . .

Because *language allows culture to exist,* its significance for human life is difficult to overstate. Consider the following effects of language.

LANGUAGE ALLOWS HUMAN EXPERIENCE TO BE CUMULATIVE

By means of language, we pass ideas, knowledge, and even attitudes on to the next generation. As a result, humans are able to modify their behavior in light of what earlier generations learned. This takes us to the central sociological significance of language: *Language allows culture to develop by freeing people to move beyond their immediate experiences.*

The symbolic aspect of social life is obvious in this photo, but symbolic interactionists see something similar in all social interaction.

events we have experienced, we develop shared understandings about what those events mean. In short, through talk, people develop a shared past.

LANGUAGE PROVIDES A SOCIAL OR SHARED FUTURE

Language also extends our time horizons forward. Because language enables us to agree on times, dates, and places, it allows us to plan activities with one another. Think about it for a moment. Without language, how could you ever plan a future event? How could you possibly communicate goals, times, and plans? Whatever planning could exist would be limited to rudimentary communications, perhaps to an agreement to meet at a certain place when the sun is in a certain position. But think of the difficulty, perhaps the impossibility, of conveying just a slight change in this simple arrangement, such as "I can't make it tomorrow, but my neighbor can take my place, if that's all right with you."

Without language, human culture would be little more advanced than that of the lower primates. If we communicated by grunts and gestures, we would be limited to a short time span—to events now taking place, those that have just taken place, or those that will take place immediately—a sort of slightly extended present. You could grunt and gesture, for example, that you want a drink of water, but in the absence of language how could you share ideas concerning past or future events? There would be little or no way to communicate to others what event you had in mind, much less your ideas and feelings about events.

LANGUAGE PROVIDES A SOCIAL OR SHARED PAST

Without language, we would have few memories, for we associate experiences with words and then use those words to recall the experience. In the absence of language, how would we communicate the few memories we had to others? By attaching words to an event, however, and then using those words to recall it, we are able to discuss the event. This is highly significant, for our talking is not "just talk." As we talk about

LANGUAGE ALLOWS SHARED PERSPECTIVES

Our ability to speak, then, provides us with a social (or shared) past and future. This is vital for humanity. It is a watershed that distinguishes us from other life forms. But speech does much more than this. When we talk with one another, we exchange ideas about events; that is, we share perspectives. *Talking about events allows us to arrive at the shared understandings that form the basis of social life.*

To not be able to talk about events because you don't share a language invites suspicion and misunderstanding. Let's explore this situation in the Miami Language box on the next page.

LANGUAGE ALLOWS SHARED, GOAL-DIRECTED BEHAVIOR

Common understandings enable us to establish a *purpose* for getting together and allow us to work toward goals. Take a look at *Making It Personal* on page 56.

MIAMI: CONTINUING CONTROVERSY OVER LANGUAGE

Immigration from Cuba and other Spanish-speaking countries has been so vast that most residents of Miami are Latinos. Half of Miami's 385,000 residents have trouble speaking English. Only one-*fourth* of Miamians speak English at home. Many English-only speakers are leaving Miami, saying that not being able to speak Spanish is a handicap to getting work. "They should learn Spanish," some reply. As Pedro Falcon, an immigrant from Nicaragua, said, "Miami is the capital of Latin America. The population speaks Spanish."

As the English-speakers see it, this pinpoints the problem: Miami is in the United States, not in Latin America.

Controversy over immigrants and language isn't new. The millions of Germans who moved to the United States in the 1800s brought their language with them. Not only did they hold their religious services in German but they also opened private schools in which the teachers taught in German, published German-language newspapers, and spoke German at home, in the stores, and in the taverns.

Some of their English-speaking neighbors didn't like this a bit. "Why don't those Germans assimilate?" they wondered. "Just whose side would they fight on if we had a war?"

This question was answered, of course, with the participation of German Americans in two world wars. It was even a general descended from German immigrants (Eisenhower) who led the armed forces that defeated Hitler.

But what happened to all this German language? The first generation of immigrants spoke German almost exclusively. The second generation assimilated, speaking English at home, but also speaking German when they visited their parents. For the most part, the third generation knew German only as "that language" that their grandparents spoke.

The same thing is happening with the Latino immigrants. Spanish is being kept alive longer, however, because Mexico borders the United States, and there is constant traffic between the countries. The continuing migration from Mexico and other Spanish-speaking countries also feeds the language.

If Germany bordered the United States, there would still be a lot of German spoken here.

Immigrants find themselves caught between two worlds, their language(s) sometimes indicating the cross pressures they experience.

Sources: Based on Sharp 1992; Usdansky 1992; Kent and Lalasz 2007; Salomon 2008; Nelson 2011.

IN SUM: The sociological significance of language is that it takes us beyond the world of apes and allows culture to develop. Language frees us from the present, actually giving us a social past and a social future. That is, language gives us the capacity to share understandings about the past and to develop shared perceptions about the future. Language also allows us to establish underlying purposes for our activities. In short, *language is the basis of culture.*

LANGUAGE AND PERCEPTION: THE SAPIR-WHORF HYPOTHESIS

In the 1930s, two anthropologists, Edward Sapir and Benjamin Whorf, noticed that the Hopi Indians of the southwestern United States had no words to distinguish the past, the present, and the future. English, in contrast—as well as French, Spanish, Swahili, and other languages—distinguish among these three time frames. From this observation, Sapir and Whorf began to think that words might be more than labels that people attach to things. They concluded that *language has embedded within it ways of looking at the world.* In other words, language not only expresses our thoughts and perceptions but language also shapes the way we think and perceive (Sapir 1949; Whorf 1956).

The **Sapir-Whorf hypothesis** challenges our common sense. It indicates that rather than objects and events forcing themselves into our minds, our language

Sapir-Whorf hypothesis Edward Sapir and Benjamin Whorf's hypothesis that language creates ways of thinking and perceiving

MAKING IT PERSONAL

Let's suppose you want to go on a picnic. You use language not only to plan the picnic but also to decide on reasons for having the picnic—which may be anything from "because it's a nice day and it shouldn't be wasted studying" to "because it's my birthday." In other words, through discussion with your friends you decide where you will go; who will drive; who will bring the hamburgers, the potato chips, the soda; and where you will meet.

Planning events is a common part of our everyday lives. We get together to go shopping with friends, to meet for lunch, to go to a movie, to do so many things. So why am I even mentioning it? Because these simple events illustrate a fundamental principle of social life, one that we usually don't notice. Only because of language can you participate in such a common yet complex event as a picnic or get together to go shopping with friends—or—and now you'll see the point—build roads and bridges or attend college classes. *Both your individual life and society itself are built on language.*

We all carve out little worlds for ourselves, although most are not as extreme as that depicted here. Those "little worlds" involve the use of unique terms.

IF YOU WANT TO LEARN MORE about how racial–ethnic terms influence how we see both ourselves and others,

Read more from the author: Race and Language: Searching for Self-Labels in **mysoclab**

determines how we perceive objects and events. This can be a difficult point to grasp because it is so abstract, so let's bring it down to earth. An observation made by sociologist Eviatar Zerubavel (1991) can help. He says that his native language, Hebrew, does not have separate words for jam and jelly. Both go by the same term, and only when Zerubavel learned English could he "see" this difference, which is "obvious" to native English speakers.

When I lived in Spain, I was struck by the relevance of the Sapir-Whorf hypothesis. (Yes, I know. Only a sociologist would say something like this.) As a native English speaker, I learned that the term *dried fruits* refers to apricots, apples, and so on. In Spain, I found that *frutos secos* (dried fruits) refers not only to such objects but also to things like almonds, walnuts, and pecans. Because of English, I see fruits and nuts as separate types of objects. This seems "natural" to me, while combining them into one unit seems "natural" to Spanish speakers. If I had learned Spanish as a child, my perception of these objects would be different.

Consider how you classify students. If you learn to think of them as Jocks, Goths, Stoners, Skaters, Band Geeks, and Preps, you will perceive students in entirely different ways from someone who has not learned these classifications.

It turns out that Sapir and Whorf's observation that the Hopi do not have tenses was wrong (Edgerton 1992:27). But this was one of those mistakes that work out anyway. They stumbled onto a major truth about social life. Learning a language means not only learning words but also acquiring the perceptions embedded in that language. In other words, language both reflects and shapes our cultural experiences (Boroditsky 2010).

4. Symbols that can be combined in an infinite number of ways to communicate abstract thought is a definition of

   a. language
   b. symbolic culture
   c. communication
   d. numbers

5. Sociologists would not say that "talk is just talk" because talk

   a. is more than just talk
   b. is never finished—some people can go on forever
   c. is a way that people express themselves
   d. allows us to build shared understandings of events

6. The sociological significance of language is that it

   a. consists of words that communicate abstract thought
   b. provides an endless flow of information
   c. allows culture to develop
   d. can be translated from one language to another

7. The Sapir-Whorf hypothesis challenges our common sense because it indicates that rather than objects and events forcing themselves into our minds

   a. we make sense of our world by classifying objects and events
   b. our language contains ways of perceiving objects and events
   c. our thought process is based on collective experiences
   d. we do the perceiving as we navigate our everyday lives

8. Sociologist Eviatar Zerubavel says that his native language, Hebrew, does not have separate words for jam and jelly. When he learned English, he understood the Sapir-Whorf hypothesis better because he

   a. was able to see the difference between jam and jelly
   b. learned that they existed
   c. learned that one comes from trees and the other from bushes
   d. found out that his native language was wrong

9. Fred thinks of girls as pretty, plain, and ugly. Bob thinks of girls as smart and dumb. Harry thinks of girls as big, just right, and skinny. (Phil just thinks of girls all the time, so we won't count him.) Fred, Bob, and Harry

   a. could broaden their categories, and life will be better for them
   b. will not approve of one another's girlfriends
   c. could put their heads together and have a more complete perception of girls
   d. will have different perceptions of the same girl

UNIT 3.4

Symbolic Culture: Gestures

WHAT AM I SUPPOSED TO LEARN?

After you have read this unit, you should be able to

State what gestures are and to what extent they are universal.

In addition to language, we use **gestures,** movements of the body, to communicate with others. Gestures are shorthand ways to convey messages without using words. Although people in every culture of the world use gestures, a gesture's meaning may change completely from one culture to another. North Americans, for example, communicate a succinct message by raising the middle finger in a short, upward stabbing motion. I wish to stress "North Americans," for this gesture does not convey the same message everywhere.

I was surprised to find that this particular gesture was not universal. I had internalized it to such an extent that I thought everyone knew what it meant. When I was comparing gestures with friends in Mexico, however, this gesture drew a blank look. After I explained its intended meaning, they laughed and showed me their rudest gesture—placing the hand under the armpit and moving the upper arm up and down. To me, they simply looked as if they were imitating monkeys, but to them the gesture meant "Your mother is a whore"—the worst possible insult in that culture.

Gestures not only facilitate communication but they can also, because they differ around the world, lead to misunderstanding, embarrassment, or worse. One time in Mexico, for example, I raised my hand to a certain height to indicate how tall a child was. My hosts began to laugh. It turned out that Mexicans use three hand gestures to indicate height: one for people, a second for animals, and yet another for plants. They were amused because I had used the plant gesture to indicate the child's height. (See Figure 3.1.)

gestures the ways in which people use their bodies to communicate with one another

FIGURE 3.1 Gestures to Indicate Height, Southern Mexico

Source: By the author.

To get along in another culture, then, it is important to learn the gestures of that culture. If you don't, you will fail to achieve the simplicity of communication that gestures allow and run the risk of appearing foolish, and possibly offend people. In some cultures, for example, you would provoke deep offense if you were to offer food or a gift with your left hand, because the left hand is reserved for dirty tasks, such as wiping after going to the toilet. Left-handed Americans visiting Arabs, please note!

Suppose for a moment that you are visiting southern Italy. After eating one of the best meals in your life, you are so pleased that when you catch the waiter's eye, you smile broadly and use the standard U.S. "A-OK" gesture of putting your thumb and forefinger together and making a large "O." The waiter looks horrified, and you are struck speechless when the manager asks you to leave. What have you done? Nothing on purpose, of course, but in that culture this gesture refers to a lower rear part of the human body that is not mentioned in polite company (Ekman et al. 1984).

Is it really true that there are no universal gestures? Some anthropologists claim that no gesture is universal. They point out that even nodding the head up and down to indicate "yes" is not universal, that in some parts of the world, such as areas of Turkey, nodding the head up and down means "no" (Ekman et al. 1984). Apparently, though, certain facial expressions are attached to some fundamental emotions. Ethologists, researchers who study biological bases of behavior, have found that expressions of anger, fear, pouting, and sadness are built into our biological makeup and are universal (Eibl-Eibesfeldt 1970: 404; Horwitz and Wakefield 2007). They point out that even infants who are born blind and deaf, who have had no chance to *learn* these gestures, express themselves in the same way.

Gestures, a significant form of our communication, differ from one culture to another. The gesture shown here would be meaningless in most cultures.

UNIT 3.4 // TESTING MYSELF
DID I LEARN IT? ANSWERS ARE AT THE END OF THE CHAPTER

1. Gestures, movements of the body to communicate with others,
   a. are more flexible than language
   b. go back to the time when people had no language and they had to use their hands to communicate with one another
   c. may differ from culture to culture
   d. are basically the same from one culture to another

2. The example of the American "A-OK" gesture being used in a restaurant in Italy illustrates that a gesture in one culture that indicates something highly positive
   a. must be translated in order to be understood
   b. can indicate something highly negative in another culture
   c. can have different meaning for men and women
   d. almost always indicates something positive in other cultures

3. Nodding the head up and down to indicate "yes"
   a. is not universal
   b. is universal
   c. depends on language
   d. communicates different things in different cultures

4. Ethologists, researchers who study biological bases of human behavior, report that expressions of anger, pouting, fear, and sadness are
   a. each represented by two basic gestures
   b. different from one culture to another
   c. related to one another
   d. built into our biological makeup and are universal

UNIT 3.5

Symbolic Culture: Values, Norms, Sanctions, Folkways, and Mores

Now that we have looked at language and gestures, let's examine the other essential elements of *symbolic culture*—its values, norms, sanctions, folkways, and mores.

Values, Norms, and Sanctions

Whenever you learn a culture—whether it's the one you learn as a baby or another that you learn later in life—you are learning a people's **values,** their ideas of what is desirable in life. To uncover people's values is to learn a great deal about them, for values are the standards by which we define what is good and bad, beautiful and ugly. Values underlie our preferences, guide our choices, and indicate what we hold worthwhile in life.

Every group develops ideas about the "right" way to follow its values. The term **norms** refers to these expectations (or rules of behavior). People's reactions when others follow or break norms are called **sanctions.** A **positive sanction** expresses approval for following a norm, and a **negative sanction** reflects disapproval for breaking a norm. Positive sanctions can be material, such as a prize, a trophy, or money, but in everyday life they usually consist of hugs, smiles, a pat on the back, or even handshakes and "high fives." Negative sanctions can also be material—being fined in court is one example—but negative sanctions, too, are more likely to be symbolic: harsh words, or gestures such as frowns, stares, clenched jaws, or raised fists. Getting a raise at work is a positive sanction, indicating that you have followed the norms clustering around work values. Getting fired, however, is a negative sanction, indicating that you have violated these norms. The North American finger gesture discussed earlier is, of course, a negative sanction.

Because people can find norms stifling, some cultures relieve the pressure through *moral holidays,* specified times when people are

values the standards by which people define what is desirable or undesirable, good or bad, beautiful or ugly

norms expectations of "right" behavior

sanctions either expressions of approval given to people for upholding norms or expressions of disapproval for violating them

positive sanction a positive reaction for following norms, ranging from a smile to a material reward

negative sanction an expression of disapproval for breaking a norm, ranging from a mild, informal reaction such as a frown to a formal reaction such as a prize or a prison sentence

allowed to break norms. Moral holidays such as Mardi Gras often center on getting rowdy. Some activities for which people would otherwise be arrested are permitted—and expected—including public drunkenness and some nudity. The norms are never completely dropped, however—just loosened a bit. Go too far, and the police step in.

Some societies have *moral holiday places,* locations where norms are expected to be broken. Red-light districts of our cities are examples. There, prostitutes are allowed to work the streets, bothered only when political pressure builds to "clean up" the area. If these same prostitutes attempt to solicit customers in adjacent areas, however, they are promptly arrested. Each year, the hometown of the team that wins the Super Bowl becomes a moral holiday place—for one night.

3.5

WHAT AM I SUPPOSED TO LEARN?

After you have read this unit, you should be able to

1 State how values, norms, and sanctions are related to one another.

2 Explain what folkways, mores, and taboos are.

Mardi Gras, in the many places it is held, is a moral holiday. This photo was taken in New Orleans.

FROM ANOTHER STUDENT . . .

I love learning sociology! I enjoy your book! It forces me to think and I love it. I cannot thank you enough for helping me to learn something that I actually enjoy learning. I actually think about sociology outside of school. Thank you so much for improving the way I see the world.

With amazement,
Charlie Diehl
St Louis College of Pharmacy

One of the more interesting examples is "Party Cove" at Lake of the Ozarks in Missouri, a fairly conservative area of the country. During the summer, hundreds of boaters—those operating everything from cabin cruisers to jet skis—moor their vessels together in a highly publicized cove, where many get drunk, take off their clothes, and dance on the boats. In one of the more humorous incidents, boaters complained that a nude woman was riding a jet ski outside of the cove. The water patrol investigated but refused to arrest the woman because she was within the law—she had sprayed shaving cream on certain parts of her body. The Missouri Water Patrol has even given a green light to Party Cove, announcing in the local newspaper that officers will not enter this cove, supposedly because "there is so much traffic that they might not be able to get out in time to handle an emergency elsewhere."

Folkways and Mores

Norms that are not strictly enforced are called **folkways.** We expect people to comply with folkways, but we are likely to shrug our shoulders and not make a big deal about it if they don't. If someone insists on passing you on the right side of the sidewalk, for example, you are unlikely to take corrective action, although if the sidewalk is crowded and you must move out of the way, you might give the person a dirty look.

Other norms, however, are taken much more seriously. We think of them as essential to our core values, and we insist on conformity. These are called **mores** (MORE-rays). A person who steals, rapes, or kills has violated some of society's most important mores. As sociologist Ian Robertson (1987:62) put it,

A man who walks down a street wearing nothing on the upper half of his body is violating a folkway; a man who walks down the street wearing nothing on the lower half of his body is violating one of our most important mores, the requirement that people cover their genitals and buttocks in public.

It should also be noted that one group's folkways may be another group's mores. Although a man walking down the street with the upper half of his body uncovered is violating a folkway, a woman doing the same thing is violating the mores. In addition, the folkways and mores of a subculture (discussed in the next section) may be the opposite of mainstream culture. For example, to walk down the sidewalk in a nudist camp with the entire body uncovered would conform to that subculture's folkways.

A **taboo** refers to a norm so strongly ingrained that even the thought of its violation is greeted with revulsion. Eating human flesh and parents having sex with their children are examples of such behaviors. When someone breaks a taboo, the individual is usually judged unfit to live in the same society as others. The sanctions are severe and may include prison, banishment, or death.

folkways norms that are not strictly enforced

mores norms that are strictly enforced because they are thought essential to core values or the well-being of the group

taboo a norm so strong that it often brings revulsion if violated

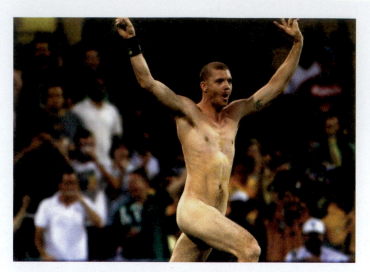

The violation of mores is considered a serious matter. This streaker at a cricket match in Brisbane, Australia, was knocked to the ground and arrested.

UNIT 3.5 // TESTING MYSELF
DID I LEARN IT? ANSWERS ARE AT THE END OF THE CHAPTER

1. Leticia was shocked when her friend showed her a pornographic magazine. She said, "I don't understand how anyone can pose for photos like that!" Leticia was expressing
   a. a positive sanction   **b.** a subcultural standard
   c. her standards of beauty   **d.** values

2. When Leticia found a pornographic magazine in her son's bedroom, she grounded her son for a week. He couldn't leave home, he couldn't have friends over, and he couldn't watch television. Leticia's actions are an example of a
   a. positive sanction   **b.** negative sanction
   c. norm   **d.** subcultural standard

3. Leticia told her son, "I don't care how you feel about it. You will not look at pornography in this house again." Leticia's statement expresses a
   a. positive sanction   **b.** narrow opinion
   c. norm   **d.** culture

4. After Leticia's son was grounded for three days, he told his mother that he was sorry and he wouldn't look at any more pornography. Leticia said that she was going to reduce his grounding by two days. Leticia's action is an example of a
   a. positive sanction   **b.** negative sanction
   c. norm   **d.** value

5. At Mardi Gras in New Orleans and Rio de Janeiro, Brazil, a lot of people get drunk. There is also a lot of nudity. Unless things get too far out of line, the

police just smile and tell the people to have fun. At other times of the year, they will arrest people for these same behaviors. This is an example of

a. the flexibility of norms and values
b. what happens when the police are corrupt
c. the police failing to uphold the law
d. moral holidays

6. The air conditioner wasn't working in the summer heat, and it was stifling hot in the office. Ben said he didn't care if people stared. He took off his shirt. (Ben was not wearing an undershirt.) Ben violated

a. an ethnocentrism **b.** a sanction
c. a folkway. **d.** one of the mores

7. The air conditioner wasn't working in the summer heat, and it was stifling hot in the office. Jenn said she didn't care if people stared. She took off her blouse. (Jenn was not wearing a slip or a bra.) Jenn violated

a. an ethnocentrism **b.** a sanction
c. a folkway **d.** one of the mores

8. Mary was photographed, fingerprinted, and booked. Later the judge sentenced her to 7 years in prison for having sex with her teenaged son. Mary had violated

a. a taboo **b.** a sanction
c. a folkway **d.** one of the mores

UNIT 3.6

Many Cultural Worlds

WHAT AM I SUPPOSED TO LEARN?

After you have read this unit, you should be able to

Explain the difference between subcultures and countercultures.

Subcultures

People who participate in the same activity, whether snowboarding or stamp collecting, tend to develop specialized ways to communicate with one another. To outsiders, their talk, even if it is in English, can seem like a foreign language. Here is one of my favorite quotes by a politician:

There are things we know that we know. There are known unknowns; that is to say, there are things that we now know we don't know. But there are also unknown unknowns; there are things we do not know we don't know. (Donald Rumsfeld, quoted in Dickey and Barry 2006:38)

Whatever Rumsfeld, the former secretary of defense under George W. Bush, meant by his statement probably will remain a known unknown. (Or would it be an unknown known?)

The same thing occurs in the subculture of sociology. Try to figure out what this means:

Path analysis showed that parental involvement fully mediated the effect of parental acculturation on intergenerational relationship, whereas intergenerational relationship mediated the effect of parental involvement on child outcomes. (Ying and Han 2008)

As much as possible, I will try to spare you from such "insider's" talk.

People who specialize in an occupation—from cabbies to politicians—tend to develop a **subculture,** *a world within the larger world of the dominant culture.* Subcultures are not limited to occupations. They can originate anywhere that people's experiences lead them to have distinctive ways of looking at the world. Even if we cannot understand the quotation from Donald Rumsfeld, it makes us aware that politicians don't view life in quite the same way most of us do. Nor do sociologists.

Watch the **Video**
The Big Picture:
Culture in **mysoclab**

U.S. society contains *thousands* of subcultures. Some are as broad as the way of life we associate with teenagers, others are as narrow as those we associate with body builders. Some U.S. ethnic groups also form subcultures: Their values, norms, and foods set them apart. So might their religion, music, language, and clothing. As you are learning, sociologists also use a unique language in their efforts to understand the world.

Some subcultures can be illustrated by photos. Take a look at the photo essay on the next two pages.

Countercultures

Consider this quote from another subculture:

If everyone applying for welfare had to supply a doctor's certificate of sterilization, if everyone who had committed a felony were sterilized, if anyone who had mental illness to any degree were sterilized—then our

subculture the values and related behaviors of a group that distinguish its members from the larger culture; a world within a world

Looking at Subcultures

Each subculture provides its members with values and distinctive ways of viewing the world. What values and perceptions do you think are common among body builders? What other subculture do you see in this photo?

Subcultures can form around any interest or activity. Each subculture has its own values and norms that its members share, giving them a common identity. Each also has special terms that pinpoint the group's corner of life and that its members use to communicate with one another. Some of us belong to several subcultures.

As you can see from this photo essay, most subcultures are compatible with the values and norms of the mainstream culture. They represent specialized interests around which its members have chosen to build tiny worlds. Some subcultures, however, conflict with the mainstream culture. Sociologists give the name *counter-cultures* to subcultures whose values (such as those of outlaw motorcyclists) or activities and goals (such as those of terrorists) are opposed to the mainstream culture. Countercultures, however, are exceptional, and few of us belong to them.

Membership in this subculture is not easily awarded. Not only must high-steel ironworkers prove that they are able to work at great heights but also that they fit into the group socially. Newcomers are tested by members of the group, and they must demonstrate that they can take joking without offense.

Specialized values and interests are two of the characteristics that mark subcultures. What values and interests distinguish the modeling subculture?

The subculture that centers around tattooing previously existed on the fringes of society, with seamen and circus folk its main participants. It now has entered mainstream society, but not to this extreme.

The cabbie subculture, centering on their occupational activities and interests, is also broken into smaller subcultures that reflect their experiences of race–ethnicity.

Can you identify this subculture?

Why would people decorate themselves like this? Among the many reasons, one is to show solidarity with the football subculture.

Even subcultures can have subcultures. The rodeo subculture is a subculture of "cowboy" subculture, which is a subculture of "western" subculture. The values that unite its members are reflected in their speech, clothing, and specialized activities, such as the one shown here.

Why are the Hell's Angels not a subculture but a counterculture?

economy could easily take care of these people for the rest of their lives, giving them a decent living standard—but getting them out of the way. That way there would be no children abused, no surplus population, and, after a while, no pollution . . . .

When the . . . present world system collapses, it'll be good people like you who will be shooting people in the streets to feed their families. (Zellner 1995:58, 65)

Welcome to the world of the Aryan supremacist survivalists, where the message is much clearer than that of politicians—and much more disturbing.

The values and norms of most subcultures blend in with mainstream society. In some cases, however, as with the survivalist quoted here, some of the group's values and norms place it at odds with the dominant culture. Sociologists use the term **counterculture** to refer to these groups. To better see this distinction, consider motorcycle enthusiasts and motorcycle gangs. Motorcycle enthusiasts—who emphasize personal freedom and speed *and* affirm cultural values of success through work or education—are members of a subculture. In contrast, the Hell's Angels, Pagans, and Bandidos not only stress freedom and speed but also value dirtiness and contempt toward women, work, and education. This makes them a counterculture.

Any challenge to core values is met with resistance, often with hostility, and sometimes with violence. To affirm their own values, members of the mainstream culture may ridicule, isolate, or even attack members of the counterculture. The Mormons, for example, were driven out of several states before they finally settled in Utah, which was at that time a wilderness. Even there, the federal government would not let them practice *polygyny* (one man having more than one wife), and Utah's statehood was made conditional on its acceptance of monogamy (Anderson 1942/1966; Williams 2007).

> **counterculture** a group whose values, beliefs, norms, and related behaviors place its members in opposition to the broader culture

UNIT 3.6 // TESTING MYSELF
DID I LEARN IT? ANSWERS ARE AT THE END OF THE CHAPTER

1. Nancy was invited to a meeting at someone's house in the country. She was curious about what the group taught, and she went. She made friends with some of the members, and she joined the group, which taught that aliens were the original inhabitants of Earth. The members didn't look weird. They voted and worked at all sorts of regular jobs. This group is an example of a
   a. monoculture
   b. neoculture
   c. counterculture
   d. subculture

2. Nancy was invited to another meeting. She went and after making friends with some of the members, she joined this group, too. This group taught that the U.S. government had been taken over by insane people who were leading the country to destruction. The members were told to keep their jobs so no one would suspect them, and to store weapons for their coming attack on the government. This group is an example of a
   a. nanoculture
   b. neoculture
   c. counterculture
   d. subculture

3. Nancy was a busy woman. This time she joined a group that taught that work and bathing were corrupting the world. What people should do is beg from the corrupters and stay away from water. Nancy's friends ridiculed her for joining this group, and they stopped seeing her. The reason her former friends acted like this was because
   a. they were heartless and unsympathetic
   b. Nancy was assaulting core values
   c. Nancy stank
   d. Nancy was asking them for money

UNIT 3.7 Values in U.S. Society

3.7

An Overview of U.S. Values

As you know, the United States is a **pluralistic society,** made up of many different groups. The United States has numerous religious and racial–ethnic groups, as well as countless interest groups that focus on activities as divergent as hunting deer or collecting Barbie dolls. Within this huge diversity, sociologists have tried to identify the underlying core values that are shared by most of the groups that make up U.S. society. Here are ten that sociologist Robin Williams (1965) identified:

Watch the **Video**
The Basics: Culture
in **mysoclab**

1. *Achievement and success.* Americans praise personal achievement, especially outdoing others. This value includes getting ahead at work and school, and attaining wealth, power, and prestige.

2. *Individualism.* Americans cherish the ideal that an individual can rise from the bottom of society to its very top. If someone fails to "get ahead," Americans generally find fault with that individual rather than with the social system for placing roadblocks in his or her path.

3. *Hard work.* Americans expect people to work hard to achieve financial success and material comfort.

4. *Efficiency and practicality.* Americans award high marks for getting things done efficiently. Even in everyday life, Americans consider it important to do things fast, and they seek ways to increase efficiency.

5. *Science and technology.* Americans have a passion for applied science, for using science to control nature—to tame rivers and harness winds—and to develop new technology, from iPads to pedal-electric hybrid vehicles.

6. *Material comfort.* Americans expect a high level of material comfort. This includes not only good nutrition, medical care, and housing but also late-model cars and recreational playthings—from iPhones to motor homes.

7. *Freedom.* This core value pervades U.S. life. It underscored the American Revolution, and Americans pride themselves on their personal freedom.

WHAT AM I SUPPOSED TO LEARN?

After you have read this unit, you should be able to

1 Summarize some of the core values of U.S. society and know how they relate to one another.

2 Know how values are lenses that shape perception and distinguish between ideal culture and real culture.

8. *Democracy.* By this term, Americans refer to majority rule, to the right of everyone to express an opinion, and to representative government.

9. *Equality.* It is impossible to understand Americans without being aware of the central role that the value of equality plays in their lives. Equality of opportunity (part of the ideal culture discussed later) has significantly influenced U.S. history and continues to mark relations among the groups that make up U.S. society.

10. *Group superiority.* Although it contradicts the values of freedom, democracy, and equality, Americans regard some groups more highly than others and have done so throughout their history. The denial of the vote to women, the slaughter of Native Americans, and the enslavement of Africans are a few examples of how groups in power considered themselves superior and denied equality and freedom to others.

In an earlier publication, I updated Williams' analysis by adding these three values:

11. *Education.* Americans are expected to go as far in school as their abilities and finances allow. Over the years, the definition of an "adequate" education has changed, and today a college education is considered an appropriate goal for most Americans. Those who have an opportunity for higher education and do not take it are sometimes viewed as doing something "wrong"—not merely as making a bad choice, but as somehow being involved in an immoral act.

12. *Religiosity.* There is a feeling that "every true American ought to be religious." This does not mean that everyone is expected to

pluralistic society a society made up of many different groups

join a church, synagogue, or mosque, but that everyone ought to acknowledge a belief in a Supreme Being and follow some set of matching precepts. This value is so pervasive that Americans stamp "In God We Trust" on their money and declare in their national pledge of allegiance that they are "one nation under God."

13. *Romantic love.* Americans feel that the only proper basis for marriage is romantic love. Songs, literature, mass media, and "folk beliefs" all stress this value. Americans grow misty-eyed at the theme that "love conquers all."

Value Clusters

As you can see, values are not independent units. Some cluster together to form a larger whole. In the **value cluster** that surrounds success, for example, we find hard work, education, material comfort, and individualism bound together. Americans are expected to go far in school, to work hard afterward, and then to attain a high level of material comfort, which, in turn, demonstrates success. Success is attributed to the individual's efforts; lack of success is blamed on his or her faults.

Values as Distorting Lenses

Values and their supporting beliefs are lenses through which we see the world. The views these lenses produce are often of what life

value cluster values that together form a larger whole

ought to be like, not what it is. For example, Americans value individualism so highly that they tend to see almost everyone as free and equal in pursuing the goal of success. This value blinds them to the significance of the circumstances that keep people from achieving success. The dire consequences of family poverty, parents' low education, and dead-end jobs tend to drop from sight. Instead, Americans see the unsuccessful as not putting out enough effort. And they "know" they are right, for the mass media dangles before their eyes enticing stories of individuals who have succeeded despite the greatest of handicaps.

"Ideal" Versus "Real" Culture

As we saw, norms develop to support cultural values, but many of these norms are followed only partially. There is always a gap between a group's ideals and what its members actually do. Sociologists use the term **ideal culture** to refer to the values, norms, and goals that a group considers ideal, desirable, and worth aiming for. Success, for example, is part of ideal culture. Americans glorify academic progress, hard work, and the display of material goods as signs of individual achievement. What people actually do, however, usually falls short of the cultural ideal. Compared with their abilities, for example, most people don't work as hard as they could or go as far as they could in school. Sociologists call the norms and values that people actually follow **real culture.**

ideal culture a people's ideal values and norms; the goals held out for them

real culture the norms and values that people actually follow; as opposed to ideal *culture*

DID I LEARN IT? ANSWERS ARE AT THE END OF THE CHAPTER

1. The United States is made up of many groups: racial–ethnic groups, religious groups, political associations for the conservative and liberal, unions that demand rights and privileges, and on and on. Some of the groups come into conflict with one another. In sociological terms, this makes the United States a
   a. conflictual society
   b. comparative society
   c. place that represents the world's future
   d. pluralistic society

2. To specify the core values of a pluralistic society is difficult because
   a. the many values of the many groups means that there are no core values
   b. one value cancels another out
   c. this type of society has many competing values
   d. the values change rapidly as the many groups interact with one another

3. Sociologist Robin Williams analyzed some of the core values of the United States. On his list are hard work, education, material comfort, and individualism. These four values are tied together into a larger whole that sociologists call a
   a. value tie
   b. value cluster
   c. core value integrator
   d. value unit

UNIT 3.8

Changing Values

WHAT AM I SUPPOSED TO LEARN?

After you have read this unit, you should be able to

1 State why value contradictions and clashes are a source of social change.

2 Identify an emerging value cluster and an emerging fifth value in the United States.

Value Contradictions

You probably were surprised to see group superiority on the list of dominant American values. This is an example of what I mentioned in Chapter 1, how sociology upsets people and creates resistance. Few people want to bring something like this into the open. It violates today's *ideal* culture, a concept we discussed on the previous page. But this is what sociologists do—they look beyond the façade to penetrate what is really going on. And when you look at our history, there is no doubt that group superiority has been a dominant value. It still is, but values change, and this one is diminishing.

Value contradictions, then, are part of culture. Not all values come wrapped in neat packages, and you can see how group superiority contradicts freedom, democracy, and equality. There simply cannot be full expression of freedom, democracy, and equality along with racism and sexism. Something has to give. One way in which Americans in the past sidestepped this contradiction was to say that freedom, democracy, and equality applied only to some groups. The contradiction was bound to surface over time, however, and so it did with the Civil War and the women's liberation movement. *It is precisely at the point of value contradictions, then, that you can see a major force for social change.*

When Values Clash

In a pluralistic society, the values of different groups can clash. This can be a force for change or a force for reaffirming the dominant values. Core values represent a way of life to people who hold them dear. They see change as an undermining of both their present and their future. Efforts to change gender roles, for example, arouse intense controversy, as do same-sex marriages. Alarmed at such onslaughts against their values, traditionalists fiercely defend historical family relationships and the gender roles they grew up with. Some use the term *culture wars* to refer to the clash in values between traditionalists and those who are advocating change. The term, though, is highly exaggerated. Compared with the violence directed against the Mormons who challenged the core value of monogamy, today's culture clashes are mild.

value contradictions values that contradict one another, such as equality and group superiority

Emerging Values

As society changes, new values emerge to support these changes. These emerging values sometimes produce new value clusters. In the United States, we can see an emerging value cluster that consists of four interrelated core values—leisure, self-fulfillment, physical fitness, and youthfulness.

1. *Leisure.* The emergence of leisure as a value is reflected in a huge recreation industry—from computer games, boats, vacation homes, and spa retreats to sports arenas, home theaters, adventure vacations, and luxury cruises.

2. *Self-fulfillment.* This value is reflected in the "human potential" movement, which emphasizes becoming "all you can be," and in magazine articles, books, and talk shows that focus on "self-help," "relating," and "personal development."

3. *Physical fitness.* Physical fitness is not a new U.S. value, but the greater emphasis on it is moving it

How does this photo reflect the four values in the emerging value cluster?

into this emerging cluster. You can see this trend in the publicity given to nutrition, organic foods, weight, and diet; the joggers, cyclists, and backpackers; and the countless health clubs and physical fitness centers.

4. *Youthfulness.* Valuing youth and disparaging old age are also not new, but some analysts note a sense of urgency in today's emphasis on youthfulness. They attribute this to the huge number of aging baby boomers, who, aghast at the physical changes that accompany their advancing years, are attempting to deny or at least postpone their biological fate. One physician even claimed that "aging is not a normal life event, but a disease" (Cowley 1996). As you age, you will be bombarded with techniques for maintaining and enhancing a youthful appearance—from cosmetic surgery to exotic creams and Botox injections.

Values don't "just happen." They are related to conditions of society, and this emerging value cluster is a response to fundamental change. Earlier generations of Americans were focused on forging a nation and fighting for economic survival. But today, millions of Americans are freed from long hours of work, and millions retire from work at an age when they anticipate

decades of life ahead of them. This value cluster centers on helping people to maintain their health and vigor during their younger years and enabling them to enjoy their many years of retirement.

We can also identify a fifth emerging value, one that is separate from this new value cluster.

5. *Concern for the environment.* During most of U.S. history, the environment was viewed as something to be exploited—a wilderness to be settled, forests to be cleared for farm land and lumber, rivers and lakes to be fished, and animals to be hunted. One result was the near extinction of the bison and the extinction in 1914 of the passenger pigeon, a species of bird previously so numerous that its annual migration would darken the skies for days. Today, Americans have developed a genuine and apparently long-term concern for the environment.

This emerging value of environmental concern is related to the current stage of U.S. economic development: Preventing pollution, cleaning it up, and protecting wildlife are expensive. People act on environmental concerns only *after* they have met their basic needs, a value that the world's poor nations have a difficult time "affording" at this point in their development (Gokhale 2009).

UNIT 3.8 // TESTING MYSELF
DID I LEARN IT? ANSWERS ARE AT THE END OF THE CHAPTER

1. Value contradictions are a source of social change. They produce a tension that leads to an attempt to resolve the contradiction. The value contradiction discussed in this unit is
   a. education and leisure
   b. hard work and leisure
   c. achievement and efficiency
   d. group superiority and equality

2. Where we have value contradictions, we also have
   a. a careless construction of society
   b. elements of society that are like trying to fit a square peg in a round hole
   c. a force for social change
   d. sociologists who point them out

3. Another force for social change is a clash in the values of different groups. The clash, sometimes

called culture wars, can result in a change in the core value or
   a. a new value cluster
   b. a reaffirming of the core value
   c. a general increase in satisfaction with the change
   d. an invasion

4. Emerging values in the United States include leisure, self-fulfillment, physical fitness, and youthfulness. These four values are interrelated, which makes them an example of
   a. a value cluster
   b. a value pack
   c. social change
   d. what happens when hard work is abandoned as a core value

5. The emerging value, concern for the environment, is an example of
   a. a value clash
   b. a culture war
   c. a value contradiction
   d. how an emerging value can depend on the state of economic development

UNIT 3.9 — Cultural Universals

With the amazing variety of human cultures around the world, are there any **cultural universals**—values, norms, or other cultural traits that are found everywhere?

To answer this question, anthropologist George Murdock (1945) combed through the data that anthropologists had gathered on hundreds of groups around the world. He compared their customs concerning courtship, marriage, funerals, games, laws, music, myths, incest taboos, and even toilet training. He found that these activities are present in all cultures, but *the specific customs differ from one group to another*. There is no universal form of the family, no universal way of toilet training children, no universal way of disposing of the dead.

Incest is a remarkable example. Groups even differ on their view of what incest is. The Mundugumors of New Guinea extend the incest taboo so far that for each man, *seven* of every eight women are ineligible marriage partners (Mead 1935/1950). Other groups go in the opposite direction and allow some men to marry their own daughters (La Barre 1954). Some groups even *require* that brothers and sisters marry one another, although only in certain circumstances (Beals and Hoijer 1965). The Burundi of Africa even insist that a mother and son have sex—but only to remove a certain curse (Albert 1963). Such sexual relations, so surprising to us, are limited to special people (royalty) or to extraordinary situations (such as when a lion hunter faces a dangerous hunt). No society permits generalized incest for its members.

> **cultural universal** a value, norm, or other cultural trait that is found in every group

The need to dispose of people's bodies is universal, but the form of doing so differs markedly around the world.

WHAT AM I SUPPOSED TO LEARN?

After you have read this unit, you should be able to

1 State whether there are cultural universals and give the reason for your answer.

2 Explain why the incest taboo is not a cultural universal.

IN SUM: Although there are universal human activities (singing, playing games, storytelling, preparing food, marrying, child rearing, disposing of the dead, and so on), there is no universal way of doing any of them.

UNIT 3.9 // TESTING MYSELF
DID I LEARN IT? ANSWERS ARE AT THE END OF THE CHAPTER

1. Anthropologist George Murdock analyzed customs around the world. He found
   a. cultural universals
   b. cultural clusters
   c. universal challenges
   d. universal activities

2. When anthropologist George Murdock analyzed customs around the world, he did not find
   a. cultural universals
   b. cultural customs
   c. that all groups around the world played games
   d. universal variances

3. The Mundugumors of New Guinea extend the incest taboo so far that for each man
   a. the only eligible marriage partners are other men
   b. marriage is not allowed until the age of 35
   c. *seven* of every eight women are ineligible marriage partners
   d. a minimum of 10 cattle and 20 sheep are required to pay the bride price

4. The Burundi of Africa require that a mother and son have sex in order to
   a. remove a curse
   b. start a new generation
   c. offer sacrifice to the sun god
   d. make the father jealous

UNIT 3.10

Technology in the Global Village

WHAT AM I SUPPOSED TO LEARN?

After you have read this unit, you should be able to

1 Summarize how and why changes in technology lead to changes in culture.

2 Explain cultural lag, cultural diffusion, and cultural leveling.

Throughout history, cultures have changed slowly. Except for catastrophes such as war, a culture would remain much the same for hundreds of years. People were farmers, and their lives were ruled by the rhythms of the season, times of planting and harvesting, and the customs that had grown up around these events. Or people were hunters and gatherers, and the ways they hunted and gathered remained the same year after year. The customs were set, with parents teaching them to the children, who continued their parent's way of life.

When technology changes, however, so does culture. People adjust their way of life to match the changed technology. Let's conclude the chapter by looking at this aspect of cultural change.

The New Technology

Now that we have looked at symbolic culture in detail, let's turn the focus onto nonmaterial culture, a group's *things,* from its houses to its toys. Central to a group's material culture is its technology. In its simplest sense, **technology** can be equated with tools. In a broader sense, technology also includes the skills or procedures necessary to make and use those tools.

We can use the term **new technology** to refer to an emerging technology that has a significant impact on social life. Although people develop minor technologies all the time, most are only slight modifications of existing technologies. Occasionally, however, they develop a technology that makes a major impact on human life. It is to these innovations that the term *new technology* refers. Five hundred years ago, the new technology was the printing press. For us, the new technology consists of satellites, computers, software programs, and the Internet.

The sociological significance of technology goes far beyond the tool itself. *Technology sets the framework for a group's symbolic culture.* When technology

technology in its narrow sense, tools; its broader sense includes the skills or procedures necessary to make and use those tools

new technology the emerging technologies of an era that have a significant impact on social life

changes, so do the ways people think and how they relate to one another. An example is gender relations. Through the centuries and throughout the world, it has been the custom (symbolic culture) for men to dominate women. Today's global communications (material culture) make this custom difficult to maintain. For example, when Arab women watch Western television, they observe an unfamiliar freedom in male–female relations. Using e-mail and telephones, these women talk about what they have seen. As they do so, they both express and create discontent, as well as stimulate feelings of sisterhood. These communications motivate some of them to agitate for social change.

We are seeing a revolutionary change in culture. The long-accepted idea that it is proper to withhold rights on the basis of someone's sex can no longer be sustained. We see the change, and even follow it in news reports, but what lies beyond our awareness in these remarkable events is the new technology, how it is joining the world's nations into a global communications network.

Cultural Lag and Cultural Change

Three or four generations ago, sociologist William Ogburn (1922/1938) coined the term **cultural lag.** By this term, Ogburn meant that not all parts of a culture change at the same pace. When one part of a culture changes, other parts lag behind.

Ogburn pointed out that *a group's material culture usually changes first, with the symbolic culture lagging behind.* The symbolic culture then plays a game of catch-up. For example, when we get sick, we can type our symptoms into a computer and get an instant diagnosis and recommended course of treatment. In some tests, computer programs

cultural lag Ogburn's term for human behavior lagging behind technological innovations

outperform physicians. Yet our customs (symbolic culture) have not caught up with our technology (nonmaterial culture), and we continue to visit the doctor's office.

Sometimes symbolic culture never does catch up, and we rigorously hold onto some custom long ago bypassed by technology. Have you ever wondered why our "school year" is nine months long, and why we take summers off? For most of us, this is "just the way it's always been," and we have never questioned it. But there is more to this custom than meets the eye. In the late 1800s, when universal schooling came about, the school year matched the technology of the time. Most parents were farmers, and for survival they needed their children's help at the crucial times of planting and harvesting. Today, generations later, when few people farm and there is no need for the "school year" to be so short, we still live with this cultural lag.

What examples of cultural leveling can you see in this photo from Beijing, China?

Technology and Cultural Leveling

For most of human history, communication was limited and travel was slow. In their relative isolation, human groups developed highly distinctive ways of life as they responded to the particular situations they faced. The unique characteristics they developed that distinguished one culture from another tended to change little over time. The Tasmanians, who live on a remote island off the coast of Australia, provide an extreme example. For thousands of years, they had no contact with other people. They were so isolated that they did not even know how to make clothing or fire (Edgerton 1992).

Except in such rare instances, humans have always had *some* contact with other groups. During these contacts, people learned from one another, adopting things they found desirable. In this process, called **cultural diffusion,** groups are most open to changes in their technology or material culture. They usually are eager, for example, to adopt superior weapons and tools. In remote jungles in South America you can find metal cooking pots, steel axes, and even bits of clothing spun in mills in South Carolina. Although the direction of today's cultural diffusion is primarily from the West to other parts of the world, cultural diffusion is not a one-way street—as you can see from bagels, woks, hammocks, and sushi in the United States.

With today's fast travel and communications, cultural diffusion is occurring rapidly. Air travel has made it possible to journey around the globe in a matter of hours. In the not-so-distant past, a trip from the United States

cultural diffusion the spread of material and symbolic culture from one group to another

to Africa was so unusual that only a few adventurous people made it, and newspapers would herald their feat. Today, hundreds of thousands of Americans make the trip each year.

The changes in communication are no less vast. Communication used to be limited to face-to-face speech, written messages that were passed from hand to hand, and visual signals such as smoke or light that was reflected from mirrors. Despite newspapers and even the telegraph, people in some parts of the United States did not hear that the Civil War had ended until weeks and even months after it was over. Today's electronic communications transmit messages across the globe in a matter of seconds, and we learn almost instantaneously what is happening on the other side of the world. During the Gulf War, reporters traveled with U.S. soldiers, and for the first time in history, the public viewed live video reports of battles as they took place and of people as they died.

Travel and communication bridge time and space to such an extent that there is almost no "other side of the world" anymore. One result is **cultural leveling,** a process in which cultures become more and more similar to one another. Not only is technology changing, but so is symbolic culture. Japan, for example, has adopted not only capitalism but also Western forms of dress and music, transforming it into a blend of Western and Eastern cultures.

Cultural leveling is apparent to any traveler. The golden arches of McDonald's welcome visitors to Beijing, Hong Kong, London,

cultural leveling the process by which cultures become similar to one another; refers especially to the process by which Western culture is being exported and diffused into other nations

Madrid, Moscow, Paris, and Tokyo. When I visited a jungle village in India—no electricity, no running water, and so remote that the only entrance was by a footpath—I saw a young man sporting a cap with the Nike emblem.

Although the bridging of geography, time, and culture by electronic signals and the adoption of Western icons do not in and of themselves mark the end of traditional cultures, the inevitable result is some degree of *cultural leveling*. We are producing blander, less distinctive ways of life—U.S. culture with French, Japanese, and Brazilian accents, so to speak. Although the "cultural accent" remains, something vital is lost forever.

UNIT 3.10 // TESTING MYSELF
DID I LEARN IT? ANSWERS ARE AT THE END OF THE CHAPTER

1. This is a basic principle of cultural change
   a. There can't be change without culture.
   b. When one part of a culture changes, the other parts resist change.
   c. The symbolic culture usually changes first.
   d. When technology changes, culture changes.

2. The term technology means about the same as
   a. a group's way of life
   b. symbolic culture
   c. tools
   d. culture change

3. The term new technology refers to
   a. something new
   b. an emerging technology that has a significant impact on a group's way of life
   c. a changed aspect of the symbolic culture
   d. a part of the ideal culture

4. Technology sets the framework for
   a. a group's symbolic culture
   b. launching changes in the material culture
   c. changing perception of reality
   d. trying to improve human society

5. The long-accepted idea that it is proper to withhold rights on the basis of someone's sex can no longer be sustained. We follow these changes in news reports, but what lies beyond our awareness is
   a. the struggle of men to maintain their dominance
   b. the role of education
   c. the vast amount of money being funneled in behind the scenes to bring this about
   d. how the new technology of communication and transportation allows it to come about

6. Sociologist William Ogburn coined the term cultural lag. By this term, Ogburn meant that
   a. we need to watch out that we don't fall behind other cultures that are changing faster than ours is
   b. some groups change faster than others, and the others lag behind
   c. when one part of a culture changes, other parts of the culture lag behind
   d. cultures tend not to change, but when they do, they can change rapidly

7. The nine-month-long school year in the United States is based on patterns of our previous agricultural society when most people were farmers and they needed the children to help with planting and harvesting. This is an example of
   a. the material culture lagging behind the symbolic culture
   b. cultural lag
   c. how far behind the U.S. educational system is
   d. the power of teacher's unions in maintaining a short work year

8. When groups come in contact, they learn from one another. This results in cultural diffusion. Groups are most open to change in
   a. their technology or material culture
   b. things that work
   c. their symbolic culture
   d. things that are suggested by their leaders

9. With today's extensive and rapid travel and communications, cultures around the world are tending to become similar to one another. This process is called
   a. cultural change
   b. changing symbolic culture
   c. changing material culture
   d. cultural leveling

PULLING IT ALL TOGETHER REVIEWING THE LEARNING GOALS

Unit 3.1 What Is Culture?

1. State what culture is.

- Culture is a group's way of life—its language, beliefs, values, norms, behaviors, and even material objects that people pass from one generation to the next.

2. Explain the difference between material culture and nonmaterial culture.

- Material culture refers to a group's material things, such as its jewelry, art, buildings, weapons, machines, hairstyles, and clothing. Nonmaterial culture refers to a group's ways of thinking (its beliefs, values, and other assumptions about the world) and doing (its common patterns of behavior, including language, gestures, and other forms of interaction).

Unit 3.2 Culture and Orientations to Life

1. Explain how culture is the lens through which you view life.

- Culture's learned and shared ways of believing and doing penetrate us at an early age, becoming part of our taken-for-granted assumptions about what normal life is. This is referred to as "culture within us."

2. Know what culture shock, ethnocentrism, and cultural relativism are.

- Culture shock is a disorientation people feel when they are exposed to a culture in which their assumptions about the way the world is, or should be, no longer work. Ethnocentrism is our tendency to judge others by the way our own group does things. Cultural relativism is an attempt to overcome ethnocentrism by understanding a culture on its own terms.

✳️━[**Explore** the **Concept**
The Asian American Population of the United States – The Diversity of Cultures in **mysoclab**]

👁️━[**Watch** the **Video**
Sociology on the Job: Culture in **mysoclab**]

📖━[**Read** the **Document**
"Body Ritual Among the Nacirema" by Horace Miner in **mysoclab**]

Unit 3.3 Symbolic Culture: Language

1. Explain how language is the basis of culture and even makes a past and future possible.

- Through language, we pass ideas, knowledge, and attitudes to the next generation, develop meanings of events and purposes, and produce memories. This process extends time from our present to the past and future.

2. Summarize the Sapir-Whorf hypothesis and know how language contains ways of viewing the world.

- The Sapir-Whorf hypothesis points out that words are more than just labels that we attach to things. Words are ways of dividing up the world. When we learn a language, we learn to perceive the world according to the way that our language divides up the world.

Pulling It All Together **73**

Unit 3.4 Symbolic Culture: Gestures

1. State what gestures are and to what extent they are universal.
   - Gestures vary from one culture to another. The basic emotions of anger, fear, pouting, and sadness, however, are built into our biological makeup and are universal.

Unit 3.5 Symbolic Culture: Values, Norms, and More

1. State how values, norms, and sanctions are related to one another.
   - People develop norms, expectations of behavior that support values, the standards they use to define what they hold dear in life. They award positive sanctions for following the norms, negative ones for breaking the norms.

2. Explain what folkways, mores, and taboos are.
   - Folkways are norms that receive little or no negative sanctions when they are violated. Mores are norms held so firmly that their violation is met with strong negative sanctions. Taboos are norms held so strongly that their violation is met with anger, revulsion, and such negative sanctions as prison or even death.

Unit 3.6 Many Cultural Worlds

1. Explain the difference between subcultures and countercultures.
   - Members of a subculture, who often develop distinctive forms of communication, occupy a specific world within the dominant culture. They agree with the norms and values of the mainstream culture. The members of a counterculture also develop distinctive forms of communication in their specific corners of life, but some of their values and norms place it at odds with the dominant subculture.

⊙ **Watch** the **Video**
The Big Picture:
Culture in **mysoclab**

Unit 3.7 Values in U.S. Society

1. Summarize some core values of U.S. society and know how they relate to one another.
   - It is difficult to specify the core values of a pluralistic society, one made up of many groups, as it has many competing values. But a summary of 13 core values of the United States was presented, from achievement and success to education and religiosity. Some of the values are tied together in value clusters.

2. Know how values are lenses that shape perception and distinguish between ideal culture and real culture.
   - To view social life through core values, such as equality, blinds us to aspects of life that contradict the value. There is always a gap between ideal culture, what is held out as desirable, and real culture, what people actually do.

⊙ **Watch** the **Video**
The Basics: Culture
in **mysoclab**

Unit 3.8 Changing Values

1. State why value contradictions and clashes are a source of social change.
   - When one value contradicts another, it produces pressure to resolve the contradiction. This also occurs when groups promote values that clash with core values. The result can be a change in the core value or in the contradictory or competing value.

2. Identify an emerging value cluster and an emerging fifth value in the United States.
   - As society changes, values change. A value cluster is emerging that consists of leisure, self-fulfillment, physical fitness, and youthfulness. A fifth emerging value, concern for the environment, depends on the stage of economic development.

Unit 3.9 Cultural Universals

1. State whether there are cultural universals and give the reason for your answer.
   - There are universal activities; that is, all human groups have games, ways of disposing of their dead, marriage, and so on. But there are no cultural universals; that is, there is no universal way of doing these things: games differ from group to group, as do ways of disposing of the dead and forms of marriage. Customs differ for all human activities.

2. Explain why the incest taboo is not a cultural universal.
   - It is the same with the incest taboo. All groups have an incest taboo, but what is considered incest—who one is forbidden to have sex with or to marry—varies around the world.

Unit 3.10 Technology in the Global Village

1. Summarize how and why changes in technology lead to changes in culture.
   - Technology sets a framework for a group's way of life. When technology is unchanged, cultures change slowly, if at all. When technology changes, people adapt their behavior (customs, symbolic culture) to match the technology.

2. Explain cultural lag, cultural diffusion, and cultural leveling.
   - Cultural lag refers to one part of culture changing (usually the technology) while other parts (usually the symbolic culture) lag behind. Cultural diffusion refers to groups adopting some part of another group's culture (especially its technology). Cultural leveling refers to cultures becoming similar to one another because of today's rapid transportation and communication.

UNIT 3.1 // TESTING MYSELF
DID I LEARN IT? ANSWERS

1. **d** language, beliefs, values, norms, behaviors, and material objects

2. **c** material and nonmaterial

3. **b** material culture

UNIT 3.2 // TESTING MYSELF
DID I LEARN IT? ANSWERS

1. **d** we tend to take the culture we are reared in for granted

2. **c** becomes our taken-for-granted assumptions about what normal life is

3. **a** culture is the lens through which we perceive and evaluate the world

4. **d** judge others by the way our own group does things

UNIT 3.3 // TESTING MYSELF
DID I LEARN IT? ANSWERS

1. **d** nonmaterial culture

2. **c** to which we attach meaning and use to communicate with one another

3. **b** language and gestures

UNIT 3.4 // TESTING MYSELF
DID I LEARN IT? ANSWERS

1. **c** may differ from culture to culture

2. **b** can indicate something highly negative in another culture

UNIT 3.5 // TESTING MYSELF
DID I LEARN IT? ANSWERS

1. **d** values

2. **b** negative sanction

3. **c** norm

4. **a** nonmaterial culture

5. **c** nonmaterial culture

6. **c** nonmaterial culture

7. **a** material culture

8. **c** nonmaterial culture

5. **a** are exposed to a culture that differs fundamentally from their own

6. **c** creates in-group loyalties

7. **b** leads to discrimination

8. **c** trying to understand a culture on its own terms

9. **b** items viewed as food in one culture can be seen as repulsive in another culture

10. **d** cultures that have less exploitation represent a better quality of life

4. **a** language

5. **d** allows us to build shared understandings of events

6. **c** allows culture to develop

7. **b** our language determines how we perceive objects and events

8. **a** found out that his native language was wrong

9. **d** will have different perceptions of the same girl

3. **a** is not universal

4. **d** built into our biological makeup and are universal

4. **a** positive sanction

5. **d** moral holidays

6. **c** a folkway

7. **d** one of the mores

8. **a** a taboo

1. **d** subculture

1. **d** pluralistic society

1. **d** group superiority and equality
2. **c** a force for social change

1. **d** universal activities
2. **a** cultural universals

1. **d** When technology changes, culture changes
2. **c** tools
3. **b** an emerging technology that has a significant impact on a group's way of life
4. **a** a group's symbolic culture

2. **c** counterculture
3. **b** Nancy was assaulting core values

2. **c** this type of society has many competing values
3. **b** value cluster

3. **b** a reaffirming of the core value
4. **a** a value cluster
5. **d** how an emerging value can depend on the state of economic development

3. **c** *seven* of every eight women are ineligible marriage partners
4. **a** remove a curse

5. **d** how the new technology of communication and transportation allows it to come about
6. **c** when one part of a culture changes, other parts of the culture lag behind
7. **b** cultural lag
8. **d** their technology or material culture
9. **d** cultural leveling

CHAPTER 4
SOCIALIZATION

▶ **Watch** the **Video** in **mysoclab**

((•—▶ **Listen** to the **Chapter Audio** in **mysoclab**

GETTING STARTED

Did you know that society makes us human? I can just hear your response: "That's ridiculous. I was born a human. I think you sociologists push the envelope a little bit too far."

I don't blame you if your response is something like this. I remember when I was first introduced to this idea. It just didn't seem reasonable. So let's see why sociologists say that society makes us human.

As we explore this fascinating idea, we'll be looking at what *you* would be like if animals raised you or if you had bad parents who locked you up in an attic when you were just a baby. We will also look at how you developed your mind, personality, emotions, and ideas. In other words, let's try to understand how YOU became YOU.

A market in Panama City, Panama

77

UNIT 4.1

Extremes in Socialization

Let's begin by introducing the major term of this chapter, **socialization,** how we learn the ways of society. Socialization refers both to our childhood experiences and to all the learning we go through in life. When our mother explains why we need to be polite to our neighbor, she is socializing us. When our teacher tells us to be quiet in class, we are being socialized. When we watch television and learn that it would be nice to have some new computer, car, or cola, we are being socialized. Socialization is an ongoing experience, one that ends only with our death.

This lifetime process of socialization began when you were a baby. Let's ask this question: What would you be like today if you had been raised by animals? Let's see if we can find an answer to this provocative question.

> 📖 **Read** the **Document**
> "Final Note on a Case of Extreme Isolation" by Kingsley Davis in **mysoclab**

Feral Children

The naked child was found in the forest, walking on all fours, eating grass, and lapping water from the river. When he saw a small animal, he would growl and pounce on it. He would rip the animal with his teeth and ferociously tear chunks from its body.

One of the reasons I went to Cambodia was to interview a feral child—the boy shown here—who supposedly had been raised by monkeys. When I arrived at the remote location where the boy was living, I was disappointed to find that the story was only partially true. When Mathay was about two months old, the Khmer Rouge killed his parents and left him to starve. Months later, villagers saw a female monkey carrying a human baby. They shot the monkey and took the baby to an orphanage. Only briefly a feral child, but an actual feral child, and the only one I'm likely to interview.

WHAT AM I SUPPOSED TO LEARN?

After you have read this unit, you should be able to

1 Explain how "society makes us human."

2 Summarize the effects of low human contact (isolation, institutionalization) on human development.

3 Use the case of Jack and Oskar to illustrate how our attitudes come from social experiences.

You might find this hard to believe, but this is probably what you would be like if you had been raised by animals. At least, this is what **feral children** were like, the wild children who were occasionally found in past centuries.

Why am I even mentioning stories that sound so exaggerated? It is because of what happened in 1798. In that year, a feral child was found in the forests of Aveyron, France. We could ignore "The wild boy of Aveyron," as he became known, writing him off as just another folk myth, except for this—French scientists took the child to a laboratory and studied him. Like the feral children that people heard about from time to time, this child, too, gave no indication of feeling the cold. Most startling, though, the boy would growl when he saw a small animal, pounce on it, and devour it uncooked.

Ever since I read Itard's (1962) account of this boy, I've been fascinated by the seemingly fantastic possibility that animals could raise human children. In 2002, I received a report from a contact in Cambodia that a feral child had been found in the jungles. When I had the opportunity the following year to visit the child and interview his caregivers, I grabbed it. The boy's photo is on the left.

Another way to see what you would be like if you were untouched by society is to study the pitiful accounts of isolated children. Let's see what we can learn from them.

socialization the process by which people learn the characteristics of their group— the knowledge, skills, attitudes, values, norms, and actions thought appropriate for them

feral children children assumed to have been raised by animals, in the wilderness, isolated from humans

Isolated Children

In 1938, Isabelle, a 6½-year-old girl in Ohio, was discovered living in a dark room with her deaf-mute mother. Isabelle couldn't talk, but she did use gestures to communicate with her mother. An inadequate diet and lack of sunshine had given Isabelle a disease called rickets.

and went to the bathroom wherever she wanted. At the age of 21, Genie was sent to a home for adults who cannot live alone. (Pines 1981)

Add Genie's pathetic story to that of Isabelle's, and we can conclude that the basic human traits of intelligence and the ability to establish close bonds with others depend on early interaction with other humans. Genie's experience also indicates that there is a period prior to age 13 in which children must learn language or they cannot become intelligent or grasp the basics of human relationships.

What would you be like, then, if you had the misfortune of having evil parents who kept you locked up in a dark attic and no one talked to you? Language is the key to human development, and language allows you to develop thought and communicate your experiences. From your world of internal silence, you would have no shared ideas, and you would lack connections to others.

In *Making It Personal,* let's consider a little more how culture has influenced you.

[Her legs] were so bowed that as she stood erect the soles of her shoes came nearly flat together, and she got about with a skittering gait. Her behavior toward strangers, especially men, was almost that of a wild animal, manifesting much fear and hostility. In lieu of speech she made only a strange croaking sound. (Davis 1940/2012:156–157)

Isabelle couldn't talk, and some thought she was mentally impaired. It certainly looked that way—she scored practically zero on her first intelligence test. But after a few months of language training, Isabelle was able to speak in short sentences. In just a year, she could write a few words, do simple addition, and retell stories after hearing them. Seven months later, she had a vocabulary of almost 2,000 words. In just two years, Isabelle reached the intellectual level that is normal for her age. Sociologist Kingsley Davis, who followed this case, said that Isabelle then went to school where she was "bright, cheerful, energetic . . . and participated in all school activities as normally as other children" (Davis 1940/2007:157–158).

Another isolated child who came to the public's attention is Genie, who was 13 when she was discovered. She had been locked in a small room and tied to a chair since she was 20 months old:

Apparently Genie's father (70 years old when Genie was discovered in 1970) hated children. He probably had caused the death of two of Genie's siblings. Her 50-year-old mother was partially blind and frightened of her husband. Genie could not speak, did not know how to chew, was unable to stand upright, and could not straighten her hands and legs. On intelligence tests, she scored at the level of a 1-year-old. After intensive training, Genie learned to walk and to say simple sentences (although they were garbled). Genie's language remained primitive as she grew up. She could not make friends, would take anyone's property if it appealed to her,

MAKING IT PERSONAL
Biology, Language, and You

The body you were born with is certainly your biological heritage. Society doesn't give you arms and legs or skin color. But your biological heritage does not determine your behaviors, attitudes, or values. Your culture—which depends on language—superimposes the specifics of what you become onto your biological heritage.

Try to trace one of your behaviors, one of your attitudes, and one of your values to specific social experiences.

Isolated Animals

Monkeys that are deprived of normal "monkey interaction" also suffer in their development. Psychologists Harry and Margaret Harlow (1962) isolated baby rhesus monkeys for different lengths of time and then put them in with the other monkeys. Monkeys that had been isolated for shorter periods (about three months) were able to adjust to normal monkey life. They learned to play and engage in pretend fights. Those isolated for six months or more, however, couldn't make the adjustment, and the other monkeys rejected them. In other words, the longer the period of isolation, the more difficult its effects are to overcome. In addition, if too much time passes after a learning stage is missed, it may be impossible to make it up. This seems to have been the case with Genie, too.

Because humans are not monkeys, we must be careful about how we apply animal studies to human behavior. The Harlow experiments, however, support what we know about children who are reared in isolation.

Institutionalized Children

Other than language, what else does a child need to develop into what we consider a healthy, balanced, intelligent human being? Part of the answer comes from an intriguing experiment from the 1930s. Back then, orphanages were common because parents were more likely than now to die before their children were grown. Children reared in orphanages tended to have low IQs. "Common sense" made it seem obvious that their low intelligence was because of poor brains ("They're just born this way"). But two psychologists, H. M. Skeels and H. B. Dye (1939), began to suspect a social cause.

Skeels (1966) provides this account of a "good" orphanage in Iowa, one where he and Dye were consultants:

Until about six months, they were cared for in the infant nursery. The babies were kept in standard hospital cribs that often had protective sheeting on the sides, thus effectively limiting visual stimulation; no toys or other objects were hung in the infants' line of vision. Human interactions were limited to busy nurses who, with the speed

born of practice and necessity, changed diapers or bedding, bathed and medicated the infants, and fed them efficiently with propped bottles.

Perhaps, thought Skeels and Dye, the problem wasn't poor brains. Maybe the cause of the babies' low intelligence was their lack of social interaction. To test their controversial idea, they placed thirteen infants who were so slow mentally that no one wanted to adopt them in an institution for women who were quite slow mentally. Although these women had celebrated 18 to 50 birthdays, their mental age was only 5 to 12. Each infant, about 19 months old, was assigned to a separate ward of women.

The women were pleased to have the babies. They enjoyed taking care of the infants' physical needs—diapering, feeding, and so on. And they loved to play with the children. They cuddled them and showered them with attention. They even competed to see which ward would have "its baby" walking or talking first. In each ward, one woman became particularly attached to the child and figuratively adopted him or her:

As a consequence, an intense one-to-one adult–child relationship developed, which was supplemented by the less intense but frequent interactions with the other adults in the environment. Each child had some one person with whom he [or she] was identified and who was particularly interested in him [or her] and his [or her] achievements. (Skeels 1966)

The researchers left a control group of twelve low-IQ infants at the orphanage. These infants received the usual care. Two and a half years later, at age 4, Skeels and Dye tested all the children's intelligence. Their findings are startling: The children cared for by the women in the institution gained an average of 28 IQ points while those who remained in the orphanage lost 30 points.

What happened after these children were grown? Did these initial differences matter? Twenty-one years later, Skeels and Dye did a follow-up study. The twelve in the control group, those who had remained in the orphanage, averaged less than a third-grade education. Four still lived in state institutions, and the others held low-level jobs. Only two had married. The thirteen in the experimental group, those cared for by the institutionalized women, had an average education of twelve grades (about normal for that period). Five had completed one or more years of college. One had even gone to graduate school. Eleven had married. All thirteen were self-supporting or were homemakers

An orphanage in Mumbai, India.

(Skeels 1966). Apparently, "high intelligence" depends on early, close relations with other humans.

A recent experiment in India confirms this early research. Some of India's orphanages are like those that Skeels and Dye studied—dismal places where unattended children lie in bed all day. When experimenters added stimulating play and interaction to the children's activities, not only did the children's motor skills improve, but so did their IQs (Taneja et al. 2002). The longer that children lack stimulating interaction, though, the more difficulty they have intellectually (Meese 2005). If this continues, like Genie, the damage can't be repaired.

There is another fascinating case for you to think about and apply to your own life in the following *Making It Personal*.

IF YOU WANT TO LEARN MORE *about identical twins Jack and Oskar,*

Read more from the author: Heredity or Environment? The Case of Jack and Oskar, Identical Twins in **mysoclab**

MAKING IT PERSONAL
Why Are You More Than a Big Animal?

Jack Yufe and Oskar Stohr are identical twins. Born in 1932 to a Roman Catholic mother and a Jewish father, they were separated as babies after their parents divorced. Jack was reared in Trinidad by his father. There, he learned loyalty to Jews and hatred of Hitler and the Nazis. After World War II, Jack and his father moved to Israel. When he was 17, Jack joined a kibbutz and later served in the Israeli army.

Oskar's upbringing was the mirror image of Jack's. Oskar was reared in Czechoslovakia by his mother's mother, who was a strict Catholic. When Oskar was a toddler, Hitler annexed this area of Czechoslovakia. As a boy, Oskar joined the Hitler Youth where he learned to love Hitler and to hate Jews. (Begley 1979; Chen 1979)

In this remarkable case, you can see how society (social experiences) trumps heredity. Jack and Oskar's sharply contrasting attitudes toward Hitler and Jews did not come from their heredity, which was identical, but from their stunningly different social experiences. Your ideas and attitudes, too, such an essential part of who you are, do not come from your biology, but from your experiences in society.

You have also seen that babies do not develop "naturally" into social adults. If children are reared in isolation, their bodies grow, but they become little more than big animals. Without language, they can't grasp relationships between people (the "connections" you call brother, sister, parent, friend, teacher, and so on). And without warm, friendly interactions, they can't bond with others. They don't become "friendly" or cooperate with others.

Now does the statement that "society makes us human" make more sense?

UNIT 4.1 // TESTING MYSELF
DID I LEARN IT? ANSWERS ARE AT THE END OF THE CHAPTER

1. This chapter is about socialization. This term refers to
   a. learning to be sociable
   b. mental processes being greater than biological ones
   c. how we learn to control our body with our mind
   d. how we learn the ways of society

2. As strange as it sounds, we know that feral children (children thought to be raised by animals) are not just folk myths because
   a. French scientists studied a feral child in 1798
   b. there are many feral children in Bosnia
   c. the Latvians sometimes use animals to socialize their children
   d. the U.S. Academy of Sciences has authorized and funded research on feral children

3. Isabelle was an isolated child studied by sociologist Kingsley Davis in the 1930s. Isabelle, who could not speak, scored practically zero on her first IQ test. After this, she
   a. was placed in a dark attic to live
   b. was placed in an orphanage to live
   c. learned how to communicate by sign language
   d. was given intensive training and developed like a normal child

4. Genie was an isolated child who was discovered in 1970 when she was 13 years old. Genie could neither walk nor talk. With intensive training, she learned to walk, but she could speak only in garbled sentences. She also went to the bathroom anywhere she felt like it. Genie's experience indicates that there is a period prior to age 13
   a. that controls bathroom functions
   b. in which personal hygiene must be learned
   c. in which children must learn language or they cannot become intelligent
   d. in which the area of the brain that governs morality must be stimulated

5. From the cases of Isabelle and Genie, it seems fair to conclude that
   a. most isolated children are girls
   b. the human traits of intelligence and the ability to establish close bonds with others depend on early interaction with other humans
   c. it is unethical for sociologists to study isolated children
   d. personal hygiene is a matter of individual preference

6. Psychologists Harry and Margaret Harlow did experiments with baby rhesus monkeys. Their experiments confirm the conclusion from the cases of Isabelle and Genie that
   a. if too much time passes after a learning stage is missed, it may be impossible to make it up
   b. learning pretend play (pretend fights for monkeys) is difficult for isolated children
   c. it is better for a child to be raised by a village of people than by a pair of parents
   d. children need two parents in order to become normal

7. Psychologists Skeels and Dye did an experiment with low-IQ babies in an orphanage (an experiment that would be prohibited today). Those in the experimental group were raised by institutionalized, low-IQ mothers, while those in the control group remained in the orphanage. The IQs of the children in the control group dropped, while the IQs of the children in the experimental group
   a. were almost identical to those in the control group
   b. dropped for a while, but then went up
   c. went up for a while, but then dropped
   d. increased

8. After their experiment with the orphanage children, Skeels and Dye concluded that
   a. they made an ethical error in research and apologized to the American Sociological Association
   b. intelligence is fixed at birth
   c. the development of intelligence depends on stimulating interaction
   d. low-IQ women make good mothers

9. Jack and Oskar were identical twins who were reared apart. Jack learned to hate Hitler and love Jews, while Oskar learned to love Hitler and hate Jews. From this case, it seems fair to conclude that
   a. some people still don't understand that Hitler was evil
   b. identical twins have different attitudes about Hitler and Jews
   c. you never know how identical twins are going to feel about things in life
   d. social experiences mold our ideas and attitudes

10. When sociologists say that "society makes us human," they mean that
   a. conception takes two people, which is a form of society
   b. humans make society
   c. our social experiences form such essential characteristics as our behaviors, ideas, attitudes, and intelligence
   d. there is nothing as social as humans

UNIT 4.2
Socialization into the Self and Mind

Besides what we have already covered, what else do you think is part of "being human"? Certainly essential to who you are is your **self,** your image of who you are. It might seem surprising, but sociologists point out that the self also comes from society. Let's see how this happens.

Cooley and the Looking-Glass Self

About a hundred years ago, Charles Horton Cooley (1864–1929), a symbolic interactionist, concluded that one way society makes us human is by producing our *self,* our image of who we are. This might sound strange to you, as most people think that the self just naturally unfolds from within us. Cooley pointed out that the *self develops from interaction with others. As we see ourselves in the eyes of others, we internalize that reflection.*

In other words, the people around us are a sort of mirror that reflects an image back to us, For this reason, Cooley (1902) coined the term **looking-glass self.** Here is how he said the looking-glass self works:

First, we imagine what people think about us. For example, we may think that others perceive us as witty or dull.

Then we interpret people's reactions. We figure out if they like us for being witty. Or do they dislike us for being dull?

Out of this comes our self-concept. How we interpret others' reactions to us frames our feelings and ideas about ourselves. A favorable reflection in this *social mirror* leads to a positive self-concept; a negative reflection leads to a negative self-concept.

In *Making It Personal* in the next column, let's consider how this applies to you.

Mead and Role Taking

Another symbolic interactionist, George Herbert Mead (1863–1931), pointed out that play is an essential way you develop a self. As you play

self the unique human capacity of being able to see ourselves "from the outside"; the views we internalize of how others see us

looking-glass self a term coined by Charles Horton Cooley to refer to the process by which our self develops through internalizing others' reactions to us

taking the role of the other putting yourself in someone else's shoes; understanding how someone else feels and thinks, so you anticipate how that person will act

in mysoclab

WHAT AM I SUPPOSED TO LEARN?

After you have read this unit, you should be able to

1 Explain the looking-glass self and why it is essential to the development of the self.

2 Explain how we develop the ability to take the role of the other and why this is essential to our socialization.

MAKING IT PERSONAL
Your Social Mirror

Your self begins in childhood, but its development is a life-long, ongoing process that is never complete. During your everyday life, you monitor how others react to you. As you evaluate their reactions, you continually modify the self. Your ideas of what others think about you can be totally inaccurate, but they still become part of your self concept.

Think about people who have been influential in your life. How did you evaluate their reactions to you? How do you think this has become part of your self concept?

with others, you learn to **take the role of the other.** That is, you learn to put yourself in someone else's shoes—to understand how that person feels and thinks and to anticipate how he or she will act.

This doesn't happen overnight. At first you can only take the role of **significant others,** individuals who significantly influence your life, such as one of your parents or a brother or sister. By assuming that person's role during play, such as dressing up in your parents' clothing, you cultivate the ability to put yourself in the place of someone else.

As your self develops, your ability to take the role of others expands. As you learn to take the role of many people, you eventually get an idea of how "people in general" think of you. Mead used the term **generalized other** to refer to our perception of how people in general think of us.

Taking the role of others is essential for you to become a

Watch the **Video**
The Basics: Socialization

significant other an individual who significantly influences someone else

generalized other the norms, values, attitudes, and expectations of people "in general"; the child's ability to take the role of the generalized other is a significant step in the development of a self

Why did Cooley use the term *looking-glass self?*

cooperative member of human groups—whether this is your family, friends, or co-workers. This ability allows you to modify your behavior by anticipating how others will react—something Genie never learned.

As Figure 4.1 illustrates, you went through three stages as you learned to take the role of the other. Let's look at these.

1. *Imitation.* Under the age of 3, you didn't have a sense of self separate from others. You could only imitate people's gestures and words. (This stage is actually not role taking, but it prepared you for it.)

FIGURE 4.1 **How We Learn to Take the Role of the Other: Mead's Three**

Stage 1: Imitation
Children under age 3
No sense of self
Imitate others

Stage 2: Play
Ages 3 to 6
Play "pretend" others
(princess, Spider-Man, etc.)

Stage 3: Team Games
After about age 6 or 7
Team games
("organized play")
Learn to take multiple roles

Stages

Source: By the author.

2. *Play.* During the second stage, from the ages of about 3 to 6, you pretended to take the roles of specific people. You might have pretended that you were a firefighter, a wrestler, a nurse, Supergirl, Spider-Man, a princess, and so on. You might have put on your parents' clothing or tied a towel around your neck to "become" Superman or Wonder Woman.

3. *Team Games.* This third stage, organized play, or team games, began about the time you entered school. The significance for the self is that to play these games you had to be able to take several roles. One of Mead's favorite examples was baseball. To play baseball, it isn't enough to know your own role. You also must be able to take the role of others, to anticipate what everyone else on the field will do when the ball is hit or thrown.

Mead also said that the self has two parts, the "I" and the "me." The "I" is *the self as subject,* the active, spontaneous, creative part of your self. In contrast, the "me" is *the self as object.* It is made up of attitudes you internalize from your interactions with others. Mead chose these pronouns because in English "I" is the active agent, as in "I shoved him," while "me" is the object of action, as in "He shoved me." It is important to stress that you are not passive in this process of forming a self. Rather, your "I" actively evaluates the reactions of others and organizes them into a unified whole.

To make these ideas clearer, let's apply them to yourself in the following *Making It Personal.*

MAKING IT PERSONAL
Your Self and Mind as Gifts from Society

You could easily get lost in the many details here, and they all are important. But I want to stress a main point of Mead's theory, which some find startling: *Your self is a social product.* Your self-image has come from interaction with others. It is important to stress that you have been active in this process. Your "I" has been busy putting these many reactions of others together.

There is another major point, which some find even more startling: *Your mind is also a social product.* In graduate school, I read Mead's book, *Mind, Self, and Society,* in which Mead stresses this point. This was hard to understand—especially the way Mead wrote—that society gives us our mind. I always thought of my mind as developing within me, not as something imposed on me from the outside.

Actually, Mead did not mean that your mind is shoved into you. Rather, your mind developed (and is developing) as a process. Again, we go back to language. Simply put, you cannot think without symbols. And where do these symbols

How is play part of learning to take the role of the other?

come from? Society gives you these symbols by giving you language. If society did not provide these symbols, you would not be able to think—and so you would not possess that entity we call the mind. Like language, both your self and mind are products of society.

UNIT 4.2 // TESTING MYSELF
DID I LEARN IT? ANSWERS ARE AT THE END OF THE CHAPTER

1. Tricia, a six-year-old, has been sulking in her room for the past two hours. Her nine-year-old brother told her that she was dumb. He shouted it over and over. And he did this in front of his two friends. Tricia feels stupid. This is part of what Charles Horton Cooley called the
   a. greater difficulty in socializing boys
   b. problem of rearing two children who are close in age
   c. reflective self
   d. looking-glass self

2. In the looking-glass self, we don't actually internalize the reactions of others to us. Instead, we internalize
   a. the behavior of others
   b. the messages that others give us through their behavior
   c. our evaluations of the reactions of others to us
   d. the elements that match our self concept

3. To be able to get along with others, it is essential that we are able to put ourselves in the shoes of other people. George Herbert Mead called this being able to
   a. follow the thinking of the other
   b. take the role of the other
   c. develop a self
   d. see ourselves in the looking-glass mirror

4. Five-year old Alicia loves to tie a towel around her neck and pretend she can fly like Wonder Woman. She also likes putting on a pink princess dress that her mother bought her for her birthday, waving a little wand and pretending that she can turn the dog into a cat. Alicia is in this stage of learning to take the role of the other
   a. play
   b. imitation
   c. team games
   d. mastery of the self

5. Five-year-old Jarmaine loves to put his little feet into his father's shoes and clunk around the house. He also pretends to shave. Jarmaine is
   a. going through a phase
   b. trying to take the role of the generalized other
   c. reflecting his developing self concept
   d. taking the role of a significant other

6. It is twelve-year-old Barbara's turn at bat. As she prepares for the pitch, she can practically see the ball flying into the air and herself running the bases and making it home. She can imagine the opposing team looking stunned and her own team clapping, shouting, and lifting her onto their shoulders. Barbara is taking the role of
   a. her team
   b. a significant other
   c. the generalized other
   d. the winner

7. Little Teddy is just six months old. If you raise your hands, he'll raise his hands. If you smile, he will smile. Teddy is in this stage of learning to take the role of the other
   a. trial and error
   b. imitation
   c. significant others
   d. infancy

8. Mead said that the self has both an "I" and a "me." The "me" is the
   a. self as object
   b. same as the "I"
   c. part that becomes active when it is threatened
   d. less important part of the self

9. From Mead's analysis of the self, we can conclude that the self
   a. comes into being only with difficulty
   b. comes into being primarily during team games
   c. arises spontaneously from within
   d. is a product of society

10. From Mead's analysis of the self, we can also conclude that the mind
    a. is the inquiring part of the self
    b. is different for men and women
    c. arises spontaneously from within
    d. is a product of society

UNIT 4.3

Socialization into Emotions

WHAT AM I SUPPOSED TO LEARN?

After you have read this unit, you should be able to

1 Explain which emotions and facial expressions are universal and why.

2 Explain what sociology has to do with emotions.

3 Explain why the phrase "society within us" applies to emotions.

Emotions, too, are an essential aspect of who we become. And like the mind, our emotions depend on socialization (Hochschild 2008). This might also sound strange. Don't all people get angry? Doesn't everyone cry? Don't we all feel guilt, shame, and fear? What has socialization to do with our emotions? Let's find out.

Expressing Emotions: Biology

At first, it may look as though socialization is not relevant for our emotions. Paul Ekman (1980), a psychologist who studied emotions in several countries, concluded that everyone experiences six basic emotions: disgust, anger, sadness, happiness, surprise, and fear. He also found that people around the world show the same facial expressions when they feel these emotions. A person from Peru, for example, could tell from the look on your face that you are angry, disgusted, or fearful, and you could tell from the Peruvian's face that he is happy, sad, or surprised. These facial expressions, Ekman concluded, are hard-wired into our brains.

Research on facial expressions at the Paralympics supports Ekman's conclusion (Matsumoto and Willingham 2009). Both people who were blind from birth and sighted people showed the same facial expressions when they learned that they had won (or lost) an event. Those blind from birth could never have learned these facial expressions.

Expressing Emotions: "Feeling Rules"

If we have universal facial expressions to express certain emotions, then this is biology, something that Darwin noted back in the 1800s (Horwitz and Wakefield 2007:41). What, then, does sociology have to do with how we express emotions? Facial expressions are only one way by which we show our feelings. We also use our bodies, voices, and gestures.

Best friends since high school, Jane and Sushana were hardly ever apart until Sushana married and moved to another state a year ago. Jane has been waiting eagerly at the arrival gate for Sushana's flight, which has been delayed. When Sushana exits, she and Jane hug one another, making "squeals of glee" and even jumping a bit.

If you couldn't tell from their names that these were women, you could tell from their behavior. To express delighted surprise, U.S. women are allowed to make "squeals of glee" in public places and to jump as they hug. But in the exact circumstances, U.S. men are expected to shake hands or to give a brief hug. If the men gave out "squeals of glee," they would be violating a fundamental "gender rule" of emotions.

Feeling rules for expressing emotions go far beyond gender. We also have "rules" of culture, social class, relationships, and settings. Consider *culture*. Two close Japanese friends who meet after a long separation don't shake hands or hug—they bow. Two Arab men will kiss. *Social class* is so significant that it cuts across other lines, even gender. Upon seeing a friend after a long absence, upper-class women and men are likely to be more reserved in expressing their delight than are working-class

What "gender rule" does this photo depict?

women and men. And you know that feeling rules change with *relationships*. You will express your feelings more openly if you are with close friends, more guardedly if you are being interviewed for a job. The *setting*, then, is also important. If you are at a rock concert, you will express your emotions quite differently than if you are in a classroom. Although you didn't realize it, a good part of your socialization during childhood centered on learning feeling rules.

What We Feel

Joan, a U.S. woman who had been married for seven years, had no children. When she finally gave birth and the doctor handed her a healthy baby girl, she was almost overcome with joy.

Tafadzwa, in Zimbabwe, had been married for seven years and had no children. When the doctor handed her a healthy baby girl, she was almost overcome with sadness.

You can easily understand why the U.S. woman felt happy. But why did the woman in Zimbabwe feel sad? In Zimbabwe culture, male children are so prized that to not give birth to a baby boy provides a reason for her husband to divorce her (Horwitz and Wakefield 2007:43). Socialization goes much deeper within us than simply guiding how, where, and when we express our feelings. It also affects *what* we feel as we go through life (Clark 1997; Shields 2002).

In the next *Making It Personal*, let's consider how feelings that society has placed in you help keep you in line.

MAKING IT PERSONAL
What Keeps You in Line?

If in a moment of intense frustration, or out of a devilish desire to shock people, you felt like tearing off your clothes and running naked down the street, what would stop you?

The answer is your socialization—*society within you*. Because of your socialization, you think along certain lines and feel particular emotions. This helps keep you in line. Thoughts such as "Would I get kicked out of school?" or "What would my friends (parents) think if they found out?" represent an awareness of the self in relationship to others. So does a desire to avoid shame or embarrassment. *Both your self and your emotions are internal controls that mold your behavior, fulfilling a primary goal of socialization to turn you into a conforming member of society.* Socialization into self and emotions is so effective that some people feel embarrassed just thinking about running naked in public!

Socialization is essential for your development as a human being. From your interaction with others, you learn how to think, reason, and feel. The net result is the shaping of your behavior—including your thinking and emotions—according to cultural standards. This is what sociologists mean when they refer to "*society within us.*"

1. You can tell from the facial expressions of a woman from Angola or Canada or Brazil that she is happy, sad, surprised, angry, disgusted, or fearful. This means that these six expressions of emotion are
   a. learned all over the world
   b. not universal
   c. learned at an early age
   d. part of our biology

2. Compared with sighted people, when people at the Paralympics who were blind from birth learned that they had won or lost an event, they showed
   a. more control of their emotions
   b. less control of their emotions
   c. the same facial expressions
   d. that they were better sports

3. "I just learned that your salary is going to be doubled when you get the promotion," Darlene's friend and co-worker told her. As she entered her boss's office to get the news, Darlene kept telling herself, "Now don't get excited and start jumping up and down." Darlene is trying to follow
   a. an office rule
   b. a feeling rule
   c. good advice
   d. common sense

4. Research shows that when women first hold a child to which they have just given birth, their emotional reactions
   a. are the same around the world
   b. depend on their hormones
   c. are different if they are married or unmarried
   d. differ from one culture to another

5. That a woman in Zimbabwe who has given birth to a baby girl is likely to react differently than an American woman who has just given birth to a baby girl indicates that socialization
   a. has reached its limits
   b. no longer applies
   c. affects what we feel
   d. has greater effects on women than on men

6. Shirley's frustration at her job has been growing by the week. Today it was just too much. She got up from her desk to tell her boss just how she felt. Then she thought about how her family needs the money she is earning. She sat back down, quietly seething within as she continued her work. Sociologists say that this is an example of
   a. second thoughts
   b. society within us
   c. putting monetary concerns ahead of emotional ones
   d. worker alienation

7. In the example just given of Shirley deciding not to tell her boss off, you can see how the self is a form of
   a. internal control
   b. socialization
   c. emotion
   d. dynamic intervention

8. A primary goal of socialization is to
   a. try to change the world
   b. get people to strive for higher goals in life
   c. overcome people's weak points
   d. turn us into conforming members of society

UNIT 4.4

Getting the Message: Learning Gender

WHAT AM I SUPPOSED TO LEARN?

After you have read this unit, you should be able to

1 Explain what gender and gender socialization are.

2 Describe the Goldberg and Lewis study.

3 Explain how the family, peers, and the mass media socialize us into gender.

I'm sure you'll agree that an essential part of who you are is your "maleness" or your "femaleness." These characteristics seem to flow from within—the way you express yourself, from your gestures to your laugh. They seem to be a natural part of you, something you were born with.

"Are you going to tell me that these are a 'gift' from society, too?" I can practically hear you ask, anticipating what is coming next.

And right you would be if you wondered this. Let's find out why.

Learning the Gender Map

For children, society is unexplored territory. But children don't explore this wilderness on their own. They are given a social map that let's them know where to go and how to act. A major signpost on society's map is **gender,** the attitudes and behaviors expected of us because we are male or female. As we learn the attitudes and behaviors assigned to our sex (called **gender socialization**), we are nudged into different lanes in life. We take direction so well that, as adults, most of us act, think, and even feel according to the guidelines on this gender map. Let's get a glimpse of how this happens.

Gender Messages in the Family

Our parents are the first significant others to show us the gender map. Sometimes they do this consciously, perhaps by wrapping our newborn bodies in pink or blue, colors that have no meaning in themselves but that are now associated with gender. Our parents' own gender ideas are embedded so firmly, however, that as this classic research illustrates, they do most of their gender teaching without being aware of what they are doing.

Psychologists Susan Goldberg and Michael Lewis (1969) asked mothers to bring their 6-month-old infants into their laboratory, supposedly to observe the infants' development. Covertly, however, they also observed the mothers. They found that the mothers kept their daughters closer to them. They also touched their daughters more than their sons and spoke to them more frequently. By the time the children were 13 months old, the girls stayed closer to their mothers during play, and they returned to their mothers sooner and more often than the boys did.

Then Goldberg and Lewis did a little experiment. They set up a barrier to separate the children from their mothers, who were holding toys. The girls were more likely to cry and motion for help; the boys were more likely to try to climb over the barrier.

Goldberg and Lewis concluded that the mothers had subconsciously rewarded their daughters for being passive and dependent, and their sons for being active and independent. These results have been confirmed by other researchers (Connors 1996; Clearfield and Nelson 2006; Best 2010).

On the basis of our sex, then, our parents treat us differently. On a conscious level, they give us different kinds of toys. Boys are more likely to get guns and "action figures" that destroy enemies. Girls are more likely to be given dolls and jewelry. Some parents try to choose "gender neutral" toys, but kids know what is popular, and they feel left out if they don't have

gender the behaviors and attitudes that a society considers proper for its males and females; masculinity or femininity

gender socialization learning society's "gender map," the paths in life set out for us because we are male or female

what the other kids have. The significance of toys in gender socialization can be summarized this way: Most parents would be upset if someone gave their son Barbie dolls.

Play also teaches gender. In ways we haven't yet studied, parents subtly "signal" to their sons that is okay for them to participate in more rough-and-tumble play. In general, parents expect their sons to get dirtier and to be more defiant, and their daughters to stay cleaner and to be more compliant (Gilman 1911/1971; Nordberg 2010; Henslin 2012). And in large part, parents get what they expect. Such experiences in socialization lie at the heart of the sociological explanation of male–female differences.

IF YOU WANT TO LEARN MORE about how socialization is so powerful that it can turn girls into boys, you might be interested in the sworn virgins

Read more from the author: Women Becoming Men: The Sworn Virgins-For Your Consideration in **mysoclab**

Gender Messages from Peers

This sorting process into gender that begins in the family continues as we are exposed to other aspects of society. Especially powerful is our **peer group,** individuals of roughly the same age who are linked by common interests. Examples of peer groups are our friends, classmates, and "the kids in the neighborhood."

During your childhood, you saw girls and boys teach one another what it means to be a female or a male. You might not have recognized what was happening, however, so let's eavesdrop on a conversation between two eighth-grade girls studied by sociologist Donna Eder (2007).

CINDY: The only thing that makes her look anything is all the makeup . . .

PENNY: She had a picture, and she's standing like this. (Poses with one hand on her hip and one by her head)

CINDY: Her face is probably this skinny, but it looks that big 'cause of all the makeup she has on it.

PENNY: She's ugly, ugly, ugly.

Do you see how these girls were giving gender lessons? They were teaching one another images of appearance and behavior that they thought were appropriate for females.

And boys? They do the same thing. Sociologist Melissa Milkie (1994), who studied junior high school boys, found that much of their talk centered on movies and TV. Although the boys had seen many images, they would single

peer group a group of individuals, often of roughly the same age, who are linked by common interests and orientations

out those associated with sex and violence. They amused one another by repeating lines, acting out parts, and joking and laughing at what they had seen.

If you know boys in their early teens, you've probably seen a lot of behavior like this. You may have been amused, or you might have shaken your head in disapproval. But did you peek beneath the surface? Milkie did. What is really going on? The boys, she concluded, were using media images to develop their identity as males. They had gotten the message: "Real" males are obsessed with sex and violence. Not to joke and laugh about murder and promiscuous sex would have marked a boy as a "weenie," a label to be avoided at all costs.

In *Making It Personal*, let's consider how you learned gender.

MAKING IT PERSONAL
Your Gender Lessons

It is time to step back and reflect some more on your childhood. You've read about parents, peers, and toys. How did your parents nudge you into gender? What were your favorite toys? Looking back, what gender messages came with your toys?

Your particular experiences in your preteen and teen groups might have been different from those you just reviewed, but your groups, too, gave you strong lessons in gender. What were they? Gender socialization doesn't stop at the end of the teens, so what gender messages are your friends giving you today?

Gender Messages in the Mass Media

▶ **Watch** the **Video**
The Big Picture: Socialization in **mysoclab**

From the boys Milkie studied, another guide to our gender map is the **mass media,** forms of communication that are directed to large audiences. Let's look at how media images help teach us gender.

ADVERTISING

From an early age, the media bombard us with stereotypical images. If you are average, you are exposed to a blistering 30,000 commercials a year (Larson 2001). In children's commercials, boys are more likely to be shown as competing in outdoor settings, while girls are more likely to be portrayed as

mass media forms of communication, such as radio, newspapers, and television, that are directed to mass audiences

cooperating in indoor settings. Action figures are pitched to little boys, and dolls are pitched to little girls (Kahlenberg and Hein 2010).

As adults, we are still peppered with ads. Although their purpose is to sell products—from booze and bras to cigarettes and cell phones—these ads continue our lessons in gender. I'm sure you have noticed the many ads that portray men as dominant and rugged and women as sexy and submissive. The stereotypical images—from cowboys who roam the wide-open spaces to scantily clad women whose physical assets couldn't possibly be real—seep into our subconscious and become part of our own images of the sexes. So do the stereotype-breaking images that are emerging. Whether overt and exaggerated or subtle and below our awareness, the mass media continue our gender lessons.

MOVIES AND TELEVISION

Movies and television also give us gender lessons. Male characters outnumber female characters in prime-time television, pointing to the greater importance of males in society. But the times are changing, and more dominant, aggressive females are also being portrayed. In cartoons, Kim Possible divides her time between cheerleading practice and saving the world from evil. With tongue in cheek, the Powerpuff Girls are touted as "the most elite kindergarten crime-fighting force ever assembled." This changed gender portrayal is especially evident in the females who play violent characters in action movies, from the assassin in *Kill Bill* to Angelina Jolie in *Salt* (Gilpatric 2010).

The gender messages, however, are mixed. Although girls are presented as more powerful than they used to be, they have to be skinny and gorgeous and wear the latest fashions. Such messages present a dilemma for girls, for continuously thrust before them is a model that is almost impossible to replicate in real life.

The mass media both reflect and stimulate gender change. Shown here is Angelina Jolie in Salt.

VIDEO GAMES

The movement, color, virtual dangers, unexpected dilemmas, and ability to control the action make video games highly appealing. High school and college students find video games a seductive way of escaping from the demands of life. The first members of the "Nintendo Generation," now in their 30s, are still playing video games—with babies on their laps.

Sociologists have begun to study how video games portray the sexes, but we still know little about their influence on the players' ideas of gender. Females are even more underrepresented in video games than on television, with 90 percent of the main characters being male (Williams et al. 2009).

IF YOU WANT TO LEARN MORE about cutting-edge changes in sex roles, you might be interested in the box on video games

Read more from the author: Lara Croft, Tomb Raider: Changing Images of Women in the Mass Media in **mysoclab**

In the next *Making It Personal*, let's briefly consider how significant gender is.

MAKING IT PERSONAL

Gender and Your View of the World

There are two reasons for an emphasis on gender. First, the powerful cultural symbols of "female" and "male" have vital effects on your life. At an early age, you learned that different behaviors and attitudes are expected of boys and girls, lessons

Why is gender a topic of sociology?

that your social experiences have constantly reinforced. These symbols, which guide your behavior, have become integrated into your view of the world, forming a picture of "how" you think males and females naturally "are."

The second reason is that gender is a primary basis for **social inequality**. That is, some people are given privileges because of their gender, while others are denied those same privileges because of theirs. This makes your socialization into gender significant on a level that reaches far beyond your personal experiences.

UNIT 4.4 // TESTING MYSELF
DID I LEARN IT? ANSWERS ARE AT THE END OF THE CHAPTER

1. If in some culture, males are expected to be passive and females dominant, this would be an example of
   a. cultural change
   b. a peer group
   c. gender reversal
   d. gender

2. Her mother told 8-year-old Geneva to stop picking on her 6-year-old brother. "That isn't lady-like, Geneva," said her exasperated mother. This is an example of
   a. a mother who is behind the times
   b. a protective mother
   c. gender socialization
   d. gender

3. Psychologists Goldberg and Lewis observed babies and mothers in their laboratory. They noticed that the mothers held their little girls more than the boys, and they also talked more to them. In a few months, the boys were more likely to try to climb over a barrier to get toys, while the girls were more likely to cry and signal for help from their mothers. Goldberg and Lewis conclude that this difference in the children's behavior
   a. came about because of the artificiality of the laboratory setting
   b. was produced by the mother's behavior
   c. reflected inborn differences between girls and boys
   d. reflected the inequality of society

4. Children's toys are
   a. a way that parents socialize their children
   b. like a puff of smoke from a campfire, present for a moment, perhaps attention getting, but irrelevant for life
   c. so different from one culture to another that we can't draw any conclusions about them
   d. a way that advertisers take advantage of the poor

5. From sociologist Donna Eder's research on eighth-grade girls, we can see that girls
   a. who are entering adolescence need a lot of guidance to become good women
   b. are envious of one another
   c. tell others what their mothers have told them in confidence
   d. socialize one another into gender

6. From sociologist Melissa Milkie's research on boys in junior high school, we can see that boys
   a. prefer action videos and movies to any other type of mass media
   b. who are entering adolescence need a lot of guidance to become good men
   c. socialize one another into gender
   d. like to be with girls but don't want their peers to know it

7. The images of the sexes portrayed in the mass media—whether stereotypical or stereotype-breaking—
   a. seldom reflect the daily lives of real people
   b. help teach what is expected of men and women in our culture
   c. are irrelevant to the product being advertised
   d. reflect the ideas of a Hollywood elite

8. On television and in video games, male characters
   a. outnumber female characters
   b. are more likely to be portrayed as sexy
   c. are more likely to be portrayed as evil
   d. are more likely to be portrayed as having lower intelligence

9. Movies and videos are now portraying this stereo-type-breaking character
   a. the sexy younger woman
   b. the aggressive and unhappy female CEO
   c. the mom who, torn between home and work, fails at both
   d. the more dominant, aggressive woman

10. The statement that gender is a primary basis for social inequality means that
    a. gender inequality is growing
    b. gender inequality is decreasing
    c. some people are given privileges because of their gender, while others are denied those same privileges because of theirs
    d. we live in what is called a zero/sum society, so if women gain something such as jobs, their gain comes at the expense of men

UNIT 4.5

Agents of Socialization

WHAT AM I SUPPOSED TO LEARN?

After you have read this unit, you should be able to

1 State what agents of socialization are.

2 Explain how social class makes a difference in socializing children.

3 Summarize findings on day care, peer groups, and the workplace.

By now, you have a good idea of how socialization has given you direction in life. Let's pursue this further by focusing on **agents of socialization,** the individuals and groups that influence people. As we considered gender messages, we already looked at the family, peers, and the mass media. Now let's look at how agents of socialization prepare us in other ways to take our place in society. We shall consider the family, then day care, school, peers, and the workplace.

The Family

The first group to have a major impact on you was your family.

agents of socialization people or groups that affect our self-concept, attitudes, behaviors, or other orientations toward life

Your experiences in the family were and are so intense that their influence is lifelong. These experiences laid down your initial motivations, values, and beliefs. In the family, you received your basic sense of self, ideas about who you are and what you deserve in life. It is here that you began to think of yourself as strong or weak, smart or dumb, good-looking or ugly—or more likely, somewhere in between. And as already noted, the lifelong process of defining yourself as feminine or masculine also began in the family.

As you already know, there are huge differences in lifestyle between families in poverty and those in wealth. Sociologists have refined this idea considerably. Let's look at some of their findings on social class and how families socialize their children.

SOCIAL CLASS AND TYPE OF WORK

Sociologist Melvin Kohn (1959, 1977, 2006) found that a main concern of working-class parents is that their children stay out of trouble. They tend to use physical punishment to keep them in line. Middle-class parents, in contrast, focus more on developing their children's curiosity, self-expression, and self-control. They are more likely to reason with their children than to use physical punishment.

These contrasts puzzled Kohn. As a sociologist, he sought the answer in life experiences, which turned out to be differences in the world of work. In their work, blue-collar workers are usually told exactly what to do. Since they expect their children's lives to be like theirs, they stress obedience. The work of middle-class parents, in contrast, requires making more decisions, and they socialize their children into the qualities they find valuable.

Kohn was still puzzled. Some working-class parents act more like middle-class parents, and vice versa. As Kohn probed this puzzle, the pieces fell into place. This time, the key turned out to be the parents' type of job. Middle-class office workers, for example, are supervised closely, and Kohn found that they follow the working-class pattern of child rearing, emphasizing conformity. And some blue-collar workers, such as those who do home repairs, have a good deal of freedom. These workers follow the middle-class model in rearing their children (Pearlin and Kohn 1966; Kohn and Schooler 1969).

SOCIAL CLASS AND PLAY

Working-class and middle-class parents also have different ideas of how children develop, ideas that have fascinating consequences for how their children play (Lareau 2002; Bodovsky and Farkas 2008). For working-class parents, children are like wild flowers—they develop naturally. Since the child's development will take care of itself, good parenting primarily means to provide food, shelter, and comfort. These parents set limits on their children's play ("Don't go near the railroad tracks") and let them play as they wish. To middle-class parents, in contrast, children are like tender house plants—they need a lot of guidance to develop correctly. These parents want their children's play to help them reach goals. They may want them

Research on how day care affects children has provoked controversy.

to play baseball, for example, not for the enjoyment of the sport, but to help them learn how to be team players.

Day Care

It is rare for social science research to make national news, but occasionally it does. This is what happened when researchers published their findings on 1,200 kindergarten children they had studied since they were a month old. They observed each child multiple times, both at home and at day care. They also videotaped and made detailed notes on how the children interacted with their mothers (National Institute of Child Health and Human Development 1999; Guensburg 2001).

What caught the media's attention? Children who spend more time in day care have weaker bonds with their mothers and are less affectionate to them. They are also less cooperative with others and more likely to fight and to be "mean." By the time they get to kindergarten, they are more likely to talk back to teachers and to disrupt the classroom. This holds true regardless of the quality of the day care, the family's social class, or whether the child is a girl or a boy (Belsky 2006). On the positive side, the children scored higher on language tests.

Are we producing a generation of "smart but mean" children? This is not an unreasonable question, since the study was designed well and an even larger study of children in England has come up with similar findings (Belsky 2006). Some point out that the differences are slight between children who spend a lot of time in day care and those who spend less time. Others respond that there are 5 million children in day care, so slight differences can be significant for society (*Statistical Abstract* 2012:Table 566).

Did these initial effects of day care follow the children, or did they wash out? To find out, the researchers continued to test these same children as they went through school. At age 15, the children who had spent more time in child care did slightly worse academically than the children who spent less time in child care. They still had slightly more behavioral problems. It was the same for children who had lower quality care (Vandell et al. 2010).

The School and Peer Groups

Let's turn back to you again. As your experiences with agents of socialization broadened, your family's influence decreased. Starting school marked only one of many steps in your transfer of allegiance, but it was significant. It exposed you to peer groups that helped you resist the efforts of your parents to socialize you. I don't know how closely your experience follows this, but here is what sociologists Patricia and Peter Adler (1998) found when they observed children at two elementary schools in Colorado:

The children separated themselves by sex and developed separate gender worlds. The norms that made boys popular were athletic ability, coolness, and toughness. Popularity for girls was based on family background, physical appearance (clothing and makeup), and the ability to attract popular boys. In this children's subculture, academic achievement pulled in opposite directions: Good grades lowered the popularity of boys, but they increased a girl's standing among her peers.

You know from your own experience how compelling peer groups are. It is almost impossible to go against a peer group, whose cardinal rule seems to be "conformity or rejection." Anyone who doesn't do what the others want becomes an "outsider" and is cast aside. For preteens and teens just learning their way around in the world, it is not surprising that the peer group rules.

As a result, peer groups tend to dominate our lives. If your peers listen to rap, Nortec, death metal, rock and roll, country, or gospel, it is almost inevitable that you also prefer that kind of music. In high school, if your friends took math courses, you probably did, too (Crosnoe et al. 2008). If they specialized in physical education, you probably did, too. As you know, it is the same for clothing styles and dating standards. Peer influences also extend to behaviors that violate social norms. If your peers were college-bound and upwardly striving, that is most likely what you were. And if they used drugs, cheated, and stole, you were likely to do so, too.

IF YOU WANT TO LEARN MORE about how socialization in school can replace old values and ways of looking at the world with new ones,

📖 **Read** more from the author: Immigrants and Their Children: Caught Between Two Worlds in **mysoclab**

The Workplace

Another significant agent of socialization is the workplace. Those initial jobs that we take in high school and college are much more than just a way to earn a few dollars. From the people we rub shoulders with at work, we learn not only a set of skills but also perspectives on the world.

Most of us eventually become committed to some particular line of work, often after trying out many jobs. This may involve **anticipatory socialization,** learning to play a role before we enter it. Anticipatory socialization is a sort of mental rehearsal for some future activity. If you are interested in a particular career, you might talk to people who do that type of work, read novels about it, or take a summer internship in that field. This allows you to become aware of what would be expected of you and to gradually identify with the role. This helps some people avoid committing themselves to an empty career, as with some of my students who tried student teaching, found that they couldn't stand it, and then moved on to jobs more to their liking.

An intriguing aspect of work as a socializing agent is that the more you participate in a line of work, the more this work becomes part of your self-concept. Eventually you will come to think of yourself so much in terms of the job that if someone asks you to describe yourself, you are likely to include the job in your self-description. You might say, "I'm a teacher," "I'm a nurse," or, as you might expect in this text, "I'm a sociologist."

> **anticipatory socialization** the process of learning in advance a role or status one anticipates having

---

1. When Dominique started school, she entered a bewildering world. The ideas of her teachers and classmates stood in sharp contrast to what she had learned at home. For Dominique, her family, her teachers, and her peers
   a. are in conflict
   b. are challenging her thought world
   c. reflect dominant and subdominant orientations to life
   d. are agents of socialization

2. Working-class parents expect their children to do work similar to their own, which is closely supervised and centers on taking orders. These parents are mainly concerned that their children
   a. do well in school
   b. develop their total potential
   c. stay out of trouble
   d. get part-time jobs to provide their own spending money

3. Working-class parents expect their children to do work similar to their own, which is closely supervised and centers on taking orders. To discipline their children, they tend to
   a. reason with their children
   b. use physical punishment
   c. make their kids sit in the corner
   d. send their kids to bed without dinner

4. Middle-class parents expect their children to do work similar to their own, which is flexible and involves making decisions. These parents are mainly concerned that their children
   a. develop their curiosity, self-expression, and self-control
   b. take school seriously
   c. get in the right schools so they can get good jobs
   d. watch less television

5. Middle-class parents expect their children to do work similar to their own, which is flexible and involves making decisions. To keep their children in line, they tend to
   a. deprive their children of television
   b. physically punish their children
   c. take away their children's dessert
   d. reason with their children

6. Research on 1,200 children in day care and their mothers shows that the children who spend more time in day care
   a. score lower on IQ tests
   b. have weaker bonds with their mothers and are less affectionate to them
   c. score lower on language tests
   d. are lazier

7. Research on 1,200 children in day care shows that the children who spend more time in day care tend to
   a. be meaner and smarter
   b. aim for higher positions in life
   c. be more motivated when they become workers
   d. have poorer health

8. When it comes to grades, peer groups tend to push grade school boys and girls in different directions. For girls, good grades
   a. come easier than they do for boys
   b. are related to the amount of television they watch
   c. make them more popular with other girls but less popular with boys
   d. increase popularity

9. The research by Patty and Peter Adler indicates that these characteristics make grade school boys popular
   a. good grades and having money to spend
   b. family background, physical appearance, and the ability to attract girls
   c. athletic ability, coolness, and toughness
   d. good looks and being able to ask intelligent questions in class

10. Carmen, who wants to be a doctor, loves reading medical novels. She has just applied for a summer internship at a local hospital. Although the internship won't pay anything, she is excited about the coming experience. This term applies to Carmen's activities
    a. delusional endeavor
    b. anticipatory socialization
    c. volunteer work
    d. escape from reality

FROM ANOTHER STUDENT

"The information that you share makes me stop and think deeply about life and society, makes me question long-held beliefs, and makes me look at issues from other points of view."

Kelly Haywood
Kaplan University

UNIT 4.6 Resocialization

WHAT AM I SUPPOSED TO LEARN?

After you have read this unit, you should be able to

1 State what resocialization is.

2 Explain how total institutions work.

What does a woman who just became a nun have in common with a man who just divorced? The answer is that they both are undergoing **resocialization**; that is, they are learning new norms, values, attitudes, and behaviors

resocialization the process of learning new norms, values, attitudes, and behaviors to match their new situation in life. In its most common form, resocialization occurs each time you learn something contrary to your previous experiences. A new boss or teacher who insists that you do things a different way is resocializing you. Most resocialization is mild—only a slight modification of things you have already learned.

Resocialization can also be intense. If you were to join Alcoholics Anonymous (AA), for example, you would be surrounded by reformed drinkers who affirm the destructive effects of alcohol. If you were to join a cult or begin psychotherapy, your resocialization would be even more profound, for you would learn views that conflict with your earlier socialization. If these new ideas "take," not only would your behavior change but also you would learn a fundamentally different way of looking at life.

Total Institutions

Relatively few of us experience the powerful agent of socialization that sociologist Erving Goffman (1961) called the **total institution.** He coined this term to refer to a place in which people are cut off from the rest of society and where they come under almost total control of the officials who are in charge. Boot camp, prisons, concentration camps, convents, some mental hospitals, some religious cults, and some military schools, such as West Point, are total institutions.

If you enter a total institution, you will be greeted with a **degradation ceremony** (Garfinkel 1956), an attempt to strip away your current identity and stamp a new one in its place. This unwelcome greeting may involve fingerprinting, photographing, or

total institution a place that is almost totally controlled by those who run it, in which people are cut off from the rest of society and the society is mostly cut off from them

degradation ceremony a term coined by Harold Garfinkel to refer to a ritual whose goal is to remake someone's self by stripping away that individual's self-identity and stamping a new identity in its place

shaving your head. You might be ordered to strip, undergo an examination (often in a humiliating, semipublic setting), and then put on a uniform that designates your new status. Officials will take away your *personal identity kit*, items such as jewelry, hairstyle, clothing, and other body decorations you use to express individuality.

If you become a resident of a total institution, you will be isolated from the public. The bars, walls, gates, and guards will not only keep you in but also keep outsiders out. Staff members will supervise your day-to-day life. Your eating, sleeping, showering, recreation—all will be standardized. You will learn that your previous statuses—student, worker, spouse, parent—mean nothing. The only thing that counts is your current status.

You won't leave a total institution unscathed, for the experience will brand an indelible mark on your self and color the way you see the world. Boot camp is brutal but swift, while prison, in contrast, is brutal and prolonged. If you ever end up in either one, you will have no difficulty in knowing how the institution profoundly marked your attitudes and orientations to life.

IF YOU WANT TO LEARN MORE about how the Marines can transform civilians into soldiers ready to kill,

📖 **Read** more from the author: Boot Camp as a Total Institution in **mysoclab**

A topic of research in sociology is total institutions, which have profound effects on people's lives.

UNIT 4.6 // TESTING MYSELF
DID I LEARN IT? ANSWERS ARE AT THE END OF THE CHAPTER

1. A woman just entered boot camp and a man was just admitted to a locked ward in a mental hospital. They are both
   a. trying anticipatory socialization
   b. trying to get help
   c. challenging norms
   d. being resocialized

2. The woman who entered boot camp and the man who was admitted to the locked ward in a mental hospital are both residents of
   a. anticipatory socialization centers
   b. a totalitarian country
   c. total institutions
   d. places where social control is loosening

3. Joan was sent to prison for forgery. When she got there, she found herself in a large room with other new inmates. She was stripped, her body cavities

were examined, she was weighed, and she was sprayed with a liquid to kill body lice. In sociological terms, Joan underwent a

a. mental breakdown
b. degradation ceremony
c. classic change in her self concept
d. soul-searching, new experience

4. Which of these is not a total institution?
   a. a college
   b. a prison
   c. West Point
   d. boot camp

UNIT 4.7

Socialization through the Life Course

The historical setting sets the stage for the life course.

WHAT AM I SUPPOSED TO LEARN?

After you have read this unit, you should be able to

1 Explain how views of children change with history, citing the Ariès controversy.

2 Summarize the stages of the life course.

3 Explain how social factors influence the life course.

4 Analyze your experience with the life course, past, present, and anticipated future.

Watch the Video
Sociology on the Job:
Socialization in **mysoclab**

You are at a particular stage in your life now, and college is a good part of it. You know that you have more stages ahead as you go through life. These stages, from birth to death, are called the **life course** (Elder 1975, 1999). *The sociological significance of the life course* is twofold. *First*, as you pass through a stage, it influences your behavior and orientations. You simply don't think about life in the same way when you are 30, are married,

life course the stages of our life as we go from birth to death

and have a baby and a mortgage, as you do when you are 18 or 20, single, and in college. (Actually, you don't even see life the same way as a freshman and as a senior.) *Second*, your life course differs by social location. Your social class, race–ethnicity, and gender, for example, map out distinctive worlds of experience.

This means that the typical life course differs for males and females, the rich and the poor, and so on. To emphasize this major sociological point, I will present a "life sketch" in which I will stress the *historical* setting of people's lives. Because of your particular social location, your own life course may differ from this sketch, which is a composite of stages that others have suggested (Levinson 1978; Carr et al. 1995; Quadagno 2007).

Childhood (from birth to about age 12)

Consider how different your childhood would have been if you had grown up at another historical time. Historian Philippe Ariès (1965) noticed that in European paintings from about A.D. 1000 to 1800, children were always dressed in adult clothing. If they were not depicted stiffly posed, as in a family portrait, they were shown doing adult activities.

From this, Ariès drew a conclusion that sparked a debate among historians. He said that Europeans of this period did not regard childhood as a special time of life. They viewed children as miniature adults and put them to work at an early age. At the age of 7, for example, a boy might leave home for good to learn to be a jeweler or a stonecutter. A girl, in contrast, stayed home until she married, but by the age of 7 she assumed her share of the household tasks. Historians agree that these were the customs of that time, but some say that Ariès' conclusion is ridiculous, that other evidence indicates that these people viewed childhood as a special time of life (Orme 2002).

Having children work like adults did not disappear with the Middle Ages. In the 1800s, this practice was still common around the world. Even today, children in the Least Industrialized Nations work in many occupations—from blacksmiths to waiters. As tourists are shocked to discover, children in these nations work as street peddlers, hawking everything from shoelaces to chewing gum. The photo below reflects a view of children that is remarkably different from the one common in the Most Industrialized Nations.

Child rearing, too, used to be remarkably different. Three hundred years ago, parents and teachers considered it their *moral* duty to *terrorize* children. To keep children in line, they would frighten them with bedtime stories of death and hellfire, lock them in dark closets, and force them to witness events like this:

> A common moral lesson involved taking children to visit the gibbet [jib-bit, an upraised post on which executed bodies were left hanging], where they were forced to inspect the rotting corpses as an example of what happens to bad children when they grow up. Whole classes were taken out of school to witness hangings, and parents would often whip their children afterwards to make them remember what they had seen. (DeMause 1975)

Industrialization transformed the way we perceive children. When children had the leisure to go to school and postpone taking on adult roles, parents and officials came to think of them as tender and innocent, as needing more care, comfort,

and protection. Such attitudes of dependency grew, and today we view children as needing the gentle guidance of adults if they are to develop emotionally, intellectually, and morally. We take our view for granted—after all, it is only "common sense." Yet, as you can see, our view of children is not "natural." It is, instead, rooted in society—in geography, history, and economic development.

Let's explore this idea in *Making It Personal.*

MAKING IT PERSONAL
How Did Culture Shape Your Childhood?

Sociologists say that *childhood varies from culture to culture.* Think about your childhood. How did the point in history in which your childhood occurred set the stage for what people expected of you and for how you were treated as a child? How about your specific social locations, especially social class and gender? Although your *biological* characteristics as a child (being small and unable to survive on your own) are universal, the way you were treated because you were a child depended on your *social location.*

If you really want to get into this—and it is fascinating—ask your grandparents, or great-grandparents if you have them, what life was like when they were kids. The remarkable differences from your own childhood that you will uncover will reveal not just different behaviors but also different views of what children are.

Adolescence (ages 13–17)

It might seem strange to you, but adolescence is not a "natural" age division. It is a *social invention.* In earlier centuries, people simply moved from childhood to young adulthood, with no stopover in between. Then came the Industrial Revolution, which allowed adolescence to be invented. Industrialization brought such an abundance of material surpluses that for the first time in history people in their teens were not needed as workers. At the same time, education became more important for achieving success. As these two forces in industrialized societies converged, they created a gap between childhood and adulthood. The term *adolescence* was coined to indicate this new stage in life (Hall 1904), one that has become renowned for uncertainty, rebellion, and inner turmoil.

The direct transition from childhood to adulthood still occurs in tribal societies. At roughly the time when our society marks off adolescence, tribal children go through *initiation rites* that mark their transition into adulthood. This grounds the self-identity, showing these young people how they fit in their society. In contrast, adolescents in the industrialized world must "find" themselves. They grapple with the dilemma of "I am neither a child nor an adult. Who am I?" As they attempt to carve out an identity that is distinct from both the "younger" world

In some places, children still do adult work. This photo was taken in India.

being left behind and the "older" world that still lingers out of reach, adolescents develop their own subcultures, with distinctive clothing, hairstyles, language, gestures, and music. We usually fail to realize that contemporary society, not biology, created this period of inner turmoil that we call *adolescence*.

Transitional Adulthood (ages 18–29)

If society invented adolescence, can it also invent other periods of life? As Figure 4.2 illustrates, this is actually happening now. Postindustrial societies are adding another period of extended youth to the life course, which sociologists call **transitional adulthood.** (Some call it *adultolescence.*)

After high school, millions of young adults postpone adult responsibilities by going to college. They are mostly freed from the control of their parents, yet they don't have to support themselves. After college, many move back home, where they live cheaply while they establish themselves in a career—and, of course, continue to "find themselves." During this time, they are "neither psychological adolescents nor sociological adults" (Keniston 1971). At some point during this period of extended youth, young adults ease into adult responsibilities. They take a full-time job, become serious about a career, engage in courtship rituals, get married— and go into debt.

> **transitional adulthood** a term that refers to a period following high school when young adults have not yet taken on the responsibilities ordinarily associated with adulthood; also called *adultolescence*

FIGURE 4.2

Transitional Adulthood: A New Stage in the Life Course

Who has completed the transition?

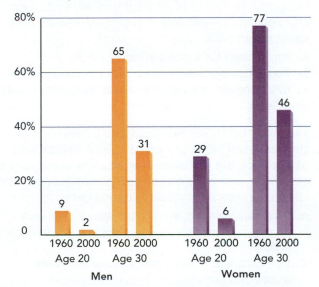

The bars show the percentage who have completed the transition to adulthood, as measured by leaving home, finishing school, getting married, having a child, and being financially independent.

Source: Furstenberg et al. 2004

The Middle Years (ages 30–65)

THE EARLY MIDDLE YEARS (AGES 30–49)

During the early middle years, most people feel more certain about "who" they are and of their goals in life. As at any point in the life course, however, the self can receive severe jolts, often coming from divorce, losing a job, or health problems. It may take years for the self to stabilize after such ruptures.

The early middle years pose a special challenge for many U.S. women who have been given the message that they can "have it all." They can be superworkers, superwives, and supermoms—all rolled into one superwoman. Reality, however, slaps them in the face: too little time, too many demands, even too little sleep. Something has to give, and attempts to resolve this dilemma are anything but easy.

THE LATER MIDDLE YEARS (AGES 50–65)

During the later middle years, people feel their bodies change, and health issues often appear. Many experience a fundamental change in thinking—*from time since birth to time left to live* (Neugarten 1976). They compare what they have accomplished with what they had hoped to achieve. Many people find themselves caring not only for their own children but also for their aging parents. Because of this double burden, people in the later middle years sometimes are called the "sandwich generation."

Some people experience few of these stresses. They find late middle age to be the most comfortable period of their entire lives. They enjoy good jobs and marriages and a standard of living higher than ever before. They have bigger houses (perhaps even paid for), drive newer cars, and take longer and more exotic vacations. Their children are grown, the self is firmly planted, and life seems good.

As they anticipate the next stage of life, however, most people do not like what they see.

The Older Years (about age 65 on)

THE TRANSITIONAL OLDER YEARS

In agricultural societies, most people died early, and old age was thought to begin at around age 40. As industrialization brought better nutrition, medicine, and public health, more people lived longer, and the beginning of "old age" gradually stretched out. Today, people who enjoy good health don't think of their 60s as old age, but as an extension of their middle years. This change is bringing *another new*

The transitional older years are a new stage in the life course.

stage of life, the period between retirement (averaging about age 63) and old age—which people are coming to see as beginning around age 75 ("Schwab Study . . ." 2008). We can call this stage the **transitional older years.**

THE LATER OLDER YEARS

As with the preceding periods of life, except the first one, there is no precise beginning point to this last stage. For some, the 75th birthday marks entry into this period of life. For others, that marker may be the 80th or even the 85th birthday. For most, this stage is marked by growing frailty and illness. For all who reach this stage, it is ended by death. For some, the physical decline is slow, and a rare few manage to see their 100th birthday mentally alert and in good physical health.

In *Making It Personal*, let's look at where you are in the life course.

> **transitional older years** an emerging stage of the life course between retirement and when people are considered old; approximately age 65 to 75

MAKING IT PERSONAL
Social Location and Your Life Course

You have already experienced some stages of the life course, and you anticipate stages ahead of you. These stages go far beyond biology, things that naturally occur to you as you add years to your life. Especially significant is your *social location,* such as your social class, gender, and race–ethnicity. You experience society's events in ways similar to those of people who share your social location, but different from those of people who do not.

And how significant this is. If you are poor, for example, you are likely to feel older sooner than wealthy people for whom life is less demanding. Your health and the choices you make—such as marrying early, entering college late, or getting in trouble with the law—can also throw your life course "out of sequence."

For all these reasons, this sketch of the life course may not reflect your own past, present, or future. Being born just ten years earlier or later may mean that you experience war or peace, an expanding economy or a depression—factors that vitally affect what happens to you. As sociologist C. Wright Mills (1959) would say, because employers are beating a path to your door, or failing to do so, you are more inclined to marry, to buy a house, and to start a family—or to postpone these life course events. In short, changing times steer your life course, sometimes into surprising directions.

1. The sociological significance of the life course is two-fold. One is that
   a. the life course has a peculiar effect on gender
   b. sociology has revealed the transitional stages of the life course
   c. the life course changes society
   d. as you pass through a stage of the life course, it influences your behavior and orientations

2. The sociological significance of the life course is two-fold. One is that
   a. society changes so quickly that you never know what you will experience when you reach the next stage in your life course
   b. the life course puts pressure on society to change
   c. a person's life course depends on social location
   d. childhood is the same the world over

3. Three hundred years ago, European parents and teachers would frighten children with bedtime stories of death and hellfire, lock them in dark closets, and force them to look at the rotting bodies of executed criminals. They did this because
   a. society was less civilized back then
   b. they considered these activities as ways to make children moral
   c. they lacked the violent entertainment we have today, such as slasher films and the Freddy Krueger horror series
   d. children back then were harder to control

4. We consider it "common sense" that children need the gentle guidance of adults if they are to develop emotionally, intellectually, and morally. This attitude toward children is
   a. not "natural," but is rooted in society
   b. the same as that held by the Europeans that Ariès studied
   c. now changing to the view that children are miniature adults
   d. universal

5. The Industrial Revolution produced a new view of children, from miniature adults to little beings who need the gentle guidance of adults. The result was a new stage in the life course called adolescence. Adolescence came with industrialization because
   a. there were more jobs, allowing teenagers to go to work
   b. people possessed more material goods than at any other time in history
   c. for the first time in history people in their teens were not needed as workers
   d. prosperity increased and parents could afford to give allowances to their teenagers

6. Before the Industrial Revolution, children
   a. were less rebellious than they are now
   b. went straight from childhood to adulthood, with no stopover called adolescence
   c. matured earlier
   d. matured later

7. In tribal societies, children still go directly to adulthood. To help them in this process, tribal societies use a transitional device called
   a. initiation rites
   b. maturity measures
   c. celebratory change
   d. relational shifts

8. Adolescence developed when teenagers were no longer needed in the workforce and they became dependent on their parents. Today, fewer young adults in their twenties are needed in the workforce, and the dependency period is being lengthened further. This is producing a new stage in the life course called
   a. post-adolescence
   b. anticipatory socialization

   c. pre-adulthood
   d. transitional adulthood

9. During the later middle years (ages 50–65), as people feel their bodies change and health issues appear, many experience a fundamental change in their thinking that can be summarized as
   a. it's time to take early retirement
   b. youth has passed me by
   c. from time since birth to time left to live
   d. I missed the boat

10. In agricultural societies, most people died early, and old age was thought to begin at around age 40. Industrialization brought better nutrition, better health, and longer lives. Today, people are living longer than ever, which is producing another new stage in the life course. This period, from about age 63 to 75 or even 80, is called the
    a. post–baby boomers
    b. transitional older years
    c. post-retirement period
    d. pre-elderly period

✓•⎯ **Study** and **Review** in **mysoclab**

PULLING IT ALL TOGETHER REVIEWING THE LEARNING GOALS

You have just reviewed the major elements of the area of sociology called socialization. These materials should help you to better understand how socialization is vital for what people, including yourself, "become." You should also have a better idea of how your orientations to life, your ideas and attitudes, depend on your social experiences.

Again, it is time to "lock in" what you have learned. As you review this chapter, keep asking yourself, "Do I understand this?" If something isn't clear, please go back to the section where it was presented. There is a lot of material here, and it certainly is OK not to get everything the first time. Using this chapter review can help you find out what isn't clear.

Unit 4.1 Extremes in Socialization

1. Explain how "society makes us human."
   - The characteristics that distinguish us as humans—high intelligence, language, having ideas—come from socialization.

2. Summarize the effects of low human contact (isolation, institutionalization) on human development.
   - Isolated children who don't learn language don't learn relationships or the capacity to share ideas.

Institutionalized children with little social interaction develop low intelligence. If caught early enough, the learning can be made up.

3. Use the case of Jack and Oskar to illustrate how social experiences shape our attitudes.
   - The almost polar opposite experiences of these identical twins led to almost polar opposite views of Jews and Hitler.

📖•⎯ **Read** the **Document**
"Final Note on a Case of Extreme Isolation" by Kingsley Davis in **mysoclab**

Unit 4.2 Socialization into the Self and Mind

1. Explain the looking-glass self and why it is essential to the development of the self.
   - We see ourselves in the eyes of others. As we evaluate this reflection, we internalize our ideas of how people are reacting to us. These images come into a more or less coherent whole called the self.

2. Explain how we develop the ability to take the role of the other and why this is essential to our socialization.

- At first, our ability to take the role of the other—to stand in someone else's shoes and see the world as he or she does—is limited to that of significant others (individuals who are important to us). Our ability gradually expands so we can take the role of the generalized other (people in general). Team games are significant in developing this ability. Taking the role of the other is essential to our socialization, as our ability to get along with others depends on it.

👁 **Watch** the **Video**
The Basics: Socialization
in **mysoclab**

Unit 4.3   Socialization into Emotions

1. Explain which emotions and facial expressions are universal and why.

- Disgust, anger, sadness, happiness, shame, and fear are universal emotions, and all people show the same facial expressions when they experience these emotions. This indicates that they are part of human biology.

2. Explain what sociology has to do with emotions.

- We are socialized to express our emotions in certain ways. The "feeling rules" we learn are based on gender, culture, social class, relationships, and settings.

3. Explain why the phrase "society within us" applies to emotions.

- Our socialization affects not just how and where we express emotions, but even what emotions we feel. This is society within us. Our self monitors our emotional expressions to help keep us conforming to social norms, another instance of society within us.

Unit 4.4   Getting the Message: Learning Gender

1. Explain what gender and gender socialization are.

- *Gender* refers to the attitudes and behaviors expected of us because of our sex. *Gender socialization* refers to our learning these attitudes and behaviors.

2. Describe the Goldberg and Lewis study.

- Mothers who were observed in the laboratory held their girl babies more than their boy babies and talked more to them. The girl babies became more passive than the boy babies, which Goldberg and Lewis conclude was due to the mothers' behavior.

3. Explain how the family, peers, and the mass media socialize us into gender.

- The messages that our family, peers, and the mass media give of what is culturally appropriate for the sexes become part of our internal images of the sexes. These guide our behavior and our orientations to life.

👁 **Watch** the **Video**
The Big Picture: Socialization
in **mysoclab**

Unit 4.5   Agents of Socialization

1. State what agents of socialization are.

- Agents of socialization are individuals and groups that influence people.

2. Explain how social class makes a difference in socializing children.

- Working-class parents are focused on keeping their children out of trouble and likely to use physical punishment. Middle-class parents, more focused on developing their children's curiosity and self-control, are more likely to reason with their children. These patterns reflect the parents' type of work. They also show up in the children's play.

3. Summarize findings on day care, peer groups, and the workplace.

- Children who spend more time in day care have weaker bonds with their mothers and are more likely to be disruptive at school and to be mean to other children. The influence of peer groups on children is often in opposition to the family. Anticipatory socialization helps us prepare for future jobs.

✳ **Explore** the **Concept**
Single Parent
Households in **mysoclab**

Unit 4.6   Resocialization

1. State what resocialization is.

- Resocialization, which ranges from mild to intense, is learning new norms, values, attitudes, and behaviors to match a new situation in life.

2. Explain how total institutions work.

- Total institutions—from prisons and mental hospitals to convents and military schools—are places where the individual is cut off from the rest of society and made captive to the organization. The staff supervises the individual's daily life, from eating to work and recreation. Total institutions have profound effects on people's attitudes and orientations to life.

Unit 4.7   Socialization through the Life Course

1. Explain how views of children change with history, citing the Ariès controversy.

- Analyzing paintings from A.D. 1000 to 1800, Ariès concluded that childhood in Europe was not a special time of life. Views of what children" are" and how they are treated vary from historical period and culture to culture.

2. **Summarize the stages of the life course.**
   - These stages are childhood, adolescence, transitional adulthood, the middle years, and the older years. The middle and older years are divided into older and later substages.

3. **Explain how social factors influence the life course.**
   - The historical period sets the stage for what happens to people during their life course. Within this setting, other aspects of social location, such as gender and social class, come into play. Social factors even produce new stages in the life course, such as adolescence and transitional adulthood.

4. **Analyze your experience with the life course, past, present, and anticipated future.**
   - This is purely personal.

Watch the Video
Sociology on the Job:
Socialization in **mysoclab**

UNIT 4.1 // TESTING MYSELF
DID I LEARN IT? ANSWERS

1. **d** how we learn the ways of society

2. **a** French scientists studied a feral child in 1798

3. **d** was given intensive training and developed like a normal child

4. **c** in which children must learn language or they cannot become intelligent

5. **b** the human traits of intelligence and the ability to establish close bonds with others depend on early interaction with other humans

6. **a** if too much time passes after a learning stage is missed, it may be impossible to make it up

7. **d** increased

8. **c.** the development of intelligence depends on stimulating interaction

9. **d.** social experiences mold our ideas and attitudes

10. **c** our social experiences form such essential characteristics as our behaviors, ideas, attitudes, and intelligence

UNIT 4.2 // TESTING MYSELF
DID I LEARN IT? ANSWERS

1. **d** looking-glass self

2. **c** our evaluations of the reactions of others to us

3. **b** take the role of the other

4. **a** play

5. **d** taking the role of a significant other

6. **c** the generalized other

7. **b** imitiation

8. **a** self as object

9. **d** is a product of society

10. **d** is a product of society

UNIT 4.3 // TESTING MYSELF
DID I LEARN IT? ANSWERS

1. **d** part of our biology

2. **c** the same facial expressions

3. **b** a feeling rule

4. **d** differ from one culture to another

5. **c** affects what we feel

6. **b** society within us

7. **a** internal control

8. **d** turn us into conforming members of society

UNIT 4.4 // TESTING MYSELF
DID I LEARN IT? ANSWERS

1. **d** gender

2. **c** gender socialization

3. **b** was produced by the mother's behavior

4. **a** a way that parents socialize their children

UNIT 4.5 // TESTING MYSELF
DID I LEARN IT? ANSWERS

1. **d.** are agents of socialization

2. **c.** stay out of trouble

3. **b.** use physical punishment

4. **a.** develop their curiosity, self-expression, and self-control

5. **d.** reason with their children

UNIT 4.6 // TESTING MYSELF
DID I LEARN IT? ANSWERS

1. **d** being resocialized

UNIT 4.7 // TESTING MYSELF
DID I LEARN IT? ANSWERS

1. **d** as you pass through a stage of the life course, it influences your behavior and orientations

2. **c** a person's life course depends on social location

3. **b** they considered these activities as ways to make children moral

4. **a** not "natural," but is rooted in society

5. **d** socialize one another into gender

6. **c** socialize one another into gender

7. **b** help teach what is expected of men and women in our culture

8. **a** outnumber female characters

9. **d** the more dominant, aggressive woman

10. **c** some people are given privileges because of their gender, while others are denied those same privileges because of theirs

6. **b.** have weaker bonds with their mothers and are less affectionate to them

7. **a.** be meaner and smarter

8. **d.** increase popularity

9. **c.** athletic ability, coolness, and toughness

10. **b.** anticipatory socialization

2. **c** total institutions

3. **b** degradation ceremony

4. **a** a college

5. **c** for the first time in history people in their teens were not needed as workers

6. **b** went straight from childhood to adulthood, with no stopover called adolescence

7. **a** initiation rites

8. **d** transitional adulthood

9. **c** from time since birth to time left to live

10. **b** transitional older years

CHAPTER 5
SOCIAL STRUCTURE AND SOCIAL INTERACTION

Listen to the **Chapter Audio** in **mysoclab**

Watch the **Video** in **mysoclab**

GETTING STARTED

Let's start this chapter a little differently. I'd like to share with you a little sociological adventure I had. Like other professionals, sociologists hold annual conventions where they share their latest research and catch up with their friends' activities.

This particular convention was held in Washington, D.C. I decided to spend the night after the convention to do a little research. I didn't know what that research would be—or where—but I figured I would find something worthwhile. When the convention was over, I climbed aboard the first city bus that came along. I didn't know where the bus was going, and I didn't know where I would spend the night.

"Maybe I overdid it this time," I thought, as the bus began winding down streets I had never seen before. Actually, this was my first visit to Washington, D.C., so everything was unfamiliar to me. I had no destination, not even a map. I carried no billfold, just a driver's license shoved into my jeans for emergency identification, some pocket change, and a $10 bill tucked into a sock. My plan was simple: If I saw something interesting, I would get off the bus and check it out.

(continued on the next page)

Los Angeles, California

(continued from the previous page)

"Nothing but the usual things," I mused, as we passed row after row of apartment buildings and stores. I could see myself riding buses the entire night. Then something caught my eye. Nothing spectacular—just groups of people clustered around a large circular area where several streets intersected.

I got off the bus and made my way to what turned out to be Dupont Circle. I took a seat on a sidewalk bench and began to observe what was going on around me. As the scene came into focus, I noticed several streetcorner men drinking and joking with one another. One of the men left his companions and sat down next to me. As we talked, I mostly listened.

As night fell, the men said that they wanted to get another bottle of wine. I contributed. They counted their money and asked if I wanted to go with them.

Although I felt my stomach churning—a combination of hesitation and fear—I heard a confident "Sure!" come out of my mouth. As we left the circle, the three men began to cut through an alley. "Oh, no," I thought. "This isn't what I had in mind."

I had but a split second to make a decision. I found myself continuing to walk with the men, but holding back half a step so that none of the three was behind me. As we walked, they passed around the remnants of their bottle. When my turn came, I didn't know what to do. I shuddered to think about the diseases lurking within that bottle. I made another quick decision. In the semidarkness I faked it, letting only my thumb and forefinger touch my lips and nothing enter my mouth.

When we returned to Dupont Circle, we sat on the benches, and the men passed around their new bottle of Thunderbird. I couldn't fake it in the light, so I passed, pointing at my stomach to indicate that I was having digestive problems.

Suddenly one of the men jumped up, smashed the emptied bottle against the sidewalk, and thrust the jagged neck outward in a menacing gesture. He glared straight ahead at another bench, where he had spotted someone with whom he had some sort of unfinished business. As the other men told him to cool it, I moved slightly to one side of the group—ready to flee, just in case.

You can see that on this sociological adventure, I almost got in over my head. Fortunately, it turned out all right. The man's "enemy" didn't look our way, the man put the broken bottle next to the bench "in case he needed it," and my intriguing introduction to a life that up until then I had only read about continued until dawn.

Sharing this story is NOT intended as an example of how to do sociological research (although you can see how fun doing research can be). Rather, I want to use this event to teach you about the two levels of sociological analysis: social structure and social interaction.

UNIT 5.1

Levels of Sociological Analysis: Macrosociology and Microsociology

WHAT AM I SUPPOSED TO LEARN?

After you have read this unit, you should be able to

1 Summarize the distinction between macrosociology and microsociology.

2 Explain why we need both macrosociology and microsociology to understand social life.

Streetcorner men seem to simply do whatever feels good at the moment. They don't have to show up at work or school, like you and I do, and they appear to come and go as they feel like it. When you look behind the scenes, though, a different picture emerges. This is apparent from the fascinating accounts that sociologists have written about men like my companions from that evening in Washington, D.C. (Liebow 1967/1999; Duneier 2001; Anderson 1978, 1990, 2006). Like us, these men are influenced by the norms and beliefs of our society.

This will become more apparent as we examine the two levels of analysis that sociologists use: macrosociology and microsociology.

Macrosociology and Microsociology: A Brief Overview

The first level is **macrosociology**. "Macro" means large, so macro–sociologists focus on the large, or broad, features of society. Sociologists who use the conflict and functionalist perspectives are macrosociologists. They analyze such things as social class and how the groups that make up society are related to one another.

How would macrosociologists analyze streetcorner men? They would examine how these men

macrosociology
analysis of social life that focuses on broad features of society, such as social class and the relationships of groups to one another; usually used by functionalists and conflict theorists

Why do we need both macrosociology and microsociology to understand this person's life?

fit into the U.S. social class system. As you would expect, they would stress that these men are located at the bottom, with few opportunities open to them. Who wants to hire streetcorner men? They have few job skills, little education, really hardly anything to offer an employer. The focus, then, is how these men fit into this broader system that makes up U.S. society.

The second level is **microsociology.** "Micro" means small, so the focus of microsociologists is on a much smaller level. Symbolic interactionists use this approach. They focus on **social interaction,** what people do when they come together. With no jobs open to them, these men hustle to survive. They spend their lives on the streets looking for something—almost anything, legal or illegal, that will give them a few bucks. Symbolic interactionists analyze the men's rules, or "codes," for getting along. They look at their survival strategies ("hustles"); how they divide up money, wine, or whatever other resources they have. They analyze the men's relationships with girlfriends, family, and friends. They even study the men's language and their pecking order.

You can see how different macrosociology and microsociology are. With their contrasting approaches, each yields a distinctive perspective. How could you understand streetcorner men without *macrosociology,* seeing how these men fit within the groups that make up U.S. society? As is true for ourselves, the social class of these men helps to shape their attitudes and behavior. And how could you understand these men without *microsociology,*

microsociology

analysis of social life that focuses on social interaction; typically used by symbolic interactionists

social interaction

what people do when they are in one another's presence; includes communications at a distance

seeing how the men live out their everyday lives? As is true for you and me, their everyday situations also form a significant part of their lives. To understand streetcorner men—or anything else in society—we need both perspectives. With only one or the other, we would have a distorted picture.

UNIT 5.1 // TESTING MYSELF
DID I LEARN IT? ANSWERS ARE AT THE END OF THE CHAPTER

1. The purpose of opening this chapter with the story of the author's experience with streetcorner men in Washington, D.C. is to introduce
   a. a method of sociological research
   b. the idea that an entire group can be overlooked in sociological research
   c. the need of social work to help streetcorner men
   d. the two levels of sociological analysis, macrosociology and microsociology

2. If macrosociologists were to do research on streetcorner men, they would focus on
   a. why these men deserve to receive welfare
   b. how these men interact with one another
   c. how these men fit into the structure of society
   d. why these men commit more crime than most men

3. If microsociologists were to do research on streetcorner men, they would focus on how
   a. changes in international relations affect the U.S. job market
   b. these men interact with one another
   c. these men fit into the structure of society
   d. the change to an information society has left these men without work

4. The ways that streetcorner men divide up the money they hustle from passersby would be a focus of
   a. conflict theorists   b. macrosociologists
   c. social workers   d. microsociologists

5. How streetcorner men fit within the groups that make up U.S. society would be a focus of
   a. symbolic interactionists b. social workers
   c. macrosociologists   d. microsociologists

6. What streetcorner men do during their everyday lives would be a focus of
   a. functionalists   b. microsociologists
   c. conflict theorists   d. macrosociologists

7. To understand social life, both macrosociology and microsociology are needed because
   a. each approach yields a distinctive perspective, part of the picture
   b. sociologists have a code that both perspectives be used
   c. this provides a balance in departments of sociology
   d. without this, we couldn't apply all three theoretical perspectives: functionalism, conflict theory, and symbolic interactionism

THE MACROSOCIOLOGICAL PERSPECTIVE

UNIT 5.2

The Macrosociological Perspective: Social Structure

How does this photo illustrate macrosociology?

WHAT AM I SUPPOSED TO LEARN?

After you have read this unit, you should be able to

1 Explain what social structure is and why it is important.

2 Explain how social structure influences the lives of street people, your instructor, and yourself.

FROM ANOTHER STUDENT

I really enjoyed the questions at the end of each unit. It helped me keep an eye on what I just learned.

—*Nandi Taggart*

Why did the street people in our opening story act as they did, staying up all night drinking wine, prepared to use a lethal weapon? Why don't *we* act like this? Social structure helps us answer such questions.

The Sociological Significance of Social Structure

I would guess that the term **social structure** doesn't ring a bell with you. Let's explore this term, which refers to the framework of society that was laid out before you were born, a framework that guides your behavior.

Let's try to put some flesh and blood on this verbal skeleton. Another way to say *social structure* is to say *the typical patterns*

of a group. This probably seems vague, too, but here's a typical pattern that you know backwards and forwards: Teachers usually stand at the front of a class where they lecture, while students usually sit facing the teacher while they take notes. If you are a student in a classroom, you follow this pattern. Are you starting to see the influence of social structure?

Let's look at another way that social structure guides your life. As I write this, I do not know your race–ethnicity. I do not know whether you are young or old, tall or short, male or female. I do not know whether you were reared on a farm, in the suburbs, or in the inner city. I do not know whether you went to a public high school or to an exclusive prep school. But I do know that you are in college. And this helps me to place you within social structure, which tells me a great deal about you.

From this one piece of information, I can assume that the social structure of your college is now shaping what you do. For example, let's suppose that today you felt euphoric over some great news. I can be fairly certain (not absolutely, mind you, but relatively confident) that when you entered the classroom, social structure overrode your mood. That is, instead of shouting at the top of your lungs, text you entered the classroom in a fairly subdued manner and took your seat.

The same social structure influences your instructor, even if he or she, on the one hand, is facing a divorce or, on the other, has just been awarded a million-dollar grant. For the first, your instructor might feel like retreating into seclusion, or for the second, she or he might feel like celebrating wildly. But most likely, your instructor will conduct class in the usual manner. *In short, social structure guides our behavior, tending to override our personal feelings.*

social structure
the framework of society that surrounds us; consists of the ways that people and groups are related to one another; this framework gives direction to and sets limits on our behavior

Now let's carry this idea back to street people. Just as social structure influences you and your instructor, so it also influences them. Like you, street people are in a specific location in the U.S. social structure. Theirs is quite different from yours or your instructor's, so it affects them in different ways. Their behaviors, although different, are as logical an outcome of where they find themselves in the social structure as are your own. Certainly nothing about their social location leads them to take notes or to lecture. In their position in the social structure, it is just as "natural" for them to drink wine all night as it is for you to stay up studying all night for a crucial examination. It is just as "natural" for you to nod and say, "Excuse me," if you enter a crowded classroom late and have to claim a desk on which someone has placed books as it is for them to break off the neck of a wine bottle and glare at an enemy.

IN SUM: People learn their behaviors and attitudes because of their location in the social structure (whether that location is privileged, deprived, or in between), and they act accordingly. This is as true of street people as it is of yourself. *The differences in behavior and attitudes are due not to biology (race–ethnicity, sex, or any other supposed genetic factors), but to people's location in the social structure.* Switch places with street people and watch your behaviors and attitudes change!

It is important to understand social structure, so I'd like to introduce this term in still another way. Please take a look at *Making It Personal.*

MAKING IT PERSONAL
Football as Social Structure

Although *social structure* surrounds you, directing your behavior, it is usually invisible. Let's see if football can make it more visible (Dobriner 1969a). You probably know the various positions on the team: center, guards, tackles, ends, quarterback, running backs, and the like. Each is a *status;* that is, each is a social position. For each of the statuses shown in Figure 5.1, there is a *role;* that is, each of these positions has certain expectations attached to it. The center is expected to snap the ball, the quarterback to pass it, the guards to block, the tackles to tackle or block, the ends to receive passes, and so on. Those role expectations guide each player's actions; in other words, the players try to do what their particular role requires.

Let's suppose that football is your favorite sport and you never miss a home game at your college. Let's also suppose that you graduate, get a great job, and move across the country. Five years later, you return to your campus for a nostalgic visit. The climax of your visit is the biggest football game of the season. When you get to the game, you might be surprised to see a different coach, but you are not surprised that each playing position is occupied by people you don't know, for all the players you knew have graduated, and their places have been filled by others.

This scenario mirrors *social structure,* the framework that surrounds us. In football, this framework consists of the coaching staff and the eleven playing positions. The game does not depend on any particular individual, but, rather, on *social statuses,* the positions that the individuals occupy. When someone leaves a position, the game can go on because someone else takes that position or status and plays the role. The game will continue even though not a single individual remains from one period of time to the next. Notre Dame's football team endures today even though Knute Rockne, the Gipper, and his teammates are long dead.

You may not play football, but you are like a football player. You live your everyday life within a clearly established social structure. The statuses that you occupy and the roles that you play were already in place before you were born. You take your particular positions in life, others do the same, and society goes about its business. Although the specifics change with time, the game—whether of life or of football—goes on.

Let's try to be more explicit. Can you answer this question: How does social structure influence your life? A good place to begin is to analyze your social statuses.

FIGURE 5.1 **Team Positions (Statuses) in Football**

Source: By the author.

UNIT 5.2 // TESTING MYSELF
DID I LEARN IT? ANSWERS ARE AT THE END OF THE CHAPTER

1. A simple definition of social structure is
   a. what people do in one another's presence
   b. the way people act
   c. street people staying up all night drinking wine
   d. the framework of society that was laid out before you were born

2. Another simple definition of social structure is
   a. teachers lecturing despite personal problems
   b. students staying quiet when they would like to be celebrating
   c. the typical patterns of a group
   d. the changes that occur in society over time

3. From this unit, it is apparent that street people
   a. are immoral
   b. are influenced by social structure
   c. should get help from social workers
   d. don't care about other people

4. If you enter a crowded classroom late and say "Excuse me" when you claim a desk on which someone has placed books, from the framework of social structure this is the same as a sreetcorner man
   a. breaking off the neck of a wine bottle and glaring at an enemy
   b. trying to break out of social structure
   c. remembering what life used to be like before bad luck hit
   d. getting married

5. The differences in behavior between yourself and streetcorner men can be traced to differences in
   a. morality   b. age
   c. race–ethnicity   d. social structure

6. In football and other team sports, the positions on the team are social statuses. The person who occupies a status has a role to perform. If you think of an entire team's positions, you have an example of
   a. a football game
   b. social statuses
   c. social structure
   d. the various positions on a football team

UNIT 5.3

The Components of Social Structure: Culture, Social Class, Groups, Social Status, and Roles

WHAT AM I SUPPOSED TO LEARN?

After you have read this unit, you should be able to

1 Explain how the components of social structure influence your life.

2 Distinguish between ascribed and achieved social statuses, master statuses, and status symbols.

3 Explain how roles are related to statuses and how they influence your life.

At this point, you should be gaining a sense that social structure provides guidelines and sets limits for your behavior. Social structure does this—and more. It also directly affects what you are like as a person. This will become more apparent as we look at five major components of social structure: culture, social class, groups, social status, and roles.

Culture

In this chapter, we consider culture's main impact. As you know, *culture* refers to a group's language, beliefs, values, behaviors, and even gestures. Culture also includes the material objects that a group uses. Culture is the *broadest framework* that determines

Culture's guidance of behavior pervades our lives. This photo was taken in China.

Try to identify some of the statuses in the status set of each of the individuals in this photo.

what kind of person you become. If you are reared in Chinese, Arab, or U.S. culture, you will grow up to be like most Chinese, Arabs, or Americans. On the outside, you will look and act like them; and on the inside, you will think and feel like them.

Social Class

All social locations influence people's lives, but especially significant is *social class,* which is based on income, education, and occupational prestige. Large numbers of people who have similar amounts of income and education and who work at jobs that are roughly comparable in prestige make up a **social class.** It is hard to overemphasize this aspect of social structure, for your social class influences not only your behaviors but even your ideas and attitudes. As stressed in the first unit, you have this in common with the street people described in our opening story: You both are influenced by social class. Their social class may be considerably less privileged, but it has no less influence on their lives.

Groups

A **group** consists of people who interact with one another and who feel that the values, interests, and norms they have in common are important. The groups to which you belong are powerful forces in your life. By belonging to a group, you assume an obligation to affirm the group's values, interests, and norms. To remain a member in good standing, you need to show that you share those characteristics. This means that *when you belong to a group you yield to others the right to judge your behavior—* even though you don't like it!

Although this principle holds true for all groups, some groups wield influence over only small segments of our lives. For example, if you belong to a stamp collector's club, the group's influence may center on your display of knowledge about stamps and perhaps your fairness in trading

social class large numbers of people who have similar amounts of income and education and who work at jobs that are roughly comparable in prestige

group people who have something in common and who believe that what they have in common is significant; also called a social group

them. Other groups, in contrast, such as your family, control many aspects of your behavior. When parents say to their 15-year-old daughter, "As long as you are living under our roof, you had better be home by midnight," they show their expectation that their daughter, as a member of the family, will conform to their ideas about many aspects of life, including their views on curfew. They are saying that as long as the daughter wants to remain a member of the family in good standing, her behavior must conform to their expectations.

Social Status

When you hear the word *status,* you are likely to think of prestige. These two words are wedded together in people's minds. As you saw in the discussion of football in *Making It Personal,* however, sociologists use **status** in a different way—to refer to the *position* that someone occupies. The position may carry a great deal of prestige, as in the case of a judge or an astronaut, or it may bring little prestige, as in the case of a convenience store clerk or a waitress at the local truck stop. The status may also be looked down on, as in the case of a streetcorner man, an ex-convict, or a thief.

All of us occupy several positions at the same time. You may simultaneously be a son or daughter, a worker, a date, and a student. Sociologists use the term **status set** to refer to all the statuses or positions that you occupy. Obviously your status set changes as your particular statuses change. Let's assume that you graduate from college. You then land a good full-time job, get married, buy a home, and have children. If this happens, your status set will then include worker, spouse, homeowner, and parent.

Like other aspects of social structure, statuses are part of our basic framework of living in society. The example I gave earlier of students and teachers who come to class and do what others expect of them despite their particular circumstances and moods illustrates how statuses affect our actions—and those of the people around us.

For more on how social status guides *your* behavior, read *Making It Personal.*

status the position that someone occupies in a social group (also called social status)

status set all the statuses or positions that an individual occupies

MAKING IT PERSONAL
Guiding Your Actions

You are surrounded by social structure, with each component guiding your behavior and even your thoughts and attitudes. The process is so continuous that you generally are unaware of how deeply this "guidance" goes.

Consider this common event: Your friends ask you to join them in doing something fun, and you say, "I really want to go with you, but I've got to (fill in the blank: go to work, help my dad, study for a soc exam)." When something like this happens, you are feeling the "gentle guidance" of a social status.

ASCRIBED AND ACHIEVED STATUSES

An **ascribed status** is involuntary. You do not ask for it, nor can you choose it. Here are some ascribed statuses that you inherited at birth: your sex, race–ethnicity, and the social class of your parents Other statuses are related to the life course and given later in life, such as teenager, "middle-aged," and senior citizen.

Achieved statuses, in contrast, are voluntary. These you earn or accomplish. As a result of your efforts, you become a student, a friend, a spouse, or a lawyer. Or, for lack of effort (or for efforts that others fail to appreciate), you become a school dropout, a former friend, an ex-spouse, or a debarred lawyer. Notice that achieved statuses can be positive or negative. Both college president and bank robber are achieved statuses.

Each status provides guidelines for how we are to act and feel. Like other aspects of social structure, statuses set limits on what we can and cannot do. Because social statuses are an essential part of the social structure, all human groups have them.

STATUS SYMBOLS

As you know, people who are pleased with their social status want others to recognize their position. To help get this recognition, they use status symbols, things that identify a status. Many people wear wedding rings to announce their marital status. Some wear uniforms, guns, and badges to proclaim that they are police officers (and not so subtly, to let you know that their status gives them authority over you). Others wear "backward" collars to declare that they are Lutheran ministers or Roman Catholic or Episcopal priests.

In contrast, people who have negative statuses try to hide the particular status symbol, but sometimes they can't. The scarlet letter in Nathaniel Hawthorne's book by the same title is one example. Another is the CONVICTED DUI (Driving Under the Influence) bumper sticker that some U.S. courts require convicted drunk drivers to display if they wish to avoid a jail sentence.

How about your own status symbols? Look at the following *Making It Personal.*

ascribed status
a position an individual either inherits at birth or receives involuntarily later in life

achieved status
a position that is earned, accomplished, or involves at least some effort or activity on the individual's part

MAKING IT PERSONAL
Your Status Symbols

All of us use status symbols to announce our statuses to others. Knowing someone's status helps us know how to interact with that person. Can you identify your own status symbols and what they communicate? For example, how does your clothing announce your statuses of sex, age, and college student?

MASTER STATUSES

A **master status** cuts across your other statuses. Some master statuses are ascribed. One example is your sex. Whatever you do, people perceive you as a male or as a female. If you are working your way through college by flipping burgers, people see you not only as a burger flipper and a student but also as a *male* or *female* burger flipper and a *male* or *female* college student. Other master statuses are race–ethnicity and age.

Some master statuses are achieved. If you become wealthy (and it doesn't matter whether your wealth comes from a successful invention, a hit song, or winning the lottery—it is still *achieved* as far as sociologists are concerned), your wealth is likely to become a master status. For example, people might say, "She is a very rich burger flipper"—or, more likely, "She's very rich, and she used to flip burgers!"

Similarly, people who become disfigured find, to their dismay, that their condition becomes a master status. For example, a person whose face is scarred from severe burns will be viewed through this unwelcome master status regardless of occupation or accomplishments. In the same way, people who are confined to wheelchairs can attest to how their wheelchair overrides all their other statuses and influences others' perceptions of everything they do. For an example of this, see the photo on the next page.

status symbols things that identify a status, such as titles (professor, doctor), a wedding ring, or a uniform

master status a status that cuts across or dominates someone's other statuses

A status symbol that no one wants. This photo of a man convicted of drunk driving was taken in Arizona.

Master statuses *overshadow our other statuses. Shown here is Stephen Hawking, who is disabled by Lou Gehrig's disease. For some, his* master status *is that of a person with disabilities. Because Hawking is one of the greatest physicists who has ever lived, however, his other* master status *is, that of a world-class physicist in the ranking of Einstein.*

Our statuses usually fit together fairly well, but some people have a mismatch among their statuses. This is known as **status inconsistency** (or discrepancy). A 14-year-old college student is an example. So is a 40-year-old married woman who is dating a 19-year-old college sophomore.

Let's consider these examples in *Making It Personal*.

status inconsistency ranking high on some dimensions of social status and low on others; also called status discrepancy

MAKING IT PERSONAL

How Would You React?

Social statuses come with built-in *norms* (expectations) that guide behavior. Since a social status gives us cues about how to interact, when people's statuses match well, it helps interaction to unfold smoothly.

People who are status inconsistent, however, throw a little wrench into society's smoothly running machinery (or so a functionalist might phrase it). That is, status-inconsistent people make it difficult to know what to expect of someone

or how to interact with that person. Consider the 14-year-old college student I just mentioned. Would you treat this person as you would a young teenager or as you would a college classmate? Or how about the 40-year-old married woman who is dating a 19-year-old college sophomore? Assume that the 19-year-old is a good friend. Would you react to the woman as you would to a friend's date? To how you would react to most women of this age? Or perhaps in some other status entirely?

Do you see how social statuses serve as guides for your behavior?

Roles

All the world's a stage
And all the men and women merely players.
They have their exits and their entrances;
And one man in his time plays many parts . . .

(William Shakespeare, *As You Like It*, Act II, Scene 7)

When you were born, society was waiting with outstretched arms to tell you how you should act. The ascribed statuses you received came with **roles**—behaviors, obligations, and privileges. Your sex is one of the best examples, as one of the first things you learned was how to act as a boy or a girl. And whether you were born poor, rich, or somewhere in between, that, too, came with certain behaviors, obligations, and privileges.

Role and *status* can seem confusing, but here is the difference: You *occupy* a status, but you *play* a role (Linton 1936). Being a son or daughter is a status that you occupy. But look at the roles that are attached to this status. As a child, you expected to receive food and shelter from your parents. And part of your role was to meet your parents' expectation that you show them respect. Or, again, your status is student, but your role is to attend class, take notes, do homework, and take tests.

Almost all of us follow the guidelines for what is "appropriate" for our roles. Few of us are bothered by these constraints, for our socialization is thorough. For most of us, socialization penetrates us so deeply that we usually *want* to do what our roles indicate is appropriate.

The sociological significance of roles is that they lay out what is expected of people. As you and the many individuals throughout society perform their roles, those many roles mesh together to form this thing called *society.* As Shakespeare put it in the preceding quote, your roles provide "your exits and your entrances" on the stage of life. In short, roles are remarkably effective at keeping you in line—telling you when you should "enter" and when you should "exit," as well as what to do in between.

Roles are powerful. In the next *Making It Personal,* let's consider how they influence your behavior.

roles the behaviors, obligations, and privileges attached to a status

MAKING IT PERSONAL
Doing What You Don't Want to Do

Roles are like fences. They allow you a certain amount of freedom, but that freedom doesn't go very far. If you are a woman, suppose that you decide that you will never again wear a dress. If you are a man, suppose that you have decided not to ever wear a suit and tie—regardless of what anyone says. In most situations, you'll stick to your decision. But what about when a formal occasion comes along? You'll probably hold out concerning some dinner, but what if you are chosen as the bridesmaid or groomsman of your best and lifelong friend who is planning a formal wedding? It is likely that you will cave in to norms that you find overwhelming.

Can you recall times when you didn't want to do something and you ended up doing it anyway because your role required it? (You should have no problem answering this. The question is probably more like "When? This morning or yesterday?")

Because of our roles, which provide the routines on which life is based, we often do things that we don't feel like doing.

1. When Clarissa joined Xi Alpha Alpha, the other members evaluated her wardrobe and suggested changes for her hair and makeup. While this reaction is more focused than most, whenever you join a group you
   a. know that others are going to look you over
   b. never know what will happen because people often switch their statuses and roles
   c. yield to others the right to judge your behavior
   d. become a member of a social status

2. Marcellus and Francisca were furious when their 15-year-old daughter came home after midnight. They told her, "As long as you are living under our roof, you had better be home by 9 o'clock on a school night and no later than 11 on a weekend." These parents are
   a. being too strict
   b. expressing similar concerns that parents the world over have
   c. following general middle-class norms, which have eased up during the past ten years
   d. saying that as long as their daughter wants to remain a member of the family in good standing, her behavior must conform to their expectations

3. To demonstrate your growing knowledge of sociology, you say to a friend, "I found out that sociologists use status in a different way. They don't mean prestige. When they use status, they are referring to"
   a. how people strive to get ahead, even when they face severe obstacles to their advancement
   b. the position that someone occupies, such as a waitress
   c. large numbers of people who have similar amounts of income and education
   d. people who interact with one another

4. social class of your parents when you were a child are examples of
   a. how society sets up controls that make it difficult to attain a higher social class
   b. how inherited factors must be overcome in order to attain a higher social class
   c. achieved statuses
   d. ascribed statuses

5. Jamele was determined not to be like his father, who could never hold a job. He studied hard, graduated from college, and then went to law school. He

became a successful lawyer, specializing in corporate acquisitions. Jamele's change in life is an example of

a. how individuals can overcome the controls that society sets up that make it difficult to attain a higher social class

b. how inherited factors must be overcome in order to attain a higher social class

c. achieved status

d. ascribed status

6. Stanton was an average student when he started to hang around a group of boys who had a shady reputation. He was later arrested for drugs and sent to a reformatory. Stanton's status as a juvenile delinquent is an example of

a. how society fails students with low grades

b. how schools fail marginal students

c. achieved status

d. ascribed status

7. The security officer at the bank stands tall and proud as she surveys the customers, her gun at the ready and her polished badge gleaming in the reflected sunlight. This person is displaying

a. pride in her work

b. status symbols

c. an excess of authority

d. what is wrong with this country

8. Teachers and bosses always got on Phil's nerves. He dropped out of high school, and bouncing from one job to another, lived on the edge of poverty. Down on his luck as usual, Phil spent his last $5 on a lottery ticket. To his amazement, Phil won $10 million. Phil's low education and background of low-paying and low-prestige jobs (he doesn't work anymore) combined with his mansion and fancy cars are an example of

a. how the American dream can come true if you keep working hard

b. the development of motivation

c. social class

d. status inconsistency

9. Everyone around town is talking about Phil's new wealth. Wherever he goes, people point to him. The waitresses at "The Dew Drop Inn" rush to serve Phil. Phil used to have trouble getting dates, but now women flock to him. Phil's wealth is a

a. role

b. status set

c. master status

d. status envy

10. Janie is disappointed with her job as a waitress at "The Dew Drop Inn." She knew she would be expected to take orders from customers, deliver their food, and put up with jokes from people like Phil, but

she didn't know that she would be expected to mop floors. This expectation is part of a

a. social class

b. role

c. growing inequality in society

d. status inconsistency

UNIT 5.4

Another Component of Social Structure: Social Institutions

WHAT AM I SUPPOSED TO LEARN?

After you have read this unit, you should be able to

1 State what the social institutions are.

2 Explain why social institutions have such powerful effects on our lives.

3 Compare functionalist and conflict views of whose interests the mass media represent.

How does this photo illustrate social institution?

What Social Institutions Are

Explore the Concept Congregational Membership, Primary Groups and Secondary Groups in **mysoclab**

Social institutions, another component of social structure, are vital for what you become—for how you view yourself and for the goals you have in life.

At first glance, the term *social institution* may seem cold and abstract—with little relevance to your life. In fact, however, **social institutions**—the standard or usual ways that a society meets its basic needs—not only shape your behavior but they even color your thoughts. How can this be?

social institutions the organized, usual, or standard ways by which society meets its basic needs

To see the answer, look at Figure 5.2. You can see that the

FIGURE 5.2 **Social Institutions in Industrial and Postindustrial Societies**

Social Institution	Basic Needs of Society	Some Groups or Organizations	Some Statuses	Some Values	Some Norms
Family	Regulate reproduction, socialize and protect children	Relatives, kinship groups	Daughter, son, father, mother, brother, sister, aunt, uncle, grandparent	Sexual fidelity, providing for your family, keeping a clean house, respect for parents	Have only as many children as you can afford, be faithful to your spouse
Religion	Concerns about life after death, the meaning of suffering and loss; desire to connect with the Creator	Congregation, synagogue, mosque, denomination, charity, clergy associations	Priest, minister, rabbi, imam, worshipper, teacher, disciple, missionary, prophet, convert	God and the holy texts such as the Torah, the Bible, and the Qur'an should be honored	Go to worship services, follow the teachings, contribute money
Education	Transmit knowledge and skills across generations	School, college, student senate, sports team, PTA, teachers' union	Teacher, student, dean, principal, football player, cheerleader	Academic honesty, good grades, being "cool"	Do homework, prepare lectures, don't snitch on classmates
Economy	Produce and distribute goods and services	Credit unions, banks, credit card companies, buying clubs	Worker, boss, buyer, seller, creditor, debtor, advertiser	Making money, paying bills on time, producing efficiently	Maximize profits, "the customer is always right," work hard
Medicine	Heal the sick and injured, care for the dying	AMA, hospitals, pharmacies, HMOs, insurance companies	Doctor, nurse, patient, pharmacist, medical insurer	Hippocratic oath, staying in good health, following doctor's orders	Don't exploit patients, give best medical care available
Politics	Allocate power, determine authority, prevent chaos	Political party, congress, parliament, monarchy	President, senator, lobbyist, voter, candidate, spin doctor	Majority rule, the right to vote as a privilege and a sacred trust	One vote per person, be informed about candidates
Law	Maintain social order, enforce norms	Police, courts, prisons	Judge, police officer, lawyer, defendant, prison guard	Trial by one's peers, innocence until proven guilty	Give true testimony, follow the rules of evidence
Science	Master the environment	Local, state, regional, national, and international associations	Scientist, researcher, technician, administrator, journal editor	Unbiased research, open dissemination of research findings, originality	Follow scientific method, be objective, disclose findings, don't plagiarize
Military	Protection from enemies, enforce national interests	Army, navy, air force, marines, coast guard, national guard	Soldier, recruit, enlisted person, officer, veteran, prisoner, spy	To die for one's country is an honor, obedience unto death	Follow orders, be ready to go to war, sacrifice for your buddies
Mass Media	Disseminate information, report events, mold public opinion	TV networks, radio stations, publishers, association of bloggers	Journalist, newscaster, author, editor, publisher, blogger	Timeliness, accuracy, freedom of the press	Be accurate, fair, timely, and profitable

Source: By the author.

social institutions are the family, religion, education, economics, medicine, politics, law, science, the military, and the mass media. The social institutions weave the fabric of society, setting the context for your behavior and orientations to life. From this figure you can see that each social institution satisfies a basic need and has its own groups, statuses, values, and norms.

We could go into great detail about each of the social institutions outlined in Figure 5.2, but at this point I simply want to stress that *the influence of social institutions is so profound that if they were different, your orientations to life would be different.* To catch just a glimpse of the depth to which they pervade your orientations to life, read the following *Making It Personal.*

MAKING IT PERSONAL

The Rhythm of Your Days

I have stressed that the social institutions profoundly affect your life. Much of this is apparent, especially when you consider that the family is one of the social institutions. The impact of the social institutions, however, goes far beyond the obvious. For example, because of our economic institution, it is common for people to work eight hours a day, five days a week. But there is nothing normal or natural about this pattern. This rhythm is an arbitrary arrangement for dividing work and leisure. Yet this one aspect of a single social institution determines how you divide up your days and lays out a structure for your interaction with family and friends and for how you meet your personal needs.

Each of the social institutions has deep implications for your life. Like most of your perception of time, most of these effects lie beyond your awareness.

UNIT 5.4 // TESTING MYSELF
DID I LEARN IT? ANSWERS ARE AT THE END OF THE CHAPTER

1. This is a definition of social institutions
   a. people who interact with one another
   b. the change of ascribed statuses into achieved statuses
   c. large numbers of people who have similar amounts of income and education
   d. a society's standard or usual way of meeting its basic needs

2. The family, religion, education, economics, medicine, politics, law, science, the military, and the mass media are
   a. similar in most societies
   b. changing in the same direction around the world
   c. social institutions
   d. separated by law and custom

3. The social institutions
   a. the antislavery movement in the 1600s
   b. are a means of transferring wealth to the needy
   c. are becoming less relevant to our lives
   d. have their own groups, statuses, values, and norms

UNIT 5.5 Comparing Functionalist and Conflict Perspectives

WHAT AM I SUPPOSED TO LEARN?

After you have read this unit, you should be able to

1 Summarize the functionalist perspective on social institutions.

2 Summarize the conflict perspective on social institutions.

Just as the functionalist and conflict perspectives of the mass media differ, so do their views of the nature of social institutions. Let's compare these views.

The Functionalist Perspective

Because the first priority of a society is to survive, all societies establish customary ways to meet their basic needs. As a result, no society is without social institutions. In tribal societies, some social institutions are less visible because the group meets its basic social needs in more informal ways. A society may be too small to have people specialize in education, for example, but it will have established ways of teaching skills and ideas to the young. It may be too small to have a military, but it will have some mechanism of self-defense.

What are society's basic needs? Functionalists identify five basic needs, which they call *functional requisites,* that each society

Functionalists call society's basic needs its functional requisites. What functional requisites does religion meet?

must meet if it is to survive (Aberle et al. 1950; Mack and Bradford 1979).

1. *Replacing members.* Obviously, if a society does not replace its members, it will not continue to exist. With reproduction fundamental to a society's existence, and the need to protect infants and children universal, all groups have developed some version of the family. The family gives the newcomer to society a sense of belonging by providing a *lineage,* an account of how he or she is related to others. The family also functions to control people's sex drive and to maintain orderly reproduction.

2. *Socializing new members.* Each baby must be taught what it means to be a member of the group into which it is born. To accomplish this, each human group develops devices to ensure that its newcomers learn the group's basic expectations. As the primary "bearer of culture," the family is essential to this process, but other social institutions, such as religion and education, also help meet this basic need.

3. *Producing and distributing goods and services.* Every society must produce and distribute basic resources, from food and clothing to shelter and education. To do this, every society establishes an *economic* institution, a means of producing goods and services along with routine ways of distributing them.

4. *Preserving order.* Societies face two threats of disorder: one internal, the potential for chaos, and the other external, the possibility of attack. To protect themselves from internal threat, they develop ways to police themselves, ranging from informal means such as gossip to formal means such as armed groups. To defend themselves against external threat, they develop a means of defense, some form of the military.

5. *Providing a sense of purpose.* Every society must get people to yield self-interest in favor of the needs of the group. To convince people to sacrifice personal gains, societies instill a sense of purpose. Human groups develop many ways to implant such beliefs, but a primary one is religion, which attempts to answer questions about ultimate meaning. Actually, all of a society's institutions are involved in meeting this functional requisite; the family provides one set of answers about the sense of purpose, education another, and so on.

The Conflict Perspective

Conflict theorists agree with the functionalists that social institutions were designed originally to meet basic survival needs. However, they do not view social institutions as working harmoniously for the common good. On the contrary, conflict theorists stress that powerful groups control our society's institutions. These groups manipulate the social institutions in order to maintain their own privileged position of wealth and power (Useem 1984; Domhoff 1999a, 1999b, 2006, 2007).

Gaining control of society's resources is central to attaining power and privilege. In the United States, a fairly small group of people gets the lion's share of our nation's wealth. Members of this elite group sit on the boards of our major corporations and our most prestigious universities. They make strategic campaign contributions to influence (or control) our lawmakers. It is they who are behind the nation's major decisions: to go to war or to refrain from war; to increase or to decrease taxes; to raise or to lower interest rates; and to pass laws that favor or impede moving capital, technology, and jobs out of the country.

How would conflict theorists explain what these British soldiers are doing in Iraq?

Feminist sociologists (both women and men) have used conflict theory to gain an understanding of how social institutions affect gender relations. *Their basic insight is that gender is an element of social structure, not simply a characteristic of individuals.* In other words, throughout the world, social institutions divide males and females into separate groups, giving them unequal access to society's resources.

IN SUM: Functionalists view social institutions as working together to meet universal human needs. Conflict theorists regard social institutions as having a single primary purpose—to preserve the social order so the wealthy and powerful can maintain their positions of privilege.

UNIT 5.5 // TESTING MYSELF
DID I LEARN IT? ANSWERS ARE AT THE END OF THE CHAPTER

1. Functionalists point out that no society is without social institutions because
   a. the powerful of each society use social institutions to control society
   b. social institutions are the ways that a society meets its basic needs
   c. they change from one society to another
   d. all societies have a need to be controlled by a superior elite

2. A functionalist was speaking to an intro class in sociology. She described five basic needs that societies have: to replace its members, socialize new members, produce and distribute goods and services, preserve order, and provide a sense of purpose. She was referring to what functionalists call
   a. new social institutions
   b. the socializing function of social institutions
   c. the need to preserve social order
   d. functional requisites

3. Except for the mass media, a recent development historically, all societies have some form of the ten social institutions outlined in Figure 5.2. In industrial and postindustrial societies, these social institutions are formal, highly visible, and specialized. In tribal societies, in contrast, some social institutions are
   a. merged into their formal system of law
   b. taken over by more powerful groups
   c. less visible because they meet their basic needs more informally
   d. discarded because the chief and elders are threatened by more democratic forms

4. Conflict theorists agree with the functionalists that social institutions were developed originally to meet basic survival needs. However, they do not

   a. view social institutions as working harmoniously for the common good
   b. think that powerful groups manipulate the social institutions
   c. view social institutions as changing
   d. think that tribal groups have social institutions

5. In support of their view that powerful groups control our society's social institutions, conflict theorists point out that
   a. some members of Congress get arrested
   b. few governors' sons and daughters serve in the military
   c. most primary teachers are women
   d. a fairly small group of people gets the lion's share of our nation's wealth

6. According to conflict theorists, an elite group
   a. works untiringly for the welfare of the majority of the country's citizens
   b. is elected to major positions because they have Hollywood contacts and know how to use the media effectively
   c. is behind the nation's major decisions, including whether or not to go to war and to move capital, technology, and jobs out of the country
   d. meets together secretly and makes the country's major decisions

7. Feminist sociologists (both women and men) have used conflict theory to gain an understanding of how social institutions affect gender relations. Their basic insight is that
   a. men and women are born with different characteristics that guide them into distinctive directions in life
   b. gender is an element of social structure, with social institutions dividing males and females into separate groups, each with unequal access to society's resources
   c. housework is not naturally women's work and should be shared by women and men
   d. for reasons we don't yet fully understand, men are more attracted to positions of power than are women

8. The basic view of functionalists is that social institutions
   a. work together to meet universal human needs
   b. are ways that the wealthy and powerful preserve the social order so they can maintain their positions of privilege
   c. change as society changes
   d. change, but slowly and only reluctantly

9. The basic view of conflict theorists is that social institutions
   a. constantly change as a society adopts new technology
   b. work together to meet universal human needs
   c. exist in industrial and postindustrial societies but not in tribal societies
   d. are ways that the wealthy and powerful preserve the social order so they can maintain their positions of privilege

UNIT 5.6

What Holds Society Together?

WHAT AM I SUPPOSED TO LEARN?

After you have read this unit, you should be able to

1 Distinguish between mechanical and organic solidarity.

2 State the difference between *Gemeinschaft* and *Gesellschaft*.

3 Explain why people change as society changes.

How do the people in this photo illustrate what Durkheim called organic solidarity?

You live in a large, pluralistic society. That is, your society is made up of many groups, each with its own interests. Some of these groups are so antagonistic they would love to get at one another's throats. On top of this, we are in the midst of rapid social change, some of which is so extensive that it threatens to rip our society apart. With both antagonistic groups and profound social change, how does society manage to hold together? Why doesn't it just rip apart? Let's examine two answers that macrosociologists have proposed. This will take us back in history a little bit—and introduce you to four strange terms.

Mechanical and Organic Solidarity

Sociologist Emile Durkheim (1893/1933) was interested in how societies manage to have **social integration**—their members being united by shared values and other social bonds. For smaller groups, he found the answer in what he called **mechanical solidarity.** By this term, Durkheim meant that people

social integration the degree to which members of a group or a society are united by shared values and other social bonds; also known as social cohesion

mechanical solidarity Durkheim's term for the unity (a shared consciousness) that people feel as a result of performing the same or similar tasks

who perform similar tasks develop similar views, a shared consciousness. Think of a farming community in which everyone is involved in growing crops—planting, cultivating, and harvesting. Because these people have so much in common, their views about life are similar. With their unity depending on sharing similar views, societies with mechanical solidarity tolerate little diversity in behavior, thinking, or attitudes.

As societies get larger, a specialized **division of labor** develops. Some people mine gold, others turn it into jewelry, and still others sell it. This division of labor disperses people into different interest groups. In these separate groups, people develop different ideas about life. No longer do they depend on one another to have similar ideas and to act alike. Rather, they depend on one another to contribute to the group through their specific work. Durkheim called this new form of solidarity **organic solidarity.**

To see why Durkheim used the term *organic solidarity,* think about your body. The *organs* of your body need one another. Your lungs depend on your heart to pump your blood, and your heart depends on your lungs to oxygenate your blood. It is the same with the social world. You need your teacher to guide you through this course but to have a job your teacher also needs students. You and your teacher are *like two organs in the same body.* (The "body" in this case is your college.) Like the heart and lungs, you each perform different tasks, but you each need one another.

Let's explore this further in *Making It Personal.*

division of labor the splitting of a group's or a society's tasks into specialties

organic solidarity Durkheim's term for the interdependence that results from the division of labor; as part of the same unit, we all depend on others to fulfill their jobs

MAKING IT PERSONAL
You and Your Car

I don't want you to miss the main point here: The change to organic solidarity brought a new basis for people's unity (their social integration). In centuries past, your views would have been similar to those of your neighbors because you lived in the same village, farmed together, and had relatives in common. But no longer does your unity depend on thinking alike. Rather, like organs in a body, you do your work while others do theirs. Society functions because each person's specialized job contributes its part to the group. You don't care what workers on an assembly line in Kentucky think, just that they put your car together well. With this change from mechanical to organic solidarity, society can tolerate a wide variety of orientations to life and still manage to work as a whole.

(By the way, if you don't have a car, it is the same point regarding the bus you ride or your refrigerator at home.)

Why are the Amish an example of what Durkheim called mechanical solidarity?

Gemeinschaft and *Gesellschaft*

Another early sociologist, Ferdinand Tönnies, also analyzed how society was changing. He (1887/1988) used *Gemeinschaft* (guh-MINE-shoft), or "intimate community," to describe village life. This is the type of society in which everyone knows everyone else. Tönnies noted that the personal ties, kinship connections, and lifelong friendships that marked village life were being crowded out by short-term relationships, individual accomplishments, and self-interest. Tönnies called this new type of society *Gesellschaft* (guh-ZELL-shoft), or "impersonal association." He did not mean that we no longer have intimate ties to family and friends but, rather, that our lives no longer center on them. Unlike the past, few of us work in a family business, for example. Contracts have replaced trusted handshakes. And unlike village life, much of our time is spent with strangers and short-term acquaintances.

> ***Gemeinschaft*** a type of society in which life is intimate; a community in which everyone knows everyone else and people share a sense of togetherness
>
> ***Gesellschaft*** a type of society that is dominated by impersonal relationships, individual accomplishments, and self-interest

IF YOU WANT TO LEARN MORE *about how social solidarity is different in village life,*

Read more from the author: The Amish: Gemeinschaft Community in a Gesellschaft Society in **mysoclab**

Changes in Social Structure

I know that *Gemeinschaft*, *Gesellschaft*, and *mechanical* and *organic solidarity* are strange terms and that Durkheim's and Tönnies' observations must seem like a dead issue. The observations that these sociologists expressed, however, are important. Beyond our families and a couple of close friends, few of us live in a community in which people are united by close ties and shared ideas and feelings. In its place, we are surrounded by associations built around impersonal, short-term contacts.

Again, I don't want you to get lost in terms and lose sight of what lies behind the terms *Gemeinschaft* and *Gesellschaft* and *mechanical* and *organic solidarity*: As societies change, so do people's orientations to life. *Social structure sets the context for what we do, feel, and think, and ultimately, then, for the kind of people we become.*

Let's explore this in the following *Making It Personal*.

MAKING IT PERSONAL
You Can Expect to Be Pushed and Pulled

It is easy for the main ideas to get lost as you try to learn these four new and rather strange terms, so let's apply the idea that lies behind them. Durkheim and Tönnies found that people changed as their associations were transformed from the intimate relationships of village life to the short-term, more anonymous life of cities. Today's social structure is continuing to evolve as it responds to new technology and to contact with different cultures. As your society changes, so will your behaviors and orientations to life.

You can expect to be pushed and pulled in one direction or another. As our economy responds to globalization, for example, it will either open or close opportunities for you. New groups such as the Department of Homeland Security will continue to come into being, unexpectedly wielding extraordinary power over your life. In short, the corner in life that you occupy, though small and seemingly private, is not closed off. Rather, just as our current social structure gives shape to your life, so it will stretch you in different directions as that social structure changes.

UNIT 5.6 // TESTING MYSELF
DID I LEARN IT? ANSWERS ARE AT THE END OF THE CHAPTER

1. To say that we live in a large, pluralistic society is to say that our society
   a. might be ripped apart one day as groups fight one another
   b. is a *Gemeinschaft* society
   c. is based on mechanical solidarity
   d. is made up of many groups, each with its own interests

2. The social solidarity of village life is based on people identifying with one another because they do similar work and share similar orientations to life. Sociologist Emile Durkheim called this form of social solidarity
   a. division of labor
   b. *Gesellschaft*
   c. organic solidarity
   d. mechanical solidarity

3. In contemporary society, social solidarity is based on a division of labor. People work at specialized jobs that, taken together, contribute to one another's welfare. Sociologist Emile Durkheim called this form of social solidarity
   a. labor reductionist
   b. the new contemporary society
   c. organic solidarity
   d. mechanical solidarity

4. This kind of society has greater tolerance for diverse orientations to life (behaviors, attitudes, beliefs) because solidarity depends on a division of labor, not on living close to one another and sharing the same kind of work
   a. mechanical solidarity
   b. organic solidarity
   c. *Gemeinschaft*
   d. village society

5. Sociologist Ferdinand Tönnies analyzed the fundamental change from village to urban life. The term he gave to intimate village life where everyone knows everyone else and people think alike is
   a. *Gemeinschaft* society
   b. *Gesellschaft* society
   c. social solidarity
   d. organic solidarity

6. This main point lies behind the terms *Gemeinschaft* and *Gesellschaft* and *mechanical* and *organic solidarity*
   a. *Gesellschaft* society changed into *Gemeinschaft* society
   b. we live in a large, pluralistic society that is based on mechanical solidarity
   c. because social structure sets the context for what we do, feel, and think, as societies change, so do people's orientations to life
   d. social solidarity comes in many forms

UNIT 5.7

The Microsociological Perspective: Social Interaction in Everyday Life

What do you think microsociologists would be likely to study in this common urban scene? How about macrosociologists?

WHAT AM I SUPPOSED TO LEARN?

After you have read this unit, you should be able to

1 Explain what personal space is and how we use four basic distance zones.

2 Understand why eye contact, smiling, and body language are topics of research by symbolic interactionists.

THE MICROSOCIOLOGICAL PERSPECTIVE

As you have seen, macrosociologists examine the broad features of society. Microsociologists, in contrast, examine narrower slices of social life. Their primary focus is *face-to-face interaction*—what people do when they are in one another's presence. Before you study the main features of social interaction, look at the photo essay on the next two pages. See if you can identify both social structure and social interaction in the photos.

Symbolic Interaction

Symbolic interactionists are especially interested in how people view things and how this, in turn, affects their behavior and orientations. Of the many areas of social life that symbolic interactionists study, let's look at just a few aspects of social interaction: personal space, eye contact, smiling, and body language.

> **Watch the Video**
> Sociology on the Job:
> Social Interaction in
> **mysoclab**

PERSONAL SPACE

We all surround ourselves with a "personal bubble" that we go to great lengths to protect. We open the bubble to intimates—to our friends, children, and parents—but we're careful to keep most people out of this space. In a crowded hallway between classes, we might walk with our books clasped in front of us (a strategy often chosen by females). When we stand in line, we make certain there is enough space so that we don't touch the person in front of us and aren't touched by the person behind us.

The amount of space that people prefer varies from one culture to another. South Americans, for example, like to be closer when they talk than do people reared in the United States. Anthropologist Edward Hall (1959; Hall and Hall 2012) recounts a conversation with a man from South America who had attended one of his lectures.

> *He came to the front of the class at the end of the lecture . . . . We started out facing each other, and as he talked I became dimly aware that he was standing a little too close and that I was beginning to back up. Fortunately I was able to suppress my first impulse and remain stationary because there was nothing to communicate aggression in his behavior except the conversational distance . . . .*
>
> *By experimenting I was able to observe that as I moved away slightly, there was an associated shift in the pattern of interaction. He had more trouble expressing himself. If I shifted to where I felt comfortable (about twenty-one inches), he looked somewhat puzzled and hurt, almost as though he were saying, "Why is he acting that way? Here I am doing everything I can to talk to him in a friendly manner and he suddenly withdraws. Have I done anything wrong? Said something I shouldn't?" Having ascertained that distance had a direct effect on his conversation, I stood my ground, letting him set the distance.*

As you can see, despite Hall's extensive knowledge of other cultures, he still felt uncomfortable in this conversation. He first interpreted the invasion of his personal space as possible

VIENNA: SOCIAL STRUCTURE AND SOCIAL INTERACTION

We live our lives within social structure. Just as a road is to a car, providing limits to where it can go, so social structure limits our behavior. Social structure—our culture, social class, statuses, roles, group memberships, and social institutions—points us in particular directions in life. Most of this direction-giving is beyond our awareness. But it is highly effective, giving shape to our social interactions, as well as to what we expect from life.

These photos that I took in Vienna, Austria, make visible some of social structure's limiting, shaping, and direction-giving. Most of the social structure that affects our lives is not physical, as with streets and buildings, but social, as with norms, belief systems, obligations, and the goals held out for us because of our ascribed statuses. In these photos, you should be able to see how social interaction takes form within social structure.

Vienna provides a mixture of the old and the new. Stephan's Dom (Cathedral) dates back to 1230, the carousel to now.

And what would Vienna be without its wieners? The word wiener actually comes from the name Vienna, which is Wien in German. Wiener means "from Vienna."

The main square in Vienna, Stephan Platz, provides a place to have a cup of coffee, read the newspaper, enjoy the architecture, or just watch the hustle and bustle of the city.

© James M. Henslin, all photos

Part of the pull of the city is its offering of rich culture. I took this photo at one of the many operas held in Vienna each night.

In the appealing street cafes of Vienna, social structure and social interaction are especially evident. Can you see both in this photo?

And what would Vienna be without its world-famous beers? The city's entrepreneurs make sure that the beer is within easy reach.

The city offers something for everyone, including unusual places for people to rest and to talk and to flirt with one another.

To be able to hang out with friends, not doing much, but doing it in the midst of stimulating sounds and sights— this is the vibrant city.

aggression, for people get close (and jut out their chins and chests) when they are hostile. But when he realized that this was not the case, Hall resisted his impulse to move.

After Hall (1969; Hall and Hall 2012) analyzed situations like this, he observed that North Americans use four different "distance zones."

1. *Intimate distance.* This is the zone that the South American unwittingly invaded. It extends about 18 inches from our bodies. We reserve this space for comforting, protecting, hugging, intimate touching, and lovemaking.

2. *Personal distance.* This zone extends from 18 inches to 4 feet. We reserve it for friends and acquaintances and ordinary conversations. This is the zone in which Hall would have preferred speaking with the South American.

3. *Social distance.* This zone, extending out from us about 4 to 12 feet, marks impersonal or formal relationships. We use this zone for such things as job interviews.

4. *Public distance.* This zone, extending beyond 12 feet, marks even more formal relationships. It is used to separate dignitaries and public speakers from the general public.

EYE CONTACT

One way that we protect our personal bubble is by controlling eye contact. Letting someone gaze into your eyes—unless the person is an eye doctor—can be taken as a sign that you are attracted to that person, even as an invitation to intimacy. Wanting to become "the friendliest store in town," a chain of supermarkets in Illinois ordered its checkout clerks to make direct eye contact with each customer. Female clerks complained that male customers were taking their eye contact the wrong way, as an invitation to intimacy. Management said they were exaggerating. The clerks' reply was, "We know the kind of looks we're getting back from men," and they refused to continue making direct eye contact with them.

SMILING

In the United States, we take it for granted that clerks will smile as they wait on us. But it isn't this way in all cultures. Apparently, Germans aren't used to smiling employees, and when Wal-Mart expanded into Germany, it brought its American ways with it. The company ordered its German employees to smile at their customers. They did—and the customers complained. The German customers interpreted the smiles as flirting (Samor et al. 2006).

BODY LANGUAGE

While we are still little children, we learn to interpret **body language,** the ways people use their bodies to give messages to others. This skill in interpreting facial expressions, posture, and gestures is essential for getting through everyday life. Without it—as is the case for people with Asperger's syndrome—we wouldn't know how to react to others. It would even be difficult to know whether someone were serious or joking.

In an interesting twist, this common skill of interpreting body language has become one of the government's tools in its fight against terrorism. Because many of our body messages lie beneath our consciousness, airport personnel and interrogators are being trained to look for telltale facial signs—from a quick downturn of the mouth to rapid blinking—that might indicate nervousness or lying (Davis et al. 2002). The U.S. army is also trying to determine how to apply body language to alert soldiers to danger when interacting wth civilians in a military zone (Yager et al. 2009).

body language the ways in which people use their bodies to give messages to others

1. In contrast to macrosociologists who examine broad features of society, microsociologists examine narrower slices of social life. The primary focus of microsociologists is
   a. social change
   b. global stratification
   c. social structure
   d. face-to-face interaction

2. How people view things (the meaning that things have for people) is a primary focus of
   a. conflict theorists
   b. functionalists
   c. microsociologists
   d. macrosociologists

3. How people use personal space, eye contact, and body language are most likely to be topics of research by
   a. conflict theorists
   b. functionalists
   c. microsociologists
   d. macrosociologists

4. The term "personal bubble" refers to
   a. the amount of space that people prefer when they interact with others
   b. changes in our ideas over time
   c. the idea that as the population increases we each have limited space
   d. an interchange of values between generations

5. The "personal bubble" is not the same in all cultures. Anthropologist Edward Hall recounts an incident in which he talked with a student from South America. Hall was surprised at how
   a. the individual used his body to express hostility
   b. loudly the individual spoke
   c. quickly this person understood cultural differences
   d. close this individual wanted to be whle they were talking

6. Hall uncovered four "distance zones" used by North Americans. This space extends about 18 inches from our bodies and is used for comforting, protecting, hugging, intimate touching, and lovemaking
   a. intimate distance
   b. personal distance
   c. social distance
   d. public distance

7. Extending about 4 to 12 feet from us, we use this zone for such things as job interviews
   a. intimate distance
   b. personal distance
   c. social distance
   d. public distance

8. Ideas of proper face-to-face interaction can differ from one society to another. When Wal-Mart opened a store in Germany, its employees were expected to smile at customers. The reaction of German customers was negative. They felt that the employees were
   a. flirting with them
   b. pressuring them to buy more merchandise
   c. not sincere
   d. wasting time

9. Interpreting body language, the ways people use their bodies to give messages to others, is a skill that we learn as children. The government has now applied body language in its fight against
   a. music and video piracy
   b. tax evasion
   c. false advertising
   d. terrorism

UNIT 5.8

Dramaturgy: The Presentation of Self in Everyday Life

WHAT AM I SUPPOSED TO LEARN?

After you have read this unit, you should be able to

1 Explain dramaturgy: stages, role performance, sign-vehicles, and teamwork.

2 Understand the difference between role conflict and role strain.

3 Explain this statement: "We become the roles we play."

4 Understand how you are an actor on the stage of life.

Introducing Dramaturgy

Let's now turn to dramaturgy, a special area of symbolic interactionism.

It was their big day, two years in the making. Jennifer Mackey wore a white wedding gown adorned with an 11-foot train and 24,000 seed pearls that she and her mother had sewn onto the dress. Next to her at the altar in Lexington, Kentucky, stood her intended, Jeffrey Degler, in black tie. They said their vows, then turned to gaze for a moment at the four hundred guests.

 Watch the **Video**
The Basics: Social Interaction in **mysoclab**

How does this photo from Brooklyn, New York, illustrate dramaturgy?

present, the self. Although you present different facets of this character to different audiences, this character lies at the center of all your performances. You have ideas about how you want others to think of you, and you use your roles in everyday life to communicate these ideas. Goffman called your efforts to manage the impressions that others receive of you **impression management.**

This makes you an actor, an idea we explore in the following *Making It Personal.*

> **impression management** people's efforts to control the impressions that others receive of them

MAKING IT PERSONAL

You, the Actor

I'm certain there have been times when you felt that some piece of clothing just didn't "feel" right for some occasion. There probably have been numerous times that you changed your mind about something you had just put on and decided to change into something else. And those times when things were "almost" right, but not quite? Perhaps then you switched shirts, changed a belt, or added a necklace.

What you were doing on these occasions was fine-tuning the impression you wanted to make. Usually you are so used to the roles you play in everyday life that you tend to think you are "just doing" things, not that you are an actor going on stage to manage impressions. Yet every time you dress for school, or for any other activity, you are preparing for impression management. Although most of your role performances are so practiced that they are routine, and you perform them without much thought, some occasions can bring you to the abrupt realization that you are an actor on stage. Try to recall your first date. How about your first day in college? If you have ever visited the parents of a loved one for the first time, that was probably another of those occasions that raised your dramaturgical awareness.

And you are an excellent actor! After all, you have gotten this far on the stage of life.

That's when groomsman Daniel Mackey collapsed. As the shocked organist struggled to play Mendelssohn's "Wedding March," Mr. Mackey's unconscious body was dragged away, his feet striking—loudly—every step of the altar stairs.

"I couldn't believe he would die at my wedding," the bride said. (Hughes 1990)

> ▶ **Read** the **Document**
> "The Presentation of Self in Everyday Life" by Erving Goffman in
> **mysoclab**

Sociologist Erving Goffman (1922–1982) added a new twist to microsociology when he recast the theatrical term *dramaturgy* into a sociological term. By **dramaturgy,** Goffman (1959/1999) meant that social life is like a drama or a stage play.

IMPRESSION MANAGEMENT

Let's follow this idea. Birth ushers you onto the stage—which is everyday life—and your socialization consists of learning to perform on this stage. You have a character to

> **dramaturgy** an approach, pioneered by Erving Goffman, in which social life is analyzed in terms of drama or the stage; also called dramaturgical analysis

STAGES

In your everyday life, you play your assigned roles. You have **front stages** on which you perform them, as did Jennifer and Jeffrey. (By the way, Daniel Mackey didn't really die—he had just fainted.) But you don't have to look at weddings to find front stages. Your everyday life is filled with them. Where your teacher lectures is a front stage. And if you wait until your parents are in a good

> **front stages** places where people give performances

According to dramaturgical analysis, how is your everyday life like a stage performance? What impression management do you see in this photo?

how you play your role as a son or daughter—which might be "ideal daughter" or "respectful son"—coming home at the hours your parents set, volunteering to help around the house, and so forth. Of course, this description may not even come close to your particular role performance.

Ordinarily, your statuses are separated sufficiently so that you find little conflict between your role performances. Occasionally, however, they clash, and you can't perform your roles when others expect you to. This problem, known as **role conflict,** is illustrated in Figure 5.3, in which family, friendship, student, and work roles come crashing together. We usually manage to avoid role conflict by segregating our statuses, although doing so sometimes requires an intense juggling act.

Occasionally, the *same* status will contain incompatible roles, a conflict known as **role strain.** Suppose that you are exceptionally well prepared for a particular class assignment. Although the instructor asks an unusually difficult question, you find yourself knowing the answer when no one else does. If you want to raise your hand, yet don't want to make your fellow students look bad, you will experience role strain. As illustrated in Figure 5.3, the difference between role conflict and role strain is that role conflict is conflict *between roles*, while role strain is conflict *within* a role.

SIGN-VEHICLES

Throughout your everyday life, then, you move from one stage to another, performing your assigned roles and delivering your lines. As you selectively communicate information about the self, you use three types of **sign-vehicles:** the social setting, your appearance, and your manner. The *social setting* is your stage, the place where the action unfolds. This is where the curtain goes up on your performance, where you find yourself playing parts and delivering lines. A social setting might be a dorm or an office, a living room or a classroom, a church or a bar. It is wherever you interact with others. The social setting includes *scenery*, the furnishings you use to communicate messages, such as desks, blackboards, chairs, couches, and so on.

The second sign-vehicle is your *appearance*, how you look when you play your roles. On the most obvious level is your choice of hairstyle to communicate messages about yourself. On some particular stage, you might be proclaiming "I'm wild and sexy," while in another setting your message might be "I'm serious and professional." Your appearance also includes *props*, which are like scenery except that they decorate your body rather than the setting.

mood to tell them some bad news, you are using a front stage. In fact, you spend most of your time on front stages, for a front stage is wherever you deliver your lines. You also have **back stages,** places where you can retreat and let your hair down. When you close the bathroom or bedroom door for privacy, for example, you are entering a back stage.

The same setting can serve as both a back and a front stage. For example, when you get into your car and look over your hair in the mirror or check your makeup, you are using the car as a back stage. But when you wave at friends or if you give that familiar gesture to someone who has just cut in front of you in traffic, you are using your car as a front stage.

ROLE PERFORMANCE, CONFLICT, AND STRAIN

As discussed earlier, everyday life brings many *statuses*. Think about your statuses. You may be a student, a shopper, a worker, and a date, as well as a daughter or a son. The *roles* attached to your statuses lay down the basic outline for your **role performance.** You have performed these roles so many times that you know them backwards and forwards. But your roles are not rigid. They allow you a great deal of flexibility. As you "interpret" them in different ways for different audiences, you can shift your message: "sexy student," "thrifty shopper," "belligerent guy," "fast driver," and so on. Consider

back stages places where people rest from their performances, discuss their presentations, and plan future performances

role performance the ways in which someone performs a role; showing a particular "style" or "personality"

role conflict conflicts that someone feels *between* roles because the expectations are at odds with one another

role strain conflicts that someone feels *within* a role

sign-vehicle the term used by Goffman to refer to the social setting, appearance, and manner, which people use to communicate information about the self

FIGURE 5.3   **Role Strain and Role Conflict**

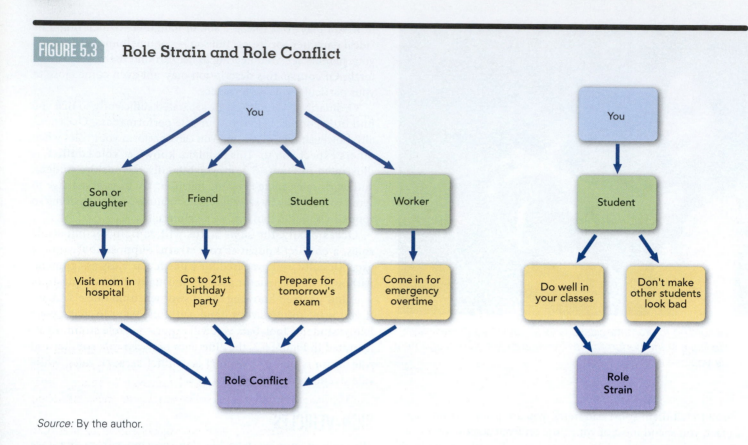

Source: By the author.

Your most obvious prop is your costume, which most people call clothing. Like any good actor, you switch costumes as you play different roles. You wear quite different costumes for attending class, swimming, jogging, working out at the gym, and dating.

Your appearance lets others know what to expect from you and how they should react. Think of the messages that props communicate. Some people use clothing to say they are college students, others to say they are older adults. Some use clothing to let you know they are clergy, others to give the message that they are prostitutes. In the same way, people choose makes of cars and brands of liquor to convey messages about the self.

Your body itself is a sign-vehicle, its shape proclaiming messages about the self. The messages that are attached to various shapes change over time, with thinness currently screaming desirability. Ours, though, is a pluralistic society. Although it has dominant body images carefully crafted by the media, there also are subthemes that follow racial–ethnic lines. How people use the body in the presentation of self varies, then, among African Americans, Latinos, and whites. Although the specific performance may differ, the principles behind that performance are the same.

In the following *Making It Personal*, let's consider what your body means.

Like Jennifer Hudson, you are an actor, but your stage is everyday life. (And you don't get paid!) How do you manage to give successful performances?

MAKING IT PERSONAL
The Meaning of Your Body

When you stand before a mirror, do you like what you see? Do you watch your weight or work out? Where did you get your ideas about what you *should* look like?

You certainly weren't born with these ideas, so where do they come from? If you read a magazine, listen to the radio, or watch television, you are bombarded with this message: "Your body isn't good enough!" The way to improve your body, of course, is to buy some product: hair extensions, magic creams, and "uplifting" bras for women—or diet programs and exercise equipment for all.

You can try to shrug off these messages, but they will still penetrate your thinking and feelings. They become part of an ideal image you hold of how you "ought" to look. Those models so attractively clothed and coiffed as they walk down the runway—could they be any thinner? For women, the message is clear: You can't be thin enough. The men's message is also clear: You can't be muscular enough.

Where are you in this process? Your options of escaping the need to perform on the stage of everyday life—locking yourself in an apartment or living in a remote cave—probably don't seem realistic. So how are you applying these mass media messages about "ideal" bodies? How do you use *your* body to communicate messages on the stages where you perform?

The third sign-vehicle is *manner*, the attitudes you show as you play your roles. You use manner to communicate messages about your feelings and moods. If you show anger or indifference, sincerity or good humor, for example, you are indicating what others can expect of you as you play your roles.

TEAMWORK

Being a good role player brings positive recognition from others, something we all covet. To accomplish this, we use **teamwork**—two or more people working together to help a performance come off as planned. If you laugh at your boss's jokes, even though you don't find them funny, you are doing teamwork to help your boss give a good performance.

It sometimes happens that a performance doesn't come off quite right. To salvage it, the team might use **face-saving behavior.**

Suppose your teacher is about to make an important point. Suppose also that her lecturing has been outstanding and the class is

teamwork two or more people working together to manage impressions jointly

face-saving behavior techniques used to salvage a performance (interaction) that is going sour

hanging on every word. Just as she pauses for emphasis, her stomach lets out a loud growl. She might then use a face-saving technique by remarking, "I was so busy preparing for class that I didn't get breakfast this morning."

It is more likely, however, that both the teacher and class will simply ignore the sound, giving the impression that no one heard a thing—a face-saving technique called *studied nonobservance*. This allows the teacher to make the point or, as Goffman would say, it allows the performance to go on.

BECOMING THE ROLES WE PLAY

A fascinating characteristic of roles is that *we tend to become the roles we play.* That is, roles become incorporated into our self-concept, especially roles for which we prepare long and hard and that become part of our everyday lives. Helen Ebaugh (1988) experienced this firsthand when she quit being a nun to become a sociologist. With her own heightened awareness of *role exit*, she interviewed people who had left marriages, police work, the military, medicine, and religious vocations. Just as she had experienced, these roles had become so intertwined with the individual's self-concept that leaving it threatened the person's identity. The question these people struggled with was "Who am I, now that I am not a nun (or wife, police officer, colonel, physician, and so on)?"

A statement made by one of my respondents illustrates how roles become part of the person. Notice how a role can linger even after the individual is no longer playing that role:

After I left the ministry, I felt like a fish out of water. Wearing that backward collar had become a part of me. It was especially strange on Sunday mornings when I'd listen to someone else give the sermon. I knew that I should be up there preaching. I felt as though I had left God.

Let's get real practical. Since you are an actor who plays roles on the stage of life, can you use your role playing ability to increase your income? You can. Interested in how? Then read the following *Making It Personal.*

MAKING IT PERSONAL
How to Advance Your Career

You can apply a lot of sociology to make your life better, including impression management, which is so significant that it can make a vital difference in your career. Let's consider how dramaturgy can affect your future. I know one individual who applied impression management to become a college president, so this is not just an abstract exercise.

Here is the principle to keep in mind: To be promoted in whatever your job or career after college, you must be perceived as someone who *should* be promoted. You must appear as someone who can take charge. You certainly cannot shrink into a corner and go unnoticed. But how you manage to give this impression makes a crucial difference.

Let's consider female executives, who must walk a finer line than men, exhibiting both dominance and femininity at the same time. If she tries to appear dominant by cursing and wearing loud clothing, this certainly will get her noticed—but it will not put her on the path to promotion. To help women walk this fine line between femininity and dominance, career counselors advise women to wear clothing that doesn't wrinkle and makeup that doesn't have to be reapplied during the day—and not to carry a purse. Stash the purse inside a briefcase, a symbol of professional dominance. And during executive sessions, place your hands on the table, not in your lap. Hands in the lap are a sign of submissiveness, but hands on the table are a sign of dominance (Needham 2006; Brinkley 2008; Agins 2009).

As you can see, all of this is impression management, in this case learning how to use your body and props to convey subtle but significant messages. Whether you are male or female, to get promoted you must look like someone who should be promoted. Much success in the work world depends not on what you know but, instead, on your ability to give the impression that you know what you should know.

What impression management do you see in this photo?

1. Dramaturgy, a term adopted from the theater by Erving Goffman, refers to social life being like a performance on a stage. Another term used in this unit for dramaturgy is
   a. stage analysis **b.** symbolic interaction
   c. sign-vehicle **d.** impression management

2. If social life is like a stage performance, then where is the stage?
   a. wherever people gather to watch a performance
   b. it is a portable concept that we carry with us
   c. wherever we give our performances
   d. there is no stage

3. In the theater, there is a front stage where performances are given and a back stage where actors get away from the prying eyes of their audience. In everyday life, this is the best example of a back stage
   a. a kitchen
   b. a bathroom
   c. a living room
   d. the hallway that runs between offices or classrooms

4. Brenda decided that she would try to get Jeb interested in her. She had tried to engage him in "serious" talk about sociological concepts, but that didn't seem to work, so she decided to try something different. That morning she put on a shorter skirt, a lower-cut blouse, and, unusual for her, makeup. Brenda is about to engage in
   a. a role performance **b.** role strain
   c. a bad move **d.** insincerity

5. Just as Brenda was talking to Jeb—and she could see his new interest—her cell phone rang. It was her mother, who said that she (her mom) had just been called into work on an emergency and Brenda needed to come home right away to take care of her little brother. Caught between the roles of "flirtatious girlfriend" and "good daughter," Brenda is experiencing
   a. a role performance **b.** teamwork
   c. role strain **d.** role conflict

6. Disappointed, but back at home, Brenda is taking care of her 10-year old brother. She notices that he has turned on a TV program that he is not allowed to watch, thinking that his sister will let him get away with it. When he begs her to let him watch the

program, Brenda is torn between being the "good, understanding, nice sister" and the "older, responsible sister." Brenda is experiencing

a. the failure of props
b. a role performance
c. role strain
d. role conflict

7. Brenda's brother spilled soda on the carpet, and both Brenda and her brother know they will be in trouble, the brother for spilling the soda and Brenda for not watching him more carefully. Both Brenda and her brother work furiously to clean up the soda so it doesn't leave a stain. When the mother returns and asks if there was any trouble, both Brenda and her brother smile and say that everything went well. Brenda and her brother have just engaged in

a. a sign-vehicle
b. teamwork
c. role strain
d. role conflict

8. The mother smiles at her children's rush to say that everything went well, knowing that something isn't quite right. As she takes off her shoes in the living room, she feels a damp spot. She immediately knows what has happened, but impressed that the

children had cleaned up whatever the mess was, she just smiles and says nothing. The mother has just engaged in

a. face-saving behavior
b. role strain
c. role conflict
d. back stage behavior

9. At school the next day, Brenda decides to change strategies concerning Jeb. When she sees him walking toward her, she reaches into her locker, making it appear that she is so intent on getting something out of it that she doesn't notice him. In dramaturgical terms, the locker Brenda was using is called

a. role performance
b. a back stage
c. a sign-vehicle
d. scenery

10. Brenda decides to continue the strategy of ignoring Jeb. This time, when she sees him walking toward her, she turns away and begins to adjust her necklace, seeming so intent on the task that she doesn't notice Jeb. In dramaturgical terms, the necklace Brenda was using is called

a. a back stage
b. teamwork
c. a prop
d. a social setting

UNIT 5.9
Ethnomethodology: Uncovering Background Assumptions

WHAT AM I SUPPOSED TO LEARN?

After you have read this unit, you should be able to

1 State what ethnomethodology is.

2 Explain what background assumptions are and how they help us navigate everyday life.

3 Be familiar with some of the exercises Garfinkel conducted with his students.

Introducing Ethnomethodology

One of the strangest words in sociology is *ethnomethodology*. To better understand this term, consider the word's three components. *Ethno* means "folk" or "people"; *method* means how people do something; *ology* means "the study of." Putting them together, then, *ethno–method–ology* means "the study of how people do things." Specifically, **ethnomethodology** is the study of how people use commonsense understandings to make sense out of life.

Let's suppose that during a routine office visit, your doctor remarks that your hair is rather long, then takes out a pair of scissors and starts to give you a haircut.

If this happened to you, you would feel strange about it. Your doctor would be violating your **background assumptions**—your ideas about the way life is, how people should act, and, in general, the way things ought to work in life. Although background assumptions lie at the root of your everyday life, they are embedded so deeply in your consciousness that you are seldom aware of them. They are part of what you assume life is, so you follow them without thinking. In this instance, your doctor does not offer you a haircut, even if he or she is good at cutting hair and you need one!

BREAKING BACKGROUND ASSUMPTIONS

The founder of ethnomethodology, sociologist Harold Garfinkel, conducted exercises to reveal our

ethnomethodology the study of how people use background assumptions to make sense out of life

background assumption a deeply embedded, common understanding of how the world operates and of how people ought to act

No one has difficulty identifying the background assumptions being violated here.

background assumptions. In one exercise, Garfinkel (1967, 2002) asked his students to act as though they did not understand the basic rules of social life. Some tried to bargain with supermarket clerks; others inched close to people and stared at them. They were met with surprise, bewilderment, even indignation and anger. In another exercise, Garfinkel asked students to act as though they were boarders in their own homes. They addressed their

People sometimes break background assumptions for the thrill of doing so, to get attention, or to express solidarity with people of similar views. This photo was taken at the Summer Solstice Parade in Seattle, Washington.

parents as "Mr." and "Mrs.," asked permission to use the bathroom, sat stiffly, were courteous, and spoke only when spoken to. As you can imagine, the other family members didn't know what to make of this (Garfinkel 1967):

> They vigorously sought to make the strange actions intelligible and to restore the situation to normal appearances. Reports (by the students) were filled with accounts of astonishment, bewilderment, shock, anxiety, embarrassment, and anger, and with charges by various family members that the student was mean, inconsiderate, selfish, nasty, or impolite. Family members demanded explanations: What's the matter? What's gotten into you? . . . Are you sick? . . . Are you out of your mind or are you just stupid?

Garfinkel also asked students to take words and phrases literally. When a student asked his girlfriend what she meant when she said that she had a flat tire, she said:

> What do you mean, "What do you mean?" A flat tire is a flat tire. That is what I meant. Nothing special. What a crazy question!

Another conversation went like this:

ACQUAINTANCE: How are you?
STUDENT: How am I in regard to what? My health, my finances, my schoolwork, my peace of mind, my . . . ?
ACQUAINTANCE: (red in the face): Look! I was just trying to be polite. Frankly, I don't give a damn how you are.

Students can be highly creative when they are asked to break background assumptions. The young children of one of my students were surprised one morning when they came down for breakfast to find a sheet spread on the living room floor. On it were dishes, silverware, lit candles—and bowls of ice cream. They, too, wondered what was going on, but they dug eagerly into the ice cream before their mother could change her mind.

This is a risky assignment to give students, however, for breaking some background assumptions can make people suspicious. When a colleague of mine gave this assignment, a couple of his students began to wash dollar bills in a laundromat. By the time they put the bills in the dryer, the police had arrived.

IN SUM: Ethnomethodologists explore *background assumptions*, the taken-for-granted ideas about the world that underlie our behavior. Most of these assumptions, or basic rules of social life, are unstated. We learn them as we learn our culture, and we violate them only with risk. Deeply embedded in our minds, background assumptions give us basic guidance for how we should live everyday life and for what we can expect from others.

UNIT 5.9 // TESTING MYSELF
DID I LEARN IT? ANSWERS ARE AT THE END OF THE CHAPTER

1. The term ethnomethodology means the study of the assumptions that people use as they go through everyday life. Another way to phrase this is to say ethnomethodology is the study of
   a. ethnos
   b. methods
   c. ologies
   d. how people use commonsense understandings to make sense of life

2. If ethnomethodology is the study of people's background assumptions, what are background assumptions?
   a. the myths that hold a society together
   b. ideas that people are discussing

   c. ideas about the way life is and how things ought to work
   d. trial and error solutions to complex problems

3. When Kathy took her son to the Rainbow Gardens preschool, she expected that he would be treated politely, given wholesome food, and play active games. Instead, he was treated rudely, given Kool-Aid and crackers, and plopped in front of a TV. These actions violated Kathy's
   a. morals
   b. background assumptions
   c. educational background
   d. research on preschools

4. Two common reactions when Garfinkel's students broke background assumptions, such as acting as though they were boarders in their own homes, were
   a. bewilderment and shock
   b. humor and laughter
   c. sadness and tears
   d. friendliness and helpfulness

UNIT 5.10
The Social Construction of Reality

WHAT AM I SUPPOSED TO LEARN?

After you have read this unit, you should be able to

1 Explain the social construction of reality and summarize the Thomas theorem.

2 Explain how our behavior is based not on what is real but on our views of what is real.

3 Explain how the gynecological examination is socially constructed to provide a definition of nonsexuality.

Introducing the Social Construction of Reality

> **Watch** the **Video**
> The Big Picture: Social Interaction in **mysoclab**

On a visit to Morocco, in northern Africa, I decided to buy a watermelon. When I indicated to the street vendor that the knife he was going to use to cut the watermelon was dirty (encrusted with filth would be more apt), he was very obliging. He immediately bent down and began to swish the knife in a puddle on the street. I shuddered as I looked at the passing burros that were urinating and defecating as they went by. Quickly, I indicated by gesture that I preferred my melon uncut after all.

"If people define situations as real, they are real in their consequences," said sociologists W. I. and Dorothy S. Thomas in what has become known as *the definition of the situation*, or the **Thomas theorem.** For that vendor of watermelons, germs did not exist. For me, they did. And each of us acted according to our definition of the situation.

It is important to note that my perception and behavior did not come from the fact that germs are real but, rather, from *my having grown up in a society that teaches they are real.* Microbes *objectively* exist, and whether or not germs are part of our thought world makes no difference as to whether we are infected by them. Our behavior, however, does not depend on what is real but, rather, on how we interpret what is real, on what sociologists call our

Thomas theorem
William I. and Dorothy S. Thomas' classic formulation of the definition of the situation: "If people define situations as real, they are real in their consequences"

A marketplace in Fes, Morocco.

definition of reality. In other words, it is not the reality of microbes that impresses itself on us, but society that impresses the reality of microbes on us.

Let's use another example. Do you remember the identical twins, Oskar and Jack, who grew up so differently? As discussed in the chapter on socialization, Jack was reared in Trinidad and learned to hate Hitler, while Oskar was reared in Germany and learned to love Hitler. As you can see, what Hitler meant to Oskar and Jack depended not on Hitler's acts, but, rather, on how they learned to view his acts—that is, on the definition of the situation.

Sociologists call this the **social construction of reality.** From the social groups to which you belong (the *social* part of this process), you learn ways of looking at life. You learn ways to view Hitler and Osama bin Laden (they're good, they're evil), germs (they exist, they don't exist), and *just about everything else in life.* In short, through your interaction with others, you learn certain ways to *construct reality;* that is, you learn ways of interpreting your experiences in life.

To better understand the social construction of reality, I want to share with you some research I did on pelvic examinations.

GYNECOLOGICAL EXAMINATIONS

When I interviewed a gynecological nurse who had been present at about 14,000 vaginal examinations, I focused on *how doctors construct social reality in order to define the examination as nonsexual* (Henslin and Biggs 1971/2012). The pelvic examination unfolds much as a stage play does. I will use "he" to refer to the physician because only male physicians were part of this study. The situation could differ in some details with female gynecologists, but it would unfold about the same.

Let's begin with the opening performance.

Scene 1 (the patient as person) In this scene, the doctor maintains eye contact with his patient, calls her by name, and discusses her problems in a professional

the social construction of reality the use of background assumptions and life experiences to define what is real

manner. If he decides that a vaginal examination is necessary, he tells a nurse, "Pelvic in room 1." By this statement, he is announcing that a major change will occur in the next scene.

Scene 2 (from person to pelvic) This scene is the depersonalizing stage. In line with the doctor's announcement, the patient begins the transition from a "person" to a "pelvic." The doctor leaves the room, and a female nurse enters to help the patient make the transition. The nurse prepares the "props" for the coming examination and answers any questions the woman might have.

What occurs at this opening point is essential for the social construction of reality, for *the doctor's absence removes even the suggestion of sexuality.* To undress in front of him could suggest either a striptease or intimacy, thus undermining the reality that the team is so carefully defining: that of nonsexuality.

The patient, too, wants to remove any hint of sexuality, and during this scene she may express concern about what to do with her panties that she has removed. Some mutter to the nurse, "I don't want him to see these." Most women solve the problem by either slipping their panties under their other clothes or placing them in their purse.

Scene 3 (the person as pelvic) This scene opens when the doctor enters the room. Before him is a woman lying on a table, her feet in stirrups, her knees tightly together, and her body covered by a drape sheet. The doctor seats himself on a low stool before the woman and says, "Let your knees fall apart" (rather than the sexually loaded "Spread your legs"), and begins the examination.

The drape sheet is crucial in this process of desexualization, for it *dissociates the pelvic area from the person:* Leaning forward and with the drape sheet above his head, the physician can see only the vagina, not the patient's face. Thus dissociated from the individual, the vagina is transformed dramaturgically into an object of analysis. If the doctor examines the patient's breasts, he also dissociates them from her person by examining them one at a time, with a towel covering the unexamined breast. Like the vagina, each breast becomes an isolated item dissociated from the person.

In this third scene, the patient cooperates in being an object, becoming, for all practical purposes, a pelvis to be examined. She withdraws eye contact from the doctor, and usually from the nurse, is likely to stare at the wall or at the ceiling, and avoids initiating conversation.

Scene 4 (from pelvic to person) In this scene, the patient becomes "repersonalized." The doctor has left the examining room; the patient dresses and fixes her hair and makeup. Her reemergence as a person is indicated by such statements to the nurse as "My clothes aren't too wrinkled, are they?" showing a need for reassurance that the metamorphosis from "pelvic" back to "person" has been completed satisfactorily.

Scene 5 (the patient as person) In this final scene, sometimes with the doctor seated at a desk, the patient is once *again treated as a person rather than as an object. The doctor makes eye contact with her and addresses her by name. She, too, makes eye contact with the doctor, and they both follow the usual middle-class interaction patterns. She has been fully restored.*

IN SUM: For an outsider to our culture, the custom of women going to male strangers for a vaginal examination might seem bizarre. But not to us. We learn that pelvic examinations are nonsexual. To sustain this definition requires teamwork—patients, doctors, and nurses working together to *socially construct reality*.

It is not just pelvic examinations or our views of germs that make up our definitions of reality. Rather, *our behavior depends on how we define reality.* Our definitions (or constructions) provide the basis for what we do and how we view life. To understand human behavior, then, we must know how people define their worlds.

But microsociology, including its social construction of reality, is not sufficient by itself. We also need the broader perspective that macrosociology provides. With each providing part of the picture, sociologists stress both approaches to understanding life in society. .

Pelvic examinations are an excellent illustration of the social construction of reality.

UNIT 5.10 // TESTING MYSELF
DID I LEARN IT? ANSWERS ARE AT THE END OF THE CHAPTER

1. The statement "If people define situations as real, they are real in their consequences" is known as
   a. the situational response
   b. sociological relativity
   c. a background assumption
   d. the Thomas theorem

2. According to the Thomas theorem (developed by W. I. and Dorothy Thomas), also called the definition of the situation, we do not act on facts (reality) but on
   a. how facts are related to one another
   b. the challenges we face in our everyday lives
   c. our interpretation of facts (reality)
   d. an attempt to improve our lives

3. What Hitler or Osama bin Laden or any other historical figure means to us depends on
   a. their acts
   b. our interpretation of their acts
   c. what we read in history books
   d. the context of related historical events

4. Gynecological examinations were used to illustrate
   a. the social construction of reality
   b. the advancement of the medical profession
   c. the high cost of current medical treatment
   d. changes in the practice of medicine

5. The main point of this unit is that to understand human behavior, we
   a. need to do research
   b. should go to college
   c. should get away from books and see how people really deal with life
   d. must know how people define reality

We'll close this chapter a little differently. First, to better see why we need both macrosociology and microsociology, look at the photos on the next two pages that I took after a tornado hit a little town in Georgia. After this, on the next page, you will have a chance to meet some delinquent boys in *Making It Personal*.

WHEN A TORNADO STRIKES: SOCIAL ORGANIZATION FOLLOWING A NATURAL DISASTER

GEORGIA

As I was watching television on March 20, 2003, I heard a report that a tornado had hit Camilla, Georgia. "Like a big lawn mower," the report said, it had cut a path of destruction through this little town. In its fury, the tornado had left behind six dead and about 200 injured.

From sociological studies of natural disasters, I knew that immediately after the initial shock the survivors of natural disasters work together to try to restore order to their disrupted lives. I wanted to see this restructuring process first-hand. The next morning, I took off for Georgia.

These photos, taken the day after the tornado struck, tell the story of people in the midst of trying to put their lives back together. I was impressed at how little time people spent commiserating about their misfortune and how quickly they took practical steps to restore their lives.

As we look at these photos, try to determine why we need both microsociology and macrosociology to understand what occurs after a natural disaster.

After making sure that their loved ones are safe, one of the next steps people take is to recover their possessions. The cooperation that emerges among people, as documented in the sociological literature on natural disasters, is illustrated here.

Personal relationships are essential in putting lives together. Consequently, reminders of these relationships are one of the main possessions that people attempt to salvage. This young man, having just recovered the family photo album, is eagerly reviewing the photos.

For children, family photos are not as important as toys. This girl has managed to salvage a favorite toy, which will help anchor her to her previous life.

© James M. Henslin, all photos

In addition to the inquiring sociologist, television teams also were interviewing survivors and photographing the damage. This was the second time in just three years that a tornado had hit this neighborhood.

Formal organizations also help the survivors of natural disasters recover. In this neighborhood, I saw representatives of insurance companies, the police, the fire department, and an electrical co-op. The Salvation Army brought meals to the neighborhood.

No building or social institution escapes a tornado as it follows its path of destruction. Just the night before, members of this church had held evening worship service. After the tornado, someone mounted a U.S. flag on top of the cross, symbolic of the church members' patriotism and religiosity—and of their enduring hope.

The owners of this house invited me inside to see what the tornado had done to their home. In what had been her dining room, this woman is trying to salvage whatever she can from the rubble. She and her family survived by taking refuge in the bathroom. They had been there only five seconds, she said, when the tornado struck.

Like electricity and gas, cable television is also restored as soon as possible.

MAKING IT PERSONAL

Saints and Roughnecks

I opened this chapter with a little story, and now I'd like to share another. I would like you to think along with me so you can better grasp why we need both macrosociology and microsociology.

In a little town in Missouri, there were two groups of boys. In one group were eight boys who were perceived by townspeople—teachers and police—as "saints" with a bright future. In the other group were six boys that the community perceived as "roughnecks," juvenile delinquents headed for no place but trouble.

The facts were a little different than the perception. The saints actually skipped school more often and did more vandalism than the roughnecks, points out sociologist William Chambliss (1973/2012), who at that time went to high school with these boys.

Why didn't the facts square up with the perception? There are two answers. The first is social structure. The saints were middle-class boys who came from "good" families. The roughnecks, in contrast, came from working-class families that did not have this sterling reputation. And because of social class, the saints had cars. They spread their vandalism around, even into neighboring communities. And the roughnecks? They couldn't afford cars. Their troublemaking was concentrated in their own neighborhood, putting them squarely in the center of the eye of the local cops.

There was still another factor. Socialized into different social classes, the boys learned distinct attitudes and ways of interacting. The roughnecks were surly and hostile to the police and teachers. But when the saints were questioned, the police and teachers found them pleasant and respectful.

This early start in life followed the boys. The boys perceived to have a bright future did have exactly that. They entered the professions and management. The one exception was a boy whose parents divorced. And the boys thought to be headed toward a dead-end future? That's just the direction they went. They ended up with low-paying jobs, and some went to prison. The two exceptions were outstanding athletes who won scholarships to college and became coaches.

Can you see how background assumptions were at work here? The teachers and the police had ideas about the boys based on their ideas about social class. Their definition of the situation influenced their reactions to the boys.

Did you see anything like this in your high school? How has social class (a part of social structure) been an overarching influence in your own life? How about your style of interaction with people in authority?

I hope that from this short account of the saints and roughnecks you can better see why we need *both* macrosociology (social structure) and microsociology (social interaction) in order to understand human behavior.

How would you use both macrosociology and microsociology to understand this group of high school boys?

✓—[**Study** and **Review** in **mysoclab**

PULLING IT ALL TOGETHER REVIEWING THE LEARNING GOALS

Unit 5.1 Introducing Macrosociology and Microsociology

1. **Summarize the distinction between macrosociology and microsociology.**
   - Macrosociology focuses on the broad features of society, from international relations to factors that

affect the unemployment rate. Microsociology focuses on social interaction, how people interact with one another.

2. **Explain why we need both macrosociology and microsociology to understand social life.**
   - Each provides part of the picture of human behavior. The broad features of social life (social structure)

set the context for people's behavior, but people develop their orientations and forms of interaction within their particular groups.

Unit 5.2 The Macrosociological Perspective: Social Structure

1. Explain what social structure is and why it is important.
   - Social structure is the framework of society: the ways its groups are related to one another and its typical patterns. Social structure sets limits and provides guidance for your behavior.

2. Explain how social structure influences the lives of street people, your instructor, and yourself.
   - All of us live our lives within the particular structure that our society provides. This pushes our behavior into certain directions, and along with it influences our orientations to life, including our ideas, attitudes, and emotions.

Unit 5.3 The Components of Social Structure: Culture, Social Class, Social Status, Roles, and Groups

1. Explain how the components of social structure influence your life.
   - Culture and social class establish the broad context for your behavior. Your group memberships, statuses, and roles provide more specific contexts, setting limits and giving more specific direction for how you should act and even feel.

2. Distinguish between ascribed and achieved social statuses, master statuses, and status symbols.
   - At birth, you are assigned ascribed statuses, such as your sex and race–ethnicity. Later in life, you attain achieved statuses such as college graduate, teacher, and married. Master statuses such as your sex and wealth or poverty cut across all your other statuses. You use status symbols to announce to others what your statuses are. They set the stage for interaction.

3. Explain how roles are related to statuses and how they influence your life.
   - Each status comes with a role—expectations of behavior and attitudes. You tend to become the roles you play.

Unit 5.4 Another Component of Social Structure: Social Institutions

1. State what the social institutions are.
   - As summarized in Figure 5.2, social institutions are family, religion, education, economy,

medicine, politics, law, science, military, and mass media.

2. Explain why social institutions have such powerful effects on our lives.
   - Social institutions surround us from birth to death. We are born within them, socialized within them, and live our lives within them.

✳ **Explore** the **Concept**
Congregational Membership, Primary Groups and Secondary Groups in **mysoclab**

Unit 5.5 Comparing Functionalist and Conflict Perspectives

1. Summarize the functionalist perspective on social institutions.
   - The functionalist view is that the social institutions work together to meet the basic needs of society: replacing members, socializing new members, producing and distributing goods and services, preserving order, and providing a sense of purpose.

2. Summarize the conflict perspective on social institutions.
   - The conflict view is that powerful groups control the social institutions, using them to maintain their places of privilege.

Unit 5.6 What Holds Society Together?

1. Distinguish between mechanical and organic solidarity.
   - Mechanical solidarity refers to community life, where people are united by shared activities and orientations to life. Little diversity of views and behavior is tolerated. Organic solidarity refers to people being united by a division of labor, in which the labor of each contributes to their society. This does not require similarity of orientations, and greater diversity is tolerated.

2. State the difference between *Gemeinschaft* and *Gesellschaft*.
   - Gemeinschaft refers to intimate village life marked by strong kinship links and lifelong associations. Gesellschaft refers to urban life marked by self-interested, impersonal, short-term associations.

3. Explain why people change as society changes.
   - Our orientations to life (ideas, beliefs, attitudes, goals) come from our associating (contacts) with others. As society changes, so do its orientations, and along with it, our own.

Unit 5.7   The Microsociological Perspective: Social Interaction

1. **Explain what personal space is and how we use four basic distance zones,**
   - We all have a "personal bubble" that we protect from intrusion. The size of people's personal bubbles varies from one culture to another. Americans have four "distance zones," ranging from where they hug to where they listen to public speakers. The distance zones are the intimate, personal, social, and public.

2. **Understand why eye contact, smiling, and body language are topics of research by symbolic interactionists.**
   - Because symbolic interactionists focus on face-to-face interaction--what people do in one another's presence—such behaviors as smiling, making eye contact, touching, and so on are their natural areas of interest.

◉ Watch the Video
Sociology on the Job: Social Interaction in **mysoclab**

Unit 5.8   Dramaturgy: The Presentation of Self in Everyday Life

1. **Explain dramaturgy: stages, role performance, sign-vehicles, and teamwork.**
   - Dramaturgy compares social interaction to a stage performance. The stage is wherever we perform our roles. We use the sign-vehicles of setting, appearance, and manner to manage impressions. Teamwork is people working together to give certain messages.

2. **Understand the difference between role conflict and role strain.**
   - Role conflict refers to incompatible expectations between roles. Role strain refers to incompatible expectations within a role.

3. **Explain this statement: "We become the roles we play."**
   - We tend to incorporate roles into our self-concept, especially roles we play repetitively.

4. **Understand how you are an actor on the stage of life.**
   - Like everyone else, you use sign-vehicles to try to manage the impressions others receive of you.

◉ Watch the Video
The Basics: Social Interaction in **mysoclab**

📖 Read the Document
"The Presentation of Self in Everyday Life" by Erving Goffman in **mysoclab**

Unit 5.9   Ethnomethodology: Uncovering Background Assumptions

1. **State what ethnomethodology is.**
   - Ethnomethodology refers to studying how people go about doing their everyday lives, how people use background assumptions to make sense of life.

2. **Explain what background assumptions are and how they help us navigate everyday life.**
   - Background assumptions are the things we assume to be normal, the way life "is." They serve as unexamined guidelines for our behavior.

3. **Be familiar with some of the exercises Garfinkel conducted with his students.**
   - The students violated background assumptions of intimate relations at home, fixed prices at stores, and moving inside the "intimate distance zone" while talking to strangers.

Unit 5.10   The Social Construction of Reality

1. **Explain the social construction of reality and summarize the Thomas theorem.**
   - Social construction of reality refers to ways we have learned to view life. We act on our views, not on what is actually "out there." The Thomas theorem, also called the definition of the situation, summarizes this: "If people define situations as real, they are real in their consequences."

2. **Explain how our behavior is based not on what is real but on our views of what is real.**
   - If we think a tiger is prowling outside our house, we likely will stay inside. It does not matter that there is no tiger out there. We act on our definitions (views of reality), not on reality.

3. **Explain how gynecological examinations are socially constructed to provide a definition of nonsexuality.**
   - In gynecological examinations, team players work together to promote the definition of nonsexuality. They use the sign-vehicles of setting, appearance, and manner—from where the patient undresses to the use of the drape sheet.

◉ Watch the Video
The Big Picture: Social Interaction in **mysoclab**

1. **d** the two levels of sociological analysis, macrosociology and microsociology

2. **c** how these men fit into the structure of society

3. **b** these men interact with one another

1. **d** the framework of society that was laid out before you were born

2. **c** the typical patterns of a group

1. **c** yield to others the right to judge your behavior

2. **d** saying that as long as their daughter wants to remain a member of the family in good standing, her behavior must conform to their expectations

3. **b** the position that someone occupies, such as a waitress

1. **d** a society's standard or usual way of meeting its basic needs

1. **b** social institutions are the ways that a society meets its basic needs

2. **d** functional requisites

3. **c** less visible because they meet their basic needs more informally

4. **a** view social institutions as working harmoniously for the common good

4. **d** microsociologists

5. **c** macrosociologists

6. **b** microsociologists

7. **a** each approach yields a distinctive perspective, just part of the picture

3. **b** are influenced by social structure

4. **a** breaking off the neck of a wine bottle and glaring at an enemy

5. **d** social structure

6. **c** social structure

4. **d.** ascribed statuses

5. **c.** achieved status

6. **c.** achieved status

7. **b.** status symbols

8. **d.** status inconsistency

9. **c.** master status

10. **b.** role

2. **c** social institutions

3. **d** have their own groups, statuses, values, and norms

5. **d** a fairly small group of people gets the lion's share of our nation's wealth

6. **c** is behind the nation's major decisions, including whether or not to go to war and to move capital, technology, and jobs out of the country

7. **b** gender is an element of social structure, with social institutions dividing males and females into separate groups, each with unequal access to society's resources

8. **a** work together to meet universal human needs

9. **d** are ways that the wealthy and powerful preserve the social order so they can maintain their positions of privilege

1. **d** is made up of many groups, each with its own interests

2. **d** mechanical solidarity

1. **d** face-to-face interaction

2. **c** microsociologists

3. **c** microsociologists

4. **a** the amount of space that people prefer when they interact with others

1. **d** impression management

2. **c** wherever we give our performances

3. **b** a bathroom

4. **a** a role performance

1. **d** how people use commonsense understandings to make sense of life

2. **c** ideas about the way life is and how things ought to work

1. **d** the Thomas theorem

2. **c** our interpretation of facts (reality)

3. **c** organic solidarity

4. **b** organic solidarity

5. **a** *Gemeinschaft* society

6. **c** because social structure sets the context for what we do, feel, and think, as societies change, so do people's orientations to life

5. **d** close this individual wanted to be while they were talking

6. **a** intimate distance

7. **c** social distance

8. **a** flirting with them

9. **d** terrorism

5. **d** role conflict

6. **c** role strain

7. **b** teamwork

8. **a** face-saving behavior

9. **d** scenery

10. **c** a prop

3. **b** background assumptions

4. **a** bewilderment and shock

3. **b** our interpretation of their acts

4. **a** the social construction of reality

5. **d** must know how people define reality

CHAPTER 6
DEVIANCE AND SOCIAL CONTROL

(((•—[**Listen** to the **Chapter Audio** in **mysoclab**

👁 **Watch** the **Video** in **mysoclab**

GETTING STARTED

Just like the last chapter, let's start this one with a little story.

In just a few moments I was to meet my first Yanomamö, my first primitive man. What would it be like? ... I looked up [from my canoe] and gasped when I saw a dozen burly, naked, filthy, hideous men staring at us down the shafts of their drawn arrows. Immense wads of green tobacco were stuck between their lower teeth and lips, making them look even more hideous, and strands of dark-green slime dripped or hung from their noses. We arrived at the village while the men were blowing a hallucinogenic drug up their noses. One of the side effects of the drug is a runny nose. The mucus is always saturated with the green powder, and the Indians usually let it run freely from their nostrils... . I just sat there holding my notebook, helpless and pathetic ...

(*continued on next page*)

Tattoo Convention, Berlin, Germany

(continued from previous page)

The whole situation was depressing, and I wondered why I ever decided to switch from civil engineering to anthropology in the first place... . [Soon] I was covered with red pigment, the result of a dozen or so complete examinations.... These examinations capped an otherwise grim day. The Indians would blow their noses into their hands, flick as much of the mucus off that would separate in a snap of the wrist, wipe the residue into their hair, and then carefully examine my face, arms, legs, hair, and the contents of my pockets. I said [in their language], "Your hands are dirty"; my comments were met by the Indians in the following way: they would "clean" their hands by spitting a quantity of slimy tobacco juice into them, rub them together, and then proceed with the examination.

This is how Napoleon Chagnon described the culture shock he felt when he met the Yanomamö tribe of the rain forests of Brazil. The following months of fieldwork brought surprise after surprise, and often Chagnon (1977) could hardly believe his eyes—or his nose.

If you were to list the deviant behaviors of the Yanomamö, what would you include? The way they appear naked in public? Their use of hallucinogenic drugs? The mucus they allowed to hang from their noses? Or the way they rub hands filled with mucus, spittle, and tobacco juice over a frightened stranger who doesn't dare to protest? Perhaps. But it isn't this simple, for as we shall see, deviance is relative. ■

UNIT 6.1

What Is Deviance?

WHAT AM I SUPPOSED TO LEARN?

After you have read this unit, you should be able to

1 Explain what deviance is and why it is relative.

2 Explain what stigma is.

3 Explain why norms and sanctions are necessary for social life to exist.

Sociologists use the term **deviance** to refer to *any* violation of norms, whether the infraction is as minor as driving over the speed limit or as serious as murder. Deviance can also be as humorous as Chagnon's encounter with the Yanomamö. This deceptively simple definition takes us to the heart of the sociological perspective on deviance, which sociologist Howard S. Becker (1966) described this way: *It is not the act itself, but the reactions to the act, that make something deviant.*

You can see that what Chagnon saw disturbed him—and you can understand why—but to the Yanomamö

deviance the violation of norms (or rules or expectations)

IF YOU WANT TO LEARN MORE *about how sexual deviance is relative,*

Read more from the author: Human Sexuality in Cross-Cultural Perspective in **mysoclab**

Violating background assumptions is a common form of deviance. Although we have no explicit rule that says, "Do not put snakes through your nose," we all know that it exists. Is this act also deviant for this man in Chennai, India?

those same behaviors were part of their normal, everyday life. What was deviant to Chagnon was *conformist* to the Yanomamö. From their viewpoint, you *should* check out strangers the way they did—and nakedness is good, as are hallucinogenic drugs. And it is natural to let mucus flow. Chagnon's experience allows us to see the *relativity of deviance*, a major point made by symbolic interactionists.

To see this principle in action, look at the photos on this page and the next.

I took this photo in Hyderabad, India. Is this man deviant? If this were a U.S. street, he would be. But here? No houses have running water in his neighborhood, and the men, women, and children bathe at the neighborhood water pump. This man, then, would not be deviant in this culture.

I can just hear you say, "OK. I get it. And that idea is fine regarding a guy who bathes in public and one who has snakes coming out his nose, but what about *crime*? Here, too, the principle applies. **Crime** is simply the violation of rules that have been written into law. I can choose from hundreds of examples to illustrate this, but let's look at this one: An act that one group applauds can be so despised by another group that they punish it by death. In the United States, people who make huge profits on a business deal are admired. Like Donald Trump and Warren Buffet, they may even write books about their exploits. In China, in contrast, until recently this same act was considered a crime called *profiteering*. Those found guilty were hanged in a public square as a lesson to all.

Unlike the general public, sociologists are *not* judging anything when they use the term *deviance*. To them, deviance simply refers to *any* act to which people respond negatively. They are not agreeing that an act is bad, just that people judge it negatively. To sociologists, then, both you and I are deviants of one sort or another, for we all violate norms from time to time.

To be considered deviant, a person does not even have to *do* anything. Some people have a **stigma,** a characteristic that discredits them. Stigma is like a huge black mark next to their name, a negative master status that marks them as "different" or even as "not one of us." People view the individual through this negative lens, which minimizes, or even wipes out, the person's positive characteristics.

crime the violation of norms written into law

stigma "blemishes" that discredit a person's claim to a "normal" identity

Stigma, analyzed by sociologist Erving Goffman (1963), comes in a variety of forms. It includes violations of norms of appearance (a huge facial birthmark) and norms of ability (blindness, deafness, mental handicaps). Stigma also includes involuntary memberships, such as being the brother of a rapist.

How Norms Make Social Life Possible

What would life be like if you could not predict what others would do? Imagine for a moment that you have gone to a store to purchase milk:

> Suppose the clerk says, "I won't sell you any milk. We're overstocked with soda, and I'm not going to sell anyone milk until our soda inventory is reduced."
>
> You don't like it, but you decide to buy a case of soda. At the checkout, the clerk says, "I hope you don't mind, but there's a $5 service charge on every fifteenth customer." You, of course, are the fifteenth.
>
> Just as you start to leave, another clerk stops you and says, "We're not working any more. We decided to have a party." Suddenly a CD player begins to blast, and everyone in the store begins to dance. "Oh, good, you've brought the soda," says a different clerk, who takes your package and passes sodas all around.

Life is not like this, of course. You can depend on grocery clerks to sell you milk. You can also depend on paying the same price as everyone else. And, of course, no one is going to force you to attend a party in the store.

Why can you be certain of this? Because we are socialized to follow norms, to play the basic roles that society assigns to us. *Norms make social life possible by making behavior predictable.* No human group can exist without norms.

Without norms, the basic order on which you depend to get through your everyday life would disappear. Instead, you would find yourself in a mass of swirling social chaos, unable to depend on anything. Norms lay out the basic guidelines for how you should play your roles and interact with others. In short, norms bring about **social order,** a group's customary social arrangements. Your life is based on these arrangements, which is why deviance often is perceived as threatening: *Deviance undermines predictability, the foundation of social life.* Consequently, human groups develop a system of **social control**— formal and informal— means of enforcing norms.

Sanctions

As we discussed in Chapter 3, people do not enforce folkways strictly, but they become upset when people break mores (MOR-ays).

social order a group's usual and customary social arrangements, on which its members depend and on which they base their lives

social control a group's formal and informal means of enforcing its norms

Expressions of disapproval for deviance, called **negative sanctions,** range from frowns and gossip for breaking folkways to imprisonment and capital punishment for violating mores. In general, the more seriously the group takes a norm, the harsher the penalty for violating it. In contrast, **positive sanctions**—from smiles to cash awards—are used to reward people for conforming to norms.

negative sanction an expression of disapproval for breaking a norm, ranging from an informal reaction such as a frown to a formal reaction such as a prize or a prison sentence

positive sanction a reward or positive reaction for following norms, ranging from a smile to a material reward

Getting a raise is a positive sanction; being fired is a negative sanction. Getting an A in intro to sociology is a positive sanction; getting an F is a negative one.

In *Making It Personal*, you can see how your use of sanctions helps to maintain the social order.

Watch the **Video**
The Basics: Deviance in **mysoclab**

MAKING IT PERSONAL
How Your Frowns Help to Maintain the Social Order

Did you know that you are part of this process of maintaining the social order? Every time you use a sanction, negative or positive, you are reinforcing norms. You do this all the time, as a regular, unthinking part of your everyday life. If you think I'm exaggerating a bit, think about how you might stare if you observe someone dressed in what you consider to be inappropriate clothing. Do you think you might gossip if a married person you know spends the night with someone other than his or her spouse?

Whether you consider the breaking of a norm merely an amusing matter or a serious infraction, however, depends on your perspective—which takes us once again to the relativity of deviance. Let's suppose that a woman appeared at your high school graduation in a bikini. You might have stared, laughed, and nudged the person next to you, but if this had been *your mother,* then what? You likely would have felt that different sanctions were called for. Similarly, if it is *your father* who spends the night with an 18-year-old college freshman, you are likely to do more than gossip.

Informal sanctions are remarkably effective. Think about how your own behavior is influenced by them—even by the *possibility* that people will gossip about you, frown at you, or stare at you. This helps keep you in line.

Then, of course, if you violate some norms, there is the possibility that someone will hit you, another informal—and rather effective–sanction.

Gossip, an informal sanction, is most effective among people who know one another or who are part of the same communication network.

UNIT 6.1 // TESTING MYSELF
DID I LEARN IT? ANSWERS ARE AT THE END OF THE CHAPTER

1. When he tried to hold up the 7-11 convenience store, Heinrich shot the clerk. An ambulance crew took her to the hospital, where she died the next day. According to sociologists, Heinrich is a
   a. transgressor
   b. sinner
   c. robber
   d. deviant

2. Angelina was drawing a blank. She knew that she knew the answer to the question, but she couldn't think of it. The soc test was important. If her GPA fell lower, she would lose her scholarship. Angelina pretended to be scratching her head as she peered at the student's answer to the side of her. She quickly scribbled down the same answer. According to sociologists, Angelina is a
   a. transgressor
   b. sinner
   c. cheater
   d. deviant

3. From Chagnon's experience with the Yanomamö, you can see that different groups have different norms, that what is deviant to some is not deviant to others. This is called the
   a. confounding variable
   b. relativity of deviance
   c. mystique of deviance
   d. shifting sands of deviance

4. At the heart of the sociological perspective on deviance is this idea
   a. It is not the act itself, but the reactions to the act, that make something deviant.
   b. Although there are many norms, there are relatively few sanctions.
   c. Rehabilitation, not punishment, is the more effective response to deviants.
   d. What goes around comes around.

5. It is easy to see the relativity of deviance when it comes to little things, such as clothing thought inappropriate by some but considered just fine by others. When it comes to crime, though, it can be more difficult to perceive this point. Yet crime is so relative that
   a. sociologists can't define crime
   b. men are usually the lawbreakers
   c. few societies operate prisons
   d. an act admired in one society can be punished by death in another society

6. Sociologists do not use the term deviant as a way to judge people's behavior. They use deviance to refer to
   a. behavior that they don't like
   b. changes in norms
   c. any act to which people respond negatively
   d. changes in sanctions

7. Freddie was born with a cleft lip. The surgeons did a bad job in trying to fix it, and Freddy has been left disfigured. Everyone who meets Freddie immediately sees the disfigurement. In sociological terms, Freddy has
   a. norm failure
   b. a stigma
   c. deviance transference
   d. AIDS—Acquired Infernal Disfigurement Syndrome

8. Deviance is often perceived as threatening because it
   a. undermines predictability, the foundation of social life
   b. is done by deviants
   c. challenges sanctions
   d. rests on shifting foundations

9. If you get an A in this class, you are receiving a
   a. deviance pass
   b. deviance bypass
   c. negative sanction
   d. positive sanction

10. Your friend tells you that when JoAnne, the mother of a mutual friend, went to a convention this past weekend she slept with her boss. Her husband who stayed home taking care of their child does not know about this. You shake your head and mutter that you never thought she was that kind of person. You have just engaged in what sociologists call
    a. a formal positive sanction
    b. an informal positive sanction
    c. an informal negative sanction
    d. a formal negative sanction

UNIT 6.2

Comparing Sociobiology, Psychology, and Sociology

WHAT AM I SUPPOSED TO LEARN?

After you have read this unit, you should be able to

1 Contrast sociobiological, psychological, and sociological explanations of deviance.

Explanations for Violating Norms

Why do people violate norms? Let's see how sociological explanations differ from biological and psychological ones.

SOCIOBIOLOGICAL EXPLANATIONS

Sociobiologists look for explanations *within* people. They assume that *inherited characteristics* are why people become juvenile delinquents and criminals (Lombroso 1911; Wilson and Herrnstein 1985; Goozen et al. 2007). An early explanation was that men with an extra Y chromosome (the "XYY" theory) were predisposed to become criminals. Another was that people with "squarish, muscular" bodies were more likely to commit **street crime**—acts such as mugging, rape, and burglary. These theories were abandoned when research did not support them.

Today, biological explanations are again being proposed (Walsh and Beaver 2009). The basic idea is that over the millennia people with certain characteristics were more likely to survive. As a result, some groups (generally women) inherit greater tendency for empathy (ability to identify with or feel another's emotions or problems) and self-control while other groups (generally men) inherit less of this and greater tendency for risk-taking.

Can you compare sociobiological, psychological, and sociological perspectives on deviance?

This explanation does fit the finding that in *all* societies, men commit more violent crime than women do. Sociobiologists stress that it took only a few pelvic thrusts for men to pass on their genes. After that, they could leave if they wanted to. The women, in contrast, became pregnant and gave birth. Women who were less empathetic (not inclined to nurture their children) engaged in more dangerous behavior. Over time, there were less of these women. In contrast, women who were more empathetic (inclined to nurture their children) engaged in less dangerous behavior. More of them survived. These women passed genes for more empathy, greater self-control, and less risk-taking to their female children. As a result, all over the world, men engage in more violent behavior, including crime, which comes from their lesser empathy, lower self-control, and greater tendency for taking risks.

Biosocial theorists stress that deviant behavior does not depend on genes alone. Inherited tendencies (the *bio* part) are modified and

> **street crime** crimes such as mugging, rape, and burglary

stimulated by the environment (the *social* part). With advances in research on genetics, biosocial research could open a new understanding of deviance.

PSYCHOLOGICAL EXPLANATIONS

Psychologists also look for explanations *within* people. Instead of genes, they examine **personality disorders.** Their supposition is that people who deviate are driven by subconscious motives (motives they are not aware of) (Barnes 2001; Mayer 2007).

The search for childhood experiences that lead to deviance has turned up dead ends. "Bad toilet training," "suffocating mothers," and "emotionally aloof fathers"—thought at one time to be keys to personality disorders—led nowhere. Some individuals with these childhood backgrounds do become embezzling bookkeepers, but others become good accountants. Just as college students and police officers represent a variety of good—and bad—childhood experiences, so do deviants. People with "suppressed anger" can become freeway snipers or military heroes—or anything else. In short, deviance is not associated with any particular personality.

SOCIOLOGICAL EXPLANATIONS

In contrast with sociobiologists and psychologists, sociologists search for factors *outside* people. They look for social influences that "recruit" people to break norms. For example, to account for why people commit crimes, sociologists examine socialization, subcultures, and social class. *Social class,* a concept that we will discuss in depth in the next chapter, refers to people's relative standing in terms of education, occupation, and especially income and wealth.

In the following units, we'll explore the sociological explanation of deviance. As we do so, we'll apply the three sociological perspectives—symbolic interactionism, functionalism, and conflict theory.

> **personality disorders** the view that a personality disturbance of some sort causes an individual to violate social norms

---

UNIT 6.2 // TESTING MYSELF
DID I LEARN IT? ANSWERS ARE AT THE END OF THE CHAPTER

1. "Pregnant women who took fewer risks were more likely to survive and pass on characteristics of empathy and self-control." Such a statement is likely to be made by a
   - **a.** sociobiologist
   - **b.** psychologist
   - **c.** sociologist
   - **d.** entomologist

2. "This boy is getting in trouble with the police because his parents were too strict and demanding when they were toilet training him. He now has unresolved conflicts that he is working out by violating the law." Such a statement is likely to be made by a
   - **a.** sociobiologist
   - **b.** psychologist
   - **c.** sociologist
   - **d.** ethnologist

3. "The ideas and norms dominant in this group of girls encourage their member to break laws." Such a statement is likely to be made by a
   - **a.** sociobiologist
   - **b.** psychologist
   - **c.** sociologist
   - **d.** ethnologist

4. Some explanations of deviance point to factors within people, others to factors outside the individual. Which of these four is most likely to stress factors outside the individual?
   - **a.** sociology
   - **b.** sociobiology
   - **c.** psychology
   - **d.** ethnology

UNIT 6.3
The Symbolic Interactionist Perspective

To help you understand the sociological explanation of deviance, we'll begin with symbolic interactionism. You will see why sociologists are not satisfied with explanations rooted in sociobiology or psychology. As you read this unit, keep this basic principle of symbolic interactionism in mind: *We are thinking beings who act according to the way we interpret situations.*

Symbolic interactionists stress that to understand what people do we must know how they interpret their situation in life. Can you apply this perspective to this photo?

WHAT AM I SUPPOSED TO LEARN?

After you have read this unit, you should be able to

1 Explain differential association theory.

2 Explain control theory.

3 Explain labeling theory.

As we consider how our membership in groups influences how we view life and, from there, our behavior, we will look at three symbolic interactionist theories: differential association, control, and labeling.

Differential Association Theory

THE THEORY

As you have seen over and over in this text, sociologists stress how groups influence us. This includes our tendency to get in trouble or to follow the rules (Deflem 2006; Chambliss 1973/2012). A major term sociologists use is **differential association,** which means that the *different* groups we *associate* with influence us in different ways. Consider an extreme: boys and girls who join street gangs and those who join the Scouts. Obviously, each will learn different attitudes and behaviors concerning deviance and conformity.

Differential association theory was developed by Edwin Sutherland (Sutherland 1924, 1947; Sutherland et al. 1992). It, is more complicated than this, but he basically said that the different groups with which you associate (your "*different*al association") give you messages about conformity and deviance. You may receive mixed messages, but you end up with more of one than the other (an "excess of definitions," as Sutherland put it). The end result is an imbalance—attitudes that tilt you toward deviance or conformity.

FAMILIES

You know how important your family has been in shaping your attitudes. It's the same with all of us. How significant the family actually is, however, might surprise you. I know that I'm impressed by this statistic: Of all prison inmates across the United States, about *half* have a father, mother, brother, sister, or spouse who has served time in prison (*Criminal Justice Statistics*

differential association Edwin Sutherland's term to indicate that people who associate with some groups learn an "excess of definitions" of deviance, increasing the likelihood that they will become deviant

2003: Table 6.0011; Glaze and Maruschak 2008:Table 11). In short, families that are involved in crime tend to set their children on a lawbreaking path. Conforming families do the same, but in a different direction.

FRIENDS, NEIGHBORHOODS, AND SUBCULTURES

Most people don't know the term *differential association*, but they do know how it works. Parents try to move out of "bad" neighborhoods because they know that if their kids have delinquent friends, they are likely to become delinquent, too. And they are right (Chung and Steinberg 2006; Church et al. 2009).

Differential association is so significant that it can even make violence seem good.

> *When sociologist Ruth Horowitz (1983, 2005) did participant observation in a lower-class Chicano neighborhood in Chicago, she discovered how the concept of "honor" propels young men to deviance. The formula is simple. "A real man has honor. An insult is a threat to that honor. Therefore, not to stand up to someone is to be less than a real man."*
>
> *Suppose you are a young man growing up in this neighborhood. You likely would do a fair amount of fighting, for you would interpret many things as attacks on your honor. You might even carry a knife or a gun, for words and fists wouldn't always be enough. Along with members of your group, you would think of fighting, knifing, and shooting quite differently from the way most people do.*

Another group, the Mafia, also connects honor and manliness with violence. This group even has an informal rating scale on killing and manliness: "The more awesome and potent the victim, the more worthy and meritorious the killer" (Arlacchi 1980).

For members of the Mafia, being willing *to kill is a measure of manhood.* For example, if someone in the Mafia were foolish enough to seduce the *capo's* (top-ranking member's) wife or girlfriend, the seduction would slash at the *capo's* manliness and honor. There is just one course open—to kill the offender. His body would be found with a powerful message—the man's penis stuffed in his mouth.

From this example, you can see how relative deviance is. Although killing is deviant in mainstream society, for members of the Mafia, *not* to kill after certain rules are broken is the deviant act.

Control Theory

Do you ever feel the urge to do something that you know you shouldn't, something that would get you in trouble? Most of us do. We find that we have to stifle things inside us—urges, hostilities, raunchy desires of various sorts. And most of the time, we manage to keep ourselves out of trouble. The basic question that control theory tries to answer is: With the desire to deviate so common, why don't we all just "bust loose"?

THE THEORY

Sociologist Walter Reckless (1973), who developed control theory, stressed that two control systems work against your motivations to deviate. Your *inner controls* include your internalized morality—your conscience, religious principles, ideas of right and wrong. Inner controls also include your fears of punishment, feelings of integrity, and desire to be a "good" person (Hirschi 1969; McShane and Williams 2007). Your *outer controls* consist of people—such as your family, friends, and the police—who influence you not to deviate.

The stronger your bonds with society, the more effective your inner controls are (Hirschi 1969). Your bonds are based on *attachments* (your affection or respect for people who conform to mainstream norms), *commitments* (having a stake in society that you don't want to risk, such as a respected place in your family or your standing at college), *involvements* (participating in approved activities), and *beliefs* (convictions that certain actions are morally wrong).

If this theory sounds like *self-*control, this is because it is. From what you read in Chapter 4, as well as what you knew before you read that chapter, the key to learning self-control is socialization during childhood. Parents help their children develop self-control by supervising them and punishing their deviant acts (Gottfredson and Hirschi 1990; Church et al. 2009). They sometimes use shame to keep their children in line. You probably had that forefinger shaken at you. I certainly recall it aimed at me.

The Mafia is a favorite topic of the mass media. The creators of The Sopranos *did a good job of illustrating the norms that operate within this group.*

IF YOU WANT TO LEARN MORE about a current application of shaming to increase self control,

📖 **Read** more from the author: Shaming: Making a Comeback? in **mysoclab**

Labeling Theory

Labeling theory focuses on the significance of reputations, how they help set us on paths that propel us into deviance or that divert us away from it.

Suppose for one undesirable moment that people around you thought of you as a "whore," a "pervert," or a "cheat." (Pick one.) Can you see the power such a reputation would have—both on how others would see you and on how you would see yourself? How about if you became known as "very intelligent," "truthful in everything," or "honest to the core"? (Choose one.) These contrasting labels would certainly give people different expectations of your character and behavior. They would also give you a different idea about who you are.

Not many of us want to be called "whore," "pervert," "cheat," and so on. We resist negative labels, even lesser ones than these that someone might try to pin on us. Did you know that some people are so successful at rejecting labels that even though they beat people up and vandalize property, they consider themselves to be conforming members of society? Let's see how they do it.

REJECTING LABELS: HOW PEOPLE NEUTRALIZE DEVIANCE

Sociologists Gresham Sykes and David Matza (1957/1988), who studied delinquent boys, found that the boys used five **techniques of neutralization** to deflect society's norms.

Denial of responsibility. Some boys said, "I'm not responsible for what happened because …" and they were quite creative about the "becauses." Some said that what happened was an "accident." Other boys saw themselves as "victims" of society. What else can you expect? "We're like billiard balls shot around the pool table of life."

> **techniques of neutralization** ways of thinking or rationalizing that help people deflect (or neutralize) society's norms

Hells Angels funeral.

Denial of injury. Another favorite explanation was "What I did wasn't wrong because no one got hurt." The boys would refer to vandalism as "mischief," call gang fights "private quarrels," and say that stealing cars was "borrowing." They might acknowledge that what they did was illegal, but claim that they were "just having a little fun."

Denial of a victim. Some boys thought of themselves as avengers. They vandalized a teacher's car to get revenge for an "unfair" grade. They shoplifted to even the score with "crooked" store owners. In short, even if the boys did accept responsibility and admit that someone had gotten hurt, they protected their self-concept by claiming that the people "deserved what they got."

Condemnation of the condemners. The boys also denied that others had the right to judge them. They accused people who pointed their fingers at them of being "a bunch of hypocrites": The police were "on the take," teachers had "pets," and parents cheated on their taxes. In short, they said, "Who are *they* to accuse *me* of something?"

Appeal to higher loyalties. The boys also justified their actions by saying that loyalty to the gang was more important than the norms of society. They might say, "I had to help my friends. That's why I got in the fight." Not incidentally, the boys may have shot a member of a rival group, maybe even a bystander!

For a discussion about how *you* neutralize your deviance, see *Making It Personal.*

MAKING IT PERSONAL
How Do You Neutralize Your Deviance?

Don't the five techniques of neutralization that the delinquent boys used sound familiar? Can you see yourself here?

1. "I couldn't help myself."
2. "Who really got hurt?"
3. "Don't you think she deserved that, after what *she* did?"
4. "Who are *you* to talk?"
5. "I had to help my friends—wouldn't you have done the same thing?"

It certainly isn't only delinquents who use techniques of neutralization. You, too, break norms, and you, too, have a need to reconcile your acts with your sense of a "good self." To do this, you, too, use some variation of these five techniques, applying them to yourself just as creatively as the boys Sykes and Matza studied many years ago.

Think of a norm you broke—from a law, such as speeding, to a "white lie" you might have told to cover your tracks in some matter. What techniques did you use to neutralize your act?

EMBRACING LABELS: TAKING PLEASURE IN DEVIANCE

Although most of us resist deviant labels, some people strive for a deviant identity and revel in it. Some teenagers, for example, make certain by their clothing, music, hairstyles, and body art that no one misses their rejection of adult norms. Their status among fellow members of a subculture—within which they are almost obsessive conformists—is vastly more important than any status outside it.

Sociologist Mark Watson (1980/2006) did participant observation with outlaw bikers. He rebuilt Harleys with them, hung around their bars and homes, and went on "runs" (trips) with them. He concluded that outlaw bikers see the world as "hostile, weak, and effeminate." Holding this conventional world in contempt, gang members pride themselves on breaking its norms and getting in trouble, laughing at death, and treating women as lesser beings whose primary value is to provide them with services—especially sex. They pride themselves in looking "dirty, mean, and generally undesirable," taking pleasure in shocking people by their appearance and behavior. Outlaw bikers also regard themselves as losers, a view that becomes woven into their unusual embrace of deviance.

UNIT 6.3 // TESTING MYSELF
DID I LEARN IT? ANSWERS ARE AT THE END OF THE CHAPTER

1. This is a basic principle of symbolic interactionism
   a. Juvenile delinquents don't have a realistic view of their acts.
   b. Unless people change, deviance will increase and threaten society.
   c. Those in control of society force their rules (norms) onto others.
   d. We are thinking beings who act according to our definition of the situation.

2. When she entered college, Betty had a hard time making friends. Finally, she found a group of girls who accepted her. The girls shoplifted on a fairly regular basis. Betty had never shoplifted before, but she began to do so. This statement best matches this theoretical perspective
   a. labeling theory
   b. control theory
   c. differential association
   d. conflict perspective

3. The term differential association applies to all groups we associate with, including our family. Different families have different effects on their children. One of the most remarkable statistics that demonstrates how differential association applies to the family is this: Of all prison inmates across the United States, about how many have a father, mother, brother, sister, or spouse who has served time in prison?
   a. one of ten
   b. two of ten
   c. one-third
   d. half

4. Hank could hardly stand the temptation. The teacher had left her purse on her desk, and he knew she had just cashed her check. Hank needed the money, but he heard his conscience shouting at him, and he didn't go near the purse. This statement best matches this theoretical perspective
   a. labeling theory
   b. control theory
   c. differential association
   d. conflict perspective

5. Control theory stresses that you have two control systems that work against your motivations to deviate. These are your
   a. inner and outer controls
   b. basic and complex controls
   c. early and later controls
   d. fast and slow controls

6. Angela is a member of a girl's gang. She steals, fights, and sells drugs. Angela thinks of herself as a good citizen, and in her best moments, as a model for other girls. It is likely that Angela
   a. does not know what a role model is
   b. will change her mind as she matures
   c. is using techniques of neutralization
   d. has been rejected by her mother

7. Ricardo's parents were upset by the neighborhood they were living in. They were especially bothered by Ricardo's friends. When Ricardo's dad received a promotion at work and a higher salary, the family moved to a better neighborhood. This statement best matches this theoretical perspective
   a. labeling theory
   b. sociobiological theory
   c. differential association
   d. conflict perspective

8. Philomena was defiant when she was accused of letting a friend copy her sociology paper. She said. "Who really got hurt? I had to help my friend." Philomena is using
   a. a technique of neutralization
   b. her friend as an excuse
   c. reverse psychology
   d. the offensive challenge

9. The girls gossiped about Annette, shaking their heads at the way she dressed. They began to call her a whore behind her back. Gradually, her reputation spread throughout the school. This statement best matches this theoretical perspective
   a. labeling theory
   b. conflict theory
   c. differential association
   d. conflict perspective

UNIT 6.4

The Functionalist Perspective

WHAT AM I SUPPOSED TO LEARN?

After you have read this unit, you should be able to

1 Explain how deviance can be functional for society.

2 Explain how strain theory illustrates how mainstream values produce deviance.

3 List four deviant paths highlighted by strain theory.

4 Explain illegitimate opportunity structures.

When we think of deviance, its dysfunctions are likely to come to mind. Functionalists point out that deviance also has functions.

Can Deviance Really Be Functional for Society?

Most of us are upset by deviance, especially crime, and assume that society would be better off without it. The classic functionalist theorist Emile Durkheim (1893/1933, 1895/1964), however, came to a surprising conclusion. Deviance, he said—including crime—is functional for society. It actually contributes to the social order. The four main functions of deviance are:

1. *Deviance clarifies moral boundaries.* Each group has ideas about how people should think and act. This is the group's *moral boundaries.* Deviant acts challenge those boundaries. To punish members who violate these boundaries affirms the group's norms and clarifies what it means to be a member of the group.

2. *Deviance affirms norms.* To sanction deviants is to declare "You can't get away with that. Our norms are right, and we are keeping them."

3. *Deviance encourages unity.* Punishing deviants fosters a "we" feeling among the group's members.

4. *Deviance promotes social change.* Not all group members agree with the norms or on what to do with people who push beyond them. Some may even approve of the rule-breaking. If boundary violations gain enough support, they become new, accepted ways of doing things. Deviance, then, can force a group to rethink and redefine its moral boundaries. This helps groups—even whole societies—to adapt to changing circumstances.

Perhaps you can apply Durkheim's four functions of deviance to this photo of Lady GaGa.

IF YOU WANT TO LEARN MORE *about the functions of deviance, as well as the central point of symbolic interactionism, that deviance involves a clash of definitions,*

Read more from the author: Pornography and the Mainstream: Freedom Versus Censorship and The Naked Pumpkin in Runner and the Naked Bike Riders: Deviance or Freedom of Self-Expression in **mysoclab**

Strain Theory: How Mainstream Values Produce Deviance

Functionalists also analyze how mainstream values generate crime. Explaining how this happens will involve a few new terms (of course!), but the idea is fairly simple.

Let's begin with what sociologists Richard Cloward and Lloyd Ohlin (1960) identified as the crucial need of the industrialized world: to locate and train people—whether they are born into wealth or into poverty—to take over society's key technical jobs. To get the most talented people to compete for these positions—to become dentists, nuclear physicists, teachers, engineers, and so on—society tries to motivate *everyone* to strive for success. It does this by making people feel dissatisfied with what they have so they will try to "better" themselves.

We succeed in getting almost everyone to want **cultural goals,** success of some sort, such as wealth and prestige. But we fail miserably in providing equal access to the **institutionalized means,** the legitimate (or acceptable) ways to reach these goals. People who want success (the cultural goal) but find that they can't get a good job (one of the institutionalized means) feel frustrated. Sociologist Robert Merton (1956, 1949/1968) developed a theory based around this situation. He called the frustration that people feel in such a situation *strain,* and his theory is called **strain theory.**

cultural goals the objectives held out as legitimate or desirable for the members of a society to achieve

institutionalized means approved ways of reaching cultural goals

strain theory Robert Merton's term for the strain engendered when a society socializes large numbers of people to desire a cultural goal (such as success), but withholds from some the approved means of reaching that goal; one adaptation to the strain is crime, the choice of an innovative means (one outside the approved system) to attain the cultural goal

People who find their legitimate access to the cultural goals blocked can feel a huge gap between themselves and mainstream society and its rules. Many in this situation feel like they don't belong, an experience Merton called *anomie* (AN-uh-me), a sense of normlessness.

Look at Table 6.1, which compares the ways that people react to the cultural goals and the institutionalized means. The most common reaction is *conformity.* Most people accept the cultural goals and use socially acceptable means to try to reach them. In industrialized societies, they try to get good jobs, a quality education, and so on. If well-paid jobs are not available, they take less desirable jobs. If they are denied access to Harvard or Stanford, they go to a state university. Others take night classes and go to vocational schools. In short, most people follow socially acceptable paths.

But when people find their legitimate way to success blocked, four deviant paths are open to them. Let's look at these paths.

FOUR DEVIANT PATHS

Those who take the first deviant path, *innovation,* accept the goals of society, but they use illegitimate means to try to reach them. Drug dealers, for example, accept the goal of achieving wealth, but they reject the legitimate avenues for doing so. So do embezzlers, robbers, and con artists. You get the idea.

Look at the second deviant path. Some people get so frustrated at getting nowhere that they give up on the cultural goals, yet they cling to conventional rules of conduct. Merton called this response *ritualism.* Although ritualists have given up on getting ahead at work, they keep their jobs by rigorously following work rules. Teachers whose idealism is shattered (who are said to suffer from "burnout") remain in the classroom, where they go through the motions and teach without enthusiasm. They cling to the job even though they have abandoned the goal, which may have been to stimulate young minds or to make the world a better place.

TABLE 6.1 How People Match Their Goals to Their Means

Do They Feel the Strain That Leads to Anomie?	Mode of Adaptation	Cultural Goals	Institutionalized Means
No	Conformity	Accept	Accept
	Deviant Paths:		
Yes	1. Innovation	Accept	Reject
	2. Ritualism	Reject	Accept
	3. Retreatism	Reject	Reject
	4. Rebellion	Reject/Replace	Reject/Replace

Source: Based on Merton 1968.

Charlie Sheen certainly felt strain when he was fired from Two and A Half Men. *Although strain theory might help explain Sheen's embrace of deviance, it likely is inadequate for this purpose.*

Those who take the third deviant path, *retreatism*, reject both the cultural goals and the institutionalized means for achieving them. Dropping the pursuit of success, they retreat into alcohol or drugs. Although their form of withdrawal is considerably different, women who enter a convent or men a monastery are also retreatists.

The final deviant response is *rebellion*. Convinced that their society is corrupt, rebels reject both society's goals and its institutionalized means. Unlike retreatists, though, they don't retreat. Instead, rebels seek to give society new goals, as well as new means for reaching them. Revolutionaries are the most committed type of rebels.

Illegitimate Opportunity Structures: Social Class, Gender, and Crime

Social class has a huge impact on our lives, some of it in surprising ways. Let's look at how social class produces distinct styles of crime.

STREET CRIME

As mentioned, industrialized societies have no trouble socializing the poor into wanting to own things. Like others, the poor are bombarded with messages urging them to buy everything from Xboxes and iPods to designer jeans and new cars. Television, videos, and movies spew out endless images of middle-class people enjoying luxurious lives. The poor get the message—Americans can afford society's many goods and services.

Yet for the poor, the most common route to success, the school system, is a bewildering world. Run by the middle class, the schools question and mock what the poor take for granted. Their speech, for example, is built around nonstandard grammar and is often laced with what the middle class considers obscenities. Their ideas of punctuality and their poor preparation in reading and paper-and-pencil skills also make it difficult to fit in. Facing such barriers, the poor are more likely than their more privileged counterparts to drop out of school. Educational failure, of course, slams the door on most legitimate avenues to financial success.

It is not that this leaves the poor without opportunities for financial success. Woven into life in urban slums is what Cloward and Ohlin (1960) called an **illegitimate opportunity structure.** An alternative door to success opens: robbery, burglary, drug dealing, prostitution, pimping, gambling, and other crimes (Sánchez-Jankowski 2003; Anderson 1978, 1990/2006). Pimps and drug dealers, for example, present an image of a glamorous life—people who are in control and have plenty of "easy money." For many of the poor, the "hustler" becomes a role model.

IF YOU WANT TO LEARN MORE about how gangs are part of the illegitimate opportunity structure that beckons disadvantaged youth,

Read more from the author: Islands in the Street: Urban Gangs in the United States in **mysoclab**

WHITE-COLLAR CRIME

The types of crime of the more privileged classes also match their life situation. And how different their illegitimate opportunities are! Physicians don't hold up cabbies, but they do cheat Medicare. Investment managers like Bernie Madoff run fraudulent schemes that cheat clients around the world. Mugging, pimping, and burgling are not part of this more privileged world, but evading income tax, bribing public officials, and embezzling are. Sociologist Edwin Sutherland (1949) coined the term **white-collar crime** to refer to crimes

illegitimate opportunity structure opportunities for crimes that are woven into the texture of life

white-collar crime Edwin Sutherland's term for crimes committed by people of respectable and high social status in the course of their occupations; for example, bribery of public officials, embezzlement, false advertising, and price fixing

White collar crime usually involves only the loss of property, but not always. To save money, Ford executives kept faulty Firestone tires on their Explorers. Shown here in Houston is one of their victims. She survived a needless accident, but was left a quadriplegic.

that people of respectable and high social status commit in the course of their occupations.

A special form of white-collar crime is **corporate crime,** crimes committed by executives in order to benefit their corporation. For example, to increase corporate profits, Sears executives defrauded $100 million from victims so poor that they had filed for bankruptcy. To avoid a criminal trial, Sears pleaded guilty. This frightened the parent companies of Macy's and Bloomingdales, which were doing similar things, and they settled out of court (McCormick 1999). Citigroup is notorious for stealing from the poor. In 2004, this firm had to pay $70 million for its crimes (O'Brien 2004). But like a career criminal, Citigroup continued its law-breaking ways. The firm "swept" money from its customers' credit cards,

corporate crime crimes committed by executives in order to benefit their corporation

even from the cards of people who had died. Caught red-handed once again—even stealing from the dead—in 2008 this company was forced to pay another $18 million (Read 2008). *Not one of the corporate thieves at Sears, Macy's, Bloomingdales, or Citigroup spent a day in jail.*

Seldom is corporate crime taken seriously, even when it results in death. In the 1930s, workers were hired to blast a tunnel through a mountain in West Virginia. The company knew the silica dust would kill the miners, and in just three months about 600 died (Dunaway 2008). No owner went to jail. In the 1980s, Firestone executives recalled faulty tires in Saudi Arabia and Venezuela but allowed them to remain on U.S. vehicles. When their tires blew out, about 200 Americans died (White et al. 2001). The photo put correct location, wherever it ends up—above? shows another human cost. *Not a single Firestone executive went to jail.*

Consider this: Under federal law, causing the death of a worker by *willfully* violating safety rules is a misdemeanor punishable by up to six months in prison. Yet to harass a wild burro on federal lands is punishable by a year in prison (Barstow and Bergman 2003). Don't you find this contrast both amazing and upsetting?

At $500 billion a year, the cost of white-collar crime costs more than street crime (Reiman and Leighton 2010). This refers only to dollar costs. No one has yet figured out a way to compare, for example, the suffering experienced by a rape victim with the pain felt by an elderly couple who have lost their life savings to white-collar fraud.

Fear, however, centers on street crime, especially the violent stranger who can change your life forever. As the social map on the next page shows, the chance of such an encounter depends on where you live. You can see that entire regions are safer—or more dangerous—than others. In general, the northern states are safer, and the southern states more dangerous.

GENDER AND CRIME

Gender is not just something we are or something we do. Gender is a feature of society that surrounds us from birth, pushing us as male or female, into different corners in life. Just as social class opens and closes the opportunity to commit crime, so does gender. Look at Table 6.2. You can see how remarkably women's involvement in crime has increased. As ideas of gender (not biology!) changed, opening business and the professions to women, it also brought new opportunities for women to commit crime. From car theft to illegal weapons, Table 6.2 shows how women have taken advantage of this new opportunity.

FIGURE 6.1 — How Safe Is Your State? Violent Crime in the United States

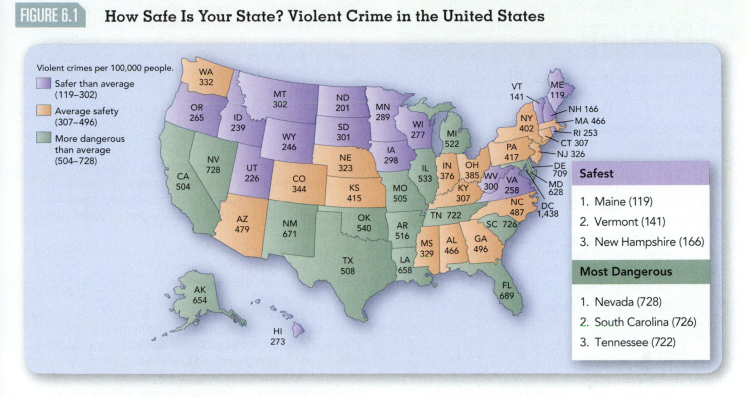

Note: Violent crimes are murder, rape, robbery, and aggravated assault. The chance of becoming a victim of these crimes is six times higher in Nevada, the most dangerous state, than in Maine, the safest state. Washington, D.C., not a state, is in a class by itself. Its rate of 1,438 is twelve times higher than Maine's rate

Source: By the author. Based on Statistical Abstract of the United States 2011. Table 304.

TABLE 6.2 — Women and Crime: What a Difference a Few Years Make

Of all those arrested, what percentage are women?			
Crime	**1992**	**2009**	**Change**
Stolen property	12.5%	20.9%	+67%
Car theft	10.8%	17.8%	+65%
Drunken driving	13.8%	22.7%	+64%
Burglary	9.2%	14.9%	+62%
Aggravated assault	14.8%	22.0%	+49%
Robbery	8.5%	11.9%	+40%
Larceny/theft	32.1%	43.6%	+36%
Arson	13.4%	17.3%	+29%
Illegal drugs	16.4%	18.7%	+14%
Forgery and counterfeiting	34.7%	37.7%	+9%
Illegal Weapons	7.5%	8.1%	+8%
Fraud	42.1%	44.3%	+5%

Source: By the author. Based on Statistical Abstract of the United States 2012: Table 324.

UNIT 6.4 // TESTING MYSELF
DID I LEARN IT? ANSWERS ARE AT THE END OF THE CHAPTER

1. Functionalists say that deviance is functional for society. Which of these is not one of the functions they identify?
   a. clarifies moral boundaries
   b. encourages unity
   c. promotes social change
   d. provides a better future

2. The term cultural goals refers to the goals held out for people. The term institutionalized means refers to the legitimate (or acceptable) ways to reach these goals. When people who try to reach cultural goals find their legitimate means blocked, they feel frustration. In strain theory, what is this frustration called?
   a. illegitimate means
   b. deviant paths
   c. strain
   d. motivators

3. Frankie's job didn't pay enough to buy the things he saw on television—things that many of his friends had, and that he felt he deserved. He began to steal from his employer. In strain theory, Frankie is following this deviant path
   a. innovation   b. ritualism
   c. retreatism   d. rebellion

4. The job that Hortense (yes, this is a woman's name) had didn't pay enough to buy the things she saw on television—things that many of her friends had, and that she thought she deserved. Out of frustration, she gave up trying to get ahead at work. She showed up each day, but she did only what she had to, making sure she followed the rules so she wouldn't be fired. Hortense is following this deviant path
   a. innovation   b. ritualism
   c. retreatism   d. rebellion

5. Manny felt more and more frustrated in school. No matter how hard he tried, the teachers always seemed negative. When Manny used drugs, he forgot about his frustrations. Using drugs more and more frequently, Manny dropped out of school and began to build his life around drugs. Manny is following this deviant path
   a. innovation   b. ritualism
   c. retreatism   d. rebellion

6. Clarissa grew increasingly upset about what she saw as the control of society by the wealthy, their corruption, and the lack of opportunities for the poor. Clarissa joined an underground group that wants to overthrow what its members see as the government of the wealthy, by the wealthy, and for the wealthy and replace it with one that offers equal opportunities for all. Clarissa is following this deviant path
   a. innovation
   b. ritualism
   c. retreatism
   d. rebellion

7. Even though Sammy dropped out of school, he had no trouble finding "work." A local drug dealer gave him a job selling drugs. Sammy's underground opportunity for financial success is part of what sociologists call
   a. an underground movement
   b. an illegitimate opportunity structure
   c. an alternative financial structure
   d. social change

8. Henrietta worked her way up to vice-president of financial affairs. In this position, she saw how sloppy the record keeping was. As she tried to straighten things out, she saw an opportunity to direct money into her personal account, a way that she was sure could not be detected. She did so. Sociologists use this term to refer to what Henrietta did
   a. white-collar crime
   b. employee advantage
   c. street crime
   d. gender change

9. Henry worked his way up to vice-president of financial affairs. In this position, he experienced intense pressure to show high profit for the corporation. To produce a better report for the stockholders, Henry devised a plan to hide some of the corporate debt. What Henry did was a crime. Sociologists use this term to refer to what Henry did
   a. misplaced goals
   b. gender crime
   c. street crime
   d. corporate crime

10. Just as social class opens and closes doors of opportunity—to both legal and illegal activities—so does gender. As ideas of gender changed, opening education, business, and the professions to women, it also brought this new opportunity for women, which they seized
   a. making better marriages
   b. retiring early
   c. committing crime
   d. having more children

UNIT 6.5
The Conflict Perspective

Class, Crime, and the Criminal Justice System

TRW sold transistors to the federal government to use in its satellites. When the transistors failed, the government had to shut down its satellite program. TRW said that the failure was a surprise, that it was due to some unknown defect. U.S. officials then paid TRW millions of dollars to investigate the failure.

Then a whistle blower appeared, informing the government that TRW knew even before it sold the transistors that they would fail in satellites. The government sued Northrop Grumman Corporation, which had bought TRW, and the corporation was found guilty (Drew 2009).

What was the punishment for a crime this serious? These are military satellites, and they compromised the defense of the United States. When the executives of TRW were put on trial and convicted, how long were they sentenced to prison? Actually, these criminals weren't even put on trial, and not one spent even a single night in jail. Northrop Grumman was fined $325 million. Then—and this is hard to believe—on the same day, the government settled a lawsuit that Northrop Grumman had brought against it for $325 million. Certainly a rare coincidence.

What view does the conflict perspective provide of what goes on behind these walls?

WHAT AM I SUPPOSED TO LEARN?

After you have read this unit, you should be able to

1 Explain the conflict view of class, crime, and the criminal justice system.

Contrast this with poor people who are caught stealing cars and sent to prison for years. How can a legal system that proudly boasts "justice for all" be so inconsistent? According to conflict theory, this question is central to the analysis of crime and the **criminal justice system**—the police, courts, and prisons that deal with people who are accused of having committed crimes. Let's see what conflict theorists have to say about this.

> 📖 **Read** the **Document**
> "The Saints and the Roughnecks" by William J. Chambliss in **mysoclab**

The Law as an Instrument of Oppression

The idea that the law operates impartially to bring justice, stress conflict theorists, is a myth promoted by the capitalist class. Instead, they view the criminal justice system as a tool used by the powerful to maintain their privileged position (Spitzer 1975; Reiman 2010; Chambliss 2000, 1973/2012). For this reason, conflict theorists refer to the law an *instrument of oppression*.

The working class and those below them pose a special threat to the power elite. They are the least rooted in society. They have few skills and only low-paying, part-time, or seasonal work—if they have jobs at all. Receiving the least of society's material rewards, they hold the potential to rebel and overthrow the current social order. To prevent this, the law comes down hard on poor people who get out of line. From this class come *most* of the prison inmates in the United States.

The criminal justice system, then, does not focus on the executives of corporations and the harm they do through manufacturing unsafe products, creating pollution, and manipulating prices. Yet the violations of the capitalist class cannot be ignored totally, for if they become too outrageous they might upset the working class and provoke revolution. To prevent this, a flagrant violation by a member of the capitalist class is occasionally prosecuted. The publicity given to the case helps to stabilize the social system by providing evidence of the "fairness" of the criminal justice system.

The powerful are usually able to bypass the courts altogether. They

criminal justice system the system of police, courts, and prisons set up to deal with people who are accused of having committed a crime

and the harm they do through manufacturing unsafe products, creating pollution, and manipulating prices. Yet the violations of the capitalist class cannot be ignored totally because

a. if they become too outrageous or oppressive they might encourage the working class to revolt
b. the quotas (the allotted spaces by social class in our jails and prisons) must be met
c. reporters are always snooping around looking for a good story
d. of recent laws passed by Congress

appear instead before civil agencies that have no power to imprison (such as the Federal Trade Commission). These agencies are often directed by people from wealthy backgrounds who sympathize with the intricacies of the corporate world. It is they who oversee most cases of price manipulation of stocks, insider trading, violations of fiduciary duty, and so on. Is it surprising, then, ask conflict theorists, that the typical sanction for corporate crime is a token fine?

👁 **Watch** the **Video** Sociology on the Job: Deviance in **mysoclab**

UNIT 6.5 // TESTING MYSELF
DID I LEARN IT? ANSWERS ARE AT THE END OF THE CHAPTER

1. According to conflict theorists, the idea that the law operates impartially to bring justice is
   a. true in the United States and most of the West, but not true in most Asian countries
   b. the basic principle on which freedom rests
   c. an idea that has to be interpreted according to changing historical situations
   d. a cultural myth promoted by the capitalist class

2. The working class and those below it pose a special threat to the power elite because they
   a. don't like the wealthy
   b. have little education
   c. are the least rooted in society
   d. are more likely to commit crimes

3. According to conflict theorists, the power elite uses the legal system to control workers and to stabilize the social order, all with the goal of
   a. creating a fairer society
   b. keeping itself in power
   c. increasing opportunities for the poor
   d. making the police more efficient

4. According to conflict theory, the criminal justice system does not focus on the executives of corporations

UNIT 6.6
Reactions to Deviance: Prisons

WHAT AM I SUPPOSED TO LEARN?

After you have read this unit, you should be able to

1 Discuss the increase in imprisonment and who the prisoners are.

2 Explain the "three-strikes" laws and their dysfunctions.

3 Summarize suggested reasons for the drop in violent crime.

4 Give basic statistics on recidivism.

Whether it is cheating on a sociology quiz or holding up a liquor store, any violation of norms invites reaction. Sanctions vary from mild, informal reactions such as frowns and stares to severe, formal responses such as imprisonment and death. Let's look at imprisonment in the United States.

Photo taken in Maricopa County jail in Phoenix, Arizona

IF YOU WANT TO LEARN MORE about the difficulty of imposing sanctions for some deviant acts, I think you'll enjoy a little
excursion to England

Read more from the author: "Dogging" in
England in **mysoclab**

Street Crime and Prisons

To see one of the most dramatic changes in the United States, look at Figure 6.2 below. The increase in the U.S. prison population is so great that the governments have not been able to build prisons fast enough to hold all the incoming prisoners. Both the state and federal governments have hired private companies to handle this overflow. About 130,000 prisoners are held in these private, "for-profit" prisons (*Source-book of Criminal Justice Statistics* 2009: Table 6.32.2008). Actually, the United States has even more prisoners than shown in Figure 6.2, since this total does not include people who are in jail. If we add them, the total comes to about 2.3 million—about one out of every 135 U.S. citizens. The United States has the unfortunate distinction of having more prisoners than any other nation in the world. And of all nations, it also has a larger percentage of its population in prison (Warren et al. 2008).

Who are these prisoners? Let's compare them with the U.S. population. As you look at Table 6.3 on the next page, several things may strike you. Half (50 percent) of all prisoners are younger than age 35, and almost all prisoners are men. Then there is this remarkable statistic: Although African Americans make up just 12.8 percent of the U.S. population, nearly two of five prisoners are African Americans. On any given day, *one out of every nine* African American men ages 20 to 34 is in jail or prison. For Latinos, the rate is one of twenty-six; for whites one of one hundred (Warren et al. 2008).

Finally, note how marriage and education—two of the major ways that society "anchors" people into mainstream norms—keep people out of prison. *Most* prisoners have never married. And look at the power of education, a major component of social class. As I mentioned earlier, social class funnels some people into the criminal justice system while it detours others around it. You can see how people who drop out of high school have a high chance of ending up in prison—and how unlikely it is for a college graduate to arrive at this unwelcome destination in life.

FIGURE 6.2

How Much is Enough? The Explosion in the Number of U.S. Prisoners

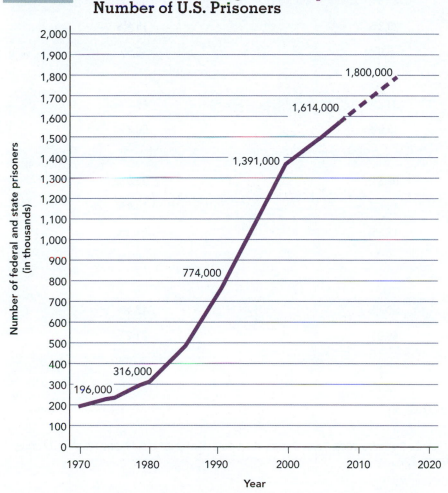

Between 1970 and 2009, the U.S. population increased 50 percent, while the number of prisoners increased 823 percent, a rate that is sixteen times greater than population growth. If the number of prisoners had grown at the same rate as the U.S. population, we would have about 294,000 prisoners, only one-fifth to one-sixth of today's total. Or if the U.S. population had increased at the same rate as that of U.S. prisoners, the U.S. population would be 1,688,000,000—approximately the population of China and all of Europe combined.

Sources: By the author. Based on Statistical Abstract of the United States 1995:Table 349; 2012:Tables 2, 347. The broken line is the author's estimate.

TABLE 6.3   Inmates in U.S. State and Federal Prisons

Characteristics	Percentage of Prisoners with These Characteristics	Percentage of U.S. Population with These Characteristics
Age		
18–24	15.9%	9.8%
25–34	33.6%	13.5%
35–44	29.1%	14.0%
45–54	14.8%	14.6%
55 and older	6.7%	23.9%
Race–Ethnicity		
African American	38.4%	12.8%
White	34.3%	65.6%
Latino	20.3%	15.4%
Other[a]	6.9%	5.5%
Sex		
Male	93.2%	49.2%
Female	6.8%	50.8%
Marital Status		
Never married	59.8%	26.0%
Divorced	15.5%	10.4%
Married	17.3%	57.3%
Widowed	1.1%	6.4%
Education		
Less than high school	39.7%	13.4%
High school graduate	49.0%	31.2%
Some college[b]	9.0%	26.0%
College graduate	2.4%	29.4%

[a]Asian Americans and Native Americans are included in this category.

[b]Includes associate's degrees.

Source: By the author. Based on Sourcebook of Criminal Justice Statistics 2003:Tables 6.000b, 6.28; 2006:Tables 6.34, 6.45; 2009:Table 6.33.2008; Statistical Abstract of the United States 2011:Tables 8, 10, 56, 227.

IF YOU WANT TO LEARN MORE about where prisoners are allowed to have guns,

Read more from the author: What Kind of Prison Is This? in **mysoclab**

Street Crime and the "Three-Strikes" Laws

As violent crime soared in the 1980s, Americans grew fearful. They demanded that their lawmakers do something. Politicians heard the message, and many responded by passing "three-strikes-and-you're-out" laws in their states. Anyone who is convicted of a third felony receives an automatic mandatory sentence.

These laws have had unanticipated consequences. Although some mandatory sentences carry life imprisonment, judges are not allowed to consider the circumstances of the individual or the crime. While few of us would feel sympathy if a man convicted of a third brutal rape or a third murder were sent to prison for life, in their haste to appease the public the politicians did not limit the three-strikes laws to *violent* crimes. And they did not consider that some minor crimes are considered felonies.

Here are some actual cases:

- In Los Angeles, a 27-year-old man who stole a pizza was sentenced to 25 years in prison (Cloud 1998).
- In Sacramento, a man passed himself off as Tiger Woods and went on a $17,000 shopping spree. He was sentenced to 200 years in prison (Reuters 2001).
- Also in California, Michael James passed a bad check for $94. He was sentenced to 25 years to life (Jones 2008).
- In Utah, a 25-year-old sold small bags of marijuana to a police informant. The judge who sentenced the man to 55 years in prison said the sentence was unjust, but he had no choice (Madigan 2004).
- In New York City, a man who was about to be sentenced for selling crack said to the judge, "I'm only 19. This is terrible." He then hurled himself out of a courtroom window, plunging to his death sixteen stories below (Cloud 1998).

In *Making It Personal*, you have a chance to analyze the three-strikes laws.

MAKING IT PERSONAL
"Three Strikes and You're Out"

To make the "three-strikes" laws personal, I could ask you to think about the last time you were convicted of a felony. This, however, is not likely to apply to you, so instead, I will ask you to apply the theoretical perspective to the "three-strikes" laws.

Let me give you some guidelines for doing this. For *symbolic interactionism,* what do these laws represent to the public? How does your answer differ depending on what part of "the public" you are referring to? For *functionalism,* who benefits from these laws? What are some of their functions? Their dysfunctions? For the *conflict perspective,* which groups are in conflict? Who has the power to enforce their will on others?

Do you know anyone who has been sentenced under a "three-strikes" law? What happened?

The Decline in Violent Crime

As you have seen, judges have sent more and more people to prison, and legislators have passed the three-strikes laws. As "getting tough" on crime took place, the rate of violent crime dropped sharply. The reason for the decline in violent crime

FROM ANOTHER STUDENT

Dear Mr. Henslin,
I cannot thank you enough for your insightful and fascinating book. I am hooked on sociology and feel like my life has taken a dramatic turn since first opening the pages of your book. I am sure you already know this, but you should be very proud of the amazing journey that you take students on every time they read your book.

Many, many thanks for the wonderful textbook!

Jennifer Sanchez
American Public University
Charles Town
West Virginia

was obvious to the public: "If you lock 'em up, they aren't on the street committing crimes." But obvious answers are not always correct, which has led to a controversy in sociology. Some sociologists agree with the public's perception that getting tough on criminals reduced violent crime (Conklin 2003). Others, in contrast, point to higher employment, a drop in drug use, and even abortion (Rosenfeld 2002; Blumstein and Wallman 2006; Reiman 2010). We can rule out unemployment, for when the unemployment rate shot up with the economic crisis the lower crime rates continued (Oppel 2011). This matter is not yet settled. We'll see what answers future research brings.

Recidivism

If a goal of prisons is to teach their clients to stay away from crime, they are colossal failures. We know this because of the **recidivism rate**—the percentage of former prisoners who are rearrested. For people sent to prison for crimes of violence, within just three years of their release, two out of three (62 percent) are rearrested, and half (52 percent) are back in prison (*Sourcebook of Criminal Justice Statistics* 2003: Table 6.52). Looking at Figure 6.3, which gives a breakdown of three-year recidivism by type of crime, do you think that prisons teach people that crime doesn't pay?

recidivism rate the percentage of released convicts who are rearrested

FIGURE 6.3 Recidivism of U.S. Prisoners

Of 272,000 prisoners released from U.S. prisons, what percentage were rearrested within three years?

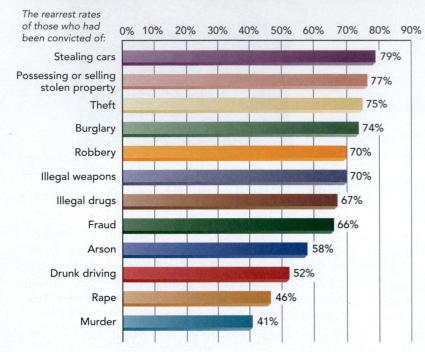

The rearrest rates of those who had been convicted of:

Stealing cars	79%
Possessing or selling stolen property	77%
Theft	75%
Burglary	74%
Robbery	70%
Illegal weapons	70%
Illegal drugs	67%
Fraud	66%
Arson	58%
Drunk driving	52%
Rape	46%
Murder	41%

Note: The individuals were not necessarily rearrested for the same crime for which they had originally been imprisoned.

Source: By the author. Based on Sourcebook of Criminal Justice Statistics 2003:Table 6.50

Watch the **Video** Sociology on the Job: Deviance in **mysoclab**

UNIT 6.6 // TESTING MYSELF
DID I LEARN IT? ANSWERS ARE AT THE END OF THE CHAPTER

1. Which of these descriptions best summarizes the trend in the number of U.S. prisoners?
   a. an increase until about year 2000, and a sharp drop since then
   b. flat—about the same number for the past 30 or 40 years
   c. an almost continual decline since 1970
   d. a sharp increase since 1970, from about 200,000 to almost 2 million

2. African Americans, who make up 12.8 percent of the U.S. population, make up this percentage of prisoners
   a. 13   b. 20
   c. 38   d. 72

3. Many "anchors" tie people into mainstream norms and behaviors. Most prisoners are missing this "anchor"
   a. goals
   b. marriage
   c. relatives
   d. divorce

4. Which of these characteristics would best predict that someone will go to prison?
   a. dropped out of high school
   b. married before age 21
   c. started college after age 20
   d. has no brother or sister

5. The "three-strikes" laws are modeled after baseball. After being convicted of a third felony, an individual is
   a. sent home
   b. forced to do long-term community service
   c. ordered to report to a parole officer
   d. given a mandatory prison sentence

6. The rate of violent crime has dropped drastically since some states passed the three-strikes laws and more offenders have been put in prison. Some sociologists disagree with this common-sense explanation for the decrease in violent crime. Among the explanations they suggest is
   a. more education
   b. a decrease in employment
   c. less drug use
   d. more police

7. If a goal of prisons is to teach their clients to stay away from crime, U.S. prisons
   a. could serve as a model for other countries
   b. are colossal failures
   c. have improved during the past 20 years
   d. are worse now than they were 20 years ago

8. Try to recall the recidivism rate of former prisoners who had served time for crimes of violence. Within three years of their release from prison, this percentage had been rearrested
   a. 12   b. 22
   c. 42   d. 62

UNIT 6.7

Reactions to Deviance: The Death Penalty

The Death Penalty and Serial Killers

As you know, **capital punishment,** the death penalty, is the most extreme measure the state takes. As you also know, the death penalty arouses both impassioned opposition and support. Advances in DNA testing have given opponents of the death penalty a strong argument: Innocent people have been sent to death row, and some have been executed. Those who are passionate about retaining the death penalty point to such crimes as these, which drew me to Texas:

As I was watching television, I was stunned by the images coming from Houston, Texas. Television cameras showed the police digging up dozens of bodies that had been buried in a boat storage shed. Fascinated, I waited impatiently for spring break. A few days later, I drove from Illinois, where I was teaching, to Houston, where 33-year-old Dean Corll had befriended Elmer Wayne Henley and David Brooks, two teenagers from broken homes. Together, they had killed twenty-seven boys. Elmer and David would pick up young hitchhikers and deliver them to Corll to rape and kill. They even brought him their own high school classmates.

| **capital punishment** the death penalty

Capital punishment arouses intense emotions—in both those who favor and those who oppose it.

WHAT AM I SUPPOSED TO LEARN?

After you have read this unit, you should be able to

1 State if serial murder has become more common.

2 Summarize geographical, social class, gender, and race–ethnic biases in the death penalty.

I decided to spend my coming sabbatical writing a novel on this case. I knew that I would have to get into the minds of the killers. I would have to "become" them day after day for months. Corll kept a piece of plywood in his apartment. In each of its corners, he had cut a hole. He and the boys would spread-eagle their handcuffed victims on this board and torture and rape them for hours. The details were bloody and gruesome. Sometimes, they would even pause to order pizza. I began to wonder about immersing myself in torture and human degradation. I was plagued with this question: Would I be the same person afterwards? I decided not to write the book.

The three killers led double lives so successfully that their friends and family were unaware of their criminal activities. Henley's mother swore to me that her son couldn't possibly be guilty—he was a good boy. Some of Elmer's high school friends told me that that his being involved in homosexual rape and murder was ridiculous—he was interested only in girls. I was interviewing them in Henley's bedroom, and for proof they pointed to a pair of girls' panties that were draped across a lamp shade.

Serial murder is the killing of victims in three or more separate events. The murders may occur over several days, weeks, or years. The elapsed time between murders distinguishes serial killers from *mass murderers,* those who do their killing all at once. Here are some infamous examples:

- During the 1960s and 1970s, Ted Bundy raped and killed dozens of women in four states. Bundy would return to the scenes of his killings and have sex with the dead bodies of his victims.
- Between 1974 and 1991, Dennis Rader killed ten people in Wichita, Kansas. Rader had written to the newspapers, proudly calling himself the BTK (Bind, Torture, and Kill) strangler.
- In the late 1980s and early 1990s, Aileen Wuornos hitchhiked along Florida's freeways. She killed seven men after having had sex with them.

| **serial murder** the killing of several victims in three or more separate events

- The serial killer with the most victims appears to be Harold Shipman, a physician in Manchester, England. From 1977 to 2000, during house calls Shipman gave lethal injections to 230 to 275 of his elderly female patients.
- In 2009, Anthony Sowell of Cleveland, Ohio, was discovered living with eleven decomposing bodies of women he had raped and strangled.

Is serial murder more common now than it used to be? Some think so because serial killers are in the news a lot. But this is primarily because of changes in technology. In the past, police departments had little communication with one another, and seldom did anyone connect killings in different jurisdictions. Today's more efficient communications, investigative techniques, and DNA matching make it easier for the police to know when a serial killer is operating in an area. Part of the perception that there are more serial killers today is also due to ignorance of our history: In our frontier past, for example, serial killers went from ranch to ranch.

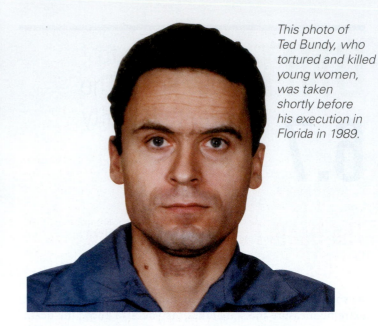

This photo of Ted Bundy, who tortured and killed young women, was taken shortly before his execution in Florida in 1989.

Bias in the Death Penalty

The arguments for and against capital punishment can go on forever, with neither side convincing the other. On the one hand, it certainly is true that there are monstrously evil people in our midst. On the other hand, the death penalty is not administered evenly. On the contrary, the death penalty is marked by strong biases. Consider *geography*: In this Social Map below, you can see how the place where people commit murder affects their chances of being put to death.

FIGURE 6.4 **Executions in the United States**

Source: By the author. Based on Statistical Abstract of the United States *2012:Table 353.*

Then, too, there is *social class bias*. As you know from news reports, it is rare for a rich person to be sentenced to death. Although the government does not collect statistics on social class and the death penalty, this common observation is borne out by the education of the prisoners on death row. *Half* of the prisoners on death row (50 percent) have not finished high school (*Sourcebook of Criminal Justice Statistics* 2009: Table 6.81).

There is also a *gender bias*—so strong that it is almost unheard of for a woman to be sentenced to death, much less executed. Although women commit 9.6 percent of the murders, they make up only 1.8 percent of death row inmates (*Sourcebook of Criminal Justice Statistics* 2009:Table 6.81). Even on death row, the gender bias continues, for the state is more likely to execute a man than a woman. As Figure 6.5 shows, only 0.9 percent of the 5,093 prisoners executed in the United States since 1930 have been women. Perhaps this gender bias reflects the relative brutality of their murders, but we need research to find out.

Racal bias was once so flagrant that it put a stop to the death penalty. Donald Partington (1965), a lawyer in Virginia, was shocked by the bias he saw in the courtroom, and he decided to document it. He found that 2,798 men had been convicted for rape and attempted rape in Virginia between 1908 and 1963—56 percent whites and 44 percent blacks. For attempted rape, 13 had been executed. For rape, 41 men had been executed. *All those executed were black.* Not one of the whites was executed.

After listening to evidence like this, in 1972 the Supreme Court ruled in *Furman v. Georgia* that the death penalty, as applied, was unconstitutional. The execution of prisoners stopped—but not for long. The states wrote new laws, and in 1977 they again began to execute prisoners. Since then, 66 percent of those put to death have been white and 34 percent African American (*Statistical Abstract* 2012: Table 352). (Latinos are evidently counted as whites in this statistic.) Living on death row is risky for anyone, but the risk is higher for some—and here is where the current bias comes in. Those most likely to be executed are African Americans and Latinos who killed whites (Jacobs et al. 2007).

To see the race–ethnicity of the prisoners on death row, see Table 6.4 on the next page.

FIGURE 6.5

Who Gets Executed? Gender Bias in Capital Punishment

99.1%

0.9%

| 5,049 | 44 |
| Men | Women |

Source: By the author. Based on Statistical Abstract of the United States 2012:Table 352.

✳ **Explore** the **Concept**
The Death Penalty in **mysoclab**

TABLE 6.4 The Race–Ethnicity of the 3,316 Prisoners on Death Row

	Percentage	
	on Death Row	in U.S. Population
Whites	44%	65%
African Americans	41%	13%
Latinos	12%	15%
Asian Americans	1%	5%
Native Americans	1%	1%

Source: By the author. Based on Sourcebook of Criminal Justice Statistics *2010:Table 6.80 and Figure 8.5 of this text.*

UNIT 6.7 // TESTING MYSELF
DID I LEARN IT? ANSWERS ARE AT THE END OF THE CHAPTER

1. Opponents and proponents of the death penalty are passionate about their positions. One argument of those who support capital punishment concerns
   a. bias in the death penalty
   b. the equality of death
   c. the inevitability of death
   d. serial killers

2. A major argument of those who oppose capital punishment concerns
   a. bias in the death penalty
   b. the equality of death
   c. the inevitability of death
   d. serial killers

3. The author says that although serial killers receive more publicity today than in the past, this is not because serial killing has grown more common. Rather, it is because
   a. there used to be more people like Jack the Ripper
   b. people today are more interested in serial killers
   c. technological change makes it easier to detect serial killers
   d. today's newspapers place more focus on lurid and startling news events

4. Although not stated in the text, killers with less education are more likely to receive the death penalty. And on death row, those with less education are more likely to be executed. These findings are examples of what kind of bias in the death penalty?
   a. gender
   b. social class
   c. race–ethnicity
   d. geography

5. Men who kill are more likely than female killers to receive the death penalty. On death row, men are also more likely than women to be executed. These findings are examples of what kind of bias in the death penalty?
   a. gender
   b. social class
   c. race–ethnicity
   d. geography

6. Those on death row most likely to be executed are African Americans and Latinos who killed whites. This finding is an example of what kind of bias?
   a. gender
   b. social class
   c. race–ethnicity
   d. geography

UNIT 6.8

On Laws and Crime Statistics

Did you know that it is a crime in Saudi Arabia for a woman to drive a car (Murphy 2011)? A crime in Florida to sell alcohol before 1 P.M. on Sundays? Or illegal in Wells, Maine, to advertise on tombstones? As I have stressed in this chapter, deviance, including the form called *crime,* is so relative that it varies from one society to another, even from one group to another within the same society. Crime also varies from one time period to another, as opinions change or as different groups gain access to power. Let's look at one of these changes.

Because crime consists of whatever acts authorities decide to declare illegal, new crimes emerge from time to time. A prime example is juvenile delinquency, which Illinois lawmakers designated a separate type of crime in 1899. Juveniles committed crimes before 1899, of course, but youths were not considered to be a separate type of lawbreaker. They were just young people who committed crimes, and they were treated the same as adults who committed the same crime. Sometimes new technology leads to new crimes. Motor vehicle theft, a separate crime in the United States, obviously did not exist before the automobile was invented.

Painting swastikas on synagogues or Jewish tombstones is a hate crime that brings back chilling memories of the Holocaust.

WHAT AM I SUPPOSED TO LEARN?

After you have read this unit, you should be able to

1 Discuss the relativity of crime.

2 Take and explain a position on hate crimes.

3 Summarize the problem with official crime statistics.

In the 1980s, another new crime was born when state governments developed the classification **hate crime,** crimes motivated by *bias* (dislike, hatred) against someone's race–ethnicity, religion, sexual orientation, disability, or national origin. Before this, people attacked others or destroyed their property out of these same motivations, but when authorities dealt with the crime the motivation was not the issue. If someone injured or killed another person because of that person's race–ethnicity, religion sexual orientation, national origin, or disability, he or she was charged with assault or murder. Today, motivation has become a central issue, and hate crimes carry more severe sanctions than acts that do not have hatred as their motive. Table 6.5 on the next page summarizes the victims of hate crimes.

We can be certain that the "evolution" of crime is not yet complete. As society changes and as different groups gain access to power, we can expect the definitions of crime to change accordingly.

Before you go to the next section, pause and consider hate crimes in a different light in *Making It Personal* on the next page.

The Trouble with Crime Statistics

What besides the number of crimes being committed affects crime statistics? The most obvious is the classifications being used. If there is no category of hate crime, for example, then the hate crime rate will be zero. There are other reasons to be wary of official crime statistics. Both the findings of symbolic interactionists (that stereotypes operate when authorities deal with people) and the assumption of conflict theorists (that the criminal justice system serves the ruling elite) indicate the need for caution.

Crime statistics do not have an objective, independent existence.

hate crime a crime that is punished more severely because it is motivated by hatred (dislike, hostility, animosity) of someone's race–ethnicity, religion, sexual orientation, disability, or national origin

MAKING IT PERSONAL
Thinking about Hate Crimes

Do you think we should have a separate classification called hate crime? Why aren't the crimes of assault, robbery, vandalism, and murder adequate? Here is one example: Gay college student Matthew Shepard was brutally murdered in Laramie, Wyoming, in 1998. This was a hate crime because Shepard was killed because he was a homosexual. In the same year in that same city, an eight-year-old girl was abducted, raped, and murdered of by a pedophile. This was not a hate crime because it was not motivated by hatred or dislike (Sullivan 1999).

Now that you have formed your opinion about whether the hate crime of murder is worse than the other crime of murder and does or does not deserves a more severe punishment, I want you to ask yourself this: How do you think your social location (race–ethnicity, gender, social class, religion, sexual orientation, or physical ability) affects your opinion? (Go back to page 171.)

They are not like oranges that you pick out in a grocery store. Rather, crime statistics are a human creation. Besides the particular laws and stereotypes, there is also the matter of how prosecutors classify a particular act. Depending on how a police report is written and its purpose (to speed things along or to motivate a suspect to talk), for a single act prosecutors can choose between burglary, breaking and entering, larceny, and even property damage. In addition, when the police are ordered to "clean up" an area, they enforce laws severely. Change these factors, and the statistics also change.

Consider this: According to official statistics, working-class boys are more delinquent than middle-class boys. Yet, who actually gets arrested for what is influenced by social class, a point that has far-reaching implications. As symbolic interactionists point out, the police follow a symbolic system (their background assumptions, or basic ideas) as they enforce the law. They interview people and investigate crimes with ideas of "typical criminals" and "typical good citizens" in mind. The more a suspect matches their stereotypes of a lawbreaker (which they call "criminal profiles"), the more likely that person is to be arrested. **Police discretion,** the

police discretion the practice of the police, in the normal course of their duties, to either arrest or ticket someone for an offense or to overlook the matter

decision whether to arrest someone or even to ignore a matter, is a routine part of police work. It is inevitable that official crime statistics reflect these and many other biases.

TABLE 6.5	Hate Crimes

Directed Against	Number of Victims
Race–Ethnicity	
African Americans	3,596
Whites	829
Latinos	792
Multiracial	276
Asian Americans	170
Native Americans	63
Religion	
Jews	1,145
Muslims	130
Catholics	89
Protestants	62
Sexual Orientation	
Homosexual	1,706
Male Homosexual	981
Female Homosexual	198
General	466
Heterosexual	34
Bisexual	27
Disabilities	
Mental	57
Physical	28

Note: The number is the cumulative victims from 2000 to 2008, the latest year available.

Source: By the author. Based on Statistical Abstract of the United States 2012: Table 322.

1. At the time of this writing, it is a crime in Saudi Arabia for a woman to drive a car. (Technically, this is not a crime, but you can't drive without a driver's license—and women cannot get drivers' licenses!) It is legal for women to drive cars in Canada. This is an example of
   a. discrimination against women
   b. the backwardness of laws in some places
   c. customs not catching up to changing technology
   d. the relativity of crime

2. Hazel was harassed by her classmates because she was a Muslim. One of her classmates became so angry when Hazel defended her religion that the classmate hit her. Hazel is a victim of
   a. a mob
   b. peer punishment
   c. a hate crime
   d. legal discrimination

3. The police saw Johnny urinating against a building. They ignored the matter because they thought Johnny was dealing drugs and if they kept observing him they would see a drug deal go down. They didn't, so they had to call it a night, but they still watch Johnny from time to time, hoping to catch him with drugs. This is an example of
   a. good police work
   b. police discretion
   c. police discrimination
   d. the war on drugs

UNIT 6.9

The Medicalization of Deviance

WHAT AM I SUPPOSED TO LEARN?

After you have read this unit, you should be able to

1 State what the medicalization of deviance is and summarize Szasz's objection to it.

2 Explain how being homeless can lead to "mental illness."

Another way in which society deals with deviance is to "medicalize" it. Let's look at what this entails.

Neither Mental Nor Illness?

To *medicalize* something is to classify it as a form of illness that properly belongs in the care of physicians. For the past hundred years or so, especially since the time of Sigmund Freud (1856–1939), the Viennese physician who founded psychoanalysis, there has been increasing **medicalization of deviance.** In this view, deviance, including crime, is a sign of mental sickness. Rape, murder, stealing, cheating, and so on are external symptoms of internal disorders, consequences of a confused or tortured mind.

Medicalization applies not just to crime but also to "unusual" behaviors that disturb people. When people cannot find a satisfying explanation for why someone is "like that," they often say that a "sickness in the head" is causing the unacceptable behavior. Psychiatrists, psychologists, and counselors love this view, as it extends their boundaries over more and more human behavior. Thomas Szasz a renegade psychiatrist, challenges this view. He (1986, 1996, 1998) argues that what are called *mental illnesses are neither mental nor illnesses. They are simply problem behaviors.*

Some behaviors that are called mental illnesses have physical causes. That is, something in an individual's body results in unusual perceptions or behavior. Some depression, for example, is caused by a chemical imbalance in the brain, which can be treated by drugs. The behaviors—crying, long-term sadness, and lack of interest in family, work, school, or grooming that are associated with depression—are symptoms of a physical problem.

Attention-deficit disorder (ADD) is an example of a new "mental illness" that has come out of nowhere. As Szasz says, "No one explains where this disease came from or why it didn't exist 50 years ago. No one is able to diagnose it with objective tests." ADD is diagnosed because a teacher or parent complained about a child misbehaving.

medicalization of deviance to make deviance a medical matter, a symptom of some underlying illness that needs to be treated by physicians

Can you apply the medicalization of deviance to this photo? How about Thomas Szasz's controversial analysis?

Misbehaving children have been a problem throughout history, but now, with doctors looking to expand their territory, this problem behavior has become a sign of "mental illness."

All of us have troubles. Some of us face a constant barrage of problems as we go through life. Most of us continue the struggle, perhaps encouraged by relatives and friends and motivated by job, family responsibilities, religious faith or philosophical views, and life goals. Even when the odds seem hopeless, we carry on, not perfectly, but as best we can.

Some people, however, fail to cope well with life's challenges. They feel overwhelmed and become depressed, uncooperative, or hostile. Some strike out at others; and some, in Merton's (1949/1968) terms, become retreatists and withdraw into their apartments or homes, refusing to come out. Although these ways of coping create problems, they are *behaviors, not mental illnesses,* stresses Szasz. "Mental illness," Szasz concludes, is a myth foisted on a naive public. Our medical profession uses pseudoscientific jargon that people don't understand so it can expand its area of control and force nonconforming people to accept society's definitions of "normal."

Szasz's controversial claim forces us to look anew at the forms of deviance that we usually refer to as mental illness. To explain behavior that people find bizarre, he directs our attention not to causes hidden deep within the "subconscious," but, instead, to how people learn such behaviors. To ask, "What is the origin of someone's inappropriate or bizarre behavior?" then becomes similar to asking "Why do some women steal?" "Why do some men rape?" "Why do some teenagers cuss their parents and stalk out of the room, slamming the door?" *The answers depend on those people's particular experiences in life, not on an illness in their minds.* In short, some sociologists find Szasz's renegade analysis refreshing because it indicates that *social experiences,* not an illness of the mind, underlie bizarre behaviors—as well as deviance in general.

Consider Jamie.

The Homeless Mentally Ill

Jamie was sitting on a low wall surrounding the landscaped courtyard of an exclusive restaurant. She appeared unaware of the stares elicited by her layers of mismatched clothing, her matted hair and dirty face, and the shopping cart that overflowed with her meager possessions.

After sitting next to Jamie for a few minutes, I saw her point to the street and concentrate, slowly moving her finger horizontally. I asked her what she was doing.

"I'm directing traffic," she replied. "I control where the cars go. Look, that one turned right there," she said, now withdrawing her finger.

"Really?" I said.

After a while she confided that her cart talked to her.

"Really?" I said again.

"Yes," she replied. "You can hear it, too." At that, she pushed the shopping cart a bit.

"Did you hear that?" she asked.

When I shook my head, she demonstrated again. Then it hit me. She was referring to the squeaking wheels!

I nodded.

When I left Jamie, she was pointing to the sky, for, as she told me, she also controlled the flight of airplanes.

To most of us, Jamie's behavior and thinking are bizarre. They simply do not match any reality we know. Could you or I become like Jamie?

Suppose for a bitter moment that you are homeless and have to live on the streets. You have no money, no place to sleep, no bathroom. You do not know *if* you are going to eat, much less where. You have no friends or anyone you can trust. You live in constant fear of rape and other violence. Do you think this might be enough to drive you over the edge?

Consider just the problems involved in not having a place to bathe. (Shelters are often so dangerous that many homeless people prefer to sleep in public settings.) At first, you try to wash in the restrooms of gas stations, bars, the bus station, or a shopping center. But you are dirty, and people stare when you enter and call the management when they see you wash your feet in the sink. You are thrown out and told in no uncertain terms never to come back. So you get dirtier and dirtier. Eventually, you come to think of being dirty as a fact of life. Soon, maybe, you don't even care. The stares no longer bother you—at least not as much as they once did.

No one will talk to you, and you withdraw more and more into yourself. You begin to build a fantasy life. You talk openly to yourself. People stare, but so what? They stare anyway. Besides, they are no longer important to you.

Jamie might be mentally ill. Some organic problem, such as a chemical imbalance in her brain, might underlie her behavior. But perhaps not. How long would it take you to exhibit bizarre behaviors if you were homeless—and hopeless? The point is that *living on the streets can cause mental illness*—or whatever we want to label socially inappropriate behaviors that we find difficult to classify. *Homelessness and mental illness are reciprocal:* Just as "mental illness" can cause homelessness, so the trials of being homeless, of living on cold, hostile streets, can lead to unusual thinking and behaviors.

Let's consider this just a little more in *Making It Personal.*

MAKING IT PERSONAL
If You Lived on the Streets

Think about what you just read. Don't let it just fly by, but really think about it. Jamie is a real person. I didn't make her up. All examples in this book that I mention my involvement with are real events.

We don't know what led to Jamie having the idea that she can control the path of cars and airplanes and that her shopping cart talks to her. It could be a chemical imbalance. Such imbalances do cause depression. Or there could be neural misfirings of some sort in her brain.

But think about the *social* challenges, the things that come with not having a home—no place to shower, no clean clothes, no regular food, no kitchen or living room or bedroom, no family or friends to help you through a crisis. If you are a woman, rape is always a threat, but on the streets rape goes far beyond a nagging potential. And if you are a man on the streets, being mugged and left crippled or brain damaged is a constant threat.

How do you think you would survive in this situation? And how do you think that living on the streets would affect your mental state? Do you think that in your isolation you would be better off than Jamie?

I do hope you've thought this through with me. It will help you see how the "social" can produce this thing we call "mental" illness.

How can mental illness be both a cause and a consequence of homelessness?

UNIT 6.9 // TESTING MYSELF
DID I LEARN IT? ANSWERS ARE AT THE END OF THE CHAPTER

1. Cindy was caught shoplifting. The school counselor told Cindy's parents that their daughter has a problem identifying with her mother and that Cindy is "acting out." The counselor recommends that Cindy see a psychiatrist for treatment. This is an example of
   a. schools taking over functions of the family
   b. middle-class paranoia
   c. the results of the no-spanking movement
   d. the medicalization of deviance

2. The author interviewed family members and friends of a teenaged serial killer who participated in the rape and murder of numerous teenagers. According to the medicalization of deviance, the crimes of this killer are
   a. deserving of the death penalty
   b. a sign that society is getting worse
   c. a sign of mental illness
   d. an example of why we need more psychiatrists

3. A renegade psychiatrist, Thomas Szasz, challenges the medicalization of deviance. He says that problem behaviors, including crime, are not a sign of mental illness. They are neither mental nor illness, he claims. Instead, they are
   a. a cry for help
   b. problem behaviors
   c. not crimes
   d. transfers of inappropriate affection into misguided behavior

4. In his challenge to the medicalization of deviance, Szasz says that the problem behaviors usually taken as a sign of mental illness are not caused by an illness in people's minds. Instead, he says they come from
   a. people's experiences
   b. internal desires, sometimes called the id
   c. bad parenting
   d. the suppressive nature of contemporary society

5. The reason that the medical profession pushes the medicalization of deviance, says Szasz, is
   a. to try to help more people
   b. because more and more people are mentally ill
   c. because the influence of the family and religion has declined
   d. to expand their territory

6. The author claims that just as mental illness can cause homelessness so
   a. problem behavior can cause both homelessness and mental illness
   b. the involvement of the medical profession in homelessness can cause mental illness
   c. homelessness can cause mental illness
   d. psychiatric treatment can cause mental illness

UNIT 6.10

The Need for a More Humane Approach

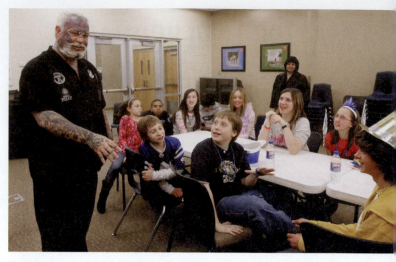

A different function of deviance: Scary Guy (his legal name) visits schools to promote understanding and acceptance of people who are different.

WHAT AM I SUPPOSED TO LEARN?

After you have read this unit, you should be able to

1 Explain why we need a more humane approach to deviants.

A More Humane Approach

As Durkheim (1895/1964:68) pointed out, deviance is inevitable—even in a group of saints.

Imagine a society of saints, a perfect cloister of exemplary individuals. Crimes, properly so called, will there be unknown; but faults which appear invisible to the layman will create there the same scandal that the ordinary offense does in ordinary society.

With deviance inevitable, one measure of a society is how it treats its deviants. Our prisons certainly don't say much good about U.S. society. Filled with the poor, uneducated, and unskilled, they are warehouses of the unwanted. White-collar criminals continue to get by with a slap on the wrist while street criminals are punished severely. Some deviants, who fail to meet current standards of admission to either prison or a mental hospital, take refuge in shelters, as well as in cardboard boxes tucked away in urban recesses. Although no one has *the* answer, it doesn't take much reflection to see that there are more humane approaches than these.

Because deviance is a certainty, the larger issues are to find ways to protect people from deviant behaviors that are harmful to themselves or others, to tolerate behaviors that are not harmful, and to develop systems of fairer treatment for deviants. In the absence of fundamental changes that would bring about an equitable social system, most efforts are, unfortunately, like putting a Band-Aid on a gunshot wound. What we need is a more humane social system, one that would prevent the social inequalities that are the focus of the next three chapters.

UNIT 6.10 // TESTING MYSELF

DID I LEARN IT? ANSWERS ARE AT THE END OF THE CHAPTER

1. The quote from Emile Durkheim about norm violations in a society of saints was intended to illustrate that
   a. there aren't many saints in this life
   b. deviance is inevitable
   c. even in Durkheim's time there were deviants
   d. we have come a long way since Durkheim's time

2. The author uses this example to indicate that we need a more humane approach to deviants
   a. the homeless
   b. shoplifters
   c. drug use by celebrities
   d. car theft by teenagers

PULLING IT ALL TOGETHER REVIEWING THE LEARNING GOALS

Unit 6.1 What Is Deviance?

1. Explain what deviance is and why it is relative.
- Norms change from one society to another. Because deviance is the violation of norms, what is deviant also changes from one group to another, making deviance relative.

2. Explain what stigma is.
- Stigma is a violation of norms so serious that it discredits an individual. As a negative master status, stigma overrides a person's other characteristics.

3. Explain why norms and sanctions are necessary for social life to exist.
- For interaction to proceed smoothly, people must know what to expect of one another. Norms lay down those expectations, and sanctions help to keep people in line.

👁—[Watch the Video
The Basics: Deviance
in **mysoclab**

Unit 6.2 Comparing Sociobiology, Psychology, and Sociology

1. Contrast sociobiological, psychological, and sociological explanations of deviance.
- The main difference is that sociological explanations look for influences for deviance outside the individual, such as socialization and peer groups. The other two look for causes within the individual, sociobiological in inherited characteristics and psychological in personality defects.

Unit 6.3 The Symbolic Interactionist Perspective

1. Explain differential association theory.
- The different groups with which we associate give us messages about conformity and deviance. We receive an excess of definitions that tilts us toward conformance or deviance. In this process are families, friends, neighborhoods, and subcultures.

2. Explain control theory.
- We all have desires to deviate. Working against these desires are inner controls (internalized morality—conscience, ideas of right and wrong) and outer controls (people—from friends to the police). The stronger our bonds to society, the more effective are our inner controls. Basic self-control develops during childhood.

3. Explain labeling theory.
- We use techniques of neutralization to reject negative labels. Some groups, such as teenagers and outlaw bikers, seek specific negative labels.

Unit 6.4 The Functionalist Perspective

1. Explain how deviance can be functional for society.
- Deviance clarifies moral boundaries, affirms norms, encourages unity, and promotes social change.

2. Explain how strain theory illustrates how mainstream values produce deviance.
- Socializing everyone into wanting success encourages people whose legitimate means to success are blocked to take deviant paths to success.

3. List the four deviant paths highlighted by strain theory.
- Innovation, ritualization, retreatism, and rebellion.

4. Explain illegitimate opportunity structures.
- This term refers to the opportunity to commit different types of crime, a door that social class opens and closes. Gender also holds a key to this door.

Unit 6.5 The Conflict Perspective

1. Explain the conflict view of class, crime, and the criminal justice system.
- The wealthy control the criminal justice system (the police, courts, and prisons designed to deal with law breakers). Because the poor pose the threat of rebellion, overthrowing the elite from their positions of privilege, the law comes down hard on the crimes of the poor, while the wealthy get a slap on the wrist.

Read the **Document**
"The Saints and the Roughnecks" by William J. Chambliss in **mysoclab**

Watch the **Video** Sociology on the Job: Deviance in **mysoclab**

Unit 6.6   Reactions to Deviance: Prisons

1. Discuss the increase in imprisonment and who the prisoners are.

- Since 1970, the number of prisoners has increased roughly from 200,000 to 2 million. Most prisoners are under age 35, never married, with low education. African Americans make up 38 percent of prisoners but only 13 percent of the population.

2. Explain the "three-strikes" laws and their dysfunctions.

- Some states require a set prison term after conviction of a third felony. Some people who have committed small offenses end up with harsh penalties, even life imprisonment.

3. Summarize suggested reasons for the drop in violent crime.

- The common assumption is longer prison sentences, but other explanations include abortion, higher employment, and less drug use.

4. Give basic statistics on recidivism.

- Measured by rearrests of former prisoners within three years, recidivism is high—from 41 percent for murder to 79 percent for car theft.

Watch the **Video** Sociology on the Job: Deviance in **mysoclab**

Unit 6.7   Reactions to Deviance: The Death Penalty

1. State if serial murder has become more common.

- There are no statistics on this, so the answer is unknown. But it is unlikely.

2. Summarize the geographical, social class, gender, and race–ethnic biases in the death penalty.

- *Geography:* Only some states have the death penalty. *Social class:* The uneducated are more likely to be on death row. *Gender:* Women are less likely to be sentenced to death and to be executed. *Race-ethnicity:* African Americans and Latinos who killed whites are more likely to be executed.

Explore the **Concept**
The Death Penalty in **mysoclab**

Unit 6.8   On Laws and Crime Statistics

1. Discuss the relativity of crime.

- What crime is varies from one society to another (women driving cars in Saudi Arabia) and in the same society from one time period to another (passage of new laws).

2. Take a position on hate crimes.

- Hate crimes carry extra penalties because they are motivated by hate or dislike. You should have applied your social location to try to understand whatever position you took on hate crimes.

3. Summarize the problem with crime statistics.

- Unlike oranges, crime statistics do not have an objective existence. They depend on the classifications being used, how acts are fit into the classification, and police discretion.

Unit 6.9   The Medicalization of Deviance

1. State what the medicalization of deviance is and summarize Szasz's objection to it.

- To medicalize deviance is to say that the behavior is a sign of mental illness that needs to be treated by a physician. Thomas Szasz's position is that problem behavior is behavior. It is not mental and it is not illness. People have learned ways of coping with problems in such a way that their coping behavior is a problem to others. It is problematic, but it remains behavior.

2. Explain how "mental illness" can lead to being homeless and how being homeless can lead to "mental illness."

- Being mentally ill can lead to someone losing a job and home and ending up on the streets. But being on the streets, with all of its problems, can lead to bizarre thinking and withdrawal into a private mental world.

Unit 6.10   The Need for a More Humane Approach

1. Explain why we need a more humane approach to deviants.

- Actually the need for a humane approach to deviants has run through the chapter. This section just reinforces it. Our court system and prisons are in special need of overhaul.

UNIT 6.1 // TESTING MYSELF
DID I LEARN IT? ANSWERS

1. **d** deviant

2. **d** deviant

3. **b** relativity of deviance

4. **a** It is not the act itself, but the reactions to the act, that make something deviant

5. **d** an act admired in one society can be punished by death in another society

6. **c** any act to which people respond negatively

7. **b** a stigma

8. **a** undermines predictability, the foundation of social life

9. **d** positive sanction

10. **c** an informal negative sanction

UNIT 6.2 // TESTING MYSELF
DID I LEARN IT? ANSWERS

1. **a** sociobiologist

2. **b** psychologist

3. **c** sociologist

4. **a** sociology

UNIT 6.3 // TESTING MYSELF
DID I LEARN IT? ANSWERS

1. **d** We are thinking beings who act according to our definition of the situation.

2. **c** differential association

3. **d** half

4. **b** control theory

5. **a** inner and outer controls

6. **c** is using techniques of neutralization

7. **c** differential association

8. **a** a technique of neutralization

9. **a** labeling theory

UNIT 6.4 // TESTING MYSELF
DID I LEARN IT? ANSWERS

1. **d** provides a better future

2. **c** strain

3. **a** innovation

4. **b** ritualism

5. **c** retreatism

6. **d** rebellion

7. **b** an illegitimate opportunity structure

8. **a** white-collar crime

9. **d** corporate crime

10. **c** committing crime

UNIT 6.5 // TESTING MYSELF
DID I LEARN IT? ANSWERS

1. **d** a cultural myth promoted by the capitalist class

2. **c** are the least rooted in society

3. **b** keeping itself in power

4. **a** if they become too outrageous or oppressive they might encourage the working class to revolt

UNIT 6.6 // TESTING MYSELF
DID I LEARN IT? ANSWERS

1. **d** a sharp increase since 1970, from about 200,000 to almost 2 million

2. **c** 38

3. **b** marriage

4. **a** dropped out of high school

5. **d** given a mandatory prison sentence

6. **c** less drug use

7. **b** are colossal failures

8. **d** 62

UNIT 6.7 // TESTING MYSELF
DID I LEARN IT? ANSWERS

1. **d** serial killers

2. **a** bias in the death penalty

3. **c** technological change makes it easier to detect serial killers

4. **b** social class

5. **a** gender

6. **c** race-ethnicity

UNIT 6.8 // TESTING MYSELF
DID I LEARN IT? ANSWERS

1. **d** the relativity of crime

2. **c** a hate crime

3. **b** police discretion

UNIT 6.9 // TESTING MYSELF
DID I LEARN IT? ANSWERS

1. **d** the medicalization of deviance

2. **a** sign of mental illness

3. **b** problem behaviors

4. **a** people's experiences

5. **d** to expand their territory

6. **c** homelessness can cause mental illness

UNIT 6.10 // TESTING MYSELF
DID I LEARN IT? ANSWERS

1. **b** deviance is inevitable

2. **a** the homeless

CHAPTER 7
SOCIAL STRATIFICATION

((•⊑ **Listen** to the **Chapter Audio** in **mysoclab**

GETTING STARTED

"How much money do you make?"

Few are going to ask you this question when they first meet you, but it is one of the main things that people wonder about others. In this chapter, we'll look at some of the differences that having money makes. We'll also explore many other things that affect your life.

We'll begin on the broadest level—the world. This will set the context to help you understand the situation in the United States, and, ultimately, your place in it.

👁 **Watch** the **Video** in **mysoclab**

Blenheim Palace, Stafforshire, England

UNIT 7.1

Global Stratification: From Slavery to Social Class

Here is a statement that will come as no surprise: Some people in the United States are wealthy, others are poor, and some are in between. Now let's build on this common knowledge. If you rank large groups of people according to how much money or property they possess, you have what sociologists call **social stratification**. It isn't just money and property. The ranking can be based on any way that people access the privileges available in their society.

Stratification doesn't occur only in the United States. *Every society stratifies its members.* Some societies have more equality than others, but all societies have inequality. The basis for stratifying people is different in tribal societies—such as who can shoot arrows accurately—but social stratification is universal. In addition, every society of the world uses *gender* to stratify its members. Because of their gender, people are either allowed or denied access to the good things their society offers.

This ranking of large groups of people according to their relative privileges is one of the most significant topics you will read about in this book, for it affects your life chances—from where you live and what you own to the age at which you are likely to die. We'll come back to this in a moment, but first let's consider three systems of social stratification: slavery, caste, and class.

> **social stratification** the division of large numbers of people into layers according to their relative property, power, and prestige; applies to both nations and to people within a nation, society, or other group

In a caste system, status is determined by birth and is lifelong. At birth, these women received not only membership in a lower caste but also, because of their gender, a predetermined position in that caste. When I photographed these women, they were carrying sand to the second floor of a house being constructed in Andhra Pradesh, India.

WHAT AM I SUPPOSED TO LEARN?

After you have read this unit, you should be able to

1 Explain variations in slavery, its causes and conditions, and slavery today.

2 Summarize India's caste system and the U.S. racial caste system.

3 State how social class systems differ from slavery and caste systems.

4 Explain how gender fits into stratification.

Slavery

Slavery, whose essential characteristic is that *some individuals own other people,* has been common throughout world history. The Old Testament even lays out rules for how owners should treat their slaves. So does the Koran. The Romans also had slaves, as did Africans and Greeks. In classical Greece and Rome, slaves did the work, freeing citizens to engage in politics and the arts. Slavery was most widespread in agricultural societies and least common among nomads, especially hunters and gatherers (Landtman 1938/1968).

You probably have many ideas about what slavery used to be like. Let's see how they compare with the remarkable forms that slavery took around the world. We'll begin by looking at the major causes and conditions of slavery.

CAUSES OF SLAVERY

Most people assume that slavery was based on race. This was seldom the case, however. There were three main factors. The first was *debt*. In some societies, creditors would enslave people who could not pay their debts. The second was *crime*. Instead of being killed, a murderer or thief might be enslaved by the victim's family as compensation for their loss. The third was *war*. Those who won wars often enslaved some of their enemies. Historian Gerda Lerner (1986) notes that women were the first people to be enslaved. When tribal men raided another group, they killed the men, raped the women, and then brought the women back as slaves. The women were valued for sexual purposes, for reproduction, and for their labor.

Roughly 2,500 years ago, when Greece was a collection of city-states, slavery was common. A city that became powerful and conquered another city would enslave some of the vanquished. Both slaves and slaveholders were Greek. About 2,000 years ago, when Rome became the supreme power of the Mediterranean area, Romans enslaved some of the Greeks they had conquered. More educated than their conquerors, some of these slaves served as tutors in Roman homes. Slavery, then, was a sign of debt, of crime, or of defeat in battle. It was not a sign that the slave was viewed as inherently inferior.

CONDITIONS OF SLAVERY

The conditions of slavery have also varied widely around the world. *In some places, slavery was temporary.* Slaves of the Israelites were set free in the year of jubilee, which occurred every fifty years. Roman slaves ordinarily had the right to buy themselves out of slavery. They knew what their purchase price was, and some were able to meet this price by striking a bargain with their owner and selling their services to others. In most instances, however, slavery was a lifelong condition. Some criminals, for example, became slaves when they were given life sentences as oarsmen on Roman war ships. There they served until death, which often came quickly to those in this exhausting service.

Slavery was not necessarily inheritable. In most places, the children of slaves were slaves themselves, but in ancient Mexico the children of slaves were free. In some places, a rich family that grew fond of the child of a slave would adopt the child. That child became an heir who bore the family name along with the other sons or daughters of the household (Landtman 1938/1968:271).

Slaves were not necessarily powerless and poor. In almost all instances, slaves owned no property and had no power. Among some groups, however, slaves could accumulate property and even rise to high positions in the community. Occasionally, a slave might even become wealthy, loan money to the master, and, while still a slave, own slaves himself or herself (Landtman 1938/1968).

SLAVERY IN THE NEW WORLD

Because slavery has a broad range of causes, some analysts conclude that racism didn't lead to slavery, but, rather, that slavery led to racism. Finding it profitable to make people slaves for life, U.S. slave owners developed an **ideology**, beliefs that justify social arrangements. Ideology paints the world in such a way that current social arrangements seem necessary and fair. U.S. colonists developed the view that their slaves were inferior. Some even said that they were not fully human. In short, the colonists wove elaborate justifications for slavery, built on the presumed superiority of their own group.

To make slavery even more profitable, slave states passed laws that made slavery *inheritable;* that is, the babies born to slaves became the property of the slave owners (Stampp 1956). These children could be sold, bartered, or traded. To strengthen their control, slave states passed laws making it illegal for slaves to hold meetings or to be away from the master's premises without carrying a pass (Lerner 1972). Sociologist W. E. B. Du Bois (1935/1992:12) noted that "gradually the entire white South became an armed camp to keep Negroes in slavery and to kill the black rebel."

The Civil War did not end legal discrimination. For example, until 1954, many states operated separate school systems for blacks and whites. Until the 1950s, in order to keep the races from "mixing," it was illegal in Mississippi for a white and an African American to sit together on the same seat of a car! There was no outright ban on blacks and whites

ideology beliefs about the way things ought to be that justify social arrangements

TO BE SOLD on board the Ship *Bance-Island*, on tuesday the 6th of *May* next, at *Aſhley-Ferry*; a choice cargo of about 250 fine healthy NEGROES, juſt arrived from the Windward & Rice Coaſt. —The utmoſt care has already been taken, and ſhall be continued, to keep them free from the leaſt danger of being infected with the SMALL-POX, no boat having been on board, and all other communication with people from *Charles-Town* prevented.
Auſtin, Laurens, & Appleby.

N. B. Full one Half of the above Negroes have had the SMALL-POX in their own Country.

being in the same car, however, so whites could employ African American chauffeurs.

SLAVERY TODAY

Slavery has again reared its ugly head in several parts of the world (Appiah and Bunzl 2007). The Ivory Coast, Mauritania, Niger, and Sudan have a long history of slavery, and not until the 1980s was slavery made illegal in Mauritania and Sudan (Ayittey 1998). It took until 2003 for slavery to be banned in Niger (Polgreen 2008).

The enslavement of children for work and sex is a problem in Africa, Asia, and South America (Trafficking in Persons Report 2010). A unique form of child slavery in some Mideast countries is buying little boys around the age of 5 or 6 to race camels. Their screams of terror are thought to make the camels run faster. In Qatar and the United Arab Emirates, which recently banned this practice, robots are supposed to replace the children (de Pastino 2005; Nelson 2009).

IF YOU WANT TO LEARN MORE about slavery today,

▶ **Read** more from the author: What Price Freedom? Slavery Today in **mysoclab**

Caste

The second system of social stratification is caste. In a **caste system**, birth determines status, which is lifelong. Someone who is born into a low-status group will always have low status, no matter how much that person may accomplish in life. In sociological terms, a caste system is built on ascribed status (discussed in Chapter 5, page 113). Achieved status cannot change an individual's place in this system.

Societies with this form of stratification try to make certain that the

caste system a form of social stratification in which people's statuses are determined by birth and are lifelong

boundaries between castes remain firm. They practice **endo-gamy**, marriage within their own group, and prohibit marriage between castes. They also believe that touching an inferior caste contaminates the superior caste. This keeps contact between castes to a minimum.

INDIA'S RELIGIOUS CASTES

India provides the best example of a caste system. Based not on race but on religion, India's caste system has existed for about 3,000 years (Chandra 1993a; Jaffrelot 2006). India's four main castes are depicted in Table 7.1.

These four castes are subdivided into about 3,000 subcastes, or *jati*. Each *jati* specializes in a particular

> **endogamy** the practice of marrying within one's own group

TABLE 7.1	India's Caste System
Caste	**Occupation**
Brahman	Priests and teachers
Kshatriya	Rulers and soldiers
Vaishya	Merchants and traders
Shudra	Peasants and laborers
Dalit (untouchables)	The outcastes; degrading or polluting labor

occupation. For example, one subcaste washes clothes, another sharpens knives, and yet another repairs shoes.

The lowest group listed in Table 7.1, the Dalit, is also called India's "untouchables." If a Dalit touches someone of a higher caste, that person becomes unclean. Even the shadow of an untouchable can contaminate. Early morning and late afternoons are especially risky, for the long shadows of these periods pose a danger to everyone higher up the caste system. Consequently, Dalits are not allowed in some villages during these times. Anyone who becomes contaminated must follow *ablution,* or washing rituals, to restore purity.

Although the Indian government abolished the caste system in 1949, centuries-old practices cannot be eliminated so easily, and the caste system remains part of everyday life in India (Beckett 2007). The ceremonies people follow at births, marriages, and deaths, for example, are dictated by caste (Chandra 1993a). The upper castes dread the upward mobility of the untouchables, sometimes resisting it even with murder and ritual suicide (Crossette 1996; Trofimov 2007). From personal observations in India, I can add that in some villages Dalit children are not allowed in the government schools. If they try to enroll, they are beaten.

A U.S. RACIAL CASTE SYSTEM

Before leaving the subject of caste, we should note that when slavery ended in the United States, it was replaced by a *racial caste system.* From the moment of birth, everyone was marked for life (Berger 1963/2012). In this system, *all* whites, even if they were poor and uneducated, considered themselves to have a higher status than *all* African Americans. As in India and South Africa, the upper caste, fearing pollution from the lower caste, prohibited intermarriage and insisted on separate schools, hotels, restaurants, and even toilets and drinking fountains in public facilities. In the South, when any white met any African American on a sidewalk, the African American had to move aside—which the untouchables of India still must do when they meet someone of a higher caste (Deliege 2001).

During my research in India, I interviewed this 8-year-old girl. Mahashury is a bonded laborer who was exchanged by her parents for a 2,000 rupee loan (about $14). To repay the loan, Mahashury must do construction work for one year. She will receive one meal a day and one set of clothing for the year. Because this centuries-old practice is now illegal, the master bribes Indian officials, who inform him when they are going to inspect the construction site. He then hides his bonded laborers. I was able to interview and photograph Mahashury because her master was absent the day I visited the construction site.

> **Watch** The Big Picture: Social Stratification the **Video** in **mysoclab**

Although a social class system has fluid boundaries (upward and downward mobility), Jennifer Lopez and this homeless woman are unlikely to move very far from where they now are.

Social Class

As you have seen, stratification systems based on slavery and caste are rigid. The lines drawn between people are firm, and there is little or no movement from one group to another. A **class system**, in contrast, is much more open, for it is based primarily on money or material possessions, which can be acquired. This system, too, is in place at birth, when children are ascribed the status of their parents. In a class system, though, individuals can change their social class by what they achieve (or fail to achieve). In addition, no laws specify people's occupations on the basis of their birth or prohibit marriage between the classes.

FLUID BOUNDARIES

A major characteristic of the class system, then, is its relatively fluid boundaries. A class system allows **social mobility**, movement up or down the class ladder. The potential for improving one's life—or for falling down the class ladder—is a major force that drives people to go far in school and to work hard. In the extreme, the family background that children inherit at birth may present such severe obstacles that they have little chance of climbing very far—or the family background may provide such privileges that it makes it difficult to fall down the class ladder.

Global Stratification and the Status of Females

In *every* society of the world, gender is a basis for social stratification. In no society is gender the sole basis for stratifying people, but gender cuts across *all* systems of social stratification (Huber 1990). Whether in

class system a form of social stratification based primarily on the possession of money or material possessions

social mobility movement up or down the social class ladder

slavery, caste, or class, people are sorted into categories on the basis of their gender and given different access to the good things available in their society.

Apparently these distinctions always favor males. It is remarkable, for example, that in *every* society of the world men's earnings are higher than women's. That most of the world's illiterate are females also drives home women's relative position in society. Of the several hundred million adults who cannot read, about two-thirds are women (UNESCO 2011). Because gender is such a significant factor in what happens to us in life, we shall focus on it more closely in Chapter 9.

Watch the **Video**
Sociology on the Job:
Social Stratification in
mysoclab

UNIT 7.1 // TESTING MYSELF
DID I LEARN IT? ANSWERS ARE AT THE END OF THE CHAPTER

1. If you divide large groups of people into layers based on some characteristic, such as their wealth, or their access to some other privilege, you have what sociologists call
   a. social power
   b. equality
   c. inherited rights
   d. social stratification

2. In every society of the world, gender is a basis for stratifying people. This means that because of their gender, people are
   a. viewed as male or female
   b. classified as male or female
   c. allowed or denied access to the good things offered by their society
   d. fearful of others, although they use various devices to disguise their feelings

3. Throughout the history of the world, slavery, the system of social stratification in which some individuals own other individuals, has been common. Which of the following was not the usual reason for slavery?

a. race
b. debt
c. crime
d. war

4. Slavery was usually a lifelong condition, but not always. In this place, slaves had the right to buy themselves out of slavery. They knew what their purchase price was, and some were able to meet this price by striking a bargain with their owner and selling their services to others.

a. Greece
b. Tripoli
c. Rome
d. United States

5. The U.S. colonists developed ideas and beliefs that justified their practice of slavery. Part of their view that helped them see slavery as fair, and even necessary, was that slaves were inferior humans. Sociologists call such beliefs

a. ideology
b. rationalization
c. stereotypes
d. denial of reality

6. Slavery has a broad range of causes. Which of these statements is stressed in the text? Some analysts conclude that

a. Racism didn't lead to slavery, but, rather, slavery led racism.
b. Slavery brought benefits to slaves.
c. Skin color has almost always been the underlying reason for slavery.
d. In most past societies, the superior people enslaved the inferior people.

7. Sociologist W. E. B. Du Bois, the first African American to get a Ph.D. from Harvard, made this statement

a. Slavery was evil, but out of it arose a nation of proud Negroes who will change the world.
b. Because we Negroes are the descendants of Africans, we all should move back to Africa, our mother continent.
c. We owe a debt of gratitude to the white slave owners.
d. Gradually the entire white South became an armed camp to keep Negroes in slavery and to kill the black rebel.

8. The Indian government abolished the caste system in 1949. Today, caste in India

a. no longer exists
b. is practically nonexistent
c. is part of the ceremonies people follow at births, marriages, and deaths
d. has become so popular that it has spread to Tibet and Sri Lanka

9. After slavery ended in the United States, it was replaced by a stratification system which marked everyone from birth and in which all whites, even if they were poor and uneducated, considered themselves to have a higher status than all African Americans. This is an example of

a. a racial caste
b. a transitory system
c. slavery
d. social class

10. A primary difference between social class and stratification systems based on slavery and caste is that social class

a. originated long before the other two
b. is superior
c. is a response to changing social conditions while the other two are not
d. is more fluid, allowing movement up and down the class ladder

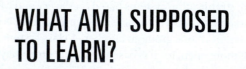

UNIT 7.2

Three Worlds of Stratification

WHAT AM I SUPPOSED TO LEARN?

After you have read this unit, you should be able to

1 Specify broad differences between the Most Industrialized, Industrializing, and Least Industrialized Nations.

2 Explain what the new global superclass is.

Just as the people within a nation are stratified, so are the world's nations. About twenty years ago, a simple model was used to depict global stratification: The term *First World* referred to the industrialized capitalist nations, *Second World* designated the communist (or socialist) countries, and *Third World* was assigned to any nation that did not fit into the first two categories. The breakup of the Soviet Union in 1989 made these terms outdated. An alternative classification that some now use—developed, developing, and undeveloped—makes it sound as though the "developed" nations are mature, while the "undeveloped" nations are somehow retarded.

To resolve this problem, I use more neutral, descriptive terms: *Most Industrialized, Industrializing,* and *Least Industrialized* nations. We can measure industrialization with no judgment implied as to whether a nation's industrialization represents "development," ranks it "first," or is even desirable at all.

The intention is to depict on a global level the three primary dimensions of social stratification: property, power, and prestige. The Most Industrialized Nations have much greater property (wealth), power (they usually get their way in international relations), and prestige (they are looked up to as world leaders).

The social map on pages 194–195 gives you a snapshot of the relative wealth and poverty of the world's nations. Let's take an overview of these three worlds of stratification.

The Most Industrialized Nations

The Most Industrialized Nations are the United States and Canada in North America; Great Britain, France, Germany, Switzerland, and the other industrialized countries of western Europe; Japan in Asia; and Australia and New Zealand in the area of the world known as Oceania. Although there are variations in their economic systems, these nations are capitalistic. As Table 7.2 shows, although these nations have only 16 percent of the world's people, they possess 31 percent of the earth's land. Their wealth is so enormous that even their poor live better and longer lives than do the average citizens of the Least Industrialized Nations.

The Industrializing Nations

The Industrializing Nations include most of the nations of the former Soviet Union and its former satellites in eastern Europe. As Table 7.2 shows, these nations account for 20 percent of the earth's land and 16 percent of its people.

There is no exact dividing point between these three "worlds," making it difficult to classify some nations. This is especially the case with the Industrializing Nations. Exactly how much industrialization must a nation have to be in this category? Although soft, these categories do point to essential differences among nations. Most people who live in the Industrializing Nations have much lower incomes and standards of living than do those who live in the Most Industrialized Nations. The majority, however, are better off than those who live in the Least Industrialized Nations. They have more access to electricity, indoor plumbing,

TABLE 7.2	Distribution of the World's Land and Population	
	Land	Population
Most Industrialized Nations	31%	16%
Industrializing Nations	20%	16%
Least Industrialized Nations	49%	68%

Sources: By the author. Computed from Kurian 1990, 1991, 1992.

automobiles, telephones, and even food than those in the Least Industrialized Nations, but less of these things than people who live in the Most Industrialized Nations.

Keep in mind that these are comparisons of nations. Just as in the United States, every nation, no matter its classification, has wealthy and poor people.

The Least Industrialized Nations

In the Least Industrialized Nations, most people live on small farms or in villages, have large families, and barely survive. These nations account for 68 percent of the world's people but only 49 percent of the earth's land.

Poverty plagues these nations to such an extent that some families actually *live* in city dumps. This is hard to believe, but look at the photos on the next two pages, which I took in Phnom Penh, the capital of Cambodia. Although wealthy nations have their pockets of poverty, *most* people in the Least Industrialized Nations are poor. *Most* have no running water, indoor plumbing, or access to trained teachers or doctors. And it is in these nations that most of the world's population growth is occurring, placing even greater burdens on their limited resources and causing them to fall farther behind each year. We'll explore this further in Chapter 13.

I'm sure that you must have played "What if?" games as a child. Pause for a moment and do this now in *Making It Personal*.

IF YOU WANT TO LEARN MORE about how price tags are being put on children's heads,

Read more from the author: Open Season: Children as Prey in **mysoclab**

MAKING IT PERSONAL

What If?

How do you think your life would be different if you had been born and reared as an average person in a Least Industrialized Nation? How would your picture of the world be different from what it is today? What would be your view of what you can expect out of life? How else do you think this would have affected your life?

From this photo of the Ginza shopping district in Tokyo, you can see why Japan is counted as a Most Industrialized Nation.

CAMBODIA

THE DUMP PEOPLE: WORKING AND LIVING AND PLAYING IN THE CITY DUMP OF PHNOM PENH, CAMBODIA

I went to Cambodia to inspect orphanages, to see how well the children are being cared for. While in Phnom Penh, Cambodia's capital, I was told about people who live in the city dump. Live there? I could hardly believe my ears. I knew that people made their living by picking scraps from the city dump, but I didn't know they actually lived among the garbage. This I had to see for myself.

I did. And there I found a highly developed social organization—an intricate support system. Because words are inadequate to depict the abject poverty of the Least Industrialized Nations, these photos can provide more insight into these people's lives than anything I could say.

The children who live in the dump also play there. These children are riding bicycles on a "road," a packed, leveled area of garbage that leads to their huts. The huge stacks in the background are piled trash. Note the ubiquitous Nike.

After the garbage arrives by truck, people stream around it, struggling to be the first to discover something of value. To sift through the trash, the workers use metal picks, like the one this child is holding. Note that children work alongside the adults.

This is a typical sight—family and friends working together. The trash, which is constantly burning, contains harmful chemicals. Why do people work under such conditions? Because they have few options. It is either this or starve.

The people live at the edge of the dump, in homemade huts (visible in the background). This woman, who was on her way home after a day's work, put down her sack of salvaged items to let me take her picture.

One of my many surprises was to find food stands in the dump. Although this one primarily offers drinks and snacks, others serve more substantial food. One even has chairs for its customers.

I was surprised to learn that ice is delivered to the dump. This woman is using a hand grinder to crush ice for drinks for her customers. The customers, of course, are other people who also live in the dump.

At the day's end, the workers wash at the community pump. This hand pump serves all their water needs—drinking, washing, and cooking. There is no indoor plumbing. The weeds in the background serve that purpose. Can you imagine drinking water that comes from below this garbage dump?

Not too many visitors to Phnom Penh tell a cab driver to take them to the city dump. The cabbie looked a bit perplexed, but he did as I asked. Two cabs are shown here because my friends insisted on accompanying me. I know they were curious themselves, but my friends had also discovered that the destinations I want to visit are usually not in the tourist guides, and they wanted to protect me.

Cutting across the Three Worlds: The New Global Superclass

No matter which world of stratification the wealthy and powerful come from, their interests run together. Today's technology, which has brought faster communications and travel than the world has ever seen, has produced growing interconnections among the world's wealthiest people. The result is a new **global superclass**. In this group, wealth and power are more concentrated than ever in the history of the world. This superclass has only about 6,000 members. *The richest 1,000 of this superclass have more wealth than the entire 2½ billion poorest people on this planet* (Rothkopf 2008:37). Almost all members of the superclass are white, and except as wives and daughters, few women take an active part in it. The sociological significance of this development is this: The growing interconnections and interrelated decision-making give this small group increasing power over world affairs.

Look at Figure 7.1. There is nothing in the history of the world to compare with this concentration of wealth.

> **global superclass** a small group of people who make the major decisions that affect the rest of the world

---

FIGURE 7.1 **The Distribution of the Earth's Wealth**

The wealthiest 10 percent of adults worldwide...

10%
90%

...own 85 percent of the earth's wealth

85%
15%

The wealthiest 1 percent of adults worldwide...

1%
99%

...own 40 percent of the earth's wealth

40%
60%

Source: By the author. Based on Rofthkopf 2008:37.

UNIT 7.2 // TESTING MYSELF
DID I LEARN IT? ANSWERS ARE AT THE END OF THE CHAPTER

1. Just as the people within a nation are stratified, so are the world's nations. Before the breakup of the Soviet empire in 1989, this model was used to refer to the three major groups of nations
   a. First World, Second World, and Third World
   b. Developed Nations, Developing Nations, and Undeveloped Nations
   c. Most Industrialized, Industrializing, and Least Industrialized Nations
   d. Wealthy Nations, Average Nations, and Poor Nations

2. Today, this model is often used instead of First, Second, and Third Worlds (but it is not used in this text)
   a. Most Powerful Nations, Nations of Average Power, and Least Powerful Nations
   b. Developed Nations, Developing Nations, and Undeveloped Nations
   c. Most Industrialized, Industrializing, and Least Industrialized Nations
   d. Wealthy Nations, Average Nations, and Poor Nations

3. The author has chosen this model to refer to the three worlds of global stratification
   a. First World, Second World, and Third World
   b. Developed Nations, Developing Nations, and Undeveloped Nations
   c. Most Industrialized, Industrializing, and Least Industrialized Nations
   d. Wealthy Nations, Average Nations, and Poor Nations

4. The United States and Canada in North America; Great Britain, France, Germany, and Switzerland in western Europe; Japan in Asia; and Australia and New Zealand in Oceania are part of this group of nations
   a. Most Industrialized   **b.** Industrializing
   c. Least Industrialized   **d.** Second World

5. Most of the nations of the former Soviet Union and its former satellites in eastern Europe are part of this group of nations
   a. Most Industrialized   **b.** Industrializing
   c. Least Industrialized   **d.** Second World

6. Most of the world's people live in this group of nations
   a. Most Industrialized   **b.** Industrializing
   c. Least Industrialized   **d.** Second World

7. With today's fast communications and travel, a new social class has emerged, one that unites its members around the globe. This group is small, with only about 6,000 members. The richest 1,000 of this class have more wealth than the 2½ billion poorest people on this planet. This group is called the
   a. new rich   **b.** old, powerful super-rich
   c. new global superclass   **d.** global controllers

UNIT 7.3

How Did the World's Nations Become Stratified?

Three distinct worlds! How did the globe become stratified like this? The commonsense answer is that the poorer nations have fewer resources than the richer nations. As with many common-sense answers, however, this one, too, falls short. Many of the Industrializing and Least Industrialized Nations are rich in natural resources, while Japan, a Most Industrialized Nation, has few.

Which of three theories of global stratification—colonialism, world system theory, or the culture of poverty—do you think best explains the livng conditions you see in this photo from Nairobi, Kenya?

WHAT AM I SUPPOSED TO LEARN?

After you have read this unit, you should be able to

1 Contrast three theories of global stratification: colonialism, world system theory, and the culture of poverty.

2 Explain why most sociologists reject the culture of poverty explanation.

Let's look at three theories that explain how global stratification came about.

Colonialism

The first theory, **colonialism**, stresses that the countries that industrialized first got the jump on the rest of the world. Industrialization, which began in Great Britain about 1750, spread throughout western Europe. Plowing some of their profits into powerful armaments and fast ships, these countries invaded weaker nations, making colonies out of them (Harrison 1993). After subduing these weaker nations, the more powerful countries left behind a controlling force in order to exploit the nations' labor and natural resources. At one point, there was even a free-for-all among the industrialized European countries as they rushed to divide up an entire continent. As they sliced Africa into pieces, even tiny Belgium got into the act and acquired the Congo, which was *seventy-five* times larger than itself.

The purpose of colonialism was to establish *economic colonies*—to exploit the nation's people and resources for the benefit of the "mother" country. The more powerful European countries would plant their national flags in a colony and send their representatives to run the government. In contrast, the United States usually chose to plant corporate flags in a colony and let those corporations dominate the territory's government. This was a common practice in Central and South America. There were exceptions, such as the conquest of the Philippines, which President McKinley said was motivated by the desire "to educate the Filipinos, and uplift and civilize and Christianize them" (Krugman 2002).

Historical events like this seem like—well, old stuff from history—but they continue to have consequences for the present, affecting your life. Look at *Making It Personal* on the next page.

colonialism the process by which one nation takes over another nation, usually for the purpose of exploiting its labor and natural resources

MAKING IT PERSONAL
Gasoline and Lines on a Map

Have you ever wondered why the national boundaries of Libya, Saudi Arabia, Kuwait, and other countries are so straight? Maybe not, but take a look at the map of Africa in Figure 7.2 on page 195. Many boundaries look like someone took a ruler and drew lines across a map. And this is just what happened. Britain and France had both invaded this area, and instead of quarreling about the spoils of their conquests, they decided there was enough to go around for both of them. They divided up North Africa and parts of the Middle East, creating new states without regard for tribes or cultures (Kifner 1999). They even chose the men who would head their newly created countries.

How significant is this for your life today? Actions of the past often come back to haunt us, and this one does continuously. This legacy of European conquests is a background factor in much of today's racial–ethnic and tribal violence in these areas: By arbitrarily incorporating groups with no history of national identity into the same political boundaries, these Most Industrialized Nations laid the groundwork for future revolutions and wars.

And your life? For starters, think about how your life has been affected—from the price you pay for a gallon of gasoline to the interruption of your life, or the lives of friends and relatives, due to fighting wars in this area of the world.

World System Theory

Let's look at the second explanation of how global stratification came about. Immanuel Wallerstein (1974, 1979, 1990) developed **world system theory**, saying that industrialization led to the world being divided into four groups of nations. The first group consists of the *core nations*, the countries that industrialized first (Britain, France, Holland, and later Germany), which grew rich and powerful. The second group he called the *semiperiphery*. The economies of these nations, located around the Mediterranean, stagnated because they grew dependent on trade with the core nations. The economies of the third group, the *periphery*, or fringe nations, developed even less. These are the eastern European countries that sold cash crops to the core nations. The fourth group of nations includes most of Africa and Asia. Called the *external area*, these nations were left out of the development of capitalism. The current expansion of capitalism has changed this situation, and eastern Europe and Asia are developing capitalism.

The **globalization of capitalism**—the adoption of capitalism around the world—has created extensive ties among the world's nations. Production and trade are now so interconnected that events around the globe affect us all. Sometimes this is immediate, as happens when a civil war disrupts the flow of oil, or—perish the thought—as would be the case if terrorists managed to get their hands on nuclear or biological weapons. At other times, the effects are like a slow ripple, as when a government adopts some policy that gradually reduces its ability to compete in world markets. All of today's societies, then, no matter where they are located, are part of a *world system*.

> **world system theory** economic and political connections that tie the world's countries together

> **globalization of capitalism** capitalism (investing to make profits within a rational system) becoming the globe's dominant economic system

IF YOU WANT TO LEARN MORE about how the globalization of capitalism is connecting Mexico and the United States,

📖 **Read** more from the author: Thinking Critically—When Globalization Comes Home: Maquiladoras South of the Border in **mysoclab**

Culture of Poverty

The third explanation of global stratification is quite unlike the other two. Economist John Kenneth Galbraith (1979) claimed that the cultures of the Least Industrialized Nations hold them back. He argued that some nations are crippled by a **culture of poverty**, a way of life that perpetuates poverty from one generation to the next. He explained it this way: Most of the world's poor people are farmers who live on little plots of land. They barely produce enough food to survive. To experiment with new farming techniques is to court disaster, for failure would lead to hunger and death.

> **culture of poverty** the assumption that the values and behaviors of the poor make them fundamentally different from other people, that these factors are largely responsible for their poverty, and that parents perpetuate poverty across generations by passing these characteristics to their children

Their religion also encourages them to avoid change, for it teaches fatalism: the belief that an individual's position in life is God's will. For example, in India, the Dalit are taught that they must have done very bad things in a previous life to suffer so. They are supposed to submit to their humiliation and suffering—and in the next life maybe they'll come back in a more desirable state.

Evaluating the Theories

Most sociologists prefer colonialism and world system theory. To them, an explanation based on a culture of poverty places blame on the victim—the poor nations themselves. It points to characteristics of the poor nations, rather than to international political arrangements that benefit the Most Industrialized Nations at the expense of the poor nations. But even taken together, these theories yield only part of the picture. None of these theories, for example, would have led anyone to expect that after World War II, Japan would become an economic powerhouse: Japan had a religion that stressed fatalism, two of its major cities had been destroyed by atomic bombs, and it had been stripped of its colonies.

Each theory, then, yields but a partial explanation, and the grand theorist who will put the many pieces of this puzzle together has yet to appear.

UNIT 7.3 // TESTING MYSELF
DID I LEARN IT? ANSWERS ARE AT THE END OF THE CHAPTER

1. This explanation of how the world's nations became stratified stresses that the countries that industrialized first got the jump on the rest of the world. They used their new wealth to produce armaments and exploit weaker nations
   a. amount of resources   b. culture of poverty
   c. world system theory   d. colonialism

2. This explanation of how the world's nations became stratified stresses that industrialization led to the world being divided into four groups of nations: the core, semiperiphery, periphery, and external areas, with the core exploiting the resources of the others
   a. amount of resources   b. culture of poverty
   c. world system theory   d. colonialism

3. This explanation of how the world's nations became stratified stresses that the characteristics of some nations (such as poverty, a religion of fatalism) hold them back
   a. amount of resources   b. culture of poverty
   c. world system theory   d. colonialism

4. Most sociologists prefer colonialism and world system theory to the culture of poverty because
   a. the culture of poverty places blame on the poor nations themselves
   b. the culture of poverty does not consider the role of religion
   c. colonialism took place first
   d. world system theory places the emphasis on global development

UNIT 7.4
Why Is Social Stratification Universal?

WHAT AM I SUPPOSED TO LEARN?

After you have read this unit, you should be able to

1 Compare the functionalist and conflict views of social stratification.

Colonialism, world system theory, and a culture of poverty offer keys to understand *how* global stratification came about. But regardless of how it occurred, *why* are all societies stratified? Are there basic sociological processes involved? Let's first consider the explanation proposed by functionalists, which has aroused much controversy in sociology, and then explanations proposed by conflict theorists.

The Functionalist View: Motivating Qualified People

Functionalists take this basic position: The patterns of society that are not functional disappear, while those that are functional

FIGURE 7.2 Global Stratification: Income[1] of the World's Nations

The Most Industrialized Nations

	Nation	Income per Person
1	Luxembourg	$84,700
2	Singapore	$59,900
3	Norway	$53,300
4	Hong Kong	$49,300
5	United States	$48,100
6	Switzerland	$43,400
7	Netherlands	$42,300
8	Austria	$41,700
9	Australia	$40,800
10	Sweden	$40,600
11	Canada	$40,300
12	Denmark	$40,200
13	Finland	$38,300
14	Iceland	$38,000
15	Germany	$37,900
16	Taiwan	$37,900
17	Belgium	$37,600
18	United Kingdom	$35,900
19	France	$35,000
20	Japan	$34,300
21	Korea, South	$31,700
22	Israel	$31,000
23	Italy	$30,100
24	Slovenia	$29,100
25	New Zealand	$27,900
26	Czech Republic	$25,900

The Industrializing Nations

	Nation	Income per Person
27	Ireland	$39,500
28	Greenland	$36,500
29	Spain	$30,600
30	Greece	$27,600
31	Slovakia	$23,400
32	Portugal	$23,200
33	Estonia	$20,200
34	Poland	$20,100
35	Hungary	$19,600
36	Lithuania	$18,700
37	Croatia	$18,300
38	Argentina	$17,400
39	Russia	$16,700
40	Chile	$16,100
41	Gabon	$16,000
42	Malaysia	$15,600
43	Latvia	$15,400
44	Mexico	$15,100
45	Mauritius	$15,000
46	Turkey	$14,600
47	Libya	$14,100
48	Bulgaria	$13,500
49	Venezuela	$12,400
50	Romania	$12,300
51	Brazil	$11,600
52	Costa Rica	$11,500
53	South Africa	$11,000
54	Cuba	$9,900
55	China	$8,400

The Least Industrialized Nations

	Nation	Income per Person		Nation	Income per Person
56	Botswana[2]	$16,300	72	Ecuador	$8,300
57	Lebanon	$15,600	73	Bosnia	$8,200
58	Uruguay	$15,400	74	Albania	$7,800
59	Belarus	$14,900	75	El Salvador	$7,600
60	Panama	$13,600	76	Guyana	$7,500
61	Kazakhstan	$13,000	77	Turkmenistan	$7,500
62	Macedonia	$10,400	78	Namibia	$7,300
63	Azerbaijan	$10,200	79	Algeria	$7,200
64	Colombia	$10,100	80	Ukraine	$7,200
65	Peru	$10,000	81	Egypt	$6,500
66	Thailand	$9,700	82	Bhutan	$6,000
67	Suriname	$9,500	83	Angola	$5,900
68	Tunisia	$9,500	84	Jordan	$5,900
69	Dominican Republic	$9,300	85	Sri Lanka	$5,600
70	Jamaica	$9,000	86	Paraguay	$5,500
71	Belize	$8,300	87	Armenia	$5,400
			88	Georgia	$5,400

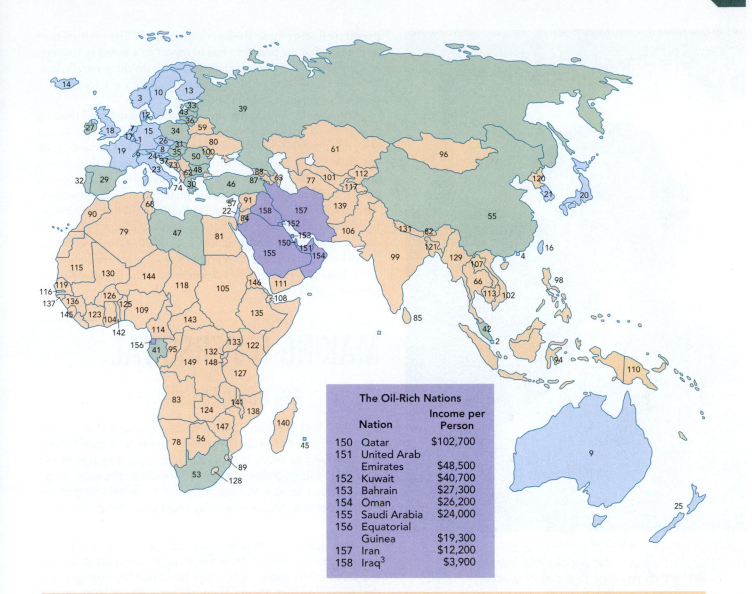

The Oil-Rich Nations

	Nation	Income per Person
150	Qatar	$102,700
151	United Arab Emirates	$48,500
152	Kuwait	$40,700
153	Bahrain	$27,300
154	Oman	$26,200
155	Saudi Arabia	$24,000
156	Equatorial Guinea	$19,300
157	Iran	$12,200
158	Iraq[3]	$3,900

The Least Industrialized Nations

	Nation	Income per Person		Nation	Income per Person		Nation	Income per Person		Nation	Income per Person
89	Swaziland	$5,200	106	Pakistan	$2,800	122	Kenya	$1,700	139	Afghanistan	$1,000
90	Morocco	$5,100	107	Laos	$2,700	123	Cote d'Ivoire	$1,600	140	Madagascar	$1,000
91	Syria	$5,100	108	Djibouti	$2,600	124	Zambia	$1,600	141	Malawi	$900
92	Guatemala	$5,000	109	Nigeria	$2,600	125	Benin	$1,500	142	Togo	$900
93	Bolivia	$4,800	110	Papua-New Guinea	$2,500	126	Burkina Faso	$1,500	143	Central African Republic	$800
94	Indonesia	$4,700	111	Yemen	$2,500	127	Tanzania	$1,500	144	Niger	$800
95	Congo	$4,600	112	Krygyzstan	$2,400	128	Lesotho	$1,400	145	Sierra Leone	$800
96	Mongolia	$4,500	113	Cambodia	$2,300	129	Burma	$1,300	146	Eritrea	$700
97	Honduras	$4,300	114	Cameroon	$2,300	130	Mali	$1,300	147	Zimbabwe	$500
98	Philippines	$4,100	115	Mauritania	$2,200	131	Nepal	$1,300	148	Burundi	$400
99	India	$3,700	116	Gambia	$2,100	132	Rwanda	$1,300	149	Congo, Dem. Rep.	$300
100	Moldova	$3,400	117	Tajikistan	$2,000	133	Uganda	$1,300			
101	Uzbekistan	$3,300	118	Chad	$1,900	134	Haiti	$1,200			
102	Vietnam	$3,300	119	Senegal	$1,900	135	Ethiopia	$1,100			
103	Nicaragua	$3,200	120	Korea, North	$1,800	136	Guinea	$1,100			
104	Ghana	$3,100	121	Bangladesh	$1,700	137	Guinea-Bissau	$1,100			
105	Sudan	$3,000				138	Mozambique	$1,100			

[1]Income is a country's purchasing power parity based on a country's Gross Domestic Product, where the value of a country's goods and services are valued at prices prevailing in the United States. Totals vary from year to year and should be considered as approximations.
[2]Botswana's income is based largely on its diamond mines.
[3]Iraq's oil wealth has been disrupted by war.
Source: By the author. Based on CIA World Factbook 2012.

To ask why there is social stratification is to ask why this pilot is paid more than most people. Which of the theories presented here do you think provides the best explanation? Why?

continue. Because social inequality is universal, present all around the world, it must help societies survive. But how?

DAVIS AND MOORE'S EXPLANATION

Two functionalists, Kingsley Davis and Wilbert Moore (1945, 1953), wrestled with this question. They concluded that stratification of society is inevitable because:

1. Some of a society's positions are more important than others.

2. The more important positions must be filled by the more qualified people.

3. To motivate the more qualified people to fill these positions, they carry greater rewards.

To flesh out this functionalist argument, consider students and college presidents. You know that the position of college president is more important than that of student. You also know the reason, that the president's decisions affect a large number of

people, including many students and teachers. The position is so important that the president has to report to a board of trustees. It is the same with generals and privates. With the general's decisions able to determine life and death, generals are accountable to superior generals and to the country's leaders.

With their high pressure—heavy responsibilities and needing to account to higher-ups—why do people accept these positions? Why don't they just take less demanding jobs? You can anticipate the answer that Davis and Moore gave: The more demanding and accountable positions offer greater rewards—more property, power, and prestige. To get highly qualified people to compete with one another, some positions offer $2 million a year, country club membership, a chauffeured limousine, and a private jet and pilot. For less demanding positions, a $30,000 salary without fringe benefits is enough to get hundreds of people to compete.

In *Making It Personal,* let's consider how the functionalist argument applies to you.

MAKING IT PERSONAL
Why Are You Going to College?

I know that there are probably many reasons that you are in college, but it is likely that one of them is to qualify for a higher-paying or more prestigious job. If so, this hits at the heart of the functionalist position on social stratification. To get more capable people to endure the rigorous training that the more important jobs require, they must offer more salary and benefits.

Or you can put it this way: If you can get the same pay with a high school diploma, why suffer through the costs and many tests and term papers that college requires? My best guess is that you agree with the functionalist position—at least on this point.

TUMIN'S CRITIQUE OF DAVIS AND MOORE

Davis and Moore were not attempting to justify social inequality; rather, they were just trying to explain *why* social stratification is universal. Nevertheless, their view makes many sociologists uncomfortable, for they see it as coming close to justifying the inequalities in society. Its bottom line seems to be: The people who contribute more to society are paid more, while those who contribute less are paid less.

Melvin Tumin (1953) pointed out what he saw as major flaws in the functionalist position. Here are three of his arguments.

First, how do we know that the positions that offer the higher rewards are more important? A heart surgeon, for example, saves lives and earns much more than a garbage collector, but this doesn't mean that garbage collectors are less important to society. By helping to prevent contagious diseases, garbage collectors save more lives than heart surgeons do. We need independent methods of measuring importance, and we don't have them.

Second, if stratification worked as Davis and Moore described, society would be a **meritocracy**; that is, positions would be awarded on the basis of merit, of ability. But life is not like this. For example, the best predictor of who goes to college is not ability but income: The more a family earns, the more likely their children will go to college (Bailey and Dynarski 2011). This doesn't show merit, but money—a form of inequality. In short, people's positions in society are based on many factors other than merit.

Third, if social stratification is so functional, it ought to benefit almost everyone. Yet social stratification is *dysfunctional* for many. Think of the people who could have made valuable contributions to society had they not been born in slums, dropped out of school, and taken menial jobs to help support their families. Then there are the many who, born female, are assigned "women's work," ensuring that they do not maximize their mental abilities.

Before we turn to the conflict perspective, look at Table 7.3 below. This table compares the functionalist and conflict views on how society's resources are divided.

TABLE 7.3   **Views of Social Stratification: The Distribution of Society's Resources**

	Who Receive the Most Resources?	Who Receive the Least Resources?
The Functionalist View	Those who perform the most important functions (the more capable and more industrious)	Those who perform the least important functions (the less capable and less industrious)
The Conflict View	Those who occupy the most powerful positions	Those who occupy the least powerful positions

Source: By the author.

The Conflict Perspective: Class Conflict and Scarce Resources

The functionalist argument infuriates conflict theorists. They don't just criticize its details, but rather, they go for the throat and attack its basic premise. Conflict, not function, they stress, is at the center of social stratification. Let's look at their major arguments.

MARX'S ARGUMENT

If he were alive to hear the functionalists, Karl Marx would be enraged. From his point of view, the people in

meritocracy a form of social stratification in which all positions are awarded on the basis of merit

power are not there because of superior traits, as the functionalists would have us believe. This view is an ideology that the elite use to justify their positions of privilege. They use this argument to seduce the oppressed into believing that their welfare depends on keeping quiet and following authorities. What is the engine of human history, Marx asked? It is class conflict, he replied to his own question. Human history consists of two parts. One part is small groups of people using their power to control society's resources to benefit themselves. They also use those resources to oppress those beneath them. The other part is the oppressed groups that are trying to overcome that domination.

Marx predicted that the workers will rip off this capitalist ideology. They will gain *class consciousness*, the realization that they are all workers united by a common oppressor. They will then fight to take over the means of production. The struggle may be covert at first, taking such forms as work slowdowns and industrial sabotage, but ultimately resistance will break out into the open. The revolution will not be easy, for the capitalists control the police and the military. They also control the educational system, where they implant *false class consciousness* in the minds of the workers' children.

CURRENT APPLICATIONS OF CONFLICT THEORY

Marx focused on overarching historic events—the accumulation of capital and power and the struggle between workers and owners. This is true of some of today's conflict sociologists, as well. Analyzing global stratification and global capitalism, they look at power relations among nations, how national elites control workers, and how power shifts as capital is shuffled among nations (Jessop 2010).

In contrast, other conflict sociologists examine conflict wherever it is found, not just as it relates to owners and workers. They examine how groups *within the same class* compete with one another for a larger slice of the pie (Collins 1999; King et al. 2010). Even within the same industry, for example, union will fight against union for higher salaries, shorter hours, and more power. A special focus is conflict between racial–ethnic groups as they compete for jobs, education, and housing—or whatever

A focus of conflict sociologists is relations of workers with their employers.

other benefits society has to offer. Another focus is relations between women and men, which conflict theorists say are best understood as conflict over power—over who controls society's resources. Unlike functionalists, conflict theorists say that just beneath the surface of what may appear to be a tranquil society lies conflict that is barely held in check.

◉ **Watch** the **Video**
The Basics: Social Class in the U.S. in **mysoclab**

UNIT 7.4 // TESTING MYSELF
DID I LEARN IT? ANSWERS ARE AT THE END OF THE CHAPTER

1. This is the basic position of functionalists
   a. Life is constantly changing so any functional analysis must be temporary.
   b. Social stratification benefits mainly those in power.
   c. Once we determine what works in a society, we have the key to explaining social stratification.
   d. The patterns of society that are not functional disappear, while those that are functional continue.

2. It is inevitable that society will be stratified, said functionalists Kingsley Davis and Wilbert Moore, because
   a. There are always people who will take advantage of others.
   b. Some people work hard, but others slack off.
   c. The more important positions must offer greater rewards to get more qualified people to take the greater responsibilities.
   d. The engine of human history is class struggle.

3. Sociologist Melvin Tumin criticized the functionalist argument. One of his points was that if stratification worked the way functionalists say, then
   a. Everyone would fail.
   b. Society would be a meritocracy.
   c. The United States would be more powerful than it is.
   d. There would be little or no unemployment.

4. Another criticism that Tumin made of the functionalist argument is that
   a. We have no independent measures of the importance of society's positions.
   b. Garbage collectors are more important than college teachers.
   c. Physicians are overpaid.
   d. The government should not set a minimum wage.

5. Conflict theorists disagree with the functionalist position. Karl Marx argued that social stratification comes about because
   a. the important positions have to be filled by the most qualified people
   b. capitalists interfere with the natural solutions to class conflict
   c. there aren't enough resources to be divided equally
   d. one group gains control over society's resources

6. Marx said that human history consists of two parts. One part is small groups of people using their power to control society's resources to benefit themselves and to oppress those beneath them. The other part is
   a. trying to motivate the more qualified people to take the more demanding positions
   b. providing more educational opportunities for the poor
   c. the oppressed groups trying to overcome their domination
   d. recognizing ability and accomplishments on a wide level in society, not just in the smaller groups in power

7. Wilbert, a greeter at Wal-Mart, was trying to form a union. Afraid of getting fired, he talked to his fellow workers privately, one by one. He told them that they were all oppressed, that the managers represented the interest of the company's owners. Only by uniting could they overcome their oppression. Conflict theorists would say that Wilbert was trying to
   a. get a raise
   b. raise class consciousness
   c. raise morale
   d. make trouble

8. Not all of today's conflict theorists focus on the class struggle between owners and workers. They
   a. also analyze conflict among workers
   b. try to find functions wherever they are
   c. try to look to the future, rather than relying on past situations
   d. are doing research on how men are coming to have less power than women

UNIT 7.5
What Determines Social Class?

WHAT AM I SUPPOSED TO LEARN?

After you have read this unit, you should be able to

1 Compare the views of Marx and Weber on social class.

I've stressed the significance of social class throughout this book, and from time to time we've looked at how it affects your life. Now we'll explore social class in greater detail. Let's begin by looking at a disagreement that arose in the early days of sociology between Marx and Weber.

Karl Marx: The Means of Production

A couple hundred years ago, masses of farmers were displaced as agricultural society began to give way to an industrial one. Fleeing to cities, they competed for the few available jobs. Paid only a pittance for their labor, they wore rags, went hungry, and slept under bridges and in shacks. In contrast, the factory owners made fortunes, built mansions, hired servants, and lived in the lap of luxury. Seeing this great disparity between owners and workers, Karl Marx (1818–1883) concluded that social class depends on a single factor: people's relationship to the **means of production**—the tools, factories, land, and investment capital used to produce wealth (Marx 1844/1964; Marx and Engels 1848/1967).

When you and I talk about differences among people, we often refer to their clothing, speech, manners, education, and income, even the car they drive. These are superficial differences, said Marx. They camouflage the only distinction that counts. There are just two classes of people: the **bourgeoisie** (*capitalists*), those who own the means of production, and the **proletariat** (*workers*), those who work for the owners. This distinction—people's relationship to the means of production—determines their social class.

Marx did recognize other groups: farmers and peasants; a *lumpenproletariat* (people living on the margin of society, such as beggars, vagrants, and criminals); and a middle group of self-employed professionals. Marx did not consider these groups to be social classes, however, for they lack **class consciousness**—a shared identity based on their position in the means of production. In other words, they did not perceive themselves as exploited workers whose plight could be resolved by collective action. Marx thought of these groups as insignificant in the future he foresaw—a workers' revolution that would overthrow capitalism.

As capitalism continues to develop, the capitalists will grow even wealthier, Marx said. When workers come to realize that capitalists are the source of their oppression, they will unite and throw off the chains of their oppressors. In a bloody revolution, they will seize the means of production and usher in a classless society. When this happens, no longer will the few grow rich at the

How do these textile workers in Fanchang, China, fit in Marx's analysis of social stratification?

expense of the many. What holds back the workers' unity and their revolution is **false class consciousness**, workers mistakenly thinking of themselves as capitalists. Workers with a few dollars in the bank often see themselves as investors, or as capitalists who are about to launch a successful business.

The only distinction worth mentioning, then, is whether a person is an owner or a worker. This decides everything else, Marx stressed, for property determines people's lifestyles, establishes their relationships with one another, and even shapes their ideas.

Max Weber: Property, Power, and Prestige

Max Weber (1864–1920) was an outspoken critic of Marx. He agreed that property is important, but said that it was only part of the picture. *Social class*, he said, has three components: property, power, and prestige (Gerth and Mills 1958; Weber 1922/1978). Some call these the three P's of social class. (Although Weber used the terms *class, power,* and *status,* some sociologists find *property, power,* and *prestige* to be clearer terms. To make them even clearer, you may want to substitute *wealth* for *property.*)

Property (or wealth), said Weber, is certainly significant in determining a person's standing in society. On that point he agreed with Marx. But, added Weber, ownership is not the only significant aspect of property. For example, some powerful people, such as managers of corporations, *control* the means of production even though they do not *own* them. If managers can control the means of production for their own benefit—awarding themselves huge

means of production the tools, factories, land, and investment capital used to produce wealth

bourgeoisie Marx's term for capitalists, those who own the means of production

proletariat Marx's term for the exploited class, the mass of workers who do not own the means of production

class consciousness Marx's term for awareness of a common identity based on one's position in the means of production

false class consciousness Marx's term to refer to workers identifying with the interests of capitalists

bonuses and magnificent perks—it makes no practical difference that they do not own the property that they use so generously for their own benefit.

Power, the second element of social class, is the ability to control others, even over their objections. Weber agreed with Marx that property is a major source of power, but he added that it is not the only source. For example, prestige can be turned into power. Two actors provide well-known examples: Arnold Schwarzenegger who became governor of California, and Ronald Reagan who was elected governor of California and then president of the United States.

Prestige, the third element in Weber's analysis, is often derived from property and power, for people tend to admire the wealthy and powerful. Prestige, however, can be based on other factors. Olympic gold medalists, for example, might not own property or be powerful, yet they have high prestige. Some are even able to exchange their prestige for property—such as those who are paid a small fortune for endorsing a certain brand of sportswear or for claiming that they start their day with "the breakfast of champions." In other words, property and prestige are not one-way streets: Although property can bring prestige, prestige can also bring property. Figure 7.3 shows how property, power, and prestige are interrelated.

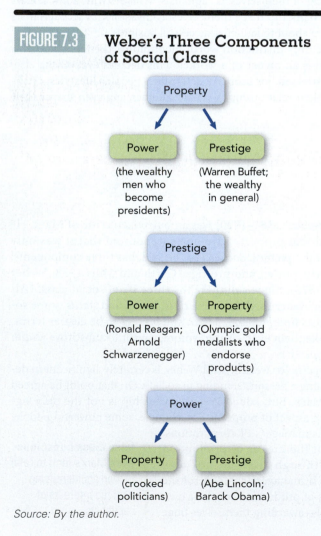

FIGURE 7.3 **Weber's Three Components of Social Class**

Property
→ Power
(the wealthy men who become presidents)
→ Prestige
(Warren Buffet; the wealthy in general)

Prestige
→ Power
(Ronald Reagan; Arnold Schwarzenegger)
→ Property
(Olympic gold medalists who endorse products)

Power
→ Property
(crooked politicians)
→ Prestige
(Abe Lincoln; Barack Obama)

Source: By the author.

1. This is Karl Marx's term for tools, factories, land, and investment capital
   a. investments
   b. the means of investments
   c. the fabric of society
   d. the means of production

2. According to Marx, the only basis for determining social class is someone's position in
   a. the means of production
   b. property, power, and prestige
   c. whatever distinguishes one group from another
   d. the social class scale

3. According to Marx's analysis, the two social classes are the bourgeoisie (capitalists), those who own the means of production, and the workers, those who work for the owners. His term for workers was
   a. unknown except for a select few in his conspiracy against the capitalists
   b. always changing
   c. proletariat
   d. changed by his followers from workers to working people

4. Marx did not consider farmers, peasants, beggars, and self-employed professionals as social classes because he said they lacked
   a. the money to buy class
   b. class consciousness
   c. the education that class requires
   d. a strong enough desire to get ahead

5. At work in the nail factory, Buzz was talking to a friend about his plans. He said he had saved $5,000 and was gong to rent a small place on Baltimore Avenue, where he was going to open a little sandwich shop. If it was successful, as he was sure it would be, he was going to open a larger one. He might even franchise his idea. He said he could imagine "Buzz's Sandwiches" all across the country. In Marx's terms, Buzz is illustrating
   a. false class consciousness
   b. an inadequate business plan
   c. undercapitalization
   d. megalomania

6. Max Weber agreed with Marx that property is important, but he said that it was only part of the picture. Social class, Weber said, is made up of these three elements
   a. the means of production, capitalists, and the bourgeoisie
   b. money, education, ad property
   c. property, power, and prestige
   d. reputation, prestige, and property

7. Ronald Reagan, an actor, was elected governor of California and then to two terms as president of the United States. His election illustrates this reason that Weber disagreed with Marx

   a. power can be exchanged for prestige
   b. prestige can be exchanged for power
   c. immigrants can succeed in the United States
   d. property can be exchanged for prestige

UNIT 7.6

Social Class in the United States

WHAT AM I SUPPOSED TO LEARN?

After you have read this unit, you should be able to

1 Distinguish between wealth and income, and state how property and income are distributed in the United States.

2 Explain the term power elite and the controversy that surrounds this term.

3 Summarize the bases for occupational prestige and how status inconsistency works.

If you ask most Americans about their country's social classes, you are likely to get a blank look. If you press the matter, you are likely to get an answer something like: "Well, there's the poor and the rich—and then there's you and me. We aren't either poor or rich." This is just about as far as most Americans' consciousness of social class goes. Let's try to flesh out this idea.

Sociologists have no clear-cut, agreed-on definition of *social class* (Crompton 2010). Few agree with Marx that there are only two social classes, those who own the means of production and those who do not. They feel that this lumps too many people together. Teenage "order takers" at McDonald's who work for

$15,000 a year are lumped together with that company's executives who make $500,000 a year—because they both are workers at McDonald's, not owners. Most sociologists use the components Weber identified and define **social class** as a large group of people who rank closely to one another in property, power, and prestige. They look at how these three elements separate people into different lifestyles, give them different chances in life, and provide them with distinct ways of looking at the self and the world.

Let's see how sociologists measure these three components of social class.

Property

Property comes in many forms, such as buildings, land, animals, machinery, cars, stocks, bonds, businesses, furniture, jewelry, and bank accounts. When you add up the value of someone's property and subtract that person's debts, you have what sociologists call **wealth**. (Others call this *net worth*.) This term can be misleading, as some of us have little wealth—especially most college students. Nevertheless, if your total comes to $10, then that is your wealth. (Obviously, *wealth* as a sociological term does not mean wealthy.)

DISTINGUISHING BETWEEN WEALTH AND INCOME

Wealth and income are sometimes confused, but they are not the same. Where *wealth* is a person's net worth, **income** is a flow of money. Income

> **social class** according to Weber, a large group of people who rank close to one another in property, power, and prestige; according to Marx, one of two groups: capitalists who own the means of production or workers who sell their labor
>
> **wealth** the total value of everything someone owns, minus the debts
>
> **income** money received, usually from a job, business, or assets

What do sociologists mean when they say that this man can have much wealth but little income?

also has many sources: The most common is wages or a business, but other sources are rent, interest, or royalties, even alimony, gambling, or an allowance. Some people have much wealth and little income. For example, a farmer may own a lot of land (a form of wealth), but bad weather and low prices for crops can cause the income to dry up. Others have much income and little wealth. An executive with a $250,000 annual salary may be debt-ridden. Below the surface prosperity—the exotic vacations, country club membership, private schools for the children, sports cars, and an elegant home—the credit cards may be maxed out, the sports cars in danger of being repossessed, and the mortgage payments "past due." Typically, however, wealth and income go together.

DISTRIBUTION OF PROPERTY

Who owns the property in the United States? One answer, of course, is "everyone." Although this statement has some merit, it overlooks how the nation's property is divided among "everyone."

Overall, Americans are worth a hefty sum, about $49 trillion (*Statistical Abstract* 2012:Table 723). This includes all real estate, stocks, bonds, and business assets in the entire country. This wealth is highly concentrated. From Figure 7.4, you can see that 70 percent, is owned by only *10 percent* of the nation's families. As you can also see from this figure, 1 percent of Americans own one-third of all U.S. assets.

DISTRIBUTION OF INCOME

How is income distributed in the United States? Economist Paul Samuelson (Samuelson and Nordhaus 2005) put it this way: "If we made an income pyramid out of a child's blocks, with each layer portraying $500 of income, the peak would be far higher than Mount Everest, but most people would be within a few feet of the ground."

I became intrigued by this statement and decided to illustrate it. Look at Figure 7.5. You can see that if each block were

FIGURE 7.4 **Distribution of the Property of Americans**

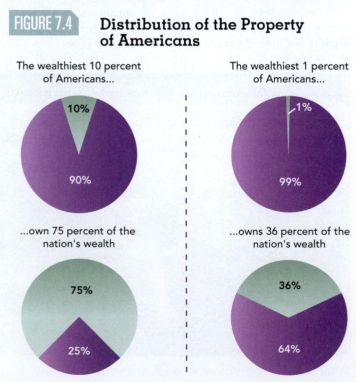

The wealthiest 10 percent of Americans...

10%
90%

...own 75 percent of the nation's wealth

75%
25%

The wealthiest 1 percent of Americans...

1%
99%

...owns 36 percent of the nation's wealth

36%
64%

Source: By the author. Based on Allegretto 2011:Table 2.

FIGURE 7.5 **Distribution of the Income of Americans**

Some U.S. families have incomes that exceed the height of Mt. Everest, 29,028 feet

Average U.S. family income $60,000 or 15 feet

Average U.S. individual income $41,000 or 10 feet

If a 1½-inch child's block equals $500 of income, the average individual's annual income of $41,000 would represent a height of 10 feet, and the average family's annual income of $60,000 would represent a height of 15 feet. The income of some families, in contrast, would represent a height greater than that of Mt. Everest.

Source: By the author. Based on Statistical Abstract of the United States 2012: Tables 681, 696.

1½ inches tall, the typical American would be just *10 feet off the ground,* for the average per capita income in the United States is about $41,000 per year. (This average income includes every American, even children.) The typical family climbs a little higher, for most families have more than one worker. Their average of $60,000 a year takes them to just 15 feet off the ground.

That some Americans enjoy the peaks of Mount Everest while most—despite their efforts—don't even make it to a tree top at the bottom of the mountain presents a striking image of income inequality in the United States.

Another picture emerges if we divide the entire U.S. population into five equal groups. As Figure 7.6 shows, the top fifth of the population receives *half* (50.3 percent) of all the income in the entire country. In contrast, the bottom fifth receives only 3.4 percent of the nation's income.

Two other features of Figure 7.6 are outstanding. First, notice how little change there has been in the distribution of income through the years. Second, look at how income inequality decreased from 1935 to 1970. *Since 1970, the richest 20 percent of U.S. families have grown richer, while the poorest 20 percent have grown poorer.* Despite numerous government antipoverty programs, the poorest 20 percent of Americans receive *less* of the nation's income today than they did decades ago. The richest 20 percent, in contrast, are receiving more, almost as much as they did in 1935.

The chief executive officers (CEOs) of the nation's largest corporations are especially affluent. The *Wall Street Journal* surveyed the 350 largest U.S. companies with the largest revenues to find out what they paid their CEOs (Lublin 2011). Their median compensation (including salaries, bonuses, and stock options) came to $9,300,000 a year. (*Median* means that half received more than this amount, and half less.)

These CEOs' average income is *225 times* higher than the average pay of U.S. workers (*Statistical Abstract* 2012:Table 681). This does *not* include their income from interest, dividends, or rents. Nor does it include the value of company-paid limousines and chauffeurs, airplanes and pilots, and private boxes at the symphony and sporting events. To really see the disparity, consider this:

> *Let's suppose that you started working the year Jesus was born and that you worked full time every year from then until now. Let's also assume that you earned today's average pay of $41,000 every year for all those years. You would still have to work another 100 years or so to earn the amount received by the highest-paid executive listed in Table 7.4.*

Imagine how you could live with an income like this. And this is precisely the point. Beyond these cold numbers lies a dynamic reality that profoundly affects people's lives. The difference in wealth between those at the top and those at the bottom of the U.S. class structure means that people experience vastly different lifestyles. For example,

> *a colleague of mine who was teaching at an exclusive Eastern university piqued his students' curiosity when he lectured on poverty in Latin America. That weekend, one of the students borrowed his parents' corporate jet and pilot, and in class on Monday, he and his friends related their personal observations on poverty in Latin America.*

TABLE 7.4 **The Five Highest-Paid CEOs**

Executive	Company	Compensation
Philippe Dauman	Viacom	$84,300,000
Lawrence Ellison	Oracle	$68,600,000
Leslie Moonves	CBS	$53,900,000
Martin Franklin	Jarden	$45,200,000
Michael White	DirectTV	$32,600,000

Note: Compensation includes salary, bonuses, and stock options.
Source: Lublin 2011.

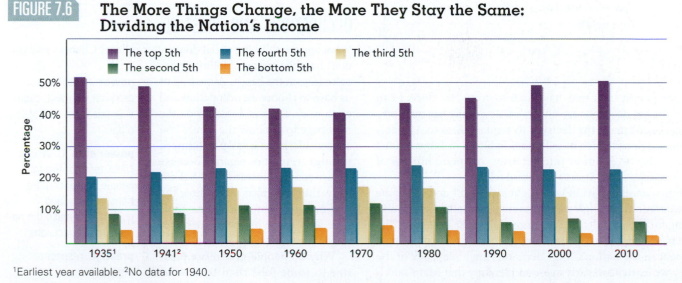

FIGURE 7.6 **The More Things Change, the More They Stay the Same: Dividing the Nation's Income**

¹Earliest year available. ²No data for 1940.

Source: By the author. Based on *Statisitcal Abstract of the United States* 1960:Table 417; 1970:Table 489; 2012:Table 694.

Sociologists find it easy to make contact with the poor. We know less about the lives of the CEOs and the power elite. They don't stand in lines like this, ready to talk to researchers.

Few of us could ever say, "Mom and Dad, I've got to do a report for my soc class, so I need to borrow the jet—and the pilot—to run down to South America for the weekend." What a lifestyle! Contrast this with Americans at the low end of the income ladder who lack the funds to travel even to a neighboring town for the weekend. For parents in poverty, choices may revolve around whether to spend the little they have at the laundromat or on milk for the baby. The elderly might have to choose between paying the rent or purchasing the medicines they need. In short, divisions of wealth represent not "mere" numbers, but choices that make vital differences in people's lives.

> **IF YOU WANT TO LEARN MORE** about how the super-rich live,
>
> **Read** more from the author: How the Super-Rich Live in **mysoclab**

Power

Like many people, you may have said to yourself, "Sure, I can vote, but the big decisions are always made despite my opinions. Certainly *I* don't make the decision to send soldiers to Afghanistan or Iraq. *I* don't launch missiles into Pakistan or Libya. *I* don't decide to raise taxes, lower interest rates, or spend billions of dollars to bail out Wall Street's fools and felons."

And then another part of you might say, "But I do participate in these decisions through my representatives in Congress, and by voting for the president." True enough—as far as it goes. The trouble is, it just doesn't go far enough. Such views of being a participant in the nation's "big" decisions are a playback of the ideology we learn at an early age—an ideology that Marx said is promoted by the elites to both legitimate and perpetuate their power. Sociologists Daniel Hellinger and Dennis Judd (1991) call this the "democratic facade" that conceals the real source of power in the United States.

THE POWER ELITE

In Chapter 1, I mentioned that in the 1950s, sociologist C. Wright Mills (1956) pointed out that **power**—the ability to get your way despite resistance—was concentrated in the hands of a few. Mills met heavy criticism, for his analysis contradicted the dominant ideology of equality. This ideology is still dominant, and many don't like Mills' term **power elite**, which he coined to refer to those who make the big decisions in U.S. society.

Mills and others have stressed how wealth and power coalesce in a group of people who view themselves as an elite. They belong to the same private clubs, vacation at the same exclusive resorts, and even hire the same bands for their daughters' debutante balls (Domhoff 1999a, 2006, 2010). This elite wields extraordinary power in U.S. society, so much so that *most* U.S. presidents have come from this group—millionaire white men from families with "old money" (Baltzell and Schneiderman 1988).

Continuing in the tradition of Mills, sociologist William Domhoff (2006, 2010) argues that this group is so powerful that the U.S. government makes no major decision without its approval. He analyzed how this elite works behind the scenes with elected officials to determine both foreign and domestic policy—from setting Social Security taxes to imposing trade tariffs. Although Mills' and Domhoff's conclusions are controversial—and alarming—they certainly follow logically from the principle that wealth brings power, and extreme wealth brings extreme power.

> **Read** the **Document** "The Power Elite" by C. Wright Mills in **mysoclab**

Prestige

OCCUPATIONS AND PRESTIGE

What are you thinking about doing after college? Chances are, you don't have the option of lolling under palm trees at the beach. Almost all of us have to choose an occupation and go to work. Look at Table 7.5 on the next page to see how the career you are considering stacks up in terms of **prestige** (respect or regard). Because we are moving toward a global society, this table also shows how the rankings given by Americans compare with those of the residents of sixty other countries.

Why do people give more prestige to some jobs than to others?

power the ability to carry out your will, even over the resistance of others

power elite C. Wright Mills' term for the top people in U.S. corporations, military, and politics who make the nation's major decisions

prestige respect or regard

TABLE 7.5 · Occupational Prestige: How the United States Compares with 60 Countries

Occupation	United States	Average of Sixty Countries
Physician	86	78
Supreme Court judge	85	82
College president	81	86
Astronaut	80	80
Lawyer	75	73
College professor	74	78
Airline pilot	73	66
Architect	73	72
Biologist	73	69
Dentist	72	70
Civil engineer	69	70
Clergy	69	60
Psychologist	69	66
Pharmacist	68	64
High school teacher	66	64
Registered nurse	66	54
Professional athlete	65	48
Electrical engineer	64	65
Author	63	62
Banker	63	67
Veterinarian	62	61
Police officer	61	40
Sociologist	61	67
Journalist	60	55
Classical musician	59	56
Actor or actress	58	52
Chiropractor	57	62
Athletic coach	53	50
Social worker	52	56
Electrician	51	44
Undertaker	49	34
Jazz musician	48	38
Real estate agent	48	49
Mail carrier	47	33
Secretary	46	53
Plumber	45	34
Carpenter	43	37
Farmer	40	47
Barber	36	30
Store sales clerk	36	34
Truck driver	30	33
Cab driver	28	28
Garbage collector	28	13
Waiter or waitress	28	23
Bartender	25	23
Lives on public aid	25	16
Bill collector	24	27
Factory worker	24	29
Janitor	22	21
Shoe shiner	17	12
Street sweeper	11	13

Note. For five occupations not located in the 1994 source, the 1991 ratings were used: Supreme Court judge, astronaut, athletic coach, lives on public aid, and street sweeper.

Sources: Treiman 1977:Appendices A and D; Nakao and Treas 1990, 1994:Appendix D.

Look carefully at Table 7.5 to see what features the jobs with the highest and lowest prestige have. You will notice that the jobs at the top share four features:

1. They pay more.

2. They require more education.

3. They require more abstract thought.

4. They offer more independence (less supervision).

Now look at the bottom jobs on this list. You can see that people give less prestige to jobs with the opposite characteristics: These jobs pay lttle, require less education, involve more physical labor, and are closely supervised. In short, the professions and the white-collar jobs are at the top of the list, the blue-collar jobs at the bottom.

One of the more interesting aspects of these rankings is how consistent they are across countries and over time. For example, people in every country rank college professors higher than nurses, nurses higher than social workers, and social workers higher than janitors. Similarly, the occupations that were ranked high twenty-five years ago still rank high today—and likely will rank high in the years to come.

Status Inconsistency

Most people have a similar rank on all three dimensions of social class—property, power, and prestige. This is referred to as **status consistency**. Some people, however, have a mixture of high and low ranks. This condition, called **status inconsistency**, leads to some interesting situations.

Sociologist Gerhard Lenski (1954, 1966) analyzed how people try to maximize their **status**, their position in a social group. People

status consistency
ranking high or low on all three dimensions of social class

status inconsistency
ranking high on some dimensions of social class and low on others; also called *status discrepancy*

What is the source of Mark Zuckerberg's prestige? How is this related to social stratification?

who rank high on one dimension of social class but lower on others want others to judge them on the basis of their highest status. Those others, however, are trying to maximize their own position, so they often respond according to these people's lowest ranking.

Back in 1952, sociologist Ray Gold did classic research on apartment-house janitors in Chicago. After they unionized, they made more money than some of the tenants whose garbage they carried out. Residents became upset when they saw the "garbage carriers" driving more expensive cars than they did. Some attempted to "put the janitor in his place" by making "snotty" remarks to him. For their part, the janitors took delight in knowing "dirty" secrets about the tenants, gleaned from their garbage.

People who are status inconsistent, then, are likely to confront one frustrating situation after another (Heames et al. 2006). They claim the higher status, but are handed the lower one. This situation, said Lenski (1954), tends to make people more politically radical. An example is college professors. Their prestige is very high, as you can see in Table 7.5, but their incomes are relatively low. Hardly anyone in the United States is more educated, and yet college professors don't even come close to the top of the income pyramid. In line with Lenski's prediction, the politics of most college professors are left of center. This hypothesis may also hold true among academic departments; that is, the higher a department's average pay, the more conservative are the members' politics. Teachers in departments of business and medicine, for example, are among the most highly paid in the university—and they also are the most politically conservative.

> **status** the position that someone occupies in a social group

---

IF YOU WANT TO LEARN MORE about how hitting it big in the lottery leads to status inconsisteny,

📖 **Read** more from the author: The Big Win: Life After the Lottery in **mysoclab**

👁 **Watch** the **Video**
Social Class in the U.S. in **mysoclab**

UNIT 7.6 // TESTING MYSELF
DID I LEARN IT? ANSWERS ARE AT THE END OF THE CHAPTER

1. Constantina, who just worked out her financial statement, was shaking her head. Her 500 acres of land carry a heavy mortgage, and the region is undergoing a drought. When she totalled the value of her land and machinery minus what she owes, her net worth came to just $329. Sociologists call this $329 her
   - **a.** ideological facade
   - **b.** shrinking assets
   - **c.** debt
   - **d.** wealth

2. When William read this chapter, he was shocked. (OK, William gets shocked easily.) He could hardly believe how unequally property is distributed in the United States, that 10 percent of the nation's families own this percentage of the nation's wealth
   - **a.** 40
   - **b.** 50
   - **c.** 60
   - **d.** 70

3. If we make an income pyramid out of a child's blocks, with each layer portraying $500 of income, the peak would be far higher than Mount Everest. A few families would be there, but the average U.S. family would be
   - **a.** half way to the top of Mount Everest
   - **b.** one fourth the way up Mount Everest
   - **c.** one tenth the way up Mount Everest
   - **d.** 10 feet off the ground

4. Income inequality decreased from 1935 to 1970. Since 1970, income inequality has
   - **a.** continued to decrease
   - **b.** increased
   - **c.** evened out
   - **d.** disappeared

5. In support of C. Wright Mills' analysis that a power elite makes the big decisions, some sociologists point out that that most U.S. presidents have come from this group
   - **a.** CEOs
   - **b.** lawyers
   - **c.** millionaire white men from families with "old money"
   - **d.** entrepreneurs

6. Researchers have studied the characteristics of jobs that give high prestige. Which of these is not one of these characteristics? The jobs
   - **a.** pay more
   - **b.** have been in the family a long time
   - **c.** require more education
   - **d.** require more abstract thought

7. After Helmuth earned his M.D. degree at Harvard, he began a successful private practice and became an investor in innovative medical products. His net worth is now in the millions. Helmuth is
   - **a.** status consistent
   - **b.** status inconsistent
   - **c.** status conscious
   - **d.** trying to climb the social class ladder

8. Unfortunately, Helmuth was also fraudulently billing Medicare. It was front page news when he was arrested and brought to trial. Found guilty, he was given probation. He can keep his medical license, but he must provide 1,000 hours of community service, giving free medical care for the poor. Helmuth is
   - **a.** status consistent
   - **b.** status inconsistent
   - **c.** status conscious
   - **d.** barely holding onto the social class ladder

9. From Ray Gold's study of apartment-house janitors who unionized and made more money than some of their tenants, we can conclude this: Because people are trying to maximize their own position, when they interact with people who are status inconsistent, they may respond according to

   a. how they feel at the moment
   b. the cues they receive during the particular interaction
   c. these people's lowest ranking
   d. these people's highest ranking

10. Individuals who are status inconsistent confront one frustrating situation after another. They claim the higher status, but are handed the lower one. This situation tends to make status-inconsistent people

   a. intolerant of others
   b. politically radical
   c. depressed
   d. fearful of interacting with others

UNIT 7.7

A Social Class Model

A mere one-half percent of Americans owns over a quarter of the entire nations' wealth. Very few minorities are numbered among this 0.5 percent. An exception is Oprah Winfrey, who has had an ultra-successful career in entertainment and investing. Worth $2.7 billion, she is the 215th richest person in the United States. Winfrey has given millions of dollars to help minority children.

WHAT AM I SUPPOSED TO LEARN?

After you have read this unit, you should be able to

1   Summarize the six-tier social class model developed by Kahl and Gilbert.

I mentioned that sociologists have no standard, agreed-on model of the social classes of the United States. In Figure 7.7 on the next page, you can see a model developed by sociologists Joseph Kahl and Dennis Gilbert (Gilbert and Kahl 1998; Gilbert 2008). Think of this model as a ladder. We'll discuss it by starting with the highest rung and moving downward. In line with Weber, on each lower rung you find less property (wealth), less power, and less prestige. Note that in this model education is also a primary measure of class.

The Capitalist Class

Sitting on the top rung of the class ladder is a powerful, wealthy, prestigious elite that consists of just 1 percent of the U.S. population. As you saw in Figure 7.4 on page 202, this capitalist class is so wealthy that it owns one–third of all the nation's assets. *This tiny 1 percent is worth more than the entire bottom 90 percent of the country* (Beeghley 2008).

Power and influence cling to this small elite. They have direct access to top politicians, and their decisions open or close job opportunities for millions of people. They even help shape the views of the nation: They own our major media and entertainment outlets—newspapers, magazines, radio and television stations, and sports franchises. They also control the boards of directors of our most influential colleges and universities. The

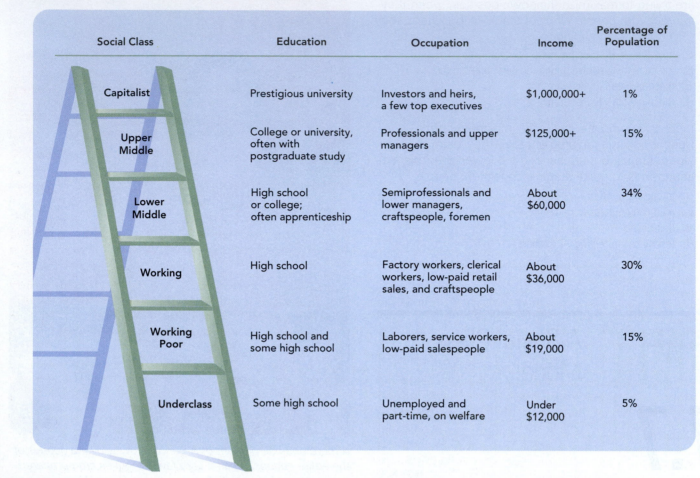

FIGURE 7.7 **The U.S. Social Class Ladder**

Social Class	Education	Occupation	Income	Percentage of Population
Capitalist	Prestigious university	Investors and heirs, a few top executives	$1,000,000+	1%
Upper Middle	College or university, often with postgraduate study	Professionals and upper managers	$125,000+	15%
Lower Middle	High school or college; often apprenticeship	Semiprofessionals and lower managers, craftspeople, foremen	About $60,000	34%
Working	High school	Factory workers, clerical workers, low-paid retail sales, and craftspeople	About $36,000	30%
Working Poor	High school and some high school	Laborers, service workers, low-paid salespeople	About $19,000	15%
Underclass	Some high school	Unemployed and part-time, on welfare	Under $12,000	5%

Source: By the author. Based on Gilbert and Kahl 1998 and Gilbert 2008; income estimates are modified from Duff 1995.

super-rich perpetuate themselves in privilege by passing on their assets and social networks to their children.

The capitalist class can be divided into "old" and "new" money. The longer that wealth has been in a family, the more it adds to the family's prestige. The children of "old" money seldom mingle with "common" folk. Instead, they attend private schools where they learn views of life that support their privileged position. They don't work for wages; instead, many study business or become lawyers so that they can manage the family fortune. These old-money capitalists (also called "blue-bloods") use their extensive political connections to protect their economic empires (Sklair 2001; Domhoff 1990, 2006, 2010).

At the lower end of the capitalist class are the *nouveau riche* (a fancy term for the new rich). Although those with "new money" have made fortunes in business, the stock market, inventions, entertainment, or sports, they are outsiders to the upper class. They have not attended the "right" schools, and they don't share the social networks that come with old money. Not

blue-bloods, they aren't trusted to have the right orientations to life. Even their "taste" in clothing and status symbols is suspect (Fabrikant 2005). Donald Trump, whose money is "new," is not listed in the *Social Register,* the "White Pages" of the blue-bloods that lists the most prestigious and wealthy one-tenth of 1 percent of the U.S. population. Trump says he "doesn't care," but he reveals his true feelings by adding that his heirs will be in it (Kaufman 1996). He could be right. The children of the new-moneyed can ascend to the top part of the capitalist class—but they have to go to the right schools *and* marry old money.

Many in the capitalist class are philanthropic. They establish foundations and give huge sums to "causes." Their motives vary. Some feel guilty because they have so much while others have so little. Others seek prestige, acclaim, or fame. Still others feel a responsibility—even a sense of fate or purpose—to use their money for doing good. Bill Gates, who has given more money to the poor and to medical research than has anyone in history, seems to fall into this latter category.

The Upper Middle Class

Of all the classes, the upper middle class is the one most shaped by education. Almost all members of this class have at least a bachelor's degree, and many have postgraduate degrees in business, management, law, or medicine. These people manage the corporations owned by the capitalist class, run their own businesses, or pursue professions. As Gilbert and Kahl (1998) say,

> [These positions] may not grant prestige equivalent to a title of nobility in the Germany of Max Weber, but they certainly represent the sign of having "made it" in contemporary America… . Their income is sufficient to purchase houses and cars and travel that become public symbols for all to see and for advertisers to portray with words and pictures that connote success, glamour, and high style.

Consequently, parents and teachers push children to prepare for upper-middle-class jobs. About 15 percent of the population belong to this class.

The Lower Middle Class

About 34 percent of the population are members of the lower middle class. In their jobs, they follow orders given by members of the upper middle class. With their technical and lower-level management positions, they can afford a mainstream lifestyle, although they struggle to maintain it. Many anticipate being able to move up the social class ladder. Feelings of insecurity are common, however, with the threat of inflation, recession, and job insecurity bringing a nagging sense that they might fall down the class ladder (Kefalas 2007).

The distinctions between the lower middle class and the working class on the next rung below are more blurred than those between other classes. In general, however, members of the lower middle class work at jobs that have slightly more prestige, and their incomes are generally higher.

The Working Class

About 30 percent of the U.S. population belong to this class of relatively unskilled blue-collar and white-collar workers. Compared with the lower middle class, they have less education and lower incomes. Their jobs are also less secure, more routine, and more closely supervised. One of their greatest fears is that of being laid off during a recession. With only a high school diploma, the average member of the working class has little hope of climbing up the class ladder. With job changes usually bringing "more of the same," most concentrate on getting ahead by achieving seniority on the job rather than by changing their type of work. They tend to think of themselves as having "real jobs" and regard the "suits" above them as paper pushers who have no practical experience (Morris and Grimes 2005).

The Working Poor

Members of this class, about 15 percent of the population, work at unskilled, low-paying, temporary and seasonal jobs, such as sharecropping, migrant farm work, housecleaning, and day labor. Most are high school dropouts. Many are functionally illiterate, finding it difficult to read even the want ads. They are not likely to vote (Beeghley 2008), for they believe that no matter what party is elected to office, their situation won't change.

Although they work full time, millions of the working poor depend on food stamps and donations from local food pantries to survive on their meager incomes (O'Hare 1996b). How can they work full time and still be poor? Suppose that you are married and have a baby 3 months old and another child 4 years old. Your spouse stays home to care for them, so earning the income is up to you. But as a high-school dropout, all you can get is a minimum wage job. At $7.25 an hour, you earn $290 for 40 hours. In a year, this comes to $15,080—before deductions. Your nagging fear— and recurring nightmare—is of ending up "on the streets."

The Underclass

On the lowest rung, and with next to no chance of climbing anywhere, is the **underclass**. Concentrated in the inner city, this group has little or no connection with the job market. Those who are

underclass a group of people for whom poverty persists year after year and across generations

In the social class divisions summarized here, where do you think these two workers fit?

employed—and some are—do menial, low-paying, temporary work. Welfare, if it is available, along with food stamps and food pantries, is their main support. Most members of other classes consider these people the "ne'er-do-wells" of society. Filled with despair, life is the toughest in this class. About 5 percent of the population fall into this class.

The homeless are part of the underclass. Their presence on our city streets bothers passersby from the more privileged social classes—which includes just about everyone. "What are those obnoxious, dirty, foul-smelling people doing here, cluttering up my city?" appears to be a common response. Some people react with sympathy and a desire to do something. But what? Almost all of us shrug our shoulders and look the other way, despairing of a solution and somewhat intimidated by their presence.

The homeless are the "fallout" of our postindustrial economy. In another era, they would have had plenty of work. They would have tended horses, worked on farms, dug ditches, shoveled coal, and run the factory looms. Some would have explored and settled the West. The prospect of gold would have lured others to California, Alaska, and Australia. Today, however, with no frontiers to settle, factory jobs scarce, and farms that are becoming technological marvels, we have little need for unskilled labor.

✳ Explore the Concept
Collars and Colors in
America in **mysoclab**

UNIT 7.7 // TESTING MYSELF
DID I LEARN IT? ANSWERS ARE AT THE END OF THE CHAPTER

1. At the top of the U.S. social class is a tiny 1 percent that is worth more than the entire bottom 90 percent of the country. In the social class model developed by Kahl and Gilbert, this group is called the
   a. decision makers
   b. oppressors
   c. controllers
   d. capitalist class

2. Almost all members of the capitalist class graduate from college, where many have studied law or business. After college, they tend to
   a. try for the highest-paying job they can find
   b. manage the family fortune
   c. take a year off and travel around Europe or Asia
   d. withdraw from public life

3. The capitalist class is divided into two groups, those with "old" and "new" money. Those with "old" money don't trust those with "new" money because those

with "new" money have not attended the "right" schools, and they don't
   a. participate in the same social networks
   b. read the same books or watch the same movies
   c. ask the right questions
   d. give to the same charities

4. The children of the new-moneyed can ascend into the top part of the capitalist class— if they go to the right schools and
   a. give to the right charities
   b. learn how to dress according to new standards
   c. send their children to old-money schools
   d. marry old money

5. This class is the most shaped by education.
   a. capitalist   b. upper middle
   c. lower middle   d. working

6. Members of this class follow orders given by members of the upper middle class. Filling the technical and lower-level management positions, they can afford mainstream lifestyles, but they feel a lot of insecurity.
   a. upper middle   b. lower middle
   c. working   d. working poor

7. One of the greatest fears of this class is being laid off. With only a high school diploma, the average member of this class has little hope of climbing up the class ladder. Job changes usually bring "more of the same," so most concentrate on getting ahead by achieving seniority on the job rather than by changing their type of work.
   a. upper middle   b. lower middle
   c. working   d. working poor

8. Although they work full time, millions from this class depend on food stamps and local food pantries to survive on their meager incomes.
   a. lower middle   b. working
   c. working poor   d. underclass

9. Members of this class are on the lowest rung of the social class ladder. Most members of other classes consider these people the "ne'er-do-wells" of society.
   a. lower middle   b. working
   c. working poor   d. underclass

10. The homeless are part of this class
    a. lower middle   b. working
    c. working poor   d. underclass

UNIT
Consequences of Social Class

7.8

The man was a C student throughout school. As a businessman, he ran Arbusto, an oil company, into the ground. An alcoholic until age forty, he was arrested for drunk driving. With this background, how did he become president of the United States?

Accompanying these personal factors was the power of social class. George W. Bush was born the grandson of a wealthy senator and the son of a businessman who himself became president of the United States after serving as a member of the House of Representatives, director of the CIA, and head of the Republican party. For high school, he went to Andover, an elite private prep school. He received his bachelor's degree from Yale and his MBA from Harvard. He was given $1 million to start his own business. When that business (Arbusto) failed, Bush fell softly, landing on the boards of several corporations. Taken care of even further, he was made the managing director of the Texas Rangers, a professional baseball team, and allowed to buy a share of the team for $600,000–which he sold for $15 million.

When it was time for him to get into politics, Bush's connections financed his run for governor of Texas and then for the presidency.

Does social class matter? And how! Think of each social class as a broad subculture with a distinct approach to life. Social class is so significant that it affects almost every aspect of our lives—our health, family life, education, religion, politics, and even our experiences with crime and the criminal justice system. Let's look at some of these effects.

Physical Health

If you want to get a sense of how social class affects health, take a ride on Washington's Metro system. Start in the blighted Southeast section of downtown D.C. For every mile you travel to where the wealthy live in Montgomery County in Maryland, life expectancy rises about a year and a half. By the time you get off, you will find a twenty-year gap between the poor blacks where you started your trip and the rich whites where you ended it. (Cohen 2004)

The principle is simple: As you go up the social class ladder, health improves. As you go down the ladder, health gets worse (Hout 2008). Age makes no difference. Infants born to the poor are more likely to die before their first birthday, and a larger percentage of poor people in their old age—whether 75 or 95—die each year than the wealthy elderly.

How can social class have such dramatic effects on health? A fundamental reason is that health care in the United States is not a citizen's right but a commodity for sale. People with good incomes or with good medical insurance are able to choose their doctors and pay for whatever treatment and medications the doctors prescribe. The poor, in contrast, don't have the money or insurance to afford this type of medical care. How much difference the new health reform will make is yet to be seen.

A second reason is lifestyles, which are shaped by social class. People in the lower classes are more likely to smoke, eat a lot of fats and sugars, be overweight, abuse drugs and alcohol, get less exercise, and practice unsafe scx (Chin et al. 2000; Dolnick 2010). This, to understate the matter, does not improve people's health.

There is a third reason, too. Life is hard on the poor. The persistent stresses they face cause their bodies to wear out faster (Geronimus et al. 2010). The rich find life better. They have

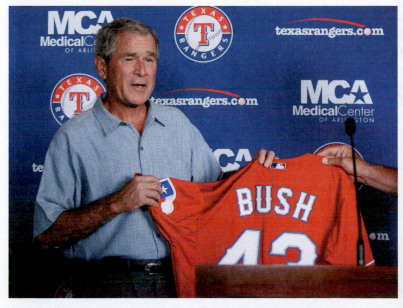

What difference has social class made in President George W. Bush's life? Why is he likely to live longer than most men his age?

fewer problems and more resources to deal with the ones they have. This gives them a sense of control over their lives, a source of both physical and mental health.

Mental Health

Sociological studies from as far back as the 1930s have found that the mental health of the lower classes is worse than that of the higher classes (Faris and Dunham 1939; Srole et al. 1978; Peltham 2009). Greater mental problems are part of the higher stress that comes with poverty. Compared with middle- and upper-class Americans, the poor have less job security and lower wages. They are more likely to divorce, to be the victims of crime, and to have more physical illnesses. Couple these conditions with bill collectors and the threat of eviction, and you can see how they can deal severe blows to people's emotional well-being.

People higher up the social class ladder experience stress in daily life, of course, but their stress is generally less, and their coping resources are greater. Not only can they afford vacations, psychiatrists, and counselors, but *their class position also gives them greater control over their lives, a key to good mental health.*

How social class underlies the care that people receive for their mental problems was driven home to me the first time I visited a homeless shelter.

> *When I entered the building, I saw a naked elderly man standing among the police. Looking confused, he was struggling to put on his clothing. The man had ripped the wires out of the homeless shelter's electrical box and then led the police on a merry chase as he had run from room to room.*
>
> *I asked the officers where they were going to take the man, and he replied, "To Malcolm Bliss" (the state mental hospital). When I commented, "I guess he'll be in there for a quite a while," they replied, "Probably just a day or two. We picked him up last week—he was crawling under cars stopped at a traffic light—and they let him out in two days."*
>
> *The police explained that a person must be a danger to others or to oneself to be admitted as a long-term patient. Visualizing this old man crawling under cars in traffic and the possibility of electrocuting himself by ripping out electrical wires with his bare hands, I marveled at the definition of "danger" that the hospital psychiatrists must be using.*

Stripped of its veil, the two-tier system of medical care is readily visible. The poor—such as this confused naked man—find it difficult to get into mental hospitals. If they are admitted, they are sent to the dreaded state hospitals. In contrast, private hospitals serve the wealthy and those who have good insurance. The rich are likely to be treated with "talk therapy" (forms of psychotherapy), the poor with "drug therapy" (tranquilizers to make them docile, sometimes known as "medicinal straitjackets").

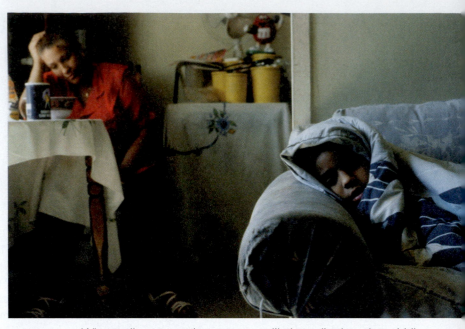

Why at all ages are the poor more likely to die than the middle class or the wealthy? This photo provides some insight into the answer.

Family Life

Social class also makes a significant difference in family life. In Chapter 11, we will look at how social class influences how we rear our children, but for now we'll just mention the influence of social class in our choice of spouse and our chances of getting divorced.

CHOICE OF HUSBAND OR WIFE

Members of the capitalist class place strong emphasis on family tradition. They stress the family's history, even a sense of purpose or destiny in life (Aldrich 1989). Children of this class learn that their choice of husband or wife affects not just them but the entire family, that it will have an impact on the "family line." These background expectations shrink the field of "eligible" marriage partners, making it narrower than it is for the children of any other social class. As a result, parents in this class play a strong role in their children's mate selection.

DIVORCE

The more difficult life of the lower social classes, especially the many tensions that come from insecure jobs and inadequate incomes, leads to higher marital friction and a greater likelihood of divorce. Consequently, children of the poor are more likely to grow up in broken homes.

Education

As you saw in Figure 7.7 on page 208, education increases as one goes up the social class ladder. It is not just the amount of

Why at all ages are the poor more likely to die than the middle class or the wealthy? This photo provides insight into the answer.

education that changes but also the type of education. Children of the capitalist class bypass public schools. They attend exclusive private prep schools such as Andover, Groton, and Phillips Exeter Academy, where they learn upper-class values and get the academic background they need for prestigious universities (Beeghley 2008; Stevens 2009). The bottom line is that they are trained to take a commanding role in society.

The exclusive prep schools are fed by a select group of prestigious preschools. Keenly aware that private schools can be a key to upward social mobility, some upper-middle-class parents make every effort to get their children into these preschools. Although some cost $37,000 a year, they have a waiting list (Anderson 2011). Not able to afford this kind of tuition, some parents hire tutors to train their 4-year olds in test-taking skills so they can get into public kindergartens for gifted students. They even hire experts to teach these preschoolers to look adults in the eye while they are being interviewed for these limited positions (Banjo 2010). You can see how such parental involvement and resources make it more likely that children from the more privileged classes go to college—and graduate.

Religion

One area of social life that we might think would not be affected by social class is religion. ("People are either religious, or they aren't. What does social class have to do with it?") Social class, however, is a significant sorter of people in all areas of social life, and religion is no exception. The social classes tend to cluster in different denominations. Episcopalians, for example, are more likely to attract the middle and upper classes, while Baptists and the Assemblies of God draw heavily from the lower classes. Patterns of worship also follow class lines: The lower classes are

attracted to more expressive worship services and louder music, while the middle and upper classes prefer more "subdued" worship. We'll explore religion and social class further in Chapter 12.

Politics

As I have stressed throughout this text, people perceive events from their own corner in life. Political views are no exception to this principle of symbolic interaction, and the rich and the poor walk different political paths. The higher that people are on the social class ladder, the more likely they are to vote for Republicans (Hout 2008). In contrast, most members of the working class believe that the government should intervene in the economy to provide jobs and to make citizens financially secure. They are more likely to vote for Democrats. Although the working class is more liberal on *economic* issues (policies that increase government spending), its members are more conservative on *social* issues (such as opposing abortion) (Houtman 1995; Hout 2008). People toward the bottom of the class structure are also less likely to be politically active—to campaign for candidates or even to vote (Gilbert 2003; Beeghley 2008).

Crime and Criminal Justice

If justice is supposed to be blind, it certainly is not when it comes to your chances of being arrested. On pages 161–162 of the chapter on Deviance and Social Control, we discussed how the social classes commit different types of crime. The white-collar crimes of the more privileged classes are more likely to be dealt with outside the criminal justice system, while the police and courts deal with the street crimes of the lower classes. One consequence of this class standard is that members of the lower classes are more likely to be in prison, on probation, or on parole. In addition, since those who commit street crimes tend to do so in or near their own neighborhoods, the lower classes are more likely to be robbed, burglarized, or murdered.

To relate social class to your own life, look at the little *Making It Personal* below.

MAKING IT PERSONAL
Your Social Class

As you read about how extensively social class affects people's lives, I'm sure you are wondering about your own life. Now is the time to make this explicit. Do a quick review of your life, asking, What difference has social class made in my life? How has it affected my life so that I am exactly where I am at this point in life? And, finally, ask yourself, How do I think that social class will continue to influence me as I go through life?

DID I LEARN IT? ANSWERS ARE AT THE END OF THE CHAPTER

1. As you go up the social class ladder, health improves. As you go down the ladder, health gets worse. Which of these was NOT given as a reason for the worse health of the poor?
   a. a two-tier system of medical care
   b. lifestyles of the poor
   c. life being harder for the poor
   d. more birth defects among the poor

2. Melinda's parents were concerned that she was seeing Tommy, who lives with his mom, who cleans houses for a living. To put distance between them, they sent Melinda on a summer study tour of the capitals of Europe. One of her classmates was Philippe from Paris, with whom she now talks almost daily. Melinda wonders why she was ever interested in Tommy. Melinda's parents are probably members of this class
   a. capitalist
   b. lower middle
   c. working
   d. working poor

3. Betty and John would love to get their daughter, Jayne, into Andover, but their chances are between slim and next to none. They know their chances will improve if they can get Jayne into a private preschool that feeds into Andover. They have just hired a tutor to teach Jayne, now 4 years old, to look the preschool interviewer in the eye when she talks to her. Betty and John are probably members of this class
   a. capitalist
   b. upper middle
   c. lower middle
   d. working

4. Dick and Jane are upset that the federal government did not extend the period of unemployment benefits and that some state governments are trying to limit union activities. Dick and Jane just went to the polls. It is likely that they voted for the
   a. Democrats
   b. Republicans
   c. Independents
   d. Greens

5. Jake was arrested for holding up a McDonald's. It is likely that Jake is a member of this class
   a. capitalist
   b. upper middle
   c. lower middle
   d. working poor

6. Gerald was arrested for securities fraud. He had faked the income in his company's annual report, whose stock is sold on the New York Stock Exchange. Gerald is probably a member of this class
   a. capitalist
   b. upper middle
   c. lower middle
   d. working poor

7. It has been several years since Myrna lost her job. After her husband left her and she lost her house, she has been bouncing from one homeless shelter to another. Myrna is probably a member of this class.
   a. lower middle
   b. working
   c. working poor
   d. underclass

UNIT 7.9

Social Mobility

WHAT AM I SUPPOSED TO LEARN?

After you have read this unit, you should be able to

1 Describe the three types of social mobility.

2 Explain where women fit in studies of social mobility.

No aspect of your life, then—from marriage to politics—goes untouched by social class. Because life is so much more satisfying in the more privileged classes, people strive to climb the social class ladder. What affects their chances of making it?

Three Types of Social Mobility

There are three basic types of social mobility: intergenerational, structural, and exchange. **Intergenerational mobility** refers to a change that occurs between generations—when grown-up children end up on a different rung of the social class ladder from the one occupied by their parents. If the daughter of someone who sells used cars for a living graduates from college and buys a Toyota dealership, she experiences

intergenerational mobility the change that family members make in social class from one generation to the next

upward social mobility. Conversely, if the son of the dealership's owner parties too much, drops out of college, and ends up selling cars, he experiences **downward social mobility**.

IF YOU WANT TO LEARN MORE about the social mobility of African Americans and the pain it brings,

Read more from the author: Social Class and the Upward Social Mobility of African Americans in **mysoclab**

We like to think that individual efforts are the reason people move up the class ladder—and their faults the reason they move down. In these examples, we can identify hard work, sacrifice, and ambition on the one hand, and lack of drive and substance abuse on the other. Although individual factors such as these do underlie social mobility, sociologists consider **structural mobility** to be the crucial factor—changes in society that cause large numbers of people to move up or down the class ladder.

To understand *structural mobility,* think about how changes in society (its *structure*) drive some people down the social class ladder and lift others up. When computers were invented, for example, new types of jobs appeared. Huge numbers of people attended workshops and took crash courses, switching from blue-collar to white-collar work. In contrast, others were thrown out of work as technology bypassed their jobs. Individual effort was certainly involved—for some seized the opportunity while others did not—but the underlying cause was a huge social change that transformed the *structure* of work. The same thing happens during depressions. Good jobs dry up, forcing millions of people downward on the class ladder. You can see how their changed status is due less to individual behavior than to *structural* changes in society.

The third type of social mobility, **exchange mobility**, occurs when large numbers of people move up and down the social class ladder, but, on balance, the proportions of the social classes remain about the same. Suppose that a million or so working-class people are trained in some new technology, and they move up the class ladder. Suppose also that because of a surge in imports, about a million skilled workers have to take lower-status jobs. Although millions of people change their social class, there is, in effect, an *exchange* among them. The net result more or less balances out, and the class system remains basically untouched.

upward social mobility movement up the social class ladder

downward social mobility movement down the social class ladder

structural mobility movement up or down the social class ladder that is due more to changes in the structure of society than to the actions of individuals

exchange mobility about the same number of people moving up and down the social class ladder, such that, on balance, the social class system shows little change

Why do we need both micro and macro approaches in sociology to explain women's increased social mobility?

Women in Studies of Social Mobility

About half of sons pass their fathers on the social class ladder, about one-third stay at the same level, and about one-sixth fall down the ladder (Blau and Duncan 1967; Featherman 1979).

"Only sons!" said feminists in response to this classic study on social mobility. "Do you think it is good science to ignore daughters? And why do you assign women the class of their husbands? Do you think that wives have no social class position of their own?" (Davis and Robinson 1988). The male sociologists who did research such as this one brushed off these objections, replying that there were too few women in the labor force to make a difference.

The sociologists simply hadn't caught up with the times. The gradual but steady increase of women working for pay had caught them unprepared. Although sociologists now include women in their research on social mobility, how to determine the social class of married women is still undecided (Beller 2009).

Upwardly mobile women report how important their parents were in their success, how when they were just children their parents encouraged them to achieve. For upwardly mobile African American women, strong mothers are especially significant (Robinson and Nelson 2010). In their study of women from working-class backgrounds who became managers and professionals, sociologists Elizabeth Higginbotham and Lynn Weber (1992) found this recurring theme: parents encouraging their daughters to postpone marriage and get an education. To these understandings from the micro approach, we need to add the macro level. Had there not been a *structural* change in society, the millions of new positions that women occupy would not exist.

UNIT 7.9 // TESTING MYSELF

DID I LEARN IT? ANSWERS ARE AT THE END OF THE CHAPTER

1. Vickie could hardly wait to leave home. Since she was a child, she had been dissatisfied with her mother's housekeeping and bothered by her father's drinking. More times than she cares to recall, she had been embarrassed by food stamps. After Vickie graduated from college, she took a position as an accountant. From there, she became treasurer of the company. Vickie's change in social class is an example of what kind of mobility?

   a. opportunity   **b.** exchange
   c. structural   **d.** intergenerational

2. Jules was one of the millions of the working and lower-middle classes who took advantage of the new computer opportunities. He took night classes in programming and became a programmer in 3-D technology. The huge change in social class brought about by the new technology represents what kind of social mobility?

   a. opportunity   **b.** exchange
   c. structural   **d.** intergenerational

3. Where Jules found opportunity and moved up the social class ladder, Gloria's experience took her in the other direction. Gloria was one of the millions of people who moved down the social class ladder when the economy deteriorated. The millions up and the millions down have left the class structure intact. What type of social mobility is this?

   a. opportunity   **b.** exchange
   c. structural   **d.** intergenerational

4. Research on the social mobility of women has uncovered this theme—that of parents

   a. encouraging their daughters to postpone marriage and get an education
   b. buying computers for their daughters
   c. hiring tutors for their daughters
   d. spending time teaching them sports

UNIT 7.10

Poverty

WHAT AM I SUPPOSED TO LEARN?

After you have read this unit, you should be able to

1 Explain what the poverty line is and why it is inadequate.

2 List some stereotypes of poverty and explain why they are true or untrue.

3 Discuss causes of poverty of children of single mothers and functions of the Horatio Alger myth.

The "American Dream" is held out to all of us, an inspiring idea that motivates us to work hard and achieve more than our parents did. Many of us succeed, but at the same time many of us find that the "limitless possibilities" of the Dream elude us. The American Dream remains out of reach for many members of the working class, and especially for those in poverty, the working poor and the underclass. As you saw in Figure 7.7 on page 208, these two classes together form about one-fifth of the U.S. population, about 60 million people. Who are these people?

Drawing the Poverty Line

To determine who is poor, the U.S. government draws a **poverty line**. This measure was set in the 1960s, when poor people were thought to spend about one-third of their incomes on food. Based on this assumption, each year the government computes a low-cost food budget and multiplies it by 3. Families whose incomes are less than this amount are classified as poor; those whose incomes are higher—even by a dollar— are considered "not poor."

poverty line the official measure of poverty; calculated to include incomes that are less than three times a low-cost food budget

However you end up measuring the poverty line, this family will fall below it. This photo was taken in Venice, California.

This official measure of poverty is grossly inadequate. Poor people actually spend only about 20 percent of their incomes on food, so to determine a poverty line, we ought to multiply their food budget by 5 instead of 3 (Uchitelle 2001). Another problem is that mothers who work outside the home and have to pay for child care are treated the same as mothers who don't have this expense. Still another problem is that the poverty line is the same for everyone across the nation, even though the cost of living is much higher in New York than in Alabama. On the other hand, much of the income of the poor goes uncounted: food stamps, rent assistance, subsidized child care, and the earned income tax credit (DeNavas-Walt et al. 2010).

That a change in the poverty line would instantly make millions of people poor—or take away their poverty—would be laughable, if it weren't so serious. (The absurdity has not been lost on Parker and Hart, as you can see from their cartoon on the next page.) Although the poverty line is arbitrary, because it is the official measure of poverty, we'll use it to see who in the United States is officially poor. Before we do this, though, let's consider some stereotypes of the poor.

Stereotypes of the Poor

All of us have stereotypes of just about everything in life, and the poor are certainly not excluded from our list. Sometimes we get the chance to compare our ideas with research, and this is one of those times. As you read *Making It Personal,* compare your ideas of the poor with common stereotypes and with sociological research.

MAKING IT PERSONAL
Testing Your Stereotypes

The word *stereotype* has a bad reputation, but in sociology it simply means the ideas we gain from our experiences that we generalize to similar things. This process is so essential for getting us through everyday life that without stereotyping we couldn't survive. From this sociological perspective, then, our stereotypes can be good or bad, adequate or inadequate. So, then, here is your chance to test your ideas against common stereotypes of the poor.

Poverty is unusual. *False.* Over a 4-year period, *one-third* (32 percent) of all Americans experience poverty for at least two months (DeNavas-Walt et al. 2010). About half the population will experience poverty at some point before they reach age 65 (Cellini et al. 2008).

People with less education are more likely to be poor. *True.* Most definitely.

Most poor people are poor because they do not want to work. *False.* About 40 percent of the poor are under age 18, and another 10 percent are age 65 or older. About 30 percent of the working-age poor work at least half the year (O'Hare 1996a, 1996b).

The poor are trapped in a cycle of poverty. *We have to go true and false on this one.* Most poverty lasts less than a year (Lichter and Crowley 2002), but just over half of those who escape poverty will return to poverty within 5 years (Ratcliffe and McKernan 2010).

Most children who are born in poverty are poor as adults. *False* By the time they grow up, most Americans who were poor as children are no longer poor (Ratcliffe and McKernan 2010).

Most African Americans are poor. *False.* More than half of all African American adults work at white-collar jobs, about 22 percent at the professional or managerial level (Beeghley 2008).

Most of the poor are African Americans. *False.* There are more poor whites than any other group.

Most of the poor are single mothers and their children. *False.* About 38 percent of the poor match this stereotype, but 34 percent of the poor live in married-couple families, 22 percent live alone or with

This cartoon pinpoints the arbitrary nature of the poverty line. This almost makes me think that the creators of the Wizard of Id have been studying sociology.

WIZARD OF ID

nonrelatives, and 6 percent live in other settings (O'Hare 1996a, 1996b).

Most of the poor live on welfare. *False.* Only about 25 percent of the income of poor adults comes from welfare. About half comes from wages and pensions, and about 22 percent from Social Security (O'Hare 1996a, 1996b).

Well, which of these stereotypes of the poor did you hold?

Isn't this a nice aspect of sociology—it lets you check your ideas of the world, which you pick up here and there and who knows where, against research.

Race–Ethnicity and Poverty

Let's take a deeper look at one of the stereotypes mentioned in the *Making It Personal* that you just read. Although most African Americans are not poor, there is a strong clustering of poverty by race–ethnicity. Look at Figure 7.8. You can see that only 12 percent of whites are poor, followed closely by Asian Americans at 13 percent. In contrast, 25 percent of Latinos live in poverty, while the total jumps even higher, to 26 percent for African Americans and 27 percent for Native Americans. However, because whites are, by far, the largest group in the United States, their lower rate of poverty translates into larger numbers. As a

result, there are more poor whites than poor people of any other racial–ethnic group. As part 2 of Figure 7.8 shows, 46 percent of all the poor are white.

Suburbanization of Poverty

Throughout the history of the United States, poverty has been more common in rural areas than in the cities or suburbs. But we have just had a major historical shift. The collapse of the housing market plunged many suburbanites into the depths of poverty. Combined with extensive migration of poor people from the cities to the suburbs, this has caused poverty to hit the suburbs so hard that *most* of the nation's poor now live in them (Kneebone and Garr 2010).

Children of Poverty

Children are more likely to live in poverty than are adults or the elderly. This holds true regardless of race–ethnicity, but from Figure 7.8, you can see how much greater poverty is among Latino, African American, and Native American children. These percentages translate into incredible numbers—approximately *14 million* children. That millions of U.S. children are reared in poverty is shocking when you consider the

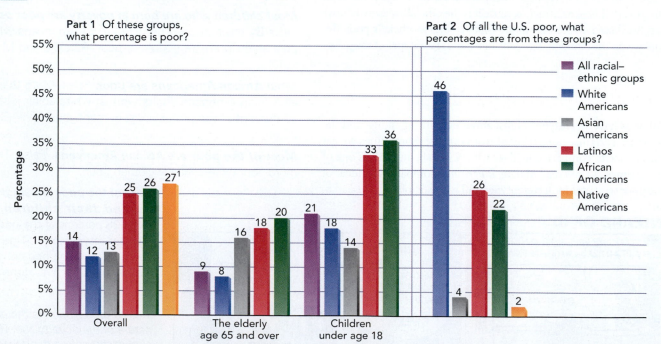

FIGURE 7.8 **Race–Ethnicity and U.S. Poverty**

[1]The source does not break this total down by age.
Note: Only these groups are listed in the source. The poverty line is $22,025 for a family of four.
Source: By the author. Based on Statistical Abstract of the United States 2011: Tables 709 and 712.

wealth of this country and our supposed concern for the well-being of children.

Why do so many U.S. children live in poverty? A major reason that many point to is that unmarried women give birth to about 1.5 million babies a year. Look at how sharply this number has increased: In 1960, 1 of 20 U.S. children was born to a single woman. Today this total is *eight times higher,* and single women now account for 8 of 20 (41 percent) of all U.S. births (*Statistical Abstract* 2012:Table 86). Let's consider this reason in the *Making It Personal* below.

MAKING IT PERSONAL

And How about This Assumption?

Do you think that births to single women cause children to live in poverty? This seems so obvious that you might be wondering why I'm even asking it. Well, read on. Let's start with something else that is obvious: Children born to wealthy single women aren't reared in poverty, are they? And you know why—because the mother has money.

And here is another one: In some industrialized countries, the birth rate of single women is higher than ours, but *our rate of child poverty is higher than theirs. (Our rate of child poverty is the highest of all industrialized nations* [Garfinkel et al. 2010]). Do you know the *why* of this one? It is simple—Even though the rate of childbirth to single women is higher in these countries, their poverty rate of children is lower because the government provides extensive support for rearing these children—from providing day care to health checkups.

To identify the cause of the poverty of children born to single women, then, why can't we point to the lack of government support for children? Interesting, isn't it, how probing a little deeper brings new information that can change our basic assumptions. Again, this is one of the fascinating beauties of sociology.

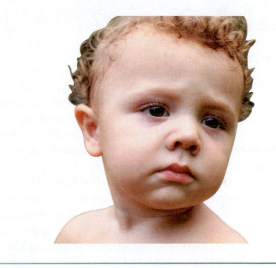

The Penalties of Poverty

Children in poverty face severe obstacles to building a satisfying life. They are more likely to die in infancy, go hungry, be malnourished, develop more slowly, and have more health problems. They also are more likely to drop out of school, become involved in criminal activities, and have children while still in their teens—thus perpetuating a cycle of poverty.

Now look at Figure 7.9 on the next page You will see that the less education that single women have, the more likely they are to bear children. As you can see, births to single women drop with each gain in education. As you know, people with lower education earn less, so this means that the single women who can least afford children are those most likely to give birth.

Let's take another look at this in *Making It Personal.*

MAKING IT PERSONAL

What Would You Do?

Let's try to tie a couple of things together here. Education opens doors to better-paying jobs, the kind that can lift people out of poverty, So what programs would you suggest for helping single women in poverty attain more education? What other policies would you suggest for reducing child poverty? Can you be specific and practical?

I'm not asking easy questions here. Policy makers have struggled with these issues for decades. But this doesn't mean that you can't come up with something better than they have.

FIGURE 7.9 Births to Single Mothers

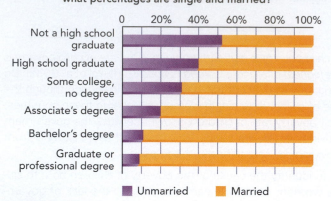

Of women with this education who give birth, what percentages are single and married?

Note: Based on a national sample of all U.S. births in the preceding 12 months.

Source: Dye 2005.

Where Is Horatio Alger? The Social Functions of a Myth

In the late 1800s, Horatio Alger was one of the country's most popular authors. The rags-to-riches exploits of his fictional boy heroes and their amazing successes in overcoming severe odds motivated thousands of boys of that period. Although Alger's characters have disappeared from U.S. literature, they remain alive and well in the American psyche. From real-life examples of people of humble origin who climbed the social class ladder, Americans, deep down, have a sense that anyone who really tries can get ahead. In fact, they believe that most Americans, including minorities and the working poor, have an average or better-than-average chance of getting ahead—obviously a statistical impossibility (Kluegel and Smith 1986).

The accuracy of the **Horatio Alger myth** is less important than the belief that limitless possibilities exist for everyone. Functionalists would stress that this belief is functional for society. It encourages people to compete for higher positions, or, as the song says, "to reach for the highest star." It also places blame for failure squarely on the individual. If you don't make it—in the face of ample opportunities to get ahead—the fault must be your own. The Horatio Alger myth helps to stabilize society: Since the fault is viewed as the individual's, not society's, current social arrangements can be regarded as satisfactory. This reduces pressures to change the system.

> **Horatio Alger myth** the belief that due to limitless possibilities anyone can get ahead if he or she tries hard enough

As both Marx and Weber pointed out, social class penetrates our consciousness, shaping our ideas of life and our "proper" place in society. When the rich look at the world around them, they sense superiority and anticipate control over their own destiny. When the poor look around them, they are more likely to sense defeat and to anticipate that unpredictable forces will batter their lives. Both rich and poor know the dominant ideology, that their particular niche in life is due to their own efforts, that the reasons for success—or failure—lie with the self. Like fish that don't notice the water, people tend not to perceive the effects of social class on their own lives.

In *Making It Personal*, let's once again consider the influence of social class on your life.

MAKING IT PERSONAL
You and Social Class Again

You've now had a glimpse into how powerfully social class impacts your life—from presenting both opportunities and obstacles to laying down channels for your marital choice, from setting the stage for your health and education to your chances of living in poverty or occupational security. You've also had a glimpse of how social class influences your values, ideas, and perception of the world and even of your own self. In the chapters to come, we will flesh out this fleeting glimpse to provide you more insight into how this general thing called "society" has a fundamental and lifelong impact on your life.

UNIT 7.10 // TESTING MYSELF
DID I LEARN IT? ANSWERS ARE AT THE END OF THE CHAPTER

1. Which of these was not pointed out as an inadequacy of the poverty line?
   a. The poor spend about one-fifth of their income on food, not the one-third assumed when the poverty line was drawn up.
   b. The poverty line is the same throughout the country, regardless of a region's cost of living.
   c. The poverty line violates the basic American value that people should support themselves.
   d. The poverty line does not count food stamps, rent assistance, and subsidized child care as income.

2. In sociology, the word stereotype refers to
   a. wrong, negative ideas
   b. ideas we gain from our experiences that we generalize to similar things
   c. changes in ideas, from positive to negative
   d. generalizations that, when tested, prove to be wrong

3. Is poverty unusual or common? Which of these statements is true?
   a. About half of Americans will experience poverty at some time before they reach age 65.
   b. This year, about half of Americans are poor.

c. About one of five Americans will be poor at some time during their lives.

d. About one of ten Americans will be poor at some time during their lives.

4. Which statement is true?
   a. Most of the poor live on welfare.
   b. Most children who are born in poverty are poor as adults.
   c. There are more poor whites than poor people of any other racial–ethnic group.
   d. Most poor people are poor because they do not want to work.

5. This group has the lowest rate of poverty
   a. African Americans
   b. Native Americans
   c. Whites
   d. Asian Americans

6. We have just had a major historical shift in the physical location of poverty. Today, poverty is most common in
   a. the suburbs
   b. cities over 100,000 people
   c. rural areas
   d. cities over 500,000 people

7. Which group of Americans is the most likely to be living in poverty?
   a. children
   b. teenagers
   c. young adults, between the ages of 20 and 25
   d. college students

8. In 1960, a different era to be sure, about 1 of 20 U.S. children was born to a single woman. Today this total runs about
   a. 2 of 20
   b. 4 of 20
   c. 5 of 20
   d. 8 of 20

9. To make the point that the birth of children to single mothers is not the cause of the children's poverty, the author stresses that
   a. single mothers all over the world give birth to children
   b. some countries have a higher birth rate to single mothers and a lower rate of child poverty
   c. the U.S. rate of birth to single mothers is the highest in the industrialized world
   d. the U.S. rate of child poverty is the highest in the industrialized world

10. In the 1800s, Horatio Alger wrote popular stories of boys who overcame severe obstacles to reach success. The Horatio Alger Myth is functional for society because it
    a. encourages people to strive for success and places blame for failure on the individual
    b. places its emphasis on the efforts of boys, who are being overlooked in the school system
    c. tells stories of success in a compelling way
    d. stresses the need for education, encouraging people to sacrifice so they can go farther in school

✓● Study and Review in mysoclab

PULLING IT ALL TOGETHER REVIEWING THE LEARNING GOALS

Unit 7.1 **Global Stratification: From Slavery to Social Class**

1. **Explain variations in slavery, its causes and conditions, and slavery today.**
   - Slavery was common and was based on debt, crime, and war, not race. In some places, slavery was temporary. In others, it was permanent and inheritable. Some slaves had power and wealth. Slavery still exists.

2. **Summarize India's caste system and the U.S. racial caste system.**
   - Caste comes with birth, is lifelong, and is maintained by rules of pollution and marriage. India's system, based on religion, has four main castes. U.S. slavery, based on race, was followed by a racial caste system, in which all whites were treated as superior to all blacks.

3. **State how a social class system differs from slavery and caste systems.**
   - Social class is based on things that can be acquired, so it is more fluid than the other systems.

4. **Explain how gender fits into stratification.**
   - Gender cuts across all systems of social stratification, with people being given or denied access to privileges based on their gender.

 Watch The Big Picture: Social Stratification the **Video** in **mysoclab**

Watch the **Video**
Sociology on the Job:
Social Stratification in
mysoclab

Unit 7.2   Three Worlds of Stratification

1. Specify broad differences between the Most Industrialized, Industrializing, and Least Industrialized Nations.
   - The *Most Industrialized Nations* rank higher than the other two on measures of property, power, and prestige—the three main elements of social stratification. The average person in the *Industrializing Nations* has more access to basic indicators of well-being—from electricity to food—than does the average person in the Least Industrialized Nation but less than those who live in the Most Industrialized Nations.

2. Explain what the new global superclass is.
   - A super-wealthy group of about 6,000 people, from all three worlds of stratification, whose interests run together, form a new global superclass. Their influence in world affairs appears to be growing.

Unit 7.3   How Did the World's Nations Become Stratified?

1. Contrast three theories of global stratification: colonialism, world system theory, and the culture of poverty.
   - *Colonialism:* the countries that industrialized first got the jump on the rest of the world, conquering areas and exploiting their resources. *World system theory:* industrialization led to the world being divided into four groups of nations: the core, semiperiphery, periphery, and external areas, with the core exploiting the resources of the others. *Culture of poverty:* the culture of some nations (poverty, fatalism) holds some nations back.

2. Explain why most sociologists reject the culture of poverty explanation.
   - Sociologists reject the culture of poverty because it places blame on the nations not on their exploitation.

Unit 7.4   Why Is Social Stratification Universal?

1. Compare the functionalist and conflict views of social stratification.
   - *Functionalists* say that the stratification of a society is inevitable because the important positions of society must offer more benefits in order to recruit more capable people to fill them. The criticism is that we don't have an independent measure of "importance."
   - *Conflict theorists* agree that the stratification of society is inevitable, but that it comes about when one group gains power and uses it to benefit themselves and to oppress those beneath them. In

the classic view of conflict theory, this process will end only when the workers gain class consciousness, rebel, and take over the means of production. Some conflict theorists analyze conflict not just between owners and workers, but wherever it occurs.

Watch the **Video**
The Basics: Social Class
in the U.S. in **mysoclab**

Unit 7.5   What Determines Social Class?

1. Compare the views of Marx and Weber on social class.
   - Marx said there was just one basis for social class: People's position in the means of production, which makes them either a capitalist (owner) or a worker. Weber said there are three bases of social class: power, property, and prestige. As Figure 7.3 shows, each of these three can lead to the others.

Unit 7.6   Social Class in the United States

1. Distinguish between wealth and income, and state how property and income are distributed in the United States.
   - *Wealth* is the value of someone's property minus the debts, while *income* is a flow of money. Wealth is concentrated. Ten percent U.S. families own 70 percent of the nation's wealth. Income inequality is growing.

2. Explain the term power elite and the controversy that surrounds this term.
   - Mills used the term "power elite" to refer to the small group that makes the country's major decisions. This analysis violates the dominant ideology of equality.

3. Summarize the bases for occupational prestige and how status inconsistency works.
   - Higher prestige goes to occupations that pay more, require more education and abstract thought, and offer more independence. The status inconsistent, who are likely to be interacted with on the basis of their lower status, tend to become politically radical.

Read the **Document**
"The Power Elite" by
C. Wright Mills in **mysoclab**

Watch the **Video**
Social Class in the
U.S. in **mysoclab**

Unit 7.7   A Social Class Model

1. Summarize the six-tier social class model developed by Kahl and Gilbert.
   - *The capitalist class,* the wealthiest 1 percent, is divided into "old" and "new" money. *The upper*

middle class (15 percent), the most shaped by education, manage the corporations owned by the capitalist class, run their own businesses, or pursue professions. *The lower middle class* (34 percent), which hold the technical and lower-level management positions, have mainstream lifestyles but are plagued by insecurity. *The working class* (30 percent) have low education and highly insecure jobs. *The working poor* (15 percent) have the least education and depend on food stamps and local food pantries to survive. The *underclass* (5 percent) live on welfare, food stamps, and food pantries. Life is toughest here.

✳ **Explore** the **Concept**
Collars and Colors in America in **mysoclab**

Unit 7.8 // Consequences of Social Class

1. Explain how social class affects people's lives.

- Social class leaves hardly any aspect of life untouched. Health: Both physical and mental health improve as you go up the social class ladder, as does health care. Family life: Wealthy parents have more input into their children's choice of spouse, and the poor are more likely to divorce. Education: The wealthy send their children to exclusive prep schools and colleges. Religion: The social classes tend to go to different denominations, with Episcopalians and Baptists as examples. Politics: The farther up the social class ladder, the more likely people are to be Republican. The working class is more liberal on economic issues and more conservative on social issues. Crime and the criminal justice system: The classes commit different types of crime, street and white-collar, which are reacted to differently by law enforcement.

Unit 7.9 // Social Mobility

1. Describe the three types of social mobility.

- *Intergenerational mobility* refers to children moving to a social class different than that of their parents. *Structural mobility* refers to large numbers of people changing their social class when changes in the structure of society open and close opportunities. *Exchange mobility* refers to an exchange among classes—that is, large numbers of people going up and down the social class ladder with little change in the social class structure.

2. Explain where women fit in studies of social mobility.

- Only sons used to be included in research on social mobility. Daughters are now included, but sociologists have not determined how to classify the social class of wives.

Unit 7.10 // Poverty

1. Explain what the poverty line is and why it is inadequate.

- The poverty line is the official measurement of where poverty begins. Inadequacies: based on a wrong assumption, that the poor spend one-third of their incomes on food; the line is the same regardless of an area's cost of living; food stamps, rent subsidies, and welfare are not counted as income.

2. List some stereotypes of poverty and explain why they are true or untrue.

- Many are listed and can be reviewed in *Making It Personal* on pages 217–218.

3. Discuss causes of poverty of children of single mothers and functions of the Horatio Alger myth.

- The cause is often assumed to be births to single mothers, but children born to wealthy single mothers are not poor. Nor are those in countries where the governments offer extensive support systems. The Horatio Alger myth, which motivates people to achieve, stabilizes society by placing the blame for failure on the individual, not the structure of society.

UNIT 7.1 // TESTING MYSELF
DID I LEARN IT? ANSWERS

1. **d** social stratification

2. **c** allowed or denied access to the good things offered by their society

3. **a** race

4. **c** Rome

5. **a** ideology

6. **a** Racism didn't lead to slavery, but, rather, slavery led racism.

7. **d** Gradually the entire white South became an armed camp to keep Negroes in slavery and to kill the black rebel

8. **c** is part of the ceremonies people follow at births, marriages, and deaths

9. **a** a racial caste

10. **d** is more fluid, allowing movement up and down the class ladder

1. **a** First World, Second World, and Third World

2. **b** Developed Nations, Developing Nations, and Undeveloped Nations

3. **c** Most Industrialized, Industrializing, and Least Industrialized Nations

4. **a** Most Industrialized

5. **b** Industrializing

6. **c** Least Industrialized

7. **c** new global superclass

1. **d** colonialism

2. **c** world system theory

3. **b** culture of poverty

4. **a** the culture of poverty places blame on the poor nations themselves

1. **d** The patterns of society that are not functional disappear, while those that are functional continue.

2. **c** the more important positions must offer greater rewards to get more qualified people to take the greater responsibilities

3. **b** society would be a meritocracy

4. **a** we have no independent measures of the importance of society's positions

5. **d** one group gains control over society's resources

6. **c** the oppressed groups trying to overcome their domination

7. **b** raise class consciousness

8. **a** also analyze conflict among workers

1. **d** the means of production

2. **a** the means of production

3. **c** proletariat

4. **b** class consciousness

5. **a** false class consciousness

6. **c** property, power, and prestige

7. **b** prestige can be exchanged for power

1. **d** wealth

2. **d** 70

3. **d** 10 feet off the ground

4. **b** increased

5. **c** millionaire white men from families with "old money"

6. **b** have been in the family a long time

7. **a** status consistent

8. **b** status inconsistent

9. **c** these people's lowest ranking

10. **b** politically radical

UNIT 7.7 // TESTING MYSELF
DID I LEARN IT? ANSWERS

1. **d** capitalist class

2. **b** manage the family fortune

3. **a** participate in the same social networks

4. **d** marry old money

UNIT 7.8 // TESTING MYSELF
DID I LEARN IT? ANSWERS

1. **d** more birth defects among the poor

2. **a** capitalist

3. **b** upper middle

UNIT 7.9 // TESTING MYSELF
DID I LEARN IT? ANSWERS

1. **d** intergenerational

2. **c** structural

UNIT 7.10 // TESTING MYSELF
DID I LEARN IT? ANSWERS

1. **c** The poverty line violates the basic American value that people should support themselves.

2. **b** ideas we gain from our experiences that we generalize to similar things

3. **a** About half of Americans will experience poverty at some time before they reach age 65.

4. **c** There are more poor whites than poor people of any other racial–ethnic group.

5. **b** upper middle

6. **b** lower middle

7. **c** working

8. **c** working poor

9. **d** underclass

10. **d** underclass

4. **a** Democrats

5. **d** working poor

6. **a** capitalist

7. **d** underclass

3. **b** exchange

4. **a** encouraging their daughters to postpone marriage and get an education

5. **d** whites

6. **a** the suburbs

7. **a** children

8. **d** 8 of 20

9. **b** some countries have a higher birth rate to single mothers and a lower rate of child poverty

10. **a** encourages people to strive for success and places blame for failure on the individual

CHAPTER 8
RACE AND ETHNICITY

Watch the **Video** in **mysoclab**

((•—[**Listen** to the **Chapter Audio** in **mysoclab**

GETTING STARTED

Did you know that a plane ride can change someone's race?

My guess is that you didn't know this. It certainly surprised me when I found out. We all think we know a lot of things about race. And we do. But a good part of what we know is just plain wrong. And most of the rest is a mixture of wrong mingled with a just a little bit of right.

I know that this is a strong statement, so read on and see why I made it. And I'll explain about that amazing plane ride, too.

Comanche Tribe, Gallup, New Mexico

UNIT 8.1

Race: Myth and Reality

Human Variety

With its population of 7 billion, the world offers a fascinating variety of human shapes and colors. Skin colors come in all shades between black and white, heightened by reddish and yellowish hues. Eyes come in shades of blue, brown, and green. Lips are thick and thin. Hair is straight, curly, kinky, black, blonde, and red—and, of course, all shades of brown.

As humans spread throughout the world, their adaptations to diverse climates and other living conditions resulted in this profusion of colors, hair textures, and other physical variations. Genetic mutations added distinct characteristics to the peoples of the globe. In this sense, the concept of **race**—a group of people with inherited physical characteristics that distinguish it from another group—is a reality. Humans do, indeed, come in a variety of colors and shapes.

People also hold a variety of myths about other groups. Let's look at some of these false beliefs.

THE MYTH OF PURE RACES

Some people think there are "pure" races, but humans show such a mixture of physical characteristics that

> **race** a group whose inherited physical characteristics distinguish it from other groups

What "race" do you think these three people are? Why? How do your ideas compare with those expressed in this chapter?

there are none. Instead of falling into distinct types that are clearly separate from one another, people's skin color, hair texture, nose shape, head shape, eye color, and so on, flow endlessly together. The mapping of the human genome system shows that the so-called racial groups differ from one another only once in a thousand subunits of the genome (Angler 2000, Frank 2007). These tiny gradations make any attempt to draw lines of pure race purely arbitrary.

> **IF YOU WANT TO LEARN MORE** about how inadequately our racial–ethnic categories reflect people's lives,
>
> **Read** more from the author: Tiger Woods: Mapping the Changing Ethnic Terrain in **mysoclab**

THE MYTH OF A FIXED NUMBER OF RACES

There have been many attempts to determine race, including classifying people by blood type and gene frequencies. But even these classifications do not uncover "race." Rather, the term is so arbitrary that biologists and anthropologists cannot even agree on how many "races" there are (Smedley and Smedley 2005). Ashley Montagu (1964, 1999), a physical anthropologist, pointed out that some scientists have classified humans into only two "races," while others have found as many as two thousand. Montagu (1960) himself classified humans into forty "racial groups."

The concept of "race" is so flexible that, well, this takes us to what I mentioned earlier, the plane ride that can change someone's race. Let's see how this could possibly, even in anyone's wildest imagination, be true. Imagine then, that you are flying from some place—anyplace—in the United States to the city of Salvador in Brazil. In that area, people classify one another not only by the color of their skin, but also by the color of their eyes, the width of their nose, the thickness of their lips, and the color and curliness of their hair. They use at least seven terms for what we call white and black. Now consider a U.S. child whose grandmother is "white" and whose parents are "black." She flies to Salvador. When she gets there, she is no longer "black." She will belong to one of their several "whiter" categories (Fish 1995).

I know that you are probably thinking, "She might fly there, but her race didn't change. It's just the same as when she got on the plane." Our common sense revolts at this, I know, but the girl's race actually did change. We want to argue this way:

"Because the girl's biological characteristics remain unchanged, her race remains unchanged." This is because we think of race as biological. *Race, however, is actually a label we use to describe perceived biological characteristics.* If one group perceives biological characteristics in one way and has certain labels for those perceptions, then that is the "race" that people are.

I know that this is difficult to accept, because from childhood we are immersed in a different idea. So let's approach this from another angle. Let's reverse the plane ride and assume that a Salvadoran girl flies to the United States. In Salvador, she is classified as a "Moreno," but when she lands in the United States, others will classify her as Hispanic. Which is she? It all depends on where she is.

Simply put, the race we "are" depends on our social location—on who is doing the classifying.

If you still aren't convinced, then consider how Americans usually classify a child born to a "black" mother and a "white" father. Why do they usually say that the child is "black"? Wouldn't it be equally as logical to classify the child as "white"? Isn't the child "black" simply because of a classification, and a highly arbitrary one at that?

Let's apply these ideas to yourself. Take a look at *Making It Personal.*

MAKING IT PERSONAL

What Race Are You?

I want to ask you two questions. The first: What "race" are you? The second: Why do you classify yourself this way?

You might want to say "This is what I am," but let's go beyond this. How about this answer?: "I learned this during my childhood." Isn't this where you got this idea, from people around you when you were little? Didn't you grow up with this idea? Where else did you get your idea of your race other than from the way that people classify you?

Most of us simply accept the labels that our groups assign us. We adopt them without thinking. They seem right, they match what we "see," and they become part of our unexamined self. Some people question the label they are assigned, however, and for them, the situation is much more complicated. Basically, it then becomes, "Who am I, then, if I'm not X?"

So where are you in this process?

What "race" are these two Brazilians? Is the child's "race" different from her mother's "race"? The text explains why "race" is such an unreliable concept that it changes even with geography.

THE MYTH OF RACIAL SUPERIORITY

Regardless of what anthropologists, biologists, and sociologists tell us, people do divide one another into races, and we are stuck with this term. People also tend to see some races (mostly their own) as superior and others as inferior. As with language, however, no race is better than another. All races have their geniuses—and their idiots. Yet the myth of racial superiority abounds. Most myths have no practical consequence, but this one is particularly dangerous. Adolf Hitler, for example, believed that the Aryans were a superior race, destined to establish a superior culture and a new world order. This destiny required them to avoid the "racial contamination" that would come from breeding with inferior races. The Aryans, then, had the "cultural duty" to isolate or destroy races that threatened their racial purity and culture.

Put into practice, Hitler's views brought the *holocaust*—the Nazi slaughter of those they deemed inferior: Jews, Slavs, gypsies, homosexuals, and people with mental and physical disabilities. Horrific images of gas ovens and emaciated bodies stacked like cordwood haunted the world's nations. At Nuremberg, the Allies, flush with victory, put the top Nazis on trial, exposing their heinous deeds to a shocked world. Their public executions, everyone assumed, marked the end of such grisly acts.

Obviously, they didn't. In the summer of 1994 in Rwanda, Hutus slaughtered about 800,000 Tutsis—mostly with machetes (Gettleman and Kron 2010). A few years later, Serbs in Bosnia massacred Muslims, giving us a new term, *ethnic cleansing.* As these events sadly attest, **genocide,** the attempt to destroy a group of people because of their presumed race or ethnicity, remains alive and well. Although more recent killings are not accompanied by swastikas and gas ovens, the perpetrators' goal is the same.

THE MYTH CONTINUES

The *idea* of race, of course, is far from a myth. Firmly embedded in our culture, this idea is a powerful force in our everyday lives. That no race is superior and that even biologists cannot decide how people should be

genocide the systematic annihilation or attempted annihilation of a people because of their presumed race or ethnicity

The reason I selected these photos is to illustrate how seriously we must take all preaching of hatred and of racial supremacy, even though it comes from harmless or even humorous sources. The strange-looking person with his hands on his hips, who is wearing lederhosen, traditional clothing of Bavaria, Germany, is Adolf Hitler. He caused this horrific scene at the Landsberg concentration camp.

People often confuse the terms *race* and *ethnic group*. For example, many people, including many Jews, consider Jews a race. Jews, however, are more properly considered an ethnic group, for it is their cultural characteristics, especially their religion, that bind them together. Wherever Jews have lived in the world, they have intermarried. Consequently, Jews in China may have Chinese features, while some Swedish Jews are blue-eyed blonds. The confusion of race and ethnicity is illustrated in the photo below.

This photo illustrates the difficulty that assumptions about race and ethnicity posed for Israel. The Ethiopian Jews look so different from other Jews that it took several years for Israeli authorities to acknowledge their "true Jewishness" and allow them to immigrate.

classified into races is not what counts. "I know what I see, and you can't tell me any different" seems to be the common attitude. As was noted in Chapter 5, sociologists W. I. and D. S. Thomas (1928) observed, "If people define situations as real, they are real in their consequences." In other words, people act on perceptions and beliefs, not facts. As a result, we will always have people like Hitler. Although few people hold such extreme views, most people appear to be ethnocentric enough to believe that their own race is—at least just a little—superior to others.

Ethnic Groups

Before ending this unit, let me introduce *ethnicity,* a significant term. In contrast to *race,* which people use to refer to supposed biological characteristics that distinguish one group of people from another, **ethnicity** and **ethnic** refer to cultural characteristics. Derived from the word *ethnos* (a Greek word meaning "people" or "nation"), *ethnicity* and *ethnic* refer to people who identify with one another on the basis of common ancestry and cultural heritage. Their sense of belonging may center on their nation or region of origin, distinctive foods, clothing, language, music, religion, or family names and relationships.

ethnicity (and ethnic) having distinctive cultural characteristics

UNIT 8.1 // TESTING MYSELF

DID I LEARN IT? ANSWERS ARE AT THE END OF THE CHAPTER

1. This unit made the point that there are no pure races because
   a. the races used to be different than they are today
   b. climate changes have changed the races
   c. the biological characteristics of groups flow endlessly together
   d. new genetic research shows that there are just three different causes of skin color

2. As Ashley Montagu, a physical anthropologist, stressed, the belief that there is a fixed number of races is a myth. He pointed out that even scientists can't agree how to classify "race." They have classified humans into these many "races"
   a. 2 to 2,000   b. 6 to 60
   c. 4 to 40   d. 2 to 20

3. The author points out that the idea of race is so arbitrary that even
   a. slavery changed people's idea of race
   b. some government officials disagree on how to classify people
   c. some parents don't know what race their children are
   d. a plane ride can change someone's race

4. Sociologists point out that race is
   a. unchanging
   b. a fixed biological characteristic
   c. a label we use to describe perceived biological characteristics
   d. a major reason that people act the way they do

5. The race you "are" depends on
   a. your birth
   b. who is doing the classifying
   c. your mother more than your father
   d. genetic mutations

6. The Nazi slaughter of those they deemed inferior—Jews, Slavs, gypsies, homosexuals, and people with mental and physical disabilities—is called
   a. the cleansing   b. World War II
   c. the burning   d. the holocaust

7. The attempt to destroy a group of people because of their presumed race or ethnicity is called
   a. phenocide   b. raceicide
   c. genocide   d. geneticide

8. When it comes to race relations, this is an important principle to understand
   a. race is one of the most important reasons that people do what they do
   b. people act on perceptions and beliefs, not facts
   c. in interracial marriage, the superior race gets inferior traits
   d. there are only four pure races

9. The author says that most people appear to believe that their own race is—at least just a little—superior to others. Most people, then, are
   a. ethnocentric
   b. biocentric
   c. centrocentric
   d. unaware of historic events that show different races getting ahead at different times

10. Sociologists use this term to refer to cultural characteristics that distinguish one group of people from another
    a. race   b. symbolic interaction
    c. culturism   d. ethnicity

UNIT 8.2

Minority Groups and Dominant Groups

WHAT AM I SUPPOSED TO LEARN?

After you have read this unit, you should be able to

1 Contrast minority and dominant groups and list the origin of minority groups.

2 Summarize the six ways that dominant groups treat minority groups.

3 Explain what leads to a high or low sense of racial–ethnic identity.

You are already familiar with the broad outline: Some racial–ethnic groups have greater power, privilege, and property. Other groups have less. It is important to understand that this is true around the world, not just in the United States. This chapter is designed to give you a much better understanding of this condition in society. Let's start by going back a few years.

GETTING A LITTLE BACKGROUND

Back in the 1940s, race relations in the United States were in turmoil. African American soldiers had served overseas in huge numbers. Seeing there a different way of life, they caught a vision of what race relations could be back home. Emboldened by these returning veterans of World War II, African Americans demanded change. Within this turbulent context, sociologists studied race–ethnic relations. The concepts they developed can help give us a broad view for understanding racial-ethnic relations today.

Louis Wirth (1945) defined a **minority group** as people who are singled out for unequal treatment and who regard themselves as objects of collective discrimination. Worldwide, minority groups share several conditions: Their physical or cultural traits are held in low esteem by the dominant group, which treats them unfairly, and they tend to marry within their own group (Wagley and Harris 1958). With these conditions, minorities tend to feel a sense of common identity (a feeling of "we-ness"). In some instances, even a sense of common destiny emerges (Chandra 1993b).

THE QUESTION OF NUMBERS

Surprisingly, a minority group is not necessarily a *numerical* minority. For example, before India's independence in 1947, a handful of British colonial rulers dominated tens of millions of Indians. Similarly, when South Africa practiced *apartheid* (ah-PAR-tate), a smaller group of Afrikaners, primarily Dutch, discriminated against a much larger number of blacks. And all over the world, as we will discuss in the next chapter, females are a minority group. Accordingly, sociologists refer to those who do the discriminating not as the *majority,* but, rather, as the **dominant group,** for regardless of their numbers, this is the group that has the greater power and privilege.

Possessing political power and unified by shared physical and cultural traits, the dominant group uses its position to discriminate against those who have different—and supposedly inferior—traits. The dominant group considers its privileged position to be the result of its own innate superiority.

BECOMING A MINORITY GROUP

How does a group become a minority? This occurs in one of two ways. The *first*

is through the expansion of political boundaries. With the exception of females, tribal societies contain no minority groups. Everyone shares the same culture, including the same language, and belongs to the same small group. A minority is produced when a group expands its political boundaries and incorporates people with different customs, languages, values, or physical characteristics into the same political entity *and* discriminates against them. For example, in 1848, after defeating Mexico in war, the United States took over the Southwest. The Mexicans living there, who had been the dominant group before the war, were transformed into a minority group, a master status that has influenced their lives ever since. Referring to his ancestors, one Latino said, "We didn't move across the border—the border moved across us."

A *second* way in which a group becomes a minority is by *migration*. This can be voluntary, as with the millions of people who have chosen to move from Mexico to the United States, or involuntary, as with the millions of Africans who were brought in chains to the United States. (The way females became a minority group represents a third way, but no one knows just how this occurred.)

How Dominant Groups Treat Minority Groups

As sociologists have studied racial–ethnic relations around the world, they have found six basic ways that dominant groups treat minority groups. These patterns are shown in Figure 8.1 on the next page. Let's look at each.

GENOCIDE

When gold was discovered in northern California in 1849, the fabled "Forty-Niners" rushed in. In this region lived 150,000 Native Americans. To get rid of them, the white government put a bounty on their heads. It even reimbursed the whites for their bullets. The result was the slaughter of 120,000 Native American men, women, and children. (Schaefer 2004)

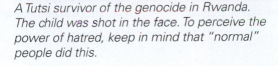

A Tutsi survivor of the genocide in Rwanda. The child was shot in the face. To perceive the power of hatred, keep in mind that "normal" people did this.

minority group people who are singled out for unequal treatment and who regard themselves as objects of collective discrimination

dominant group the group with the most power, greatest privileges, and highest social status

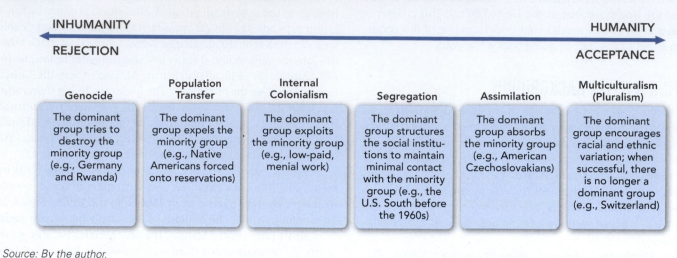

FIGURE 8.1 Global Patterns of Intergroup Relations: A Continuum

INHUMANITY ← → HUMANITY

REJECTION ← → ACCEPTANCE

Genocide	Population Transfer	Internal Colonialism	Segregation	Assimilation	Multiculturalism (Pluralism)
The dominant group tries to destroy the minority group (e.g., Germany and Rwanda)	The dominant group expels the minority group (e.g., Native Americans forced onto reservations)	The dominant group exploits the minority group (e.g., low-paid, menial work)	The dominant group structures the social institutions to maintain minimal contact with the minority group (e.g., the U.S. South before the 1960s)	The dominant group absorbs the minority group (e.g., American Czechoslovakians)	The dominant group encourages racial and ethnic variation; when successful, there is no longer a dominant group (e.g., Switzerland)

Source: By the author.

Could you ever participate in genocide? Don't be too quick to answer. We are going to try to understand how ordinary, good people like yourself can take part in genocide. In the events depicted in the little vignette above, those who did the killing were regular people—people like you and I. The killing was promoted by calling the Native Americans "savages," making them appear inferior, as somehow less than human. Killing them, then, didn't seem the same as killing whites in order to take their property.

Most Native Americans died not from bullets but from the diseases the whites brought with them. Measles, smallpox, and the flu came from another continent, and the Native Americans had no immunity against them (Dobyns 1983; Schaefer 2004). But to accomplish the takeover of their resources, the settlers and soldiers destroyed the Native Americans' food supply (buffalos, crops). From all causes, about *95 percent* of Native Americans died (Thornton 1987; Churchill 1997). Ordinary, "good" people were intent on destroying the "savages."

Now consider last century's two most notorious examples of genocide. In Germany during the 1930s and 1940s, Hitler and the Nazis attempted to destroy all Jews. In the 1990s, in Rwanda, the Hutus tried to destroy all Tutsis. One of the horrifying aspects of these two slaughters is that the killers did not crawl out from under a rock someplace. In some cases, it was the victims' neighbors and friends who did the killing. Even teachers killed their students (Huttenbach 1991; Browning 1993; Gross 2001).

Labels are powerful, dehumanizing ones even more so. They help people to **compartmentalize**—to separate their acts of cruelty from their sense of being good and decent people. To regard members of some group as inferior opens the door to treating them

compartmentalize to separate acts from feelings or attitudes

inhumanely. In some cases, as with whites and Native Americans, Germans and Jews, and Hutus and Tutsis, labels help people to kill—and to still retain a good self-concept (Bernard et al. 1971). In short, *labeling a targeted group as "inferior," "less than fully human," or even as "bad" or an "enemy" facilitates genocide.*

POPULATION TRANSFER

There are two types of **population transfer:** indirect and direct. *Indirect transfer* is achieved by making life so miserable for members of a minority that they leave "voluntarily." Under the bitter conditions of czarist Russia, for example, millions of Jews made this "choice." *Direct transfer* occurs when a dominant group expels a minority. Examples include the U.S. government relocating Native Americans to reservations in the 1800s and transferring Americans of Japanese descent to internment camps during World War II.

In the 1990s, a combination of genocide and population transfer occurred in Bosnia and Kosovo, parts of the former Yugoslavia. A hatred nurtured for centuries had been kept under wraps by Tito's iron-fisted rule from 1944 to 1980. After Tito's death, these suppressed, smoldering hostilities soared to the surface, and Yugoslavia split into warring factions. When the Serbs gained power, Muslims rebelled and began guerilla warfare. The Serbs vented their hatred by what they termed **ethnic cleansing:** They terrorized villages with killing and rape, forcing survivors to flee in fear.

population transfer the forced transfer of a minority group

INTERNAL COLONIALISM

Conflict theorists use the term **internal colonialism** to describe how a country's dominant group exploits

ethnic cleansing a policy of eliminating a population; includes forcible expulsion and genocide

minority groups for its economic advantage. The dominant group manipulates the social institutions to suppress minorities and deny them full access to their society's benefits. Slavery, reviewed in Chapter 7, is an extreme example of internal colonialism, as was the South African system of *apartheid*. Although the dominant Afrikaners despised the minority, they found its presence necessary. As Simpson and Yinger (1972) put it, who else would do the hard work?

SEGREGATION

Internal colonialism is often accompanied by **segregation**— the separation of racial–ethnic groups. Segregation allows the dominant group to maintain social distance from the minority and yet exploit their labor as cooks, cleaners, chauffeurs, nannies, farm workers, and so on. In the U.S. South until the 1960s, by law African Americans and whites had to use separate public facilities such as hotels, schools, swimming pools, bathrooms, and drinking fountains. In thirty-eight states, laws prohibited marriage between blacks and whites. Violators could be sent to prison (Mahoney and Kooistra 1995). The last law of this type was repealed in 1967 (Spickard 1989). In the villages of India, an ethnic group, the Dalits (untouchables), is forbidden to use the village pump. Dalit women must walk long distances to streams or pumps outside the village to fetch their water (author's notes).

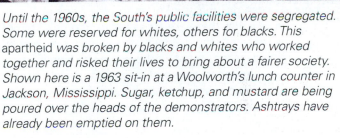

Until the 1960s, the South's public facilities were segregated. Some were reserved for whites, others for blacks. This apartheid was broken by blacks and whites who worked together and risked their lives to bring about a fairer society. Shown here is a 1963 sit-in at a Woolworth's lunch counter in Jackson, Mississippi. Sugar, ketchup, and mustard are being poured over the heads of the demonstrators. Ashtrays have already been emptied on them.

could celebrate only Russian holidays, not Armenian ones. *Permissible assimilation*, in contrast, allows the minority to adopt the dominant group's patterns in its own way and at its own speed.

ASSIMILATION

Assimilation is the process by which a minority group is absorbed into the mainstream culture. There are two types. In *forced assimilation*, the dominant group refuses to allow the minority to practice its religion, to speak its language, or to follow its customs. Before the fall of the Soviet Union, for example, the dominant group, the Russians, required that Armenian children attend schools where they were taught in Russian. Armenians

internal colonialism the policy of exploiting minority groups for economic gain

segregation the policy of keeping racial–ethnic groups apart

assimilation the process of being absorbed into the mainstream culture

MULTICULTURALISM (PLURALISM)

A policy of **multiculturalism**, also called **pluralism**, permits or even encourages racial–ethnic variation. The minority groups are able to maintain their separate identities, yet participate freely in the country's social institutions, from education to politics. Switzerland provides an outstanding example

multiculturalism (also called pluralism) a policy that permits or encourages ethnic differences; also called pluralism

pluralism the diffusion of power among many interest groups that prevents any single group from gaining control of the government

of multiculturalism. The Swiss population includes four ethnic groups: French, Italians, Germans, and Romansh. These groups have kept their own languages, and they live peacefully in political and economic unity. Multiculturalism has been so successful that none of these groups can properly be called a minority.

Minority group or dominant group? Do you feel a high sense of race–ethnicity, or hardly any? To see why, take a look at *Making It Personal*.

MAKING IT PERSONAL

Why Do You Think You Are What You Think You Are?

Not all of us have the same sense of ethnicity. Some of us feel firm boundaries between "us" and "them." Our race–ethnicity is a burning matter, constantly before us. Others have assimilated so extensively into the mainstream culture that they are only vaguely aware of their ethnic origins. If asked to identify themselves ethnically, they respond with something like "I'm Heinz 57—German and Irish, with a little Italian and French thrown in—and I think someone said something about being one-sixteenth Indian, too."

How about you? Do you feel an intense sense of racial–ethnic identity, or do you feel hardly any? Either way, here is where you can get the answer as to why. Look at Figure 8.2. You can see that there are four factors that heighten or reduce your sense of ethnic identity, the relative size, power, appearance, and discrimination of the group you identify with. If you have a heightened sense of racial–ethnic identity, it is likely that your group is smaller than the dominant group, has little power, looks different from most people in society, and

FIGURE 8.2   **A Sense of Ethnicity**

A Low Sense	A Heightened Sense
Part of the majority	Smaller numbers
Greater power	Lesser power
Similar to the "national identity"	Different from the "national identity"
No discrimination	Discrimination

Source: By the author. Based on Doane 1997.

perhaps is discriminated against. In contrast, if you belong to the dominant group that holds most of the power, look like most people in your society, and feel no discrimination, you are likely to experience a sense of "belonging"—and to wonder why ethnic identity is such a big deal.

With these keys to understanding, you should now have more insight into how you construct your racial–ethnic identity. You might want to follow this up and look at the *Making It Personal* below.

MAKING IT PERSONAL

Are You Doing Ethnic Work?

Ethnic work refers to the way people construct their ethnicity. For people who have a strong ethnic identity, this term refers to how they enhance and maintain their group's distinctions—from clothing, food, and language to religious practices and holidays. For people whose ethnic identity is not as firm, it refers to attempts to recover an ethnic heritage. Some try to trace family lines or visit the country or region of their family's origin.

ethnic work activities designed to discover, enhance, maintain, or transmit an ethnic or racial identity

Are you doing ethnic work? Is someone in your family tracing your family history or has someone produced a "family tree"? Has anyone suggested that it would be nice to visit the "home country"? Or meet some "cousins" or other relatives "over there" to see what they are like? Ethnic work has confounded the experts, who thought that the United States would be a melting pot, with most of its groups blending into a sort of ethnic stew. Because so many Americans have become fascinated with their "roots" and are not identifying themselves simply as "American," some analysts suggest that "tossed salad" is a more appropriate term than "melting pot."

The photo essay on the next page illustrates some of the ways that Americans are engaged in ethnic work.

Ethnic Work

Explorations in Cultural Identity

Ethnic work refers to the ways that people establish, maintain, and transmit their ethnic identity. As shown here, among the techniques people use to forge ties with their roots are dress, dance, and music.

Wearing traditional clothing and participating in a parade help to maintain the ethnic identity of these Americans who trace their origin to the Philippines.

Many African Americans are trying to get in closer contact with their roots. To do this, some use musical performances, as with this group in Philadelphia, Pennsylvania. Note the five-year old who is participating.

Many European Americans are also involved in ethnic work, attempting to maintain an identity more precise than "from Europe." These women of Czech ancestry are performing for a Czech community in a small town in Nebraska.

The Cinco de Mayo celebration is used to recall roots and renew ethnic identities. This one was held in Los Angeles, California.

Many Native Americans have maintained continuous identity with their tribal roots. You can see the blending of cultures in this photo taken at the March Pow Wow in Denver, Colorado.

UNIT 8.2 // TESTING MYSELF
DID I LEARN IT? ANSWERS ARE AT THE END OF THE CHAPTER

1. MaryAnn belongs to a group whose physical and cultural traits are held in low esteem by the dominant group. Members of her group tend to identify with one another and to marry within their own group. MaryAnn belongs to a
   a. sect
   b. cult
   c. dominant group
   d. minority group

2. KeishaAnn belongs to a group that discriminates against those who have different—and supposedly inferior—traits. Her group considers its privileged position to be the result of its own innate superiority. KeishaAnn belongs to a
   a. power group
   b. pure racial group
   c. dominant group
   d. minority group

3. Until 1848, the Mexicans who were living in what is now the Southwest United States were the dominant group. After defeating Mexico in war in 1848, the United States took over the Southwest. The Mexicans living there were transformed into a
   a. power group
   b. pure racial group
   c. dominant group
   d. minority group

4. In Germany during the 1930s and 1940s, the Nazis attempted to destroy all Jews. In the 1990s, in Rwanda, the Hutus tried to destroy all Tutsis. These are examples of
   a. population transfer
   b. segregation
   c. internal colonialism
   d. genocide

5. In the 1800s, the U.S. government relocated Native Americans to reservations and during World War II transferred Americans of Japanese descent to internment camps. These are examples of
   a. segregation
   b. multiculturalism (pluralism)
   c. population transfer
   d. internal colonialism

6. The South African system of apartheid can fit more than one type, but regarding its aspect of having blacks doing the hard manual labor, it fits this type
   a. multiculturalism (pluralism)
   b. internal colonialism
   c. genocide
   d. segregation

7. In thirty-eight U.S. states, whites passed laws that prohibited marriage between blacks and whites. The penalties for violating the law included prison sentences. This is an example of
   a. segregation
   b. assimilation
   c. multiculturalism (pluralism)
   d. internal colonialism

8. In this policy, the minority group is able to maintain its separate identity, yet participate freely in the country's social institutions.
   a. population transfer
   b. segregation
   c. multiculturalism (pluralism)
   d. internal colonialism

9. MaryAnn, who belongs to a group that does not have much power or prestige or privilege and whose members regard themselves as discriminated against is likely to feel a
   a. high sense of opportunity
   b. heightened sense of power
   c. heightened sense of racial–ethnic identity
   d. low sense of racial–ethnic identity

10. MaryAnn decided to investigate her roots. She traveled back to her family's country of origin, and she bought a cookbook that features food from the "old country." MaryAnn is doing
    a. follow up
    b. ethnic work
    c. ancestral research
    d. minority group research

UNIT 8.3
Prejudice and Discrimination

WHAT AM I SUPPOSED TO LEARN?

After you have read this unit, you should be able to

1 Distinguish between discrimination and prejudice and explain the origin of prejudice.

2 Explain what internalizing dominant norms means.

3 Contrast individual and institutional discrimination.

Those who preach hatred often find a receptive audience in people who see themselves as victims.

We've discussed how discrimination is one of the essential characteristics in defining dominant and minority groups, and that without discrimination you don't have a minority group. So let's look at how people learn prejudice and how extensive prejudice and discrimination are.

Learning Prejudice

DISTINGUISHING BETWEEN PREJUDICE AND DISCRIMINATION

Discrimination is common around the world. In Mexico, Mexicans of Hispanic descent discriminate against Mexicans of Native American descent. In Israel, Ashkenazi Jews, primarily of European descent, discriminate against Sephardi Jews from the Middle East. In China, the Han and the Uighurs discriminate against each other. In some places, the elderly discriminate against the young; in others, the young discriminate against the elderly. And all around the world, men discriminate against women.

Discrimination is an *action*—unfair treatment directed against someone. Discrimination is based on many characteristics: age, sex, height, weight, skin color, clothing, speech, income, education, marital

> **discrimination** an act of unfair treatment directed against an individual or a group
>
> **racism** prejudice and discrimination on the basis of race
>
> **prejudice** an attitude or prejudging, usually in a negative way

status, sexual orientation, disease, disability, religion, and politics. When the reason for discrimination is someone's perception of race, it is known as **racism.** Discrimination is often the result of an *attitude* called **prejudice**—a prejudging of some sort, usually in a negative way. It usually involves prejudging a group as inferior.

LEARNING PREJUDICE FROM OTHERS

We are not born with beliefs, ideas, or attitudes. These we learn from others. So it is with prejudice. Like our other attitudes, we learn this one from the people around us. You know that some highly prejudiced people are attracted to the neo-Nazis. Nothing new there. But here is a twist. Sociologist Michael Kimmel (2007), who interviewed neo-Nazi skinheads in Sweden, found that young men were attracted mostly by the group's tough masculinity, not its hatred of immigrants. When they join, they learn the hatred. Similarly, Kathleen Blee (2005, 2011), who interviewed female members of the KKK and Aryan Nations in the United States, found that they were attracted to the hate group because someone they liked belonged to it. They learned to be racists *after* they joined the group. In both the Blee and Kimmel studies, the members' racism was not the *cause* of their joining but, rather, joining was the cause of their racism.

Just as our associations can increase prejudice, they can also reduce prejudice. Not just any association will do it, though. Certain conditions reduce prejudice, increase mutual understandings, and improve relations. What leads to these results? They are more likely to happen if people from different racial–ethnic groups are of equal status, and if they interact frequently while working toward a goal they both want (Riley 2009). An example is parents who form committees to improve their children's schools. Sociologists have a shorthand name for these findings: *contact theory*.

THE FAR-REACHING NATURE OF PREJUDICE

It is amazing how much prejudice people can learn. In classic research, psychologist Eugene Hartley (1946) asked people how they felt about several racial–ethnic groups. Besides Negroes, Jews, and so on, he included the Wallonians, Pireneans, and Danireans—names he had made up. Most people who expressed dislike for Jews and Negroes also showed similar contempt for these three fictitious groups.

Hartley's study shows that prejudice does not depend on negative experiences with others. It also reveals that people who are prejudiced against one racial–ethnic group tend to be prejudiced against other groups. People can be prejudiced against people they have never met—and even against groups that do not exist!

"ETHNIC MAPS" AND INTERNALIZING DOMINANT NORMS

Prejudice is so extensive that people even learn to be prejudiced against their *own* group. A national survey found that African Americans think that lighter-skinned African American women are more attractive than those with darker skin (Hill 2002). Participant observation in the ghetto also reveals a preference for lighter skin (Jones 2010). Sociologists call this *the internalization of the norms of the dominant group.*

To study the internalization of dominant norms, psychologists Mahzarin Banaji and Anthony Greenwald created the *Implicit Association Test.* In one version of this test, good and bad words are flashed on a screen along with photos of African Americans and whites. Most subjects are quicker to associate positive words (such as *love, peace,* and *baby*) with whites and negative words (such as *cancer, bomb,* and *devil*) with blacks. Here's the clincher: This is true for *both* whites and blacks (Dasgupta et al. 2000; Greenwald and Krieger 2006). Apparently, we all learn the *ethnic maps* of our culture and, along with them, their route to biased perception.

Groups Based on Prejudice

Some groups, such as the neo-Nazis and the Ku Klux Klan, even base their existence on prejudice. These groups believe that race is real, that white is best, and that beneath society's surface is a murky river of mingling conspiracies (Ezekiel 1995). What would happen if a Jew attended their meetings? Would he or she survive? By now, you've learned that the drive to know takes sociologists to some interesting places. Sociologist Raphael Ezekiel (1995) told leaders of these groups that he was a Jew and that he wanted to interview them and to attend their meetings. Amazingly, they let him do so. Here are some of the insights he gained during his fascinating sociological adventure:

CORE BELIEFS

Ezekiel found that the organizations are based on fundamental ideas that the members keep affirming to one another.

> [The leader has a] belief in exclusive categories. For the white racist leader, it is profoundly true . . . that the socially defined collections we call races represent fundamental categories. A man is black or a man is white; there are no in-betweens. Every human belongs to a racial category, and all the members of one category are radically different from all the members of other categories. Moreover, race represents the essence of the person. A truck is a truck, a car is a car, a cat is a cat, a dog is a dog, a black is a black, a white is a white. . . . These axioms have a rock-hard quality in the leaders' minds; the world is made up of racial groups. That is what exists for them. (In addition), life is about the war between these groups. (Finally), events have secret causes, (and) . . . any myth is plausible, as long as it involves intricate plotting. (pp. 66–67)

WHO IS ATTRACTED TO THESE GROUPS?

Here is what Ezekiel discovered:

> [There is a] ready pool of whites who will respond to the racist signal. . . . This population [is] always hungry for activity—or for the talk of activity—that promises dignity and meaning to lives that are working poorly in a highly competitive world. . . . Much as I don't want to believe it, [this] movement brings a sense of meaning—at least for a while—to some of the discontented. To struggle in a cause that transcends the individual lends meaning to life, no matter how ill-founded or narrowing the cause. . . . I often found myself driving with them past the closed factories, the idled plants of our shrinking manufacturing base. These fatherless Nazi youths, these high-school dropouts, will find little place in the emerging economy . . . a permanently underemployed white underclass is taking its place alongside the permanent black underclass. The struggle over race merely diverts youth from confronting the real issues of their lives. (pp. 32–33)

Individual and Institutional Discrimination

Sociologists stress that we should move beyond thinking in terms of **individual discrimination,** the negative treatment of one person by another. Although such behavior creates problems, it is primarily an issue between individuals. With their focus on the broader picture, sociologists encourage us to examine

individual discrimination person-to-person or face-to-face discrimination; the negative treatment of people by other individuals

Messages of supremacy can provide a sense of hope and the promise of a better future for those who feel they have been wronged and rejected.

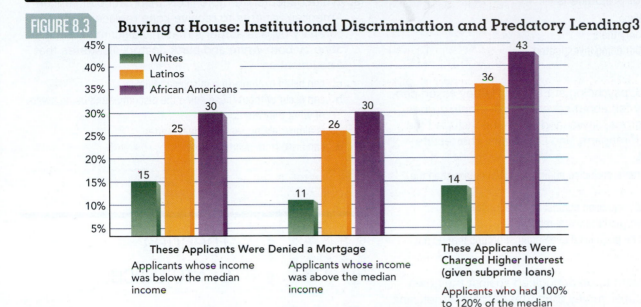

FIGURE 8.3 Buying a House: Institutional Discrimination and Predatory Lending[3]

These Applicants Were Denied a Mortgage

Applicants whose income was below the median income

Applicants whose income was above the median income

These Applicants Were Charged Higher Interest (given subprime loans)

Applicants who had 100% to 120% of the median income

Legend: Whites, Latinos, African Americans

Source: By the author. Based on Kochbar and Gonzalez-Barrera 2009.

institutional discrimination—that is, to see how discrimination is woven into the fabric of society. Let's look at two examples.

HOME MORTGAGES

Bank lending provides an excellent example of institutional discrimination. Earlier studies using national samples showed that bankers were more likely to reject the loan applications of minorities. When bankers defended themselves by saying that whites had better credit history, researchers retested their data. They found that even when applicants had identical credit, African Americans and Latinos were *60 percent* more likely to be rejected (Thomas 1991, 1992).

The subprime debacle that threw the stock market into a tailspin brought new revelations. Look at Figure 8.3 above. You can see that *minorities are still more likely to be turned down for a loan—whether their incomes are below or above the average income of their community.* Beyond this hard finding lies another just as devastating. In the credit crisis that caused so many to lose their homes, African Americans and Latinos were hit harder than whites. The last set of bars on Figure 8.3 shows a major reason for this: *Banks purposely targeted minorities to charge higher interest rates.* Over the lifetime of a loan, these higher monthly payments can come to an extra $100,000 to $200,000 (Powell and Roberts 2009).

HEALTH CARE

It is important to understand that discrimination does not have to be deliberate. In some cases, no one is aware of it—neither those being discriminated against *nor* those doing the discriminating. Consider knee replacements and coronary bypass

institutional discrimination
negative treatment of a minority group that is built into a society's institutions; also called *systemic discrimination*

surgery. White patients are more likely than either Latino or African American patients to receive these procedures (Skinner et al. 2003; Popescu et al. 2007). Treatment after a heart attack follows a similar pattern: Whites are more likely than blacks to be given cardiac catheterization, a test to detect blockage of blood vessels. This study of 40,000 patients holds a surprise: Both black *and* white doctors are more likely to give this preventive care to whites (Stolberg 2001).

Researchers do not know why race–ethnicity is a factor in medical decisions. With both white and black doctors involved, we can be certain that physicians *do not intend* to discriminate. Apparently, the implicit bias that comes with the internalization of dominant norms becomes a subconscious motivation for giving or denying access to advanced medical procedures.

Watch the **Video**
The Basics: Race and Ethnicity in **mysoclab**

UNIT 8.3 // TESTING MYSELF
DID I LEARN IT? ANSWERS ARE AT THE END OF THE CHAPTER

1. Juan, who owns a dry cleaners, cannot stand Pireneans. Whenever a Pirenean enters his shop, he goes into the back room and stays there until the Pirenean leaves. Juan's action is an example of
   - **a.** shortchanging a customer
   - **b.** preferential customering
   - **c.** prejudice
   - **d.** discrimination

2. Juan told a friend about what he does when Pireneans come into his shop. His friend said that you can't trust Pireneans, that they steal and won't work. Juan's and his friend's feelings and ideas are examples of
   - **a.** erroneous ideas
   - **b.** preferential customering
   - **c.** prejudice
   - **d.** discrimination

3. The source of prejudice is
   a. inborn feelings
   b. learning from others
   c. unknown, but being investigated
   d. changing

4. Back in 1946, psychologist Eugene Hartley asked people how they felt about several racial–ethnic groups. Besides Negroes, Jews, and so on, he included the Wallonians, Pireneans, and Danireans. The results showed that
   a. there was more prejudice against the Wallonians than the Danireans
   b. no one was prejudiced against the Wallonians
   c. the Pireneans had the worst reputation
   d. people can be prejudiced even against groups that do not exist

5. People can learn to be prejudiced against their own group. A national survey found that African Americans think that lighter-skinned African American women are more attractive than those with darker skin. This is an example of
   a. the white skin fallacy
   b. internalizing dominant norms
   c. dominant group prejudice
   d. in-group prejudice

6. In the Implicit Association Test, words are flashed on a screen along with photos of African Americans and whites. Most subjects, both blacks and whites, are quicker to associate positive words with whites and negative words with blacks. This is an example of
   a. the white skin fallacy
   b. internalizing dominant norms
   c. dominant group prejudice
   d. in-group prejudice

7. To get through a course in calculus, Clarissa and her friends formed a study group. They refused to let Clara join them because Clara is a Wallonian. This is an example of
   a. a misplaced fallacy
   b. institutional discrimination
   c. individual discrimination
   d. prejudice

8. If sociologists did national or statewide research on the acceptance rates of mortgage applicants and found that Wallonians with the same credit history as others are more likely to be turned down for loans, this would be an example of
   a. a misplaced fallacy
   b. institutional discrimination
   c. individual discrimination
   d. prejudice

9. White patients are more likely than Latino or African American patients to receive knee replacements and coronary bypass surgery. That this discrimination is done by both white and black doctors illustrates that discrimination
   a. can be an example of a misplaced fallacy
   b. can occur without those doing the discriminating being aware of what they are doing
   c. is almost always an individual matter
   d. can arise from positive traits

UNIT 8.4

Theories of Prejudice

WHAT AM I SUPPOSED TO LEARN?

After you have read this unit, you should be able to

1 Summarize psychological theories of prejudice: scapegoats, frustration, and the authoritarian personality.

2 Explain the sociological perspectives of prejudice: functionalism, conflict, and symbolic interactionism.

Social scientists have developed several theories to explain prejudice. Let's first look at psychological explanations, then at sociological ones.

Psychological Perspectives
FRUSTRATION AND SCAPEGOATS

"Why are we having a depression? The Jews have taken over the banking system, and they want to suck every dollar out of us."

Racial-ethnic relations are troubled throughout the world. This photo is from England.

They're always talking with their hands. I don't like the Walloneans, either. They're always smiling at something. And I don't like librarians. And my job sucks. Hitler might have had his faults, but he put people to work during the Great Depression."

Have you ever wondered whether some people's personalities make them more inclined to be prejudiced, and others more fair-minded? For psychologist Theodor Adorno, who had fled from the Nazis, this was no idle speculation. With the horrors he had observed still fresh in his mind, Adorno wondered whether there might be a certain type of person who is more likely to fall for the racist spewings of people like Hitler, Goebbels, and those in the Ku Klux Klan.

To find out, Adorno and associates (1950) gave three tests to about 2,000 people, ranging from college professors to prison inmates (Adorno et al. 1950). He measured their ethnocentrism, anti-Semitism (bias against Jews), and support for strong, authoritarian leaders. People who scored high on one test also scored high on the other two. For example, people who agreed with anti-Semitic statements also said that governments should be authoritarian and that foreign customs pose a threat to the "American" way.

Adorno concluded that highly prejudiced people have deep respect for authority and are submissive to authority figures. He termed this the **authoritarian personality.** These people believe that things are either right or wrong. Ambiguity disturbs them, especially in matters of religion or sex. They become anxious when they confront norms and values that are different from their own. To view people who differ from themselves as inferior assures them that their own positions are right.

Adorno's research stimulated more than 1,000 research studies. In general, the researchers found that people who are older, less educated, less intelligent, and from a lower social class are more likely to be authoritarian. Critics say that this doesn't indicate a particular personality, just that the less educated are more prejudiced—which we already knew (Yinger 1965; Ray 1991). Nevertheless, researchers continue to study this concept (McFarland 2010).

This is what Hitler shouted in the 1930s. Germany was in the midst of a depression so severe that it was wiping out the middle class. Inflation soared so greatly that it took a wheelbarrow of currency to buy groceries. Who caused these severe problems? every German wondered. Hitler said he had the answer: the Jews. Amidst Hitler's inflamed speeches, the Germans grasped at straws and elected Hitler to restore prosperity to Germany.

Like Hitler, people often unfairly blame their troubles on a **scapegoat**—often a racial–ethnic or religious minority. Why do they do this? Psychologist John Dollard and colleagues (1939) suggested that prejudice is the result of frustration. People who are unable to strike out at the real source of their frustration (such as not having a job) look for someone to blame. This person or group becomes a target on which they vent their frustrations.

Frustration and prejudice often go together. A team of psychologists led by Emory Cowen (1959) measured the prejudice of a group of students. They then gave the students two puzzles to solve, making sure the students did not have enough time to solve them. After the students had worked furiously on the puzzles, the experimenters shook their heads in disgust and said that they couldn't believe the students hadn't finished such a simple task. They then retested the students. The results? Their scores on prejudice increased. The students had directed their frustrations outward, transferring them to people who had nothing to do with the contempt they had experienced.

THE AUTHORITARIAN PERSONALITY

"I don't like Swedes. They're too rigid. And I don't like the Italians.

Sociological Perspectives

Sociologists find psychological explanations inadequate. They stress that the key to understanding prejudice cannot be found by looking *inside* people, but, rather, by examining conditions *outside* them. For this reason, sociologists focus on how social environments influence prejudice. With this background, let's compare functionalist, conflict, and symbolic interactionist perspectives on prejudice.

scapegoat an individual or group unfairly blamed for someone else's troubles

authoritarian personality Theodor Adorno's term for people who are prejudiced and rank high on measures of conformity, intolerance, insecurity, respect for authority, and submissiveness to superiors

This photo, taken in Birmingham, Alabama, provides a glimpse into the intensity and bravery of the civil rights demonstrators of the 1960s.

FUNCTIONALISM

In a television documentary, journalist Bill Moyers interviewed Fritz Hippler, a Nazi who at age 29 was put in charge of the entire German film industry. When Hitler came to power, Hippler said, the Germans were no more anti-Semitic than the French. Hippler was told to increase anti-Semitism in Germany. Obediently, he produced movies that contained vivid scenes comparing Jews to rats—with their breeding threatening to infest the population.

Why was Hippler told to create hatred? Prejudice and discrimination were functional for the Nazis. Defeated in World War I and devastated by fines levied by the victors, Germany was on its knees. Runaway inflation was destroying its middle class. To help unite this fractured Germany, the Nazis created a scapegoat to blame for their troubles. In addition, the Jews owned businesses, homes, bank accounts, jewelry, fine art, and other property that the Nazis could confiscate. Jews also held key positions (as university professors, reporters, judges, and so on), which the Nazis could give as prizes to their followers. In the end, hatred also showed its dysfunctional face, as the Nazi officials hanged at Nuremberg discovered.

Prejudice becomes practically irresistible when state machinery is used to advance the cause of hatred. To produce prejudice, the Nazis harnessed government agencies, the schools, police, courts, and mass media. A pair of identical twins, Jack and Oskar, who had been separated as babies, illustrates how thorough and devastating the results were. Jack was brought up as a Jew in Trinidad, while Oskar was reared as a Catholic

in Czechoslovakia. Under the Nazi regime, Oskar learned to hate Jews, unaware that he himself was a Jew.

Be sure that you don't miss the significance of what the Nazis did. *The social environment can be set up to increase or decrease prejudice.* This is also illustrated by a little experiment performed by psychologists Muzafer Sherif and Carolyn Sherif (1953). In a boys' summer camp, the Sherifs assigned friends to different cabins and then had the cabin groups compete in sports. In just a few days, strong in-groups had formed. Even lifelong friends began to taunt one another, calling each other "crybaby" and "sissy."

IN SUM: Functionalists stress that the social environment can be arranged to generate positive or negative feelings about people. Note especially how prejudice arises if we pit groups against one another in an "I win, you lose" situation. In both the Nazis' action and in the little summer camp experiment, you can also see that prejudice is functional, that it creates in-group solidarity. And, of course, it is obvious how dysfunctional prejudice is, when you observe the way it destroys human relationships.

CONFLICT THEORY

"The Japanese have gone on strike? They're demanding a raise? And they even want a rest period? We'll show them who's boss. Hire those Koreans who've been trying to get work."

This did happen. When Japanese workers in Hawaii struck, owners of plantations replaced them with Koreans (Jeong and You 2008). What the owners did, say conflict theorists, was to exploit a **split labor market,** the division of workers along racial–ethnic (and gender) lines (Du Bois 1935/1992; Roediger 2002). Today's exploitation of these divisions is more subtle than what occurred in Hawaii, but the split labor market is far from dead. It is still vibrant in its more subdued form. White workers are keenly aware that members of other racial–ethnic groups are ready to take their jobs. African Americans and Latinos often perceive the other as competitors (Cose 2006). Men certainly know that women are eager to get promoted. And elderly workers know that an army of unemployed young people is knocking at the door eager to take their jobs. You can see how today's split labor market creates fears of competition and of being replaced, and how this helps to keep workers in line.

split labor market workers split along racial–ethnic, gender, age, or any other lines; this split is exploited by owners to weaken the bargaining power of workers

reserve labor force the unemployed; unemployed workers are thought of as being "in reserve"—capitalists take them "out of reserve" (put them back to work) during times of high production and then put them "back in reserve" (lay them off) when they are no longer needed

Another tactic that owners use is the **reserve labor force.** This is simply another term for the unemployed. To expand production during economic booms, companies hire people who don't have jobs. When the economy revives, they lay off these workers. That desperate people are "out there" looking for work is a lesson not lost on those who have jobs. Many workers are just one or two paychecks away from ending up "on the streets," and haunting them is the fear of eviction and having their cars and furniture repossessed.

IN SUM: Conflict theorists stress that divisions among workers deflect anger and hostility away from those in power, redirecting these powerful emotions toward racial-ethnic groups. Instead of recognizing their common class interests and working for their mutual welfare, workers learn to fear and distrust one another.

SYMBOLIC INTERACTIONISM

Note the connection between labels and prejudice in this statement:

> "I know her qualifications are OK, but yikes! She's ugly. I don't want to have to look at her every day. Let's hire the one with the nice curves."

How does reserve labor force *fit into explanations of prejudice? This photo was taken in Laguna Beach, California.*

> **IF YOU WANT TO LEARN MORE** *about how prejudice used to be strong that whites kept a black man in a zoo,*
>
> **Read** more from the author: The Man in the Zoo in **mysoclab**

While conflict theorists focus on how owners (or capitalists) exploit racial and ethnic divisions, symbolic interactionists examine how labels affect perception and create prejudice.

HOW LABELS CREATE SELECTIVE PERCEPTION: Symbolic interactionists stress that *the labels we learn affect how we perceive people.* Labels create **selective perception.** That is, labels lead us to see certain things while they blind us to others. When a group is given a label, we tend to perceive its members as all alike. We shake off evidence that doesn't fit (Simpson and Yinger 1972). Shorthand for emotionally charged stereotypes, some racial and ethnic labels are especially powerful. As you know, the term *nigger* is not neutral. Nor are *honky, cracker, spic, mick, kike, limey, kraut, dago, guinea,* or any of the other scornful words people use to belittle ethnic groups.

And it is not just racial-ethnic labels that create selective perception. Consider the label *ugly* in the short statement above, as well as *whore, rapist,* and *child molester.* Such words work in a similar way. They overpower us with emotions, blocking out rational thought about the people to whom they refer (Allport 1954).

selective perception
seeing certain features of an object or situation, but remaining blind to others

LABELS AND SELF-FULFILLING STEREOTYPES: Some stereotypes have another amazing capacity. They not only create selective perception, but they also produce the very behavior depicted in the stereotype. To see how this is possible, let's consider Group X. You know this group. Your stereotype tells you that its members are lazy. This means they don't deserve good jobs. ("They are lazy and wouldn't do the job well.") Denied the better jobs, most members of Group X do "dirty work," the jobs few people want. ("That's the right kind of work for that kind of people.") Since much "dirty work" is temporary, members of Group X are often seen "on the streets." Seeing them just "hanging around" reinforces the original stereotype of laziness. ("Look at them. They just hang around the streets. They don't want to work.") In such a *self-fulfilling stereotype,* the discrimination that created the "laziness" in the first place passes unnoticed.

IN SUM: The primary focus of symbolic interactionists is meaning—what things mean to people and how people use those meanings (symbols) to build their worlds. Negative stereotypes underlie prejudice. These stereotypes affect what people "see" when they look at others. This, in turn, creates or reinforces prejudice and encourages and justifies discrimination.

In the following *Making It Personal,* let's try to make these ideas a little more personal.

> **Read** the **Document**
> "Racism in Toyland" by Christine L. Williams in **mysoclab**

MAKING IT PERSONAL
Your Negative Stereotypes and Prejudices

We all have a dark side when it comes to prejudice. As much as many of us don't like to admit it, there is ample evidence that this is true. Recall the bias by both white and African American physicians that we reviewed in Unit 8.3. And recall that *Implicit Association Test* in Unit 8.2 that reveals people's deep stereotypes, many of which they don't even know they have.

So, now let's really get personal. And you don't have to share this with anyone, so feel free to explore your own deep prejudices. Consider what you just reviewed in this symbolic interactionist section. To apply it is to see that we all have stereotypes of groups of people, and some of them are negative. Which ones do you have? When you see someone from some particular racial–ethnic group—a stranger about whom you know nothing—what comes to mind? If this question is too threatening, then think about other groups that we stereotype: body size (both very thin and very heavy) or social class. What images come to mind when you see an ultra thin or obese person? How about when you see someone who is wearing shabby, out-of-date clothing? How about a homeless person?

The bottom line is that prejudice is not just something "out there" that "bad" people have. We all have prejudices. We learn prejudice as we learn society

Watch the **Video**
Sociology on the Job:
Race and Ethnicity in
mysoclab

UNIT 8.4 // TESTING MYSELF
DID I LEARN IT? ANSWERS ARE AT THE END OF THE CHAPTER

1. In the 1930s, Germany was in an inflationary depression so severe that it was wiping out the middle class. Hitler said that the Jews were profiting from good people's problems, arousing prejudice and discrimination against Jews. Hitler was using the Jews as a
   a. reintegrative target   b. passive prejudice probe
   c. reactionary model   d. scapegoat

2. Psychologist Theodor Adorno tested people on their levels of ethnocentrism, anti-Semitism (bias against Jews), and support for strong, authoritarian leaders. He gave this name to people who scored high on all three tests
   a. Hitlerites
   b. the authoritarian personality
   c. the prejudiced personality
   d. the exploited

3. When sociologists study prejudice, they are interested in learning about the consequences of prejudice for social interaction and
   a. how prejudice creates wealth for some
   b. the origin of prejudice
   c. how prejudice creates inner turmoil for people who are prejudiced
   d. how the social environment increases or decreases prejudice

4. At a boys' summer camp, psychologists Muzafer Sherif and Carolyn Sherif assigned friends to different cabins and then had the cabin groups compete in sports. In just a few days
   a. the cabin groups formed alliances with one another
   b. three boys had to be sent home because they could not stand competing with their friends
   c. parents demanded that the living arrangements be changed to conform to what they had agreed to when they signed the summer camp application
   d. strong in-groups formed and even lifelong friends began to call one another "crybaby" and "sissy"

5. The social environment can be set up to increase or decrease prejudice. This environment produces high prejudice
   a. requiring football players to spend long hours doing library research
   b. having people who recently broke up go on blind dates
   c. an "I win, you lose" situation
   d. women and men college students working on the same research teams

6. "The Nazis gained from anti-Semitism. They seized businesses, bank accounts, fine art, and other property from Jews They also replaced Jews in key positions (university professors, reporters, judges, and so on), giving these positions as prizes to their followers." This statement is likely to be made by a
   a. psychologist
   b. functionalist
   c. conflict theorist
   d. symbolic interactionist

7. When the all-male workforce at the cannery threatened to go on strike, management said, "Go ahead if you want to. A lot of women want your jobs, and they can run those machines just as good as you—and cheaper." The managers were trying to break worker solidarity by taking advantage of
   a. a split labor market
   b. a reserve labor force
   c. a weak union
   d. labor opportunities

8. A year later, workers at the cannery could not stand their working conditions any longer and they again threatened to strike. This time, management said, "If you strike, we'll replace you with all those unemployed men down at the labor office begging for

work." The managers were trying to break worker solidarity by threatening to use a

a. labor disparity   **b.** recession
c. split labor market   **d.** reserve labor force

9. Labels lead us to see certain things while they blind us to others. When a group is labeled, we tend to perceive its members as all alike. We shake off evidence that doesn't fit. This characteristic of labeling is called

a. an open venue   **b.** selective perception
c. label blindness   **d.** deep prejudice

10. Members of Group A think that members of Group X are lazy. They never offer jobs to members of Group X. Many members of Group X are poor and unemployed and hang around the street. Members of Group A take the idleness of Group X as proof that their ideas about Group X are right. This is an example of

a. job lockup
b. prejudice without discrimination
c. discrimination without prejudice
d. a self-fulfilling stereotype

UNIT 8.5

Racial–Ethnic Relations: European Americans

WHAT AM I SUPPOSED TO LEARN?

After you have read this unit, you should be able to

1 Specify the major racial–ethnic groups and their percentage of the U.S. population.

2 Summarize the relationship of Anglos to white ethnics in the early years of the United States and indicate how racism showed up in an early law.

Racial–ethnic identity is constantly changing, and the use of any term carries a risk as it takes on politically charged meanings. This means that no term that refers to specific groups satisfies

USA—the land of diversity.

everyone. If we had no separate racial–ethnic identities, this problem would not exist. But as part of everyday life we do classify ourselves and one another as belonging to distinct racial–ethnic groups.

As Figures 8.4 and 8.5 illustrate, on the basis of these self-identities whites make up 65 percent of the U.S. population, minorities (African Americans, Asian Americans, Latinos, and Native Americans) add up to 34 percent. Between 1 and 2 percent claim membership in two or more racial–ethnic groups.

FIGURE 8.4   **Race–Ethnicity of the U.S. Population**

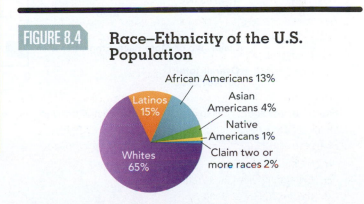

Source: By the author. See Figure 8.5.

As you can see from the social map on the next page, the distribution of dominant and minority groups among the states seldom comes close to the national average. This is because minority groups tend to be clustered in regions. The extreme distributions are represented by Maine and Vermont, where whites outnumber minorities 19 to 1, and by Hawaii where minorities outnumber whites 3 to 1.

With this as background, let's review the major groups in the United States, going from the largest to the smallest.

White Anglo Saxon Protestants

Benjamin Franklin said, "Why should the Palatine (German) boors be suffered (allowed) to swarm into our settlements and by herding together establish their language and manners to the exclusion of ours? Why should Pennsylvania, founded by the English, become a colony of aliens, who will shortly be so numerous as to germanize us instead of our anglifying them?" (in Alba and Nee 2003:17)

FIGURE 8.5 **U.S. Racial–Ethnic Groups**

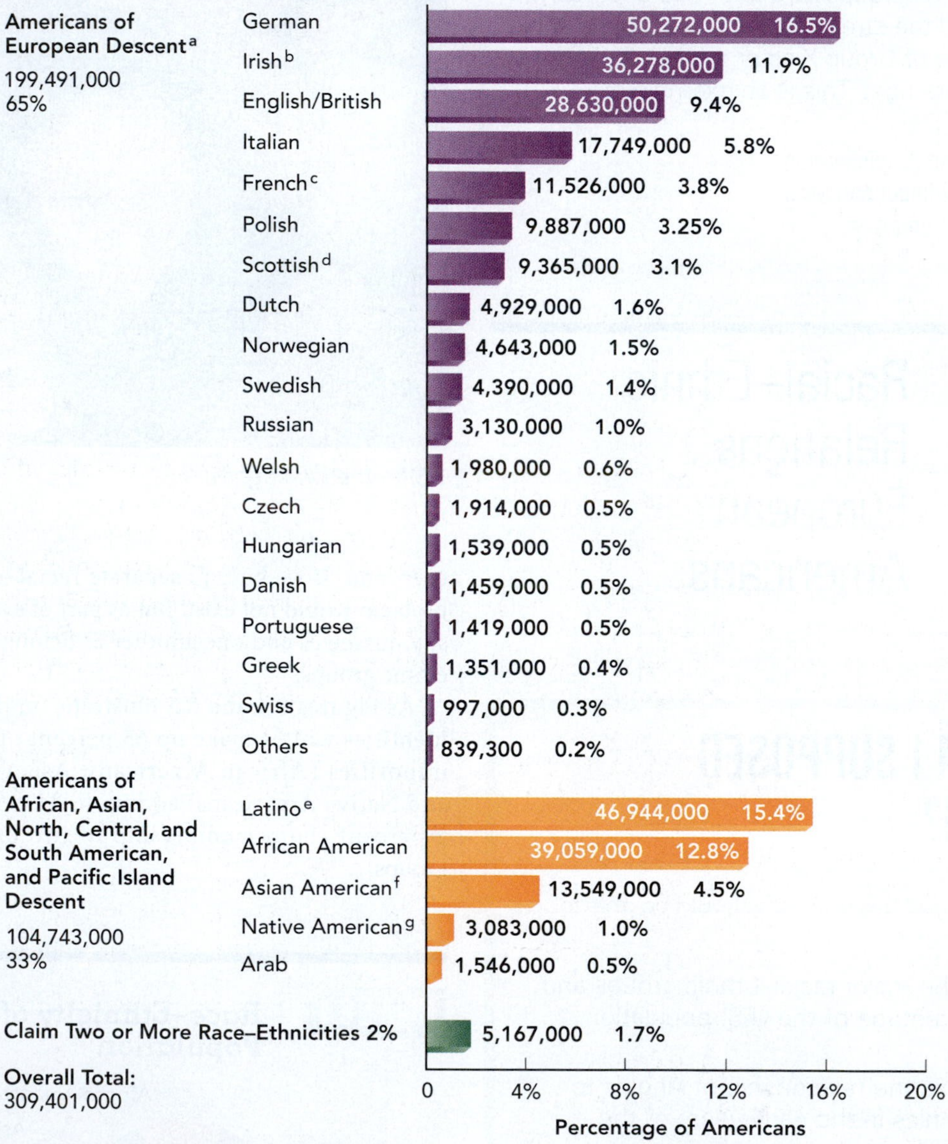

Americans of European Descent[a] 199,491,000 65%		
German	50,272,000	16.5%
Irish[b]	36,278,000	11.9%
English/British	28,630,000	9.4%
Italian	17,749,000	5.8%
French[c]	11,526,000	3.8%
Polish	9,887,000	3.25%
Scottish[d]	9,365,000	3.1%
Dutch	4,929,000	1.6%
Norwegian	4,643,000	1.5%
Swedish	4,390,000	1.4%
Russian	3,130,000	1.0%
Welsh	1,980,000	0.6%
Czech	1,914,000	0.5%
Hungarian	1,539,000	0.5%
Danish	1,459,000	0.5%
Portuguese	1,419,000	0.5%
Greek	1,351,000	0.4%
Swiss	997,000	0.3%
Others	839,300	0.2%

Americans of African, Asian, North, Central, and South American, and Pacific Island Descent 104,743,000 33%		
Latino[e]	46,944,000	15.4%
African American	39,059,000	12.8%
Asian American[f]	13,549,000	4.5%
Native American[g]	3,083,000	1.0%
Arab	1,546,000	0.5%

Claim Two or More Race–Ethnicities 2%		
	5,167,000	1.7%

Overall Total: 309,401,000

Percentage of Americans

Source: By the author. Based on Statistical Abstract of the United States 2010:Table 10; 2011:Table 52.

FIGURE 8.6 The Distribution of Dominant and Minority Groups

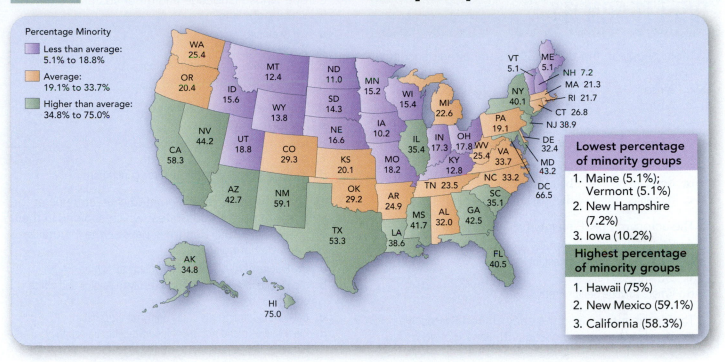

Percentage Minority

- Less than average: 5.1% to 18.8%
- Average: 19.1% to 33.7%
- Higher than average: 34.8% to 75.0%

WA 25.4
OR 20.4
ID 15.6
MT 12.4
ND 11.0
MN 15.2
WI 15.4
MI 22.6
NY 40.1
VT 5.1
ME 5.1
NH 7.2
MA 21.3
RI 21.7
CT 26.8
NJ 38.9
NV 44.2
UT 18.8
WY 13.8
SD 14.3
IA 10.2
IL 35.4
IN 17.3
OH 17.8
PA 19.1
WV 25.4
DE 32.4
CA 58.3
CO 29.3
NE 16.6
KS 20.1
MO 18.2
KY 12.8
VA 33.7
MD 43.2
DC 66.5
AZ 42.7
NM 59.1
OK 29.2
AR 24.9
TN 23.5
NC 33.2
SC 35.1
GA 42.5
TX 53.3
MS 41.7
AL 32.0
LA 38.6
FL 40.5
AK 34.8
HI 75.0

Lowest percentage of minority groups

1. Maine (5.1%); Vermont (5.1%)
2. New Hampshire (7.2%)
3. Iowa (10.2%)

Highest percentage of minority groups

1. Hawaii (75%)
2. New Mexico (59.1%)
3. California (58.3%)

Source: By the author. Based on Statistical Abstract of the United States *2011:Table 19.*

At the founding of the United States, White Anglo Saxon Protestants (**WASPs**) held deep prejudices against other whites. There was practically no end to their disdainful stereotypes of **white ethnics**—immigrants from Europe whose language and other customs differed from theirs. The English despised the Irish, viewing them as dirty, lazy drunkards, but they also painted Poles, Jews, Italians, and others with similar disparaging brushstrokes. From the Franklin quote, you can see that they didn't like Germans either.

The political and cultural dominance of the WASPs placed intense pressure on immigrants to assimilate into the mainstream culture. The children of most immigrants embraced the new way of life and quickly came to think of themselves as Americans rather than as Germans, French, Hungarians, and so on. Like a heavy overcoat on a hot day, they discarded their distinctive customs, especially their language, often viewing them as symbols of shame. This second generation of immigrants was sandwiched between two worlds: "the old country" of their parents and their new home. Their children, the third generation, had an easier adjustment, for they had fewer customs to discard. As white ethnics assimilated into this

WASP white anglo saxon protestant

white ethnics white immigrants to the United States whose cultures differ from WASP culture

Anglo-American culture, the meaning of WASP expanded to include them.

And for those who weren't white? Perhaps the event that best illustrates the racial view of the nation's founders occurred when Congress passed the Naturalization Act of 1790, declaring that only white immigrants could apply for citizenship. Relationships among the various racial–ethnic groups since the founding of the nation have, at best, been a rocky one.

IN SUM: Because Protestant English immigrants settled the colonies, they established the culture—from the dominant language to the dominant religion. Highly ethnocentric, they regarded the customs of other groups as inferior. Because white Europeans took power, they determined the national agenda to which other ethnic groups had to react and conform. Their institutional and cultural dominance still sets the stage for current ethnic relations.

IF YOU WANT TO LEARN MORE about white identity and privilege in everyday life,

Read more from the author: Individual Rights vs the common Good in **mysoclab**

UNIT 8.5 // TESTING MYSELF

UNIT 8.5 // TESTING MYSELF
DID I LEARN IT? ANSWERS ARE AT THE END OF THE CHAPTER

1. Most people in the United States trace their ancestry to
   a. Africa
   b. Asia
   c. Australia
   d. Europe

2. In Maine and Vermont, whites outnumber minorities 19 to 1. In this state, minorities outnumber whites 3 to 1
   a. New Jersey
   b. Minnesota
   c. Hawaii
   d. Oregon

3. The acronym WASP stands for
   a. Why Anglos Seem Powerful
   b. White Anglo Saxon Protestant
   c. We Are Sexy People
   d. Where Anyone Seems Pretty

4. The dominant group in the early United States was the Anglos, people from England. They looked down on immigrants from other European countries, even despising them. The term for immigrants from Europe whose language and other customs differed from the Anglos is
   a. white ethnics
   b. WASPs
   c. SEEs (Southern and Eastern Europeans)
   d. USA (United Southern Anglos)

5. Which generation of immigrants has the easiest adjustment to a new culture?
   a. first
   b. second
   c. third
   d. it's about the same for these three generations

6. Prejudice was a taken-for-granted characteristic of the founders of the United States, which showed in their early laws. In 1790, Congress passed the Naturalization Act, declaring that
   a. the Pledge of Allegiance applied only to Anglos
   b. the Pledge of Allegiance applied only to Anglos and white ethnics
   c. only white immigrants could apply for citizenship
   d. black slaves could not apply for citizenship unless they passed a literacy test

---

UNIT 8.6

Racial–Ethnic Relations: Latinos (Hispanics)

WHAT AM I SUPPOSED TO LEARN?

After you have read this unit, you should be able to

1 Discuss the causes, reaction, and extent of illegal immigration and the controversy over Spanish.

2 Explain the diversity of Latinos and how this affects their political unity.

Before reviewing major characteristics of Latinos, it is important to stress that *Latino* and *Hispanic* refer not to a race but to ethnic groups. Latinos may identify themselves as blacks, whites, or Native Americans. Some Latinos who have an African heritage refer to themselves as Afro-Latinos (Navarro 2003). Some Latinos prefer the term *Hispanic American,* but others reject it, saying that it ignores the Native American side of their heritage. Some want to limit the term *Chicanos*—commonly used to refer to Americans from Mexico—to those who have a sense of ethnic oppression and unity. Others say that this term also applies to those who have assimilated.

Numbers, Origins, and Location

When birds still nested in the trees that would be used to build the *Mayflower,* Latinos had already established settlements in Florida and New Mexico (Bretos 1994). Today, Latinos are the largest minority group in the United States. As shown in Figure 8.7 on the next page, about 32 million people trace their origin to Mexico, 4 million to Puerto Rico, almost 2 million to Cuba, and about 8 million to Central and South America.

Although Latinos are officially tallied at 47 million, another 9 million Latinos are living here illegally. About 7 million are from Mexico, and the rest from Central and South America (*Statistical Abstract* 2012:Table 45). Most Latinos are citizens or legal residents, but each year about 700,000 Latinos, most from Mexico, are arrested, usually soon after crossing the border

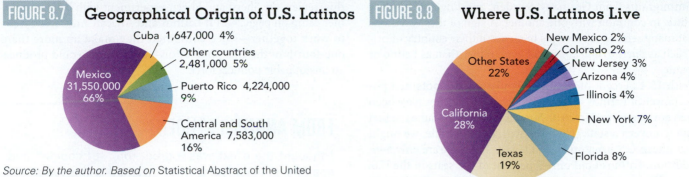

FIGURE 8.7 Geographical Origin of U.S. Latinos

- Cuba 1,647,000 4%
- Other countries 2,481,000 5%
- Mexico 31,550,000 66%
- Puerto Rico 4,224,000 9%
- Central and South America 7,583,000 16%

Source: By the author. Based on Statistical Abstract of the United States 2011:Table 37.

FIGURE 8.8 Where U.S. Latinos Live

- New Mexico 2%
- Colorado 2%
- New Jersey 3%
- Arizona 4%
- Illinois 4%
- New York 7%
- Florida 8%
- Other States 22%
- California 28%
- Texas 19%

Source: By the author. Based on Statistical Abstract of the United States 2011:Table 19.

(*Statistical Abstract* 2012:Table 531). They are returned to their home countries. Before our economic crisis when more jobs were available, the number was over a million a year. With this vast migration, about 20 million more Latinos live in the United States than Canadians (34 million) live in Canada. As Figure 8.8 shows, almost half live in just the states of California and Texas.

The massive unauthorized entry into the United States has aroused public concern. Arizona passed a law that gives its police the power to detain anyone suspected of being in the country illegally (Archibold 2010). This law aroused bitter opposition across the nation, as well as intense support for it. Another response was to build a wall along the 2,000 mile border between Mexico and the United States. After building just 53 miles of the wall at the horrendous cost of $1 billion, the wall was canceled (Preston 2011). Civilian groups such as the Minutemen also patrol the border, but unofficially. To avoid conflict with the U.S. Border Patrol, the Minutemen do not carry guns. A second unofficial group, the Techno Patriots, also patrols the border, using computers and thermal imaging cameras. When they confirm illegal crossings, they call the Border Patrol, whose agents make the arrests (Archibold and Preston 2008; Marino 2008).

Despite laws, walls, technology, and patrols, as long as there is a need for unskilled labor and millions of people live in grinding poverty, this flow of undocumented workers will continue. To gain insight into why, let me share this with you.

When I was living in Colima, Mexico, I met Manuel, who had lived in the United States for seven years. When Manuel invited me to go on a business trip with him, I accepted. As we traveled from one remote village to another, Manuel would sell used clothing that he had heaped in the back of his older-model Ford station wagon.

At one stop, Manuel took me into a dirt-floored, thatched-roof hut. While chickens ran in and out, Manuel whispered to a slender man who was about 23 years old. Juan, as his name turned out to be, had a partial grade school education. He also had a wife, four hungry children under the age of 5, and two pigs—his main food supply. Although eager to work, Juan had no job, for there was simply no work available in this remote village.

Manuel explained to me that he was not only selling clothing—he was also lining up migrants to the United States. For a fee, he would take a man to the border and introduce him to a "wolf," who would help him cross into the promised land.

Looking up from the children playing on the dirt floor with chickens pecking about them, I saw a man who loved his family. In order to make the desperate bid for a better life, he would suffer an enforced absence from them, as well as the uncertainties of a foreign culture whose language he did not know.

Juan opened his billfold, took something out, and slowly handed it to me. I felt tears as I saw the tenderness with which he handled this piece of paper. It was his passport to the land of opportunity: a Social Security card made out in his name, sent by a friend who had already made the trip and who was waiting for Juan on the other side of the border.

It was then that I realized that the thousands of Manuels scurrying about Mexico and the millions of Juans they are transporting can never be stopped, for only the United States can fulfill their dreams of a better life.

SPANISH LANGUAGE

The Spanish language distinguishes most Latinos from other U.S. ethnic groups. With 35 million people speaking Spanish at home, the United States has become one of the largest Spanish-speaking nations in the world (*Statistical Abstract* 2012: Table 53). Because about half of Latinos are unable to speak English, or can do so only with difficulty, many millions face a huge obstacle to getting good jobs.

The growing use of Spanish has stoked controversy (Fund 2007). Perceiving the prevalence of Spanish as a threat, Senator S. I. Hayakawa of California initiated an "English-only" movement in 1981. The constitutional amendment that he sponsored never got off the ground, but thirty states have passed laws that declare English their official language.

DIVERSITY

For Latinos, country of origin is highly significant. Those from Puerto Rico, for example, feel that they have little in common with people from Mexico, Venezuela, or El Salvador—just as earlier immigrants from Germany, Sweden, and England felt they had little in common with one another. A sign of these divisions is that many refer to themselves in terms of their country of origin, such as *puertorriqueños* or *cubanos,* rather than as Latino or Hispanic.

With 15.4 percent of the U.S. population, the potential political power of Latinos is remarkable. Several Latinos have been elected governors, and in 2010, Susana Martinez became the first Latina to govern a state (New Mexico). In the Senate, we might expect fifteen U.S. senators to be Latino—but there are only *four.* In addition, Latinos hold only 5 percent of the seats in the U.S. House of Representatives (*Statistical Abstract* 2012:Table 413). Among the reasons that keep the potential from becoming real is a lack of unity based on country of origin.

As Latinos have become more visible in the United States and more vocal in their demands for equality, they have come face to face with African Americans who fear that Latino gains in employment and at the ballot box come at their expense (Hutchinson 2008). This rivalry even shows up in prison, where hostility between Latino and African American gangs sometimes escalates into violence (Thompson 2009). (To better understand this, review the Sherif and Sherif experiment with boys at summer camp on page 242.) If Latinos and African Americans were to work together—since combined they make up more than one-fourth of the U.S. population—their unity would produce an unstoppable political force.

FROM ANOTHER STUDENT . . .

I thought the eText was a great tool. If I couldn't find something, I just typed what I wanted in the search bar and it brought up great results.

—*Jaclyn Nickerson*

COMPARATIVE CONDITIONS

To see how Latinos are doing on major indicators of well-being, look at Table 8.1. As you can see, compared with white

TABLE 8.1   **Race–Ethnicity and Comparative Well-Being[1]**

Racial–Ethnic Group	Income		Unemployment		Poverty		Home Ownership	
	Median Family Income	Compared to Whites	Percentage Unemployed	Compared to Whites	Percentage Below Poverty Line	Compared to Whites	Percentage Who Own Their Homes	Compared to Whites
Whites	$70,835	—	7.0%	—	9.3%	—	73%	—
Latinos	$43,437	39% lower	10.0%	43% higher	21.3%	129% higher	49%	33% lower
Country or Area of Origin								
Cuba	NA[2]	NA	NA	NA	16.8%	81% higher	58%	21% lower
Central/ South America	NA	NA	NA	NA	18.9%	103% higher	40%	45% lower
Mexico	NA	NA	NA	NA	24.8%	166% higher	49%	33% lower
Puerto Rico	NA	NA	NA	NA	25.2%	171% higher	38%	48% lower
African Americans	$41,874	41% lower	14.3%	104% higher	24.1%	159% higher	46%	37% lower
Asian Americans[3]	$80,101	13% higher	4.9%	30% lower	10.5%	13% higher	60%	14% lower
Native Americans	$43,190	39% lower	NA	NA	24.2%	160% higher	55%	25% lower

[1] Data are from 2005 and 2006.
[2] NA=Not Available
[3] Includes Pacific Islanders

Source: By the author. Based on Statistical Abstract of the United States *2012:Tables 36, 37, 627. Bureau of Labor Statistics 2012.*

TABLE 8.2   Race–Ethnicity and Education

Racial–Ethnic Group	Education Completed				Doctorates		
	Less Than High School	High School	Some College	College (BA or Higher)	Number Awarded	Percentage of all U.S. Doctorates[1]	Percentage of U.S. Population
Whites	9.6%	29.2%	21.9%	31.1%	39,648	78.0%	65.0%
Latinos	39.1%	26.1%	16.8%	12.6%	2,540	5.0%	15.4%
African Americans	18.6%	31.6%	24.8%	17.6%	4,434	8.7%	12.8%
Asian Americans	14.7%	16.0%	13.0%	49.7%	3,875	7.6%	4.5%
Native Americans	23.5%	30.4%	25.6%	13.0%	332	0.6%	1.0%

[1]Percentage after the doctorates awarded to nonresidents are deducted from the total.

Source: By the author. Based on Statistical Abstract of the United States 2012:Tables 36, 300, and Figure 8.5 of this text.

Photo taken just across the U.S. border, between Tijuana and San Diego.

Americans and Asian Americans, Latinos have less income, higher unemployment, and more poverty. They are also less likely to own their homes. We get another view if we focus on education. In Table 8.2, you can see that Latinos are the most likely to drop out of high school and the least likely to graduate from college. In a postindustrial society that increasingly requires advanced skills, these totals indicate that huge numbers of Latinos will be left behind.

IN SUM: The umbrella term of *Latino* (or *Hispanic*) conceals as much as it reveals. To understand comparative conditions, we need to also look at people's country of origin, which remains highly significant not only for self-identity but also for determining life chances. As you can see from Table 8.1, Latinos who trace their roots to Cuba have less poverty and are more likely to own their homes. In contrast, those who trace their origin to Puerto Rico score lower on these indicators of well-being.

UNIT 8.6 // TESTING MYSELF
DID I LEARN IT?   ANSWERS ARE AT THE END OF THE CHAPTER

1. The terms Latino and Hispanic refer to
   a. a race
   b. people from Mexico who are legal immigrants
   c. Americans from Mexico who have a sense of ethnic oppression and unity
   d. an ethnic group

2. Some Latinos want to limit the term Chicanos—commonly used to refer to Americans from Mexico—to those who
   a. are legal immigrants
   b. bypassed legal channels when they moved to the United States

   c. are from Mexico and have been in the United States for a second generation or longer
   d. have a sense of ethnic oppression and unity

3. With about 47 million people and making up about 15 percent of the population, the largest minority group in the United States is
   a. African Americans
   b. Asian Americans
   c. Latinos
   d. European Americans

4. Comparing the number of Latinos in the United States with the population of Canada, we find that
   a. more Canadians live in Canada than there are Latinos living in the United States
   b. millions more Latinos live in the United States than there are Canadians in Canada

c. the number of Latinos in the United States is about the same as the number of Canadians in Canada

d. there is no way to compare these totals

5. The primary reason for the massive migration of Mexicans to the United States is

a. jobs

b. education

c. freedom of association

d. a free press

6. This country has become one of the largest Spanish-speaking nations in the world

a. France

b. Germany

c. Paraguay

d. the United States

7. Earlier immigrants from Germany, Sweden, and England felt they had little in common with one another. This feeling is shared by Latinos who

a. are coming in huge numbers from Germany, Sweden, and England

b. believe that their country of origin is no longer relevant

c. are divided by country of origin

d. generally refuse to vote for candidates whose background is German or Swedish

8. In a postindustrial society that increasingly requires advanced skills, the statistics in Table 8.1 indicate that huge numbers of Latinos will be left behind. This is because Latinos

a. dislike education

b. are the most likely to drop out of high school and the least likely to graduate from college

c. are taking more theoretical than practical courses in high school and college

d. are not willing to move where the jobs are

UNIT 8.7

Racial–Ethnic Relations: African Americans

WHAT AM I SUPPOSED TO LEARN?

After you have read this unit, you should be able to

1 Explain the conditions of African Americans in the South after slavery.

2 Discuss the economic and political gains and losses of African Americans.

3 Summarize the sociological debate about race-ethnicity and social class.

It was 1955, in Montgomery, Alabama. As specified by law, whites took the front seats of the bus, and blacks went to the back. As the bus filled up, blacks had to give up their seats to whites.

When Rosa Parks, a 42-year-old African American woman and secretary of the Montgomery NAACP, was told that she would have to stand so that white folks could sit, she refused (Bray 1995). She stubbornly sat there while the bus driver raged and whites felt insulted. Her arrest touched off mass demonstrations, led 50,000 blacks to boycott the city's buses for a year, and thrust an otherwise unknown preacher into a historic role.

Reverend Martin Luther King, Jr., who had majored in sociology at Morehouse College in Atlanta, Georgia, took control. He organized car pools and preached nonviolence. Incensed at this radical organizer and at the stirrings in the normally compliant black community, segregationists also put their beliefs into practice—by bombing the homes of blacks and dynamiting their churches.

After slavery was abolished, the Southern states passed laws (*Jim Crow* laws) to segregate blacks and whites. The segregation included separate schools for blacks and whites. A challenge to these laws reached the U.S. Supreme Court, which ruled in 1896 in *Plessy v. Ferguson* that it was a reasonable use of state power to require "separate but equal" accommodations for blacks. Never mind that the facilities, including public schools were certainly separate, but never equal. Whites used

Rising Expectations and Civil Strife

The barriers came down, but they came down slowly. In 1964, Congress passed the Civil Rights Act, making it illegal to discriminate on the basis of race. African Americans were finally allowed in "white" restaurants, hotels, theaters, and other public places. Then in 1965, Congress passed the Voting Rights Act, banning the fraudulent literacy tests that the Southern states had used to keep African Americans from voting.

African Americans then experienced what sociologists call **rising expectations**. They expected that these sweeping legal changes would usher in better conditions in life. However, the lives of the poor among them changed little, if at all. Frustrations built up, exploding in Watts in 1965, when people living in that ghetto of central Los Angeles took to the streets in the first of what were termed the *urban revolts*. When a white supremacist assassinated King on April 4, 1968, inner cities across the nation erupted in fiery violence. Under threat of the destruction of U.S. cities, Congress passed the sweeping Civil Rights Act of 1968.

CONTINUED GAINS

Since then, African Americans have made remarkable gains in politics, education, and jobs. At 9 percent, the number of African Americans in the U.S. House of Representatives is *two to three times* what it was a generation ago (*Statistical Abstract* 1989:Table 423; 2012:Table 413). As college enrollments increased, the middle class expanded, and today 40 percent of all African American families make more than $50,000 a year. One in four earns over $75000, and one in eight over $100,000 (*Statistical Abstract* 2012:Table 696).

African Americans have become prominent in politics. Jesse Jackson (a sociology major) competed for the Democratic presidential nomination in 1984 and 1988. In 1989, L. Douglas Wilder was elected governor of Virginia, and in 2006, Deval Patrick became governor of Massachusetts. These accomplishments, of course, pale in comparison to the election of Barack Obama as president of the United States in 2008.

CURRENT LOSSES

Despite these remarkable gains, African Americans continue to lag behind in politics, economics, and education. Only *one* U.S. senator is African American, but we would expect twelve or thirteen on the basis of the percentage of African Americans in the U.S. population. As Tables 8.1 and 8.2 on pages 250 and 251 show, African Americans average only 59 percent of white income, have much more unemployment and poverty, and are less likely to own their home or to have a college education. That two of five African American families have incomes over $50,000 is only part of

> **rising expectations** the sense that better conditions are soon to follow, which, if unfulfilled, increases frustration

Taken at one of the most famous speeches in U.S. history, when in 1963 at the Lincoln Memorial in Washington, D.C. Martin Luther King, Jr. inspired Americans with his refrain, "I Have a Dream."

this ruling to strip blacks of the political power they had gained after the Civil War. Declaring political primaries to be "white," they prohibited blacks from voting in them. Not until 1944 did the Supreme Court rule that political primaries weren't "white" and were open to all voters. White politicians then passed laws that restricted voting only to people who could read—and they determined that most African Americans were illiterate. Not until 1954 did African Americans gain the legal right to attend the same public schools as whites, and, as recounted in the vignette, even later to sit where they wanted on a bus.

President Barack Obama with Queen Elizabeth II in London, England, in 2011.

Julius Wilson (1978, 2000, 2007) ignited the controversy when he proposed that social class has become more important than race in determining the life chances of African Americans. Before civil rights legislation, he says, the African American experience was dominated by race. Throughout the United States, African Americans were excluded from avenues of economic advancement: good schools and good jobs. When civil rights laws opened new opportunities, African Americans seized them. However, as legislation was opening doors to African Americans, the United States was in a transition to a post-industrial society: Manufacturing jobs dried up, and many blue-collar jobs were moved to the suburbs. As better-educated African Americans obtained white-collar jobs, they moved out of the inner city. Left behind were those with poor education and few skills.

Wilson stresses how significant these two worlds of African American experience are. The group that is stuck in the inner city lives in deep poverty, attends failing schools, and faces dead-end jobs or welfare. This group is filled with hopelessness and despair, combined with apathy or hostility. In contrast, those who moved up the social class ladder live in comfortable homes in secure neighborhoods. Their jobs provide decent incomes, and they send their children to good schools. With their middle-class experiences shaping their views on life, their aspirations and values have little in common with those of African Americans who remain poor. According to Wilson, then, social class—not race—is the more significant factor in the lives of African Americans.

Some sociologists reply that this analysis overlooks the discrimination that continues to underlie the African American experience. They note that African Americans who do the same work as whites average less pay (Willie 1991; Herring 2002) and even receive fewer tips (Lynn et al. 2008). This, they argue, points to racial discrimination, not to social class.

the story. Table 8.3 shows the other part—that one of every five or six African American families makes less than $15,000 a year.

The upward mobility of millions of African Americans into the middle class has created two worlds of African American experience—one educated and affluent, the other uneducated and poor. Concentrated among the poor are those with the least hope, the most despair, and the violence that so often dominates the evening news. Although homicide rates have dropped to their lowest point in thirty-five years, African Americans are *six* times more likely to be murdered than whites (*Statistical Abstract* 2012:Table 312).

RACE OR SOCIAL CLASS? A SOCIOLOGICAL DEBATE

This division of African Americans into "haves" and "have-nots" has fueled a sociological controversy. Sociologist William

TABLE 8.3	Race–Ethnicity and Income Extremes

	Less than $15,000	Over $100,000
Asian Americans	6.9%	37.7%
Whites	7.2%	27.0%
African Americans	17.9%	12.1%
Latinos	15.3%	12.4%

Note: These are family incomes. Only these groups are listed in the source.
Source: By the author: Based on Statistical Abstract of the United States 2012:Table 695.

What is the answer to this debate? Wilson would reply that it is not an either-or question. "My book is titled *The **Declining** Significance of Race*," he would say, "not *The **Absence** of Race*." Certainly racism is still alive, he would add, but today social class is more central to the African American experience than is racial discrimination. He stresses that we need to provide jobs for the poor in the inner city—for work provides an anchor to a responsible life (Wilson, 2007, 2012).

RACISM AS AN EVERYDAY BURDEN

Researchers sent out 5,000 résumés in response to help-wanted ads in the Boston and Chicago Sunday papers. The résumés were identical—except some applicants had white-sounding names, such as Emily and Brandon, while others had black-sounding names, such as Lakisha and Jamal. Although the qualifications of these supposed job applicants were identical, the white-sounding names received 50 percent more callbacks than the black-sounding names. (Bertrand and Mullainathan 2002)

Certainly racism continues as a regular feature of society, often something that whites, who are not hit by its sting, are only vaguely aware of. But for those on the receiving end, racism can be an everyday burden. Here is how an African American professor describes his experiences:

[One problem with] being black in America is that you have to spend so much time thinking about stuff that most white people just don't even have to think about. I worry when I get pulled over by a cop... . I worry what some white cop is going to think when he walks over to our car, because he's holding on to a gun. And I'm very aware of how many black folks accidentally get shot by cops. I worry when I walk into a store that someone's going to think I'm in there shoplifting... . And I get resentful that I have to think about things that a lot of people, even my very close white friends whose politics are similar to mine, simply don't have to worry about. (Feagin 1999:398)

UNIT 8.7 // TESTING MYSELF
DID I LEARN IT? ANSWERS ARE AT THE END OF THE CHAPTER

1. After slavery was abolished, the southern states passed laws to segregate blacks and whites. These laws were called
   a. separation laws
   b. Martin Luther King laws
   c. Henry Mack laws
   d. Jim Crow laws

2. In this infamous 1896 decision, the U.S. Supreme Court ruled that it was a reasonable use of state power to require "separate but equal" accommodations for blacks
   a. Martin Luther King v. James Shepherd
   b. Du Bois v. The State of Georgia
   c. Plessy v. Ferguson
   d. The American Sociological Association v. The American Psychological Association

3. The southern states passed laws to limit voting in political primaries to whites. When, in 1944, the U.S. Supreme Court ruled that political primaries weren't "white" and were open to all voters, African Americans became eligible to vote in southern states. In response, southern states passed laws that limited voting to people who could pass these tests
   a. constitutional knowledge
   b. literacy
   c. illiteracy
   d. reciting the Bill of Rights

4. After a series of sweeping legal changes, African Americans thought that better conditions would come soon, a condition that often precedes revolution. Riots erupted when the lives of the poor among them changed little, if at all. Sociologists use this term to refer to rising expectations that good changes will come soon
   a. rising expectations
   b. standard change
   c. challenging change
   d. frustration-deficit syndrome

5. As college enrollments increased, the middle class expanded, and today 40 percent of all African American families make more than $50,000 a year. The other part of the picture is that almost one of every five or six African American families
   a. is not putting money away for the college education of their children
   b. makes $200,000 or more per year
   c. is a college graduate
   d. makes less than $15,000 a year

6. The chances of African Americans being murdered is this much higher than that of whites
   a. two times
   b. four times
   c. six times
   d. there is no difference in the murder rates of whites and blacks

7. Sociologist William Julius Wilson ignited a debate in sociology when he proposed that this has become more important than race in determining the life chances of African Americans

   a. poverty
   b. social class
   c. the region of the country in which African Americans live
   d. whether people live in urban or rural areas

8. Sociologists analyze how racism is an everyday burden for minorities. In one of their studies, they mailed 5,000 résumés in response to help-wanted ads. The résumés were identical, except some applicants had black-sounding names and others had white-sounding names. Applicants with white-sounding names received

   a. 50 percent more callbacks
   b. 10 percent more callbacks
   c. 10 percent fewer callbacks
   d. 50 percent fewer callbacks

UNIT 8.8

Racial–Ethnic Relations: Asian Americans

WHAT AM I SUPPOSED TO LEARN?

After you have read this unit, you should be able to

1 Explain why the term Asian American does not refer to a race.

2 Discuss the success of Asian Americans.

I have stressed in this chapter that our racial–ethnic categories are based more on social factors than on biological ones. This point is again obvious when we examine the category of Asian American. As Figure 8.9 shows, those who are called Asian Americans came to the United States from many countries. *With no unifying culture or "race," why should people from so many backgrounds be clustered together and assigned a single*

label? Think about it. What culture or race–ethnicity do Samoans and Vietnamese have in common? Or Laotians and Pakistanis? Or people from Guam and those from China? Those from Japan and those from India? Yet *all* these groups—and more—are lumped together and called Asian Americans. You might want to keep this in mind as you look at the photos on the next page.

Since *Asian American* is a standard term, however, let's look at the characteristics of the 14 million people who are lumped together and assigned this label.

A Background of Discrimination

Lured by gold strikes in the West and an urgent need for unskilled workers to build the railroads, 200,000 Chinese immigrated between 1850 and 1880. When the famous golden spike was driven at Promontory, Utah, in 1869 to mark the completion of the railroad to the West Coast, white workers prevented Chinese workers from being in the photo—even though Chinese made up 90 percent of Central Pacific Railroad's labor force. (Hsu 1971)

After the railroad was complete, the Chinese competed with whites for other jobs. Anglos then formed vigilante groups to intimidate them. They also used the law. In 1850, California passed the Foreign Miner's Act, which required Chinese (and Latinos) to pay $20 a month in order to work. Wages at that time were a dollar a day. The California Supreme Court ruled that Chinese could not testify against whites (Carlson and Colburn 1972). In 1882, Congress passed the Chinese Exclusion Act, suspending all Chinese immigration for ten years. Four years later, the Statue of Liberty was dedicated. The tired, the poor, and the huddled masses it was intended to welcome were obviously not Chinese.

When immigrants from Japan arrived, they encountered *spillover bigotry,* a stereotype that lumped Asians together, depicting them as sneaky, lazy, and untrustworthy. After Japan attacked Pearl Harbor in 1941, conditions grew worse for the 110,000 Japanese Americans who called the United States their

FIGURE 8.9 **The Country of Origin of Asian Americans**

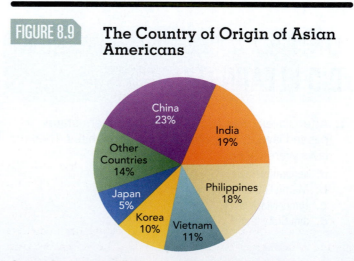

China 23%
India 19%
Philippines 18%
Vietnam 11%
Korea 10%
Japan 5%
Other Countries 14%

Source: By the author. Based on U.S. Census Bureau 2010.

The classification "Asian American" is a catch-all category, as these photos of "Asian Americans" illustrate.

home. U.S. authorities feared that Japan would invade the United States and that the Japanese Americans would fight on Japan's side. They also feared that Japanese Americans would sabotage military installations on the West Coast. Although no Japanese American had been involved in even a single act of sabotage, on February 19, 1942, President Franklin D. Roosevelt ordered that everyone who was *one-eighth Japanese or more* be confined in detention centers (called "internment camps"). These people were charged with no crime, and they had no trials. Japanese ancestry was sufficient cause for being imprisoned.

DIVERSITY

As you can see from Tables 8.1 and 8.2 on pages 250 and 251, the income of Asian Americans has outstripped that of all groups, including whites. This has led to the stereotype that all Asian Americans are successful. Are they? As you can also see from Table 8.1, their poverty rate is actually *higher* than that of whites. As with Latinos, country of origin is significant: Poverty is unusual among Chinese and Japanese Americans, but it clusters among Americans from Southeast Asia. Altogether, between 1 and 2 million Asian Americans live in poverty.

REASONS FOR SUCCESS

The high average income of Asian Americans can be traced to three major factors: family life, educational achievement, and assimilation into mainstream culture. Of all racial–ethnic groups, including whites, Asian American children are the most likely to grow up with two parents and the least likely to be born to either a teenaged or single mother (*Statistical Abstract* 2012: Tables 69, 86). Common in these families is a stress on self-discipline, thrift, and hard work (Suzuki 1985; Bell 1991). This early socialization provides strong impetus for the other two factors.

The second factor is an unprecedented rate of college graduation. As Table 8.2 on page 251 shows, 50 percent of Asian Americans complete college. To realize how stunning this is, compare their rate with those of the other groups shown on this table. Educational achievement, in turn, opens doors to economic success.

The third factor is assimilation. The most striking indication of assimilation is a high rate of intermarriage. Of Asian Americans who graduate from college, about 40 percent of the men and 60 percent of the women marry a non-Asian American (Qian and Lichter 2007). The intermarriage of Japanese Americans is so extensive that two of every three of their children have one parent who is not of Japanese descent (Schaefer 2004). The Chinese are close behind (Alba and Nee 2003).

Asian Americans are becoming more prominent in politics. With more than half of its citizens being Asian American, Hawaii has elected Asian American governors and sent several Asian American senators to Washington. In 2012, Mazie Hirono became the first Asian American woman to be elected to the U. S. Senate. The first Asian American governor outside of Hawaii was Gary Locke, who served from 1997 to 2005 as governor of Washington, a state in which Asian Americans make up less than 6 percent of the population. In 2008, in Louisiana, Piyush Jindal became the first Indian American governor.

UNIT 8.8 // TESTING MYSELF
DID I LEARN IT? ANSWERS ARE AT THE END OF THE CHAPTER

1. Laotians and Pakistanis, people from Guam and those from China, people from Japan and India, Nepal and Thailand, Malaysia and Vietnam: These and many other people are lumped together and given this single label
   - **a.** African Americans
   - **b.** European Americans
   - **c.** Native Americans
   - **d.** Asian Americans

2. To unify the country, the U.S. government gave away huge amounts of land to build railroads to the West Coast. About 90 percent of the Central Pacific Railroad's workers were Chinese. When a photo of the completion of the railroad to the West Coast was taken,
   - **a.** the Chinese workers went on strike
   - **b.** the white workers went on strike
   - **c.** the Chinese workers were not allowed in the photo
   - **d.** the photographer, a secret agent of the railroad, assassinated the top Chinese leader, who was forming a workers' union

3. The U.S. legal system used to be openly racist. Here is one example. California's 1850 Foreign Miner's Act required Chinese (and Latinos) to pay $20 a month in order to work—when wages were a dollar a day. Here is another: The California Supreme Court ruled that Chinese
   - **a.** were not citizens
   - **b.** could not testify against whites
   - **c.** had to return to China by the age of 30
   - **d.** women had to use birth control

4. During World War II, U.S. authorities feared that Japanese Americans would sabotage military installations on the West Coast. On February 19, 1942, President Franklin D. Roosevelt ordered that everyone who was one-eighth Japanese or more
   - **a.** be confined in detention centers
   - **b.** be sent to Alaska
   - **c.** had to serve in the U.S. armed forces and fight Japan
   - **d.** had to take an oath of allegiance if they were going to work for the government, including teaching school

5. Asian Americans have faced severe prejudice and discrimination. Today, their average incomes are
   - **a.** declining
   - **b.** about the same as that of African Americans
   - **c.** less than that of Native Americans
   - **d.** considerably higher than that of whites

6. Despite the overall success of Asian Americans, their poverty rate is higher than that of whites, especially for Americans from Southeast Asia. Poverty is especially low for Americans from
   - **a.** Vietnam
   - **b.** Thailand
   - **c.** China and Japan
   - **d.** Cambodia

7. There are several reasons that Asian Americans have been so successful. This is not one of them.
   - **a.** a high rate of college graduation
   - **b.** their refusal to own guns
   - **c.** low rates of childbirth to single women
   - **d.** assimilation

UNIT 8.9

Racial–Ethnic Relations: Native Americans

WHAT AM I SUPPOSED TO LEARN?

After you have read this unit, you should be able to

1 Explain the diversity of Native Americans.

2 Summarize the U.S. government's historical relationship with Native Americans.

3 Explain the situation of Native Americans today.

I don't go so far as to think that the only good Indians are dead Indians, but I believe nine out of ten are—and I shouldn't inquire too closely in the case of the tenth. The most vicious cowboy has more moral principle than the average Indian. (Teddy Roosevelt, 1886, President of the United States 1901–1909)

Diversity of Groups

This quote from Teddy Roosevelt provides insight into the rampant racism of earlier generations. Yet, even today, thanks to countless grade B Westerns, some Americans view the original inhabitants of what became the United States as uncivilized savages, a single group of people subdivided into separate tribes. The European immigrants to the colonies, however, encountered diverse groups of people who spoke over 700 languages. Their variety of cultures ranged from nomadic hunters and gatherers to farmers who lived in wooden houses (Schaefer 2004). Each group had its own norms and values—and the usual ethnocentric pride in its own culture. Consider what happened in 1744 when the colonists of Virginia offered college scholarships for "savage lads." The Iroquois replied:

Native Americans do ethnic work to help maintain their cultural heritage. Photo taken in Scottsdale, Arizona.

Several of our young people were formerly brought up at the colleges of Northern Provinces. They were instructed in all your sciences. But when they came back to us, they were bad runners, ignorant of every means of living in the woods, unable to bear either cold or hunger, knew neither how to build a cabin, take a deer, or kill an enemy . . . . They were totally good for nothing.

They added:

If the English gentlemen would send a dozen or two of their children to Onondaga, the great Council would take care of their education, bring them up in really what was the best manner and make men of them. (Nash 1974, in McLemore 1994)

Native Americans, who numbered about 10 million when the Colonists began to arrive, had no immunity to the diseases the Europeans brought with them. With deaths due to disease—and warfare, a much lesser cause—their population plunged. The low point came in 1890, when the census reported only 250,000 Native Americans. If the census and the estimate of the original population are accurate, Native Americans had been reduced to about *one-fortieth* their original size. The population has never recovered, but Native Americans now number about 3 million (see Figure 8.5 on page 246). Native Americans, who today speak 150 different languages, do not think of themselves as a single people who fit neatly within a single label (McLemore 1994).

From Treaties to Genocide and Population Transfer

At first, the Native Americans tried to accommodate the strangers, since there was plenty of land for both the few newcomers and themselves. Soon, however, the settlers began to raid Indian villages and pillage their food supplies (Horn 2006). As wave after wave of settlers arrived, Pontiac, an Ottawa chief, saw the future—and didn't like it. He convinced several tribes to unite in an effort to push the Europeans into the sea. He almost succeeded, but failed when the English were reinforced by fresh troops (McLemore 1994).

A pattern of deception evolved. The U.S. government would make treaties to buy some of a tribe's land, with the promise to honor forever the tribe's right to what it had not sold. European immigrants, who continued to pour into the United States, would then disregard these boundaries. The tribes would resist, with death tolls on both sides. The U.S. government would then intervene—not to enforce the treaty, but to force the tribe off the lands it had been promised "forever"—obviously not a very long time in the government's reckoning. In its relentless drive westward, the U.S. government embarked on a policy of genocide. It assigned the U.S. cavalry the task of "pacification," which translated into slaughtering Native Americans who "stood in the way" of this territorial expansion.

The acts of cruelty perpetrated by the Europeans against Native Americans appear endless, but two are especially notable. The first is the Trail of Tears. The U.S. government adopted a policy of population transfer (see Figure 8.1 on page 232), which it called *Indian Removal*. The goal was to confine Native Americans to specified areas called *reservations*. In the winter of 1838–1839, the U.S. Army rounded up 15,000 Cherokees and forced them to walk 1,000 miles from the Carolinas and Georgia to Oklahoma. Conditions were so brutal that about 4,000 of those who were forced to make this midwinter march died along the way. The second notable act of cruelty also marked the symbolic end to Native American resistance to the European expansion. It took place in 1890 at Wounded Knee, South Dakota. There the U.S. cavalry gunned down 300 men, women, and children of the Dakota Sioux tribe. After the massacre, the soldiers threw the bodies into a mass grave (Thornton 1987; Lind 1995; DiSilvestro 2006).

THE INVISIBLE MINORITY AND SELF-DETERMINATION

Native Americans can truly be called the invisible minority. Because about half live in rural areas and one-third in just three states—Oklahoma, California, and Arizona—most other Americans are hardly aware of a Native American presence in the United States. The isolation of more than a third of Native Americans on 550 reservations further reduces their visibility (Schaefer 2012) Table 8.2 on page 251 shows their very high rate of poverty and how their educational attainment lags behind most groups: Only 13 percent graduate from college.

Native Americans are experiencing major changes. In the 1800s, U.S. courts ruled that Native Americans did not own the land on which they had been settled and had no right to develop its resources. They made Native Americans wards of the state, and the Bureau of Indian Affairs treated them like children (Mohawk 1991; Schaefer 2004). Then, in the 1960s, Native Americans won a series of legal victories that gave them control over reservation lands. With this legal change, many Native American tribes have opened businesses—ranging from fish canneries to industrial parks that serve metropolitan areas. The Skywalk, opened by the Hualapai, which offers breathtaking views of the Grand Canyon, gives an idea of the varieties of businesses to come.

It is the casinos, though, that have attracted the most attention. In 1988, the federal government passed a law that allowed Native Americans to operate gambling establishments on reservations. Now over 200 tribes have casinos. *They bring in $26 billion a year, more than all the casinos in Las Vegas* (Pratt 2011; *Statistical Abstract* 2012:Table 1258). The Oneida tribe of New York, which has only 1,000 members, runs a casino that nets $232,000 a year for each man, woman, and child (Peterson 2003). This huge amount, however, pales in comparison with that of the Mashantucket Pequot tribe of Connecticut. With only 700 members, the tribe brings in more than $2 million a day just from slot machines (Rivlin 2007). Incredibly, one tribe has only *one* member: She has her own casino (Bartlett and Steele 2002).

Preferring to travel a different road entirely, some tribes embrace the highly controversial idea of *separatism*. Because Native Americans were independent peoples when the Europeans arrived and they never willingly joined the United States, many tribes maintain the right to remain separate from the U.S. government.

The Lucky Eagle Casino, Eagle Pass, Texas, owned by the Kickapoo.

The chief of the Onondaga tribe in New York, a member of the Iroquois Federation, summarized the issue this way:

> For the whole history of the Iroquois, we have maintained that we are a separate nation. We have never lost a war. Our government still operates. We have refused the U.S. government's reorganization plans for us. We have kept our language and our traditions, and when we fly to Geneva to UN meetings, we carry Hau de no sau nee passports. We made some treaties that lost some land, but that also confirmed our separate-nation status. That the U.S. denies all this doesn't make it any less the case. (Mander 1992)

One of the most significant changes for Native Americans is **pan-Indianism**. This emphasis on common elements that run through their

pan-Indianism a movement that focuses on common elements in the cultures of Native Americans in order to develop a cross-tribal self-identity and to work toward the welfare of all Native Americans

cultures is an attempt to develop an identity that goes beyond the tribe. Pan-Indianism ("We are all Indians") is a remarkable example of the plasticity of ethnicity. It embraces and substitutes for individual tribal identities the label "Indian"—originally imposed by Spanish and Italian sailors, who thought they had reached the shores of India. As sociologist Irwin Deutscher (2002:61) put it, "The peoples who have accepted the larger definition of who they are, have, in fact, little else in common with each other than the stereotypes of the dominant group which labels them."

Native Americans say that it is they who must determine whether they want to establish a common identity and work together as in pan-Indianism or to stress separatism and identify solely with their own tribe. It is up to us, they say, whether we want to assimilate into the dominant culture or to stand apart from it; to move to cities or to remain on reservations; or to operate casinos or to engage only in traditional activities. "We are sovereign nations," they point out, "and we will not take orders from the victors of past wars."

UNIT 8.9 // TESTING MYSELF
DID I LEARN IT?
ANSWERS ARE AT THE END OF THE CHAPTER

1. The European immigrants to the colonies encountered groups of people so diverse that they spoke over 700 languages and had contrasting systems of norms and sanctions. Most were nomadic hunters, but some
   a. traded horses for a living
   b. sold fish at a weekly market
   c. raised birds for a living
   d. were farmers who lived in wooden houses

2. When the Europeans arrived in North America, there were about this many million Native Americans
   a. 1   b. 5
   c. 10   d. 50

3. By 1890, there were about this many Native Americans in the United States
   a. 250,000   b. 1 million
   c. 2 million   d. 5 million

4. In the U.S. government's dealing with the Native Americans, this was the common pattern. The government would make treaties to buy some of a tribe's land, with the promise to honor forever the tribe's right to what it had not sold. European immigrants would disregard these boundaries, and the U.S. government would
   a. enforce the treaty
   b. force the tribe off its lands
   c. instruct the settlers to move west where there was still plenty of land
   d. promise to give leaders of the tribe tax-free U.S. citizenship

5. In a process called Indian removal, the U.S. government
   a. forced about 10 percent of Native Americans to move to Canada
   b. separated Native American children from their parents and sent them to boarding schools
   c. declared it illegal for Native Americans to live in the federal district, Washington, D.C.
   d. moved Native Americans to reservations

6. In the winter of 1838–1839, the U.S. Army rounded up 15,000 Cherokees and forced them to walk 1,000 miles from the Carolinas and Georgia to Oklahoma. This event is called
   a. The Cherokee Roundup   b. The Warning Shot
   c. The Trail of Tears   d. The Impediment to Unity

7. In general, the Native American casinos are doing well. Compared with the casinos in Las Vegas, the Native American casinos bring in
   a. one-tenth as much   b. more
   c. about the same amount   d. half as much

8. The emphasis on common elements that run through the Native American cultures in an attempt to develop an identity that goes beyond the tribe is called
   a. pan-Indianism   b. tribalism
   c. Native American unity   d. The Reconciliation

UNIT
8.10
Looking Toward the Future

WHAT AM I SUPPOSED TO LEARN?

After you have read this unit, you should be able to

1 Discuss major trends in immigration and affirmative action and how they might influence your future.

Education opens doors of opportunity. What is your opinion of affirmative action in college admissions?

The Immigration Debate

Throughout its history, the United States has both welcomed immigration and feared its consequences. The gates opened wide (numerically, if not in attitude) for waves of immigrants in the 1800s and early 1900s. During the past twenty years, a new wave of immigration has brought close to a million new residents to the United States each year. Today, more immigrants (38 million) live in the United States than at any other time in the country's history (*Statistical Abstract* 2007:Table 5; 2012:Table 40).

In contrast to earlier waves, in which immigrants came almost exclusively from western Europe, the current wave of immigrants is so diverse that it is changing the U.S. racial–ethnic mix. If current trends in immigration (and birth) persist, in less than fifty years the "average" American will trace his or her ancestry to Africa, Asia, South America, the Pacific Islands, the Middle East—almost anywhere but white Europe. For a picture of this remarkable change, look at Figure 8.10. You can see that by the middle of this century members of minority groups will outnumber white Americans.

In some states, the future is already arriving. In California, racial–ethnic minorities have become the majority. California has 21 million minorities and 15 million whites (*Statistical Abstract* 2012:Table 18). Californians who request new telephone service can speak to customer service representatives in Spanish, Korean, Vietnamese, Mandarin, or Cantonese. If they want, they can also press a button for English.

As in the past, there is concern that "too many" immigrants will change the character of the United States. "Throughout the history of U.S. immigration," write sociologists Alejandro Portes and Rubén Rumbaut (1990), "a consistent thread has been the fear that the 'alien element' would somehow undermine the institutions of the country and would lead it down the path of disintegration and decay." A hundred years ago, the widespread fear was that the immigrants from southern Europe would bring

Back in 1903, sociologist W. E. B. Du Bois said, "The problem of the twentieth century is the problem of the color line—the relation of the darker to the lighter races." Incredibly, over a hundred years later, the color line remains one of the most volatile topics facing the United States. From time to time, the color line takes on a different complexion, as with the war on terrorism and the corresponding discrimination directed against people of Middle Eastern descent.

In another hundred years, will yet another sociologist lament that the color of people's skin still affects human relationships? Given our past, it seems that although racial–ethnic walls will diminish, even crumble at some points, the color line is not likely to disappear. Let's close this chapter by looking at two issues we are currently grappling with: immigration and affirmative action.

FIGURE 8.10   **Projections of the Racial–Ethnic Makeup of the U.S. Population**

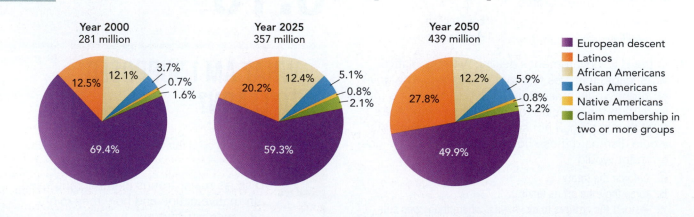

Year 2000
281 million

- 69.4%
- 12.5%
- 12.1%
- 3.7%
- 0.7%
- 1.6%

Year 2025
357 million

- 59.3%
- 20.2%
- 12.4%
- 5.1%
- 0.8%
- 2.1%

Year 2050
439 million

- 49.9%
- 27.8%
- 12.2%
- 5.9%
- 0.8%
- 3.2%

- ■ European descent
- ■ Latinos
- ■ African Americans
- ■ Asian Americans
- ■ Native Americans
- ■ Claim membership in two or more groups

Source: By the author. Based on U. S. Census Bureau 2009; *Statistical Abstract of the United States* 2012:Table 12. I modified the projections based on the new census category of membership in two or more groups and trends in interethnic marriage.

communism with them. Today, some fear that Spanish-speaking immigrants threaten the primacy of the English language. In addition, the age-old fear that immigrants will take jobs away from native-born Americans remains strong. Finally, minority groups that struggled for political representation fear that newer groups will gain political power at their expense.

It's time to go to another *Making It Personal*, this time to consider your ideas about the country's changing racial–ethnic mix.

MAKING IT PERSONAL

What Do You Think about the Changing Racial–Ethnic Mix?

What do you think about the projected future indicated in Figure 8.10 on the previous page where minorities outnumber whites?

A primary sociological principle is that our ideas and attitudes are "socially rooted"—that is, they depend on our social location. Our social locations provide experiences that give us particular ideas. We end up having world views similar to the people who share our social location.

How do *your* social locations, especially your identifying with a racial–ethnic group, influence your answer to the question with which I opened this *Making It Personal?*

Affirmative Action

Affirmative action in our multicultural society lies at the center of a national debate about racial–ethnic relations. In this policy, initiated by President Kennedy in 1961, goals based on race (and sex) are used in hiring, promotion, and college admissions. Sociologist Barbara Reskin (1998) examined the results of affirmative action. She concluded that although it is difficult to separate the results of affirmative action from economic booms and busts and the greater numbers of women in the workforce, affirmative action has had a modest impact.

The results may have been modest, but the reactions to this program have been anything but modest. Affirmative action has been at the center of controversy for almost two generations. Liberals, both white and minority, say that this program is the most direct way to level the playing field of economic opportunity. If whites are passed over, this is an unfortunate cost that we must pay if we are to make up for past discrimination. In contrast, conservatives, both white and minority, agree that opportunity should be open to all, but claim that putting race (or sex) ahead of an individual's training and ability to perform a job is reverse discrimination. Because of their race (or sex), qualified people who had nothing to do with past inequality are discriminated against. They add that affirmative action stigmatizes the people who benefit from it, because it suggests that they hold their jobs because of race (or sex), rather than merit.

This national debate crystallized with a series of controversial rulings. One of the most significant was *Proposition 209,* a 1996 amendment to the California state constitution. This amendment made it illegal to give preference to minorities and women in hiring, promotion, and college admissions. Despite appeals, the U.S. Supreme Court upheld this California law.

A second significant ruling was made by the U.S. Supreme Court in 2003. White students who had been denied admission to the University of Michigan claimed that they had been discriminated against because less qualified applicants had been admitted on the basis of their race. The Court ruled that universities can give minorities an edge in admissions, but there must be a meaningful review of individual applicants. Mechanical systems, such as giving extra points because of race, are unconstitutional. This murky message satisfied no one, as no one knew what it really meant.

To remove ambiguity, opponents of affirmative action followed California's lead and put amendments to their state constitutions on the ballot. The amendment, passed by Michigan voters, makes it illegal for public institutions to even consider race or sex in hiring, in awarding contracts, or in college admissions. Colorado and Nebraska have passed similar amendments to their constitutions (Lewin 2007; Kaufman and Fields 2008). Despite these court rulings, proponents of affirmative action have not given up and are still pursuing court cases. As I write this, another case, *Fisher v. The University of Texas,* is before the U.S. Supreme Court.

With constitutional battles continuing, the issue of affirmative action in a multicultural society is likely to remain center stage for quite some time.

You probably have your own ideas about affirmative action. Let's explore them in *Making It Personal.*

MAKING IT PERSONAL

What Is Your Opinion of Affirmative Action?

What is your opinion of affirmative action? As in the previous *Making It Personal,* try to analyze how your social location has led you to have your opinion. We have just discussed major racial–ethnic groups. How do you think your opinion would change if you were a member of a different group?

Toward a True Multicultural Society

The United States has the potential to become a society in which racial–ethnic groups not only coexist but also respect one another—and thrive—as they work together for mutually beneficial goals. In a true multicultural society, the minority groups that make up the United States would participate fully in the nation's social institutions while maintaining their cultural integrity.

Reaching this goal will require that we understand that "the biological differences that divide one race from another add up to a drop in the genetic ocean." For a long time, we have given racial categories an importance they never merited. Now we need to figure out how to reduce them to the irrelevance they deserve. In short, we need to make real the abstraction called equality that we profess to believe (Cose 2000).

Many find the potential of a united diverse society an inspiration. Whether ours will be a "united" society or simply a "diverse" one remains an open question.

Watch the **Video**
The Big Picture: Race and Ethnicity in **mysoclab**

Explore the **Concept**
How Diverse is American Society? in **mysoclab**

1. In 1903, this sociologist (introduced in Chapter 1) made this statement: "The problem of the twentieth century is the problem of the color line—the relation of the darker to the lighter races."
   a. Max Weber
   b. Emile Durkheim
   c. Harriet Martineau
   d. W. E. B. Du Bois

2. Today, more immigrants live in the United States than at any other time in the country's history. In earlier waves of immigration, immigrants came almost exclusively from western Europe. The current wave is so diverse that it is changing the U.S. racial–ethnic mix. If current trends persist, in less than fifty years
   a. there will be more immigrants than people who were born in the United States
   b. more Asian Americans will live in the United States than Chinese who live in China
   c. minorities will outnumber whites
   d. a major third political party will be formed to represent the interests of immigrants

3. "I know I was turned down because of a minority," moaned Barbara who had just received news that her application to a top college had been rejected. Without naming it, Barbara was referring to a program called
   a. affirmative action
   b. equal opportunity
   c. Making Things Right
   d. Opportunity For All

4. The topic of affirmative action touches an emotional hot spot and arouses strong reactions. After sociologist Barbara Reskin examined the results of affirmative action, she concluded that
   a. it was unfair, a form of reverse discrimination
   b. the results were modest
   c. corporations were being forced to hire unqualified people
   d. affirmative action programs should be dropped in university admissions but kept in government hiring

PULLING IT ALL TOGETHER REVIEWING THE LEARNING GOALS

Unit 8.1 Race: Myth and Reality

1. Explain why three beliefs about race are myths.

- *The myth of pure races:* Races are an endless mixture of biological characteristics, not distinct types. *The myth of a fixed number of races:* There is no agreement on how many races there are. Using different characteristics, some biologists and anthropologists have concluded that there are just two races, others that there are 2,000. *The myth of racial superiority:* All races have their geniuses and idiots. This ethnocentric belief is particularly dangerous and has led to the holocaust and other forms of organized murder.

2. Explain how ethnicity differs from race.

- People use the term *race* to refer to supposed biological characteristics that distinguish one group of people from another. The terms *ethnicity* and *ethnic* refer to cultural characteristics that distinguish one group of people from another.

Unit 8.2 Minority Groups and Dominant Groups

1. Contrast minority and dominant groups and list the origin of minority groups.

- *Minority groups* receive unequal treatment, and their members regard themselves as objects of collective discrimination. *Dominant groups* have greater power and privilege and discriminate against minority groups. A dominant group can be smaller than a minority group. Minority groups are created when a group expands, incorporating groups with different racial–ethnic characteristics into a political unit or when a group migrates to an area dominated by a group with different characteristics.

2. Summarize the six ways that dominant groups treat minority groups.

- These are summarized in Figure 8.1 on page 232.

3. Explain what leads to a high or low sense of racial–ethnic identity.

- Groups that feel discrimination, have less power, and look different than most are likely to feel a heightened sense of ethnicity. People who belong to groups with more power, look like most people, and feel no discrimination are likely to experience a sense of "belonging."

Unit 8.3 Prejudice and Discrimination

1. Distinguish between prejudice and discrimination and explain the origin of prejudice.

- *Prejudice* is an attitude, a prejudging of some sort, generally based on feelings about the superiority of one's own group. Like other attitudes, prejudice is learned. *Discrimination* is an action, negative treatment of an individual or a group.

2. Explain what internalizing dominant norms means.

- Dominant ideas—negative and positive—exist about racial–ethnic groups. Members of minority groups also learn their culture's "road map" of ethnic relations, with some internalizing negative ideas about their own group.

3. Contrast individual and institutional discrimination.

- *Individual discrimination* is one individual treating another unfairly. As with mortgages and health care, *institutional discrimination* is unfairness that is built into society. Institutional discrimination can occur without either the one discriminating or the one being discriminated against being aware of it.

> 👁–| **Watch** the **Video**
> The Basics: Race and Ethnicity in **mysoclab**

Unit 8.4 Theories of Prejudice

1. Summarize psychological theories of prejudice: frustration, scapegoats, and the authoritarian personality.

- *Frustration* can be directed outward, onto *scapegoats*, groups that have nothing to do with the cause of the frustration. The *authoritarian personality* refers to people who have a high respect for authority, see things as black or white, and tend to be prejudiced.

2. Explain the sociological perspectives of prejudice: functionalism, conflict, and symbolic interactionism.

- *Functionalism:* Some politicians find prejudice useful; using scapegoats helps them accomplish goals. Prejudice increases when groups are pitted against one another. The dysfunctions of prejudice include destroyed human relationships. *Conflict theory:* Owners use the split labor market and the reserve labor force to pit worker against worker in order to control workers and increase their profits. *Symbolic interactionism:* Labels lead to selective perception. Some labels can even produce the behavior depicted by a stereotype.

Read the Document
"Racism in Toyland" by
Christine L. Williams in
mysoclab

Watch the Video
Sociology on the Job:
Race and Ethnicity in
mysoclab

Unit 8.5   Racial–Ethnic Relations: European Americans

1. Specify the major racial–ethnic groups and their percentage of the U.S. population.
   - The groups are whites (65%), Latinos (Hispanics) (15%), African Americans (13%), Asian Americans (4%), and Native Americans (1%). From 1 to 2 percent claim membership in more than one of these groups.

2. Summarize the relationship of Anglos to white ethnics in the early years of the United States and indicate how racism showed up in an early law.
   - The Anglos (the English) held negative stereotypes of other groups, including white ethnics, immigrants from European countries other than England. The taken-for-granted prejudice of that period is indicated by the Naturalization Act Congress passed in 1790, declaring that only white immigrants could apply for citizenship.

Unit 8.6   Racial–Ethnic Relations: Latinos (Hispanics)

1. Discuss the causes, reaction, and extent of illegal immigration and the controversy over Spanish.
   - Poverty in Mexico and Central and South America is the cause. Most Latinos have been born in the United States or are legal immigrants. About 9 million are living here illegally, which is an explosive political issue. In reaction, civilian volunteers also patrol the border with Mexico. With controversy over the use of Spanish, 30 states have declared English their official language.

2. Explain the diversity of Latinos and how this affects their political unity.
   - In addition to the usual social class divisions, Latinos are divided by country of origin. Most think of themselves not as Latino or Hispanic (classifications placed on them) but identify with people who come from the same country. This splits Latinos politically.

Unit 8.7   Racial–Ethnic Relations: African Americans

1. Explain the conditions of African Americans in the South after slavery.
   - Among other conditions, African Americans were segregated: the back of buses, separate and inferior schools, and no voting. When the segregationist (Jim Crow) laws were banned, rising expectations accompanied by little change led to riots.

2. Discuss the economic and political gains and losses of African Americans.
   - *Economic gains:* Forty percent of families make over $50,000 a year. *Political gains:* Two African American governors and a president. *The losses:* One of five or six makes less than $15,000 a year. And only one African American is a senator.

3. Summarize the sociological debate about race–ethnicity and social class.
   - With African Americans increasingly divided into the "haves" and the "have nots," some sociologists suggest that African American life is now shaped more by social class than by race. Others disagree. All agree that race remains an everyday burden for African Americans.

Unit 8.8   Racial–Ethnic Relations: Asian Americans

1. Explain why the term *Asian American* does not refer to a race.
   - Laotians and Pakistanis, people from Guam and those from China, people from Japan and India, Laos and Thailand—these and many other groups are lumped together and given this single label.

2. Discuss the success of Asian Americans.
   - The average income of Asian Americans is the highest of all racial–ethnic groups, including that of whites. The basic reasons include low rates of divorce and teenage childbirth combined with a high rate of assimilation and college graduation. Asian Americans have cautiously entered politics, where they are seeing some success.

Unit 8.9   Racial–Ethnic Relations: Native Americans

1. Explain the diversity of Native Americans.
   - The European immigrants to the colonies encountered groups of people so diverse that they spoke over 700 languages and had many systems of norms and sanctions. Most were nomadic hunters, but some were farmers who lived in wooden houses. The tribes did not identify with one another.

2. Summarize the U.S. government's historical relationship with Native Americans.
   - The government viewed Native Americans as enemies who stood in the way of their continental expansion. They slaughtered them, destroyed their food supply, made treaties and systematically broke them, and moved the Native Americans to reservations.

3. Explain the situation of Native Americans today.
   - Native Americans speak 150 languages and do not think of themselves as a single people. Their casinos are bringing prosperity to some poor areas. Main issues are self-determination tribal identity, and pan-Indianism.

Unit 8.10 Looking Toward the Future

1. Discuss major trends in immigration and affirmative action and how they might influence your future.
   - If the present pattern of immigration continues, by the year 2050 minorities will outnumber whites. A widespread fear is that the new immigrants will change the culture negatively, take away jobs, and dilute the political power of those who are already citizens. Estimating how this trend will affect your life is up to you.

2. Present both sides of the affirmative action debate.
   - Affirmative action has given preference to minorities in some hiring and promotion and in college admissions. Proponents argue that affirmative action is needed to make up for past wrongs, that it helps to level the playing field of opportunity. Opponents claim that affirmative action is reverse discrimination, that it discriminates against qualified people who are not guilty of discrimination

Watch the **Video** The Big Picture: Race and Ethnicity in **mysoclab**

Explore the **Concept** How Diverse is American Society? in **mysoclab**

UNIT 8.1 // TESTING MYSELF
DID I LEARN IT? ANSWERS

1. **c** the biological characteristics of groups flow endlessly together
2. **a** 2 to 2,000
3. **d** a plane ride can change someone's race
4. **c** a label we use to describe perceived biological characteristics

5. **b** who is doing the classifying
6. **d** the holocaust
7. **c** genocide
8. **b** people act on perceptions and beliefs, not facts
9. **a** ethnocentric
10. **d** ethnicity

UNIT 8.2 // TESTING MYSELF
DID I LEARN IT? ANSWERS

1. **d** minority group
2. **c** dominant group
3. **d** minority group
4. **d** genocide

5. **c** population transfer
6. **b** internal colonialism
7. **a** segregation
8. **c** multiculturalism (pluralism)
9. **c** heightened sense of racial–ethnic identity
10. **b** ethnic work

UNIT 8.3 // TESTING MYSELF
DID I LEARN IT? ANSWERS

1. **d** discrimination
2. **c** prejudice
3. **b** learning from others
4. **d** people can be prejudiced even against groups that do not exist

5. **b** internalizing dominant norms
6. **b** internalizing dominant norms
7. **c** individual discrimination
8. **b** institutional discrimination
9. **b** can occur without those doing the discriminating being aware of what they are doing

UNIT 8.4 // TESTING MYSELF
DID I LEARN IT? ANSWERS

1. **d** scapegoat
2. **b** the authoritarian personality
3. **d** how the social environment increases or decreases prejudice
4. **d** strong in-groups formed and even lifelong friends began to call one another "crybaby" and "sissy"

5. **c** an "I win, you lose" situation
6. **b** functionalist
7. **a** a split labor market
8. **d** reserve labor force
9. **b** selective perception
10. **d** a self-fulfilling stereotype

1. d Europe

2. c Hawaii

1. d an ethnic group

2. d have a sense of ethnic oppression and unity

3. c Latinos

4. b millions more Latinos live in the United States than there are Canadians in Canada

1. d Jim Crow laws

2. c Plessy v. Ferguson

3. b literacy

1. d Asian Americans

2. c the Chinese workers were not allowed in the photo

3. b could not testify against whites

1. d were farmers who lived in wooden houses

2. c 10

3. a 250,000

1. d W. E. B. Du Bois

3. b White Anglo Saxon Protestant

4. a white ethnics

5. c third

6. c only white immigrants could apply for citizenship

5. a jobs

6. d the United States

7. c are divided by country of origin

8. b are the most likely to drop out of high school and the least likely to graduate from college

4. a rising expectations

5. d makes less than $15,000 a year

6. c six times

7. b social class

8. a 50 percent more callbacks

4. a be confined in detention centers

5. d considerably higher than that of whites

6. c China and Japan

7. b their refusal to own guns

4. b force the tribe off its lands

5. d moved Native Americans to reservations

6. c The Trail of Tears

7. b more

8. a pan-Indianism

2. c minorities will outnumber whites

3. a affirmative action

4. b the results were modest

CHAPTER 9
SEX AND GENDER

((•—|Listen to the **Chapter Audio** in **mysoclab**

◉—|**Watch** the **Video** in **mysoclab**

GETTING STARTED

In your everyday life, you constantly send messages about your "femaleness" or "maleness." You are aware that certain gestures are "feminine" and others "masculine," and you use or avoid gestures because of this. A major reason you choose or reject a piece of clothing is how you think it reflects your "masculinity" or "femininity." Do you know, too, that you avoid certain words and expressions because they are too "feminine" or too "masculine"? It is the same with your laugh—the way you laugh shows others how "masculine" or "feminine" you are. This chapter will open a world of sociological analysis on "doing gender." And we will go far beyond this, and look at how gender is significant for distributing power and prestige, for determining who gets paid more at work—and for helping to decide your sociological fate in life.

Get ready for a fascinating journey.

Girls powderpuff football in Harper Woods, Michigan

UNIT 9.1

Differences between Sex and Gender

Learning to do gender. Photo taken in the Cook Islands in the South Pacific.

Sex and Gender

If someone asks you what the difference is between females and males, probably the first thing you will think of is **sex,** the *biological characteristics* that distinguish males and females. As you know, you are born with your sex—and

sex biological characteristics that distinguish females and males, consisting of primary and secondary sex characteristics

your parents were happy to tell everyone that they had a new little girl or a new little boy.

You were born with what are called the *primary sex characteristic*—a vagina or a penis and other organs related to reproduction. Later, you developed your *secondary sex characteristics*—the physical distinctions between males and females that are not directly connected with reproduction. These characteristics became evident when you reached puberty. If you are a male, you developed more muscles and a lower voice, as well as more body hair and height. If you are a female, you developed breasts and formed more fatty tissue and broader hips.

Your gender, in contrast, is *not* a biological characteristic. Gender is something *social*. **Gender** refers to masculinity or femininity. Gender consists of whatever behaviors and attitudes a group considers proper for its males and females. *Although you were born with your sex, you learned your gender.* In other words, you learn (and still are learning) the behaviors and attitudes your culture asserts are appropriate for your sex.

Let's explore your sex and gender in *Making It Personal.*

gender the behaviors and attitudes that a society considers proper for its males and females; masculinity or femininity

MAKING IT PERSONAL
Your Sex and Gender

The distinction between sex and gender should help you see that your (feminine or masculine) behaviors do not flow from the fact that you were born a female or a male. So, then, how did you learn to be masculine or feminine? Can you think of events from your childhood in which you learned that certain behaviors were "not appropriate" for you? Peers are especially effective in teaching sex-linked behaviors. What "gender lessons" can you recall from your peers?

Today, of course, you are quite accomplished at "doing gender," and you show your gender as a regular part of your everyday life.

How is this woman doing gender? Is this biological or learned?

It is important to note that different groups have different ideas of how males and females should act. The sociological significance of this is that *gender differs from one society to another.* You can catch a glimpse of these differences in the photo montage on the next page.

Different Ideas About Gender

As you can see from these photos of four women and four men, standards of gender are arbitrary and vary from one culture to another. Yet, in its ethnocentrism, each group thinks that its preferences reflect what gender "really" is. As indicated here, around the world men and women try to make themselves appealing by aspiring to their group's standards of gender.

👁 **Watch** the **Video**
Sociology on the Job:
Gender in **mysoclab**

UNIT 9.1 // TESTING MYSELF
DID I LEARN IT? ANSWERS ARE AT THE END OF THE CHAPTER

1. The penis and the vagina are examples of
   a. primary sex characteristics
   b. secondary sex characteristics
   c. changing expectations
   d. biological constructions of sexuality

2. At puberty, Mary developed breasts and her hips grew larger. This is an example of
   a. primary sex characteristics
   b. secondary sex characteristics
   c. sex
   d. gender

3. At puberty, Joe's voice became much lower and his thin arms began to show more muscle. This is an example of
   a. primary sex characteristics
   b. secondary sex characteristics
   c. environmental factors bringing earlier maturation
   d. boys' greater strength

4. The term sex refers to characteristics that are
   a. learned
   b. inherited
   c. demonstrated by some people, but not by others
   d. banned in many countries

5. The term gender refers to characteristics that are
   a. learned
   b. inherited
   c. demonstrated by some people, but not by others
   d. banned in many countries

6. Mary, age 8, likes to dress up in her mother's dress and carry her purse. This is an example of
   a. sex
   b. gender
   c. primary sex characteristics
   d. secondary sex characteristics

7. Joe will play with his little sister at home, even putting her in her little stroller and pushing her around the living room. If his friends come over, he won't do this. This is an example of
   a. sex
   b. gender
   c. primary sex characteristics
   d. secondary sex characteristics

8. Mary likes to jump rope with the girls. Joe likes to play soccer with the boys. This is an example of
   a. sex
   b. gender
   c. primary sex characteristics
   d. secondary sex characteristics

9. From the photo montage on page 272, "Standards of Gender," you can see that gender, what is considered masculine or feminine,
   a. is inborn, separating males and females into distinct groups
   b. does not exist
   c. is probably no different than what the term sex refers to
   d. varies around the world

Standards of Gender

Each human group determines its ideas of "maleness" and "femaleness." As you can see from these photos of four women and four men, standards of gender are arbitrary and vary from one culture to another. Yet, in its ethnocentrism, each group thinks that its preferences reflect what gender "really" is. As indicated here, around the world men and women try to make themselves appealing by aspiring to their group's standards of gender.

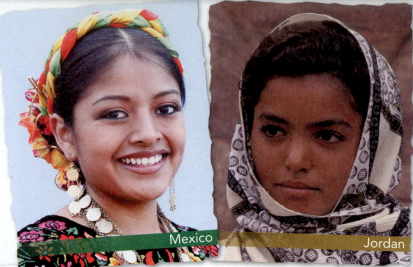
Mexico
Jordan

Kenya

Ethiopia

Brazil

New Guinea

India

Tibet

UNIT 9.2
Human Behavior: Biological or Social Factors?

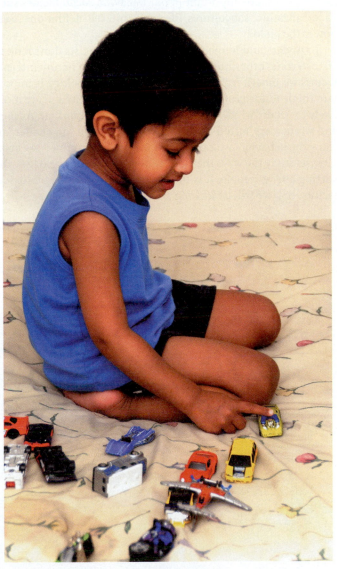

Boys greater desire to play with cars, trucks, and hammers– biological or learned? A combination of both?

The Dominant Position in Sociology

Are you like a rat, penguin, or spider that behaves the way it does because of genetics? Some form of this question keeps coming up. It usually is asked more like this: Do the genes you inherited from your parents determine your behavior? Here is the quick

WHAT AM I SUPPOSED TO LEARN?

After you have read this unit, you should be able to

1 Summarize the dominant position in sociology on genetic factors in human behavior.

2 Summarize the minority position in sociology on genetic factors in human behavior.

3 Give the basic findings on the Vietnam Veterans Study and explain how social factors override testosterone.

4 Understand why sociologists focus on social factors rather than on biological factors in human behavior.

sociological answer: The dominant sociological position is that *social* factors, not biology, are the reasons people do what they do.

Let's apply this position to gender. If biology were the principal factor in human behavior, all around the world we would find women behaving in one way and men in another. Men and women would be just like male spiders and female spiders, whose genes tell them what to do. In fact, however, ideas of gender vary greatly from one culture to another—and, as a result, so do male–female behaviors.

Sociologists do acknowledge that biological factors are involved in some human behavior other than reproduction and childbearing (Udry 2000). Alice Rossi, a feminist sociologist and former president of the American Sociological Association, suggested that women are better prepared biologically for "mothering" than are men. Rossi (1977, 1984) said that women are more sensitive to the infant's soft skin and to their nonverbal communications. Perhaps Rossi expressed it best when she said that the issue is not either biology or society. Instead, culture gives shape to whatever predispositions nature provides.

FROM ANOTHER STUDENT . . .

This is the first booktext I have read where the author speaks directly to the reader and it really made the reading flow and you felt as if you were talking to someone. I enjoy it so much that I am sharing the material with my husband. This creates a great time for us to communicate and grow with each other….I am learning and I am having fun.

Denise Brinkman, LPN
Ivy Tech Community College

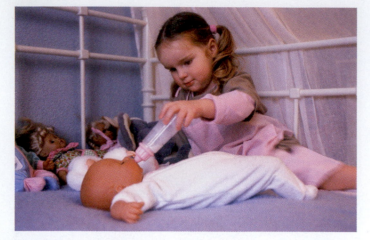

The greater tendency of girls to play with dolls—biological or learned? A combination of both?

The Minority Position in Sociology

A few sociologists take a more extreme view. Steven Goldberg (1993, 2003) asks, "Why do men dominate all societies around the globe?" The reason, he says, is because men are born with a greater drive to dominate social life. Around the world, men are more willing than women "to sacrifice the rewards of other motivations—the desire for affection, health, family life, safety, relaxation, vacation and the like—in order to attain dominance and status." The result, he says, is plain to anyone who wants to look at social life with an unbiased view.

Goldberg's position is hotly debated, however, and not many sociologists accept it. Most sociologists take the position that men are socialized (learn) to be more dominant than women. They point out that today's women are experiencing a different socialization, and they are becoming more dominant. They are arguing cases in court, campaigning for political office, and taking leadership in corporations (Epstein 1999, 2007). These are changed social factors, not changed biology.

So what's the answer? Let's look at some fascinating research on Vietnam veterans and see if this helps.

The Vietnam Veterans Study

In 1985, the U.S. government began a health study of Vietnam veterans. To be certain that the study was representative, the researchers chose a random sample of 4,462 men. (As you'll recall from Chapter 2, A random sample allows us to generalize beyond the sample.) Among the data the researchers collected was a measurement of testosterone. When the veterans who had the higher testosterone levels were boys, they were more likely to get in trouble with parents and teachers and to become delinquents. As adults, they were more likely to use hard drugs, to get into fights, to end up in lower-status jobs, and to have more sexual partners. Those who married were more likely to have affairs, to

hit their wives, and, it follows, to get divorced (Dabbs and Morris 1990; Booth and Dabbs 1993).

This makes it sound like biology is the reason for their behavior. Fortunately for us sociologists, there is another side to this research, and here is where *social class*, which we reviewed in Chapter 7, comes into play. *Compared with the high-testosterone men from the higher social classes, the high-testosterone men from the lower social classes got in more trouble with the law, did worse in school, and were more likely to mistreat their wives* (Dabbs and Morris 1990). Don't let the significance of this last sentence get by you. It means that social factors—in this case social class—overrode biology. Although biological factors, such as hormones, are important in our behavior, *social* factors such as socialization, subcultures, life goals, and self-definitions overpower the biology.

To understand human behavior, we sociologists don't look to testosterone, other hormones, genetic markers, or any internal factors we inherit from our parents. Although biology is important (high-testosterone men do get into more fights and are more likely to get divorced), social factors are more important. As men and women are sorted into groups, they learn to "do gender," or show the behaviors we call "masculine" and "feminine." We sociologists study the ways that society does this sorting and how the sorting affects people. It is the social factors, not the biological factors, that we will be looking at in this chapter.

> 👁 **Watch** the **Video**
> The Big Picture:
> Gender in **mysoclab**

Sociologists study the social factors that underlie human behavior, the experiences that mold us, funneling us into different directions in life. The research on Vietnam veterans discussed in the text indicates how the sociological door is opening slowly to also consider biological factors in human behavior. This March 31, 1967, photo shows soldiers of the 1st Cavalry Division carrying a buddy who had just been shot.

UNIT 9.2 // TESTING MYSELF
DID I LEARN IT? ANSWERS ARE AT THE END OF THE CHAPTER

1. The dominant position in sociology is
   a. People's behavior is like that of rats, penguins, and spiders.
   b. The genes we inherit from our parents determine our behavior.
   c. Women are better than men at being fair in politics.
   d. Social factors are the primary reasons people do what they do.

2. This statement best describes the position of sociologists who acknowledge some biological factors in human behavior other than reproduction.
   a. Biology has nothing to do with human behavior.
   b. Biology has almost everything to do with human behavior.
   c. Culture shapes our biological predispositions.
   d. There are a lot of factors we must consider in human behavior, including the Zodiac.

3. According to what you read, this statement is true
   a. In the matter of nature versus nurture, sociologists prefer the nurture explanation.
   b. Biology is the primary reason that people do what they do.
   c. Biological factors override our social experiences.
   d. Men arc born with a weaker drive than women to dominate social relations, but their socialization overpowers this inborn tendency.

4. The minority position in sociology is
   a. Men are born with a greater drive to dominate social life.
   b. Men are born with a weaker drive than women to dominate life, but their socialization overpowers this tendency.
   c. Women are about the same as men when it comes to being fair in politics.
   d. Men and women have biological predispositions that lead to them being separated into doing "women's work" and "men's work."

5. Sociologist Steven Goldberg takes the position that men are born with a greater drive to dominate social life. For evidence, he points out that men dominate all societies around the world. He says this is because men are more willing "to sacrifice the rewards of other motivations—the desire for affection, health, family life, safety, relaxation, vacation and the like—in order to attain dominance and status." Most sociologists
   a. disagree with Goldberg
   b. agree with Goldberg

   c. aren't sure what position to take
   d. say that it is time to move on to more important research questions

6. In the Vietnam Veteran's Study, researchers found that men with high testosterone
   a. got into more fights than did men with low testosterone
   b. were more likely to get killed in combat than were men with low testosterone
   c. were more stratified than were men with low testosterone
   d. confused the researchers, and they concluded that human behavior is so diverse (varied) that we can't come up with any solid generalizations

7. In the Vietnam Veterans Study, researchers found that compared with men with low testosterone, men with high testosterone were
   a. not sick as often
   b. more likely to play football and other competitive games
   c. more satisfied with life
   d. more likely to mistreat their wives

8. In the Vietnam Veterans Study, researchers found that compared with men with low testosterone, men with high testosterone were
   a. more likely to cheat on their wives
   b. more likely to marry Vietnamese women
   c. less likely to make telephone calls home to their families
   d. more likely to vote

9. In the Vietnam Veterans Study, researchers found that compared with high-testosterone men from higher social classes, high-testosterone men from lower social classes were more likely to
   a. have problems sleeping
   b. do well in school
   c. mistreat their wives
   d. claim biology as a defense for their actions

10. The most accurate conclusion of the sociological position on biological and social factors in human behavior would be
    a. Biological and social factors are about equal in importance.
    b. Biology is important, but social factors override it.
    c. Biology sorts people into two types, and the rest follows.
    d. People with more biology are more likely to get in trouble with the law.

UNIT 9.3

How Females Became a Minority Group

How does this photo illustrate the primary theory of how women became a minority group?

Females as a Minority Group

Around the world, gender is *the* primary division between people. Every society sorts men and women into separate groups and gives them different access to property, power, and prestige. These divisions *always* favor men-as-a-group. After reviewing the historical record, historian and feminist Gerda Lerner (1986) concluded that *"there is not a single society known where women-as-a-group have decision-making power over men (as-a-group)."* Consequently, sociologists classify females as a *minority group*.

Because females outnumber males, you may find this strange. Recall from our previous chapter on race–ethnicity, However, that the term *minority group* is used even when the group being discriminated against is larger than the dominant group. A classic example occurred when England ruled India. A few thousand British dominated the country and discriminated against 300 million Indians. The term *minority group* applies to women because it refers to people who are discriminated against on the basis of physical or cultural characteristics, regardless of their numbers (Hacker 1951).

Have females always been a minority group? Some analysts speculate that in earlier societies, when people survived by hunting and gathering, women and men were social equals (Leacock 1981; Hendrix 1994). Others point out that in small farming (horticultural) societies there was less gender discrimination than is common today (Collins et al. 1993). In these societies, women may have contributed about 60 percent of the group's total food. Yet, around the world, gender is the basis for discrimination. Why?

How Did Females Become a Minority Group?

How, then, did it happen that women became a minority group? Let's consider two theories that have been proposed to explain the origin of **patriarchy**—men dominating society.

patriarchy a society in which men-as-a-group dominate women-as-a-group; authority is vested in males

HUMAN REPRODUCTION

The *first* theory—the major one—points to human reproduction (Lerner 1986; Friedl 1990). In early human history, life was short. Because people died young, for the group to survive women had to give birth to many children. This brought severe consequences for women. To survive, an infant needed a nursing mother. If there were no women to nurse the child, it died. With a child at her breast or in her uterus, or one carried on her hip or on her back, women were not able to move as quickly as men. Nor could they be away from camp for as long as the men could. Around the world, then, women assumed the tasks that were associated with the home and child care, while men hunted the large animals and did other tasks that required both greater speed and longer absences from the base camp (Huber 1990).

This led to men becoming dominant. When the men left the camp to hunt animals, they made contact with other tribes. They traded with them, gaining new possessions—and they also quarreled and waged war with them. It was also the men who made and controlled the instruments of power and death, the weapons that were used for hunting and warfare. The men heaped prestige upon themselves as they returned to the camp triumphantly, leading captured prisoners and displaying their new possessions or the large animals they had killed to feed the women and children.

Contrast this with the women. Their activities were routine, dull, and taken-for-granted. The women kept the fire going, took care of the children, and did the cooking. There was nothing triumphant about what they did—and they were not perceived as risking their lives for the group. The women were "simply there," awaiting the return of their men, ready to acclaim their accomplishments.

Men, then, took control of society. Their sources of power were their weapons, items of trade, and the knowledge they gained from their contact with other groups. Women did not have access to these sources of power, which the men enshrouded in secrecy. The women became second-class citizens, subject to whatever the men decided.

HAND-TO-HAND COMBAT

Here is the *second* theory. It is short and simple, built around warfare and body strength. Anthropologist Marvin Harris (1977) pointed out that tribal groups did a lot of fighting with one another. Their warfare was personal and bloody. Unlike today, their battles were hand-to-hand, with groups fighting fiercely, trying to kill one another with clubs, stones, spears, and arrows. And when these weapons failed, they beat and strangled one another.

It is obvious, said Harris, that women were at a disadvantage in hand-to-hand combat. Because most men are stronger than most women, men became the warriors. And the women?

How does this photo of a spear fight in Tanzania illustrate the second major theory of how women became a minority group?

The men needed strong motivation to risk their lives in combat, rather than just running into the bush when an enemy attacked. The women became the reward that enticed men to risk their lives in battle. The bravest men were given more wives from the women at home—and the choice of the women they captured when they defeated an enemy. The women, in effect, became prisoners for sex and labor.

IN SUM: Is either theory correct—the one built around human reproduction or the one built around warfare? The answer lies buried in human history, and there is no way to test these theories. Male dominance could be the result of some entirely different cause. Gerda Lerner (1986) suggests that patriarchy could have even had different origins in different places.

CONTINUING DOMINANCE

We don't know the origins of patriarchy, then, but whatever its origins, circular thinking evolved. Men came to think of themselves as inherently superior. And the evidence for their superiority? Their domination of society. (You can see how circular this reasoning is: Men dominate society because they are superior, and they know they are superior because they dominate society.) The men kept many of their activities secret and constructed rules and rituals to avoid "contamination" by females, whom they viewed as inferior by this time. Even today, patriarchy is accompanied by cultural supports designed to justify male dominance. A common form is to designate certain activities as "not appropriate" for women, such as playing football, driving race cars, mining coal, or being a soldier or astronaut.

Tribal societies eventually developed into larger groups, and the hunting and hand-to-hand combat ceased to be routine. Did the men then celebrate the end of their risky hunting and fighting and welcome the women as equals? You know the answer. Men enjoyed their power and privileges, and they didn't want to give them up. They held onto them. Male dominance of contemporary societies, then, is a continuation of a millennia-old pattern whose origin is lost in history.

FROM ANOTHER STUDENT . . .

Mr. Henslin,
I just wanted to quickly shoot you a note to tell you how much I looked forward to each and every chapter of your text. I loved the conversational style, the interesting personal anecdotes, creative analogies, and everything else you did to bring the material to life. I thoroughly enjoyed it.

Thanks,
Kate Luna
Grand Canyon University
Phoenix, Arizona

UNIT 9.3 // TESTING MYSELF
DID I LEARN IT? ANSWERS ARE AT THE END OF THE CHAPTER

1. Historian and feminist Gerda Lerner (1986) concluded that there
   a. are two societies where women-as-a-group have decision-making power over men as-a-group
   b. are only a few societies where women-as-a-group have decision-making power over men as-a-group
   c. are many societies where women-as-a-group have decision-making power over men as-a-group
   d. is not a single society where women-as-a-group have decision-making power over men as-a-group

2. Around the world, gender is the primary division between people. Every society sorts men and women into separate groups and gives them different access to property, power, and prestige. These divisions
   a. always favor men-as-a-group
   b. sometimes favor men-as-a-group
   c. usually favor men-as-a-group
   d. usually favor women-as-a-group

3. Applying the term minority group to women
   a. does not make sense because there are more women than men
   b. is rejected by sociologists because there are more women than men
   c. is done by sociologists because the term has nothing to do with numbers
   d. is a custom primarily among sociologists in Asia

4. Some analysts speculate that in hunting and gathering societies, women and men
   a. were social equals
   b. were more likely to hunt than to gather
   c. had fewer children than tribal groups do today
   d. found more satisfaction in nature than people do in modern societies

5. This statement refers to the central idea of the main theory of the origin of patriarchy
   a. With a child at her breast or in her uterus, or one carried on her hip or on her back, women were not able to move as quickly as men or leave the base camp as long as men could.
   b. The challenges of post-menopausal life created divisions between the sexes that ultimately resulted in gender cleavages.
   c. Because women are weaker than men, they took over child care and homemaking responsibilities, while the men took over the hunting.
   d. Male–female divisions are part of nature, occurring universally throughout the world.

6. According to the main theory of patriarchy, the source(s) of power of tribal men was (were) their
   a. greater strength by which they subdued women
   b. larger brain, which allowed them to dominate women
   c. genetic predisposition to violence
   d. weapons, items of trade, and knowledge gained from contact with other groups

7. Anthropologist Marvin Harris (1977) proposed a second theory of the origin of patriarchy. His theory centers on the need for hand-to-hand combat for survival in tribal groups. Because most men are stronger than most women, he says that men became the warriors, and women became
   a. the ones who made the weapons
   b. those who did the encouraging
   c. the reward that enticed men to risk their lives in battle
   d. weaker, as they didn't do the activities that build strength that the men did as they prepared for combat

8. Whatever the origins of men's dominance of society, this circular system of thought evolved
   a. Men came to think of themselves as inherently superior—based on the evidence that they dominated society.
   b. Trade was considered essential to the welfare of the group, and this required that men spend more time away from home.

c. The care of children was seen as essential to the welfare of the group, and more resources were given this task.

d. Women increasingly dropped out of public life as they saw men take over trade and warfare.

9. Patriarchy is always accompanied by cultural supports designed to justify male dominance. One of these supports is

a. the monuments to war often found in public parks

b. designating certain activities as "not appropriate" for women

c. the traditional view of keeping men away from homemaking activities

d. making weapons for war

10. Male dominance of contemporary societies is

a. seen by social analysts as necessary if we are to survive terrorism and potential wars

b. likely to get stronger as global capitalism becomes more dominant

c. a continuation of a millennia-old pattern whose origin is lost in history

d. likely to decrease as we experience global warming

UNIT 9.4

Fighting Back: The Rise of Feminism

The women's rights which we take for granted today came through long, bitter struggle. This photo was taken in 1906.

WHAT AM I SUPPOSED TO LEARN?

After you have read this unit, you should be able to

1 Explain what it means to say that a husband and wife used to be legally one person.

2 Know what "using cultural supports to justify dominance" means.

3 Summarize the three waves of feminism.

Cultural Supports to Maintain Dominance

In the early history of the United States, the second-class status of women was taken for granted. A husband and wife were legally one person—him (Chafetz and Dworkin 1986). Wives (and single women) could not vote, buy property in their own name, make legal contracts, or serve on juries. How could things have changed so much in the past hundred years or so that these examples sound like fiction?

As we just saw, in some way that is lost in history, men took control of society. That control included their domination of women. After society changed from hunting and gathering to agricultural and industrial, men tenaciously held on to their power and privileges. As I mentioned in the previous unit, men always use "cultural supports" to justify their dominance. To maintain their position, men used the social institutions—the law, religion, politics, business, education, and the family. There, children learned their "proper" roles as boys and girls—and what they should expect as adults. In other words, the social institutions reinforced the dominance of men.

The Struggle

Women broke through these cultural supports to win basic rights, but only through a prolonged and bitter struggle. Let's take a brief look at how this came about in the United States.

Feminism—the view that biology is not destiny and that stratification by gender is wrong and should be resisted—met with strong opposition, both by men who had power and privilege to lose and by women who accepted their status as morally correct. In 1894, for example, Jeannette Gilder said that women should not be given the right to vote because "politics is too public, too wearing, and too unfitted to the nature of women" (Crossen 2003).

Feminists, then known as *suffragists,* struggled against such views. In 1916, they founded the National Woman's Party, and in 1917 they began to picket the White House, demanding the right to vote. The men in power thought that "the nonsense" would go away, but the women continued to picket and draw attention to their grievances. After six months, the men's patience had worn thin and they had the women arrested. Hundreds were sent to prison, including Lucy Burns, a leader of the National Woman's Party. The extent to which these women had threatened male privilege is demonstrated by how they were treated in prison.

Two men brought in Dorothy Day [the editor of a periodical that promoted women's rights], twisting her arms above her head. Suddenly they lifted her and brought her body down twice over the back of an iron bench. . . . They had been there a few minutes when Mrs. Lewis, all doubled over like a sack of flour, was thrown in. Her head struck the iron bed and she fell to the floor senseless. As for Lucy Burns, they handcuffed her wrists and fastened the handcuffs over [her] head to the cell door. (Cowley 1969)

This was what is called the *first wave* of the women's movement. This first wave had a radical branch whose concern was very broad—to reform all the institutions of society. It also had a conservative branch whose concern

feminism the philosophy that men and women should be politically, economically, and socially equal; also organized activities on behalf of this principle

was much more focused—to win the vote for women (Freedman 2001). The conservative branch dominated the movement, and after the right to vote was won in 1920, the women's movement basically dissolved.

Then in the 1960s, the *second wave* of the women's movement began. Sociologist Janet Chafetz (1990) points out that up to this time most women thought of work as a temporary activity. Work for them was intended to fill the time between completing high school (and, for a few, completing college) and getting married. From Figure 9.1 on the next page, you can see how children's books reinforced such thinking.

As more women took jobs, however, women began to regard their work as careers. When they did this, they began to compare their working conditions with those of men. Before this, it didn't bother them much that men were given advantages at work, such as more pay. This seemed right because the men were supporting families and the women were just passing time until they married. As the women shifted their reference group, though, it transformed their view of work and of their place in it. The result was a second wave of protest against gender inequalities. The goals of this second wave (which continues today) are broad, ranging from raising women's pay to changing social policies on violence against women.

And now, a *third wave* of feminism has emerged. In addition to the broad goal of gender equality in all areas of life, three main aspects are apparent. The first is a greater focus on the problems of women in the Least Industrialized Nations (Spivak 2000; Hamid 2006). In these countries, women are fighting battles against conditions that women in the Most Industrialized Nations overcame long ago. The second is a criticism of the values that dominate work and society. Some feminists argue that the values so prized at work—competition, toughness, calloused emotions, and independence—represent "male" qualities. These, they say, should be replaced with cooperation, connection, openness, and interdependence (England 2000). A third aspect of this current wave is the need to challenge gender roles and to remove impediments to women's love and sexual pleasure (Crawford 2009). We need, they stress, to remove all double standards, so women have the same rights to sexual pleasure that men do. Part of the third wave is younger feminists challenging the ideas of older feminists.

Although U.S. women enjoy fundamental rights today, gender inequality continues to play a central role in social life. In the pages that follow, we will look at several areas of gender inequality, beginning with the world of work, one that will have a direct effect on your life.

> ***IF YOU WANT TO LEARN MORE*** *about the women's movement in Iran, a country where women enjoy few rights and women who protest face danger,*
>
> **Read** more from the author: Women in Iran: The Times are Changing, Ever so Slowly in **mysoclab**

FIGURE 9.1 **Teaching Gender**

Mother and Sally

Mother can sew.
Jane can sew.

Father

"I will help," said Dick.
"I will help you with the pigs."

Source: From *Dick and Jane: Fun with Our Family,* Illustrations © copyright 1951, 1979, *and Dick and Jane: We Play Outside,* copyright © 1965, Pearson Education, Inc., published by Scott, Foresman and Company. Used with permission.

UNIT 9.4 // TESTING MYSELF
DID I LEARN IT? ANSWERS ARE AT THE END OF THE CHAPTER

1. To say that a husband and wife used to be legally one person refers to all these except this one.
   a. Property was in the name of the husband only.
   b. Women had to get written permission from their mothers to marry, and they had to show this to a judge, who then granted written authorization for the marriage.
   c. Only the husband, not the wife, could make legal contracts.
   d. Only the husband, not the wife, could vote.

2. This statement best summarizes what it means to say that men use "cultural supports" to maintain their dominance.
   a. Feminists have been trying to change the social institutions because they disagree with both their philosophy and approach.
   b. Men were never certain that their dominance was firm enough, and they constantly were on the alert for ways to strengthen it.
   c. Although some women were satisfied with their position in society, and even viewed it as morally right, others agitated for social reform.
   d. The social institutions—the law, religion, politics, business, education, and the family—teach children their "proper" roles as boys and girls, and what they should expect as adults.

3. Feminism is defined in the text as
   a. an attempt to take social control from men
   b. the goal of equality in pay, medical care, and maintaining hard-won rights
   c. the breaking down of barriers that prevent men and women from having equal social interaction
   d. the view that biology is not destiny and that stratification by gender is wrong and should be resisted

4. In the 1800s and early 1900s, feminists were called
   a. the women who wanted to change the world
   b. the hands that rock the cradle—and the world
   c. suffragists
   d. the left-wing militants of Washington, D.C.

5. What happened after women picketed the White House for six months in 1917?
   a. Winter came and they had to give up.
   b. The police locked arms, forming a barrier around the White House that prevented the women from approaching it.
   c. They were arrested and sent to prison.
   d. They won a new law and in triumph called an end to their protest.

6. There are three waves of feminism. The goal of the conservatives in the first wave, in the late 1800s and the early 1900s, was to

a. strike down the laws that made it illegal for women to drive

b. make same-sex marriages legal

c. get the president to announce in a State of the Union address to Congress that gender inequality was a problem

d. win the vote for women

7. Figure 9.1 illustrates gender lessons that school readers taught children in the 1950s and 1960s. A main gender lesson girls were taught in these readers was to

a. be a good student

b. feed the animals

c. help mom with housework

d. be attractive to boys

8. There are three waves of feminism. Until the second wave that began in the 1960s, most women thought of work as

a. a temporary activity to fill the time between completing high school (and, for a few, completing college) and getting married

b. their contribution to making society a better place

c. a disagreeable activity that interfered with their broader vision of improving society

d. wage slavery

9. There are three waves of feminism. During the second wave that began in the 1960s, women shifted their reference group. This statement refers to

a. fewer women wanting to get married, which has resulted in more cohabitation and a lower birth rate

b. women rejecting negative stereotypes of femininity

c. women thinking of jobs as careers and challenging the greater privileges men had at work

d. women wanting to adopt "male" values

10. There are three waves of feminism. The third and current wave of feminism has the broad goal of gaining gender equality in all areas of life. This goal has three main aspects. Which of these is not one of these aspects?

a. a criticism of the values that dominate work and society

b. the removal of impediments to women's love and sexual pleasure

c. a greater focus on the problems of women in the Least Industrialized Nations

d. locating weaknesses in social institutions and developing strategies for exploiting them

UNIT 9.5

Global Inequality in the World of Work

WHAT AM I SUPPOSED TO LEARN?

After you have read this unit, you should be able to

 1 Know what the "sex typing" of work means.

 2 Summarize the basic findings from Murdock's survey of work and gender in 324 societies around the world.

3 Explain why anatomy is not destiny when it comes to work.

4 State the basic principle about gender and the prestige of work.

Gender roles have changed remarkably during the past few decades.

In the rest of this chapter, we will review many areas of **gender discrimination** (also called **sexual discrimination**), people being singled out for unequal treatment because of their sex. One of the most common forms, and one that you are destined to face in one way or another, is discrimination at work. Let's begin, then, with gender in the world of work.

We will first look at gender discrimination on a global level. This will give us a background for understanding gender discrimination at work in the United States.

Sex Typing of Work around the World

THE MURDOCK RESEARCH

First, let's look at work around the world and try to find out what kind of work is always "men's work" or always "women's work." When anthropologists report on the people they study, they include information on how those people divide up work. Anthropologist George Murdock (1937) reviewed these reports, which included research on 324 societies around the world. He found that in all of them work is *sex typed*; that is, they associate some activities with men and other activities with women. In other words, in all societies, some work is "women's work," and other work is "men's work."

This wasn't the surprise. From what we know about gender, we could expect this. But here is the surprise. Murdock also found that the work that one society considers "women's work" can be considered "men's work" in another society. He reports this example: In some groups, women take care of cattle, but in other groups this is "men's work."

Murdock did find a clustering around gender. Around the world, three types of work are usually considered "men's work"—not always, but generally. These are making weapons, pursuing sea mammals, and hunting. In a few societies, though, women also did this work. As for "women's work," cooking, making clothing, carrying water, and grinding grain were almost always assigned to women. A few societies, however, regarded these activities as men's work.

Murdock found one exception to work being assigned to either men or women. This was metalworking, which in all of the 324 societies was considered "men's work." In contrast, no specific work was universally assigned only to women.

ANATOMY AND DESTINY

Does anatomy equal destiny when it comes to work? From this research, we can see that the answer is a loud *no* when it comes to men's and women's capacity for work. Although in some societies women and men are locked into particular types of work, this is *social*, not biological. It is just the way a group chooses to divide up work. Men and women are not "naturally" cut out for particular work because of their

gender discrimination people being given or denied resources and privileges on the basis of their sex; also called *sexual discrimination*

biology. Work that is considered feminine in one society may be deemed masculine in another, and vice versa.

All of us learn to think about "men's work" and "women's work" based on our experiences in the society in which we grow up. Let's explore your ideas in *Making It Personal*.

MAKING IT PERSONAL
Your Stereotypes

We all have stereotypes. These are general ideas about aspects of our social world (people, things, and even different kinds of work). We all pick ideas up from our parents, friends, conversations, the media, and personal experiences. What stereotypes of "men's work" and "women's work" do you hold? Can you recall how you learned these ideas?

It is enlightening to go beyond our own society to see how people "do gender" in other places in the world. Look at the photo essay on next two pages. I think you'll be struck at how different gender and work are in India. As I traveled about the country, I was surprised by what I saw, which is why I took these photos.

Gender and the Prestige of Work

As sociologists examined gender and work, they found this fascinating principle: *Universally, greater prestige is given to male activities—regardless of what those activities are* (Linton 1936; Rosaldo 1974). If taking care of goats is "men's work," then the care of goats is considered important and brings high prestige. But if taking care of goats is "women's work," then the care of goats is considered less important and brings less prestige.

You should note that this is not just the way it is in some small tribal groups. This is a universal principle. Let's take an example closer to home. Delivering babies used to be "women's work." Midwives or neighborhood women and female relatives delivered the new baby. Men had nothing to do with it. They were even kicked out of the house during the delivery, or at least not allowed in the bedroom where the woman was having a baby. What kind of prestige did delivering babies have? Very low—it was just one of those "women things."

Then doctors (men) started to look for ways to expand their work, and they decided that delivering babies would be a good way to make more money. This wasn't easy for them to accomplish, since while she was giving birth a woman wouldn't let even her husband in the room, much less some strange man. To learn how to do the job, the men bribed midwives to sneak them into the bedroom. The men crawled on their hands and knees. They hid, watched, listened, and learned. Eventually, male doctors succeeded in making childbirth a medical matter, and they took over. What happened to the prestige of delivering babies? It shot through the roof (Ehrenreich and English 1973; Wertz and Wertz 1981; Rothman 1994).

WORK AND GENDER: WOMEN AT WORK IN INDIA

Traveling through India was both a pleasant and an eye-opening experience. The country is incredibly diverse, the people friendly, and the land culturally rich. For this photo essay, wherever I went—whether city, village, or country-side— I took photos of women at work.

From these photos, you can see that Indian women work in a wide variety of occupations. Some of their jobs match traditional Western expectations, and some diverge sharply from our gender stereotypes. Although women in India remain subservient to men—with the women's movement hardly able to break the cultural surface—women's occupations are hardly limited to the home. I was surprised at some of the hard, heavy labor that Indian women do.

Sweeping the house is traditional work for Western women. So it is in India, but the sweeping has been extended to areas outside the home. These women are sweeping a major intersection in Chennai. When the traffic light changes here, the women will continue sweeping, with the drivers swerving around them. This was one of the few occupations that seems to be limited to women.

Women also take care of livestock. It looks as though this woman dressed up and posed for her photo, but this is what she was wearing and doing when I saw her in the field and stopped to talk to her. While the sheep are feeding, her job is primarily to "be" there, to make certain the sheep don't wander off or that no one steals them.

I visited quarries in different parts of India, where I found men, women, and children hard at work in the tropical sun. This woman works 8-1/2 hours a day, six days a week. She earns 40 rupees a day (about ninety cents). Men make 60 rupees a day (about $1.35). Like many quarry workers, this woman is a bonded laborer. She must give half of her wages to her master.

Indian women are highly visible in public places. A storekeeper is as likely to be a woman as a man. This woman is selling glasses of water at a beach on the Bay of Bengal. The structure on which her glasses rest is built of sand.

This woman belongs to the Dhobi sub caste, whose occupation is washing clothes. She stands waist deep at this same spot doing the same thing day after day. The banks of this canal in Hyderabad are lined with men and women of her caste, who are washing linens for hotels and clothing for more well-to-do families.

A common sight in India is women working on construction crews. As they work on buildings and on highways, they mix cement, unload trucks, carry rubble, and, following Indian culture, carry loads of bricks atop their heads. This photo was taken in Raipur, Chhattisgarh.

As in the West, food preparation in India is traditional women's work. Here, however, food preparation takes an unexpected twist. Having poured rice from the 60-pound sack onto the floor, these women in Chittoor search for pebbles or other foreign objects that might be in the rice.

When I saw this unusual sight, I had to stop and talk to the workers. From historical pictures, I knew that belt-driven machines were common on U.S. farms 100 years ago. This one in Tamil Nadu processes sugar cane. The woman feeds sugar cane into the machine, which disgorges the stalks on one side and sugar cane juice on the other.

The villages of India have no indoor plumbing. Instead, each village has a well with a hand pump, and it is the women's job to fetch the water. This is backbreaking work, for, after pumping the water, the women wrestle the heavy buckets onto their heads and carry them home. This was one of the few tasks I saw that was limited to women.

© James M. Henslin, all photos

This principle is breathtaking in its significance for social life. *It is not the work that provides the prestige, but the sex with which the work is associated.* You might not grasp the full significance of this principle now—and not find it breathtaking—but it is significant. And it will affect your life.

UNIT 9.5 // TESTING MYSELF
DID I LEARN IT? ANSWERS ARE AT THE END OF THE CHAPTER

1. The phrase "sex typing of work" refers to
   a. associating some work (such as cooking or taking care of cattle) with one sex or the other
   b. giving examinations to determine if someone is masculine or feminine enough for a particular type of work
   c. having sex at work
   d. Hollywood's practice of casting rugged men as leads in Western movies and glamorous, but weak, women as their romantic leads

2. When George Murdock reviewed the reports of anthropologists on 324 societies around the world, he found that
   a. the West is much fairer in the way it divides work
   b. most anthropologists had not reported on how work is divided in the groups they studied
   c. very few of the societies sex type work
   d. all societies associate some work with men and other work with women

3. From Murdock's review of research on 324 societies, which statement is true?
   a. In most societies, women do more work than men.
   b. In most societies, most hard or heavy work is assigned to men.
   c. Work that one society considers "women's work" can be considered "men's work" in another society.
   d. The sex typing of work is undergoing fundamental change.

4. In his review of research on 324 societies, Murdock found that three types of work are usually considered "men's work"—not always, but generally. These are
   a. hunting lions, making traps, and stalking enemies
   b. making weapons, pursuing sea mammals, and hunting
   c. fishing, lumbering, and mining
   d. farming, exploring, and fighting enemies

5. In his review of research on 324 societies, Murdock found that four types of work are usually considered "women's work"—not always, but generally. These are
   a. cooking, making clothing, carrying water, and grinding grain
   b. taking care of cattle, taking care of goats, cooking, and cleaning
   c. supervising children, canoe making, pottery making, and making fishing nets
   d. food storage, doing laundry, cleaning fish, and preserving animal hides

6. From Murdock's review of work around the world, we can conclude that
   a. in most societies, women do more work than men
   b. most hard or heavy work is assigned to men
   c. anatomy is not destiny
   d. child care should be divided more evenly between husband and wife

7. From the photo essay on women and work in India, you can see that women in India
   a. do about the same work that women do in the United States
   b. don't do much work outside the home
   c. are limited primarily to what we would call "easy" work
   d. do a lot of work that is usually considered "men's work" in the United States

8. Sociologists have discovered this principle regarding work and prestige.
   a. Greater prestige is given to activities that involve self-sacrifice.
   b. It is not the work that provides the prestige, but the sex with which the work is associated.
   c. People who fail at work receive such low prestige that few recover from the loss.
   d. In tribal societies, taking care of goats brings low prestige.

9. When delivering babies was "women's work,"
   a. there were few male doctors
   b. cabdrivers refused to pick up pregnant women for fear they would deliver a baby in their cab
   c. delivering babies brought low prestige
   d. few babies survived

10. To expand their business, physicians, who at that time in our history were men, wanted to branch out into delivering babies. Because they did not know how to deliver babies, they
    a. bribed midwives to sneak them into the bedroom where a woman was having a baby
    b. simply gave up
    c. hired midwives as instructors at the medical colleges
    d. observed as their own wives gave birth and wrote reports for their colleagues

UNIT 9.6

Gender Inequality in the American Workplace

The relative positions of men and women in the world of work underlie part of the gender pay gap.

This global overview through Murdock's research provides us an excellent context for considering the world of work in the United States. Let's begin with one of the most remarkable areas of gender inequality at work, the pay gap.

The Pay Gap

After college, you might like to take a few years off, travel around Europe, sail the oceans, or maybe sit on a beach in some South American paradise and drink piña coladas. But chances are, you are going to go to work instead. Since you have to work, how would you like to make an extra $700,000 on your job? If this sounds appealing, read on. I'm going to reveal how you can make an extra $1,458 a month between the ages of 25 and 65.

I know that you are sitting on the edge of your chair by now, ready for me to reveal the secret. I hate to break the news, but this financial bonanza is impossible for some, although it certainly is simple for others. Look at Figure 9.2 on the next page. From it, you can see that to tap into this fortune, all you have to do is be born a boy. This figure is not a mistake. If we compare full-time workers, based on current differences in earnings, this is how much more money the *average man* can expect to earn over the course of his career.

How about boosting the pay up a bit more, say to $2,550 a month for a whopping career total of $1,225,000? How can you do this? Be both a male and a college graduate. Hardly any single

After you have read this unit, you should be able to

1 Summarize the gender pay gap.

2 Explain reasons for the gender pay gap.

3 Explain what keeps the glass ceiling in place.

factor pinpoints gender discrimination better than these totals. As you can see from Figure 9.2 on the next page, the pay gap shows up at *all* levels of education. But as I'm sure you'll notice, the pay gap is the worst for college graduates.

For college students, the gender gap in pay begins with the first job after graduation. You might know of a particular woman who was offered a higher salary than most men in her class, but she would be an exception. On average, men enjoy a "testosterone bonus," and employers start them out at higher salaries than women (Harris et al. 2005; Carter 2010). *Depending on your sex, then, you will either benefit from the pay gap or be victimized by it.*

Perhaps you would like to get a higher starting salary when you finish college? Read *Making It Personal.*

MAKING IT PERSONAL

How to Get a Higher Salary

A consistent research finding is that when college students take their first jobs, most women start at lower salaries than men do. Another finding is that women aren't as good as men at negotiating salaries. Women are more likely to accept the first offer, or to negotiate a little and be happy with the little increase that comes with a second offer.

Why settle for less than the company is willing to pay? If you are a woman, remember that the first offer is almost always negotiable. The hiring agent will be happy if you accept the offer, but usually is willing to add considerably to it if you negotiate strongly. Negotiation is a skill. Learn it. Read books on how to negotiate—and practice with a partner.

If you are a man, hone up on your negotiating skills. You can increase your starting salary, too. For both men and women, the time you put into improving this skill will pay off in cold cash.

The pay gap is so great that U.S. women who work full-time average *only 72 percent* of what men are paid. As you can see from Figure 9.3 on the next page, the pay gap used to be even

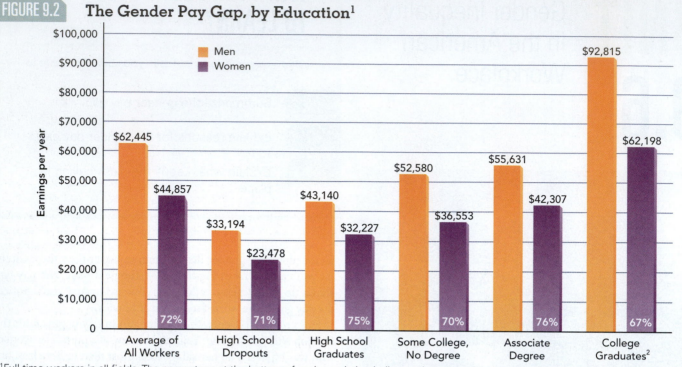

FIGURE 9.2 | The Gender Pay Gap, by Education[1]

[1]Full-time workers in all fields. The percentage at the bottom of each purple bar indicates the women's average percentage of the men's income.
[2]Bachelor's and all higher degrees, including professional degrees.
Source: By the author. Based on Statistical Abstract of the United States *2012:Table 703.*

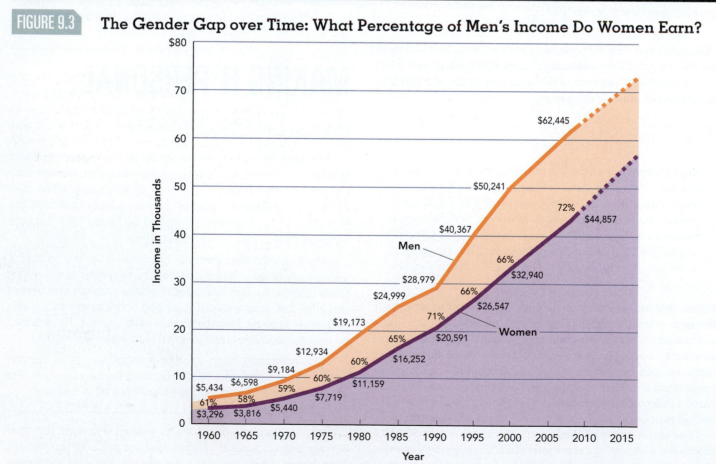

FIGURE 9.3 | The Gender Gap over Time: What Percentage of Men's Income Do Women Earn?

Source: Based on Statistical Abstract of the United States *1995:Table 739; 2002:Table 666; 2012:Table 703, and earlier years. Broken lines indicate author's estimate.*

Ginni Rometty, CEO of IBM, is one of the women who have broken through the glass ceiling. What keeps the glass ceiling from being broken wide open?

The Slowly Cracking Glass Ceiling

"First comes love, then comes marriage, then comes flex time and a baby carriage."

Said by a supervisor at Novartis who refused to hire women (Carter 2010)

This supervisor's statement reflects open, blatant discrimination. In contrast, most gender discrimination in the workplace is covert (hidden). Much of it is unintentional, flowing from **gender stereotypes**—assumptions about what men and women are like.

Apart from overt discrimination and the "child penalty," what keeps women from breaking through the **glass ceiling,** the mostly invisible barriers that prevent women from reaching the executive suite? Here is where the "pipelines" that lead to the top of a company come into play. These pipelines are its marketing, sales, and production positions, those that directly affect the corporate bottom line (Hymowitz 2004; DeCrow 2005). Men, who dominate the executive suite, stereotype women as being good at "support" but less capable than men of leadership (Belkin 2007). They steer women into human resources or public relations. In these positions, successful projects are not appreciated in the same way as projects that bring corporate profits—and bonuses for their managers.

Another reason the glass ceiling is so powerful is that women lack strong mentors—successful executives who take an interest in them and teach them the ropes. This lack is no trivial matter, for strong mentors provide opportunities to develop leadership skills that open the door to the executive suite (Hymowitz 2007; Yakaboski and Reinert 2011). Some men are afraid to mentor women for fear of later accusations of sexual harassment.

worse. A gender gap in pay occurs not only in the United States but also in *all* industrialized nations.

REASONS FOR THE GENDER PAY GAP

What logic can underlie the gender pay gap? Maybe it is due to career choices. Perhaps women are more likely to choose lower-paying jobs, such as teaching grade school, while men are more likely to go into better-paying areas of work, such as business and engineering. Actually, this is true, and researchers have found that about *half* of the gender pay gap is due to such factors. And the balance? It consists of a combination of gender discrimination (Jacobs 2003; Roth 2003) and what is called the "child penalty"—women missing out on work experience and opportunities while they care for children (Hundley 2001; Wade et al. 2010).

THE CEO GAP

As a final indication of the extent of the U.S. gender pay gap, consider this. Of the nation's top 500 corporations (the Fortune 500), only 12 are headed by women (VanderMey 2011). I examined the names of the CEOs of the 350 largest U.S. corporations, and I found that your best chance to reach the top is to be named (in this order) John, Robert, James, William, or Charles. Edward, Lawrence, and Richard are also advantageous names. Amber, Katherine, Leticia, and Maria apparently draw a severe penalty. Naming your baby girl John or Robert might seem a little severe, but it could help her reach the top. (I say this only slightly tongue-in-cheek. One of the few women to head a Fortune 500 company—before she was fired and given $21 million severance pay—had a man's first name: Carleton Fiorina of Hewlett-Packard. Carleton's first name is actually Cara, but knowing what she was facing in the business culture, she dropped this feminine name to go by her masculine middle name.)

Explore the **Concept**
The Occupations of Females and Males in **mysoclab**

THE WOMEN WHO BREAK THROUGH

As you would expect, the women who break through the glass ceiling are highly motivated individuals with a fierce competitive spirit. They are willing to give up sleep, recreation, and family responsibilities for the sake of advancing their careers. What you might not have expected, but which makes sense when you consider the work environment, is that these women have also learned to play by "men's rules," developing a style that makes men comfortable.

AND THE FUTURE?

Will the glass ceiling crack open? Some think so. They point out that women who began their careers twenty to thirty years ago are now running major divisions within the largest companies, and from them, some will emerge as the new CEOs. Others reply that these optimists have been saying this same thing for years, that the glass ceiling continues to be so strong that most of these women they refer to have already reached their top positions (Carter 2010).

We'll have to see what the future brings, but the growing number of women who are majoring in law and business is certainly a promising indication of positive change.

Watch the **Video**
The Basics: Gender in **mysoclab**

gender stereotypes
Ideas or assumptions about how men and women "are"

glass ceiling the mostly invisible barrier that keeps women from advancing to the top levels at work

UNIT 9.6 // TESTING MYSELF
DID I LEARN IT?

1. Comparing full-time female and male workers who graduate from college, over his lifetime the average man can expect to earn an additional
   - **a.** $250,000
   - **b.** $500,000
   - **c.** $700,000
   - **d.** $1,000,000

2. Figure 9.3 shows that in 1960, full-time working women averaged 61 percent of what full-time working men earned. After 50 years of trying to achieve equal pay, full-time working women now average this percentage of what full-time working men earn.
   - **a.** 72 percent
   - **b.** 82 percent
   - **c.** 92 percent
   - **d.** 102 percent

3. Researchers have found several causes for the gender pay gap. Which of these is not one of those causes?
   - **a.** Men are more likely to go into better-paying areas of work, such as engineering, while women are more likely to go into lower-paying areas of work, such as teaching.
   - **b.** Gender discrimination
   - **c.** The "child penalty"—women miss out on work experience and opportunities while they care for children.
   - **d.** Women don't work as hard as men.

4. For their first job after college, men, on average, are offered
   - **a.** higher starting salaries than women
   - **b.** lower starting salaries than women
   - **c.** the same average starting salaries as women
   - **d.** lower salaries in teaching but higher salaries in engineering

5. Of the nation's top 500 corporations (the Fortune 500), women head
   - **a.** 12
   - **b.** 82
   - **c.** 112
   - **d.** 212

6. The term glass ceiling refers to
   - **a.** the different starting salaries offered to men and women who graduate from college
   - **b.** the tendency of women to quit their jobs or to go to part-time work after they marry
   - **c.** the mostly invisible barriers that prevent women from reaching the executive suite
   - **d.** the difficulty women have in getting adequate child care, which holds them back at work

7. The "pipelines" that lead to being promoted to the top positions of a company are in
   - **a.** marketing, sales, and production
   - **b.** the support roles
   - **c.** human resources and public relations
   - **d.** advertising

8. One reason the glass ceiling is so powerful is that
   - **a.** Men don't want to compete with women.
   - **b.** Women tend to be seen as being good at "support" but less capable than men of leadership, so they are steered to human resources and public relations.
   - **c.** The laws regarding equal pay are not enforced.
   - **d.** Women, though few want to admit it, are less capable than men.

9. One reason the glass ceiling is so powerful is that women
   - **a.** are more competitive than men
   - **b.** have a covert preference to be homemakers
   - **c.** lack mentors—successful executives who take an interest in them and teach them the ropes
   - **d.** don't make as good leaders as men do

10. All of these are true except one. The women who are breaking through the glass ceiling are women who
    - **a.** have a fierce competitive spirit
    - **b.** are willing to give up sleep and recreation for the sake of career advancement
    - **c.** have learned to play by "men's rules," developing a style that makes men comfortable
    - **d.** have husbands who take over most of the household tasks

UNIT 9.7
Sexual Harassment

WHAT AM I SUPPOSED TO LEARN?

After you have read this unit, you should be able to

1 Define sexual harassment.

2 Explain how the perception of social structure was essential to the development of the term sexual harassment.

3 Explain how the term sexual harassment has changed the perception of behavior.

What would determine if this is flirting or sexual harassment?

As we consider sexual harassment in this brief unit, we will take a symbolic interactionist perspective and look at how terms affect perception. I know that this sounds abstract, but what this means will become clear.

From Personal to Structural

Another problem that sometimes comes up at work and school is **sexual harassment**—unwelcome sexual attention that can affect a person's job or school performance or create a hostile environment. This term is so common today that it might surprise you to learn that the term didn't exist until the 1970s. Until then, sexual harassment was not recognized as a problem. Women considered unwanted sexual comments, touches, looks, and pressure to have sex to be a personal matter. It was something done by a "turned on" man, or maybe by an obnoxious one.

With the prodding of feminists, women began to look at things differently. They began to see that unwanted sexual advances were part of a much larger issue, that it was not simply men doing obnoxious things because they were attracted to women. They started to view the problem in terms of *social structure*—men in positions of authority and women working under that authority. This was a vital change in perception—from individual, personal attraction to men using their positions of authority to pressure women to have sex.

Today, we take this view for granted, but seeing this underlying *structural* basis was a breakthrough in perception. It changed the way men and women view unwanted sexual advances at work and school. Because we have the term *sexual harassment,* we are now more apt to perceive a supervisor who makes sexual advances to a worker not as sexual attraction but as a misuse of authority.

It is important to add that sexual harassment is not just a "man thing." When the term was developed in the 1970s, it was almost exclusively men who occupied positions of authority. The change has been so far-reaching since then that throughout today's

sexual harassment the abuse of one's position of authority to force unwanted sexual demands on someone

society women are in positions of authority. In those positions they, too, sexually harass their subordinates (Settles et al. 2011), and men now file one of every six legal claims (Mattioli 2010). With most authority still vested in men, however, most sexual harassers are men.

> **IF YOU WANT TO LEARN MORE** *about sexual harassment as an abuse of power, and how this occurs in the military,*
>
> **Read** more from the author: Sexual Harassment and Rape of Women in the Military in **mysoclab**

UNIT 9.7 // TESTING MYSELF
DID I LEARN IT? ANSWERS ARE AT THE END OF THE CHAPTER

1. Sexual harassment refers to
   a. sex games at work and school
   b. the laws that provide punishment for illegal sex acts at work or school
   c. women who are not interested in sex getting offended when a man makes a sexual advance
   d. unwelcome sexual attention that can affect a person's job or school performance or create a hostile environment

2. Sexual harassment was not recognized as a problem until the 1970s because
   a. There was little sex going on at that time, especially at work.
   b. The laws of that time were quite explicit, and the punishment for sexual harassment was severe.
   c. Women of that period were much more welcoming of sexual advances than women are today.
   d. Before this, women considered unwanted sexual comments, touches, looks, and pressure to have sex to be a personal matter.

3. Underlying the development of the term sexual harassment is this essential change
   a. With the prodding of feminists, women began to perceive unwanted sexual advances at work and school to be part of a structural problem.
   b. Fewer men used their positions of authority to pressure women to have sex.
   c. The behavior changed, but the perception did not.
   d. Men and women began to view unwanted sexual advances at work and school as undesirable.

4. With many women in positions of authority today
   a. Sexual harassment has become mostly a thing of the past.
   b. Women, too, have become sexual harassers.
   c. Men have become much more careful about how they approach women sexually.
   d. The laws of sexual harassment no longer apply.

UNIT 9.8

Gender Inequality in Everyday Life and Health Care

Let's turn to two more areas of gender inequality—everyday life, where inequality is routine and taken for granted, and health care, where gender inequality can be a matter of life and death.

Gender Inequality in Everyday Life

In everyday life, the devaluation of femininity (placing a lower value on things feminine) is often invisible. It quietly lurks in our thinking, serving as a background assumption for what we do in everyday life. Could this possibly be true? Or do you think I am exaggerating? Let's find out. Let's see if we can bring this form of gender inequality into the light, where, perhaps, it can become less assumed as a background factor in our social interaction.

DEVALUATION OF THINGS FEMININE

In general, a higher value is placed on things considered masculine, for masculinity is a cultural symbol of strength and success. Femininity, in contrast, is often perceived in terms of weakness and lack of accomplishment.

Are you aware of this? Most people don't seem to be, or at least they can't put their finger on it. But all you have to do is listen carefully as people talk. You can hear these relative evaluations pop up in everyday speech. Let's begin with a quick historical glance. You might even have said something like this—or at least heard someone say something like it:

Sociologist Samuel Stouffer headed a research team that produced The American Soldier *(1949), a classic study of World War II combat soldiers. To motivate their men, officers used feminine terms as insults. If a man showed less-than-expected courage or endurance, an officer might say, "Whatsa matter, Bud—got lace on your drawers?" (Drawers was a term for women's undergarments—the same as asking if the men were wearing panties.) A generation later, officers who trained soldiers to fight in Vietnam still used accusations of femininity to motivate their men. Drill sergeants would mock their troops by saying, "Can't hack it, little girls?" (Eisenhart 1975).*

"This is all historical," you might say. And it is. But the practice continues. Male soldiers who show hesitation during maneuvers are still mocked by others, who call them girls (Miller 1997/2007).

And it isn't just the military. It is the same in sports. Anthropologist Douglas Foley (1990/2006), who studied high school football in Texas, reports that coaches insult boys who don't play well by shouting that they are "wearing skirts." In her research,

sociologist Donna Eder (1995) heard junior high boys call one another "girl" when they didn't hit hard enough in football. When they play basketball, boys of this age also call one another a "woman" when they miss a basket (Stockard and Johnson 1980). In professional hockey, if players are not rough enough on the ice, their teammates call them "girls" (Gallmeier 1988:227).

These insults roll so easily off the tongues of men in sports and war that it is easy to lose sight of their significance, that they represent a devaluation of females. How do these insults show a devaluation of femininity? Sociologists Stockard and Johnson (1980:12) hit the nail on the head when they pointed out, "There is no comparable phenomenon among women, for young girls do not insult each other by calling each other 'man.'"

Our background assumptions focus our perception, making some things invisible to us. Much of our male–female interaction in everyday life is like this, containing a devaluation of things feminine so taken-for-granted that it drops below our level of awareness.

Let's pursue this form of insult a little more in *Making It Personal.*

MAKING IT PERSONAL

Insulting Terms for Women

Can you see the significance of this informal observation of men calling men who underperform girls? The researchers didn't go out to find this. They simply heard such comments as they watched soldiers in training and boys and men playing sports. Do you see how these little statements hit at the heart of the different values placed on masculinity and femininity?

If you have personally heard or made such comments, I would appreciate it if you would share them with me—the exact comment and the circumstances under which it was said. My email address is located in the Preface.

Let's turn to another area of gender inequality, one that is also below our level of awareness, but so severe that it brings death.

Gender Inequality in Health Care

Medical researchers were perplexed. Reports were coming in from all over the country: Women were twice *as likely as men to die after coronary bypass surgery. Researchers at Cedars-Sinai Medical Center in Los Angeles checked their own records. They found that of 2,300 coronary bypass patients, 4.6 percent of the women died as a result of the surgery, compared with 2.6 percent of the men.*

These findings were a sociological puzzle. To solve it, researchers first turned to biology (Bishop 1990). In coronary bypass surgery, surgeons take a blood vessel from one part of the body and stitch it to an artery on the surface of the heart. Perhaps, thought the researchers, the surgery is more difficult to do on women because of their smaller arteries. To find out, they timed surgeons, finding out how long they kept patients on the heart-lung machine while they operated. They were quite surprised at what they found: Women spent *less* time on the machine than men. This indicated that the surgery was not more difficult to perform on women, maybe even a bit easier.

Since this idea (called a hypothesis when it is part of research) didn't work out, the researchers had to probe further. As they did so, a surprising answer unfolded: unintended gender discrimination. When women complained of chest pains, their doctors took them only *one-tenth as seriously* as when men made the same complaints. How do we know this? Doctors were *ten* times more likely to give men exercise stress tests and radioactive heart scans. They also sent men to surgery on the basis of abnormal stress tests, but they waited until their women patients showed clear-cut symptoms of heart disease before sending them to surgery. After heart disease is more advanced, patients are more likely to die during and after surgery.

No one knows why this form of gender discrimination exists, even though it is so severe that life and death hang in the balance. The physicians, both male and female, do not *intend* to discriminate against their female patients. They just do, without being aware of it. Underlying this discrimination somehow are background assumptions—ways the doctors perceive men, women, and pain. No one has yet determined just what these assumptions are.

These findings about unintended gender discrimination have been publicized among physicians. Did the discrimination stop? Unfortunately, the problem continues (Jneid et al. 2008). Perhaps as more women become physicians, the situation will change, since female doctors are more sensitive to women's health problems. For example, they are more likely to order Pap smears and mammograms (Lurie et al. 1993). In addition, as more women join the faculties of medical schools, we can expect women's health problems to receive more attention in the training of physicians. Even this might not do it, however, as no one knows how stereotyping of the sexes produces this deadly discrimination, and women, too, hold our cultural stereotypes.

You, too, have assumptions of the sexes, of course. Let's explore them in *Making It Personal.*

MAKING IT PERSONAL
Your Background Assumptions

Physicians work within what sociologists call "a framework of background assumptions." This means that doctors have ideas, many of which they are unaware, that influence their choices in giving medical treatment. We all have background assumptions, and for us, too, they are an essential part of our everyday lives.

What background assumptions do you think you have that influence your perception of men and women? Their abilities? Their "proper" place in life?

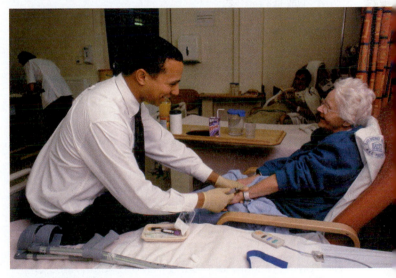

How do background assumptions influence patient care?

IF YOU WANT TO LEARN MORE about how women are discriminated against in the practice of medicine—sometimes even purposely chosen as victims

UNIT 9.8 // TESTING MYSELF
DID I LEARN IT? ANSWERS ARE AT THE END OF THE CHAPTER

1. In everyday life, the devaluation of femininity is often
   a. a background assumption, so taken for granted that it is largely invisible

   b. discussed by columnists, sometimes even making the front page of newspapers

   c. part of ordinary discussions over coffee

   d. perceived as something that we have to get rid of

2. In everyday life, masculinity often

   a. is exchanged with femininity

   b. symbolizes strength and success

   c. is perceived as a problem to be overcome

   d. presents a challenge for sports coaches

3. In everyday life, femininity is often

   a. a planned device

   b. part of the dynamic wardrobe of cultural attainments

   c. perceived in terms of weakness and lack of accomplishment

   d. a way that men seek to cover their weaknesses

4. In training soldiers, officers often insult the performance of their trainees by saying they

   a. need to go back to school

   b. should beef up more

   c. are performing like girls

   d. look like kids

5. In sports, coaches insult players and players insult one another by saying that someone is acting like

   a. he or she doesn't know what is going on

   b. an idiot

   c. a woman or girl

   d. a kid

6. Regarding the insults in sports and among soldiers that represent gender inequality, Stockard and Johnson pointed out, "There is no comparable phenomenon among women, for young girls do not insult each other by calling each other

   a. a dog."   **b.** dumb."

   c. clumsy."   **d.** a man."

7. Medical researchers found that the death rates of women during coronary bypass surgery were higher than those of men. The reason was that

   a. The women were afraid of surgery and kept postponing it.

   b. Doctors were ten times more likely to give men exercise stress tests and radioactive heart scans, which allowed them to have surgery before their heart disease became more advanced.

   c. Doctors were fearful of being sued for malpractice by women who would exaggerate their heart symptoms, so they kept postponing the women's surgery.

   d. The women were less likely to have insurance.

8. That the death rates of women during coronary bypass surgery are higher than those of men is an example of

   a. persistent discrimination

   b. unintended discrimination

   c. blatant discrimination

   d. improper teaching in our medical schools

9. When the reason for the higher death rates of women during coronary bypass surgery was publicized—that physicians were referring women for surgery later than the men—what happened?

   a. The news shocked the nation, and the medical profession made fundamental changes in the training of physicians.

   b. The U.S. Senate held hearings, calling some of the most well known doctors to testify.

   c. The death rates of women during coronary bypass surgery dropped to almost the same as the men's rate.

   d. Not much—the problem continues.

10. The author suggests that the higher death rates of women during coronary bypass surgery are the consequence of

   a. stereotyping of the sexes in ways that are below our level of awareness

   b. blatant and unconscionable discrimination

   c. inadequate training in our medical schools

   d. the masculine orientation of the medical profession

UNIT 9.9

Violence against Women

WHAT AM I SUPPOSED TO LEARN?

After you have read this unit, you should be able to

1 Know what suttee and "honor killings" are and how they are examples of gendered violence.

2 Summarize the general patterns of rape in the United States, including the most common age of victims, frequency of acquaintance rape, and the reasons so few victims of date rape report the crime.

3 Know the gendered pattern in murder.

4 Explain why it is difficult to break gendered violence.

Let's turn, now, to another area of gender discrimination: violence against women. Around the world, one of the consistent characteristics of violence is its gender inequality. That is, females are more likely to be the victims of males, not the other way around. In this brief review we'll look first at the global level and then at the United States.

Violence against Women on a Global Level

Violence against women is a global human rights issue. Throughout history, women have suffered horribly at the hands of men. One of the most brutal examples is *suttee,* which was practiced by some Hindu communities in India and banned by the British in 1829. It was the custom to burn a man's body when he died. This is actually a custom in several parts of the world, but in *suttee* when a man died, his widow was also burned with his body—even though she was quite alive and the idea of being burned alive didn't appeal to her.

No longer do we have this particular form of **gendered violence,** violence directed by one sex against the other. But in various parts of the world women are still kidnapped to be brides, they are forced into prostitution, and we still have female infanticide, female circumcision, and "honor killings."

> *IF YOU WANT TO LEARN MORE about the violence directed against females around the world—females being selected for abortion and the circumcision of girls*
>
> **Read** more from the author: Killing Little Girls: An Ancient and Thriving Practice and Female Circumcision in **mysoclab**

What are *"honor killings"*? A woman who is thought to have brought disgrace on her family is killed by a male relative—usually a brother or her husband, but sometimes her father or uncles. This form of violence against women is built into some societies

gendered violence
violence directed by one sex against the other

Painting of a suttee in an Italian encyclopedia from the 1800s. The term comes from sati, a sanskrit term meaning faithful wife.

One form of gendered violence is the prostitution of girls, as in this photo taken in Phnom Penh, the capital of Cambodia. Unlike these girls, some children who are prostituted have not yet reached puberty.

(Yardley 2010a), a custom that developed centuries, perhaps millennia, ago. It is still followed in a few countries, such as India, Jordan, Kurdistan, and Pakistan.

What threat to a family's honor can be so severe that the men in the family kill their own daughter, wife, sister, or mother? The usual reason is sex outside of marriage. Virginity at marriage is so prized in these societies that even a woman who has been raped is in danger of becoming the victim of an honor killing (Zoepf 2007; Falkenberg 2008). It is the same with a married woman who is thought to have had sex with a lover. Killing the girl or woman—even one's own sister or mother—removes the "stain" she has brought to the family and restores its honor in the community. Sharing this view, the police in these countries generally ignore honor killings, regarding them as private family matters.

With the slogan, "There is no honor in honor killings," groups of Arabs and Muslims are trying to change ideas about honor. A sign of changing views is that the national legislature of Pakistan passed laws making honor killing illegal (Appiah 2010).

Violence against Women in the United States

The history of the United States has never provided a cultural setting that would develop such customs as *suttee* or "honor killings." But the United States does not lack in violence against women. In considering gendered violence in the United States, we have only enough space to take a brief look at rape and murder.

FORCIBLE RAPE

Being raped is a common fear of U.S. women, a fear that is far from groundless. The U.S. rape rate is 0.59 per 1,000 females

TABLE 9.1	Age of Rape Victims

Age	Rate per 1,000 Females
12–15	1.9
16–19	3.3
20–24	2.3
25–34	1.3
35–49	0.8
50–64	0.3
65 and Older	0.09

Sources: By the author. A ten-year average, based on Statistical Abstract of the United States 2002:Table 303; 2003:Table 295; 2004:Table 322; 2005:Table 306; 2006:Table 308; 2007:Table 312; 2008:Table 316; 2009:Table 305; 2010:Table 305; 2012:Table 316.

TABLE 9.2	Relationship of Victims and Rapists

Relationship	Percentage
Relative	7%
Knows Well	33%
Casual Acquaintance	23%
Stranger	34%
Not Reported	2%

Sources: By the author. A ten-year average, based on Statistical Abstract of the United States 2002:Table 296; 2003:Table 323; 2004-2005:Table 307; 2006:Table 311; 2007:Table 315; 2008:Table 316; 2009:Table 306;. 2010:Table 306; 2011:Table 313.

(*Statistical Abstract 2012:Table 314*). If we exclude the very young and women over age 50, those who are the least likely to be rape victims, the rate comes to about 1 per 1,000. This means that 1 of every 1,000 U.S. girls and women between the ages of 12 and 50 is raped *each year*. Despite this high rate, women are safer now than they were ten and twenty years ago. The rape rate then was even higher than today.

Although any woman can be a victim of sexual assault—and victims include babies and elderly women—the typical victim is 16 to 19 years old. As you can see from Table 9.1, sexual assault peaks at those ages and then declines.

Women's most common fear seems to be that of strangers—who, appearing as though from nowhere, abduct and beat and rape them. Contrary to the stereotypes that underlie these fears, two of every three (63 percent) victims know their attacker. As you can see from Table 9.2, strangers commit just one of three rapes.

DATE (ACQUAINTANCE) RAPE

What has shocked so many about date rape (also known as *acquaintance rape*) are studies showing that it is common (Littleton et al. 2008). Researchers who used a nationally representative sample of women enrolled in U.S. colleges and universities with 1,000 students or more found that 1.7 percent had been raped during the preceding six months. Another 1.1 percent had been victims of attempted rape (Fisher et al. 2000).

Think about how huge these numbers are. With 11 million women enrolled in college, 2.8 percent (1.7 plus 1.1) means that about 300,000 college women were victims of rape or of attempted rape *in just the past six months*. (This conclusion assumes that the rate is the same in colleges with fewer than 1,000 students, which has not been verified.)

Most of the women told a friend what happened, but only 5 *percent* reported the crime to the police (Fisher et al. 2003). The most common reason for not reporting was thinking that the event "was not serious enough." The next most common reason was being unsure whether a crime had been committed. Many women were embarrassed and didn't want others, especially their family, to know what happened. Others felt there was no proof ("it would be my word against his"). Still others feared reprisal from the man or feared the police (Fisher et al. 2000). Sometimes a rape victim feels partially responsible because she knows the person, was drinking with him, went to his place voluntarily, or invited him to her place. As a physician who treats victims of date rape said, "Would you feel responsible if someone hit you over the head with a shovel—just because you knew the person?" (Carpenito 1999).

MURDER

Figure 9.4 on the next page gives you a good summary of the gendered pattern of murder, a pattern similar to what we find all over the world. In every country, men are more likely than women to be killers. Although females make up about 51 percent of the U.S. population, you can see that don't even come close to making up 51 percent of the nation's killers. As you can also see from this figure, when women are murdered, about 9 times out of 10 the killer is a man.

FEMINISM AND GENDERED VIOLENCE

Feminist sociologists have been especially effective in bringing violence against women to the public's attention. Some use symbolic interactionism, pointing out that to associate strength and virility with violence—as is done in many cultures—is to promote violence. Others use conflict theory. They argue that men are losing power, and that some men turn violently against women as a way to reassert their declining power and status (Reiser 1999; Meltzer 2002).

FIGURE 9.4 — Killers and Their Victims

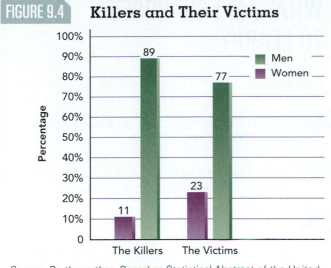

Source: By the author. Based on *Statistical Abstract of the United States 2012: Tables 311, 324.*

SOLUTIONS

There is no magic bullet for this problem of gendered violence, but to be effective, any solution must break the connection between violence and masculinity. This would require an educational program that encompasses schools, churches, homes, and the media. Given the gun-slinging heroes of the Wild West and other American icons, as well as the violent messages that are thrown at us in the mass media, including video games, it is difficult to be optimistic that a change will come any time soon.

UNIT 9.9 // TESTING MYSELF
DID I LEARN IT? ANSWERS ARE AT THE END OF THE CHAPTER

1. The term gendered violence refers to violence that
   a. is directed by one sex against the other
   b. has no gender (it has been degenderized)
   c. is forced upon someone
   d. existed in the past, but today has disappeared or has only remnants left

2. The term *suttee* refers to
   a. a canopy placed over bodies as they are burned in India
   b. the firewood, built to precise specifications, lit when bodies are burned in India
   c. a past practice in India of burning a living widow along with the body of her dead husband
   d. widows in India having to wear black clothing until they either remarry or die

3. The term honor killings refers to
   a. receiving honor for killing, such as medals in war
   b. killing for the purpose of revenge
   c. killing that is done by honorable people
   d. male relatives killing a woman who has brought disgrace to the family

4. What threat to a family's honor is so severe that the men do "honor killing"? The usual reason is
   a. sex outside of marriage
   b. that the victim committed robbery or some other felony
   c. that the individual was extremely sick and had little chance of getting well
   d. to please the mother

5. About 1 of every 1,000 girls and women in the United States between the ages of 12 and 50 is raped each year. Despite this high number, women
   a. take few precautions against being raped
   b. refuse to carry guns
   c. are safer now than they were ten and twenty years ago—the rape rate then was higher than today
   d. who talk to their friends and listen to the news know that the rape rate is much higher than this

6. Although any woman can be a victim of sexual assault—and victims include babies and elderly women—the typical victim is
   a. 12 to 15 years old   b. 16 to 19 years old
   c. 19 to 25 years old   d. 25 to 35 years old

7. You looked at Table 9.1 (or at least I hope you did). According to what you saw there, women are
   a. most likely to be assaulted by a relative
   b. most afraid of being attacked by someone they meet online
   c. more likely to be attacked by someone they know than by a stranger
   d. more likely to be raped at home than at any other location

8. Only about 5 percent of victims of date (acquaintance) rape report the assault to the police. Those who did not report the assault gave these reasons—except this one.
   a. They felt sorry for the individual who had attacked them.
   b. They felt partially responsible for the attack.
   c. They felt embarrassed.
   d. They were not sure that a crime had taken place.

9. Figure 9.4 provides a summary of gendered murder. When women are murdered, about what percentage die at the hands of men?
   a. 25   b. 40   c. 70   d. 90

10. The author says that there is no magic bullet for the problem of gendered violence, but to be effective, any solution must
   a. stop men from killing so many women
   b. get women to take self-defensive measures, perhaps even arm themselves
   c. break the connection between violence and masculinity
   d. take into account that we have violent video games

UNIT 9.10
The Changing Face of Politics

Cultural Supports of Gender Discrimination

As we conclude this chapter, I want to make explicit this general principle of gender inequality, which has run through the topics we have reviewed. Gender inequality is not some accidental, hit-or-miss affair. I mentioned cultural supports of gender inequality. This means that a society's institutions work together to maintain the group's particular forms of inequality. Customs, often venerated throughout history, both justify and maintain these arrangements. In some cases, the prejudice and discrimination directed at females are so extreme that they result in their death.

Politics is one of the areas of global gender discrimination. Men have used politics—the power it brings—to enforce their ideas of gender in their society. As the women's movement has grown more powerful and global, major changes are occurring

in this area of social life. Let's look at what is happening in the United States.

Women's Potential Political Power

Eight million more women than men are of voting age, and more women than men vote in U.S. national elections. As Table 9.3 shows, however, men greatly outnumber women in political office. Despite the gains women have made in recent elections, since 1789 almost 2,000 men have served in the U.S. Senate, but only 42 women have served, including the 20 current senators. Not until 1992 was the first African American woman (Carol Moseley-Braun) elected to the U.S. Senate. No Latina or Asian American woman has yet been elected to the Senate (National Women's Political Caucus 1998, 2011; *Statistical Abstract* 2012:Table 413; election results 2012).

We are in the midst of extensive change. In 2002, Nancy Pelosi was the first woman to be elected by her colleagues as minority leader of the House of Representatives. Five years later, in 2007, they chose her as the first female Speaker of the House. These posts made Pelosi the most powerful woman ever in Congress. Another significant event occurred in 2008 when Hillary Clinton came within a hair's breadth of becoming the presidential nominee of the Democratic party. That same year, Sarah Palin was chosen as the Republican vice-presidential candidate. We can also note that more women are becoming corporate executives and lawyers (*Statistical Abstract* 2012:Table 303). In these positions, women are traveling more and making statewide and national contacts. Another change is that child care is increasingly seen as a responsibility of both mother and father. With these changes, it is only a matter of time until a woman occupies the Oval Office.

Women have become increasingly active and dominant in U.S. politics. Shown here is Hillary Clinton meeting with leaders in Singapore.

TABLE 9.3   U.S. Women in Political Office

	Offices Held by Women (Percentage)	Offices Held By Women (Number)
National Office		
U.S. Senate	20%	20
U.S. House of Representatives	17%	73
State Office		
Governors	12%	6
Lt. Governors	18%	9
Attorneys General	8%	4
Secretaries of State	24%	12
Treasurers	20%	10
State Auditors	16%	8
State Legislators	24%	1,800

Source: Center for American Women and Politics 2010; Hook 2012

UNIT 9.10 // TESTING MYSELF
DID I LEARN IT? ANSWERS ARE AT THE END OF THE CHAPTER

1. Gender inequality is
   a. accidental
   b. a hit-or-miss affair
   c. part of how society's institutions work together
   d. hard to study because it is changing so rapidly

2. This is why women could take political control of the United States
   a. The U.S. Senate and House of Representatives are vulnerable because of eligibility rules passed about ten years ago.
   b. Female candidates have received tutoring from previous office holders and skilled political consultants.
   c. There is nothing in the U.S. Constitution that would prevent this from happening.
   d. Eight million more women than men are of voting age, and more women than men vote in U.S. national elections.

3. Since 1789, almost 2,000 men have served in the U.S. Senate. During this time, how many women have served in the Senate?
   a. 42   b. 127
   c. 211   d. 398

4. Only one African American woman has ever been elected to the U.S. Senate. How many Latina or Asian American women have been elected to the Senate?
   a. 0   b. 2
   c. 4   d. 8

5. In 2002, Nancy Pelosi was elected by her colleagues as minority leader of the House of Representatives. Five years later, in 2007, she was chosen as the Speaker of the House. Before this, how many women had served as minority leader of the House of Representatives and the Speaker of the House?
   a. 0   b. 1
   c. 3   d. 5

6. The author says that it is only a matter of time before a woman is elected President of the United States. In addition to women having achieved high political office, having come close to becoming the presidential nominee, and being chosen by a major political party as the vice-presidential nominee, the author also states that
   a. The schools are stressing greater gender equality.
   b. A major study shows that women hold greater wealth than men.
   c. More women are becoming corporate executives and lawyers.
   d. Men are so disgusted with the current political situation that they are willing to give women a try.

PULLING IT ALL TOGETHER REVIEWING THE LEARNING GOALS

Unit 9.1   Differences between Sex and Gender

1. Distinguish between primary and secondary sex characteristics.

- *Primary sex characteristics*—a vagina or a penis and other organs related to reproduction. *Secondary sex characteristics*—physical distinctions between males and females not directly connected with reproduction.

2. Distinguish between sex and gender.

- *Sex* refers to the biological characteristics that distinguish males and female. *Gender* refers to learned behaviors called masculinity and femininity.

👁 **Watch** the **Video**
Sociology on the Job:
Gender in **mysoclab**

Unit 9.2   Human Behavior: Biological or Social Factors?

1. Summarize the dominant position in sociology on genetic factors in human behavior.

- Social factors are the primary reasons people do what they do. Any biological predispositions of humans to behavior are overlaid with culture.

2. Summarize the minority position in sociology on genetic factors in human behavior.

- Men dominate all societies of the world because of their biological predispositions.

3. Give the basic findings on the Vietnam Veterans Study and explain how social factors override testosterone.

- As boys, the higher-testosterone men got into more trouble with parents, teachers, and the law. As adults, they were more likely to use hard drugs, get into fights, have lower-status jobs, have more sexual partners, have affairs, and get divorced. Higher-testosterone men from higher social classes did less of these things.

4. Understand why sociologists focus on social factors rather than on biological factors in human behavior.

- Social factors override biology.

👁 **Watch** the **Video** The Big
Picture: Gender in **mysoclab**

Unit 9.3   How Females Became a Minority Group

1. Explain why the term minority group applies to women.

- *Minority group* refers to people who are discriminated against on the basis of physical or cultural characteristics, regardless of their numbers.

2. Explain how females became a minority group.

- The origin is lost in history. The two main theories are based on human reproduction and hand-to-hand combat.

3. Summarize two theories of the origins of patriarchy.

- The first is that having babies limited women's activities. With men doing the hunting, trading, and warfare, they took over society. The second is that because men are stronger, they did the fighting and women became their reward.

4. Know the circular system of thought used to prove male "superiority."

- Men dominate society because they are superior, and they know they are superior because they dominate society.

Unit 9.4   Fighting Back: The Rise of Feminism

1. Explain what it means to say that a husband and wife used to be legally one person.

- Wives (and single women) could not vote, buy property in their own name, make legal contracts, or serve on juries.

2. Know what "using cultural supports to justify dominance" means.

- The social institutions—the law, religion politics, business, education, and the family—teach children their "proper" roles as boys and girls and what they should expect as adults.

3. Summarize the three waves of feminism.

- *First wave:* late 1800s and early 1900s: won women's right to vote. *Second wave:* 1960s and continuing:

primary concerns—working conditions and sexual harassment. *Third wave:* 1990s and continuing: primary concerns—conditions of women around the world, changed values at work, and sexuality.

Unit 9.5 **Global Inequality in the World of Work**

1. **Know what the "sex typing" of work means.**
   - Associating some activities with men and other activities with women.

2. **Summarize the basic findings from Murdock's survey of work and gender in 324 societies around the world.**
   - The work that one society considers "women's work" can be considered "men's work" in another society. The one exception is metal working.

3. **Explain why anatomy is not destiny when it comes to work.**
   - In one society, a certain type of work is assigned to women; in another society, that same work is assigned to men.

4. **State the basic principle about gender and the prestige of work.**
   - Greater prestige is given to male activities—regardless of what those activities are.

Unit 9.6 **Gender Inequality in the American Workplace**

1. **Summarize the gender pay gap.**
   - Around the world, men average more pay than women. In the United States full-time working women average 72 percent of what full-time working men earn.

2. **Explain reasons for the gender pay gap.**
   - There are three: Women are less likely to go into better-paying areas of work, gender discrimination, and the "child penalty."

3. **Explain what keeps the glass ceiling in place.**
   - There are four: Overt discrimination, the "child penalty," women being directed to "support" positions, and lack of effective mentors.

✳ Explore the Concept
The Occupations of Females and Males in
mysoclab

👁 Watch the Video
The Basics: Gender in
mysoclab

Unit 9.7 **Sexual Harassment**

1. **Define sexual harassment.**
   - Unwelcome sexual attention that can affect a person's job or school performance or create a hostile environment.

2. **Explain how the perception of social structure was essential to the development of the term sexual harassment.**
   - From seeing the problem in personal terms, a man here or there doing obnoxious things, to viewing the underlying problem as men using their positions of authority to pressure women to have sex.

3. **Explain how the term sexual harassment has changed the perception of behavior.**
   - People are now more apt to perceive a supervisor who makes sexual advances to a worker not as sexual attraction but as a misuse of authority.

Unit 9.8 **Gender Inequality in Everyday Life and Health Care**

1. **Explain how statements made during the training of soldiers and in sports illustrate the devaluation of femininity.**
   - Boys and men insult under performers by referring to them in feminine terms or calling them girls.

2. **Explain how gender inequality can be a life-and-death matter in the practice of medicine.**
   - Women are more likely to die in coronary bypass surgery because doctors wait until a woman's heart disease is more advanced than a man's before recommending surgery.

📖 Read the Document
"Health Care Reform—A Woman's Issue" by Catherine DeLorey in
mysoclab

Unit 9.9 **Violence against Women**

1. **Know what *suttee* and "honor killings" are and how they are examples of gendered violence.**
   - *Suttee* is burning a living widow with the body of her dead husband. "Honor killing" refers to relatives killing a woman who has brought them shame. Both are directed by men against women.

2. **Summarize the most common age of victims, frequency of acquaintance rape, and the reasons so few victims of date rape report the crime.**
   - The typical rape victim is 16 to 19 years old, and the average rapist is someone the victim knows. About 1.7 percent of female college students have been raped during the past six months. Reasons for not reporting the rape: uncertainty, feeling responsible, embarrassment, and fear.

3. **Know the gendered pattern in murder.**
   - Of all killers, 90 percent are men. Of all victims, one-fifth are women.

4. State why it is difficult to break gendered violence.
- Violence is associated with masculinity.

Unit 9.10 **The Changing Face of Politics**

1. Know why women could take political control of the United States.
- Eight million more women than men are of voting age, and more women than men vote in U.S. national elections.

2. State how extensively the U.S. Senate has been a political organization of men.
- Since 1789 almost 2,000 men have served in the U.S. Senate, but only 38 women have served, including the 17 current senators.

3. Summarize the gender change in U.S. politics.
- The growing prominence of women in politics is indicated by women being elected Speaker of the House, running for president, and being the vice-presidential nominee of a major political party.

UNIT 9.1 / / TESTING MYSELF
DID I LEARN IT? ANSWERS

1. a primary sex characteristics

2. b secondary sex characteristics

3. b secondary sex characteristics

UNIT 9.2 / / TESTING MYSELF
DID I LEARN IT? ANSWERS

1. d Social factors are the primary reasons people do what they do.

2. c Culture shapes our biological predispositions.

3. a In the matter of *nature* versus *nurture*, sociologists prefer the nurture explanation.

UNIT 9.3 / / TESTING MYSELF
DID I LEARN IT? ANSWERS

1. d There is not a single society where women-as-a-group have decision-making power over men (as-a-group).

2. a always favor men-as-a-group

3. c is done by sociologists because the term has nothing to do with numbers

4. a were social equals

4. b inherited

5. a learned

6. b gender

7. b gender

8. b gender

9. d varies around the world

4. a Men are born with a greater drive to dominate social life.

5. a disagree with Goldberg

6. a got into more fights than did men with low testosterone

7. d more likely to mistreat their wives

8. a more likely to cheat on their wives

9. c mistreat their wives

10. b Biology is important, but social factors override it.

5. a With a child at her breast or in her uterus, or one carried on her hip or on her back, women were not able to move as quickly as men or leave the base camp as long as men could.

6. d weapons, items of trade, and knowledge gained from contact with other groups

7. c the reward that enticed men to risk their lives in battle

8. a Men came to think of themselves as inherently superior—based on the evidence that they dominated society.

9. b designating certain activities as "not appropriate" for women

10. c a continuation of a millennia-old pattern whose origin is lost in history

1. **b** Women had to get written permission from their mothers to marry, and they had to show this to a judge, who then granted written authorization for the marriage.

2. **d** The social institutions—the law, religion, politics, business, education, and the family—teach children their "proper" roles as boys and girls, and what they should expect as adults.

3. **d** the view that biology is not destiny and that stratification by gender is wrong and should be resisted

1. **a** associating some work (such as cooking or taking care of cattle) with one sex or the other

2. **d** all societies associate some work with men and other work with women

3. **c** Work that one society considers "women's work" can be considered "men's work" in another society.

4. **b** making weapons, pursuing sea mammals, and hunting

1. **c** $700,000

2. **a** 72 percent

3. **d** Women don't work as hard as men.

4. **a** higher starting salaries than women

5. **a** 12

1. **d** unwelcome sexual attention that can affect a person's job or school performance or create a hostile environment

2. **d** Before this, women considered unwanted sexual comments, touches, looks, and pressure to have sex to be a personal matter.

4. **c** suffragists

5. **c** They were arrested and sent to prison.

6. **d** win the vote for women

7. **c** help mom with housework

8. **a** a temporary activity to fill the time between completing high school (and, for a few, completing college) and getting married

9. **c** women thinking of jobs as careers and challenging the greater privileges men had at work

10. **d** locating weaknesses in social institutions and developing strategies for exploiting them

5. **a** cooking, making clothing, carrying water, and grinding grain

6. **c** anatomy is not destiny

7. **d** do a lot of work that is usually considered "men's work" in the United States

8. **b** It is not the work that provides the prestige, but the sex with which the work is associated.

9. **c** delivering babies brought low prestige

10. **a** bribed midwives to sneak them into the bedroom where a woman was having a baby

6. **c** the mostly invisible barriers that prevent women from reaching the executive suite

7. **a** in marketing, sales, and production

8. **b** Women tend to be seen as being good at "support" but less capable than men of leadership, so they are steered to human resources and public relations.

9. **c** lack mentors—successful executives who take an interest in them and teach them the ropes

10. **d** have husbands who take over most of the household tasks

3. **a** With the prodding of feminists, women began to perceive unwanted sexual advances at work and school as part of a *structural* problem.

4. **b** Women, too, have become sexual harassers.

1. **a** a background assumption, so taken for granted that it is largely invisible

2. **b** symbolizes strength and success

3. **c** perceived in terms of weakness and lack of accomplishment

4. **c** are performing like girls

5. **c** a woman or girl

6. **d** a man."

7. **b** Doctors were *ten* times more likely to give men exercise stress tests and radioactive heart scans, which allowed them to have surgery before their heart disease became more advanced.

8. **b** unintended discrimination

9. **d** Not much—the problem continues.

10. **a** stereotyping of the sexes in ways that are below our level of awareness

1. **a** directed by one sex against the other

2. **c** a past practice in India of burning a living widow along with the body of her dead husband

3. **d** male relatives killing a woman who has brought disgrace to the family

4. **a** sex outside of marriage

5. **c** are safer now than they were ten and twenty years ago—the rape rate then was higher than today

6. **b** 16 to 19 years old

7. **c** more likely to be attacked by someone they know than by a stranger

8. **a** They felt sorry for the individual who had attacked them.

9. **d** 90

10. **c** break the connection between violence and masculinity

1. **c** part of how society's institutions work together

2. **d** Eight million more women than men are of voting age, and more women than men vote in U.S. national elections.

3. **a** 42

4. **a** 0

5. **a** 0

6. **c** More women are becoming corporate executives and lawyers.

CHAPTER 10
POLITICS AND THE ECONOMY

👁 **Watch** the **Video** in **mysoclab**

((•— **Listen** to the **Chapter Audio** in **mysoclab**

GETTING STARTED

I don't know if you ever read *1984*, a book about the future that George Orwell wrote in 1949. "Big Brother," as Orwell called the government that he saw coming, dictated almost every aspect of each person's life. Loving someone was forbidden, a betrayal of the supreme love and total allegiance that all citizens owed Big Brother.

Despite the danger, Winston and Julia fall in love and meet secretly. When informers turn them in, interrogators separate Julia and Winston and try to destroy their affection and restore their loyalty to Big Brother.

(*continued on next page*)

Washington D.C.

(continued from previous page)

Winston's tormentor is O'Brien, who straps Winston into a chair so tightly that he can't even move his head. O'Brien then sets a cage with two starving sewer rats on the table next to Winston. He picks up a hood connected to the door of the cage and places it over Winston's head. He explains that when he presses the lever, the door of the cage will slide up, and the rats will shoot out like bullets and bore straight into Winston's face. Winston's eyes, the only part of his body that he can move, dart back and forth, revealing his terror. O'Brien adds that the rats sometimes attack the eyes first, but sometimes they burrow through the cheeks and devour the tongue. When O'Brien places his hand on the lever, Winston realizes that the only way out is for someone to take his place. But who? Then he hears his own voice screaming, "Do it to Julia! . . . Tear her face off. Strip her to the bones. Not me! Julia! Not me!"

Orwell does not describe Julia's interrogation, but when Julia and Winston see each other later, they realize that each has betrayed the other. Their love is gone. Big Brother has won.

Although seldom this dramatic, politics is always about power and authority. Let's explore this topic that is so significant to your life. ◼

POLITICS: ESTABLISHING LEADERSHIP

UNIT 10.1

Power, Authority, and Violence

WHAT AM I SUPPOSED TO LEARN?

After you have read this unit, you should be able to

1 Explain the difference between authority and coercion.

2 Explain the three types of authority and give an example of each.

3 Explain how leadership is transferred in each of the three types of authority.

Whether you and I like it or not, some people have power over us. As Max Weber (1913/1947) pointed out, we perceive some of that power as legitimate, others as illegitimate. *Legitimate* power is called **authority**. This is power that we accept as right. In contrast, *illegitimate* power—called **coercion**—is power that we consider wrong.

Let's compare these two types of power.

Imagine that you are on your way to buy a hot new cell phone–iPad combination that just came on sale for $250. As you approach the store, a man shoves a gun in your face and demands your money. Frightened for your life, you hand over your $250. After filing a police report, you head back to college to take a sociology exam. Still shaken and running late, you step on the gas. As you hit 85, you see flashing blue and red lights in your rear-view mirror. Your explanation about the robbery doesn't faze the officer—or the judge who hears your case a few weeks later. She first lectures you on safety and then orders you to pay $50 in court costs plus $10 for every mile over 65. You pay the $250.

The mugger, the police officer, and the judge—all have power, and in each case you part with $250. What, then, is the difference? The difference is that the mugger has no authority. His power is *illegitimate*—he has no *right* to do what he did. In contrast, you acknowledge that the officer has the right to stop you and that the judge has the right to fine you. They have authority, or *legitimate* power.

Authority and Legitimate Violence

As sociologist Peter Berger remarked, in the end it makes little difference whether you willingly pay the fine that the judge levies against you or refuse to pay it. The court will get its money one way or another.

There may be innumerable steps before its application [of violence], in the way of warnings and reprimands. But if all the warnings are disregarded, even in so slight a matter as paying a traffic ticket, the last thing that will happen is that a couple of cops show up at the door with handcuffs and a Black Maria [police van]. Even the moderately

Authority power that people consider legitimate, as rightly exercised over them; also called legitimate power

Coercion power that people do not accept as rightly exercised over them; also called illegitimate power

Traditional Authority

Throughout history, the most common basis for authority has been tradition. **Traditional authority**, which is based on custom, is the hallmark of tribal groups and clans. In these societies, custom dictates basic relationships. For example, birth into a particular family makes an individual the chief, king, or queen. As far as members of that society are concerned, this is the right way to determine who shall rule because "We've always done it this way."

Although traditional authority declines with industrialization, it never dies out. Even though we live in a postindustrial society, not a little tribal group, parents continue to exercise authority over their children *because* parents always have had such authority. From generations past, we inherit the idea that parents should discipline their children, choose their doctors and schools, and teach them religion and morality.

How does traditional authority apply to your life? Take a look at *Making It Personal.*

> **State** a political entity that claims monopoly on the use of violence in some particular territory; commonly known as a country
>
> **traditional authority** authority based on custom

Adolph Hitler with two generals at the Nazi Party Day, Nuremberg, Germany, 1937. Of the three types of authority, which applies to Hitler?

courteous cop who hands out the initial traffic ticket is likely to wear a gun—just in case. (Berger 1963)

You know that if someone owes you money, you can't take the money by force. And you can't put that person in prison. But the government can. The *government*, also called the **state**, claims the exclusive right to use violence—and the right to punish everyone else who uses violence (Weber 1946, 1922/1978). And here's the ultimate proof of the state's monopoly on violence: You cannot kill someone because that person has done something you consider absolutely horrible—but the state can. As Berger (1963) summarized this matter, *"Violence is the ultimate foundation of any political order."*

But just why do we accept some power as legitimate? Max Weber (1922/1978) identified three sources of authority: traditional, rational–legal, and charismatic. Let's look at each.

MAKING IT PERSONAL

You and Traditional Authority

Traditional authority is the first of three types of authority that we are reviewing in this unit. It is the one that you learned from infancy. Your parents are the best example. Consider the extent of authority they exercised over you. When you were a little child, they decided what you should wear, when you should eat, what you should eat, when you should go to bed, what you should watch on television, even when you should take a bath.

Now that's a lot of authority!

You, of course, have shrugged off that authority at this point in your life. You make those particular decisions for yourself. But are there still things that you do because you feel an obligation to your parents? If you are age 20 or less, there likely are many such things. What if you are age 40 or more? Traditional authority may be but a pale reflection of its former self, but it occasionally appears. Suppose that you have appeared for your obligatory annual Thanksgiving dinner with Mom and Dad. While there, your mom or dad tells you to get something from the kitchen. You do so.

There isn't much traditional authority left in our society, but we still have little bits and pieces of it.

Rational–Legal Authority

The second type of authority, **rational–legal authority**, is based not on custom but on written rules. *Rational* means reasonable, and *legal* means part of law. *Rational–legal,* then, refers to matters that have

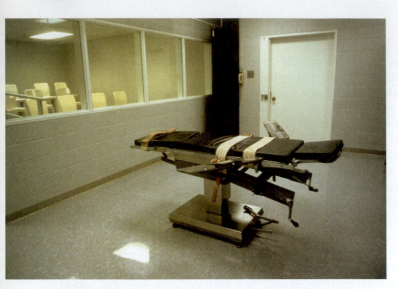

Those in political control of a society claim the right to fine, imprison, and take lives. Shown here is the lethal injection chamber in Jarrett, Virginia.

been agreed to by reasonable people and written into law (or regulations of some sort). The matters that are agreed to may be as broad as our constitution, which specifies the rights that you and I have, or as narrow as the contract you sign when you get a credit card. Because bureaucracies are based on written rules, rational–legal authority is sometimes called *bureaucratic authority.*

It is important to understand that *rational–legal authority comes from the position that someone holds, not from the person who holds that position.* The U.S. president's authority, for example, does not come from custom or the individual's personal characteristics. It comes from the legal power assigned to that office, as specified in the Constitution. In rational–legal authority, everyone—no matter how high the office—is subject to the organization's written rules. In governments based on traditional authority, the ruler's word may be law, but in those based on rational–legal authority, the ruler's word is subject to the law.

How does rational–legal authority apply to your life? Take a look at *Making It Personal.*

> **rational–legal authority** authority based on law or written rules and regulations; also called bureaucratic authority

MAKING IT PERSONAL
You and Rational–Legal Authority

I'm not sure how you feel about the police, but many of us are uncomfortable around them. The pistol, club, and handcuffs hanging from the cop's belt make us just a little apprehensive—and often a whole lot more. You can never be absolutely sure about what is going to happen.

And we have such feelings even if we haven't done anything wrong! Anyway, this is how it is with some of us. Maybe you are more comfortable around people who carry guns at their hips while looking for evil doers.

The police are just one example—and an extreme one, at that—of rational–legal authority. You are immersed in this type of authority. Do you remember the principal of your grade school? If you were ever "sent to the office" (as I was), that tall, scowling, overpowering individual can leave lasting memories of rational–legal authority.

But this type of authority goes way beyond police and principals. It includes all the teachers you have had, all government officials, even the person who delivers your mail.

Can you see how rational–legal authority not only surrounds you but also is an essential part of what holds society together? Do you see the tremendous power rational-legal authority exerts in your life?

Charismatic Authority

A few centuries back, in 1429, the English controlled large parts of France. When they prevented the coronation of a new French king, a farmer's daughter heard a voice telling her that God had a special assignment for her—that she should put on men's clothing, recruit an army, and go to war against the English. Inspired, Joan of Arc raised an army, conquered cities, and defeated the English. Later that year, her visions were fulfilled as she stood next to Charles VII while he was crowned king of France. (Bridgwater 1953)

Joan of Arc is an example of **charismatic authority**, the third type of authority that Weber identified. *Charisma* is a Greek word that means a gift freely and graciously given (Arndt and Gingrich 1957). People are drawn to a charismatic individual because they believe that God has touched that person or that nature has given that individual exceptional qualities (Lipset 1993). The armies did not follow Joan of Arc because it was the custom to do so, as in traditional authority. (Quite the contrary: Women were supposed to stay home at this time.) Nor did the soldiers risk their lives alongside her because she held a position defined by written rules, as in rational–legal authority. Instead, people followed her because they were attracted by her outstanding traits. To them, Joan of Arc was a messenger of God, fighting on the side of justice, and they accepted her leadership because of these appealing qualities.

How does charismatic authority apply to your life? Take a look at *Making It Personal.*

> **charismatic authority** authority based on an individual's outstanding traits, which attract followers

MAKING IT PERSONAL
You and Charismatic Authority

You are not likely to have had much experience with charismatic authority. But charismatic individuals certainly can be powerful. With their compelling message and ability to attract followers, they can pull society apart or put it together. But they have to appear at the right time, or else their words fall flat. A few years ago some of the followers of Hitler listened to Hitler's speeches. They shook their heads and said that they didn't understand why they felt the way they did back then. But they did feel that way—and you know some of the consequences.

Do you think that you could never come under the influence of a charismatic individual? Why would you be different from all those regular, educated Germans? The time was right. Or very wrong.

Remember that charismatic individuals can also be good. And it doesn't take the extreme of a Joan of Arc—just someone that you feel has those tremendously outstanding characteristics.

Charismatic individuals usually appear in politics and religion. Be on your guard.

THE THREAT POSED BY CHARISMATIC LEADERS

Kings and queens owe allegiance to tradition, and presidents must follow written laws. To what, however, do charismatic leaders owe allegiance? Their authority rests in their ability to attract followers, which is often based on their sense of a special mission or calling. Because they are not regulated by tradition or law, charismatic leaders pose a threat to the established political order. As Joan of Arc did, they can inspire followers to disregard—or even to overthrow—traditional and rational–legal authorities.

As you can imagine, this threat does not go unnoticed by traditional and rational–legal authorities, who are constantly trying to protect their power. As a result, they often oppose charismatic leaders. Their opposition can backfire, however. If people perceive a charismatic leader as an underdog persecuted by the powerful, it can arouse even more positive sentiment in favor of that person. Occasionally the Roman Catholic Church faces such a threat, as when a priest claims miraculous powers that appear to be accompanied by amazing healings. As people flock to this individual, they bypass parish priests and the formal ecclesiastical structure. This transfer of allegiance from the organization to an individual threatens the church hierarchy. Consequently, church officials may encourage the priest to withdraw from the public eye, perhaps to a monastery, to rethink matters. This defuses the threat, reasserts rational–legal authority, and maintains the stability of the organization.

FROM ANOTHER STUDENT ...

Your introductions to each chapter piqued my interest and gave me the desire to read on . The layout was user friendly because of the smooth flow of information. The concepts connected one to another like links in a chain. This made the concepts easier to process and understand. Thank you for designing a great textbook.

With gratitude,
Michael Zapata
Indiana University South Bend

One of the best examples of charismatic authority is Joan of Arc, shown here mounted and armored.

The Transfer of Authority

At some point, authority must be transferred from one person to another. For an organization to be stable, this transfer must be orderly. Under traditional authority, people know who is next in line. Under rational–legal authority, people might not know who the next leader will be, but they do know how that person will be selected. South Africa provides a remarkable example of how a rational–legal organization allows the orderly transfer of authority. For decades, this white-ruled country had been ripped apart by violence between whites and blacks, with horrible killings committed by each side. Yet when blacks were allowed to vote in 1994 and Nelson Mandela, the black hero of the opposition, was elected, power was transferred peacefully from whites to blacks. This government continues to function.

Charismatic authority is quite different. Authority is built around a single individual and has no rules of succession. The death or incapacitation of a charismatic leader can mean a bitter struggle to seize the top position. To avoid this, some charismatic leaders appoint a successor. This does not guarantee orderly succession, of course, for the followers may not have the same confidence in the designated heir as did the charismatic leader. A second strategy is for the charismatic leader to build an organization. As the organization develops rules or regulations, it transforms itself into a rational–legal organization. Weber used the term **routinization of charisma** to refer to the transition of authority from a charismatic leader to either traditional or rational–legal authority.

routinization of charisma the transfer of authority from a charismatic figure to either a traditional or a rational–legal form of authority

UNIT 10.1 // TESTING MYSELF
DID I LEARN IT? ANSWERS ARE AT THE END OF THE CHAPTER

1. Ellie Mae was shopping when a woman shoved her against the wall and took her purse. That woman had this type of power over Ellie Mae
   a. charismatic authority
   b. rational-legal authority
   c. legitimate power, called authority
   d. illegitimate power, called coercion

2. Ellie Mae chased the woman who had stolen her purse. When she caught up with her, she beat the woman. A police officer saw this and arrested both the women. The judge sentenced the woman who had stolen the purse to jail and gave Ellie Mae probation. The authority of the police officer and the judge is
   a. charismatic authority
   b. traditional authority
   c. rational-legal authority
   d. illegitimate power, called coercion

3. When the judge gave Ellie Mae probation, he said, "I understand your anger, but you can't take the law in your own hands." The judge was saying that the state
   a. is never wrong
   b. claims the exclusive right to use violence——and the right to punish everyone else who uses violence
   c. will stand up against purse snatchers
   d. makes the laws

4. You might think that the ultimate foundation of a government is the consent of the governed. Sociologists, however, say that this is its foundation
   a. violence
   b. information
   c. deceit
   d. an orientation toward future possibilities

5. Howard, a single parent, decided that his son's school was inferior, so he decided to home school his son. Howard's authority over his son, which can be traced back to thousands of years of custom, is an example of
   a. charismatic authority
   b. traditional authority
   c. rational-legal authority
   d. illegitimate power, called coercion

6. At work, Howard is a lower-level manager. He gives orders to a dozen people, who report to him. He has the authority to fire those whose work he doesn't like. At the same time, Howard must turn in regular reports to a manager above him. Howard's authority is an example of
   a. charismatic authority
   b. traditional authority
   c. rational-legal authority
   d. illegitimate power, called coercion

7. Howard became fascinated by a spell-binding speaker who talked about the end of civilization as we know it and the need to prepare now for the violence that is on its way. Howard is convinced that God has appointed this woman to prepare a select group of people to survive. Howard quit his job and joined this politico-religious cult. The power that the leader of this group has over Howard is an example of
   a. charismatic authority
   b. traditional authority
   c. rational-legal authority
   d. illegitimate power, called coercion

8. The leader of the cult that Howard joined had a heart attack. As she was dying, the followers quarrelled about who would take over. After her death, they broke into two rival groups, with each taking about half the members. Each group claims to represent the true message of the founder. This is an example of
   a. the problem of the transfer of authority in charismatic groups
   b. trying to discover truth in a poly-diverse society
   c. charismatic authority changing into traditional authority
   d. the acid test of charisma

9. For an organization to be stable, its transfer of leadership must be orderly. Under traditional authority, people know who is next in line. Under rational–legal authority, people might not know who the next leader will be, but they do know
   a. that the present leader will appoint someone
   b. that someone with appealing characteristics will take over
   c. that checks and balances will make sure that the next leader is competent
   d. how that person will be selected

10. Affairs in Howard's politico-religious cult turned out all right after all. Among the leader's personal papers was a declaration that Nancy should be the next leader. Although the two rival factions thought that Nancy lacked charisma, they agreed that they should honor the wishes of the charismatic founder. They joined forces behind Nancy. To prevent quarrels, Nancy immediately wrote up a set of rules and had everyone sign them. Weber used this term to refer to what happened
    a. charismatic succession
    b. the failure of charisma
    c. the routinization of charisma
    d. politico-religious group leadership transition

UNIT 10.2

Types of Government

You are familiar with your country's government, and you know that yours is just one of several types that exist around the world. Let's compare the main types of government: monarchies, democracies, dictatorships, and oligarchies. As we do so, let's also look at how the state arose and why an idea that you take for granted—citizenship—was revolutionary.

WHAT AM I SUPPOSED TO LEARN?

After you have read this unit, you should be able to

1 Explain how political power expanded.

2 Explain the differences between monarchies, democracies, dictatorships, and oligarchies.

3 Explain why citizenship is a revolutionary idea.

Monarchies: The Rise of the State

Early societies were small. Instead of having an extensive political system, they operated more like an extended family. As surpluses developed, societies grew larger. Cities then evolved—perhaps as early as 3500 B.C. (Fischer 1976). This was followed by **city-states**, where power radiated outward from a city like a spider's web. The ruler of each city controlled the immediate surrounding area, but the land between cities remained in dispute. Each city-state had its own **monarchy**, a king or queen whose right to rule was passed on to the monarch's children. If you drive through Spain, France, or Germany, you can still see evidence of former city-states. In the countryside, you will see only scattered villages. Farther on, your eye will be drawn to the outline of a castle on a faraway hill. As you get closer, you will see that the castle is surrounded by a city. Several miles farther, you will see another city, also dominated by a castle. Each city, with its castle, was once a center of power.

City-states often quarreled, and wars were common. The victors extended their rule, and eventually a single city-state was able to wield power over an entire region. As the size of these regions grew, the people slowly began to identify with the larger region. That is, they began to see distant inhabitants as "we" instead of "they." What we call the *state*—the political entity that claims a monopoly on the use of violence within a territory—came into being.

Saddam Hussein celebrating his birthday in Baghdad, Iraq, in 1999. Of the four types of leaders discussed here, what type was Hussein?

Democracies: Citizenship as a Revolutionary Idea

The United States had no city-states. Each colony, however, was small and independent like a city-state. After the American Revolution, the colonies united. With the greater strength and resources that came from political unity, they conquered almost all of North America, bringing it under the power of a central government.

The government formed in this new country was called a **democracy**. (Derived from two Greek words—*demos* [common people] and *kratos* [power]—democracy literally means "power to the people.") Because of the bitter antagonisms

city-state an independent city whose power radiates outward, bringing the adjacent area under its rule

monarchy a form of government headed by a king or queen

democracy a government whose authority comes from the people; the term, based on two Greek words, translates literally as "power to the people"

associated with the **revolution** against the British king, the founders of the new country distrusted monarchies. They wanted to put political decisions into the hands of the people.

This was not the first democracy the world had seen. Such a system had been tried before, but only with smaller groups. Athens, a city-state of Greece, practiced democracy 2,500 years ago, with each free male above a certain age having the right to be heard and to vote. Members of some Native American tribes, such as the Iroquois, also elected their chiefs, and in some, women were able to vote and to hold the office of chief. (The Incas and Aztecs of Mexico and Central America had monarchies.)

Because they were small, tribes and cities were able to practice **direct democracy**. That is, they were small enough for the eligible voters to meet together, express their opinions, and then vote publicly—much like a town hall meeting today. As populous and spread out as the United States was, however, direct democracy was impossible, and the founders invented **representative democracy**. Certain citizens (at first only white men who owned land) voted for other white men to represent them in Washington. Later, the vote was extended to men who didn't own property, then to African American men, and, finally, to women.

Unless you are an immigrant, you probably take the concept of citizenship for granted. But this idea didn't always exist. It had to be envisioned or invented. There is nothing natural about citizenship; it is simply one way in which people define themselves. Throughout most of human history, people were thought to *belong* to a clan, to a tribe, or even to a ruler. The idea of **citizenship**—that by virtue of birth and residence people have basic rights—is quite new to the human scene.

The concept of representative democracy based on citizenship—perhaps the greatest gift the United States has given to the world—was revolutionary. Power was to be vested in the people themselves, and government was to flow from the people. That this concept was revolutionary is generally forgotten. It meant *the reversal of traditional ideas. It made the government responsive to the people's will, rather than the people being responsive to the government's will.* To keep the government responsive to the needs of its citizens, people were expected to express dissent. In a widely quoted statement, Thomas Jefferson observed:

A little rebellion now and then is a good thing . . . . It is a medicine necessary for the sound health of government . . . . God forbid that we should ever be twenty years without such a rebellion . . . . The tree of liberty must be refreshed from time to time with the blood of patriots and tyrants. (In Hellinger and Judd 1991)

Let's consider Jefferson's statement in the following *Making It Personal.*

MAKING IT PERSONAL
On Rebellion

What a powerful statement Thomas Jefferson made!

Our society has changed so much since Jefferson said these words that today he might be arrested for saying them. If you think I'm exaggerating, read Jefferson's statement aloud. Now imagine yourself before a large crowd of people shouting these same words.

Get what I mean? Don't you think that Homeland Security would be interested in anyone who did this? These words certainly come close to inciting rebellion against the government. And Homeland Security is always a bit nervous, seeing enemies around every corner.

How could our society have changed so greatly that what a major founder of the country said could be the basis for his arrest today? The answer goes far beyond this text, but it does give you something quite significant to think about. How much democracy—"power to the people"—remains?

The idea of **universal citizenship**—*everyone* having the same basic rights because they were born in a country (or immigrated and became a naturalized citizen)—flowered slowly. And it came into practice only through fierce struggle. When the United States was founded, this idea was still in its infancy. Today, it seems inconceivable to Americans that sex or race–ethnicity should be the basis for denying anyone the right to vote, hold office, make a contract, testify in court, or own property. For earlier generations of property-owning white American men, however, it seemed just as inconceivable that women, racial–ethnic minorities, and the poor should be *allowed* such rights.

Dictatorships and Oligarchies: The Seizure of Power

If an individual seizes power, the government is known as a **dictatorship**. If a small group takes control,

---

revolution armed resistance designed to overthrow and replace a government

direct democracy a form of democracy in which the eligible voters meet together to discuss issues and make their decisions

representative democracy a form of democracy in which voters elect representatives to meet together to discuss issues and make decisions on their behalf

citizenship the concept that birth (and residence or naturalization) in a country imparts basic rights

universal citizenship everyone having the same basic rights by virtue of being born in a country (or by immigrating and becoming naturalized citizen)

dictatorship a form of government in which an individual has seized power

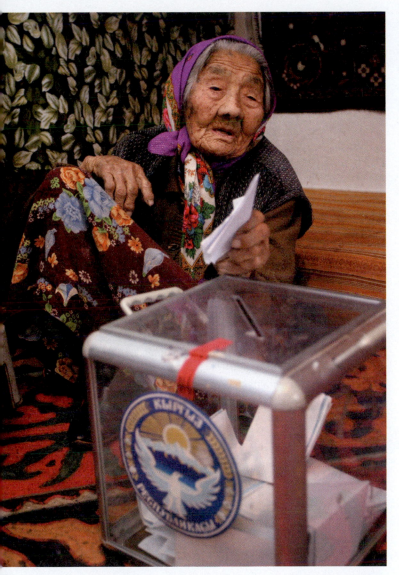

Patriotism is unleashed when dictators are deposed. This photo of boys painted in their country's colors was taken in Cairo, Egypt, in 2011 after their long-ruling dictator was overthrown.

Citizenship in a democracy is appealing to people around the world. This elderly woman is voting in Kyrgyzstan, a country previously ruled by the Soviets.

the government is called an **oligarchy**. The occasional coups in Central and South America and Africa, in which military leaders seize control of a country, are often oligarchies. Although one individual may be named president, often it is military officers, working behind the scenes, who make the decisions. If their designated president becomes uncooperative, they remove that person from office and appoint another.

Some monarchies, dictatorships, and oligarchies are ruthless as they exercise control over their citizens, while others are gentle. **Totalitarianism** is almost

> **oligarchy** a form of government in which a small group of individuals holds power; the rule of the many by the few
>
> **totalitarianism** a form of government that exerts almost total control over people

total control of a people by the government. In Nazi Germany, Hitler organized a ruthless secret police force, the Gestapo, which searched for any sign of dissent. Spies even watched how moviegoers reacted to newsreels, reporting those who did not respond "appropriately" (Hippler 1987). Saddam Hussein acted just as ruthlessly toward Iraqis. The lucky ones who opposed Hussein were shot; the unlucky ones had their eyes gouged out, were bled to death, or were buried alive (Amnesty International 2005). The punishment for telling a joke about Hussein was to have your tongue cut out.

People around the world find great appeal in the freedom that comes with citizenship and representative democracy. Those who have no say in their government's decisions, or who face prison or even death for expressing dissent, find in these ideas the hope for a brighter future. With today's electronic communications, people no longer remain ignorant of whether they are more or less politically privileged than others. This knowledge produces pressure for governments to allow greater citizen participation—and for governments to respond to their citizens' concerns. Even the communist rulers of China are sensitive to online communications and are known to change course if they sense strong sentiment in some direction (Areddy 2012). As electronic communications develop further, this pressure will increase.

Watch the **Video**
The Basics: Politics and Government in **mysoclab**

UNIT 10.2 // TESTING MYSELF
DID I LEARN IT? ANSWERS ARE AT THE END OF THE CHAPTER

1. Early societies were small. Instead of having an extensive political system, they operated more like an extended family. The following factor allowed societies to grow and cities to develop, bringing about larger political systems
   a. armies
   b. the denial of the vote to women
   c. surpluses
   d. the demand for citizenship

2. Minola was taking a sociology course. She was interested in radical political movements and became excited about something she read in her text. She called her boyfriend and said, "Guess what the word democracy means!" Her question was met with silence. She said, "It comes from two Greek words—*demos*, common people, and *kratos*, power. So democracy actually means
   a. We have arrived!
   b. Power is on its way!
   c. Power to the people!
   d. Power taken away from the people

3. Minola said to her boyfriend, "If you want to understand politics (and you'd better if you are going to be with me), you've got to get this background. Democracy isn't new. Twenty-five hundred years ago, this city-state practiced democracy
   a. Rome
   b. Athens
   c. Constantinople
   d. New York City

4. Minola added, "You know those town hall meetings that some of our politicians are using to drum up support? Well, past groups that practiced democracy were small enough for the eligible voters to meet together, express their opinions, and then vote publicly. This is called
   a. direct democracy
   b. indirect democracy
   c. misdirected democracy
   d. representative democracy

5. "But today," Minola added, pausing to make sure her boyfriend was following along, "direct democracy is impossible because the United States is large and spread out. So the founders of this country, who were disgusted with monarchies, invented
   a. indirect monarchy
   b. direct democracy
   c. indirect democracy
   d. representative democracy

6. Minola added, "And you know what else I learned? When the United States was founded, only white male landowners had the right to vote. And they could vote only for men to represent them. Later, men who didn't own property were able to vote. Then the vote was given to African American men. Well, guess who then finally got the right to vote! It was
   a. all men over the age of 21
   b. all men over the age of 18
   c. women
   d. immigrants

7. "Sometimes you think you know it all, Minola," said her boyfriend. "I've been reading the text, too. Tell me why citizenship was a revolutionary idea—and why it still is in some countries." "Of course, I know that," Minola replied. "It's because the idea of citizenship
   a. made the kings and queens of that time rethink their monarchical duties (Minola loved throwing that word around)
   b. reversed traditional ideas. Instead of the people being responsive to the government's will, it made the government responsive to the people's will
   c. allowed immigrants to become citizens, which extended voting rights far beyond the original intention
   d. was a new idea

8. "Okay, you got that one," said Minola's boyfriend. "But do you know the term for a group that seizes control of a government?" (He shouldn't have even bothered asking this of someone who knows the word monarchical.) "Of course," Minola replied. "It is an
   a. oligarchy
   b. monarchy
   c. dictatorship
   d. democracy

9. Taking the offensive again, Minola said, "How about Hitler's form of government? If you don't use the word dictatorship, which it was, what word would you use?" Her boyfriend quickly replied, "It took total control over the citizens, so it was
   a. a plutocracy
   b. an oligarchy
   c. a monarchy
   d. totalitarianism

10. "That's right" said Minola's boyfriend. "Just one more. All over the world, governments that don't have democracy are experiencing pressure to change. This is because people are attracted to the idea of freedom that democracy brings. And with today's electronic communications, people
   a. are likely to follow the affairs of celebrities rather than think about political matters
   b. are lulled into a stupor by the media's emphasis on sports
   c. know whether they are more or less politically privileged than others
   d. become confused by the many political talk shows

UNIT
The U.S. Political System
10.3

Now you have a global background about the types of government and why the idea of citizenship is so important for today's politics. Let's turn to the U.S. political system. We shall consider the two major political parties, try to understand today's voting patterns, and look at the role of lobbyists and PACs.

Political Parties and Elections

After the founding of the United States, numerous political parties emerged. By the time of the Civil War, however, just two parties dominated U.S. politics: the Democrats, who in the public mind are associated with the working class, and the Republicans, who are associated with wealthier people (Burnham 1983). In pre-elections, called *primaries,* the voters decide who

WHAT AM I SUPPOSED TO LEARN?

After you have read this unit, you should be able to

1 Explain why Democrats and Republicans are centrist and why third parties do poorly.

2 Explain the major patterns in U.S. voting.

3 Summarize and criticize the role of lobbyists in U.S. politics.

will represent their party. The candidates chosen by each party then campaign, trying to appeal to the most voters. The social map below shows how Americans align themselves with political parties.

SLICES FROM THE CENTER

Regardless of their differences and their public quarrels, the Democrats and Republicans represent *different slices from the*

FIGURE 10.1 **Which Political Party Dominates**

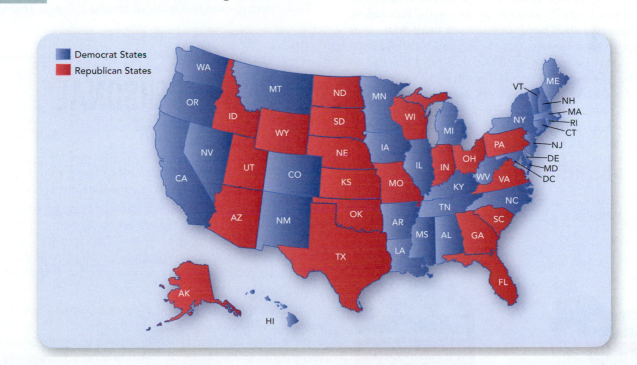

Note: Domination by a political party does not refer to votes for president or Congress. This social map is based on the composition of each states' upper and lower houses. When different parties dominate a state's houses, the total number of legislators was used. In Nebraska, where no parties are designated, the percentage vote for president was the determining factor.

Source: By the author. Based on Statistical Abstract of the United States 2011:Table 411.

center. Although each party may ridicule the opposing party and promote different legislation—and they do fight hard battles—they both support the same fundamentals of U.S. political philosophy, such as free public education, a strong military, and freedom of religion, speech, and assembly. And they both promote capitalism—especially profits and the private ownership of property.

This makes it difficult to distinguish a conservative Democrat from a liberal Republican. The extremes are easy to discern, however. Deeply committed Democrats support legislation that transfers income from those who are richer to those who are poorer or that controls wages, working conditions, and competition. Deeply committed Republicans, in contrast, oppose such legislation, preferring a freer market.

Those who are elected to Congress may cross party lines. That is, some Democrats vote for legislation proposed by Republicans, and vice versa. This happens because officeholders support their party's philosophy, but not necessarily its specific proposals. When it comes to a particular bill, such as raising the minimum wage, some conservative Democrats may view the measure as unfair to small employers and vote with the Republicans against the bill. At the same time, liberal Republicans—feeling that the proposal is just, or sensing a dominant sentiment in voters back home—may side with its Democratic backers.

THIRD PARTIES

Third parties sometimes play a role in U.S. politics, but to gain power, they must also support these centrist themes. Any party that advocates radical change is doomed to a short life. Because most Americans consider votes for them as wasted, third parties do not do well at the polls. Two exceptions are the Bull Moose party, whose candidate, Theodore Roosevelt, won more votes in 1912 than William Howard Taft, the Republican presidential candidate, and the United We Stand (Reform) party, founded by billionaire Ross Perot, which won 19 percent of the vote in 1992. Amidst internal bickering, the Reform Party declined rapidly and fell off the political map (Bridgwater 1953; *Statistical Abstract* 1995:Table 437; 2012:Table 403).

Voting Patterns

Like most behaviors we have looked at in this book, we can trace major voting patterns to age, race–ethnicity, education, income,

These two parties dominate U.S. politics. The success rate of other parties falls between zero and zero.

The power of lobbyists, which represent specific interests, lies in their ability to raise money and votes for politicians. Do you think we should ban lobbyists? Limit them? Expand their power?

and sex. Look at Table 10.1 on next page. You can see how the percentage of people who vote increases with age and how much more likely non-Hispanic whites are to vote than any other group. The exception was 2008, when Barack Obama ran for president.

You can also see how voting increases with each level of education. Education is so significant that college graduates are twice as likely to vote as are high school dropouts. Notice, too, how much more likely the employed are to vote. And look at how powerful income is, how at each higher income level people are more likely to vote. Finally, note that women are more likely than men to vote.

How about *you* and voting? Read *Making It Personal* below.

MAKING IT PERSONAL
You and Voting

Looking at voting patterns can make you a little drowsy—sort of like the bedtime reading you want if you are having trouble falling asleep. But these dry facts do represent people's behavior, which is what we are looking at in this book. And you fit into this picture. Where? On Table 10.1, you can find your social locations—especially your age, race–ethnicity, sex, and education. Can you see how your social locations are background factors in your own voting?

This really isn't just dry stuff—once you see how these larger social forces are influencing your life to such an extent that they even lay down channels for how you vote. Of course, you might be the maverick, the one who goes against the flow. After all, 1 percent of African Americans voted for the candidate who opposed Barack Obama. So let's go one step farther. If you are an exception to your social locations, what are the social forces driving this behavior?

SOCIAL INTEGRATION

How can we explain these voting patterns? It is useful to look at the extremes. You can see from Table 10.1 that the people who are most likely to vote are older, more educated, affluent, and employed. Those who are least likely to vote are younger, less educated, poorer, and unemployed. From these extremes, we can draw this principle: The more that people feel they have a stake in the political system, the more likely they are to vote. They have more to protect, and they feel that voting can make a difference. In effect, people who have been rewarded more by the political and economic system

TABLE 10.1 **Who Votes for President?**

	1988	1992	1996	2000	2004	2008	2012
Overall							
Americans Who Voted	57%	61%	54%	55%	58%	58%	57%
Age							
18–20	33%	39%	31%	28%	41%	41%	33%
21–24	46%	46%	33%	35%	43%	47%	47%
25–34	48%	53%	43%	44%	47%	49%	46%
35–44	61%	64%	55%	55%	57%	55%	53%
45–64	68%	70%	64%	64%	67%	65%	63%
65 and older	69%	70%	67%	68%	69%	68%	69%
Sex							
Male	56%	60%	53%	53%	56%	56%	54%
Female	58%	62%	56%	56%	60%	60%	59%
Race–Ethnicity							
Whites	64%	70%	56%	56%	60%	60%	58%
African Americans	55%	59%	51%	54%	56%	61%	62%
Asian Americans	NA	54%	NA	25%	30%	32%	31%
Latinos	48%	52%	27%	28%	28%	32%	32%
Education							
High school dropouts	41%	41%	34%	34%	35%	34%	32%
High school graduates	55%	58%	49%	49%	52%	51%	49%
College dropouts	65%	69%	61%	60%	66%	65%	62%
College graduates	78%	81%	73%	72%	74%	73%	72%
Marital Status							
Married	NA	NA	66%	67%	71%	70%	69%
Divorced	NA	NA	50%	53%	58%	59%	59%
Labor Force							
Employed	58%	64%	55%	56%	60%	60%	59%
Unemployed	39%	46%	37%	35%	46%	49%	46%
Income[1]							
Under $20,000	NA	NA	NA	NA	48%	52%	48%
$20,000 to $30,000	NA	NA	NA	NA	58%	56%	56%
$30,000 to $40,000	NA	NA	NA	NA	62%	62%	58%
$40,000 to $50,000	NA	NA	NA	NA	69%	65%	63%
$50,000 to $75,000	NA	NA	NA	NA	72%	71%	68%
$75,000 to $100,000	NA	NA	NA	NA	78%	76%	74%
Over $100,000	NA	NA	NA	NA	81%	92%	79%

[1] *The primary source used different income categories for 2004, making the data from earlier presidential election years incompatible.*

Sources: By the author. Based on Casper and Bass 1998; Jamieson et al. 2002; Holder 2006; *Current Population Survey*: Voting and Registration Supplement, 2012; *Statistical Abstract of the United States* 1991: Table 450; 1997: Table 462; 2013: Table 407.

feel more socially integrated. They vote because they perceive that elections make a difference in their lives, including the type of society in which they and their children live.

ALIENATION

In contrast, those who gain less from the system—in terms of education, income, and jobs—are more likely to feel alienated from politics. Perceiving themselves as outsiders, many feel hostile toward the government. Some feel betrayed, believing that politicians have sold out to special-interest groups. They ask, "How can you tell if politicians are lying?" and reply cynically, "When you see their lips moving."

APATHY

But we must go beyond this. From Table 10.1, you can see that many highly educated people with good incomes also stay away from the polls. They do not vote because of **voter apathy**, or indifference. Seeing little difference between the two major political parties, their view is that "next year will bring more of the same, regardless of who is in office." A common attitude behind voter apathy is "What difference will my one vote make when there are millions of voters?" Only about *half* of the nation's eligible voters cast ballots in presidential and congressional elections (*Statistical Abstract* 2012:Table 398).

The low voter turnout of Asian American is perplexing. As we reviewed in Chapter 8, Asian Americans have the highest education and income of all racial–ethnic groups. We would expect, then, that their voting rate would be similarly high. I do not think that apathy is the answer. There likely is a subcultural explanation of some sort.

THE GENDER AND RACIAL–ETHNIC GAPS IN VOTING

Historically, men and women voted the same way, but now we have a *political gender gap*. That is, men and women are somewhat more likely to vote for different presidential candidates. As you can see from Table 10.2 on the next page, men are more likely to favor the Republican candidate, and women are more likely to vote for the Democratic candidate. This table also illustrates the much larger racial–ethnic gap in politics. Note how few African Americans vote for a Republican presidential candidate.

As you saw in Table 10.1, voting patterns reflect life experiences, especially people's economic conditions. On average, women earn less than men, and African Americans earn less than whites. As a result, at this point in history, women and African Americans tend to look more favorably on government programs that redistribute income, and so they are more likely to vote for Democrats. As you

voter apathy indifference and inaction on the part of individuals or groups with respect to the political process

can see in Table 10.2 on the next page, Asian American voters, with their higher average incomes, are an exception to this pattern. Attempted explanations are far from satisfactory (Wong et al. 2011), but the reason could be a lesser emphasis on individualism in the Asian American subculture.

Lobbyists and Special-Interest Groups

Suppose that you are president of the United States, and you want to make milk more affordable for the poor. As you check into the matter, you find that part of the reason that prices are high is because the government is paying farmers billions of dollars in price supports. You propose to eliminate these subsidies.

Immediately, large numbers of people leap into action. They contact their senators and representatives and hold news conferences. Your office is flooded with calls, faxes, and e-mail.

Reuters and the Associated Press distribute pictures of farm families—their Holsteins grazing contentedly in the background—and inform readers that your harsh proposal will destroy these hard-working, healthy, happy, good Americans who are struggling to make a living. President or not, you have little chance of getting your legislation passed.

What happened? The dairy industry went to work to protect its special interests. A **special-interest group** consists of people who think alike on a particular issue and who can be mobilized for political action. The dairy industry is just one of thousands of such groups that employ **lobbyists**, people who are paid to influence legislation on behalf of their clients. Special-interest groups and lobbyists have become a major force in U.S. politics. Members of Congress who want to be reelected must pay attention to them, for they represent blocs of voters who share a vital interest in the outcome of specific bills. Well financed and able to contribute huge sums, lobbyists can deliver votes to you—or to your opponent.

THE REVOLVING DOOR

Some members of Congress who lose an election find a pot of gold waiting for them. So do people who have served in the White House as assistants to the president. Their contacts swing open the doors of the powerful, and they are sought after as lobbyists (Vidal et al. 2010). Some go to work for the same companies they regulated when they worked for the president (Delaney 2010).

special-interest group a group of people who support a particular issue and who can be mobilized for political action

lobbyists people who influence legislation on behalf of their clients

TABLE 10.2 How the Two-Party Presidential Vote Is Split

	1988	1992	1996	2000	2004	2008	2012[1]
Women							
Democrat	50%	61%	65%	56%	53%	57%	55%
Republican	50%	39%	35%	44%	47%	43%	45%
Men							
Democrat	44%	55%	51%	47%	46%	52%	45%
Republican	56%	45%	49%	53%	54%	48%	52%
African Americans							
Democrat	92%	94%	99%	92%	90%	99%	93%
Republican	8%	6%	1%	8%	10%	1%	6%
Whites							
Democrat	41%	53%	54%	46%	42%	44%	39%
Republican	59%	47%	46%	54%	58%	56%	59%
Latinos							
Democrat	NA	NA	NA	61%	58%	66%	71%
Republican	NA	NA	NA	39%	42%	34%	27%
Asian Americans							
Democrat	NA	NA	NA	62%	77%	62%	TK
Republican	NA	NA	NA	38%	23%	38%	TK

[1]The totals can be less than 100 percent because of votes for other candidates.

Sources: By the author. Based on Gallup Poll 2008; *Statistical Abstract of the United States* 1999:Table 464; 2002:Table 372; 2012:Table 404. "PEW Exit Poll." Washington, D.C.: PEW Research Center. November 2012.

To try to reign in some of this influence peddling, Congress made it illegal for former senators to lobby for two years after they leave office. Yet these individuals do lobby. How do you suppose they get around this law? It's all in the name. They hire themselves out to lobbying firms as *strategic advisors*. They then lobby—excuse me—"strategically advise" their former colleagues ("It's So Much Nicer …" 2008).

THE MONEY

With information like this getting out, the media put pressure on Congress. Congress then passed a law to limit the amount of money that any individual or organization can donate to a candidate. All contributions over $500 must be made public. The politicians didn't want their bankroll cut, of course, so they immediately looked for ways to get around the law they had just passed. It didn't take long to find the loophole—which they might have built in purposely. "Handlers" solicit donations from hundreds or even thousands of donors—each contribution within the legal limit—and turn the large amount over to the candidate. Special-interest groups use the same technique. They form **political action committees (PACs)** to solicit contributions from many, and then use that large amount to influence legislation.

Political action committees are powerful, for they bankroll lobbyists and legislators. To influence the passage of laws, about 4,500 PACs shell out a half billion dollars to politicians (*Statistical Abstract* 2012:Tables 422, 423). These committees give money to candidates to help get them elected, and after their election give "honoraria" (gifts of money) to senators who agree to say a few words at a breakfast. A few PACs represent broad social interests such as environmental protection. Most, however, represent the financial interests of specific groups, such as the banking, dairy, defense, and oil industries.

CRITICISM OF LOBBYISTS AND PACs

The major criticism leveled against lobbyists and PACs is that their money, in effect, buys votes. Rather than representing the people who elected them, legislators support the special interests of groups that have the ability to help them stay in power. The PACs that have the most clout in terms of money and votes gain the ear

political action committee (PAC) an organization formed by one or more special-interest groups to solicit and spend funds for the purpose of influencing legislation

THE INTRICATE MECHANICS OF GOVERNMENT

PUBLIC ENTRANCE

LOBBYIST ENTRANCE

©'06 WILEY INK, INC.
DIST. BY UNIVERSAL PRESS SYNDICATE 9-22 WILEYINK@EARTHLINK.NET
GOCOMICS.COM

of Congress. To politicians, the sound of money talking apparently sounds like the voice of the people.

Even if the United States were to outlaw PACs, special-interest groups would not disappear from U.S. politics. Lobbyists walked the corridors of the Senate long before PACs, and since the time of Alexander Graham Bell they have carried the unlisted numbers of members of Congress. For good or for ill, lobbyists play an essential role in the U.S. political system.

Watch the **Video**
The Big Picture: Politics and Government in **mysoclab**

UNIT 10.3 // TESTING MYSELF
DID I LEARN IT? ANSWERS ARE AT THE END OF THE CHAPTER

1. This term refers to pre-elections in which voters decide who will represent their party
   a. pre-elections   **b.** samples
   c. primaries   **d.** the first vote

2. When Nicole read this chapter, she was surprised that the author made the statement that despite their public quarrels, the Democrats and Republicans represent different slices from the center. Although this upset some of her ideas, she knew this meant that these two parties
   a. have grown closer over time
   b. have stopped much of their quarreling so they can cooperate on getting the economy moving

   c. make backroom deals that they don't want the public to know about
   d. support the same fundamentals of U.S. political philosophy, such as capitalism, free public education, a strong military, and freedom of religion, speech, and assembly

3. One reason that third parties do poorly in U.S. politics is they
   a. lack the "name recognition" that the two major political parties have
   b. violate commonly agreed-on (centrist) political philosophy
   c. seldom have good speakers
   d. get bad publicity

4. In the political gender gap, women are more likely than men to vote for a
   a. Democrat
   b. Republican
   c. third party
   d. Universalist

5. This group is likely to look more favorably on government programs that redistribute income
   a. Americans whose ancestry is in Europe
   b. environmentalists
   c. Republicans
   d. African Americans

6. This is the exception to high rates of voting by people with higher incomes and education
   a. white Americans
   b. Latinos
   c. Asian Americans
   d. African Americans

7. People who are paid to influence legislation on behalf of their clients are called
   a. vote getters
   b. lobbyists
   c. anti-democrats
   d. fund raisers

8. To bypass campaign limitation laws, special-interest groups collect money from many individuals, all within the legal limit. "Handlers" then give these contributions to favored candidates. The groups that solicit and distribute these donations are
   a. political action committees (PACs)
   b. money solicitation committees (MSCs)
   c. campaign finance committees (CFCs)
   d. fund management committees (FMCs)

9. The major criticism leveled against lobbyists and PACs is that
   a. they favor conservative candidates
   b. they favor liberal candidates
   c. their influence is one-sided
   d. their money, in effect, buys votes

UNIT 10.4

Who Rules the United States?

You might be wondering about this: With lobbyists and PACs wielding such influence, just whom do U.S. senators and representatives really represent? This question has led to a lively debate among sociologists. In this short unit, we'll look at the two main arguments.

The Functionalist Perspective: Pluralism

Functionalists view the state as having arisen out of the basic needs of the social group. To protect themselves from oppressors, people formed a government and gave it the monopoly on violence. The risk is that the state can turn that force against its own citizens. To return to the example used at the beginning of this chapter, states have a tendency to become muggers. Thus, people must find a balance between having no government—which would lead to **anarchy**, a condition of disorder and violence — and having a government that protects them from violence, but that also may turn against them. When functioning well, then, the state is a balanced system that protects its citizens both from one another *and* from itself.

What keeps the U.S. government from turning against its citizens? Functionalists say that **pluralism**, a diffusion of power among many special-interest groups, prevents any one group from gaining control of the government and using it to oppress the people (Bentley 1908; Dahl 1961, 1982; Lemann 2008). To keep the government from coming under the control of any one group, the founders of the United States set up three branches of government: the executive branch (the president), the judiciary branch (the courts), and the legislative branch (the Senate and House of Representatives). Each is sworn to uphold the Constitution, which guarantees rights to citizens, and each can nullify the actions of the other two. This system, known as **checks and balances**, was

anarchy a condition of lawlessness or political disorder caused by the absence or collapse of governmental authority

pluralism the diffusion of power among many interest groups that prevents any single group from gaining control of the government

checks and balances the separation of powers among the three branches of U.S.government—legislative, executive, and judicial—so that each is able to nullify the actions of the other two, thus preventing any single branch from dominating the government

WHAT AM I SUPPOSED TO LEARN?

After you have read this unit, you should be able to

1 Summarize the functionalist and conflict views on power in the United States.

2 State whether the functionalist or conflict view is correct and why.

designed to ensure that no one branch of government dominates the others.

IN SUM: Our pluralist society has many parts—women, men, racial–ethnic groups, farmers, factory and office workers, religious organizations, bankers, bosses, the unemployed, the retired—as well as such broad categories as the rich, middle class, and poor. No group dominates. Rather, as each group pursues its own interests, it is balanced by other groups that are pursuing theirs. To attain their goals, groups must negotiate with one another and make compromises. This minimizes conflict. Because these groups have political muscle to flex at the polls, politicians try to design policies that please as many groups as they can. This, say functionalists, makes the political system responsive to the people, and no one group rules.

The United States Senate

The Conflict Perspective: The Power Elite

If you focus on the lobbyists scurrying around Washington, stress conflict theorists, you get a blurred image of superficial activities. What really counts is the big picture, not its fragments. The important question is: Who holds the power that determines the country's overarching policies? For example, who determines interest rates—and their impact on the price of our homes? Who sets policies that encourage the transfer of jobs from the United States to countries where labor costs less? And the ultimate question of power: Who is behind the decision to go to war?

Sociologist C. Wright Mills (1956) took the position that the country's most important matters are not decided by lobbyists or even by Congress. Rather, the decisions that have the greatest impact on your life—and people across the globe—are made by a **power elite**. As depicted in Figure 10.2, the power elite consists of the top leaders of the largest corporations, the most powerful generals and admirals of the armed forces, and certain elite politicians—the president, the president's cabinet, and senior members of Congress who chair the major committees. It is they who wield power, who make the decisions that direct the country and shake the world.

Are the three groups that make up the power elite—the top business, political, and military leaders—equal in power? Mills said that they were not, but he didn't point to the president and his staff or even to the generals and admirals as the most powerful. Instead, he said that the corporate (business) leaders are the most dominant. Because all three segments of the power elite view capitalism as essential to the welfare of the country, Mills said that business interests take center stage in setting national policy.

Sociologist William Domhoff (1990, 2006) uses the term **ruling class** to refer to the power elite. He focuses on the 1 percent of Americans who belong to the super-rich, the powerful capitalist class analyzed in Chapter 7 (pages 202–205). Members of this class control our top corporations and foundations, even the boards that oversee our major universities. It is no accident, says Domhoff, that from this group come most members of the president's cabinet and the ambassadors to the most powerful countries of the world.

IN SUM: Conflict theorists take the position that a *power elite*, whose connections extend to the highest centers of power, determines the economic and political conditions under which the rest of the country operates (Domhoff 1990, 1998, 2007). They stress that

power elite C. Wright Mills' term for the top people in U.S. corporations, military, and politics who make the nation's major decisions

ruling class another term for the power elite

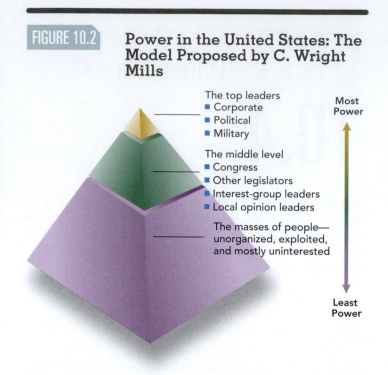

FIGURE 10.2 Power in the United States: The Model Proposed by C. Wright Mills

The top leaders
- Corporate
- Political
- Military

The middle level
- Congress
- Other legislators
- Interest-group leaders
- Local opinion leaders

The masses of people—unorganized, exploited, and mostly uninterested

Most Power

Least Power

Source: By the author. Based on Mills 1956.

we should not think of the power elite (or ruling class) as some secret group that meets to agree on specific matters. Rather, the group's unity springs from people having similar backgrounds and orientations to life. All have attended prestigious private schools, belong to exclusive clubs, and are millionaires many

Did Mills identify the military as the most powerful group in the United States?

times over. Their behavior stems not from some grand conspiracy to control the country but from a mutual interest in solving the problems that face big business.

Which View Is Right?

The functionalist and conflict views of power in U.S. society cannot be reconciled. Either competing interests block any single group from being dominant, as functionalists assert, or a power elite oversees the major decisions of the United States, as conflict theorists maintain. The answer may have to do with the level you look at. Perhaps at the middle level of power depicted in Figure 10.2, the competing groups do keep each other at bay, and none is able to dominate. If so, the functionalist view would apply to this level. But which level holds the key to U.S. power? Perhaps the functionalists have not looked high enough, and activities at the peak remain invisible to them. On that level, does an elite dominate? To protect its mutual interests, does a small group make the major decisions of the United States?

Sociologists passionately argue this issue, but with mixed data, we don't yet know the answer. We await further research.

Watch the **Video**
Sociology on the Job:
Politics and Government
in **mysoclab**

DID I LEARN IT? ANSWERS ARE AT THE END OF THE CHAPTER

1. "Too many rules!" complained Nicole, as she reviewed the "rules of the road" for her driving test. "I wish we didn't have a government. I could just drive how I wanted." In a moment, she added, "But I know we have to have rules or else we'd have disorder and violence." Nicole was referring to

   a. misanthropy
   b. archeology
   c. archaicism
   d. anarchy

2. "At least there's no one group in control of society," said Hank, "or else we would be in a lot of trouble. We have a lot of laws because there are lots of groups promoting their ideas." Hank is taking this position

   a. conflict   b. anarchist
   c. functionalist   d. powerist

3. "I know another name for the position you're arguing," said Nicole. "It is

   a. symbolic interactionism
   b. pluralism
   c. conflict
   d. anarchism

4. "Well, whatever you call it, I know I'm right," said Hank. "Remember our old social studies class? We learned that there is a system set up to prevent any one of the three branches of government from taking over? As I recall, this is called

   a. checks and balances
   b. constitutional prerogative
   c. tripartite rule
   d. mutual submissiveness

5. Frank had grown increasingly impatient and a bit irritated as he listened to Nicole and Hank. He finally blurted out, "You're so wrong I can't stand it. There *is* a power elite that makes the country's major decisions. Did you ever hear of any of us voting on going to war in Iraq? Or Afghanistan? Or Libya? Or bombing some other place?" Practically shouting now, he said, "No! It's the power elite, just like C. Wright Mills said. And the ones who run it are the

   a. generals and admirals
   b. top political leaders
   c. women
   d. top corporate leaders

6. Frank is taking this position

   a. conflict
   b. pluralist
   c. functionalist
   d. powerist

7. Another name that some sociologists use for power elite is

   a. dominant group
   b. ruling class
   c. functionalist
   d. the wealthy

8. With the functionalist/conflict debate among sociologists continuing regarding the source of power in the United States, the best conclusion is

   a. there is evidence on both sides, so we don't know
   b. the conflict perspective wins
   c. the functionalist perspective wins
   d. the pluralist perspective wins

UNIT 10.5

War and Terrorism: Implementing Political Objectives

You might be wondering why I am including war and terrorism as topics of politics. The reason is simply this: War and terrorism are tools politicians use to try to accomplish goals. The Prussian military analyst Carl von Clausewitz, who entered the military at the age of 12 and rose to the rank of major-general, put it best when he said, "War is merely a continuation of politics by other means."

Let's look at this aspect of politics.

Why Countries Go to War

War, armed conflict between nations (or politically distinct groups) is simply *one option* that groups choose for dealing with disagreements. Why do nations choose this option? As usual, sociologists answer this question not by focusing on factors *within* humans, such as aggressive impulses, but by looking for *social* causes—conditions in society that encourage or discourage combat between nations.

> **war** armed conflict between nations or politically distinct groups

War, including terrorism, is part of politics, a way to reach political goals.

WHAT AM I SUPPOSED TO LEARN?

After you have read this unit, you should be able to

1 Explain why war is a topic that belongs in a chapter on politics.

2 Explain why nations go to war—its essential conditions and fuels.

3 Explain why some groups choose terrorism.

THE CONDITIONS AND FUELS OF WAR

As he searched for an answer to what causes war, sociologist Nicholas Timasheff (1965) identified three essential conditions. The first is an antagonistic situation in which two or more states confront incompatible objectives. For example, each may want the same land or oil. The second is a cultural tradition of war. Because their nation has fought wars in the past, the leaders of a group see war as an option for dealing with serious disputes with other nations. The third is a "fuel" that heats the antagonistic situation to a boiling point, so that politicians cross the line from thinking about war to actually waging it.

Timasheff identified seven "fuels" of war. He found that war is likely if a country's leaders see the antagonistic situation as an opportunity to achieve one or more of these objectives:

1. *Beliefs:* forcibly converting others to religious or political beliefs

2. *Unity:* uniting rival groups within their country

3. *Revenge:* settling "old scores" from earlier conflicts

4. *Power:* dominating a weaker nation

5. *Prestige:* defending the nation's "honor"

6. *Ethnicity:* bringing under their rule "our people" who are living in another country

7. *Position:* protecting or exalting the leaders' positions

You can use these three essential conditions and seven fuels to analyze any war. They will help you understand why politicians at that time chose war as their political action.

To better understand today's wars, read the next *Making It Personal*.

MAKING IT PERSONAL

The Flesh and Blood of War

Sociological analysis can be cold and dispassionate. The "fuels" of war that you just read about are like this: a list of conditions that is accurate and insightful, but cold. Throughout this book, I've tried to bring you the flesh and blood of topics, to help you see the ways that people experience life. So let's do this again.

Behind these "fuels" are politicians who make the bloody choice to go to war. You know that they don't pick up a gun and fight the war themselves. Instead, they sit back and watch it from the comfort of their homes and offices. Some even profit from the war, making investments in the weapons industry. For most politicians, the deaths are bloodless affairs. It is young men, and increasingly young women, who do the killing—and dying—for the politicians.

Some soldiers are killed on the battlefield; others survive but are mutilated for the rest of their lives. Many who survive with their bodies intact suffer emotionally. Some of my students have shared their suffering with me. One who became my friend, a highly intelligent and interesting individual, took his life before he graduated. One day he left his wife and children, walked into a country field, and shot himself. But let me share one of the most powerful statements I have come across. Just before he put a bullet through his brain, a soldier from California wrote this:

I can't sleep anymore. When I was in Vietnam, we came across a North Vietnamese soldier with a man, a woman, and a three- or four-year-old girl. We had to shoot them all. I can't get the little girl's face out of my mind. I hope that God will forgive me ... I can't. (Smith 1980)

I apologize for leaving this *Making It Personal* on such a negative note, but war is certainly one of the most negative aspects of the human condition. I can't think of much positive about it to share with you.

Terrorism

Mustafa Jabbar, in Najaf, Iraq, is proud of his first born, a baby boy. Yet he said, "I will put mines in the baby and blow him up." (Sengupta 2004)

How can feelings run so deeply that a father would sacrifice his only son? Some groups nourish hatred, endlessly chronicling the injustices and atrocities of their archenemy. Stirred in a cauldron of bitterness, and mixed liberally with perceived injustice, righteous hatred boils until it overflows and dominates people's lives.

How would you apply the analysis of terrorism in the text to this photo?

Its antagonisms, so bitter, can span generations; its embers, ever renewed, sometimes burn for centuries.

But what can a group do if it is weaker than its enemy? Unable to meet its more powerful opponent on the battlefield, one option is **terrorism**, violence intended to create fear in order to bring about political objectives. And, yes, if the hatred is strong enough, that can mean blowing up your only child.

Suicide terrorism, a weapon sometimes chosen by the weaker group, captures headlines around the world. Among the groups that have used suicide terrorism are the Palestinians against the Israelis and the Iraqis and Afghanistanis against U.S. troops. The suicide attack that has had the most profound effects on your life was launched on the World Trade Center and the Pentagon

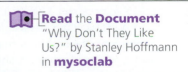

Read the **Document** "Why Don't They Like Us?" by Stanley Hoffmann in **mysoclab**

terrorism the use of violence or the threat of violence to produce fear in order to attain political objectives

under the direction of Osama bin Laden. You might have wondered what kind of sick people become suicide terrorists?

Let's find out in the following *Making It Personal.*

MAKING IT PERSONAL

Testing Your Stereotypes of Suicide Terrorists

What kind of sick people become suicide terrorists? A lot of people wonder about this. How could anyone blow themselves or their children up?

Sociologist Marc Sageman (2008a, 2008b) wondered this same thing, and he decided that research might provide the answer. To do his research, Sageman had a much greater advantage than you or I would have. Sageman had been in the CIA, and through his contacts he was able to study 400 al-Qaeda terrorists who had targeted the United States. He was able to examine thousands of pages of their trial records.

Here is what he found. Contrary to stereotypes, suicide terrorists are not uneducated, mentally unbalanced loners. On the contrary. most are well educated, socially integrated, in good mental health, and highly aware of what they are doing. These individuals are convinced about the justice of their cause, and they are willing to sacrifice their lives for it.

These findings certainly blew away my stereotypes of suicide terrorists, and I think they probably do the same for yours. What a different picture emerges when we do research on the general, unsystematic ideas that we form as we go through life. Highly patriotic individuals who are willing to die for "the cause." Sounds like every general's dream of a fighting force, doesn't it?

IF YOU WANT TO LEARN MORE about suicide terrorists,

 **Read** more from the author: Who Are the Suicide Terrorists? Testing Your Stereotypes in **mysoclab**

The suicide attacks on New York and Washington, D.C., are tiny in comparison with the threat of weapons of mass destruction (WMDs). If terrorists unleash biological, nuclear, or chemical weapons, the death toll could run in the millions. There have been a couple of scares. A shipment of enriched uranium that was being smuggled out of Europe was intercepted just before it landed in terrorists' hands (Sheets and Broad 2007a,b). The public didn't know about this. But the chilling possibility of biological weapons was brought home to Americans in 2001 when the media reported that anthrax powder had been mailed to a few select victims. People all over the country became upset and called the police when they saw spilled flour or talcum powder. If the real thing happens…

It is sometimes difficult to tell the difference between war and terrorism. This is especially so in civil wars when the opposing sides attack civilians and don't wear uniforms. Among the many unfortunate aspects of these wars is the chilling use of children as soldiers and sex slaves.

IF YOU WANT TO LEARN MORE about child soldiers,

Read more from the author: Child Soldiers in **mysoclab**

UNIT 10.5 // TESTING MYSELF
DID I LEARN IT? ANSWERS ARE AT THE END OF THE CHAPTER

1. "I wonder why war is a topic in a chapter on politics. Usually this is about voting and stuff," thought Jaime. After he read the unit, he knew the answer. War is
   a. hell
   b. slowly disappearing
   c. a remnant left over from mankind's primitive past
   d. a tool politicians use to try to accomplish goals

2. Juan especially liked this quote from Carl von Clausewitz
   a. "War is hell."
   b. "Go to war slowly, but don't let anyone despoil your honor."
   c. "War is merely a continuation of politics by other means."
   d. "Wars may come and go, but some hang on forever."

3. "It's the sociological perspective again," said Juan as he was reading. "I see that to explain war, sociologists focus on
   a. factors within humans, such as aggressive impulses
   b. social causes, conditions in society
   c. people's changing life situations
   d. the percentage of the male population that is below the age of 25

4. As Juan read further, he found there were three essential conditions of war: an antagonistic situation with incompatible objectives, a cultural tradition of war, and
   a. a "fuel" that heats the antagonistic situation to a boiling point
   b. leaders who have made calculations about the likelihood of victory
   c. leaders who care more about themselves than about the people
   d. propaganda to create hatred of the enemy

5. Juan decided that he wanted to memorize the seven fuels of war, so he developed a mnemonic device, BURP PEP, which stand for
   a. Bombs, Unity, Rigidity, Pressure, Performance, Entrance, and Prey

b. Boots, Unicorns, Raspberry, Peach, Plum, Essences, and Prison
c. Battlefield, Universal, Retaliation, Power, Peace, Espionage, and People
d. Beliefs, Unity, Revenge, Power, Prestige, Ethnicity, and Position

6. Suicide terrorism is a weapon or strategy of war that is sometimes chosen by a weaker group. Research by sociologist Marc Sageman, who had access to CIA files and trial transcripts, reveals that suicide terrorists are

a. unhappy loners
b. mostly from families in poverty
c. educated, socially integrated, and in good mental health
d. mentally ill

One aspect of the intricately interrelated, multifaceted U.S. economy, its market forces increasingly dependent on political decisions.

THE ECONOMY: WORK IN THE GLOBAL VILLAGE

UNIT 10.6

The Transformation of Economic Systems

WHAT AM I SUPPOSED TO LEARN?

After you have read this unit, you should be able to

1 Explain the transformation of societies through history.

If you are like most students, you are wondering how changes in the economy are going to affect your chances of getting a good job. As we switch topics in this part of the chapter, let's see if we can shed some light on this question. We'll begin with this story:

The sound of her alarm rang in Kim's ears. "Not Monday already," she groaned. "There must be a better way of starting the week." She pressed the snooze button on the clock (from Germany) to sneak another ten minutes' sleep. In what seemed like just thirty seconds, the alarm shrilly insisted that she get up and face the week.

Still bleary-eyed after her shower, Kim peered into her closet and picked out a silk blouse (from China), a plaid wool skirt (from Scotland), and leather shoes (from Italy). She nodded, satisfied, as she added a pair of simulated pearls (from Taiwan). Running late, she hurriedly ran a brush (from Mexico) through her hair. As Kim wolfed down a bowl of cereal (from Canada) topped with milk (from the United States), bananas (from Costa Rica), and sugar (from the Dominican Republic), she turned on her kitchen television (from Korea) to listen to the weather forecast.

Gulping the last of her coffee (from Brazil), Kim grabbed her briefcase (from India), purse (from Spain), and jacket (from Malaysia), left her house, and quickly climbed into her car (from Japan). As she glanced at her watch (from Switzerland), she hoped that the traffic would be in her favor. She muttered to herself as she pulled up at a stoplight (from Great Britain) and eyed her gas gauge. She grumbled again when she pulled into a station and paid for gas (from Saudi Arabia), for the price had risen over the weekend. "My paycheck never keeps up with prices," she moaned.

Today's **economy**—our system of producing and distributing goods and services—differs radically from past economies. From the products that you (and Kim) use, you can see that today's economy knows no national boundaries. With so many items flowing into the United States from countries that have much cheaper labor, many of us are concerned that our country is losing its ability to compete in global markets. We'll come back to this, but first we need to get a broad view of how global forces affect the U.S. economy—and your life. To do so, let's go back just a little bit—to early humans. A *quick* review of sweeping historical changes will help you see what has led to your current situation. For a visual overview of what we are going to discuss, see Figure 10.3.

economy a system of producing and distributing goods and services

FIGURE 10.3   Social Transformations of Society

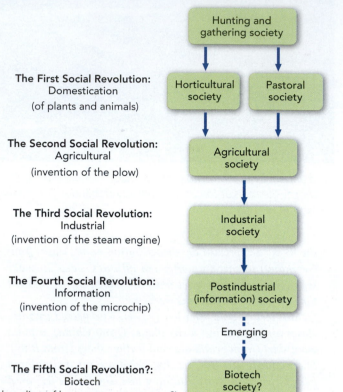

The First Social Revolution:
Domestication
(of plants and animals)

The Second Social Revolution:
Agricultural
(invention of the plow)

The Third Social Revolution:
Industrial
(invention of the steam engine)

The Fourth Social Revolution:
Information
(invention of the microchip)

The Fifth Social Revolution?:
Biotech
(decoding of human genome system?)

Hunting and gathering society

Horticultural society → Pastoral society

Agricultural society

Industrial society

Postindustrial (information) society

Emerging

Biotech society?

Not all the world's societies will go through the transformations shown in this figure. Whether any hunting and gathering societies will survive, however, remains to be seen. A few might, perhaps kept on "small reserves" that will be off limit to developers but open to guided "ethno-tours" at a hefty fee.

Source: By the author.

Preindustrial Societies: The Birth of Inequality

The earliest human groups lived in **hunting and gathering societies**. In small groups of about twenty-five to forty, people lived off the land. They gathered plants and hunted animals in one location and then moved to another place as these sources of food ran low. Having few possessions, these people did little trading with one another. With no excess to accumulate, everybody owned as much (or, really, as little) as everyone else.

When people discovered how to breed animals and cultivate plants, societies split in two directions. Groups that built their lives around taking care of animals are called

hunting and gathering societies a human group that depends on hunting and gathering for its survival

pastoral societies. Those that built their lives around growing crops are called **horticultural societies**. The more dependable food supply in pastoral and horticultural societies allowed humans to settle down in a single place. Human groups grew larger, and for the first time in history, it was no longer necessary for everyone to work at producing food. Some people became leather workers, others made weapons, and so on. This new division of labor produced a surplus, and groups traded items with one another. The primary sociological significance of surplus and trade is this: They fostered *social inequality,* for some people accumulated more possessions than others. The effects of that change remain with us today.

The plow brought the next major change, ushering in **agricultural societies**. Plowing the land made it more productive, allowing even more people to specialize in activities other than producing food. More specialized divisions of labor followed, and trade expanded. Trading centers then developed, which turned into cities, and as you just saw, into city-states. As power passed from the heads of families and clans to a ruling elite, social, political, and economic inequalities continued to grow.

Industrial Societies: The Birth of the Machine

The steam engine, invented in 1765, brought with it **industrial societies**. Based on machines powered by fuels, these societies created a surplus unlike anything the world had ever seen. This, too, stimulated trade among nations and led to even greater social inequality. A handful of individuals opened factories and exploited the labor of many.

This was followed by even more efficient machines. As the surpluses continued to grow, the emphasis gradually changed—from producing goods to consuming them. In 1912, sociologist Thorstein Veblen coined the term **conspicuous consumption** to describe this fundamental change in people's orientations. By this term, Veblen meant that the Protestant ethic identified by Weber—an emphasis on hard work, savings, and a concern for salvation (discussed on pages 7–8)—was being replaced by an eagerness to show off wealth by the "elaborate consumption of goods."

To see how this works in your own life, read the following *Making It Personal.*

pastoral societies a society based on the pasturing of animals

horticultural societies a society based on cultivating plants by the use of hand tools

agricultural societies a society based largely on agriculture

industrial societies a society based on the harnessing of machines powered by fuels

conspicuous consumption Thorstein Veblen's term for a change from the Protestant ethic to an eagerness to show off wealth by the consumption of goods

MAKING IT PERSONAL
Your Conspicuous Consumption

What Veblen noticed was just the beginning of a fundamental change. Conspicuous consumption has so transformed our lives that Veblen wouldn't recognize today's society. Our economy depends on Americans consuming more and more. When consumers slow up, the economy swoons.

Advertisers specialize in creating the need to consume conspicuously. "You don't want your neighbors to be driving a newer or more expensive car than yours, do you?" Advertisers continuously shout some version of this question/statement at us. It comes in various forms—your jeans, your shirts, your blouses, your shoes. These items can't be "less" than those of the student sitting alongside you, can they? Of course not. So no matter your reservations, you buy. You have to keep up with trends and remain stylish. And you show off. You don't really mean to show off, perhaps, but you can't really be shown up by someone else, either.

Ah, conspicuous consumption at work.

Some people, like those I know in Washington, D.C., have rejected conspicuous consumption entirely. Although they have good jobs, they go "dumpster diving" for their fruits and vegetables. They put on dark clothing at night and search dumpsters behind food stores.

How is conspicuous consumption at work in your life?

Postindustrial Societies: The Birth of the Information Age

In 1973, sociologist Daniel Bell noted that a new type of society was emerging. This new society, which he called the **postindustrial society**, has six characteristics: (1) a service sector so large that *most* people work in it, (2) a vast surplus of goods, (3) even more extensive trade among nations, (4) a wider variety and quantity of goods available to the average person, (5) an information explosion, and (6) a **global village**—that is, the world's nations are linked by fast communications, transportation, and trade.

To see why analysts use the term *postindustrial society* to describe the United States, look at Figure 10.4. The change in work shown in this figure is without parallel in human history. In the 1800s, most U.S. workers were farmers. Today, farmers make up only about 1 percent

postindustrial society
a society based on information, services, and high technology, rather than on raw materials and manufacturing; also called *postmodern* and *information society*.

global village refers to the world's nations being so interconnected that what happens in one nation affects others, much like what happens to people who live in the same village

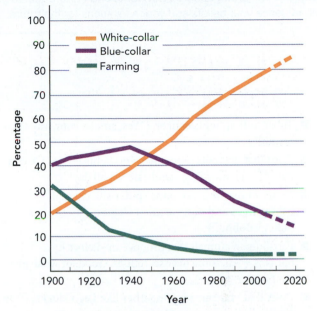

FIGURE 10.4 **The Revolutionary Change in the U.S. Workforce**

Source: By the author. Based on Statistical Abstract of the United States, various years, and 2012:Tables 616, 620.

of the workforce. With the technology of the 1800s, a typical farmer produced enough food to feed five people. With today's powerful machinery and hybrid seeds, a farmer now feeds about eighty people. In 1940, about half of U.S. workers wore a blue collar; then changing technology shrank the market for blue-collar jobs. White-collar work continued its ascent, reaching the dominant position it holds today. For more on how changing society affects your life, see *Making It Personal*.

MAKING IT PERSONAL
Shaping Your World

The broad changes in societies that I just sketched may seem to be abstract matters, but they are far from irrelevant for your life. Think for a moment how your world would be different if you had grown up in an agricultural society. You would have different ideas about who you are (a farmer or a farmer's wife) and what you should expect out of life (God's will; at the mercy of the seasons). You would have sharply contrasting ideas about the number of children you should have (many). Your relationship with your spouse would be vastly different (dominant men and submissive women). In short, practically nothing would be the same.

When society changes, then, so do people's lives. Consider the information explosion that has had such a powerful effect on your life. When you graduate from college, you will most likely do some form of "knowledge work." Instead of working on a farm or in a factory, you will manage information or design, sell, or service products. As with any type of employment, this work will have profound effects on how you live, think, and relate to people. It will produce social networks and nurture attitudes. It will influence your beliefs and your aspirations for the future.

Biotech Societies: Is a New Type of Society Emerging?

- Tobacco that fights cancer. ("Yes, smoke your way to health!")
- Corn that prevents pregnancy and fights herpes ("Corn flakes in the morning—and safe sex all day!")
- Goats whose milk contains spider silk (to make fishing lines and body armor) ("Got milk? The best bulletproofing.")
- Part-human animals that produce medicines for humans. ("Ah, those liver secretions. Good for what ails you.")
- DNA that you can snap together like Lego blocks. ("Our BioBricks build better life forms.")
- Bacteria that excrete diesel fuel. ("Put our germ droppings in your gas tank.")

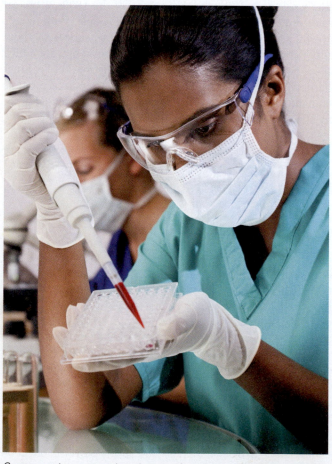

Some analysts surmise that we have entered a new type of society, sometimes called a biotech society.

I know that such products sound like science fiction, but we *already* have the goats that make spider silk. Human genes have been inserted into animals, and they do produce medicine (Elias 2001; Kristoff 2002; Osborne 2002). The snap-together BioBricks should be available soon (Mooallem 2010). Perhaps one day, you will be able to design your own bacterium—or elephant. We already have the bacteria that produce diesel fuel, but it isn't harvestable yet (Mooallem 2010).

The changes in which we are immersed are so extensive that we may be stepping into another new type of society. In this new **biotech society**, the economy will center on applying and altering genetic structures—both plant and animal—to produce food, medicine, and materials.

If there is a new society—and this is not certain—when did it begin? There are no firm edges to new societies, for each new one overlaps the one it is replacing. The opening to a biotech society could have been 1953, when Francis Crick and James Watson identified the double-helix structure of DNA. Or perhaps historians will trace the date to the decoding of the human genome in 2001.

Whether or not we are entering a new society is not important for our main point: The changes that our society is going through will affect the type of work you do—and even whether there will be work available for you in the first place.

In *Making It Personal*, let's look more closely at your place in the global village.

> **biotech society** a society whose economy increasingly centers on the application of genetics—human genetics for medicine, and plant and animal genetics for the production of food and materials.

MAKING IT PERSONAL

Where in the Village Do You Live?

To apply these ideas to your life, let's explore the concept of the global village. Think of the globe as divided into three neighborhoods—the three worlds of industrialization and postindustrialization that we reviewed in Chapter 7. Some nations are located in the poor part of the global village. Their citizens do menial work and barely eke out a living. Life is so precarious that some people even starve to death—while the global villagers in the rich neighborhood feast on the best cuts of meat, the fanciest desserts, and the finest wines that the globe has to offer. It's the same global village, but what a difference the neighborhood makes.

Now visualize any one of the three neighborhoods. Again you will see gross inequalities within them. Not everyone who lives in the poor neighborhood is poor, and some areas of the rich neighborhood, where the United States is, are packed with poor people.

Where do you live in this global village? How does this influence how you think about yourself? What you can expect out of life? What you anticipate that you will be doing for a living?

UNIT 10.6 // TESTING MYSELF
DID I LEARN IT? ANSWERS ARE AT THE END OF THE CHAPTER

1. In this type of society, groups of about twenty-five to forty people gather plants and hunt animals in one location and then move to another place as these sources of food run low. There is little inequality.
   - **a.** postindustrial
   - **b.** biotech
   - **c.** agricultural
   - **d.** hunting and gathering

2. After people discovered how to breed animals and cultivate plants, these two types of society developed. In them, the more dependable food supply allowed humans to settle down in a single place. Human groups grew larger, and for the first time in history, it was no longer necessary for everyone to work at producing food.
   - **a.** industrial and postindustrial
   - **b.** pastoral and horticultural
   - **c.** agricultural and pastoral
   - **d.** hunting and gathering

3. The plow allowed this society to develop. Even more people were able to specialize in activities other than producing food. Surpluses developed, as did trading centers and cities.
   - **a.** postindustrial
   - **b.** biotech
   - **c.** agricultural
   - **d.** hunting and gathering

4. The steam engine ushered in this typ e of society, creating a surplus unlike anything the world had ever seen. This stimulated trade among nations and brought even greater social inequality.
   - **a.** industrial
   - **b.** biotech
   - **c.** agricultural
   - **d.** hunting and gathering

5. In 1912, sociologist Thorstein Veblen noted that the Protestant ethic—an emphasis on hard work, savings, and a concern for salvation—was being replaced by an eagerness to show off wealth by the "elaborate consumption of goods." He used this term to refer to this elaborate consumption
   - **a.** elaborate consumption
   - **b.** showing off
   - **c.** spectacular consumption
   - **d.** conspicuous consumption

6. In 1973, sociologist Daniel Bell noted that this new type of society was emerging. Three of its characteristics are a service sector so large that most people work in it, an information explosion, and a global village.
   - **a.** postindustrial
   - **b.** biotech
   - **c.** agricultural
   - **d.** postinformation

7. I don't like to ask little questions about statistics, but this one is stunning. With the technology of the 1800s, a typical farmer produced enough food to feed five people. With today's powerful machinery and hybrid seeds, today's typical farmer feeds this many people.
   - **a.** 10
   - **b.** 25
   - **c.** 50
   - **d.** 80

8. This term refers to the world's nations being linked by fast communications, transportation, and trade.
   - **a.** high-speed rail transportation
   - **b.** satellite communications
   - **c.** global village
   - **d.** the Internet

9. In this new type of society, which seems to be emerging now, the economy will center on applying and altering genetic structures—both plant and animal—to produce food, medicine, and materials.
   - **a.** biotech
   - **b.** postindustrial
   - **c.** industrial
   - **d.** postagricultural

10. Perhaps historians will trace the starting date of this new type of society to 1953 when Francis Crick and James Watson identified the double-helix structure of DNA, or maybe to the decoding of the human genome in 2001
    - **a.** biotech
    - **b.** postindustrial
    - **c.** industrial
    - **d.** postagricultural

UNIT 10.7

Principles and Criticisms of Capitalism and Socialism

WHAT AM I SUPPOSED TO LEARN?

After you have read this unit, you should be able to

1 Explain the three principles of capitalism and the three principles of socialism.

2 Summarize the major criticisms of capitalism and socialism.

How does this indoor mall in Las Vegas illustrate the three principles of capitalism?

Now that we have sketched the main historical changes in economic systems, let's compare capitalism and socialism, the two main economic systems in force today. This will help us to understand where the United States stands in the world economic order.

Capitalism

WHAT CAPITALISM IS

Although you live in a capitalist society, you may not understand its basic features. What most people see is a jumble of local shopping malls and fast-food chains and Internet stores, not the principles that lie behind them. So let's see what they are. Look at Table 10.3, which distills the many businesses of the United States down to their basic components. As you can see, **capitalism** has

TABLE 10.3 — Comparing Capitalism and Socialism

Capitalism	Socialism
1. Individuals own the means of production.	1. The public owns the means of production.
2. Based on competition, the owners determine production and set prices.	2. Central committees plan production and set prices; no competition.
3. The pursuit of profit is the reason for distributing goods and services.	3. No profit motive in the distribution of goods and services.

Source: By the author

three essential features: (1) *private ownership of the means of production* (individuals own the land, machines, and factories); (2) *market competition* (the owners compete with one another, decide what to produce, and set the prices for their products); and (3) *the pursuit of profit* (the owners try to sell their products for more than what they cost).

These are the principles, but it is also important to know that no country has pure capitalism. Pure capitalism, known as **laissez-faire capitalism** (literally "hands off" capitalism), means that the government doesn't interfere in the market. The current form of U.S. capitalism is **welfare** or **state capitalism**. Private citizens own the means of production and pursue profits, but they do so within a vast system of laws designed to protect the welfare of the population and make sure that the government can collect taxes. Consider this example:

Suppose that you've been working for years to develop the perfect drink. After countless experiments, you've discovered it. You have produced a miracle tonic that will grow hair, erase wrinkles, and dissolve excess fat. You envision yourself as an overnight sensation—not only a multimillionaire but also the toast of television talk shows and the darling of Hollywood.

But don't count on your money or fame just yet. You still have to deal with the laws and regulations of welfare capitalism. They limit your capacity to produce and sell. First, you must comply with local and state laws. You must apply for a business license and a state tax number that allows you to buy your ingredients without paying sales taxes. Then come the federal regulations. You cannot simply take your product to local stores and ask them to sell it; you first must seek approval from federal agencies that monitor compliance with the Pure Food and Drug Act. This means that you must prove that your product will not cause harm to the public. Your manufacturing process is also subject to federal, state, and local laws concerning fraud, hygiene, and the disposal of hazardous wastes.

Suppose that you overcome these obstacles, and your business prospers. Other federal agencies will monitor your compliance with laws concerning minimum wages, Social Security taxes, and gender, racial, religious, and disability discrimination. State agencies will examine your records to see whether you have paid unemployment taxes and sales taxes and make sure that you carry the required insurance. Inspectors will even check the temperature of your refrigerators. Finally, as your shadowy but ever-present business partner, the Internal Revenue Service will look over your shoulder and demand about 35 percent of your profits.

In short, the U.S. economic system is highly regulated and is far from an example of laissez-faire capitalism.

capitalism an economic system characterized by the private ownership of the means of production, the pursuit of profit, and market competition

laissez-faire capitalism unrestrained manufacture and trade (literally "hands off" capitalism)

welfare (or state) capitalism an economic system in which individuals own the means of production but the state regulates many economic activities for the welfare of the population

Socialism

WHAT SOCIALISM IS

From Table 10.3, you can see that **socialism** also has three essential components: (1) public ownership of the means of production, (2) central planning, and (3) the distribution of goods without a profit motive.

In socialist economies, the government owns the means of production—not only the factories but also the land, railroads, oil wells, and gold mines. Unlike capitalism, in which **market forces**—supply and demand—determine both what will be produced and the prices that will be charged, a central committee decides that the country needs x number of toothbrushes, y toilets, and z shoes. The committee decides how many of each will be produced, which factories will produce them, what price will be charged for the items, and where they will be distributed.

Socialism is designed to eliminate competition, for goods are sold at predetermined prices regardless of the demand for an item or the cost of producing it. The goal is not to make a profit, nor is it to encourage the consumption of goods that are in low demand (by lowering the price) or to limit the consumption of hard-to-get goods (by raising the price). Rather, the goal is to produce goods for the general welfare and to distribute them according to people's needs, not their ability to pay.

In a socialist economy *everyone* in the economic chain works for the government. The members of the central committee who set production goals are government employees, as are the supervisors who implement their plans, the factory workers who produce the merchandise, the truck drivers who move it, and the clerks who sell it. Those who buy the items may work at different jobs—in offices, on farms, or in day care centers—but they, too, are government employees.

Just as capitalism does not exist in a pure form, neither does socialism. Although the ideology of socialism calls for resources to be distributed according to need and not the ability to pay, socialist countries found it necessary to pay higher salaries for some jobs in order to entice people to take on greater responsibilities. Factory managers, for example, always earned more than factory workers. These differences in pay follow the functionalist argument of social stratification presented in Chapter 7 (pages 193–197). By narrowing the huge pay gaps that are part of capitalist nations, however, socialist nations did establish considerably greater equality of income.

Dissatisfied with the greed and exploitation of capitalism and the lack of freedom and individuality of socialism, Sweden and Denmark developed **democratic socialism** (also called *welfare socialism*). In

socialism an economic system characterized by the public ownership of the means of production, central planning and the distribution of goods without a profit motive

market forces the law of supply and demand

democratic socialism a hybrid economic system in which the individual ownership of businesses is mixed with the state ownership of industries thought essential to the public welfare, such as the postal service and the delivery of medicine and utilities

this form of socialism, both the state and individuals produce and distribute goods and services. The government owns and runs the steel, mining, forestry, and energy concerns, as well as the country's telephones, television stations, and airlines. Remaining in private hands are the retail stores, farms, factories, and most service industries.

Criticisms of Capitalism and Socialism

In India, an up-and-coming capitalist giant, the construction of a 27-story building is almost complete (Yardley 2010b). It comes with a grand ballroom, nine elevators, a 50-seat theater, a six-story garage and three helipads on the roof. The occupants are ready to move in—all five of them— a husband, wife, and their three children. From their perch, they will be able to view the teeming mass of destitute people below.

The tallest building in the world, the Burj Khalifa, is located in Dubai. Dubai's wealth is based on oil, not capitalism.

The primary criticism leveled against capitalism is that it leads to social inequality. Capitalism, say its critics, produces a tiny top layer of wealthy people who exploit an immense bottom layer of poorly paid workers. Another criticism is that the tiny top layer wields vast political power. Those few who own the means of production reap huge profits, build up political power, and get legislation passed that goes against the public good.

The primary criticism leveled against socialism is that it does not respect individual rights. Others (in the form of some government body) control people's lives. The government decides where people will live, work, and go to school. In China, the government even determines how many children women may bear (Mosher 1983, 2006). Critics argue that central planning is grossly inefficient and that socialism is not capable of producing much wealth. They maintain that its greater equality really amounts to giving almost everyone an equal chance to be poor.

UNIT 10.7 // TESTING MYSELF
DID I LEARN IT? ANSWERS ARE AT THE END OF THE CHAPTER

1. The term market competition means that the owners
   a. compete with one another and decide what to produce and set the prices for their products
   b. leave advertising and other marketing up to professionals
   c. advertise their products to get people to buy them
   d. of small businesses are directly involved with the market, but the shareholders of large businesses have managers who are responsible for the day-to-day work

2. Essential to capitalism is the pursuit of profit. The simple meaning of this statement is that
   a. the owners exploit workers
   b. everyone benefits as this gives people a strong reason to produce goods and get others to buy them
   c. the owners try to sell their products for more than what they cost
   d. people take a risk of loss as they invest in products to sell

3. Essential to capitalism is the private ownership of the means of production. This term means that
   a. people own the gold mines, but not the gold
   b. individuals own the land, machines, and factories
   c. people own the gold, but not the gold mines
   d. the government owns the land, machines, and factories

4. Capitalism is built on supply and demand. This means that production is geared toward goods that are in high demand, while production drops for goods that are not in high demand. The term for this is

   a. market forces
   b. socialism
   c. advertising and consumption
   d. conspicuous consumption

5. "I didn't know there were different types of capitalism. I thought there was just capitalism," said Dennis. "In the United States private citizens own the means of production and pursue profits, but there is a vast system to protect the welfare of the population. They call this
   a. laissez-faire capitalism
   b. Cap-Soc (capitalism/socialism)
   c. individualistic socialism
   d. welfare or state capitalism

6. Dennis added, "I just learned that the three essential components of socialism are the public ownership of the means of production, central planning, and
   a. market competition
   b. the pursuit of profit
   c. individuals owning the land, machines, and factories
   d. the distribution of goods without a profit motive

7. "Wow!" said Denise. "I just learned something, too. I didn't know that in a socialist economy everyone of working age
   a. has a home
   b. distributes goods without a profit motive
   c. works for the government
   d. is active in market competition

8. "But there is no pure socialism," said Dennis. "And there isn't any pure capitalism either. Pure capitalism, or 'hands off' capitalism means that the government doesn't interfere in the market. They call this
   a. let-it-loose capitalism   b. laissez-faire capitalism
   c. freedom capitalism   d. handy capitalism

9. "There is a lot of criticism against both capitalism and socialism," said Dennis. "The main criticism of capitalism is that it
   a. harms the environment
   b. is risky and too many individuals lose money
   c. leads to social inequality
   d. does not respect individual rights

10. "And how about the criticism of socialism?" added Denise. "I read that the main one is that it
    a. leads to social inequality
    b. does not respect individual rights
    c. harms the environment
    d. leads to too much self-reflection, reducing production

UNIT 10.8
Belief Systems and the Convergence of Capitalism and Socialism

WHAT AM I SUPPOSED TO LEARN?

After you have read this unit, you should be able to

1 Explain the main belief systems of capitalism and socialism.

2 Apply convergence theory to capitalism and socialism.

Belief Systems of Capitalism and Socialism

Not only do capitalism and socialism have different approaches to producing and distributing goods but they also represent opposing belief systems. *Capitalists* believe that market forces should determine both products and prices. They also believe that profits are good for humanity. The potential to make money stimulates people to produce and distribute goods, as well as to develop new products. Society benefits, as the result is a more abundant supply of goods at cheaper prices.

Socialists take an opposite view of profits. They consider them to be immoral. An item's value is based on the work that goes into it, said Karl Marx. The only way there can be profit, he stressed, is by paying workers less than the value of their labor. Profit, then, is an *excess value* that has been withheld from workers. Socialists believe that the government should protect workers from this exploitation. To do so, the government should own the means of production, using them not to generate profit but to produce items that match people's needs, not their ability to pay.

Capitalists and socialists paint each other in such stark colors that *each perceives the other system as one of exploitation.* Capitalists believe that socialists violate people's basic right to make their own decisions and to pursue opportunity. Socialists believe that capitalists violate people's basic right to be free from poverty. With each side claiming moral superiority while viewing the other as a threat to its very existence, the last century witnessed the world split into two main blocs. In what was known as the *Cold War,* the West armed itself to defend and promote capitalism, the East to defend and promote socialism. During the Cold War, the world came close to being wiped out by nuclear weapons that each aimed at the other.

The Convergence of Capitalism and Socialism

Regardless of the validity of the criticisms that each side threw at the other, an amazing thing happened: *Capitalism and socialism have come to resemble one another.* As societies industrialize, they grow similar. They urbanize, encourage higher education, and produce similar divisions of labor (such as professionals and skilled technicians; factory workers and factory managers). Similar values also emerge (Kerr 1983). By itself, this tendency would make capitalist and socialist nations grow more alike, but another factor has also brought them closer to one another (Form 1979): Despite their incompatible beliefs, both capitalist and socialist systems have adopted features from the other.

That capitalism and socialism are growing similar is known as **convergence theory**. Fundamental changes in socialist countries give evidence for this coming hybrid, or mixed, economy. For example, Russians suffered from the production of shoddy goods, they were plagued by shortages, and their standard of living lagged severely behind that of the West. To try to catch up, in the 1980s and 1990s, the rulers of Russia made the private ownership of property legal and abandoned communism. Making a profit—which had been a crime—was encouraged. China joined the change, but kept a communist government. In its converged form, capitalists were even invited to join the Communist party. The

convergence theory the view that as capitalist and socialist economic systems each adopt features of the other, a hybrid (or mixed) economic system will emerge

This stock exchange is in Hangzhou, China, is an example of the convergence of capitalism and socialism.

convergence is so great that when the Western governments implemented stimulus plans to counter the economic crisis, China joined in with a huge stimulus plan of its own (Batson 2009). Even Western banks are welcomed in China, so they can provide specialized services to China's 960,000 new millionaires (Yenfang 2011)—and to China's 115 new billionaires (Flannery 2011). Perhaps the point that best summarizes this remarkable change is that some textbooks in China now give more space to Bill Gates than to Mao (Guthrie 2008).

IF YOU WANT TO LEARN MORE about the new capitalism in China,

Read more from the author: The New Capitalism in China in **mysoclab**

Changes in capitalism also support this theory. The United States has adopted many socialist practices based on the government taking money from some individuals to pay for the benefits it gives to others. Look at these examples:

Unemployment compensation: taxes paid by workers are distributed to those who no longer produce a profit

Subsidized housing: shelter, paid for by the many, is given to the poor and elderly, with no motive of profit

Subsidized medicine: the government takes money from some to pay for the medical treatment of others

Welfare: taxes from the many are distributed to the needy

Minimum wage: the government, not the employer, determines the minimum that workers are paid

Social Security: the retired do not receive what they paid into the system, but, rather, money that the government collects from current workers.

Finally, in 2008, when Wall Street and auto firms started to buckle, the U.S. government stepped in to shore up these businesses. In some cases, the government even bought the companies, fired the CEOs, and set salary limits. Such an extended embrace of socialist principles indicates that the United States has produced its own version of a mixed economy.

IN SUM: Convergence is unfolding before our very eyes. On the one hand, capitalists have assumed, reluctantly, that their system should provide workers with at least minimal support during unemployment, extended illness, and old age—and in some instances that the government should buy company stock. On the other hand, socialist leaders have admitted, also reluctantly, that profit and private ownership do motivate people to work harder.

UNIT 10.8 // TESTING MYSELF
DID I LEARN IT? ANSWERS ARE AT THE END OF THE CHAPTER

1. These people believe that profits are good for humanity, that they stimulate people to produce goods and to develop new products. They say that society benefits, as the result is a more abundant supply of goods at cheaper prices.
   a. socialists
   b. democratic socialists
   c. capitalists
   d. cap-socs

2. These people believe that profits are evil, that they are an excess value that has been withheld from workers.
   a. socialists
   b. democratic socialists
   c. capitalists
   d. cap-socs

3. Both capitalists and socialists believe that they are morally superior and view the other as a threat to its existence. From about 1945 to 1990, the capitalists and socialists threatened each other with nuclear destruction. This period is known as the
   a. Stalemate Time
   b. Cold War
   c. Danger Zone
   d. Threat Time

4. Both capitalists and socialists believe that they are morally superior and view the other as a threat to its existence. This group believes that the other violates people's basic right to make their own decisions and to pursue opportunity.
   a. socialists
   b. democratic socialists
   c. capitalists
   d. cap-socs

5. Both capitalists and socialists believe that they are morally superior and view the other as a threat to its existence. This group believes that the other violates people's basic right to be free from poverty.
   a. socialists
   b. democratic socialists
   c. capitalists
   d. cap-socs

6. Over the years, capitalism and socialism have grown similar to one another as each has adopted features of the other. That this is happening matches

a. capitalism
b. socialism
c. convergence theory
d. democratic socialism

7. An indication that socialism has come closer to capitalism is that socialist countries have adopted

a. centralized planning of the production and distribution of goods
b. Social Security
c. the private ownership of property
d. communism

8. An indication that capitalism has come closer to socialism is that capitalist countries have adopted

a. the profit motive
b. Social Security
c. the private ownership of property
d. communism

For an economy to exist, there must be established ways to exchange goods and services. All modern economies use paper money as one these ways.

UNIT 10.9

The Globalization of Capitalism

WHAT AM I SUPPOSED TO LEARN?

After you have read this unit, you should be able to

 1 Describe the new global structure and how it is related to capitalism.

2 Summarize the change in worker pay over the past approximately forty years and explain how the nation's income is divided.

3 Describe the global superclass.

Capitalism has integrated the world's countries, making them all part of the same broader economic unit. When the economic crisis hit the United States, it spread quickly around the world. Leaders from the top 20 countries that produce consumer goods met in Washington to see what steps they could take to head off the crisis. Chinese leaders said that no one should worry about them not being a team player, that they realized that any action they took would affect other nations. (Yardley and Bradsher 2008)

The globalization of capitalism may be the most significant economic change in the past 100 years. Its impact on our lives may rival that of the Industrial Revolution. As Louis Gallambos, a historian of business, says, "This new global business system will change the way everyone lives and works" (Zachary 1995).

Let's look, then, at how capitalism is changing the face of the globe. As you read this unit, you should have no problem seeing how this is affecting your life.

A New Global Structure

The globalization of capitalism has forged a new world structure. Three primary trading blocs have emerged: North and South America, dominated by the United States; Europe, dominated by Germany; and Asia, dominated by China and Japan.

In this structure, trade among nations is now more extensive than it has ever been. This has increased competition, which combined with the search for greater profits, has brought greater productivity. The result is the lower prices and higher standard of living that you enjoy. But as production has moved to countries where labor costs are lower, millions of U.S., U.K., French, and German workers have lost their jobs. And millions of workers in the Least Industrialized Nations work in sweatshop conditions as they produce the products you enjoy. Some point out that this is merely a temporary dislocation. As the economies of the Least Industrialized Nations advance, their workers will receive more pay and better working conditions. They also point out that as the Most Industrialized Nations lose factory jobs, their workers shift into service and high-tech jobs. Today's millions of workers searching in vain for jobs that no longer exist would disagree.

To see how the globalization of capitalism applies to your life, read *Making It Personal*.

MAKING IT PERSONAL

Your Standard of Living

I realize that when I said you were enjoying lower prices and a higher standard of living, you may have thought that I missed this one. You know how much is in your wallet or purse, how much is in the bank (if you have a bank account), and how many bills are yet to be paid. "What lower prices and higher standard of living are you talking about?" could very well have been your response.

But you do experience these benefits. When? Every time you shop. The prices might not seem lower to you, but they are—much, much lower than they would be without the globalization of capitalism. Clothing from India, for example, costs a fraction of the cost of what clothing used to cost when it was made by U.S. workers in Boston and Charlotte. It is the same with household gadgets, cars, and computers. The global competition has increased productivity and lowered prices. And whether or not you think you have lower prices, you really do.

Just two more quick examples: A generation ago, you would have paid double for new tires for your car than now, and the tires would have lasted just half as long as the ones you buy now. And a generation ago, it would have cost you something like a dollar a minute to talk long distance—and you would have been reluctant to pick up the phone. Today, you can make that same call over Skype for no cost at all.

Certainly the adjustment has been anything but easy. As the U.S. steel industry lost out to global competition, for example, the plant closings created "rust belts" in the northern states. The globalization of capitalism has also brought special challenges to small towns across the country, which were already suffering long-term losses because of urbanization. Their struggle to survive is the topic of the photo essay on pages 340–341.

Stagnant Paychecks

With our extensive automation, the productivity of U.S. workers has increased year after year, making them some of the most productive in the world (*Statistical Abstract* 2012:Tables 1353, 1355). Is their pay keeping pace?

Look at Figure 10.5. The gold bars show current dollars. These are the dollars the average worker finds in his or her paycheck. You can see that since 1970, the average pay of U.S. workers has soared from just over $3 an hour to over $19 an hour. Workers today are bringing home about *six* times as many dollars as workers used to.

But let's strip away the illusion. Look at the purple bars, which show the dollars adjusted for inflation, the buying power of those paychecks. You can see how inflation has shredded the value of the dollars that workers earn. With their $19 an hour, today's workers can buy little more than workers in 1970 could with their "measly" $3 an hour. The question is not "How could workers live on just $3 an hour back then?" but, rather, *"How can workers get by on a 62-cent-an-hour raise that it took 40 years to get?"* That's less than two cents an hour per year! Incredibly, despite workers having more college and technical training,

FIGURE 10.5

Average Hourly Earnings of U.S. Workers in Current and Constant Dollars

Source: By the author. Based on Statistical Abstract of the United States *1992:Table 650; 1999:Table 698; 2012:Table 644*

despite the use of computers and much higher productivity, the purchasing power of workers increased just 62 cents an hour between 1970 and 2010.

What can you buy with those 62 cents?

Actually, after taxes and Social Security deductions, we should ask, What can you buy with the 40 cents?

The New Economic System and the Old Divisions of Wealth

Let's begin by looking at the dilemma that capitalists face.

Suppose that you own a business that manufactures widgets. You are paying your workers $150 a day ($18.88 an hour, which includes their vacation pay, medical and unemployment benefits, and Social Security). Widgets similar to yours are being manufactured in Thailand, where workers are paid $8 a day. Those imported widgets are being sold in the same stores that feature your widgets.

How long do you think you could stay in business? Even if your workers were willing to drop their pay in half—which they aren't willing to do—you still couldn't compete.

What do you do? Your choices are simple. You can continue as you are and go broke, try to find some other product to manufacture (which, if successful, will soon be made in Thailand or India or China)—or you can close up your plants here and manufacture your widgets in Thailand.

I don't want to give the impression that all owners and bosses are evil capitalists out to fleece their workers. The vignette above is meant to illustrate that the global economic system is a force far beyond the reach of individual owners or individual corporations. The stark choices they face don't make for easy times for them either. One wrong decision can destroy a generation of wealth and privilege—or small family-run businesses that have barely sputtered along.

And workers? They are faced with high insecurity with layoffs and plant closings. You probably are familiar with this on a personal basis—from what someone in your family or a friend is going through. The insecurity is especially hard-hitting on the most desperate of workers, the less-skilled and those who live from paycheck to paycheck. No matter how hard they work, how can they compete with workers overseas who work for peanuts? They suffer the wrenching adjustments that come from having their jobs pulled out from under them, looking for work and finding only jobs that pay lower wages—if that. They watch their savings go down the drain, postpone their retirement, lose their cars and homes, and see their children disillusioned about the future.

What about the wealthy? With the shifting economy, aren't they, perhaps, being hurt like the workers are? Some rich individuals do get on the wrong side of investments and lose their collective shirts. In general, though, the wealthy do just fine in our challenging economic times.

How can I be so sure? you might be wondering. Take a look at Figure 10.6. Each rectangle on the left of this figure represents a fifth of the U.S. population, about 62 million people. The rectangles of the inverted pyramid on the right show the percentage of the nation's income that goes to each fifth of the population. You can see that half of the entire country's income goes to the richest fifth of Americans. In sharp contrast, the bottom fifth of the nation, the poorest among us, receive only 3 percent of the nation's wealth. This income inequality has been growing for decades, and it now is the largest we have had in generations.

Let's consider these divisions of income in *Making It Personal*.

MAKING IT PERSONAL
Your Share of the Nation's Income

You probably know this common folk saying, "The rich get richer, and the poor get poorer." As you have just seen, this saying is insightful. Look again at Figure 10.6. This division of the nation's income has not been more extreme since before the Great Depression of the 1930s.

What implications of this division of the nation's income do you see for the nation's future? For your future?

FIGURE 10.6 The Inverted Income Pyramid: The Proportion of Income Received by Each Fifth of the U.S. Population

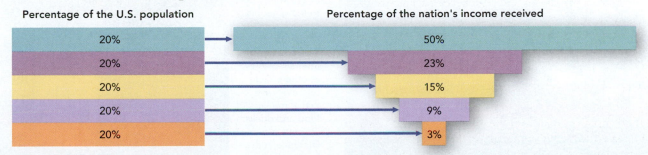

Source: By the author. Based on Statistical Abstract of the United States *2012:Table 694.*

SMALL TOWN USA: STRUGGLING TO SURVIVE

SOUTHEASTERN USA

All across the nation, small towns are struggling to survive. Parents and town officials are concerned because so few young adults remain in their home town . There is little to keep them there, and when they graduate from high school, most move to the city. With young people leaving and old ones dying, the small towns are shriveling .

How can small towns contend with cutthroat global competition when workers in some countries are paid a couple of dollars a day? Even if you open a store, down the road Wal-Mart sells the same products for about what you pay for them—and offers much greater variety.

There are exceptions: Some small towns are located close to a city, and they receive the city's spillover. A few possess a rare treasure—some unique historical event or a natural attraction—that draws visitors with money to spend . Most of the others, though, are drying up, left in a time warp as history shifts around them. This photo essay tells the story.

People do whatever they can to survive. This enterprising proprietor uses the building for an unusual combination of purposes: a "plant world," along with the sale of milk, eggs, bread, and, in a quaint southern touch, cracking pecans.

I was struck by the grandiosity of people's dreams, at least as reflected in the names that some small-towners give their businesses. Donut Palace has a nice ring to it—inspiring thoughts of wealth and royalty (note the crowns). Unfortunately, like so many others, this business didn't make it.

The small towns are filled with places like this—small businesses, locally owned, that have enough clientele for the owner and family to eke out a living. They have to offer low prices because there is a fast-food chain down the road. Fixing the sign? That's one of those "I'll get-to-its."

In striking contrast to the grandiosity of some small town business names is the utter simplicity of others. Cafe tells everyone that some type of food and drinks are served here. Everyone in this small town knows the details.

© James M. Henslin, all photos

One of the few buildings consistently in good repair in the small towns is the U.S. Post Office. Although its importance has declined in the face of telecommunications, for "small towners" the post office still provides a vital link with the outside world.

With little work available, it is difficult to afford adequate housing. This house, although cobbled together and in disrepair, is a family's residence.

There is no global competition for this home-grown business. Shirley has located her sign on a main highway just outside Niceville, Florida. By the looks of the building, business could be better.

This general store used to be the main business in the area: it even has a walk-in safe. It has been owned by the same family since the 1920s, but is no longer successful. To get into the building, I had to find out where the owner (shown here) lived, knock on her door, and then wait while she called around to find out who had the keys.

This is a successful business. The store goes back to the early 1900s, and the proprietors have capitalized on the "old timey" atmosphere.

The Global Superclass

The leaders of the globe's top multinational companies and major investors overlap to such an extent that they form a small circle, one that we can call the global superclass (Rothkopf 2008). The superclass is not only extremely wealthy, but it is also extremely powerful. These people have access to the top circles of political power around the globe.

The global superclass has only recently emerged, and as of yet sociologists don't know a great deal about this group—except that its members are extremely rich and powerful. The members of the global superclass don't like sociologists or anyone else doing research on them. Privacy suits them just fine—and they can afford the world's tightest privacy, keeping them away from prying eyes.

One member of the global superclass, though, has given us insight into how the group works. He said that every country has major financial institutions that are central to its development. Members of the superclass use their connections in this financial network to make contact with government officials around the globe. Ultimately, says this individual, there are just twenty to fifty people worldwide who drive the globe's major decisions.

Can we really believe this—just *twenty to fifty individuals who make the world's major decisions!?* The individual who described the way things work at the top is Stephen Schwarzman, an insider in this group. How much of an insider? Pay attention to this real-life example of how this interconnected circle of global power works out in practice:

> When Schwarzman, the head of a major U.S. investment company, had a problem with some policy of the German government, he called a German friend. The friend arranged for Schwarzman to meet with the Chancellor of Germany. After listening to Schwarzman, the Chancellor agreed to support a change in Germany's policy.

Do you see the immense power that is concentrated in this small group? The U.S. members can call the U.S. president, the English members can call the British prime minister, and so on. They know how to get and give favors, to move vast amounts of capital, and to open and close doors to investments around the world. This concentration of power is new to the world scene, and we have much to learn about it. But this we can say for sure: Working behind the scenes, the global superclass affects your present and your future.

The faces of the individuals who head the world's most powerful nations change with elections, deaths, and appointments, but the interests that they represent remain the same.

UNIT 10. 9 // TESTING MYSELF

DID I LEARN IT? ANSWERS ARE AT THE END OF THE CHAPTER

1. The author uses the term "new global structure" to refer to new
   a. communications and transportation
   b. forms of science that are creating a biotech society
   c. forms of currency exchange
   d. trading blocs of nations

2. The globalization of capitalism has led to millions of
   a. U.S. workers getting new jobs
   b. Americans getting raises
   c. U.S. jobs being transferred to other countries
   d. women taking postgraduate courses in business

3. Extensive automation has made U.S. workers some of the most productive in the world. In current dollars, the average pay of U.S. workers over the past approximately forty years has gone from $3.23 an hour to
   a. $10.50   b. $19.07
   c. $22.50   d. $31.75

4. U.S. workers make more than they used to. In current dollars, the average pay of U.S. workers over the past approximately forty years has gone from $3.23 an hour to $19.07. In constant dollars (dollars adjusted

for inflation), worker pay has gone from $8.29 an hour to

a. $8.91 **b.** $9.99
c. $10.70 **d.** $12.10

5. If we divide the U.S. population into fifths and look at the percentage of the nation's income that each fifth receives, we find that the bottom fifth gets this percentage

a. 50 **b.** 20
c. 15 **d.** 3

6. If we divide the U.S. population into fifths and look at the percentage of the nation's income that each fifth receives, we find that the top fifth gets this percentage

a. 3 **b.** 25
c. 35 **d.** 50

7. Just as each country has a top class of wealthy, powerful people, so does the world. That is, the leaders of the globe's top multinational companies and major investors form a small circle that is becoming known as the

a. Global 500 **b.** global superclass
c. capitalist elite **d.** Chosen

8. This is the number of people who make up the global superclass, the one that apparently makes the world's major decisions

a. 20 to 50 **b.** 500 to 700
c. 2,000 to 3,000 **d.** 5000 to 10,000

UNIT 10.10
A New World Order?

WHAT AM I SUPPOSED TO LEARN?

After you have read this unit, you should be able to

1 Explain major developments in trading blocs of nations and how this is related to a New World Order.

2 Explain strains in global capitalism and a possible shift in global leadership.

To close this chapter, let's look at an aspect of our changing political and economic order that has far-reaching implications for your life. You know that some groups use war and terrorism to try to dominate the globe. These have always failed. Yet a New World Order might be on its way, ushered in not by the weapons of war, but by changing economic-political conditions.

Current arrangements of power carry contradictions that must be resolved. The rise of China is a major contradiction. Shown here is China's first aircraft carrier.

Trends Toward Unity

Perhaps the key *political* event of our era is the globalization of capitalism. Why am I using the term *political*? Isn't capitalism a type of economics? The reason is that politics and economics are twins, with each setting the stage for the other. Look at the economic–political units being developed. The United States, Canada, and Mexico have formed a North American Free-Trade Association (NAFTA). Ten Asian countries with a combined population of a half billion people have formed a regional trading partnership called ASEAN (Association of South East Asian Nations). Struggling for dominance is an even more encompassing group called the *World* Trade Organization. These coalitions of trading partners are making national borders increasingly insignificant.

The European Union (EU) might be pointing to our future. Transcending their national boundaries, twenty-seven European countries (with a combined population of 450 million) formed this economic–political unit. These nations have adopted a single, cross-national currency, the euro, which has replaced the marks, francs, liras, lats, and pesetas of the individual countries. The EU has also set up a military staff in Brussels, Belgium.

Could this process continue until there is just one state or empire that envelops the earth? It is possible. The United Nations is striving to become the legislative body of the world, wanting its decisions to supersede those of any individual nation. The UN operates a World Court (formally titled the International Court of Justice). It has also sent "peacekeeping" troops to several nations.

Strains in the Global System

Although the globalization of capitalism and its encompassing trade organizations could lead to a single world government, the developing global system is experiencing strains that threaten to rip the system apart. Unresolved items constantly rear up, demanding realignments of the current arrangements of power. Although these pressures are resolved on a short-term basis, over time their cumulative weight leads to a gradual shift in global stratification.

The dominance of any nation or coalition of nations always comes to an end. It is always replaced by another group or culture. The process of decline is usually slow and can last hundreds of years (Toynbee 1946), but in our speeded-up world, the future bursts into the present at a furious rate. If the events of the past century indicate the future, the decline of U.S. dominance—like that of Great Britain—will come fairly suddenly, although certainly not without resistance and bloodshed. With bases around the world, in enormous debt, and fighting one war after another, it appears that the United States is overspent and overextended. As it declines, the shape of the new economic and political arrangement of world power is anyone's guess. Certainly, however, it will include an ascendant China.

As the economic and political arrangements of the present give way, you will face a new world. Whatever the particular shape of future stratification, economic–political elites will be directing it. They will use their resources to bolster their positions, making alliances across international boundaries designed to continue their dominance. Perhaps this process will lead to a one-world government, perhaps to a dictatorship or an oligarchy that controls the world's resources and people. If so, you could end up living under a government like that of Winston and Julia in our opening vignette.

Only time will tell.

UNIT 10.10 // TESTING MYSELF
DID I LEARN IT? ANSWERS ARE AT THE END OF THE CHAPTER

1. This term refers to the developing alignment of the world's nations, where the potential is that the world's nations will be members of the same political system
   a. Developing World Order
   b. Realignment of Power Relations
   c. global superclass
   d. New World Order

2. Indications are that the United States will lose power in world leadership and this country will gain power
   a. Germany
   b. Great Britain
   c. China
   d. South Africa

3. No nation or group of nations remains in power forever. Each dominant power eventually overextends itself and fails. Regarding the coming new dominant power, you can be sure that it will be
   a. part of a conspiracy
   b. better than what we have had in the past
   c. motivated by the desire to bring peace and rid the world of poverty
   d. directed by economic–political elites

PULLING IT ALL TOGETHER REVIEWING THE LEARNING GOALS

Unit 10.1 Power, Authority, and Violence

1. Explain the difference between authority and coercion.

- *Authority* is power that we consider legitimate. *Coercion* is power we consider illegitimate. Governments claim a monopoly on violence, the foundation of a political order.

2. Explain the three types of authority and give an example of each.

- *Traditional authority* is based on custom, *rational-legal authority* on written rules, and *charismatic authority* on people's perception that an individual has been touched by God or has almost irresistible qualities.

3. Explain how leadership is transferred in each of the three types of authority.

- In *traditional authority*, the transition of leadership follows custom. In *rational-legal authority*, it follows written rules. In *charismatic authority*, there is no fixed way. If charismatic authority changes into one of the other two types, it is called the *routinization of charisma*.

Unit 10.2 Types of Government

1. Explain how political power expanded.

- Human groups used to be small, with political power similar to what we find in an extended family. As populations grew, political power expanded. Early power was centered in city-states, expanding from there to larger groups.

2. Explain the differences between monarchies, democracies, dictatorships, and oligarchies.

- Monarchies are governments ruled by kings and queens; in democracies, citizens can vote their will; a dictatorship is the seizure of power by an individual; and in an oligarchy a group has seized power.

3. Explain why citizenship is a revolutionary idea.

- During most of history, the government forced its will on the people. Democracies reverse this traditional idea by making the government responsive to the people's will.

👁‍|**Watch** the **Video**
The Basics: Politics and Government in **mysoclab**

Unit 10.3 The U.S. Political System

1. Explain why Democrats and Republicans are centrist and why third parties do poorly.

- Both the Democrats and Republicans support the same political philosophy of capitalism, free speech, U.S. dominance and a strong military, and so on. If a third party violates these centrist themes, it loses appeal.

2. Explain the major patterns in U.S. voting.

- Voting follows patterns of age, race–ethnicity, education, income, and sex. In general, people who benefit more from the political system are more likely to vote. Alienation and apathy are common, and half of Americans do not vote in federal elections.

3. Summarize and criticize the role of lobbyists in U.S. politics.

- Lobbyists use PACs (political action committees) to solicit money and distribute it to favored candidates. The major criticism is that they are buying votes.

❋|**Explore** the **Concept**
Majority-Minority States in **mysoclab**

👁|**Watch** the **Video**
The Big Picture: Politics and Government in **mysoclab**

Unit 10.4 Who Rules the United States?

1. Summarize the functionalist and conflict views on power in the United States.

- *The functionalist view*: The answer is pluralism. Like the three branches of government, many special-interest groups compete for power and resources. Power is diffused among them, and none is in control. *The conflict view*: A power elite—consisting of the top leaders of the largest corporations, the most powerful generals and admirals of the armed forces, and certain elite politicians—make the big decisions. They share similar interests in promoting capitalism. The corporate leaders dominate this group.

2. State whether the functionalist or conflict view is correct and why.

- Sociologists are debating this issue, and currently there is no answer.

Unit 10.5   War and Terrorism

1. Explain why war is a topic that belongs in a chapter on politics.
   - As Carl von Clausewitz said, "War is merely a continuation of politics by other means."

2. Explain why nations go to war—its essential conditions and fuels.
   - The three essential conditions are an antagonistic situation with incompatible objectives, a cultural tradition of war, and a "fuel" that heats the antagonistic situation to a boiling point. The seven fuels are revenge, power, prestige, unity, position, ethnicity, and beliefs. They are explained in more detail on page 000.

3. Explain why some groups choose terrorism.
   - Terrorism, which can be highly effective, is a tactic of war chosen by weaker groups that are unable to compete on the battlefield.

▐■▌Read the Document
"Why Don't They Like
Us?" by Stanley Hoffmann
in mysoclab

Unit 10.6   The Transformation of Economic Systems

1. Explain the transformation of societies through history.
   - Early humans lived in *hunting and gathering societies*, moving on when food became scarce. After learning to breed animals and cultivate plants, societies branched in one of two directions: *pastoral societies*, taking care of animals, or *horticultural societies*, growing crops. The plow ushered in *agricultural society*, and the steam engine brought *industrial society*. A characteristic of industrial societies is a changed emphasis from production to consumption. In *postindustrial societies*, most people work at service jobs. A *biotech society* seems to be emerging. If so, the economy will center on applying and altering genetic structures—both plant and animal—to produce food, medicine, and materials.

Unit 10.7   Principles and Criticisms of Capitalism and Socialism

1. Explain the three principles of capitalism and the three principles of socialism.
   - The basic features of capitalism are (1) *private ownership of the means of production* (individuals own the land, machines, and factories), (2) *market competition* (the owners compete with one another and decide what to produce and set the prices for their products), and (3) *the pursuit of profit* (the owners try to sell their products for more than what they cost). The basic features of socialism are: (1) *public ownership of the means of production*, (2) *central planning*, and (3) *the distribution of goods without a profit motive*.

2. Summarize the major criticisms of capitalism and socialism.
   - The main criticism of capitalism is that it leads to social inequality. The main criticism of socialism is that it does not respect individual rights.

Unit 10.8   Belief Systems and the Convergence of Capitalism and Socialism

1. Explain the main belief systems of capitalism and socialism.
   - *Capitalists* believe that market forces should determine products and prices. Profits are good, motivating people to produce and distribute goods and to develop new products. *Socialists* believe that profits are bad, an excess value withheld from workers. The government should protect workers from this exploitation by producing items that match people's needs, not their ability to pay.

2. Apply convergence theory to capitalism and socialism.
   - Both capitalism and socialism have adopted features of the other. Capitalist governments collect money from some individuals to pay for the benefits they give to others: unemployment compensation, subsidized housing and medicine, welfare, a minimum wage, and Social Security. Socialistic governments now allow people to make a profit in producing and distributing goods.

Unit 10.9   The Globalization of Capitalism

1. Describe the new global structure and how it is related to capitalism.
   - Blocs of trading partners have emerged, from regional to a developing global bloc. This has increased global trade and competition, lowered prices, and sent jobs to countries where labor costs less.

2. Summarize the change in worker pay over the past approximately forty years and explain how the nation's income is divided.
   - The average U.S. worker's pay went from $3.23 an hour in 1970 to $19.07 now. In constant dollars, the increase was from $8.03 to $8.91. The bottom fifth gets 3 percent of the nation's income, while the top fifth receives half of the nation's income.

3. Describe the global superclass.
   - A small group of just 20 to 50 people is apparently behind the world's major decisions.

Unit 10.10 A New World Order?

1. Explain major developments in trading blocs of nations and how this is related to a New World Order.
   - Huge regional economic–political units are being knitted together, from NAFTA in North America to ASEAN in Asia. National currencies are being replaced with regional currencies. The United Nations is attempting to become the legislative body of the world. The potential is for this process to continue, ending with a one-world government.

2. Explain strains in global capitalism and a possible shift in global leadership.
   - The economic crisis has revealed huge flaws in the global banking system. With the United States overextended and overspent, it is likely that U.S. power will decline. No one knows the future shape of global politics, but there are indications that power will pass to the East. Whatever form it takes, it will be directed by political elites.

UNIT 10.1 // TESTING MYSELF
DID I LEARN IT? ANSWERS

1. **d** illegitimate power, called coercion

2. **c** rational-legal authority

3. **b** claims the exclusive right to use violence—and the right to punish everyone else who uses violence

4. **a** violence

5. **b** traditional authority

6. **c** rational-legal authority

7. **a** charismatic authority

8. **a** the problem of the transfer of authority in charismatic groups

9. **d** how that person will be selected

10. **c** the routinization of charisma

UNIT 10.2 // TESTING MYSELF
DID I LEARN IT? ANSWERS

1. **c** surpluses

2. **c** Power to the people!

3. **b** Athens

4. **a** direct democracy

5. **d** representative democracy

6. **c** women

7. **b** reversed traditional ideas. Instead of the people being responsive to the government's will, it made the government responsive to the people's will

8. **a** oligarchy

9. **d** totalitarianism

10. **c** know whether they are more or less politically privileged than others

UNIT 10.3 // TESTING MYSELF
DID I LEARN IT? ANSWERS

1. **c** primaries

2. **d** support the same fundamentals of U.S. political philosophy, such as capitalism, free public education, a strong military, and freedom of religion, speech, and assembly

3. **b** violate commonly agreed-on (centrist) political philosophy

4. **a** Democrat

5. **d** African Americans

6. **c** Asian Americans

7. **b** lobbyists

8. **a** political action committees (PACs)

9. **d** their money, in effect, buys votes

UNIT 10.4 // TESTING MYSELF
DID I LEARN IT? ANSWERS

1. d anarchy

2. c functionalist

3. b pluralism

4. a checks and balances

5. d top corporate leaders

6. a conflict

7. b ruling class

8. a there is evidence on both sides, so we don't know

UNIT 10.5 // TESTING MYSELF
DID I LEARN IT? ANSWERS

1. d a tool politicians use to try to accomplish goals

2. c "War is merely a continuation of politics by other means."

3. b social causes, conditions in society

4. a a "fuel" that heats the antagonistic situation to a boiling point

5. d Beliefs, Unity, Revenge, Power, Prestige, Ethnicity, and Position

6. c educated, socially integrated, and in good mental health

UNIT 10.6 // TESTING MYSELF
DID I LEARN IT? ANSWERS

1. d hunting and gathering

2. b pastoral and horticultural

3. c agricultural

4. a industrial

5. d conspicuous consumption

6. a postindustrial

7. d 80

8. c global village

9. a biotech

10. a biotech

UNIT 10.7 // TESTING MYSELF
DID I LEARN IT? ANSWERS

1. a compete with one another and decide what to produce and set the prices for their products

2. c the owners try to sell their products for more than what they cost

3. b individuals own the land, machines, and factories

4. a market forces

5. d welfare of state capitalism

6. d the distribution of goods without a profit motive

7. c works for the government

8. b laissez-faire capitalism

9. c leads to social inequality

10. b does not respect individual rights

UNIT 10.8 // TESTING MYSELF
DID I LEARN IT? ANSWERS

1. **c** capitalists

2. **a** socialists

3. **b** Cold War

4. **c** capitalists

5. **a** socialists

6. **c** convergence theory

7. **c** the private ownership of property

8. **b** Social Security

UNIT 10.9 // TESTING MYSELF
DID I LEARN IT? ANSWERS

1. **d** trading blocs of nations

2. **c** U.S. jobs being transferred to other countries

3. **b** $19.07

4. **a** $8.91

5. **d** 3

6. **d** 50

7. **b** global superclass

8. **a** 20 to 50

UNIT 10.10 // TESTING MYSELF
DID I LEARN IT? ANSWERS

1. **d** New World Order

2. **c** China

3. **d** directed by economic-political elites

CHAPTER 11
MARRIAGE AND FAMILY

Watch the **Video** in **mysoclab**

((•—[**Listen** to the **Chapter Audio** in **mysoclab**

GETTING STARTED

You know how important your family has been to you. Whether you were reared with both parents or just one, or even with a relative, your family has given you a basic introduction to social life. They have taught you a language and laid down your basic values. You've also picked up many other deep-rooted things from your family, matters quite significant but that mostly lie buried below your awareness. For example, from seeing how your parents and others interact, you have learned basic ideas about how husbands and wives should relate to one another. (Or perhaps from seeing how they interact, you have learned how husbands and wives should *not* relate to one another.)

So, based on your experience, maybe you already know everything about marriage and family. Just joking. But you do come to this chapter with years of experience and a lot of ideas. So let's see how the research matches your experience and ideas.

Jakarta, Indonesia

UNIT 11.1

Marriage and Family in Global Perspective

Let's begin by looking at how marriage and family customs differ around the world. This will give you a context for interpreting your own experiences with this vital social institution.

What Is a Family?

You might think it strange to ask what a family is, but it isn't easy to define. Even though the family is so significant to humanity that it is universal, the world's cultures display so much variety that it is difficult to locate common elements. The Western world, for example, regards a family as a husband, wife, and children. Other groups, though, have family forms in which men have more than one wife (**polygyny**) or women more than one husband (**polyandry**). How about the obvious? Perhaps we can define the family as the approved group into which children are born? Then we would be overlooking the Banaro of New Guinea. A Banaro woman

> **Polygyny** a form of marriage in which men have more than one wife
>
> **polyandry** a form of marriage in which women have more than one husband

The family is universal, but its form varies around the world. Shown here is a man in Malaysia with his four wives.

WHAT AM I SUPPOSED TO LEARN?

After you have read this unit, you should be able to

1 Explain why it is difficult to define marriage and family.

2 List the common cultural themes that run through marriage and family.

must give birth *before* she can marry—and she *cannot* marry the father of her child (Murdock 1949).

You can see that such remarkable variety makes it difficult to define *family*. So let's use a broad definition. A **family** consists of people who consider themselves related by blood, marriage, or adoption. Sometimes people mix this up with the term **household**, but a household simply refers to people who occupy the same housing unit—a house, apartment, or other living quarters.

We can classify families as **nuclear** (husband, wife, and children) and **extended** (including people such as grandparents, aunts, uncles, and cousins in addition to the nuclear unit). Sociologists also refer to the **family of orientation** (the family in which an individual grows up) and the **family of procreation** (the family that is formed when a couple has its first child).

> **Watch** the **Video**
> The Basics: Families in **mysoclab**

What Is Marriage?

To try to define marriage brings the same problem. For just about every element you might regard as essential to marriage, some group has a different custom.

Consider the sex of the bride and groom. Until recently, opposite sex was taken for granted when defining marriage. Then in the 1980s and 1990s, several European countries legalized same-sex marriages. Canada and several U.S. states soon followed.

Same-sex marriages sound so new. But let's go back in history a bit. When Columbus landed in the Americas, some Native American tribes already had same-sex marriages. Through a ceremony called the *berdache,* a man or woman who wanted to be a member of the opposite sex was officially *declared*

> **family** two or more people who consider themselves related by blood, marriage, or adoption
>
> **household** people who occupy the same housing unit
>
> **nuclear family** a family consisting of a husband, wife, and child(ren)
>
> **extended**
>
> **family of orientation** the family in which a person grows up
>
> **family of procreation** the family formed when a couple's first child is born

to have his or her sex changed. The "new" man or woman put on the clothing and performed the tasks associated with his or her new sex, and was allowed to marry.

I'm sure you can think of one thing that has to be universal in marriage—that the bride and groom are alive. So you would think. But even here we find an exception. On the Loess Plateau in China, if a son dies without a wife, his parents look for a dead woman to be his bride. After finding one—from parents willing to sell their dead unmarried daughter—the dead man and woman are married and then buried together. Happy that their son will have intimacy in the afterlife, the parents throw a party to celebrate the marriage (Fremson 2006).

With such wide, encompassing cultural variety, let's use a broad definition here, too. We will define **marriage** as a group's approved mating arrangements, usually marked by a ritual of some sort (the wedding) to indicate the couple's new public status.

Common Cultural Themes

Despite this amazing diversity, we can locate several themes that run through marriage and family. Look at Table 11.1. All societies use marriage and family to establish patterns of mate selection, descent,

inheritance, and authority. Let's look at these patterns.

MATE SELECTION

Each human group establishes rules to govern who marries whom. Some groups have norms of **endogamy**. Their members must marry *within* their group. For example, some groups prohibit interracial marriage, which makes them select partners within their own racial–ethnic group. In contrast, norms of **exogamy** specify that people must marry *outside* their group. The best example of exogamy is the **incest taboo**, which prohibits sex and marriage among designated relatives.

As you can see from Table 11.1, how people find spouses varies around the world. In some groups, fathers select the children's mates, with no input from the children. Other groups are highly individualistic, as is common in Western cultures where the individuals choose their spouses. In *Making It Personal*, we look at changes in mate selection that are taking place in our culture.

marriage a group's approved mating arrangements, usually marked by a ritual of some sort

endogamy the practice of marrying within one's own group

exogamy the practice of marrying outside one's own group

incest taboo the rule that prohibits sex and marriage among designated relatives

---

TABLE 11.1 **Common Cultural Themes: Marriage in Traditional and Industrialized Societies**

Characteristic	Traditional Societies	Industrial (and Postindustrial) Societies
What is the structure of marriage?	*Extended* (marriage embeds spouses in a large kinship network of explicit obligations)	*Nuclear* (marriage brings fewer obligations toward the spouse's relatives)
What are the functions of marriage?	Encompassing (see the six functions listed in Unit 2)	More limited (many functions are fulfilled by other social institutions)
Who holds authority?	*Patriarchal* (authority is held by males)	Although some patriarchal features remain, authority is divided more equally
How many spouses at one time?	Most have one spouse (*monogamy*), while some have several (*polygamy*)	One spouse
Who selects the spouse?	Parents, usually the father, select the spouse	Individuals choose their own spouses
Where does the couple live?	Couples usually reside with the groom's family (*patrilocal residence*), less commonly with the bride's family (*matrilocal residence*)	Couples establish a new home (*neolocal residence*)
How is descent figured?	Usually figured from male ancestors (*patrilineal kinship*), less commonly from female ancestors (*matrilineal kinship*)	Figured from male and female ancestors equally (*bilineal kinship*)
How is inheritance figured?	Rigid system of rules; usually patrilineal, but can be matrilineal	Highly individualistic; usually bilineal

Source: By the author.

MAKING IT PERSONAL
Electronic Matchmaking

I'm sure that you have noticed the dating sites on the Internet. They began as general sites ("Everyone sign up here") and then branched into specializations that feature matches based on age, religion, race–ethnicity, sexual orientation, and body size. On one site, you even have to qualify as "beautiful." All dating sites promise discretion, especially the sites promoting themselves for married people who are looking for variety.

You might not be able to believe some of the claims, such as "We'll find your perfect match scientifically." Many people, though, are using these sites for dating, and a good number are finding their marriage partners through them. Do you recall the point made in Chapter 2 that our behavior changes to match new technology? This particular change is remarkable, illustrating how deeply changes in technology penetrate, reaching even into our intimate lives.

What do you think about electronic dating sites? Have you used one? Would you? If you did, what concerns would you have and what would you watch out for?

Snapshots

Tall, Dark, and Handsome chats with Buxom Blonde.

IF YOU WANT TO LEARN MORE about electronic matchmaking,

Read more from the author: Finding a Mate: Not the Same as It Used to Be in **mysoclab**

DESCENT

I know that you have a quick answer for this question: How are you related to your father's father or to your mother's mother? You might think that people all over the world would give the same answer. But no. There are many **systems of descent**, the ways people trace kinship over generations. We use a **bilineal system**, for we think of ourselves as related to *both* our mother's and our father's sides of the family. "Doesn't everyone?" you might ask. Ours, however, is only one logical way to reckon descent. Some groups use a **patrilineal system**, tracing descent only on the father's side. They don't think of children as being related to their mother's relatives. Others follow a **matrilineal system**, tracing descent only on the mother's side, and not considering children to be related to their father's relatives. The Naxi of China, for example, don't even have a word for father (Hong 1999).

INHERITANCE

Marriage and family—in whatever form is customary in a society—are also used to determine the rights of inheritance. In a bilineal system, property is passed to both males and females, in a patrilineal system only to males, and in a matrilineal system (the rarest form), only to females. No system is natural. Rather, each matches a group's ideas of justice and logic.

system of descent how kinship is traced over the generations

bilineal (system of descent) a system of reckoning descent that counts both the mother's and the father's side

patrilineal (system of descent) a system of reckoning descent that counts only the father's side

matrilineal (system of descent) a system of reckoning descent that counts only the mother's side

Read the **Document** "'Night to His Day': The Social Construction of Gender" by Judith Lorber in **mysoclab**

AUTHORITY

Historically, the thread of **patriarchy** has run through all societies. This term refers to men-as-a-group dominating women-as-a-group. Contrary to what some think, there are no historical records of a true **matriarchy**, a society in which women-as-a-group dominate men-as-a-group. Although U.S. marriage and family customs are becoming more **egalitarian**, or equal, they developed within a framework of patriarchy. If you look closely, you can still see the patriarchal reflection.

patriarchy a society in which men-as-a-group dominate women-as-a-group; authority is vested in males

matriarchy a society in which women-as-a-group dominate men-as-a-group; authority is vested in females

egalitarian authority more or less equally divided between people or groups (in marriage, for example, between husband and wife)

For example, despite some changes, the typical bride still takes the groom's last name. And you probably received your father's last name.

I should point out that naming customs aren't the same the world over. Customs in the United States are but one of many.

Children in Spain, for example, receive the last names of both their mother and father, and they are given hyphenated last names. When there is a lot of intermarrying, as in a village I have lived in, both names can be the same. In this Spanish village, a lot of people have the same last name: Barbero-Barbero.

UNIT 11.1 // TESTING MYSELF
DID I LEARN IT? ANSWERS ARE AT THE END OF THE CHAPTER

1. After Susan told Leticia that John had moved in with her, she added, "Now we are a family." Leticia said, "Just a moment. You haven't really formed a family. You and John have formed a
   - **a.** partnership
   - **b.** unit
   - **c.** mixed unit
   - **d.** household

2. "What do you mean?" asked Susan. "Why aren't we a family?" "Because," said Leticia, "a family consists of people who
   - **a.** are married
   - **b.** are married and have children
   - **c.** consider themselves related by blood, marriage, or adoption
   - **d.** plan on always staying together, even if they don't

3. "You seem to know a lot about this," said Susan. "Well, I've been reading the chapter, and I learned some interesting things about marriage and family," answered Leticia. "One of the things I learned is that in some cultures women have more than one husband. This is known as
   - **a.** polygyny
   - **b.** polyandry
   - **c.** a nuclear family
   - **d.** an extended family

4. "Well, I know that in some cultures men have more than one wife," said Susan. "But I don't know what this is called." Leticia said, "This is the only place I've come across the word so far, but it is
   - **a.** polygyny
   - **b.** polyandry
   - **c.** berdache
   - **d.** extended family

5. Susan said, "I'm living with my mom, dad, and crazy little brother, so I know that my family is nuclear." "It is also your family of orientation," said Leticia. "Well, if I do marry John and we have a child, what kind of family will we be?" "I'd like to say 'happy,'" said Leticia, "but I know you're looking for a term. It is
   - **a.** extended family
   - **b.** basic family
   - **c.** typical family
   - **d.** family of procreation

6. "In my reading, I learned that some Native American tribes had same-sex marriages," said Leticia. "They held a ceremony for someone who wanted to be a member of the opposite sex and declared that

person's sex to be changed. The person then put on the clothing and performed the tasks associated with the new sex. And this person could marry. The ceremony was called the
   - **a.** sex change
   - **b.** new person
   - **c.** berdache
   - **d.** transformation

7. "The chapter also covered the incest taboo," said Leticia. "I know what that is, said Susan. "It is rules against
   - **a.** sex and marriage
   - **b.** sex
   - **c.** marriage
   - **d.** sex and marriage among designated relatives

8. "I learned something else that was really different," said Leticia. "You know how we consider ourselves related to both our mother and father, right?" "Of course," said Susan. "There couldn't be any other way." "Well, I read that there actually is," replied Leticia. "Ours is called a bilineal system of descent, but some groups consider children to be related only to their mother, not at all to the father. This system of descent is known as
   - **a.** siblineal
   - **b.** patrilineal
   - **c.** matrilineal
   - **d.** fratrilineal

9. "Then I suppose there are groups that consider children to be related only to their father, not at all to the mother?" asked Susan. "Right," confirmed Leticia. "This system of descent is known as
   - **a.** siblineal
   - **b.** patrilineal
   - **c.** matrilineal
   - **d.** fratrilineal

10. "Overall, our system is more equal, or egalitarian," added Leticia, "but you can still see traces of patriarchy. Did you know that?" "I did," said Susan. "You can see it in
   - **a.** the way that women give in to men when they argue
   - **b.** murder, with men much more likely to kill women than women to kill men
   - **c.** the bride taking the last name of the groom
   - **d.** shoplifting, with women much more likely than men to steal perfumes

UNIT 11.2
Marriage and Family in Theoretical Perspective

As you have seen, human groups have many forms of mate selection, ways to trace descent, and methods to assign authority and pass on property. Although these patterns are arbitrary, each group perceives its own forms of marriage and family as natural. Now let's see what pictures emerge when we view marriage and family theoretically.

The Functionalist Perspective: Functions and Dysfunctions

Functionalists stress that to survive, a society must fulfill basic functions (that is, meet its basic needs). When functionalists look at marriage and family, they examine how they are related to other parts of society, especially the ways that marriage and family contribute to the well-being of society. Let's look at how marriage and family help society survive.

WHY THE FAMILY IS UNIVERSAL

As you've seen, marriage and family take dramatically different forms around the world. Yet the family is universal. The reason for this, say functionalists, is that the family fulfills six needs that are

WHAT AM I SUPPOSED TO LEARN?

After you have read this unit, you should be able to

1 Explain the main ideas of the functionalists on marriage and family.

2 Explain the main ideas of the conflict theorists on marriage and family.

3 Explain the main ideas of the symbolic interactionists on marriage and family.

basic to the survival of every society. These needs, or functions, are (1) economic production, (2) socialization of children, (3) care of the sick and aged, (4) recreation, (5) sexual control, and (6) reproduction. To make certain that these functions are performed, every human group has adopted some form of the family.

FUNCTIONS OF THE INCEST TABOO

Functionalists note that the incest taboo helps families avoid *role confusion*. This makes it easier to socialize children. For example, if father–daughter incest were allowed, how should a wife treat her daughter? Would she be her daughter or the second wife of her husband? Should the daughter consider her mother as a mother or as the first wife? Would her father be a father or a lover? And would the wife be the husband's main wife or the "mother of the other wife"? And if the daughter had a child by her father, what relationships would everyone have? Maternal incest would also lead to complications every bit as confusing as these.

The incest taboo also forces people to look outside the family for marriage partners. Anthropologists theorize that *exogamy* was especially functional for tribal societies, that it forged alliances between tribes that otherwise might have killed each other off. Exogamy still extends social networks today. It adds and builds relationships with the spouse's family and friends.

What different pictures of the family emerge when you apply the functionalist, conflict, and symbolic interactionist perspectives? Can you apply these perspectives to what you see in this photo?

FROM ANOTHER STUDENT . . .

I wish I had taken this course sooner! I loved learning about gender and norms—it explained a lot for me.

—*Zack Hamilton*

The Conflict Perspective: Struggles between Husbands and Wives

Anyone who has been married or who has seen a marriage from the inside knows that—despite a couple's best intentions—conflict is a part of marriage. Conflict is inevitable for two people who live intimately and share most everything in life—from their goals and checkbooks to their bedroom and children. At some point, their desires and approaches to life clash, sometimes mildly and sometimes quite harshly. Conflict among married people is so common that it is the grist of soap operas, movies, songs, and novels.

Power is the source of such conflict in marriage. Who has it? And who resents not having it? Throughout history, husbands have had more power, and wives have resented it. In the United States, as I'm sure you know, wives have gained more and more power in marriage. Do you think that one day wives will have more power than their husbands?

You probably are saying that such a day will never come. But could it be that wives have already reached this point? From time to time, you've seen some surprising things in this book. Before you shake your head, look at Figure 11.1. Based on a national sample, this figure shows who makes decisions concerning the family's finances and purchases, what to do on the weekends, and even what to watch on television. As you can see, wives now have more control over the family purse and make more of these decisions than do their husbands. These findings are such a surprise that we await confirmation by future studies.

The Symbolic Interactionist Perspective: Gender, Housework, and Child Care

Now let's see what light the symbolic interactionists cast on marriage and family.

FIGURE 11.1 **Who Makes the Decisions at Home?**

- Wife makes more decisions — 43%
- Husband makes more decisions — 26%
- Couples divide decisions equally — 31%

Note: Based on a nationally representative sample, with questions on who chooses weekend activities, buys things for the home, decides what to watch on television, and manages household finances.

Source: Morin and Cohn 2008.

CHANGES IN TRADITIONAL GENDER ORIENTATIONS

Throughout the generations, housework and child care have been regarded as "women's work," and men have resisted getting involved. As women put in more hours at paid work, men gradually began to do more housework and to take on more responsibility for the care of their children. Ever so slowly, cultural ideas changed, and over the past few years housework, care of children, and paid labor have come to be regarded as the responsibilities of both men and women.

Remember that symbolic interactionists focus on meaning, or ideas. To understand what responsibilities husbands and wives consider "right" for themselves is a key to understanding their behavior. When ideas of right and wrong change, it leads to new norms that guide behavior in new directions. It was once considered "right" for a wife who worked at a full-time paid job to also do all the housework. But no longer. Let's examine these changing ideas of "proper" responsibilities and relationships in the family.

WHO DOES WHAT?

Figure 11.2 illustrates several significant changes that have taken place in U.S. families. The first is likely to surprise you. If you look closely at this figure, you will see that not only are husbands spending more time taking care of the children but so are wives.

What different pictures of the family emerge when you apply the functionalist, conflict, and symbolic interactionist perspectives? Can you apply these perspectives to what you see in this photo?

FIGURE 11.2 **In Two-Paycheck Marriages, How Do Husbands and Wives Divide Their Responsibilities?**

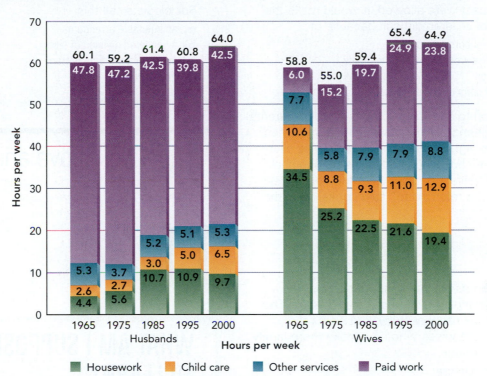

Source: *By the author. Based on Bianchi et al. 2006. Housework hours are from Table 5.1, child care from Table 4.1, and work hours and total hours from Table 3.4. "Other services" is derived by subtracting the hours for housework, child care, and paid work from the total hours.*

This is fascinating: *Both* husbands and wives are spending more time in child care.

Are children really getting *more* attention from their parents than they used to? This flies in the face of our mythical past, the *Leave-It-to-Beaver* images that color our perception of how things used to be. You know that families are not leisurely lolling through their days as huge paychecks flow in. So if parents are spending more time with their children, just where is the time coming from?

Today's parents are squeezing out more hours for their children by spending less time on social activities and by participating less in organizations. But this accounts for only some of the time. Look again at Figure 11.2, but this time focus on the hours that wives spend doing housework. You can see that the time women spend doing housework has dropped by 15 hours a week. The mothers now have a lot more time to spend with the children. Men spend about 4 more hours a week with the children than they used to, but their hours don't seem to come from a reduction elsewhere. They seem to have been added to the men's weekly total.

Finally, from Figure 11.2, you can see differences in how husbands and wives spend their time. In what sociologists call a *gendered division of labor*, husbands still take the primary responsibility for earning the income and wives take the primary responsibility for taking care of the house and children. You can also see that a shift is taking place in this traditional gender

division of labor: Wives are spending more time than they used to earning the family income, while husbands are spending more time than they used to on housework and child care. These trends are part of changing ideas of gender—of what is considered "appropriate" for husbands and wives. From these fundamental changes, we can anticipate greater marital equality in the future.

UNIT 11.2 // TESTING MYSELF
DID I LEARN IT?   ANSWERS ARE AT THE END OF THE CHAPTER

1. At this point, Susan was ahead of Letitia on her reading. She said, "Did you know that the functionalists focus on how marriage and family help societies survive?" "No, I didn't. How do they do that?" asked Letitia." "They analyze six basic functions that families perform. They are
   a. entertainment, socialization, care, recreation, status, and realization
   b. escape, study, caffeine, recreation, sex, and reproduction
   c. election, socialization, creativity, realization, status, and retrospection
   d. economic production, socialization of children, care of the sick and aged, recreation, sexual control, and reproduction

2. "Did they bring up the incest taboo again?" asked Letitia. "Yes. Functionalists say that the incest taboo helps society survive by pushing people to marry outside the family. This expands ties to other people. Besides, if incest were allowed, it would make the socialization of children difficult because of
   a. what the neighbors would say
   b. how the police would break up the family
   c. role confusion
   d. the physical harm to the children

3. Susan went on to say, "You know how Deb's parents are always fighting? Well, I have a different idea on this now. Their fighting is related to struggles over power between husbands and wives that go back thousands of years." "I know what theoretical perspective you are referring to," said Letitia. "It is the
   a. functionalist
   b. conflict
   c. symbolic interactionist
   d. power

4. "I know the times are changing, but I didn't know things were changing this much," said Susan. "The chapter quotes a national study, and it isn't the husbands but the wives who now make more family decisions regarding
   a. finances and purchases
   b. what to do on the weekends,
   c. what to watch on television
   d. finances, purchases, what to do on the weekends, and what to watch on television

5. Susan added, "Can you guess what theoretical perspective this one refers to? Ideas that associate housework and child care with women have changed to include men." "I know what that would be," said Letitia. "You're referring to changing ideas, or meaning, which is a symbol. So it is
   a. meaning theory
   b. functionalism
   c. conflict theory
   d. symbolic interactionism

6. "I've got to tell you about one of the findings that blew away a stereotype I had," said Susan. "I always thought that families in the past spent a lot more time with their children. Now I read that both mothers and fathers are spending more time with their children." "How can that be, since they are so busy?" asked Letitia. "Well, the main reason is that wives
   a. have cut down on their paid work
   b. are getting along better with their mothers-in-law and now get more help
   c. are doing less housework
   d. have pressured their husbands to take more responsibility for the children

7. "I've got to mention a term that you should know," said Susan. "Husbands and wives spend their time in different ways. Wives put in more time on child care, and husbands spend more time doing paid work. Sociologists call this
   a. an equitable arrangement
   b. a gendered division of labor
   c. an inequitable time pattern
   d. time bartering

UNIT 11.3

Love and Marriage

WHAT AM I SUPPOSED TO LEARN?

After you have read this unit, you should be able to

1 Explain how love works and what the social channels of love and marriage are.

What do sociologists mean by the phrase, the social channels of love?

Your ideas of marriage and family should be broadening at this point. Now let's see how your ideas of love hold up.

Love and Courtship in Global Perspective

Have you ever been sick over love? Some people can't eat, and they become obsessed with thoughts of the one they love. When neuroscientists studied "love sickness," they found that it is real: Love feelings light up the same area of the brain that lights up when cocaine addicts are craving coke (Fisher et al. 2010).

Evidently, then, love can be an addiction. From your own experience, you probably know the power of **romantic love**—mutual sexual attraction and idealized feelings about one another. People in most cultures talk about similar experiences (Jankowiak and Fischer 1992), but not all of them follow our pattern and make love the basis of marriage.

For more on love as the reason for marriage, read *Making It Personal*.

> **romantic love** feelings of sexual attraction accompanied by an idealization of the other

MAKING IT PERSONAL
Finding Love

You know that in our culture love is considered the only real, true basis of marriage. You also know that people get married for many reasons other than love, especially for economic security. But love is the ideal, the only true reason for marriage.

We even try to measure love, although in a rather rough way: "Do you love him?" (You see, love exists.) "How much do you love him?" (You can measure love.) "Do you love him enough to get married?" (You can even measure love so you know you have enough to build marriage on it.)

"We might not have much money, but our love will see us through." (Love is powerful.)

These are just part of the American beliefs about love. More than likely you learned them as you grew up, and they have become part of your world view.

If you had been reared in India, you would have learned that love comes *after* marriage. Your father and, to a lesser extent, your mother would have arranged your marriage, and from your culture you would know that love follows marriage. And guess what? That's just what happens.

Are you *in love*? Are you looking for *true love*? Can you see your culture at work?

> ***IF YOU WANT TO LEARN MORE*** about love in India,
>
> **Read** more from the author: East is East and West is West: Love and Arranged Marriage in India in **mysoclab**

Because love plays such a significant role in Western life—and often is regarded as the *only* proper basis for marriage—social scientists have probed this concept with the tools of the trade: experiments, questionnaires, interviews, and observations. In a fascinating experiment, psychologists Donald Dutton and Arthur Aron discovered that fear can produce romantic love (Rubin 1985). Here's what they did.

About 230 feet above the Capilano River in North Vancouver, British Columbia, a rickety footbridge sways in the wind. It makes you feel like you might fall into the rocky gorge below. A more solid footbridge crosses only ten feet above the shallow stream.

The experimenters had an attractive woman approach men who were crossing these bridges. She told them she was studying "the effects of exposure to scenic attractions on creative expression." She showed them a picture, and they wrote down their associations. The sexual imagery in their stories showed that the men on the unsteady, frightening bridge were more sexually aroused than were the men on the solid bridge. More of these men also called the young woman afterward—supposedly to get information about the study.

If you are reading closely (and I know that you might be skimming), you may have noticed that this research was really about sexual attraction, not love. And this is how romantic love usually begins. You find yourself sexually attracted to someone, and you spend time with that person. If you discover mutual interests, you may label your feelings "love." Apparently, then, *romantic love has two components*. The first is emotional, a feeling of sexual attraction. The second is cognitive, a label that you attach to your feelings. If you attach this label, you describe yourself as being "in love."

For a little more on this, read *Making It Personal* below.

MAKING IT PERSONAL
How Love Happens

Yes, I know that in doing our analyses, we sociologists can take the fun out of things. Here we change the excitement and thrill of love into two labels, and one called cognitive at that.

But think about it. Doesn't this give you more insight into how love "happens"?

Consider just this: Some people apply the cognitive label and then withdraw it. They "fall madly in love," but then get rejected. They then say, "I wasn't really in love, after all."

And then there are parents who refuse to let a child apply the label. "It's just puppy love," they say. That is, this is not real love. It is just a fleeting feeling.

Anything like this ever happen to you?

Can you see how "love" requires both the feeling and the label?

Why does romantic love require both a feeling and a label?

Marriage

In the typical case, marriage in the United States is preceded by "love," but, contrary to folklore, whatever love is, it certainly is not blind. That is, love does not hit us willy-nilly, as if Cupid had shot darts blindly into a crowd. If it did, marital patterns would be unpredictable. An examination of who marries whom, however, reveals that love follows social channels.

THE SOCIAL CHANNELS OF LOVE AND MARRIAGE

The most highly predictable social channels are age, education, social class, and race–ethnicity. For example, a Latina with a college degree whose parents are both physicians is likely to fall in love with and marry a Latino slightly older than herself who has graduated from college. Similarly, a girl who drops out of high school and whose parents are on welfare is likely to fall in love with and marry a man who comes from a background similar to hers.

Sociologists use the term **homogamy** (huh-MOG-uh-mee) to refer to the tendency of people who have similar characteristics to marry one another. (Yes, sociologists could have called this *similarity,* but for whatever reason, we prefer more technical sounding words.) Homogamy occurs largely as a result of *propinquity,* or spatial nearness. (We sociologists do talk like this. Aren't you glad that I avoid this when I

homogamy the tendency of people with similar characteristics to marry one another

can?) This simply means that you will likely "fall in love" with and marry someone who lives near you or whom you meet at school, church, or work. The people with whom you associate are far from a random sample of the population. Social filters produce neighborhoods, schools, and places of worship that follow racial–ethnic and social class lines.

As with all social patterns, there are exceptions. Although 92 percent of Americans who marry choose someone of their same racial–ethnic background, 8 percent do not. Because there are 61 million married couples in the United States, those 8 percent add up to a large number, over 4 million couples (*Statistical Abstract* 2012:Table 60).

One of the more dramatic changes in U.S. marriage patterns is the increase in marriages between African Americans and whites. It is difficult today to realize how norm-shattering such marriages used to be, but they once were illegal in 40 states (Staples 2008). People in Mississippi felt so strongly about such marriages that—and this might be hard for you to believe—their penalty for a black and white getting married was *life in prison* (Crossen 2004b). Despite the risks, a few couples crossed the "color line," but it took the social upheaval of the 1960s to break this barrier permanently. In 1967, the U.S. Supreme Court struck down the state laws that prohibited such marriages.

Figure 11.3 illustrates this change. Look at the race–ethnicity of the husbands and wives in these marriages. Can you see that here, too, Cupid's arrows don't hit random targets? Why do you think this particular pattern exists?

FIGURE 11.3 **Marriages between Whites and African Americans: The Race–Ethnicity of Husbands and Wives**

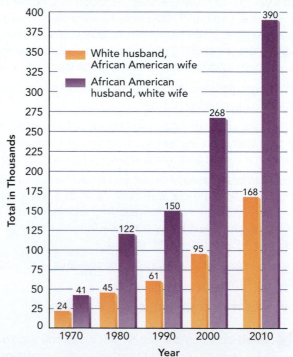

Source: By the author. Based on Statistical Abstract of the United States *1990:Table 53; 2012:Table 60.*

UNIT 11.3 // TESTING MYSELF
DID I LEARN IT? ANSWERS ARE AT THE END OF THE CHAPTER

1. Katie told Wilbur: "I just read about love." "Not again," said Wilbur. "This is different," said Katie. "It's scientific. I found out that love can be a form of addiction. This is because love feelings

   a. are real
   b. can't be turned off by will power
   c. bring both emotional highs and emotional lows
   d. light up the same area of the brain that lights up when cocaine addicts are craving coke

2. "I know what you are talking about," said Wilbur, recalling Natasha. "I remember how we had to be together all the time. Now I know that our feelings were idealized, but I didn't realize it then." "I remember," replied Katie. "You are referring to

   a. sexual addiction   b. platonic love
   c. romantic love   d. a solid basis for marriage

3. "I read that love is different in India," said Katie. "How can that be? Love is love," reasoned Wilbur. "Well," said Katie, "Here love comes before marriage, but in India

   a. they don't have love
   b. they don't have marriage
   c. love comes after marriage
   d. love comes during childhood, what we call "puppy love," but they call it real love

4. "I read about an experiment where an attractive woman met guys on a swaying foot bridge high above a river and met other guys on a steady, lower bridge. She asked the men some questions. The guys on the high bridge used more sexual imagery. And they were more likely to call the girl, too," said Katie. "What's the point?" asked Wilbur. "It is that

   a. fear can produce love
   b. bridges are dangerous places
   c. you never know what to expect on a swaying foot bridge
   d. bridges are good places to meet someone

5. "I still don't get the point," sighed Wilbur. "I don't think you are even talking about love. It sounds more like the guys on the swaying bridge had more sexual interest." "That's right," agreed Katie. "But the real point is that romantic love

   a. can happen anywhere, even on bridges
   b. does not exist
   c. frightens people
   d. is preceded by sexual interest

6. "Another way of putting this, which is what the sociologists do," said Katie, "is that romantic love has two components. The first is emotional, a feeling of sexual attraction. The second is

   a. almost like the first, but less emotional
   b. almost like the first, but even more emotional
   c. cognitive, a label that we attach to our feelings
   d. called the "recovery phase," when the individuals start to come back to their senses

7. "In my reading, I learned that it used to be illegal for blacks and whites to marry," said Katie. "In Mississippi, people who broke this law could even be sent to prison for life! Then in 1967

   a. the U.S. Supreme Court struck down the state laws that prohibited such marriages
   b. the people got fed up with these laws, and there were massive protests across the United States
   c. people began to break this law
   d. there were so many of these marriages that the states had to repeal these laws

8. "Did you learn anything else about black/white marriages?" asked Wilbur. "I learned that they follow social channels," answered Katie, pleased to use this phrase. "Their main pattern is

   a. a sharp decrease during the past five years
   b. many marriages in the North and West and few in the South and Midwest
   c. a black husband and a white wife
   d. a white husband and a black wife

UNIT 11.4   Family Transitions

WHAT AM I SUPPOSED TO LEARN?

After you have read this unit, you should be able to

1 Explain changes in preferences in number of children, what makes good day care, the empty nest, adultolescents, and widowhood.

After a couple marries, they go through a series of transitions. These transitions differ from couple to couple, including setting

How are your ideas of the ideal number of children to have related to your culture?

up housekeeping, changing jobs, moving to another community, and so on. We don't have space to follow all of these transitions, so we'll focus on just a few. Let's begin with having children.

Childbirth

IDEAL FAMILY SIZE

Figure 11.4, which shows how many children Americans consider ideal, illustrates a significant historical shift. You can trace Americans changing preference from larger to smaller families.

The research on which Figure 11.4 is based shows some interesting divides. One is by religion, not between Protestants and Roman Catholics, who give the same answers, but by church attendance. People who attend church services more often prefer larger families than those who attend less often. Recent polls have also revealed a divide that no one expected: Younger Americans (ages 18 to 34) prefer larger families more than do those who are older than age 34 (Gallup Poll, June 30, 2011). We don't have the answer to this one figured out yet, and we don't know if this is a flash in the pan or a trend that will continue.

Regarding the number of children you want, take a look at *Making It Personal* on the next page.

Child Rearing

You know that in most families it takes an income from both husband and wife to survive. With mothers and fathers spending so many hours away from home at work, we must ask: Who's minding the kids while the parents are at work?

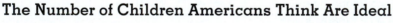

FIGURE 11.4

The Number of Children Americans Think Are Ideal

— Larger Families: Three or more children

— Smaller Families: Zero, one, or two children

Source: Gallup Poll 2011.

MAKING IT PERSONAL
How Many Children Do You Want?

Throughout this text, I have stressed *society within you*. One of the fascinating things about sociology is to learn how your experiences in society penetrate your very being, influencing both your behavior and your orientations to life. Here is another significant example–how something as intimate and personal as the number of children you want is influenced by society.

The easiest way to see this is to look at Figure 11.4 and put yourself into the past. If you had grown up in the 1940s, you very likely would have wanted three or more children. But since you are living in this current historical period, it is more likely that you consider two children to be ideal. It is also likely that you want one boy and one girl. This is not necessarily the case, of course, for these are averages.

More and more couples today prefer to have no children at all. If you are among them, this same point applies. Whatever the number of children that you see as ideal, you probably can point to experiences that have led to your having your particular idea.

The typical American family has just two children. The range is from zero to 19. Shown here are Michelle and Jim Bob Duggar of Tontitown, Arkansas, with their 19 children.

FIGURE 11.5 **Who Takes Care of Preschoolers While Their Mothers Are at Work?**

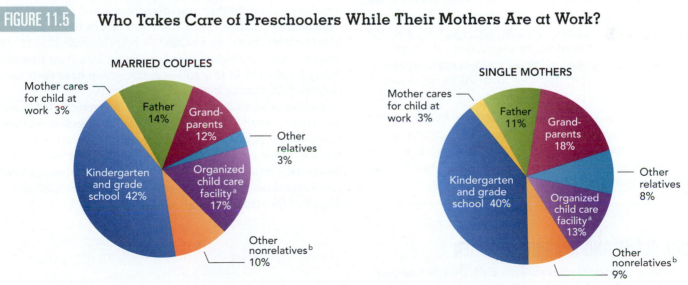

MARRIED COUPLES
- Mother cares for child at work 3%
- Father 14%
- Grandparents 12%
- Other relatives 3%
- Organized child care facility[a] 17%
- Other nonrelatives[b] 10%
- Kindergarten and grade school 42%

SINGLE MOTHERS
- Mother cares for child at work 3%
- Father 11%
- Grandparents 18%
- Other relatives 8%
- Organized child care facility[a] 13%
- Other nonrelatives[b] 9%
- Kindergarten and grade school 40%

[a]Includes day care centers, nursery schools, preschools, and Head Start programs.

[b]Includes in-home babysitters and other nonrelatives providing care in either the child's or the provider's home.

Source: America's Children in Brief 2010: Table FAM3A.

MARRIED COUPLES AND SINGLE MOTHERS

Two of five U.S. children are born to women who are not married, and many of the married women get divorced. Are there differences in the child care arrangements of single and married mothers? As you can see from Figure 11.5, their overall arrangements are similar. A main difference, though, is that when married women are at work, the child is more likely to be under the father's care or in day care. For single mothers, grandparents and other relatives are more likely to fill in for the absent father.

DAY CARE

Figure 11.5 also shows that about one of four children is in day care. Apparently only a minority of U.S. day care centers offer high-quality care as measured by whether they provide safety, stimulating learning activities, and emotional warmth (Bergmann 1995; Blau 2000; Belsky 2009). A primary reason for this dismal situation is the low salaries paid to day care workers, who average only about $17,000 a year ("Career Guide…" 2011).

To see how you can use sociology to get better care for your children, read *Making It Personal*.

MAKING IT PERSONAL
Choosing Day Care

It is difficult to judge the quality of day care. Things might look okay, but you don't know what takes place when you are not there. What can you do about it? If you ever look for day care for your children, keep these two factors in mind, the best predictors that your children will receive quality care: staff who have taken courses in early childhood development and a low ratio of children per staff member (Blau 2000; Belsky et al. 2007).

Then if you have nagging fears that your children might be neglected or even abused, choose a center that streams live Webcam images on the Internet. While at work, you can "visit" each room of the day care center via cyberspace and monitor your toddler's activities and care.

SOCIAL CLASS AND REARING CHILDREN

Do you think that social class makes a difference in how people rear their children? If you answered *yes*, you are right. But what difference? And why? Sociologists have found that working-class and middle-class parents have fundamentally different views of children. Working-class parents tend to think of children as wild flowers that develop naturally. Middle-class parents, in contrast, are more likely to think of children as garden flowers that need a lot of nurturing if they are to bloom (Lareau 2002). These contrasting views of wild flowers and

hot-house plants make a world of difference. Working-class parents are more likely to set limits on their children and then let them choose their own activities. Middle-class parents are more likely to try to push their children into activities that they think will develop their children's thinking and social skills. On a very practical level, the children of working-class parents play sports "for the fun of it," while the children of middle-class parents play sports to "learn cooperative teamwork."

Staying Home Longer

The later stages of family life bring their own pleasures and problems. One of them is older children staying home longer. Note that I was very careful not to say whether this is a pleasure or a problem.

"ADULTOLESCENTS" AND THE NOT-SO-EMPTY NEST

Adolescents, especially the young men, used to leave home after finishing high school. (My high school graduation present was a suitcase. I kid you not.) When the last child left home at about age 17 to 19, the husband and wife were left with what was called an *empty nest*. (See, sociologists don't always choose big words.) Today's nest is not as empty as it used to be. With young people expected to spend more years in school, combined with the high cost of establishing a household, U.S. children are leaving home later. Many stay home during college, and others move back after college. Some strike out on their own, but then find the cost or responsibility too great and return home. Much to their own disappointment, some of these "boomerang children" even leave and return to the parents' home several times. As a result, 18 percent of all U.S. 25- to 29-year-olds (over two million) are living with their parents. About 15 percent of this still-at-home group have their own children (U.S. Census Bureau 2010:Table A2).

Although these "adultolescents" enjoy the protection of home, they have to work out issues of remaining dependent on their parents at the same time that they are grappling with concerns and fears about establishing independent lives. For the parents, "boomerang children" mean not only a disruption of routines but also disagreements about turf, authority, and responsibilities—items they thought were long ago resolved.

Widowhood

Let's look at one more transition. As you know, women are more likely than men to become widowed. The two simple reasons are that, on average, women live longer than men, and they usually marry men older than they are. For either women or men, the death of a spouse tears at the self, clawing at identities that had merged through the years. With the one who had become an essential part of the self gone, the survivor, as in adolescence, once again confronts the perplexing question, "Who am I?"

Widow in Galicia, Spain. As in New Orleans, which was a Spanish settlement, the custom in Spain is not to bury the dead but to place them above ground.

The death of a spouse produces what is called the *widowhood effect*: The impact of the death is so strong that surviving spouses tend to die earlier than expected. The "widowhood effect" is not even across the board, however, and those who have gone through anticipatory grief suffer fewer health consequences (Elwert and Christakis 2008). Apparently learning that a spouse is going to die gives people time to make preparations that smooth the transition—from arranging finances to preparing themselves psychologically for being alone. You can see how saying goodbye and cultivating treasured last memories would help people adjust to the impending death of an intimate companion. Sudden death, in contrast, rips the loved one away, offering no chance for this predeath healing.

UNIT 11.4 // TESTING MYSELF
DID I LEARN IT? ANSWERS ARE AT THE END OF THE CHAPTER

1. "In this unit, I learned something about religion and how many children married couples want," said Katie. "Roman Catholics want more kids than the Protestants, right?" said Wilbur. "No, they want about the same number of children, which was a surprise to me, too. It's that people who attend church more often, both Protestants and Catholics,
   a. spend more time with their children
   b. have less time to take care of their children
   c. prefer larger families
   d. prefer smaller families

2. "I learned something interesting about age and preference for children," added Katie. "What about age?" asked Wilbur. "Compared with Americans over age 34, those who are 18 to 34
   a. prefer smaller families
   b. prefer larger families
   c. are more likely to want twins
   d. are more fearful of bringing children into an uncertain world

3. "I learned something I really like," said Katie. "When I have children and I choose a day care center, I want a good one. I'm going to look for
   a. friendly staff and a low cost
   b. a center located in my own neighbourhood
   c. a new building and top quality equipment
   d. staff who have taken courses in early childhood development and a low ratio of children per staff member

4. "I also learned that working-class and middle-class parents have different ideas about children," said Katie. "What are they?" asked Wilbur. "Working-class parents tend to think of children as wildflowers that develop naturally, but middle-class parents are more likely to think of children as
   a. wild bushes that need to be pruned regularly to keep them in line
   b. weeds that need to be watched or they get out of hand
   c. garden flowers that need a lot of nurturing if they are to bloom
   d. young trees that are going to grow straight and tall

5. "What difference does it make how they think of their children?" asked Wilbur. "It makes a big difference," Katie replied. "It affects their child rearing. Working-class parents are more likely to set limits on their children and then let them choose their own activities. Middle-class parents are more likely to
   a. wait and watch and be more patient
   b. push their children into activities that they think will develop the children's thinking and social skills

   c. get the children's grandparents involved
   d. keep track of their children by using cell phones

6. "Here's something you already know," said Katie. "More and more young people are going back to live with their parents—just like you." "Right," said Wilbur. "I hated doing it, but I couldn't find a job that paid enough for a good apartment. And besides, my mom washes my clothes." "Just pitiful," said Katie. "Anyway, sociologists have a word for people like you. It is
   a. the empty-nesters
   b. slobs
   c. adultolescents
   d. the home returners

7. "I learned another thing that is interesting," said Katie. "When people know that a loved one is going to die,

they make preparations and even go through grief before the person passes away. Because of this, they
   a. hardly miss the person
   b. suffer fewer health consequences
   c. are ready to move on and remarry
   d. spend less money on the funeral

8. "I leaned something else about death and the surviving spouse," said Katie. "When a spouse dies, the surviving spouse tends to die earlier than expected." "Do sociologists have a name for this?" asked Wilbur. "Of course. Those sociologists have a name for almost everything. They call this the
   a. widow maker
   b. pre-death healing factor
   c. health-destroyer
   d. widowhood effect

UNIT 11.5

Racial-Ethnic Diversity

WHAT AM I SUPPOSED TO LEARN?

After you have read this unit, you should be able to

1 Summarize major characteristics of families by racial–ethnic groups.

I know that the last unit was packed with information. There is a lot in this unit, too, but it is shorter and there aren't many terms. Before we begin, it is important for you to understand that there is no such thing as *the* American family. Family life varies widely throughout the United States. The significance of social class, mentioned earlier, will continue to be evident as you study diversity in U.S. families.

African American Families

You can see that the heading reads African American *families*, not *the* African American family. Just as there is no such thing as *the* American family, there is no such thing as *the* African American family. The primary distinction is not between African Americans and other groups, but between social classes (Willie and Reddick 2003). Upper-class African Americans follow their class interests. Because they want to preserve and increase privilege and family fortune, they are especially concerned about the family background of those whom their children marry (Gatewood 1990). To them, marriage is viewed as a merger of family lines. Children of this class marry later than children of other classes.

Middle-class African American families focus on achievement and respectability. Both husband and wife are likely to work outside the home. A central concern is that their children go to college, get good jobs, and marry well—that is, marry people like themselves, educated and hardworking, who want to get ahead in school and pursue a successful career.

African American families in poverty face all the problems that cluster around poverty (Wilson 2007; Bryant et al. 2010). Because the men are likely to be unemployed with few marketable skills, it is difficult for them to fulfill the cultural roles of husband and father. Consequently, these families are likely to be headed by a woman and to have a high rate of births to single women. Divorce and desertion are also more common than among other classes. Sharing scarce resources and "stretching kinship" are primary survival mechanisms. People who have helped out in hard times are considered brothers, sisters, or cousins to whom one owes obligations as though they were blood relatives. Men who are not the biological fathers of their children are given fatherhood status (Stack 1974; Hall 2008). Sociologists use the term *fictive kin* to refer to this stretching of kinship.

From Figure 11.6 you can see that, compared with other groups, African American families are the least likely to be headed by married couples and the most likely to be headed by women. Because African American women tend to go farther in school than African American men, they are more likely than women in other racial–ethnic groups to marry men who are less educated than themselves (Eshleman 2000; Harford 2008).

Latino Families

As Figure 11.6 shows, the proportion of Latino families headed by married couples and women falls in between that of whites and Native Americans. The effects of social class on families, which I just sketched, also apply to Latinos. In addition, families differ by country of origin. Families from Mexico, for example, are more likely to be headed by a married couple than are families from Puerto Rico (*Statistical Abstract* 2012:Table 37). The longer that Latinos have lived in the United States, the more their families resemble those of middle-class Americans (Saenz 2004).

With such wide variety, experts disagree on what is distinctive about Latino families. Some researchers have found that Latino husbands–fathers play a stronger role than husbands–fathers in white and African American families (Vega 1990; Torres et al. 2002). Others point to the Spanish language, the Roman Catholic religion, and a strong family orientation coupled with a disapproval of divorce. There may be some tendencies here, but the variety is so far-ranging that there also are Latino families who are Protestants, don't speak Spanish, and so on. Still others

As with other groups, there is no such thing as the Latino family. Some Latino families speak little or not English, while others have assimilated into U. S. culture to such an extent that they no longer speak Spanish.

emphasize loyalty to the extended family, with an obligation to support relatives in times of need (Cauce and Domenech-Rodriguez 2002), but this, too, is hardly unique to Latino families.

With such variety, you can see how difficult it is to draw generalizations. The sociological point that runs through all studies of Latino families, however, is this: Social class is more important in determining family life than is either being Latino or a family's country of origin.

FIGURE 11.6 **Family Structures: U.S. Families with Children Under Age 18 Headed by Mothers, Fathers, and Both Parents**

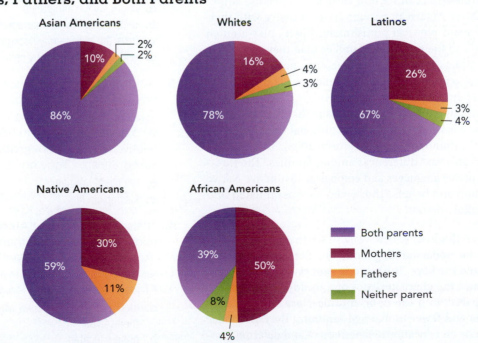

Sources: By the author. For Native Americans, Krieder and Elliot 2009:Table 1. For other groups, Statistical Abstract of the United States 2012:Table 69.

Asian American Families

As you can see from Figure 11.6 on the previous page, Asian American children are more likely than children in other racial–ethnic groups to grow up with both parents. As with the other groups, family life also reflects social class. In addition, because Asian Americans emigrated from many different countries, their family life reflects those many cultures (Jeong and You 2008). As with Latino families, the more time that has passed since their immigration, the less closely their family life reflects the patterns in their country of origin (Glenn 1994; Jeong and You 2008).

Despite such differences, sociologist Bob Suzuki (1985) identified several distinctive characteristics of Asian American families. They tend to retain Confucian values that provide a framework for family life: humanism, collectivity, self-discipline, hierarchy, respect for the elderly, moderation, and obligation. Obligation means that each member of a family owes respect to other family members and has a responsibility never to bring shame on the family. And a child's success brings honor to the family (Zamiska 2004). To control their children, Asian American parents are more likely to use shame and guilt than physical punishment.

Seldom does the ideal translate into the real, and so it is here. The children born to Asian immigrants confront a bewildering world of incompatible expectations—those of the new culture and those of their parents. As a result, they experience more family conflict and emotional problems than do children of Asian Americans who are not immigrants (Meyers 2006; Ying and Han 2008).

Native American Families

Figure 11.6 on the previous page shows the structure of Native American families. You can see how close it is to that of Latinos. In general, Native American parents are permissive with their children and avoid physical punishment. Elders play a much more active role in their children's families than they do in most U.S. families: Elders, especially grandparents, not only provide child care but also teach and discipline children. Like others, Native American families differ by social class.

Perhaps the single-most significant issue that Native American families face is whether to follow traditional values or to assimilate into the dominant culture (Frosch 2008). This primary distinction creates vast differences among families. The traditionals speak native languages and emphasize distinctive Native American values and beliefs. Those who have assimilated into the broader culture do not.

IN SUM: From this brief review, you can see that race–ethnicity signifies little for understanding family life. Rather, social class and culture hold the keys. The more resources a family has, the more it assumes the characteristics of a middle-class nuclear family. Compared with the poor, middle-class families have fewer children and fewer unmarried mothers. They also place greater emphasis on educational achievement and deferred gratification (postponing things you want).

In *Making It Personal,* let's turn to your family.

MAKING IT PERSONAL
Your Family

How does your family compare with those listed here? How does your family's social class make a difference? From what you know about the types of families in the group you identify with, you should be able to see your own family and how the characteristics described here apply to it.

Did it happen like this?

UNIT 11.5 // TESTING MYSELF
DID I LEARN IT? ANSWERS ARE AT THE END OF THE CHAPTER

1. Jorge said, "It is interesting that there is no such thing as the American family or the Latino family." "Are they all the same, then?" asked Carla. ""It isn't that," answered Jorge. "The main distinction is not race–ethnicity, but differences by
   a. length of time in the United States
   b. region of the country
   c. age of the family head
   d. social class

2. Jorge stated, "I found out that upper-class families play more of a role in who their children marry. One of the primary concerns of upper-class African American families is that the spouses of their children
   a. might switch allegiance
   b. understand how to manage the family fortune
   c. have the right family background
   d. will not have too many children themselves

3. "And you know that African American families in poverty have more divorce and desertion, right?" George asked. "Sort of," said Carla. "They also treat people who have helped out in hard times like they are blood relatives." "Do sociologists have a name for this?" asked Susan. "They do. It is
   a. nonblood relatives   b. fictive kin
   c. kinship circle   d. hard-time family

4. "I also found out that African American women tend to go farther in school than African American men." "And?" asked Carla. "Well," Jorge answered, "one result is that compared with women in other groups, African American women are
   a. more likely to marry men who are less educated than themselves
   b. more educated
   c. getting better jobs
   d. paid more

5. "What did you find out about Latino families?" asked Carla. "I found out that there is such a variety of Latino families that it is hard to generalize," Jorge stated. "But I also found out that the longer that Latinos live in the United States, the more

   a. they miss the old country
   b. likely they are to own boats and motor homes
   c. money they save
   d. their families resemble those of middle-class Americans

6. "How about Asian American families?" asked Carla. "One of the main differences," said Jorge, "is that compared with all other groups, their children are more likely to

   a. play video games   b. be on probation
   c. grow up with both parents   d. feel insecure

7. "They also have an interesting Confucian concept called obligation. By this, they mean that each member of a family

   a. owes respect to other family members and has a responsibility never to bring shame on the family
   b. is assigned duties to perform within the family
   c. must always keep the family informed of where he or she is going
   d. cannot date without getting the parent's permission

8. "What about Native American families?" asked Carla. "Well," said Jorge, "I think one of the main distinctions is that they have to make a hard decision." "What's that?" asked Carla. "They have to decide whether to

   a. count elders as part of the family unit
   b. let elders live with them
   c. grant or withhold authority to elders
   d. assimilate or to follow traditional ways

UNIT 11.6

More Diversity

WHAT AM I SUPPOSED TO LEARN?

After you have read this unit, you should be able to

1 Describe some of the diversity in U.S. families.

There certainly is much more diversity in U.S. families than racial–ethnic distinctions, which, as you just saw, is not much. Let's take a brief look at one-parent families, families without children, blended families, and gay and lesbian families.

One-Parent Families

Another indication of how extensively U.S. families are changing is the increase in one-parent families. From Figure 7, you can see that the percentage of U.S. children who live with two parents (not necessarily their biological parents) has dropped sharply. The concerns—even alarm—that are often expressed about one-parent families may have more to do with their poverty than with children being reared by one parent. Because women head most one-parent families, these families tend to be poor. Although most divorced women earn less than their former husbands, four of five (81 percent) of children of divorce live with their mothers (U.S. Census Bureau 2010:Table C3).

To understand the typical one-parent family, then, we need to view it through the lens of poverty, for that is its primary source of strain. The results are serious, not just for these parents and their children but also for society. Children from one-parent families are more likely to have behavioral problems in school, drop out of school, get arrested, have physical health problems, have emotional problems, and get divorced

(McLanahan and Sandefur 1994; McLanahan and Schwartz 2002; Amato and Cheadle 2005; Wen 2008; Waldfogel et al. 2010). If female, they are more likely to have sex at a younger age and to bear children while still unmarried teenagers.

Couples without Children

Most married women give birth, but about one of five do not (Dye 2008). This figure is *double* what it was twenty years ago. As you can see from Figure 11.8, having no children varies by racial–ethnic group, with whites and Latinas representing the extremes. Some couples are infertile, but most childless couples have made a *choice* to not have children—and they prefer the term *childfree* rather than *childless*. Some decide before marriage that they will never have children, often to attain a sense of freedom—to pursue a career, to be able to change jobs, to travel, and to have less stress (Letherby 2002; Koropeckyj-Cox 2007). Some couples take a different route: They simply postponed the date they were going to have their first child until either it was too late to have children or it seemed too uncomfortable to add a child to their lifestyle.

With trends firmly in place—more education and careers for women, advances in contraception, legal abortion, the high cost of rearing children, and an emphasis on possessing more material things—the proportion of women who never bear children is likely to increase. Consider this statement in a newsletter:

We are DINKS (Dual Incomes, No Kids). We are happily married. I am 43; my wife is 42. We have been married for

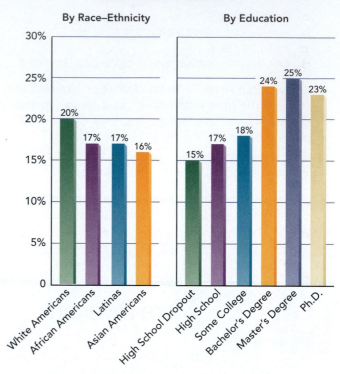

FIGURE 11.8 **What Percentage of U.S. Married Women Ages 40–44 Never Give Birth?**

Source: By the author. Based on Livingston and Cohn 2010.

almost twenty years... . Our investment strategy has a lot to do with our personal philosophy: "You can have kids—or you can have everything else!"

IF YOU WANT TO LEARN MORE about couples who can't have children but want them so much they rent uteruses,

Read more from the author: Rent-a-Womb: How Much for Your Uterus? in **mysoclab**

Blended Families

The **blended family**, one whose members were once part of other families, is an important type of family in the United States. Two divorced people who marry and each bring their children into a new family unit form a blended family. With divorce common, millions of children spend some of their childhood in blended families. One of their main characteristics is complicated relationships. I've never seen a better explanation of

blended family a family whose members were once part of other families

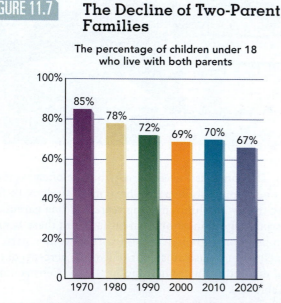

FIGURE 11.7 **The Decline of Two-Parent Families**

The percentage of children under 18 who live with both parents

*Author's estimate. 2010 is based on slight increases since 2000

Source: By the author. Based on Statistical Abstract of the United States 1995:Table 79; 2012:Table 69.

how complicated they can become than this description written by one of my freshman students:

I live with my dad. I should say that I live with my dad, my brother (whose mother and father are also my mother and father), my half sister (whose father is my dad, but whose mother is my father's last wife), and two stepbrothers and stepsisters (children of my father's current wife). My father's wife (my current stepmother, not to be confused with his second wife who, I guess, is no longer my stepmother) is pregnant, and soon we all will have a new brother or sister. Or will it be a half brother or half sister?

If you can't figure this out, I don't blame you. I have trouble myself. It gets very complicated around Christmas. Should we all stay together? Split up and go to several other homes? Who do we buy gifts for, anyway?

Gay and Lesbian Families

Although a handful of U.S. states allow people of the same sex to marry, 41 states have laws that prohibit same-sex marriages (Dematteis 2011). Walking a fine conceptual tightrope, some states recognize "registered domestic partnerships," giving legal status to same-sex unions but avoiding the term *marriage*. The result is that most gay and lesbian couples lack both legal marriage and the legal protection of registered "partnerships."

Gay and lesbian couples live throughout the United States, but about half live in just twenty cities, with the greatest concentrations in San Francisco, Los Angeles, Atlanta, New York City, and Washington, D.C. About one-fifth of gay and lesbian couples were previously married to heterosexuals. Some 22 percent of female couples and 5 percent of male couples have children from their earlier heterosexual marriages (Bianchi and Casper 2000).

What are same-sex relationships like? Like everything else in life, these couples cannot be painted with a single brush stroke. As it does for opposite-sex couples, social class significantly shapes their orientations to life. Sociologists Philip Blumstein and Pepper Schwartz (1985), who interviewed same-sex couples, found their main struggles to be housework, money, careers, problems with relatives, and sexual adjustment. If these sound familiar, they should be, as they are the same problems that heterosexual couples face. Some find that their sexual orientation brings discrimination, which can add stress to their relationship (Todosijevic et al. 2005). The children they rear have about the same adjustment as children reared by heterosexual parents (Gederen et al. 2012) and are no more likely to have a gay or lesbian sexual orientation (Farr et al. 2010; Tasker 2010). Same-sex couples are more likely to break up, and one argument for legalizing gay marriages is that this will make these relationships more stable. Where same-sex marriages are legal, like opposite-sex marriages, to break them requires negotiating around legal obstacles.

UNIT 11.6 // TESTING MYSELF
DID I LEARN IT? ANSWERS ARE AT THE END OF THE CHAPTER

1. Concerns are often expressed about one-parent families. These concerns may have more to do with this than with children being reared by one parent
   a. lack of education
   b. negative urban environments
   c. that there are so many missing fathers
   d. poverty

2. Compared with children who are reared by both parents, children from one-parent families are more likely to drop out of school, get arrested, have physical and emotional health problems, and
   a. have higher incomes
   b. complete college
   c. get divorced
   d. have higher intelligence

3. Some couples without children are infertile, but a more common reason is that couples choose not to have children. Another route to not having children is
   a. interference from in-laws
   b. postponing having children until it is too late
   c. military service
   d. separation because of prison

4. Couples who choose not to have children prefer this term to refer to themselves
   a. childfree
   b. childless
   c. childbound
   d. avante guard

5. This term refers to families whose members were once part of other families
   a. partial families
   b. impartial families
   c. homogenized families
   d. blended families

6. Of gay and lesbian couples, about this percentage had earlier heterosexual marriages
   a. 5
   b. 10
   c. 20
   d. 50

7. The primary problems experienced by gay and lesbian couples

    a. are decreasing because of greater acceptance of such relationships

    b. are the same as those of heterosexual couples

    c. create more emotional strain than those experienced by heterosexual couples

    d. focus around their sexuality

UNIT 11.7

Current Trends

Among the many changes in U.S. family life is women postponing having their first child until they are in their 30s, and for a few even their 40s.

WHAT AM I SUPPOSED TO LEARN?

After you have read this unit, you should be able to

1   Explain major changes in age at first marriage and childbirth and in cohabitation.

Nothing stays the same, or so it seems. And it certainly doesn't when it comes to marriage and family life in the United States. You have read about some of these changes already, and now we'll focus on two fundamental changes: postponing marriage and children and cohabitation.

Postponing Marriage and Childbirth

Figure 11.9 on the next page illustrates one of the most significant changes in U.S. marriages. As you can see, in 1890, the typical first-time bride was 22 years old and her husband was 4 years older. Then for 60 years the age at first marriage dropped. By 1950, the average first-time groom hadn't even celebrated his 23rd birthday. His bride had just left her teens. For about twenty years, there was little change. But then, about 1970, the average age started a sharp increase, which has continued for the past 40 years. *Today's average first-time bride and groom are older than at any other time in U.S. history.*

Postponing marriage is what you see all around you, so it may surprise you to learn that *most* U.S. women used to be married by the time they turned 24. Look at Figure 11.10 on the next page. The percentage of women ages 20 to 24 who are unmarried is now more than *double* what it was in 1970. One result is that the average U.S. woman doesn't have her first child until a couple of months after her 25th birthday, also the highest in U.S. history (Mathews and Hamilton 2009).

These are fundamental breaks with the past, and sociologists point to a simple explanation: cohabitation. Although Americans have postponed the age at which they first marry, they have *not* postponed the age at which they first set up housekeeping with someone of the opposite sex. Let's look at this trend.

Cohabitation

Figure 11.11 on page 374 shows the increase in **cohabitation**, adults living together in a sexual relationship without being married. This figure is one of the most remarkable in sociology. Hardly ever do we have totals that rise this steeply and consistently. From a furtive activity, cohabitation has moved into the mainstream, and cohabitation is *ten times* more common today than it was in the 1970s. About two-thirds of people who marry today have cohabited (Huang et al. 2011). Cohabitation is now so common that about 40 percent of U.S. children will spend some time in a cohabiting family (Scommegna 2002).

What is the difference between cohabitation and marriage? There is a one-word answer: *commitment.* In marriage, the assumption is

cohabitation unmarried couples living together in a sexual relationship

FIGURE 11.9 | **When Do Americans Marry? The Changing Age at First Marriage**

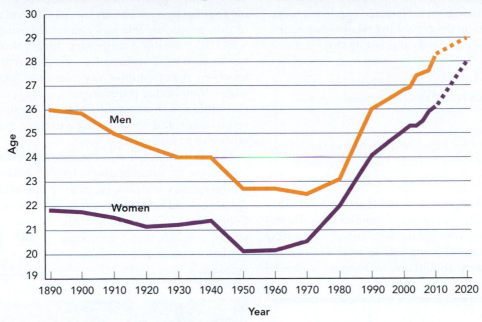

Note: This is the median age at first marriage. The broken lines indicate the author's estimate.

Source: By the author. Based on U.S. Census Bureau 2010.

FIGURE 11.10 | **Americans Ages 20 to 24 Who Are Married**

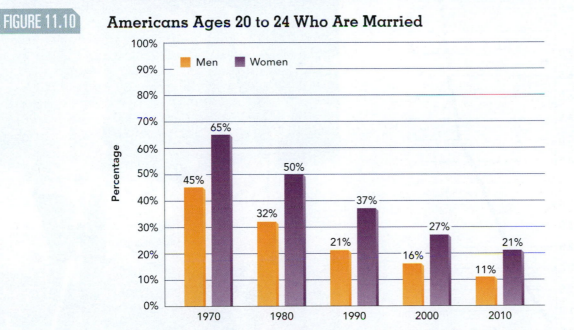

Source: By the author. Based on Statistical Abstract of the United States 1993:Table 60; 2002:Table 48; 2012:Table 57.

permanence; in cohabitation, couples agree to remain together for "as long as it works out." For marriage, individuals make public vows that legally bind them as a couple; for cohabitation, they simply move in together. Marriage requires a judge to authorize its termination; if a cohabiting relationship sours, the couple separates, telling friends and family that "it didn't work out."

> *IF YOU WANT TO LEARN MORE* about what happens to couples who cohabit,
>
> **Read** more from the author: You Want Us to Live Together? What Do You Mean by That? in **mysoclab**

Are the marriages of couples who lived together before they married stronger than the marriages of couples who did not cohabit? It would seem they would be, wouldn't it? Cohabiting couples have the advantage of being able to work out real-life problems before they marry. To find out, sociologists compared

their divorce rates. It turns out that couples who cohabit before marriage were *more* likely to divorce (Lichter and Qian 2008). The reason, suggested some sociologists, was because *cohabiting* relationships are so easy to end (Dush et al. 2003). Because of this, people are less picky about choosing someone to live with ("It's probably a temporary thing") than choosing someone to marry ("This is really serious"). After living together, however, many couples experience a "push" toward marriage—from having common possessions, pets, and children to the subtle and not-so-subtle hints of family and friends. As a result, many end up marrying a partner that they would not otherwise have chosen.

Now that cohabitation has become a part of the courtship/mating process, the initial findings of higher divorce are washing out. Of the recently married, the divorce rate of those who did and did not cohabit before marriage is about the same (Manning and Cohen 2011). If this finding holds, we can conclude that cohabitation neither weakens nor strengthens marriage.

> **Watch** the **Video**
> The Big Picture: Families in **mysoclab**

FIGURE 11.11 **Cohabitation in the United States**

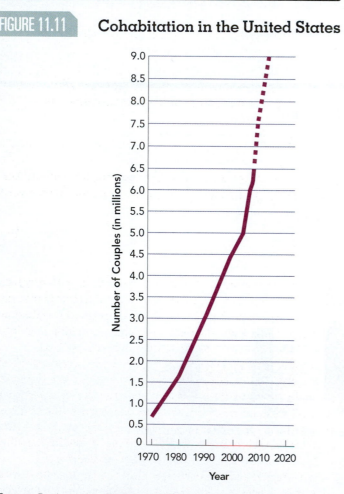

Source: By the author. Based on U.S. Bureau of the Census 2007b and Statistical Abstract of the United States 1995:2012:Table 63.

UNIT 11.7 // TESTING MYSELF
DID I LEARN IT? ANSWERS ARE AT THE END OF THE CHAPTER

1. The changes in age at first marriage are startling. Let's run through a few statistics. In 1890, the typical first-time bride was 22 years old, and her husband was about
   - **a.** 23
   - **b.** 24
   - **c.** 25
   - **d.** 26

2. By 1950, the average first-time groom hadn't yet celebrated his 23rd birthday, and the average first-time bride had just turned age
   - **a.** 20
   - **b.** 21
   - **c.** 22
   - **d.** 23

3. This is when the average first-time bride and groom were (or are) older than at any other time in U.S. history:
   - **a.** 1890
   - **b.** 1950
   - **c.** 1970
   - **d.** now

4. This is when the average age of women who give birth for the first time was (or is) older than at any other time in U.S. history:
   - **a.** 1890
   - **b.** 1950
   - **c.** 1970
   - **d.** now

5. For why the average age of first-time marriages and for women who give birth for the first time are the highest in U.S. history, sociologists have found a simple explanation. It is
   - **a.** fear
   - **b.** maturity
   - **c.** marital conflict at home
   - **d.** cohabitation

6. The primary difference between marriage and cohabitation can be summarized by this one word
   - **a.** approval
   - **b.** involvement
   - **c.** commitment
   - **d.** community

7. When sociologists compared the divorce rates of married couples who had and had not cohabitated before marriage, they found that the couples who had cohabited had higher divorce rates. The latest research shows
   - **a.** lower divorce rates among the couples who cohabited
   - **b.** higher divorce rates among the couples who cohabited
   - **c.** about the same divorce rates among couples who did and did not cohabit
   - **d.** so much divorce it shocked the researchers

UNIT 11.8

Divorce and Remarriage

WHAT AM I SUPPOSED TO LEARN?

After you have read this unit, you should be able to

1 Explain different ways of measuring divorce, and the different rates.

2 Explain the consequences of divorce for children and grandchildren.

3 Discuss divorced fathers' contact with children, relationship of ex-spouses, and remarriage.

The topic of family life would not be complete without considering divorce. Let's first try to determine how much divorce there really is.

Ways of Measuring Divorce

You probably have heard that the U.S. divorce rate is 50 percent, a figure that is popular with reporters. The statistic is true in the sense that each year almost half as many divorces are granted as there are marriages performed. The totals are roughly 2 million marriages and 1 million divorces (*Statistical Abstract* 2012:Table 133).

What is wrong, then, with saying that the divorce rate is about 50 percent? Think about it for a moment. These are the number of divorces and marriages that take place during a particular year. Why should we compare them? The couples who divorced do not—with rare exceptions—come from the group that married that year. The one number has *nothing* to do with the other, so these statistics in no way establish the divorce rate.

What figures should we compare, then? Couples who divorce come from the entire group of married people in the country. Since the United States has 61,000,000 married couples, and a little over 1 million of them get divorced in a year, the divorce rate for any given year is less than 2 percent. A couple's chances of still being married at the end of a year are over 98 percent—not bad odds—and certainly much better odds than the mass media would have us believe. As the social map below shows, the "odds"—if we want to call them that—depend on where you live.

Over time, of course, each year's small percentage adds up. A third way of measuring divorce, then, is to ask, "Of all U.S. adults, what percentage is divorced?" Figure 11.13 on page 378 answers this question. You can see how divorce has increased over the years. You can also see the difference that race–ethnicity makes for the likelihood that couples will divorce. If you look closely, you can also see that the increase in the rate of divorce has slowed down.

Figure 11.13 on page 378 shows us the percentage of Americans who are currently divorced, but we get yet another answer if we ask this question, "What percentage of Americans have *ever* been divorced?" This percentage increases with each age group, peaking when people reach their 50s. Considering people's lifetime, then, about 43 to 46 percent of marriages end in divorce (Amato 2010). A divorce rate of 50 percent, then, is actually fairly accurate.

For information on *your* chances of divorce, read the *Making It Personal* on the next page.

Children of Divorce

The news isn't good. Compared with children reared by both parents, children whose parents divorce are less likely to complete high school or to graduate from college (McLanahan and Schwartz 2002). They are also more likely to have emotional problems and to become juvenile delinquents (Amato and Sobolewski 2001; Wallerstein et al. 2001). And as adults, they are more likely to divorce, perpetuating a marriage–divorce cycle (Cui and Fincham 2010).

Not all children whose parents divorce have problems, of course. Sociologists have tried to find out why some do and some don't, and they have come up with some answers. Children who feel close to both parents make the best adjustment to their parents' divorce while those who don't feel close to either parent make the worst adjustment (Richardson and McCabe 2001). The children who adjust well experience little conflict, feel loved, live with a parent who is making a good adjustment, and have consistent routines. It also helps if their family has adequate money to meet its needs. Children also adjust better if a second adult can be counted on for support (Hayashi and Strickland 1998). Sociologist Urie Bronfenbrenner (1992) says this person is like the third leg of a stool, giving stability to the smaller family unit. Any adult can be the third leg, he says—a relative, friend, or even a former mother-in-law—but the most powerful stabilizing third leg is the father, the ex-husband.

You just read that the divorce rate of adults whose parents divorced is higher than the divorce rate of adults who grew up in intact families. But here is something else to add to this: Those who marry someone whose parents did not divorce are more

Figure 11.12   The "Where" of U.S. Divorce

Annual divorces per 1,000 people

- Lower than average: 2.2 to 3.1
- Average: 3.3 to 4.1
- Higher than average: 4.3 to 6.5

Lowest divorce rate
1. Massachusetts (2.2)
2. North Dakota (2.4)
3. Illinois (2.6)

Highest divorce rate
1. Nevada (6.5)
2. Arkansas (5.9)
3. Wyoming (5.5)

Note: Data for California, Georgia, Hawaii, Indiana, Louisiana, and Minnesota, based on the earlier editions in the source, have been decreased by the average decrease in U.S. divorce.

Source: By the author. Based on Statistical Abstract of the United States *1995:Table 149; 2002:Table 111; 2010:Table 126.*

MAKING IT PERSONAL
Your Chances of Getting Divorced

What you probably want to know is what *your* chances of divorce are. It is one thing to know that a certain percentage of Americans are divorced, but have sociologists found out anything that will tell you about your chances of divorce? Let's find out.

Look at Table 11.2, which shows some factors that reduce people's risk of divorce. As you can see, people who go to college,

TABLE 11.2	What Reduces the Risk of Divorce

Factors That Reduce People's Chances of Divorce	How Much Does This Decrease the Risk of Divorce?
Some college (vs. high-school dropout)	–13%
Affiliated with a religion (vs. none)	–14%
Parents not divorced	–14%
Age 25 or over at marriage (vs. under 18)	–24%
Having a baby 7 months or longer after marriage (vs. earlier)	–24%
Annual income over $25,000 (vs. under $25,000)	–30%

Note: These percentages apply to the first ten years of marriage.

Source: Whitehead and Popenoe 2004.

participate in a religion, wait to get married before having children, and earn higher incomes have a much better chance that their marriage will last. You can also see that having parents who did not divorce is significant. If you reverse these factors, you will see how the likelihood of divorce increases for people who marry in their teens, have a baby before they marry, and so on.

Now—and this is very important—these factors increase or reduce the risk of divorce for *groups* of people. I don't want to disappoint you, but they do not apply to you individually. Your chance of divorce does not increase by 14 percent, for example, if your parents are divorced.

To help explain why, we'll come back to this point in the next unit.

And I'll close with this. Your marriage will be what you make it. If you have that 50 percent figure dancing in your head while you are getting married, you might as well make sure that you have an escape door open even while you're saying "I do."

Divorces are often messy. To settle the question of who get the house, a couple in Cambodia sawed their house in half.

likely to have lasting marriages. Their marriages have more trust and less conflict. If both husband and wife come from broken families, however, there is less trust and more conflict. These marriages are more likely to break up (Wolfinger 2011).

Grandchildren of Divorce

You know that divorce has serious affects on children, but did you know that the effects continue across generations? Sociologists Paul Amato and Jacob Cheadle (2005) studied the grandchildren of people who had divorced. Using a national sample, they compared grandchildren—those whose grandparents had divorced with those whose grandparents had not divorced. Their findings are astounding. The grandchildren of divorce have weaker ties to their parents, don't go as far in school, and don't get along as well with their spouses. As these researchers put it,

when parents divorce, the consequences ripple through the lives of children who are not yet born.

Fathers' Contact with Children after Divorce

With most children living with their mothers after divorce, how often do fathers see their children? Look at Table 11.3 to see the four main patterns. The most common pattern is for fathers to see their children frequently after the divorce, and to keep doing so. But as you can see, a similar number of fathers have little contact with their children both right after the divorce and during the following years. After a divorce, which fathers are more likely to see and talk often to their children? It is men who were married to the mothers of the children, especially those who are older, more

11.8

FIGURE 11.13

What Percentage of Americans Are Divorced?

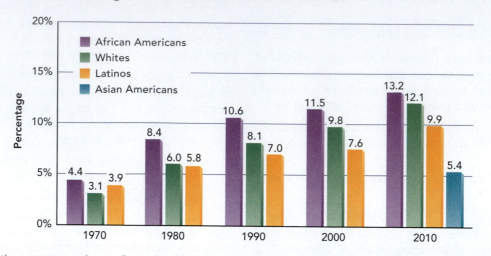

Note: This figure shows the percentage who are divorced and have not remarried, not the percentage who have ever divorced. Only these racial–ethnic groups are listed in the source. The source only recently added data on Asian Americans.

Source: By the author. Based on Statistical Abstract of the United States 1995:Table 58; 2012:Table 56.

TABLE 11.3

Fathers' Contact with Their Children After Divorce

Frequent[1]	Minimal[2]	Decreased[3]	Increased[4]
38%	32%	23%	8%

[1] Maintains contact once a week or more through the years.

[2] Little contact after the divorce, maybe 2 to 6 times a year.

[3] Has frequent contact after the divorce but decreases it through the years.

[4] Has little contact after the divorce but increases it through the years. Sometimes called the "divorce activated" father.

Source: By the author: Based on Cheadle et al. 2010.

educated, and have higher incomes. In contrast, men who were cohabiting with the mothers, as well as younger, less educated men with lower incomes, tend to have less contact with their children.

The Ex-Spouses

Women are more likely than men to feel that divorce is giving them a "new chance" in life. A few couples manage to remain friends through it all—but they are the exception. The spouse who initiates the divorce usually gets over it sooner (Kelly 1992; Wang and Amato 2000) and remarries sooner (Sweeney 2002).

Divorce does not necessarily mean the end of a couple's relationship. Many divorced couples maintain contact because of their children. For others, the *continuities*, as sociologists call them, represent lingering attachments (Vaughan 1985; Masheter 1991; author's file). The former husband may help his former wife paint a room or move furniture; she may invite him over for a meal or to watch television. They might even go to dinner or to see a movie together. Some couples even continue to make love after they divorce.

Remarriage

Remarriage is now so common that one-fourth (24 percent) of married couples are on their second (or more) marriage (Elliott and Lewis 2010). How do remarriages work out? The divorce rate of remarried people *without* children is the same as that of couples in their first marriages. But blended families—remember the earlier section on how complicated their relationships can get? Those who bring children into a new marriage also bring additional stress, and they are more likely to divorce again (MacDonald and DeMaris 1995). A lack of clear norms may also undermine these marriages (Coleman et al. 2000). As sociologist Andrew Cherlin (1989) noted, we lack satisfactory names for stepmothers, stepfathers, stepbrothers, stepsisters, stepaunts, stepuncles, stepcousins, and stepgrandparents. Not only are these awkward terms to use, but they also represent ill-defined relationships.

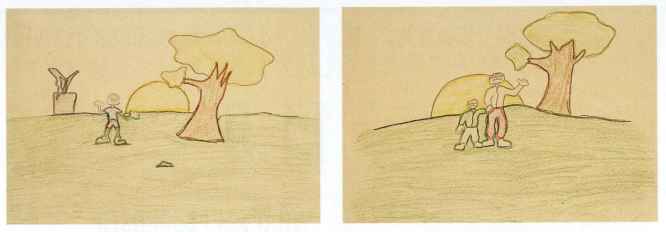

It is difficult to capture the anguish of the children of divorce, but when I read these lines by the fourth-grader who drew these two pictures, my heart was touched:

Me alone in the park . . .

All alone in the park.

My Dad and Mom are divorced

that's why I'm all alone.

This is me in the picture with my son.

We are taking a walk in the park.

I will never be like my father.

I will never divorce my wife and kid.

UNIT 11.8 // TESTING MYSELF
DID I LEARN IT?
ANSWERS ARE AT THE END OF THE CHAPTER

1. "You know my parents are divorced," said Garfield. "Mine, too," said Marsha. "I guess almost everyone's parents divorce today." "Not quite. It all depends on how you measure divorce," said Garfield. "What do you mean? Divorce is divorce," said Marsha. "Well, if you compare the number getting divorced in a year with the number getting married that same year, you get a total of
   a. 20 percent
   b. 30 percent
   c. 40 percent
   d. 50 percent

2. "Then the divorce rate is 50 percent," said Marsha. "Well," said Garfield "if you compare the number who divorce in a year with the total number of married couples, you come up with just
   a. 2 percent
   b. 5 percent
   c. 10 percent
   d. 20 percent

3. "You're making my head swim," Marsha said. "The simplest thing is to tell me what the divorce rate is for people over a lifetime." "Oh, that's a good measure," replied Garfield. "It is about
   a. 25 percent
   b. 45 percent
   c. 65 percent
   d. 85 percent

4. "Did you learn anything about the children of divorce?" asked Marsha. Garfield said, "I learned that they are less likely to complete high school or to graduate from college. They are also more likely to
   a. turn inward and read books
   b. play sports
   c. fight with their siblings
   d. get in trouble with the law

5. "What about these kids after they grow up? Did you learn anything about their chances of divorce?" asked Marsha. "Yeah, I did. Compared with those whose parents didn't divorce, it is
   a. lower
   b. higher
   c. no different
   d. higher in some years and lower in others

6. "You and I are both divorced, so this looks bad for us. But we didn't get arrested, and here we are in college," said Marsha. "Right," said Garfield. "A main point in the text was that these are group statistics. They
   a. apply only to other people's groups
   b. only work some of the time
   c. don't apply to the individual
   d. change from year to year

7. "I've got to mention one more thing," said Garfield. "The effects of divorce cross generations. Sociologists have found that the grandchildren of parents who divorce are
   a. less likely to divorce
   b. more likely to divorce
   c. less likely to marry
   d. more likely to marry

8. "You and I lived with our mothers after their divorce. We hardly ever saw our dads. Is that how it is all over?" asked Marsha. Garfield answered, "This is very common, but slightly edging it out is the pattern of fathers seeing
   a. their children frequently after the divorce, and to keep doing so
   b. their children frequently after the divorce, and then to stop seeing them
   c. little of their children after the divorce, and then to start seeing them frequently
   d. little of their children, then a lot and then a little

9. "Any info on which fathers are more likely to see their children frequently?" asked Marsha. "Good question. Sociologists have found that it is fathers who are older, more educated, and
   a. had fewer children
   b. came from larger families
   c. more religious
   d. were married to the mothers

10. "Do you remember when your dad used to come over and help fix things in the house right after the divorce?" asked Garfield. "I'll never forget it. He even took mom out on a date once. I thought they would get back together." "Sociologists have a cute term for this," said Garfield. "They call it
    a. terminations
    b. continuities
    c. closure
    d. post-divorce folly

UNIT 11.9

Two Sides of Family Life

WHAT AM I SUPPOSED TO LEARN?

After you have read this unit, you should be able to

1 Explain the dark and bright sides of family life.

The Dark Side of Family Life: Spouse Battering, Child Abuse, and Incest

The dark side of family life involves events that people would rather keep in the dark. Let's look at spouse battering, child abuse, and incest.

SPOUSE BATTERING

From his own research and his review of the research of others, sociologist Murray Straus concludes that wives attack their husbands as often as husbands attack their wives (Straus and Gelles 1988; Straus 1992; Straus 2011). Gender equality may exist in *initiating* marital violence, but it certainly vanishes when it comes to the *effects* of violence. As you know, women are much more likely to be injured. You also know that the primary reason is that most husbands are bigger and stronger than their wives, putting women at a physical disadvantage in this literal battle of the sexes.

Gender equality in initiating violence goes against the dominant idea of our society, which generally lays the blame at the feet of men. This is another of the surprising findings in sociology. And it has serious implications: If we want to curb violence,

IF YOU WANT TO LEARN MORE about why some women remain with their abusive husbands,

Read more from the author: "Why Doesn't She leave?" The Dilemma of Abused Women in **mysoclab**

we should *not* concentrate on men, but, instead, on *both* men and women. The basic sociological question, then, is how to socialize both males and females to handle frustration and disagreements without resorting to violence. We do not yet have this answer.

Watch the **Video**
Sociology on the Job:
Families in **mysoclab**

CHILD ABUSE

I answered an ad about a lakeside house in a middle-class neighborhood that was for sale by the owner. As the woman showed me through her immaculate house, I was surprised to see a plywood box in the youngest child's bedroom. About 3 feet high, 3 feet wide, and 6 feet long, the box was perforated with holes and had a little door with a padlock. Curious, I asked what it was. The woman replied matter-of-factly that her son had a behavior problem, and this was where they locked him for "time out." She added that other times they would tie him to a float, attach a line to the dock, and put him in the lake.

I left as soon as I could. With thoughts of a terrorized child filling my head, I called the state child abuse hotline.

As you can tell, what I saw upset me. Most of us are bothered by child abuse—helpless children being victimized by their parents and other adults who are supposed to love, protect, and nurture them. The most gruesome of these cases make the evening news: The 4-year-old girl who was beaten and raped by her mother's boyfriend, passed into a coma, and three days later passed out of this life; the 6- to 10-year-old children whose stepfather videotaped them engaging in sex acts. Unlike these cases, which made headlines in my area, most child abuse is never brought to our attention: the children who live in filth, who are neglected—left alone for hours or even days at a time—or who are beaten with extension cords—cases like the little boy I learned about when I went house hunting.

Child abuse is extensive. Each year, U.S. authorities receive about 2 million reports of children being abused or neglected. About 800,000 of these cases are substantiated (*Statistical Abstract* 2012:Table 343). The excuses that parents make are incredible. Of those I have read, the most fantastic is what a mother said to a Manhattan judge, "I slipped in a moment of anger, and my hands accidentally wrapped around my daughter's windpipe" (LeDuff 2003).

INCEST

Incest is most likely to occur in families that are socially isolated (Smith 1992). Sociologist Diana Russell (n.d.) found that incest victims who experience the greatest trauma are those who were victimized the most often, whose assaults occurred over longer periods of time, and whose incest was "more intrusive"—for example, sexual intercourse as opposed to sexual touching.

Apparently, the most common form of incest is sex between brothers and sisters. Most sibling incest is initiated by a brother who is five years older than his sister (Krienert and Walsh 2011). In one-fourth of cases of sibling incest, the victim is a younger brother, and in 13 percent of the cases it is the sister who is the offender. Most of those who initiate the incest are between the ages of 13 and 15, with most victims age 12 or younger. In most cases, the parents treat the incest as a family matter to be dealt with privately.

The Bright Side of Family Life: Successful Marriages
SUCCESSFUL MARRIAGES

After examining divorce and family abuse, one could easily conclude that marriages seldom work out. This would be far from the truth, however, for about three of every five married Americans report that they are "very happy" with their marriages (Whitehead and Popenoe 2004). (Keep in mind that each year divorce eliminates about a million unhappy marriages.) To find out what makes marriage successful, sociologists Jeanette and Robert Lauer (1992) interviewed 351 couples who had been married fifteen years or longer. Fifty-one of these marriages were unhappy, but the couples stayed together for religious reasons, because of family tradition, or "for the sake of the children."

Of the others, the 300 happy couples, all

1. Think of their spouses as best friends
2. Like their spouses as people
3. Think of marriage as a long-term commitment
4. Believe that marriage is sacred
5. Agree with their spouses on aims and goals
6. Believe that their spouses have grown more interesting over the years
7. Strongly want the relationship to succeed
8. Laugh together

Sociologist Nicholas Stinnett (1992) used interviews and questionnaires to study 660 families from all regions of the United States and parts of South America. He found that happy families.

1. Spend a lot of time together
2. Are quick to express appreciation
3. Are committed to promoting one another's welfare
4. Do a lot of talking and listening to one another
5. Are religious
6. Deal with crises in a positive manner

There are three more important factors: Marriages are happier when the partners get along with their in-laws (Bryant et al. 2001), find leisure activities that they both enjoy (Crawford et al. 2002), and agree on how to spend money (Bernard 2008).

To again see why your marriage, if you have one or will have one, is beyond statistics, read *Making It Personal*.

MAKING IT PERSONAL
Creating a Positive Self-Fulfilling Prophecy

In the last *Making It Personal*, I stressed that you can't apply group statistics to yourself. They apply to the group, and you are an individual. You may be part of a group, but as an individual you don't have the group's characteristics. I hope this makes sense.

So let's apply this principle by looking at divorce again. You might be concerned that high national divorce statistics decrease the odds of your marriage being successful. A lot of students think this way. But if the divorce rate were 33 percent or 50 percent, this would not mean that if you marry, your chances of getting divorced are 33 percent or 50 percent. This is a misuse of statistics—and a common one at that. Divorce statistics represent all marriages and have absolutely *nothing* to do with your marriage. Your chances depend on our own situation—especially the way you approach marriage.

To make this point clearer, let's apply symbolic interactionism. From a symbolic interactionist perspective, you create your own world. That is, you interpret your experiences in life and act accordingly. As you do this, you can create a self-fulfilling prophecy—either a negative or a positive one. For example, if you think that your marriage might fail, you are more likely to run when things become difficult. If you think that your marriage is going to work out, when trouble comes you are more likely to stick around and do things that help make your marriage successful.

The old saying "There are no guarantees in life" is certainly true, but it does help to have a vision that a good marriage is possible and that it is worth the effort to achieve.

UNIT 11.9 // TESTING MYSELF
DID I LEARN IT? ANSWERS ARE AT THE END OF THE CHAPTER

1. "I read something interesting in this last unit," said Shanice. "When it comes to initiating violence, wives
   a. are more likely to start the fight
   b. are less likely to start the fight
   c. use more threatening words
   d. and husbands are about equally likely to attack the other

2. "Wives are more likely to get hurt, though, right?" asked DeShawn. "Right," said Shanice, "so you would think that to prevent violence the focus would be on the husbands. But because of how violence is initiated, the author suggests that to reduce marital violence, we focus
   a. almost exclusively on wives
   b. mostly on wives, but some on husbands
   c. on people before they get married, especially on high school students
   d. on both husbands and wives

3. "I didn't like what I read about child abuse," said DeShawn. "It was hard to believe that the number of reports of child abuse in a year is about
   a. 100,000   b. ½ million
   c. 1 million   d. 2 million

4. "And did you read about incest?" Shanice asked. "I did," answered DeShawn. "I learned that most incest occurs between
   a. grandfathers and granddaughters
   b. fathers and daughters
   c. brothers and sisters
   d. mothers and sons

5. "And do you remember who the typical person is who initiates incest?" asked Shanice." "I sure do," said DeShawn. "It is
   a. an aunt
   b. the father
   c. an older sister
   d. an older brother

6. "That didn't surprise me when I read it," said Shanice. "And I did learn that incest is most common in families that
   a. go to church, synagogue, or mosque
   b. have no father
   c. don't go on vacations
   d. are socially isolated

7. "I found it interesting that sociologists have uncovered what kind of incest creates the most trauma for

victims," said Shanice. "Besides the most intrusive incest, another factor is incest that

a. took place with brothers
b. occurred over the longest time
c. took place at schools
d. involved more than one offender

8. "Let's move on to a more pleasant topic," DeShawn suggested. "I want to have a happy marriage, so I was interested in the factors that lead to successful marriages. There were a lot of things listed, but I liked the one that the couples laugh together." "That was good," agreed Shanice, "but I liked this one best, that the couples

a. think of their spouses as best friends
b. don't do anything that involves the other without talking it over with the other first
c. avoid talking about things on which they disagree
d. keep on talking about things they disagree until they find a solution

UNIT 11.10

The Future of Marriage and Family

WHAT AM I SUPPOSED TO LEARN?

After you have read this unit, you should be able to

1. List major trends in marriage and family that are likely to continue.

Now you can relax. You are going to read the shortest unit in the book—it's just two paragraphs.

What can we expect of marriage and family in the future? Despite its many problems, marriage is in no danger of becoming a relic of the past. Marriage is so functional that it exists in every society. We can be sure that the vast majority of Americans will continue to find marriage vital to their welfare.

Certain trends are firmly in place—cohabitation, births to single women, and age at first marriage. As more married women join the workforce, wives will continue to gain marital power. In the midst of changing marriage and family, our culture will continue to be haunted by distorted images of marriage and family: the bleak ones portrayed in the mass media and the rosy ones perpetuated by cultural myths. Sociological research can help correct these distortions and allow us to see how our own family experiences fit into the patterns of our culture. Sociological research can also help in answering the big question: How do we develop social policies that will support and enhance family life?

UNIT 11.10 // TESTING MYSELF
DID I LEARN IT? ANSWERS ARE AT THE END OF THE CHAPTER

1. With the many problems that plague marriage and family, we can expect marriage to
a. become a relic of the past
b. slowly shrink, until only about half of adults are married
c. be replaced by cohabitation for almost everyone
d. continue strong

2. The author suggests that as more married women join the workforce, they will
a. start to neglect their children
b. increase the divorce rate
c. gain more marital power
d. lower the wage rate because of the increased supply of labor

3. The author suggests that sociological research can help to answer this big question
a. How do we help women who are being abused by their husbands or mates?
b. How do we develop social policies that will support and enhance family life?
c. What is the inherent meaning of marriage and family?
d. What form will marriage and family take in the future?

PULLING IT ALL TOGETHER REVIEWING THE LEARNING GOALS

Unit 11.1   Marriage and Family in Global Perspective

1. Explain why it is difficult to define marriage and family.

- There is such cultural variety in forms of marriage and family that they are difficult to define. Family forms range from the nuclear family to extended families, from one spouse to polygyny (more than one wife) and polyandry (more than one husband). Marital forms are also broad, including brides and grooms of the opposite sex, the same sex, even those who are dead. Broad definitions, then, are: *Family,* people who consider themselves related by blood, marriage, or adoption, and *marriage,* a group's approved mating arrangements, usually marked by a ritual of some sort.

2. List the common cultural themes that run through marriage and family.

- These are listed on Table 11.1 on page 352.

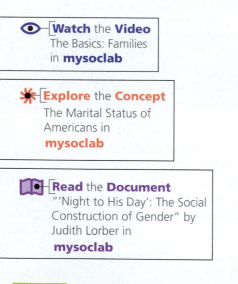

Watch the **Video**
The Basics: Families in **mysoclab**

Explore the **Concept**
The Marital Status of Americans in **mysoclab**

Read the **Document**
"'Night to His Day': The Social Construction of Gender" by Judith Lorber in **mysoclab**

Unit 11.2   Marriage and Family in Theoretical Perspective

1. Explain the main ideas of the functionalists on marriage and family.

- Marriage and family help society survive by meeting six basic functions: economic production, socialization of children, care of the sick and aged, recreation, sexual control, and reproduction. The incest taboo prevents role confusion and helps socialize children.

2. Explain the main ideas of conflict theorists on marriage and family.

- Throughout history, husbands have had more power, and wives have resented it. As indicated in Figure 11.1 (page 356), the balance of power seems to be shifting.

3. Explain the main ideas of the symbolic interactionists on marriage and family.

- Ideas about gender, what is "right" for husbands and wives when it comes to housework and child care, have changed dramatically, ushering in new norms and behavior.

Unit 11.3   Love and Marriage

1. Explain how love works and what the social channels of love and marriage are.

- Romantic love is preceded by sexual attraction. If the feelings persist after spending time together, people add the label of love. Love produces marriages that follow social channels: age, education, social class, and race–ethnicity. In India, love follows marriage.

Unit 11.4   Family Transitions

1. Explain changes in preferences in number of children, what makes good day care, the empty nest, adultolescents, and widowhood.

- Over the years, Americans have preferred fewer children. Today, those who are ages 18 to 34 prefer more children than do those over age 34. People who attend church more often prefer larger families. In child care: For single mothers, grandparents and other relatives fill in for the absent father. The best day care: where staff have taken courses in early childhood development and there is a low ratio of children per staff member. The social classes have different approaches to child rearing. More young people are returning to the home nest. The widowhood effect: When a spouse dies, surviving spouses tend to die earlier than expected.

Unit 11.5   Racial Ethnic Diversity

1. Summarize major characteristics of families by racial-ethnic groups.

- The main difference is not racial-ethnic, but, rather, social class. There is more variation within any racial–ethnic group by social class than there are differences between racial–ethnic groups. *African American:* Upper: concern that those whom their children marry come from the right family background. Poverty: likely to be headed by a woman and to have a high rate of divorce, desertion, and births to single women. *Latino:* The same, with much variety depending on country of origin. *Asian American:* The same, with the greatest likelihood of children being reared by two parents, often with an emphasis on Confucian values. *Native American:* Elders, especially grandparents, play a more important role, and a major question is to assimilate or to follow traditional patterns.

Unit 11.6 **More Diversity**

1. Describe some of the diversity in U.S. families.
   - *One-parent families:* The concerns expressed likely have more to do with their poverty than with the children being reared by one parent. Problems plague children from one-parent families: physical and emotional problems, dropping out of school, getting in trouble with the law. *Families without children:* Some couples are infertile, but most choose to not have children. Others simply postpone having children until it is too late. *Blended families,* whose members were once part of other families, have complicated relationships. *Gay and lesbian families:* About a fifth have children from previous heterosexual marriages. Their problems are basically the same as those of heterosexual couples.

Unit 11.7 **Current Trends**

1. Explain major changes in age at first marriage, age at first childbirth, and in cohabitation.
   - In 1890, the first-time bride was age 22, and her husband 26. For 60 years, these ages dropped. By 1950, the first-time bride was just out of her teens, and her husband was not quite 23 years old. Then about 1970, the age of first-time marriages began to increase, and now they are the highest in U.S. history. The age at which U.S. women now have their first child (25.2 years) is the highest in U.S. history. The basic reason is cohabitation. Couples have postponed marriage, but not the age at which they set up housekeeping. Divorce is higher among couples who live together before marriage.

◉ Watch the Video
The Big Picture: Families in **mysoclab**

Unit 11.8 **Divorce and Remarriage**

1. Explain ways of measuring divorce, and the different rates.
   - Comparing the number who divorce with the number who marry: 50 percent. Comparing the annual

number who divorce with total marriages: 2 percent. The percentage of divorced adults: from 5 percent to 12 percent, depending on the racial–ethnic group. Divorce over a lifetime: close to 50 percent.

2. Explain the consequences of divorce for children and grandchildren.
   - *Children of divorce:* more likely to drop out of school, divorce, have emotional problems, and trouble with the law. *Best adjustment:* Get along with both parents, experience low conflict, feel loved, follow routines, and have a second adult to help. *Grandchildren of divorce:* more likely to divorce.

3. Discuss divorced fathers' contact with children, ex-spouses, and remarriage.
   - *Fathers with most contact:* older, more educated, higher income, were married. Many ex-spouses have "continuities" after divorce. The divorce rate of blended families is high.

Unit 11.9 **Two Sides of Family Life**

1. Explain the dark and bright sides of family life.
   - *The dark side of family life* consists of battering, child abuse, and incest. *Battering:* Husbands and wives are about equally likely to attack one another, but 85 percent of the injured are women. *Child abuse:* About 2 million reports are made each year of U.S. children being abused or neglected, with about 800,000 substantiated. *Incest:* Victims with the greatest trauma are those who were victimized the most often, whose assaults occurred over longer periods of time, and whose incest was "more intrusive." Incest is most likely to occur in isolated families. The least common offenders are mothers. *The bright side of family life* consists of characteristics that make marriage successful. These characteristics are listed on page 381.

◉ Watch the Video
Sociology on the Job:
Families in **mysoclab**

Unit 11.10 **The Future of Marriage and Family**

1. List major trends in marriage and family that are likely to continue.
   - The future is likely to bring an increase in cohabitation, more births to single women, a higher age at first marriage, more married women in the workforce, and more marital power for women. Sociological research can help formulate policies that support and enhance family life.

1. **d** household

2. **c** consider themselves related by blood, marriage, or adoption

3. **b** polyandry

4. **a** polygyny

1. **d** economic production, socialization of children, care of the sick and aged, recreation, sexual control, and reproduction

2. **c** role confusion

1. **d** light up the same area of the brain that lights up when cocaine addicts are craving coke

2. **c** romantic love

3. **c** love comes after marriage

1. **c** prefer larger families

2. **b** prefer larger families

3. **d** staff who have taken courses in early childhood development and a low ratio of children per staff member

1. **d** social class

2. **c** have the right family background

3. **b** fictive kin

5. **d** family of procreation

6. **c** berdache

7. **d** sex and marriage among designated relatives

8. **c** matrilineal

9. **b** patrilineal

10. **c** the bride taking the last name of the groom

3. **b** conflict

4. **d** finances, purchases, what to do on the weekends, and what to watch on television

5. **d** symbolic interactionism

6. **c** are doing less housework

7. **b** a gendered division of labor

4. **a** fear can produce love

5. **d** is preceded by sexual interest

6. **c** cognitive, a label that we attach to our feelings

7. **a** the U.S. Supreme Court struck down the state laws that prohibited such marriages

8. **c** a black husband and a white wife

4. **c** garden flowers that need a lot of nurturing if they are to bloom

5. **b** push their children into activities that they think will develop the children's thinking and social skills

6. **c** adultolescents

7. **b** suffer fewer health consequences

8. **d** widowhood effect

4. **a** more likely to marry men who are less educated than themselves

5. **d** their families resemble those of middle-class Americans

6. **c** grow up with both parents

7. **a** owes respect to other family members and has a responsibility never to bring shame on the family

8. **d** assimilate or to follow traditional ways

1. **d** poverty

2. **c** get divorced

3. **b** postponing having children until it is too late

4. **a** childfree

5. **d** blended families

6. **c** 20

7. **b** are the same as those of heterosexual couples

1. **d** 26

2. **a** 20

3. **d** now

4. **d** now

5. **d** cohabitation

6. **c** commitment

7. **c** about the same divorce rates among couples who did and did not cohabit

1. **d** 50 percent

2. **a** 2 percent

3. **b** 45 percent

4. **d** get in trouble with the law

5. **b** higher

6. **c** don't apply to the individual

7. **b** more likely to divorce

8. **a** their children frequently after the divorce, and to keep doing so

9. **d** were married to the mothers

10. **b** continuities

1. **d** and husbands are about equally likely to attack the other

2. **d** on both husbands and wives

3. **d** 2 million

4. **c** brothers and sisters

5. **d** an older brother

6. **d** are socially isolated

7. **b** occurred over the longest time

8. **a** think of their spouses as best friends

1. **d** continue strong

2. **c** gain more marital power

3. **b** How do we develop social policies that will support and enhance family life?

CHAPTER 12
EDUCATION AND RELIGION

((•⃤ Listen to the **Chapter Audio** in **mysoclab**

👁 **Watch** the **Video** in **mysoclab**

GETTING STARTED

Have you ever wondered why people need a high school diploma to sell cars or to join the U.S. Marines? Why do employers insist on diplomas and degrees? Why don't they simply use on-the-job training?

In some cases, job skills must be mastered before you are allowed to do the work. On-the-job training was once adequate to become an engineer or an airline pilot, but with changes in information and technology it is no longer sufficient. This is precisely why doctors display their credentials so prominently. Their framed degrees declare that an institution of higher learning has certified them to work on your body.

But testing in algebra or paragraph construction to sell gizmos at Radio Shack? Sociologist Randall Collins (1979) observed that industrialized nations have become **credential societies**. By this, he means that employers use diplomas and degrees as *sorting devices* to determine who is eligible for a job. Because employers don't know potential workers, they depend on schools to weed out the incapable.

In *Making It Personal*, consider how this applies to you.

Bamako, Mali.

EDUCATION: TRANSFERRING KNOWLEDGE AND SKILLS

UNIT 12.1
Education in Global Perspective

WHAT AM I SUPPOSED TO LEARN?

After you have read this unit, you should be able to

1 Explain how industrialization is related to the development of education.

2 Summarize the educational systems of Japan, Russia, and Egypt.

MAKING IT PERSONAL
Your Credentials

When you graduate from college, potential employers will presume that you are a responsible person. They will assume that you have shown up for numerous classes, have taken and passed many tests, and have turned in hundreds of assignments on time. They will also presume that you have demonstrated basic writing and thinking skills. They will then graft their particular job skills onto this foundation, which has been certified by your college.

"What difference does that piece of paper make?" It makes quite a difference in a credential society. In our huge, diverse, and largely impersonal society, how else can a potential employer know who you are?

In the early years of the United States, there was no free public education. Parents with an average income could not afford to send their children even to grade school. As the country industrialized during the 1800s, political and civic leaders recognized the need for an educated workforce. They also feared the influx of "foreign" values, for this was a period of high immigration. They looked on public education as a way to reach two major goals: producing more educated workers and "Americanizing" immigrants (Hellinger and Judd 1991; Jones and Meyer 2010).

As industrialization progressed and fewer people made their living from farming, formal education came to be regarded as essential to the well-being of society. High school graduation became common, but with the distance to the nearest college too far and the cost of tuition and lodging too great, most high school graduates could not attend

credential society the use of diplomas and degrees to determine who is eligible for jobs, even though the diploma or degree may be irrelevant to the actual work

college. This predicament gave birth to community colleges. This system of colleges has become so extensive that almost two of five (38 percent) of all undergraduates in the United States are enrolled in them today (*Statistical Abstract* 2012:Table 278).

Look at Figure 12.1 on the next page. You can see that as the U.S. college system expanded, more and more people went to college. The change is so extensive that receiving a bachelor's degree in the United States is now *twice* as common as completing high school used to be.

> *IF YOU WANT TO LEARN MORE* about community colleges in the U.S. educational system,
>
> **Read** more from the author: Community Colleges: Facing Old and New Challenges in **mysoclab**

To further place our educational system in perspective, let's look at education in three countries at different levels of industrialization. This will help you see how education is related to both a nation's culture and its economy.

Watch the **Video**
The Basics: Education in **mysoclab**

Education in the Most Industrialized Nations: Japan

A central sociological principle of education is that a nation's education reflects its culture. Because a core Japanese value is solidarity with the group, the Japanese discourage competition among individuals. In the workforce, people who are hired together work as a team. They are not expected to compete with one another for promotions; instead, they are promoted as a group (Ouchi 1993). Japanese education reflects this group-centered approach to life. Children in grade school work as a group, all mastering the same skills and materials. On any one day, children all over Japan study the same page from the same textbook ("Less Rote . . ." 2000).

In a fascinating cultural contradiction, college admissions in Japan are highly competitive. The Scholastic Assessment Test

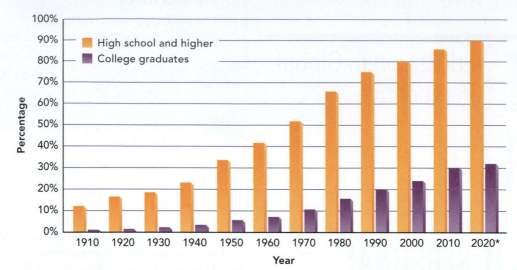

FIGURE 12.1 **Educational Achievement in the United States**

Note: Americans 25 years and over. Asterisk indicates author's estimate. College graduates are included in both categories (High school and higher, and College graduates).

Sources: By the author. Based on National Center for Education Statistics 1991:Table 8; Statistical Abstract of the United States 2012:Table 231.

(SAT), taken by college-bound high school juniors and seniors in the United States, is voluntary, but Japanese seniors who want to attend college must take a national test. U.S. students who perform poorly on their tests can usually find some college to attend—as long as their parents can pay the tuition. Until recently, in Japan only the top scorers—rich and poor alike—were admitted to college. This is changing. Because of Japan's low birth rate, the pool of students has shrunk and Japan's colleges have begun to compete for students (McNeill 2008). As in the United States, children from the richer families score higher on college admission tests and are more likely to go to college (Yamamoto and Brinton 2010). In each country, to be born into a richer family means to inherit privileges—among them having more highly educated parents, from grade school through high school being expected to bring home top grades, and enjoying cultural experiences that translate into higher test scores.

Japanese schoolchildren with a robot that is able to "exercise" along with them.

Education in the Industrializing Nations: Russia

After the Russian Revolution of 1917, the Soviet Communist party changed the nation's educational system. At that time, as in most countries, education was limited to children of the elite. The communists expanded the educational system until eventually it encompassed all children. Following the sociological principle that education reflects culture, the new government made certain that socialist values dominated its schools, for it saw education as a way to advance the new political system. As a result, schoolchildren were taught that capitalism was evil and that communism was the salvation of the world. Every classroom was required to prominently display photographs of Lenin and Stalin.

Education, including college, was free. Just as the economy was directed from central headquarters in Moscow, so was education. Schools stressed mathematics and the natural sciences. Each school followed the same state-prescribed curriculum, and all students in the same grade used the same government-approved textbooks. To prevent critical thinking, which might lead to criticisms of communism, few courses in the social sciences were taught, and students memorized course materials, repeating lectures on oral exams (Deaver 2001).

Russia's switch from communism to capitalism brought a change in culture—especially new ideas about profit, private

Schoolchildren in Egypt.

property, and personal freedom. This, in turn, meant that the educational system had to adjust to the country's changing values and views of the world. The photos of Lenin and Stalin came down, and for the first time, private, religious, and even foreign-run schools were allowed. For the first time as well, teachers were able to encourage students to think for themselves.

Because it is true of education everywhere, we can confidently predict that Russia's educational system will continue to reflect its culture. Its educational system will glorify Russia's historical exploits and reinforce its values and world views—no matter how they might change.

Education in the Least Industrialized Nations: Egypt

Education in the Least Industrialized Nations stands in sharp contrast to that in the industrialized world. Because most of the citizens of these nations work the land or take care of families, there is little emphasis on formal schooling. Mandatory attendance laws are not enforced. As you saw in Figure 7.2 (pages 193–194), millions of people in the Least Industrialized Nations live on less than $1,000 a year. In some of these nations, few children go to school beyond the first couple of grades. As was once common in the United States, it is primarily the wealthy in the Least Industrialized Nations who have the means and the leisure for formal education—especially anything beyond the basics. As an example, let's look at education in Egypt.

The Egyptian constitution guarantees five years of free grade school for all children, but many poor children receive no education at all. For those who do attend school, qualified teachers are few, and classrooms are crowded. As a result, one-third of Egyptian men and over half of Egyptian women are illiterate (UNESCO 2011). Those who go beyond the five years of grade school attend a preparatory school for three years. High school also lasts for three years. During

the first two years, all students take the same courses, and during the third year they specialize in arts, science, or mathematics (UNESCO 2012). The emphasis has been on memorizing facts to pass national tests. As concerns have grown that this approach leaves minds less capable of evaluating life and opens the door to religious extremism, some Egyptian educators have pressed for critical thinking to be added to the curriculum (Gauch 2006). So far, the government has been slow to respond, and little has changed (Dhillon et al. 2008).

1. "I've been wondering why anyone has to have a high school diploma to sack groceries at the superrmarket," said Ammon. "I read," Eboni replied, "that this is because we have become
   a. an education-crazed society
   b. a political society
   c. a global competitive society
   d. a credential society

2. "Why would we use credentials like that?" asked Ammon. "In smaller groups," said Eboni, "people knew one another and what their abilities were. It isn't like that now. So credentials have replaced this personal knowledge. Community colleges are part of this. They have grown so much that of all students in higher education, about
   a. one of twenty is in community colleges
   b. one of ten is in community colleges
   c. one of five is in community colleges
   d. two of five are in community colleges

3. "I read that this is a central sociological principle of education," said Ammon, "that a nation's education
   a. reflects its culture.
   b. is as good as the financial support that it receives
   c. moves from primitive to advanced as a society industrializes
   d. is better in democracies than in dictatorships

4. "Why was education in Japan featured?" asked Eboni. Ammon answered, "It is an example of
   a. education in a Most Industrialized Nation
   b. how education changes as society changes
   c. education in an Asian nation
   d. how teamwork can be an essential component of education

5. "Since Japanese students are admitted to the universities on the basis of national tests," said Eboni, "I was surprised that the children of the rich do better." "Why is that?" asked Ammon. "It's the same around the world. Children born into richer families
   a. have more money
   b. can figure out what is going to be asked on tests

c. are smarter

d. have more educated parents, are expected to bring home top grades, and enjoy cultural experiences that translate into higher test scores

6. "I liked this point," said Ammon. "In communist Russia, photographs of Lenin and Stalin were displayed in every classroom because

a. Lenin and Stalin didn't want anyone to forget who they were

b. they were the favorite two people of the Youth Communist Party

c. schools were seen as a way to advance the new political system

d. there was a rivalry with the czar of Russia, and the czar lost

7. "And I liked this one," said Eboni. "Schools in communist Russia stressed mathematics and the natural sciences. Few courses in the social sciences were taught because

a. there were few social scientists

b. critical thinking might lead to criticisms of communism

c. with all the courses in mathematics and natural sciences, there wasn't enough time

d. the parents insisted it be this way

8. "Then," continued Eboni. "After the fall of communism, Russian teachers

a. were able to encourage students to think for themselves

b. were paid high salaries

c. began a "no grade" system

d. lost the respect of both parents and children

9. "The author says that whatever else happens, he knows that Russia's schools will glorify Russia's historical exploits and reinforce its values and world view," said Ammon. "How does he know that?" asked Eboni. "He bases it on the sociological principle, that

a. power flows to the wealthy

b. there are never enough good schools for those who want them

c. education is a basic right, but an expensive one

d. educational systems reflect their culture

10. "Do you know why education in Egypt was featured?" asked Eboni. "Yes," replied Ammon, "it is an example of

a. education in a dictatorship

b. an educational system based on noncompetitive, dynamic principles

c. education in a Least Industrialized Nation

d. how education leads to dissatisfaction and, ultimately, even to revolution

UNIT 12.2

The Functionalist Perspective: Providing Social Benefits

WHAT AM I SUPPOSED TO LEARN?

After you have read this unit, you should be able to

1 Explain the functionalist perspective on education.

A central position of functionalism is that when the parts of society are working properly, each part contributes to the well-being or stability of that society. **Manifest functions** are the positive things that people intend their actions to accomplish. The positive consequences they did not intend are called **latent functions**. Let's look at the functions of education.

Teaching Knowledge and Skills

Education's most obvious manifest function is to teach knowledge and skills—whether the traditional three R's or their more contemporary counterparts, such as computer literacy. Each generation must train the next to fill the group's significant positions. Because our postindustrial society needs highly educated people, the schools supply them.

The Transmission of Mainstream Values

Another manifest function of education is the **transmission of mainstream values**, a process by which schools pass on a society's core values from one generation to the

manifest functions the intended beneficial consequences of people's actions

latent functions the unintended beneficial consequences of people's actions

transmission of mainstream values passing on a group's core values

Inclusion, also called mainstreaming, is one of the manifest functions of current education in the United States.

next. Because of this, schools in a socialist society stress values of socialism, while schools in a capitalist society teach values that support capitalism. U.S. schools, for example, stress competition, individualism, and people's right to private property.

Regardless of a country's economic system, loyalty to the state is a cultural value, and schools around the world teach patriotism. U.S. schools—as well as those of Russia, France, China, and other countries around the world—extol the society's founders, their struggle for freedom from oppression, and the goodness of the country's social institutions. Seldom is this function as explicit as it is in Japan, where the law requires that schools "cultivate a respect for tradition and culture, and love for the nation and homeland" (Nakamura 2006).

To help you see how the transmission of cultural values affects teaching, read *Making It Personal*.

MAKING IT PERSONAL

How Would You Teach History?

To better visualize what the functionalists mean by the transmission of mainstream values, consider how a course in U.S. history would be taught in Cuba, Iran, and Muncie, Indiana. In Cuba, a specific event would be framed through socialism. Teachers might stress the people's struggle against U.S. oppression and how socialism helps people. The same event

taught in Iran might stress the expansion of U.S. power and the superiority of Persian culture. In Muncie, Indiana, teachers would likely stress how the event represents the superiority of democracy and, perhaps, how the United States is bringing freedom to oppressed parts of the word.

Do you see how education supports mainstream values and how this central function of education works?

> ✳ **Explore** the **Concept**
> Dropping Out in the
> Information Age in
> **mysoclab**

Social Integration

Schools also bring about *social integration*. U.S. schools promote a sense of national identity by having students salute the flag and sing the national anthem. One of the best examples of how U.S. schools promote political integration is how they have taught mainstream ideas and values to tens of millions of immigrants. Coming to regard themselves as Americans, the immigrants gave up their earlier national and cultural identities (Carper 2000; Thompson 2009).

This integrative function of education makes people similar in their appearance, speech, and even ways of thinking. But it goes far beyond this. *To forge a national identity is to stabilize the political system.* If people identify with a society's institutions and *perceive them as the basis of their own welfare,* they have no reason to rebel. This function is especially significant when it comes to the lower social classes, from which most social revolutionaries emerge. Because the wealthy are getting so much from the system, they already have a vested interest in maintaining it the way it is. But getting the lower classes to identify with a social system *as it is* goes a long way toward preserving the system in its current state.

People with disabilities often find themselves left out of the mainstream of society. To overcome this, U.S. schools have added a manifest function, **inclusion** or mainstreaming. This means that educators try to incorporate students with disabilities into regular school activities. Wheelchair ramps are provided for people who cannot walk, and interpreters who use sign language attend classes with those who cannot hear. Most students who are blind attend special schools, as do people with severe learning disabilities. Most inclusion seems to go fairly smoothly, but mainstreaming students with serious emotional and behavioral problems disrupts classrooms, frustrates teachers, and increases teacher turnover (Tomsho and Golden 2007). Overall, 95 percent of students with disabilities attend school in regular classrooms at least part of the day (U.S. Department of Education 2011).

Gatekeeping (Social Placement)

Sociologists Talcott Parsons (1940), Kingsley Davis, and Wilbert Moore (Davis and Moore 1945) pioneered a view called **social placement**.

inclusion helping people to become part of the mainstream of society; also called *mainstreaming*

social placement a function of education— funneling people into a society's various positions

Unit 12.2 The Functionalist Perspective: Providing Social Benefits   **393**

They pointed out that some jobs require few skills and can be performed by people of lesser intelligence. Other jobs, such as those of engineer and physician, require higher intelligence and more education. It is up to the schools to sort the capable from the incapable. They do this on the basis of the students' abilities and ambitions.

As you can see, social placement, more commonly known as **gatekeeping**, means to open the doors of opportunity for some and to close those doors to others. The question is: What opens and closes those doors? Is it merit, as the functionalists argue? To accomplish gatekeeping, schools use some form of **tracking**, sorting students into different educational "tracks" or programs on the basis of their perceived abilities. Some U.S. high schools funnel students into one of three tracks: general, college prep, or honors. Students on the lowest track are likely to go to work after high school, or to take vocational courses. Those on the highest track usually attend prestigious colleges. Those in between usually attend a local college or regional state university.

You can also see that the impact of gatekeeping is lifelong. Tracking affects people's opportunities for jobs, income, and lifestyle. When tracking was challenged—that it is based more on social class than merit—schools retreated from formal tracking. Placing students in "ability groups" and "advanced" classes, however, serves the same purpose (Gamoran 2009).

Replacing Family Functions

Over the years, the functions of U.S. schools have expanded so greatly that they even replace some family functions. Child care is an example. Grade schools do double duty as babysitters for families in which both parents work, or for single working

gatekeeping the process by which education opens and closes doors of opportunity; another term for the social placement function of education

tracking in education, the sorting of students into different programs on the basis of perceived abilities

mothers. Child care has always been a latent function of formal education, for it was an unintended consequence. With two wage earners in most families, child care has become a manifest function, and some schools offer child care both before and after the school day. Some high schools even provide nurseries for the children of their teenaged students (Bosman 2007).

Another expanded function in this nation's schools is providing sex education, and, as in 500 school-based health centers, birth control (Elliott 2007). This has stirred controversy, for some families resent schools taking this function away from them.

IN SUM: Functionalists analyze the functions, the benefits, that schools provide society. Not only do the schools teach the knowledge and skills needed by the next generation, but they also stabilize the society by forging a national identity. A controversial function is gatekeeping, sorting students for various levels of jobs. The functions of schools have expanded, replacing some of the family's functions.

UNIT 12.2 // TESTING MYSELF
DID I LEARN IT? ANSWERS ARE AT THE END OF THE CHAPTER

1. "OK, let's test each other, and see if we've got this down. Do you know what theoretical perspective this statement represents?" asked Eboni. "When the parts of society are working properly, each contributes to the well-being or stability of that society." "Sure," said Ammon, "This is
   a. marginalization
   b. conflict
   c. symbolic interactionism
   d. functionalism

2. "Do you remember the term for the positive things that people intend their actions to accomplish?" asked Eboni. "Yes, those are
   a. dysfunctions
   b. latent functions
   c. manifest functions
   d. intentional actions

3. "How about if something positive comes out of people's actions, but they weren't intended?" asked Ammon. "Those," said Eboni, "are
   a. dysfunctions
   b. latent functions
   c. manifest functions
   d. unintentional actions

4. "And when schools pass on a society's core values from one generation to the next," continued Eboni, this function is called
   a. transmission of mainstream values
   b. teaching knowledge and skills
   c. social integration
   d. gatekeeping

5. "My grandma told me about a neighbor with disabilities who couldn't go to school when she was young," said Ammon. "My cousin is in a wheelchair, and he

With more two-paycheck families, childcare has become a manifest function of schools.

goes to regular school," said Eboni. "I know him," said Ammon. "He's in school because of a program called

a. Opportunity Bound   b. bridging
c. Reaching Out   d. inclusion

6. "Did you know that schools track some people into jobs that require few skills, which pay little, and others into jobs that require more skills and pay more?" asked Eboni. "I didn't know that," said Ammon, "but I learned about it in this unit. I think they call this gate-keeping." "Right," said Eboni. "And the other name is

a. mainstreaming
b. social integration
c. social placement
d. cultural transmission of values

7. "Schools are actually replacing some family functions," said Ammon. "This one has raised a lot of controversy

a. supervising homework
b. providing sex education
c. providing recreation
d. competitive sports

UNIT 12.3

The Conflict Perspective: Perpetuating Social Inequality

WHAT AM I SUPPOSED TO LEARN?

After you have read this unit, you should be able to

1 Explain the conflict perspective on education.

Unlike functionalists, who look at the benefits of education, conflict theorists examine how *the educational system helps to pass social inequality across generations*. They call this *reproducing*

Inequality in education shows up in many ways, such as the "nonessential" courses that schools offer or fail to offer their students.

social inequality. By this, they mean that schools perpetuate the social divisions of society and help members of the elite to maintain their dominance.

Let's look, then, at how education is related to social classes and how it helps people inherit *social capital,* the life opportunities that were laid down before they were born.

Stacking the Deck: Unequal Funding

Conflict theorists stress that the way schools are funded stacks the deck against the poor. Because public schools are supported largely by local property taxes, the richer communities (where property values and incomes are higher) have more to spend on their children, and the poorer communities have less to spend on theirs. Consequently, the richer communities can offer higher salaries and take their pick of the most highly qualified and motivated teachers. They can also afford to buy the latest textbooks, computers, and software, as well as offer courses in foreign languages, music, and the arts. This, stress conflict theorists, means that in *all* states the deck is stacked against the poor.

Tilting the Tests: Discrimination by IQ

Even intelligence tests help to keep the social class system intact. Let's look at an example. How would you answer this question?

A symphony is to a composer as a book is to a(n) ___
___ paper ___ sculptor ___ musician ___ author ___ man

You probably had no difficulty coming up with "author" as your choice. Wouldn't any intelligent person have done so?

Actually, no—and this takes us to the heart of a central issue in intelligence testing. Why wouldn't all intelligent people know the answer? This question contains *cultural biases*. Isn't it true that children from some backgrounds are more familiar with the concepts of symphonies, composers, and sculptors than are other children? This means that the test is tilted in their favor.

To make the bias clearer, I would like you to try to answer this question:

If you throw two dice and "7" is showing on the top, what is facing down?

___*seven* ___*snake eyes* ___*box cars* ___*little Joes* ___*eleven*

Adrian Dove (n.d.), a social worker in Watts, a poor area of Los Angeles, suggested this question. Its cultural bias should be obvious—that it allows children from certain social backgrounds to perform better than others. Unlike the first question, this one is not tilted to the middle-class experience. In other words, IQ (intelligence quotient) tests measure not only intelligence but also acquired knowledge.

You should now be able to perceive the bias of IQ tests that use such words as *composer* and *symphony*. A lower-class child may have heard about rap, rock, gangsta, or jazz, but not about symphonies. One consequence of this bias to the middle-class experience is that the children of the poor score lower on IQ tests. Then, to match their supposedly inferior intelligence, these children are assigned to less demanding courses. Their inferior education helps

them reach their social destiny: lower-paying jobs in adult life. As conflict theorists view them, then, IQ tests are another weapon in an arsenal designed to maintain the social class structure across the generations.

Let's pursue this main point of conflict theory.

The Bottom Line: Family Background

REPRODUCING THE SOCIAL CLASS STRUCTURE

The end result of unequal funding, IQ tests, and other factors is this: Family background is more important than test scores in predicting who attends college. In a classic study, sociologist Samuel Bowles (1977) compared the college attendance of high school students who had scored the highest and lowest on college prep tests. From Figure 12.2, you can see how social class overpowers ability. Of the high school students who scored the highest, 90 percent of those from affluent homes went to college, while only half of those from low-income homes did. Of the students who scored the lowest, 26 percent from affluent homes went to college, while only 6 percent from poorer homes did so.

Other sociologists have confirmed this classic research. Anthony Carnevale and Stephen Rose (2003) also compared students' college attendance with their intellectual abilities and their parents' social class. Regardless of personal abilities, children from more well-to-do families are more likely not only to go to college but also to attend the nation's most elite schools. This, in turn, piles advantage upon advantage, because they get higher-paying and more prestigious jobs when they graduate. The elite colleges are icing on the cake for these students of more privileged birth.

Education can be a great "leveler," offering the same advantages ... all children, regardless of their social class. In practice, it ...sn't work this way.

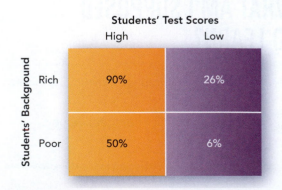

FIGURE 12.2 **Who Goes to College? Comparing Social Class and Ability in Determining College Attendance**

	Students' Test Scores	
	High	Low
Rich	90%	26%
Poor	50%	6%

Students' Background

Source: Bowles 1977.

REPRODUCING THE RACIAL–ETHNIC STRUCTURE

Conflict theorists point out that the educational system reproduces not only the U.S. social class structure but also its racial–ethnic divisions. Look at Figure 12.3. Notice that compared with whites, African Americans and Latinos are much less likely to complete high school and, of those who do, much less likely to go to college. Because adults without college degrees usually end up with low-paying, dead-end jobs, you can see how this supports the conflict view—that education is helping to reproduce the racial–ethnic structure for the next generation.

IN SUM: U.S. schools closely reflect the U.S. social class system. They equip the children of the elite with the tools they need to maintain their dominance, while they prepare the children of the poor for lower-status positions. Because education's doors of opportunity swing wide open for some but have to be pried open by others, conflict theorists say that the educational system perpetuates social inequality across generations (or, as they often phrase it, helps to reproduce the social class structure). In fact, they add, this is one of its primary purposes.

To reveal the schools' hidden curriculum, read *Making It Personal.*

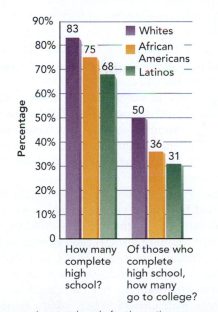

FIGURE 12.3

The Funneling Effects of Education: Race–Ethnicity

Note: The source gives totals only for these three groups.
Source: By the author. Based on Statistical Abstract of the United States *2011:Table 269.*

MAKING IT PERSONAL
You and the Hidden Curriculum

Let's look at another aspect of education that conflict theorists stress and see how it applies to you. The term **hidden curriculum** refers to the attitudes and unwritten rules of behavior that schools teach in addition to the formal curriculum. Examples are obedience to authority and conformity to mainstream norms. Conflict theorists stress that the hidden curriculum helps to perpetuate social inequalities.

To understand this central point, consider the way English is taught—and this is one of the most powerful examples you will ever come across. Schools for the middle class—whose teachers know where their students are headed—stress "proper" English and "good" manners. In contrast, the teachers in inner-city schools—who know where *their* students are headed—allow ethnic and street language in the classroom.

Each type of school helps to reproduce the social class structure. That is, each is preparing students to work in positions similar to those of their parents. The social class of some children destines them for higher positions. For these jobs, they need "refined" speech and manners. The social destiny of other students is low-status jobs. For this type of work, they need only to obey rules (Bowles and Gintis 1976,,2002). Teaching these students "refined" speech and manners would be wasted effort. In other words, even the teaching of English helps keep the social classes intact across generations.

Can you see from this example how schools help perpetuate social inequality? Whether you went to an inner-city school, a middle-class school, or an elite school, can you see how your schools were part of your "social destiny?" If you broke with that social destiny, how did it happen?

> **hidden curriculum** the unwritten goals of schools, such as teaching obedience to authority and conformity to cultural norms

DID I LEARN IT? ANSWERS ARE AT THE END OF THE CHAPTER

1. Ammon asked, "Do you know what this means? 'The educational system reproduces the social class structure.'" "Not a clue," said Eboni. "It means," replied Ammon, "that schools
   a. take their orders from the elite
   b. are not really interested in democracy
   c. have the hidden goal of keeping the poor from getting ahead
   d. perpetuate or help maintain the divisions of society

2. "It's still a little fuzzy," said Eboni. "Can you try to explain it another way?" "Sure," commented Ammon. "The text also put it this way

   a. There is no justice in life.
   b. Our society is filled with social inequalities and always will be.
   c. Schools help people inherit the life opportunities that were laid down before they were born.
   d. You can't expect teachers to do any better because the wealthy rule society.

3. "I don't understand how schools can help perpetuate social inequality. I thought they were trying to help people get ahead," said Eboni. "A lot of teachers are doing that," said Ammon, "but there are what sociologists call structural aspects of education." (Ammon had read a supplementary source.) "Schools in poor areas get less money to run their schools. IQ tests have cultural biases that discriminate against the poor. There is also this factor

   a. the anti-poor bias of teachers
   b. the hidden curriculum
   c. backstage string pulling by the elite
   d. expanding opportunities

4. "Here's the bottom line," said Ammon. "Regardless of their abilities, the children of the wealthy

   a. are more likely to go to college
   b. have more intelligence
   c. are more responsible
   d. are more likely to want to get ahead through education

UNIT 12.4
The Symbolic Interactionist Perspective: Teacher Expectations

WHAT AM I SUPPOSED TO LEARN?

After you have read this unit, you should be able to

1 Explain the symbolic interactionist perspective on education.

One of the fascinating aspects of education is how teacher expectations influence learning.

You have seen how functionalists focus on how education benefits society, and that conflict theorists examine how education perpetuates social inequality. Symbolic interactionists, in contrast, study face-to-face interaction in the classroom. They have found that the expectations of teachers have profound consequences for their students. Let's see what these are.

The Rist Research

In your high school, you probably saw some people get tracked into college prep courses and others into vocational ones. What is the basis for this separation? There is no single answer, but in what has become classic research, sociologist Ray Rist came up with some intriguing findings. Rist (1970, 2007) did participant observation in an African American grade school with an African American faculty. He found that after only eight days in the classroom, the kindergarten teacher felt that she knew the children's abilities well enough to assign them to three separate worktables. To Table 1, Mrs. Caplow assigned those she considered to be "fast learners." They sat at the front of the room, closest to her. Those whom she saw as "slow learners," she assigned to Table 3, located at the back of the classroom. She placed "average" students at Table 2, in between the other tables.

This seemed strange to Rist. He knew that the children had not been tested for ability, yet their teacher was certain that she could identify the bright and slow children. Investigating further, Rist found that social class was the basis for these assignments. Middle-class students were separated out for Table 1, and children from poorer homes were assigned to Tables 2 and 3. The teacher paid the most attention to the children at Table 1, who were closest to her, less to Table 2, and the least to Table 3. It didn't take long for the children at Table 1 to perceive that they were treated better and to come to see themselves as smarter. They became the leaders in class activities and even ridiculed children at the other tables, calling them "dumb." Eventually, the children at Table 3

How Do Teacher Expectations Work?

Sociologist George Farkas (1990a, 1990b, 1996) became interested in how teacher expectations affect grades. Using a stratified sample of students in a large school district in Texas, he found that teacher expectations produced gender and racial–ethnic biases. *On the gender level:* Even though boys and girls had the same test scores, girls on average were given higher course grades. *On the racial–ethnic level:* Asian Americans who had the same test scores as the other groups averaged higher grades than did African Americans, Latinos, and whites.

At first, this may sound like more of the same old news—another case of discrimination. But this explanation doesn't fit, which is what makes the finding fascinating. Look at who the victims are. It is unlikely that the teachers would be prejudiced against boys and whites. To interpret these unexpected findings, Farkas used symbolic interactionism. He observed that some students "signal" to their teachers that they are "good students." They show an eagerness to cooperate, and they quickly agree with what the teacher says. They also show that they are "trying hard." The teachers pick up these signals and reward these "good students" with better grades. Girls and Asian Americans, the researcher concluded, are better at giving these signals so coveted by teachers.

In the next *Making It Personal*, let's consider how "signaling" might apply to you.

The effects of self-fulfilling prophecies, a significant area of sociological research, begin early in the educational process.

disengaged themselves from many classroom activities. At the end of the year, only the children at Table 1 had completed the lessons that prepared them for reading.

This early tracking stuck. Their first-grade teacher looked at the work these students had done, and she placed students from Table 1 at her Table 1. She treated her tables much as the kindergarten teacher had, and the children at Table 1 again led the class.

The children's reputations continued to follow them. The second-grade teacher reviewed their scores and also divided her class into three groups. The first she named the "Tigers" and, befitting their name, gave them challenging readers. Not surprisingly, the Tigers came from the original Table 1 in kindergarten. The second group she called the "Cardinals." They came from the original Tables 2 and 3. Her third group consisted of children she had failed the previous year, whom she called the "Clowns." The Cardinals and Clowns were given less advanced readers.

Rist concluded that *each child's journey through school was determined by the eighth day of kindergarten!* As we saw with the Saints and Roughnecks in Chapter 5, labels can be so powerful that they set people on courses of action that affect the rest of their lives.

What occurred was a **self-fulfilling prophecy**, a term, coined by sociologist Robert Merton (1949/1968). This term refers to a false assumption of something that is going to happen but which then comes true simply because it was predicted. For example, if people believe an unfounded rumor that a credit union is going to fail because its officers have embezzled their money, they all rush to the credit union to demand their money. The prediction—although originally false—is now likely to come true.

One caveat (a fancy way of saying "warning") about the Rist research: This was one kindergarten in St. Louis, Missouri. As with other participant observation research, we do not know how far it applies to other schools.

self-fulfilling prophecy
Robert Merton's term for an originally false assertion that becomes true simply because it was predicted

MAKING IT PERSONAL

How Do You Signal?

So, grade school students "give messages" to their teachers—and, without being aware of it, teachers respond to those messages. Do you think this happens in high school? You know it does. You probably saw plenty of it. The "Saints" and the "Roughnecks" that you read about in Chapter 6 confirms that it happens in high school. Do you think, then, that this happens in college? Hmmm. Could be. But we have no data on this, so we can't say.

Think about your own "signaling." What "messages" have you tried to give teachers about yourself? Perhaps that you are a "good" student who is "really trying"? Perhaps something else. What? How?

We don't know much about how students "signal" messages to teachers. Perhaps you will become the educational sociologist who will shed more light on this significant area of human behavior.

UNIT 12.4 // TESTING MYSELF
DID I LEARN IT? ANSWERS ARE AT THE END OF THE CHAPTER

1. "I'm glad that didn't happen to me," said Eboni. "What didn't happen?" asked Ammon. "I read about a kindergarten where the teacher put the kids in different tables and treated them differently. Those who got the most attention from the teacher were kids who
   a. had transferred from other schools
   b. were from urban areas
   c. had come from foreign countries
   d. were from middle class homes

2. "So what?" shrugged Ammon. "It made a big difference," said Eboni. "The kids who got the teacher's attention completed the year's reading goals. The others didn't. And the following year
   a. The students who did well continued to do well, and those who did poorly continued to do poorly.
   b. There was no consistent pattern.
   c. The pattern set up in kindergarten was reversed.
   d. The teacher was fired.

3. "Basically," continued Eboni, "the teacher had an idea that certain students would do well, and she did

things that stimulated them to do well, and ... " "I know what that is," said Ammon. "It's
   a. bias
   b. a self-fulfilling prophecy
   c. a fake reality
   d. an amplified social class realism

4. "There was another study that was interesting," said Eboni, "because it reminded me of you." "What do you mean?" asked Ammon. "Don't forget that I went to grade school with you. I remember how you were always raising your hand and the good grades you got. I think teachers liked this because you
   a. were giving signals that you were a good student
   b. were showing them that you were middle class
   c. didn't spend as much time at video games as I did
   d. would rather be reading books than out playing sports

5. "I didn't do anything special. That's just me. Why do you bring it up?" "Because," Eboni replied, "I realize now that you
   a. were just a kid and didn't know what you were doing
   b. might have been punished by your parents if you hadn't done this
   c. have changed
   d. might have received better grades because of it

6. "Forget me," said Ammon. "Is there a general term besides self-fulfilling prophecy for all this?" "Glad you asked," said Eboni laughing. "I've been wanting to tell you. It's
   a. mental constructs
   b. reality differentiation
   c. teacher expectations
   d. symbolic scenery

UNIT 12.5
Problems in U.S. Education—And Their Solutions

Now that we've looked at some of the dynamics within the classroom, let's turn to two problems facing U.S. education—mediocrity and violence—and consider potential solutions.

WHAT AM I SUPPOSED TO LEARN?

After you have read this unit, you should be able to

1 Explain the problems of mediocrity and violence in education and their possible solutions.

One of the more obtrusive and unwelcome changes in U.S. education.

Mediocrity

THE RISING TIDE OF MEDIOCRITY

Since I know you love taking tests, let's see how you do on these three questions:

1. How many goals are on a basketball court?
   a. 1 b. 2 c. 3 d. 4

2. How many halves are in a college basketball game?
   a. 1 b. 2 c. 3 d. 4

3. How many points does a three-point field goal account for in a basketball game?
   a. 1 b. 2 c. 3 d. 4

I know that this sounds like a joke, but it isn't. Sociologist Robert Benford (2007) got his hands on a copy of a 20-question final examination given to basketball players who took a credit course on coaching principles at the University of Georgia. This is about as mediocre as mediocrity can get.

Let's move to a broader view of the mediocrity that plagues our educational system like pollution plagues gasoline engines:

- Arizona officials gave their high school sophomores a math test that covered the math that sophomores should know. *One of ten passed.*
- New York officials were so pleased with *their* test results that they called a press conference. They boasted that 80 percent of their students were proficient at math. When the students took a federal test, though, the results dropped just a bit—to 34 percent (Medina 2009).
- Pennsylvania students also did miserably, but officials figured out a solution: Students who can't pass the exit exam can do "projects" instead.
- Not to be outdone in this race to the bottom, Arkansas dropped its passing score in math to 24 out of 100 (Urbina 2010a).
- Overall, U.S. schools have reduced their standards so greatly that only *34 percent* of high school graduates are ready for college (Greene and Winters 2005).

As an educator, I find these events disturbing, disgusting, and inexcusable. As a student, I hope you do, too. You are going to be living in this country for a long time, and this kind of education does not indicate a bright future for the nation.

THE SAT TESTS

When it comes to the SAT tests, the news is mixed. First the good news. Look at Figure 12.4. You can see how the scores dropped from the 1960s to 1980. When Congress expressed concern, school officials decided they had better do something if they didn't want to lose their jobs. They raised their standards, and the SAT scores started to climb. The recovery in math is encouraging. Today's high school seniors now score the same in math as seniors did in the 1960s. Administrators are requiring more of teachers, and teachers are requiring more of students. Each is performing according to these higher expectations.

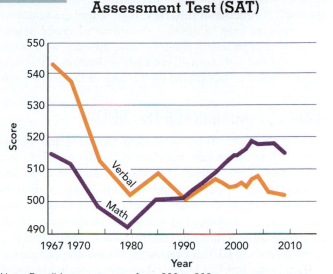

FIGURE 12.4 **National Results of the Scholastic Assessment Test (SAT)**

Note: Possible scores range from 200 to 800.
Sources: By the author. Based on Statistical Abstract of the United States 2012:Table 267.

But then there is the bad news. Look at the verbal scores on Figure 12.4. Their drop from the 1960s is even larger than the drop in math, and they have not recovered. Today's students can't handle analogies and antonyms, which demand penetrating thinking. No one knows why the verbal scores remain so low, but the usual suspects have been rounded up: "dummied down" textbooks, less rigorous teaching, and less reading because of television and video and computer games.

Rather than facing the bad news—and force schools to do a better job of teaching, as they did with math—the makers of the SAT took the easy way out: They made the SAT easier. They dropped the testing on analogies and antonyms and shortened the test. Then they gave students more time to take the shorter, easier test. The test makers then "rescored" the totals of previous years to match the easier test. This "dummying down" of the SAT is a form of grade inflation, the topic to which we shall now turn.

> ◉─ **Watch** the **Video**
> Sociology on the Job:
> Education in **mysoclab**

GRADE INFLATION, SOCIAL PROMOTION, AND FUNCTIONAL ILLITERACY

The letter grade C used to indicate average, and since more students are average than superior, high school teachers used to give about twice as many C's as A's. Now they give more A's than C's. Students aren't smarter—grading is just easier. Grades have become so inflated that some of today's A's are the C's of years past. **Grade inflation** is so pervasive that *48 percent* of all college freshmen have an overall high school grade-point average of A. This is more than *twice* what it was in 1970 (*Statistical Abstract* 2012:Table 286).

> **grade inflation** higher grades given for the same work; a general rise in student grades without a corresponding in-crease in learning

Easy grades and declining standards have been accompanied by **social promotion**, passing students from one grade to the next even though they have not learned the basic materials. One result is **functional illiteracy**, high school graduates who never mastered even things they should have learned in grade school. Some high school graduates have difficulty with reading and writing and can't even fill out a job application. Others can't figure out whether they get the right change at the grocery store.

RAISING STANDARDS FOR TEACHERS

It is one thing to identify problems, quite another to find solutions for them. How can we solve mediocrity? To offer a quality education, we need quality teachers. Don't we already have them? Most teachers are qualified and, if motivated, can do an excellent job. But a large number of teachers are not qualified. Consider just a couple of items. California requires that its teachers pass an educational skills test. California's teachers did so poorly that to get enough teachers to fill their classrooms, officials dropped the passing grade to the 10th-grade level. These are college graduates who are teachers—and they are expected to perform at the 10th-grade level (Schemo 2002). I don't know about you, but I think this situation is a national disgrace. If we want to improve teaching, we need to insist that teachers meet high standards.

RAISING STANDARDS FOR STUDENTS

What else can we do to improve the quality of education? An older study by sociologists James Coleman and Thomas Hoffer (1987) provides helpful guidelines. They wanted to see why the test scores of students in

> **social promotion** passing students on to the next level even though they have not mastered basic materials
>
> **functional illiterate** a high school graduate who has difficulty with basic reading and math

U.S. primary and high schools generally do a mediocre job. Do you think higher teacher salaries would help solve this problem?

Roman Catholic schools average 15 to 20 percent higher than those of students in public schools. Is it because Catholic schools attract better students, while public schools have to put up with everyone? To find out, they tested 15,000 students in public and Catholic high schools.

Their findings? From the sophomore through the senior years, students at Catholic schools pull ahead of public school students by a full grade in verbal and math skills. The superior test performance of students in Catholic schools, the researchers concluded, is not because of better students, but because of higher standards. Catholic schools have not watered down their teaching as have public schools. The researchers also underscored the importance of parental involvement. Parents and teachers in Catholic schools reinforce each other's commitment to learning.

To see how this might apply to you—and how the bureaucracy you might work for can devour you—read the following *Making It Personal*.

MAKING IT PERSONAL
Squashed by the Organization

Here's the basic principle that underlies the findings about Roman Catholic and public schools: Students perform better when they are expected to meet higher standards. To this, you might want to reply, "I knew that. Who wouldn't?" Somehow, however, this basic principle is lost on many teachers. They end up teaching at a low level because they expect little of their students, and they have supervisors who accept low student performance. The obvious, then, is not always so obvious, is it?

Let's probe a little deeper, though. Teachers and supervisors are probably aware of these basics. I've seen new college graduates start out teaching with enthusiasm and a desire to change the world, or at least the students in their classroom. But they get ensnared in a bureaucracy, and bit by bit, filling out forms and meeting nonsensical goals replaces their teaching. Gradually, the fire that set them on the path of teaching is replaced with the dullness of meeting requirements and qualifying for a raise.

Watch out after you graduate. Whatever you are going to do—and it doesn't have to be teaching—watch out for the organization that will engulf you, smother you, and, if possible, remove your very humanity by turning you into an unthinking, obedient machine. You might find yourself walking in a robotic stupor the rest of your life.

A WARNING ABOUT HIGHER STANDARDS

If we raise standards, we can expect protest. Which do you think upsets people? To use low standards and to tell students they are doing well? Or to do rigorous teaching and use high standards to measure student achievement? I think you know. Listen to what happened when Florida raised its standards. The state decided that high school seniors needed to pass an assessment test in order to receive a diploma. *Thirteen thousand* students failed the test. Did parents tell the kids to buckle down and study? No. The parents of failed students banded together to pressure the state to drop the new test. They even asked people to boycott Disney World and to not buy Florida orange juice (Canedy 2003). What positive steps to improve their children's learning!

Enough of this one. Let's look at a second problem in education.

> **Read the Document**
> "Race-Specific Policies and the Truly Disadvantaged" by William Julius Wilson in **mysoclab**

Violence

Some U.S. schools have deteriorated to the point that safety is an issue. In these schools, uniformed guards and metal detectors have become permanent fixtures. In an era of bomb threats, terrorists, and roaming sociopaths, school officials everywhere fear that "it could happen here." Some states require lockdown, or "Code Blue," drills: The classrooms—each equipped with a phone—are locked, the windows are locked, and the shades are drawn. The students are told to remain absolutely silent, while a school official wanders the halls, like an armed intruder, listening for the slightest sound that would indicate that someone was in a classroom (Kelley 2008).

IF YOU WANT TO LEARN MORE about school violence,

> **Read** more from the author: School Shootings: Exploring a Myth in **mysoclab**

A SECURE LEARNING ENVIRONMENT

The first step in offering good education is to keep students safe and free from fear. To minimize violence, school administrators

Police protect students as they run under cover from Columbine High School on April 20, 1999.

can expel all students who threaten the welfare of others. They also can refuse to tolerate threats, violence, and weapons. Although there have been examples of stupid enforcement, such as a second grader being expelled for having nail clippers, a zero tolerance policy for guns and other weapons on school property helps to make schools safer.

1. "I read some statistics that bother me," said Ammon. "What?" asked Eboni. "There are a lot of them, but this one sums them up. Our schools have lowered their standards so much that only this percentage of high school graduates are ready for college
   a. 34
   b. 44
   c. 54
   d. 64

2. "Ugh," said Eboni. "That can't be good for the country. By the way, how did you do on your SATs?" "I don't want to talk about that," answered Ammon. "That's what I thought," Eboni replied. "Did you see the national results, how far the scores dropped from the 1960s to 1980?" "I did," said Ammon. "Do you remember which ones went back up to where they were back in the old days?"
   a. achievement scores
   b. analogy scores
   c. math scores
   d. verbal scores

3. "Which ones are still down, then?" asked Eboni, still wondering if Ammon had read the material.
   a. achievement scores
   b. analogy scores
   c. math scores
   d. verbal scores

4. "What else was listed as part of the mediocrity of education?" asked Ammon. "Grade inflation was pretty striking," said Eboni. "C is supposed to represent average, but 48 percent of high school graduates who enter college now have
   a. an A average
   b. a B average
   c. a C average
   d. a D average

5. "How can A be average?" asked Ammon. "That doesn't make sense." "I know," agreed Eboni, "but this is the way it is. Anyway, the Roman Catholic students do much better on tests than the public school

students." "Sure," said Ammon. "They get to pick and choose their students." "That's not it," answered Eboni. "Sociologists compared the students, and the RC students kept pulling farther ahead each year." "Then what is it?" asked Ammon. "The Roman Catholic schools

a. require extracurricular activities
b. have less emphasis on sports
c. ban cell phones
d. have higher teacher expectations (standards)

6. "I agree with the author that to offer a good education, students have to be safe and free from fear," said Ammon. "The solution he suggested might be right. I don't know, but he proposed

a. probation for possessing a weapon on school property
b. jail for possessing a weapon on school property
c. zero tolerance of threats, violence, and weapons on school property
d. giving a stern warning to the student and sending a letter to the parents

RELIGION: ESTABLISHING MEANING

UNIT 12.6

Religion in Global Perspective

WHAT AM I SUPPOSED TO LEARN?

After you have read this unit, you should be able to

1 Summarize Emile Durkheim's conclusions about religion.

Let's look at the main characteristics of a second significant social institution.

Orthodox Jews at a synagogue in Jerusalem.

What Is Religion?

Sociologists who do research on religion do not try to prove that one religion is better than another. Nor is it their goal to verify or disprove anyone's faith. As was mentioned in Chapter 1, sociologists have no tools for deciding that one course of action is more moral than another, much less for determining that one religion is "the" correct one. Religion is a matter of faith—and sociologists deal with empirical matters, things they can observe or measure.

When it comes to religion, then, sociologists study the effects of religious beliefs and practices on people's lives. They also analyze how religion is related to society, especially to its stratification systems. They do not try to evaluate the truth of a religion's teachings.

Emile Durkheim was highly interested in religion, probably because he was reared in a mixed-religion family by a Protestant mother and a Jewish father. Durkheim decided to find out what all religions have in common. After surveying religions around the world, in 1912 he published his findings in *The Elementary Forms of the Religious Life*. Here are Durkheim's three main findings.

1. The world's religions are so varied that they have no specific belief or practice in common.

2. All religions develop a community centering on their beliefs and practices.

3. All religions separate the sacred from the profane. By **sacred**, Durkheim referred to aspects of life having to do with the supernatural that inspire awe, reverence, deep respect, even fear. By **profane**, he meant aspects of life that are not concerned with religion but, instead, are part of ordinary, everyday life.

> **sacred** Durkheim's term for things set apart or forbidden that inspire fear, awe, reverence, or deep respect

> **profane** Durkheim's term for common elements of everyday life

Durkheim (1912/1965) summarized his conclusions by saying:

A religion is a unified system of beliefs and practices relative to sacred things, that is to say, things set apart and forbidden—beliefs and practices which unite into one single moral community called a Church, all those who adhere to them.

Religion, then, has three elements:

1. *Beliefs* that some things are sacred (forbidden, set apart from the profane)

2. *Practices* (rituals) centering on the things considered sacred

3. *A moral community* (a church) resulting from a group's beliefs and practices

Durkheim used the word **church** in an unusual way, to refer to any

religion according to Durkheim, beliefs and practices that separate the profane from the sacred and unite its adherents into a moral community

church according to Durkheim, one of the three essential elements of religion—a moral community of believers; also refers to a large, highly organized religious group that has formal, sedate worship services with little emphasis on evangelism, intense religious experience, or personal conversion

A statue of Buddha at Ayutthaya, Thailand.

"moral community" centered on beliefs and practices regarding the sacred. In Durkheim's sense, *church* refers to Buddhists bowing before a shrine, Hindus dipping in the Ganges River, and Confucians offering food to their ancestors. Similarly, the term *moral community* does not imply morality in the sense you are familiar with—of ethical conduct. Rather, a moral community is simply a group of people who are united by their religious practices—and that would include sixteenth-century Aztec priests who each day gathered around an altar to pluck out the beating heart of a virgin.

UNIT 12.6 // TESTING MYSELF
DID I LEARN IT? ANSWERS ARE AT THE END OF THE CHAPTER

1. "Sociologists study religion," said Eboni. "I know that. They try to disprove religion," replied Ammon. "No, they don't," Eboni stated. "They study religion in order to
   a. locate the true religion
   b. find out which religions are the closest to the truth
   c. find the effects of religious participation on people's lives
   d. determine the difference between science and religion

2. "That early sociologist, Emile Durkheim, studied religion," said Eboni. "And they are still quoting him?" asked Ammon. "Yes. That's because he discovered basic principles," Eboni answered. "Like what?" asked Ammon. "Like this: Religions are so varied that they have no particular beliefs or practices in common, but they all separate the world into the sacred and the profane." "Profane? What did he mean by that?" asked Ammon. "This refers to
   a. things set apart and forbidden
   b. anti-religious things
   c. things like cussing
   d. aspects of life that are not concerned with religion, that are part of everyday life

3. "What did Durkheim mean by sacred, then?" asked Ammon. "This," said Eboni, "refers to
   a. things that inspire fear, awe, and reverence
   b. anti-religious things
   c. going to church
   d. aspects of life that are not concerned with religion, that are part of ordinary, everyday life

4. "Durkheim also said that all religions have rituals regarding the sacred, which unite its participants in a moral community," said Eboni. "Religions are moral, then," said Ammon. "Yes, but in a different way than we think of it. He simply meant that all religions are

united around their beliefs and practices. Even this was part of a moral community

    a. lions roaring after they kill an animal

    b. Aztec priests plucking the heart out of a living virgin

    c. children playing house

    d. teenagers at their first kiss

5. "That really is a different meaning of moral," said Ammon. "Yes, and he used church in a different way, too." "How?" asked Ammon. "In Durkheim's definition, this group is a church

    a. Muslims at a mosque

    b. students who are studying together

    c. an instructor lecturing to college students

    d. a family

6. "What did Durkheim say that religion is?" asked Ammon. "He said that every religion has these three elements," said Eboni

    a. beliefs, leaders, and followers

    b. place, priests, and practices

    c. practice, sacred, and profane

    d. beliefs, practices, and a moral community

UNIT 12.7
The Functionalist Perspective

WHAT AM I SUPPOSED TO LEARN?

After you have read this unit, you should be able to

1 Explain some functions of religion.

2 Explain some dysfunctions of religion.

To better understand the sociological approach to religion, let's see what pictures emerge when we apply the three theoretical perspectives. We'll begin with functionalism. Functionalists stress that religion is universal because it meets universal human needs. Let's look at some of the functions—and dysfunctions—of religion.

How do you think the six functions of religion mentioned here apply to this religious rally for teens?

Functions of Religion

QUESTIONS ABOUT ULTIMATE MEANING

Around the world, religions provide answers to perplexing questions about ultimate meaning—such as the purpose of life, why people suffer, and the existence of an afterlife. The answers give followers a sense of purpose. Instead of seeing themselves hit by random events in an aimless existence, believers see their lives as fitting into a divine plan.

EMOTIONAL COMFORT

People find comfort in the answers that religion provides about ultimate meaning. They are assured that there is a purpose to life, even to suffering. The rituals that enshroud crucial events such as illness and death also provide emotional comfort at times of crisis. The individual knows that others care and can find consolation in following familiar rituals.

SOCIAL SOLIDARITY

Religious teachings and practices unite believers into a community ("we Jews," "we Christians," "we Muslims") that is built around shared values and perspectives. The religious rituals that surround marriage, for example, link the bride and groom with a community that wishes them well. So do other religious rituals, such as those that celebrate birth and mourn death.

GUIDELINES FOR EVERYDAY LIFE

The teachings of religion are not all abstractions. They also provide practical guidelines for everyday life. For example, four of the ten commandments delivered by Moses to the Israelites concern God, but the other six contain instructions for getting along with others, from how to avoid problems with parents and neighbors to warnings about lying, stealing, and having affairs.

The consequences for people who follow these guidelines can be measured. For example, people who attend church are less likely to abuse alcohol, nicotine, and illegal drugs than are people who don't go to church (Gillum 2005; Wallace et al 2007; Gallup Poll 2010). In general, churchgoers follow a healthier lifestyle, and they live longer than people who don't go to church.

SOCIAL CONTROL

Religion not only provides guidelines for everyday life but also sets limits on behavior. Most norms of a religious group apply only to its members, but nonmembers also feel spillover. Religious teachings, for example, are incorporated into criminal law. In the United States, blasphemy and adultery were once crimes for which people could be arrested. Some states still have laws that prohibit the sale of alcohol before noon on Sunday, laws whose purpose was to get people out of the saloons and into the churches.

SOCIAL CHANGE

Although religion is often so bound up with the prevailing social order that it resists social change, religion occasionally spearheads change. In the 1960s, for example, the civil rights movement, whose goal was to desegregate public facilities and abolish racial discrimination at southern polls, was led by religious leaders, especially leaders of African American churches such as Martin Luther King, Jr. Churches also served as centers at which demonstrators were trained and rallies were organized. Other churches were centers for resisting this change.

Dysfunctions of Religion

Functionalists also examine ways in which religion is *dysfunctional*—that is, how it can bring harmful results. Two dysfunctions are religious persecution and war and terrorism.

RELIGION AS JUSTIFICATION FOR PERSECUTION

Beginning in the 1200s and continuing into the 1800s, in what has become known as the Inquisition, special commissions of the Roman Catholic Church tortured women to make them confess that they were witches. After the women confessed, they were burned at the stake. In 1692, Protestant leaders in Salem, Massachusetts,

Executing heretics—*those who disagree with someone's religious beliefs*—is a dysfunction of religion. Depicted in this woodcut is the execution of Jan Hus of Czechoslovakia on July 6, 1415.

executed twenty-one women and men who were accused of being witches. In 2001, in the Democratic Republic of the Congo, about 1,000 alleged witches were hacked to death (Jenkins 2002). In Angola, children who are accused of being witches are beaten and then killed (LaFraniere 2007). In Pakistan, women who commit adultery are stoned to death. Similarly, it seems fair to say that the Aztec religion had its dysfunctions—at least for the virgins who were offered to appease angry gods. In short, religion has been used to justify oppression and any number of brutal acts.

WAR AND TERRORISM

History is filled with wars based on religion—commingled with politics. Between the eleventh and fourteenth centuries, for example, Christian monarchs conducted nine bloody Crusades in an attempt to take the region they called the Holy Land away from the Muslims who controlled it. The suicide terrorists we discussed in Chapter 10 are a current example.

IF YOU WANT TO LEARN MORE about terrorism and religion,

Read more from the author: Terrorism and the Mind of God in **mysoclab**

UNIT 12.7 // TESTING MYSELF
DID I LEARN IT? ANSWERS ARE AT THE END OF THE CHAPTER

1. "Why are you religious, Amy?" asked LeRoy. "I don't know all the reasons, but I don't know what I would have done without my religion when my mom died. It is so good to know she is with God." Amy is referring to this function of religion: providing

   a. answers about ultimate meaning
   b. social solidarity
   c. guidelines for everyday life
   d. social control

2. "When the priest (minister, rabbi, imman) compared mom's life to a beautiful flower, it made me feel so much better," added Amy. Amy is referring to this function of religion: providing

   a. emotional comfort   **b.** social solidarity
   c. guidelines for everyday life   **d.** social control

3. "When people told me about how much my mother meant to them, I broke into tears. I really didn't know she had helped so many people," commented Amy. Amy is referring to this function of religion: providing

   a. answers about ultimate meaning
   b. social solidarity
   c. guidelines for everyday life
   d. social control

4. Amy stated, "I talked to the priest (minister, rabbi, imman), and he told me that the best thing I could do would be to follow in my mother's footsteps." Amy is referring to this function of religion: providing

   a. answers about ultimate meaning
   b. social solidarity
   c. guidelines for everyday life
   d. social stratification

5. "Before mom's death, I was using drugs and getting deeper into them. The priest (minister, rabbi, imman) had heard about this, and he explained why I had to stop. I feel a lot better now that the drugs are out of my system." Amy is referring to this function of religion: providing

   a. answers about ultimate meaning
   b. social solidarity
   c. emotional comfort
   d. social control

6. "Leaders of your religion used to march in the South, back when it was segregated, didn't they?" asked LeRoy. "Right. They even got thrown in jail." Amy is referring to this function of religion: promoting

   a. emotional comfort   **b.** social solidarity
   c. guidelines for everyday life   **d.** social change

7. "Religions aren't always so good," said LeRoy. "They used to burn witches at the stake, didn't they?" "Yes," agreed Amy. "And I saw a painting of an Aztec priest plucking out the heart of a living girl. I thought of myself when I saw it." LeRoy and Amy are referring to what sociologists call

   a. functions of religion   **b.** dysfunctions of religion
   c. persecution and terrorism   **d.** persecution, war, and terrorism

UNIT 12.8
The Conflict Perspective

WHAT AM I SUPPOSED TO LEARN?

After you have read this unit, you should be able to

1 Explain the conflict perspective on religion.

As usual, the emphasis of conflict theorists is quite different from those of the functionalists and symbolic interactionists. In general, when to comes to religion, conflict theorists are highly critical. They stress that religion supports the status quo (the existing social structure) and helps maintain social inequalities. Let's look at some of their analyses.

Opium of the People

Karl Marx, who founded conflict theory, was an avowed atheist. Believing that the existence of God was impossible, Marx set the tone for conflict theorists with this famous statement: "Religion is the sigh of the oppressed creature, the sentiment of a heartless world . . . . It is the opium of the people" (Marx 1844/1964). Marx meant that oppressed workers find escape in religion. He saw religion as similar to a drug (opium) that helps workers forget their misery. By taking their eyes off their suffering in this world and placing them on future happiness in an afterlife, religion reduces the possibility that workers will rebel against their oppressors.

Legitimating Social Inequalities

Conflict theorists say that religion legitimates the social inequalities of society. By this, they mean that religion teaches that the existing social arrangements of a society represent what God desires. For example, during the Middle Ages, Christian theologians taught the *divine right of kings*. This meant that God determined who would become king and set him on the throne. The king ruled in God's place, and it was the duty of a king's subjects to be loyal to him (and to pay their taxes). To disobey the king was to disobey God.

In what was perhaps the supreme technique of legitimating the social order (and one that went even a step farther than the divine right of kings), the religion of ancient Egypt held that the pharaoh himself was a god. The emperor of Japan was similarly declared divine. If this were so, who could ever question his decisions? Today's politicians would give their right arm for such a religious teaching.

Conflict theorists point to other examples of how religion legitimates the social order. It is part of a divine plan, say Hindus in India, that some people suffer in poverty and that others enjoy wealth and live in comfort. Anyone who tries to change caste will come back in the next life as a member of a lower caste—or even as a snake. A fascinating example comes from the United States before the Civil War. Southern ministers defended their region's view, using scripture to prove that slavery was God's will. In the North, ministers legitimated *their* region's social structure by using scripture to prove that slavery was evil (Ernst 1988; Nauta 1993; White 1995).

Hindus at an annual rite in the Ganges River at Varanasi, India. How would conflict theorists apply "legitimating the social order" to the Hindu caste system?

1. "I read that conflict theory was founded by an atheist," said LeRoy. "Who was that?" asked Amy. "It was

   a. Max Weber
   b. Emile Durkheim
   c. W. E B. DuBois
   d. Karl Marx

2. "Marx must have been hostile to religion, then," said Amy. "Yes, he was. He said that religion reduced the likelihood that workers would rebel against their oppressors. It took their eyes off their suffering and

   a. encouraged them take care of their families
   b. gave them food and helped with their rent
   c. placed their eyes on an afterlife
   d. got them to think about having fun, especially at church picnics

3. "Didn't Marx make some famous statement about this?" asked Amy. "Yes," replied LeRoy. "He said that religion was like

   a. an oceangoing ship
   b. opium
   c. a merry-go-round
   d. roller coaster

4. "Is that all? Don't conflict theorists say anything else?" asked Amy. "Sure they do," said LeRoy. "One of their main points is that

   a. Religion legitimates the social inequalities of society.
   b. There is no way to prove that there is an afterlife.
   c. Workers in poverty need to be thrifty so their savings can lift them out of poverty.
   d. If both owners and workers take their religion seriously, they will cooperate as brothers and sisters who share the same goals.

5. "What do conflict theorists mean that religion legitimates the social inequalities of society?" asked Amy. LeRoy answered, "They mean that religion teaches that

   a. Workers must rebel against their oppressors.
   b. Society should not change.
   c. There are many religions around the world, and all societies have social inequalities.
   d. The existing social arrangements of a society represent what God desires.

6. "Did you read any interesting examples?" asked Amy. "I liked the one about the pharaohs being gods," said LeRoy. "You can see how that kept people following the way things were set up in that society. Then there was one about how Hindu beliefs support

   a. the idea that the pharaohs were gods
   b. the idea that people should try their best to get ahead
   c. the caste system
   d. Vishnu as the head god

7. "And there was an example about the belief that God appointed the men who would be the kings," continued LeRoy. "I know that one," said Amy. "They called this the

   a. enlightened path
   b. rule of the nobility
   c. noble path
   d. divine right of kings

8. "And I really liked this one," said LeRoy. "When a country is divided, the same religion can divide, with each justifying its region's social inequalities." "I don't know what you mean. Was there an example?" asked Amy. "Yes. Before the War Between the States, ministers in the North condemned slavery, and those in the South

   a. defended slavery
   b. secretly plotted against the slaveholders
   c. were silent on slavery
   d. moved to the North

UNIT 12.9
The Symbolic Interactionist Perspective

WHAT AM I SUPPOSED TO LEARN?

After you have read this unit, you should be able to

 1 Explain the symbolic interactionist perspective on religion.

As you know, symbolic interactionists focus on the meanings that people give their experiences. Let's apply this perspective to religious symbols, beliefs, and rituals to see how they help to forge a community of like-minded people.

Religious Symbols

Suppose that it is about 2,000 years ago and you have just joined a new religion. You have come to believe that a recently crucified Jew named Jesus is the Messiah, the Lamb of God offered for your sins. The Roman leaders are persecuting the followers of Jesus. They hate your religion because

When I visited a Hindu temple in Chattisgargh, India, I was impressed by the colorful and expressive statues on its roof. Here is a close-up of some of those figures, which represent some of the millions of gods that Hindus worship.

you and your fellow believers will not acknowledge Caesar as God.

Christians are few in number, and you are eager to have fellowship with other believers. But how can you tell who is a believer? Spies are everywhere. The government has sworn to destroy this new religion, and you do not relish the thought of being fed to lions in the Coliseum.

You use a simple technique. While talking with a stranger, as though doodling absentmindedly in the sand or dust, you casually trace the outline of a fish. Only fellow believers know the meaning—that taken together, the first letter of each word in the Greek sentence "Jesus (is) Christ the Son of God" spell the Greek word for fish. If the other person gives no response, you rub out the outline and continue the interaction as usual. If there is a response, you eagerly talk about your new faith.

All religions use symbols to provide identity and create social solidarity for their members. For Muslims, the primary symbol is the crescent moon and star; for Jews, the Star of David; for Christians, the cross. For members, these are not ordinary symbols, but sacred emblems that evoke feelings of awe and reverence. In Durkheim's terms, religions use symbols to represent what the group considers sacred and to separate the sacred from the profane.

A symbol is a condensed way of communicating. Worn by a fundamentalist Christian, for example, the cross says, "I am a follower of Jesus Christ. I believe that he is the Messiah, the promised Son of God, that he loves me, that he died to take away my sins, that he rose from the dead and is going to return to earth, and that through him I will receive eternal life."

That is a lot to pack into one symbol—and it is only part of what this symbol means to a fundamentalist believer. To people in other traditions of Christianity, the cross conveys somewhat different meanings—but to all Christians, the cross is a way of expressing meaning. So it is with the Star of David, the crescent moon and star, the cow (expressing to Hindus the unity of all living things), and the various symbols of the world's many other religions.

Beliefs

All religions have beliefs. The belief may be vague ("God is") or highly specific ("God wants us to prostrate ourselves and face Mecca five times each day"). Religious beliefs include not only *values* (what is considered good and desirable in life—how we ought to live) but also a **cosmology**, a unified picture of the world. For example, the Jewish, Christian, and Muslim belief that there is only one God, the creator of the universe, who is concerned about the actions of humans and who will hold us accountable for what we do, is a cosmology. Such beliefs produce a unifying picture of the universe.

In the following *Making It Personal*, let's consider your cosmology.

| **cosmology** teachings or ideas that provide a unified picture of the world

MAKING IT PERSONAL
Your Cosmology

I don't know if you belong to a religious group or are religious in some other way. If you don't or are an atheist, you may skip this *Making It Personal* if you wish. All I want to ask is How do the essential elements of religion that Durkheim laid out—beliefs, practices, and moral community—apply to your experiences?

If you are religious, what is the cosmology that you are learning from your religion?

Rituals

Out of beliefs come **rituals**, ceremonies or repetitive practices. Rituals help to unite people into a moral community. Some rituals, such as the bar mitzvah of Jewish boys and the holy communion of Christians, are designed to create in devout believers a feeling of closeness with God and unity with one another. Rituals include kneeling and praying at set times; bowing; crossing oneself; singing; lighting candles and incense; reading scripture; and following prescribed traditions at processions, baptisms, weddings, and funerals. The photo essay on the next two pages features annual rituals held in Spain during Holy Week.

| **rituals** ceremonies or repetitive practices; in religion, observances or rites often intended to evoke a sense of awe of the sacred

THROUGH THE AUTHOR'S LENS
HOLY WEEK IN SPAIN

SPAIN

Religious groups develop rituals designed to evoke memories, create awe, inspire reverence, and stimulate social solidarity. One of the primary means by which groups, religious and secular, accomplish these goals is through the display of symbols.

I took these photos during Holy Week in Spain—in Malaga and Almuñecar. Throughout Spain, elaborate processions feature tronos that depict the biblical account of Jesus' suffering, death, and resurrection. During the processions in Malaga, the participants walk slowly for about two minutes; then because of the weight of the tronos, they rest for about two minutes. They repeat this process for about six hours a day.

The procession in the village was more informal. This Roman soldier has an interesting way of participating—and keeping tabs—on his little daughter. The girl is distributing candy.

Bands, sometimes several of them, are part of the processions.

A group of participants exiting the Church of the Incarnation for Malaga's Easter procession.

Parents gave a lot of attention to their children both during the preparations and during the processions. This photo was taken during one of the repetitive two-minute breaks.

Beneath the costumes are townspeople and church members who know one another well. They enjoy themselves prior to the procession. This man is preparing to put on his hood.

During the short breaks at the night processions, children from the audience would rush to collect dripping wax to make wax balls. This was one way that the audience made themselves participants in the drama.

For the Good Friday procession, I was fortunate to be able to photograph the behind-the-scenes preparations, which are seldom seen by visitors. Shown here are finishing touches being given to the Mary figure.

Some *tronos* are so heavy that they require over 100 men to carry them. This photo was taken in Malaga, on Monday of Holy Week.

The town square was packed with people awaiting the procession. From one corner of the square, the *trono* of Jesus was brought in. Then from another, that of Mary ("reuniting" them, as I was told). During this climactic scene, the priest on the balcony on the left read wa message.

Religious Experience

The term **religious experience** refers to a sudden awareness of the supernatural or a feeling of coming into contact with God. Some people undergo a mild version, such as feeling closer to God when they look at a mountain, watch a sunset, or listen to a certain piece of music. Others report a life-transforming experience. St. Francis of Assisi, for example, said that he became aware of God's presence in every living thing.

Some Protestants use the term **born again** to describe people who have undergone such a life-transforming religious experience. These people say that they came to the realization that they had sinned, that Jesus had died for their sins, and that God wants them to live a new life. Their worlds become transformed. They look forward to the Resurrection and to a new life in heaven. They also see relationships with spouses, parents, children, and even bosses in a new light. They report a need to make changes in how they interact with others so that their lives reflect their new, personal commitment to Jesus as their "Savior and Lord." They describe a feeling of beginning life anew; hence the term *born again.*

As I mentioned, there are many types of religious experiences. The following *Making It Personal* has a little different approach.

> **religious experience** a`sudden awareness of the super-natural or a feeling of coming in contact with God
>
> **born again** a term describing Christians who have undergone a religious experience so life-transforming that they feel they have become new persons

MAKING IT PERSONAL

Want to Share Something with Me?

There is no single religious experience. I'm interested in exploring the variety of religious experiences that people have. If you've had one, would you share it with me? I'll try to put the accounts that students send me together and make sense of them. If you send me something, I will be free to quote from it. Do let me know if it is okay to use your name. If you don't say so, I won't.

If you want to, then, write me at henslin@aol.com

1. "Amy, you know those things you told me about your religion?" asked LeRoy. "I remember," said Amy." "Well," said LeRoy, "I learned a word that applies to them." "What is it?" asked Amy. "They all come together and produce a picture of the world, right?" "I guess so," said Amy. "I hadn't thought about it." "And," continued LeRoy, "this is called a(n)

   a. epistemology
   b. entireology
   c. perspectology
   d. cosmology

2. "That's a big word," said Amy. "I'm not likely to use it anywhere." "Okay, but this one you will. You told me that you kneel and cross yourself in your religion, right?" "Yeah," answered Amy. "Well, those are called

   a. defacements
   b. transformations
   c. rituals
   d. religious experiences

3. "I knew that," said Amy. "Nothing new there. Why did you bring it up?" "Because," answered LeRoy, "rituals are another part of all religions, and symbolic interactionists study what rituals do." "What do rituals do?" asked Amy. "They

   a. represent incompatible cosmologies
   b. help create solidarity and produce a moral community
   c. produce enlightenment
   d. feed the fuels of controversy

4. "One more thing," added LeRoy. "You know how symbolic interactionists look at the meaning that people give their experiences, right?" "Right. We've covered that several times in the text," said Amy. "Well, there is something called a religious experience—people feeling a sudden contact or closeness with God." "I know about that," said Amy. "Do you know the term that some Christians use to refer to their religious experiences?" asked LeRoy. "Sure. It's

   a. born again
   b. transformative life
   c. reproductive technology
   d. reassertive naturalism

UNIT 12.10

Religion in the United States

Types of Religious Groups

Sociologists have identified four types of religious groups: cult, sect, church, and ecclesia. Why do some of these groups meet with hostility, while others tend to be accepted? For an explanation, look at Figure 12.5.

Let's explore what sociologists have found about these four types of religious groups. The summary that follows is a modification of analyses by sociologists Ernst Troeltsch (1931), Liston Pope (1942), and Benton Johnson (1963).

Cult (New Religion)

The word *cult* conjures up bizarre images—shaven heads, weird music, brainwashing. Even ritual suicide may come to mind. Cults, however, are not necessarily weird, and few practice

WHAT AM I SUPPOSED TO LEARN?

After you have read this unit, you should be able to

1 Describe the four types of religious groups.

2 Describe the characteristics of religious groups in the United States.

3 Explain why religion is likely to persist in any coming future.

"brainwashing" or bizarre rituals. In fact, *all religions began as cults* (Stark 1989). A **cult** is simply a new or different religion whose teachings and practices put it at odds with the dominant culture and religion. Because the term *cult* arouses such negative meanings in the public mind, however, some sociologists prefer to use the term *new religion* instead.

Cults often originate with a **charismatic leader**, an individual who has

cult a new religion with few followers, whose teachings and practices put it at odds with the dominant culture and religion

charismatic leader literally, someone to whom God has given a gift; in its extended sense, someone who exerts extraordinary appeal to a group of followers

---

FIGURE 12.5 **Religious Groups: From Hostility to Acceptance**

The more that a group has these emphases, the less it is accepted:

1. The need to reject society (the culture is a threat to true religion)
2. The group feels rejected by society (the group feels hostility)
3. Hostility toward other religions
4. Hostility from other religions
5. Personal salvation
6. Emotional expression of religious beliefs
7. Revelation (God speaks directly to people)
8. God intervenes in people's lives (such as healing or giving guidance)
9. A duty to spread the message (evangelism)
10. A literal interpretation of scripture
11. A literal heaven and hell
12. A conversion experience is necessary

Cult

Sect

Church

Ecclesia

The more that a group has these characteristics, the more the group is accepted:

1. The organization is large
2. The organization is wealthy
3. The members are well to do ("worldly success")
4. The clergy are required to have years of formal training

← Less acceptance by society

More acceptance by society →

Note: Any religious organization can be placed somewhere on this continuum, based on its having "more" or "less" of these characteristics and emphases. The sizes of the rectangles are intended to represent the group's relative characteristics and emphases.

Sources: By the author. Based on Troeltsch 1931; Pope 1942; and Johnson 1963.

charisma, an outstanding gift or some exceptional quality. People feel drawn to both the person and the message, finding the message appealing and feeling inspired by the individual. Many followers believe that God has touched the person.

The most popular religion in the world began as a cult. Its handful of followers believed that an unschooled carpenter who preached in remote villages in a backwater country was the Son of God, and that he was killed and came back to life. Those beliefs made the early Christians a cult, setting them apart from the rest of their society. Persecuted by both religious and political authorities, these early believers clung to one another for support. Many cut off associations with friends and family who didn't accept the new message. To others, the early Christians must have seemed deluded and brainwashed.

Most cults fail. Not many people believe the new message, and the cult fades into obscurity. Some, however, succeed and make history. Over time, large numbers of people may come to accept the message and become followers of the religion. If this happens, the new religion changes from a cult to a sect.

Sect

A **sect** is larger than a cult, but its members still feel tension between their views and the prevailing beliefs and values of the broader society. A sect may even be hostile to the society in which it is located. At the very least, its members remain

> **Sect** a religious group larger than a cult that still feels substantial hostility from and toward society

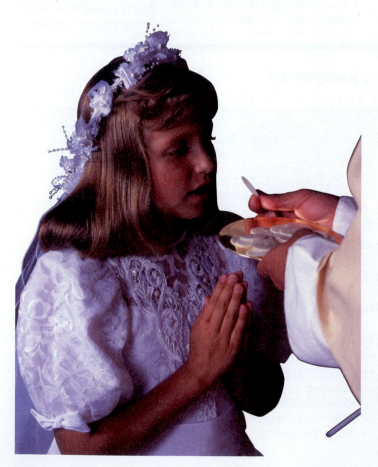

uncomfortable with many of the emphases of the dominant culture. Nonmembers, in turn, tend to be uncomfortable with members of the sect.

> *IF YOU WANT TO LEARN MORE* about Pentecostal religions in the United States,
>
> **Read** more from the author: The New Face of Religion: Pentecostals and the Spanish Speaking Immigrants, in **mysoclab**

If a sect grows, its members gradually make peace with the rest of society. To appeal to a broader base, the sect shifts some of its doctrines, redefining matters to remove some of the rough edges that create tension between it and the rest of society. As the members become more respectable in the eyes of society, they feel less hostility and little, if any, isolation. If a sect follows this course, as it grows and becomes more integrated into society, it changes into a church.

Church

At this point, the religious group is highly bureaucratized—probably with national and international headquarters that give direction to the local congregations, enforce rules about who can be ordained, and control finances. The relationship with God has grown less intense. The group is likely to have less emphasis on personal salvation and emotional expression. Worship services are likely to be more sedate, with sermons more formal, and written prayers read before the congregation. Rather than being recruited from the outside by personal evangelism, most new members now come from within, from children born to existing members. Rather than joining through conversion—seeing the new truth—children may be baptized, circumcised, or dedicated in some other way. At some designated age, children may be asked to affirm the group's beliefs in a confirmation or bar mitzvah ceremony.

Ecclesia (State Religion)

Finally, some groups become so integrated into a culture, and so strongly allied with their government, that it is difficult to tell where one leaves off and the other takes over. In these *state religions,* also called **ecclesia**, the government and religion work together to try to shape society. There is no recruitment of members, for citizenship makes everyone a member. For most people in the society, the religion is part of a cultural identity, not an eye-opening experience. Sweden provides a good example of how extensively religion and government intertwine in an ecclesia. In the 1860s, all citizens had to memorize Luther's *Small*

> **ecclesia** a religious group so integrated into the dominant culture that it is difficult to tell where the one begins and the other leaves off; also called a *state religion*

Catechism and be tested on it yearly (Anderson 1995). Today, Lutheranism is still associated with the state, but most Swedes come to church only for baptisms, marriages, and funerals.

Unlike cults and sects, which perceive God as personally involved with and concerned about an individual's life, ecclesia envision God as more impersonal and remote. Church services reflect this view of the supernatural, for they tend to be highly formal, directed by ministers or priests who, after undergoing rigorous training in approved schools or seminaries, follow prescribed rituals.

About 65 percent of Americans belong to a church, synagogue, or mosque. Let's examine the religious groups to which they belong.

FROM ANOTHER STUDENT . . .

I liked the debates we had in class. I didn't always agree with everyone, but it kept things interesting. I like that there is more than one way to think about society.

—Paul Bachman

Characteristics of Religious Groups

DIVERSITY

The first thing to note is that with about 300,000 congregations and hundreds of denominations, no religious group even comes close to being a dominant religion in the United States (*Statistical Abstract* 2011:Table 76). Table 12.1 illustrates some of this remarkable diversity.

SOCIAL CLASS

Religion in the United States is stratified by social class. As you can see from Figure 12.6 on the next page, some religious groups are "top-heavy," and others are "bottom-heavy." The most top-heavy are Jews and Episcopalians; the most bottom-heavy are Assembly of God, Southern Baptists, and Jehovah's Witnesses. This figure should help you to see that churchlike groups tend to appeal to people who have more "worldly" success, while the more sectlike groups attract people who have less "worldly" success.

From this figure, you can see how *status consistency* applies to religious groups. If a group ranks high (or low) on education, it is also likely to rank high (or low) on income and occupational

TABLE 12.1	How U.S. Adults Identify with Religion	

Religious Group	Number of Members	Percentage of U.S. Adults
Christian	**176,000,000**	**78.4%**
Protestant	115,000,000	51.3%
Evangelical churches	59,000,000	26.3%
Mainline churches	41,000,000	18.1%
Historical black churches	16,000,000	6.9%
Roman Catholic	54,000,000	23.9%
Mormon	3,800,000	1.7%
Jehovah's Witness	1,600,000	0.7%
Orthodox, Greek, Russian	1,400,000	0.6%
Other Christian	700,000	0.3%
Other Religions	**11,000,000**	**4.7%**
Jewish	3,800,000	1.7%
Buddhist	1,600,000	0.7%
Muslim	1,400,000	0.6%
Hindu	900,000	0.4%
Other faiths	2,700,000	1.2%
(Unitarians, New Age, Native American religions, Liberal)		
No Identity with a Religion	**36,000,000**	**16.1%**
Nothing in particular	27,000,000	12.1%
Agnostic	5,400,000	2.4%
Atheist	3,600,000	1.6%
Don't Know or Refused	**1,800,000**	**0.8%**

Note: Due to rounding, totals may not add to 100. Based on a sample of 35,000 of the 225 million Americans age 18 and over.
Source: U.S. Religious Landscape Survey 2008:5.

FIGURE 12.6 Social Class and Religious Affiliation

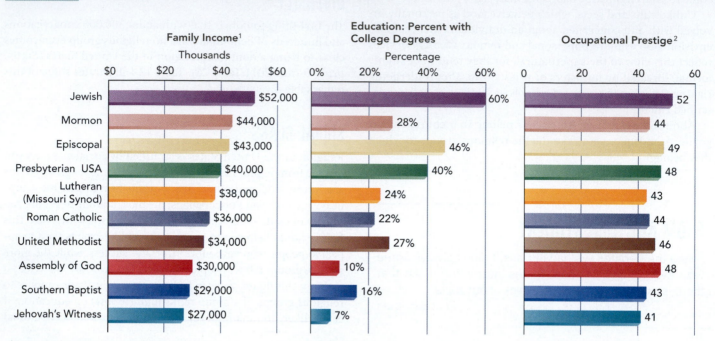

¹Since the income data were reported, inflation has run approximately 20 percent.

²Higher numbers mean that more of the group's members work at occupations that have higher prestige, generally those that require more education and offer higher pay.

Source: By the author. Based on Smith and Faris 2005.

prestige. Jews, for example, rank the highest on education, income, and occupational prestige, while Jehovah's Witnesses rank the lowest on these three measures of social class. As you can see, the Mormons are status inconsistent. They rank second in income, fourth in education, and tie for sixth in occupational prestige. Even more status inconsistent is the Assembly of God. Their members tie for third in occupational prestige but rank only eighth in income and ninth in education. This inconsistency is so jarring that there could be a problem with the sample.

> **Watch** the **Video**
> The Big Picture:
> Religion in **mysoclab**

RACE–ETHNICITY

All major religious groups draw from the nation's many racial–ethnic groups. Like social class, however, race–ethnicity tends to cluster. People of Irish descent are likely to be Roman Catholics; those with Greek ancestors are likely to belong to the Greek Orthodox Church. African Americans are likely to be Protestants—more specifically, Baptists—or to belong to fundamentalist sects.

Although many churches are integrated, it is with good reason that Sunday morning between 10 and 11 A.M. has been called "the most segregated hour in the United States." African Americans tend to belong to African American churches, while most whites see only whites in their churches. The segregation of churches is based on custom, not on law.

PLURALISM AND FREEDOM

It is the U.S. government's policy not to interfere with religions. The government's position is that its obligation is to ensure an environment in which people can worship as they see fit. Religious freedom is so extensive that anyone can start a church and proclaim himself or herself a minister, revelator, or any other desired term. The exceptions to this hands-off policy, however, are startling. The most notorious exception in recent times occurred in Waco, Texas, when armed agents of the Bureau of Alcohol, Tobacco, and Firearms attacked the compound of the Branch Davidians, an obscure religious group. Eighty-two men, women, and children were burned to death. Another is the government's infiltration of mosques to monitor the activities of Arab immigrants (Elinson 2004).

> ***IF YOU WANT TO LEARN MORE*** *about limitations to the policy of freedom when a religion that sacrifices animals moves to the United States,*
>
> **Read** more from the author: Human Heads and Animal Blood: The Toleration of Religion in **mysoclab**

TOLERATION

The general religious toleration of Americans can be illustrated by three prevailing attitudes: (1) "All religions have a right to exist—as long as they don't try to brainwash or hurt anyone." (2) "With so many religions to choose from, how can anyone tell which one—if

3. *An afterlife.* Science can offer no information on this at all, for it has no tests to prove or disprove a "hereafter."

4. *Morality.* Science can demonstrate the consequences of behavior, but not the moral superiority of one action compared with another. This means that science cannot even prove that loving your family and neighbor is superior to hurting and killing them. Science can describe death and measure consequences, but it cannot determine the moral superiority of any action, even in such an extreme example.

There is no doubt that religion will last as long as humanity lasts, for what could replace it? And if something did, and answered such questions, would it not be religion under a different name?

Joel Osteen, televangelist and senior pastor at a megachurch in Houston, Texas. The church building, a former coloseum which cost $95 million to renovate, seats 16,000 people.

any—is true?" (3) "Each of us may be convinced about the truth of our religion—and that is good—but don't be obnoxious by trying to convince others that you have the exclusive truth."

THE ELECTRONIC CHURCH

What began as a ministry to shut-ins and those who do not belong to a church blossomed into its own type of church. Its preachers, called "televangelists," reach millions of viewers and raise millions of dollars. Some of its most famous ministries are those of Joyce Meyers, Pat Robertson (the 700 Club), Benny Hinn, Creflo Dollar, and Joel Osteen.

The Future of Religion

Religion thrives in the most advanced scientific nations—and, as officials of Soviet Russia were disheartened to learn—in even the most ideologically hostile climate. Although the Soviet authorities threw believers into prison, people continued to practice their religions. Humans are inquiring creatures. As they reflect on life, they ask, What is the purpose of it all? Why are we born? Is there an afterlife? If so, where are we going? Out of these concerns arises this question: If there is a God, what does God want of us in this life? Does God have a preference about how we should live?

Science, including sociology, cannot answer such questions. By its very nature, science cannot tell us about four main concerns that many people have:

1. *The existence of God.* About this, science has nothing to say. No test tube has either isolated God or refuted God's existence.

2. *The purpose of life.* Although science can provide a definition of life and describe the characteristics of living organisms, it has nothing to say about ultimate purpose.

IF YOU WANT TO LEARN MORE about how technology is changing religion,

Read more from the author: God on the Net: The Online Marketing of Religion in **mysoclab**

UNIT 12.10 // TESTING MYSELF
DID I LEARN IT? ANSWERS ARE AT THE END OF THE CHAPTER

1. "I found out that there are four types of religious groups," said Amy. "The beliefs and practices of one type put it at odds with society." "Which one is that?" asked LeRoy. "It is a(n)
   a. cult   b. sect
   c. church   d. ecclesia

2. "Cult? Ugh. You mean like weird clothes and brainwashing?" asked LeRoy. "Sometimes, but not always. Although the word cult is standard, sociologists know that people have reactions like yours, so some of them use this term instead
   a. church   b. sect
   c. new religion   d. ecclesia

3. "Cults often begin when people are drawn to someone they think has a gift from God," said Amy. "That sounds like something we read in the chapter on politics," said LeRoy. "Good connection," Amy agreed. "Sociologists call this a
   a. gifted person
   b. charismatic leader
   c. strong religious leader
   d. founder of a new religion

4. "When a cult grows, it tends to tone down some of the sharpest things that the society doesn't like about

it," said Amy. "This brings less tension, and the group grows more comfortable with the society." "What do sociologists call this type of religious group?" asked LeRoy. "They call it a

a. church b. sect
c. new religion d. ecclesia

5. "I suppose a religious group can keep growing and keep toning down the controversial things, right?" asked LeRoy. "You're picking this up," commented Amy. "And then the group is called a

a. church b. sect
c. new religion d. ecclesia

6. "That's it, then," said LeRoy. "Not quite," Amy answered. "A religious group can grow so large and become so integrated in the society that you can't tell where one begins and the other leaves off. It's like Lutheranism in Sweden and Islam in the Arab countries." "Hmm," said LeRoy. "Do sociologists have a name for this?" "Of course," Amy smiled. "They seem to have a name for everything. They call it

a. a church b. a sect
c. a new religion d. an ecclesia

7. "What did you learn about the religious groups in the United States?" asked LeRoy. "Well," said Amy, "I found it interesting that church groups are divided by

a. social class
b. their views of the meaning of contemporary society
c. the Protestant ethic and the spirit of capitalism
d. their views of how democracy affects religious orientations

8. "Some of the groups, like the Jews, are high on income, occupational prestige, and education. Others, like the Jehovah's Witnesses, are low on all three," Amy stated. "That sounds like something else from another chapter, too," said LeRoy. "I bet it is called

a. status inconsistency
b. social class divisions
c. status consistency
d. disintegrative statuses

9. "Right," agreed Amy. "And some groups, such as the Mormons, are mixed on these three. You probably remember that term, too." "Yes," said LeRoy. "It is called

a. disintegrative statuses
b. status inconsistency
c. disintegrative statuses
d. status consistency

10. "With the advances of science, I think religion will disappear," observed LeRoy. "The text said it won't," replied Amy, "because science can't answer questions about

a. what it means to be successful
b. the internal dynamics of marriage
c. ultimate meaning
d. what causes thoughts

✔ ⎯[**Study** and **Review** in **mysoclab**

PULLING IT ALL TOGETHER REVIEWING THE LEARNING GOALS

Unit 12.1 Education in Global Perspective

1. Explain how industrialization is related to the development of education.

- As societies industrialized and fewer people farmed, the need for education grew. Industrialized societies became credential societies: Credentials replace personally knowing people's abilities.

2. Summarize the educational systems of Japan, Russia, and Egypt.

- *Japan:* Students study the same page of the same books on the same day. College is limited to the top scorers on national examinations. With fewer young people, this is changing. *Russia:* Under communism, schools were free at all levels. Emphasis was on capitalism as evil and communism the salvation of the world. No critical thinking was tolerated. After the collapse of communism, schools became less centralized and critical thinking was allowed. In *Egypt*, illiteracy is common. The poor receive little education. Emphasis is on memorization. Educators are pressing for critical thinking to be allowed.

👁 Watch the **Video**
The Basics: Education in **mysoclab**

Unit 12.2 The Functionalist Perspective: Providing Social Benefits

1. Explain the functionalist perspective on education.

- Functionalists stress education's intended benefits, its manifest functions. These include teaching knowledge and skills (so the next generation can fill the necessary positions); the transmission of values (schools pass on a society's core values to the next generation); social integration (promoting a sense of national identity; (includes inclusion or mainstreaming, incorporating students with disabilities into regular school activities); and social placement or gatekeeping (sorting students into different educational tracks or programs on the basis of their perceived abilities). The effects of gatekeeping are lifelong, for it opens and closes doors of opportunity for students. Schools also replace some family functions, such as child care and sex education.

Explore the Concept Dropping Out in the Information Age in **mysoclab**

Unit 12.3 The Conflict Perspective: Perpetuating Social Inequality

1. Explain the conflict perspective on education.

- A main point of conflict theorists is that U.S. schools help reproduce social inequality (perpetuate the social class structure). Among the ways they do this is the unequal funding of schools (schools in elite areas get more money for their programs), the cultural bias of IQ tests, and the hidden curriculum. Part of the hidden curriculum is the attitudes and behaviors that schools teach children to match their perceived destination in life. Regardless of personal abilities, children from more well-to-do families are more likely to go to college, attend elite colleges, and obtain better jobs. In these same ways, education helps reproduce the racial–ethnic structure for the next generation. The bottom line: The educational system helps the ruling class to maintain its dominance.

Unit 12.4 The Symbolic Interactionist Perspective: Teacher Expectations

1. Explain the symbolic interactionist perspective on education.

- Symbolic interactionists study face-to-face interaction. Classic research of a kindergarten classroom found that the teacher gave more favorable treatment to middle class students. This led to the middle class students progressing faster in their learning than students from homes in poverty. These initial results followed the students into their next grades. Other research indicates that some students are better than others at signaling that they are good students. Even though they score the same on tests, they are given better grades. Giving favorable treatment lies below the teachers' awareness. The shorthand term for what occurred in both these studies is teacher expectations. We know neither the extent of social class bias in kindergarten nor how students do their "signaling."

Unit 12.5 Problems in U.S. Education—And Their Solutions

1. Explain the problems of mediocrity and violence in education and their possible solutions.

- Mediocrity plagues U.S. high schools. A major reason for the low performance of students is low teacher expectations (low requirements). As student performance has dropped, teachers and administrators have lowered the passing score. The solution is high standards rigorously enforced. Violence is also intolerable. Since a safe learning environment is essential for education, the solution is zero tolerance.

Watch the Video Sociology on the Job: Education in **mysoclab**

Read the Document "Race-Specific Policies and the Truly Disadvantaged" by William Julius Wilson in **mysoclab**

Unit 12.6 Religion in Global Perspective

1. Summarize Emile Durkheim's conclusions about religion.

- Early sociologist Emile Durkheim analyzed religions around the world. The world's religions are so varied, he said, that they have no specific belief or practice in common. But they all develop a community centering on their beliefs and practices. And they all separate the sacred from the profane. By sacred, Durkheim meant aspects of life having to do with the supernatural, things that inspire awe, reverence, deep respect, even fear. By profane, he meant aspects of ordinary, everyday life. In a famous statement, Durkheim said "a religion is a unified system of beliefs and practices relative to sacred things, that is to say, things set apart and forbidden—beliefs and practices which unite into one single moral community called a Church, all those who adhere to them."

Unit 12.7 The Functionalist Perspective

1. Explain some functions of religion.

- Religions provide answers to questions about ultimate meaning—such as the purpose of life, why people suffer, and the existence of an afterlife. Religion also provides emotional comfort, social solidarity through identification with a community of believers, and social control through guidelines and rules for living. Religions both resist and promote social change.

2. Explain some dysfunctions of religion.

- Religions have been used to justify persecution, such as hunting down and killing witches. Religions are also used to promote war and terrorism.

Unit 12.8 The Conflict Perspective

1. Explain the conflict perspective on religion.

- Karl Marx, who founded conflict theory, was an avowed atheist. He set the tone for conflict theorists with his famous statement that "religion is the opium of the people." He meant that religion takes the worker's eyes off their suffering, reducing the possibility that they will rebel against their oppressors. Conflict theorists stress that religion legitimates the social inequalities of society. By this, they mean that religion teaches that society's existing social arrangements represent what God desires. They point to many examples: ancient Egypt, where the pharaoh was believed to be a god; Hindu support of the caste system; and the "divine right of kings" during Europe's middle ages.

Unit 12.9 The Symbolic Interactionist Perspective

1. Explain the symbolic interactionist perspective on religion.

- Symbolic interactionists focus on the meanings that people give their experiences. They analyze how religions use symbols to provide identity and create social solidarity for their members. What the cross means to a fundamentalist Christian was given as an example. Religious beliefs also lead to rituals, repetitive practices that help unite people into a moral community. The term religious experience refers to a sudden awareness of the supernatural or a feeling of coming into contact with God. There are many varieties of religious experiences. Some Protestants use the term born again to describe people who have undergone a life-transforming religious experience.

Unit 12.10 Religion in the United States

1. Describe the four types of religious groups.

- *Cult*: a new religion, at odds with society. *Sect*: a new religion that has grown larger and more respectable. *Church*: a bureaucratized religion that is at peace with society. *Ecclesia*: a religion that is hard to distinguish from the society. As religious groups develop, they lose the fervency of the cult.

2. Describe the characteristics of religious groups in the United States.

- No religious group dominates. Religious groups are stratified by social class. Some groups are top heavy, others bottom heavy. They are also segregated by race-ethnicity, which is voluntary. U.S. policy is pluralism, freedom, and toleration. There are exceptions when the government comes down hard. Technology has produced an electronic church.

3. Explain why religion is likely to persist in any coming future.

- Religion will continue because science can't answer questions about ultimate meaning: the purpose of life, the existence of God and an afterlife, and what morality is.

Watch the **Video**
The Big Picture:
Religion in **mysoclab**

DID I LEARN IT? ANSWERS

1. **d** a credential society

2. **d** two of five are in community colleges

3. **a** reflects its culture

4. **a** education in a Most Industrialized Nation

5. **d** have more educated parents, are expected to bring home top grades, and enjoy cultural experiences that translate into higher test scores

6. **c** schools were seen as a way to advance the new political system

7. **b** critical thinking might lead to criticisms of communism

8. **a** were able to encourage students to think for themselves

9. **d** educational systems reflect their culture

10. **c** education in a Least Industrialized Nation

DID I LEARN IT? ANSWERS

1. **d** functionalism

2. **c** manifest functions

3. **b** latent functions

4. **a** transmission of mainstream values

5. **d** inclusion

6. **c** social placement

7. **b** providing sex education

DID I LEARN IT? ANSWERS

1. **d** perpetuate or help maintain the divisions of society

2. **c** Schools help people inherit the life opportunities that were laid down before they were born.

3. **b** the hidden curriculum

4. **a** are more likely to go to college

DID I LEARN IT? ANSWERS

1. **d** were from middle class homes

2. **a** The students who did well continued to do well, and those who did poorly continued to do poorly.

3. **b** a self-fulfilling prophecy

4. **a** were giving signals that you were a good student

5. **d** might have received better grades because of it

6. **c** teacher expectations

DID I LEARN IT? ANSWERS

1. **a** 34

2. **c** math scores

3. **d** verbal scores

4. **a** an A average

5. **d** have higher teacher expectations (standards)

6. **c** zero tolerance of threats, violence, and weapons on school property

UNIT 12.6 // TESTING MYSELF
DID I LEARN IT? ANSWERS

1. **c** find the effects of religious participation on people's lives

2. **d** aspects of life that are not concerned with religion, that are part of everyday life

3. **a** things that inspire fear, awe, and reverence

4. **b** Aztec priests plucking the heart out of a living virgin

5. **a** Muslims at a mosque

6. **d** beliefs, practices, and a moral community

UNIT 12.7 // TESTING MYSELF
DID I LEARN IT? ANSWERS

1. **a** answers about ultimate meaning

2. **a** emotional comfort

3. **b** social solidarity

4. **c** guidelines for everyday life

5. **d** social control

6. **d** social change

7. **b** dysfunctions of religion

UNIT 12.8 // TESTING MYSELF
DID I LEARN IT? ANSWERS

1. **d** Karl Marx

2. **c** placed their eyes on an afterlife

3. **b** opium

4. **a** Religion legitimates the social inequalities of society.

5. **d** The existing social arrangements of a society represent what God desires.

6. **c** the caste system

7. **d** divine right of kings

8. **a** defended slavery

UNIT 12.9 // TESTING MYSELF
DID I LEARN IT? ANSWERS

1. **d** cosmology

2. **c** rituals

3. **b** help create solidarity and produce a moral community

4. **a** born again

UNIT 12.10 // TESTING MYSELF
DID I LEARN IT? ANSWERS

1. **a** cult

2. **c** new religion

3. **b** charismatic leader

4. **b** sect

5. **a** church

6. **d** an ecclesia

7. **a** social class

8. **c** status consistency

9. **b** status inconsistency

10. **c** ultimate meaning

CHAPTER 13
POPULATION AND URBANIZATION

Watch the **Video** in **mysoclab**

Listen to the **Chapter Audio** in **mysoclab**

GETTING STARTED

I want to start this chapter by sharing something that happened in Mexico. The image still haunts me.

There stood Celia, age 30, her distended stomach visible proof that her thirteenth child was on its way. Her oldest was only 14 years old! He had already gone as far in school as he ever would. Each morning, he joined the men to work in the fields. Each evening around twilight, I saw him return home, exhausted from hard labor in the subtropical sun.

I was living in Colima, Mexico, and Celia and her husband, Angel, had invited me for dinner. A thatched hut consisting of only a single room served as home for all fourteen members of the family. At night, the parents and younger children crowded into a double bed, while the eldest boy slept in a hammock. As in many homes in the village, the other children slept on mats spread on the dirt floor—despite the crawling scorpions.

(*continued on next page*)

Worli, India

425

(continued from previous page)

The home had only a gas stove, a table, and a cabinet where Celia stored her few cooking utensils and clay dishes. There were no closets; clothes hung on pegs in the walls. There also were no chairs, not even one. I was used to the poverty in the village, but this really startled me. The family was too poor to afford even a single chair.

Celia beamed as she told me how much she looked forward to the birth of her next child. Could she really mean it? It was hard to imagine that any woman would want to be in her situation.

Yet Celia meant every word. She was as full of delighted anticipation as she had been with her first child—and with all the others in between.

How could Celia have wanted so many children—especially when she lived in such poverty? That question bothered me. I couldn't let it go until I understood why.

This chapter helps to provide an answer. ■

POPULATION IN GLOBAL PERSPECTIVE

Celia—her life and her attitudes—take you into the heart of **demography.** This is the study of the size, composition, growth, and distribution of human populations. In this Unit, you will come face to face with two dramatic questions that affect your future: Are you doomed to live in a world so filled with people that there will be little space for anybody? And are chronic famine and mass starvation the sorry fate of most earthlings?

A lot of people around the world are concerned about population growth. Let's look at how this concern began.

UNIT 13.1

A Planet with No Space for Enjoying Life?

This is going to surprise you, but I'm going to start by talking about the potato. In the 1600s, the Spanish *conquistadores* found that people in the Andes Mountains were eating potatoes, which were unknown in Europe. They brought some home to cultivate. Potatoes are easy to grow, and gradually they became the main

Demography the study of the size, composition, growth, and distribution of human populations

WHAT AM I SUPPOSED TO LEARN?

After you have read this unit, you should be able to

 1 State what demography is.

 2 Explain the arguments of the New Malthusians and the Anti-Malthusians.

3 Explain the demographic transition.

The Spanish explorers of the 1500s sailed to the "New World" in ships like this. Some of their lowly discoveries, such as the potato, changed the "Old World."

food of the lower classes. With a greater abundance of food, fertility increased and the death rate dropped. Europe's population soared, almost doubling during the 1700s (McKeown 1977; McNeill 1999).

Thomas Malthus (1766–1834), an English economist, was alarmed when he saw this surging growth. In 1798, he wrote a

FIGURE 13.1 How Fast Is the World's Population Growing?

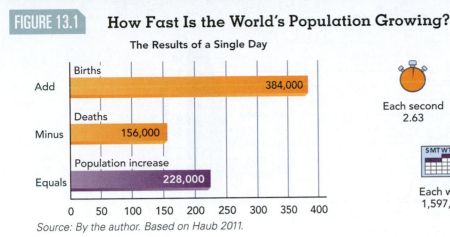

The Results of a Single Day

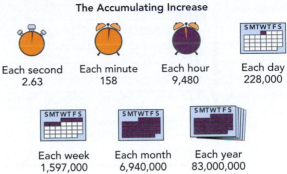

The Accumulating Increase

Each second	2.63
Each minute	158
Each hour	9,480
Each day	228,000
Each week	1,597,000
Each month	6,940,000
Each year	83,000,000

Source: By the author. Based on Haub 2011.

book that became world famous, *An Essay on the Principle of Population.* In it, Malthus proposed what became known as the **Malthus theorem.** He argued that although population grows geometrically (from 2 to 4 to 8 to 16 and so forth), the food supply increases only arithmetically (from 1 to 2 to 3 to 4 and so on). This meant, he stressed, that if births go unchecked, the population of a country, or even of the world, will outstrip its food supply.

The New Malthusians

Was Malthus right? One group, which can be called the *New Malthusians,* is convinced that today's situation is at least as grim as Malthus imagined—and probably even grimmer. For example, *the world's population is growing so fast that in just the time it takes you to read this chapter, another 20,000 to 40,000 babies will be born!* By this time tomorrow, the earth will have about 228,000 more people to feed. This increase goes on hour after hour, day after day, without letup. For an illustration of this growth, see Figure 13.1.

The New Malthusians point out that the world's population is following an **exponential growth curve.** This means that if growth doubles during approximately equal intervals of time, it suddenly accelerates. To illustrate the far-reaching implications of exponential growth, sociologist William Faunce (1981) retold an old parable about a poor man who saved a rich man's life. The rich man was grateful and said that he wanted to reward the man for his heroic deed.

The man replied that he would like his reward to be spread out over a four-week period, with each day's amount being twice what he received on the preceding day. He also said he would be happy to receive only one penny on the first day. The rich man immediately handed over the penny and congratulated himself on how cheaply he had gotten by.

At the end of the first week, the rich man checked to see how

Malthus theorem an observation by Thomas Malthus that although the food supply increases arithmetically (from 1 to 2 to 3 to 4 and so on), population grows geometrically (from 2 to 4 to 8 to 16 and so forth)

exponential growth curve a pattern of growth in which numbers double during approximately equal intervals, showing a steep acceleration in the later stages

much he owed and was pleased to find that the total was only $1.27. By the end of the second week he owed only $163.83. On the twenty-first day, however, the rich man was surprised to find that the total had grown to $20,971.51. When the twenty-eighth day arrived the rich man was shocked to discover that he owed $1,342,177.28 for that day alone and that the total reward had jumped to $2,684,354.56!

This is precisely what alarms the New Malthusians. They claim that humanity has just entered the "fourth week" of an exponential growth curve. Figure 13.2 on the next page shows why they think the day of reckoning is just around the corner. It took from the beginning of time until 1800 for the world's population to reach its first billion. To add the second billion was shortened to 130 years (1930). Then, just 30 years later (1960), the world population hit 3 billion. The time it took to reach the fourth billion was cut in half, to only 15 years (1975). Then just 12 years later (in 1987), the total reached 5 billion. In another 12 years, it hit 6 billion (in 1999). And in yet another 12 years, it hit 7 billion (in 2011).

On average, every minute of every day, 156 babies are born. As Figure 13.1 shows, at each sunset the world has 228,000 more people to feed and clothe and shelter than it did the day before. In a year, this comes to 83 million people. During the next four years, this increase will total more than the entire U.S. population. Think of it this way: *In the next 12 years, the world will add as many people as it did during the entire time from when the first humans began to walk the earth until the year 1800.*

In 43 years, the world's population doubled—going from 3.5 billion in 1968 to 7 billion in 2011. If this continues, there will be 14 billion people on earth by 2054.

These totals terrify the New Malthusians. They are convinced that we are headed for a showdown between population and food. It is obvious that we will run out of food if we don't curtail population growth. Soon we are going to see more televised images of pitiful, starving children.

The Anti-Malthusians

All of this seems obvious, and no one wants to live shoulder-to-shoulder and fight for scraps. How, then, can anyone argue with the New Malthusians?

FIGURE 13.2   World Population Growth Over 2,000 Years

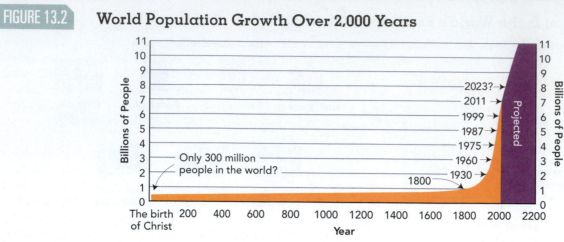

Sources: Modified from Piotrow 1973; McFalls 2007.

"We can," say an optimistic group of demographers. This group, which we can call the Anti-Malthusians, claim that the alarming predictions of the Malthusians are wrong, that their little stories are cute but misleading. The Anti-Malthusians say that Europe's **demographic transition** gives us a more accurate glimpse of the future. What do they mean by this? Look at Figure 13.3, which diagrams the demographic transition. You can see that during most of its history, Europe was in Stage 1. For centuries, Europe's population remained about the same as

> **demographic transition** a three-stage historical process of population growth: *first*, high birth rates and high death rates; *second*, high birth rates and low death rates; and *third*, low birth rates and low death rates; a *fourth* stage in which deaths outnumber births has made its appearance in the Most Industrialized Nations

its high death rates offset its high birth rates. Then came Stage 2, the "population explosion" that so upset Malthus. Europe's population surged because it birth rates remained high while its death rates went down. But look at Stage 3. Here you see a significant transition: Europe's population stabilized as people brought their birth rates in line with their lower death rates.

This, say the Anti-Malthusians, will also happen in today's Least Industrialized Nations. Their current surge in population growth simply indicates that they have reached Stage 2 of the demographic transition. When they move into Stage 3, as surely they will, we will wonder what all the fuss was about. In fact, their growth is already slowing.

The Anti-Malthusians make another startling argument—that our future will be the opposite of what the New Malthusians worry about: The world's problem will not be a population explosion, but

FIGURE 13.3   The Demographic Transition

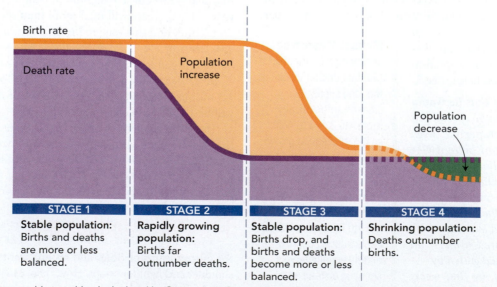

Note: The standard demographic transition is depicted by Stages 1–3. Stage 4 has been suggested by some Anti-Malthusians.

a **population shrinkage**—populations getting smaller. They point out that births in seventy-seven countries have already dropped so low that these countries no longer produce enough children to maintain their populations. If it weren't for immigration from Africa, all the countries of Europe would fill more coffins than cradles. The exception is Kosovo (Haub 2011).

Some Anti-Malthusians even predict a demographic free fall (Mosher 1997). As more nations enter Stage 4 of the demographic transition, the world's population will peak at about 8 or 9 billion, then begin to grow smaller. Two hundred years from now, they say, we will have a lot fewer people on earth.

> **◉ Watch the Video**
> The Big Picture: Population, Urbanization and Environment
> Invest in **mysoclab**

Who Is Correct?

After World War II, the West exported its hybrid seeds, herbicides, and techniques of public hygiene around the globe. Death rates plummeted in the Least Industrialized Nations as their food supply increased and health improved. Because their birth rates stayed high, their populations mushroomed.

We can use the conflict perspective to understand what happened when this message reached the leaders of the industrialized world. They saw the mushrooming populations of the Least Industrialized Nations as a threat to the global balance of power they had worked out. With swollen populations, the poorer countries might demand a larger share of the earth's resources. The leaders used the United Nations to spearhead efforts to reduce world population growth. The results have been remarkable. The annual growth of the Least Industrialized Nations has dropped 29 percent, going from an average of 2.1 percent a year in the 1960s to 1.5 percent today (Haub and Yinger 1994; Haub 2011).

The New Malthusians and Anti-Malthusians greeted this news with

> **population shrinkage**
> the process by which a country's population becomes smaller because its birth rate and immigration are too low to replace those who die and emigrate

significantly different interpretations. For the Anti-Malthusians, this slowing of growth was the signal they had been waiting for: Stage 3 of the demographic transition had begun. First, the death rates of the Least Industrialized Nations fell—now, just as they predicted, birth rates are also falling. Did you notice, they would say, if they looked at Figure 13.2, that it took twelve years to add the fifth billion to the world's population—and also twelve years to add the sixth and seventh billions? Population momentum has slowed. The New Malthusians reply that a slower growth rate still spells catastrophe—it will just take longer for it to hit.

As you can see, both the New Malthusians and the Anti-Malthusians have looked at historical trends and projected them onto the future. The New Malthusians project continued world growth and are alarmed. The Anti-Malthusians project Stage 3 of the demographic transition onto the Least Industrialized Nations and are reassured. Both sides agree that the Least Industrialized Nations are in Stage 2 of the demographic transition. The question is, Will these nations enter Stage 3?

It simply is too early to tell. Like the proverbial pessimists who see the glass of water half empty, the New Malthusians interpret changes in world population growth negatively. And like the eternal optimists who see the same glass half full, the Anti-Malthusians view the figures positively. Sometime during our lifetimes we should know the answer.

UNIT 13.1 // TESTING MYSELF
DID I LEARN IT? ANSWERS ARE AT THE END OF THE CHAPTER

1. "Carmen, did you read the next chapter?" asked José. "Not yet," said Carmen. "It's about population, isn't it?" "Yes, and they use this term for the study of population
   a. mamography
   b. reproductography
   c. graphology
   d. demography

2. "I didn't read the chapter, but I know there's a population explosion and the world is going to run out of food," said Carmen. "You sound like a Malthusian," said Jose. "What's that?" asked Carmen. "It's people who say that the population is going to outstrip the food supply. They started with Thomas Malthus in 1798 in England who wrote a book explaining that population grows faster than food. They call his idea the
   a. demographic transition
   b. Malthus theorem
   c. change maker
   d. geometric-arithmetic equation

3. "I don't know about that," said Carmen, "but did the chapter say how fast the world's population is growing?" "It did," answered José. "Every day, the world adds this many people—and this is after you subtract the deaths from the number of new babies
   a. 18,000
   b. 68,000
   c. 98,000
   d. 228,000

Can you explain why this photo from Aragon, Spain, illustrates Stage 3 of the deomographic transition?

4. "That comes to about one billion new people in 12 years," added José. "See, I was right," said Carmen. "The earth can't support that many people." "Maybe not," José replied, "but the Anti-Malthusians say that Europe's experience can give us a picture of the world's future. For centuries, Europe was in Stage 1. Its population was stable, with the number of deaths about the same as the number of births. Then came Stage 2, when the population surged. At this point, there were a lot more births than deaths. Then Europe reached Stage 3, when

   a. births were higher for a while, but then death rates grew higher

   b. the population grew even faster

   c. births dropped and got balanced with deaths again

   d. laws limited the number of children women could bear

5. "Is there a Stage 4?" asked Carmen. "Yes," said José, "and Europe has entered it. This is when

   a. births outnumber deaths and the population grows quickly

   b. deaths outnumber births and the population shrinks

   c. deaths and births outpace each other

   d. change is so uncertain that you can't predict whether population will increase or decrease

6. "Here's a special concern of the New Malthusians," said José. "They say that if growth doubles during approximately equal intervals of time, then it suddenly accelerates." "What do they call this?" asked Carmen. "They call this

   a. an exponential growth curve   **b.** a fast cycle

   c. an accelerator   **d.** the doubling factor

7. "I don't understand why there is a population explosion in the Least Industrialized Nations," said Carmen. "After all, their populations were stable for hundreds of years." "Right," commented José. "What happened was that their birth rates stayed the same, but their death rates dropped like a roller coaster. This was because after World War II, the West

   a. exported faulty birth control devices to the Least Industrialized Nations

   b. stopped abortion in the Least Industrialized Nations

   c. began to teach the value of having children

   d. exported hybrid seeds, herbicides, and techniques of public hygiene

8. "What happened then?" asked Carmen. "The annual growth of the Least Industrialized Nations dropped about 30 percent, going from an average of 2.1 percent a year in the 1960s to 1.5 percent today." "Why?" asked Carmen. "A major reason" answered José, "was that the leaders of the Most Industrialized Nations

   a. threatened war if these nations didn't reduce their population growth

   b. had the United Nations spearhead efforts to reduce world population growth

   c. threatened to stop all immigration if they didn't reduce their population growth

   d. mixed birth control substances in the food they gave as part of their foreign aid

9. "So everybody's happy about the situation now?" asked Carmen. "Not quite," replied José. "The New Malthusians still say that population growth will outstrip the food supply, and some of the Anti-Malthusians say that the world's population is

   a. going to shrink

   b. growing at the right rate but in the wrong countries

   c. losing its character

   d. starting to deteriorate

10. "So who's right?" asked Carmen. "Well," said José, "it is

   a. too early to tell

   b. the New Malthusians

   c. the Anti-Malthusians

   d. about evenly split between the New and Anti-Malthusians

UNIT 13.2

Why Are People Starving?

WHAT AM I SUPPOSED TO LEARN?

After you have read this unit, you should be able to

1   Explain why there is starvation in some parts of the world.

Pictures of starving children gnaw at our conscience. We live in such abundance, while these children and their parents starve before our very eyes. Why don't they have enough food? Is it because the earth is not producing enough food or that the abundant food the world produces does not reach them?

If food production has increased so there is more food per person in the world, why is there starvation? This photo was taken in Niger, Africa.

The Anti-Malthusians make a point that seems irrefutable. As Figure 13.4 on the next page shows, *there is more food for each person in the world now than there was in 1950.* Despite the billions of additional people who now live on this planet, improved seeds and fertilizers have made more food available for each person on earth. And even more food is on the way, for bioengineers continue to make breakthroughs in agriculture. The global production of meat, fish, and cereals (grains and rice) increases each year (State of the World 2011).

Then why do people die of hunger? From Figure 13.4 we can conclude that people don't starve because our planet produces too little food, but because particular places lack food. Droughts and wars are the main reasons. Just as droughts slow or stop food production, so does war. In nations ravaged by civil war, opposing sides either confiscate or burn crops, and farmers flee to the cities (Thurow 2005; Gettleman 2009).

The New Malthusians counter with the argument that the world's population is still growing and that we don't know how long the earth will continue to produce enough food. They add that the recent policy of turning food (such as corn and sugar cane) into biofuels (such as gasoline and diesel) is short-sighted, posing a threat to the world's food supply. A bushel of corn that goes into someone's gas tank is a bushel of corn that does not go on people's dinner plates.

Both the New Malthusians and the Anti-Malthusians have contributed significant ideas, but theories will not eliminate famines. Starving children are going to continue to peer out at us from our televisions and magazines, their tiny, shriveled bodies and bloated stomachs nagging at our consciences and imploring us to do something. Regardless of the underlying causes of this human misery, the solution is twofold: first, to transfer food from nations that have a surplus to those that have a shortage, and second, where needed, to teach more efficient farming techniques

Pictures of starving Africans leave the impression that Africa is overpopulated. Why else would all those people be starving? The truth, however, is far different. Although Africa has 23 percent of the earth's land, it has only 15 percent of the Earth's population (Haub and Kent 2008; Haub 2011). Africa even has vast areas of fertile land that have not yet been farmed. The reason for famines in Africa, then, cannot be too many people living on too little land.

FIGURE 13.4

How Much Food Does the World Produce per Person?

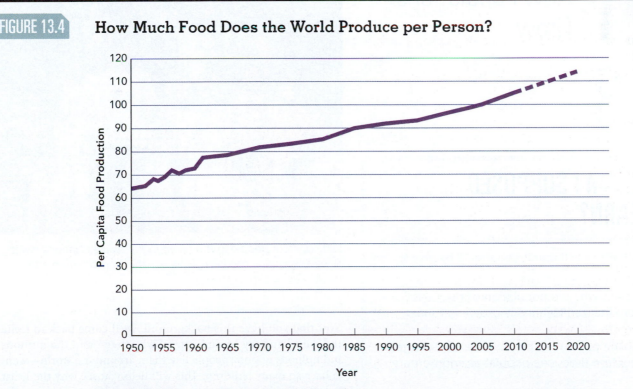

Note: 2004-2006 equals 100. Projections by the author.

Sources: By the author. *Statistical Abstract of the United States* 2010:Table 133. Food and Agricultural Organization of the United Nations, January 27, 2012.

1. "I read the unit about starvation," commented Carmen, "and I learned some interesting things." "Like what?" asked José. "Like world food production. You know that there are billions more people today than 50 or 60 years ago?" "Of course," said José. "Well, today there is

   a. more concern about health
   b. less concern about health
   c. a lot less food for each person in the world
   d. more food for each person in the world

2. "Then this means that people don't starve because the earth produces too little food, but because particular places lack food?" asked José. "Right," said Carmen. "And this is because

   a. they don't know how to farm
   b. of biofuels

   c. of droughts and wars
   d. the news reports exaggerate the problem

3. "Did you ever think that when you run your car you are taking food away from someone?" asked Carmen. "That's ridiculous," José answered. "Okay, maybe a bit exaggerated," said Carmen laughing, "but it is still true that biofuels

   a. can produce food
   b. are produced from food that someone could otherwise have eaten
   c. are made from chemicals and those chemicals could be used for food
   d. are the answer to the world's problem of running out of oil

4. "Do you think that Africa is overpopulated?" asked Carmen. "Of course. Everybody knows that. You saw that TV special about starving kids in Africa." "That's what I thought, too," said Carmen, "but I found out that Africa has 23 percent of the earth's land but it has

   a. 15 percent of the earth's population
   b. 20 percent of the earth's population
   c. 25 percent of the earth's population
   d. 30 percent of the earth's population

UNIT 13.3

How Populations Grow

Why do poor people in the Least Industrialized Nations want to have so many children? How are their life situation and world view a part of this?

WHAT AM I SUPPOSED TO LEARN?

After you have read this unit, you should be able to

1 Explain why the population of the Least Industrialized Nations is growing so fast.

2 Explain population pyramids and how age structure produces population momentum.

Now that you have this background, we'll come back to Celia and Angel and try to understand why they—and the millions and millions of poor people like them around the world—want to have so many children. This will help you see why the Least Industrialized Nations are growing *thirteen times faster* than the

FIGURE 13.5 — World Population Growth, 1750–2150

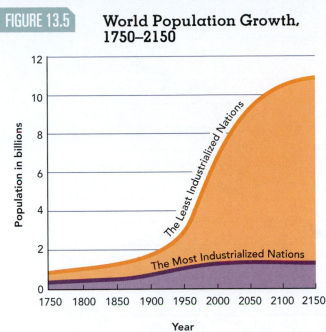

Sources: "The World of the Child 6 Billion" 2000; Haub 2011.

Most Industrialized Nations (Haub 2011). At these rates, it will take several hundred years for the average Most Industrialized Nation to double its population, but just 40 years for the average Least Industrialized Nation to do so. Figure 13.5 puts the matter in stark perspective.

> **IF YOU WANT TO LEARN MORE** about how tsunamis can help you understand the population explosion,
>
> **Read** more from the author: How the 2004 Tsunami Can Help Us to Understand Population Growth in **mysoclab**

Why Do the Least Industrialized Nations Have So Many Children?

THE SYMBOLIC INTERACTIONIST PERSPECTIVE

Why was Celia so happy about having her thirteenth child? To understand the world of Celia and Angel, we must see life as they see it—the essence of the symbolic interactionist perspective. You know that your culture provides a perspective on life that guides your choices. So it is with Celia and Angel's culture. While your culture tells you that one or two—maybe even three—children are about right, theirs tells them that twelve children are not enough. How can this be? Why is bearing children so important to them—and to poor people around the world?

The first reason is that parenthood brings status. In the Least Industrialized Nations, motherhood is the most prized status a woman can achieve. The more children a woman bears, the more she is thought to have achieved the purpose for which she was born. Similarly, a man proves his manhood by fathering children ("What a man he is! He has 15 kids."). The more children he fathers, especially sons, the better—for through them his name lives on.

Second, the community supports this view. Celia and those like her live in *Gemeinschaft* communities, where people share similar views of life. To them, children are a sign of God's blessing, so bearing children assures them that they are blessed by God. It is the barren woman, not the woman with a dozen children, who is to be pitied.

There is also another powerful incentive: As surprising as it may seem, children are *economic assets*. Like Celia and Angel's eldest son, children begin contributing to the family income at a young age. For a picture of how this can be, see Figure 13.6 on the next page. But even more important: Children are the equivalent of our Social Security. In the Least Industrialized Nations, the government does not provide social security. This motivates people to bear more children: When parents become too old to work, their children take care of them. The more children they have, the broader their base of support.

To those of us who live in the Most Industrialized Nations, it seems irrational to have many children. And for us it would be. Understanding life from the framework of people who are living it, however, reveals how it makes perfect sense to have many children. Consider this report by a government worker in India:

> *Thaman Singh (a very poor man, a water carrier) . . . welcomed me inside his home, gave me a cup of tea (with milk and "market" sugar, as he proudly pointed out later), and said: "You were trying to convince me that I shouldn't have any more sons. Now, you see, I have six sons and two daughters and I sit at home in leisure. They are grown up and they bring me money. One even works outside the village as a laborer. You told me I was a poor man and couldn't support a large family. Now, you see, because of my large family I am a rich man." (Mamdani 1973)*

THE CONFLICT PERSPECTIVE

Conflict theorists offer an entirely different view. Feminists argue that women like Celia have internalized values that support the dominance of men. In Latin America, *machismo*—an emphasis on male virility and dominance—runs through the culture. To father many children, especially sons, shows that a man is sexually potent, giving him higher status in the community. From a conflict perspective, then, the reason poor people have so many children is that men control women's reproductive choices.

Implications of Different Rates of Growth

The result of Celia and Angel's desire for many children—and of the millions of Celias and Angels like them—is that Mexico's population will double in forty years. The implications of a doubling population are mind-boggling. Just to stay even, within forty years Mexico must double the number of available jobs

FIGURE 13.6 — Why the Poor Need Children

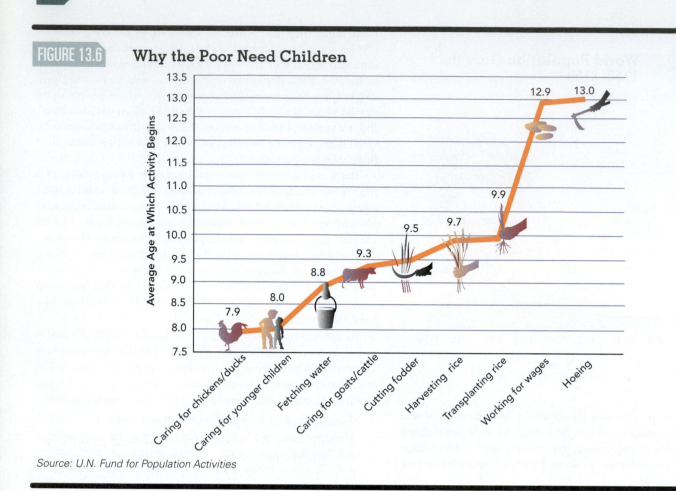

Source: U.N. Fund for Population Activities

FIGURE 13.7 — Three Population Pyramids

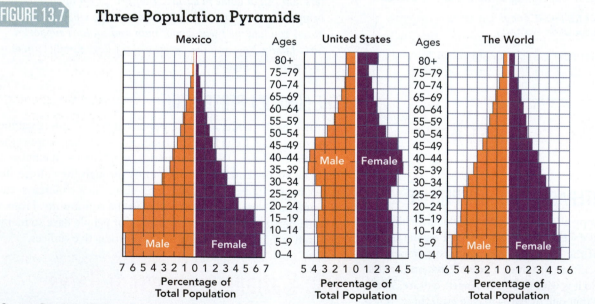

Source: Population Today, 26, 9, September 1998:4, 5.

and housing facilities; its food production; its transportation and communication facilities; its water, gas, sewer, and electrical systems; and its schools, hospitals, churches, civic buildings, theaters, stores, and parks. If Mexico fails to double them, its already meager standard of living will drop even further.

In contrast, women in the United States are having so few children that if it weren't for immigration, the U.S. population would be slowly shrinking. To illustrate population dynamics, demographers use **population pyramids.** These depict a country's population by age and sex. Look at Figure 13.7, which shows the population pyramids of the United States, Mexico, and the world.

population pyramid
a graph that represents the age and sex of a population

In *Making It Personal*, let's consider why population pyramids are so important.

MAKING IT PERSONAL

Population Pyramids

To see why population pyramids are important, I would like you to imagine a miracle. Imagine that, overnight, the average number of children per woman in Mexico drops to 2.1, the same as in the United States. If this happened, it would seem that Mexico's population would grow at the same rate as that of the United States, right?

But this isn't what would happen. Instead, the population of Mexico would grow much faster than that of the United States. To see why, look again at the population pyramids in Figure 13.7. Can you see that a much higher percentage of Mexican women are in their childbearing years? This is the key to why Mexico's population would grow faster. Even if Mexico and the United States had the same birth rate (2.1 children per woman), a larger percentage of women in Mexico would be giving birth. As demographers like to phrase this, Mexico's age structure gives it greater population momentum.

Ordinarily, a demographic statement like this one might seem like Greek, but this should make it clear. If it isn't perfectly clear, read the two paragraphs above again.

On average, the birth rate of U.S. women barely keeps up with U.S. deaths. That average includes all U.S. women, from those who never give birth to Nadya Suleman, shown here, who is often called "octomom." Using in vitro fertilization (IVF), Suleman gave birth to octuplets.

1. "I read the next unit," said Jose. "Did you know that the Least Industrialized Nations are growing 13 times faster than the Most Industrialized Nations?" "No, I didn't," Carmen replied. "And this means," continued José, "that it will take hundreds of years for the population of the Most Industrialized Nations to double, but the population of the Least Industrialized Nations will double in

   a. 100 years   b. 80 years
   c. 60 years   d. 40 years

2. "Why are they having so many children there?" asked Carmen. "The symbolic interactionists say that we need to see the world as they see it," said José. "They see children as gifts from God, a woman's purpose is to have children, and through children a man

   a. lives longer
   b. can get paid for a "father's leave" from work
   c. proves that he is a real man
   d. gets obligations from his neighbors

3. "There is another reason, too," continued José. "Children are economic assets." "What do you mean?" asked Carmen. "They start working at a young age," explained José, "helping produce food at home or bringing money to the family. Also, they

   a. help to develop the community
   b. support the parents when they are old
   c. bring prestige to the parents when they join the military
   d. bring a monthly payment from the government

4. "I suppose the conflict perspective is a little different," said Carmen. "Right," said José. "They agree with these things, but they add that women in the Least Industrialized Nations have so many children because

   a. men control women's reproductive choices
   b. children bring a monthly payment from the government
   c. the parents cannot afford birth control
   d. having obligations to many children keeps the parents from rebelling against the government

5. "I found out that the population of the United States would be shrinking," said José, "if we didn't have

   a. women marrying at such young ages
   b. our high birth rate
   c. adoption of children from other countries
   d. immigration

6. "Demographers use population pyramids," said José. "What are those?" asked Carmen. "They are illustrations of a country's

   a. wealth structure, with the smaller number of rich at the top, the larger numbers of poor at the bottom, and the others in between

b. level of education, with a few at the top, many in the middle, and most at the bottom

c. population by age and sex

d. children grouped by age

7. "What good are population pyramids?" asked Carmen. "If you read them right," said José, "you can see population dynamics." "What does that mean?" Carmen asked. "For example," replied José, "even if two countries have the same birth rate, one can be growing faster than the other because that one

a. has less birth control

b. has more women in the child bearing years

c. places more value on children

d. has more doctors and hospitals

8. "And I suppose those demographers have their own way of saying that, right?" asked Carmen. "Right," said José. "They put it this way:

a. age structure gives a country its population momentum

b. the value placed on children divided by a country's infrastructure yields an exponential growth curve

c. a country's infrastructure determines its birth rate

d. economic progression plus the child bearing ratio equals a country's birth rate

UNIT 13.4

The Three Demographic Variables

WHAT AM I SUPPOSED TO LEARN?

After you have read this unit, you should be able to

1 Explain how demographers use three demographic variables to project population growth.

2 Explain problems in forecasting population growth.

How many people will live in the United States fifty years from now? What will the world's population be then? These are important questions. Educators want to know how many schools to build. Businesses want to know how the demand for their products will change. The government needs to know how many doctors, engineers, and executives to train. Politicians want to know how many people will be paying taxes—and how many young people will be available to fight their wars.

To project the future of populations, demographers use three **demographic variables:** fertility, mortality, and migration. Let's look at each.

FERTILITY

The number of children that the average woman bears is called the **fertility rate.** The world's overall fertility rate is 2.5, which means that during her lifetime the average woman in the world gives birth to 2.5 children. At 2.1, the fertility rate of U.S. women is considerably less (Haub 2011). A term that is sometimes confused with fertility is **fecundity,** the number of children that women are capable of bearing. This number is rather high, as some women have given birth to 30 children (McFalls 2007)!

Different parts of the world have different fertility rates. The highest is in Middle Africa, where the average woman gives birth to 5.9 children; the lowest is southern Europe, where the average woman bears 1.4 children (Haub 2011). As you can see from Table 13.1 on the next page, three countries tie for the world's lowest fertility rate. There, the average woman gives birth to only 1.0 child. Six of the lowest-birth countries are in Europe, the rest in Asia. Now look at the countries with the highest birth rate. They are also clustered. All of them are in Africa. Niger in West Africa holds the record for the world's highest birth rate. There, the average woman gives birth to 7.4 children, seven

demographic variables the three factors that influence population growth: fertility, mortality, and net migration

fertility rate the number of children that the average woman bears

fecundity the number of children that women are capable of bearing

The United States takes in more immigrants each year than all other countries combined. This naturalization ceremony was held in Phoenix, Arizona.

TABLE 13.1 · Extremes in Childbirth

Where Do Women Give Birth to the Fewest Children?		Where Do Women Give Birth to the Most Children?	
Country	Number of Children	Country	Number of Children
Macao	1.0	Niger	7.4
Hong Kong	1.0	Mali	6.6
Taiwan	1.0	Somalia	6.5
Andorra	1.2	Uganda	6.5
Bosnia-Herzegovina	1.2	Congo, Dem. Republic	6.4
San Marino	1.2	Chad	6.2
South Korea	1.2	Zambia	6.2
Germany	1.3	Burkina Faso	6.0
Hungary	1.3	Liberia	5.8
Portugal	1.3	Angola	5.8

Note: Several other countries also average 1.3 children per woman.

Source: Haub 2011.

times as many children as the average woman in Macao, Hong Kong, and Taiwan.

To compute a country's fertility rate, demographers analyze the government's records of births. From these, they figure the country's **crude birth rate,** the annual number of live births per 1,000 people. There can be considerable slippage here, of course. The birth records in many of the Least Industrialized Nations are haphazard, at best.

MORTALITY

The second demographic variable is measured by the **crude death rate**, the annual number of deaths per 1,000 people. Its extremes are even higher than the extremes of the birth rate. The highest death rate is 39, a record held by Afghanistan in Asia. At 1, the world's record for the lowest death rate is held by Qatar, another Asian country (Haub 2011).

MIGRATION

The third demographic variable is the **net migration rate**—the difference between the number of immigrants (people moving into a country) and emigrants (people moving out of a country) per 1,000 people. Unlike fertility and mortality, migration does not affect the global population, for people are simply shifting their

crude birth rate the annual number of live births per 1,000 population

crude death rate the annual number of deaths per 1,000 population

net migration rate the difference between the number of immigrants and emigrants per 1,000 population

residence from one country or region to another.

What motivates people to give up the security of their family and friends to move to a country with a strange language and unfamiliar customs? To understand migration, we need to look at both push and pull factors. The *push factors* are what people want to escape: poverty, war and violence, or persecution for their religious and political ideas. The *pull factors* are the magnets that draw people to a new land, such as opportunities for education, better jobs, the freedom to worship or to discuss political ideas, and a more promising future for their children. After "migrant paths" are established, immigration often accelerates—networks of kin and friends attract more people from the same nation, even from the same villages.

Around the world, the flow of migration is from the Least Industrialized Nations to the industrialized countries. By far, the United States is the world's number-one choice. The United States admits more immigrants each year than all the other nations of the world combined. Thirty-seven million residents—one of every eight Americans—were born in other countries (*Statistical Abstract* 2012:Table 41). Table 13.2 on the next page shows where recent U.S. immigrants were born. With the economic crisis, this flow has slowed. Not only are fewer migrants arriving, but many who have lost their jobs are returning to their home countries (Chishti and Bergeron 2010).

To escape grinding poverty, such as that which surrounds Celia and Angel, millions of people enter the United States illegally. Although it may seem surprising, as Figure 13.8 shows, U.S. officials have sufficient information on these approximately 11 million people to estimate their country of origin.

> **Watch** the **Video**
> The Basics: Population, Urbanization and Environment in **mysoclab**

FIGURE 13.8 · Country of Origin of Unauthorized Immigrants to the United States

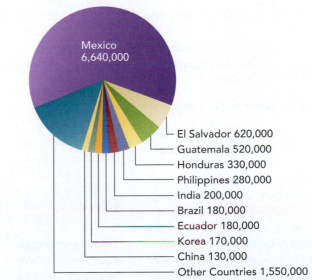

- Mexico 6,640,000
- El Salvador 620,000
- Guatemala 520,000
- Honduras 330,000
- Philippines 280,000
- India 200,000
- Brazil 180,000
- Ecuador 180,000
- Korea 170,000
- China 130,000
- Other Countries 1,550,000

Source: By the author. Based on *Statistical Abstract of the United States* 2012:Table 45.

TABLE 13.2 **Country of Birth of Authorized U.S. Immigrants**

North America	3,605,000	Pakistan	157,000	South America	906,000
Mexico	1,693,000	Iran	132,000	Colombia	251,000
Cuba	329,000	Bangladesh	107,000	Peru	146,000
Dominican Republic	318,000	Taiwan	88,000	Brazil	124,000
El Salvador	253,000	Japan	76,000	Ecuador	113,000
Haiti	214,000			Venezuela	84,000
Jamaica	181,000	**Europe**	**1,264,000**	Guyana	76,000
Canada	168,000	Ukraine	153,000	Argentina	51,000
Guatemala	161,000	United Kingdom	149,000		
		Russia	140,000	**Africa**	**860,000**
Asia	**3,785,000**	Poland	117,000	Nigeria	111,000
India	663,000	Bosnia and Herzegovina	89,000	Ethiopia	110,000
China	662,000	Germany	78,000	Egypt	73,000
Philippines	587,000	Romania	54,000	Somalia	65,000
Vietnam	306,000	Albania	51,000	Ghana	64,000
Korea	222,000				

Note: Totals are for the top countries of origin for 2001–2010, the latest years available.

Source: By the author. Based on Statistical Abstract of the United States 2012: Table 50.

Problems in Forecasting Population Growth

The total of the three demographic variables—fertility, mortality, and net migration—gives us a country's **growth rate,** the net change after people have been added to and subtracted from a population. What demographers call the **basic demographic equation** is quite simple:

Growth rate = births – deaths + net migration

If population increase depended only on biology, the demographer's job would be easy. But social factors—wars, economic booms and busts, plagues, and famines—push rates of birth and death and migration up or down. Politicians also complicate projections. Sometimes governments try to persuade women to bear fewer—or more—children. When Hitler decided

growth rate the net change in a population after adding births, subtracting deaths, and either adding or subtracting net migration

basic demographic equation the growth rate equals births minus deaths plus net migration

that Germany needed more "Aryans," the German government outlawed abortion and offered cash bonuses to women who gave birth. The population increased. Today, European leaders are alarmed that their birth rates have dropped so low that their populations will shrink. With its population dropping, Russia's leaders are offering cash payments to women who have children (Kramer 2012).

IF YOU WANT TO LEARN MORE about how even infanticide can affect population growth,

▶ **Read** more from the author: Killing Little Girls: An Ancient and Thriving Practice in **mysoclab**

In China, we find the opposite situation. Many people know that China tries to limit population growth with its "One couple, one child" policy, but few know how ruthlessly officials enforce this policy. Steven Mosher (2006), an anthropologist who did fieldwork in China, revealed that—whether she wants it or not—after the birth of her first child, each woman is fitted with an IUD (intrauterine device). If a woman has a second child, she is sterilized. The exception is rural couples, who are allowed to have a second child—if their first one was a girl (Greenhalgh 2009). If a woman gets pregnant without government permission (yes, you read that right), the fetus is aborted. If she does not consent to an abortion, one is performed on her anyway—even if she is nine months pregnant. No unmarried woman is allowed to give birth: Officials arrest any unmarried woman who gets pregnant and force her to have an abortion.

Although government policies can change a country's growth rate, the main factor is not the government, but industrialization. *In every country that industrializes, the birth rate drops.* Industrialization makes rearing children more expensive, as they require more education and remain dependent longer. The basis for conferring status also changes—from having many children to attaining education and displaying material wealth. People like Celia and Angel in our opening vignette begin to see life differently, and their motivation to have many children drops sharply. Not knowing how rapidly industrialization will progress or how quickly changes in values and reproductive behavior will follow adds to the difficulty of making accurate projections.

Consider how difficult it is to estimate the U.S. population in the year 2050. Between now and then, will we have **zero population growth?** (Every 1,000 women would give birth to 2,100 children, the extra 100 children making up for those who do not survive or reproduce.) What percentage of women will go to college? (Educated women bear fewer children.) How many immigrants will we have? Will some devastating disease appear? Because of these

zero population growth women bearing only enough children to reproduce the population

Chinese officials have become concerned about the lopsided gender ratio that their "one couple, one child" policy has produced. Their billboards continue to promote this policy, but they are now featuring a female child to try to reduce female infanticide.

many unknowns, demographers play it safe by making several projections of population growth, each depending on an "if" scenario. Figure 13.9 shows their three projections of the U.S. population.

FIGURE 13.9 **Population Projections of the United States**

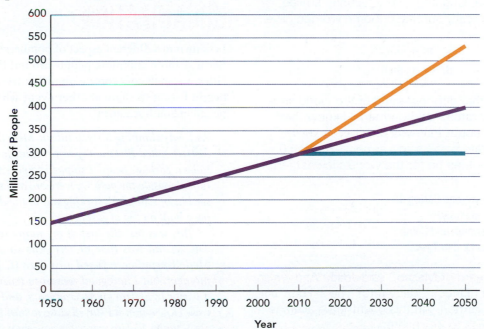

Note: The projections are based on different assumptions of fertility, mortality, and especially migration.

Source: By the author. Based on Day 2010.

UNIT 13.4 // TESTING MYSELF
DID I LEARN IT? ANSWERS ARE AT THE END OF THE CHAPTER

1. "What did you learn about demography in this unit, Carmen?" asked José. "One thing I learned is there are three demographic variables: fertility, mortality, and
   a. births **b.** deaths
   c. immigration **d.** migration

2. "The demographers don't just say 'fertility,' though," said Carmen. "They say '*fertility rate*.'" "What does fertility rate mean?" asked José. "It is," replied Carmen, "the
   a. births minus deaths plus net migration
   b. annual number of live births per 1,000 people
   c. number of children that the average woman bears
   d. annual number of deaths per 1,000 people

3. "And sometimes," said Carmen, "people mix fecundity up with fertility." "Well, yeah," said José. "It's just another strange word. It might be on the test, though, so what does it mean?" "It means," said Carmen, laughing, "the
   a. annual number of deaths per 1,000 people
   b. number of children that women are capable of bearing
   c. annual number of live births per 1,000 people
   d. births minus deaths plus net migration

4. "Okay. Now I know the word fecundity, but I'll never be able to use it. And just how fecund can women be?" asked José, laughing. "Very fecund," smiled Carmen. "I was really surprised. Some women have given birth to
   a. 10 children **b.** 20 children
   c. 30 children **d.** 40 children

5. "I also learned that different parts of the world have different fertility rates," said Carmen. "I knew that," replied José. "I doubt that–you didn't even know what a fertility rate was," said Carmen. "But at 1.0, these three countries tie for the world's lowest fertility rate
   a. Belgium, Germany, and Portugal
   b. France, Spain, and Italy
   c. Canada, Switzerland, and China
   d. Macao Hong Kong, and Taiwan

6. "I never even heard of Macao," said José. "And which country has the highest fertility rate?" he asked. "It's in Africa," said Carmen. "In this country the average woman gives birth to 7.4 children
   a. Botswana **b.** Liberia
   c. Niger **d.** Union of South Africa

7. "Demographers also study a country's annual number of live births per 1,000 people," Carmen stated. "What do they call that?" asked José. "They call it the
   a. demographic variable **b.** crude birth rate
   c. fecundity rate **d.** fertility rate

8. "If you figure the difference between a country's immigrants and emigrants," Carmen added, "you end up with a country's
   a. growth rate **b.** fertility rate
   c. net migration rate **d.** equalization rate

9. "If you put this all together," said Carmen, "you end up with this little formula: 'The growth rate equals births minus deaths plus net migration.' Demographers call this the
   a. equalization rate
   b. fertility rate
   c. demographic growth process
   d. basic demographic equation

10. "That makes sense," nodded José. "If the growth rate equals births minus deaths plus net migration, then it is easy for the demographers to predict population growth." "Not quite that easy," said Carmen. "Some things foul this up. They change the birth and death rates and the rates of migration." "Like what?" José asked. "Like wars," said Carmen, "and droughts and plagues and
    a. political decisions
    b. the weather
    c. low manufacturing standards of birth control devices
    d. changing ideas and standards of love and beauty

URBANIZATION

Let's turn to a different aspect of population—where people live. Because more and more people around the world are living in cities, we shall concentrate on urban trends and urban life. To begin, I want to share another event with you. This one happened in South America.

As I was climbing a steep hill in Medellin, Colombia, in a district called El Tiro, my informant, Jaro, said, "This used to be a garbage heap." I stopped to peer through the vegetation alongside the path we were on, and sure enough, I could see bits of refuse still sticking out of the dirt. The "town" had been built on top of garbage.

This was just the first of my many revelations that day. The second was that El Tiro was so dangerous that the Medellin police refused to enter it. I shuddered for a moment, but I had good reason to trust Jaro. He had been a pastor in El Tiro for several years, and he knew the people well. I knew that if I stayed close to him I would be safe.

Actually, El Tiro was safer now than it had been. A group of young men had banded together to make it so, Jaro told me. A sort of frontier justice prevailed. The vigilantes told the prostitutes and drug dealers that there would be no prostitution or drug dealing in El Tiro and to "take it elsewhere." They killed anyone who robbed or killed someone. And they even made families safer—they would beat up any man who got drunk and beat "his" woman. With the threat of instant justice, the area had become much safer.

Jaro then added that each household had to pay the group a monthly fee, which turned out to be less than a dollar in U.S. money. Each business had to pay a little more. For this, they received security.

As we wandered the streets of El Tiro, it did look safe—but I still stayed close to Jaro. And I wondered about this group of men who had made the area safe. What kept them from turning on the residents? Jaro had no answer. When Jaro pointed to two young men, whom he said were part of the ruling group, I asked if I could take their picture. They refused. I did not try to snap one on the sly.

My final revelation was El Tiro itself. On the next two pages you can see some of the things I saw that day.

In this second part of the chapter, you will get a context for understanding urban life—and El Tiro. Let's go back in history and find out how the city itself came about.

UNIT
The Development of Cities
13.5

WHAT AM I SUPPOSED TO LEARN?

After you have read this unit, you should be able to

1 Give a brief history of cities and urbanization.

Cities are not new to the world scene. Perhaps as early as 7,000 years ago, people built small cities with massive defensive walls, such as biblically famous Jericho (Homblin 1973). Cities on a larger scale appeared about 3500 B.C., around the time that writing was invented (Chandler and Fox 1974; Hawley 1981). At that time, cities emerged in several parts of the world—first in

FROM ANOTHER STUDENT . . .

The way this book is organized into small sections makes reading much easier. This chapter was actually fun to read.

—Kristie Carlisle

Mesopotamia (today's Iran and Iraq) and later in the Nile, Indus, and Yellow River valleys, in West Africa, along the shores of the Mediterranean, in Central America, and in the Andes (Fischer 1976; Flanagan 1990).

About 5,500 years ago, Norway was home to one of the first cities of Europe. The city, which had been buried under sand, was not discovered until 2010 (Goll 2010). In the Americas, the first city was Caral, in what is now Peru (Fountain 2001). Covered by jungle growth, it, too, was recently discovered.

The key to the origin of cities is the development of more efficient agriculture (Lenski and Lenski 1987). Only when farming produces a surplus can some people stop producing food and gather in cities to spend time in other economic pursuits. We can even define a **city** as a place in which a large number of people are permanently based and do not produce their own food. The invention of the plow about 5,000 years ago brought a jump in farming efficiency. The new food surpluses stimulated the development of towns and cities.

> **city** a place in which a large number of people are permanently based and do not pro-duce their own food

---

IF YOU WANT TO LEARN MORE about the gentrification of Harlem,

Read more from the author: Reclaiming Harlem: A Twist in the Invasion-Succession Cycle in **mysoclab**

Rio de Janeiro, Brazil, one of the larger cities of the world. Why was this city not possible two hundred years ago?

THROUGH THE AUTHOR'S LENS

MEDELLIN, COLOMBIA: A WALK THROUGH EL TIRO

These are some of the photos I took when I walked through El Tiro, an urban development built on a hill of garbage. The account of my visit is on the preceding two pages.

Almost at the top of the garbage heap, I saw this boy in front of his house. His mother has hung out the family's wash to dry.

Kids are kids the world over. These children don't know they are poor. They are having a great time playing on a pile of dirt in the street.

This is the "richer" area below El Tiro. As you can see, some of the residents own cars.

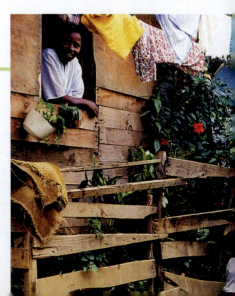

This is one of my favorite photos. The woman is happy that she has a home—and proud of what she has done with it. What I find remarkable is the flower garden she so carefully tends, and has taken great effort to protect from children and dogs. I can see the care she would take of a little suburban home.

El Tiro has home delivery.

The road to El Tiro. On the left, going up the hill, is a board walk. To the right is a meat market (*carnicería*). Note the structure above the meat market, where the family that runs the store lives.

An infrastructure has developed to serve El Tiro. This woman is waiting in line to use the only public telephone.

It doesn't take much skill to build your own house in El Tiro. A hammer and saw, some nails, and used lumber will provide most of what you need. This man is building his house on top of another house.

What do people do to make a living in El Tiro? Anything they can. This man is sharpening a saw in front of his home.

"What does an El Tiro home look like inside?," I kept wondering. Then Jaro, my guide (on the left), took me inside the home of one of his parishioners. Amelia keeps a neat house, with everything highly organized.

© James M. Henslin, all photos

Early cities were small economic centers surrounded by walls to keep out enemies. These cities had to be fortresses, for they were constantly under threat. This photo is of Avila, Spain, whose walls date from 1090.

Most early cities were small, merely a collection of a few people in agricultural centers or on major trade routes. Even Athens at the height of its power in the fifth century B.C. had only about 250,000 inhabitants. The first three cities to reach 1 million residents did so only briefly, and then they all declined. The first city to reach 1 million, Rome, lost population as the Roman Empire declined, eventually becoming only a collection of villages (Palen 2008). About A.D. 800 to 900, Changan (Xi'an) in China and Baghdad in Persia (Iraq) were the next cities to reach a million, but they, too, declined (Chandler and Fox 1974).

Two hundred years ago, the only city in the world that had a population of more than a million was Peking (Beijing), China (Chandler and Fox 1974). As Figure 13.10 shows, today the world has over 400 cities with more than a million residents. From one to 400! Why? Behind this surge lies the Industrial Revolution. It not only drew people to cities by providing work but it also stimulated fast transportation and communications. These, in turn, brought efficiency in moving people, resources, and products. These essential factors, including streets and sewers that allow large cities to exist, are called *infrastructure*. Systems to transmit information are also an essential part of the city's infrastructure.

✳ Explore the Concept
Where do Americans Live? in **mysoclab**

The Process of Urbanization

As you have seen, cities reach far back in history, but urbanization is quite recent. **Urbanization** is the movement of masses of people to cities, which

> **urbanization** the process by which an increasing proportion of a population lives in cities and has a growing influence on the culture

---

FIGURE 13.10

A Global Boom: Cities with over One Million Residents

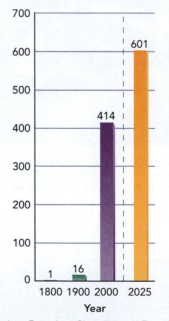

Year	Cities
1800	1
1900	16
2000	414
2025	601

Sources: By the author. Based on Chandler and Fox 1974; Brockerhoff 2000; United Nations 2008.

then have a growing influence on society. In 1800, a mere 3 percent of the world's population lived in cities (Hauser and Schnore 1965). But just a few years ago, in 2008, for the first time in history more people lived in cities than in rural areas. Urbanization is taking place around the globe, but as you can see from Table 13.3 it is quite uneven.

TABLE 13.3 — Urbanization and Industrial Development

	Percent Urban
Least Industrialized Nations	27%
Industrializing Nations	44%
Most Industrialized Nations	75%

Source: By the author. Based on Haub 2011.

Why are cities so appealing? Because of their exquisite division of labor, cities offer incredible variety—music ranging from rap and salsa to death metal and classical, shops that feature imported delicacies from around the world and those that sell special foods for vegetarians and diabetics. Cities also offer anonymity, which so many find refreshing in light of the tighter controls of village and small-town life. And, of course, cities offer work.

Some cities have grown so large and have so much influence over a region that the term *city* is no longer adequate to describe them. The term **metropolis** is used instead. This term refers to a central city surrounded by smaller cities and their suburbs. They are linked economically and by transportation and communication. Some are also linked politically, through county boards and regional governing bodies.

Some metropolises have grown so large and influential that the term **megalopolis** is used to describe them. This term refers to an overlapping area consisting of at least two metropolises and their many suburbs. Of the twenty or so megalopolises in the United States, the three largest are the eastern seaboard running from Maine to Virginia; the area in Florida between Miami, Orlando, and Tampa; and California's coastal area between San Francisco and San Diego. The California megalopolis extends into Mexico and includes Tijuana and its suburbs.

This process of urban areas turning into a metropolis, and a metropolis developing into a megalopolis, is occurring worldwide. When a city's population hits 10 million, it is called a **megacity.** In 1950, New York City and Tokyo were the only megacities in the world, but today there are twenty-two. Megacities are growing so fast that by the year 2025 there are expected to be thirty. The largest of these are shown in Figure 13.11. As you can see, most megacities are located in the Least Industrialized Nations.

metropolis a central city surrounded by smaller cities and their suburbs

megalopolis an urban area consisting of at least two metropolises and their many suburbs

megacity a city of 10 million or more residents

UNIT 13.5 // TESTING MYSELF
DID I LEARN IT? ANSWERS ARE AT THE END OF THE CHAPTER

1. "Andris, did you read Unit 13.5?" asked Evija. "Sort of. Why? "I learned some things," Evija replied. "Like what?" asked Andris. "Well, I learned that the first cities go back in history about

   a. 1,000 years   **b.** 3,000 years
   c. 5,000 years   **d.** 7,000 years

FIGURE 13.11 — The World's 22 Megacities

Tokyo 37,100,000
Istanbul 11,200,000
Moskva (Moscow) 10,600,000
Osaka-Kobe 11,400,000
New York 20,000,000
Los Angeles 13,200,000
Dhaka 16,600,000
Beijing 13,300,000
Cairo 11,700,000
Paris 10,800,000
Delhi 24,200,000
Lagos 12,400,000
Shanghai 17,800,000
Mexico City 20,100,000
Karachi 14,800,000
Rio de Janeiro 12,400,000
Manila 12,500,000
Sao Paulo 21,300,000
Kinshasa 10,700,000
Mumbai (Bombay) 21,800,000
Buenos Aires 13,400,000
Kolkata (Calcutta) 16,900,000

Note: Includes continuous cities. Los Angeles, for example include Long Beach and Santa Ana. New York includes Newark.

Source: By the author. Based on projected 2015 populations by the United Nations.

2. "Where were the first ones?" asked Andris. "They were located in Mesopotamia," answered Evija. "Mesopotamia? Where's that?" asked Andris. "It was a civilization located where these countries are today:

a. Botswana and Liberia   **b.** Egypt and Latvia
c. Iran and Iraq   **d.** China and Tibet

3. "I thought there were always cities," said Andris. "Why did they develop?" "To have a city," stated Evija, "some people have to be able to do things other than gather or produce food." "So what brought about a food surplus so cities could develop?" asked Andris. "The first major event was the

a. Industrial Revolution
b. women's liberation movement
c. discovery of grain
d. invention of the plow

4. "And the next one?" Andris asked. "This was the

a. Industrial Revolution
b. women's liberation movement
c. discovery of grain
d. invention of the plow

5. "Guess which city was probably the first to reach a million people," said Evija. Andris replied, "It was probably

a. Peking   **b.** Rome
c. London   **d.** New York City

6. "Lucky guess," smiled Evija. "No, I knew that," said Andris. "All right," said Evija. "Then do you know what a city's forms of transportation and communication, plus such things such as its sewers and streets, are called?" "I think so," Andris replied. "They are part of a city's

a. basic services   **b.** rudiments
c. underworld   **d.** infrastructure

7. "You were just kidding me, then. You studied this unit," said Evija. "Since you know so much about this, I'm going to ask you about some terms." "Go ahead," said Andris. "I'm ready." "When masses of people move to cities, and those cities have a growing influence on society, it's called

a. city growth   **b.** a megacity
c. urbanization   **d.** megalopolizing

8. "Then try this one. When a central city is surrounded by smaller cities and their suburbs, and all are connected economically and linked by transportation and communication, and sometimes politically, it's called a

a. giant city   **b.** megacity
c. metropolis   **d.** urban area

9. "How about when two or more metropolises and their many suburbs overlap and they have a powerful influence on a region?" asked Evija. Andris said, "Then they use the term

a. megalopolis   **b.** megacity
c. metropolis   **d.** urban area

10. "You did study this. You know, then, that when a city reaches 10 million or more it's called a megacity. Now," continued Evija, "in 1950, New York City and Tokyo were the only megacities in the world…" "And you want to know how many there are today, right?" interrupted Andris. "Right. Do you know the answer?" asked Evija, somewhat exasperated. "Sure," said Andris. "Today there are

a. 10   **b.** 12
c. 15   **d.** 22

UNIT 13.6

U.S. Urban Patterns

WHAT AM I SUPPOSED TO LEARN?

After you have read this unit, you should be able to

1 Summarize U.S. urban patterns.

The United States

From this global view, let's turn our focus on the United States.

FROM COUNTRY TO CITY

When the United States was founded, it was almost entirely rural. Only about 5 percent of Americans lived in cities. By 1920, this figure had jumped to 50 percent. Urbanization has continued without letup, and today about 80 percent of Americans live in cities. As you can see from the following Social Map, like our other social patterns, urbanization is uneven across the United States.

 Read the **Document**
"The Growth and Death of a Neighborhood" by Rob Gurwitt in **mysoclab**

As cities grow, they tend to spread out until they meet physical obstructions. The ocean limits the expansion of San Francisco, California, shown here.

FROM CITY TO CITY

As Americans migrate in search of work and better lifestyles, some cities grow while others shrink. Table 13.4 on the next page compares the fastest-growing cities with those that are losing people. This table reflects a major shift of people, resources, and power between regions of the United States. As you can see, five of the ten fastest-growing cities are in the West, and five are in the South. Of the ten shrinking cities, six are in the Northeast, two in the South, two in the Midwest. New Orleans, a special case, has not yet recovered from Hurricane Katrina.

BETWEEN CITIES

As Americans migrate, **edge cities** have appeared—clusters of buildings and services near the intersections of major highways. These areas of shopping malls, hotels, office parks, and apartment complexes are not cities in the traditional sense. Rather than being political units with their own mayor or city manager, they overlap political boundaries and include parts of several cities or towns. Yet, edge cities—such as Tysons Corner near Washington, D.C., and those clustering along the LBJ Freeway near Dallas, Texas—provide a sense of place to those who live or work there.

WITHIN THE CITY

Another U.S. urban pattern is **gentrification,** the movement of middle-class people into rundown areas of a city. What draws the middle class are the low prices for large houses that, although

edge city a large clustering of service facilities and residential areas near highway intersections that provides a sense of place to people who live, shop, and work there

gentrification middle-class people moving into a rundown area of a city, displacing the poor as they buy and restore homes

---

FIGURE 13.12   **How Urban Is Your State? The Rural–Urban Makeup of the United States**

The most urban states:

1. California (94.4%); New Jersey (94.4%)
2. Hawaii (91.5%); Nevada (91.5%)
3. Massachusetts (91.4%)

The most rural states:

1. Vermont (61.8% rural)
2. Maine (59.8% rural)
3. West Virginia (53.9% rural)

Legend:
- The most rural states: 38% to 62% urban
- Average states: 65% to 78% urban
- The most urban states: 80% to 94% urban

Source: By the author. Based on Statistical Abstract of the United States 2010:Table 29.

TABLE 13.4 The Shrinking and the Fastest-Growing Cities

	The Shrinking Cities			The Fastest-Growing Cities	
1. −11.3%	New Orleans, LA		1. +41.8%	Las Vegas, NV	
2. −6.2%	Youngstown, OH		2. +41.8%	Raleigh, NC	
3. −3.5%	Detroit, MI		3. +40.3%	Cape Coral–Ft. Myers, FL	
4. −3.3%	Cleveland, OH		4. +39.8%	Provo, UT	
5. −3.1%	Pittsburgh, PA		5. +39.7%	Greely, CO	
6. −3.0%	Buffalo–Niagara Falls, NY		6. +37.3%	Austin, TX	
7. −2.4%	Flint, MI		7. +37.0%	Myrtle Beach, SC	
8. −1.7%	Charleston, WV		8. +36.1%	McAllen, TX	
9. −1.2%	Toledo, OH		9. +33.5%	Fayetteville, AR	
10. −0.8%	Dayton, OH		10. +32.8%	Port St. Lucie, FL	

Note: Population change from 2000 to 2008, the latest years available.

Source: By the author. Based on *Statistical Abstract of the United States* 2012:Table 20.

deteriorated, can be restored. With gentrification comes an improvement in the appearance of the neighborhood—freshly painted buildings, well-groomed lawns, and the absence of boarded-up windows.

Gentrification received a black eye. As a neighborhood improved, property prices would go up, driving many of the poor out of their neighborhood. This created tensions between the poorer residents and the newcomers (Anderson 1990, 2006). These tensions were often tinged with racial–ethnicity antagonisms, as the middle-class newcomers were usually white. On a more positive note, sociologists have also found that gentrification draws middle-class minorities to the neighborhood and improves their incomes (McKinnish et al. 2008).

Among the exceptions to the usual pattern of the gentrifiers being whites and the earlier residents being minorities is Harlem in New York City. Here both groups are African Americans. As middle-class and professional African Americans reclaimed this area, an infrastructure—which includes everything from Starbucks coffee shops to dentists—followed. So did soaring real estate prices.

FROM CITY TO SUBURB

The term **suburbanization** refers to people moving from cities to **suburbs,** the communities located just outside a city. Suburbanization is not new. The Mayan city of Caracol (in what is now Belize) had suburbs, perhaps even with specialized subcenters, the equivalent of today's strip malls (Wilford 2000). The extent

suburbanization the migration of people from the city to the suburbs

suburb a community adjacent to a city

to which people have left U.S. cities in search of their dreams is remarkable. In 1920, only about 15 percent of Americans lived in the suburbs, but today over half of all Americans live in them (Palen 2012).

After the racial integration of U.S. schools in the 1950s and 1960s, whites fled the city. They have now begun to return (Dougherty 2008a). Although only a trickle at this point, their return to the city is significant enough that in Washington, D.C., and San Francisco, California, some black churches and businesses are making the switch to a white clientele. In a reversal of patterns, some black churches are now fleeing the city, following their parishioners to the suburbs.

SMALLER CENTERS

Another trend is the development of micropolitan areas. A *micropolis* (my-CROP-uh-lis) is a city of 10,000 to 50,000 residents that is not a suburb, such as Gallup, New Mexico, or Carbondale, Illinois. Most micropolises are located "next to nowhere." They are fairly self-contained in terms of providing work, housing, and entertainment, and few of their residents commute to urban centers for work. Micropolises are growing, as residents of both rural and urban areas find their cultural attractions and conveniences appealing, especially in the absence of the city's crime and pollution.

The Rural Rebound

The desire to retreat to a safe haven has led to a migration to rural areas that is without precedent in the history of the United States. Some small farming towns are making a comeback, their boarded-up stores and schools once again open for business and learning. In some cases, towns have even become too expensive for families that had lived there for decades (Dougherty 2008b).

The "push" factors for this fundamental shift are fears of urban crime and violence. The "pull" factors are safety, lower cost of living, and more living space. Interstate highways have made airports—and the city itself—accessible from longer distances. With satellite communications, smart phones, fax/scanning machines, and the Internet, people can be "plugged in"—connected with others around the world—even though they live in what just a short time ago were remote areas.

Listen to the wife of one of my former students as she explains why she and her husband moved to a rural area, three hours from the international airport that they fly out of each week:

I work for a Canadian company. Paul works for a French company, with headquarters in Paris. He flies around the country doing computer consulting. I give motivational seminars to businesses. When we can, we drive to the airport together, but we often leave on different days. I try to go with my husband to Paris once a year.

We almost always are home together on the weekends. We often arrange three- and four-day weekends, because I can plan seminars at home, and Paul does some of his consulting from here.

Sometimes shopping is inconvenient, but we don't have to lock our car doors when we drive, and the new Wal-Mart superstore has most of what we need. E-commerce is a big part of it. I just type in www—whatever, and they ship it right to my door. I get make-up and books online. I even bought a part for my stove.

Why do we live here? Look at the lake. It's beautiful. We enjoy boating and swimming. We love to walk in this park-like setting. We see deer and wild turkeys. We love the sunsets over the lake. (author's files)

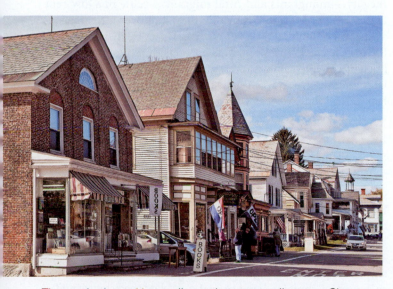

The rural rebound has enlivened many small towns. Shown here is the reinvigorated shopping district of the village of Chester, Vermont.

1. "Evija, did you read Unit 13.6?" asked Andris. "I did," said Evija. "Let me test you this time, okay?" "All right," Evija answered. "The fastest growing U.S. cities are in the
   a. West and South
   b. West and North
   c. East and South
   d. East and North

2. "Do you remember what they call clusters of buildings and services near the intersections of major highways?" asked Andris. "Yes, I do," said Evija. "I remember that they are not really cities, but they provide a sense of place to those who live or work there. They are called
   a. bent cities
   b. new cities
   c. edge cities
   d. cluster cities

3. "You know that middle-class people move into run-down areas of a city and fix up its rundown buildings, right?" asked Andris. "Of course," said Evija. "We've both seen this. We've even talked about how they displace the poorer residents." "Right," replied Andris, "but do you know what this process is called?" "No, what is it?" asked Evija. "It's called
   a. the replacement-displacement cycle
   b. gentrification
   c. urban renewal
   d. the master plan

4. "I learned that in gentrification, the usual pattern is for the gentrifiers to be whites and the earlier residents to be minorities," said Andris. "Do you know what is exceptional about the gentrification of Harlem?" "Yes, I know that," answered Evija. "In Harlem
   a. both groups are African Americans
   b. the gentrifiers are African Americans and the displaced are whites
   c. the gentrifiers are Asian Americans and the displaced are African Americans
   d. the gentrifiers are whites and the displaced are whites

5. "Here's an easy one," stated Andris. "The term for people moving from the city to the suburb is
   a. suburbing
   b. subbing
   c. subsidization
   d. suburbanization

6. "But let's make it a little tougher," said Andris. "Suburbanization isn't new. It probably reaches back to the Romans and the classic Greek cities. And in North America, we can trace suburbanization to this Mayan city
   a. Caracol
   b. Endeavor
   c. Las Playas
   d. Los Dioses Celosos

7. "Do you remember the term for a city of 10,000 to 50,000 residents that is not a suburb? It is located sort of next to nowhere." "I do," said Evija. "It is a

α. micropolis
b. macropolis
c. megacity
d. metropolis

8. "And if you can, tell me the name for this new unprecedented trend in U.S. history—migration from the city to small towns and rural areas," said Andris. "I remember that," replied Evija. "It is not one of those long names. It is the

α. rural rebound
b. move back
c. return
d. regional restratification

UNIT 13.7

Models of Urban Growth

WHAT AM I SUPPOSED TO LEARN?

After you have read this unit, you should be able to

1 Summarize the models of urban growth that sociologists have proposed.

In the 1920s, Chicago was a vivid mosaic of immigrants, gangsters, prostitutes, the homeless, the rich, and the poor—much like it is today. Sociologists at the University of Chicago studied these contrasting ways of life. One of them, Robert Park, coined the term **human ecology** to describe how people adapt to their environment (Park and Burgess 1921; Park 1936). (This concept is also known as *urban ecology*.)

Part of what sociologists have studied is how cities grow. Let's look at four main models they have developed.

human ecology Robert Park's term for the relationship between people and their environment (such as land and structures); also known as urban ecology

The Concentric Zone Model

Back in 1925, sociologist Ernest Burgess developed the classic picture of how cities expand, the *concentric-zone model*. Look at part A of Figure 13.13 on the next page. The model shows a city expanding outward from its center. Zone 1 is the central business district. Zone 2, which encircles the downtown area, is in transition. It contains rooming houses and deteriorating housing, which Burgess said breed poverty, disease, and vice. Zone 3 is the area to which thrifty workers have moved in order to escape the zone in transition and yet maintain easy access to their work. Zone 4 contains more expensive apartments, residential hotels, single-family homes, and exclusive areas where the wealthy live. Commuters live in Zone 5, which consists of suburbs or satellite cities that have grown up around transportation routes.

Burgess said that "no city fits perfectly this ideal scheme." Some cities have physical obstructions such as a lake, river, or railroad that cause their expansion to depart from the model. Burgess also noted that businesses had begun to deviate from the model by locating in outlying zones (see Zone 10). This was in 1925. Burgess didn't know it, but he was seeing the beginning of a major shift that led businesses away from downtown areas to suburban shopping malls. Today, these malls account for most of the country's retail sales.

The Sector Model

Sociologist Homer Hoyt (1939, 1971) modified Burgess' model. As shown in part B of Figure 13.13, he noted that a concentric zone can contain several sectors competing for the same land. In the same sector, there can be working-class housing, expensive homes, businesses, and so on.

An example of this dynamic competition is what sociologists call an **invasion–succession cycle.** Poor people moving into the city—immigrants and rural migrants—settle in a low-rent area. As more and more move in, they spill over into adjacent areas, where middle-class people live. Upset by their presence, the middle class moves out. This expands the sector of low-cost housing. The invasion–succession cycle is never complete, for later another group will replace this earlier one. The cycle, in fact, can go full circle, as with gentrification, where the "invaders" are the middle class.

The Multiple-Nuclei Model

Geographers Chauncey Harris and Edward Ullman noted that a city can have several centers, which they called *nuclei* (Harris and Ullman 1945; Ullman and Harris 1970). As shown in part C of Figure 13.13, each nucleus contains some specialized activity. A familiar example

invasion–succession cycle the process of one group of people displacing a group whose racial–ethnic or social class characteristics differ from their own

FIGURE 13.13   How Cities Develop: Models of Urban Growth

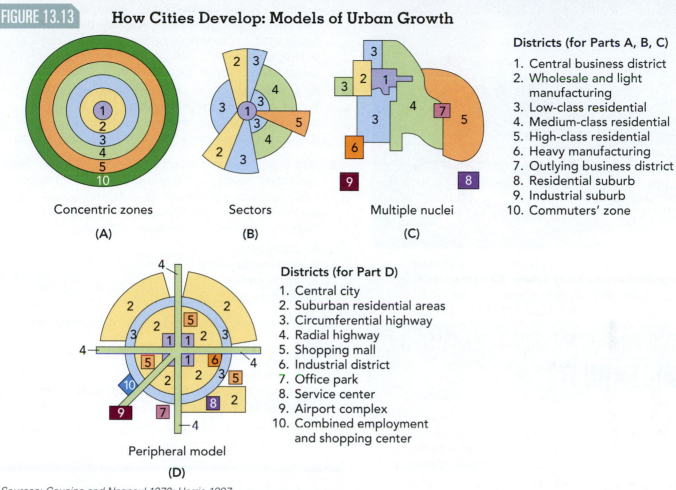

Concentric zones
(A)

Sectors
(B)

Multiple nuclei
(C)

Districts (for Parts A, B, C)

1. Central business district
2. Wholesale and light manufacturing
3. Low-class residential
4. Medium-class residential
5. High-class residential
6. Heavy manufacturing
7. Outlying business district
8. Residential suburb
9. Industrial suburb
10. Commuters' zone

Districts (for Part D)

1. Central city
2. Suburban residential areas
3. Circumferential highway
4. Radial highway
5. Shopping mall
6. Industrial district
7. Office park
8. Service center
9. Airport complex
10. Combined employment and shopping center

Peripheral model
(D)

Sources: Cousins and Nagpaul 1970; Harris 1997.

is the clustering of fast-food restaurants in one area of a city and automobile dealers in another area. One reason for this is that retail districts draw more customers if there are more stores. Other clustering occurs because some types of land use are incompatible. Factories and expensive homes, for example, don't mix very well, so they tend to be located in their separate areas. One result is that services are not spread evenly throughout the city.

The Peripheral Model

A new highway will change a city's growth. Look at part D of Figure 13.13. This model developed by Chauncey Harris (1997) shows the impact of radial highways, how people and services move away from the central city to the city's periphery, or outskirts. It also shows the development of industrial and office parks.

Critique of the Models

No models of urban growth are satisfactory. They are time bound, for medieval cities didn't follow these patterns. In addition, they do not account for urban planning. Most European cities have laws that preserve green belts (trees and farmlands) around the city. This prevents urban sprawl: Wal-Mart cannot

buy land outside the city and put up a store. Instead, it must locate in the downtown area with the other stores. Norwich, England, has 250,000 people—yet the city ends abruptly in a green belt where pheasants skitter across plowed fields while sheep graze in verdant meadows (Milbank 1995).

If you were to depend on these models, you would also be surprised when you visit the cities of the Least Industrialized Nations. The inner cities there are not filled with poor people. On the contrary, the wealthy live in the inner city, surrounded by fine restaurants and other services. Tucked behind walls and protected from public scrutiny, they enjoy luxurious homes and gardens. The poor, in contrast, especially rural migrants, settle in areas outside the city. As with El Tiro (pages 442–443), sometimes they even make their homes on top of piles of garbage.

IF YOU WANT TO LEARN MORE about why city slums are better than living in the countryside,

Read more from the author: Why City Slums are Better Than the County: Urbanization in the Least Industrialized Nations in **mysoclab**

Although most of the world's people now live in cities, many continue to live in rural towns. Few are as idyllic as Walenstadt, Switzerland, shown here.

UNIT 13.7 // TESTING MYSELF
DID I LEARN IT? ANSWERS ARE AT THE END OF THE CHAPTER

1. "Let's try it again," said Evija, "but this time I'm going to ask you questions." "Okay," agreed Andris. "Fire away." "I will. Robert Park coined a term to describe how people adapt to their environment. Some call it urban ecology, but Park called it

   a. urban environment **b.** master planning
   c. the urban cycle **d.** human ecology

2. "Back in 1925," said Evija, "Ernest Burgess developed a concentric-zone model to illustrate how a city expands away from its center. Each zone has different characteristics, from exclusive areas to rundown areas. He noted that businesses had begun to locate in outlying zones. He didn't know it, but he was noting a major shift—businesses moving from downtown areas to

   a. follow migrant paths
   b. more profitable centers
   c. suburban shopping malls
   d. retail stores

3. "Homer Hoyt modified Burgess's model of urban growth," said Evija. "He wanted to illustrate that a concentric zone can have many sectors, all competing for the same land. Sometimes one group will even displace another group." "I know what that is," said Andris. "It's called

   a. a displacement cycle
   b. an invasion-succession cycle
   c. a concentric zone
   d. a concentric cycle

4. "These models are getting a little confusing," said Andris. "I know," nodded Evija, "which is why you need to look at Figure 13.13. Anyway, the multiple-nuclei model shows how similar activities cluster in the same nucleus." "Can you give me an example?" asked Andris. "Sure, it's like when

   a. expensive homes are located in the same neighborhood
   b. factories spread throughout the city
   c. fast-food restaurants spread out
   d. public schools are located near the homes of their students

5. "Are there other urban models?" asked Andris. "Just one more," said Evija. "It shows the effect of radial highways, how people and services move away from the central city to the city's periphery, or outskirts." "What's it called?" asked Andris. "It's the

   a. concentric zone model
   b. single nucleus model
   c. outskirts model
   d. peripheral model

6. "Which one is best?" asked Andris. "Apparently," said Evija,

   a. it is the concentric zone model
   b. it is the multiple-nuclei model
   c. no model accounts for all types of urban development
   d. they all tie for first place

UNIT 13.8
City Life: From Alienation to Community

WHAT AM I SUPPOSED TO LEARN?

After you have read this unit, you should be able to

1 Describe the extremes of alienation and community in urban life.

2 Explain the types of people who live in the city.

I don't know how you feel about the city. Perhaps you are a little frightened by it, or maybe you feel totally comfortable in the city. Probably you feel a little of both, depending on what area of the city you are in. Let's look at the contrasts of alienation and community.

Alienation in the City

IMPERSONALITY AND SELF-INTEREST

In a classic essay, sociologist Louis Wirth (1938) noted how different urban life was from life in villages and small towns where most people know one another. Instead, urban dwellers live anonymous lives marked by segmented and superficial encounters. This undermines kinship and neighborhood, the traditional bases of social control and feelings of solidarity. Urbanites then focus on their own concerns and grow indifferent to other people's problems. In short, the price of the personal freedom that the city offers can be alienation. Seldom, however, does alienation get to this point:

> In crowded traffic on a bridge going into Detroit, Deletha Word bumped the car ahead of her. The damage was minor, but the driver, Martell Welch, jumped out. Cursing, he pulled Deletha from her car, pushed her onto the hood, and began to beat her. Martell's friends got out to watch. One of them held Deletha down while Martell took a car jack and smashed Deletha's car. Scared for her life, Deletha broke away, fleeing to the bridge's railing. Martell and his friends taunted her, shouting, "Jump, bitch, jump!" Deletha plunged to her death. (Newsweek, September 4, 1995). Welch was convicted of second degree murder and sentenced to 16 to 40 years in prison.

This certainly is not an everyday situation, but anyone who lives in a large city knows that even a minor traffic accident can explode into road rage. You had better be careful because you don't know who that stranger in the mall (or in the car ahead of you) is. In fact, you might not know who your next door neighbor is. The most common reason for impersonality and self-interest is not fear of danger, however, but the impossibility of dealing with crowds as individuals. In the city, stimuli come buzzing in from all directions. To find focus, we concentrate on our own concerns, retreating into more private worlds.

Community in the City

I don't want to give the impression that the city is inevitably alienating. Far from it. Here is another aspect of the attack on Deletha Word. After Deletha went over the railing, two men jumped in after her, risking injury and their own lives in a futile attempt to save her.

Many people find community in the city, sometimes in surprising places. Sociologist Herbert Gans, a symbolic interactionist who did participant observation in the West End of Boston, was so impressed with the area's sense of community that he titled his book *The Urban Villagers* (1962). In this book, which has become a classic in sociology, Gans said:

> After a few weeks of living in the West End, my observations—and my perceptions of the area—changed drastically. The

Large cities are not monoliths. Their smaller areas offer diversity, and for some a sense of community, which sometimes comes from repetitive shopping. This photo was taken in New York City.

> search for an apartment quickly indicated that the individual units were usually in much better condition than the outside or the hallways of the buildings. Subsequently, in wandering through the West End, and in using it as a resident, I developed a kind of selective perception, in which my eye focused only on those parts of the area that were actually being used by people. Vacant buildings and boarded-up stores were no longer so visible, and the totally deserted alleys or streets were outside the set of paths normally traversed, either by myself or by the West Enders. The dirt and spilled-over garbage remained, but, since they were concentrated in street gutters and empty lots, they were not really harmful to anyone and thus were not as noticeable as during my initial observations.
>
> Since much of the area's life took place on the street, faces became familiar very quickly. I met my neighbors on the stairs and in front of my building. And, once a shopping pattern developed, I saw the same storekeepers frequently, as well as the area's "characters" who wandered through the streets everyday on a fairly regular route and schedule. In short, the exotic quality of the stores and the residents also wore off as I became used to seeing them.

In this area of poverty, Gans found a **community,** people who identified with the area and with one another. Its residents enjoyed networks of friends and acquaintances. Despite the area's substandard buildings, most West Enders had chosen to live here. *To them, this was a low-rent district, not a slum.*

Most West Enders had low-paying, insecure jobs. Other residents were elderly, living on small pensions. Unlike the middle class, these people didn't care about their "address." The area's inconveniences were something they put up with in exchange for cheap housing. In general, they were content with their neighborhood.

community people who identify with an area and with one another

Who Lives in the City?

As you can expect from most things you have read in this book, social class is especially significant for how people experience the city. The city's wealthier residents enjoy greater security, which reduces alienation and increases their satisfaction with city life (Santos 2009). There also are different types of urban dwellers, each with distinctive experiences. As we review the five types that Gans (1962, 1968, 1991) identified, try to see where you fit.

THE COSMOPOLITES

The cosmopolites (cause-MOP-oh-lites) are the intellectuals, professionals, artists, and entertainers who have been attracted to the city. They value its conveniences and cultural benefits.

THE SINGLES

Usually in their early 20s to early 30s, the singles have settled in the city temporarily. For them, urban life is a stage in their life course. Businesses and services, such as singles bars and apartment complexes, cater to their needs and desires. After they marry, many move to the suburbs.

THE ETHNIC VILLAGERS

To attain a sense of identity, working-class members of the same ethnic group band together. They form tightly knit neighborhoods that resemble villages and small towns. Family- and peer-oriented, they try to isolate themselves from the dangers and problems of urban life.

THE DEPRIVED

Destitute, emotionally disturbed, and with little income, education, or work skills, the deprived live in neighborhoods that are more like urban jungles than urban villages. Some stalk their jungle in search of prey. Neither predator nor prey has much hope for anything better in life—for themselves or for their children.

THE TRAPPED

Like the deprived, these people don't live in the area by choice. Some were trapped when an ethnic group "invaded" their neighborhood and they could not afford to move. Others have been trapped in a downward spiral. They started life in a higher social class, but they drifted downward because of personal problems—mental or physical illness or addiction to alcohol or other drugs. There also are the elderly who are trapped by poverty and not wanted elsewhere. Like the deprived, the trapped suffer from high rates of assault, mugging, and rape.

In *Making It Personal,* let's pursue this discussion and see where you fit in the diversity of the city.

MAKING IT PERSONAL
Where Do You Fit?

The city is a rich mosaic of social diversity. Each group has its own lifestyle, and each has distinct experiences. Some people welcome the city's cultural diversity and mix with several groups. Others find community by retreating into the security of ethnic enclaves. Some feel trapped and deprived, living lives of fear and despair. To them, the city is an urban jungle that poses threats to their health and safety.

From a sense of community to a life of alienation. Where do you fit within all this? Why do you suppose this is your "fit," rather than somethng else?

Following Gans' analysis, what type of urban residents do you think these people represent? This scene is from the movie Sex and the City.

UNIT 13.8 // TESTING MYSELF
DID I LEARN IT? ANSWERS ARE AT THE END OF THE CHAPTER

1. "Evija," said Andris. "I read that back in the 1930s, sociologist Louis Wirth said that cities undermine community because interaction in urban life is
   a. based on money
   b. like an octopus, stretching its strangling tentacles around a city's residents
   c. like an exchange of power for prestige
   d. anonymous, segmented, and superficial

2. "I don't feel that way," said Evija. "I like the city." "You don't live in a fancy area, do you?" asked Andris. "Of course not! You know I can barely pay the rent, and I can't afford a car. The area I live in is poor, but I like

it." "Why?" asked Andris "Well, some might call it a slum, but it really isn't," answered Evija. "A lot of students live there. For me and my friends, it is a

a. dangerous area
b. refuge
c. low-rent district
d. seething cauldron of hostility

3. "I know what you mean," said Andris. "There are several types of people who live in the city. I would classify you as one of the

a. singles
b. ethnic villagers
c. deprived
d. trapped

4. "That's fine with me," said Evija. "And what about Frederico—how would you classify him?" "He lives in the Italian section with all those Italian restaurants," said Andris, "where they have that food fair every spring and fall. His parents and uncles and cousins all live nearby, so I would say he is one of the

a. singles
b. ethnic villagers
c. deprived
d. trapped

5. "How about my aunt?" asked Evija. "She's always so scared. Someone broke in down the hall and raped her neighbor. She didn't finish high school, and she's been in and out of mental hospitals." "Then," said Andris, "she would be one of the

a. singles
b. ethnic villagers
c. deprived
d. trapped

6. "And how about your aunt?" asked Evija. "She used to have a good job and then she got into drugs." "Yeah, a sad case," said Andris. "Now she can't hold a job, and she lives in this poor area with a lot of crime. She is one of the

a. singles
b. ethnic villagers
c. deprived
d. trapped

7. "And you, Andris?" asked Evija. "You know I'm a musician, Evija. I moved here for both the work and the opportunity to be around other musicians. We jam every week." "Then," said Evija, "you are one of the

a. cosmopolites
b. ethnic villagers
c. deprived
d. trapped

UNIT 13.9

The Diffusion of Responsibility

WHAT AM I SUPPOSED TO LEARN?

After you have read this unit, you should be able to

1 Explain the diffusion of responsibility.

2 Explain why the social psychology lab is not real life.

Imagine that you are taking a team-taught course in social psychology and your professors have asked you to join a few students to discuss your adjustment to college life. When you arrive, they tell you that to make the discussion anonymous they want you to sit unseen in a booth. You will participate in the discussion over an intercom, talking when your microphone comes on. The professors say that they will not listen to the conversation, and they leave.

You find the format somewhat strange, to say the least, but you go along with it. You have not seen the other students in their booths, but when they talk about their experiences, you find yourself becoming wrapped up in the problems that they begin to share. One student even mentions how frightening it is to be away from home because of his history of epileptic seizures. Later, you hear this individual breathe heavily into the microphone. Then he stammers and cries for help. A crashing noise follows, and you imagine him lying helpless on the floor.

Nothing but an eerie silence follows. What do you do?

Your professors, John Darley and Bibb Latané (1968), staged the whole thing, but you don't know this. No one had a seizure. In fact, no one was even in the other booths. Everything, except your comments, was on tape.

Some participants were told that they would be discussing the topic with just one other student, others with two, others with three, four, and five. Darley and Latané found that all students who thought they were part of a dyad (just two students) rushed out to help. If they thought they were part of a triad (three

For many people, it is easier to find community in the suburb than in the city. Shown here are neighbors helping neighbors.

students), only 80 percent went to help—and they were slower in leaving the booth. In six-person groups, only 60 percent went to see what was wrong—and they were even slower.

This experiment revealed a *diffusion of responsibility*—that the more bystanders there are, the less likely people are to help. As a group grows, people's sense of responsibility becomes diffused, with each person assuming that another will do the responsible thing. "With these other people here, it is not my responsibility," they reason.

The diffusion of responsibility helps to explain why people in a city can ignore the plight of others. Those who did nothing to intervene in the attack on Deletha Word were not uncaring people. Each felt that others might do something.

LABORATORY FINDINGS AND THE REAL WORLD:
Experiments in social psychology can give insight into human behavior—and at the same time, they can woefully miss the mark. This classic laboratory experiment has serious flaws when it comes to real life. Before you take the quiz, look at the photos on the next page that I snapped in Vienna, Austria, and you'll see something entirely different. Many people—strangers to one another—were simply passing one another on the sidewalk. But as you can see, no diffusion of responsibility stopped them from immediately helping the man who had tripped and fallen. Other norms and values that people carry within them are also at work, ones that can trump the diffusion of responsibility.

UNIT 13.9 // TESTING MYSELF
DID I LEARN IT? ANSWERS ARE AT THE END OF THE CHAPTER

1. "I read about an interesting experiment," said Evija. "What is it?" asked Andris. "You can read the details in the text, but basically the larger a group is, the less responsibility any one person feels if someone has a problem." "That makes sense," said Andris. "What do they call this?"
   a. group growth and responsibility
   b. inverse group size and diminishing responsibility
   c. diminishment of responsibility
   d. diffusion of responsibility

2. "You know that example in the book, that horrible case of the woman who was beaten after she bumped someone's car and then drowned in the river?" asked Evija. "I remember it," said Andris. "The experiment helps to explain it," said Evija. "Each person felt that
   a. he or she didn't want trouble
   b. the woman deserved it
   c. others might do something.
   d. the cops were on the way

3. "But there is more to it," added Evija. "The author took some photos on a city street of an old man being helped by a young woman. He says that this shows that laboratory experiments
   a. are about the same as real life
   b. are far from real life
   c. are better than observing real life
   d. should never be accepted

UNIT 13.10
Urban Problems and Social Policy

WHAT AM I SUPPOSED TO LEARN?

After you have read this unit, you should be able to

1   Explain why U.S. cities have declined.

2   Explain how U.S. cites can be revitalized.

THROUGH THE AUTHOR'S LENS
COMMUNITY IN THE CITY

AUSTRIA

Serendipity sometimes accompanies sociologists as they do their work, which was certainly the case here. The entire episode took no more than three minutes, and I was fortunate to capture it with my camera. Community should be a verb, as it is something people do, not just feel, as you can see in these photos.

As I was walking in Vienna, a city of almost 2 million people, I heard a crashing noise behind me. I turned, and seeing that a man had fallen to the sidewalk, quickly snapped this picture. You can see strangers beginning to help the man. This photo was taken about three seconds after the man fell.

The man is now on his feet, but still a bit shaky. The two who have helped him up are still expressing their concern, especially the young woman.

© James M. Henslin, all photos

Two strangers are helping the man, with another two ready to pitch in. They have all stopped whatever they were diding to help a man they do not know.

By this point, the police officer has noticed that I have been taking photos. You can see him coming toward me, his hand on whatever he is carrying at his hip, his shoulders back, glowering and ready for a confrontation. He asked, "What are you doing?" I said, "I am taking pictures" (as though he couldn't see this). He asked, "Do you have to take pictures of this man?" I said, "Yes," and hoping to defuse the situation, added, "I'm a sociologist, and I'm documenting how people help each other in Vienna." He grunted and turned away.

This photo really completes the series, as this individual was acting as the guardian of the community, placing a barrier of protection around the participants in this little drama.

To close this chapter, let's look at the primary reasons that U.S. cities have declined, and then consider how they can be revitalized.

Suburbanization

In the transition to the suburbs that we discussed earlier, the U.S. city has been the loser. As people moved out of the city, businesses and jobs followed. White-collar businesses, such as insurance companies, were the first to move their offices to the suburbs. They were soon followed by manufacturers. This process has continued so relentlessly that today twice as many manufacturing jobs are located in the suburbs as in the city (Palen 2012). As the city's tax base shrank, it left a budget squeeze that affected not only parks, zoos, libraries, and museums but also the city's basic services—its schools, streets, sewer and water systems, and police and fire departments.

CITY VERSUS SUBURB

Suburbanites want the city to keep its problems to itself. They reject proposals to share suburbia's revenues with the city and oppose measures that would allow urban and suburban governments joint control over what has become a contiguous mass of people and businesses. They do not mind going to the city to work, or venturing there on weekends for the diversions it offers, but they do not want to help pay the city's expenses.

It is likely that the mounting bill ultimately will come due, however, and that suburbanites will have to pay for their attitude toward the urban disadvantaged. Sociologist David Karp and colleagues (1991) put it this way:

> It may be that suburbs can insulate themselves from the problems of central cities, at least for the time being. In the long run, though, there will be a steep price to pay for the failure of those better off to care compassionately for those at the bottom of society.

Our occasional urban riots may be part of that bill—perhaps just the down payment.

SUBURBAN FLIGHT

In some places, the bill is coming due quickly. As they age, some suburbs are becoming mirror images of the city that their residents so despise. Suburban crime, the flight of the middle class, a shrinking tax base, and eroding services create a spiraling sense of insecurity, stimulating more middle-class flight (Katz and Bradley 2009; Palen 2012). Figure 13.14 on the next page illustrates this process, which is new to the urban–suburban scene.

Disinvestment and Deindustrialization

As the cities' tax base shrank and their services declined, neighborhoods deteriorated, and banks began **redlining:** Afraid of loans going

redlining a decision by the officers of a financial institution not to make loans in a particular area

bad, bankers would draw a line around a problem area on a map and refuse to make loans for housing or businesses there. This **disinvestment** (withdrawal of investment) pushed these areas into further decline. Youth gangs, muggings, and murders are common in these areas, but good jobs are not.

The globalization of capitalism has also left a heavy mark on U.S. cities. As we reviewed in Chapter 10, to compete in the global market, many U.S. companies moved their factories to countries where labor costs are lower. This process, called **deindustrialization**, eliminated millions of U.S. manufacturing jobs. Lacking training in the new information technologies, many poor people are locked out of the benefits of the postindustrial economy that is engulfing the United States. Left behind in the inner cities, many live in quiet and not so quiet despair.

The Potential of Urban Revitalization

Social policy usually takes one of two forms. The first is to tear down and rebuild—something that is fancifully termed **urban renewal.** The result is the renewal of an area—but not for the benefit of its inhabitants. Stadiums, high-rise condos, luxury hotels, and boutiques replace run-down, cheap housing. Outpriced, the area's inhabitants are displaced into adjacent areas.

The second is to attract businesses to an area by offering them reduced taxes. This program, called **enterprise zones**, usually fails because most businesses refuse to locate in high-crime areas. They know that the high costs of security and the losses from crime can eat up the tax savings.

Highly promising is a modification of the enterprise zone called the *Federal Empowerment Zone*. This program is the opposite of disinvestment. It targets the redevelopment of an area by adding low-interest loans to the tax breaks. The renaissance of Harlem was stimulated by designating Harlem a Federal Empowerment Zone. The low-interest loans brought grocery stores, dry cleaners, and video stores, attracting the middle class. As the middle class moved back in, the demand for more specialty shops followed. A self-feeding cycle of investment and hope replaced the self-feeding cycle of despair, crime, and drug use that accompanies disinvestment.

If cities become top agenda items of the government, they can be turned into safe places to live and enjoy. This will require not just huge sums of money but also creative urban planning. That we are beginning to see success in Harlem,

disinvestment the withdrawal of investments by financial institutions, which seals the fate of an urban area

deindustrialization the process of industries moving out of a country or region

urban renewal the rehabilitation of a rundown area, which usually results in the displacement of the poor who are living in that area

enterprise zone the use of economic incentives in a designated area to encourage investment

FIGURE 13.14 **Urban Growth and Urban Flight**

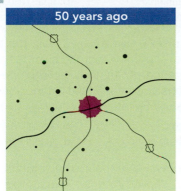

50 years ago

At first, the city and surrounding villages grew independently.

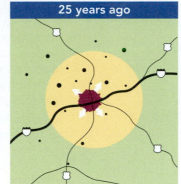

25 years ago

As city dwellers fled urban decay, they created a ring of suburbs.

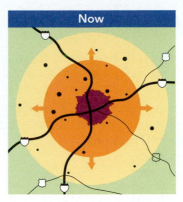

Now

As middle-class flight continues outward, urban problems are arriving in the outer rings.

👁 **Watch** the **Video**
Sociology on the Job: Population, Urbanization and Environment in **mysoclab**

PUBLIC SOCIOLOGY

Simply replacing old buildings with new ones is certainly not the answer. Instead, we need to apply sociological principles to build community. Here are three guiding principles suggested by sociologist William Flanagan (1990):

Scale. Regional and national planning is necessary. Local jurisdictions, with their many rivalries, competing goals, and limited resources, end up with a hodge-podge of mostly unworkable solutions.

Livability. Cities must be appealing and meet human needs, especially the need of community. This

Chicago's North Town, and even in formerly riot-torn East Los Angeles indicates that we can accomplish this transformation.

will attract the middle classes into the city, which will increase its tax base. In turn, this will help finance the services that make the city more livable.

Social justice. In the final analysis, social policy must be evaluated by how it affects people. "Urban renewal" programs that displace the poor for the benefit of the middle class and wealthy do not pass this standard. The same would apply to solutions that create "livability" for select groups but neglect the poor and the homeless.

Most actions taken to solve urban problems are merely window dressing. They help politicians appear as though they are doing something constructive. Band-Aids that cover up the problems that hurt our quality of life can never be adequate. We must address the root causes of urban problems—poverty, poor schools, crimes of violence, lack of jobs, and an inadequate tax base. Only then can our cities be transformed into safe and appealing places to live, environments that enhance our quality of life.

How do we solve the root causes of urban problems? If we do so, we can transform our cities into appealing places that enhance our quality of life. This photo was taken in Baltimore, Maryland.

The potential ahead of us: A dangerous slum transformed into an appealing place to live. This photo was taken in Harlem, New York City.

UNIT 13.10 // TESTING MYSELF
DID I LEARN IT? ANSWERS ARE AT THE END OF THE CHAPTER

1. "I learned why U.S. cities declined," said Andris. "What was the main reason?" asked Evija. "It was because
   a. so much money was spent on the war in Vietnam
   b. taxes were reduced after secret agreements between the Democrats and Republicans
   c. of teacher strikes
   d. of suburbanization

2. "How did suburbanization lead to the city's decline?" asked Evija. Andris answered, "It wasn't just people who moved to the suburbs, but also businesses and jobs. This
   a. left fewer people in the city
   b. meant fewer people used the public facilities such as libraries
   c. reduced the city's tax base
   d. emptied out areas of the city, and the abandoned housing deteriorated

3. "And when the city's tax base dropped," said Evija, "I suppose that
   a. the entertainment centers closed up
   b. city services deteriorated
   c. there was a reduction in patriotism
   d. fewer children went to school

4. "Right," said Andris. "But it wasn't only suburbanization. Banks played a role, too." "How?" asked Evija. "Bankers would refuse to make loans in certain areas, which brought about more decline in those

areas. Their refusal to make loans in designated areas was called
   a. disinvestment
   b. loan reconsideration
   c. a criminal conspiracy
   d. rechartering

5. "Anything else?" asked Evija. "Yes, there is another reason, too. There were broad changes, actually global rearrangements, that moved millions of manufacturing jobs overseas," said Andris. "What is that called?" asked Evija. "It is
   a. rechartering
   b. global restructuring
   c. job transfers
   d. deindustrialization

6. "Urban renewal is probably the solution," said Evija. "Not really," replied Andris. "It just replaces old buildings with new ones and
   a. costs millions and millions of dollars
   b. the new buildings deteriorate, too
   c. displaces the poor
   d. takes up more urban space

7. "What might work then?" asked Evija. "There is a program that provides tax breaks and low-interest loans to new businesses that locate in designated areas," replied Anris. "It is called a
   a. low-interest zone
   b. federal empowerment zone
   c. new business zone
   d. entrepreneur zone

8. "Whatever we do," said Evija, "I know that to have a true solution we must
   a. get at the root causes of the city's decline
   b. improve the city's schools
   c. hire more police
   d. get the children to read more and to watch less television

✓—[**Study** and **Review** in **mysoclab**

PULLING IT ALL TOGETHER REVIEWING THE LEARNING GOALS

Unit 13.1 A Planet with No Space for Enjoying Life?

1. State what demography is.
   - Demography focuses on human populations: their size, composition, growth, and distribution.

2. Explain the arguments of the New Malthusians and the Anti-Malthusians.
   - In 1798, Thomas Malthus developed the Malthus theorem, stating that population growth would outstrip the food supply. The *New Malthusians*

continue the argument: a current population growth of 228,000 people a day, one billion in 12 years. In just 43 years, the world's population has gone from 3.5 billion to 7 billion (in 2011). The *Anti-Malthusians* argue that we can see the future through Europe's Stage 3 of the demographic transition.

3. Explain the demographic transition.
   - Figure 13.3 outlines the four stages of the demographic transition.

Watch the **Video**
The Big Picture: Population,
Urbanization and Environment
Invest in **mysoclab**

Unit 13.2 Why Are People Starving?

1. Explain why there is starvation in some parts of the world.

- The obvious reason—that the earth does not produce enough food—is wrong. Despite the earth adding billions of people, there is more food available per person today than there was 50 years ago. The problem is that because of droughts and wars particular places lack food. The production of biofuels (turning food into fuel such as corn into gasoline) reduces the world's food supply. The solution is to transfer food from nations that have a surplus to those that have a shortage and to teach more efficient farming techniques. The stereotype of Africa being overpopulated is incorrect. Africa has 23 percent of the Earth's land, but only 15 percent of the Earth's population.

Unit 13.3 How Populations Grow

1. Explain why the population of the Least Industrialized Nations is growing so fast.

- Population in the Least Industrialized Nations is growing 13 times faster than in the Most Industrialized Nations. *Symbolic interactionist perspective:* In the Least Industrialized Nations, having children brings status and reflects the community's values. Children are economic assets, working at a young age and supporting the parents in their old age. *Conflict perspective*: In these nations, men control women's reproductive choices.

2. Explain population pyramids and how age structure produces population momentum.

- As in Figure 13.7, population pyramids depict a country's population by age and sex. More women in childbearing years (age structure) means a population grows faster (population momentum).

Unit 13.4 The Three Demographic Variables

1. Explain how demographers use three demographic variables to project population growth.

- The three demographic variables are fertility, mortality, and migration. The basic demographic equation is: The growth rate equals births minus deaths plus net immigration. *Fertility:* The fertility rate is the number of children that the average woman bears. The crude birth rate is the annual number of live births per 1,000 people. *Mortality:* The crude death rate is the annual number of deaths per 1,000 people. *Migration:* The net migration rate is the difference between the number of immigrants and emigrants per 1,000 people.

2. Explain problems in forecasting population growth.

- Wars, economic booms and busts, plagues, famines, and political policies push rates of birth and death and migration up or down.

Watch the **Video**
The Basics: Population,
Urbanization and
Environment in **mysoclab**

Unit 13.5 The Development of Cities

1. Give a brief history of cities and urbanization.

- The first cities go back almost 7,000 years. The earliest ones appeared in Iran and Iraq. A city can appear only when there is a food surplus, so some people can stop producing food and spend time in other economic pursuits. Two events that produced a food surplus and spurred the development of cities were the invention of the plow and the Industrial Revolution. *Urbanization*, the movement of masses of people to cities which then have a growing influence on society, is quite recent. The city attracts so many people because it provides variety, anonymity, and work. The term *metropolis* refers to large cities that have influence over a region. If metropolises and their suburbs overlap, they are called a *megalopolis*. When a city hits 10 million or more, it is called a *megacity*.

Explore the **Concept**
Where do Americans
Live? in **mysoclab**

Unit 13.6 U.S. Urban Patterns

1. Summarize U.S. urban patterns.

- When the United States was founded, it was almost entirely rural. Only about 5 percent of Americans lived in cities. Today, about 80 percent do. As Table 13.4 shows, the U.S. is experiencing major regional shifts. Edge cities have appeared—clusters of buildings and services near the intersections of major highways. In gentrification, the movement of middle-class people into rundown areas of a city, the usual pattern is for the newcomers to be whites and those displaced to be minorities. In the gentrification of Harlem, both the newcomers and the displaced are African Americans. Suburbanization reaches back in history. "White flight" seems to have ended. A *micropolis* is a city of 10,000 to 50,000 residents that is not a suburb. Without precedence in U.S. history is the current rural rebound, the flight from cities to small towns.

Unit 13.7 Models of Urban Growth

1. Summarize the models of urban growth that sociologists have proposed.
   - Figure 13.13 portrays these models. The classic concentric zone model illustrates how cities expand outward from the center. The sector model shows that a concentric zone can contain several sectors. The multiple-nuclei model shows that a city can have several centers (nuclei). The peripheral model portrays the impact of radial highways, how people and services move away from the central city to the city's periphery, or outskirts. None of these models is adequate. They don't account for medieval cities, European cities where laws prevent expansion into rural areas, or the urban patterns of the rapidly industrializing nations.

Unit 13.8 City Life: From Alienation to Community

1. Describe the extremes of alienation and community in urban life.
   - Unlike villages and small towns, urban life is marked by anonymous, segmented relationships that undermine community. One result is alienation, where people no longer identify with one another. Road rage was used as an example. Even in slum areas, though, people can find community, a sense of identifying with an area and with one another. The West End of Boston was given as an example.

2. Explain the types of people who live in the city.
   - Gans identified five types of urban dwellers: The cosmopolites, singles, ethnic villagers, deprived, and trapped. Each experiences the city differently.

> **Read** the **Document**
> "The Growth and Death of a Neighborhood" by Rob Gurwitt in **mysoclab**

Unit 13.9 The Diffusion of Responsibility

1. Explain the diffusion of responsibility.
   - Lab experiments show that as a group grows larger, people feel less responsibility for others. Their sense of responsibility becomes less personal, more diffused or spread out.

2. Explain why the social psychology lab is not real life.
   - A series of photos taken by the author of a man who fell on the sidewalk illustrates that lab experiments can fall quite short when compared with real life.

Unit 13.10 Urban Problems and Social Policy

1. Explain why U.S. cities have declined.
   - Suburbanization is not just the movement of people from cities to suburbs, but also the transfer of businesses and jobs. This reduced the city's tax base and eroded city services. Disinvestment and deindustrialization also contributed to the city's decline.

2. Explain how U.S. cities can be revitalized.
   - Replacing buildings in some form of urban renewal is not the answer, although Federal Empowerment Zones can help. The root causes must be addressed: poverty, poor schools, crimes of violence, lack of jobs, and an inadequate tax base. Public sociology in the form of applying sociological principles can guide the revitalizing of cities.

> **Watch** the **Video**
> Sociology on the Job: Population, Urbanization and Environment in **mysoclab**

UNIT 13.1 // TESTING MYSELF
DID I LEARN IT? ANSWERS

1. **d** demography

2. **b** Malthus theorem

3. **d** 228,000

4. **c** births dropped and got balanced with deaths again

5. **b** deaths outnumber births and the population shrinks

6. **a** an exponential growth curve

7. **d** exported hybrid seeds, herbicides, and techniques of public hygiene

8. **b** had the United Nations spearhead efforts to reduce world population growth

9. **a** going to shrink

10. **a** too early to tell

UNIT 13.2 / / TESTING MYSELF
DID I LEARN IT? ANSWERS

1. d more food for each person in the world

2. c of droughts and wars

UNIT 13.3 / / TESTING MYSELF
DID I LEARN IT? ANSWERS

1. d 40 years

2. c proves that he is a real man

3. b support the parents when they are old

UNIT 13.4 / / TESTING MYSELF
DID I LEARN IT? ANSWERS

1. d migration

2. b annual number of live births per 1,000 people

3. b number of children that women are capable of bearing

4. c 30 children

UNIT 13.5 / / TESTING MYSELF
DID I LEARN IT? ANSWERS

1. d 7,000 years

2. c Iran and Iraq

3. d invention of the plow

4. a Industrial Revolution

UNIT 13.6 / / TESTING MYSELF
DID I LEARN IT? ANSWERS

1. a West and South

2. c edge cities

3. b gentrification

3. b are produced from food that someone could otherwise have eaten

4. a 15 percent of the earth's population

4. a men control women's reproductive choices

5. d immigration

6. c population by age and sex

7. b has more women in the child bearing years

8. a age structure gives a country its population momentum

5. d Macao, Hong Kong, and Taiwan

6. c Niger

7. b crude birth rate

8. c net migration rate

9. d basic demographic equation

10. a political decisions

5. b Rome

6. d infrastructure

7. c urbanization

8. c metropolis

9. a megalopolis

10. d 22

4. a both groups are African Americans

5. d suburbanization

6. a Caracol

7. a micropolis

8. a rural rebound

1. **d** human ecology

2. **c** suburban shopping malls

1. **d** anonymous, segmented, and superficial

2. **c** low-rent district

3. **a** singles

1. **d** diffusion of responsibility

1. **d** of suburbanization

2. **c** reduced the city's tax base

3. **b** city services deteriorated

3. **b** an invasion-succession cycle

4. **a** expensive homes are located in the same neighborhood

5. **d** peripheral model

6. **c** no model accounts for all types of urban development

4. **b** ethnic villagers

5. **c** deprived

6. **d** trapped

7. **a** cosmopolites

2. **c** others might do something

3. **b** are far from real life

4. **a** disinvestment

5. **d** deindustrialization

6. **c** displaces the poor

7. **b** federal empowerment zone

8. **a** get at the root causes of the city's decline

CHAPTER 14
SOCIAL CHANGE AND THE ENVIRONMENT

Watch the **Video** in **mysoclab**

((•—| **Listen** to the **Chapter Audio** in **mysoclab**

GETTING STARTED

In this chapter, we will focus on social change, probably the main characteristic of social life today. Social change is another key to opening insight into the self. This is because social change has a fundamental influence on the way you think and live, just as it will for your children. We will also examine how social change is threatening our environment, that thin crust of earth, with its water and air, on which our very existence depends.

To help you understand **social change**, a shift in some characteristic of culture and society, we will begin in our usual way, by first laying a broad foundation.

Sabi Sands Reserve, South Africa

UNIT 14.1

How Social Change Transforms Social Life

Social change is such a vital part of living in society today that it has been a recurring theme throughout this book. To make this theme more explicit, let's review the main points about social change that we already looked at in the preceding chapters. This will be a whirlwind tour of things we have already covered.

The Four Social Revolutions

Change is so fast that today's society is quite different from the way it was when you started grade school. Rapid social change is also occurring around the world. Why is the world changing so quickly?

To get the answer, we have to reach back in history just a bit—to the time when humans first domesticated plants and animals. As strange as it may seem, this event of thousands of years ago set in motion forces that are still echoing through your life. This first social revolution allowed hunting and gathering societies to develop into horticultural and pastoral

social change the alteration of culture and societies over time

societies (see pp. 328–330). Then the plow brought another social revolution, and agricultural societies emerged. The third social revolution, prompted by the invention of the steam engine, ushered in the Industrial Revolution. Now you are in the midst of the fourth social revolution, stimulated by the invention of the microchip. The process of change has accelerated so greatly that the mapping of the human genome system could be introducing yet another new type of society, one based on biotechnology.

So you don't lose the thread of thought here: We would have had none of these changes if our remote ancestors had not domesticated plants and animals.

> **Watch** the **Video** The Basics: Collective Behavior and Social Movements in **mysoclab**

From *Gemeinschaft* to *Gesellschaft*

Social revolutions don't just touch the surface. When a social revolution is full-blown, little of a people's way of life remains. Consider the change from agricultural to industrial society. It was not simply that people changed where they lived, moving from the farm to the city. They certainly did this, but the change was so deep that it even transformed peoples' connections with one another. In an agricultural society, people's lives are built around obligations. Like friendship today, the rules aren't written down, but everyone knows what they owe others. Lives revolve around kinship and friendship and the exchanging of favors. When people moved to the city, many intimate relationships were replaced with impersonal associations built around paid work, contracts, and money. As you learned (page 121), sociologists use the term *Gemeinschaft* to refer to life in traditional societies and *Gesellschaft* to refer to life in industrial societies. These terms indicate a fundamental shift in the way people live and how they think about life. Table 14.1 on the next page summarizes these changes.

The Industrial Revolution

The sweeping changes shown in Table 14.1 were ushered in by the Industrial Revolution. The traits listed in this table are *ideal types* in Weber's sense of the term, for in no society do all of

Technology is transforming life across the globe. How do you think that computers will change the lives of these villagers in Ollantayambo, Peru?

TABLE 14.1 Comparing Traditional and Industrialized (and Information) Societies

Characteristics	Traditional Societies	Industrialized (and Information) Societies
General Characteristics		
Social change	Slow	Rapid
Size of group	Small	Large
Religious orientation	More	Less
Education	Informal	Formal
Place of residence	Rural	Urban
Family size	Larger	Smaller
Infant mortality	High	Low
Life expectancy	Short	Long
Health care	Home	Hospital
Temporal orientation	Past	Future
Demographic transition	First stage	Third stage (or Fourth)
Material Relations		
Industrialized	No	Yes
Technology	Simple	Complex
Division of labor	Simple	Complex
Income	Low	High
Material possessions	Few	Many
Social Relationships		
Basic organization	*Gemeinschaft*	*Gesellschaft*
Families	Extended	Nuclear
Respect for elders	More	Less
Social stratification	Rigid	More open
Statuses	More ascribed	More achieved
Gender equality	Less	More
Norms		
View of morals	Absolute	Relativistic
Social control	Informal	Formal
Tolerance of differences	Less	More

Source: By the author.

them appear to the maximum degree. Our new technology has even made countries a mixture of the traits shown in this table. For example, in Uganda most people follow a traditional way of life. But not the elite. They own computers, have smaller families, emphasize formal education, and so on. The characteristics shown in Table 14.1 should be interpreted as "more" or "less" rather than "either-or."

IN SUM: Keep the main point in mind: *When technology changes, societies change.* You have seen how domestication, the plow, and the steam engine transformed people's lives. So

the computer is changing our lives. Today's traditional societies are being transformed by the technology they import from the industrialized world. In the last chapter, you saw some of the dramatic changes that took place when the West exported medicine and hybrid seeds to the Least Industrialized Nations. Their populations exploded when their death rates dropped but their births stayed high. The world is being swept by social change. One of the most significant is that masses of people are moving to cities that have little industry to support them. You might want to look again at the photo essay on pages 442–443.

Let's consider social change in *Making It Personal.*

MAKING IT PERSONAL
You and Social Change

When I was in the seventh grade, I took my first course in physical science. The instructor, Mr. Bender, had just completed college and was interested in doing a good job in the classroom. On one test, the essay question asked for an example of physical change. As I thought about the question, I realized that almost everything changes. So—in my smart-aleck seventh grade manner—instead of a raging river washing out farmland and towns, mountain erosion, or things that my instructor expected, my answer was an ant moving a piece of food to an ant hill. Mr. Bender didn't appreciate my answer and wouldn't give me credit for it.

So let's skip ants, and let me ask you this question about social (not physical) change: What changes have you observed in society (social life, your way of life) since you were a child? As you answer this, you will start to gain a picture of how fast and extensive today's social change is.

And no ants!

UNIT 14.1 // TESTING MYSELF
DID I LEARN IT? ANSWERS ARE AT THE END OF THE CHAPTER

1. A shift in some characteristic of culture and society is known as
   a. cultural shift
   b. social shift
   c. characteristic shift
   d. social change

2. The author says that to understand today's social change, we need to go back to the
   a. Industrial Revolution
   b. invention of capitalism
   c. time when humans first domesticated plants and animals
   d. first example of slavery

3. The reason that we should look so far back in history to understand today's social change is because if the domestication of plants and animals had not occurred

  a. plants would not be cultivated
  b. animals would still be wild
  c. we could not have had the social changes that have taken place since then
  d. we would still be living in agricultural societies

4. The change from agricultural to industrial society transformed peoples' personal connections. Many intimate relationships were replaced with impersonal associations built around paid work, contracts, and money. Sociologists use these terms to summarize this change

  a. from industrial to agricultural
  b. from *Gemeinschaft* to *Gesellschaft*
  c. from personal to impersonal
  d. from intimate to contractual

5. The main point in this unit is that

  a. when technology changes, societies change
  b. you never know what the next change will be
  c. social change has slowed
  d. our society is so established that social change will have less effects on it than on traditional societies

UNIT 14.2

Global Politics: Power and Conflict

WHAT AM I SUPPOSED TO LEARN?

After you have read this unit, you should be able to

1 Give a quick overview of geopolitics since World War II.

2 Explain the two threats to the New World Order.

Geopolitics, though it might seem remote, affects your life intimately. You can glimpse part of the developing New World Order in this photo of the G8 summit in Deauville, France.

Like most of us, your main concern is probably to get through everyday life. With this close-up focus, you quite understandably lose sight of one of the most significant social changes that is affecting your life—the shifting arrangements of power among the world's nations. Because these alignments (called **geopolitics**) are so significant to your well-being and to that of your children, let's look at them in a little more detail.

A VERY BRIEF HISTORY OF GEOPOLITICS

Global divisions of power were apparent by the sixteenth century. At that time, nations with the most advanced technology (the swiftest ships and the most powerful cannons) conquered other nations and took control of their resources. In the eighteenth century, at the beginning of the Industrial Revolution, the countries that industrialized first exploited the resources of those that had not yet industrialized. The consequences of this early domination remain with us today, including the recurring conflicts over oil in the Middle East.

G7 PLUS

Before World War II, the British controlled an empire so huge that they used to proudly proclaim that the sun never set on the British flag. After World War II, a triadic (or three-part) division of the globe appeared: a Japan-centered East (soon to be dominated by China), a Germany-centered Europe, and a United States–centered western hemisphere. To maintain their global dominance, these three powers, along with Canada, France, Great Britain, and Italy, formed G7, meaning the "Group of 7." Fear of Russia's nuclear arsenal prompted G7 to let Russia join this elite club, creating G8. G8 is fragile, for it depends on Russia's cooperation, which is never certain.

This group is gradually—but reluctantly—adjusting to the growing

geopolitics shifting economic and political relationships among the world's nations

wealth and power of China. Wanting to recapture its glories of centuries past, China is expanding its area of influence. Bowing to the inevitable and attempting to reduce the likelihood of conflict as China steps on turf claimed by others, G8 has allowed China to become an observer at its annual summits. As mentioned in Chapter 7, if China cooperates adequately, the next step will be its full membership in this exclusive club, transforming it into G9.

DIVIDING UP THE WORLD

At their annual meetings, these world powers set policies to guide global economic affairs. G8's goal is to perpetuate its global dominance. Essential to this goal is access to abundant, cheap oil. This requires that G8 dominate the Middle East, not letting it become an independent power. To the degree that these nations fail to implement policies that promote their own interests, they undermine the New World Order they are trying to orchestrate.

TWO THREATS TO THIS COALITION OF POWERS

G8 faces two major threats to the global divisions it is trying to work out. The first is dissension, with Russia at the center of intrafamilial feuding. Because Russia is still stinging from the loss of its empire in the 1990s, and wants a more powerful presence on the world stage, it is quick to perceive insult and threat—and to retaliate. In the dead of winter of 2006 and again in 2009, amidst a dispute with Ukraine over the price of gas, Russia turned off the pipeline that carries its gas through Ukraine to western Europe. It made no difference that this act endangered lives in several countries (Crossland 2006; Kramer 2009). Russia also threatened to aim its missiles at cities in Europe if the United States didn't back down from its plan to put missiles in Poland as part of a missile-defense shield (Blomfield 2007). Russia even

went as far as threatening a nuclear attack on Poland (McElroy 2008). The United States did back down—ever so quietly. Despite snarling back and forth, it is likely that these nations will resolve their tensions—including those arising from China's growing economic and military might—and realign their structure of power. Unless catastrophe intervenes, the result will be a New World Order.

Ethnic rivalries are a second threat G8 faces as it divides up the world. In Europe, ethnic violence in the former Yugoslavia split the country into seven nations. The Flemish defiantly proclaim that they are not Belgian, and Turks in Germany fear the young Germans who, barely held in check, threaten their lives. In Africa, the Igbo won't let the government count them because, as they say, "We are not Nigerian." We do not know how long the lid can be kept on the seemingly bottomless ethnic antagonisms that exist around the world. The end of these hostilities will certainly not come during our lifetimes.

For global control, G8 requires political and economic stability, both in their own backyards and in those countries that provide the raw materials that fuel their industrial machine. This explains why G8 cares little when African nations self-destruct in ethnic slaughter but refuse to tolerate interethnic warfare in their own neighborhoods. To allow warfare between different groups in Bosnia, Kosovo, or Georgia would be to tolerate conflict that could spread and engulf Europe. In contrast, the deaths of hundreds of thousands of Tutsis in Rwanda carried little or no political significance for these powerful countries.

The path to the New World Order is peppered with bumps. A major bump is ethnic nationalism, ethnic groups demanding independence. Shown here is a Flemish protest in Brussels. The Flemings say they are not Belgians.

UNIT 14.2 // TESTING MYSELF
DID I LEARN IT? ANSWERS ARE AT THE END OF THE CHAPTER

1. The shifting alignments of world powers and their relationships to one another is called
   a. shifting alignments
   b. realignments
   c. world power shifts
   d. geopolitics

2. Canada, France, Great Britain, and Italy formed G7, meaning the "Group of 7," along with the United States and
   a. Germany and Japan
   b. Germany and China
   c. China and Japan
   d. Russia and Japan

3. With the addition of this country, G7 became G8
   a. China
   b. Belgium
   c. Spain
   d. Russia

4. This country has become an observer at G8's annual summits. If it cooperates to G8's satisfaction, it will become a member, changing G8 to G9.
   a. Japan
   b. Russia
   c. China
   d. Latvia

5. The goal of G8 is to
   a. help the poor nations
   b. perpetuate G8's dominance of the world
   c. help keep grains affordable for the world's poor
   d. divide up the world's resources in ways that benefit the world's nations

6. The two major threats to the New World Order being worked out by G8 are ethnic conflicts around the world that threaten political stability and
   a. quarrels among the G8 nations
   b. the economic development of the Least Industrialized Nations
   c. the financial cost of maintaining global dominance
   d. the loss of prestige on which global power is based

UNIT 14.3

Theories and Processes of Social Change

WHAT AM I SUPPOSED TO LEARN?

After you have read this unit, you should be able to

1 Use evolutionary theory, natural cycles, and conflict over power to explain social change.

Social change has always fascinated theorists. Of the many attempts to explain why societies change, in this unit we shall consider just three: the evolution of societies, natural cycles, and conflict and power.

Multilinear views of societal evolution assume that different paths lead to industrializatiion. How would China fit into this view? This photo was taken in Tiananmen Square.

Evolution from Lower to Higher

Evolutionary theories of how societies change are of two types: unilinear and multilinear. *Unilinear* theories assume that all societies follow the same path. Each society evolves from simpler to more complex forms, a journey that takes each society through the same sequences (Barnes 1935). Of the many versions of this theory, the one proposed by Lewis Morgan (1877) once dominated Western thought. Morgan said that all societies go through three stages: savagery, barbarism, and civilization. In Morgan's eyes, England, his own society, was the epitome of civilization. All other societies were destined to follow the same path.

Multilinear views of evolution replaced unilinear theories. Instead of assuming that all societies follow the same sequence, multilinear theorists proposed that different routes lead to the same stage of development. All paths lead to industrialization, but societies need not pass through the same stages on their journey (Sahlins and Service 1960; Lenski and Lenski 1987).

Central to all evolutionary theories, whether unilinear or multilinear, is the assumption of *cultural progress*. Tribal societies are assumed to have a primitive form of human culture. As these societies evolve, they reach a higher state—the supposedly advanced and superior form that characterizes the Western world. Growing appreciation of the rich diversity—and complexity—of tribal cultures has discredited this idea. In addition, Western culture is now in crisis (poverty, racism, war, terrorism, sexual assaults, unsafe streets) and no longer regarded as the top of human civilization. The idea of cultural progress has been cast aside, and evolutionary theories have been rejected (Eder 1990; Smart 1990).

Natural Cycles

Cyclical theories attempt to account for the rise of entire civilizations. Why, for example, did Egypt, Greece, and Rome wield such power and influence, only to reach a peak and then decline? Cyclical theories assume that civilizations are like organisms: They are born, enjoy an exuberant youth, come to maturity, and then decline as they reach old age. Finally, they die (Hughes 1962).

The cycle does exist, but why? Historian Arnold Toynbee (1946) said that each civilization faces challenges to its existence. Groups work out solutions to these challenges, as they must if they are to continue. But these solutions are not satisfactory to all. The ruling elite manages to keep the remaining oppositional forces under control, even though they "make trouble" now and then. At a civilization's peak, however, when it has become an empire, the ruling elite loses its capacity to keep the masses in line "by charm rather than by force." Gradually, the fabric of society rips apart. Force may hold the empire together for hundreds of years, but the civilization is doomed.

In a book that provoked widespread controversy, *The Decline of the West* (1926–1928), Oswald Spengler, a high school teacher in Germany, proposed that Western civilization had passed its peak and was in decline. Although the West succeeded in overcoming the crises provoked by Hitler and Mussolini, as Toynbee noted, civilizations don't end in sudden collapse. Because the decline can last hundreds of years, perhaps the crisis in Western civilization mentioned earlier (poverty, rape, murder, and so on) indicates that Spengler was right, and we are now in decline. If so, it appears that China is waiting on the horizon to seize global power and to forge a new civilization.

Conflict over Power

Long before Toynbee, Karl Marx identified a recurring process of social change. He said that each *thesis* (a current arrangement of power) contains its own *antithesis* (contradiction or opposition). A struggle develops between the thesis and its antithesis, leading to a *synthesis* (a new arrangement of power). This new social order, in turn, becomes a thesis that will be challenged by its own antithesis, and so on. Figure 14.1 gives a visual summary of this process.

According to Marx's view (called a **dialectical process** of history), each ruling group sows the seeds of its own destruction. Consider capitalism. Marx said that capitalism (the thesis) is built on the exploitation of workers (an antithesis—an-TITH-uh-sis, or built-in opposition). With workers and owners on a collision course, the dialectical process will not stop until workers establish a classless state (the synthesis).

The analysis of G7/G8 in the previous unit follows conflict theory. G8's current division of the globe's resources and markets is a thesis. Resentment on the part of have-not nations is an antithesis. The demand to redistribute power and resources will come from any Least Industrialized

dialectical process (of history) each arrangement of power (a thesis) contains contradictions (antitheses) which make the arrangement unstable and which must be resolved; the new arrangement of power (a synthesis) contains its own contradictions; this process of balancing and unbalancing continues throughout history as groups struggle for power and other resources

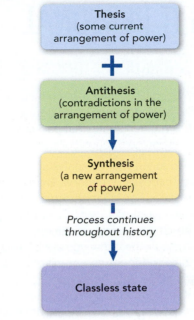

FIGURE 14.1 **Marx's Model of Historical Change**

Thesis (some current arrangement of power)

+

Antithesis (contradictions in the arrangement of power)

↓

Synthesis (a new arrangement of power)

Process continues throughout history

↓

Classless state

Source: By the author.

or Industrializing Nation that gains military power. With their nuclear weapons, China, India, Pakistan, Russia, and North Korea fit this scenario. Eventually, a new rearrangement of power will come. We don't know its shape at this point, but like the old, this new synthesis will contain its own antitheses, such as ethnic hostilities, or leaders who feel that their countries have been denied a fair share of resources. These contradictions will haunt the new rearrangement of power, and at some point another synthesis will be worked out. The process repeats, a continual cycle of thesis, antithesis, and synthesis.

Let them eat cake! Oxfam

If G8's current division of the globe's resources and markets is the thesis, what is the antithesis? What do you think the synthesis will be?

Let's try to combine geopolitics and the dialectical process of history in *Making It Personal*.

MAKING IT PERSONAL
You and the Dialectical Process of History

This *Making It Personal* is a little more difficult than usual. You will be able to answer it only to the extent that you have a background for it. If you don't have that background yet, it is okay. You will gain it as you go through college and life.

You have just read about Marx's analysis with that heavy phrase, "a dialectical process of history." By now, you know that in sociology Marx is not "that commie guy," that he is taken seriously as an analyst of society. A lot of people stumble over his ideas about a workers' revolution, but as you are wrapping up the course I expect that you are beyond this, that you've been able to consider not communism or socialism—but Marx's analyses of society. At this point, I ask that you think about his analysis of recurring cycles: thesis, antithesis, and synthesis. These cycles can provide an outstanding framework for interpreting history.

Here are the questions for you to grapple with. In today's geopolitics, what is the thesis? What is the antithesis? What do you think the coming synthesis will be? And from there, what do you think the antithesis in that new synthesis will be?

I said this would be a bit more difficult. Just let your ideas flow. As you go through college, your ideas are likely to undergo major change. But, for now, what are your answers?

UNIT 14.3 // TESTING MYSELF
DID I LEARN IT? ANSWERS ARE AT THE END OF THE CHAPTER

1. Unilinear evolutionary theories of social change assume that all societies pass through the same stages in the same order. This unilinear theory proposed by Lewis Morgan, consisting of these three stages, once dominated Western thought
   a. first stage, second stage, and third stage
   b. savagery, barbarism, and civilization
   c. simple, more complex, and advanced
   d. primitive, developing, and developed

2. This evolutionary theory of social change assumes that all societies will end up with industrialization, but in getting there they won't all go through the same stages in the same order
   a. multilinear   b. passive
   c. active   d. unilinear

3. Central to all evolutionary theories is the assumption of
   a. cultural progress
   b. the gradual emancipation of women
   c. change from more complex to simpler forms
   d. an increasing need for more educated workers

4. The idea that the West represented the height of civilization dominated evolutionary theories. These theories have been discredited because of
   a. the discovery of more advanced tribes in the Amazon jungle
   b. research on older civilizations that had declined
   c. the declining intelligence around the world
   d. the crisis in western civilization

5. This theory assumes that civilizations are like organisms: They are born, enjoy an exuberant youth, come to maturity, and then decline as they reach old age
   a. multilinear evolutionary theories
   b. unilinear evolutionary theories
   c. natural cycles
   d. progression-advancement

6. According to natural cycle theory, civilizations decline when
   a. inflation spins out of control
   b. the ruling elite loses its capacity to keep the masses in line "by charm rather than by force"
   c. the tax burden falls mainly on the rich
   d. the tax burden falls mainly on the poor

7. According to this theory of social change, each ruling group sows the seeds of its own destruction
   a. dialectical process of history
   b. monolectical process of history
   c. multilectical process of history
   d. multilineal process of history

8. According to the dialectical process of history developed by Karl Marx, a current arrangement of power is called
   a. an oppositional force   b. a synthesis
   c. an antithesis   d. a thesis

9. According to the dialectical process of history, each arrangement of power contains oppositional forces called
   a. the unsettled factors
   b. a synthesis
   c. an antithesis
   d. a thesis

10. According to the dialectical process of history, oppositional forces eventually form a new arrangement of power called
    a. the new power   b. a synthesis
    c. an antithesis   d. a symbiosis

UNIT 14.4

Ogburn's Theory

Sociologist William Ogburn (1922/1938, 1961, 1964) proposed a theory of social change that is based largely on technology. As you can see from Table 14.2, he said that technology changes society by three processes: invention, discovery, and diffusion. Let's consider each.

INVENTION

Ogburn defined **invention** as a combining of existing elements and materials to form new ones. We usually think of inventions as being only material items, such as computers, but there also are *social inventions*. We have considered many social inventions in this text, including democracy and citizenship (pages 311–312), capitalism (page 332), socialism (page 333), and in Chapter 9, gender equality. We saw how these social inventions had far-reaching consequences on people's lives. Material inventions can also affect social

> **invention** the combining of existing elements and materials to form new ones; identified by William Ogburn as one of three processes of social change

life deeply, as we have seen with the computer, which has transformed our society.

DISCOVERY

Ogburn identified **discovery**, a new way of seeing reality, as a second process of change. The reality is already present, but people see it for the first time. An example is Columbus' "discovery" of North America, which had consequences so huge that they altered the course of human history. This example also illustrates another principle: A discovery brings extensive change only if it comes at the right time. Other groups, such as the Vikings, had already "discovered" North America in the sense of learning that a new land existed—obviously no discovery to the Native Americans already living in it. Viking settlements disappeared into history, however, and Norse culture was untouched by the discovery.

> **discovery** a new way of seeing reality; identified by William Ogburn as one of three processes of social change

---

TABLE 14.2 Ogburn's Processes of Social Change

Process of Change	What It Is	Examples	Social Changes
Invention	A combining of existing elements to form new ones	1. Cars 2. Computers 3. Graphite composites	1. Urban sprawl and long commutes to work 2. Telework and Global Positioning System 3. New types of building construction
Discovery	A new way of seeing some aspect of the world	1. Columbus—North America 2. Gold in California 3. DNA	1. Realignment of global power 2. Westward expansion of United States 3. Positive identification of criminals
Diffusion	The spread of an invention or discovery	1. Airplanes 2. Money 3. Condom	1. Global tourism 2. Global trade 3. Smaller families

Note: For each example, there are many changes. You can also see that any particular change, such as global trade, depends not just on one item, but on several preceding changes.

Source: By the author.

How would you apply Ogburn's theory of social change to this photo taken in the village of Bhaktapur, Nepal?

Aborigines of Australia, it upset their whole society. How could such a simple object do this? Before this, the men controlled axe-making. They used a special stone that was available only in a remote region, and fathers passed axe-making skills on to their sons. Women had to request permission to use the axe. When steel axes became common, women also possessed them, and the men lost both status and power (Sharp 1995).

Diffusion also includes the spread of social inventions and ideas. As we saw in Chapter 10, the idea of citizenship changed political structures around the world. It swept away monarchs as an unquestioned source of authority. The idea of gender equality is now circling the globe. To those who grew up with this concept, it is surprising to think that opposition to withholding rights on the basis of someone's sex can be revolutionary. Like citizenship, gender equality is destined to transform human relationships and entire societies.

> **Watch** the **Video** The Big Picture: Collective Behavior and Social Movements in **mysoclab**

CULTURAL LAG

Ogburn coined the term **cultural lag** to refer to how some elements of a culture lag behind the changes that come from invention, discovery, and diffusion. Technology, he suggested, usually changes first, with culture lagging behind. In other words, we play catch-up with changing technology, adapting our customs and ways of life to new technology.

Let's consider Ogburn's analysis in *Making It Personal*.

cultural lag Ogburn's term for human behavior lagging behind technological innovations

FROM ANOTHER STUDENT ...

I never heard of sociology before, but it turns out this is the most interesting subject yet. There are a lot of different ways to look at the world.

—Steven Harkins

DIFFUSION

The third process of social change that Ogburn identified is **diffusion**, the spread of an invention or discovery from one area to another. He stressed how diffusion also changes people's lives. Consider an object as simple as the axe. When missionaries introduced steel axes to the

diffusion the spread of an invention or a discovery from one area to another; identified by William Ogburn as one of three processes of social change

MAKING IT PERSONAL

You and Ogburn

In the first unit, I mentioned that social change is so fast that today's society is quite different from the way it was when you started grade school. I would like you to think about the changes that have taken place in society since you started school. First, what are those changes? That is, just what is different about society (or perhaps better phrased, your own way of life) now than it was when you were a little kid? Second, I would like you to apply Ogburn's analysis of social change to your observations. How does each change you identified fit into Ogburn's outline of discovery, invention, and diffusion?

Ogburn's analysis is deceptively simple. It is easy to understand, and it provides an excellent framework for interpreting your experiences of social change.

And now, the final part of your application of Ogburn's analysis: For the social changes that you identified, what cultural lags can you pinpoint? In other words, How did your culture (behaviors, ideas, and customs) lag behind the particular social change? Did your behaviors "catch up"? How?

UNIT 14.4 // TESTING MYSELF
DID I LEARN IT? ANSWERS ARE AT THE END OF THE CHAPTER

1. Sociologist William Ogburn proposed a theory of social change that is based largely on technology. He said that societies change because of
   a. the discontent people feel when they miss out on new technology
   b. gender issues that arise when new technology replaces old technology
   c. a gradual maturing process
   d. invention, discovery, and diffusion

2. Inventions are a combining of existing elements and materials to form new ones. We usually think of material inventions, but, as with citizenship and democracy, there also are
   a. new ideas
   b. ideas that disrupt society
   c. social inventions
   d. social realignments

3. A second process of social change that Ogburn identified is a new way of seeing reality. He called this
   a. invention
   b. discovery
   c. diffusion
   d. social change

4. The spread of an invention or discovery from one area to another can also change society. Ogburn called this
   a. diffusion
   b. invention
   c. discovery
   d. social change

5. Ogburn's theory of social change is not limited to technology, because the invention, discovery, or diffusion can also be that of
   a. dreams
   b. books
   c. education
   d. ideas

6. Culture generally lags behind the changes that come from invention, discovery, and diffusion. Ogburn called this
   a. social change
   b. slow invention
   c. cultural lag
   d. slow diffusion

UNIT 14.5

Networking, Facebook, and Technology

WHAT AM I SUPPOSED TO LEARN?

After you have read this unit, you should be able to

1 Explain some ways that technology is changing social life.

As you may recall from Chapter 3, *technology* has a double meaning. It refers to both the *tools*, the items used to accomplish tasks, and the *skills* or procedures needed to make and use those tools. The tool can be as simple as a comb or as complicated as

a computer. The skill or procedure includes not only the methods used to manufacture combs and computers but also those needed to "produce" an acceptable hairdo or to go online. Apart from any particulars, then, technology always refers to *artificial means of extending human abilities*.

All human groups make and use technology, but today's *new technologies*, as they are called, allow us to do what has never

New technologies change society, often in surprising ways. This scene, which is becoming common, illustrates an unexpected effect of technology on social interaction.

been done before. We can transplant organs and communicate almost instantaneously anywhere on the globe. We can also travel greater distances faster and even probe space. Although you have grown up with these features of technology, these are all new to the human scene.

Change is so rapid that desktop computers are becoming relics destined for museums. Some laptops are being replaced by handheld devices that contain keyboards and cameras. Some cursors can be controlled by eye movements. And this is just the beginning. In our coming biotech society, you might not even be able to recognize computers. Data might be stored on holograms located in your own proteins (Guessous et al. 2004).

Although new devices are fascinating, *the sociological significance of technology is not the device but how technology changes your way of life.* Let's explore this in *Making It Personal*.

MAKING IT PERSONAL

Technology in Your Life

As we apply sociology in these *Making It Personal* features, I have sometimes become personal with you, giving you a glimpse into my life. To see effects of technology on social relationships, we'll do it again.

My wife and I sit at the same large dining room table that serves as our desk, each absorbed in our computers as we go about our individual tasks. Although we can easily talk to one another, and do, we also send emails back and forth throughout the day, even though we are within arms' reach of one another. One of us finds something interesting to forward, the latest news on Latvia or the global economic crisis, some sociological analysis, news from a friend or one of the kids, or even something humorous. By sending the message instead of talking, we don't break the other's concentration. We attend to the message when it seems convenient—and perhaps during our breaks, when we then chat with one another.

This is a personal experiencing of technological change, an example of how technology is changing social patterns, making them look quite different from the past. How is this happening with you? How are you adapting the new technology? How are you making it fit your life situation? Your particular patterns are likely to be different from mine, but you, like the rest of us, are adapting your way of life to our changing technology.

Your social destiny is a life continuously transformed by changing technology. Other than becoming a hermit, you have no way out of this evolving process. Electronic networking, such as through Facebook and its many counterparts, is part of the impact of technology on your life. Like other technology, social networking devices can bring unexpected consequences. Let's look at one that surprised almost everyone.

The Facebook of Revolution

Mohamed Bouazizi, 26, sold fruit on the street to support himself, his mother, and his five brothers and sisters in their three-room home in Sidi Bouzid, Tunisia. It was common for city inspectors to harass the fruit vendors, demanding bribes or confiscating their fruit if they didn't pay. They paid.

But not today. Bouazizi said no to the demand for a bribe. To teach him a lesson, the city inspector's assistants beat him and took his fruit. Instead of retreating, Bouazizi went to the municipal offices and demanded his property. There, more city officials beat him.

"This is how it is," everyone told him. "There's nothing you can do about it." Bouazizi decided that he could do something about it. He walked to the governor's mansion and in front of its ornate gate doused himself with paint thinner, lit a match, and set himself afire (Fahim 2011).

What does this desperate suicide in a dusty, out-of-the-way town run by corrupt officials have to do with technology?

Bouazizi didn't die immediately. Despite having burns over 90 percent of his body, he lingered for several days, barely holding onto life. There were small protests. His family and friends threw coins at those ornate gates where Bouazizi had died, shouting, "Here's your bribe!" One man posted photos and videos of these small protests on Facebook. As the word spread, the protests grew, not just in Sidi Bouzid, but throughout Tunisia. The protests turned into violent confrontations with the police and military. Two weeks later, the man who had been the dictator of Tunisia for 23 years fled the country.

This bitter resentment fanned by technology ignited what became known as the Arab Spring. Emboldened by the fall of the Tunisian government, citizens of nearby Arab nations, also under oppressive dictatorships, took to the streets. Organized and encouraged by Facebook entries and mini-blog Tweets, unarmed protestors gathered in city squares, demanding change. Soldiers firing onto the crowds infuriated even more people, turning passivity and docility into angry denunciation. As the demonstrations continued to grow, Gamal Mubarak, the dictator of Egypt, who had ruled with an iron fist for 30 years, fled the country. Other governments soon toppled.

Technology was not the cause of the Arab Spring. Facebook and Tweeting—with their vast networking that reaches out like a spider's web to encompass more and more people—were not a cause, but a tool that allowed people to bypass the government-censored mass media. These tools helped protesters fan discontent and allowed informal leaders to emerge. Sharing photos and personal accounts of government beatings, torture, and killings ignited rage. The pent-up hostilities built over the harsh decades of oppression and injustice erupted to the surface.

Seeing the power of this new technology and seemingly constantly fearful of the people, governments are striking back. To suppress information and dissent, some governments shut down the towers that carry the signals on which Tweeting depends. Going one step further, and borne out of extreme fear, Iran is going to start its own national Internet. The government says that this is to benefit the people, that it will give them more dependable and inexpensive service. What it will actually do is give the government control over this new threat. At will, officials can shut the Internet down (Rhoads and Fassihi 2011).

Information freely exchanged lies at the basis of a free people. And all governments—whether dictatorships or democracies, whether in the East or the West—fear a free exchange of ideas and opinions. Ultimately, this means that governments fear sociology—except where sociology becomes a handmaiden of the state.

Let's look at one more area of social life that is being transformed by new technology.

The Changing Face of War
CYBER WARFARE

Every country looks for an edge when it is in conflict with other nations. Combining the computer's capacity to store and retrieve information with devices to monitor human activities can provide that advantage. If these tools can be disrupted by an enemy, however, these same capacities can be turned into weaknesses, an Achilles Heel by which the weaker can bring down the powerful.

This potential of turning strength into weakness strikes fear in U.S. officials who are in charge of security and war (Sanger and Bumiller 2011). It does the same with their counterparts throughout the world. What if an enemy is able to disrupt vital communications? We could be left with a window of darkness, staring at blank screens or reading files filled with false information fed by the enemy. Military leaders would be unable to communicate with troops, while the enemy who disrupted the communications attacks. This fear pervades the military—on both sides, wherever those fluid sides line up today.

Cyber war is not merely a potential future event. Its prelude has already begun. Thousands of attacks have been launched against the military computers of the United States (Sanger et al. 2009; Bumiller and Shanker 2012). The purpose of the attacks seems to be to find chinks in the armor, the spots where malicious software can be installed unawares—to then be unleashed at some designated moment. Beyond the military, the targets are the nation's electrical grid, its banking system, the stock exchanges, oil and gas pipelines, the air traffic control system, and Internet and cell phone communications.

These initial cyber forays, with Russia and China the primary suspects, have stimulated the United States to spend billions of dollars in preparation for cyber war. We can be certain that those billions are not directed solely at defense. The United States, most assuredly, is also probing the cyber defense of its cyber enemies.

AN OMINOUS TRANSITION

We are beginning to see an ominous transition. Already there is the Pterodactyl, China's answer to the Predator. To the amazement of the Pentagon, China has advanced its technology to the point that its unmanned aerial vehicles (UAVs) have begun to rival those of the United States (Page 2010; Wall 2010). China has even begun to flaunt its space weapons in the face of the Pentagon, a not too subtle warning not to mess with China as its leaders expand their territorial ambitions.

Weapons are made to be used—despite the constant polite rhetoric about their defensive purposes. On both sides are itchy fingers, and now that China has become an ominous threat to U.S. space superiority, the Pentagon faces a new challenge. How will it be able to contain China's political ambitions if Star Wars looms?

To close this unit, read *Making It Personal*.

MAKING IT PERSONAL
Your Big Brother

You probably will not be involved in a revolution. And I certainly hope that the coming confrontations between China and the United States never break into war, that they remain matters handled by diplomats. Apart from these issues, then, do you have concerns about technology? Does it bother you, for example, that in China authorities are issuing identity cards with a chip that includes the individual's name, address, education, work history, and religion? To enforce the country's "one couple, one child" policy, the chip also includes the individual's reproductive history (Bradsher 2007).

You probably are yawning about now. "So what? That's China. I have my own concerns just getting through the day." But your future gets involved here—not in China but right here in the United States. The Federal Drug Administration has approved an identity chip the size of a grain of rice that can be injected under your skin (Stein 2004). This chip can store your

It is likely that this form of invasive search will become a thing of the past. Technologies are being perfected that can "see everything" while you stand in line–and even evaluate the look on your face.

name, address, age, weight, height, hair and skin color, and race–ethnicity. It could, of course, also include the names and addresses of your friends and associates—even any suspected acts of disloyalty.

If the government starts recording this information on the chip, people will protest, of course. And Homeland Security will scream danger—all those terrorists ready to plant bombs under your bed. If this doesn't do it, there is another way to overcome resistance. On the chip, government officials can record only the standard information—name, age, and so on. But this information can open centralized files that store the information about suspected disloyalty.

The beauty of this technology—from the perspective of government agents—is that the chip can be activated by a scanner. You would not even know that you were under surveillance.

Does this bother you? Or do you think such things are necessary if we are to have a secure society? If you haven't read George Orwell's *1984*, to raise your awareness I highly recommend this novel.

This protest in Tunisia, part of the Arab Spring, depended on communication. If the microchip had not been invented, would it have taken place?

UNIT 14.5 // TESTING MYSELF
DID I LEARN IT? ANSWERS ARE AT THE END OF THE CHAPTER

1. Technology has a double meaning. It refers to both the tools, the items used to accomplish tasks, and the
   a. history of the development of those tools
   b. relationship of those tools to other tools
   c. people who operate or use those tools
   d. skills or procedures needed to make and use those tools

2. Apart from any particular tools, technology always refers to
   a. new devices
   b. both old and new devices
   c. artificial means of extending human abilities
   d. the human capacity for creative effort and developing solutions to problems

3. The sociological significance of technology is not the device but
   a. the procedures for using the device
   b. how technology changes people's way of life
   c. how the device is related to preceding devices on which it is built
   d. how the cost of developing the device is related to other possible social uses of that money

4. Technology—in the forms of Facebook and tweeting—was a tool that helped to overthrow long-lasting dictatorships in
   a. Tunisia and Egypt
   b. China and Hong Kong
   c. Uruguay and Peru
   d. Liberia and Haiti

5. Countless attacks have been made on U.S. computers—military, banking, business, utilities. These attacks seem to be the initial forays in coming
   a. peace overtures
   b. Big Brother control of society
   c. global warfare that will destroy humanity
   d. cyber warfare

6. This country has made remarkable advancements in military weapons. It is likely that confrontations over territorial ambitions with this country and the United States will follow.
   a. Russia
   b. China
   c. Yugoslavia
   d. France

7. In a reminder that Big Brother may be watching, this country has developed—and a government agency has approved—an identity chip the size of a grain of rice that can be injected under the skin
   a. United States
   b. Russia
   c. China
   d. Canada

UNIT 14.6
The Growth Machine Versus the Earth

WHAT AM I SUPPOSED TO LEARN?

After you have read this unit, you should be able to

1 Explain how environmental problems are related to industrialization, why there can never be an energy shortage, and why rain forests should be saved.

After a frustrating struggle of twenty years, Russian environmentalists won a court order to stop Baikalsk Paper Mill from dumping its wastes into Lake Baikal. When the mill filed for bankruptcy, Vladimir Putin, the prime minister of Russia, boarded a minisub and said, "I'll see if the lake has been damaged." At the bottom of Lake Baikal, Putin said, "It's clean. I can see the bottom." He then told Oleg Deripaska, the major owner of the paper mill, "You can dump your wastes in the lake." (Boudreaux 2010)

Politicians are usually more subtle than this, but befitting his power and position, Putin doesn't have to be. He can crown himself an environmental expert and give personal permission to pollute. Although the specifics differ, in country after country similar battles are being waged. While environmentalists struggle for a clean Earth, politicians fight for jobs and votes—and while doing so, line the pockets of their friends, and their own as well.

Underlying today's environmental decay is the globalization of capitalism, which I have stressed throughout this text. To maintain their dominance and increase their wealth, the Most Industrialized Nations, spurred by multinational corporations, continue to push for economic growth. At the same time, the Industrializing Nations, playing catch-up, are striving to develop their economies. Meanwhile, the Least Industrialized Nations are anxious to enter the race: Because they start from even farther behind, they have to strive for even faster growth.

Many people are convinced that the Earth cannot withstand such an onslaught. Global economic production creates global pollution, and faster-paced production means faster-paced destruction of our environment. In this relentless pursuit of economic development, many animal species have been driven to the verge of extinction—or are already gone forever. If the goal is a **sustainable environment**, a world system in which we use our physical environment to meet our needs without destroying humanity's future, we cannot continue to trash the Earth. In short, the ecological message is incompatible with an economic message that implies it is OK to rape the Earth if it makes someone money.

Before looking at the social movement that has emerged about this issue, let's examine some major environmental problems.

> **Read the Document**
> "Sixteen Impacts of Population Growth" by Brown, Gardner, and Halweil in **mysoclab**

Environmental Problems and Industrialization

Although even tribal groups produced pollution, the frontal assault on the natural environment did not begin in earnest until nations industrialized. Industrialization was equated with progress and prosperity. For the Most Industrialized Nations, the slogan has been "Growth at any cost."

sustainable environment a world system that takes into account the limits of the environment, produces enough material goods for everyone's needs, and leaves a heritage of a sound environment for the next generation

In some countries, the deterioration of the environment and the poverty are remarkable. This girl in Mexico City, Mexico, is playing in a dump while her parents search for scraps for their survival.

FIGURE 14.2 The Worst Hazardous Waste Sites

Least waste sites: 0–12

Average waste sites: 13–29

Most waste sites: 30–116

WA	48
OR	12
MT	15
ND	0
MN	25
VT	11
ME	12
NH	21
MA	32
RI	12
CT	15
NJ	116
DE	14
MD	19
DC	1
ID	9
WY	2
SD	2
WI	38
MI	67
NY	86
PA	96
CA	97
NV	1
UT	19
CO	20
NE	13
IA	12
IL	49
IN	31
OH	40
WV	9
VA	30
NC	32
AZ	9
NM	14
KS	12
MO	29
KY	14
TN	14
SC	26
AR	9
OK	9
LA	13
MS	6
AL	15
GA	16
TX	49
FL	52
AK	5
HI	3

= 10 sites

Least hazardous sites
1. North Dakota (0)
2. Nevada (1)
3. South Dakota (2); Wyoming (2)

Most hazardous sites
1. New Jersey (116)
2. California (97)
3. Pennsylvania (96)

Note: These are the waste sites so outstandingly threatening to public health that they made the national priority list. New Jersey is in a class by itself. This small state has 20 more hazardous waste sites than its nearest competitor, Pennsylvania, with 96.

Source: By the author. Based on Statistical Abstract of the United States 2012:Table 384.

TOXIC WASTES

Industrial growth has come, but at a high cost, with toxic by-products that harm the environment and pose dangers to people's health. Much toxic waste has simply been dumped onto the land or into rivers, lakes, and the oceans. Formerly pristine streams have been turned into putrid sewers. The public water supply of some cities is unfit to drink. On the Social Map above, you can see the locations of the worst hazardous waste sites in the United States. A special problem involves nuclear power plants, supposedly a solution to the problem of the "dirty" generation of electricity. Nuclear plants produce wastes that remain deadly for thousands of years. We simply don't know what to do with these piles of lethal garbage (Vergakis 2009).

And what if a tsunami hits a nuclear plant? But that certainly is too far-fetched to even consider. With all the concerns about radiation, and after the lesson of Chernobyl, which spewed poisons over land and people, certainly adequate precautions have been taken in building nuclear plants. Certainly the world wished that this were true when a tsunami hit Japan, destroying nuclear reactors and spewing nuclear contamination.

The lesson from Japan might be summarized as: "When it comes to nuclear accidents, no matter how far-fetched, if they can happen they probably will." It is impossible however, to protect every

nuclear facility against every conceivable accident—which gives almost irrefutable ammunition to the antinuclear social movement.

Garbage so clogs this river in China that specialized ships have been built to clean up the mess. As China industrializes further, environmental issues will become more of a priority.

We can't lay the cause of our polluted Earth solely at the feet of the Most Industrialized Nations. The Industrializing Nations also do their share, with China the most striking example. This country now emits more carbon dioxide than does the United States (Rogers and Evans 2011). Of the world's forty most polluted cities, *thirty-six* are in China (World Bank 2007:Figure 5). The 9,000 chemical plants along the banks of China's Yangtze River have turned this major waterway into an industrial sewer (Zakaria 2008). Like the Russians before them, authorities imprison any Chinese who dare to speak out about pollution (Larson 2011; Wong 2011). As China secures its place in the industrialized world, its leaders will inevitably place more emphasis on controlling pollution. However, the harm done to our planet in the meantime is incalculable.

With limited space to address this issue, let's focus on fossil fuels, the energy shortage, and the rain forests.

FOSSIL FUELS AND GLOBAL WARMING

Burning fossil fuels to run motorized vehicles, factories, and power plants has been especially harmful to our Earth. One consequence, shown in Figure 14.3, is acid rain, which kills animal and plant life. The harm is so extensive that fish can no longer survive in some lakes in Canada and the northeastern United States.

Another consequence is **global warming**, an increase in the Earth's temperature. The world's glaciers and the ice caps at the North and South Poles store such incredible amounts of water that if they melt the level of the world's oceans will rise by several feet. This will devastate the world's shores and beaches. Many barrier islands off the coast of the United States will disappear. The oceans will reclaim Florida's Everglades.

As the glaciers and ice caps melt, the world's low-lying little island nations will be washed into the sea. No longer is this just theoretical, at least to these nations. One of them, Kiribati, in the South Pacific, is taking global warming seriously. Over the past few years, this nation has saved money. They have used these savings to buy land in Fiji, which is 1,500 miles away. They expect to move their entire population of 106,000 there (Perry 2012).

global warming an increase in the Earth's temperature

FIGURE 14.3　**Acid Rain**

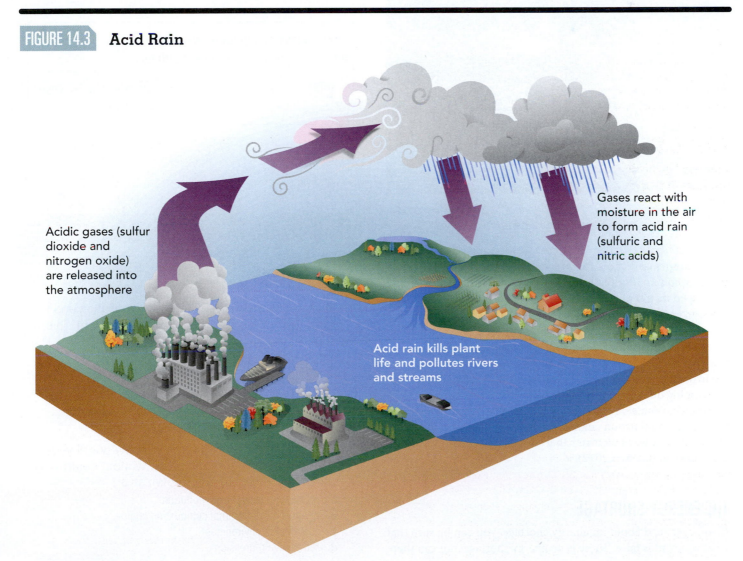

Acidic gases (sulfur dioxide and nitrogen oxide) are released into the atmosphere

Gases react with moisture in the air to form acid rain (sulfuric and nitric acids)

Acid rain kills plant life and pollutes rivers and streams

Source: By the author.

The rain forests are rapidly disappearing. In this photo from Indonesia, you can see land being cleared for a canal.

ever be. We can produce unlimited low-cost power, which can help to raise the living standards of humans across the globe. The sun, for example, produces more energy than humans could ever use. Boundless energy is also available from the tides and the winds. In some cases, we need better technology to harness these sources of energy; in others, we need only to apply the technology we already have.

THE RAIN FORESTS

Of special concern are the world's rain forests. Although they cover just 6 percent of the Earth's land area, the rain forests are home to *one-half* of all the Earth's plant and animal species (Frommer 2007). Despite knowing their essential role for humanity's welfare, we seem bent on destroying rain forests for the sake of timber and farms. In the process, we extinguish plant and animal species, perhaps thousands a year. As biologists remind us, once a species is lost, it is gone forever. Like Esau who traded his birthright for a bowl of porridge, we are exchanging our future for lumber, farms, and pastures.

> ***IF YOU WANT TO LEARN MORE*** about the disappearing rain forests and the tribes who live in them,
>
> **Read** more from the author: The Rain Forests: Lost Tribes, Lost Knowledge in **mysoclab**

Burning fossil fuels in internal combustion engines is a primary source of global warming. Of the technologies being developed to use alternative sources of energy in vehicles, the most prominent is the gas–electric hybrid. Some of these cars are expected to eventually get several hundred miles per gallon of gasoline. The hybrid, however, is but a bridge until vehicles powered by fuel cells become practical. With fuel cells converting hydrogen into electricity, it will be water, not carbon monoxide, coming out of a car's exhaust pipe.

Despite promising technology that might reduce our reliance on internal combustion engines, global warming continues. And it is rushing toward us faster than even some of the pessimists had expected (Gerken 2012).

THE ENERGY SHORTAGE

If you ever read about an energy shortage, you can be sure that what you read is false. There is no energy shortage, nor can there

UNIT 14.6 // TESTING MYSELF
DID I LEARN IT? ANSWERS ARE AT THE END OF THE CHAPTER

1. Many reasons can be given for the pollution and other destruction of our natural environment. This is a major one:
   a. competition with China
   b. the development of the Eurozone
   c. lack of enforcement of anti-pollution laws in the United States
   d. the globalization of capitalism

2. A reasonable goal seems to be to use our physical environment to meet our needs without destroying humanity's future. This is known as a
   a. paced withdrawal from pollution
   b. reversal of the internal combustion engine
   c. sustainable environment
   d. retroactive regression

3. Nuclear plants pose a special environmental problem because they produce wastes that
   a. turn deadly when they get wet
   b. remain deadly for thousands of years
   c. turn into carbon dioxide
   d. break into nonacidic components when they are exposed to the sun

4. It isn't only the Most Industrialized Nations that are polluting the Earth. The Industrializing Nations also do their share. The worst offender is
   a. China
   b. Russia
   c. Great Britain
   d. Tibet

5. If a Chinese citizen protests pollution, that person is
   a. acclaimed as a hero of the workers
   b. interviewed by local and national television stations
   c. put to work cleaning the streets
   d. put in prison

6. If the seas rise, the world's shorelines will be flooded and some island nations will be washed into the ocean. If this occurs, it will be because of
   a. the Most Industrialized Nations
   b. the little ice age
   c. global warming
   d. nuclear plants

7. There can never be an energy shortage because
   a. governments will make sure we have enough energy
   b. the sun produces more energy than humans could ever use
   c. our government has stockpiled enough energy to last for more than two generations
   d. scientists will always figure out a solution to the problem

8. To sharply reduce pollution, we can replace vehicles that are propelled by internal combustion engines with those that use fuel cells to
   a. convert hydrogen into electricity
   b. increase gasoline efficiency
   c. convert sunlight into gasoline
   d. follow the sun's path

9. When we have fuel cells that convert hydrogen into electricity, it won't be carbon monoxide coming out of a car's exhaust pipe. It will be
   a. carbon trioxide
   b. carbon dioxide
   c. ice
   d. water

10. Although the rain forests cover just 6 percent of the Earth's land area, they are home to
    a. 6 percent of all the Earth's plant and animal species
    b. 25 percent of all the Earth's plant and animal species
    c. one-half of all the Earth's plant and animal species
    d. all of the Earth's plant and animal species

UNIT 14.7

The Environmental Movement

WHAT AM I SUPPOSED TO LEARN?

After you have read this unit, you should be able to

1 Discuss the environmental movement, from green parties to radical environmentalists.

Concern about environmental problems has touched such a nerve that it has produced a worldwide social movement. In Europe, *green parties,* political groups whose central concern is the environment, have become a force for change. Germany's green party, for example, has won seats in the national legislature. In the United States, in contrast, green parties have had little success.

One concern of the environmental movement in the United States is **environmental injustice**, minorities and the poor being the ones who suffer the most from the effects of pollution (Lerner 2010). Industries locate where land is cheaper, which, as you know, is *not* where the wealthy live. Nor will the rich allow factories to spew pollution near their homes. As a result, pollution is more common in low-income communities. Sociologists have studied, formed, and joined *environmental justice* groups that fight to close polluting plants and block construction of polluting industries. Similar to the defeat at Lake Baikal that I just mentioned, this often pits environmentalists against politicians and the wealthy.

Explore the **Concept**
Riding a Bicycle to Work in **mysoclab**

Like the members of last century's civil rights movement, environmentalists are certain that they stand for what is right and just. Most activists seek quiet solutions in politics, education, and legislation. Others, in contrast, despairing that pollution continues, the rain forests are still being cleared, and species continue to become extinct, are convinced that the planet is doomed unless we take immediate action. This conviction motivates some to choose a more radical course, to use extreme tactics to try to arouse indignation among the public and to force the government to act. In *Making It Personal,* we consider such activists.

environmental injustice refers to how minorities and the poor are harmed the most by environmental pollution

In the face of opposition from government and industry, environmentalists often depend on attention-getting tactics. These individuals in Stuttgart, Germany, are protesting the cutting of trees for a railway project.

MAKING IT PERSONAL

Radical Environmentalism

Chaining oneself to a giant Douglas fir that is slated for cutting, tearing down power lines and ripping up survey stakes, driving spikes into redwood trees, sinking whaling vessels, and torching SUVs and Hummers—are these the acts of dangerous punks who have little understanding of the needs of modern society? Or are they the efforts of brave men and women who are willing to put their freedom, and even their lives, on the line on behalf of the Earth itself?

Let me make this clear up front: I am not proposing that you follow such a course of action. I do think, though, that we should understand why **ecosabotage**—actions taken to sabotage the efforts of people who are thought to be legally harming the environment—is taking place.

Consider the Medicine Tree, a 3,000-year-old redwood in the Sally Bell Grove in northern California. Georgia Pacific, a lumber company, was determined to cut down the Medicine Tree, the oldest and largest of the region's redwoods. Members of Earth First! chained themselves to the tree. After they were arrested, the sawing began. Other protesters jumped over the police-lined barricade and stood defiantly in the path of men wielding axes and chain saws. A logger swung an axe and barely missed a demonstrator. At that moment, the sheriff radioed a restraining order, and the cutting stopped.

How many 3,000-year-old trees remain on our planet? Does our desire for fences and picnic tables for backyard barbecues justify cutting

> **ecosabotage** actions taken to sabotage the efforts of people who are thought to be legally harming the environment

them down? Issues like these—as well as the slaughter of seals and whales, the destruction of the rain forests, and the drowning of dolphins in mile-long drift nets—spawned Earth First! and other organizations such as Greenpeace, the Rainforest Action Network, the Ruckus Society, and the Sea Shepherds.

Radical environmentalists are united neither on tactics nor on goals. Most envision a simpler lifestyle that will consume less energy and reduce pressure on the Earth's resources. Some try to stop specific activities, such as the killing of whales. The goal of others is to destroy all nuclear weapons and dismantle nuclear power plants. Some would like to see everyone become vegetarians. Some even want humans to return to hunting and gathering societies.

Radical groups have had some successes. They have brought a halt to the killing of dolphins off Japan's Iki Island, achieved a ban on whaling, established trash recycling programs, and saved hundreds of thousands of acres of trees, including the Medicine Tree.

But what do you think about ecosaboteurs? Should we applaud or jail them? As symbolic interactionists stress, it all depends on how you view their actions. And as conflict theorists emphasize, your view likely depends on your social location. That is, if you own a lumber company, you will see ecosaboteurs remarkably differently than a camping enthusiast will. (The preceding information came from several sources: Carpenter 1990; Eder 1990; Foote 1990; Reed and Benet 1990; Knickerbocker 2003; Gunther 2004; Fattig 2007; Agar 2011.)

So, let's apply sociology: What is your view of ecosaboteurs? How does your view depend on your life situation?

> ⊙ **Watch** the **Video** Sociology on the Job: Collective Behavior and Social Movements in **mysoclab**

An object of protest by environmentalists is the hunting of bottlenose dolphins. This hunt is occurring off the coast of Japan.

UNIT 14.7 // TESTING MYSELF
DID I LEARN IT? ANSWERS ARE AT THE END OF THE CHAPTER

1. In Europe, *green parties*, political groups whose central concern is the environment, have become a force for change. Germany's green party has won seats in the national legislature. In this country, green parties have had little success.
   a. Belgium
   b. France
   c. Spain
   d. United States

2. A major concern of the environmental movement in the United States is
   a. to form green parties
   b. to make it illegal to use internal combustion engines
   c. environmental injustice
   d. to get the American Sociological Association to promote radical environmentalism

3. Most environmental activists seek quiet solutions in politics, education, and legislation. Others, in contrast, have become
   a. editors of major newspapers
   b. radical environmentalists
   c. TV reporters specializing in the environment
   d. U.S. Senators

4. Actions taken to sabotage the efforts of people who are thought to be legally harming the environment are called
   a. ecosabotage
   b. illegal environmentalism
   c. legal environmentalism
   d. rain foresters

UNIT 14.8
Environmental Sociology

WHAT AM I SUPPOSED TO LEARN?

After you have read this unit, you should be able to

1 Explain environmental sociology.

2 Explain the goal of harmony in technology and the environment.

One of the concerns of environmentalists is the pollution that can come from deepwater oil drilling. This pelican in Louisiana is being cleaned after the Deepwater Horizon drilling platform caught on fire.

Congratulations! You have reached the very last unit of the book! We'll close with a brief overview of environmental sociology and stress the need to harmonize technology and the environment.

The Environment and Sociology

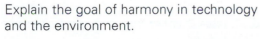

A specialization within sociology is **environmental sociology**, whose focus is the relationship between human societies and the environment (Dunlap and Catton 1979, 1983; Bell 2009). Environmental sociology is built around these key ideas:

1. The physical environment should be a significant variable in sociological investigation.

2. Human beings are but one species among many that depend on the natural environment.

3. Because of feedback to nature, human actions have many unintended consequences.

4. The world is finite, so there are physical limits to economic growth.

environmental sociology a specialty within sociology whose focus is how humans affect the environment and how the environment affects humans

5. Economic expansion requires increased extraction of resources from the environment.

6. Increased extraction of resources leads to environmental problems.

7. These environmental problems place limits on economic expansion.

8. Governments create environmental problems by encouraging the accumulation of capital.

9. For the welfare of humanity, environmental problems must be solved.

You should note that the goal of environmental sociology is not to stop pollution or nuclear power. Rather, its goal is to study how humans (their cultures, values, and behavior) affect the physical environment and how the physical environment affects human activities. Not surprisingly, environmental sociology attracts environmental activists, and the "Section on Environment and Technology" of the American Sociological Association (n.d.) tries to influence governmental policies.

TECHNOLOGY AND THE ENVIRONMENT: THE GOAL OF HARMONY

It is inevitable that humans will continue to develop new technologies. But the abuse of our environment by those technologies is not inevitable. To understate the matter, the destruction of our planet is an unwise choice.

If we are to live in a world that is worth passing on to coming generations, we must seek harmony between technology and the natural environment. This will not be easy. At one extreme are people who claim that to protect the environment we must eliminate industrialization and go back to a tribal way of life. At the other extreme are people who, blind to the harm being done to the natural environment, want the entire world to industrialize at full speed. Somewhere, there must be a middle ground, one that recognizes not only that industrialization is here to stay but also that we *can* control industrialization, for it is our creation. Controlled, industrialization can enhance our quality of life; uncontrolled, it will destroy us.

It is essential, then, that we develop ways to reduce or eliminate the harm that technology does to the environment. This includes mechanisms to monitor the production and use of technology and the disposal of its wastes. The question, of course, is whether we have the resolve to take the steps necessary to preserve the environment for future generations. What is at stake is nothing less than the welfare of planet Earth. Surely this should be enough to motivate us to make wise choices.

UNIT 14.8 // TESTING MYSELF
DID I LEARN IT? ANSWERS ARE AT THE END OF THE CHAPTER

1. The specialization within sociology whose focus is the relationship between human societies and the environment is called

Face masks won't protect these children in Japan from the radiation spewed from a nuclear plant after a tsunami hit it, but it makes people feel like they are doing something. Environmental destruction continues.

    a. relational sociology
    b. social sociology
    c. societal sociology
    d. environmental sociology

2. The goal of environmental sociology is to
    a. stop pollution
    b. stop nuclear power
    c. study how humans affect the physical environment and how the physical environment affects human activities
    d. do research on how we can improve the safety of technology

3. Apart from the many disagreements among environmentalists concerning goals and strategies, the real question is whether
    a. radical environmentalism is good or bad
    b. we have the resolve to take the steps necessary to preserve the environment for future generations
    c. we can get enough people active in order to pass laws to protect the environment
    d. how we can put teeth into the environmental laws

PULLING IT ALL TOGETHER REVIEWING THE LEARNING GOALS

Unit 14.1 How Social Change Transforms Social Life

1. Explain how social change transforms social life, using the four social revolutions, *Gemeinschaft* and *Gesellschaft*, and the Industrial Revolution.

- The main point is that when technology changes, so does social life. The first social revolution, the domestication of plants and animals, was followed millennia later by the inventions of the plow and the steam engine. All three changed people's relationships, what they expect out of life, and their views of the self. In traditional society, social life is based around the obligations of kinship and friendship. Industrialization, which stimulated cities, changed society from *Gemeinschaft* to *Gesellschaft*, moving the focus from intimate relationships to short-term, contractual relationships based on money. The fourth social revolution—our current one ushered in by the microchip—is also changing our lives fundamentally.

👁—[Watch the Video The Basics: Collective Behavior and Social Movements in **mysoclab**

Unit 14.2 Global Politics: Power and Conflict

1. Give a quick overview of geopolitics since World War II.

- World War II marked the end of the British Empire, and a new alignment of nations appeared: a Japan-centered East, a German-centered Europe, and an United States–centered Western Hemisphere. These three countries—plus Canada, France, Great Britain, and Italy—formed G7. The goal is to maintain their dominance of global affairs. Russia has been added, making it G8. China is an observer and will become a member. Dominating the Middle East to maintain supplies of oil is essential to the goals of G8.

2. Explain the two threats to the New World Order.

- The first threat is dissension among the countries that make up G8. The second is ethnic rivalries within G8 countries. Each undermines political stability.

Unit 14.3 Theories and Processes of Social Change

1. Use evolutionary theory, natural cycles, and conflict over power to explain social change.

- Unilinear evolutionary theories of how societies change assume that all societies follow the same path. Multilinear theories assume that all paths lead to industrialization, but societies need not pass through the same sequence of stages on their journey. Evolutionary theories assume cultural progress and have been discarded. Natural cycles theory assumes that civilizations are born, enjoy a youth, come to maturity, and then decline when the ruling elite can no longer keep the oppositional forces under control. The decline of a civilization can take hundreds of years. Conflict over power, a dialectical process of history, assumes that every arrangement of power (a thesis) contains oppositional forces (an antithesis) that will disrupt the arrangement of power, resulting in a new synthesis with its own built-in antithesis.

Unit 14.4 Ogburn's Theory

1. Explain Ogburn's theory of social change.

- Ogburn said that technology produces social change by three processes: invention (new things), discovery (finding existing things), and diffusion (items spreading from one group to another). The term cultural lag refers to technology changing first and culture catching up with the changed technology. Both material items (cars, computers) and social items (changed ideas of citizenship, women's rights) are forces for social change.

👁—[Watch the Video The Big Picture: Collective Behavior and Social Movements in **mysoclab**

Unit 14.5 Networking, Facebook, and Technology

1. Explain how technology is changing social life.

- All human groups use technology, which refers to both the tool and techniques for using the tool. Our lives are being transformed by technology. Social networking—through Facebook and Tweeting—were essential to the Arab revolutions that overthrew long-lasting dictatorships. Technology, as always, is transforming warfare. Cyber attacks have already begun. China's leap in financial prominence and military technology will challenge the world leadership of the United States. The potential use of technology to control citizens is a concern to many.

Unit 14.6 The Growth Machine Versus the Earth

1. Explain how environmental problems are related to industrialization, why there can never be an energy shortage, and why rain forests should be saved.

- The environment is being trashed as the world's Least Industrialized Nations rush to industrialize and the industrialized nations continue to pollute. Toxic wastes and nuclear plants are part of the problem, but the major felon is burning fossil fuels in internal combustion engines. Global warming is a major threat to producing a sustainable environment, a world system in which we meet our needs and don't destroy our children's future. There can never be an energy shortage, for the sun produces endless energy. The disappearing rain forests are a sad reminder that the Earth is being raped.

> **Read** the **Document**
> "Sixteen Impacts of Population Growth" by Brown, Gardner, and Halweil in **mysoclab**

Unit 14.7 The Environmental Movement

1. Discuss the environmental movement, from green parties to radical environmentalists.

- Concern about the environment has produced a worldwide social movement. In Europe, green parties, political groups whose central concern is the environment, have become a force for change. Green parties in the United States have had little success. A major concern of the environmental movement in the United States is environmental injustice, minorities and the poor being the ones who suffer the most from pollution. Most environmental activists seek quiet solutions in politics, education, and legislation but some have taken a radical path and become ecosaboteurs.

> **Explore** the **Concept**
> Riding a Bicycle to Work in **mysoclab**

> **Watch** the **Video** Sociology on the Job: Collective Behavior and Social Movements in **mysoclab**

Unit 14.8 Environmental Sociology

1. Explain environmental sociology.

- The goal of environmental sociology is not to stop pollution but to study the relationship of humans and the environment. Its key ideas are that human activity affects the environment, limits should be placed on economic growth so it does not hurt the environment, and for the benefit of future generations we must solve environmental problems.

2. Explain the goal of harmony in technology and the environment.

- Technology is a human creation, and, as such, it can be controlled. Uncontrolled, technology will destroy our environment. Controlled, we can have the economic development we need and enhance our quality of life. The question is whether we humans have the resolve to take the steps necessary to protect the environment.

UNIT 14.1 // TESTING MYSELF
DID I LEARN IT? ANSWERS

1. **d** social change

2. **c** time when humans first domesticated plants and animals

UNIT 14.2 // TESTING MYSELF
DID I LEARN IT? ANSWERS

1. **d** geopolitics

2. **a** Germany and Japan

3. **c** we could not have had the social changes that have taken place since then

4. **b** from *Gemeinschaft* to *Gesellschaft*

5. **a** when technology changes, societies change

3. **d** Russia

4. **c** China

5. **b** perpetuate G8's dominance of the world

6. **a** quarrels among the G8 nations

1. **b** savagery, barbarism, and civilization

2. **a** multilinear

3. **a** cultural progress

4. **d** the crisis in western civilization

1. **d** invention, discovery, and diffusion

2. **c** social inventions

1. **d** skills or procedures needed to make and use those tools

2. **c** artificial means of extending human abilities

3. **b** how technology changes people's way of life

1. **b** the globalization of capitalism

2. **c** sustainable environment

3. **b** remain deadly for thousands of years

4. **a** China

1. **d** United States

2. **c** environmental injustice

1. **d** environmental sociology

2. **c** study how humans affect the physical environment and how the physical environment affects human activities

5. **c** natural cycles

6. **b** the ruling elite loses its capacity to keep the masses in line "by charm rather than by force"

7. **a** dialectical process of history

8. **d** a thesis

9. **c** an antithesis

10. **b** a synthesis

3. **b** discovery

4. **a** diffusion

5. **d** ideas

6. **c** cultural lag

4. **a** Tunisia and Egypt

5. **d** cyber warfare

6. **b** China

7. **a** United States

5. **d** put in prison

6. **c** global warming

7. **b** the sun produces more energy than humans could ever use

8. **a** convert hydrogen into electricity

9. **d** water

10. **c** one-half of all the Earth's plant and animal species

3. **b** radical environmentalists

4. **a** ecosabotage

3. **b** we have the resolve to take the steps necessary to preserve the environment for future generations

As you explored social life in this textbook, I hope that you found yourself thinking along with me. If so, you should have gained a greater understanding of why people think, feel, and act as they do—as well as insights into why *you* view life the way you do. Developing your sociological imagination was my intention in writing this book. I have sincerely wanted to make sociology come alive for you.

Majoring in Sociology

If you feel a passion for peering beneath the surface—for seeking out the social influences in people's lives, and for seeing these influences in your own life—this is the best reason to major in sociology. As you take more courses in sociology, you will continue this enlightening process of social discovery. Your sociological perspective will grow, and you will become increasingly aware of how social factors underlie human behavior.

In addition to people who have a strong desire to continue this fascinating process of social discovery, there is a second type of person whom I also urge to major in sociology. Let's suppose that you have a strong, almost unbridled sense of wanting to explore many aspects of life. Let's also assume that because you have so many interests, you can't make up your mind about what you want to do with your life. You can think of so many things you'd like to try, but for each one there are other possibilities that you find equally as compelling. Let me share what one student who read this text wrote me:

> I'd love to say what my current major is—if only I truly knew. I know that the major you choose to study in college isn't necessarily the field of work you'll be going into. I've heard enough stories of grads who get jobs in fields that are not even related to their majors to believe it to a certain extent. My only problem is that I'm not even sure what it is I want to study, or what I truly want to be in the future for that matter.
>
> The variety of choices I have left open for myself are very wide, which creates a big problem, because I know I have to narrow it down to just one, which isn't something easy at all for me. It's like I want to be the best and do the best (medical doctor), yet I also wanna do other things (such as being a paramedic, or a cop, or firefighter, or a pilot), but I also realize I've only got one life to live. So the big question is: What's it gonna be?

This note reminded me of myself. In my reply, I said:

> You sound so much like myself when I was in college. In my senior year, I was plagued with uncertainty about what would be the right course for my life. I went to a counselor and took a vocational aptitude test. I still remember the day when I went in for the test results. I expected my future to be laid out for me, and I hung on every word. But then I heard the counselor say, "Your tests show that mortician should be one of your vocational choices."
>
> Mortician! I almost fell off my chair. That choice was so far removed from anything that I wanted that I immediately gave up on such tests.
>
> I like your list of possibilities: physician, cop, firefighter, and paramedic. In addition to these, mine included cowboy, hobo, and beach bum. One day, I was at the dry cleaners (end of my sophomore year in college), and the guy standing next to me was a cop. We talked about his job, and when I left the dry cleaners, I immediately went to the police station to get an application. I found out that I had to be 21, and I was just 20. I went back to college.
>
> I'm very happy with my choice. As a sociologist, I am able to follow my interests. I was able to become a hobo (or at least a traveler and able to experience different cultural settings). As far as being a cop, I developed and taught a course in the sociology of law.
>
> One of the many things I always wanted to be was an author. I almost skipped graduate school to move to Greenwich Village and become a novelist. The problem was that I was too timid, too scared of the unknown—and I had no support at all—to give it a try. My ultimate choice of sociologist has allowed me to fulfill this early dream.

It is sociology's breadth that is so satisfying to those of us who can't seem to find the limit to our interests, who can't pin ourselves down to just one thing in life. Sociology covers *all* of social life. Anything and everything that people do is part of sociology. For those of us who feel such broad, and perhaps changing interests, sociology is a perfect major.

But what if you already have a major picked out, yet you really like thinking sociologically? You can *minor* in sociology. Take sociology courses that continue to pique your sociological imagination. Then after college, continue to stimulate your sociological interests through your reading, including novels. This ongoing development of your sociological imagination will serve you well as you go through life.

But What Can You Do with a Sociology Major?

I can just hear someone say: "That's fine for you, since you became a sociologist. I don't want to go to graduate school, though. I just want to get my bachelor's degree and get out of college and get on with life. So, how can a bachelor's in sociology help me?"

This is a fair question. Just what can you do with a bachelor's degree in sociology?

A few years ago, in my sociology department we began to develop a concentration in applied sociology. At that time, since this would be a bachelor's degree, I explored this very question. I was surprised at the answer: *Almost anything!*

It turns out that most employers don't care what you major in. (Exceptions are some highly specialized fields such as nursing, computers, and engineering.) *Most* employers just want to make certain that you have completed college, and for most of them one degree is the same as another. *College provides the base on which the employer builds.*

Because you have your bachelor's degree—no matter what it is in—employers assume that you are a responsible person. This credential implies that you have proven yourself: You were able to stick with a four-year course, you showed up for classes, listened to lectures, took notes, passed tests, and carried out whatever assignments you were given. On top of this base of presumed responsibility, employers add the specifics necessary for you to perform their particular work, whether that be in sales or service, in insurance, banking, retailing, marketing, product development, or whatever.

If you major in sociology, you don't have to look for a job as a sociologist. If you ever decide to go on for an advanced degree, that's fine. But such plans are not necessary. The bachelor's in sociology can be your passport to most types of work in society.

Final Note

I want to conclude by stressing the reason to major in sociology that goes far beyond how you are going to make a living. It is the sociological perspective itself, the way of thinking and understanding that sociology provides. Wherever your path in life may lead, the sociological perspective will accompany you.

You are going to live in a fast-paced, rapidly changing society that, with all its conflicting crosscurrents, is going to be in turmoil. The sociological perspective will cast a different light on life's events, allowing you to perceive them in more insightful ways. As you watch television, attend a concert, converse with a friend, listen to a boss or co-worker—you will be more aware of the social contexts that underlie such behavior. The sociological perspective that you develop as you major in sociology will equip you to view what happens in life differently from someone who does not have your sociological background. Even events in the news will look different to you.

The final question that I want to leave you with, then, is, "If you enjoy sociology, why not major in it?"

With my best wishes for your success in life,

Jim Henslin

GLOSSARY

achieved statuses positions that are earned, accomplished, or involve at least some effort or activity on the individual's part

acid rain rain containing sulfuric and nitric acids (burning fossil fuels release sulfur dioxide and nitrogen oxide that become sulfuric and nitric acids when they react with moisture in the air)

agents of socialization people or groups that affect our self-concept, attitudes, behaviors, or other orientations toward life

agricultural societies a society based largely on agriculture

alienation Marx's term for workers' lack of connection to the product of their labor; caused by their being assigned repetitive tasks on a small part of a product—this leads to a sense of powerlessness and normlessness; others use the term in the general sense of not feeling a part of something

anarchy a condition of lawlessness or political disorder caused by the absence or collapse of governmental authority

anticipatory socialization the process of learning in advance a role or status one anticipates having

apartheid the enforced separation of racial–ethnic groups as was practiced in South Africa

applied sociology the use of sociology to solve problems—from the micro level of classroom interaction and family relationships to the macro level of crime and pollution

ascribed status a position an individual either inherits at birth or receives involuntarily later in life

assimilation the process of being absorbed into the mainstream culture

authoritarian personality Theodor Adorno's term for people who are prejudiced and rank high on measures of conformity, intolerance, insecurity, respect for authority, and submissiveness to superiors

authority power that people consider legitimate, as rightly exercised over them; also called *legitimate power*

back stages places where people rest from their performances, discuss their presentations, and plan future performances

background assumptions a deeply embedded, common understanding of how the world operates and of how people ought to act

basic demographic equation the growth rate equals births minus deaths plus net migration

basic or pure sociology sociological research for the purpose of making discoveries about life in human groups, not for making changes in those groups

bilineal (system of descent) a system of reckoning descent that counts both the mother's and the father's side

biotech society a society whose economy increasingly centers on the application of genetics—human genetics for medicine, and plant and animal genetics for the production of food and materials

blended family a family whose members were once part of other families

body language the ways in which people use their bodies to give messages to others

bonded labor (indentured service) a contractual system in which someone sells his or her body (services) for a specified period of time in an arrangement very close to slavery, except that it is entered into voluntarily

born again a term describing Christians who have undergone a religious experience so life-transforming that they feel they have become new persons

bourgeoisie Marx's term for capitalists, those who own the means of production

capital punishment the death penalty

capitalism an economic system characterized by the private ownership of the means of production, the pursuit of profit, and market competition

case study an intensive analysis of a single event, situation, or individual

caste system a form of social stratification in which people's statuses are determined by birth and are lifelong

charisma literally, an extraordinary gift from God; more commonly, an outstanding, "magnetic" personality

charismatic authority authority based on an individual's outstanding traits, which attract followers

charismatic leader literally, someone to whom God has given a gift; in its extended sense, someone who exerts extraordinary appeal to a group of followers

checks and balances the separation of powers among the three branches of U.S. government—legislative, executive, and judicial—so that each is able to nullify the actions of the other two, thus preventing any single branch from dominating the government

church according to Durkheim, one of the three essential elements of religion—a moral community of believers; also refers to a large, highly organized religious group that has formal, sedate worship services with little emphasis on evangelism, intense religious experience, or personal conversion

citizenship the concept that birth (and residence or naturalization) in a country imparts basic rights

city-state an independent city whose power radiates outward, bringing an adjacent area under its rule

city a place in which a large number of people are permanently based and do not produce their own food

class conflict Marx's term for the struggle between capitalists and workers

class consciousness Marx's term for awareness of a common identity based on one's position in the means of production

class system a form of social stratification based primarily on the possession of money or material possessions

closed-ended questions questions that are followed by a list of possible answers to be selected by the respondent

coercion power that people do not accept as rightly exercised over them; also called illegitimate power

cohabitation unmarried couples living together in a sexual relationship

colonialism the process by which one nation takes over another nation, usually for the purpose of exploiting its labor and natural resources

common sense those things that "everyone knows" are true

community people who identify with an area and with one another

compartmentalize to separate acts from feelings or attitudes

conflict theory a theoretical perspective in which society is viewed as composed of groups that are competing for scarce resources

conspicuous consumption Thorstein Veblen's term for a change from the Protestant ethic to an eagerness to show off wealth by the consumption of goods

control group the subjects in an experiment who are not exposed to the independent variable

control theory the idea that two control systems—inner controls and outer controls—work against our tendencies to deviate

convergence theory the view that as capitalist and socialist economic systems each adopt features of the other, a hybrid (or mixed) economic system will emerge

corporate crime crimes committed by executives in order to benefit their corporation

corporate welfare the financial incentives (tax breaks, subsidies, and even land and stadiums) given to corporations in order to attract them to an area or induce them to remain

cosmology teachings or ideas that provide a unified picture of the world

counterculture a group whose values, beliefs, norms, and related behaviors place its members in opposition to the broader culture

credential society the use of diplomas and degrees to determine who is eligible for jobs, even though the diploma or degree may be irrelevant to the actual work

crime the violation of norms written into law

criminal justice system the system of police, courts, and prisons set up to deal with people who are accused of having committed a crime

crude birth rate the annual number of live births per 1,000 population

crude death rate the annual number of deaths per 1,000 population

cult a new religion with few followers, whose teachings and practices put it at odds with the dominant culture and religion; also called a *new religion*

cultural diffusion the spread of material and symbolic culture from one group to another

cultural goals the objectives held out as legitimate or desirable for the members of a society to achieve

cultural lag Ogburn's term for human behavior lagging behind changes in technology

cultural leveling the process by which cultures become similar to one another; refers especially to the process by which Western culture is being exported and diffused into other nations

cultural relativism not judging a culture but trying to understand it on its own terms

cultural transmission (of values) the process of transmitting values from one group to another; often refers to how cultural traits are transmitted across generations and, in education, the ways in which schools transmit a group's culture, especially its core values

cultural universals a value, norm, or other cultural trait that is found in every group

culture of poverty the assumption that the values and behaviors of the poor make them fundamentally different from other people, that these factors are largely responsible for their poverty, and that parents perpetuate poverty across generations by passing these characteristics to their children

culture The language, beliefs, values, norms, behaviors, and even material objects that characterize a group and are passed from one generation to the next

culture shock the disorientation that people experience when they come in contact with a fundamentally different culture and can no longer depend on their taken-for-granted assumptions about life

degradation ceremony a term coined by Harold Garfinkel to refer to a ritual whose goal is to remake someone's self by stripping away that individual's self-identity and stamping a new identity in its place

deindustrialization the process of industries moving out of a country or region

democracy a government whose authority comes from the people; the term, based on two Greek words, translates literally as "power to the people"

democratic socialism a hybrid economic system in which the individual ownership of businesses is mixed with the state ownership of industries thought essential to the public welfare, such as the postal service and the delivery of medicine and utilities

demographic transition a three-stage historical process of population growth: *first*, high birth rates and high death rates; *second*, high birth rates and low death rates; and *third*, low birth rates and low death rates; a *fourth* stage in which deaths outnumber births has made its appearance in the Most Industrialized Nations

demographic variables the three factors that influence population growth: fertility, mortality, and net migration

demography the study of the size, composition, growth, and distribution of human populations

dependent variable a factor in an experiment that is changed by an independent variable

deviance the violation of norms (or rules or expectations)

dialectical process (of history) each arrangement of power (a thesis) contains contradictions (antitheses) which make the arrangement unstable and which must be resolved; the new arrangement of power (a synthesis) contains its own contradictions; this process of balancing and unbalancing continues throughout history as groups struggle for power and other resources

dictatorship a form of government in which an individual has seized power

differential association Edwin Sutherland's term to indicate that people who associate with some groups learn an "excess of definitions" of deviance, increasing the likelihood that they will become deviant

diffusion the spread of an invention or a discovery from one area to another; identified by William Ogburn as one of three processes of social change

direct democracy a form of democracy in which the eligible voters meet together to discuss issues and make their decisions

discovery a new way of seeing reality; identified by William Ogburn as one of three processes of social change

discrimination an act of unfair treatment directed against an individual or a group

disinvestment the withdrawal of investments by financial institutions, which seals the fate of an urban area

divine right of kings the idea that the king's authority comes from God; in an interesting gender bender, also applies to queens

division of labor the splitting of a group's or a society's tasks into specialties

documents in its narrow sense, written sources that provide data; in its extended sense, archival material of any sort, including photographs, movies, videos, CDs, DVDs, and so on

dominant group the group with the most power, greatest privileges, and highest social status

downward social mobility movement down the social class ladder

dramaturgy an approach, pioneered by Erving Goffman, in which social life is analyzed in terms of drama or the stage; also called *dramaturgical analysis*

ecclesia a religious group so integrated into the dominant culture that it is difficult to tell where the one begins and the other leaves off; also called a *state religion*

economy a system of producing and distributing goods and services

ecosabotage actions taken to sabotage the efforts of people who are thought to be legally harming the environment

edge city a large clustering of service facilities and residential areas near highway intersections that provides a sense of place to people who live, shop, and work there

egalitarian authority more or less equally divided between people or groups (in marriage, for example, between husband and wife)

endogamy the practice of marrying within one's own group

enterprise zone the use of economic incentives in a designated area to encourage investment

environmental injustice refers to how minorities and the poor are harmed the most by environmental pollution

environmental sociology a specialty within sociology whose focus is how humans affect the environment and how the environment affects humans

estate stratification system the stratification system of medieval Europe, consisting of three groups or estates: the nobility, clergy, and commoners

ethnic cleansing a policy of eliminating a population; includes forcible expulsion and genocide

ethnic work activities designed to discover, enhance, maintain, or transmit an ethnic or racial identity

ethnicity (and ethnic) having distinctive cultural characteristics

ethnocentrism the use of one's own culture as a yardstick for judging the ways of other individuals or groups, generally leading to a negative evaluation of their values, norms, and behaviors

ethnomethodology the study of how people use background assumptions to make sense out of life

evangelism an attempt to win converts

exchange mobility about the same number of people moving up and down the social class ladder, such that, on balance, the social class system shows little change

exogamy the practice of marrying outside one's own group

experiment the use of control and experimental groups and dependent and independent variables to test causation

experimental group the group of subjects in an experiment who are exposed to the independent variable

exponential growth curve a pattern of growth in which numbers double during approximately equal intervals, showing a steep acceleration in the later stages

extended family a family that includes not only the husband, wife, and children but also other relatives such as aunts or uncles or cousins or grandparents

face-saving behavior techniques used to salvage a performance (interaction) that is going sour

false class consciousness Marx's term to refer to workers identifying with the interests of capitalists

family of orientation the family in which a person grows up

family of procreation the family formed when a couple's first child is born

family two or more people who consider themselves related by blood, marriage, or adoption

fecundity the number of children that women are capable of bearing

feminism the philosophy that men and women should be politically, economically, and socially equal; organized activities on behalf of this principle

feral children children assumed to have been raised by animals, in the wilderness, isolated from humans

fertility rate the number of children that the average woman bears

fieldwork research in which the researcher participates in a research setting while observing what is happening in that setting pastoral society a society based on the pasturing of animals

folkways norms that are not strictly enforced

front stages places where people give performances

functional analysis a theoretical perspective in which society is viewed as composed of various parts. Each part has a function that, when fulfilled, contributes to society's equilibrium; also known as *functionalism* and *structural functionalism*

functional illiterate a high school graduate who has difficulty with basic reading and math

gate-keeping the process by which education opens and closes doors of opportunity; another term for the social placement function of education

Gemeinschaft a type of society in which life is intimate; a community in which everyone knows everyone else and people share a sense of togetherness

gender discrimination people being given or denied resources and privileges on the basis of their sex; also called *sexual discrimination*

gender socialization learning society's "gender map," the paths in life set out for us because we are male or female

gender stereotypes ideas of what people are like because they are female or male

gender stratification males' and females' unequal access to property, power, and prestige

gender the behaviors and attitudes that a society considers proper for its males and females; masculinity or femininity

gendered violence violence directed by one sex against the other

generalizability the extent to which the findings from one group (or sample) can be generalized or applied to other groups (or populations)

generalization a statement that goes beyond the individual case and is applied to a broader group or situation

generalized other the norms, values, attitudes, and expectations of people "in general"; the child's ability to take the role of the generalized other is a significant step in the development of a self

genetic predisposition inborn tendencies (for example, a tendency to commit deviant acts)

genocide the systematic annihilation or attempted annihilation of a people because of their presumed race or ethnicity

gentrification middle-class people moving into a rundown area of a city, displacing the poor as they buy and restore homes

geopolitics shifting economic and political relationships among the world's nations

Gesellschaft a type of society that is dominated by impersonal relationships, individual accomplishments, and self-interest

gestures the ways in which people use their bodies to communicate with one another

glass ceiling the mostly invisible barrier that keeps women from advancing to the top levels at work

global superclass a small group of people who make the major decisions that affect the rest of the world

global village refers to the world's nations being so interconnected that what happens in one nation affects people in other nations, much like what happens to people who live in the same village

global warming an increase in the Earth's temperature

globalization the growing interconnections among nations due to the expansion of capitalism

globalization of capitalism capitalism (investing to make profits within a rational system) becoming the globe's dominant economic system

grade inflation higher grades given for the same work; a general rise in student grades without a corresponding increase in learning

greenhouse effect the buildup of carbon dioxide in the earth's atmosphere that allows light to enter freely but inhibits the release of heat; believed to cause global warming

group people who have something in common and who believe that what they have in common is significant; also called a *social group*

growth rate the net change in a population after adding births, subtracting deaths, and either adding or subtracting net migration

hate crime a crime that is punished more severely because it is motivated by hatred (dislike, hostility, animosity) of someone's race–ethnicity, religion, sexual orientation, disability, or national origin

hidden curriculum the unwritten goals of schools, such as teaching obedience to authority and conformity to cultural norms

homogamy the tendency of people with similar characteristics to marry one another

household people who occupy the same housing unit

horticultural societies a society based on cultivating plants by the use of hand tools

Horatio Alger myth the belief that due to limitless possibilities anyone can get ahead if he or she tries hard enough

human ecology Robert Park's term for the relationship between people and their environment (such as land and structures); also known as *urban ecology*

hunting and gathering societies human groups that depend on hunting and gathering for their survival

hypothesis a statement of how variables are expected to be related to one another, often according to predictions from a theory

income money received, usually from a job, business, or assets

ideal culture a people's ideal values and norms; the goals held out for them

ideology beliefs about the way things ought to be that justify social arrangements

illegitimate opportunity structure opportunities for crimes that are woven into the texture of life

impression management people's efforts to control the impressions that others receive of them

incest sexual relations between specified relatives, such as brothers and sisters or parents and children

incest taboo the rule that prohibits sex and marriage among designated relatives

inclusion helping people to become part of the mainstream of society; also called *mainstreaming*

independent variable a factor that causes a change in another variable, called the dependent variable

individual discrimination person-to-person or face-to-face discrimination; the negative treatment of people by other individuals

industrial societies a society based on the harnessing of machines powered by fuels

institutional discrimination negative treatment of a minority group that is built into a society's institutions; also called *systemic discrimination*

institutionalized means approved ways of reaching cultural goals

intergenerational mobility the change that family members make in social class from one generation to the next

internal colonialism the policy of exploiting minority groups for economic gain

interview direct questioning of respondents

interviewer bias effects of interviewers on respondents that lead to biased answers

invasion–succession cycle the process of one group of people displacing a group whose racial–ethnic or social class characteristics differ from their own

invention the combining of existing elements and materials to form new ones; identified by William Ogburn as one of three processes of social change

labeling theory the view that the labels people are given affect their own and others' perceptions of them, thus channeling their behavior into either deviance or conformity

laissez-faire capitalism unrestrained manufacture and trade (literally "hands off" capitalism)

language a system of symbols that can be combined in an infinite number of ways and can represent not only objects but also abstract thought

latent functions the unintended beneficial consequences of people's actions

life course the stages of our life as we go from birth to death

lobbyists people who influence legislation on behalf of their clients

looking-glass self a term coined by Charles Horton Cooley to refer to the process by which our self develops through internalizing others' reactions to us

machismo an emphasis on male strength, high sexuality, and dominance

macro-level large-scale patterns of society

macrosociology analysis of social life that focuses on broad features of society, such as social class and the relationships of groups to one another; usually used by functionalists and conflict theorists

Malthus theorem an observation by Thomas Malthus that although the food supply increases arithmetically (from 1 to 2 to 3 to 4 and so on), population grows geometrically (from 2 to 4 to 8 to 16 and so forth)

manifest functions the intended beneficial consequences of people's actions

market forces production, prices, and distribution of goods and services; supply and demand

marriage a group's approved mating arrangements, usually marked by a ritual of some sort

mass media forms of communication, such as radio, newspapers, and television that are directed to mass audiences

master status a status that cuts across or dominates someone's other statuses

material culture The material objects that distinguish a group of people, such as their art, buildings, weapons, utensils, machines, hairstyles, clothing, and jewelry

matriarchy a society in which women-as-a-group dominate men-as-a-group; authority is vested in females

matrilineal (system of descent) a system of reckoning descent that counts only the mother's side

means of production the tools, factories, land, and investment capital used to produce wealth

mechanical solidarity Durkheim's term for the unity (a shared consciousness) that people feel as a result of performing the same or similar tasks

medicalization of deviance to make deviance a medical matter, a symptom of some underlying illness that needs to be treated by physicians

megacity a city of 10 million or more residents

megalopolis an urban area consisting of at least two metropolises and their many suburbs

meritocracy a form of social stratification in which all positions are awarded on the basis of merit

metropolis a central city surrounded by smaller cities and their suburbs

metropolitan statistical area (MSA) a central city and the urbanized counties adjacent to it

micro-level small-scale patterns of society

microsociology analysis of social life that focuses on social interaction; typically used by symbolic interactionists

minority group people who are singled out for unequal treatment and who regard themselves as objects of collective discrimination

modernization the transformation of traditional societies into industrial societies

monarchy a form of government headed by a king or queen

mores norms that are strictly enforced because they are thought essential to core values or the well-being of the group

multiculturalism a policy that permits or encourages ethnic differences; also called *pluralism*

multinational corporations companies that operate across national boundaries; also called *transnational corporations*

natural sciences the intellectual and academic disciplines designed to understand, explain, and predict events in our natural environments

negative sanction an expression of disapproval for breaking a norm, ranging from a mild, informal reaction such as a frown to a formal reaction such as a prize or a prison sentence

neocolonialism the economic and political dominance of the Least Industrialized Nations by the Most Industrialized Nations

net migration rate the difference between the number of immigrants and emigrants per 1,000 population

new technology the emerging technologies of an era that have a significant impact on social life

nonmaterial culture a group's ways of thinking (including its beliefs, values, and other assumptions about the world) and doing (its common patterns of behavior, including language and other forms of interaction); also called *symbolic culture*

nonverbal interaction communication without words—through gestures, use of space, silence, and so on

norms expectations of "right" behavior

nuclear family a family consisting of a husband, wife, and children

objectivity (in research) value neutrality in research

oligarchy a form of government in which a small group of individuals holds power; the rule of the many by the few

open-ended questions questions that respondents answer in their own words

operational definition the way in which a researcher measures a variable

organic solidarity Durkheim's term for the interdependence that results from the division of labor; as part of the same unit, we all depend on others to fulfill their jobs

pan-Indianism a movement that focuses on common elements in the cultures of Native Americans in order to develop a cross-tribal self-identity and to work toward the welfare of all Native Americans

participant observation research in which the researcher participates in a research setting while observing what is happening in that setting; also called *fieldwork*

patriarchy a group in which men-as-a-group dominate women-as-a-group; authority is vested in males

patrilineal (system of descent) a system of reckoning descent that counts only the father's side

patterns of behavior recurring characteristics or events

pastoral societies a society based on the pasturing of animals

peer group a group of individuals, often of roughly the same age, who are linked by common interests and orientations

personality disorders the view that a personality disturbance of some sort causes an individual to violate social norms

pluralism the diffusion of power among many interest groups that prevents any single group from gaining control of the government

pluralistic society a society made up of many different groups

police discretion the practice of the police, in the normal course of their duties, to either arrest or ticket someone for an offense or to overlook the matter

political action committee (PAC) an organization formed by one or more special-interest groups to solicit and spend funds for the purpose of influencing legislation

polyandry a form of marriage in which women have more than one husband

polygyny a form of marriage in which men have more than one wife

population a target group to be studied

population pyramid a graph that represents the age and sex of a population

population shrinkage the process by which a country's population becomes smaller because its birth rate and immigration are too low to replace those who die and emigrate

population transfer the forced transfer of a minority group

positive sanction a positive reaction for following norms, ranging from a smile to a material award

positivism the application of the scientific approach to the social world

postindustrial society a society based on information, services, and high technology, rather than on raw materials and manufacturing; also called *postmodern society* and *information society*

postmodern society a society whose chief characteristic is the use of tools that extend human abilities to gather and analyze information, to communicate, and to travel; also called a *postindustrial society*

poverty line the official measure of poverty; calculated to include incomes that are less than three times a low-cost food budget

power the ability to carry out your will, even over the resistance of others

power elite C. Wright Mills' term for the top people in U.S. corporations, military, and politics who make the nation's major decisions

prestige respect or regard

prejudice an attitude or prejudging, usually in a negative way

profane Durkheim's term for common elements of everyday life

proletariat Marx's term for the exploited class, the mass of workers who do not own the means of production

public sociology applying sociology for the public good; especially the use of the sociological perspective (how things are related to one another) to guide politicians and policy makers

questionnaires a list of questions to be asked of respondents

race a group whose inherited physical characteristics distinguish it from other groups

racism prejudice and discrimination on the basis of race

random sample a sample in which everyone in the target population has the same chance of being included in the study

rapport (ruh-POUR) a feeling of trust between researchers and the people they are studying

rational–legal authority authority based on law or written rules and regulations; also called *bureaucratic authority*

real culture the norms and values that people actually follow; as opposed to *ideal* culture

recidivism rate the percentage of released convicts who are rearrested

redlining a decision by the officers of a financial institution not to make loans in a particular area

reliability the extent to which research produces consistent or dependable results

religion according to Durkheim, beliefs and practices that separate the profane from the sacred and unite its adherents into a moral community

religious experience a sudden awareness of the supernatural or a feeling of coming in contact with God

replication the repetition of a study in order to test its findings

representative sample a sample that represents the target population

representative democracy a form of democracy in which voters elect representatives to meet together to discuss issues and make decisions on their behalf

research method one of six procedures that sociologists use to collect data: surveys, secondary analysis, analysis of documents, experiments, unobtrusive measures, and participant observation; also called *research design*

reserve labor force the unemployed; unemployed workers are thought of as being "in reserve"—capitalists take them "out of reserve"(put them back to work) during times of high production and then put them back "in reserve"(lay them off) when they are no longer needed

resocialization the process of learning new norms, values, attitudes, and behaviors

respondents people who respond to a survey, either in interviews or by self-administered questionnaires

revolution armed resistance designed to overthrow and replace a government

rising expectations the sense that better conditions are soon to follow, which, if unfulfilled, increases frustration

rituals ceremonies or repetitive practices; in religion, observances or rites often intended to evoke a sense of awe of the sacred

role the behaviors, obligations, and privileges attached to a status

role conflict conflicts that someone feels *between* roles because the expectations are at odds with one another

role performance the ways in which someone performs a role; showing a particular "style" or "personality"

role strain conflicts that someone feels *within* a role

romantic love feelings of sexual attraction accompanied by an idealization of the other

routinization of charisma the transfer of authority from a charismatic figure to either a traditional or a rational–legal form of authority

ruling class another term for the *power elite*

sacred Durkheim's term for things set apart or forbidden that inspire fear, awe, reverence, or deep respect

sample the individuals intended to represent the population to be studied

sanctions either expressions of approval given to people for upholding norms or expressions of disapproval for violating them

Sapir-Whorf hypothesis Edward Sapir and Benjamin Whorf's hypothesis that language creates ways of thinking and perceiving

scapegoat an individual or group unfairly blamed for someone else's troubles

science the application of systematic methods to obtain knowledge and the knowledge obtained by those methods

scientific method the use of objective, systematic observations to test theories

secondary analysis the analysis of data that have been collected by other researchers

sect a religious group larger than a cult that still feels substantial hostility from and toward society

segregation the policy of keeping racial–ethnic groups apart

selective perception seeing certain features of an object or situation, but remaining blind to others

self-administered questionnaires questionnaires that respondents fill out

self-fulfilling prophecy Robert Merton's term for an originally false assertion that becomes true simply because it was predicted

self the unique human capacity of being able to see ourselves "from the outside"; the views we internalize of how others see us

serial murder the killing of several victims in three or more separate events

serial fatherhood a pattern of parenting in which a father, after a divorce, reduces contact with his own children, serves as a father to the children of the woman he marries or lives with, then ignores these children, too, after moving in with or marrying another woman

sex biological characteristics that distinguish females and males, consisting of primary and secondary sex characteristics

sexual harassment the abuse of one's position of authority to force unwanted sexual demands on someone

sign-vehicles the term used by Goffman to refer to the social setting, appearance, and manner, which people use to communicate information about the self

significant others an individual who significantly influences someone else

slavery a form of social stratification in which some people own other people

social change the alteration of culture and societies over time

social class according to Weber, a large group of people who rank close to one another in property, power, and prestige; according to Marx, one of two groups: capitalists who own the means of production or workers who sell their labor

social construction of reality the use of background assumptions and life experiences to define what is real

social context society people who share a culture and a territory

social control a group's formal and informal means of enforcing its norms

social facts Durkheim's term for a group's patterns of behavior

social institutions the organized, usual, or standard ways by which society meets its basic needs

social integration the degree to which the members of a group or society are united by shared norms, values, behaviors, and other social bonds; also known as *social cohesion*

social interaction what people do when they are in one another's presence; includes communications at a distance

social location the group memberships that people have because of their location in history and society

social mobility movement up or down the social class ladder

social order a group's usual and customary social arrangements, on which its members depend and on which they base their lives

social placement a function of education—funneling people into a society's various positions

social promotion passing students on to the next level even though they have not mastered basic materials

social sciences the intellectual and academic disciplines designed to understand the social world objectively by means of controlled and repeated observations

social stratification the division of large numbers of people into layers according to their relative property, power, and prestige; applies to both nations and to people within a nation, society, or other group

social structure the framework of society that surrounds us; consists of the ways that people and groups are related to one another; this framework gives direction to and sets limits on our behavior

socialism an economic system characterized by the public ownership of the means of production, central planning, and the distribution of goods without a profit motive

socialization the process by which people learn the characteristics of their group—the knowledge, skills, attitudes, values, norms, and actions thought appropriate for them

society people who share a culture and a territory

sociology the scientific study of society and human behavior

sociological perspective understanding human behavior by placing it within its broader social context; also called the *sociological imagination*

special-interest group a group of people who support a particular issue and who can be mobilized for political action

split labor market workers who are divided along racial–ethnic, gender, age, or any other lines; this split is exploited by owners to weaken the bargaining power of workers

state a political entity that claims monopoly on the use of violence in some particular territory; also known as a *country*

status consistency ranking high or low on all three dimensions of social class

status inconsistency ranking high on some dimensions of social class and low on others; also called *status discrepancy*

status set all the statuses or positions that an individual occupies

status symbols things that identify a status, such as titles (professor, doctor), a wedding ring, or a uniform

status the position that someone occupies in a social group; also called *social status*

stigma "blemishes" that discredit a person's claim to a "normal" identity

strain theory Robert Merton's term for the strain engendered when a society socializes large numbers of people to desire a cultural goal (such as success), but withholds from some the approved means of reaching that goal; one adaptation to the strain is crime, the choice of an innovative means (one outside the approved system) to attain the cultural goal

stratified random sample a sample from selected subgroups of the target population in which everyone in those subgroups has an equal chance of being included in the research

street crime crimes such as mugging, rape, and burglary

structural mobility movement up or down the social class ladder that is due more to changes in the structure of society than to the actions of individuals

structured interviews interviews that use closed-ended questions

subculture the values and related behaviors of a group that distinguish its members from the larger culture; a world within a world

subjective meanings the meanings that people give their own behavior

suburb a community adjacent to a city

suburbanization the migration of people from the city to the suburbs

survey the collection of data by having people answer a series of questions

sustainable environment a world system that takes into account the limits of the environment, produces enough material goods for everyone's needs, and leaves a heritage of a sound environment for the next generation

symbol something to which people attach meaning and then use to communicate with others

symbolic culture another term for nonmaterial culture

symbolic interactionism a theoretical perspective in which society is viewed as composed of symbols that people use to establish meaning, develop their views of the world, and communicate with one another

system of descent how kinship is traced over the generations

taboo a norm so strong that it often brings revulsion if violated

target population a target group to be studied

taking the role of the other putting yourself in someone else's shoes; understanding how someone else feels and thinks, so you anticipate how that person will act

teamwork two or more people working together to manage impressions jointly

techniques of neutralization ways of thinking or rationalizing that help people deflect (or neutralize) society's norms

technology in its narrow sense, tools; its broader sense includes the skills or procedures necessary to make and use those tools

terrorism the use of violence or the threat of violence to produce fear in order to attain political objectives

theory a statement about how some parts of the world fit together, how two or more facts, conditions, or variables are related to one another

Thomas theorem William I. and Dorothy S. Thomas' classic formulation of the definition of the situation: "If people define situations as real, they are real in their consequences"

total institution a place that is almost totally controlled by those who run it, in which people are cut off from the rest of society and the society is mostly cut off from them

totalitarianism a form of government that exerts almost total control over people

tracking in education, the sorting of students into different programs on the basis of perceived abilities

traditional authority authority based on custom

transitional adulthood a term that refers to a period following high school when young adults have not yet taken on the responsibilities ordinarily associated with adulthood; also called *adultolescence*

transitional older years an emerging stage of the life course between retirement and when people are considered old; approximately age 65 to 75

transmission of mainstream values passing on a group's core values

underclass a group of people for whom poverty persists year after year and across generations

universal citizenship the idea that everyone has the same basic rights by virtue of being born in a country (or by immigrating and becoming a naturalized citizen)

unobtrusive measures ways of observing people so they do not know they are being studied

unstructured interviews interviews that use open-ended questions

upward social mobility movement up the social class ladder

urban renewal the rehabilitation of a rundown area, which usually results in the displacement of the poor who are living in that area

urbanization the process by which an increasing proportion of a population lives in cities and has a growing influence on the culture

validity the extent to which an operational definition measures what it is intended to measure

value cluster values that together form a larger whole

value the standard by which people define what is desirable or undesirable, good or bad, beautiful or ugly

value contradictions values that contradict one another, such as equality and group superiority

value free the view that a sociologist's personal values or beliefs should not influence social research

variable a factor that can vary (or change) from one person or situation to another

Verstehen a German word used by Weber that is perhaps best understood as "to have insight into someone's situation"

voter apathy indifference and inaction on the part of individuals or groups with respect to the political process

war armed conflict between nations or politically distinct groups

WASP White Anglo-Saxon Protestant

wealth the total value of everything someone owns, minus the debts

welfare capitalism an economic system in which individuals own the means of production but the state regulates many economic activities for the welfare of the population; also known as *state capitalism*

white ethnics white immigrants to the United States whose cultures differ from WASP culture

white-collar crime Edwin Sutherland's term for crimes committed by people of respectable and high social status in the course of their occupations; for example, bribery of public officials, embezzlement, false advertising, and price fixing

world system theory economic and political connections that tie the world's countries together

zero population growth women bearing only enough children to reproduce the population

REFERENCES

CHAPTER 1

Addams, Jane. *Twenty Years at Hull-House*. New York: Signet, 1981. Originally published 1910.

American Sociological Association. "An Invitation to Public Sociology." 2004.

Aptheker, Herbert. "W. E. B. Du Bois: Struggle Not Despair." *Clinical Sociology Review, 8,* 1990:58–68.

Cantoni, Davide. "The Economic Effects of the Protestant Reformation: Testing the Weber Hypothesis in the German Lands." Harvard University Job Market Paper, November 10, 2009.

Coser, Lewis A. *Masters of Sociological Thought: Ideas in Historical and Social Context,* 2nd ed. New York: Harcourt Brace Jovanovich, 1977.

DeMartini, Joseph R. "Basic and Applied Sociological Work: Divergence, Convergence, or Peaceful Co-existence?" *The Journal of Applied Behavioral Science, 18,* 2, 1982:203–215.

Dobriner, William M. *Social Structures and Systems*. Pacific Palisades, Calif.: Goodyear, 1969.

Du Bois, W. E. B. *The Autobiography of W. E. B. Du Bois: A Soliloquy on Viewing My Life from the Last Decade of Its First Century*. New York: International, 1968.

Durkheim, Emile. *Suicide: A Study in Sociology,* John A. Spaulding and George Simpson, trans. New York: Free Press, 1966. Originally published 1897.

Gilman, Charlotte Perkins. *The Man-Made World; or, Our Androcentric Culture*. New York: Echo Library, 1971. Originally published 1911.

Gitlin, Todd. *The Twilight of Common Dreams: Why America Is Wracked by Culture Wars*. New York: Metropolitan Books, 1997.

Knapp, Daniel. "What Happened When I Took My Sociological Imagination to the Dump." *Footnotes,* May–June, 2005:4.

Lengermann, Madoo, and Gillian Niebrugge. *The Women Founders: Sociology and Social Theory, 1830–1930*. Prospect Heights, Ill.: Waveland Press, 2007.

Marx, Karl, and Friedrich Engels. *Communist Manifesto*. New York: Pantheon, 1967. Originally published 1848.

Mills, C. Wright. *The Sociological Imagination*. New York: Oxford University Press, 1959.

Sageman, Marc. "Explaining Terror Networks in the 21st Century." *Footnotes,* May–June 2008a:7.

Sageman, Marc. *Leaderless Jihad: Terror Networks in the Twenty-First Century*. Philadelphia: University of Pennsylvania Press, 2008b.

Stark, Rodney. *Sociology,* 3rd ed. Belmont, Calif.: Wadsworth, 1989.

Weber, Max. *The Protestant Ethic and the Spirit of Capitalism*. New York: Scribner, 1958. Originally published 1904–1905.

CHAPTER 2

Bianchi, Suzanne M., John P. Robinson, and Melissa A. Milkie. *Changing Rhythms of American Family Life*. New York: Russell Sage Foundation, 2006.

Burgess, Ernest W., and Harvey J. Locke. *The Family: From Institution to Companionship*. New York: American Book, 1945.

Edgerton, Robert B. *Sick Societies: Challenging the Myth of Primitive Harmony*. New York: Free Press, 1992.

Lee, Raymond M. *Unobtrusive Methods in Social Research*. Philadelphia, Pa.: Open University Press, 2000.

Leeson, Peter T. "Cooperation and Conflict: Evidence on Self-Enforcing Arrangements and Heterogeneous Groups." *American Journal of Economics and Sociology,* October 2006.

Piven, Frances Fox. "Can Power from Below Change the World?" *American Sociological Review, 73,* 1, February 2008:1–14.

Rosenbloom, Stephanie. "In Bid to Sway Sales, Cameras Track Shoppers." *New York Times,* March 19, 2010.

Schaefer, Richard T. *Sociology,* 3rd ed. New York: McGraw-Hill, 1989.

Singer, Natasha. "Shoppers Who Can't Have Secrets." *New York Times,* April 30, 2010.

Statistical Abstract of the United States. Washington, D.C.: U.S. Census Bureau, published annually.

Turner, Jonathan H. *The Structure of Sociological Theory*. Homewood, Ill.: Dorsey, 1978.

Venkatesh, Sudhir. *Gang Leader for a Day: A Rogue Sociologist Takes to the Streets*. New York: Penguin, 2008.

CHAPTER 3

Albert, Ethel M. "Women of Burundi: A Study of Social Values." In *Women of Tropical Africa,* Denise Paulme, ed. Berkeley: University of California Press, 1963:179–215.

Anderson, Nels. *Desert Saints: The Mormon Frontier in Utah*. Chicago: University of Chicago Press, 1966. Originally published 1942.

Bates, Marston. *Gluttons and Libertines: Human Problems of Being Natural*. New York: Vintage Books, 1967. Quoted in Crapo, Richley H. *Cultural Anthropology: Understanding Ourselves and Others,* 5th ed. Boston: McGraw Hill, 2002.

Beals, Ralph L., and Harry Hoijer. *An Introduction to Anthropology*, 3rd ed. New York: Macmillan, 1965.

Boroditsky, Lera. "Lost in Translation." *Wall Street Journal*, July 24, 2010.

Dickey, Christopher, and John Barry. "Iran: A Rummy Guide." *Newsweek*, May 8, 2006.

Edgerton, Robert B. *Sick Societies: Challenging the Myth of Primitive Harmony.* New York: Free Press, 1992.

Eibl-Eibesfeldt, Irrenäus. *Ethology: The Biology of Behavior.* New York: Holt, Rinehart, and Winston, 1970.

Ekman, Paul, Wallace V. Friesen, and John Bear. "The International Language of Gestures." *Psychology Today*, May 1984:64.

Gampbell, Jennifer. "In Northeast Thailand, a Cuisine Based on Bugs." *New York Times*, June 22, 2006.

Gokhale, Ketaki. "India Plans Focus on Environment." *Wall Street Journal*, August 14, 2009.

Horwitz, Allan V., and Jerome C. Wakefield. *The Loss of Sadness: How Psychiatry Transformed Normal Sorrow into Depressive Disorder.* New York: Oxford University Press, 2007.

Kent, Mary, and Robert Lalasz. "In the News: Speaking English in the United States." Population Reference Bureau, January 18, 2007.

La Barre, Weston. *The Human Animal.* Chicago: University of Chicago Press, 1954.

Linton, Ralph. *The Study of Man.* New York: Appleton-Century-Crofts, 1936.

Mead, Margaret. *Sex and Temperament in Three Primitive Societies.* New York: New American Library, 1950. Originally published 1935.

Murdock, George Peter. "The Common Denominator of Cultures." In *The Science of Man and the World Crisis,* Ralph Linton, ed. New York: Columbia University Press, 1945.

Nelson, Gary. "Hispanic-Only FIU Mayoral Debate Draws Harsh Criticism." *CBS Miami*, May 11, 2011.

Ogburn, William F. *Social Change with Respect to Culture and Human Nature.* New York: W. B. Huebsch, 1922. (Other editions by Viking in 1927, 1938, and 1950.)

Robertson, Ian. *Sociology*, 3rd ed. New York: Worth, 1987.

Salomon, Gisela, "In Miami, Spanish Is Becoming the Primary Language." Associated Press, May 29, 2008.

Sapir, Edward. *Selected Writings of Edward Sapir in Language, Culture, and Personality,* David G. Mandelbaum, ed. Berkeley: University of California Press, 1949.

Sharp, Deborah. "Miami's Language Gap Widens." *USA Today*, April 3, 1992:A1, A3.

Sumner, William Graham. *Folkways: A Study in the Sociological Importance of Usages, Manners, Customs, Mores, and Morals.* New York: Ginn, 1906.

Usdansky, Margaret L. "English a Problem for Half of Miami." *USA Today*, April 3, 1992:A1, A3, A30.

Whorf, Benjamin. *Language, Thought, and Reality,* J. B. Carroll, ed. Cambridge, MA: MIT Press, 1956.

Williams, Jasmin K. "Utah—The Beehive State." *New York Post*, June 12, 2007.

Williams, Robin M., Jr. *American Society: A Sociological Interpretation,* 2nd ed. New York: Knopf, 1965.

Ying, Yu-Wen, and Meekyung Han. "Parental Contributions to Southeast Asian American Adolescents' Well-Being." *Youth and Society, 40,* 2, December 2008:289–306.

Zellner, William W. *Countercultures: A Sociological Analysis.* New York: St. Martin's, 1995.

Zerubavel, Eviatar. *The Fine Line: Making Distinctions in Everyday Life.* New York: Free Press, 1991.

CHAPTER 4

Adler, Patricia A., and Peter Adler. *Peer Power: Preadolescent Culture and Identity.* New Brunswick, N.J.: Rutgers University Press, 1998.

Ariès, Philippe. *Centuries of Childhood*, R. Baldick, trans. New York: Vintage Books, 1965.

Begley, Sharon. "Twins: Nazi and Jew." *Newsweek, 94,* December 3, 1979:139.

Belsky, Jay. "Early Child Care and Early Child Development: Major Findings of the NICHD Study of Early Child Care." *European Journal of Developmental Psychology, 3,* 1, 2006:95–110.

Best, Deborah L. "The Contribution of the Whitings to the Study of the Socialization of Gender." *Journal of Cross-Cultural Psychology, 41,* 2010:534–545.

Bodovski, Katerina, and George Farkas. "'Concerted Cultivation' and Unequal Achievement in Elementary School." *Social Science Research, 37,* 2008:903–919.

Carr, Deborah, Carol D. Ryff, Burton Singer, and William J. Magee. "Bringing the 'Life' Back into Life Course Research: A 'Person-Centered' Approach to Studying the Life Course." Paper presented at the annual meetings of the American Sociological Association, 1995.

Chen, Edwin. "Twins Reared Apart: A Living Lab." *New York Times Magazine*, December 9, 1979:112.

Clark, Candace. *Misery and Company: Sympathy in Everyday Life.* Chicago: University of Chicago Press, 1997.

Clearfield, Melissa W., and Naree M. Nelson. "Sex Differences in Mothers' Speech and Play Behavior with 6-, 9-, and 14-Month-Old Infants." *Sex Roles, 54,* 1–2, January 2006:127–137.

Connors, L. "Gender of Infant Differences in Attachment: Associations with Temperament and Caregiving Experiences."

Paper presented at the Annual Conference of the British Psychological Society, Oxford, UK, 1996.

Cooley, Charles Horton. *Human Nature and the Social Order.* New York: Scribner's, 1902.

Crosnoe, Robert, Catherine Riegle-Crumb, Sam Field, Kenneth Frank, and Chandra Muller. "Peer Group Contexts of Girls' and Boys' Academic Experiences." *Child Development, 79,* 1, February 2008:139–155.

DeMause, Lloyd. "Our Forebears Made Childhood a Nightmare." *Psychology Today 8,* 11, April 1975:85–88.

Eder, Donna. "On Becoming Female: Lessons Learned in School." In *Down to Earth Sociology: Introductory Readings,* 14th ed., James M. Henslin, ed. New York: Free Press, 2007.

Ekman, Paul. *Faces of Man: Universal Expression in a New Guinea Village.* New York: Garland Press, 1980.

Elder, Glen H., Jr. "Age Differentiation and Life Course." *Annual Review of Sociology, 1,* 1975:165–190.

Elder, Glen H., Jr. *Children of the Great Depression: Social Change in Life Experience.* Boulder, Colo.: Westview Press, 1999.

Furstenberg, Frank F., Jr., Sheela Kennedy, Vonnie C. McLoyd, Ruben G. Rumbaut, and Richard A. Settersten, Jr. "Growing Up Is Harder to Do." *Contexts, 3,* 3, Summer 2004:33–41.

Garfinkel, Harold. "Conditions of Successful Degradation Ceremonies." *American Journal of Sociology, 61,* 2, March 1956:420–424.

Gilman, Charlotte Perkins. *The Man-Made World; or, Our Androcentric Culture.* New York: 1971. Originally published 1911.

Gilpatric, Katy. "Violent Female Action Characters in Contemporary American Cinema." *Sex Roles, 62,* 2010:734–746.

Goffman, Erving. *Asylums: Essays on the Social Situation of Mental Patients and Other Inmates.* Chicago: Aldine, 1961.

Goldberg, Susan, and Michael Lewis. "Play Behavior in the Year-Old Infant: Early Sex Differences." *Child Development, 40,* March 1969:21–31.

Guensburg, Carol. "Bully Factories." *American Journalism Review, 23,* 6, 2001:51–59.

Hall, G. Stanley. *Adolescence: Its Psychology and Its Relations to Physiology, Anthropology, Sociology, Sex, Crime, Religion, and Education.* New York: Appleton, 1904.

Harlow, Harry F., and Margaret K. Harlow. "Social Deprivation in Monkeys." *Scientific American, 207,* 1962:137–147.

Henslin, James M. "On Becoming Male: Reflections of a Sociologist on Childhood and Early Socialization." In *Down to Earth Sociology: Introductory Readings,* 15th ed., James M. Henslin, ed. New York: The Free Press, 2012.

Hochschild, Arlie. "Feelings around the World." *Contexts, 7,* 2, Spring 2008:80.

Horwitz, Allan V., and Jerome C. Wakefield. *The Loss of Sadness: How Psychiatry Transformed Normal Sorrow into Depressive Disorder.* New York: Oxford University Press, 2007.

Itard, Jean Marc Gospard. *The Wild Boy of Aveyron,* George and Muriel Humphrey, trans. New York: Appleton-Century-Crofts, 1962.

Kahlenberg, Susan G., and Michelle M. Hein, "Progression on Nickelodeon? Gender-Role Stereotypes in Toy Commercials." *Sex Roles, 62,* 2010:830–847.

Keniston, Kenneth. *Youth and Dissent: The Rise of a New Opposition.* New York: Harcourt, Brace, Jovanovich, 1971.

Kohn, Melvin L. "Social Class and Parental Values." *American Journal of Sociology, 64,* 1959:337–351.

Kohn, Melvin L. *Class and Conformity: A Study in Values,* 2nd ed. Homewood, Ill.: Dorsey Press, 1977.

Kohn, Melvin L. *Change and Stability: A Cross-National Analysis of Social Structure and Personality.* Boulder, Colo.: Paradigm, 2006.

Kohn, Melvin L., and Carmi Schooler. "Class, Occupation, and Orientation." *American Sociological Review, 34,* 1969:659–678.

Lareau, Annette. "Invisible Inequality: Social Class and Childrearing in Black Families and White Families." *American Sociological Review, 67,* October 2002:747–776.

Larson, Mary Strom. "Interactions, Activities and Gender in Children's Television Commercials: A Content Analysis." *Journal of Broadcasting and Electronic Media, 45,* Winter 2001:41–51.

Levinson, D. J. *The Seasons of a Man's Life.* New York: Knopf, 1978.

Matsumoto, D., and B. Willingham. "Spontaneous Facial Expressions of Emotion of Congenitally and Noncongenitally Blind Individuals." *Journal of Personality and Social Psychology, 96,* 2009:1–10.

Meese, Ruth Lyn. "A Few New Children: Postinstitutionalized Children of Intercountry Adoption." *Journal of Special Education, 39,* 3, 2005:157–167.

Milkie, Melissa A. "Social World Approach to Cultural Studies." *Journal of Contemporary Ethnography, 23,* 3, October 1994:354–380.

National Institute of Child Health and Human Development. "Child Care and Mother–Child Interaction in the First 3 Years of Life." *Developmental Psychology, 35,* 6, November 1999:1399–1413.

Neugarten, Bernice L. "Middle Age and Aging." In *Growing Old in America,* Beth B. Hess, ed. New Brunswick, N.J.: Transaction, 1976:180–197.

Nordberg, Jenny. "In Afghanistan, Boys Are Prized and Girls Live the Part." *New York Times,* September 20, 2010.

Orme, Nicholas. *Medieval Children.* New Haven, Conn.: Yale University Press, 2002.

Pearlin, L. I., and Melvin L. Kohn. "Social Class, Occupation, and Parental Values: A Cross-National Study." *American Sociological Review, 31,* 1966:466–479.

Pines, Maya. "The Civilizing of Genie." *Psychology Today, 15,* September 1981:28–34.

Quadagno, Jill. *Aging and the Life Course: An Introduction to Gerontology,* 4th ed. New York: McGraw-Hill, 2007.

"Schwab Study Finds Four Generations of American Adults Fundamentally Rethinking Planning for Retirement." Reuters, July 15, 2008.

Shields, Stephanie A. *Speaking from the Heart: Gender and the Social Meaning of Emotion.* New York: Cambridge University Press, 2002.

Skeels, H. M. "*Adult Status of Children with Contrasting Early Life Experiences: A Follow-up Study.*" *Monograph of the Society for Research in Child Development, 31, 3,* 1966.

Skeels, H. M., and H. B. Dye. "A Study of the Effects of Differential Stimulation on Mentally Retarded Children." *Proceedings and Addresses of the American Association on Mental Deficiency, 44,* 1939:114–136.

Statistical Abstract of the United States. Washington D.C.: U.S. Census Bureau, published annually.

Taneja, V., S. Sriram, R. S. Beri, V. Sreenivas, R. Aggarwal, R. Kaur, and J. M. Puliyel. "'Not by Bread Alone': Impact of a Structured 90-Minute Play Session on Development of Children in an Orphanage." *Child Care, Health & Development, 28, 1,* 2002:95–100.

Vandell, Deborah Lowe, Jay Belsky, Margaret Burchinal, Laurence Steinberg, and Nathan Vandergrift. "No Effects of Early Child Care Extend to Age 15 Years? Results from the NICHD Study of Early Child Care and Youth Development." *Child Development, 81, 3,* May/June 2010:737–756.

Williams, Dmitri, Nicole Martins, Mia Consalvo, and James D. Ivory. "The Virtual Census: Representations of Gender, Race, and Age in Video Games." *New Media & Society, 11, 5,* 2009:815–834.

CHAPTER 5

Aberle, David F., A. K. Cohen, A. K. David, M. J. Leng, Jr., and F. N. Sutton. "The Functional Prerequisites of a Society." *Ethics, 60,* January 1950:100–111.

Agins, Teri. "When to Carry a Purse to a Meeting." *Wall Street Journal,* October 1, 2009.

Anderson, Elijah. *A Place on the Corner.* Chicago: University of Chicago Press, 1978.

Anderson, Elijah. *Streetwise: Race, Class, and Change in an Urban Community.* Chicago: University of Chicago Press, 1990.

Anderson, Elijah. "Streetwise." In *Exploring Social Life: Readings to Accompany Essentials of Sociology, Sixth Edition,* 2nd ed., James M. Henslin, ed. Boston: Allyn and Bacon, 2006:147–156. Originally published 1990.

Brinkley, Christina. "Women in Power: Finding Balance in the Wardrobe." *Wall Street Journal,* January 24, 2008.

Chambliss, William J. "The Saints and the Roughnecks." In *Down to Earth Sociology: Introductory Readings,* 15th ed., James M. Henslin, ed. New York: The Free Press, 2012. First published in 1973.

Davis, Ann, Joseph Pereira, and William M. Bulkeley. "Security Concerns Bring Focus on Translating Body Language." *Wall Street Journal,* August 15, 2002.

Dobriner, William M. "The Football Team as Social Structure and Social System." In *Social Structures and Systems: A Sociological Overview.* Pacific Palisades, Calif.: Goodyear, 1969:116–120.

Domhoff, G. William. "The Bohemian Grove and Other Retreats." In *Down to Earth Sociology: Introductory Readings,* 10th ed., James M. Henslin, ed. New York: Free Press, 1999a:391–403.

Domhoff, G. William. "State and Ruling Class in Corporate America (1974): Reflections, Corrections, and New Directions." *Critical Sociology, 25, 2–3,* July 1999b:260–265.

Domhoff, G. William. *Who Rules America? Power, Politics, and Social Change,* 5th ed. New York: McGraw-Hill, 2006.

Domhoff, G. William. "C. Wright Mills, Power Structure Research, and the Failures of Mainstream Political Science." *New Political Science, 29,* 2007:97–114.

Duneier, Mitchell. *Sidewalk.* New York: Farrar, Straus and Giroux, 1999.

Durkheim, Emile. *The Division of Labor in Society,* George Simpson, trans. New York: Free Press, 1933. Originally published 1893.

Ebaugh, Helen Rose Fuchs. *Becoming an Ex: The Process of Role Exit.* Chicago: University of Chicago Press, 1988.

Garfinkel, Harold. *Studies in Ethnomethodology.* Englewood Cliffs, N.J.: Prentice Hall, 1967.

Garfinkel, Harold. *Ethnomethodology's Program: Working Out Durkheim's Aphorism.* Lanham, Md.: Rowman & Littlefield, 2002.

Goffman, Erving. *The Presentation of Self in Everyday Life.* New York: Peter Smith, 1999. Originally published 1959.

Hall, Edward T. *The Silent Language.* New York: Doubleday, 1959.

Hall, Edward T. *The Hidden Dimension.* Garden City, N.Y.: Anchor Books, 1969.

Hall, Edward T., and Mildred R. Hall. "The Sounds of Silence." In *Down to Earth Sociology: Introductory Readings,* 15th ed., James M. Henslin, ed. New York: Free Press, 2012.

Henslin, James M., and Mae A. Biggs. "Behavior in Pubic Places: The Sociology of the Vaginal Examination." In *Down to Earth Sociology: Introductory Readings,* 15th ed., James M. Henslin, ed. New York: Free Press, 2012. Originally published 1971.

Hughes, Kathleen A. "Even Tiki Torches Don't Guarantee a Perfect Wedding." *Wall Street Journal,* February 20, 1990:A1, A16.

Liebow, Elliott. *Tally's Corner: A Study of Negro Streetcorner Men.* Boston: Little, Brown, 1999. Originally published 1967.

Linton, Ralph. *The Study of Man.* New York: Appleton-Century-Crofts, 1936.

Mack, Raymond W., and Calvin P. Bradford. *Transforming America: Patterns of Social Change,* 2nd ed. New York: Random House, 1979.

Needham, Sarah E. "Grooming Women for the Top: Tips from Executive Coaches." *Wall Street Journal,* October 31, 2006.

Samor, Geraldo, Cecilie Rohwedder, and Ann Zimmerman. "Innocents Abroad?" *Wall Street Journal,* May 5, 2006.

Tönnies, Ferdinand. *Community and Society (Gemeinschaft und Gesellschaft),* with a new introduction by John Samples. New Brunswick, N.J.: Transaction, 1988. Originally published 1887.

Useem, Michael. *The Inner Circle: Large Corporations and the Rise of Business Political Activity in the U.S. and U.K.* New York: Oxford University Press, 1984.

Yager, Mark, Beret Strong, Linda Roan, David Matsumoto, and Kimberly A. Metcalf. "Nonverbal Communication in the Operating Environment." United States Army Research Institute for the Behavioral and Social Sciences, Technical Report 1238, January 2009.

CHAPTER 6

Anderson, Elijah. *A Place on the Corner.* Chicago: University of Chicago Press, 1978.

Anderson, Elijah. "Streetwise." In *Exploring Social Life: Readings to Accompany Essentials of Sociology, Sixth Edition,* 2nd ed., James M. Henslin, ed. Boston: Allyn and Bacon, 2006:147–156. Originally published 1990.

Arlacchi, P. *Peasants and Great Estates: Society in Traditional Calabria.* Cambridge, UK: Cambridge University Press, 1980.

Barnes, Helen. "A Comment on Stroud and Pritchard: Child Homicide, Psychiatric Disorder and Dangerousness." *British Journal of Social Work, 31,* 3, June 2001.

Barstow, David, and Lowell Bergman. "Death on the Job, Slaps on the Wrist." *Wall Street Journal,* January 10, 2003.

Becker, Howard S. *Outsiders: Studies in the Sociology of Deviance.* New York: Free Press, 1966.

Blumstein, Alfred, and Joel Wallman. "The Crime Drop and Beyond." *Annual Review of Law and Social Science, 2,* December 2006:125–146.

Chagnon, Napoleon A. *Yanomamo: The Fierce People,* 2nd ed. New York: Holt, Rinehart and Winston, 1977.

Chambliss, William J. *Power, Politics, and Crime.* Boulder, Colo.: Westview Press, 2000.

Chambliss, William J. "The Saints and the Roughnecks." In *Down to Earth Sociology: Introductory Readings,* 15th ed., James M. Henslin, ed. New York: The Free Press, 2012.

Chung, He Len, and Laurence Steinberg. "Relations between Neighborhood Factors, Parenting Behaviors, Peer Deviance, and Delinquency among Serious Juvenile Offenders." *Developmental Psychology, 42,* 2, 2006:319–331.

Church, Wesley T., II, Tracy Wharton, and Julie K. Taylor. "An Examination of Differential Association and Social Control Theory: Family Systems and Delinquency." *Youth Violence and Juvenile Justice, 7,* 1, January 2009:3–15.

Cloud, John. "For Better or Worse." *Time,* October 26, 1998:43–44.

Cloward, Richard A., and Lloyd E. Ohlin. *Delinquency and Opportunity: A Theory of Delinquent Gangs.* New York: Free Press, 1960.

Conklin, John E. *Why Crime Rates Fell.* Boston: Allyn and Bacon, 2003.

Deflem, Mathieu, ed. *Sociological Theory and Criminological Research: Views from Europe and the United States.* San Diego: JAI Press, 2006.

Drew, Christopher. "Military Contractor Agrees to Pay $325 Million to Settle Whistle-Blower Lawsuit." *New York Times,* April 2, 2009.

Dunaway, Wilma A. *Women, Work, and Family in the Antebellum Mountain South.* New York: Cambridge University Press, 2008.

Durkheim, Emile. *The Division of Labor in Society,* George Simpson, trans. New York: Free Press, 1933. Originally published 1893.

Durkheim, Emile. *The Rules of Sociological Method,* Sarah A. Solovay and John H. Mueller, trans. New York: Free Press, 1938, 1958, 1964. Originally published 1895.

Glaze, Lauren E., and Laura M. Maruschak. "Parents in Prison and Their Minor Children." Bureau of Justice Statistics Special Report, August 2008:1–25.

Goffman, Erving. *Stigma: Notes on the Management of Spoiled Identity.* Englewood Cliffs, N.J.: Prentice Hall, 1963.

Goozen, Stephanie H. M. van, Graeme Fairchild, Heddeke Snoek, and Gordon T. Harold. "The Evidence for a Neurobiological Model of Childhood Antisocial Behavior." *Psychological Bulletin, 133,* 1, 2007:149–182.

Gottfredson, Michael R., and Travis Hirschi. *A General Theory of Crime.* Stanford, Calif.: Stanford University Press, 1990.

Hirschi, Travis. *Causes of Delinquency.* Berkeley: University of California Press, 1969.

Horowitz, Ruth. *Honor and the American Dream: Culture and Identity in a Chicano Community.* New Brunswick, N.J.: Rutgers University Press, 1983.

Horowitz, Ruth. "Studying Violence among the 'Lions.'" In *Social Problems*, James M. Henslin, ed. Upper Saddle River, N.J.: Prentice Hall, 2005:135.

Jacobs, David, Zhenchao Qian, Jason T. Carmichael, and Stephanie L. Kent. "Who Survives on Death Row? An Individual and Contextual Analysis." *American Sociological Review, 72*, August 2007:610–632.

Jones, Allen. "Let Nonviolent Prisoners Out." *Los Angeles Times*, June 12, 2008.

Lombroso, Cesare. *Crime: Its Causes and Remedies*, H. P. Horton, trans. Boston: Little, Brown, 1911.

Madigan, Nick. "Judge Questions Long Sentence in Drug Case." *New York Times*, November 17, 2004.

Mayer, John D. *Personality: A Systems Approach.* Boston: Allyn and Bacon, 2007.

McCormick, John. "The Sorry Side of Sears." *Newsweek*, February 22, 1999:36–39.

McShane, Marilyn, and Frank P. Williams, III., eds. *Criminological Theory.* Upper Saddle River, N.J.: Prentice Hall, 2007.

Merton, Robert K. *Social Theory and Social Structure.* Glencoe, Ill.: Free Press, 1949. Enlarged ed., 1968.

Merton, Robert K. "The Social-Cultural Environment and Anomie." In *New Perspectives for Research on Juvenile Delinquency*, Helen L. Witmer and Ruth Kotinsky, eds. Washington, D.C.: U.S. Department of Health, Education, and Welfare, 1956:24–50.

Murphy, Caryle. "Women's Rights Key to Kingdom's Future." *Global Post, September 6, 2011.*

O'Brien, Timothy L. "Fed Assesses Citigroup Unit $70 Million in Loan Abuse." *New York Times*, May 28, 2004.

Oppel, Richard A., Jr. "Steady Decline in Major Crimes Baffles Experts." *New York Times*, May 23, 2011.

Partington, Donald H. "The Incidence of the Death Penalty for Rape in Virginia." *Washington and Lee Law Review, 22*, 1965:43–75.

Read, Madlen. "Citi Pays $18M for Questioned Credit Card Practice." Associated Press, August 26, 2008.

Reckless, Walter C. *The Crime Problem*, 5th ed. New York: Appleton, 1973.

Reiman, Jeffrey. *The Rich Get Richer and the Poor Get Prison: Ideology, Class, and Criminal Justice*, 9th ed. Boston: Allyn and Bacon, 2010.

Reuters. "Fake Tiger Woods Gets 200-Years-to-Life in Prison." April 28, 2001.

Rosenfeld, Richard. "Crime Decline in Context." *Contexts, 1, 1*, Spring 2002:25–34.

Sánchez-Jankowski, Martín. "Gangs and Social Change." *Theoretical Criminology, 7, 2*, 2003:191–216.

Sourcebook of Criminal Justice Statistics. Washington, D.C.: U.S. Government Printing Office, published annually.

Spitzer, Steven. "Toward a Marxian Theory of Deviance." *Social Problems, 22*, June 1975:608–619.

Statistical Abstract of the United States. Washington, D.C.: U.S. Census Bureau, published annually.

Sullivan, Andrew. "What's So Bad about Hate?" *New York Times Magazine,* September 26, 1999.

Sutherland, Edwin H. *Criminology.* Philadelphia: Lippincott, 1924.

Sutherland, Edwin H. *Principles of Criminology*, 4th ed. Philadelphia: Lippincott, 1947.

Sutherland, Edwin H. *White Collar Crime.* New York: Dryden Press, 1949.

Sutherland, Edwin H., Donald R. Cressey, and David F. Luckenbill. *Principles of Criminology*, 11th ed. Dix Hills, N.Y.: General Hall, 1992.

Sykes, Gresham M., and David Matza. "Techniques of Neutralization." In *Down to Earth Sociology: Introductory Readings*, 5th ed., James M. Henslin, ed. New York: Free Press, 1988:225–231. Originally published 1957.

Szasz, Thomas S. *The Myth of Mental Illness*, rev. ed. New York: Harper & Row, 1986.

Szasz, Thomas S. "Mental Illness Is Still a Myth." In *Deviant Behavior 96/97*, Lawrence M. Salinger, ed. Guilford, Conn.: Dushkin, 1996:200–205.

Szasz, Thomas S. *Cruel Compassion: Psychiatric Control of Society's Unwanted.* Syracuse, N.Y.: Syracuse University Press, 1998.

Walsh, Anthony, and Kevin M. Beaver. "Biosocial Criminology." In *Handbook on Crime and Deviance*, M. D. Krohn et al., eds. Dordrecht, N.Y.: Springer, 2009:79–101.

Warren, Jennifer, Adam Gelb, Jake Horowitz, and Jessica Riordan. "One in 100: Behind Bars in America 2008." Washington, D.C.: Pew Charitable Trust, February 2008.

Watson, J. Mark. "Outlaw Motorcyclists." In *Society: Readings to Accompany Sociology: A Down-to-Earth Approach, Core Concepts*, James M. Henslin ed. Boston: Allyn and Bacon, 2006:105–114. Originally published 1980 in *Deviant Behavior, 2, 1.*

White, Joseph B., Stephen Power, and Timothy Aeppel. "Death Count Linked to Failures of Firestone Tires Rises to 203." *Wall Street Journal,* June 19, 2001:A4.

Wilson, James Q., and Richard J. Herrnstein. *Crime and Human Nature.* New York: Simon & Schuster, 1985.

CHAPTER 7

Aldrich, Nelson W., Jr. *Old Money: The Mythology of America's Upper Class.* New York: Vintage Books, 1989.

Appiah, Kwame Anthony, and Martin Bunzl, eds. *Buying Freedom: The Ethics and Economics of Slave Redemption.* Princeton, N.J.: Princeton University Press, 2007.

Ayittey, George B. N. "Black Africans Are Enraged at Arabs." *Wall Street Journal*, interactive edition, September 4, 1998.

Bailey, Martha J., and Susan M. Dynarski. "Gains and Gaps: Changing Inequality in U.S. College Entry and Completion." In *Whither Opportunity?: Rising Inequality, Schools, and Children's Life Chances*, Greg J. Duncan and Richard J. Murnane, eds. New York: Russell Sage, September 2011.

Baltzell, E. Digby, and Howard G. Schneiderman. "Social Class in the Oval Office." *Society, 25,* September/October 1988:42–49.

Banjo, Shelly. "Prepping for the Playdate Test." *Wall Street Journal,* August 19, 2010.

Beeghley, Leonard. *The Structure of Social Stratification in the United States,* 5th ed. Boston: Allyn& Bacon, 2008.

Beller, Emily. "Bringing Intergenerational Social Mobility Research into the Twenty-First Century: Why Mothers Matter." *American Sociological Review, 74,* August 2009:507–528.

Blau, Peter M., and Otis Dudley Duncan. *The American Occupational Structure.* New York: John Wiley, 1967.

Blee, Kathleen M. "Trajectories of Ideologies and Action in US Organized Racism." In *Identity and Participation in Culturally Diverse Societies: A Multidisciplinary Perspective*, Assaad E. Azzi, Xenia Chryssochoou, Bert Klandermans, and Bernd Simon, eds. Oxford, UK: Blackwell Publishing, 2011.

Cellini, Stephanie R., Signe-Mary McKernan, and Caroline Ratcliffe. "The Dynamics of Poverty in the United States: A Review of Data, Methods, and Findings." *Journal of Policy Analysis and Management, 27,* 2008:577–605.

Chandra, Vibha P. "Fragmented Identities: The Social Construction of Ethnicity, 1885–1947." Unpublished paper, 1993.

Chin, Nancy P., Alicia Monroe, and Kevin Fiscella. "Social Determinants of (Un)Healthy Behaviors." *Education for Health: Change in Learning and Practice, 13,* 3, November 2000:317–328.

Cohen, Patricia. "Forget Lonely. Life Is Healthy at the Top." *New York Times,* May 15, 2004.

Collins, Randall. "Socially Unrecognized Cumulation." *American Sociologist, 30,* 2, Summer 1999:41–61.

Crompton, Rosemary. "Class and Employment." *Work, Employment and Society, 24,* 2010:9–26.

Davis, Kingsley, and Wilbert E. Moore. "Some Principles of Stratification." *American Sociological Review, 10,* 1945:242–249.

Davis, Kingsley, and Wilbert E. Moore. "Reply to Tumin." *American Sociological Review, 18,* 1953:394–396.

Davis, Nancy J., and Robert V. Robinson. "Class Identification of Men and Women in the 1970s and 1980s." *American Sociological Review, 53,* February 1988:103–112.

DeNavas-Walt, Carmen, Bernadette D. Proctor, and Jessica C. Smith. "Income, Poverty, and Health Insurance Coverage in the United States: 2009." *Current Population Reports P60-238,* Washington, D.C.: U.S. Census Bureau, September 2010.

dePastino, Blake. "Photo in the News: Robot Jockeys Race Camels in Qatar." *National Geographic,* July 15, 2005.

Dolnick, Sam. "The Obesity-Hunger Paradox." *New York Times,* March 12, 2010.

Domhoff, G. William. *The Power Elite and the State: How Policy Is Made in America.* Hawthorne, N.Y.: Aldine de Gruyter, 1990.

Domhoff, G. William. "The Bohemian Grove and Other Retreats." In *Down to Earth Sociology: Introductory Readings,* 10th ed., James M. Henslin, ed. New York: Free Press, 1999:391–403.

Domhoff, G. William. *Who Rules America? Power, Politics, and Social Change*, 5th ed. New York: McGraw-Hill, 2006.

Domhoff, G. William. "Wealth, Income, and Power." Website: Who Rules America, September 2010. http://sociology.ucsc.edu/whorulesamerica/

Du Bois, W. E. B. *Black Reconstruction in America: An Essay toward a History of the Part Which Black Folk Played in the Attempt to Reconstruct Democracy in America, 1860–1880.* New York: Atheneum, 1992. Originally published 1935.

Fabrikant, Geraldine. "Old Nantucket Warily Meets the New." *New York Times,* June 5, 2005.

Faris, Robert E. L., and Warren Dunham. *Mental Disorders in Urban Areas.* Chicago: University of Chicago Press, 1939.

Featherman, David L. "Opportunities Are Expanding." *Society, 13,* 1979:4–11.

Galbraith, John Kenneth. *The Nature of Mass Poverty.* Cambridge Mass.: Harvard University Press, 1979.

Garfinkel, Irwin, Lee Rainwater, and Timothy Smeeding. *Wealth and Welfare States: Is America a Laggard or a Leader?* New York: Oxford University Press, 2010.

Geronimus, Arline T., Margaret T. Hicken, Jay A. Pearson, Sarah J. Seashols, Kelly L. Brown, and Tracy Dawson Cruz. "Do US Black Women Experience Stress-Related Accelerated Biological Aging?" *Human Nature, 21,* 2010:19–38.

Gerth, H. H., and C. Wright Mills. *From Max Weber: Essays in Sociology.* New York: Galaxy, 1958.

Gilbert, Dennis L. *The American Class Structure in an Age of Growing Inequality,* 6th ed. Belmont, Calif.: Wadsworth Publishing, 2003.

Gilbert, Dennis L. *The American Class Structure in an Age of Growing Inequality,* 7th ed. Los Angeles, Calif: Pine Forge Press, 2008.

Gilbert, Dennis, and Joseph A. Kahl. *The American Class Structure: A New Synthesis,* 4th ed. Belmont, Calif.: Wadsworth Publishing, 1998.

Gold, Ray. "Janitors versus Tenants: A Status-Income Dilemma." *American Journal of Sociology, 58,* 1952:486–493.

Harrison, Paul. *Inside the Third World: The Anatomy of Poverty,* 3rd ed. London: Penguin Books, 1993.

Heames, Joyce Thompson, Michael G. Harvey, and Darren Treadway. "Status Inconsistency: An Antecedent to Bullying Behavior in Groups." *International Journal of Human Resource Management,* 17, 2, February 2006:348–361.

Hellinger, Daniel, and Dennis R. Judd. *The Democratic Facade.* Pacific Grove, Calif.: Brooks/Cole, 1991.

Higginbotham, Elizabeth, and Lynn Weber. "Moving with Kin and Community: Upward Social Mobility for Black and White Women." *Gender and Society, 6,* 3, September 1992:416–440.

Hout, Michael. "How Class Works: Objective and Subjective Aspects of Class Since the 1970s." In *Social Class: How Does It Work?* Annette Lareau and Dalton Conley, eds. New York: Russell Sage, 2008:52–64.

Houtman, Dick. "What Exactly Is a 'Social Class'?: On the Economic Liberalism and Cultural Conservatism of the 'Working Class.'" Paper presented at the annual meetings of the American Sociological Association, 1995.

Huber, Joan. "Micro-Macro Links in Gender Stratification." *American Sociological Review, 55,* February 1990:1–10.

Jaffrelot, Christophe. "The Impact of Affirmative Action in India: More Political than Socioeconomic." *India Review, 5,* 2, April 2006:173–189.

Jessop, Bob, "The Return of the National State in the Current Crisis of the World Market." *Capital and Class, 34,* 1, 2010:38–43.

Kaufman, Joanne. "Married Maidens and Dilatory Domiciles." *Wall Street Journal,* May 7, 1996:A16.

Kefalas, Maria. "Looking for the Lower Middle Class." *City and Community, 6,* 1, March 2007:63–68.

Kifner, John. "Building Modernity on Desert Mirages." *New York Times,* February 7, 1999.

King, Eden B., Jennifer L. Knight, and Michelle R. Hebl. "The Influence of Economic Conditions on Aspects of Stigmatization." *Journal of Social Issues, 66,* 3, September 2010:446–460.

Kluegel, James R., and Eliot R. Smith. *Beliefs about Inequality: America's Views of What Is and What Ought to Be.* Hawthorne, N.Y.: Aldine de Gruyter, 1986.

Kneebone, Elizabeth, and Emily Garr. "The Suburbanization of Poverty: Trends in Metropolitan America, 2000 to 2008." Washington, D.C.: Brookings, January 2010.

Krugman, Paul. "White Man's Burden." *New York Times,* September 24, 2002.

Landtman, Gunnar. *The Origin of the Inequality of the Social Classes.* New York: Greenwood Press, 1968. Originally published 1938.

Lenski, Gerhard. "Status Crystallization: A Nonvertical Dimension of Social Status." *American Sociological Review, 19,* 1954:405–413.

Lenski, Gerhard. *Power and Privilege: A Theory of Social Stratification.* New York: McGraw-Hill, 1966.

Lerner, Gerda. *Black Women in White America: A Documentary History.* New York: Pantheon Books, 1972.

Lerner, Gerda. *The Creation of Patriarchy.* New York: Oxford, 1986.

Lichter, Daniel T., and Martha L. Crowley. "Poverty in America: Beyond Welfare Reform." *Population Bulletin, 57,* 2, June 2002:1–36.

Lublin, Joann S. "CEO Pay in 2010 Jumped 11%." *Wall Street Journal,* May 9, 2011.

Marx, Karl. "Contribution to the Critique of Hegel's Philosophy of Right." In *Karl Marx: Early Writings,* T. B. Bottomore, ed. New York: McGraw-Hill, 1964:45. Originally published 1844.

Marx, Karl, and Friedrich Engels. *Communist Manifesto.* New York: Pantheon, 1967. Originally published 1848.

Mills, C. Wright. *The Power Elite.* New York: Oxford University Press, 1956.

Morris, Joan M., and Michael D. Grimes. "Moving Up from the Working Class." In *Down to Earth Sociology: Introductory Readings,* 13th ed., James M. Henslin, ed. New York: Free Press, 2005:365–376.

Nelson, Dean. "Former Camel Jockeys Compensated by UAE." *Telegraph,* May 5, 2009.

O'Hare, William P. "A New Look at Poverty in America." *Population Bulletin, 51,* 2, September 1996a:1–47.

O'Hare, William P. "U.S. Poverty Myths Explored: Many Poor Work Year-Round, Few Still Poor after Five Years." *Population Today: News, Numbers, and Analysis, 24,* 10, October 1996b:1–2.

Peltham, Brett W. "About One in Six Americans Report History of Depression." *Gallup Poll,* October 20, 2009.

Polgreen, Lydia. "Court Rules Niger Failed by Allowing Girl's Slavery." *New York Times,* October 27, 2008.

Ratcliffe, Caroline, and Signe-Mary McKernan. "Childhood Poverty Persistence: Facts and Consequences." The Urban Institute, Brief 14, June 2010:1–10.

Robinson, Gail, and Barbara Mullins Nelson. "Pursuing Upward Mobility: African American Professional Women Reflect on Their Journey." *Journal of Black Studies, 40,* 6, 2010:1168–1188.

Rothkopf, David. *Superclass: The Global Power Elite and the World They Are Making.* New York: Farrar, Straus and Giroux, 2008.

Samuelson, Paul Anthony, and William D. Nordhaus. *Economics,* 18th ed. New York: McGraw Hill, 2005.

Sklair, Leslie. *Globalization: Capitalism and Its Alternatives,* 3rd ed. New York: Oxford: University Press, 2001.

Srole, Leo, et al. *Mental Health in the Metropolis: The Midtown Manhattan Study.* Albany: New York University Press, 1978.

Stampp, Kenneth M. *The Peculiar Institution: Slavery in the Ante-Bellum South.* New York: Vintage Books, 1956.

Statistical Abstract of the United States. Washington D.C.: U.S. Census Bureau, published annually.

Stevens, Mitchell. *Creating a Class: College Admissions and the Education of Elites.* Cambridge, Mass.: Harvard University Press, 2009.

Trafficking in Persons Report. Washington, D.C.: U.S. Department of State, June 14, 2010.

Tumin, Melvin M. "Some Principles of Social Stratification: A Critical Analysis." *American Sociological Review, 18,* August 1953:394.

Uchitelle, Louis. "How to Define Poverty? Let Us Count the Ways." *New York Times,* May 28, 2001.

UNESCO. "UNESCO Launches Global Partnership for Girls and Women's Education." June 2011.

Wallerstein, Immanuel. *The Modern World System: Capitalist Agriculture and the Origins of the European World-Economy in the Sixteenth Century.* New York: Academic Press, 1974.

Wallerstein, Immanuel. *The Capitalist World-Economy.* New York: Cambridge University Press, 1979.

Wallerstein, Immanuel. "Culture as the Ideological Battleground of the Modern World-System." In *Global Culture: Nationalism, Globalization, and Modernity,* Mike Featherstone, ed. London: Sage, 1990:31–55.

Weber, Max. *Economy and Society,* G. Roth and C. Wittich, eds. Berkeley: University of California Press, 1978. Originally published 1922.

CHAPTER 8

Adorno, Theodor W., Else Frenkel-Brunswick, D. J. Levinson, and R. N. Sanford. *The Authoritarian Personality.* New York: Harper & Row, 1950.

Alba, Richard, and Victor Nee. *Remaking the American Mainstream: Assimilation and Contemporary Immigration.* Cambridge, Mass.: Harvard University Press, 2003.

Allport, Floyd. *Social Psychology.* Boston: Houghton Mifflin, 1954.

Angler, Natalie. "Do Races Differ? Not Really, DNA Shows." *New York Times,* August 22, 2000.

Archibold, Randal C., and Julia Preston. "Homeland Security Stands by Its Fence." *New York Times,* May 21, 2008.

Archibold, Randal C. "Arizona Enacts Stringent Law on Immigration." *New York Times,* April 23, 2010.

Bartlett, Donald L., and James B. Steele. "Wheel of Misfortune." *Time,* December 16, 2002:44–58.

Bell, David A. "An American Success Story: The Triumph of Asian-Americans." In *Sociological Footprints: Introductory Readings in Sociology,* 5th ed., Leonard Cargan and Jeanne H. Ballantine, eds. Belmont, Calif.: Wadsworth, 1991:308–316.

Bernard, Viola W., Perry Ottenberg, and Fritz Redl. "Dehumanization: A Composite Psychological Defense in Relation to Modern War." In *The Triple Revolution Emerging: Social Problems in Depth,* Robert Perucci and Marc Pilisuk, eds. Boston: Little, Brown, 1971:17–34.

Bertrand, Marianne, and Sendhil Mullainathan. "Are Emily and Brendan More Employable than Lakish and Jamal? A Field Experiment on Labor Market Discrimination." Unpublished paper, November 18, 2002.

Blee, Kathleen M. "Inside Organized Racism." In *Life in Society: Readings to Accompany Sociology: A Down-to-Earth Approach,* 7TH *Edition,* James M. Henslin, ed. Boston: Allyn and Bacon, 2005:46–57.

Bray, Rosemary L. "Rosa Parks: A Legendary Moment, a Lifetime of Activism." *Ms., 6,* 3, November–December 1995:45–47.

Bretos, Miguel A. "Hispanics Face Institutional Exclusion." *Miami Herald,* May 22, 1994.

Browning, Christopher R. *Ordinary Men: Reserve Police Battalion 101 and the Final Solution in Poland.* New York: HarperPerennial, 1993.

Bureau of Labor Statistics. "The Unemployment Situation." November 2012.

Carlson, Lewis H., and George A. Colburn. *In Their Place: White America Defines Her Minorities, 1850–1950.* New York: Wiley, 1972.

Chandra, Vibha P. "The Present Moment of the Past: The Metamorphosis." Unpublished paper, 1993.

Churchill, Ward. *A Little Matter of Genocide: Holocaust and Denial in the Americas, 1492 to the Present.* San Francisco, Calif.: City Lights Books, 1997.

Cose, Ellis. "What's White Anyway?" *Newsweek,* September 18, 2000:64–65.

Cose, Ellis. "Black versus Brown." *Newsweek,* July 3, 2006:44–45.

Cowen, Emory L., Judah Landes, and Donald E. Schaet. "The Effects of Mild Frustration on the Expression of Prejudiced Attitudes." *Journal of Abnormal and Social Psychology.* January 1959:33–38.

Dasgupta, Nilanjana, Debbie E. McGhee, Anthony G. Greenwald, and Mahzarin R. Banaji. "Automatic Preference for White Americans: Eliminating the Familiarity Explanation." *Journal of Experimental Social Psychology, 36,* 3, May 2000:316–328.

Deutscher, Irwin. *Accommodating Diversity: National Policies that Prevent Ethnic Conflict.* Lanham, Md.: Lexington Books, 2002.

DiSilvestro, Roger L. *In the Shadow of Wounded Knee: The Untold Final Chapter of the Indian Wars.* New York: Walker & Co., 2006.

Dobyns, Henry F. *Their Numbers Became Thinned: Native American Population Dynamics in Eastern North America.* Knoxville: University of Tennessee Press, 1983.

Dollard, John, et al. *Frustration and Aggression.* New Haven, Conn.: Yale University Press, 1939.

Du Bois, W. E. B. *Black Reconstruction in America: An Essay toward a History of the Part Which Black Folk Played in the Attempt to Reconstruct Democracy in America, 1860–1880.* New York: Atheneum, 1992. Originally published 1935.

Ezekiel, Raphael S. *The Racist Mind: Portraits of American Neo-Nazis and Klansmen.* New York: Viking, 1995.

Feagin, Joe R. "The Continuing Significance of Race: Antiblack Discrimination in Public Places." In *Majority and Minority: The Dynamics of Race and Ethnicity in American Life,* 6th ed., Norman R. Yetman, ed. Boston: Allyn and Bacon, 1999:384–399.

Fish, Jefferson M. "Mixed Blood." *Psychology Today, 28,* 6, November–December 1995:55–58, 60, 61, 76, 80.

Frank, Reanne. "What to Make of It? The (Re)emergence of a Biological Conceptualization of Race in Health Disparities Research." *Social Science & Medicine, 64,* 2007:1977–1983.

Fund, John. "English-Only Showdown." *Wall Street Journal,* November 28, 2007.

Gettleman, Jeffrey, and Josh Kron, "U.N. Report on Congo Massacres Draws Anger." *New York Times,* October 1, 2010.

Greenwald, Anthony G., and Linda Hamilton Krieger. "Implicit Bias: Scientific Foundations." *California Law Review,* July 2006.

Gross, Jan T. *Neighbors.* New Haven, Conn.: Yale University Press, 2001.

Hartley, Eugene. *Problems in Prejudice.* New York: King's Crown Press, 1946.

Herring, Cedric. "Is Job Discrimination Dead?" *Contexts,* Summer 2002: 13–18.

Hill, Mark E. "Skin Color and the Perception of Attractiveness among African Americans: Does Gender Make a Difference?" *Social Psychology Quarterly, 65,* 1, 2002:77–91.

Horn, James P. *Land As God Made It: Jamestown and the Birth of America.* New York: Basic Books, 2006.

Hsu, Francis L. K. *The Challenge of the American Dream: The Chinese in the United States.* Belmont, Calif.: Wadsworth, 1971.

Hutchinson, Earl Ofari. "The Latino Challenge to Black America." *Washington Post,* January 11, 2008.

Huttenbach, Henry R. "The Roman *Porajmos:* The Nazi Genocide of Europe's Gypsies." *Nationalities Papers, 19,* 3, Winter 1991:373–394.

Jeong, Yu-Jin, and Hyun-Kyung You. "Different Historical Trajectories and Family Diversity among Chinese, Japanese, and Koreans in the United States." *Journal of Family History, 33,* 3, July 2008:346–356.

Jones, Jeffrey Owen, and Peter Meyer. *The Pledge: A History of the Pledge of Allegiance.* New York: St. Martin's Press, 2010.

Kaufman, Jonathan, and Gary Fields. "Election of Obama Recasts National Conversation on Race." *Wall Street Journal,* November 10, 2008.

Kimmel, Michael. "Racism as Adolescent Male Rite of Passage." *Journal of Contemporary Ethnography, 36,* 2, April 2007:202–218.

Lee, Sharon M. "Asian Americans: Diverse and Growing." *Population Bulletin, 53,* 2, June 1998:1–39.

Lewin, Tamar. "Colleges Regroup after Voters Ban Race Preferences." *New York Times,* January 26, 2007.

Lind, Michael. *The Next American Nation: The New Nationalism and the Fourth American Revolution.* New York: Free Press, 1995.

Lynn, Michael, Michael Sturman, Christie Ganley, Elizabeth Adams, Mathew Douglas, and Jessica McNeil. "Consumer Racial Discrimination in Tipping: A Replication and Extension." *Journal of Applied Social Psychology, 38,* 4, 2008:1045–1060.

Mahoney, John S., Jr., and Paul G. Kooistra. "Policing the Races: Structural Factors Enforcing Racial Purity in Virginia (1630–1930)." Paper presented at the annual meetings of the American Sociological Association, 1995.

Mander, Jerry. *In the Absence of the Sacred: The Failure of Technology and the Survival of the Indian Nations.* San Francisco, Calif.: Sierra Club Books, 1992.

Marino, David. "Border Watch Group 'Techno Patriots' Still Growing." Tucson, Ariz.: KVOA News 4, February 14, 2008.

McFarland, Sam. "Authoritarianism, Social Dominance, and Other Roots of Generalized Prejudice." *Political Psychology, 31,* 3, June 2010:453–477.

McLemore, S. Dale. *Racial and Ethnic Relations in America.* Boston: Allyn and Bacon, 1994.

Mohawk, John C. "Indian Economic Development: An Evolving Concept of Sovereignty." *Buffalo Law Review, 39,* 2, Spring 1991:495–503.

Montagu, M. F. Ashley. *Introduction to Physical Anthropology,* 3rd ed. Springfield, Ill.: Thomas, 1960.

Montagu, M. F. Ashley. *The Concept of Race.* New York: Free Press, 1964.

Montagu, M. F. Ashley, ed. *Race and IQ: Expanded Edition.* New York: Oxford University Press, 1999.

Nash, Gary B. *Red, White, and Black.* Englewood Cliffs, N.J.: Prentice Hall, 1974.

Navarro, Mireya. "For New York's Black Latinos, a Growing Racial Awareness." *New York Times,* April 28, 2003.

Peterson, Iver. "1993 Deal for Indian Casino Is Called a Model to Avoid." *New York Times,* June 30, 2003.

Popescu, Ioana, Mary S. Vaughan-Sarrazin, and Gary E. Rosenthal. "Differences in Mortality and Use of Revascularization in Black and White Patients With Acute MI Admitted to Hospitals With and Without Revascularization Services." *Journal of the American Medical Association, 297,* 22, June 13, 2007:2489–2495.

Portes, Alejandro, and Rubén G. Rumbaut. *Immigrant America.* Berkeley: University of California Press, 1990.

Powell, Michael, and Janet Roberts. "Minorities Hit Hardest by Foreclosures in New York." *New York Times,* May 15, 2009.

Pratt, Timothy. "Nevada's Gambling Revenue Rises After Two Year Slump." Reuters, February 10, 2011.

Preston, Julia. "Homeland Security Cancels 'Virtual Fence' after Billion Is Spent." *New York Times,* January 14, 2011.

Qian, Zhenchao, and Daniel T. Lichter. "Social Boundaries and Marital Assimilation: Interpreting Trends in Racial and Ethnic Intermarriage." *American Sociological Review, 72,* February 2007:68–94.

Ray, J. J. "Authoritarianism Is a Dodo: Comment on Scheepers, Felling and Peters." *European Sociological Review, 7,* 1, May 1991:73–75.

Reskin, Barbara F. *The Realities of Affirmative Action in Employment.* Washington, D.C.: American Sociological Association, 1998.

Riley, Naomi Schaefer. "The Real Path to Racial Harmony." *Wall Street Journal,* August 14, 2009.

Rivlin, Gary. "Beyond the Reservation." *New York Times,* September 22, 2007.

Roediger, David R. *Colored White: Transcending the Racial Past.* Berkeley: University of California Press, 2002.

Schaefer, Richard T. *Racial and Ethnic Groups,* 9th ed. Upper Saddle River, N.J.: Prentice Hall, 2004.

Schaefer, Richard T. *Racial and Ethnic Groups,* 13th ed. Boston: Pearson Education, 2012.

Sherif, Muzafer, and Carolyn Sherif. *Groups in Harmony and Tension.* New York: Harper & Row, 1953.

Simpson, George Eaton, and J. Milton Yinger. *Racial and Cultural Minorities: An Analysis of Prejudice and Discrimination,* 4th ed. New York: Harper & Row, 1972.

Skinner, Jonathan, James N. Weinstein, Scott M. Sporer, and John E. Wennberg. "Racial, Ethnic, and Geographic Disparities in Rates of Knee Arthroplasty among Medicare Patients." *New England Journal of Medicine, 349, 14,* October 2, 2003:1350–1359.

Smedley, Audrey, and Brian D. Smedley. "Race as Biology Is Fiction, Racism as a Social Problem Is Real: Anthropological and Historical Perspectives on the Social Construction of Race." *American Psychologist, 60, 1,* January 2005:16–26.

Spickard, P. R. S. *Mixed Blood: Intermarriage and Ethnic Identity in Twentieth Century America.* Madison: University of Wisconsin Press, 1989.

Statistical Abstract of the United States. Washington, D.C.: U.S. Census Bureau, published annually.

Stolberg, Sheryl Gay. "Blacks Found on Short End of Heart Attack Procedure." *New York Times,* May 10, 2001.

Suzuki, Bob H. "Asian-American Families." In *Marriage and Family in a Changing Society,* 2nd ed., James M. Henslin, ed. New York: Free Press, 1985:104–119.

Thomas, Paulette. "U.S. Examiners Will Scrutinize Banks with Poor Minority-Lending Histories." *Wall Street Journal,* October 22, 1991:A2.

Thomas, Paulette. "Boston Fed Finds Racial Discrimination in Mortgage Lending Is Still Widespread." *Wall Street Journal,* October 9, 1992:A3.

Thomas, W. I., and Dorothy Swaine Thomas. *The Child in America: Behavior Problems and Programs.* New York: Alfred A. Knopf, 1928.

Thompson, Don. "Officials: Gang Rivalry Led to Calif. Prison Riot." Associated Press, December 10, 2009.

Thornton, Russell. *American Indian Holocaust and Survival: A Population History Since 1492.* Norman: University of Oklahoma Press, 1987.

Wagley, Charles, and Marvin Harris. *Minorities in the New World.* New York: Columbia University Press, 1958.

Willie, Charles Vert. "Caste, Class, and Family Life Experiences." *Research in Race and Ethnic Relations, 6,* 1991:65–84.

Wilson, William Julius. *The Declining Significance of Race: Blacks and Changing American Institutions.* Chicago: University of Chicago Press, 1978.

Wilson, William Julius. *When Work Disappears: The World of the New Urban Poor.* Chicago: University of Chicago Press, 1996.

Wilson, William Julius. *The Bridge over the Racial Divide: Rising Inequality and Coalition Politics.* Berkeley: University of California Press, 2000.

Wilson, William Julius. "Jobless Poverty: A New Form of Social Dislocation in the Inner-City Ghetto." In *The Inequality Reader: Contemporary and Foundational Readings in Race, Class and Gender,* David B. Grusky and Szonja Szelenyi, eds. Boulder, Calif.: Westview Press, 2007:142–152.

Wilson, William Julius. *The Truly Disadvantaged: The Inner City, The Underclass, and Public Policy,* 2nd edition. Chicago: University of Chicago Press, 2012.

Wirth, Louis. "The Problem of Minority Groups." In *The Science of Man in the World Crisis,* Ralph Linton, ed. New York: Columbia University Press, 1945.

Yinger, J. Milton. *Toward a Field Theory of Behavior: Personality and Social Structure.* New York: McGraw-Hill, 1965.

CHAPTER 9

Appiah, Kwame Anthony. "Best Weapon Against Honor Killers: Shame." *Wall Street Journal,* September 25, 2010.

Belkin, Lisa. "The Feminine Critique." *New York Times,* November 1, 2007.

Bishop, Jerry E. "Study Finds Doctors Tend to Postpone Heart Surgery for Women, Raising Risk." *Wall Street Journal,* April 16, 1990:B4.

Booth, Alan, and James M. Dabbs, Jr. "Testosterone and Men's Marriages." *Social Forces, 72,* 2, December 1993:463–477.

Carpenito, Lynda Juall. "The Myths of Acquaintance Rape." *Nursing Forum, 34,* 4, October–December 1999:3.

Carter, Nancy M. "Pipeline's Broken Promise." New York: *Catalyst,* 2010.

Chafetz, Janet Saltzman. *Gender Equity: An Integrated Theory of Stability and Change.* Newbury Park, Calif.: Sage, 1990.

Chafetz, Janet Saltzman, and Anthony Gary Dworkin. *Female Revolt: Women's Movements in World and Historical Perspective.* Totowa, N.J.: Rowman & Allanheld, 1986.

Collins, Randall, Janet Saltzman Chafetz, Rae Lesser Blumberg, Scott Coltrane, and Jonathan H. Turner. "Toward an Integrated Theory of Gender Stratification." *Sociological Perspectives, 36,* 3, 1993:185–216.

Cowley, Joyce. *Pioneers of Women's Liberation.* New York: Merit, 1969.

Crawford, Bridget J. "The Third Wave's Break from Feminism." *International Law in Context,* 2009.

Crossen, Cynthia. "Deja Vu." *Wall Street Journal,* March 5, 2003.

Dabbs, James M., Jr., and Robin Morris. "Testosterone, Social Class, and Antisocial Behavior in a Sample of 4,462 Men." *Psychological Science, 1,* 3, May 1990:209–211.

DeCrow, Karen. Foreword to *Why Men Earn More* by Warren Farrell. New York: AMACOM, 2005:xi–xii.

Eder, Donna. *School Talk: Gender and Adolescent Culture.* New Brunswick, N.J.: Rutgers University Press, 1995.

Ehrenreich, Barbara, and Deidre English. *Witches, Midwives, and Nurses: A History of Women Healers.* Old Westbury, N.Y.: Feminist Press, 1973.

Eisenhart, R. Wayne. "You Can't Hack It, Little Girl: A Discussion of the Covert Psychological Agenda of Modern Combat Training." *Journal of Social Issues, 31,* Fall 1975:13–23.

England, Paula. "The Impact of Feminist Thought on Sociology." *Contemporary Sociology: A Journal of Reviews,* 2000:263–267.

Falkenberg, Katie. "Pakistani Women Victims of 'Honor.'" *Washington Times,* July 23, 2008.

Fisher, Bonnie S., Francis T. Cullen, and Michael G. Turner. *The Sexual Victimization of College Women.* Washington, D.C.: U.S. Department of Justice, 2000.

Fisher, Bonnie S., Leah E. Daigle, Francis T. Cullen, and Michael G. Turner. "Reporting Sexual Victimization to the Police and Others: Results from a National-Level Study of College Women." *Criminal Justice and Behavior, 30,* 1, February 2003:6–38.

Foley, Douglas E. "The Great American Football Ritual." In *Society: Readings to Accompany Sociology: A Down-to-Earth Approach, Core Concepts,* James M. Henslin, ed. Boston: Allyn and Bacon, 2006: 64–76. Originally published 1990.

Freedman, Jane. *Feminism.* Philadelphia: Open University Press, 2001.

Friedl, Ernestine. "Society and Sex Roles." In *Conformity and Conflict: Readings in Cultural Anthropology,* James P. Spradley and David W. McCurdy, eds. Glenview, Ill.: Scott, Foresman, 1990:229–238.

Gallmeier, Charles P. "Methodological Issues in Qualitative Sport Research: Participant Observation among Hockey Players." *Sociological Spectrum, 8,* 1988:213–235.

Goldberg, Steven. *Why Men Rule: A Theory of Male Dominance.* Chicago: Open Court, 1993.

Goldberg, Steven. *Fads and Fallacies in the Social Sciences.* Amherst, N.Y.: Humanity/Prometheus, 2003.

Hacker, Helen Mayer. "Women as a Minority Group." *Social Forces, 30,* October 1951:60–69.

Hamid, Shadi. "Between Orientalism and Postmodernism: The Changing Nature of Western Feminist Thought towards the Middle East." *HAWWA, 4,* 1, 2006:76–92.

Harris, Kim, Dwight R. Sanders, Shaun Gress, and Nick Kuhns. "Starting Salaries for Agribusiness Graduates from an AAS-CARR Institution: The Case of Southern Illinois University." *Agribusiness, 21,* 1, 2005:65–80.

Harris, Marvin. "Why Men Dominate Women." *New York Times Magazine,* November 13, 1977:46, 115, 117–123.

Hendrix, Lewellyn. "What Is Sexual Inequality? On the Definition and Range of Variation." *Gender and Society, 28,* 3, August 1994:287–307.

Henslin, James, M. *Essentials of Sociology: A Down-to-Earth Approach,* 10th edition, Boston: Pearson, 2013.

Hook, Janet. "Another 'Year of Women' in Congress." *Wall Street Journal,* November 9, 2012.

Huber, Joan. "Micro-Macro Links in Gender Stratification." *American Sociological Review, 55,* February 1990:1–10.

Hundley, Greg. "Why Women Earn Less Than Men in Self-Employment." *Journal of Labor Research, 22,* 4, Fall 2001:817–827.

Hymowitz, Carol. "Through the Glass Ceiling." *Wall Street Journal,* November 8, 2004.

Hymowitz, Carol. "Raising Women to Be Leaders." *Wall Street Journal,* February 12, 2007.

Jacobs, Jerry A. "Detours on the Road to Equality: Women, Work and Higher Education." *Contexts,* Winter 2003:32–41.

Jneid, Hani, Gregg C. Fonarow, Christopher P. Cannon, et al. "Sex Differences in Medical Care and Early Death after Acute Myocardial Infarction." *Circulation,* December 8, 2008.

Leacock, Eleanor. *Myths of Male Dominance.* New York: Monthly Review Press, 1981.

Lerner, Gerda. *The Creation of Patriarchy.* New York: Oxford, 1986.

Linton, Ralph. *The Study of Man.* New York: Appleton-Century-Crofts, 1936.

Littleton, Heather, Carmen Radecki Breitkopf, and Abbey Berenson. "Women Beyond the Campus: Unacknowledged Rape among Low-Income Women." *Violence against Women, 14,* 3, March 2008:269–286.

Lurie, Nicole, Jonathan Slater, Paul McGovern, Jacqueline Ekstrum, Lois Quam, and Karen Margolis. "Preventive Care for Women: Does the Sex of the Physician Matter?" *New England Journal of Medicine, 329,* August 12, 1993:478–482.

Mattioli, Dana. "More Men Make Harassment Claims." *Wall Street Journal,* March 23, 2010.

Meltzer, Scott A. "Gender, Work, and Intimate Violence: Men's Occupational Spillover and Compensatory Violence." *Journal of Marriage and the Family, 64,* 2, November 2002:820–832.

Miller, Laura L. "Women in the Military." In *Down to Earth Sociology: Introductory Readings,* 14th ed., James M. Henslin, ed. New York: Free Press, 2007. Originally published 1997.

Murdock, George Peter. "Comparative Data on the Division of Labor by Sex." *Social Forces, 15,* 4, May 1937:551–553.

National Women's Political Caucus. "Factsheet on Women's Political Progress." Washington, D.C., June 1998.

National Women's Political Caucus. "Women in Congress," 2011.

Reiser, Christa. *Reflections on Anger: Women and Men in a Changing Society.* Westport, Conn.: Praeger Publishers, 1999.

Rosaldo, Michelle Zimbalist. "Women, Culture and Society: A Theoretical Overview." In *Women, Culture, and Society,* Michelle Zimbalist Rosaldo and Louise Lamphere, eds. Palo Alto, Calif.: Stanford University Press, 1974.

Rossi, Alice S. "A Biosocial Perspective on Parenting." *Daedalus, 106,* 1977:1–31.

Rossi, Alice S. "Gender and Parenthood." *American Sociological Review, 49,* 1984:1–18.

Roth, Louise Marie. "Selling Women Short: A Research Note on Gender Differences in Compensation on Wall Street." *Social Forces, 82,* 2, December 2003:783–802.

Rothman, Barbara Katz. "Midwives in Transition: The Structure of a Clinical Revolution." In *Dominant Issues in Medical Sociology,* 3rd ed., Howard D. Schwartz, ed. New York: McGraw-Hill, 1994:104–112.

Settles, Isis H., Zaje A. T. Harrell, NiCole T. Buchanan, and Stevie C. Y. Yap. "Frightened or Bothered: Two Types of Sexual Harassment Appraisals." *Social Psychological and Personality Science,* March 29, 2011.

Spivak, Gayatri Chakravorty. "Feminism 2000: One Step Beyond." *Feminist Review, 64,* Spring 2000:113.

Statistical Abstract of the United States. Washington, D.C.: U.S. Census Bureau, published annually.

Stockard, Jean, and Miriam M. Johnson. *Sex Roles: Sex Inequality and Sex Role Development.* Englewood Cliffs, N.J.: Prentice Hall, 1980.

Udry, J. Richard. "Biological Limits of Gender Construction." *American Sociological Review, 65,* June 2000:443–457.

VanderMey, Anne. "Fortune 500 Women CEOs." *CNN Money,* May 5, 2011.

Wade, Lisa. "Separate and Unequal." *Ms. Magazine,* April 12, 2011.

Wertz, Richard W., and Dorothy C. Wertz. "Notes on the Decline of Midwives and the Rise of Medical Obstetricians." In *The Sociology of Health and Illness: Critical Perspectives,* Peter Conrad and Rochelle Kern, eds. New York: St. Martin's Press, 1981:165–183.

Yakaboski, Tamara, and Leah Reinert, "Review of Women in Academic Leadership: Professional Strategies, Personal Choices." *Women in Higher Education, 4,* 1, 2011.

Yardley, Jim. "In India, Caste, Honor, and Killings Intertwine." *New York Times,* July 9, 2010a.

Zoepf, Katherine. "A Dishonorable Affair." *New York Times,* September 23, 2007.

CHAPTER 10

Amnesty International. "Decades of Human Rights Abuse in Iraq." www.amnestyusa.org, 2005.

Areddy, James T. "Chinese Concern on Inequality Rises." *Wall Street Journal,* October 17, 2012.

Arndt, William F., and F. Wilbur Gingrich. *A Greek-English Lexicon of the New Testament and Other Early Christian Literature.* Chicago: University of Chicago Press, 1957.

Batson, Andrew. "China Stimulus Tweaks Don't Redress Imbalances." *Wall Street Journal,* March 9, 2009.

Bell, Daniel. *The Coming of Post-Industrial Society: A Venture in Social Forecasting.* New York: Basic Books, 1973.

Bentley, Arthur Fisher. *The Process of Government: A Study of Social Pressures.* Chicago: University of Chicago Press, 1908.

Berger, Peter L. *Invitation to Sociology: A Humanistic Perspective.* New York: Doubleday, 1963.

Bridgwater, William, ed. *The Columbia Viking Desk Encyclopedia.* New York: Viking Press, 1953.

Burnham, Walter Dean. *Democracy in the Making: American Government and Politics.* Englewood Cliffs, N.J.: Prentice Hall, 1983.

Dahl, Robert A. *Who Governs?* New Haven, Conn.: Yale University Press, 1961.

Dahl, Robert A. *Dilemmas of Pluralist Democracy: Autonomy vs. Control.* New Haven, Conn.: Yale University Press, 1982.

Delaney, Arthur. "Revolving Door: 1447 Former Government Workers Lobby for Wall Street." *Huffington Post,* June 3, 2010.

Domhoff, G. William. *The Power Elite and the State: How Policy Is Made in America.* Hawthorne, N.Y.: Aldine de Gruyter, 1990.

Domhoff, G. William. *Who Rules America? Power and Politics in the Year 2000,* 3rd ed. Mountain View, Calif.: Mayfield Publishing, 1998.

Domhoff, G. William. *Who Rules America? Power, Politics, and Social Change,* 5th ed. New York: McGraw-Hill, 2006.

Domhoff, G. William. "C. Wright Mills, Power Structure Research, and the Failures of Mainstream Political Science." *New Political Science, 29,* 2007:97–114.

Elias, Paul. "'Molecular Pharmers' Hope to Raise Human Proteins in Crop Plants." *St. Louis Post-Dispatch,* October 28, 2001:F7.

Fischer, Claude S. *The Urban Experience.* New York: Harcourt, 1976.

Flannery, Russell. "Chinese Businessman Billionaire Days Don't Last Long." *Forbes,* June 2, 2011.

Form, William. "Comparative Industrial Sociology and the Convergence Hypothesis." *Annual Review of Sociology, 5,* 1, 1979.

Guthrie, Doug. "The Great Helmsman's Cultural Death." *Contexts, 7,* 3, Summer 2008:26–31.

Hellinger, Daniel, and Dennis R. Judd. *The Democratic Facade.* Pacific Grove, Calif.: Brooks/Cole, 1991.

Hippler, Fritz. Interview in a television documentary with Bill Moyers in *Propaganda,* in the series "Walk through the 20th Century," 1987.

"It's So Much Nicer on K Street." *New York Times,* June 8, 2008.

Kerr, Clark. *The Future of Industrialized Societies.* Cambridge, Mass.: Harvard University Press, 1983.

Kristoff, Nicholas D. "Interview with a Humanoid." *New York Times,* July 23, 2002.

Lemann, Nicholas. "Conflict of Interests." *New Yorker,* August 11, 2008.

Lipset, Seymour Martin. "The Social Requisites of Democracy Revisited." Presidential address to the American Sociological Association, Boston, Massachusetts, 1993.

Mills, C. Wright. *The Power Elite.* New York: Oxford University Press, 1956.

Mooallem, Jon. "Do-It-Yourself Genetic Engineering." *New York Times,* February 14, 2010.

Mosher, Steven W. "Why Are Baby Girls Being Killed in China?" *Wall Street Journal,* July 25, 1983:9.

Mosher, Steven W. "China's One-Child Policy: Twenty-Five Years Later." *Human Life Review,* Winter 2006:76–101.

Osborne, Lawrence. "Got Silk." *New York Times Magazine,* June 15, 2002.

"Pew Exit Poll." Washington D.C.: PEW Research Center. November 2012.

Rothkopf, David. *Superclass: The Global Power Elite and the World They Are Making.* New York: Farrar, Straus and Giroux, 2008.

Sageman, Marc. "Explaining Terror Networks in the 21st Century." *Footnotes,* May–June 2008a:7.

Sageman, Marc. *Leaderless Jihad: Terror Networks in the Twenty-First Century.* Philadelphia: University of Pennsylvania Press, 2008b.

Sengupta, Somini. "In the Ancient Streets of Najaf, Pledges of Martyrdom for Cleric." *New York Times,* July 10, 2004.

Sheets, Lawrence Scott, and William Broad. "Georgia Says It Blocked Smuggling of Arms-Grade Uranium." *New York Times,* January 25, 2007a.

Sheets, Lawrence Scott, and William J. Broad. "Smuggler's Plot Highlights Fear over Uranium." *New York Times,* January 25, 2007b.

Smith, Clark. "Oral History as 'Therapy': Combatants' Account of the Vietnam War." In *Strangers at Home: Vietnam Veterans Since the War,* Charles R. Figley and Seymore Leventman, eds. New York: Praeger, 1980:9–34.

Statistical Abstract of the United States. Washington D.C.: U.S. Census Bureau, published annually.

Timasheff, Nicholas S. *War and Revolution.* Joseph F. Scheuer, ed. New York: Sheed & Ward, 1965.

Toynbee, Arnold. *A Study of History,* D. C. Somervell, abridger and ed. New York: Oxford University Press, 1946.

Vidal, Jordi Blanes, Mirko Draca, and Christian Fons-Rosen. "Revolving Door Lobbyists." Center for Economic Performance, Discussion Paper 993, August 2010.

Weber, Max. *From Max Weber: Essays in Sociology,* Hans Gerth and C. Wright Mills, trans. and ed. New York: Oxford University Press, 1946.

Weber, Max. *The Theory of Social and Economic Organization,* A. M. Henderson and Talcott Parsons, trans., Talcott Parsons, ed. Glencoe, Ill.: Free Press, 1947. Originally published 1913.

Weber, Max. *Economy and Society,* G. Roth and C. Wittich, eds. Berkeley: University of California Press, 1978. Originally published 1922.

Wong, Janelle, S. Karthick Ramakrishnan, Taeku Lee, and Jane Junn. Asian American Political Participation: Emerging Constituents and Their Political Identities. New York: Russell Sage, 2011.

Yardley, Jim. "Soaring above India's Poverty, a 27-Story Home." *New York Times,* October 28, 2010b.

Yardley, Jim, and Keith Bradsher. "China, an Engine of Growth, Faces a Global Slump." *New York Times,* October 22, 2008.

Yenfang, Qian. "Fast Growth of Economy, Fast Rise of Wealthiest." *China Daily,* March 4, 2011.

Zachary, G. Pascal. "Behind Stocks' Surge Is an Economy in Which Big U.S. Firms Thrive." *Wall Street Journal,* November 22, 1995:A1, A5.

CHAPTER 11

Amato, Paul. "Research on Divorce: Continuing Trends and New Developments." *Journal of Marriage and Family, 72,* 3, June 2010: 650–666.

Amato, Paul R., and Jacob Cheadle. "The Long Reach of Divorce: Divorce and Child Well-Being across Three Generations." *Journal of Marriage and Family, 67,* February 2005:191–206.

Amato, Paul R., and Juliana M. Sobolewski. "The Effects of Divorce and Marital Discord on Adult Children's Psychological Well-Being." *American Sociological Review, 66,* 6, December 2001:900–921.

Belsky, Jay, Deborah Lowe Vandell, Margaret Burchinall, K. Alison Clarke-Stewart, Kathleen McCartney, and Margaret Tresch Owen. "Are There Long-Term Effects of Early Child Care?" *Child Development, 78,* 2, March/April 2007:681–701.

Bergmann, Barbara R. "The Future of Child Care." Paper presented at the annual meetings of the American Sociological Association, 1995.

Bernard, Tara Siegel. "The Key to Wedded Bliss? Money Matters." *New York Times,* September 10, 2008.

Bianchi, Suzanne M., and Lynne M. Casper. "American Families." *Population Bulletin, 55,* 4, December 2000:1–42.

Blau, David M. "The Production of Quality in Child-Care Centers: Another Look." *Applied Developmental Science, 4,* 3, 2000:136–148.

Blumstein, Philip, and Pepper Schwartz. *American Couples: Money, Work, Sex.* New York: Pocket Books, 1985.

Bronfenbrenner, Urie. "Principles for the Healthy Growth and Development of Children." In *Marriage and Family in a Changing Society,* 4th ed., James M. Henslin, ed. New York: Free Press, 1992:243–249.

Bryant, Chalandra M., R., D. Conger, and Jennifer M. Meehan. "The Influence of In-Laws on Changes in Marital Success." *Journal of Marriage and the Family, 63, 3,* August 2001:614–626.

Bryant, Chalandra M., K.A.S. Wickrama, John Boland, et al. "Race Matters, Even in Marriage: Identifying Factors Linked to Marital Outcomes for African Americans." *Journal of Family Theory and Review, 2,* 3, September 2010:157–174.

"Career Guide to Industries: 2010–11 Edition." Washington, D.C. Bureau of Labor Statistics 2011.

Cauce, Ana Mari, and Melanie Domenech-Rodriguez. "Latino Families: Myths and Realities." In *Latino Children and Families in the United States: Current Research and Future Directions,* Josefina M. Contreras, Kathryn A. Kerns, and Angela M. Neal-Barnett, eds. Westport, Conn.: Praeger, 2002:3–25.

Cherlin, J. Andrew. "Remarriage as an Incomplete Institution." In *Marriage and Family in a Changing Society,* 3rd ed., James M. Henslin, ed. New York: Free Press, 1989:492–501.

Coleman, Marilyn, Lawrence Ganong, and Mark Fine. "Reinvestigating Remarriage: Another Decade of Progress." *Journal of Marriage and the Family, 62,* 4, November 2000:1288–1307.

Crawford, Duane W., Renate M. Houts, Ted L. Huston, and Laura J. George. "Compatibility, Leisure, and Satisfaction in Marital Relationships." *Journal of Marriage and Family, 64,* May 2002:433–449.

Crossen, Cynthia. "Before Social Security, Most Americans Faced Very Bleak Retirement." *Wall Street Journal,* September 15, 2004b.

Cui, Ming, and Frank D. Fincham. "The Differential Effects of Parental Divorce and Marital Conflict on Young Adult Romantic Relationships." *Personal Relationships, 17,* 3, September 2010:331–343.

Dematteis, Lou. "Same-Sex Marriages, Civil Unions, and Domestic Partnerships." *New York Times,* July 11, 2011.

Dush, Claire M. Kamp, Catherine L. Cohan, and Paul R. Amato. "The Relationship between Cohabitation and Marital Quality and Stability: Change across Cohorts?" *Journal of Marriage and Family, 65,* 3, August 2003:539–549.

Dye, Jane Lawler. "Fertility of American Women: 2006." Washington, D.C. U.S. Census Bureau, August 2008.

Elliott, Diana B., and Jamie M. Lewis. "Embracing the Institution of Marriage: The Characteristics of Remarried Americans." Paper presented at the annual meetings of Population Association of America, April 17, 2010.

Elwert, Felix, and Nicholas A. Christakis. "The Effect of Widowhood on Mortality by the Causes of Death of Both Spouses." *American Journal of Public Health, 98,* 11, November 2008:2092–2098.

Eshleman, J. Ross. *The Family,* 9th ed. Boston: Allyn and Bacon, 2000.

Farr, Rachel H., Stephen L. Forssell, and Charlotte J. Patterson. "Parenting and Child Development in Adoptive Families: Does Parental Sexual Orientation Matter?" *Applied Developmental Science, 14,* 3, 2010:164–178.

Fisher, Helen E., Lucy L. Brown, Arthur Aron, Greg Strong, and Deborah Masek. "Reward, Addiction, and Emotion Regulation Systems Associated with Rejection in Love." *Journal of Neurophysiology, 104,* 2010:51–60.

Fremson, Ruth. "Dead Bachelors in Remote China Still Find Wives." *New York Times,* October 5, 2006.

Frosch, Dan. "Its Native Tongue Facing Extinction, Arapaho Tribe Teaches the Young." *New York Times,* October 17, 2008.

Gallup Poll. "America's Preference for Smaller Families Edge Higher." Princeton, N. J. Gallup Organization, June 30, 2011.

Gatewood, Willard B. *Aristocrats of Color: The Black Elite, 1880–1920.* Bloomington, Ind.: Indiana University Press, 1990.

Glenn, Evelyn Nakano. "Chinese American Families." In *Minority Families in the United States: A Multicultural Perspective,* Ronald L. Taylor, ed. Englewood Cliffs, N.J.: Prentice Hall, 1994:115–145.

Hall, J. Camille. "The Impact of Kin and Fictive Kin Relationships on the Mental Health of Black Adult Children of Alcoholics." *Health and Social Work, 33,* 4, November 2008:259–266.

Harford, Tim. "Why Divorce Is Good for Women." The Undercover Economist, *Slate,* January 16, 2008.

Hayashi, Gina M., and Bonnie R. Strickland. "Long-Term Effects of Parental Divorce on Love Relationships: Divorce as Attachment Disruption." *Journal of Social and Personal Relationships, 15*, 1, February 1998:23–38.

Hong, Lawrence. "Marriage in China." In *Til Death Do Us Part: A Multicultural Anthology on Marriage,* Sandra Lee Browning and R. Robin Miller, eds. Stamford, Conn.: JAI Press, 1999.

Huang, Penelope M., Pamela J. Smock, Wendy D. Manning, and Cara A. Bergstrom-Lynch. "He Says, She Says: Gender and Cohabitation." *Journal of Family Issues, 32,* February 2011.

Jankowiak, William R., and Edward F. Fischer. "A Cross-Cultural Perspective on Romantic Love." *Journal of Ethnology, 31,* 2, April 1992:149–155.

Jeong, Yu-Jin, and Hyun-Kyung You. "Different Historical Trajectories and Family Diversity among Chinese, Japanese, and Koreans in the United States." *Journal of Family History, 33,* 3, July 2008:346–356.

Kelly, Joan B. "How Adults React to Divorce." In *Marriage and Family in a Changing Society,* 4th ed., James M. Henslin, ed. New York: Free Press, 1992:410–423.

Koropeckyj-Cox, Tanya. "Attitudes about Childlessness in the United States." *Journal of Family Issues, 28,* 8, August 2007:1054–1082.

Lareau, Annette. "Invisible Inequality: Social Class and Childrearing in Black Families and White Families." *American Sociological Review, 67,* October 2002:747–776.

Lauer, Jeanette, and Robert Lauer. "Marriages Made to Last." In *Marriage and Family in a Changing Society,* 4th ed., James M. Henslin, ed. New York: Free Press, 1992:481–486.

LeDuff, Charlie. "Handling the Meltdowns of the Nuclear Family." *New York Times,* May 28, 2003.

Letherby, Gayle. "Childless and Bereft? Stereotypes and Realities in Relation to 'Voluntary' and 'Involuntary' Childlessness and Womanhood." *Sociological Inquiry, 72,* 1, Winter 2002:7–20.

Lichter, Daniel T., and ZhenchaoQian. "Serial Cohabitation and the Marital Life Course." *Journal of Marriage and Family, 70,* November 2008:861–878.

MacDonald, William L., and Alfred DeMaris. "Remarriage, Stepchildren, and Marital Conflict: Challenges to the Incomplete Institutionalization Hypothesis." *Journal of Marriage and the Family, 57,* May 1995:387–398.

Manning, Wendy D., and Jessica Cohen. "Premarital Cohabitation and Marital Dissolution: An Examination of Recent Marriages." Bowling Green State University: The Center for Family and Demographic Research, Working Paper Series 2010–11.

Masheter, Carol. "Postdivorce Relationships between Ex-Spouses: The Role of Attachment and Interpersonal Conflict." *Journal of Marriage and the Family, 53,* February 1991:103–110.

Mathews, T. J., and Brady E. Hamilton. "Delayed Childbearing: More Women Are Having Their First Child Later in Life." *NCHS Data Brief,* 21, Hyattsville, Md.: National Center for Health Statistics, August 2009:1–7.

McLanahan, Sara, and Gary Sandefur. *Growing Up with a Single Parent: What Hurts, What Helps.* Cambridge, Mass.: Harvard University Press, 1994.

McLanahan, Sara, and Dona Schwartz. "Life without Father: What Happens to the Children?" *Contexts, 1,* 1, Spring 2002:35–44.

Meyers, Laurie. "Asian-American Mental Health." *APA Online,* February 2006.

Murdock, George Peter. *Social Structure.* New York: Macmillan, 1949.

Richardson, Stacey, and Marita P. McCabe. "Parental Divorce during Adolescence and Adjustment in Early Adulthood." *Adolescence, 36,* Fall 2001:467–489.

Rubin, Zick. "The Love Research." In *Marriage and Family in a Changing Society,* 2nd ed., James M. Henslin, ed. New York: Free Press, 1985.

Russell, Diana E. H. "Preliminary Report on Some Findings Relating to the Trauma and Long-Term Effects of Intrafamily Childhood Sexual Abuse." Unpublished paper, no date.

Saenz, Rogelio. "Latinos and the Changing Face of America." Washington, D.C.: Population Reference Bureau, 2004:1–28.

Scommegna, Paola. "Increased Cohabitation Changing Children's Family Settings." *Population Today, 30,* 7, October 2002:3, 6.

Smith, Beverly A. "An Incest Case in an Early 20th-Century Rural Community." *Deviant Behavior, 13,* 1992:127–153.

Stack, Carol B. *All Our Kin: Strategies for Survival in a Black Community.* New York: Harper, 1974.

Staples, Brent. "Loving v. Virginia and the Secret History of Race." *New York Times,* May 14, 2008.

Statistical Abstract of the United States. Washington, D.C.: U.S. Census Bureau, published annually.

Stinnett, Nicholas. "Strong Families." In *Marriage and Family in a Changing Society,* 4th ed., James M. Henslin, ed. New York: Free Press, 1992:496–507.

Straus, Murray A. "Explaining Family Violence." In *Marriage and Family in a Changing Society,* 4th ed., James M. Henslin, ed. New York: Free Press, 1992:344–356.

Straus, Murray A. "Gender Symmetry and Mutuality in Perpetration of Clinical-level Partner Violence: Empirical Evidence and Implications for Prevention and Treatment." *Aggression and Violent Behavior, 16,* 2011:279–288.

Straus, Murray A., and Richard J. Gelles. "Violence in American Families: How Much Is There and Why Does It Occur?" In *Troubled Relationships,* Elam W. Nunnally, Catherine S. Chilman, and Fred M. Cox, eds. Newbury Park, Calif.: Sage, 1988:141–162.

Suzuki, Bob H. "Asian-American Families." In *Marriage and Family in a Changing Society,* 2nd ed., James M. Henslin, ed. New York: Free Press, 1985:104–119.

Sweeney, Megan M. "Remarriage and the Nature of Divorce: Does It Matter Which Spouse Chose to Leave?" *Journal of Family Issues, 23,* 3, April 2002:410–440.

Tasker, Fiona. "Same-Sex Parenting and Child Development: Reviewing the Contribution of Parental Gender." *Journal of Marriage and Family, 72,* 1, February 2010:35–40.

Todosijevic, Jelica, Esther D. Rothblum, and Sondra E. Solomon. "Relationship Satisfaction, Affectivity, and Specific Stressors in Same-Sex Couples Joined in Civil Unions." *Psychology of Women Quarterly, 29,* 2005:158–166.

Torres, Jose B., V. Scott H. Solberg, and Aaron H. Carlstrom. "The Myth of Sameness among Latino Men and Their Machismo." *American Journal of Orthopsychiatry, 72,* 2, 2002:163–181.

U.S. Census Bureau. "Annual Social and Economic Supplement to Current Population Survey." Washington, D.C.: U.S. Government Printing Office, 2010.

Vaughan, Diane. "Uncoupling: The Social Construction of Divorce." In *Marriage and Family in a Changing Society,* 2nd ed., James M. Henslin, ed. New York: Free Press, 1985:429–439.

Vega, William A. "Hispanic Families in the 1980s: A Decade of Research." *Journal of Marriage and the Family, 52,* November 1990:1015–1024.

Waldfogel, Jane, Terry-Ann Craigie, and Jeanne Brooks-Gunn. "Fragile Families and Child Wellbeing." In *Fragile Families, 20,* 2, Fall 2010:87–112.

Wallerstein, Judith S., Sandra Blakeslee, and Julia M. Lewis. *The Unexpected Legacy of Divorce: A 25-Year Landmark Study.* Concord, N.H.: Hyperion Press, 2001.

Wang, Hongyu, and Paul R. Amato. "Predictors of Divorce Adjustment: Stressors, Resources, and Definitions." *Journal of Marriage and the Family, 62,* 3, August 2000:655–668.

Wen, Ming. "Family Structure and Children's Health and Behavior." *Journal of Family Issues, 29,* 11, November 2008:1492–1519.

Whitehead, Barbara Dafoe, and David Popenoe. "The Marrying Kind: Which Men Marry and Why." Rutgers University: The State of Our Unions: The Social Health of Marriage in America, 2004.

Willie, Charles Vert, and Richard J. Reddick. *A New Look at Black Families,* 5th ed. Walnut Creek, Calif.: AltaMira Press, 2003.

Wilson, William Julius. "Jobless Poverty: A New Form of Social Dislocation in the Inner-City Ghetto." In *The Inequality Reader: Contemporary and Foundational Readings in Race, Class and Gender,* David B. Grusky and SzonjaSzelenyi, eds. Boulder, Calif.: Westview Press, 2007:142–152.

Wolfinger, Nicholas H. "More Evidence for Trends in the Intergenerational Transmission of Divorce: A Completed Cohort Approach Using Data from the General Social Survey." *Demography, 48,* 2011:581–592.

Ying, Yu-Wen, and Meekyung Han. "Parental Contributions to Southeast Asian American Adolescents' Well-Being." *Youth and Society, 40,* 2, December 2008:289–306.

Zamiska, Nicholas. "Pressed to Do Well on Admissions Tests, Students Take Drugs." *Wall Street Journal,* November 8, 2004.

CHAPTER 12

Anderson, Philip. "God and the Swedish Immigrants." *Sweden and America,* Autumn 1995:17–20.

Benford, Robert D. "The College Sports Reform Movement: Reframing the 'Educational' Industry." *The Sociological Quarterly, 48,* 2007:1–28.

Bosman, Julie. "New York Schools for Pregnant Girls Will Close." *New York Times,* May 24, 2007.

Bowles, Samuel. "Unequal Education and the Reproduction of the Social Division of Labor." In *Power and Ideology in Education,* J. Karabel and A. H. Halsely, eds. New York: Oxford University Press, 1977.

Bowles, Samuel, and Herbert Gintis. *Schooling in Capitalist America.* New York: Basic Books, 1976.

Bowles, Samuel, and Herbert Gintis. "*Schooling in Capitalist America* Revisited." *Sociology of Education, 75,* 2002:1–18.

Canedy, Dana. "Critics of Graduation Exam Threaten Boycott in Florida." *New York Times,* May 13, 2003.

Carnevale, Anthony P., and Stephen J. Rose. "Socioeconomic Status, Race/Ethnicity, and Selective College Admissions." New York: The Century Foundation, March 2003.

Carper, James C. "Pluralism to Establishment to Dissent: The Religious and Educational Context of Home Schooling." *Peabody Journal of Education, 75,* 1–2, 2000:8–19.

Coleman, James S., and Thomas Hoffer. *Public and Private Schools: The Impact of Communities.* New York: Basic Books, 1987.

Collins, Randall. *The Credential Society: An Historical Sociology of Education.* New York: Academic Press, 1979.

Davis, Kingsley, and Wilbert E. Moore. "Some Principles of Stratification." *American Sociological Review, 10,* 1945:242–249.

Deaver, Michael V. "Democratizing Russian Higher Education." *Demokratizatsiya, 9,* 3, Summer 2001:350–366.

Dhillon, Navtej, Amina Fahmy, and Djavad Salehi-Isfahani. "Egypt's Education System: Parents and Students Emerge as a New Force for Reform." Brookings, December 4, 2008.

Dove, Adrian. "Soul Folk 'Chitling' Test or the Dove Counterbalance Intelligence Test." Mimeo, no date.

Durkheim, Emile. *The Elementary Forms of the Religious Life.* New York: Free Press, 1965. Originally published 1912.

Elinson, Elaine. "Lifting the Veil on Government Surveillance." *ACLU News,* Spring 2004.

Elliott, Joel. "Birth Control Allowed for Maine Middle Schoolers." *New York Times,* October 18, 2007.

Ernst, Eldon G. "The Baptists." In *Encyclopedia of the American Religious Experience: Studies of Traditions and Movements,* Vol. 1, Charles H. Lippy and Peter W. Williams, eds. New York: Scribners, 1988:555–577.

Farkas, George. *Human Capital or Cultural Capital?: Ethnicity and Poverty Groups in an Urban School District.* New York: Walter DeGruyter, 1996.

Farkas, George, Robert P. Grobe, Daniel Sheehan, and Yuan Shuan. "Cultural Resources and School Success: Gender, Ethnicity, and Poverty Groups within an Urban School District." *American Sociological Review, 55,* February 1990a:127–142.

Farkas, George, Daniel Sheehan, and Robert P. Grobe. "Coursework Mastery and School Success: Gender, Ethnicity, and Poverty Groups within an Urban School District." *American Educational Research Journal, 27,* 4, Winter 1990b:807–827.

Gallup Poll. "Very Religious Americans Lead Healthier Lives." Princeton, N.J.: Gallup Organization, December 23, 2010.

Gamoran, Adam. "Tracking and Inequality: New Directions for Research and Practice." WCER, Working Paper 2009-6. Madison: University of Wisconsin–Madison: Wisconsin Center for Education Research, August 20, 2009.

Gauch, Sarah. "In Egyptian Schools, a Push for Critical Thinking." *Christian Science Monitor,* February 9, 2006.

Gillum, R. F. "Frequency of Attendance at Religious Services and Smoking: The Third National Health and Nutrition Examination Survey." *Preventive Medicine, 41,* 2005:607–613.

Greene, Jay P., and Marcus A. Winters. "Public High School Graduation and College-Readiness Rates, 1991–2002." Center for Civic Innovation at the Manhattan Institute. *Education Working Paper, 8,* 2005.

Hellinger, Daniel, and Dennis R. Judd. *The Democratic Facade.* Pacific Grove, Calif.: Brooks/Cole, 1991.

Jenkins, Philip. "The Next Christianity." *Atlantic Monthly,* October 2002:53–68.

Johnson, Benton. "On Church and Sect." *American Sociological Review, 28,* 1963:539–549.

Jones, Jeffrey Owen, and Peter Meyer. *The Pledge: A History of the Pledge of Allegiance.* New York: St. Martin's Press, 2010.

Kelley, Tina. "In an Era of School Shootings, a New Drill." *New York Times,* March 25, 2008.

LaFraniere, Sharon. "African Crucible: Cast as Witches, Then Cast Out." *New York Times,* November 15, 2007.

"Less Rote, More Variety: Reforming Japan's Schools." *The Economist,* December 16, 2000:8.

Marx, Karl. "Contribution to the Critique of Hegel's Philosophy of Right." In *Karl Marx: Early Writings,* T. B. Bottomore, ed. New York: McGraw-Hill, 1964:45. Originally published 1844.

McNeill, David. "Facing Enrollment Crisis, Japanese Universities Fight to Attract Students." *Chronicle of Higher Education,* July 11, 2008.

Medina, Jennifer. "U.S. Math Tests Find Scant Gains across New York." *New York Times,* October 14, 2009.

Merton, Robert K. *Social Theory and Social Structure.* Glencoe, Ill.: Free Press, 1949. Enlarged ed., 1968.

Nakamura, Akemi. "Abe to Play Hardball with Soft Education System." *The Japan Times,* October 27, 2006.

Nauta, André. "That They All May Be One: Can Denominationalism Die?" Paper presented at the annual meetings of the American Sociological Association, 1993.

Ouchi, William. "Decision-Making in Japanese Organizations." In *Down to Earth Sociology: Introductory Readings,* 7th ed., James M. Henslin, ed. New York: Free Press, 1993:503–507.

Parsons, Talcott. "An Analytic Approach to the Theory of Social Stratification." *American Journal of Sociology, 45,* 1940:841–862.

Pope, Liston. *Millhands and Preachers: A Study of Gastonia.* New Haven, Conn.: Yale University Press, 1942.

Rist, Ray C. "Student Social Class and Teacher Expectations: The Self-Fulfilling Prophecy in Ghetto Education." *Harvard Educational Review, 40,* 3, August 1970:411–451.

Rist, Ray C. "Student Social Class and Teacher Expectations: The Self-Fulfilling Prophecy in Ghetto Education." *Harvard Educational Review,* reprinted in *Opportunity Gap: Achievement and Inequality in Education,* Carol DeShano, James Philip Huguley, ZenubKakli, RadhikaRao, and Ronald F. Ferguson, eds. Cambridge, Mass.: Harvard Education Publishing Group, 2007:187–225.

Schemo, Diana Jean. "Education Dept. Says States Have Lax Standard for Teachers." *New York Times,* June 13, 2002.

Stark, Rodney. *Sociology,* 3rd ed. Belmont, Calif.: Wadsworth, 1989.

Statistical Abstract of the United States. Washington, D.C.: U.S. Census Bureau, published annually.

Thompson, Ginger. "Where Education and Assimilation Collide." *New York Times,* March 14, 2009.

Tomsho, Robert, and Daniel Golden. "Educating Eric." *Wall Street Journal,* May 12, 2007.

Troeltsch, Ernst. *The Social Teachings of the Christian Churches.* New York: Macmillan, 1931.

UNESCO. "UNESCO Launches Global Partnership for Girls and Women's Education." June 2011.

UNESCO. "Egypt." World Data on Education, 7th ed., May 2012.

U.S. Department of Education, National Center for Education Statistics. "Projections of Education Statistics to 2017," September 2008:Table 10.

Urbina, Ian. "As School Exit Tests Prove Tough, States Ease Standards." *New York Times,* January 11, 2010a.

Wallace, John M., Ryoko Yamaguchi, Jerald G. Bachman, Patrick M. O'Malley, John E. Schulenberg, and Lloyd D. Johnston. "Religiosity and Adolescent Substance Use: The Role of Individual and Contextual Influences." *Social Problems, 54*, 2, 2007:308–327.

White, Jack E. "Forgive Us Our Sins." *Time,* July 3, 1995:29.

Yamamoto, Yoko, and Mary C. Brinton. "Cultural Capital in East Asian Educational Systems: The Case of Japan." *Sociology of Education, 83*, 1, 2010:67–83.

CHAPTER 13

Anderson, Elijah. *Streetwise: Race, Class, and Change in an Urban Community.* Chicago: University of Chicago Press, 1990.

Anderson, Elizabeth. "Recent Thinking about Sexual Harassment: A Review Essay." *Philosophy & Public Affairs, 34*, 3, 2006:284–312.

Burgess, Ernest W. "The Growth of the City: An Introduction to a Research Project." In *The City,* Robert E. Park et al., eds. Chicago: University of Chicago Press, 1925:47–62.

Chandler, Tertius, and Gerald Fox. *3000 Years of Urban Growth.* New York: Academic Press, 1974.

Chishti, Muzaffar, and Claire Bergeron. "Increasing Evidence That Recession Has Caused Number of Unauthorized Immigrants in US to Drop." Washington, D.C.: Migration Policy Institute, March 15, 2010.

Darley, John M., and Bibb Latané. "Bystander Intervention in Emergencies: Diffusion of Responsibility." *Journal of Personality and Social Psychology, 8, 4*, 1968:377–383.

Dougherty, Conor. "The End of White Flight." *Wall Street Journal,* July 19, 2008a.

Dougherty, Conor. "The New American Gentry." *Wall Street Journal,* January 19, 2008b.

Faunce, William A. *Problems of an Industrial Society,* 2nd ed. New York: McGraw-Hill, 1981.

Fischer, Claude S. *The Urban Experience.* New York: Harcourt, 1976.

Flanagan, William G. *Urban Sociology: Images and Structure.* Boston: Allyn and Bacon, 1990.

Fountain, Henry. "Archaeological Site in Peru Is Called Oldest City in Americas." *New York Times,* April 27, 2001.

Gans, Herbert J. *The Urban Villagers.* New York: Free Press, 1962.

Gans, Herbert J. *People and Plans: Essays on Urban Problems and Solutions.* New York: Basic Books, 1968.

Gans, Herbert J. *People, Plans, and Policies: Essays on Poverty, Racism, and Other National Urban Problems.* New York: Columbia University Press, 1991.

Gettleman, Jeffrey. "Starvation and Strife Menace Torn Kenya." *New York Times,* February 28, 2009.

Goll, Sven. "Archaeologists Find 'Mini-Pompeii.'" *Views and News from Norway,* October 1, 2010.

Greenhalgh, Susan. "The Chinese Biopolitical: Facing the Twenty-First Century." *New Genetics and Society, 28*, 3, September 2009:205–222.

Harris, Chauncey D. "The Nature of Cities and Urban Geography in the Last Half Century." *Urban Geography, 18*, 1997.

Harris, Chauncey D., and Edward Ullman. "The Nature of Cities." *Annals of the American Academy of Political and Social Science, 242*, 1945:7–17.

Haub, Carl. "Population Data Sheet." Washington, D.C.: Population Reference Bureau, 2011.

Haub, Carl, and Mary Mederlos Kent. "World Population Data Sheet." Washington, D.C.: Population Reference Bureau, 2008.

Haub, Carl, and Nancy Yinger. "*The U.N. Long-Range Population Projections: What They Tell Us.*" Washington, D.C.: Population Reference Bureau, 1994.

Hauser, Philip, and Leo Schnore, eds. *The Study of Urbanization.* New York: Wiley, 1965.

Hawley, Amos H. *Urban Society: An Ecological Approach.* New York: Wiley, 1981.

Homblin, Dora Jane. *The First Cities.* Boston: Little, Brown, Time-Life Books, 1973.

Hoyt, Homer. *The Structure and Growth of Residential Neighborhoods in American Cities.* Washington, D.C.: Federal Housing Administration, 1939.

Hoyt, Homer. "Recent Distortions of the Classical Models of Urban Structure." In *Internal Structure of the City: Readings on Space and Environment,* Larry S. Bourne, ed. New York: Oxford University Press, 1971:84–96.

Karp, David A., Gregory P. Stone, and William C. Yoels. *Being Urban: A Sociology of City Life,* 2nd ed. New York: Praeger, 1991.

Kramer, Andrew E. "Putin Needs Higher Oil Prices to Pay for Campaign Promises." New York Times, March 16, 2012.

Katz, Bruce, and Jennifer Bradley. "The Suburban Challenge." *Newsweek,* January 26, 2009.

Kramer, Andrew E. "Putin Needs Higher Oil Prices to Pay for Campaign Promises." *New York Times*, March 16, 2012.

Lenski, Gerhard, and Jean Lenski. *Human Societies: An Introduction to Macrosociology,* 5th ed. New York: McGraw-Hill, 1987.

Malthus, Thomas Robert. *First Essay on Population 1798.* London: Macmillan, 1926. Originally published 1798.

Mamdani, Mahmood. "The Myth of Population Control: Family, Caste, and Class in an Urban Village." New York: Monthly Review Press, 1973.

McFalls, Joseph A., Jr. "Population: A Lively Introduction, 5th ed." *Population Bulletin, 62*, 1, March 2007:1–30.

McKeown, Thomas. *The Modern Rise of Population.* New York: Academic Press, 1977.

McKinnish, Terra, Randall Walsh, and Kirk White. "Who Gentrifies Low-Income Neighborhoods?" National Bureau of Economic Research, Working Paper 14036, May 2008.

McNeill, William H. "How the Potato Changed the World's History." *Social Research, 66,* 1, Spring 1999:67–83.

Milbank, Dana. "Guarded by Greenbelts, Europe's Town Centers Thrive." *Wall Street Journal,* May 3, 1995:B1, B4.

Mosher, Steven W. "Too Many People? Not by a Long Shot." *Wall Street Journal,* February 10, 1997:A18.

Mosher, Steven W. "China's One-Child Policy: Twenty-Five Years Later." *Human Life Review,* Winter 2006:76–101.

Palen, J. John. *The Urban World,* 9th ed. Boulder, Colo.: Paradigm Publishers, 2012.

Park, Robert Ezra. "Human Ecology." *American Journal of Sociology, 42,* 1, July 1936:1–15.

Park, Robert Ezra, and Ernest W. Burgess. *Human Ecology.* Chicago: University of Chicago Press, 1921.

Santos, Fernanda. "Are New Yorkers Satisfied? That Depends." *New York Times,* March 7, 2009.

State of the World: Innovations that Nourish the Planet. Washington, D.C.: Worldwatch Institute, 2011.

Statistical Abstract of the United States. Washington, D.C.: U.S. Census Bureau, published annually.

Thurow, Roger. "Farms Destroyed, Stricken Sudan Faces Food Crisis." *Wall Street Journal,* February 7, 2005.

Ullman, Edward, and Chauncey Harris. "The Nature of Cities." In *Urban Man and Society: A Reader in Urban Ecology,* Albert N. Cousins and Hans Nagpaul, eds. New York: Knopf, 1970:91–100.

Wilford, John Noble. "In Maya Ruins, Scholars See Evidence of Urban Sprawl." *New York Times,* December 19, 2000.

Wirth, Louis. "Urbanism as a Way of Life." *American Journal of Sociology, 44,* July 1938:1–24.

CHAPTER 14

Adam, David. "Climate: The Hottest Year." *Nature, 468,* November 15, 2010:362–364.

Agar, John. "Man Linked to Earth Liberation Front Members Accused in Wexford County Arson." *Grand Rapids Press,* April 12, 2011.

American Sociological Association. "Section on Environment and Technology." Pamphlet, no date.

Barnes, Harry Elmer. *The History of Western Civilization,* Vol. 1. New York: Harcourt, Brace, 1935.

Bell, Michael Mayerfeld. *An Invitation to Environmental Sociology.* Los Angeles: Pine Forge Press, 2009.

Blomfield, Adrian. "Putin Vows to Aim Nukes at Europe." *London Daily Telegraph,* June 4, 2007.

Boudreaux, Richard. "Putin Move Stirs Russian Environmentalist Row." *New York Times,* January 20, 2010.

Bradsher, Keith. "China Enacting a High-Tech Plan to Track People." *New York Times,* August 12, 2007.

Bumiller, Elisabeth, and Thom Shanker. "Panetta Warns of Dire Threat of Cyberattack on U.S." *New York Times,* October 11, 2012.

Carpenter, Betsy. "Redwood Radicals." *U.S. News & World Report, 109,* 11, September 17, 1990:50–51

Crossland, David. "Gas Dispute Has Europe Trembling." *Spiegel Online,* January 2, 2006.

Dunlap, Riley E., and William R. Catton, Jr. "Environmental Sociology." *Annual Review of Sociology, 5,* 1979:243–273.

Dunlap, Riley E., and William R. Catton, Jr. "What Environmental Sociologists Have in Common Whether Concerned with 'Built' or 'Natural' Environments." *Sociological Inquiry, 53,* 2–3, 1983:113–135.

Eder, Klaus. "The Rise of Counter-Culture Movements against Modernity: Nature as a New Field of Class Struggle." *Theory, Culture & Society, 7,* 1990:21–47.

Fahim, Kareem. "Slap to a Man's Pride Set Off Tumult in Tunisia." *New York Times,* January 22, 2011.

Fattig, Paul. "Good Intentions Gone Bad." *Mail Tribune,* June 6, 2007.

Foote, Jennifer. "Trying to Take Back the Planet." *Newsweek, 115,* 6, February 5, 1990:24–25.

Frommer, Arthur. *Peru.* New York: Wiley, 2007.

Gerken, James. "Arctic Ice Melt, Sea Level Rise May Pose Imminent Threat to Island Nations, Climate Scientist Says." Huffington Post, October 5, 2012.

Guessous, Fouad, Thorsten Juchem, and Norbert A. Hampp. In *Optical Security and Counterfeit Deterrence Techniques,* Rudolf L. vanRenesse, ed. Proceedings of the SPIE, *5310,* 2004.

Gunther, Marc. "The Mosquito in the Tent." *Fortune, 149,* 11, May 31, 2004:158.

Hughes, H. Stuart. *Oswald Spengler: A Critical Estimate,* rev. ed. New York: Scribner's, 1962.

Knickerbocker, Brad. "Firebrands of 'Ecoterrorism' Set Sights on Urban Sprawl." *Christian Science Monitor,* August 6, 2003.

Kramer, Andrew E. "Putin's Grasp of Energy Drives Russian Agenda." *New York Times,* January 29, 2009.

Larson, Christina. "Green Activists Feel Sting of Chinese Government Crackdown." Yale 360, June 30, 2011.

Lenski, Gerhard, and Jean Lenski. *Human Societies: An Introduction to Macrosociology,* 5th ed. New York: McGraw-Hill, 1987.

Lerner, Steve. *Sacrifice Zones: The Front Lines of Toxic Chemical Exposure in the United States.* Cambridge, Mass.: MIT Press, 2010.

McElroy, Damien. "Russian General Says Poland a Nuclear 'Target.'" *Telegraph,* August 15, 2008.

Morgan, Lewis Henry. *Ancient Society.* New York: Holt, 1877.

Ogburn, William F. *Social Change with Respect to Culture and Human Nature.* New York: W. B. Huebsch, 1922. (Other editions by Viking in 1927, 1938, and 1950.)

Ogburn, William F. "The Hypothesis of Cultural Lag." In *Theories of Society: Foundations of Modern Sociological Theory,* Vol. 2, Talcott Parsons, Edward Shils, Kaspar D. Naegele, and Jesse R. Pitts, eds. New York: Free Press, 1961:1270–1273.

Ogburn, William F. *On Culture and Social Change: Selected Papers,* Otis Dudley Duncan, ed. Chicago: University of Chicago Press, 1964.

Page, Jeremy. "China's New Drones Raise Eyebrows." *Wall Street Journal,* November 18, 2010.

Perry, Nick. "Kiribati Global Warming Fears: Entire Nation May Move to Fiji." *Huffington Post,* March 9, 2012.

Reed, Susan, and Lorenzo Benet. "Ecowarrior Dave Foreman Will Do Whatever It Takes in His Fight to Save Mother Earth." *People Weekly, 33,* 15, April 16, 1990:113–116.

Rhoads, Christopher, and Farnaz Fassihi. "Iran Vows to Unplug Internet." *Wall Street Journal,* May 28, 2011.

Rogers, Simon, and Lisa Evans. "World Carbon Dioxide Emissions Data by Country: China Speeds Ahead of the Rest." *Guardian,* January 31, 2011.

Sahlins, Marshall D., and Elman R. Service. *Evolution and Culture.* Ann Arbor: University of Michigan Press, 1960.

Sanger, David E., and Elisabeth Bumiller. "Pentagon to Consider Cyberattacks Acts of War." *New York Times,* May 31, 2011.

Sanger, David E., John Markoff, and Thom Shanker. "U.S. Plans Attack and Defense in Cyberspace Warfare." *New York Times,* April 27, 2009.

Sharp, Lauriston. "Steel Axes for Stone-Age Australians." In *Down to Earth Sociology: Introductory Readings,* 8th ed., James M. Henslin, ed. New York: Free Press, 1995:453–462.

Smart, Barry. "On the Disorder of Things: Sociology, Postmodernity and the 'End of the Social.'" *Sociology, 24,* 3, August 1990:397–416.

Spengler, Oswald. *The Decline of the West,* 2 vols., Charles F. Atkinson, trans. New York: Knopf, 1926–1928. Originally published 1919–1922.

Stein, Rob. "FDA Approves Implantable Identity Chip." *Washington Post,* October 14, 2004.

"Threatened Island Nations: Legal Implications of Rising Seas and a Changing Climate." New York: Columbia University, Conference at Columbia Law School, May 23–25, 2011.

Toynbee, Arnold. *A Study of History,* D. C. Somervell, abridged and ed. New York: Oxford University Press, 1946.

Vergakis, Brock. "Bill Would Limit Future Utah Nuclear Power Plants." Associated Press, February 12, 2009.

Wall, Robert. "China's Armed Predator." *Aviation Week,* November 17, 2010.

Wong, Gillian. "Wife Visits Jailed China Activist Ahead of Release." Associated Press, June 20, 2011.

World Bank. "Cost of Pollution in China: Economic Estimates of Physical Damages." Washington, D.C: World Bank, February 2007.

Zakaria, Fareed. *The Post-American World.* New York: W. W. Norton, 2008.

CREDITS

Newscom; 184, James Henslin; 185L, Everett Collection; 185R, David Urbina/PhotoEdit; 187, Tibor Bognar/Alamy; 188–189, James Henslin; 191, Borderland/Alamy; 192, hc/Fotolia LLC; 196, REB Images/Blend Images/Alamy; 199, Wu Fong/EyePress EyePress/Newscom; 201, Brocreative,/Shutterstock; 204, Robin Nelson/PhotoEdit; 205, Paul Sakuma/AP Photos; 207, George Burns/AFP/Getty Images/Newscom; 209, Ivanova Inga/Shutterstock; 211, Ron T. Ennis/MCT/Newscom; 212, Imagestate Media Partners Limited—Impact Photos/Alamy; 213, Andreas Gebert/dpa/picture-alliance/Newscom; 215, Comstock/Jupiter Images/Getty Images/Thinkstock; 217T, ZUMA Press/Newscom; 217B, Creators Syndicate; 219L, altanaka/Shutterstock; 219R, Sascha Burkard/Shutterstock.

CHAPTER 8

226, Dick Doughty/HAGA/The Image Works; 227, Peter Titmuss/Alamy; 228, Celia Mannings/Alamy; 229TL, Time Life Pictures/National Archives/Time Life Pictures/Getty Images; 229TR, akg-images/Newscom; 229B, Les Stone/ZUMA Press/Newscom; 231, Jenny Matthews/Alamy; 233, Fred Blackwell; 235, Jesicca Griffin/AP Images, Lincoln Journal Star, Ken Blackbird/AP Images, Robert Galbraith/Reuters/Corbis, Rick Wilking/Reuters/Landov, Lee Snider/The Image Works; 237, Mike Fox/ZUMA Press/Newscom; 238, Keith Wood/Stone/Getty Images; 241, Mario Mitsis/Alamy; 242, Bill Hudson/AP Images; 243, o44/ZUMA Press/Newscom; 245, PhotosToGo/Index Stock Imagery; 251, PASSEMARD/CL2P/SIPA/Newscom; 253, files UPI Photo Service/Newscom; 254, Photoshot/Newscom; 257L, Richard Maschmeyer/Robert Harding World Imagery/Alamy; 257R, Alain Evrard/Glow Images; 259, Doug James/Alamy; 260, ZUMA Wire Service/Alamy; 262, Tom McCarthy/PhotoEdit; 264, maxstockphoto/Shutterstock.

CHAPTER 9

269, Jim West/The Image Works; 270, Chad Ehlers/Alamy; 271, STOCK4B-RF/Glow Images; 272, Claudia Adams/Danita Delimont/Alamy, Ajit Solanki/AP Images, Jake Warga/Corbis, Reuters/Corbis, Marco Simoni/Robert Harding World Imagery/Corbis, Robert Harding Picture Library/SuperStock, Pacific Stock/SuperStock; 273, Arvind Balaraman/Shutterstock; 274L, Picture Partners/Alamy; 274R, Bettmann/Corbis; 276, Dr. Margorius 2010/Shutterstock; 277, Bildagentur-online/McPhoto/Alamy; 279, Trinity Mirror/Mirrorpix/Alamy; 282, AVAVA/Fotolia; 284–285, James Henslin; 287, Angela Hampton Picture Library/Alamy; 289, Zhang jusheng—Imaginechina/AP Images; 291, Cultura Creative/Alamy; 293, Photofusion Picture Library/Alamy; 295L, Luca Tettoni/Robert Harding Picture Library Ltd./Alamy; 295R, Dan Vincent/Alamy; 298, Mandel Ngan/AFP/Getty Images/Newscom.

CHAPTER 10

305, SFC/Shutterstock; 307, Everett Collection; 308, Dennis Brack/Newscom; 309, Ivy Close Images/Alamy; 311, SIPA/Newscom; 313L, Chris Hondros/Getty Images News/Getty Images; 313R, Igor Kovalenko/EPA/Newscom; 316T, Bill Clark/Roll Call Photos/Newscom; 316B, Matt Trommer/Shutterstock; 320, Universal UClick; 321, Scott J. Ferrell/Congressional Quarterly/Newscom; 322, Department of Defense; 324, DoD photo by Sgt. Cooper T. Cash, U.S. Army; 325, Stacy Walsh Rosenstock/Alamy; 327, Jim Bryant/UPI/Newscom; 330, Darren Baker/Shutterstock; 332, JTB Photo/SuperStock; 333, Gavin Hellier/Robert Harding Picture Library Ltd/Alamy; 335, Ju Huanzong/Xinhua/Photoshot/Newscom; 337, Voloh/Fotolia; 340–341, James Henslin; 342, Mark Johnston/dpa/picture-alliance/Newscom; 343, Kerim Okten/EPA/Newscom.

CHAPTER 11

350, Dita Alangkara/AP Photos; 351, Mark Baker/AP Photos; 353, Jason Love/CartoonStock Ltd.; 355, Ariel Skelley/Blend Images/Alamy; 356, John Dowland/PhotoAlto sas/Alamy; 360, Mark Scott/Alamy; 362, Monkey Business Images/Shutterstock; 365, Maria Galan/age fotostock/Robert Harding World Imagery; 367, Mark Burnett/Alamy; 369, rSnapshotPhotos/Shutterstock; 372, Janie Airey Cultura/Newscom; 374, Monkey Business Images/Shutterstock; 377, HO/AFP/Getty Images/Newscom; 379, Center for Talent Innovation; 382, Jiang Jin/Purestock/Alamy; 383, Bob D'Amico/ABC via Getty Images.

CHAPTER 12

388, Pascal Deloche/Godong/picture alliance/Godong/Newscom; 390, Yoshikazu Tsuno/AFP/GETTY IMAGES/Newscom; 391, frans lemmens/Alamy; 393, Bob Daemmrich/PhotoEdit; 394, WpN/UPPA/Photoshot; 395, Allan Munsie/Alamy; 396, Bob Daemmrich/PhotoEdit; 398, Ciro CesarR/La Opinion/Newscom; 399, ZUMA Press/Newscom; 400, Bob Daemmrich/PhotoEdit; 402, Ruaridh Stewart/ZUMA Press/Newscom; 403, Jose Luis Gonzalez/Stringer Mexico/Reuters; 404, Hanan Isachar/Alamy; 405, Steve Vidler/SuperStock; 406, Jim West/Alamy; 407, North Wind/North Wind Picture Archives; 409, David Pearson/Alamy; 410, James Henslin; 411, casejustin/Shutterstock, Christopher Poliquin/Shutterstock, Georgios Kollidas/Shutterstock; 412–413, James Henslin; 416, Myrleen Ferguson Cate/PhotoEdit.

CHAPTER 13

425, India Images/Dinodia Photos/Alamy; 426, Antonio S/Shutterstock; 429, Jeffrey Blackler/Alamy; 431, The Guardian/Alamy; 432, Allan Ivy/Alamy; 435, BSA/ZOJ WENN Photos/Newscom; 436, k94/ZUMA Press/Newscom; 439, Heritage Imagestate/Glow Images; 441, Photo Researchers/Photoshot; 442–443, James Henslin; 444, age fotostock/SuperStock; 447, Kim Karpeles/Alamy; 449, Mira/Alamy; 452, David R. Frazier Photolibrary, Inc./Alamy; 453, Richard Lord/PhotoEdit; 454, AF archive/Alamy; 456, Gerry Rousseau/Alamy; 457, James Henslin; 459L, Kevin Lamarque/Reuters/Landov; 459R, Ambient Images/Peter BennettAmbient Images/Peter Bennett/Glow Images.

CHAPTER 14

465, Dave Pusey/Shutterstock; 466, Phil Borges/DanitaDelimont.com "Danita Delimont; 468, Markus Schreiber/AFP/Getty

Images/Newscom; 469, Yves Herman/Reuters/Landov; 470, STR/AFP/Getty Images/Newscom; 471, Meunie Pierre/ABACA/ Newscom; 474, Bill Bachmann/DanitaDelimont.com "Danita Delimont Photography"/Newscom; 475, Joseph Reid/Alamy; 477, Gary C. Caskey/UPI/Newscom; 478, Salah Habibi/AP Photos; 479, Science Faction/SuperStock; 480, ChinaFotoPress/ Liu Yanmin/ChinFotoPress/Newscom; 482, Romeo Gacad/AFP/ Getty Images/Newscom; 484T, Marijan Murat/dpa/picture-alliance/Newscom; 484B, Kyodo/Newscom; 485, Mira Oberman/ AFP/Getty Images/Newscom; 486, jn1/ZUMA Press/Newscom.

TEXT CREDITS
CHAPTER 1

8, Fig. 1.1, Table adapted from *2010 World Population Data Sheet* by Carl Haub, 2010. Copyright © 2010 by The Population Reference Bureau. Reprinted with permission; 13, Fig 1.3, Based on DeMartini 1982.

CHAPTER 2

33, Fig. 2.3, Based on Statistical Abstract of the United States 1998: Table 92 and 2010: Tables 78, 129.

CHAPTER 3

60, "A man who walks down a street . . ." Ian Robertson (1987:62); 61, "There are things we know that we know . . ." Donald Rumsfeld quoted in Dickey and Barry 2006: 38; 61, Excerpt from *Countercultures: A Sociological Analysis* by William W. Zellner, 1995. Copyright © 1995 by St. Martins Press. Reprinted with permission of Worth Publishers.

CHAPTER 4

78, "The naked child was found in the forest . . ." Itard 1962; 79, Excerpt from "Extreme Isolation of a Child" by Kingsley Davis, from *American Journal of Sociology,* January 4, 1940, Volume 45. Copyright © 1940 by the Kingsley David Estate. Reprinted with permission; 79, "Apparently Genie's father was 70 years old when . . ." based on The Civilizing of Genie by Maya Pines in Psychology Today, September 1981; 80, Excerpt from "A Study of the Effects of Differential Stimulation on Mentally Retarded Children" by H.M. Skeels and H.B. Dye, from Proceedings and Addresses of the American Association on Mental Deficiency, 1939, Volume 44. Copyright © 1939 by AAID. Reprinted with permission; 80, Excerpt from "A Study of the Effects of Differential Stimulation on Mentally Retarded Children" by H.M. Skeels and H.B. Dye, from Proceedings and Addresses of the American Association on Mental Deficiency, 1939, Volume 44. Copyright © 1939 by AAID. Reprinted with permission; 89, "Goldberg and Lewis asked mothers to bring their . . ." based on Play Behavior in the Year-Old Infant: Early Sex Differences by Goldberg and Lewis in *Child Development* 1969; 89, Hannamariah/Shutterstock; 89, Excerpt from *School Talk: Gender and Adolescent Culture* by Donna Eder. Copyright © 1995 by Donna Eder. Reprinted with permission of Rutgers University Press; 94, Patricia

and Peter Adler, 1998; 98, "A common moral lesson involved taking children . . ." based on Our Forebears Made Childhood a Nightmare by Lloyd DeMause in Psychology Today, April 197; 99, Fig. 4.2, Figure from "Growing up is Harder to do" by Frank F. Furstenburg, Sheela Kennedy, Vonnie C. McLoyd, Ruben G. Rumbaut and Richard A. Settersten, JR., from *Contexts,* Volume 3(2), Summer 2004. Copyright © 2004 by SAGE.

CHAPTER 5

123, Excerpt from *The Sounds of Silence* by Edward T. Hall and Mildred R. Hall, originally published by Playboy Magazine, 1971. Copyright © by Edward T. Hall Associates. Reprinted with permission; 127, "It was their big day, two years in the making . . ." based on Even Tiki Torches Don't Guarantee a Perfect Wedding by Kathleen A. Hughes in *The Wall Street Journal;* 134, *Studies in Ethnomethodology,* 1967.

CHAPTER 6

145, Excerpt from *Yanomano,* 2nd Edition, by Napoleon Chagnon. Copyright © 1997 by Wadsworth, a part of Cengage Learning, Inc. Reprinted with permission. www.cengage.com/ permissions; 152, Based on Ruth Horowitz (1983, 2005); 156, Table 6.1, Based on Merton, 1968; 159, Fig. 6.1, Based on Statistical Abstract of the United States, Table 304, 2011; 159, Table 6.2, Table 330 from Statistical Abstract of the United States; 161, Based on Military Contractor Agrees to Pay $325 Million to Settle Whistle-Blower Lawsuit in the *New York Times;* 163, Fig. 6.2, Based on Statistical Abstract of the United States, Table 349 (1995); TABLE 335 (2010; 164, Table 6.3, Based on *Sourcebook of Criminal Justice Statistics* 2003: Tables 6.000b, 6.28; 2006: Tables 6.34, 6.45; 2009: Table 6.33; 2008; 166, Fig. 6.3, Based on *Sourcebook of Criminal Justice Statistics,* Table 6.5; 168, Fig. 6.4, Statistical Abstract of the United States, Table 341; 169, Based on Statistical Abstract of the United States, Table 340, 2010; 170, Table 6.4, Based on *Sourcebook of Criminal Justice Statistics* 2010: Table 6.80 and Figure 12.5; 172, Table 318 from Statistical Abstract of the United States, 2011; 176, "Imagine a society of saints, a perfect cloister . . ." Durkheim (1895/1964:68) Originally published 1893; 176, Susan Pfannmuller/MCT/Newscom.

CHAPTER 7

190, Fig. 7.1, Based on CIA World Factbook 2010; 194–195, Fig. 7.2, Based on Beeghley, 2008; 197, John James/Alamy; 202, Fig. 7.4. Based on Beeghley, 2008.; 202, Fig 7.5, Based on *Statistical Abstract of the United States,* 2011.; 203, Fig. 7.6, Based on DeNavas-Walt, et al., 2010: Table 3 and *Statistical Abstract of the United States,* Table 417; 1970: Table 489; 2011: Table 693, 1960; 205, Table 7.5, Based on Treiman 1977: Appendices A and D; Nakao and Treas 1990, 1994: Appendix D; 208, Fig. 7.7, Based on Gilbert and Kahl 1998 and Gilbert 2008; income estimates are modified from Duff, 1995; 209, Excerpt from *The American Class Structure: A New Synthesis* by Dennis Gilbert and Joseph A. Kahl, 4th Ed. Copyright © by Dennis Gilbert. Reprinted with permission; 211, Cohen, 2004; 218, Fig. 7.8, based on *Statistical Abstract of the United States,* 2010: Table 36, 694, and 697; 220, Fig. 7.9, Based on Fertility of American Women: June 2008, Current Population Reports, by Jane Lawler Dye, U.S. Census Bureau, Washington, DC, 2010, Table 3.

CHAPTER 8

231, Excerpt from *Racial and Ethnic Groups* by Richard T. Schaefer, 9th Ed. Copyright © 2004 by Richard T. Schaefer. Reprinted with permission by Pearson Education, Inc. Upper Saddle River, NJ; 234, Fig. 8.2, Based on Doane, 1997; 238, Excerpt from *The Racist Mind* by Raphael Ezekiel. Copyright © 1995 by Raphael S. Ezekiel; 238, Excerpt from *The Racist Mind* by Raphael Ezekiel. Copyright © 1995 by Raphael S. Ezekiel. Reprinted by permission of Viking Penguin, a division of Penguin Group (USA) Inc. and Kathi J. Paton Literary Agenc; 239, Fig. 8.3, Based on Kochbar and Gonzalez-Barrera, 2009; 246, Alba, Richard, and Victor Nee. *Remaking the American Mainstream: Assimilation and Contemporary Immigration.* Cambridge, Mass.: Harvard University Press, 200; 246, Statistical Abstract of the United States 2010: Tables 10, 52; 247, Statistical Abstract of the United States 2011: Table 19; 249, Fig. 8.7, Statistical Abstract, 2011: Table 37; 249, Fig. 8.8, Statistical Abstract of the United States 2010: Table 19; 250, Table 8.1, Statistical Abstract of the United States 2010: Tables 36, 39, 2010; 251, Table 8.2, Statistical Abstract of the United States 2010: Tables 36, 39, 289, and figure 12.5, 2010; 254, Table 8.3, Statistical Abstract of the United States 2010: Table 679, 2010; 255, Excerpt from *Majority and Minority: The Dynamics of Race and Ethnicity in American Life* by Norman R. Yetman, 6th Ed. Copyright © 1999 by Norman R. Yetman. Reprinted with permission by Pearson Education, Inc. Upper Saddle River, NJ; 256, Fig. 8.9, U.S. Census Bureau, 2010; 259, Theodore Roosevelt, 1886; 259, Excerpt from *Racial and Ethnic Relations in America* by Dale S. McLemore, 4th Ed. Copyright © 1994 by Dale S. McLemore. Reprinted with permission by Pearson Education, Inc. Upper Saddle River, NJ; 260, Excerpt from *Daybreak* by Oren Lyons. Copyright © by Oren Lyons. Reprinted with permission; 262, Fig 8.10, U.S. Census Bureau 2009; Statistical Abstract of the United States 2010: Table 3.I.

CHAPTER 9

288, Figure 9.2, Statistical Abstract of the United States 1995: Table 739; 2002: Table 666; 2011: Table 702, and earlier years; 292, *Down to Earth Sociology: Introductory Readings,* 2007; 293, Based on Bishop, 1990; 296, Table 9.1, Statistical Abstract of the United States 2001: Table 341; 2002: Table 303; 2003: Table 295; 2004: Table 322; 2005: Table 306; 2006: Table 308; 2007: Table 311; 2008: Table 313; 2009: Table 305; 2010: Table 305; 296, Table 9.2, Statistical Abstract of the United States 2000: Table 342; 2001: Table 304; 2002: Table 296; 2003: Table 323; 2004–2005: Table 307; 2006: Table 311; 2007: Table 315; 2008: Table 316; 2009: Table 306; 2010: Table 306; 297, Fig. 9.4, Statistical Abstract of the United States 2011: Tables 309, 320; 299, Table 9.3, Table from "Women in Elected Office" from the Center for American Women and Politics website. Copyright © 2010 by the Center for American Women and Politics. Reprinted with permission.

CHAPTER 10

306, *Invitation to Sociology: A Humanistic Perspective,* 1963; 308, Based on *The Columbia Viking Desk Encyclopedia* edited by William Bridgwater, 1953; 312, Hellinger and Judd, 1991; 315, Fig. 10.1, Statistical Abstract of the United States 2010: Table 401, 2010; 317, Table 10.1, Based on Casper and Bass 1998; Jamieson et al. 2002; Holder 2006; File and Crissey 2010: Table 1; Statistical Abstract of the United States 1991: Table 450; 1997: Table 462; 2010: Table 406; 319, Gallup Poll 2008; Statistical Abstract of the United States 1999: Table 464; 2002: Table 372; 2010: Table 38; 322, Fig. 10.2, Based on Mills, 1956; 325, Excerpt from "Oral History as 'Therapy': Combatants' Account of the Vietnam War" by Clark Smith, from *Strangers at Home: Vietnam Veterans Since the War,* Edited by Charles R. Figley and Seymore Leventman. Copyright © 1980 by Charles R. Figley. Reprinted with permission; 329, Fig. 10.4, Statistical Abstract of the United States, Various years, and 2010: Tables 603, 1332; 337, Based on "China, an Engine of Growth, Faces a Global Slump," by Jim Yardley and Keith Bradshe; 338, Fig. 10.5, Statistical Abstract of the United States 1992: Table 650; 1999: Table 698; 2011: Table 643; 339, Fig. 10.6, Statistical Abstract of the United States 2010: Table 675, 2010.

CHAPTER 11

356, Fig. 11.1, ; Figure from "Women Call the Shots at Home; Public Mixed on Gender Roles in Jobs" by Pew Social Trends Staff from the Pew Research Center website. Copyright © 2008 by Social & Demographic Trends, a Pew Research Center project. Reprinted with permission. http://pewsocialtrends.org; 357, Fig. 11.2, Based on Bianchi, et al. 2006; 358, Oscar Knott/Glow Images; 358, *Marriage and Family in a Changing Society,* 1985; 360, Fig. 11.3, *Statistical Abstract of the United States* 1990: Table 53; 2011: Table 60; 362, Fig. 11.4, Figure from "Americans: 2.5 Children is 'Ideal' Family Size" by Joseph Carroll from the Gallup website, June 26, 2007. Copyright © 2007 by The Gallup Organization. Reprinted with permission; 363, Doug Meszle/Newscom; 363, Fig. 11.5, Adapted from "America's Children in Brief: Key National Indicators of Well-Being 2010"; 367, Fig. 11.6, *Statistical Abstract of the United States* 1990: Table 53; 2011: Table 60; 370, Fig. 11.7, Statistical Abstract of the United States 1995: Table 79; 2011: Table 69; 370, Fig. 11.8, Based on "Women Ages 40–44," in Dye, 2008; 373, Fig. 11.9, U.S. Census Bureau, 2010; 374, Fig 11.11, Based on U.S. Census Bureau 2007 and Statistical Abstract of the United States 1995: Table 60; 2010: Table 63; Kreider 2010; 376, Fig. 11.12, Statistical Abstract of the United States 1995: Table 149; 2002: Table 111, 2010: Table 126; 377, Table 11.2, From "The Marrying Kind: Which Men Marry and Why" by David Popenhoe and Barbara Dafoe Whitehead, from *The State of Our Unions: The Social Health of Marriage in America,* July 2004. Copyright © 2004 by National Marriage

Project at the University of Virginia. Reprinted with permission; 378, Fig. 11.13, Statistical Abstract of the United States 1995: Table 58; 2011: Table 56; 378, Table 11.3, Based on *Demography* by Cheadle et. Al, 2010.

CHAPTER 12

390, Fig. 12.1, Based on National Center for Education Statistics 1991: Table 8; Statistical Abstract of the United States 2011: Table 227; 396, Fig. 12.2, Based on Unequal Education and the Reproduction of the Social Division of Labor in *Power and Ideology in Education* by Bowles, Karabel and Halsely, 1977; 397, Fig. 12.3, Statistical Abstract of the United States 2010: Table 264; 401, Fig. 12.4, Statistical Abstract of the United States 2011: Table 263; 405, Durkheim (1912/1965); 415, Fig. 12.5, Based on Troeltsch 1931; Pope 1942; and Johnson 1963; 417, Table 12.1, Adapted from "Religious Affiliation: Diverse and Dynamic," U.S. Religious Landscape Survey, February 2008; 418, Fig. 12.6, Based on Smith and Faris, 2005; 419, Frank E. Lockwood/MCT/Newscom.

CHAPTER 13

427, Fig. 13.1, Based on Haub, 2011; 427, Excerpt from *Problems of an Industrial Society,* 2nd Edition, by William Faunce. Copyright © 1981 by William Faunce. Reprinted with permission by McGraw Hill, Inc.; 431, Fig. 13.4, Based on Simon 1981; Food and Agriculture Organization of the United Nations 2006; Statistical Abstract of the United States 2010: Table 1335; 433, Fig. 13.5, Based on "The World of the Child 6 Billion" 2000; Haub 2011; 433, *The Myth of Population Control: Family, Caste,* *and Class in an Urban Village,* 1973; 434, Fig. 13.6, Based on "An Overview of Urbanization, Internal Migration, Population Distribution and Development in the World" in U.N. Fund for Population Activities (Based on a survey in Indonesia) January 14, 2008; 434, Fig. 13.7, Figure adapted from *Population Today,* Volume 26, Number 9, September, 1998. Copyright © 1998 by The Population Reference Bureau. Reprinted with permission; 437, Table 13.1, Table adapted from 2010 World Population Data Sheet by Carl Haub, 2010. Copyright © 2010 by The Population Reference Bureau. Reprinted with permission; 437, Fig. 13.8, Statistical Abstract of the United States 2011: Table 45; 438, Table 13.2, Statistical Abstract of the United States 2010: Table 50, 2010; 439, Fig. 13.9, Based on Day, 2010; 444, Fig. 13.10, Based on Chandler and Fox 1974; Brockerhoff 2000; United Nations 2008; 445, Table 13.3, Based on Haub, 2011; 445, Fig. 13.11, Based on United Nations 2008: Table 3; 447, Fig. 13.12, Statistical Abstract of the United States 2010: Table 29, 2010; 448, Table 13.4, Statistical Abstract of the United States 2010: Table 20, 2010; 451, Fig. 13.13, Urban Man and Society: A Reader in Urban Ecology (Cousins and Nagpaul 1970); The Nature of Cities and Urban Geography in the Last Half Century (Harris 1997); 453, "The Urban Villagers" by Herbert J. Gans. Copyright © 1962 by The Free Press. Copyright © by Herbert J. Gans. Reprinted with the permission of Free Press, a Division of Simon & Schuster, Inc. All rights reserved; 458, *Being Urban: A Sociology of City Life,* 1991.

CHAPTER 14

480, Fig. 14.2, Statistical Abstract of the United States 2010: Table 371, 2010.

NAME INDEX

Note: Pages followed by an (f) indicate a figure; by a (t) indicate a table.

A

Abbott, Grace, 10, 11f
Aberle, David, 118
Addams, Jane, 12
Adler, Patricia, 94
Adler, Peter, 94
Adorno, Theodor, 241, 492
Agins, Teri, 132
Alba, Richard, 258
Albert, Ethel M., 69
Aldrich, Nelson W., Jr., 212
Alger, Horatio, 219–220
Allport, Floyd, 243
Amato, Paul R., 376, 378
Anderson, 64, 157, 213, 417, 448
Angler, Natalie, 227
Appiah, Kwame Anthony, 183, 295
Aptheker, Herbert, 12
Archibold, Randal C., 249
Areddy, 313
Ariès, Philippe, 97–98
Arlacchi, P., 152
Arndt, William F., 308
Aron, Arthur, 359
Ayittey, George B. N., 183

B

Bailey, Joseph, 197
Balch, Emily Greene, 11f
Baltzell, E. Digby, 204
Banaji, Mahzarin R., 238
Banjo, Shelly, 213
Banks, Laurie, 14
Barnes, 150, 470
Barry, John, 81
Barstow, David, 158
Bartlett, Donald L., 260
Bass, Loretta E., 317
Bates, Marston, 52
Beah, Ishmael, 336
Beals, 69
Beaver, Kevin M., 150
Becker, Howard S., 146
Becker, Selwyn, 184
Beckett, Paul, 184
Beeghley, Leonard, 207, 209, 213, 217
Begley, Sharon, 81

Belkin, Lisa, 289
Bell, Alexander Graham, 320
Bell, Daniel, 329, 331
Bell, Michael Mayerfeld, 485
Beller, Emily, 215
Belsky, Jay, 93, 364
Benet, Lorenzo, 484
Benet, Sula, 484
Benford, Robert D., 401
Bentley, Arthur Fisher, 321
Berger, Peter, 306–307
Bergeron, 437
Bergman, Lowell, 158, 364
Bergmann, Barbara R., 364
Bernard, 232, 381
Bertrand, Merianne, 255
Best, 89
Bianchi, Suzanne M., 371
Biggs, Mae, 136
bin Laden, Osama, 136
Bishop, Jerry E., 293
Blau, 215, 364
Blee, Kathleen, 237
Blomfield, Adrian, 469
Blumstein, Alfred, 165
Blumstein, Philip, 371
Bodovski, Katerina, 93
Booth, Alan, 274
Boroditsky, Lera, 56
Bosman, Julie, 394
Boudreaux, Richard, 479
Bowles, Samuel, 396, 397
Bradford, 118
Bradley, Jennifer, 458
Bradsher, Keith, 477
Bray, Rosemary L., 252
Bretos, Miguel A., 248
Bridgwater, William, 308, 316
Brinkley, Christina, 132
Brinton, 390
Broad, William J., 326
Brockerhoff, Martin P., 444
Bronfenbrenner, Urie, 376
Brooks, David, 167
Browning, Christopher R., 232
Bryant, Chalandra M., 366, 381
Buffet, Warren, 200
Bumiller, Elisabeth, 477
Bundy, Ted, 167, 168
Bunzl, Martin, 183
Burgess, Ernest W., 33, 34, 450, 452

Burnham, Walter Dean, 315
Burns, Lucy, 280
Bush, George W., 61, 211

C

Canedy, Dana, 403
Cantoni, Davide, 8
Capela, Stanley, 14
Carlson, 256
Carnevale, Anthony P., 396
Carpenito, Lynda Juall, 296
Carpenter, Betsy, 484
Carper, James C., 393
Carr, Deborah, 97
Carter, Nancy M., 287, 289
Casper, 371
Catton, William R., Jr., 485
Cauce, Ana Mari, 367
Cellini, Stephani R., 217
Chafetz, Janet, 280
Chagnon, Napoleon, 146, 148
Chambliss, William J., 138, 151, 161
Chandler, Tertius, 441, 444
Chandra, Vibha P., 184, 231
Cheadle, Jacob, 370, 377
Cheang, Sopheng, 377
Chen, 81
Cherlin, Andrew, 379
Chin, Nancy P., 211
Chishti, Muzaffar, 437
Chivers, C. J., 437, 438
Christakis, Nicholas A., 364
Chung, He Len, 152
Church, Wesley T., II, 152
Churchill, Ward, 232
Clark, Candace, 87
Clearfield, Melissa W., 89
Clinton, Hillary, 298
Cloud, John, 165
Cloward, Richard, 156, 157
Cohen, Patricia, 211, 374
Cohn, D'Vera, 356
Colburn, George A., 256
Coleman, James, 379, 402
Collins, Randall, 276, 388
Collymore, Yvette, 197
Comte, Auguste, 5–6
Conklin, John E., 165
Connors, 89
Cooley, Charles Horton, 32, 83
Cooper, Anna Julia, 11f

Corll, Dean, 167
Cose, Ellis, 242, 264
Coser, Lewis A., 7, 38
Cousins, Albert H., 451
Cowen, Emory, 241
Cowley, Geoffrey, 68, 280
Crawford, 280, 381
Crick, Francis, 330, 331
Crompton, Rosemary, 201
Crosnoe, Robert, 94
Crossen, Cynthia, 280, 360
Crossette, Barbara, 184
Crossland, David, 469
Crowley, Martha L., 217
Cui, Ming, 376

D

Dabbs, James M., Jr., 274
Dahl, 321
Darley, John, 455
Darwin, Charles, 6, 86
Dasgupta, Nilanjana, 238
Dauman, Philippe, 203
Davis, Ann, 126
Davis, Kingsley, 196–198, 393–394
Davis, Nancy, 215
Day, Dorothy, 280
de Pastino, Blake, 183
Deaver, Michael V., 390
DeCrow, Karen, 289
Deflem, Mathieu, 151
Degler, Jeffrey, 127
Delaney, Arthur, 319
Deliege, Robert, 184
DeMaris, Alfred, 379
DeMartini, Joseph R., 13
Dematteis, Lou, 371
DeMause, Lloyd, 98
DeNavas-Walt, Carmen, 217
Deripaska, Oleg, 479
Deutscher, Irwin, 261
Dhillon, Navtej, 391
Dickey, Christopher, 81
DiSilvestro, Roger L., 260
Doane, Ashley, 234
Dobriner, William M., 7, 109
Dobyns, Henry F., 7, 109, 232
Dollard, Creflo, 419
Dollard, John, 241
Dolnick, Sam, 211
Domenech-Rodriguez, Melanie, 367
Domhoff, William, 118, 204, 208, 322
Dougherty, Conor, 448, 449
Dove, Adrian, 396
Drew, Christopher, 161
Du Bois, W. E. B., 12, 183, 242

Duff, Christina, 208
Dunaway, Wilma A., 158
Duncan, Otis Dudley, 158, 215
Duneier, Mitchell, 106
Dunham, Warren, 212
Dunlap, Riley E., 485
Durkheim, Emile, 7, 8, 9, 120, 155, 176, 405, 492, 496, 497, 498
Dush, Claire M. Kamp, 374
Dutton, Donald, 359
Dworkin, Anthony Gary, 279
Dye, H. B., 80
Dye, Jane Lawler, 370
Dynarski, 197

E

Ebaugh, Helen, 131
Eckholm, Erik, 131
Eder, Donna, 89, 91, 292
Eder, Klaus, 470, 484
Edgerton, Robert B., 38, 50, 56, 71
Ehrenreich, Barbara, 283
Eibl-Eibesfeldt, Irrenäus, 58
Eisenhart, R. Wayne, 292
Eisenhower, 55
Ekman, Paul, 58, 86
Elder, Glen H., Jr., 97
Elias, Paul, 330
Elinson, Elaine, 418
Elliott, 379, 394
Ellison, Lawrence, 203
Elwert, Felix, 364
Engels, Friedrich, 6
England, Paula, 280
English, Deidre, 283
Epstein, Cynthia Fuchs, 274
Ernst, Eldon G., 409
Eshleman, J. Ross, 367
Evans, Lisa, 481
Ezekiel, Raphael, 238

F

Fabrikant, Geraldine, 208
Fahim, 476
Falcon, Pedro, 55
Falkenberg, Katie, 295
Faris, Robert E. L., 212
Farkas, George, 93, 399
Farr, Rachel H., 371
Fassihi, 477
Fattig, Paul, 484
Faunce, William, 427
Feagin, Joe R., 255
Featherman, David L., 215
Fields, Gary, 263

Fincham, Frank D., 376
Fiorina, Carleton, 289
Fischer, 311, 359, 441
Fish, Jefferson M., 227
Fisher, 263, 296, 359
Flanagan, William G., 441, 459
Flannery, Russell, 336
Foley, Douglas, 292
Foote, Jennifer, 484
Form, William, 335
Fountain, Henry, 441
Fox, 441, 444
Francis of Asisi, St., 414
Frank, Reanne, 227
Franklin, Benjamin, 246
Franklin, Martin, 203
Freedman, Jane, 280
Fremson, Ruth, 352
Freud, Sigmund, 173
Friedl, Ernestine, 277
Friedman, Dusty, 52
Frommer, Arthur, 482
Frosch, Dan, 368
Fund, John, 249
Furstenberg, Frank, Jr., 99

G

Galbraith, John Kenneth, 192
Gallmeier, Charles P., 292
Gamoran, Adam, 394
Gampbell, Jennifer, 52
Gans, Herbert J., 453, 454, 462
Garfinkel, Harold, 96, 134
Garr, Emily, 218
Gates, Bill, 208, 236
Gatewood, Willard B., 366
Gauch, Sarah, 391
Gederen, 371
Gelles, 380
Genie (isolated child), 79, 82
Gerken, 482
Geronimus, Arlene T., 211
Gerth, H. H., 199
Gettleman, Jeffrey, 228, 431
Gilbert, Dennis, 207, 209, 213
Gilder, Jeannette, 280
Gillum, R. F., 407
Gilman, Charlotte Perkins, 11f, 89
Gilpatric, Katy, 90
Gingrich, F. Wilber, 308
Gintis, Herbert, 397
Gitlin, Todd, 7
Glaze, Lauren E., 152
Glenn, 368
Goffman, Erving, 96, 128, 147
Gokhale, Ketaki, 68

Gold, Ray, 206, 207
Goldberg, Steven, 274
Goldberg, Susan, 89, 91
Golden, Daniel, 393
Goll, 441
Goozen, Stephanie H., 150
Gottfriedson, Michael R., 152
Green, Leslie, 14, 488
Greene, Jay P., 401
Greenhalgh, Susan, 438
Greenwald, Anthony G., 238
Grimes, Michael D., 209
Gross, 232
Guessous, Fouad, 476
Gunther, Marc, 484
Guthrie, Doug, 336
Guy, Scary, 176

H

Hacker, Helen Mayer, 276
Hall, Edward T., 123, 127
Hall, G. Stanley, 98, 123, 126
Hall, J. Camille, 366
Hamid, Shadi, 280
Hamilton, Brady E., 372
Han, Meekyung, 61
Harford, Tim, 367
Harlow, Harry, 80
Harlow, Margaret, 80
Harris, Chauncey, 450, 451
Harris, Kim, 287
Harris, Marvin, 231, 277, 278
Harrison, Paul, 191
Hart, 217
Hartley, Eugene, 237
Haub, Carl, 429, 431, 433, 436, 437
Hauser, Philip, 444
Hawking, Stephen, 113
Hawley, Amos H., 441
Hayakawa, S. I., 249
Hayashi, Gina M., 376
Haywood, Kelly, 95
Heames, 206
Hein, Michelle M., 90
Hellinger, Daniel, 204, 312, 389
Hendrix, Lewellyn, 276
Henley, Elmer Wayne, 167
Henslin, James M., 19, 89, 136
Herring, Cedric, 254
Herrnstein, Richard J., 150
Higgenbotham, Elizabeth, 216
Hill, 238
Hinn, Benny, 419
Hippler, Fritz, 313
Hirschi, Travis, 152
Hitler, Adolf, 228, 229, 232, 241, 242, 244

Hochschild, Arlie, 86
Hoffer, Thomas, 402
Hoijer, Harry, 69
Holder, Kelly, 317
Homblin, Dora Jane, 441
Hong, Lawrence, 353
Horn, James P., 259
Horowitz, Ruth, 152
Horwitz, Allan V., 58, 86, 87
Hout, Michael, 211, 213
Houtman, Dick, 213
Hoyt, Homer, 450
Hsu, Francis K. L., 256
Huang, 372
Huber, Joan, 185, 277
Hughes, Everett C., 128
Hughes, H. Stuart, 471
Hundley, Greg, 288
Hussein, Saddam, 313
Hutchinson, Earl Ofari, 250
Huttenbach, Henry R., 232
Hymowitz, Carol, 289

I

Isabelle (isolated child), 78–79, 82
Itard, Jean Marc Gospard, 78

J

Jabbar, Mustafa, 325
Jackson, Jesse, 253
Jacobs, 169, 288
James, Michael, 165
Jamieson, 174–175
Jankowiak, William R., 359
Jefferson, Thomas, 312
Jenkins, Philip, 407
Jeong, Yu-Jin, 242, 367
Jessop, Bob, 197
Jesus, 203, 410, 412, 414
Jindal, Piyush, 258
Jneid, Hani, 293
Joan of Arc, 308
Johnson, 292
Johnson, Benton, 415
Jones, 165, 238
Judd, Dennis R., 204, 312, 389

K

Kahl, Joseph, 207, 209
Kahlenberg, Susan G., 90
Karp, David A., 458
Katz, 458
Kaufman, Joanne, 263
Kaufman, Jonathan, 208

Kefalas, Maria, 209
Kelley, Tina, 403
Kelly, Joan, 378
Kelly, Florence, 11f
Keniston, Kenneth, 99
Kennedy, John F., 263
Kent, Mary, 55, 431
Kerr, Clark, 335
Kifner, John, 192
Kimmel, Michael, 237
King, Eden, 197
King, Martin Luther, Jr., 252, 253
Kluegel, James R., 220
Knapp, Daniel, 14
Kneebone, Elizabeth, 218
Kochbar, Rakesh, 239
Kohn, Melvin, 93
Kooistra, Paul G., 233
Koropeckyj-Cox, Tanya, 370
Kramer, 469
Krieger, Linda Hamilton, 238
Krienert, 381
Kron, Josh, 228
Krugman, Paul, 191

L

La Barre, Weston, 69
Lady Gaga, 155
LaFraniere, Sharon, 407
Lalasz, Robert, 55
Landtman, Gunnar, 182, 183
Lareau, Annette, 93, 364
Larson, 90, 481
Latané, Bibb, 455
Lauer, Robert, 381
Leacock, Eleanor, 276
LeDuff, Charlie, 381
Lee, 28, 258
Leeson, Peter T., 38
Leighton, 158
Lemann, Nicholas, 321
Lengermann, Madoo, 10
Lenin, Vladimir Ilyich, 390, 391, 392
Lenski, Gerhard, 205, 206, 441, 470
Lenski, Jean, 441, 470
Lerner, Gerda, 182, 276, 277, 278
Lerner, Steve, 483
Letherby, Gayle, 370
Levinson, D. J., 97
Lewin, 263
Lewis, Jamie, 379
Lewis, Michael, 89, 91, 102
Lichter, Daniel T., 217, 257, 374
Liebow, Elliot, 106
Lincoln, Abe, 200
Lind, Michael, 260

Linton, Ralph, 49, 113, 283
Lipchik, Ella, 30
Lipset, Seymour Martin, 308
Littleton, Heather, 296
Locke, Gary, 258
Locke, Harvey, 33, 34
Lombroso, Cesare, 150
Lopez, Jennifer, 317
Lublin, Joann S., 203
Lurie, Nicole, 293
Lynn, Michael, 254

M

MacDonald, William L., 379
Mack, Raymond W., 118
Mackey, Daniel, 128
Mackey, Jennifer, 127
Madigan, Nick, 165
Mahashury, (bonded laborer), 184
Mahoney, John, 233
Malthus, Thomas Robert, 426–430, 496
Mamdani, Mahmood, 433
Mandela, Nelson, 309
Mander, Jerry, 260
Manning, 374
Marino, 249
Martineau, Harriet, 11–12
Martinez, Susana, 250
Maruschak, Laura M., 152
Marx, Karl, 6–7, 38, 197, 408, 471, 492, 493, 494, 497, 498
Mary (mother of Jesus), 413
Masheter, Carol, 378
Mathay (feral child), 78
Mathews, T. J., 372
Matsumoto, D., 86
Mattioli, 291
Matza, David, 153
Mayer, John, 150, 199
McCabe, 376
McCormick, John, 158
McElroy, Damien, 469
McFalls, Joseph A., Jr., 436
McFarland, Sam, 241
McKeown, Thomas, 426
McKernan, Signe-Mary, 217
McKinley, William, 191
McKinnish, Terra G., 448
McLanahan, Sara, 370, 376
McLemore, S. Dale, 259, 376
McNeill, 390, 426–429
McShane, 152
Mead, George Herbert, 32, 69, 83–84, 85
Medina, Jennifer, 401
Meese, Ruth Lyn, 81

Meltzer, Scott A., 296
Merton, Robert K., 35–36, 156, 174, 399, 498, 499
Meyer, Peter, 389
Meyers, Laurie, 368
Meyers, Joyce, 419
Milbank, Dana, 451
Milkie, Melissa, 89–90, 91
Miller, 292
Mills, C. Wright, 2, 3, 4, 13, 100, 199, 204, 322, 497
Mohawk, John C., 260
Montagu, Ashley, 227
Mooallem, Jon, 330
Moonves, Leslie, 203
Moore, Wilbert, 196–197, 198, 393–394
Morgan, Lewis, 470
Morin, 356
Morris, 209, 274
Moseley-Braun, Carol, 298
Moses (biblical character), 407
Mosher, Steven W., 334, 429, 438
Moyers, Bill, 242
Mullainathan, Sendhil, 255
Murdock, George Peter, 69, 283, 351
Murphy, John, 171
Mussolini, Benito, 471

N

Nagpaul, Hans, 451
Nakamura, Akemi, 393
Nakao, Keiko, 204
Nash, Gary B., 259
Nauta, André, 409
Navarro, Mireya, 248
Nee, Victor, 258
Needham, Sarah E., 132
Nelson, 55, 89, 183, 216
Neugarten, Bernice L., 99
Niebrugge, Gillian, 10
Nordberg, Jenny, 89
Nordhaus, William D., 202
Nordland, Rod, 202

O

Obama, Barack, 200, 254
O'Brien, 22, 158, 306
Ogburn, William, 70, 473–475, 493, 494, 496
O'Hare, William P., 209, 217, 218
Ohlin, Lloyd, 156, 157
Oppel, Richard A., Jr., 165
Orme, Nicholas, 98
Orwell, George, 305–306

Osborne, 330
Osteen, Joel, 419
Ouchi, William, 390

P

Page, 477
Palen, J. John, 444, 448, 458
Palin, Sarah, 298
Park, Robert Ezra, 450
Parks, Rosa, 252
Parsons, Talcott, 13, 393–394
Partington, Donald, 169
Patrick, Deval, 253
Paul, Alice, 11f
Pearlin, L. I., 93
Pelosi, Nancy, 298
Peltham, Brett W., 212
Perkins, Frances, 10, 11f
Perot, Ross, 316
Perry, William J., 481
Peterson, 260
Pines, Maya, 79
Piotrow, Phylis Tilson, 428
Piven, Frances Fox, 38
Polgreen, Lydia, 183
Pontiac, Ottawa Chief, 259
Pope, Liston, 415
Popenoe, David, 381
Popescu, Ioana, 239
Portés, Alejandro, 262
Possible, Kim, 90, 147, 401
Powell, 239
Powerpuff Girls, 90
Preston, 249
Putin, Vladimir, 479

Q

Qian, Zhenchao, 257, 374
Quadagno, Jill, 97

R

Rader, Dennis, 167
Ratcliffe, Caroline, 217
Ray, J. J., 241
Read, Madlen, 158
Reagan, Ronald, 200
Reckless, Walter, 152
Reddick, Richard J., 364
Reed, 484
Reiman, Jeffrey, 158, 161, 165
Reinert, Leah, 289
Reiser, Christa, 296
Reitz, Jeffrey G., 296
Reskin, Barbara, 263, 264
Rhoads, Christopher, 477

Richardson, Stacey, 376
Riley, 237
Rist, Ray, 398–399
Rivlin, Gary, 260
Roberts, Janet, 239
Robertson, Ian, 60
Robertson, Pat, 419
Robinson, 215, 216
Rockne, Knute, 109
Roediger, David R., 242
Rogers, Simon, 481
Rometty, Ginni, 289
Roosevelt, Franklin D., 257
Roosevelt, Theodore, 10, 259
Rose, Stephen J., 396
Rosenberg, Charles E., 28
Rosenfeld, Richard, 165
Rossi, Alice, 273
Roth, Louise Marie, 288
Rothkopf, David, 190, 342
Rothman, Barbara Katz, 283
Rubin, Zick, 359
Rumbaut, Rubén, 262
Rumsfeld, Donald, 61
Russell, Diana, 381

S

Saenz, Rogelio, 367
Sageman, Marc, 13, 326
Sahlins, Marshall D., 470
Salomon, Gisela, 55
Samor, Geraldo, 126
Samuelson, Paul A., 202
Sánchez-Jankowski, Martin, 157
Sandefur, Gary, 370
Sanger, David E., 477
Santos, Fernanda, 454
Sapir, Edward, 55, 498
Schaefer, Richard T., 231, 232, 257, 259, 260
Schemo, Diana Jean, 402
Schmitt, Eric, 402
Schneiderman, Howard G., 204
Schnore, Leo, 444
Schooler, Carmi, 93
Schwartz, Pepper, 371, 376
Schwarzenegger, Arnold, 200
Schwarzman, Stephen, 342
Scommegna, Paola, 372
Scott, 281
Sengupta, Simini, 325
Service, Elman R., 470
Settles, Isis H., 291
Shanker, Thom, 477
Sharp, 55, 474
Sheets, Lawrence Scott, 326

Shepard, Matthew, 172
Sherif, Carolyn, 242
Sherif, Muzafer, 242
Shields, Stephanie A., 87
Shipman, Harold, 168
Simpson, George Eaton, 233, 243
Singer, Natasha, 28
Singh, Thaman, 433
Skeels, H. M., 80, 81
Skinner, Jonathan, 239
Sklair, Leslie, 208
Smart, 470
Smedley, Audrey, 227
Smedley, Brian D., 227
Sobolewski, Juliana M., 376
Sowell, Anthony, 168
Spencer, Herbert, 6, 9
Spengler, Oswald, 471
Spickard, P. R. S., 233
Spitzer, Steven, 161
Spivak, Gayatri Chakravorty, 280
Sprecher, Susan, 280
Srole, Leo, 212
Stack, Carol B., 366
Stalin, Joseph, 390, 391, 392
Stampp, Kenneth M., 183
Staples, 360
Stark, Rodney, 12
Stark, Roger, 415
Starr, Ellen Gates, 12
Steele, James B., 260
Stein, Rob, 477
Steinberg, Laurence, 152
Stevens, 213
Stinnett, Nicholas, 381
Stockard, Jean, 292
Stohr, Oskar, 81
Stolberg, Sheryl Gay, 239
Stone, Kathy, 10
Stouffer, Samuel, 292
Straus, Murray, 380
Strickland, Bonnie R., 376
Sullivan, 172
Sumner, William, 50
Sutherland, Edwin, 151, 157, 494
Suzuki, Bob H., 257, 368
Sweeney, Megan M., 378
Sykes, Gresham, 153
Szasz, Thomas, 174

T

Talbot, Marion, 10, 11f
Taneja, V., 81
Tasker, Fiona, 371
Taylor, 317

Thomas, Dorothy Swaine, 137, 229, 232, 239, 500
Thomas, W. I., 32, 137, 229, 500
Thompson, 250, 393
Thornton, Russell, 232
Thurow, Roger, 431
Timasheff, Nicholas, 324
Todosijevic, 371
Tomsho, Robert, 393
Tönnies, Ferdinand, 121
Torres, Jose B., 367
Toynbee, Arnold, 471
Treas, Judith, 205
Treiman, Donald J., 205
Troeltsch, Ernst, 415
Trofimov, Yaroslav, 184
Trump, Donald, 208
Tumin, Melvin, 196–197, 198
Turner, 38

U

Uchitelle, Louis, 217
Udry, J. Richard, 273
Ullman, Edward, 450
Urbina, Ian, 401
Usdansky, Margaret L., 55
Useem, Michael, 118
Utar, Hale, 118

V

Vandell, Deborah Lowe, 93
VanderMey, 289
Vaughan, Diane, 378
Veblen, Thorstein, 328–329, 493
Vega, William A., 367
Venkatesh, Sudhir, 29
Vergakis, Brock, 480
Vidal, Jordi Blanes, 319
Vishnu, 410
von Clausewitz, Carl, 324, 326, 345

W

Wade, 288
Wagley, Charles, 231
Wakefield, Jerome C., 58, 86, 87
Wall, Robert, 477
Wallace, John M., 407
Wallerstein, Immanuel, 191
Wallerstein, Judith, 376
Wallman, Joel, 165
Walsh, Anthony, 150, 381
Wang, Hongyu, 378
Warren, Jennifer, 163
Watson, James, 330, 331

Watson, John, 330, 331
Watson, Mark, 154
Webb, Beatrice Potter, 11f
Weber, Lynn, 216
Weber, Max, 7, 10, 199–200, 306, 307
Welch, Martell, 453
Wells-Barnett, Ida B., 11f
Wen, Ming, 370
Wertz, Dorothy C., 283
Wertz, Richard W., 283
White, Joseph, 158
White, Michael, 203
Whitehead, 377, 381
Whorf, Benjamin, 55, 498
Wilder, L. Douglas, 253
Wilford, John Noble, 448
Williams, Christine L., 243
Williams, Dimitri, 91

Williams, Frank, 152
Williams, Robin, 64, 65, 66
Willie, 254, 364
Willingham, B., 86
Wilson, James, 150
Wilson, William Julius, 253, 255, 366
Winfrey, Oprah, 207
Winters, Marcus A., 401
Wirth, Louis, 231, 453
Wolfinger, Nicholas H., 376
Wong, Gillian, 318, 481
Woods, Tiger, 165, 227, 265
Word, Deletha, 453, 456
Wuornos, Aileeen, 167

Y

Yager, 126
Yakaboski, Tamara, 289

Yamamoto, Yoko, 390
Yardley, Jim, 295, 333, 337
Yenfang, Quan, 336
Ying, Yu-Wen, 61, 368
Yinger, 61, 233, 241, 243, 429
You, Hyun-Kyung, 242, 367
Yufe, Jack, 81

Z

Zachary, G. Pascal, 337
Zakaria, Fareed, 337, 481
Zamiska, Nicholas, 368
Zellner, William W., 64
Zerubavel, Eviatar, 55, 56, 57
Zetsche, Dieter, 57
Zoepf, Katherine, 295
Zuckerberg, Mark, 205

Note: Pages followed by an (f) indicate a figure; by a (t) indicate a table.

A

Aborigines, of Australia, 474
Abortion, 165, 178, 295, 370, 438, 439
Achieved status, 112, 492
Acid rain, 481, 492
Adolescence, 98, 100, 101, 102
Adoption, 351, 384
Adulthood, 99–100, 101
    transitional, 98, 99, 102
"Adultolescents," 364
Advertising
    billboards, 439
    body image in, 130
    of cigarettes, 90
    in early capitalism, 90
    and gender, 90, 439
    in the global village, 3
    by religious groups, 419
Affirmative action, 262, 263
Afghanistan, 194, 204, 325, 437
Africa. See also specific countries
    author's visit to, 47–48
    birth rate in, 437
    caste in, 184, 186
    child labor, 183
    colonialism in, 191
    culture in, 47–48
    ethnic conflicts in, 228, 231, 233, 236
    fertility rate in, 436
    genocide in, 228, 232
    and Most Industrialized Nations, 187, 193f, 194
    population growth in, 436, 437, 461
    poverty in, 431
    slavery in, 183
    starvation in, 431
    world system theory, 192
African Americans, 252–256. See also Race–ethnicity
    and capital punishment, 169, 178
    and caste system, 184
    and civil rights movement, 253
    comparative well-being statistics, 250t
    on death row, 170t
    discrimination against, 183, 231, 233, 239, 240, 252–256
    and education, 251t, 253
    ethnic identity, 245–246
    and expectations of, 253–254
    family structure of, 366, 367
    and Harlem, 441, 448, 449, 458, 461–462
    hate crimes against, 172t
    and health care, 239
    income, 239, 250, 251, 253, 254
    and internalization of norms, 238, 239
    interracial marriage, 360
    Jim Crow laws, 252
    middle class, 366
    migration by, 231
    and mortgages, 250t
    murder of, 254, 255
    number of, 253
    overview, 266
    and politics, 253
    and poverty, 217, 218f–219, 250t, 366
    prejudice, 252–253
    in prisons, 163–164t, 177
    professionals, 12
    race vs. social class, 12, 16, 254–255
    racism, as everyday burden, 255–256
    riots, 253, 266
    and single parent households, 367
    and slavery, 182, 183, 186
    social class of, 12, 16, 182–183, 184, 254–255
    social mobility of, 215, 216, 217–219, 254
    stereotypes, 217, 218
    and street crimes, 163
    suicide and, 8
    terms for, 56, 227, 229
    and tornado, 140
    and unemployment, 250t, 253
    upper class, 366
    in U.S. population, 245f, 246f
    in various sectors, 163, 164, 170t, 217, 218, 219, 231, 262f, 245f, 250t, 251, 254, 266
Age. See also Children and childhood; Elderly; Life course; specific categories of
    and culture, 49, 52, 73, 89, 90
    and divorce, 377t
    at first marriage, median, in U.S., 373f
    old, attitudes toward, 68
    of rape victims, 296t
    and social context, 2, 4, 23
    and voting, 317t
    and wealth, 38
Agents of socialization, 92–94, 102, 492
Aging. See Elderly
Agricultural revolution, 328, 466
Agricultural societies, 36, 72, 99, 328
    deaths in, 99, 101
    defined, 328, 492
    divorce rate, 36
    and nine-month year, 72
    relationships in, 466, 468
    slavery, 182
    work in, 466
AIDS, 13, 14
Albania, 193f, 438t
Alcohol as a drug, 96, 157, 211, 454
Alcoholics Anonymous, 96
Alienation
    and city life, 453
    defined, 492
    described, 453
    of voters, 318, 345
    in the workplace, 88
Al-Qaeda, 326
American Civil Liberties Union (ACLU), 12
American Medical Association, 116f
American Sociological Association, 12, 14, 15, 273, 486
Amish, 121
Anarchy, 321, 492
Andhra Pradesh, India, 182
Anglo Saxon Protestants, 246–248, 500
Animals
    deprived, 80
    domestication of, 328f, 467, 468, 487
    extinction of, 68, 479
    as food, 52
    and genetics, 330
    isolated, 80
    religious sacrifices, 418, 422
    in subcultures, 63
Anomie, 156
Anthrax, 326
Anthropology, 145
Anticipatory socialization, 94, 102, 492
Anti-Malthusians, 427–429
Anti-Semitism, 241, 242, 244
Apartheid, 231, 233, 236, 492
Appearance, and self image, 130

Applied sociology, 13–14, 492
Arabs, in U.S. population, 246f
Aragon, Spain, 429
Armenians, 233
Aryan Nations, 237
Aryans, 64, 228, 438
Ascribed status, 112, 492
ASEAN (Association of South East Asian Nations), 343, 346
Asian Americans. *See also* Race–ethnicity
    assimilation of, 257–258
    background of, 256–257
    characteristics, 368
    comparative well-being statistics, 250t
    country of origin of, 256
    discrimination against, 256–257
    diversity among, 257
    and education, 251t, 257
    family structure of, 257, 368
    and hate crimes, 172t
    home ownership, 250t
    income, 250t
    interracial marriage of, 257–258
    overview, 266
    in politics, 258
    and poverty, 250t
    and relocation camps, 232, 236, 257
    and spillover bigotry, 256
    success of, 257–258
    and teacher expectations, 399
    and two parent households, 368
    unemployment of, 250t
    in U.S. population, 245f, 246f
Assimilation
    of Asian Americans, 257–258, 266
    defined, 233, 492
    through education, 257
    and family life, 257
    and intermarriage, 257–258
    and language, 233
    global patterns of, 232f
    and politics of immigrants, 247
    types of, 233
    and WASP culture, 247
Athens, 312, 444
Atlanta University, 12
Attention deficit disorder (ADD), 174
Australia, 60, 71, 187, 193f, 474
Authoritarian leaders, 241
Authoritarian personality, 241, 492
Authority
    in bureaucracies, 308
    in cults, 415–416
    defined, 306, 492
    the family, 307, 353–354

and industrialization, 307
in marriage, 353–354
power of, 306
transfer of, 309
types of, 307–309
and violence, 306–307
Automobiles and social change, 473t, 482, 487
Average, ways to measure, 25t
Aveyron, France, 78
Ayutthaya, Thailand, 405
Aztecs, 312, 405, 407, 408

B

Back stages, 129, 492
Background assumptions
    and assumptions of normality, 133–135
    breaking, 133–134
    defined, 133, 492
    and deviance, 146, 172
    and discrimination, 256–258, 293
    and ethnomethodology, 133–135, 142
    and family, 296
    and microsociological perspective, 133–134
    and physicians, 293
    and race–ethnicity, 231
    and social construction of reality, 136, 138, 500
    and sociology, 5–9
Banking system, 240, 477, 478
Baseball, 84, 93, 211
Basketball, 292, 401
Basic demographic equation, 438, 492
Basic sociology. *See* Sociology
Bavaria, Germany, 229
Behavior, goal directed, 54
Beauty/looks
    and advertising, 90, 131
    and culture, 51
    effects of, 359, 361
    and skin color, 238, 240
    and socialization, 51, 89, 90, 130, 131
    and standards of gender, 51
    and stereotypes, 243
Berdache, 351
Bias
    in crime statistics, 171–172
    in criminal justice, 161
    in death penalty, 168–169, 178
    gender, 169
    in intelligence (IQ) tests, 395–396
    in mass media, 66, 90–92
    in medicine, 301, 239
    racial, 169

in research, 25, 43
social class, 169
Big Brother, 305. *See also* War, cyber war and cyber defense
Bikers, 154
Bilineal system of descent, 353, 492
Billboards, 439
BioBricks, 330
Bioengineering, 431
Biofuels, and food supply, 431, 432, 461
Biography, 3
Biology and human behavior. *See* Nature vs. nurture
Biotech society, 330–331, 492
Birth control, and education, 3945
Births/birth rates. *See also* Childbirth
    changes in, 372, 385
    crude birth rate, 437
    fertility rate, 436–437f
    and industrialization, 219–220, 221
    and population, 437
    to single mothers, 363f
    in U.S., 435
Bisexuals, hate crimes and, 172t
Blaming the victim, 195
Blended families, 370–371, 385, 492
Bloomingdale's, 158
Blue-collar workers. *See* Working class
Boards of directors, 207
Body image, 130–131
Body language, 126, 492
Body weight, and image, 131, 211, 237
Bonded laborers, 184, 284, 492
Boot camp, 96
Born again, 414, 492
Botswana, 193f
Bouazizi, Mohamed, 476
Bourgeoisie, 6, 38, 39, 43, 199, 200, 492
Branch Davidians, 418
Brazil, 228
Brooklyn, New York, 128
Brooks, David, 167
Buddhism, 405
Bull Moose Party, 316
Bullfighting, 46, 50
Bundy, Ted, 168
Bureau of Indian Affairs, 260
Bureaucracies
    and alienation, 318
    church as, 309, 416, 422
    defined/characteristics of, 308
    and disaster assistance, 140
    dysfunctions of, 402
    and education, 402
    ideal versus real, 66
    incompetence in, 402
    and rational-legal authority, 308

and schools, 402
structure of universities, 207
Bureaucratic authority, 308
Burial, and the family, 365
Business, and culture, 208, 209, 210, 211
Bush, George W., 211

C

Cairo, Egypt, 313
California, 29, 165, 200, 210, 231, 247,
    and affirmative action, 261
    divorce in, 376f
    "English-only" movement, 249
    Foreign Miner's Act, 256, 258
    gold rush in, 210, 231
    hazardous waste sites in, 480f
    labor discrimination in, 243
    and the invisible minority, 260
    and megacities, 445, 447
    and Ogburn's processes, 473t
    population of, 249f
    poverty in, 217
    prestige and politics in, 200, 201
    race-ethnic minorities of, 247, 262
    radical environmentalism in, 484
    rural-urban makeup of, 447f, 448
    and sociology careers, 14, 29
    teaching standards, 402
    "three-strikes" law, 163
Calvinism, 8
Cambodia, 1, 78, 187
Cameras, surveillance, 28, 249
Campaign funding, 118, 316, 318–320
Capital punishment, 167, 168–169, 492
Capitalism. See also Globalization of
    capitalism
    belief systems of, 335
    characteristics of, 332
    in China, 335–336
    and class conflict, 207–208, 322–333
    and competition, 332, 334, 346
    conflict perspective on, 322–333
    corporate, 322, 345
    and crime, 157–158
    criticisms of, 333–334
    and cultural leveling, 71
    defined, 332, 492
    and dialectical process of history,
        471–472
    and economic crisis, 337,
        340–341, 347
    as economic system, 327–331, 339
    and education, 316, 317t, 318, 393
    and exploitation, of workers, 471
    and global stratification, 337–338
    ideology of, 335

and Industrial Revolution, 337,
    466–468
laissez-faire, 332
and market forces, 333
principles of, 332
and rationalization of society, 308
regulation of, 332
and religion, 7–10, 308
in Russia, 335
socialism, convergence with, 332t,
    335–337
spirit of, 8, 10
welfare or state, 332
and workers' revolution, 6–7, 199,
    472
working conditions and, 38, 338–339
Capitalist class. See also Corporations
    characteristics of, 207–208
    and class, 207–208
    and exploitation of workers, 333,
        335, 346
    and marriage, 208, 317t
    model of, 207–209
    workers, thinking of self as, 208,
        209, 223
Caracol, 448
Caral, 441
Card stacking, as unequal funding, 395
Careers, advancement of, 131–132
Case studies, 21, 492
Casinos, 260–261
Caste, 182, 183–184, 492
Catastrophes, 70, 429, 469
Cause and effect, 27
Census, and race, 256f, 259
Centrist parties, 316, 345
CEOs (Chief Executive Officers), 203t,
    289
Charisma, defined, 308, 492
Charismatic authority, 308, 492
Charismatic leaders, 309, 415, 492
Chattisgargh, India, 410
Checks and balances, 321, 492
Chennai, India, 146
Chernobyl, 480
Cherokee, the, 260, 261
Chester, Vermont, 449
Child abuse, 381
Child labor
    in Africa, 183
    in Asia, 183
    8-hour work day, 12
    in history, 12, 15, 98
    in India, 184
    in Least Industrialized Nations, 98
    and slavery, 183
    in South America, 183

Child rearing. See also Parenthood
    changes in, 356–358
    extending home life, 364
    by grandparents, 362, 363f, 368,
        377
    in history, 69
    by married couples, 362
    and preschoolers, 363f
    and race–ethnicity, 366–369
    by single mothers, 362
    and social class, 364
    in U.S., 362–364, 367f
Childbirth, 361–362. See also Births/birth
    rates; Reproduction of humans
    emotions on birth of girl, 87, 88
    and family size, 361–362, 363
    global extremes in, 437
    infants, and women, 273
    in least industrialized nations, 433
    midwives vs. doctors, 283
    and motherhood, 272
    postponing, 372
    and social facts, 87, 88, 128, 141,
        158, 183, 184, 185
Children and childhood. See also Births/
    birth rates
    attention, from parents, 357
    bonding with mothers, 93, 102
    counseling, 14
    in day care, 93
    and divorce, 376–378
    in earlier societies, 97–98
    as economic assets, 433
    enslavement of, 183
    family size, 361–362, 363
    feral, 78
    gay/lesbian adoptions, 371
    and gender socialization, 14, 89–92
    historical views of, 97–98
    infant mortality, 467t
    infanticide, 295, 438, 439, 461
    institutionalized, 80
    isolated, 78–79, 80
    labor of (See Child labor)
    in Least Industrialized Nations, 187,
        189, 433
    and the life course, 97–98
    living with both parents, 357, 364,
        367f, 370f
    and marital satisfaction, 87
    meaning of, 33
    morality of babies, 49
    parents, influence on, 19, 33
    play of, 83, 84, 89, 90, 93, 102
    and poverty, 218–219, 434f
    preschoolers, 213, 363f
    reasoning skills of, 389–392

Children and childhood (*Continued*)
  of single mothers, 362
  socialization, 97–98
  as a social unit, 36
  as soldiers, 326
  time spent with, 357
  in tribal societies, 98, 101
  tutors for preschoolers, 213
  and work, 97–98
China
  abortion in, 437
  beauty standards, 51
  billionaires in, 336
  brides for dead sons, 352
  capitalism in, 335–336, 346
  carbon dioxide/pollution in, 480, 481
  childbirth in, 334
  and cities, 444
  culture in, 110
  cyber war, 477
  economy of, 336, 469
  education in, 393
  and electronic communication, 313,
    336
  and elders, 368, 385
  environmental issues in, 480, 481
  racial-ethnicity, 256f, 257
  and gender ratios, 439
  and geopolitics, 468–469, 487
  as a global power, 337, 471
  identity cards, 477
  immigrants, 437f, 438f
  income, global stratification in, 193f
  and industrialization, 193f
  infanticide in, 439
  and Internet, control of, 477
  and Japan, 468
  Jew's in, 229
  nuclear weapons, 471
  one-child policy, 438–439
  political system of, 335–336
  and power, 343, 344, 471
  profiteering in, 147
  Pterodactyl (military plane), 477
  social stratification, 199
  textile workers, 199
Chinese Americans. *See* Asian
  Americans
Chinese Exclusion Act of 1882, 256
Christianity, 411. *See also* specific
  denominations
Chromosomes, 150
Church(es), 404, 416, 492
CIA (Central Intelligence Agency), 211,
  326, 327
  reaction, 278, 300
  ision, female, 50, 295, 301

Cities. *See also* Inner city; Urbanization
  alienation in, 453, 454
  community in, 453–454, 457
  composition of, 454
  defined, 492
  development of, 441–446
  diffusion of responsibility for,
    455–456
  edge cities, 447, 461
  fastest growing, 448t
  growth of, 440, 444f
  life in, 12, 453
  megacities, 445–446
  photo essay on, 442–443, 457
  population, percentage of, 445, 448t
  revitalization of, 458–459
  shrinking, 448t
  social interaction in, 12, 124–125,
    452–455
  structures of, 447–448
  suburbanization, 218, 458
  urbanization, influence of, 444–445
  in U.S., 446–450
  world's largest, 445f
Citigroup, 158
Citizenship, 311–312, 313, 492
City-states, 311–312, 492
Civil rights
  of corporations, 263
  demonstrators, 242
  and education, 253
  and female circumcision, 50, 295
  free speech, 65, 345
  and gender, 70, 72, 280
  health care and, 211
  in Iran, 280, 301
  racial discrimination, 253, 254
  and social change, 401, 407
  voting, 116, 253
  of women, 12, 279, 280
  of workers, 38, 66
Civil Rights Act of 1964, 253
Civil Rights Act of 1968, 253
Civil rights movement
  brief history of, 407
  participants in, 407
  photo of, 253
  and racial discrimination, 407
  and religion, 316, 418
Civil strife, and rising expectations,
  253–255
Civilization, natural cycles of, 470–471
Class. *See* Social class
Class conflict, 6–7, 493
Class consciousness, 199, 493
Class system, defined, 493
Classless state, 471

Closed-ended questions, 25, 26t, 43, 493
Clothing, 47–48, 61, 94, 96, 132
Coalition government, 343–344, 469
Coalitions, 469
Coercion, 306, 345, 493
Cohabitation, 372–375, 493
Cold War, 335
Collective behavior
  acting crowds, 199
  and diffusion, 474
  and discrimination, 231, 265
  and environmentalism, 484
  and groups, 265
  rumors, 399
  and social revolutions, 466, 474, 484
  thought processes, 55–56
College. *See also* specific universities
  affirmative action, 263
  attendance, and pay gap, 287, 288f
  attendance, by race–ethnicity, 251,
    253, 255, 257
  attendance, by social class, 396
  as bureaucracies, 402
  community colleges, 389, 391, 420
  and date rape, 296
  drug use, 30
  graduation statistics, 251t, 266
  in Japan, 390
  and prisons, 164
  private vs. public, 202, 208, 213, 322
  professors, 205, 206, 241
  and race-ethnicity, 251t
  in Russia, 390
  and SATs, 390, 401
  and working women, 288–289
Colonialism, 191, 493
Colonies, 191, 246, 311
Comanche tribe, 226
Commitment
  in marriage vs. cohabitation, 33, 43,
    372–373, 381
  to religion, 414
  to a social movement, 152
Common sense
  and bias, 80
  and children, 98, 100
  defined, 493
  and ethnomethodology, 133–135
  language and perception, 55–57
  and race, 227–228
  and research, 19, 42
  and sociology, 19, 20
  and violent crime, 166
Communication. *See also* Language;
  Mass media
  and Arab Spring, 478
  by body language, 126

and cities, 445, 446
and cultural leveling, 71–72, 74
and cyber warfare, 477
gestures in, 57–58, 273
global, 70, 74, 313, 444
information age, 329, 331
and mass media, 90
and nonmaterial culture, 48, 53–54
nonverbal, 40, 57–58
online, 313, 314, 449, 477
and politics, 71, 313
in society, 54, 107, 148
in subcultures, 190
telecommunications, 341, 477
Communism, 7, 263, 390, 392, 420
Communist Party, 335, 390, 392
Community. *See also* Gemeinschaft;
    "Moral community"
    building of, 459
    in cities, 453–454, 457
    compared with alienation, 453
    defined, 453, 493
    elderly, support for, 368, 385
    and religion, 404, 405, 406–407,
        422
    significance of, 120–121, 141
Community colleges, 389, 391, 420
Compartmentalization, 232, 493
Computers. *See also* Internet
    and Big Brother, 477–478
    in business and finance, 339
    consulting, 449
    and cultural change, 70–71, 473
    in education, 392, 395, 401
    as an invention, 473
    and leisure, 67
    math and reading scores, 401
    in medicine, 70
    new technology of, 70, 466, 487
    in research, 25
    as social communication, 475–477
    and social inequality, 395, 466, 467
    and statistics, 25
    and surveillance, 249
    in war and terrorism, 477, 478
    and work, 215, 216, 338, 339
Concentric zone model, 450
Conflict perspective
    application of, 39, 43
    chart summarizing, 41t
    explained, 38
    as macrosociology, 41t
    Marx, Karl and, 38, 197
Conflict perspective on
    capitalism, 38–39
    and children, 433
    class conflict, 197–198

crime and criminal justice system,
    161–162
and internal colonialism, 233
divorce, 41t
ecosabotage, 484–485
education, 395–398
the elderly, 242
family size, 361–362
and feminists, 38–39
vs. functionalist perspective, 117–
    118, 141
gendered violence, 295, 296–297
global birth control, 430
globalization of capitalism, 192, 337–
    338, 344, 458
health care, 423
the homeless, 90–41
marriage and family, 356
the mass media, 117
medicalization, 173–174, 175
midwives, defeat of, 283
modern applications, 38, 39
politics in U.S., 322–323
power, 322–323, 468
power elite, 322–323
prejudice, 242–243
religion, 408–410
reproduction, 118–119
resources, 197–198
and role performance, 129–130
social institutions, 118–119
Social Security, 38
social stratification, 197–198
and strain, 129–130
welfare, 332
work, 38–39, 242–243
Conflict sociologists, 197
Conflict theory, defined, 493
Conformity, 38, 60, 93, 94, 151, 156
Confucianism, 38, 60, 93, 94, 156,
    369
Congress, U.S., 316, 318, 320, 322
Conspicuous consumption,
    328–329, 493
Construction of reality. *See* Reality, social
    construction of
Contact theory, 237
Control groups, 27, 493
Control theory, 152, 154, 493
Controversy
    in capitalism, 7–8, 38
    in colonialism, 195–197
    and day care, 93
    deception, 259
    due to protecting the subjects, 27
    over group values, 67
    over language, 55

due to manipulating the subjects,
    26, 28, 42
and power elite, 222
due to protecting the subjects, 27
and Philippe Ariès, 97–98, 102
social reform vs. social theory,
    10–15
violent crime, decline of, 165
Convergence theory, 335–336, 346, 493
Core nations, 192
Core values, 64
    conflict in, 67, 74
    and conformity, 60
    emerging, 67–68
    and mores, 60
    resistance to, 64
    and society, 68
    transmission of, 392–393
    in U.S., 65–66, 74
Corll, Dean, 167
Corporate crime, 158, 162, 493
Corporations. *See also* Bureaucracies;
    Multinational
    bailouts, 204
    boards of directors, 207
    CEOs, 203, 289
    and colonialism, 191
    and criminal justice system, 161, 162
    diversity in, 274
    drug companies, 332
    and economic colonies, 191
    as elite group, 118, 204, 322
    funding politicians, 318–320
    in Japan, 337–338
    multinational, 479
    and power, 199, 322, 345
    and production, 199
    and "sandwich generation," 99
    and upper middle class, 209
    and wealth, 211, 222–223, 339
    women in management of, 289
Corporate welfare, defined, 493
Cosmology, 411, 493
Cosmopolites, 454
Countercultures, 61, 64, 493. *See also*
    Subculture
Courtship, 359, 360
"Covering up" of problems, 459
Credential societies/credentialing, 388,
    389, 493
Credit cards, 389
Crime. *See also* Criminal justice system;
    Delinquents/delinquency; Deviance;
    Gangs; Murder; Rape
    conflict perspective on, 161
    corporate, 158
    decline in, 165

Crime (*Continued*)
 defined, 147, 493
 functionalist perspective on,
   155–160, 177
 and gender, 158–159
 genetic predispositions, 150
 hate crimes, 172–173
 and illegitimate opportunity, 157–160
 and police discretion, 172, 178
 relativity of, 146, 148, 149
 and social class, 157–160, 213
 statistics on, 171–173
 street, 157
 symbolic interactionist perspective
   on, 151–154
 violent, 159f, 165
 white-collar, 157–158
Criminal justice system. *See also*
   Prisoners
 and class, 161
 conflict perspective on, 161
 death penalty, 167–170, 178, 307
 defined, 161, 493
 and race–ethnicity, 164t, 170t
 reaction to deviance, 162–166
 and social class, 157–160, 213
 "three strikes" laws, 164–165
 women in, 158–159
Criminal records, 26, 27
Crude birth rate, defined, 493
Crusades, the, 407
Crying, 174
Cuban Americans, 250t. *See also* Latinos
Cults, 415–416, 493
Cultural diffusion, 71–72, 74, 493
Cultural diversity. *See* Diversity
Cultural evolution, 470
Cultural goals, 54, 62, 66, 156, 493
Cultural identity, 235
Cultural lag, 70–71, 74, 474, 493
Cultural leveling, 71–72, 74, 493
Cultural privilege, 38, 66, 111, 113, 182
Cultural relativism, 50, 52, 53, 73, 493
Cultural transmission of values, 59–61,
   392–393, 493
Cultural universals, 69, 493
Culture, 46–76. *See also* Subcultures
 in Africa, 47
 and assumptions, 49
 and beauty, 51
 and biological explanations, 58, 73
 and body image, 90, 130, 131
 and business/corporations, 118,
   199–120, 203, 204–205
 change in, 70–71, 74
 and childhood, 48, 98
 and children, number of, 361–363

in China, 110
as component of social structure, 110
countercultures, 61–64, 74
defined, 48, 73, 493
discrimination, support of, 298
in education, 64, 65, 66
and emotions, 58, 73
in everyday life, 52
evolutionary theories of, 470
as framework, 110
and gender changes, 67, 70
and gestures, 48, 49, 53, 54, 57–58, 73
and global capitalism, 70
in global village, 70–72, 74
health, views on, 68
hidden, 289
ideal, 65, 66, 67, 74
identity, 235
influence of, 49
internalization of, 49, 53, 57, 238, 239
and IQ testing, 395–396
judgment of others, 50
and language, 53–57, 61, 71, 73
leveling of, 71–72
life orientation and, 49–53, 73
mainstream, 63, 64, 74, 156–157
male, 277–278, 279, 280, 283, 300
material, 48, 49, 70, 71, 72, 73
and morality, 49, 74, 152, 177, 307,
   405, 419
and new technology, 70
nonmaterial, 48, 49, 53, 70, 73
overview, 47–48, 49–50
photo essay on, 235
and privilege, 38, 66, 116f, 118–119,
   141, 177, 197, 208, 231, 236, 247,
   265, 266, 280, 339, 366
and quality of life, 50
real, 66
and religious beliefs, 55, 65–66, 411
relativism of, 40
residing within us, 52
secularization of, 412
as social structure, 110–111
symbolic, 53–57
and tribal progress, 470
and taken-for-granted assumptions,
   49, 52, 73
and universals, 69, 74
and values, 50, 59–60 , 74
Culture clash (or conflict), 62, 66,
   67, 68, 74
Culture of poverty, 192–195, 493
Culture shock, 49–50, 52, 73, 493
Culture wars, 67–68
Currency, 241, 344
Customs, 69

Cyber war and cyber defense, 477
Cycle of poverty, 217, 219
Czechoslovakia, 407

D

Dating, online, 353
Day care
 effects on children, 93
 grade schools as, 394
 and the Internet, 364
 moral concern about, 93
 numbers of children in, 93, 363f, 364
 ND socialization, 93
 quality of, 93, 364
Death. *See also* Murder
 adjusting to, 78, 364
 in agricultural societies, 101
 and corporate decisions, 158
 crude rate, 437
 and customs for, 69, 301, 365
 and gender, 293–294, 298, 301
 global, 437
 industrialization and technology, 467t
 infant mortality, 467t
 and medical errors, 239–240
 and poverty, 192, 212, 213
 process of, 36, 97, 100
 and race–ethnicity, 259, 437
 and religion, 116f, 184
 at school, 19
 and sexism, 293–294, 298, 301
 and social class, 426
 sociology of, 14, 97, 141
 of spouse, 264–365, 366
 as a stage, 97, 100
 of students, 19
 by suicide, 8
 from unsafe products, 161–162
 in wars, 325
Death penalty
 bias in, 168–169
 and gender, 169
 geography of, 168, 178
 and race-ethnicity of, 169–170
 and serial killers, 167–168
 by state, 168f
Death rates, 169f
Death row, 167, 169–170t, 178
Death squads, 232
Debutante balls, 204
Decent, system of familial, 353
Declining privilege, 296
Declining Significance of Race, The
   (Wilson), 255
Deepwater Horizon, 484
Deferred gratification, 368

Definition of the situation. *See* Reality, social construction of; Thomas theorem

Degradation ceremony, 96, 493

Dehumanization, 232

Deindustrialization, 458, 493

Delinquents/delinquency
and children of divorce, 376
and differential association, 152
and labeling, 137, 153–154
as separate type of crime, 171
and social class, 172, 275
and social structure, 137
sociobiological explanation, 150
study of, 153, 274
and subcultures, 152
and techniques of neutralization, 153, 499
and testosterone levels, 274, 274, 275, 300

Democracy
background of, 311
citizenship in, 312
as a core value, 65
defined, 311, 493
direct, 312, 494
in Europe, 311–312, 314
and the mass media, 116f, 117, 119
and rebellion, 312
representative, 312, 498

Democratic façade, 204

Democratic leaders, 253, 298, 315–316, 345

Democratic socialism, 333, 493

Democrats, 315–316, 345

Demographic equation, basic, 438

Demographic transition, 428–429, 460, 493

Demographic variables, 436–440, 493

Demography, defined, 426, 494

Denominations (religious), 116f, 213, 223, 417

Dependency ratio, 98, 101

Dependent variable, 27, 494

Depersonalization, 136

Deprived, in cities, 454

Descent, systems of, 353

Deviance, 145–180. *See also* Crime
background assumptions, 146–147
conflict perspective on, 161–162
control theory of, 152
defined, 146, 494
and differential association, 151–152
explanations of, 146
and the family, 152–152
and friends, neighborhoods, subcultures, 152

functionalist perspective on, 155
functions of, 155
and the homeless, 174
and honor, 152
humane approach to, 176, 178
labeling theory of, 153–154
and the mafia, 152
medicalization of, 173–175
and mental illness, 174
and moral holidays, 173
naked runs/rides, 87, 212
neutralization of, 153, 499
overview, 145–146, 177
paths to, 156–157
pleasure in, 153–154
and psychological explanations, 149
reactions to, 162–166
relativity of, 146, 148, 149, 178
sexual, 146, 167–168
and social change, 155
and social class, 157, 160
and sociobiological explanations, 149
and sociological explanations, 149
and strain theory, 156
symbolic interactionist perspective on, 146, 151–154
and unity, 155
and values, 156–157
and Yanomamö Indians, 145–146, 148

Dialectical process of history, 471–472

Dictatorships, 312–314, 494

Differential association theory, 151–152, 494

Diffusion
of culture, 71, 72, 74
defined, 474, 494
of ideas, 473t, 474, 475
of inventions, 473t, 474, 475, 487
of responsibility, 455–456

Direct democracy, 494

Direct transfer, of minorities, 232

"Dirty work," 243

Disabilities, people with, 113, 172t, 228, 393, 421

Disasters, 139, 140

Discovery, defined, 473, 494

Discrimination. *See also* Prejudice; Racism; specific racial–ethnic groups
defined, 237, 494
ethnic conflicts, 227–230, 231–236, 237–240, 244, 265
as an everyday burden, 255
and gender/women, 283, 287–290, 293, 298
and hate crimes, 172–173
in health care, 239

and the homeless, 40–41
in housing/mortgages, 239
individual and institutional, 238–240
and in-/out-groups, 242
and intelligence (IQ) tests, 395–396
vs. prejudice, 237
and segregation, 232, 233, 252–253, 266
and stereotypes, 217, 243, 247, 282, 283, 289
systemic, 239
unintentional, 289

Disengagement theory, 399

Disinvestment, and cities, 458, 494

Distance learning, 10

"Distance zones," 126, 127, 141

Diversity. *See also* Homosexuals; Minority group(s); Race–ethnicity
and African Americans, 366
and Asian Americans, 257, 368
and blended families, 370–371
and childless couples, 370
in the corporation, 202, 203, 209, 211, 222–223, 274
and culture, 352
and gay and lesbian families, 371
of groups, 259
and Latinos, 249–250, 266, 367
and Native Americans, 259, 266, 368
and one-parent families, 369–370
and religious groups, 417
in united society, 264
in U.S. families, 369–372
in U.S. population, 245, 257

Divine right of kings, 409, 422, 494

Division of labor
and capitalism/socialism convergence, 335
in cities, 445
defined, 120, 494
and gender, 289, 357
on a global scale, 298, 301
in hunting and gathering societies, 328
modern/traditional comparison, 328, 328–331
in pastoral and horticultural societies, 120, 328
in social movement organizations, 280, 284–285, 298
and social solidarity, 120, 141

Divorce
and blended families, 370, 379, 385
children of, 376, 379
and cohabitation, 19, 374, 375
conflict perspective on, 356
and ex-spouses, 378

Divorce (*Continued*)
   factors in, 377
   fatherhood after, 377–378
   functionalist perspective on, 36, 37
   geographic patterns of, 376f
   and grandchildren, 377
   husbands and, 22t, 378
   measuring, 375
   and race–ethnicity, 378
   reduction of, 377t
   and remarriage, 379–380
   and social class, 212
   spousal abuse, 26t, 380–381
   statistics on, 382
   symbolic interactionist perspective
      on, 33, 382
   in the U.S. 33f, 375–376, 378f
   and voting, 317t
   in Zimbabwe, 87
Documents, in research, 26–27, 494
Dollar (U.S.), hourly earnings, 338
Domestic partnerships, 371
Domestication revolution, 467,
   468, 487
Dominant groups, 231–234, 265,
   279–280, 494
Double standard, 280
Downward social mobility, 215, 494
Dramaturgy, 127–133
   and actors, 128
   and body image, 131
   and careers, 131–132
   and conflict, 129
   defined, 494
   impression management, 128, 129
   overview, 127–128, 141–142
   role performance, 129
   sign-vehicles, 129
   stages of, 128–129
   and strain, 129–130
   teamwork, 131
Drugs
   alcohol, 96, 157, 171, 211, 407, 454
   cocaine, 359
   hallucinogenic, 145, 146
   and mental illness, 174
   monitoring, by government, 332
   nicotine, 407
   and prisoners, 166f
   and religion, 407
   and social class, 211
   student use of, 30, 94, 115
   and testosterone levels, 300
   as therapy for the poor, 212
   in underground economy, 156,
      157, 160
   and veterans, 274

   and women, 159t
Dubai, 333
Dump people, 188–189, 329, 479
Dupont Circle, 106
Dyads, 455
Dysfunctions
   of bureaucracies, 402
   defined, 35
   and deviance, 155, 165, 178
   in functional analysis, 35–36, 41t, 43
   globalization of capitalism, 337–338,
      344, 346, 458, 479
   latent, defined, 35
   of nuclear family, 355
   of prejudice, 242, 265
   of religion, 407–408, 422
   and social stratification, 197
   and society, 36

E

Earth First!, 484
Ecclesia, 416–417, 494
Economic crisis, 165, 249, 336, 337, 347,
   437, 476
Economics, field of, 327–331
Economy, the, 305–349. *See also*
   Capitalism
   biotech society, 328, 330–331, 346
   convergence theory, 335–336, 346
   defined, 327, 494
   depression and discrimination, 174,
      175, 241, 244, 339
   global power rearrangement,
      327–331
   and home mortgages, 239
   and immigration, 262–263
   mediums of exchange, 241, 337, 344
   modern, 327
   and oil, 194f
   of small towns, 340–341
   as a social institution, 116f, 122, 141
   socialism, 333–334
   transformation of, 327–331
   underground, 160, 156, 157
   wealth divisions, 339
Ecosabotage, 484–485, 494
Edge cities, 447, 494
Education, 389–404 *See also* College;
   Schools
   achievement, in the U.S., 390f
   and capitalism, 390, 392, 420
   and computers, 395, 467
   conflict perspective on, 395–398
   credentials/diplomas, 389
   and crime, 163, 164t
   and culture, 389, 390, 391

   curriculum, 392, 393, 397
   distance learning, 10
   and divorce, 212, 223
   doctorates earned, 251t, 388
   in earlier societies, 10
   in Egypt, 391
   in the 1800s, 10, 71
   and family functions, 394
   functional illiteracy, 402
   functionalist perspective on, 117–118,
      392–395
   funding for, 395
   future of, 400–404, 421
   and gender, 399
   in global perspective, 389–392
   grade inflation, 401
   "hidden curriculum" in, 397, 421
   home schooling, 310
   and ideology, 64, 65, 66, 74
   and income, 219, 220
   and industrialization, 389–392
   in Industrializing Nations, 116, 390–
      391, 392–392
   in Japan, 390
   learning environments, 403
   in Least Industrialized Nations, 98,
      187, 391–392
   math and reading scores, 401
   and mediocrity in, 401
   in medicine, 206, 209
   in Most Industrialized Nations, 390
   and patriotism, 393
   and pay gap, 287
   and peer group influence, 93–94
   and poverty, 217, 220
   and pregnancy, 219, 220f
   problems and solutions, in U.S.,
      400–404
   purpose of, 392, 393–394
   quality of, 401
   racial–ethnic relations, 197–198,
      251t, 397
   research on, 398–399
   and religious affiliation, 417, 418f, 420
   in Russia, 390–391
   and SAT tests, 401
   and the school year, 391, 400
   and single mothers, 220f
   and social class, 107, 111, 207, 208,
      209, 212–213, 222–223, 396
   and social integration, 393
   as a social institution, 117, 393, 394
   and social mobility, 215, 216
   and social placement, 392–393
   and social promotion, 402
   standards, raising, 402–403
   for success, 98

and suicide terrorists, 326
symbolic interactionist perspective, 398–400
on teacher expectations, 398, 399
teachers, 399, 402
and technology, 392, 395
tests, discrimination in, 395–396
and transmission of values, 392–393, 421
tutors for preschoolers, 213, 214
unequal funding for, 395
in U.S., in earlier years, 389–390f
and values, 65, 66, 74, 392–393
and violence, 403
and voting patterns, 316–318
and work, 205
Egalitarian, defined, 353, 494
Ego, defined, 353
Egypt, 391
El Tiro, 440–441, 442–443
Elderly
abuse of, 296, 297
ascribed status of, 112
care of, 36, 368, 461
changing sentiment about, 99–100
conflict perspective on, 242
defining "old," 100 , 101
and dependency, 36, 368, 461
discrimination, 237
functionalist perspective on, 36
and industrialization, 467t
and income, 37, 204, 211
and the life course, 99–100
population, percentage of, 218f
and poverty, 211, 217, 336, 454
and race–ethnicity, 218f
and retirement, 453
and sandwich generation, 99
and Social Security, 218, 249, 336, 433
and socialization, 99–100
stereotypes of, 68
suicide of, 67
and work, 242
and values, 68
Electronic church, 419
Elite. *See* Power elite
Emergent values, 67–68
Emotions, 86–87, 102, 406
and childbirth, 87
and biology, 86
in everyday life, 87
expression, 86–87
and relationships, 87
Empty nest, 364, 384
Endangered species, 479, 482, 483
Endogamy, 352, 494

Energy shortage, 482–483, 487–488
England, 241, 250
"English only" movement, 55, 249
Enterprise zones, 458, 494
Environment, 479–486, 487–488
Chernobyl, 480
and ecosabotage, 484–485
energy shortages, 482–483, 487–488
and fossil fuels, 481–482
global perspective on, 479, 481–482, 487–488
and globalization of capitalism, 479
and industrialization, 479–483
internal combustion engines, 482
Medicine Tree protest, 484
as a social movement, 483–485
rain forests, 482
recycling, 484
and radical movements, 484–485
and sociology, 485–486
sustainability of, 479
and technology, 482, 485–488
toxic wastes, 480–481
and tribal societies, 479, 486
as a value, 68
Environmental injustice, 483, 488, 494
Environmental justice groups, 483
Environmental movement, 483–485
Environmental sociology, 485–486, 494
Essay on the Principle of Population, An, 427
Estate stratification system, 494
Ethics in research, 28, 78–79, 82
Ethiopia, 194, 271, 438t
Ethiopian Jews, 229
Ethnic, defined, 494
Ethnic cleansing, 228, 230, 232, 494. *See also* Genocide
Ethnic maps, 238
Ethnic villagers, 233, 454
Ethnic work, 234–235, 494
Ethnicity. *See also* Race–ethnicity
background of, 229–230
and cancer, 14, 238
construction of, 234–235
defined, 229, 494
future of, 263
vs. race, 229
U.S. diversity, 245–247
Ethnocentrism, 50–52, 494
Ethnomethodology, 133–135, 142, 494
Europe, 38, 97, 100, 191, 430, 460
European Americans, relations with, 245–248, 266
European Union (EU), 344
Evangelism, 405, 415f, 416, 494

Everyday life. *See also* Reality, social construction of
and beauty, 50, 51
and body image, 130, 131
and changing culture, 49
dramaturgy, 127–131
and ethnomethodology, 133–135,
and eye contact, 126
gender inequality in, 292–293
and gestures, 57–58
and height, 237, 270
impression management in, 128, 129, 132
personal space in, 123, 126
racial–ethnic relations, 263
and religion, 407
and research, 31, 43
rhythm of, 117
roles in, 125–133
social interaction, 83, 109, 123–127
standardization of, 59
stereotypes in, 217–218, 244, 283, 326
symbols in, 32
Exchange mobility, 215, 494
Exogamy, 352, 494
Experimental groups, 27, 494
Experiment(s), 27. *See also* Research
and cause and effect, 27
defined, 27, 494
diffusion of responsibility, 455–456, 462
and gender messages, 89
by Harlow, 80, 82
morality of babies, 49, 59, 98
on orphanages, 81, 82
on personal space, 123
prejudice in, 241, 242
and the real world, 456
as a research method, 21f, 27
on romantic love, 359, 361
on social unity, 250
unethical, 78–79, 82
Exponential growth curve, 427, 494
Extended, defined, 494
Extinction of species, 68, 479
Eye contact, 126

F

Facebook, 476–477, 478, 487
Face-saving behavior, 131, 494
Face-to-face interaction, 41, 71, 123, 127, 421
Facial expressions, 58, 86, 87, 102, 126, 148

Factories, 199, 328, 333, 458, 418. *See also* Industrialization
False class consciousness, 199, 494
Family of orientation, defined, 494
Family of procreation, defined, 494
Families, 366–367. *See also* Children and childhood; Divorce; Marriage
    abuse/violence in, 380–381
    of African Americans, 366
    as agent of socialization, 92–93
    of Asian Americans, 367, 376f
    authority in, 352t, 353–354
    blended, 370–371
    and burial, 365
    childless, 369, 370f
    conflict perspective on, 356
    and decision making, 356f
    defined, 351, 494
    and deviance, 151–152
    diversity in, 366–367
    and education, 394, 396–398
    extended, 351, 352t, 367, 384
    and fatherhood, 366
    fathers, absent, 362, 384
    functionalist perspective on, 355
    functions of, 355
    future of, 356, 357, 383
    gay and lesbian, 371, 385
    gender messages in, 89
    grandparents, 363f, 368, 377, 384, 385
    in hunting and gathering societies, 276
    income and college attendance, 396
    and industrialization, 36
    and intergenerational relationships, 61
    of Latinos, 367
    mate selection, 212
    of Native Americans, 367
    nuclear, 351, 352t, 368, 384
    one-parent, 369–370, 384. *See also* Single mothers
    of orientation, 351
    as a primary group, 116f
    of procreation, 351
    and "sandwich generation," 99
    size of, 361–362
    and social class, 212, 364, 366, 367, 368, 384
    as a social institution, 92–93
    and social mobility, 185, 213, 214–215
    symbolic interactionist perspective on, 151–152
    trends in, 357, 370, 372–375, 385
    two-parent households, 367f, 394
    universality of, 355

Famines, 426, 431, 461
Fanchang, China, 199
Fashions, 90
Fatherhood, 366
Fecundity, defined, 436, 494
Feelings, 86–87. *See also* Emotions
Female circumcision, 295, 302
Female infanticide, 295
Femininities, emerging, 270, 274, 283, 300
Femininity, devaluation of, 292, 301
Feminism and feminists
    and circumcision, 295, 302
    and conflict perspective, 119, 356
    defined, 280, 494
    early research, 10–12
    evolution of, 279–282
    feminism, defined, 280, 300
    and gender, 38–39, 279–281
    and global stratification, 185
    and population growth, 439
    and sexual harassment, 291
    and social theory, 10
    sociologists, 273, 276
    stratification status of, 185
    symbolic interactionist perspective on, 291
    three waves of, 280, 282, 300
    and violence, 296
Feral children, 78, 494
Fertility rate, defined, 436, 494
Fes, Morocco, 136
Fieldwork. *See* Participant observation
Firestone tires, 158
Fisher v. the University of Texas, 263
Flu virus, 232
Folkways, 60, 494
Food
    bioengineering of, 431
    and biofuels, 431, 432, 461
    and cancer, 14
    customs, 52
    and population growth, 430–432
    world production of, 431f
Football, 108
Ford Explorers, 158
Ford Motor Company, 158
Foreign Miner's Act of 1850, 256, 258
Formal organizations. *See* Bureaucracies
Fossil fuels, 481–482. *See also* Oil
Framework of ideas, 31
Fraud, 157, 158, 159t, 166f, 206, 214
Free trade, 343
Friends, 152. *See also* Peers
Front stages, 128–129, 494
Frustration, 240–241

Functional analysis. *See also* Functionalist perspective on
    application of, 36, 43
    chart summarizing, 41t
    defined, 494–495
    explained, 35
    latent functions, 392, 496
    as macrosociology, 41t
    manifest functions, 392, 496
    Merton, Robert and, 35–36
    origins of, 35
Functional illiteracy, 402
Functional requisites, 117–118
Functionalist perspective on
    benefits of society, 392–393, 421
    vs. conflict perspective, 117–118, 141
    crime and deviance, 155, 156, 160, 177
    deviance, 155
    divorce, 36, 37, 41t
    education, 392–395
    the elderly, 36
    the family, 355, 394–395
    the homeless, 40–41
    incest taboo, 355, 358, 384
    industrialization, 36, 37
    macro level, 40, 43, 106
    marriage, 355, 357
    and mass media, 117–118
    and motivation, 195–197
    on pluralism, 321
    politics in U.S., 321
    power elite, 323
    prejudice, 242
    religion, 406–408
    social environment, 242
    social integration, 393
    social institutions, 118, 119
    social placement, 393–394
    social stratification, 113, 195–197, 220, 222
    society, 38
    structure and function, 37
    unskilled jobs, 40
    and values, 156
    workers, 195–197
Functions, 35. *See also* Functional analysis
Fundamentalist, 411, 418, 422
Furman v. Georgia, 169

G

G 7/G 8, 468–469 , 471
Gambling, 157, 202
Games, 69, 84, 91

Gangs
    biker, 154
    in everyday life, 29
    and disinvestment, 458
    functions of, 64
    and honor, 153
    as in-/out-groups, 242
    Mafia, 152
    norms in, 154
    and opportunity structure, 157
    participant observation of, 28
    research, 29
    rivalry between, 250
Gasoline, and stratification, 192
Gatekeeping, 393–394, 495
Gemeinschaft, 121, 141, 466, 495
Gender, 269–304. See also Feminism;
    Masculinity; Women
    and advertising, 90, 283, 297
    affirmative action, 263
    and authority, 276, 291, 301
    author's experience with, 28
    awareness of, 88–89
    and background assumptions, 293
    and beauty, 51
    and biology, 273–275, 283. See also
        Childbirth
    and body images, 90, 130
    in capital punishment, 169
    and caste, 184
    in childhood, 89–90
    and conflict theory, 119
    and crime, 158–159
    defined, 89, 270, 495
    and discrimination, 282, 283–290
    and division of labor, 357
    and domination, 274
    double standard of, 280
    in earlier societies, 276
    and education, 160, 288f
    and effects on life, 91
    and the elderly, 296, 297
    and emotions, 280
    and equality, concept of, 280–282
    in everyday life, 269, 272, 292–294
    and eye contact, 126
    and the family, 89, 281, 295, 300
    and feminist sociologists, 119,
        273, 296
    future of, 273, 296
    and gender, 158–159
    and global stratification, 282–286
    hand-to-hand combat, 277–278
    and health care, 293–294
    and housework, 282
    in hunting and gathering societies,
        276, 278, 280

identification with, 235, 250, 261, 266
illegitimate opportunities, 157–160
and illiteracy, 185
in India, 271, 284–286, 295, 297
and infanticide, 295
and isolation, 21, 23
and mass media, 90
as a master status, 112
and medicine/health care, 293–294
orientations, changes in, 356–358
overview, 88
and pay, 287–290
and peers, 89–90
photo essay on, 284–285
and play, 272, 273, 274, 275, 278,
    281f, 292
and politics, 274, 275, 280, 298–299
and poverty, 384
and prestige, 283
and reproduction, 270, 273, 277, 300
in research, 28, 274–275, 283, 286,
    287, 288, 292, 293, 296
and segregation, 242
vs. sex, 270
and sex-selection abortion, 295, 302
and social change, 289, 291, 298,
    467t, 474
and social class, 93, 274, 275
and social inequality, 91, 280, 282–
    286, 292–294, 298, 301
as a social location, 100
as social structure, 291, 301
socialization into, 89, 274, 275
and societal changes, 272
and sports, 292, 294
stereotypes of, 283, 289
symbolic interactionist perspective
    on, 290–291, 356
and teacher expectations, 399
and testertone, 274–275
and toys, 89, 90, 91
and transition to adulthood, 99
and video games, 91
and violence (See under Violence)
and voting, 298, 302, 317t
and work, 283–290
worldview of, 91
Gender age, 242
Gender discrimination, defined, 282, 495
Gender gap
    in pay, 287–288
    in politics, 318, 320
    in voting, 317t
Gender messages, 89–90, 102
Gender roles, 10, 50, 90, 91, 113
Gender socialization, defined, 89, 495
Gender stereotypes, defined, 289, 495

Gender stratification
    in agricultural societies, 280
    biology vs. culture, 86, 109, 273
    crime, 169f
    defined, v
    future of, 39, 298
    global perspective on, 185–186
    and master statuses, 112
    in politics, 280, 298–299
    in sociological research, 28, 215–216
    in the U.S., 288f
    and violence, 295–297
    in the workplace, 215, 263, 282,
        283–286
Gendered violence, 495. See also
    Conflict perspective on; Symbolic
    interactionist perspective on; Violence
Generalizability, 495
Generalizations, 367, 495
Generalized other, 84, 495
Gendered violence, defined, 295
Genes and human behavior. See Nature
    vs. nurture
Genetic engineering, 330–331, 346
Genetic predispositions, 273, 274,
    300, 495
Geneva Convention, 260
Genocide
    defined, 228, 495
    Holocaust, 228, 230, 232, 265
    of Native Americans, 231–232
    by ordinary people, 232
    in Rwanda, 228, 231, 232, 236
Gentrification, 232, 441, 447–448, 449,
    461, 495
Geopolitics, 468–470, 487, 495. See also
    G 7/G 8; Global stratification
Germany, 468, 469, 483. See also
    Nazis
Gesellschaft, 121, 141, 495
Gestapo, 313
Gestures, 57–58, 495
Ghettoes, 238, 253. See also Inner city;
    Slums
Glass ceiling, 289–290, 495
Global competition, 338, 340–341
Global perspective on
    banking, 344, 347
    beauty, 51
    capitalism (See Globalization of
        capitalism)
    cities, 444f
    dominant and minority groups,
        231–234
    education, 389–392
    gender inequality, 38–39
    love and courtship, 359

Global perspective on (*Continued*)
marriage and family, 351–354, 384
population growth, 426
power/geopolitics, 468–470
racial–ethnic relations, 231f
religion, 404–406
reasoning, 278
self, the, 83–85, 101–102
technology, 467, 475–478
trade, 346, 473t
Global stratification. *See also* Capitalism;
Social stratification
and balance of power, 321
distribution of land, income, and
population, 193f
and the environment, 427–430,
479–483
and families, 355, 359
and females, 185
income, 193
maintaining, 468–469
origin of, 185
poverty, 192, 195
power/geopolitics, 468–470
slavery and social class,
182–183, 221
and social class, 185
and social stratification, 191–195
and the superclass, 190
strains in system of, 344
and technology, 70
theory of, 186–190, 191–192
unity, trends toward, 343–344
wealth, divisions of, 315, 334, 339
and women, 295
Global superclass, 190, 342, 343,
346, 495
Global village
and culture, 70–72
defined, 329, 495
economy and work in the, 327–328
technology and, 70–71
Global warming, 481–482, 487–488, 495
Globalization
and communication, 192
defined, 192, 495
of disease, 232
McDonaldization of society, 71
power/geopolitics, 468–470
of social movements, 479–483
and social structure, 337–338
and sociology, effects on, 337–338
and the superclass, 190
and technology, 70
of work, 190, 338–339, 344, 346
Globalization of capitalism. *See also*
Multinational corporations

alienation and, 318
conflict perspective on, 322–323
and cultural leveling, 71–72
defined, 495
described, 337
and divisions of wealth, 339
economic crisis and, 336, 337, 347
effect on small towns, 340–341
and environmental degradation,
483–487
and ethics, 328, 331
in everyday life, 338
functionalist perspective on, 321
investments, 325, 339, 342
and jobs, 322, 329, 333, 337–338,
339, 346
and New World Order, 343–344
and ownership of businesses, 333
and paychecks, 338–339
photo essay on, 340–341
and power elites, 322–323
structure of, 337–338
and trade, 328, 329, 332, 337, 343–
344, 346
and wealth, 339
and work, 338–339
world system theory, 191–192
Goal-directed behavior, 54
Goals vs. means, 156t
Gossip, 148
Government. *See also* Politics
checks and balances, 321
coalition, 343–344
corporate bailouts, 204
and corporations, 322, 345
and the military, 322
and religion, 316
types of, 311–314
in the U.S., 315f, 320, 321–323
Grade inflation, 401, 495
Grandparents, 351, 362, 363f, 368, 385
Great Britain, 11, 118, 190, 191, 344, 468
Greece, 182, 193, 213, 470
Green belts, 451
Green parties, 483, 485t, 488
Greenhouse, 495
Group size, 467t
Groups
control, 27f
defined, 111, 495
dominant, 38, 231–234
experimental, 27, 80
in-groups, 242
labeling and prejudice, 153–154
minority, 231–234
organized, 152
patterns of, 108

primary, 116
reference, 280, 282
secondary, 116
small, defined,
social networks, 476–477
and social structure, 108–109, 111
stability of, 309
Growth rate, defined, 438, 495
Guatemala, 194, 437f, 438t
Guilt, 49, 86, 208, 368
Gulf Wars, 71
Gush Katif beach, Israel, 1
Gynecological examinations, 136–137

H

Handlers, 319
Hangzhou, China, 335
Harlem, 459
Harlow experiments, 80, 82
Harvard University, 12, 156, 186, 206, 211
Hate crimes, 171–173, 495
Hate groups, 236. *See also* Ku Klux Klan;
Neo-Nazis
Hatred, 171, 172, 232, 237, 242, 325
Hazardous waste sites, 480–481
Health and health care. *See also* Life
expectancy; Medicine
clubs, 68
conflict perspective on, 429
costs of care, 137, 336
and depersonalization, 136
discrimination in, 239, 293–294, 301
disease, infectious, 14, 232, 259
in everyday life, 292–294
illness, 212, 336, 406, 454
functionalist perspective on, 394,
407, 429
gender discrimination in, 293–294
in global perspective, 426–430
heart disease, 293, 301
and industrialization, 116f, 219, 467t
inequality in, 211, 223, 239,
293–294, 301
and lifestyles, 100, 211, 407
mental health (*See* Mental illness)
physical health, 211–212
race-ethnicity, 239
reform of, 211, 293
and religion, 407
as a right versus a commodity, 211
and smoking, 211, 330
and social class, 211, 219, 223
and social institutions, 116f, 239, 265
and sociology, applied, 136
study on, 274
and technology, 70

threats to, 454

treatment versus prevention, 70, 175, 211, 239, 293, 336

two-tier system of, 212

values, 68

Health Maintenance Organizations (HMOs), 116f

Height, 237, 270

Hell's Angels, 64, 153

Henley, Elmer Wayne, 167

Heredity. *See* Genetic predispositions; Nature vs. nurture

Heterosexual, hate crimes and, 172t

Hidden corporate culture, 289

"Hidden curriculum," 397, 421, 495

High schools, 394, 402, 421

Hindus, 405, 409, 410, 411

Hispanics. *See* Latinos

History

and biography, 2–4, 16

of childhood, 97

of cities, 441–446, 461

as class struggle, 208

components of, 198

dialectical process of, 471–472

of education, 10

of geopolitics, 468

of money, 7

natural cycles of civilization, 470–471

teaching of, 393

of urbanization, 440–441, 461

Hmong, 49

HMOs (Health Maintenance Organizations), 116f

Holocaust, 171, 228, 265

Holy Week in Spain, 412–413

Home schooling, 310

Homeland Security, 122, 312, 393, 478

Homeless, the

author's experience with, 28, 40–41

boundaries of, 185

conflict perspective on, 39

and deviance, 174

doing research on, 174

functionalist perspective on, 40–41

medicalization of, 172–175

and mental illness, 174, 178

in shelters, 40, 174, 176

social challenges of, 175

sociological perspectives on, 40, 174–175, 178, 185, 212

streetcorner men, 106–107, 110, 111

as underclass, 210

Homogamy, 360, 495

Homosexuals, 172t, 228, 230, 371, 385

Honor, and killing, 152, 295

"Honor killings," 295, 297, 301

Hopi, the, 55, 56

Horatio Alger myth, 219–220, 495

Horticultural societies, 328, 495

Households, defined, 351, 495

Housework, 356–358

Housing segregation, 250

Hualapai, the, 260

Hudson, Jennifer, 130

Hull-House, 12, 15

Human ecology, 450, 495

Human genome, decoding of, 227, 330, 331, 466

Human heads, in religion, 418, 422

Hunting and gathering societies, 276, 280, 328f, 466, 484, 495

Husbands, violent and nonviolent, 22t

Hutus, 228, 232, 236

Hyderabad, India, 147

Hygiene, 50, 332, 429

Hypothesis, 21–22, 495

I

Id, defined, 175

Ideal culture, 65, 66, 67, 74, 495

Idealized traits, of societies, 466–467

Identity. *See also* Self (the)

and initiation rites, 98

and labels, 153–154

national, 192, 234f, 393–394, 421

personal identity kit, 96

racial–ethnic, 234, 245

and religion, 411, 417t

and roles, 10, 67, 84, 90, 91, 109, 113–115

and total institutions, 96

and work, 454

Ideology

of capitalism and socialism, 332–334

defined, 183, 495

and education, 280, 300

of equality, 220, 222

to justify slavery, 183

to justify stratification, 197, 204

of opportunity, 219–221

and power, 204

and socialism, 333

and suicide terrorists, 326

and work, 220

Illegitimate opportunity structure, 157–160, 495

Illiteracy, functional, 402

Immigrants

and Arizona law, 249

assimilation of, 233

birthplace of, 249f

and border fence, 248–249, 251

Chinese, 256–258

debate, 262–263

and Hull-House, 12, 15

illegal/unauthorized, 248, 249, 266, 437

Irish, 246f, 247

Lativians, 30

Latinos, 55, 249

politics of, 12, 262–263

push and pull factors, 437

racial–ethnic mix in U.S., 245–246, 249

socialization of, 185, 209

Immigrants in U.S., country of origin, 437f, 438f

Immigration debate, 262–263

Impersonality, and cities, 453

Implicit Association Test, 238, 240, 244

Impression management, 128, 129, 132, 495

Incarceration. *See* Prisoners

Incas, 312

Incest and incest taboo, 69, 352, 355, 382–383, 495

Inclusion, defined, 393, 495

Income. *See also* Poverty; Social class; Social inequality, Wealth

average hourly, 338f

of CEOs, 203t

defined, 201, 495

distribution of, 202–204

division of, 203

and divorce, 366, 368, 377t

and education, 251t, 257, 298f

extremes, in U.S., 255t

and gender, 287–290

global stratification of, 193f, 337–343

inequality of, 338–343

and inflation, 338, 343

of Native Americans, 367f

and race–ethnicity, 239, 250–251, 253, 254, 257, 266

and religious affiliation, 418f

of teachers, 206

"testosterone" bonus, 273

in underground economy, 156, 158, 160

in the U.S., 33f, 203f

and voting patterns, 316–318

vs. wealth, 201–202

Indentured service, 184, 284

Independent variables, 27, 496

India

author's visit to, 72, 147

background assumptions, 146

British rule of, 276

caste system in, 182, 184, 186

India (*Continued*)
  child labor in, 98, 184
  and deviance, 147
  marriage in, 32
  megacities in, 445f
  norms in, 50
  as nuclear power, 471
  orphanages in, 80, 81
  photos of, 284–285
  population growth in, 433, 437
  poverty in, 29, 192–193
  religion in, 184, 295, 297, 405, 409,
      410, 411, 422
  sex-selection abortion in, 295
  and technology, 72
  traditional life in, 284–285
Individual discrimination, 238, 496
Individualism, 65, 66, 393
Individualistic vs. structural explanations
    of poverty, 214–215, 223
Indonesia, 194f, 350, 482
Industrial Revolution, 466–467. *See also*
    Industrialization
  and adolescence, 98, 100
  and cities, 444, 461
  defined, 5
  effects on society, 466–468
  and origin of sociology, 5
  as social revolution, 466–467, 487
  theories, 38
Industrial societies, 328, 496
Industrialization. *See also* Industrial
    Revolution
  and aging/elderly, 37, 454
  and birth rate, 390, 428f–429
  and capitalism/modernization, 329,
      337–342
  and childhood, 98
  and cities/urbanization, 444–445, 461
  and consumption, 329
  development of, 36–37
  and development of sociology, 5
  and death, 428f
  and economy, 116f, 328–329
  and education, 116f
  and the environment, 479–483
  in everyday life, 329–330
  and the family, 116f
  and global stratification, 187–190
  and law, 116f
  and leisure, 98
  machine, birth of, 328
  and mass media, 116f
  and marriage in, 352t
  and meaning of "old age," 99, 101, 211
  and medicine, 116f
  and military, 116f
    and politics, 116f
    and pollution, 161, 162, 479–483
    post-, 329
    and production, 199
    and rationality, 308
    and relationships, 466, 467t
    and religion, 116f
    and science, 116f
    as social institution, 116f
    and social stratification, 187
    traditional authority in, 307
    vs. traditional societies, 467t
    and types of society, 327–331
    and urbanization, 445t
Industrializing Nations
    and credential societies, 388, 389
    distribution of land, income,
        population, 203–204
    education in, 390–392
    environmental problems in,
        479–483
    income, 187, 193f
    lifestyles in, 222
    map of, 193f
    power in, 471
    urbanization in, 445t, 462
Inequality. *See* Social inequality
Infant mortality, 467
Infanticide, 295, 438, 439, 461
Inflation, 209
Information age, 329–330, 393
Information societies. *See* Postindustrial
    societies
In-groups, 242
Inheritance, 353
Initiation rites, 98
Inner city, 108, 209, 254–255, 397
Inquisition, the, 407
Institutional discrimination, 496
Institutionalized, 156, 496
Insurance, health, 116f, 211, 212
Intel, 116f, 140, 211, 212, 458
Intelligence, 79, 80, 101
Intelligence (IQ) tests, 395–396
Interaction. *See* Social interaction
Intergenerational conflict, 61
Intergenerational mobility, 214–215, 495
Intergroup relations
    global patterns of, 232f
    and parental involvement in, 61
Internal colonialism, 232–233, 496
Internet
    and capitalism, 332
    cyber war/defense, 477
    dating/mate selection, 352–353
    Iran, 476
    personal photos, effects of, 476
    and politics, 476, 477
    in research, 28
    religion on, 419
    sociological significance of, 3, 70,
        449, 476
    and war, 477
    web coupons with personal informa-
        tion, 28
Interview direct, defined, 496
Interviewer bias effects, 25–26, 496
Interviews, 25–26
Institutional discrimination, 239
Invasion–succession cycle, 450–451, 496
Inventions. *See also* New technology;
    Social inventions
    defined, 473, 496
    diffusion of, 473t, 474, 475, 487
    mediums of exchange, 477
    microchip, 466, 478, 487
    plow, 466, 467, 487
    and social change, 473, 474, 487
    and social revolutions, 466
    steam engine, 466, 467, 487
Investments, global, 325, 342
IQ tests, 395–396
Iran, 194f, 280, 301, 411, 461
Iraq, 118, 194f, 311, 313, 325, 441
Iraq War, 118, 325
Iroquois, the, 259, 260, 312
Islam, 19, 420. *See also* Muslims
Israel, 489, 183, 193f, 229, 325
Italy, 58, 193f, 468, 469, 487

J

Jackson, Mississippi, 233
Japan
    and China, 468
    culture of, 71, 86
    discrimination of, 256–257
    economy of, 337
    education in, 389, 390, 420
    emperor as a god, 409
    environmental issues in, 480,
        481, 486
    and geopolitics, 468, 487
    group identity in, 390
    income stratification in, 193f
    megacity in, 445f
    as Most Industrialized Nation, 187
    religion in, 195
    resources in, 191
    values in, 390, 393
Japanese Americans. *See* Asian
    Americans
Jews
    anti-Semitism, 240, 241, 242, 244

of Ethiopia, 229
as ethnic group, 228, 229
genocide/Holocaust, 230, 232, 236, 241
and hate crimes, 172t
and labels, 232
learning prejudice, 237
Nazis creating prejudice against, 228, 242
Orthodox, 404
as an out-group, 242
population transfer of, 232
and religion, 404, 411, 417
and social class, 418, 420
Jim Crow laws, 252, 266
Jolie, Angelina, 90

K

Kenya, 51, 191, 194f, 271
Khmer Rouge, 78
Kindergarten, 90, 93, 363f, 398–399
King, Martin Luther, Jr. 252, 253, 407
"Knowledge work," 329
Koran (Qur'an), 116, f182
Kosovo, 232, 469
Ku Klux Klan, 238, 241
Kurds, 295
Kuwait, 192, 194f
Kyrgyzstan, 313

L

Labeling
    and delinquents, 153
    and deviance, 153–154
    in education, 74, 398–399
    embracing as identity, 153
    and growing old, 68
    and perception, 243
    and prejudice, 232, 245
    and self-labeling, 243–244
Labeling theory, 153–154, 496
Labor. See Division of labor; Work and workers
Laissez-faire capitalism, 332, 496
Lake of the Ozarks, Missouri, 60
Land, income and population distribution, 187
Language, 53–57
    body language, 126
    controversy of, 55
    cumulative experiences, 54
    and culture, 53–57
    defined, 53, 496
    embedded, within us, 55
    "English only" movement, 55–56

and ethnic relations, 231, 247, 249, 263
in everyday life, 56
feminine terms as insults, 292
functions of, 54
goal-directed behavior, 54
and perception, 54, 55–56
and perspectives, 54
and shared past, 54
and social class, 397
Sapir-Whorf hypothesis, 55
Spanish in U.S., 55, 249
and symbolic culture, 53–54
Las Vegas, 332
Latent functions, 392, 496
Latinos. See also Race–ethnicity
    and capital punishment, 169, 178
    comparative well-being statistics, 250–251
    and crime, 163, 164t
    and culture, 55, 130, 242, 248, 249
    on death row, 170t
    defined, 248
    diversity among, 249–250
    and education, 251t
    as fathers, 367
    family structure of, 367
    in government, 250
    hate crimes against, 172t
    and health care, 239
    and housing, 250t
    income, 250t
    location of, 248–249
    and mortgages, 239
    numbers of, 55, 248–249
    origins of, 248, 249, 250
    overview, 266
    and politics, 250
    poverty/income, 217, 218f, 219, 250t, 251
    in prisons, 163–164t, 250
    residence patterns of, 249f
    and social class, 366, 367
    and Spanish language, 249
    terms for, 250, 251
    undocumented workers, 249
    unemployment of, 250t
    in U.S. population, 246f
Latvia, 30, 193f, 476
Law. See also Criminal justice system
    conflict perspective on, 161
    mandatory education, 391
    and oppression, 161–162
    as social institution, 280, 300
    unintended consequences of, 35, 165
    unusual laws, 158

Leaders. See also Authority
    authoritarian, 241, 244
    charismatic, 308, 309, 415
    in corporations, 274, 322, 345
    military, 313, 322, 477
    opinion, 322
    religious, 407, 408, 410
    transfer of authority, 309
Leadership, 306
Leadership styles, 306–309
Learning environments. See Education
Least Industrialized Nations
    on births in, 437
    children in, 432–433
    cities/urbanization, 445, 451, 462
    and colonialism/neocolonialism, 191, 222, 232–233
    conflict perspective on, 433
    and debt, 344
    defined, 186
    described, 187
    distribution of land, income, 193f
    education in, 391
    and elitism, 41, 204
    environmental problems in, 479
    food in, 429
    and global stratification, 193f, 222
    income of, 193f
    map of, 194f
    migration from, 437
    and oil-rich nations, 194f
    overview, 187
    population, 187t
    population growth in, 187, 428f, 430, 432f, 433, 439, 461
    poverty in, 187, 192
    and power, 471
    resources of, 191
    stratification of, 222
    symbolic interactionist perspective on, 433
    and the U.N., 434f
    women in, 280
    workers in, 337–338
Legal system, 161, 162, 258
Leisure, 67, 68, 74, 98, 381
Lesbians. See Homosexuals
Liberia, 437, 446
Libya, 192, 193f, 204
Life, meaning of, 406
Life chances, 182, 251, 254, 256
Life course, 97–100, 102. See also Culture
    adolescence, 98
    childhood, 97–98
    cultural influences on, 98
    defined, 496
    during adolescence, 98

Life course (*Continued*)
during childhood, 97–98
middle years, 99
older years, 99–100
and social location, 98, 100
social significance of, 97
and socialization, 97–100
transitional adulthood, 99
Life expectancy, 211, 467t
Lifestyles
and the environment, 484
and health, 211, 407
of the super-rich, 203–204, 208
and relationships, 199, 203
Livability, and urbanization, 459
Living together. *See* Cohabitation
Living-dying interval, 36, 100
Loans, 238–239
Lobbyists, 316, 318–320, 496
Longevity, 99, 101. *See also* Life
expectancy
Looking-glass self, 83, 496
Looks. *See* Beauty/looks
Los Angeles, 235, 253, 371, 445f, 459
Lottery winners, 112, 115, 206
Louisiana, 258, 376f, 485. *See also* New
Orleans
Love/romance. *See also* Courtship
brain's response to, 359
emergence of, 359
in global perspective, 359
finding, 359
in India, 359, 361, 364
and marriage, 358–359
research on attraction, 33, 359, 384
and social channels, 360–361
symbolic interactionist perspective
on, 33–34
Lower middle class, 209
Loyalty, 50, 153, 367, 393
Lumpenproletariat, 199
Lutheranism, as ecclesia, 417
Lynching, 10, 12

M

Machismo, 433, 496
Macro-level analysis, 40–41,
106–107, 496
Macrosociological perspective on
and culture, 110–111
defined, 106, 496
and groups, 111
and microsociology, 40–41, 43–44,
106–107, 141
and social class, 111
and social status, 111–113

and social structure, 108–110
and sports, 109
and streetcorner men, 106–107, 109
theories, types of, 41t
Macrosociology, defined, 106, 107
Macy's, 158
Mafia, 152
Mainstreaming, 156–157
Malawi, 194f
Male dominance, 277–279, 300
Malthus theorem, 427, 429, 496
Malaysia, 351
Mandatory education laws, 391
Manifest functions, 392, 496
Mardi Gras, 59, 60
Marines, U.S., 96, 116f, 388
Market forces, 333, 496
Marketing research, 14
Marriage, 350–387. *See also*
Cohabitation; Courtship; Decent,
system of familial; Divorce; Families;
Mate selection
age at, 372, 373f, 385
arranged, 359, 384
and authority, 354
and caste, 184
changing meanings of, 372–375
and childbirth, 87
child care responsibilities, 356–357,
362–364, 384
childless, 370
children, effect of, 364
and commitment, 33, 356, 357,
372–373, 381
conflict perspective on, 356
cultural themes of, 352–354
of dead sons in China, 352
decision making in, 356
defined, 351, 496
and divorce, 375–380
electronic matchmaking, 353
and empty nest, 364, 384
functionalist perspective on, 355
future of, 383
and gender roles, 356–358, 384
global perspective on, 351–354
happiness, children and, 433
and housework, 356–358
and incest, 352, 355, 381, 382–383,
385, 355
and inheritance, 353
interracial, 230, 233, 236, 257–258,
352, 360
and love, 358–361
mate selection, 352
in the 1970s, 372
norms in, 360

overview, 350
polygyny/polyandry, 351, 384
postponing, 372–375
and remarriage, 379–380
same-sex, 351–352, 354, 371
social channels of, 360–361
and social class, 212, 364
spouse abuse, 380–381
statistics on, 370f, 373f, 375f
successful, 381–383
symbolic interactionist perspective
on, 33, 355, 356–358
and testosterone levels, 274, 300
theoretical perspective on, 355–358
two-paycheck, 357f
variety in, 351–352
and women in labor force, 383, 385
Marxism, Marx on, 197
Masculinities, emerging, 88, 91, 269,
270, 271
Masculinity, 237, 270, 292, 297, 300
Mass media. *See also* Advertising
and advertising, 90
and body image, 131
conflict perspective on, 118–119
control of, 242
and culture, 102
defined, 90, 496
and disasters, 140
functionalist perspective on, 117–118
and gender, 70, 90–92, 102
in Iran, 476–477
and love, 66
and marriage, 376, 383
in movies, 90
and norms, 152
and propaganda, 242
and religion, 419
and slavery today, 183
as a social institution, 116f, 117, 119, 141
and social movements, 476
and stereotypes, 90, 91
and street crime, 157
in television, 90
and values, 66, 152
video games as, 91
Master status, 112, 113, 496
Matchmaking, 353
Mate selection. *See also* Marriage
changes in, 352–353
as cultural theme, 352
Internet dating sites, 353, 384
and love, 360–361
polygyny, 351, 384
and social class, 360
Material culture, 48, 49, 70, 71, 72,
73, 496

Math education, 401, 402
Matriarchy, 353, 496
Matrilineal system of descent, 353, 496
McDonald's, 71, 201
Means, explained, 25t
Means of production, defined, 496. See also Production
Mechanical solidarity, 120–121, 141, 496
Medellin, Colombia, 440–443
Medians, explained, 25t
Medical insurance, 211
Medicalization. of deviance, 173–175, 178, 496
Medicare, 206
Medicine. See also Health and health care; Surgery
    and American Medical Association, 116f
    and biotech societies, 330, 331
    and computers, 70, 174
    and cultural lag, 70–71, 474
    and the elderly, 204
    exported, 467
    fraud in, 206
    future of, 330, 331
    gender in, 292–294, 301
    gynecological examinations, 136–137
    HMOs, 116f
    and midwives, 283
    professionalization of, 206
    sexism in, 292–294, 301
    as a social institution, 116f, 117, 141
    subsidized, 336, 346
Mediocrity, in education, 401, 402
Mediums of exchange, 241, 337, 344
Megacities, 445–446, 496
Megalopolis, 445, 496
Melting pot, 234–235
Mental illness
    and ADD, 174
    and hate crimes, 172t
    and the homeless, 174, 175
    and medicalization, 173–174, 178
    personality disorders, 174
    in present vs. past, 150
    and social class, 212
    and subcultures, 63–64
Meritocracy, 197
Methodists, 418f
Metropolis, 445, 496
Metropolitan, defined, 496
Mexico, 55, 57, 192, 231, 249, 251
Miami, 54, 445
Microchip, effects on society, 328f, 466, 478, 487. See also Computers
Micro-level analysis, 40–41, 106–107, 496

Micropolis, 448, 462
Microsociological perspective
    and background assumptions, 133–134
    defined, 107, 496
    described, 40–41
    and macrosociology, 40–41, 43–44, 106–107
    and presentation of self, 123127
    and social construction of reality, 135–136, 500
    and symbolic interaction, 41t, 123–127, 141
Microsociology, defined, 107
Middle age, 99
Middle class, 209
Midwives, 283
Migration, 437
Military. See also War
    and computers, 476, 478
    and control of, 197, 313, 417
    and crime, 161
    functionalist perspective on, 117, 118
    and industrialization, 116f
    and New World Order, 469
    political philosophy in U.S., 316
    as power elite, 13, 204, 322
    and resocialization, 96, 102
    Saddam Hussein, 311, 313
    and sexual harassment, 291, 301
    schools, 96, 102
    as a social institution, 117, 141
    soldiers, 71, 96, 204, 260, 274, 292, 325, 326
    war and terrorism, 324, 344, 476
Mind, development of, 83–86
Miners in West Virginia, 158
Minority group(s). See also Multicultural-ism; Race–ethnicity; specific groups
    assimilation of, 233
    and access to power, 231, 233, 234
    becoming a, 231
    defined, 231, 496
    distribution in U.S., 232, 247f
    and dominant groups, 230–236, 265, 274–275, 277–278
    emergence of, 231
    exploitation of, 232–233
    females as, 237, 276–279
    and genocide–232, 231
    gentrification and, 276–279
    and hand-to-hand combat, 277
    and human reproduction, 277
    identification with, 234
    invisible, 260–261
    and migration, 231
    numbers of, 231

overview, 231
    shared characteristics of, 231
    in tribal societies, 231
Minutemen (border patrol), 249
Modernization, 496
Modes, 25t
Monarchies, 311, 496
Money. See Income; Property; Wealth
Monkeys, 78–80, 82
Monogamy, 64, 67, 352t
Monopolies, 307, 311, 321, 345
Monotheism, 411
"Moral community," 405–406, 414, 421, 422
Moral holidays, 59
Morality. See also Ethics in research
    of babies, 49
    control theory, 152, 177
    development of, 49
    and deviance, 155
    vs. moral community, 405
    and religion, 405
    and science, 419
    and terrorists, 326
    and traditional authority, 307
    universality and, 60
    and war, 477–478
Mores, defined, 60, 496
Mormons, 417t, 418f
Morocco, culture of, Morocco, 47, 49, 135, 136
Mortgage loans, 238–239
Most Industrialized Nations. See also G 7/G 8
    children in, 98
    defined, 186
    distribution of land, income, population, 187
    education in, 390
    environmental problems in, 479–483
    geopolitics, 468–470
    and global stratification, 187
    and Japan, 187
    map of, 193f
    migration to, 437
    overview, 187, 222
    population growth of, 433f
    power of, 187
    theories on, 195
Motherhood, 273, 433. See also Single mothers
Motorcyclists, 62, 64
Movies, 90
Multiculturalism, 233–234, 496
Multicultural society, 263–264
Multinational corporations. See also Globalization of capitalism

Multinational corporations (*Continued*)
　　defined, 496
　　and division of wealth, 339
　　and energy shortage, 482
　　and global domination, 468–470
　　global investing by, 192
　　and global superclass, 190, 342, 343
　　nation's largest, 203, 289, 345
　　ownership vs. management of, 342
　　and pollution, 479–483
　　power of, 203–204
　　and social stratification, 199, 203,
　　　　204, 209, 222–223
Multiple-nuclei model, 450–451
Mumbai, India, 80
Murder. *See also* Genocide; Terror(ism)
　　of African Americans, 254, 255
　　and alienation in cities, 458
　　and DNA matching, 168
　　gender bias, 90, 169
　　gendered, 296–297, 301
　　hate crimes, 172
　　and honor, 152, 295, 297, 301
　　infanticide, 295
　　and medicalization of deviance, 175
　　and mental illness, 173
　　organized, 265
　　and recidivism, 166f, 178
　　school shootings, 19, 403, 421
　　serial, 167–168, 178
　　sex of victims and killers, 296
　　statistics in U.S., 159f
Muslims, 172t, 228, 232, 407, 411. *See
　　also* Islam
Myths
　　and core beliefs, 238
　　folk, 78, 81
　　Horatio Alger, 219–220, 221, 223
　　of an idyllic past, 357
　　and law as oppressive instrument, 161
　　of marriage and family, 383
　　of mental illness, 174
　　about the poor, 218, 219–220
　　of race, 227–228, 265
　　about school shootings, 403, 421
　　social functions of, 219–221
　　and sociology, 5, 69
　　about welfare, 218

N

1984, (Orwell), 305, 306
NAACP (National Association for the
　　Advancement of Colored People), 12,
　　13, 15, 252
NAFTA (North American Free Trade
　　Association), 343, 346

Naked run, 87
Name calling, 292
Nannies, 233
Nation vs. state, 249, 253
National Women's Party, 298
Nationalism, 469
Native Americans, 258–261. *See also*
　　Race–ethnicity; specific tribes/nations
　　American population of, 259
　　berdache among, 351
　　and casinos, 260, 261, 266
　　comparative well-being statistics, 251t
　　democracy among, 312
　　discrimination against, 232, 236
　　diversity among, 259
　　and education, 251
　　in the 1800s, 259
　　ethnic identity, 235, 245
　　family structure of, 368
　　and genocide, 231, 259–260
　　and hate crimes, 172t
　　home ownership, 250t
　　income, 250t
　　as invisible minority, 260–261
　　number of, 246f, 251t
　　overview, 266
　　and pan-Indianism, 260–261
　　as parents, 368
　　population transfer of, 232, 259–260
　　and poverty, 250t
　　and segregation, 232, 236, 260–261
　　and separatism, 260–261
　　treaties with, 259–260
　　unemployment of, 250t
　　in U.S. population, 245f, 246f
Natural disasters, 139–140
Natural sciences, 390, 392, 496
Nature vs. nurture (biology and behavior)
　　and deviance, 149–150
　　and gender, 273–275
　　genetics-informed sociology, 273
　　and human characteristics, 273
　　and race–ethnicity, 264
　　social structure, 273
　　sociobiology, 86, 150
Nazis. *See also* Neo-Nazis
　　authoritarian personality, 241, 307
　　creating prejudice, 242, 244
　　Gestapo, 313
　　hate groups, 238
　　Hitler as charismatic leader, 307, 309
　　Hitler Youth, 238
　　Holocaust, 232, 236, 244
　　and New World Order, 237
　　origins of, 228
　　propaganda, 242
　　and racial superiority, 228, 238

and social environment, 242
　　support of, 241
Negative sanctions, 59, 148, 496
Neighborhoods, 152
Neocolonialism, defined, 496
Neo-Nazis, 237, 238
Net migration rate, 437, 496
Networks, social, 476–477
Neutralization, 153, 499
Nevada, 159f, 376f, 378f, 447f, 480f
New-Malthusians, 427, 429, 460
New Orleans, 59, 60, 365, 447, 448t
New technology. *See also* Computers;
　　Internet; Mass media; Surveillance
　　and aging, 99–100
　　automobile, effects of, 482
　　and communication, 70, 475–477
　　and crimes, 171
　　and cultural lag, 70–71, 74, 474
　　and cultural leveling, 71–72
　　defined, 70, 497
　　electronic matchmaking, 353
　　and the global village, 70–71
　　and industrialization, 467
　　and marriage, 353
　　and restructuring of work, 215–216
　　and serial killers, 168
　　social control by, 70, 122, 215
　　social structure, 122, 215–216
　　in Uganda, 467
　　and values, 65
　　and war, 477–478
New World Order
　　and geopolitics, 468, 469, 470, 487
　　and globalization of capitalism,
　　　　343–344
　　and nationalism, 469
　　and Nazis, 237
New York, 453
News reporting, 70, 72, 93, 116f, 313
Nicotine, 407
Nike, 72, 189
"Nintendo Generation," 91
Nonmaterial (symbolic) culture, 48, 53,
　　70–71, 73, 497
Nonverbal interaction, 40, 497
Norms. *See also* Deviance
　　and culture, 3, 59–60
　　defined, 59, 497
　　and deviance, 155
　　and facial expressions, 148
　　functions of, 59
　　and gossip, 148
　　internalization of, 49, 53, 238, 239
　　making social life possible, 49, 74, 147
　　and moral holidays, 59
　　of noninvolvement, 80–81, 101

and peer groups, 89–90, 93–95
and sanctions, 147–148
and social institutions, 106, 111, 113, 114, 116f, 117
and social interactions, 147
in traditional and modern societies, 67, 72
violation of, 149–150
North Korea, 417
Northrop Grumman, 161
Norway, ancient city in, 441
Novartis, 289
Nuclear family, 497
Nuclear proliferation, 468, 471, 480, 483, 487
Nuremberg Trials, 228, 242

O

Obedience, 93, 116f, 397
Objectivity, 5, 10, 116f
Objectivity value, 497
Ociological perspective, 497
Ogburn's theory, 33, 70–71, 473–475
Oil
    and environmentalism, 485
    fossil fuels, 481–482
    and geopolitics, 319, 469, 470, 487
    nations, 194f
    ownership of, 333
    and war, 324, 477
    and wealth, 333
Oil-rich nations, 194f
Oligarchy, 312–314, 497
Ollantayambo, Peru, 466
One world, 344, 347
Oneida, the, 260
One-parent families, 369–370. See also Single mothers
Open-ended questions, 25, 26, 43, 497
Operational definitions, 21, 497
"Opium of the people," 408
Opportunity, illegitimate, 157–160
Organic solidarity, 120–121, 141, 497
Organizations. See Bureaucracies
Orphanages, 78, 80–81, 82

P

PACs (Political Action Committees), 319–320
Pakistan, 194f, 258, 266, 295, 407, 471
Palestinians, 325
Pan-Indianism, 260–261, 266, 497
Paralympics, 86, 87
Parenthood. See also Child rearing; Single mothers
    child care responsibilities, 356–358

fatherhood, 366
grandparents as parents, 363, 368, 377
and marriage, 33, 34
meaning of, 33
motherhood, status of, 433
symbolic interactionist perspective on, 33
Participant observation
    of abused victims, 28
    of bikers, 154
    of communities, 453
    defined, 497
    of dominant norms, 238
    as fieldwork, 28
    of friends, neighborhoods and sub-cultures, 152
    of gangs, 28
    in gender research, 29
    of the homeless, 40
    of honor and violence, 152
    of kindergarten, 93, 398–399
    of medicine, 136–137
    of pelvic examinations, 136–137
    of racists, 12
    as a research method, 20, 21, 23, 28, 42
    of restaurant workers, 36
    of the Yanomamö, 3, 145–146, 148
Party Cove, Missouri, 50
Passenger pigeons, 68
Pastoral and horticultural societies, 328, 497
Path analysis, 61
Patriarchy, 276, 277–278, 279, 300, 497
Patrilineal system of descent, 353, 497
Patriotism, 313
Patterns of behavior, 8–10, 497
Paychecks, stagnant, 338–339
Pay gap, 287–289
Pearl Harbor, 256
Peer groups, 93–94, 497
Peer pressure, 93–94, 102
Peers, 89–90
Pelvic examinations, 136–137
Pentagon, 325, 477
Pentecostalism, 416, 419, 422
Pequot, the, 260
Perception
    cultural influences on, 49, 62, 74
    and generalized other, 84
    and in-groups/out-groups, 50, 242
    and labels, 153–154
    and language, 55–57
    selective, 112, 243, 453
    sex and gender, 290–291, 292, 301
    and social construction, 135, 137–138
Peripheral model, 451

Periphery nations, 192, 195, 222
Persecution, by religions, 407–408, 422
Personal identity kit, 96
Personal space, 123, 126
Personality, 129
Personality disorders, 150, 497
Phnom Penh, Cambodia, 187
Philippines, 191, 194f, 256f, 257, 437f
Photo essays, by the author
    community in the city, 457
    and cultural identity, 235
    and ethnic work, 235
    Holy Week in Spain, 412–413
    India, gender and work, 284–285
    Medellin, Colombia, 442–443
    of social structure/interaction, 124–125, 138–140
    of subcultures, 62–63
    towns, struggle of survival, 340–341
Physical fitness, as a value, 67–68
Play, 93
Plessy v. Ferguson, 252
Plow, the, effects on society, 328, 331, 346, 441, 461
Pluralism. See also Multiculturalism
    as characteristic of U.S. society, 65, 321, 345
    defined, 321, 497
    explained, 233–234
    global patterns of, 232
    and power in U.S., 321
    and religious freedom, 418
Pluralistic society, 65, 120, 122, 130, 497
Poland, 193f, 438, 469
Police discretion, 172, 178, 497
Political Action Committees (PACs), 319–320, 497
Political parties. See also Politics
    Bull Moose Party, 316
    centrist parties, 316, 345
    Communist Party, 335, 390
    Democrats and Republicans, 315–316, 345
    and elections, 315–316
    gender and race, 317t, 319t
    green parties, 483, 484, 485, 488
    oligarchy, 313
    Reform Party, 316
    third parties, 316
Politics, 305–349. See also G 7/G 8; Power
    African Americans in, 253
    Asian Americans in, 258
    authority of the state, 116, 306–307, 310, 311
    and birth control, 394

Politics (*Continued*)
campaign contributions, 118, 319, 320
conflict perspective of, 322–323
and divine right of kings, 409
emergence of, 315
European systems, 344
functionalist perspective, 321
and gender, 298–299, 318
geopolitics, 468–470
green parties, 483, 484, 485, 488
and identity chips, 477, 478
and immigrants, 262–263
Latinos in, 250, 266
lobbyists and PACs, 319–320
micro- vs. macropolitics, 40–41
and multinational corporations, 342, 343, 479
parties, differences, 315–316
power, 468–470
pluralistic perspective of, 321
and race–ethnicity, 253, 258, 266, 318
and social class, 213
as a social institution, 116f, 117, 141
and Social Security funds, 38, 204, 336
and status inconsistency, 206
as a subculture, 318
and terrorism, 324–327
third parties, 315
types of government, 321–323
U.S. political system, 315–320, 345
and war, 324–327
and women, 287–290, 298–299
Pollution. *See* Environment
Polyandry, 351, 384, 497
Polygyny, 351, 497
Polytheism, 410
Poor, the. *See* Poverty
Population, 425–430
demographic variables of, 426–427, 436–441
distribution of world, 426
in 1800s, 262f, 428f, 433f, 444f
elderly, percentage of, 218f
global perspective of, 426–430
projection of, 438–439
U.S., 439f
world, 427–428, 433f
Population explosion, 428–429, 430, 433, 461
Population growth, 428, 430, 433, 461
anti-Malthusians' perspective on, 427–430
and balance of power, 429
conflict perspective on, 433

and demographic transition, 428–429, 460
factors in, 432–433
forecasting, 438–440
and immigration, 429, 434, 461
and industrialization, 439
in Least Industrialized Nations, 428, 429, 430, 432, 433–435
New Malthusians' perspective on, 427
rates of, 433–435
reasons for, 428, 436–440
shrinkage, 429
symbolic interactionist perspective, 433
world's, 427–428, 433f
Population pyramids, 434, 435–436, 461, 497
Population shrinkage, 429, 497
Population transfer, 232, 462, 497
Populations (in research), 24–25, 497
Positive sanctions, 59, 148, 497
Positivism, 5–6, 497
Postindustrial societies, 116f, 329–330, 497
Postmodern societies, 329, 497
Potato, the, 426
Poverty. *See also* Homeless; Income; Inner city; Social class
antipoverty programs, 203
and assumptions, 219
author's experience with, 40, 212
blaming the victim, 195, 220, 222
characteristics of the poor, 195
and child labor, 15
and children, 218–219, 434f
in China's new capitalism, 335–336, 346
culture of, 192–195
cycle of, 217, 219
determination of, 216–217
duration of, 192, 209–210
dynamics of, 66, 192–195
in early U.S., 218
and education, 217, 220, 221, 223
and the elderly, 204, 211, 217, 218f, 336, 454
in everyday life, 220
explanations of, 191–195
factors in, 430–432
facts/myths about, 219–220
and gender, 384
geographical patterns of, 187–190, 221
globalization of, 193–195
and health, 211, 214, 219
and Horatio Alger myth, 219–220
and illegal immigration, 266

illegitimate opportunities, 157–160
income stratification, 191–195
individualistic vs. structural explanations of poverty, 214–215, 223
in inner city, 209
in Least Industrialized Nations, 187, 432
as a myth, 219–220, 223
oil-rich nations, 194f
in one-parent families, 218, 219f, 221
penalties of, 219
by race–ethnic group, 217–218
and religion, 192–193, 409
rural, 218
and single mothers, 219, 220f
and social class, 220
and social Darwinism, 6, 9, 86
and social stratification, 192–195
and starvation, 430–431
and stereotypes, 217–218, 223
suburbanization of, 218
theories of, 195
underclass, 210
and welfare reform, 35, 37
working poor, the, 208f, 209, 220, 223
Poverty line, 216–217, 223, 497
Power. *See also* Authority; Leaders; Leadership
and authority, 38, 241, 306–310
and class, 204, 222, 322–323
conflict perspective on, 468–470
conflicts in U.S. over, 323
of corporations, 204, 209, 211, 222–223, 289
declining privilege theory, 296–297
defined, 204, 497
functionalist perspective on, 6–9, 197–198
geopolitics, 468–470
of global superclass, 190, 342, 343, 346
male dominance, 39, 277, 278–279
of peer pressure, 93–94
property and prestige, 199–201
and rape, 296–297
seizure of, 312–313
and social stratification, 185, 186–190
strains in global system of, 344
thesis and antithesis, 471–472, 487
transfer of, 309
Power elite
in China, 335–336, 346
conflict perspective on, 322–323
and criminal justice system, 161, 307
defined, 204, 322, 497

global superclass, 190, 342
in government, 322, 342
and ideology, 197
in Least Industrialized Nations, 191, 193f, 194f, 222
maintaining power, 161, 322, 468–470
in maintaining stratification, 393
and multinational corporations, 322
as social class, 204
and social movements, 483, 488
and working class, 161–162
Powerpuff Girls, 90
Prayer, 416
Predator, the, 477
Predatory lending 239f
Pregnancy. See Reproduction of humans
Prejudice. See also Discrimination; Hatred; Racism; Sexism
ageism, 67, 68
anti-Semitism, 241, 242, 244
and the authoritarian personality, 241
core beliefs of, 238
defined, 237, 497
and hate groups, 238
and frustration, 240–241
learning of, 237–238
nature of, 237
sociological perspective on, 241–245
theories of, 240–245, 265
Preschools, 363f
Prestige
defined, 204, 497
and occupations, 204–205
power and prestige, 199–200
Primary groups, 116
Prisons
as deviance control, 162–166, 177–178
population growth, 163f, 164t
recidivism, 165–166f
and street crime, 163–164
"three strikes" law, 164–165
Prisoners. See also Criminal justice system
characteristics of, 163, 164f
on death row, 167, 169, 170, 178
and education, 163
Japanese Americans as, 232, 236, 257
and marriage, 163
numbers of, in U.S., 163f, 164t
race–ethnicity of, 163, 164f
recidivism of, 165–166f
resocialization of, 96
treatment of, 163
Privacy. See Surveillance
Production

means of, 199
in nontraditional societies, 466, 467
in traditional societies, 466, 467
Profane, defined, 404, 497
Professions, 138, 158, 205. See also Work and workers
Proletariat, 6, 199, 497
Propaganda, 242
Property
described, 201
distribution of, 202
vs. income and wealth, 201–204
power and prestige, 199–201
Proposition 209, 263
Prostitution, 50, 157, 295, 441
Protestant ethic, 7–8, 246, 247
Protests, 280, 301, 469, 478, 484
Pure sociology. See Sociology
Psychological perspective
and diffusion of responsibility, 456
on prejudice, 240–241
and real life experimentation, 456
Psychology, 150, 177. See also Personality disorders
Public opinion, 33, 116f
Public sociology, 459, 497
Puerto Rican Americans, 250t. See also Latinos
Push and pull effect, 122

Q

Questionnaires, 25, 29, 497
Questions
and establishing rapport, 26
formulating for research, 25–26
neutral, 25
types of, 25
Qur'an (Koran), 116f

R

Race, defined, 227
Race–ethnicity, 226–268. See also Discrimination; Minority group, Prejudice; Racism; specific groups
in Africa, 231, 233, 236
and Aryans, 64, 228, 236, 438
background assumptions of, 231
biological differences, 264
and blended families, 370–371
and cancer, 238
in the census, 259
and childless couples, 370
and common sense, 227–228
conflict among groups, 228, 232
contact theory, 237

on death row, 170t
defined, 497
diversity in U.S., 245–252, 257, 259, 266, 366–369
and divorce, 266
in early U.S., 231
and education, 251, 260, 397
in the 1800s, 232, 236
and ethnic group, 229
and the elderly, 237
and European Americans relations, 245–248, 266
and family, 366–369
in the future, 262–272
and gay and lesbian families, 371
and hate crimes, 172–173
and health care, 239
and immigration, 256, 262–263, 264, 266, 267
and income, 239, 250–251, 253, 254, 257, 258, 266
and interracial marriage, 230, 233, 236, 257–258
and job discrimination, 256
and labels, 228, 232
and language, 229, 231, 233–234, 247, 249, 266
and medical care, 239
and mother/child deaths, 437
as myth and reality, 227–228, 265
and one-parent families, 369–370
and politics, 253, 258, 266
population statistics, 245–247
and poverty, 217–218
and prison population, 250
and religion, 229, 247, 418
self-label, 243
segregation by, 232f, 233, 252, 266
and self-labels, 243
as subcultures, 274
and teacher expectations, 399
and voting, 253, 255, 317t
Race, pure, 227
Racism. See also Discrimination; Prejudice; Race–ethnicity
as an everyday burden, 255
anti-Semitism. See Holocaust; Nazis
defined, 237, 497
and early sociologists, 12
in earlier U.S., 231
learning of, 237–238
and murder, 254, 255, 265
and slavery, 183
as a value, 231
Radicalization, 484–485
Rain forests, 482
Random samples, 25, 497

Rape
  acquaintance, 296
  authors observations on, 167
  and conquest/war, 182, 232
  date, 296
  and death penalty, 167–168, 169
  homeless and, 174, 175
  and "honor killings," 152, 295
  and mental illness, 173, 175
  as nonviolent crime, 159f
  and power, 296–297
  and racial bias, 169
  recidivism and, 166f
  rate in U.S., 169, 295–296
  relationship of victim to rapist,
      296, 301
  research on, 26
  and serial murder, 167–168
  sociobiological explanations, 150
  statistics on, 26, 166f
Rapists, 243, 296, 301
Rapport, 26, 497
Rationalization of society, 153, 308
Rational–legal authority, 308, 497
Real culture, defined, 497
Reality, social construction of
  and abortion, 439
  aging, 68
  defined, 136, 498, 500
  definition of the situation, 135–136
  of gender, 353
  germs, 135–136
  gynecological examinations,
      136–137
  health and illness, 136, 137
  and medicalization of human
      conditions, 173–175
  overview, 136–137, 142, 146
  photo essay on, 139–140
  and racial–ethnic identity, 227–228
  and saints and roughnecks, 137–138
  and social movements, 466
  and Thomas theorem, 135–136
Recidivism rate, 165–166, 497
Redlining, 458, 497
Redwoods, 484
Reference groups, 280, 282
Reform. See Social reform
Reform Party, 316
Reincarnation, 48
Reliability (of data), 21, 498
Religion, 404–420. See also specific
    religions
  as agent of socialization, 213
  American attitudes toward, 418
  author's request for reader's spiritual
      perceptions, 414

basic components of, 404–405
and beliefs, 411
and capitalism, 7–8
and charismatic leaders, 308, 309
and community, 406–407
conflict perspective on, 408–410
as a church, 416
as a cult, 415–416. See also
    Charismatic leaders
and death, 406, 407
defined, 405, 498
described, 404–406
diversity in, 417
and divorce, 367, 377
dysfunctions of, 407–408
electronic church/televangelists, 419
family size and, 362, 365
functional perspective on, 406–408
fundamentalism in, 411
future of, 419
global perspective, 404–406
and hate crimes, 172–173
and health, 407
Holy Week in Spain, 412–413
and ideology, 411
identification with, in the U.S., 417t
and industrialization, 116f
and Internet, 419
membership statistics, 417t
as "opium of the people", 408
photo essay on, 412–413
pluralism and freedom of, 418
and poverty, 409
and prayer, 416
purpose of, 406–407
and race-ethnicity, 418
rituals of, 414
and sects, 416
secularization of, 412–413
and social class, 213, 418f
and social control, 213
and social inequalities, 409
as a social institution, 116f,
    417–418
and social mobility, 409–410
as a state religion, 416–417
and subjective experiences, 414
symbolic interactionist perspective
    on, 410–414
symbols of, 410–411
and terrorism, 407–408
toleration of, 415f, 418–419
types of groups in, 415–419
in U.S., 415–420
and U.S. government, 418
and values, 411
and Waco, Texas, 418

Religious experience, 414, 498
Relocation camps, 232, 236, 260,
    261
Replication, defined, 498
Representative democracy, 312, 498
Representative sample, 25, 498
Reproduction of humans. See also
    Childbirth
  and behavior, 273, 439
  and family, 355, 384
  functionalist perspective on, 118
  and gender stratification, 277
  and male dominance, 277, 300
  payments for pregnancy, 438
  and sex, 270, 300
  social control of, 116f, 118
  social structure, 116f
  women's reproductive choices, 433,
      435
Reproduction of social structure, 118
Republicans, 315–316, 345
Research, 18–31. See also Experiment(s);
    Participant observation; specific
    topics
  analysis of results, 23, 26–27
  and bias, 25, 43
  causation and correlation in, 27
  and common sense, 19
  on education, 398–399
  ethics in, 28
  framework of ideas, 31
  and gender, 28
  on the homeless, 40–41
  importance of, 19, 42
  interviewer effect in, 25
  levels of analysis, 40–42
  methods of (design), 21, 24–30,
      42–43, 498
  models, 20–23, 42
  overview, 18
  on peer pressure, 89–90
  on suicide terrorists, 326
  tables, summarizing, 22t
  terms for, 20–23
  and theory, 38–39, 43
  topics, 39, 123, 126, 141
  validity, 21, 23, 42
  vs. reform, 10–16
Research findings, 19
Research methods, defined, 498. See
    also Research
Reserve labor force, 242–243, 498
Resocialization, 95–96, 102, 498
Resources
  conflict perspective on, 38, 41t, 43
  distribution of, 118
Respondents, 25, 498

Retirement, 68, 100, 339. *See also* Social Security
Revolution(s)
    agricultural, 328f, 466, 468
    American, 311–312
    and authority, 306–307
    biotech, 330–331
    defined, 312, 498
    domestication, 328f, 467, 468, 487
    French, 5
    Industrial (*See* Industrial Revolution)
    information, 328f, 329–330
    and liberty, 312
    Marx on, 197
    and rising expectations, 253
    social, 328f
Revolving door policy, and congress, 319
Russian
    industrialization, 390–391
    race-ethnicity, 233, 246f
    social, 335
    as social movements, 479
    Thomas Jefferson on rebellion, 312
    of workers, 6, 199, 472
Rights. *See* Civil rights
Rio de Janeiro, Brazil, 441
Riots, 255, 266, 459
Rising expectations, defined, 253, 498
Rites of passage, 98
Ritualism, 156
Rituals, 99, 184, 278, 405, 412–413, 414, 498
Role conflict, 130, 498
Role confusion, 355, 394
Role exit, 131
Role expectations, 109, 141
Role performance, 129, 498
Role strain, 129–130, 498
Role taking, 83
Roles, 113–114, 130, 131, 498. *See also* Gender roles
Roman Catholic Church
    and capitalism, 8
    charismatic leaders, 309
    and children, 362, 365
    dysfunction of, 407
    as ecclesia, 416–417
    and education, 402, 403–404
    and hate crimes, 172t
    member characteristics, 417t
    and persecution, 407
    race-ethnicity, 367, 418
    school system of, 402, 403–404
    and social class, 418f
    and status symbols, 112
    statistics on, 417t
Romantic love, 359, 360, 498

"Roughnecks," the, 137–138
Routinization of charisma, 309, 345, 498
Ruling class, 322, 498. *See also* Power elite
Rumors, 399
Rural patterns, 447f
Rural rebound, 448–450
Russia
    capitalism in, 335
    cyber war, 477
    economy of, 335
    and education, 390–391
    environmentalism, 481
    and G 7, 468
    and geopolitics, 468, 469, 471, 487
    and Poland, 469
    population, 246f
    and religious persecution, 232, 233
    revolution in, 390
    social stratification in, 194f
    and Ukraine, 469
    and wars, 232, 390, 469
Rwanda, 194f, 228, 231–232, 236, 469

S

Sacred, defined, 404, 498
"Saints," the, 137–138
Samples, 24–25, 498
Sanctions, 59–60, 147–149, 498
San Diego, 251
"Sandwich generation," 99
San Francisco, California, 28, 40, 447
Sapir-Whorf hypothesis, 55, 498
SATs, 401
Saudi Arabia, 158, 171, 178, 194f, 327
Scale, and urbanization planning, 459
Scapegoats, 240–241, 498
Schools. *See also* College; Education
    as agent of socialization, 93–94
    and caste in India, 184
    cheating by administrations of, 401–402
    and cultural lag, 70–71, 474
    functions of, 65, 116f, 389–390
    funding of, 395, 396, 421
    and gender, 89, 95, 281f, 282, 298f, 399
    graduation/dropout rates, 288f
    homeschool, 310
    parental involvement in, 213
    preschools, 213, 363f
    private, 55, 202, 208, 213, 322
    segregated, 233, 252–253
    as stabilizers of the social system, 394
    tracking in, 394, 399
    violence in, 19, 403, 421

Science. *See also* Experiment(s); Research
    and common sense, 19, 20, 42, 55, 57
    as a core value, 65
    defined, 5, 498
    goals of, 5, 116f
    in industrial and postindustrial societies, 116f
    and morality, 152, 177
    natural sciences, 65
    and religion, 7–8, 10
    as a social institution, 117, 141
    social sciences compared, 5–7
    and technology, 65
    and theory, 5
    vs. tradition, 5
Scientific method, 5, 498
Sears, 158
Seattle, Washington, 134
Secondary analysis, 26, 498
Secondary groups, 116
Sector model, 450
Sects, 416, 498
Secularization, 412–413
Segregation. *See also* Apartheid; Caste
    defined, 233, 498
    in education, 233, 252–253
    extent of, 232f
    in regions, 233
    in the South, 233, 252, 266
    and the split labor market, 242
Selective perception, 243, 498
Self (the), 83–86. *See also* Identity
    components of, 84
    defined, 83, 498
    development of, 83–87
    and labels, 153–154
    origin of concept, 83
    presentation of, 127–133
    and role playing, 84
    as a social product, 85
    Social mirrors, 83–84
    sign-vehicles, 129
    as a symbol, 83–84, 85
Self-administered questionnaires, 25, 498
Self-concept. *See* Self (the)
Self-control, 93, 102, 150, 152, 177
Self-fulfilling prophecies
    creating positive, 382
    defined, 399, 498
    and education, 399
    in marriage, 382
    and stereotypes, 243
Self-fulfilling stereotypes, 243
Self-interest, and cities, 453
Semiperiphery nations, 192, 195, 222
Senior citizens. *See* Elderly

Serial, 498
Serial murder, 167–168, 498
Sex. *See also* Gender; Masculinity;
    Women
    and culture. *See* Gender; Gender
      roles
    defined, 270, 498
    vs. gender, 89–90, 94, 269–272
    in public places, 284–285
    roles, 10, 50, 90, 91, 113, 280, 281,
      282, 300
    as status, 112, 141, 274, 275,
      279, 280
    and work, 282
Sex change, 352
Sexism
    and death, 292, 293, 294, 298, 301
    in everyday life, 10
    and infanticide, 295
    in medicine, 293, 301
    in sociology, 10–12
    and values, 67
    and violence, 294–297, 301
    at work, 289, 291
Sex-selective abortion, 295, 302
Sexual assault. *See* Rape
Sexual attraction, 291, 301
Sexual behavior, 272–275, 300
Sexual discrimination. *See* Gender,
    discrimination
Sexual harassment, 289, 290–291, 498
Shaming, 152
Sheen, Charlie, 157
Sick Societies (Edgerton), 50
Sign-vehicles, 129, 498
Significant others, 84, 498
Single mothers
    births to, 220f, 221
    and child rearing, 362
    and poverty, 218, 221
Skywalk, 260
Slavery. *See also* Caste
    buying freedom from, 183, 187
    causes of, 182–183, 221–222
    conditions of, 183
    defined, 182, 498
    in earlier societies, 182–183
    and global stratification, 182–186
    ideology of, 183
    in the modern world, 183
    in the new world, 183
    and religion, 182
    today, 183
    in tribal societies, 182
    in the United States, 183
Slums, 12, 15, 157, 451, 452, 453, 459.
    See also Dump people

Single population, in cities, 454
Small towns, 340–341
Smiling, cultural diversity in, 126
Social, defined, 499
Social capital, 395
Social change, 465–478. *See also* Social
    movements
    and the automobile, 473t, 482, 487
    and the computer, 467, 473, 475–476,
      477, 478, 487
    defined, 465, 498
    and deviance, 155, 177
    and divorce, 41t
    early history of, 466
    emerging masculinities/femininities,
      270, 274, 283, 300
    evolutionary theories of, 470
    and gender relations, 70, 119,
      467t, 474
    and geopolitics, 468–470
    in India, 417
    in Iran, 476
    medicine and technology, 467
    and mediums of exchange, 477
    natural cycles of, 470–471, 487
    Ogburn's processes of, 473–475
    and religion, 407
    and social revolutions, 466–468
    and sociology, 4, 6, 7, 476, 477, 484
    and technology, 475–478
    theories of, 470–472
    and urban problems, 456–460
    and value contradictions, 67
Social class, 93, 157. *See also* Social
    stratification; specific classes
    and African Americans, 12, 16, 182–
      183, 184, 254–255
    capitalist (*See* Capitalist class)
    and child rearing, 364
    class system, defined, 185
    and college attendance, 396
    components of, 199–201
    and conflict, 6–7, 38, 197–198
    consequences of, 211–214, 223
    contradictory locations in, 97, 100
    and crime, 161, 213
    and crime statistics, 171–173, 177
    in criminal justice system, 161, 213
    and death penalty, 169
    defined, 111, 201, 498
    and delinquency, 157–160
    determination of, 198–200, 222
    and deviance, 150, 157–160
    and divorce, 212
    and education, 212–213, 396
    and emotions, 86
    and environmental injustice, 483, 488

    in everyday life, 213
    and the family, 212, 367
    global superclass, 190, 342, 343, 346
    and health and health care, 211–212
    of the homeless, 185, 210
    illegitimate opportunities, 157–160
    of immigrants, 247
    and income, 201–204
    ladder of, 208f
    among Latinos, 248–252, 266
    macrosociology and, 138
    and marriage, 212
    and mental illness, 212
    microsociology and, 138, 141
    models of, 207–209, 222–223
    and neighborhoods, 152
    and opportunities, 160, 214–216, 223
    and play, 93
    and politics, 213
    and power, 199–200, 204–205
    and power elite, 204
    and prestige, 199–200, 204–205
    and property, 199–200, 201–204
    and production, 199
    vs. race, 254–255
    of religious groups, 213, 417–418
    reproducing, 395, 396, 397
    as social structure, 111
    and socialization, 86, 93
    and streetcorner men, 106–107,
      110, 111
    theories of, 199–200
    in the U.S., 201–207
    and voting, 317t
    wealth vs. income, 201–203
    and work, 93
    and workers' revolution, 6, 199, 472
Social class ladder, 208f
Social construction of reality, defined,
    498, 500. *See also* Reality, social
    construction of
Social context, 2–4, 16
Social control
    of citizens, 112, 172
    conflict perspective on, 118–119
    control theory, 118–119, 152
    defined, 147, 498
    as a function of religion, 8, 116f,
      213, 407
    functionalist perspective on, 117–118
    and gender, 88–92
    of information, 116f
    mass media, influence of, 90
    and norms, 50, 59
    reactions to deviance, 162–166
    and religion, 407
    of reproduction, 116f, 118

and self and emotions, 83–88
symbolic interactionist perspective on, 151–154
of technology, 70–72, 74
of workers, 93, 94–95
Social context, 2, 16
Social Darwinism, 6
Social environment, 242, 244
Social facts, 7, 102, 273, 274, 300, 498
Social inequality. *See also* Gender stratification; Global stratification; Social stratification
in agricultural societies, 328
birth of, 328
and capitalism, 334, 346
and computers, 395, 466, 467
in criminal justice system, 161–162, 176
defined, 91
in different societies, 182
in education, 395–396, 398, 421
in health care, 211, 219, 223
and gender, 91, 93, 274, 275
and income, 203, 206, 222, 338–343
in India, 221
and industrialization, 328, 331
in marriage, 185, 216
origin of, 328
perpetuating, 395–398
and plant/animal domestication, 328f, 467, 487
in preindustrial societies, 328
and religion, 409
and social networks, 476–477
and social stratification, 196–197
Social institutions, 115–117, 119, 141, 498. *See also* specific institutions
Social integration, 7, 120, 317–318, 393, 499
Social interaction, 123–127. *See also* Communication; Community; Social structure
animals deprived of, 80
children deprived of, 78–79
defined, 107, 499
and microsociology, 106–107, 123, 126, 141
and norms, 147
and roles, 83, 129, 130, 131
and social structure in cities, 124–125
and technology, 475–477, 478
Social inventions
adolescence as, 98
capitalism, 7–9
citizenship, 311–312
democracy, 311–312

effect on social life, 473
material, 473
money, 337
and revolutions, 328
and social change, 466, 473, 474, 487
socialism, 333–334
Social isolation, 21, 23
Social justice, and urbanization, 459
Social location, 2, 98, 100, 499. *See also* Social class
Social mirror, 83–84
Social mobility
of African Americans, 215
and class, 185, 213
defined, 185, 499
and education, 213
and gender, 215–216
myth of, 219–221
and pain, 215
and race-ethnicity, 184
and religion, 184, 221
types of, 214–215, 223
and women, 215–216
Social movement organizations, 446
Social movements
anti-nuclear, 480
civil rights, 253–254, 407
collective behavior, 484
environmental, 483–485
Social networks, 476–477. *See also* Groups
Social order, 147, 148, 499
Social placement, 393–394, 499
Social policies, and urban problems, 456–460
Social promotion, 402, 499
Social reform. *See also* Social change; Social movements
Addams, Jane and, 12–13
vs. analysis, 16
health care, 293
as risky, 14
role of sociology in, 10–14, 16
vs. research, 10–14
vs. theory, 13
Social Register, 208
Social research. *See* Research
Social revolutions. *See* Revolution(s)
Social sciences, 499
Social Security, 93, 390, 392
Social setting, 129
Social solidarity, 406–407
Social status, 111–112
Social stratification, 181–225. *See also* Gender stratification; Global stratification; Power elite; Social class
caste system, 183–184

and Communist Party, 390
comparative, 187, 197t, 205t
conflict perspective on, 196–198
defined, 182, 499
determination of, 216–217
and females, 185
functionalist perspective on, 195–196
global superclass, 190, 342, 343, 346
in Great Britain, 187
in everyday life, 196
functionalist perspective on, 196–197
and ideology, 183, 186, 197, 204, 220, 222
inevitability of, 196
in India, 188–189
and industrialization, 186–190, 222
in Japan, 187
and Marx's argument, 197
overview, 181–182
and poverty, 216–221
resources, distribution of, 187, 191, 195, 197–198, 223
in Russia, 194f
slavery, 182–183, 221–222
and social mobility, 185
in South Africa, 184, 194f
systems of, 191–195
theories of, 195
universality of, 195–198, 222
Social structure, 108–122
changes in, 121–122
components of, 141
culture as, 110–111
defined, 108, 499
Gemeinshaft and Gesellshaft, 121, 141, 466
and globalization, 337–338
and macrosociology, 40, 106–107, 138–141
and microsociology, 40–41, 106–107, 138
overview, 105
and personal relationships, 139
reproduction of, 396–398
social institutions, 115–117
and social interaction in cities, 124–125, 140
and social mobility, 185, 213
sociological significance of, 108
and sports, 109
Social workers, 11f, 205, 396
Socialism, 332, 333–334, 499
Socialization
agents of, 92–95, 102
animals vs., 81
anticipatory, 92, 94, 102
of children, 78–79, 80

Socialization (*Continued*)
  and conformity, 38, 60, 87, 93, 94, 151, 156
  and day care, 93
  defined, 78, 499
  into emotions, 86–88
  extremes in, 78–82, 101
  and the family, 92–93
  into gender, 88–92
  of immigrants, 233
  into the mind/self, 83, 85, 87, 101–102
  and neighborhoods, 89, 152
  overview, 77
  and peer groups, 93–94
  and play, 93
  prisoners of, 163, 169
  and religion, 213
  in schools, 93–94
  and social class, 93
  and work, 93
  and workplace, 94
Societies
  culture and, 3
  defined, 2, 499
  dependent on norms, 59–60
  future of, 330, 331
  and industrialization, 116f, 328–331, 352t, 467
  mechanical, 120–121, 141
  medicalization of, 173–175
  organic solidarity of, 120–121, 141
  personalization of, 3
  technology, influence upon, 467
  theories of, 470–471
  traditional, 352t, 467t, 487
  transformation of, 327–331
  types of, 120–121
  urbanization, influence of, 444–445
Sociobiology, 86, 150, 177
Sociological analysis, 106–107
  levels of, 106–107
  macrosociological perspective in, 40–41, 106–107
  microsociological perspective in, 40–41, 106–107
  versus social reform, 10–14, 16
Sociological imagination. *See* Sociological perspective, the
Sociological perspective
  defined, 499
  overview, 1–2
  on prejudice, 241–245
Sociological theory, 1–17. *See also* Conflict, Feminist, Functionalist, and Symbolic interactionist perspectives
Sociology
  applied, 13

basic (pure), 13
  and biology, 79, 86
  careers in, 14
  and common sense, 19, 42
  defined, 31
  on the dominant position, 273
  early female sociologists, 10–11
  and the environment, 242, 244, 483, 488
  and feminists, 38–39
  in the future, 289
  genetics-informed, 330
  and globalization, 41, 192, 337–343
  and industrialization, 36, 39, 98, 99, 100, 101, 186–187
  levels of analysis, 40–42
  on the minority position, 273
  norms, 150
  in North America, 10–15
  origins/development of, 5–10, 16
  and positivism, 5–6
  and protestant ethic, 7
  public, 13–14
  religion, and capitalism, 7–8
  and research (*See* Research)
  risks of, 14
  rogue gang research, 29
  sexism in, 10–11
  and science, 5
  and social Darwinism, 6–7
  and social reform, 10–15
  social environments, 241–242
  and social integration, 7
  and the social sciences, 5
  and society, 2–4
  stages in its development, 84. *See also* Life course
  and study of religion, 7–8
  theory in, 12–13, 31–43
  and values, 59
Sociologists, 29, 204
Sociology
  basic, 492
  defined, 5, 177, 499
  majoring in, 490
  pure, 492
  reasons for, 491
  uses for, 490–491
Soldiers, 96, 126, 184t, 231, 232. *See also* Military
Solidarity, 120
South Africa, 123, 184, 193f
Soviet Union, 313. *See also* Russia
Space
  exploration of, 476
  personal, 123–124
  and war, 477

Spain, 36, 56, 426
Spanish, use of in U.S., 249
Special-interest groups, 318, 319–320, 499
"Spin doctors," 116f
Spirit of capitalism. *See* Capitalism
Split labor market, 242, 499
Sports
  and academics, 116f
  as agent of socialization, 109
  and gender, 242, 292
  and leisure, as value, 67
  and social class, 207, 208, 364
  as social status, 110
  as social structure, 109
  and taking role of the other, 83
Spousal abuse, 380–381
Sri Lanka, 193f
St. Louis, Missouri, 23, 399
Star Wars weapons, 477
Staring, 47, 48
Starvation, 430–431
State, defined, 307, 499
State religions, 416–417
Statistics, interpreting
  analysis of, 14
  averages, measuring, 25t
  and chances of marital success/failure, 381–382
  on crime, 171–173
  means, medians, modes, 25t
  misuse of, 382
  of death certificates, 14
Status, defined, 111, 205, 499
Status, types of, 111, 205–206
Status consistent, 205, 499
Status inconsistency, 113, 205–207, 499
Status set, 111–113, 499
Status symbols, 111, 499
Steam engine, 328, 331, 346, 467, 487
Stereotypes
  of Asians, 257
  and beauty, 51
  and corporate culture, 289
  defined, 217
  and discrimination, 247, 256–257
  in everyday life, 283
  and gangs, 29
  and hate crimes, 171, 172
  and health care, 293
  held by police, 138, 172
  and mass media, 90
  of Native Americans, 261
  negative, 244
  of the poor, 217–218, 461
  and prejudice, 244, 265
  and rapists, 296
  and race-ethnicity, 217, 243, 266

self-fulfilling, 243
  of suicide terrorists, 326
  of women, 284–285, 289
Stigma, 147, 499
Stock markets, 239
Strain theory, 156–157, 499
Stratification. *See* Gender stratification;
  Global stratification; Social stratification
Stratified random samples, 399, 499
Street crime, 150, 157, 499
Streetcorner men, 106–107, 110, 111. *See also* Homeless, the
Structural mobility, 215, 499
Structured interviews, 499
Students'
  alcohol/drug use, 30, 94, 11
  educational standards, 402–403
Studied nonobservance, 131
Stuttgart, Germany, 484
Subcultures
  and African Americans, 8
  and Asian Americans, 318
  of children, 94
  vs. counterculture, 61, 64, 74
  defined, 499
  of deviance, 154
  in everyday life, 61
  explained, 61
  military, 322
  motorcycle gangs, 64
  of neighborhoods and friends, 152, 177
  in occupations, 61
  photo essay on, 62–63
  and self image, 99
  and social class, 211
  and social integration, 7
  of sociology, 16
  in sports, 62, 63
  of terrorists, 326, 327, 346
  in U.S., 61
  values and norms, 64
  and whites, 8
Subjective meanings, defined, 499
Suburban flight, 458
Suburbanization, 218, 448, 449, 458, 462, 499
Suburbs, 448, 499
Sudan, 52, 183, 194f
Suicide
  methods of, 8f
  and race–ethnicity, 8
  and religion, 7, 9
  ritual, 184
  and social integration, 7, 8
  sociological perspective on, 7, 9, 16
  by soldiers, 325–326, 327, 346
Suicide terrorism, 326, 327, 346

Superiority, 228, 238
Super-rich, the, 204, 208, 322. *See also* Power elite
Surgery, 36, 239, 293, 301
Surveillance, 478
Surveys, 24–26, 499
"Survival of the fittest," 6, 9
Survivalists, 64
Sustainable environment, 479, 499
Sweden, 193f, 237, 250, 333, 416
Sworn virgins, 89
Symbol, defined, 499
Symbolic culture, 53–57
  defined, 53, 499
  language, 53–57
Symbolic interactionism
  application of, 33–34, 43
  chart summarizing, 41t
  defined, 32, 499
  explained, 32
  and fossils,
  as microsociology, 41t, 123–127
  and social construction of reality, 135–136, 500
Symbolic interactionist perspective on
  application of, 33–34
  births in Least Industrialized Nations, 433
  body language, 126, 141
  deviance, 146–147, 151–154, 177
  divorce, 33, 41t
  ecosabotage, 484–485
  education, 398–400, 421
  in everyday life, 32
  eye contact, 126, 141
  families, 151–152, 356–358
  gender roles, 356–358
  gendered violence, 296–297
  the homeless, 107
  love, 33–34
  macro and micro approaches, 40, 43, 123, 126
  marriage and family, 33, 356–358
  midwives, defeat of, 283
  parenthood, 33
  personal space, 123–125
  population growth, 433, 453, 461
  prejudice, 243–244
  remarriage, 379–380
  religion, 410, 414
  and self-concept, 83–84
  smiling, 126, 141
  sexual harassment, 290–291
  statistics, 171–172
  symbols, 33, 34
Symbols
  defined, 32, 53

and development of self, 32
  Holy Week in Spain, 412–413
  religious, 32, 410–411
  status, 112
  and technology, 70
Synthesis, and theories, 471
Systems of descent, 353, 499

T

Tables, how to read, 22t
Taboos, 60, 499
Taken-for-granted assumptions. *See* Background assumptions
Taking the role of the other, 83, 499
Target population, 25, 499
Tasmania, 71
Tattooing, 63
Teachers
  expectations, 398, 399
  raising standards for, 402–403
Teamwork, 131, 499
Techniques of neutralization, 153, 499
Techno Patriots, 249
Technological life, 70, 210
Technology. *See also* Inventions; New technology
  and birth of machine, 328–329
  and control of workers, 338, 342–343
  as a core value, 65
  and cultural leveling, 71–72, 74
  defined, 70, 475, 499
  and divorce, 36
  and the environment, 482, 485–488
  and gender, 70
  and global domination, 337–338, 468–469
  and global inequality, 215, 216, 249, 329
  and health, 99
  identity chips, 478
  and ideology, 204
  and life span, 99–100, 101
  and medical diagnoses, 70–71
  and religion, 419, 422
  significance of, 476
  and social change, 467, 473, 474, 475–478, 488
  and social interaction, 475–477, 478
  and social organization, 476–477
  and social relationships, 475–477
  and surveillance, 478
  and symbolic culture, 70
  3-D, 216
  and war and terrorism, 477–478
Televangelists, 419
Television, 90

Terror(ism)
   and Al-Qaeda, 326
   and body language, 126
   cyber defense, 477
   defined, 325, 499
   and the future, 477, 487
   international, 325, 407
   and religion, 407–408
   stereotypes, 326
   suicide, 326
   and technology, 477
   of weaker enemies, 325–326
Testosterone, 274, 275, 300
"Testosterone bonus," 273
Thailand, 51, 52, 193f, 339, 405
Theory in sociology, 31, 499. *See also*
   Conflict, Feminist, Functionalist, and
   Symbolic interactionist perspectives
Thesis, and antithesis, 471–472, 487
Thinness, 130
Third parties, 316, 320, 345
Thomas theorem, 135–136, 500
"Three-strikes" laws, 164–165
Tijuana, 251
Tobacco, 145, 146
Tokyo, Japan, 187
Torah, the, 116f
Tornado photo essay, 140
Torture, 407, 476
Total institutions, 96, 500
Totalitarianism, 313, 500
Toxic wastes, 480–481
Toys, 89, 90, 91, 139
Tracking in schools, 394, 500
Trading blocs, 337, 346
Tradition and science, 5
Traditional authority
   basis for, 345
   and charismatic authority, 308
   defined, 307, 500
   governments based upon, 308
   and industrialization, 307
   and rationalization, 308
   and transfer of authority, 309, 310, 345
   and tribal societies, 307
   in U.S. society, 308
Traditional societies, 352t, 467t
Trail of Tears, 260
Transformative social movements,
   466–468
Transitional adulthood, 99, 100, 500
Transitional older years, defined, 99–100,
   500
Transmission of mainstream values, 500
Trapped population, in cities, 454
Triads, 455–456, 468
Tribal societies

adolescence in, 98, 101
and cultural progress, 470
and the environment, 486
and gender prestige, 283
hand-to-hand combat, and women,
   277–278
identification with, 235, 250, 261, 266
and incest, 355
minority groups in, 231
and pollution, 479
and slavery, 182
social institutions, 117, 119
and traditional authority, 307
TRW/Northrop Grumman, 161
Tsunamis, 433, 461, 480, 486
Tunisia, 478
Tutsis, 228, 231, 232
Twin studies, 81, 136, 242

U

Underclass, 209–210, 500. *See also*
   Homeless
Underground opportunity, 160
Unemployment, 40, 43, 138, 250t, 251
United Arab Emirates, 183
United Nations, 344, 347, 429, 444f
Unity, trends in, 343–344
Universal citizenship, 312, 500
Universals, cultural, 69
University of Chicago, 11, 12, 29, 450
University of Georgia, 401
University of Michigan, 263
University of Virginia, 2
Unobtrusive measures, 28, 500
Unstructured interviews, defined, 500
Upper middle class, 209
Upward social mobility, 215, 500
Urban flight, 459
Urban renewal, 458, 459, 460, 462,
   500
Urban revolts, 253
Urban sprawl, 451, 473t
Urban Villagers, The (Gans), 453
Urbanization, 440–441. *See also* Cities
   defined, 444, 500
   early history of, 444
   and industrialization, 445t
   infrastructure, 444
   in the Least Industrialized Nations,
     445, 451, 462
   models of growth, 450–452
   overview, 440–441
   process of, 444–446
   structures of, 446–448
   in U.S., 446–450
Utah, 64, 165, 256

V

Vaginal examinations, 136–137
Validity, 21, 500
Value clusters, 66, 500
Value contradictions, 67, 500
Value free, defined, 500
Values. *See also* Core values
   changing, 67–68
   clusters, 66
   Confucian, 368, 369, 384, 405
   contradictions in, 67
   core, 60, 64, 65, 66, 67, 74
   cultural transmission of, 59–61,
     392–393, 421
   defined, 59, 500
   and deviance, 156–157
   as distorting lenses, 66
   and education, 65, 66, 74
   emerging, 67–68
   and the environment, 68, 74
   and individualism, 65, 66
   and religion, 407, 411, 416
   research of, 59–60
   in social institutions, 392–393
   and subcultures, 60, 61, 62–64,
     74
   and technology, 70
   transformation of, 71
   transmission of, 392–393
   universal, 50, 69, 74
   in U.S., 50, 65–66
   and work, 59, 64, 65, 66, 68
Varanasi, India, 409
Variables, 21, 500
Verstehen, 500
Veterans, study on, 274–275
Video games, 91
Vienna, Austria, 124–125
Vietnam, 194f, 256, 292, 325, 438t
Vietnam Veterans Study, 274–275
Violence. *See also* Murder; Rape
   and authority, 306–307
   and crime, 165
   in the family, 380–381
   female circumcision as, 295, 302
   and feminists, 296
   and gangs, 152
   and husband's achievement, 22t
   and male identity, 89–90, 295, 296,
     297, 301, 302
   legitimate, 306–307
   and religion, 407
   riots, 253, 266
   in schools, 19, 403, 421
   against women, and violence,
     167–168, 294–297, 301

by women, 159t, 380
    in the U.S., 159f
Virgins, sworn ("social men"), 89
Voter apathy, defined, 500
Voting
    and alienation, 318
    and apathy, 318, 500
    in early democracies, 318
    in early U.S., 40, 253
    and education, 316–318
    and employment, 317t
    and gender, 318
    influences of life on, 318
    patterns in U.S., 316–318
    and race–ethnicity, 253, 255, 266,
        316–318
    and social class, 317t
    and social integration, 317
    two-party presidential vote, 319t
Voting Rights Act of 1965, 253

W

Waco, Texas, 418
Walenstadt, Switzerland, 452
War, 324–327, 477. *See also* Genocide;
    Military; specific wars
    child soldiers, 326, 346
    combat and gender inequality, 277
    and computers, 477
    and conflicts, 471–472
    conditions leading to, 324–325
    costs of, 468–469
    cyber war and cyber defense, 477
    defined, 324, 500
    and dehumanization, 232
    as dysfunction of religion, 407–408
    and ethnic conflicts, 228, 469
    and the future, 477
    and politics, 324–325, 468–469, 487
    reasons for, 324–325
    and religion, 407–408
    and slavery, 182, 183
    in space, 477
    and starvation, 431
    and technology, 477–478
    and terrorism, 325–326
Washington, D.C., 105–106
WASPs (white Anglo-Saxon Protestant),
    defined, 247, 500. *See also* Whites
Wealth, 190f, 201–202, 500
Weapons of mass destruction, 326
Weight, body, 14, 68, 211, 237, 478
Welfare
    conflict perspective on, 342
    functionalist perspective on, 35
    funding, 336

myths about, 218
    reform of, 35, 37
    social class, 208, 210, 254
Welfare (state) capitalism, 332, 500
Welfare socialism, 333–334
Whales, 484
Winfrey, Oprah, 207
White ethnics, 247, 500
"White flight," 247, 266
White-collar crime, 157–158, 500
Whites. *See also* Race–ethnicity
    Anglo Saxon Protestants, 246–248,
        500
    comparative well-being
        statistics, 250
    and crime, 163
    and death penalty, 169, 170t
    and education, 251, 397, 399
    ethnic background of, 245–247
    family structure of, 367, 370, 378f
    hate crimes, 172t
    income extremes, 254t
    interracial marriage of, 233,
        236, 360f
    and marriage, 360
    numbers of, 248
    and politics, 316, 317t, 318, 319t
    and poverty, 217, 218, 250t
    and suicide, 8
    and voting, 253, 255
Widowhood and widows, 364, 365
Witches, 407, 408, 422
Women. *See also* Gender; Sexism;
    Single mothers
    and abortion, 295, 302, 370,
        438, 439
    and authority, 353
    and background assumptions, 293
    circumcision of, 295, 302
    in crime, 158–159t, 169
    and death penalty, 169, 178
    discrimination against, 276–279,
        283, 298
    early female sociologists, 10–11
    and education, 39, 164t, 220f,
        288f, 391
    female infanticide, 295
    and gynecology, 136–137
    impression management, for
        actors, 128
    impression management, and
        careers, 131–132
    impression management, for
        executives, 132
    as a minority group, 233, 237
    and pay gap, 287–289
    in politics, 287–290, 298–299

and power, 190, 289–290
    pregnancy, medicalization of, 438
    in prostitution, 50, 157, 295, 441
    and retreatism, 157
    as "social men"/taking men's
        roles, 89
    social mobility of, 215–216
    social stratification of, 274
    and sociobiological explanations, 150,
        273–275
    sociologists, 11f
    and stereotypes, 283
    terms for, 292
    violence against, 167–168, 294–297
    violence by, 159t
    and voting, 298–299, 302
    and work (*See* under Gender)
Women's movement, 280, 301. *See also*
    Feminism
Woolworth's, 233
Work and workers. *See also* Division
    of labor
    affirmative action, 262, 263
    blue- vs. white-collar, 205, 215,
        329f
    bonded laborers, 184, 284
    by children (*See* Child labor)
    in childhood, 97–98
    conflict perspective on, 197–198
    control of, 265
    and credential societies, 389
    discrimination, 232f, 233, 242–243,
        263, 265
    exploitation of, 333, 335, 346
    and gender, 282–286, 287–290,
        356–358
    global division of labor, 328, 335
    and globalization, 337–343
    hourly earnings in U.S., 338f
    and identity, 199, 454
    and Industrial Revolution, 5, 38, 337,
        444, 466–467
    Japanese, 242
    and leisure, 67, 68, 74, 98, 381
    motivation of, 195–197
    in new economic system, 339–341
    prestige of, 204–205
    reserve labor force, 242–243
    revolution of, 329–330
    rights, struggle for, 6, 197–198
    sex typing of occupations, 283
    and social class, 93, 209
    and socialization, 93
    and split labor market, 242
    telework, 473t
    traditional, and women, 356–358
    in types of societies, 327–330

Work and workers. (*Continued*)
in underground opportunities, 156, 157, 160
in U.S. society, 339
Working class. *See also* Work and workers
and child rearing, 363–364
defined, 209
and deviance, 172
exploitation of, 335, 339, 346
law and oppression of, 161–162
and power elite, 161–162
Marx on, 197
and prestige of work, 204–205, 283
and socialization of children, 93
Working poor, the, 209

Workplace
alienation/isolation, 318
and anticipatory socialization, 94, 102
as agents of socialization, 94
computers in, 215, 216, 338, 339
gender inequality, 287–290, 301
humanizing of, 287–290
and new technology, 70
racial–ethnic diversity in, 250
racism in, 255, 256
sexual harassment in, 290–291
subcultures in, 62, 63
World Court, 344
World system theory, 191–192, 500
World Trade Center, 325
World Trade Organization, 343

World Wars I and II, 195, 232, 242, 429, 468
Wounded Knee, 260

X

"XYY" theory, 150

Y

Yanomamö Indians, 3, 145–146, 148
Youthfulness, as a value, 68, 74
Yugoslavia, 232, 469

Z

Zero population growth, 439, 500
Zimbabwe, 87, 88, 194f
Zuckerberg, Mark, 205